Linux: The Complete Reference, Second Edition

Richard Petersen

Osborne **McGraw-Hill**

Berkeley   New York   St. Louis   San Francisco
Auckland   Bogotá   Hamburg   London   Madrid
Mexico City   Milan   Montreal   New Delhi   Panama City
Paris   São Paulo   Singapore   Sydney
Tokyo   Toronto

Osborne/**McGraw-Hill**
2600 Tenth Street
Berkeley, California 94710
U.S.A.

For information on translations or book distributors outside the U.S.A., or to arrange
bulk purchase discounts for sales promotions, premiums, or fund-raisers, please
contact Osborne/**McGraw-Hill** at the above address.

Linux: The Complete Reference, Second Edition

1234567890 AGM AGM 901987654321098

ISBN 0-07-882461-3

> **To my brothers,**
> **George, Robert, and Mark**

Publisher
   Brandon A. Nordin

Editor-in-Chief
   Scott Rogers

Acquisitions Editor
   Wendy Rinaldi

Project Editor
   Heidi Poulin

Editorial Assistant
   Ann Sellers

Copy Editors
   Gary Morris
   Dennis Weaver

Proofreader
   Stefany Otis

Indexer
   Valerie Robbins

Computer Designer
   Roberta Steele

Illustrator
   Lance Ravella

Contents

Acknowledgments xix
Introduction xxiii

Part I

Introduction to Linux

1 The Linux Operating System 3

Operating Systems and Linux 5
History of Linux and Unix 6
Linux Overview 8
    Shell: Bourne, Korn, and C-Shell 9
    File Structure: Directories and Files 10
    Utilities: Editors, Filters, and Communications 11
Linux Software and Information Sources on the Internet 12
Linux Releases 14
OpenLinux 14
Summary: The Linux Operating System 15

IIIII 2 Installing Linux 21
    Hardware, Software, Information Requirements 22
        Hardware Requirements 23
        Software Requirements 23
        Information Requirements 24
        Upgrade Information for Already Installed
        Linux Systems 26
    Opening Disk Space for Linux Partitions 27
        Deleting Partitions 28
        Nondestructive Repartition 29
        Destructive Repartitioning of Your Entire
        Hard Drive 30
    Creating the OpenLinux Install Disks 32
    Installing Linux 33
        Booting the Computer and Creating Linux Partitions 34
        Installing Your Linux System: OpenLinux Lite 40
        Network Configuration 42
        Final Configuration 44
        Installing LILO 44
        Finishing Configuration 45
    Installing and Configuring X-Windows 47
        The Virtual Desktop 52
    Installing Sound Drivers: sound 54
    Lisa 55

IIIII 3 Linux Startup and Setup 57
    User Accounts 58
    Accessing Your Linux System 59
        Starting and Shutting Down Linux 60
        Logging into and out of Linux:
        The Command Line 61
        Starting and Exiting the Window Manager: X-Windows . . . 63
    Linux Commands and Command
    Line Editing 64
    Online Manual 66
        whatis and apropos 68
        Xman and tkman 69
    Online Documentation 71
    Configuring Your System: Easy Setup with Lisa 71
    Installing Software Packages 75
        Command and Program Directories: PATH 76
        Lisa: Software Package Management 77
        Linux Installation Manager: glint 77

Command Line Installation: Redhat Package Manager 81
Installing Software from Online Sources 83
Remote Communications 85
Modem Setup 86
Telecommunication Programs: minicom and Seyon 87
Internet Connections with Modems: pppd and ezppp 88
pppd 88
EzPPP 92
Email: XFMail 99
X-Windows and Network Configuration 100
Summary: Getting Started with Linux 100

IIIII 4 Window Managers and Desktops: X-Windows 107
Window, File, and Program Managers 108
Starting and Exiting X-Windows Window Managers and
File Desktops 109
System Configuration Tools 110
Windows and Icons 111
The Terminal Window: Xterm 112
X-Windows Multitasking 114
The fvwm Window Manager and Desktop 115
The fvwm Workplace Menu 116
The GoodStuff Taskbar 116
Virtual Desktops: fvwm 117
The Caldera Desktop 118
Directory Windows 120
Managing the Caldera Desktop 122
Installing Window Managers and
File Managers 123
Starting Window Managers 124
fvwm and fvwm2 125
Xview: olwm and olvwm 125
fvwm95 and qvwm 128
LessTif: mwm 130
AfterStep 130
Motif 131
The Crisplite and XEmacs Editors 131
Summary: X-Windows 133

Part II

Linux Operations

▌▌▌▌▌ 5 Shell Operations 139
The Command Line 140
Options and Arguments 141
Command Line Features 142
Special Characters and File Name Arguments: *, ?, [ ] 143
Standard Input/Output and Redirection 147
Redirecting the Standard Output: > and >> 149
The Standard Input 151
Redirecting the Standard Input: < 152
Pipes: | 153
Pipes and Redirection: tee 156
Redirecting and Piping the Standard Error: >&, 2> 158
Shell Variables 161
Definition and Evaluation of Variables: =, $, set, unset 161
TCSH Shell Variables 163
Shell Scripts: User-Defined Commands 164
Jobs: Background, Kills, and Interruptions 166
Background and Foreground: &, fg, bg 167
Canceling Jobs: kill 168
Interruptions: CTRL-Z *169*
Delayed Execution: at 170
Summary: Shell Operations 173

▌▌▌▌▌ 6 The Linux File Structure 181
Linux Files 182
File Types 183
File Classifications: the file and od Commands 183
The File Structure 184
Home Directories 185
Path Names 186
System Directories 187
Listing, Displaying, and Printing Files: ls, cat, more, and
lpr 188
Displaying Files: cat and more 189
Printing Files: lpr, lpq, and lprm 189
Managing Directories: mkdir, rmdir, ls, cd, and pwd 191
Creating and Removing Directories:
mkdir and rmdir 191
Listing Directories: ls 191
Path Names: the pwd Command 192

Change Directory: the cd Command 192
Nested Directories 195
Referencing the Working and Parent Directories: .
and 195
Using Absolute and Relative Path Names: ~ 197
File and Directory Operations: find, cp, mv, rm, and ln 199
Searching Directories: find 199
Copying Files 203
Moving Files 206
Moving and Copying Directories 209
The ~ Special Character 210
Erasing a File: the rm Command 211
Links: the ln Command 212
Summary: The Linux File Structure 217

7   File Management Operations 225
Displaying File Information: ls -l 226
File and Directory Permissions: chmod 227
Setting Permissions: Permission Symbols 229
Absolute Permissions: Binary Masks 231
Directory Permissions 235
Changing a File's Owner or Group: chown and chgrp . . . 237
File Systems: mount and umount 237
Mounting and Formatting Floppy Disks 240
Mounting CD-ROMs 241
Mounting Hard Drive Partitions: Linux and MS-DOS 243
Automatically Mounting File Systems: the fstab file 244
Linux File System Manager: Lisa and fstool 247
Network File Systems: NFS and /etc/exports 249
NIS 251
Archive Files and Devices: tar 251
XTar 254
File Compression: gzip 255
Installing Software from Compressed Archives: .tar.gz 257
Downloading Compressed Archives from
Online Sites 258
Compiling Software 260
The mtools Utilities: msdos 261
DOS and Windows Emulators: DOSemu, Wine, and
Willow 264
Summary: File Management 265

‖‖ **8**	**Electronic Mail**	**279**
	Local and Internet Addresses	280
	Mail Transport Agents: deliver, sendmail, smail	281
	Accessing Mail on Remote POP Mail Servers: popclient	282
	The Mail Utility	284
	Sending Messages	284
	Editing Mail Messages: The Tilde Commands	287
	Receiving Mail: The Mail Shell	292
	Mail Aliases, Options, and the Mail Shell Initialization File: .mailrc	304
	The Elm Utility	308
	Sending Mail with Elm	308
	Receiving Mail Using Elm	310
	Quitting the Elm Utility	313
	Deleting and Undeleting Messages: d and u	314
	Replying to Messages	315
	Sending Messages from Elm	315
	Saving Messages in Elm	315
	Reading Mailbox Files with Elm	316
	Elm Aliases: Alias Menu and aliases.text	317
	Elm Options: .elmrc	319
	Pine	320
	Mailing Binaries and Archives	322
	Notifications of Received Mail: From and biff	325
	Communications with Other Logged-in Users: Write and Talk	326
	Direct Connections: The Write Utility	326
	Interactive Communication: The Talk Utility	327
	Summary: Mail	328
‖‖ **9**	**Usenet and Newsreaders**	**339**
	Usenet News	340
	Installing trn and tin	342
	News Transport Agents	342
	INN	343
	The trn Newsreader	344
	Newsgroup List	345
	The trn Selector	347

Selector Display Modes: Article, Subject,
and Thread 349
Displaying Articles: trn Thread Trees 352
Saving Articles 357
Replying to Articles in trn: Follow-ups and Messages 358
Marking Articles 359
Article Selections 359
trn Options 361
Article List : the rn Newsreader 361
Posting Articles: Pnews 363
Pnews Signatures: The .signature File 364
The tin Newsreader 364
Encoded Binaries: uuencode and uudecode 367
Summary: Usenet and Newsreaders 368

||||| 10 Internet Tools 379
Internet Addresses 381
Remote Login: telnet 383
Network File Transfer: ftp 386
Archie 390
Archie Client 391
Archie Servers 393
Xarchie 394
An Internet User Interface: Gopher 395
Gopher Menus 397
Using Gopher to Access Services 398
Gopher Bookmark Menu 399
Veronica 402
WAIS 403
Summary: Accessing the Internet 404

||||| 11 The World Wide Web 413
URL Addresses 414
Web Pages 416
Web Browsers 417
Netscape Navigator 419
Mosaic 422
Arena 424
Lynx: Line-Mode Browser 426
HotJava 428
Web Search Utilities 429
JAVA for Linux 430
Java Development Kit: JDK 430

JDK 1.0.2 431

JDK 1.1.1 431

Java Applets 433

Using Linux as a Web Server 434

Network Configuration as a Web Server 434

Creating Your Own Web Site 434

Creating Web Pages with HTML 435

Common Gateway Interfaces 442

Summary: WWW 443

12 Internet Servers 451

Starting Servers 453

Server init Scripts 454

inetd Server Management 457

ftp Server 459

The Ftp Server Configuration Files 460

The ftp User Account 462

ftp Server Directories 466

Permissions 468

ftp Files 469

Web Server 469

Configuring Your Web Server 471

Starting the Web Server 476

Gopher Server 478

The Gopher User Account and Data Directory 480

The University of Minnesota Gopher 481

GN Gopher Server 493

Testing the Gopher Server 497

Gopher Directories 498

Gopher Indexes: gopherindex 502

A Gopher Example 502

WAIS Server 505

Configuring and Installing freeWAIS Source Code:

Makefile and ir.h 508

Creating Indexes 510

Your WAIS Sources 512

Testing Your WAIS Server 514

Starting freeWAIS 514

Summary: Internet Servers 515

13 Remote Access 517

TCP/IP Remote Access Operations: rwho, rlogin, rcp,

and rsh 518

TCP/IP Network System Information: rwho, ruptime,
and ping 519
Remote Access Permission: .rhosts 520
Remote Login: rlogin 521
Remote File Copy: rcp 521
Remote Execution: rsh 523
Unix to Unix CoPy: uucp 525
Installing and Configuring UUCP 525
UUCP Addressing 527
Connected Systems: uname 529
Making UUCP Connections: uucico and uuxqt 530
Mail File Transfer: uuto and uupick 530
Direct File Copy: uucp and uustat 532
Remote Execution: uux 534
Summary: Remote Access 535

Part IV

Shells

14   Filters and Regular Expressions 543
Using Redirection and Pipes with Filters: cat, tee,
head, and tail 544
Outputting the Beginning and End of a File:
head and tail 546
Types of Filter Output: wc, spell, and sort 547
Counting Words: wc 548
Spell Checking: spell 548
Sorting Files: sort 549
Searching Files: grep and fgrep 550
grep 550
fgrep 551
Editing Filters 552
The Stream Editor: sed 553
Differences and Changes: diff 555
Regular Expressions 557
Matching the Beginning and End of a Line: ^, $ 557
Matching Any Character: 557
Matching Repeated Characters: * 558
Classes of Characters: [ ] 560
grep and Regular Expressions 563
Full Regular Expressions and Extended Special
Characters: |, ( ), +, and ? 564

Summary: Filters 566
    File Filters 567
    Edit Filters 567
    Regular Expressions 568
    Data Filters 569

▌▌▌▌ 15 The Bourne Again Shell (BASH) **577**
Command and File Name Completion 578
Command Line Editing 579
History 579
    History Event Editing 581
    Configuring History: HISTFILE and HISTSAVE 582
Aliases 583
Controlling Shell Operations 585
    ignoreeof 585
    noclobber 585
    noglob 586
Environment Variables and Subshells: export 586
Configuring Your Login Shell with Special Shell Variables . . . 588
    System-determined Special Variables 590
    BASH Shell Redefinable Special Variables 591
    BASH Shell User-defined Special Variables 596
    BASH Shell Login Initialization File: .profile 598
    The BASH Shell Initialization File: .bashrc 601
    The BASH Shell Logout Initialization File: .bash_logout . . 603
BASH Shell Programming 603
    Shell Scripts: Commands and Comments 604
Variables and Scripts 606
    Definition and Evaluation of Variables: =, $, set, unset . . . 606
    Variable Values: Strings 607
    Values from Linux Commands: Back Quotes 609
    Quoting Commands: Single Quotes 610
    Script Input and Output: echo, read, and << 611
    Script Command Line Arguments 613
    Export Variables and Script Shells 614
Arithmetic Shell Operations: let 615
Control Structures 617
    The test Command 617
    Conditions: if, if-else, elif, case 618
    Loops: while, for-in, for 623
Summary: BASH Shell 627

||||| 16   The TCSH Shell 637

     Command Line Completion 638
     History 639
        History Event Substitutions 641
     Aliases 643
     TCSH Shell Feature Variables:
        Shell Features 644
           echo 644
           ignoreeof 644
           noclobber 645
           noglob 645
     TCSH Special Shell Variables for Configuring Your System . . . 646
        prompt, prompt2, prompt3 646
        cdpath 647
        history and savehist 647
        mail 648
     TCSH Shell Initialization Files: .login, .tcshrc, .logout 649
        .login 649
        .tcshrc 650
        .logout 652
     TCSH Shell Programming 652
        TCSH Shell Variables, Scripts, and Arguments 652
        Control Structures 658
     Summary 667

Part V

Editors and Utilities

||||| 17   The Vi Editor 679

     Vi Command, Input, and Line Editing Modes 680
     Creating, Saving, and Quitting a File in Vi 681
     Managing Editing Modes in Vi 684
     Vi Editing Commands: Common Operations 685
        Moving Through the Text in Vi 685
        Modifying Text in Vi: Input, Deletions,
          and Changes 688
        Copying, Moving, and Searching Text in Vi 691
     Advanced Vi Editing Commands 692
        Advanced Cursor Movement 693
     Line Editing Commands 694

Options in Vi: set and .exrc 695
 The Vi Initialization File: .exrc 696
Summary: the Vi Editor 698

|||||| 18   The Emacs Editor 709
Creating a File Using Emacs 710
Meta-Keys, Line Commands, and Modes 711
Emacs Editing Commands 712
 Movement Commands 713
 Deletions 713
 Kill Buffers and Moving Text 714
 Regions: Point and Mark 715
 Incremental Searches 715
 Substitutions: Replace and Query-Replace 716
Using Windows in Emacs 717
Buffers and Files 718
 File Buffers 718
 Unattached Buffers 719
Help 721
XEmacs 721
Summary: Emacs 722

Part VI

Administration

|||||| 19   Systems Administration 731
System Management: Superuser 732
 The Root User Desktop 733
 System Time and Date 734
 Scheduling Tasks: crontab 735
 System States: init and shutdown 736
 System Initialization Files: /etc/rc.d 738
Managing Users 738
 Adding and Removing Users with usercfg 739
 The /etc/passwd File 741
 Managing User Environments: /etc/skel 742
 Adding Users with adduser 743
 Adding and Removing Users with useradd, usermod,
  and userdel 744
 Adding and Deleting Groups 745
Installing and Managing Devices 748
 Creating Device Files: mknod 749

Installing and Managing Printers 749
Installing and Managing Terminals and Modems 754
LILO 756
Summary: System Administration 757

|||||| 20 Network Administration 767
TCP/IP Network Addresses 768
Network Address 769
Broadcast Address 769
Gateway Address 769
Nameserver Addresses 769
Netmask 770
TCP/IP Configuration Files 770
Identifying Hostnames: /etc/hosts 771
Network Name: /etc/networks 771
Network Initialization: /etc/rc.d/init.d/inet 772
/etc/HOSTNAME 772
Network Interfaces and Routes: ifconfig and route 772
Netcfg and Lisa 773
ifconfig 774
Routing 776
Monitoring Your Network: ping and netstat 778
Domain Name Service (DNS) 780
host.conf 781
/etc/resolv.conf 782
Setting Up Your Own Nameserver: named 783
SLIP and PPP 783
Preparations for Connecting to SLIP or PPP 784
PPP 784
SLIP and CSLIP: dip 794
Summary: Network Administration 800

|||||| 21 Configuring the X-Windows System 813
XFree86 Servers 814
/etc/XF86Config file 815
Screen 817
Files, Modules, ServerFlags, and Keyboard 818
Pointer 819
Monitor 819
Device 820
X-Windows and Window Managers 821
fvwm Configuration Files 822
The Taskbar: system.fvwmrc.goodstuff 822

The Workplace Menu: system.fvwmrc.menu 823
Icon Styles and Device Bindings: .styles and .bindings . . . 824
Startup Applications: system.fvwmdesk 825
X-Windows Command Line Arguments 825
X-Windows Configuration Files 826
Fonts 831
Compiling X-Windows Applications 833
Summary: Configuring X-Windows 833

||||| 22   Typesetting: TeX, LaTeX, and Ghostscript 841
Typesetting 845
TeX Files 847
TeX commands 848
Paragraphs 849
Spacing 849
Headers and Footers 850
Fonts 850
Mathematical Formulas 853
LaTeX 855
Document Classes 855
Packages 857
Page Format 857
Fonts 858
Sectioning 858
Footnotes and Cross-References 859
Environments 859
Counters 861
Lists 861
Tables 863
Mathematical Formulas: math Mode 865
Graphics 867
Letters 870
Defining New Commands,
Environments, and Fonts 872
TeX Applications 872
Ghostscript and Ghostview 873
Ghostview and GV 875

||||| 23   Compilers and Libraries: gcc, g++, and gdb 893
Getting Information: info 894
The C Compiler: gcc 894
ELF and a.out Binary Formats 896
C++ and Objective C: g++ 896

Other Compilers: Pascal, ADA, Lisp, and Fortran 897
Creating and Using Libraries: Static, Shared, and Dynamic . . . 897
The gdb Symbolic Debugger 899
    xxgdb 901
Programming Tools 902
Development Tools 902
    The make Utility 903
    The Revision Control System: RCS 905
Online Manuals for Applications: man 907

24   Perl 917

Perl Command Line Operations 919
Perl Scripts 919
Perl Input and Output: <> and print 921
Perl File Handles 923
Perl Variables and Expressions 924
Arrays and Lists 926
    Array Management Functions: List Operations 928
    Associative Arrays 929
Control Structures 930
    Loops 930
    Conditions: if, elsif, unless, and switch 932
String Functions 933
Pattern Matching 933
Functions: sub 934

25   Tcl, Tk, and Expect 949

Tcl/Tk Products and Versions 951
Tcl 953
    The tclsh Shell and Scripts 953
    Expressions 954
    Embedded Commands 955
    Variables 955
    Arrays 956
    Lists 957
    Control Structures 958
    Tcl Procedures: proc 960
    Tcl String Commands: string 961
    Tcl Input and Output: gets and puts 962
    Tcl File Handles 963
Tk 965
    The wish Shell and Scripts 965
    Tk Widgets 966

Events and Bindings 970
SpecTcl 973
Expect 974

||||| 26 gawk 983
The gawk Command 984
Pattern Searches and Special Characters 986
Variables, Constants, and Patterns 987
Pattern Search Operators 989
BEGIN and END Patterns 990
gawk Instruction Files 990
Control Structures 991
gawk as User-Defined Filters 991

Part VII

Appendixes

||||| A Hardware Parameters 999
CD-ROM Parameters 1001
ISP16/MAD16/Mozart Soft Configurable CD-ROM 1001
Sony CDU31A/CDU33A 1001
Mitsumi FX001S/D (non IDE/ATAPI) 1001
Mitsumi XA/MultiSession (non IDE/ATAPI) 1002
Matsushita/Panasonic/Teac/CreativeLabs on SBPRO
(non IDE/ATAPI) 1002
Aztech/Orchid/Okano/Wearnes/Conrad/TXC/CyDRO
M (non IDE) 1002
Sony CDU535 1002
GoldStar R420 1003
Philips/LMS CM206/226 on CM260 1003
Optics Storage DOLPHIN 8000AT 1003
Sanyo CDR-H94A 1003
SCSI Parameters 1004
AdvanSys ABPxxx 1004
BusLogic 1004
Ultrastor 14f (ISA), 24f (EISA), 34f (VLB) 1005
UltraStore 1005
Adaptec AHA152X 1005
Adaptec 154x, AMI FastDisk VLB, DTC 329x
(Standard) 1006
Adaptec AHA1740 1006
Adaptec AHA274X/284X/294X 1006

Future Domain 16xx 1006
Always IN2000 1007
Generic NCR5380/53c400 SCSI 1007
NCR53c406a 1008
Qlogicfas Driver Version 0.45, chip ... at ..., IRQ ...,
    TPdma: 1008
QLogic ISP1020 Intelligent SCSI Processor
    Driver (PCI) 1008
Pro Audio Spektrum Studio 16 1008
Seagate ST0x/Future Domain TMC-8xx/TMC-9xx 1009
Trantor T128/T128F/T228 1009
DTC 3180/3280 1009
NCR53c{7,8}xx (rel 17) 1009
NCR 53C810, 53C815, 53C820, 53C825 1010
EATA-DMA (DPT, NEC, AT&T, SNI, AST, Olivetti,
    Alphatronix) 1010
EATA-PIO (old DPT PM2001, PM2012A) 1010
Western Digital WD 7000 (FASST/ASC/xX) 1011
EATA ISA/EISA (DPT PM2011/021/012/022/122/322) . . 1011
AM53C974 1011
PPA 1012
Network Card Parameters 1012
Using Other Parameters 1012

B   Software Packages Index 1013

C   XFree86-Supported Chipsets for X-Windows 1041
Standard SVGA Chipsets 1042
Accelerated SVGA Chipsets 1042

D   About the CD-ROM 1045

    Index 1047

Acknowledgments

I would like to thank all those at Osborne/McGraw-Hill who made this book a reality, particularly Wendy Rinaldi, acquisitions editor, for her continued encouragement and management of such a complex project; Ann Sellers, editorial assistant, who provided resources and helpful advice; Gary Morris and Dennis Weaver, copy editors, for their excellent job with editing; and project editor Heidi Poulin who coordinated the intricate task of generating the final version. Thanks also to Scott Rogers who initiated the project.

I would also like to thank Caldera for their advice and support, and for the OpenLinux Linux system that they provided for this book. Thanks to Ransome Love, Nick Wells, and Allan Smart for their technical advice and support.

Special thanks to Linus Torvalds, the creator of Linux, and to those who continue to develop Linux as an open, professional, and accessible operating system. I would also like to thank professors and students at the University of California, Berkeley, for the experience and support in developing new and different ways of understanding operating system technologies.

I would also like to thank my parents, George and Cecelia, and my brothers, George, Robert, and Mark, for their support and encouragement with such a difficult project. Also Valerie and Marylou and my nieces and nephews, Aleina, Larisa, Justin, Christopher, and Dylan, for their support and deadline reminders.

Introduction

The Linux operating system has become a viable alternative for anyone with a PC. It brings all the power and flexibility of a Unix workstation, as well as a complete set of Internet applications and a fully-functional desktop interface. All of this can easily be installed on any 486 or Pentium PC. This book is designed not only to be a complete reference on Linux, but also to provide clear and detailed explanations of Linux features. No prior knowledge of Unix is assumed; Linux is an operating system anyone can use.

The second edition of this book identifies four major Linux topics: the Internet, Unix, System Administration, and Programming. For the Internet, Linux has become a platform for very powerful Internet applications. Not only can you use the Internet, but, with Linux, become a part of it, creating your own Web, ftp, Gopher, and WAIS sites. Other users can access your Linux systems, several at the same time, using different services. You can also use very powerful Unix-based applications for mail and news.

But Linux systems are not limited to the Internet. You can use it on any local intranet, setting up an ftp or Web site for your network. The OpenLinux Linux system provided with this book comes equipped with fully functional ftp and Web servers already installed and ready to use. All you need to do is add the files you want onto your site.

Linux is also a fully-functional Unix operating system. It has all the standard features of a powerful Unix system. There are shells for managing your commands.

Linux uses two of the more advanced Unix shells: the Bourne Again Shell and the TCSH shell. Each supports a complete shell programming language that you can use to create your own shell scripts. A wide array of Unix applications operates on Linux. The GNU public licensed software provides professional level applications such as programming development tools, editors and word processors, as well as numerous specialized applications such as those for graphics and sound. A massive amount of software is available at online Linux sites where you can download applications and then easily install them onto your system.

Linux has the same level of system administration features that you find on standard Unix systems. It has the same multiuser and multitasking capabilities. You can set up accounts for different users and each can access your system at the same time. Each user can have several programs running concurrently. With Linux you can control access, set up network connections, and install new devices. Your OpenLinux Linux system includes several easy-to-use, window-based configuration utilities that you can use to perform system administration tasks such as installing printers, adding users, and establishing new network connections.

Linux also has very powerful development tools for creating your own Linux applications. These include the GNU C compiler with a large number of programming tools such as debuggers and revision managers. There are also Perl and Tcl/Tk versions for Linux included on the book's CD-ROM. With Perl you can quickly develop powerful applications. Tcl/Tk lets you easily create programs with very sophisticated graphical user interfaces. As interpreted languages, both the Perl and Tcl/Tk programs that you develop on your Linux system will also run on other systems such as Macs and Windows 95. With the shell programming capabilities of the different shells and the gawk filter, you can create your own Linux commands. In the area of document processing, you can use the TeX and LaTeX formatters to easily generate technically complex postscript documents.

Since this book is really four books in one—an Internet book, a Unix book, a System Administration book, and a Linux Programming book—how you choose to use it depends upon how you want to use your Linux system. If you only want to use Linux for its Internet services, then you only have to learn a simple set of Unix operations and concentrate on the Internet applications, most of which are already installed for you. If you want to use Linux as a Unix workstation, the book provides a detailed presentation of Unix features such as shell programming, file management, filters and editors, as well as Unix mailers and newsreaders. If you want to use Linux as a multiuser system servicing many users or integrate it into a local network, you can use the detailed system, file, and network administration information provided in the administration chapters. If you want to develop your own Linux applications, you can use the programming chapters on Perl, Tcl/Tk, and C programming. None of these tasks are in any way exclusive. If you are working in a business environment, you will probably make use of all four aspects. Single users may concentrate more on the Internet features, whereas programmers may make more use of the Unix features.

The book is designed to help you start using Linux quickly. After a streamlined installation procedure taking about 40 minutes in Part I, you are introduced to the easy-to-use window-based interface that is installed with OpenLinux. You can run all your applications from here using icons, menus, and windows. A window-based text editor, CRiSPlite, is provided as part of the OpenLinux installation. At any time, you can open up a terminal window through which you can enter standard Unix commands on a command line. Linux window-based interfaces consist of two separate components: a window manager and a desktop. The window manager handles windows and the desktop handles file management using icons and menus. Different desktops will run on the same window manager, and vice versa. OpenLinux, as well as many other distributions, use the fvwm window manager. fvwm is a free, stable, and easy-to-use window manager that not only handles windows but includes a program menu and taskbar for starting programs. OpenLinux also provides a trial use (90 days) of its commercial desktop, called the Caldera Desktop, that includes an icon bar and desktop layouts.

Linux supports a large number of window managers and desktops that you can easily download and install on your system. Several of the more commonly used ones are described in Chapter 4. Many of these interfaces have the same look and feel of popular interfaces such as fvwm95 for Windows 95, AfterStep for Next, mlvwm for Mac, amiwn for Amiga, and LessTif for Motif. Others are either native Linux versions like OpenLook and Motif, or have their own customized interfaces such as the K desktop or Freedom.

You are then introduced to a set of basic Unix operations in Part II that you will need in order to work on your Linux system. Many of these can also be performed using the desktop interface, but others require that you know how the Unix command line interface works. In particular, you will need Unix commands for accessing your CD-ROM or floppy drive, downloading software from Internet sites, and creating shell scripts for customized operations.

The book then discusses in detail the many Internet applications you can use on your Linux system. OpenLinux automatically installs mail, ftp, and Web Browser applications, as well as ftp and Web servers. On your CD-ROM, there are also other mail applications, newsreaders, and Internet tools such as Gopher clients that you can easily install from your desktop. In addition, you'll find instructions on how to download and install Internet applications such as the Netscape and Mosaic Web Browsers, Gopher and Archie clients, and Gopher and WAIS servers. Chapter 11 is devoted entirely to the Web, discussing the major Web Browsers including Hot Java and how to create your own Web pages. Chapter 12 discusses the four different types of Internet servers: ftp, Web, Gopher, and WAIS. Although ftp and Web servers are already installed for you, this chapter describes how they are set up. A discussion follows on how to download and install Gopher and WAIS servers, setting up your own Gopher and WAIS Internet sites.

Part IV of the book discusses the more complex features of Linux as a Unix system. The very powerful set of Unix filters is described in Chapter 14. Shell programming for both Bourne and C-shells are presented with examples of the different programming commands in Chapters 15 and 16. Chapters 17 and 18 cover the standard editors, Vi and Emacs, and include techniques designed to start you using these editors quickly and easily.

Chapters 19, 20, and 21 discuss system, network, and X-Windows administration, respectively. These chapters emphasize the use of special system management utilities that you can operate from the desktop and use to set up your network easily, add users, and configure devices such as printers. There is also a detailed description of the configuration files used in management and how to make entries in them. Various aspects of network administration, such as network connections and routes, Domain Name services, Network File Servers, and Hostname designations are discussed. For those using modems to connect to networks such as the Internet, the SLIP and PPP protocols are discussed in detail, including how to use the dip and pppd program to make SLIP and PPP connections. X-Windows topics cover the XFree86 servers, window manager configuration, X-Windows startup files, and X-Windows configuration commands. The discussion of XFree86 servers includes a detailed explanation of the **/etc/XF86Config** configuration file used to configure your card. You are shown how to customize your fvwm window manger using its system configuration files. You also learn how to setup your own .xinitrc X-Windows startup file to startup your whatever window manager, desktop, or applications you might prefer.

The last part of the book discusses programming topics. Chapter 23 covers C programming tools beginning with the C compiler and including tasks such as managing libraries. The development tools make, the gdb debugger, and RCS revision manager are covered. Chapter 24 deals with Perl programming, beginning with a discussion of Perl Internet resources where you can find information, help, and programs. Perl's file management, string manipulation, and control structures are explained. Extensive tables for Perl commands are provided. Chapter 25 covers the Tcl, Tk, and Expect development languages. Internet resources are discussed including a list of several Tcl/Tk products freely available such as the SpecTel GUI builder and the Tcl/Tk Web server. Tcl and Tk commands are then both used to create GUI interfaces in sample Tcl/Tk programs. Chapter 26 shows how to use gawk to create powerful shell applications. Document formatting using Tex and LaTeX are covered in Chapter 22, including Internet resources for TeX and LaTeX support and applications.

Finally, there are four appendixes covering hardware boot parameters: the software packages included on the Caldera CD-ROM, a list of XFree86 supported chips, and a section about the CD included with this book.

NOTE: *The book includes numerous tables that list different commands and their options. In most cases, you will find the tables placed at the end of the chapters where you can easily locate and refer to them. For example, the end of Chapter 1 holds tables listing Internet sites where you can obtain information about Linux and sites that hold Linux software that you can download and install.*

PART ONE

Introduction to Linux

Chapter One

The Linux Operating System

3

L   inux is an operating system for PC computers that use 386, 486, or Pentium processors, such as IBM compatibles. There are also versions for DEC Alpha systems, Macintosh computers, and Sun systems. Linux was developed in the early 1990s by Linus Torvald along with other programmers around the world. As an operating system, it performs many of the same functions as DOS or Windows. However, Linux is distinguished by its power and flexibility. Most PC operating systems, such as DOS, began their development within the confines of small restricted personal computers, which have only recently become more versatile machines. Such operating systems are constantly being upgraded to keep up with the ever-changing capabilities of PC hardware. Linux, on the other hand, was developed in a very different context. Linux is a PC version of the Unix operating system that has been used for decades on mainframes and minicomputers and is currently the system of choice for workstations. Linux brings the speed, efficiency, and flexibility of Unix to your PC, taking advantage of all the capabilities that personal computers can now provide.

Linux does all this at a great price. It is free. Unlike the official Unix operating system, Linux is distributed freely under a GNU general public license as specified by the Free Software Foundation, making it available to anyone who wants to use it. Linux is copyrighted and is not public domain. However, a GNU public license has much the same effect as being in the public domain. The license is designed to ensure that Linux remains free, and, at the same time, standardized. There is only one official Linux.

The fact that Linux is free sometimes gives people the mistaken impression that it is somehow less than a professional operating system. Linux is, in fact, a PC version of Unix. To truly appreciate Linux, you need to understand the special context in which the Unix operating system was developed. Unix, unlike most other operating systems, was developed in a research and academic environment. In universities and research laboratories, Unix is the system of choice. Its development paralleled the entire computer and communications revolution over the past several decades. Computer professionals often developed new computer technologies on Unix, such as those developed for the Internet. Though a very sophisticated system, Unix was designed from the beginning to be flexible. The Unix system itself can be easily modified to create different versions. In fact, many different vendors maintain official versions of Unix. IBM, Sun, and Hewlett-Packard all sell and maintain their own versions of Unix. People involved in research programs will often create their own versions of Unix, tailored to their own special needs. This inherent flexibility in the Unix design in no way detracts from its quality. In fact, it attests to its ruggedness, allowing it to adapt to practically any environment. It is in this context that Linux was developed. Linux is, in this sense, one other version of Unix—a version for the PC.

Its development by computer professionals working in a research-like environment reflects the way Unix versions have usually been developed. The fact that Linux is publicly licensed and free reflects the deep roots that Unix has in academic institutions, with their sense of public service and support. Linux is a top-rate operating system accessible to everyone, free of charge.

As a way of introducing Linux, this chapter discusses Linux as an operating system, the history of Linux and Unix, and the overall design of Linux. The chapter also discusses how best to use this book. People often come to Linux with very different backgrounds. Some features may appear familiar, while others may seem completely alien. This book presents different features of Linux within an organized context that will provide you with a clear understanding of the Linux operating system, no matter what your background.

Operating Systems and Linux

An *operating system* is a program that manages computer hardware and software for the user. Operating systems were originally designed to perform repetitive hardware tasks. These tasks centered around managing files, running programs, and receiving commands from the user. You interact with an operating system through a user interface. This user interface allows the operating system to receive and interpret instructions sent by the user. You only need to send an instruction to the operating system to perform a task, such as reading a file or printing a document. An operating system's user interface can be as simple as entering commands on a line, or as complex as selecting menus and icons.

An operating system also manages software applications. To perform different tasks, such as editing documents or performing calculations, you need specific software applications. An editor is an example of a software application. An editor allows you to edit a document, making changes and adding new text. The editor itself is a program consisting of instructions to be executed by the computer. To use the program, it must first be loaded into computer memory, and then its instructions executed. The operating system controls the loading and execution of all programs, including any software applications. When you want to use an editor, you simply instruct the operating system to load the editor application and execute it.

File management, program management, and user interaction are traditional features common to all operating systems. Linux, like all versions of Unix, adds two more features. Linux is a multiuser and multitasking system. As a multitasking system, you can ask the system to perform several tasks at the same time. While one task is being done, you can work on another. For example, you can edit a file while another file is being printed. You do not have to wait for the other file to finish printing before you edit. As a multiuser system, several users can log into the system at the same time, each interacting with the system through his or her own terminal.

Operating systems were originally designed to support hardware efficiency. When computers were first developed, their capabilities were limited and the operating system had to make the most of them. In this respect, operating systems were designed with the hardware in mind, not the user. Operating systems tended to be rigid and inflexible, forcing the user to conform to the demands of hardware efficiency.

Linux, on the other hand, is designed to be flexible, reflecting its Unix roots. As a version of Unix, Linux shares the same flexibility designed for Unix, a flexibility stemming from Unix's research origins. The Unix operating system was developed by Ken Thompson at AT&T Bell Laboratories in the late 1960s and early 1970s. It incorporated many new developments in operating system design. Originally, Unix was designed as an operating system for researchers. One major goal was to create a system that could support the researchers' changing demands. To do this, Thompson had to design a system that could deal with many different kinds of tasks. Flexibility became more important than hardware efficiency. Like Unix, Linux has the advantage of being able to deal with the variety of tasks any user may face.

This flexibility allows Linux to be an operating system that is accessible to the user. The user is not confined to limited and rigid interactions with the operating system. Instead, the operating system is thought of as providing a set of highly effective tools that the user can make use of. This user-oriented philosophy means that you can configure and program the system to meet your specific needs. With Linux, the operating system becomes an *operating environment*.

History of Linux and Unix

As a version of Unix, the history of Linux naturally begins with Unix. The story begins in the late 1960s when there was a concerted effort to develop new operating system techniques. In 1968, a consortium of researchers from General Electric, AT&T Bell Laboratories, and the Massachusetts Institute of Technology carried out a special operating system research project called Multics. Multics incorporated many new concepts in multitasking, file management, and user interaction. In 1970, Ken Thompson and Dennis Ritchie of AT&T Bell Laboratories developed the Unix operating system, incorporating many of the features of the Multics research project. He tailored the system for the needs of a research environment, designing it to run on minicomputers. From its inception, Unix was an affordable and efficient multiuser and multitasking operating system.

The Unix system became popular at Bell Labs as more and more researchers started using the system. In 1973, Dennis Ritchie collaborated with Ken Thompson to rewrite the programming code for the Unix system in the C programming language. Dennis Ritchie, a fellow researcher at Bell Labs, developed the C programming language as a flexible tool for program development. One of the advantages of C is that it can directly access the hardware architecture of a computer with a generalized set of programming commands. Up until this time, an operating system had to be specially rewritten in a hardware-specific assembly language for each type of computer. The C programming language allowed Dennis Ritchie and Ken Thompson to write only one version of the Unix operating system that could then be compiled by C compilers on different computers. In effect, the Unix operating system became transportable—able to run on a variety of different computers with little or no reprogramming.

Unix gradually grew from one person's tailored design to a standard software product distributed by many different vendors, such as Novell and IBM. Initially, Unix was treated as a research product. The first versions of Unix were distributed free to the computer science departments of many noted universities. In 1972, Bell Labs began issuing official versions of Unix and licensing the system to different users. One of these users was the computer science department of the University of California, Berkeley. Berkeley added many new features to the system that later became standard. In 1975, Berkeley released its own version of Unix known by its distribution arm, Berkeley Software Distribution (BSD). This BSD version of Unix became a major contender to the AT&T Bell Labs version. Other independently developed versions of Unix sprouted up. In 1980, Microsoft developed a PC version of Unix called Xenix. AT&T developed several research versions of Unix, and in 1983 they released the first commercial version, called System 3. This was later followed by System V, which became a seriously supported commercial software product.

At the same time, the BSD version of Unix was developing through several releases. In the late 1970s, BSD Unix became the basis of a research project by the Department of Defense's Advanced Research Projects Agency (DARPA). As a result, Berkeley released a powerful version of Unix called BSD release 4.2. It included sophisticated file management as well as networking features based on TCP/IP network protocols—the same protocols now used for the Internet. BSD release 4.2 was widely distributed and adopted by many vendors such as Sun Microsystems.

The proliferation of different versions of Unix led to a need for a Unix standard. Software developers had no way of knowing what versions of Unix their programs would actually run on. In the mid-1980s, two competing standards emerged, one based on the AT&T version of Unix, and the other on the BSD version. In bookstores today you will see many different books on Unix for one or the other version. Some specify System V Unix, others focus on BSD Unix.

AT&T moved Unix to a new organization, called Unix System Laboratories, that could focus on developing a standard system, integrating the different major versions of Unix. In 1991, Unix System Laboratories developed System V release 4, which incorporated almost all the features found in System V release 3, BSD release 4.3, SunOS, and Xenix. In response to System V release 4, several other companies, such as IBM and Hewlett-Packard, established the Open Software Foundation (OSF) to create their own standard version of Unix. There were then two commercial standard versions of Unix—the OSF version and System V release 4. In 1993 AT&T sold off its interest in Unix to Novell. Unix System Laboratories became part of Novell's UNIX System's Group. Novell issued its own versions of Unix based on System V release 4, called UnixWare, designed to interact with Novell's NetWare system. Unix System Laboratories is currently owned by the Santa Cruz Operation. With Solaris, Sun has introduced System V release 4 onto its Sun systems. Two competing graphical user interfaces (GUIs) for Unix, called Motif and OpenLook, have been merged into a new desktop standard called the Common Desktop Environment (CDE).

Throughout much of its development, Unix remained a large and demanding operating system requiring a workstation or minicomputer to be effective. Several versions of Unix were designed primarily for the workstation environment. SunOS was developed for Sun workstations, and AIX was designed for IBM workstations.

However, as personal computers became more powerful, efforts were made to develop a PC version of Unix. Xenix and System V/386 are commercial versions of Unix designed for IBM-compatible PCs. AUX is a Unix version that runs on the Macintosh. It is a testament to Unix's inherent portability that it can be found on almost any type of computer: workstations, minicomputers, and even supercomputers. This inherent portability made possible an effective PC version of Unix.

Linux is designed specifically for Intel-based personal computers. It started out as a personal project of a computer science student named Linus Torvald at the University of Helsinki. At that time, students were making use of a program called Minix that highlighted different Unix features. Minix was created by Professor Andrew Tannebaum and widely distributed over the Internet to students around the world. Linus' intention was to create an effective PC version of Unix for Minix users. He called it Linux, and in 1991 released version 0.11. Linux was widely distributed over the Internet, and in the following years other programmers refined and added to it, incorporating most of the applications and features now found in standard Unix systems. All the major window managers have been ported to Linux. Linux has all the Internet utilities, such as ftp, telnet, and slip. It also has a full set of program development utilities, such as C++ compilers and debuggers. Given all its features, the Linux operating system remains small, stable, and fast. In its simplest format, it can run effectively on just 4MB of memory.

Though Linux has developed in the free and open environment of the Internet, it adheres to official Unix standards. Due to the proliferation of Unix versions in the previous decades, the Institute of Electrical and Electronics Engineers (IEEE) developed an independent Unix standard for the American National Standards Institute (ANSI). This new ANSI standard Unix is called the Portable Operating System Interface for Computer Environments (POSIX). The standard defines how a Unix-like system needs to operate, specifying details such as system calls and interfaces. POSIX defines a universal standard that all Unix versions must adhere to. Most popular versions of Unix are now POSIX compliant. Linux was developed from the beginning according to the POSIX standard.

Linux Overview

Like Unix, Linux can be generally divided into four major components: the kernel, the shell, the file structure, and the utilities. The *kernel* is the core program that runs programs and manages hardware devices such as disks and printers. The *shell* provides an interface for the user. It receives commands from the user and sends those commands to the kernel for execution. The *file structure* organizes the way files are stored on a storage device such as a disk. Files are organized into directories. Each directory may contain any number of subdirectories, each holding files.

Together, the kernel, the shell, and the file structure form the basic operating system structure. With these three you can run programs, manage files, and interact with the system. In addition, Linux has software programs called utilities that have come to be considered standard features of the system. The *utilities* are specialized programs, such as editors, compilers, and communications programs, that perform standard computing operations. You can even create your own utilities.

Shell: Bourne, Korn, and C-Shell

The shell provides an interface between the kernel and the user. It can be described as an interpreter. It interprets commands entered by the user and sends them to the kernel. The shell interface is very simple. It usually consists of a prompt at which you type a command and then press ENTER. In a sense, you are typing the command on a line; this line is often referred to as the *command line*. You will find that the commands entered on the command line can become very complex.

As an alternative to a command line interface, Linux provides a graphical user interface (GUI) called X-Windows that has several window managers for you to use. A window manager operates much like the Windows and Mac GUIs. You have windows, icons, and menus, all managed through mouse controls. Two of the more popular window managers are the Free Virtual Window Manager (fvwm) and the OpenLook window manager (olwm). The Motif window manager is also available, but Motif is a proprietary program that you have to purchase separately. In addition to window managers, you will also need to use file and program managers. There are several different file and program managers available, and many Linux vendors supply their own. For example, the OpenLinux system included with this text provides a sophisticated file manager and program manager, making use of icon bars and directory folders.

Though a window manager makes for a flexible and engaging interface, keep in mind that it is really just a front for the shell. The window manager simply passes off the commands it receives to the shell. It is the shell that actually interprets the command and sends it to the kernel. Figure 1-1 shows the relationship of the shell to the kernel and other system components.

The shell does more than just interpret commands; it provides an environment that you can configure and program. The shell also has its own programming language that allows you to write programs that execute Linux commands in complex ways. The shell programming language has many of the features of normal programming languages, such as loop and branch control structures. You can even create complex shell programs that are as powerful as many applications programs.

Each user on a Linux system has his or her own user interface, or shell. Users can tailor their shells to their own special needs. In this sense, a user's shell functions more as an operating environment, which the user can control.

Over the years, several different kinds of shells have been developed. Currently, there are three major shells: Bourne, Korn, and C-shell. The Bourne shell was developed at Bell Labs for System V. The C-shell was developed for the BSD version of Unix. The Korn shell is a further enhancement of the Bourne shell. Current versions of Unix, including Linux, incorporate all three shells, which allows you to choose the one you prefer. However, Linux uses enhanced or public domain versions of these shells: the

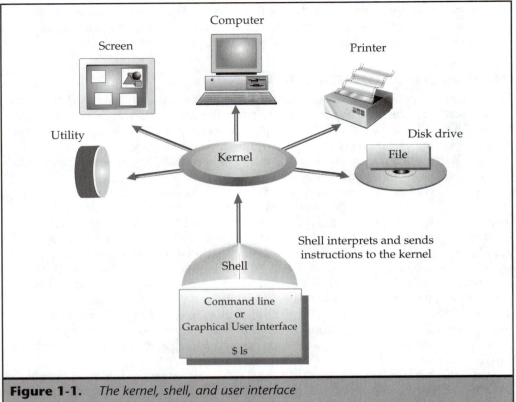

Figure 1-1. *The kernel, shell, and user interface*

Bourne Again shell, the TC-shell, and the Public Domain Korn shell. When you start your Linux system, you will be placed in the Bourne Again shell, an updated version of the Bourne shell. From there you can switch to other shells as you wish.

File Structure: Directories and Files

In Linux, files are organized into directories, much as they are in DOS. However, unlike DOS, you have much more flexibility and control over your files. The entire Linux file system is one large interconnected set of directories, each containing files. Some directories are standard directories reserved for system use. You can create your own directories for your own files, as well as easily move files from one directory to another. You can even move entire directories and share directories and files with other users on your system. With Linux, you can also set permissions on directories and files, allowing others to access them or restricting access to you alone.

The directories of each user are in fact ultimately connected to the directories of other users. Directories are organized into a hierarchical tree structure, beginning with an initial root directory. All other directories are ultimately derived from this first root directory. Figure 1-2 shows an example of this treelike, hierarchical file structure. You can actually travel throughout the system, entering any directory that may be open to you. This interconnectivity of the file structure makes it easy to share data. Several users could access the same files.

The root directory is a special directory that you will need to make use of when you first set up your Linux system. Linux is a multiuser system. You could have several users sharing the same operating system. However, the operating system itself resides in programs placed in special directories beginning with the root directory. These are sometimes referred to as *system directories*. In Figure 1-2, the system directories are those just below the root: man, bin and usr. There are many others. System directories are described in Chapter 5.

Utilities: Editors, Filters, and Communications

Linux contains a great number of utilities. Some utilities perform simple operations; others are complex programs with their own sets of commands. To begin with, many utilities can be classified into three general categories: editors, filters, and communications programs. Of course, not all utilities fit these categories. There are also utilities that perform file operations and program management.

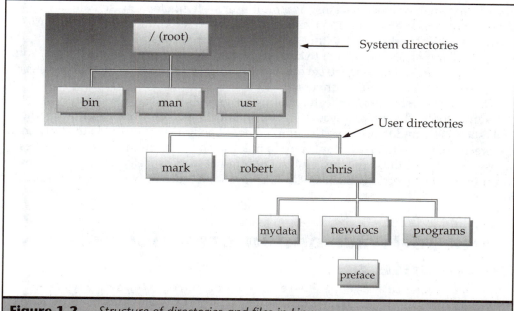

Figure 1-2.   *Structure of directories and files in Linux*

There are several standard editors available on all Unix versions, including Linux: Ed, Ex, Vi, and Emacs. Ed and Ex are line editors, whereas Vi and Emacs are full-screen editors. All the standard editors were developed for early, less powerful machines that could not handle full-screen cursor movement like today's PC word processors can. Even though Vi and Emacs have full-screen capability, they are not as fluid and easy to use as many mouse-driven word processors. Ed and Ex are line editors that display and edit only one line at a time. Even with these limitations, however, the editors are highly effective. They have a large set of commands that can be combined into complex operations.

Another set of utilities can best be described as filters. A *filter* reads input from either the user, a file, or some other source, examines and processes the data, and outputs the result. In this sense, they filter data that is passed through them. There are many different types of filters. Some use line editing commands to output edited versions of a file. Others search files for a pattern and output only that part of the data with the pattern. Still others perform word processing operations, detecting format commands in a file and outputting a formatted version of the file. The input for a filter does not have to be a file. It can be data input by the user from the keyboard. It can also be the output of another filter. Filters can be connected together, whereby the output of one filter can become the input of another filter, and so on. It is even possible to program your own filters. A filter-programming language called awk enables you to write your own filters.

Linux also has a set of utilities that allow you to communicate with other users on your own system or other systems. As a multiuser system, Linux must maintain contact with and keep track of all users. The basic need for monitoring and the basic interconnectivity of the file structure make an electronic mail system easy to implement. Messages can be sent to and received from other users on the system. You can even broadcast a message to several users at once, or directly connect to another user and carry on a real-time conversation.

One of the most important features of Linux, as well as all Unix systems, is its set of Internet tools. The Internet was designed and developed on Unix systems. Internet tools such as ftp and telnet were first implemented on BSD versions of Unix. Darpanet, the precursor to the Internet, was set up to link Unix systems at different universities across the nation. Linux contains a full set of Internet tools as well as those providing direct Internet connections, such as slip. Web Browsers, such as Netscape, are available for Linux.

Linux Software and Information Sources on the Internet

Linux was developed as a cooperative effort over the Internet. No company or institution controls Linux. Development often takes place when Linux users decide to work on a project together. When completed, the software is posted at an ftp site on the Internet. Any Linux user can then access the site and download the software.

Software can be in the form of source code that you need to compile, or binary files that are ready to run. Software packages usually include documentation and configuration files. OpenLinux makes use of a special installation utility called the Redhat Package Manager (RPM). You can install an RPM package, with all its documentation and configuration files, using one simple **rpm -i** command (see Chapter 3). Most current software is available in RPM packages. A great many of these RPM packages can be found at **ftp.redhat.com/pub/contrib/i386**. You should always check here first for the RPM version of the software you want. One of the major ftp sites for both Linux software and documentation is **sunsite.unc.edu** in the directory **/pub/Linux**. Homesites are where Linux software is originally posted. Mirror sites are copies of these homesites. Both **ftp.caldera.com** and **ftp.redhat.com** maintain extensive archives of Linux documentation and software. Table 1-1 lists different ftp sites. You can find other sites through resource pages that hold links to other Web sites, for example, the Linux on the World Wide Web at **www.ssc.com/linux/ resources/web.html**. Of particular interest is the Linux Game Tome listing most of the popular games available for Linux. In Chapter 3, Table 3-2 lists several Resource pages.

Most Linux software is copyrighted under a GNU public license provided by the Free Software Foundation, and is often referred to as GNU software. GNU software is distributed free provided it is freely distributed to others. GNU software has proven to be very reliable and effective. Many of the popular Linux utilities such as C compilers, shells, and editors are all GNU software applications. You will find installed with your Caldera OpenLinux system the GNU C++ and Lisp compilers, Vi and Emacs editors, BASH and TCSH shells, as well as Tex and Ghostscript document formatters. Many other GNU software applications are available at different ftp sites on the Internet listed in Table 1-2. Chapter 7 describes in detail the process of downloading software applications from Internet sites and installing them on your system.

Lately, major software companies are also developing Linux versions of their most popular applications. Netscape provides a Linux version of their popular Web Browser that you can download from the Caldera ftp site at **ftp.caldera.com**. There is also a Linux version of Sun's Java available through **ftp.blackdown.org**. A Linux version of WordPerfect is also available.

Linux documentation has also been developed over the Internet. Much of the documentation currently available for Linux can be downloaded from Internet ftp sites. A special Linux project called the Linux Documentation Project headed by Matt Welsh is currently developing a complete set of Linux manuals. The documentation, at its current level, is available at this URL: **http://sunsite.unc.edu/mdw**. The documentation includes a user's guide, an introduction, and administration guides. They are available in text, PostScript, or Web page format. Table 1-3 lists these guides. You can find briefer explanations in what are referred to as HOW-TO documents. HOW-TO documents are available for different subjects such as installation, printing, and email. The documents are available at Linux ftp sites usually in the directory **/pub/Linux/doc/HOW-TO**.

You can find a listing of different Linux information sites in the file META-FAQ located at Linux ftp sites, usually in the directory **/pub/Linux/doc**. On the same site and directory, you can also download the Linux Software Map, LSM. This is a listing of most of the software currently available for Linux. Also, many software companies have Web sites that provide information about their Linux applications. Some of these are listed in Table 1-4.

In addition to ftp sites, there are also Linux Usenet newsgroups. Through your Internet connection, you can access Linux newsgroups to read the comments of other Linux users and post messages of your own. There are several Linux newsgroups, each beginning with comp.os.linux. One of particular interest to the beginner is **comp.os.linux. help**, where you can post questions. Table 1-5 lists the different Linux newsgroups available on Usenet.

Most of the standard Linux software and documentation currently available is already included on your OpenLinux Lite CD-ROM. HOW-TO documents are all accessible in HTML format, so you can view them easily with your Web Browser. However, in the future, you may need to directly access Linux Internet sites for up-to-date information and software.

Currently, the only publication dealing with Linux is the *Linux Journal*. You can obtain information about it from the following address or at their Web site at **www.ssc.com/lg**

Linux Journal
P.O. Box 85867
Seattle, WA 98145
206-527-3385

Linux Releases

Although there is only one standard version of Linux, there are actually several different releases. Different companies and groups have packaged Linux and Linux software in slightly different ways. Each company or group then releases the Linux package, usually on a CD-ROM. Later releases may include updated versions of programs or new software. Some of the more popular releases are Slackware, Redhat, TAMU, Yggdrasil, and Infomagic. The OpenLinux Lite CD-ROM included in this text contains Caldera's complete OpenLinux Linux system. Several distributions, such as Caldera and Redhat, also offer their systems bundled with commercial software such as word processors or commercial Internet servers such as Netscape.

OpenLinux

The OpenLinux Lite CD-ROM included with this book contains Caldera's complete OpenLinux Linux system and software packages including all the GNU software packages, as well as the X-Windows window managers and Internet tools. It is POSIX compliant, adhering to Unix standards. Caldera distributes its OpenLinux system free of charge. The CD-ROM is only referred to as "lite" because Caldera also offers an extensive line of commercial and proprietary Linux packages that are not included here. Such proprietary, licensed software packages are not freely distributable. They include such products as WordPerfect, the Netscape Internet server, and the Novell Netware client. See the Caldera Web site at **www.caldera.com** for more information.

Summary: The Linux Operating System

Linux is a version of the Unix operating system that was developed by Linus Torvald for PCs with 386, 486, or Pentium processors. Linux is distinguished by its power and flexibility, bringing all the features of Unix, including multitasking and multiuser capabilities, to your PC. Linux is available free under a GNU public license. It is a carefully maintained operating system adhering to POSIX standards.

Your Linux software package includes not only the Linux operating system but also a series of software applications such as compilers and editors. It also includes the X-Windows GUI with several window managers, allowing you to use windows, icons, and menus to interact with the system.

The Linux system is made up of a kernel, the shell, a file structure, and utilities. The kernel is the heart of the system. It contains the control programs that directly manage the computer hardware. The shell is the user interface. The shell receives commands from the user and sends them to the kernel for execution. The shell can be tailored to an individual user's needs. The shell even has a programming language that can be used to program commands. The file structure consists of directories within which files are placed. Directories provide you with a convenient way to organize your files. You can move from one directory to another and set permissions on directories, opening up and sharing the files in them with other users.

A set of programs that is standard for the Linux system are commonly called utilities. Utilities can be generally categorized as editors, filters, or communications programs. Some of the editors, though powerful, are not as easy to use as many current PC editors. Filters are specialized utilities that receive data and generate a modified form of that data. Communications utilities allow you to send messages to and receive messages from other users. Internet tools allow you easy access to information services such as Usenet and the Web.

Linux ftp Sites	Directory	
sunsite.unc.edu	/pub/linux	
tsx-11.mit.edu	/pub/linux	
nic.funet.fi	/pub/os/linux	
Mirror Sites		
ftp.mcc.ac.uk	/pub/linux	Britain
ftp.ibp.fr	/pub/linux	France
ftp.dfv.rwth-aachen.de	/pub/linux	Germany
kirk.bu.oz.au	/pub/linux	Australia
ftp.uu.net	/systems/unix/linux	
ftp.stack.nl	/pub/linux	
ftp.caldera.com	/pub/linux	
ftp.redhat.com	/pub/	
ftp.cdrom.com	/pub/linux/	Concord, CA
ftp.siriuscc.com	/pub/linux/	Dallas, TX
lss.afit.af.mil	/pub/linux/	Dayton, OH
ftp.engr.uark.edu	/pub/linux/	Fayetteville, AR
ftp.spin.ad.jp	/pub/linux/sunsite.unc.edu/	Tokyo
ftp.funet.fi	/pub/linux/	
ftp.ba-mannheim.de	/pub/linux/	Mannheim
ftp.nuri.net	/pub/linux/	Seoul

Table 1-1. *Linux ftp Sites* (continued)

ftp and Web Sites	Applications
ftp://ftpredhat.com/pub/contrib/i386	Linux applications in RPM format (shareware)
ftp://ftp.ncsa.edu	Mosaic Web Browser and Web Server software for Linux
ftp://ftp4.netscape.com ftp://ftp.caldera.com	Netscape Web Browser for Linux
ftp://ftp.blackdown.org	Sun's Java Development Kit for Linux (link to mirror sites)
http://www.redhat.com	Applixware Office Suite
http://www.sdcorp.com/wplinux.htm	WordPerfect 7
http://www.caldera.com	Netscape Web Browser for Linux, Caldera Office Suite, StarOffice
http://sunscript.sun.com	Tk/Tcl Products
http://www.uk.linux.org/LxCommercial.html	Linux Commercial Vendors Index
http://www.xnet.com/~blatura/linapps.shtml	Linux Applications and Utilites Page

Table 1-2.   *Linux Applications*

Sites	Description
http://sunsite.unc.edu/mdw	LDP Web site
ftp://sunsite.unc.edu/pub/ Linux/docs/linux-doc-project	LDP ftp site
http://www.iki.fi/liw/linux/ sag/	System Administrators' Guide Homepage
ftp://sunsite.unc.edu/pub/ Linux/docs/HOWTO	LDP HOW-TO documents

Guides	Document Format and Web Sites
Linux Installation and Getting Started Guide	DVI, PostScript, and HTML (online)
Linux User's Guide	DVI, PostScript, and PDF
Linux System Administrator's Guide	DVI, PostScript, and HTML (online)
Linux Network Adiminstrator's Guide	DVI, PostScript, and HTML (online)
Linux Programmer's Guide	**linuxwww.db.erau.edu/LPG** (link through LDP Web site), DVI, PostScript, and HTML (online)
The Linux Kernel	DVI and PostScript
Linux Kernel Hacker's Guide	**www.redhat.com/** (link through LDP Web site), DVI, PostScript, and HTML (online)

Table 1-3. *Linux Documentation Project*

Web Site	Description
www.ssc.com/linux	Linux Resources Web site
www.caldera.com	Caldera Web site
www.redhat.com	Redhat Web site
sunsite.unc.edu/mdw	Web site for Linux Documentation Project
www.ssc.com/lg	Linux Journal
www.linux.org	Linux Organization
www.li.org	Linux International Web site
www.uk.linux.org	Linux European Web site
www.blackdown.org	Web site for Linux Java
www.netscape.com	Netscape Web site
www.fokus.gmd.de/linux	Woven Goods for Linux
www.ssc.com/linux/resources/web.html	Linux on the World Wide Web

Table 1-4. *Web Sites*

Usenet Newsgroups	Description
comp.os.linux.announce	Announcements of Linux developments
comp.os.linux.devlopment.apps	For programmers developing Linux applications
comp.os.linux.devlopment.system	For programmers working on the Linux operating system
comp.os.linux.hardware	Linux hardware specifications
comp.os.linux.admin	System administration questions
comp.os.linux.misc	Special questions and issues
comp.os.linux.setup	Installation problems
comp.os.linux.answers	Answers to command problems
comp.os.linux.help	Questions and answers for particular problems
comp.os.linux.networking	Linux network questions and issues

Table 1-5. *Usenet Newsgroups*

Chapter Two

Installing Linux

This chapter describes the installation procedure for the OpenLinux Lite provided on the enclosed CD-ROM. The installation includes the Linux operating system, a great many Linux applications, and a complete set of Internet servers. Different Linux distributions usually have their own installation programs. For example, the Slackware distribution of Linux uses a very different installation program from that of OpenLinux. The Caldera OpenLinux installation program is designed to be efficient and brief while installing as many features as possible. Certain features, such as Web Server support, would ordinarily require specialized and often complex configuration operations. The OpenLinux automatically installs and configures many of these features.

Installing Linux involves several steps. First, you need to determine whether your computer meets the basic hardware requirements. These days, most Intel-based PC computers do. Then you will have to look up certain technical specifications about the hardware you use, such as your monitor type and the type of chips used in your video card. This kind of information is available in the manuals that came with the hardware.

If you want to have your Linux system share a hard drive with another operating system, you may need to repartition your hard disk. There are several different options for partitioning your hard drive, depending on whether or not it already contains data you need to preserve.

You then need to prepare a boot disk with which you will start the installation program. Once the installation program begins, you simply follow the instructions, screen by screen. Most of the time you will only need to make simple selections or provide yes and no answers. The installation program progresses through several phases. First you create Linux partitions on your hard drive, then you install the software packages. After that you can configure your network connection, and then your X-Windows server for graphical user interface support. Both X-Windows and network configurations can be performed independently at a later time.

Once your system is installed, you are ready to start it and log in. You will be logging into a simple command line interface. From the command line, you can then invoke X-Windows, which will provide you with a full graphical user interface.

You have the option of installing just the operating system, the system with a standard set of applications, or all the software available on the CD-ROM. If you choose a standard installation you can add the uninstalled software packages later. Chapter 3 describes how you can use the **glint** utility or the Redhat Package Manager to install, or even uninstall, the software packages.

Hardware, Software, Information Requirements

Before installing Linux, you need to be sure that your computer meets certain minimum hardware requirements. You will also need certain software, namely, hard disk preparation programs such as fdisk. These are standard on all DOS systems and are also provided on your OpenLinux Lite CD-ROM. There is also certain specific information that you will need to have ready concerning your monitor, video card, mouse, and CD-ROM drive. All the requirements are presented in detail in the following sections. Be sure to read them carefully before you begin installation. During the installation program, you will need to provide responses based on the configuration of your computer.

Hardware Requirements

Listed here are the minimum hardware requirements for installing a Linux system:

- A 32-bit Intel-based personal computer. An Intel or compatible 80386, 80486, or Pentium microprocessor is required. Both SX and DX CPUs are acceptable.
- A 3 1/2-inch floppy disk drive.
- At least 8MB RAM, though 16MB are recommended.
- At least 300MB free hard disk space; 300 to 400MB are recommended. You will need at least 750MB to load and make use of all the software packages on your OpenLinux CD-ROM. The Standard installation of basic software packages takes 212MB, plus 16 to 64MB for swap space. If you have less than 200MB, you can elect to perform a minimum install, installing only the Linux kernel without most of the applications. You could later install the applications you want one at a time.
- A 3 1/2-inch, DOS-formatted, high-density (HD) floppy disk, to be used to create a boot disk.
- A CD-ROM drive.
- Two empty DOS-formatted, 3 1/2-inch, high-density (HD) floppy disks.

If you plan to use the X-Windows graphical user interface, you will also need:

- A video graphics card.
- A mouse or other pointing device.

Software Requirements

There are only a few software requirements. Basically, you need an operating system from which you can create your Linux boot disk, and if you plan to have both DOS and Linux on the same hard drive, you will need DOS partition software. Accordingly, if you have OS/2, you will need OS/2 partition software.

The operating system is required to allow you to prepare your installation disks. Using a DOS system, you can access the OpenLinux CD-ROM and issue DOS-like commands to create your installation disks. Any type of DOS will do, and you can even use the same commands on OS/2. However, you do not need DOS to run Linux. Linux is a separate operating system in its own right.

If you want to have Linux share your hard disk with another operating system, DOS for example, you will need certain utilities to prepare the hard disk for sharing. For DOS, you need either the defrag and fips utilities or the fdisk utility. The fips utility is provided on your OpenLinux CD-ROM. It will perform a nondestructive partition of your hard disk, freeing up space for your Linux system. Defrag and fdisk are standard DOS utilities, usually located in your **dos** directory. Defrag is used with fips to defragment your hard disk before fips partitions it. There are, of course, other commercial utilities that can also perform the required defragmentation. Fdisk is an alternative to fips that performs a destructive partition, erasing everything on your hard disk and requiring a complete reformat and DOS installation.

Information Requirements

Part of adapting a powerful operating system like Linux to the PC entails making the most efficient use of the computer hardware at hand. To do so, Linux requires specific information about the computer components that it is dealing with. For example, special Linux configuration files are tailored to work with special makes and models of video cards and monitors. Before installing Linux, you will need to have such information on hand. The information is usually available in the manual that came with your hardware peripherals or computer.

CD-ROM, Hard Disk, and Mouse Information

If you have a SCSI CD-ROM drive, you will need the manufacturer's name and model. If you have an IDE CD-ROM drive, just make note of that fact.

Decide how much of your hard drive (in megabytes) you want to dedicate to your Linux system. If you are sharing with DOS, decide how much you want for DOS and how much for Linux.

Decide how much space you want for your swap partition. Your swap partition must be between 16MB and 64MB, with 32MB appropriate for most systems. It is used by Linux as an extension of your computer's RAM.

Find the make and model of the mouse you are using. Linux supports both serial and bus mice. Most mice are supported, including Microsoft, Logitech, and Mouse Systems.

Know what time zone you are in. If your computer is directly connected to the Internet, you may want to use Greenwich mean time (GMT) as your time zone. If, however, you are using a stand-alone computer that also runs DOS, you may want to use a local time zone.

Know which serial port your mouse is using: COM1, COM2, or none if you use the PS/2 mouse port.

Video and Monitor Information

You have the following information about your video card and monitor. X-Windows already has settings for most video cards, so you may not need to use the video card information. However you will absolutely need the monitor information including the vertical and horizontal refresh rates.

Video Card Information:

- What is the make and model of your video card?
- What chipset does your video card use?
- How much memory is on your video card?

Monitor Information:

- What is the manufacturer and model of your monitor? Linux supports several monitors. If yours is not one of them, you can choose a generic profile, or you can enter information for a custom profile. To do that, you will need the following information:

  - The horizontal refresh rate in Hz
  - The vertical refresh rate in Hz

Network Configuration Information

Except for deciding your hostname, you do not have to configure your network during installation. You can put it off to a later time and use the netcfg utility to perform network configuration. However, if the information is readily available, the installation procedure will automatically configure your network, placing needed entries in the appropriate configuration files. If you are on a network, you will have to obtain most of this information from your network administrator. If you are using an Internet service provider, they should provide you with much of this information. If you are setting up a network yourself, you will have to determine each piece of information. The installation program will prompt you to enter in these values:

- Decide on a name for your computer (this is called a hostname). Your computer will be identified by this name on the Internet.
- Your domain name.
- The IP (Internet Protocol) address assigned to your machine. Every host on the Internet is assigned an IP address. This address is a set of four numbers, separated by periods, which uniquely identifies a single location on the Internet, allowing information from other locations to reach that computer.
- Your network IP address. This address is usually the same as the IP address, but with an added 0.
- The netmask. This is usually 255.255.255.0 for class C IP addresses. If, however, you are part of a large network, check with your network administrator.
- The broadcast address for your network. Usually, your broadcast address is the same as your IP address with the number 255 added at the end.

- If you have a gateway, you will need the gateway (router) IP address for your network.
- The IP address of any nameservers that your network uses.
- NIS domain and IP address if your network uses an NIS server.

Upgrade Information for Already Installed Linux Systems

If you already have installed another version of Linux such as the Caldera Network Desktop or Redhat, you may have personalized your system with different settings that you would like to keep. These settings are held in configuration files that you can save to a floppy disk and then use on your new OpenLinux system, in effect, retaining your original configuration (if you use **mcopy** be sure to use the **-t** option). There also may be directories and files of data you may want to preserve such as Web pages used for a Web site. You may also want to save copies of software packages you have downloaded. For these and for large directories it is best to use the following **tar** operation.

```
tar cvMf /dev/fd0  directory-or-package
```

Make copies of the following configuration files and any other files you want to restore. You only need to copy the ones you want to restore.

Files	Description
/etc/XF86Config	X-Windows configuration file
/etc/lilo.conf	Boot manager configuration file
/etc/hosts	IP addresses of connected systems
/etc/resolv.conf	Domain name server addresses
/etc/fstab	File systems mounted on your system
/etc/passwd	Names and passwords of all users on your system
/home/user	Any home directories of users with their files on your sytem, where *user* is the user name. (For a large number of files use **tar cfM/dev/fd0/home/user**)
.netscape	Each home directory has its own **.netscape** subdirectory with Netscape configuration files such as your bookmark entries
Web site pages and ftp files	You may want to save any pages used for a Web site or files on an ftp site you are running. On CND versions these are located at **/home/httpd/** and **/home/ftpd**

Once you have installed OpenLinux you can mount the floppy disk and copy the saved files from the floppy to your system, overwriting those initially set up. If you use the **/etc/XF86Config** file from your previous system, you will not have to run XF86Setup to set up X-Windows. The **/etc/XF86Config** file includes all the X-Window setup information.

If you want to restore the **/etc/lilo.conf** file from your previous system, you will also have to install it using the following command.

```
# lilo /etc/lilo.conf
```

To restore archives that you saved on multiple disks using the **tar** operation, place the first disk in the floppy drive and use the following command.

```
tar xvMf  /dev/fd0
```

Opening Disk Space for Linux Partitions

If you are using an entire hard drive for your Linux system or if you are upgrading a currently installed Linux system and want to use the same partitions, you can skip this section and go on to installing Linux. If, however, your Linux system is going to share a hard drive with your DOS system, you will need to partition and format your hard drive so that part of it is used for DOS and the remaining part is free for Linux installation. How you go about this process depends on the current state of your hard disk. If you have a new hard disk and you are going to install both DOS and Linux on it, you only need to be sure to install DOS on only part of the hard drive, leaving the rest free for Linux. However, if you are already using this hard disk, you must either delete partitions you already have or repartition your entire hard disk, leaving part of it free for Linux. The objective in each situation is to free up space for Linux. When you install Linux, you will then partition and format that free space for use by Linux.

A hard disk is organized into partitions. The partitions are further formatted to the specification of a given operating system. When you installed DOS, you first needed to divide your hard disk into different partitions. You then used the DOS format operation to format each partition into a DOS disk, each identified by a letter. For example, you may have divided your disk into two partitions, one formatted as the C disk and the other as the D disk. Alternatively, you may have divided your hard disk into just one partition and formatted it as the C disk. In order to share your hard drive with Linux, you will need to free up some space by either reducing their size or deleting some of those partitions.

First, decide how much space you will need for your Linux system. You will probably need a minimum of 300MB, though more is recommended. As stated earlier, the basic set of Linux software packages takes up 212MB, whereas the entire set of software packages, including all their source code file, takes 667MB. In addition, you will need space for a Linux swap partition used to implement virtual memory. This takes between 16 and 32MB. At 300MB, you could install the basic package and have about 85MB for your own use, though you will quickly find this too limited if you need to install any other software packages. A more practical minimum would be 400MB to 500MB.

Once you have determined the space you need for your Linux system, you can then set about freeing up that space on your hard drive. Depending on how your hard disk is partitioned, you will have to take slightly different steps to free up this space. If you have several partitions already, you will probably only need to delete a few of them.

To see what options are best for you, you should first determine what your partitions are and their sizes. You can do this with the fdisk utility. To start this utility, enter **fdisk** at the DOS prompt, and press ENTER.

```
C:\> fdisk
```

This brings up the menu of fdisk options. Choose option 4 to display a list of all your current partitions and the size of each. You can determine whether you need either to reduce or repartition your disk, or whether you can get away with just deleting some unused partitions.

If you have only a couple or just one large partition covering the entire disk, you have two options. You can use the DOS defrag and Linux fips utilities to nondestructively create free space from unused space on your hard drive. You should still make a backup of your important data for safety's sake. But you would not have to reinstall DOS and restore your backups. Everything would be preserved. Alternatively, you can repartition your entire disk, erasing all your data. You will then have to reinstall DOS and restore your data from backups, as well as reformat your hard drive. If you are installing a new hard drive on which you want to have both DOS and Linux, you would follow the same steps for repartitioning your disk, though you will not need to delete any partitions, since you would have none to begin with.

Deleting Partitions

In most cases a user will have several partitions on the hard drive. If you have DOS partitions that are rarely used or have very little data on them, you may consider deleting them to free up space for your Linux system. In this case, simply determine how many and which ones you want to delete. Deleting a partition will erase all the data on it, so be sure to back up any data first. Partitions are of fixed size, so you could end up with more space than you need. If this happens you could just add a new DOS partition of a smaller size.

Bear in mind that there is a critical difference between a DOS partition and a Linux partition. If you already have a Linux system on your disk and you want to remove those Linux partitions to install a new system, you must use the Linux fdisk utility, not

DOS' fdisk. A Linux partition can only be safely removed by the Linux fdisk utility located on your Linux CD-ROM.

To delete partitions, first start the fdisk utility.

```
C:\> fdisk
```

From the fdisk menu, select option 3, "Delete partition or Logical DOS Drive." This will bring up a list of the current drives and prompt you to enter the number of the partition. Each partition entry will list the type, volume label, and the number of megabytes it uses. Do not delete a partition whose type is PRI DOS. This is usually the first partition. A safe bet is to start with the last partition.

After entering a partition's number, you will be prompted for the volume label. (The volume label is listed in the partition entry on the fdisk menu.) When you are asked to confirm, type **y** to delete the partition. If you then go back and select option 4, "Display partition information," you will see that the partition is gone and in its place is an entry specifying free space. This tells you how much free space is open for Linux to use.

If you need more space, you can delete another partition by repeating the previous steps. With each partition you delete, you will increase your free space. If deleting a partition has freed up too much space, you can use the Add option in the fdisk menu to add a new smaller DOS partition.

To add a partition, select the Partition Creation option in the fdisk menu. This displays the Partition Creation menu, from which you then select the Extended DOS Partition option, option 2. You will be prompted to set the size of the partition. After adding the partition, check the listing of partitions by selecting the fourth item in the fdisk options menu. The last entry will specify the amount of free space. Be sure you leave enough for your Linux system.

Nondestructive Repartition

If you already have a large amount of data and programs on your PC that you don't want to have to reinstall, you can attempt a nondestructive repartition using the defrag and fips utilities. You should, however, back up your data just as a precaution. To perform a nondestructive partition, you first need to know if you already have enough unused space on your hard drive that can be used for Linux. If you do not, you will have to delete some files. You can use **chkdsk** on each of the drives on your hard drive to see how much space is available. See if they add up to as much or more free space needed for Linux. If not, delete some unwanted files and check again, and repeat until you have enough space.

When DOS creates and saves files, it places them in different sectors on your hard disk. Your files are spread out across your hard disk with a lot of empty space in between. This has the effect of fragmenting the remaining unused space into smaller sections, separated by files. The defrag utility performs a defragmentation process that moves all the files into adjoining space on the hard disk, thereby leaving all the unused space as one large continuous segment. Once you have defragmented your disk, you can use the fips utility to create free space using part or all of the unused space. Fips is a version of fdisk designed to detect continuous unused space and delete it from its current DOS partition, opening unpartitioned free space that can then be used by Linux. All your DOS partitions and drives remain intact with all their data and programs. They are just smaller.

To run the defrag utility, enter the command **defrag**. This is a DOS command usually found in the **dos** directory.

```
C:\>  dos\defrag
```

Defrag will display a screen with colored blocks representing the different sectors on your hard disk. It will carry out an optimization of your hard disk, moving all your used sectors, your data and programs, together on the hard disk. This may take a few minutes. When complete, you will see the used sectors arranged together on the screen. You can then exit the defrag utility.

Now you are ready to run the fips utility to actually free up space. Fips is located on your Linux CD-ROM, also in the directory named **\col\tools\fips15**. Change to your CD-ROM drive and run the fips utility. In the following example, the CD-ROM drive is drive E.

```
C:\> e:
E:\> \col\tools\fips15\fips
```

Fips will display a screen showing the amount of free space. Use your arrow keys to make the space smaller if you do not need all your free space for Linux. You should leave some free space for your DOS programs. Then press ENTER to free the space.

Destructive Repartitioning of Your Entire Hard Drive

Instead of reducing your current DOS partitions, you could just eliminate them and start over from scratch. This process destructively partitions your hard disk, erasing all data on your hard drive. There are several situations in which you may want to do this.

The fips utility simply reduces the size of the partitions that you have; it does not eliminate any. If you have several partitions, you could end up with a lot of small partitions, whereas you may prefer a few larger partitions. If you want larger partitions, you must destructively repartition your disk, creating all new ones. You could then restore your DOS system and data from backups.

If you have a new hard drive that you just bought and are now installing, you will need to perform the same steps for destructively partitioning the hard drive (of course, without any backup or restoration of data, since with a new hard drive there is no data yet).

If you are using most of your hard drive already and there would be a great many files to erase to open up space for fips to work, you could just back up your files and then destructively repartition your hard disk. You could then later restore only those files you want.

Before you partition your entire disk, you need to back up any data to floppies or tape. Having done that, you are ready to destructively partition your disk. Again, be warned that partitioning your hard drive will erase all data on that hard drive.

The next steps describe how you create a DOS boot disk with the format and fdisk utilities. First, insert a blank floppy disk into your floppy disk drive. Use the **format** command and the option **/s** to format the disk and copy the system files to it at the same time. Be sure to specify the letter of the floppy drive; in the next example it is the A drive. Copy the **command.com**, **format.com**, and **fdisk.exe** files to the A drive. Both format and fdisk are in the **dos** directory.

```
C:\> format a: /s
C:\> copy command.com  a:
C:\> copy dos/format.com  a:
C:\> copy dos/fdisk.exe  a:
```

You now have a DOS boot disk. Restart your computer with the DOS boot disk in your floppy drive. The system will boot from that disk instead of your hard disk. You will see the A:\> prompt. Now you are ready to repartition your hard disk using fdisk. Enter the command:

```
A:\> fdisk
```

This will bring up the fdisk menu with its list of partition options. You can create, delete, or simply list your partitions.

If you are not installing a new hard disk, your hard disk will already contain partitions that you will first have to delete. In this case, select option 3 from the fdisk options menu to delete a partition. Your current partitions will be displayed, and you will be prompted to enter the number of the partition to be deleted. Then you will be prompted for the volume name. Next, you will be asked if you really want to delete it. Press **y**. You are then returned to the fdisk options menu. Select option 3 and repeat the previous steps to delete another partition. Continue this process until all your partitions are deleted. Each time you delete a partition, you will notice the list of partitions becomes smaller and a new entry specifying free space becomes larger.

Once you have deleted all the partitions, you are ready to partition your hard disk with new DOS partitions, leaving enough free space for your Linux partitions. Select option 1 from the fdisk options menu to add a partition. This will give a menu specifying three different types of partitions: a primary DOS partition, an extended DOS partition, and a logical DOS partition. Your first partition has to be a primary DOS partition, so enter 1 as your choice.

You will then have to set this DOS partition as an active partition so it can be used to boot DOS. You select the second option from the fdisk menu, and then select partition 1 as an active partition.

Now you can add another partition. For added partitions, you should select the Extended DOS Partition option in the Partition Creation menu, option 2. After adding partitions, check the listing of partitions by selecting option 4 in the fdisk options menu. The last entry will specify the amount of free space. Be sure you leave enough for your Linux system.

Once you have finished partitioning the DOS part of your hard drive, you need to format those partitions. Use the **format** command with **/s** when formatting your primary partition so the system files will be copied to it and it can boot. The primary partition is usually labeled C.

```
A:\>  format c: /s
```

The remaining partitions can be formatted with a simple **format** command. The next example formats the partition labeled D.

```
A:\>  format d:
```

Once you have finished formatting the partitions, you can remove your boot disk and restart your computer. The computer will boot from your hard drive. You can now reinstall DOS and Windows, as well as any other data you backed up and any programs you have.

Creating the OpenLinux Install Disks

You will install OpenLinux Lite using an Install disk whose image is currently located on your OpenLinux CD-ROM. You first have to create the Install disk using that disk image. The Install disk has to be created on a computer that runs DOS. Begin by first starting your computer and entering **DOS**. Then perform the following steps.

1. Insert the OpenLinux Lite CD-ROM into your CD-ROM drive.

2. At your DOS prompt, change to your CD-ROM drive, using whatever the letter for that drive may be. For example, if your CD-ROM drive is the E: drive, just type **e:** and press ENTER.

```
C:\> e:
E:\>
```

3. Once you have changed to the CD-ROM drive you then need to change to the **\col\launch\floppy** directory. The Install disk images are there, as well as the **rawrite3** command you use to create the disks. You will need to copy two disk images: **INSTALL.IMG** and **MODULES.IMG**. First change to that directory.

```
E:\> cd col\launch\floppy
E:\col\launch\floppy>
```

4. Now insert your blank DOS formatted 3 1/2-inch floppy diskette into your floppy drive.

5. Now start the **rawrite3** command. The **rawrite3** command will actually write the disk image to your floppy disk. **rawrite3** is a DOS command located in the **\col\launch\floppy** directory on the CD-ROM. The **rawrite3** command will first prompt you for the name of the disk image file you want to copy. Enter the full name of the **INSTALL.IMG** file. It will then ask you to enter the letter of the floppy drive where you put your floppy disk. On many systems this will be the **A** drive.

```
E:\col\launch\floppy > rawrite3
Enter source file name: INSTALL.IMG
Enter destination drive (A or B) and press enter: A
```

6. Press ENTER to confirm that you have a blank diskette in the drive. **rawrite3** will then copy the image file to your diskette, creating your install disk. When it finishes, remove your diskette from the floppy drive. This is the diskette that the Installation procedure described later refers to as the Install diskette.

Repeat the same process to make a disk of **MODULES.IMG**. The modules disk is only used to let you manually configure your hardware, should you need to.

Installing Linux

Installing Linux involves several processes, beginning with creating Linux partitions, then loading the Linux software, configuring your X-Windows interface, installing the Linux Loader (LILO) that will boot your system, and creating new user accounts. The installation program is a screen-based program that takes you through all these processes, step by step, as one continuous procedure. You will be able to use your mouse, as well as the arrow keys, SPACEBAR, and ENTER. You can always move back to the previous screen by pressing the ESC key. There is very little you have to do other than make selections and choose options. Some screens, such as the monitor screen, will provide a list of options from which you make a selection. Others will just ask you to choose YES or NO for which you can enter a **y** or **n**, or use the mouse click. In a few cases you will be asked for information you should already have if you followed the steps earlier in this chapter. For example, the video card screen in the X-Windows installation will present you with a list of graphics chips and ask you to select the chips used in your video card. The information you should have before you start is listed in the previous section on required information.

You are now ready to begin installation. The steps for each part of the procedure are delineated in the following sections. It should take you no more than an hour.

Booting the Computer and Creating Linux Partitions

If you followed the instructions in the first part of the chapter, you have freed up space on your hard drive and created your boot and root disks, and you are now ready to create your Linux partitions. To do this, you will need to boot your computer using the boot disk that you made earlier. When you start your computer, the installation program will begin, and through that you can access the Linux fdisk utility with which you will create your Linux partitions.

1. Insert the Linux boot disk into your floppy drive and reboot your computer. If your system also supports booting from your CD-ROM drive, you can boot directly from the OpenLinux Lite CD-ROM, instead of the boot diskette. It is best to perform a cold boot, turning off the computer completely and then turning it on again with the install disk in the floppy drive.

   The installation program will start, presenting you with an Introduction screen. After a moment, the following prompt will appear at the bottom of your screen:

   ```
   boot:
   ```

2. Press ENTER. If necessary, enter boot parameters as described on the screen. This may be needed if your CD-ROM is not being recognized. (See Appendix A.) Most systems will not need boot parameters.

Configuration information will fill your screen as the installation program attempts to detect your hardware components automatically. Should Linux have a problem identifying one of your components, that fact will be listed here. The auto-detection messages will fill up several screens. This information is, at this point, held by the installation program for you to examine. Check it to make sure the auto-detection procedure has correctly identified your hardware components. You can move back to a previous screen by holding down the left SHIFT key and pressing PAGE UP. Holding down the left SHIFT key and pressing PAGE DOWN moves you forward to the next page. Take note of the device name given to your CD-ROM. It will be something like hdc or sdc. If your hardware was not correctly detected, you may have to reboot and start over, reentering the appropriate hardware specifications at the boot prompt. For example, for an Ethernet card, you would enter the IRQ, port, starting address, ending address, and device. Appendix A lists the syntax for entering information for different devices.

3. If your system has Plug and Play cards, be sure to disable them at this point by entering **pnp**. Then press ENTER to continue. (Plug and Play cards will interfere with Linux installation.)

```
>>> init: press <Enter> to continue <<<
pnp
```

If you enter **pnp**, you will have to wait for your Plug and Play cards to be disabled. Then, the init prompt will be repeated, at which you press ENTER to continue.

4. A list of languages then appears. Choose a language and press ENTER.

5. A screen is displayed that shows a list of keyboards. Choose your keyboard from the list and press ENTER.

After a moment, a list of detected IDE and ATAPTI hardware is displayed. This screen provides a detailed description of all the hardware that the auto-detection process identified. Press ENTER to continue.

6. You are then asked if all the hardware has been correctly recognized. If all your hardware is correctly detected, select YES by pressing **y** to continue installation If not, you can select NO at the bottom of the screen. You then have the option to automatically attempt detection with the auto-probe utility or to manually detect unrecognized hardware. If you select NO to the auto-probing, then you will be placed in the Kernel Module Manager where you can load specific hardware modules used to detect and configure your hardware. In the Kernel Module Manager you first choose the type of hardware support you need and then choose a module you want loaded. If needed enter any hardware parameters. (See Appendix A.)

7. Next you are asked to create or change a Linux partition. The first time you install, you will have to create the Linux partition where your OpenLinux System is to be installed. Press **y** to choose YES to create a Linux partition. If you are upgrading a currently installed Linux system such as the Caldera Network Desktop or Redhat, you can use the partition you already have. The

partitions have to be a type 83, ext2, Linux partition. In this case, press **n** and continue on to format those partitions. Skip to step 11 and start installing OpenLinux.

8. A list of hard disks on your system is then displayed. Choose the hard disk where you want the partition. If you have more than one, use the arrow keys to move to the one you want. Press ENTER to continue.

9. You are then asked if you want to change your partition table. Press **y** to select YES.

You are now in the Linux fdisk program. You will be taking the free space that you created earlier and partitioning and formatting it for your Linux operating system. Or, if you are using your entire hard disk for Linux, you will be creating all the partitions for that hard disk.

You need to create two Linux partitions: The main partition and the swap partition. The partitions have different types that you need to specify. Linux fdisk is a line-oriented program. It has a set of one-character commands that you simply press. Then, you may be prompted to type in certain information and press ENTER. If you run into trouble during the fdisk procedure, you can press **q** at any time, and you will return to the previous screen without any changes having been made. No changes are actually made to your hard disk until you press **w**. This would be your very last command. It makes the actual changes to your hard disk and then quits fdisk, returning you to the installation program. Table 2-1 lists the commonly used fdisk commands.

Command	Action
a	Toggle a bootable flag
l	List known partition types
m	List of commands
n	Add a new partition
p	Print the partition table
q	Quit without saving changes
t	Change a partition's type
w	Write table to disk and exit

Table 2-1.   *List of Commonly Used fdisk Commands*

Perform the following steps to create your Linux partitions. You will first be creating the swap partition.

a. Press **p** to display your current partitions.

b. Press **n** to define a new partition.

You will be asked if it is a primary partition.

c. Press **p** to indicate that it is a primary partition.

d. Enter the partition number for the partition you are creating.

e. Enter the beginning cylinder for the partition. This is the first number in parentheses at the end of the prompt.

You are then prompted to enter the last cylinder number or size of the partition. This determines the size of the partition. Alternatively, you can enter the size in megabytes by entering a **+** before the number and an **M** after it; **+32M** specifies a partition of 32MB. In this case, you do not need to determine the last cylinder number.

f. Enter a size for the swap partition, between 16MB and 32MB.

g. Press **t** to indicate that you want to set the type for the Linux partition. Enter the partition number, and then at the Hex code prompt enter **82**. This is the type for the Linux swap partition.

h. Press **n** to define another new partition and **p** to mark it as a primary partition.

i. Enter the partition number for the partition you are creating.

j. Enter the beginning cylinder for the partition. This is the first number in parentheses at the end of the prompt.

k. You are then prompted to enter the last cylinder number. You can either enter the last cylinder you want for this partition or enter a size. You can enter the size as **+300M** for 300MB. Remember that a standard install uses at least 300MB. Anywhere from 300MB to 400MB would be appropriate, though, if you have the space, you can make it larger. Bear in mind that the size cannot exceed your free space. Also, recall that the full package with all source code files will take 664MB. The default type for a Linux partition is 83. You will not have to set it.

l. Press **w** to write out the changes to the hard disk, and then ENTER to continue.

The following is a sample run of the fdisk program, showing you the interface and the commands you will need to use to create your partitions. When specifying the size of main Linux partitions you can specify a cylinder number as shown in this example, or just the size you want with a preceding **+**, such as **+500** for a 500MB partition. Notice that when you are prompted to enter the first cylinder, the first available cylinder is listed in the prompt. You can use that (205 and then 238 in this example).

```
Command (m for help): p

Disk /dev/hda: 32 heads, 63 sectors, 827 cylinders
Units = cylinders of 2016 * 512 bytes

    Device Boot    Begin    Start    End    Blocks    Id    System
/dev/hda1            1        1      204    205600+   6     DOS 16-bit
                                                            >=32M

/dev/hda4          537      537      826    292320    5     Extended
/dev/hda6          543      543      826    286240+   6     DOS 16-bit
                                                            >=32M

Command (m for help): n
Command action
   l    logical (5 or over)
   p    primary partition (1-4)
p
Partition number (1-4): 2
First cylinder (205-827): 205
Last cylinder or +size or +sizeM or +sizeK ([205]-536): +32

Command (m for help): n
Command action
   l    logical (5 or over)
   p    primary partition (1-4)
p
Partition number (1-4): 3
First cylinder (238-827): 238
Last cylinder or +size or +sizeM or +sizeK ([238]-536): 536

Command (m for help): p

Disk /dev/hda: 32 heads, 63 sectors, 827 cylinders
Units = cylinders of 2016 * 512 bytes

    Device Boot    Begin    Start    End    Blocks    Id    System
/dev/hda1            1        1      204    205600+   6     DOS 16-bit
    >=32M
/dev/hda2          205      205      237    33264     83    Linux
    native
```

```
/dev/hda3          238       238      536    301392   83  Linux
     native
/dev/hda4          537       537      826    292320    5  Extended
/dev/hda6          543       543      826    286240+   6  DOS 16-bit
     >=32M

Command (m for help): t
Partition number (1-6): 2
Hex code (type L to list codes): 82
Changed system type of partition 2 to 82 (Linux swap)

Command (m for help): a
Partition number (1-6): 3

Command (m for help): p

Disk /dev/hda: 32 heads, 63 sectors, 827 cylinders
Units = cylinders of 2016 * 512 bytes

Device Boot    Begin    Start      End   Blocks    Id  System
   /dev/hda1               1        1      204   205600+   6  DOS 16-bit
     >=32M
/dev/hda2              205      205      237    33264   82  Linux swap
/dev/hda3     *        238      238      536   301392   83  Linux
     native
/dev/hda4              537      537      826   292320    5  Extended
/dev/hda6              543      543      826   286240+   6  DOS 16-bit
     >=32M

Command (m for help): w
The partition table has been altered!
Calling ioctl() to re-read partition table
(reboot to insure the partition table has been updated)
Syncing disks.
```

A screen warns you that your partition table has been changed. Press ENTER, and you then return to the screen displaying your system's hard disks. The entry "1. No further disk changes" at the top will be highlighted. At this point you can press ENTER to continue, unless you have other hard disks on your system that you also want to partition.

Note that if you already have old Linux partitions that you no longer want, you can use Linux fdisk to delete them. Remember, only a Linux fdisk can safely delete a

Linux partition. First, press **p** to display the partitions so you can determine the partition number of the Linux partition you want to remove. Then enter **d**, and you will be prompted for the partition number to delete. Be very careful to give the correct number. If you accidentally enter the one for your DOS partition, you will be instructing fdisk to delete it, erasing everything on it. If this should happen, you can always press **q** to abandon the fdisk sessions, instead of **w**. No changes will be made and nothing will be deleted. Then, at the hard disk selection screen, you can select your hard disk again and start over.

10. The next screen prompts you to reboot your computer. Recall that your Linux boot disk is still in your floppy disk drive. If it is not, insert it now. Press ENTER to reboot. You will begin installation all over again, but your hard disk partitions will now be ready. Continue with the next section to perform installation.

Installing Your Linux System: OpenLinux Lite

Now that you have created your Linux partitions, you are ready to install your Linux system. In step 10, your computer rebooted. As before, introductory information is displayed and a boot prompt appears at the bottom of the screen. You will be repeating steps 2 through 6 to again start up the installation program. But this time you will skip partitioning since it is already done, and you will continue with the actual installation of the Linux system.

11. Repeat steps 2 through 6 in the previous section. When asked to change your partition table, this time, press N or ENTER.

12. The next screen displays the partition you created for your Linux swap space. By selecting it you will format it. Be sure the Linux swap partition is selected. It will have a type of 82. Press ENTER to format your swap space.

13. In the next screen, you are given three choices—CD-ROM, hard disk, or network—from which to install Linux. Choose CD-ROM to install the OpenLinux Lite system included with this text.

    Upon choosing CD-ROM, a list of CD-ROM drives, with yours highlighted, will be displayed. You have to confirm that this is your CD-ROM drive. If not, look through the list to find yours and click on it. Recall the device name given to your CD-ROM earlier.

14. Press ENTER to confirm your CD-ROM drive. (If it is not listed, you will have to start over and enter the hardware specification for it when the boot prompt appears.)

    Alternatively, you can use the hard disk option if you should have difficulty accessing your CD-ROM. You could copy the CD-ROM to a DOS partition and then install from there. The network install allows you to access the OpenLinux CD-ROM remotely, across a network such as an NFS network. You could also have the CD-ROM copied to a hard drive partition and then load it from there across a network. If you choose a hard drive install, you have to specify the hard disk partition and the directory where the copy of the CD-ROM was placed. **/dev/hda1** indicates the first partition. If you choose a network install, you have to specify the server address and the directory path where the Linux CD-ROM is located.

15. The list of partitions on your hard disk is again displayed. The partition you created for your Linux main partition should already be highlighted, and it will have a type of 83. Be sure the main Linux partition is highlighted. Then press ENTER to format it.

16. You can have Linux check for defective sectors while it formats, if you wish. Wait a moment for the partition to be formatted.

Next, you are asked to choose an install option. There are several choices, dependent largely on the amount of space you have. There are seven options, with several options for smaller installations. Listed here are four of the more common ones:

- Standard Open Linux Lite: Standard default installation; takes 212MB.

- Minimal System: A complete Linux system without Windows support or many of the standard applications; takes only 58MB.

- Small Standard: Includes commonly used packages; takes about 91MB.

- Complete System: includes the entire set of packages on the OpenLinux CD-ROM, including tools for developers; takes about 667MB.

17. You are then asked to choose an X-Windows graphics server. You can choose more than one by simply selecting a server on the list and pressing the SPACEBAR. When you are finished, press ENTER. You can choose the standard SVGA server and a specialized accelerated server tailored to specific chipsets used in different video cards. The name of the chipset is included in the name of the accelerated server (S3 for S3 chipset). The VGA-16 server will always be loaded. (See Table 2-2 for a complete listing.) Once you have installed your system you can find detailed information about the different servers and chipsets they support in the **/usr/X11R6/lib/X11/doc** directory and in the **/usr/doc/HOWTO/XFree86-HOWTO** file. The **XFree86-HOWTO** contains a listing of all the chispsets supported.

18. Read the notice that appears and press ENTER to begin installation.

It takes approximately 15 to 30 minutes for a standard installation. During this time a screen will appear showing the progress of the installation, indicating the percentage completed and each package as it is installed. The Linux screen saver will be active, so, after awhile your monitor will go dark. To reactivate the screen, just press either the SHIFT, CTRL, or ALT key.

Server	Type
XFree86_SVGA	Color SVGA server. Includes drivers for many video cards
XFree86_VGA16	16-color SVGA and VGA non-accelerated server
XFree86_Mono	Monochrome non-accelerated server
XFree86_S3	S3 accelerated server
XFree86_S3V	S3 ViRGE and ViRGE/VX accelerated server (many 3D cards)
XFree86_I128	Number 9 Image 128 accelerated server
XFree86_8514	8514/A accelerated server
XFree86_Mach8	ATI Mach8 accelerated server
XFree86_Mach32	ATI Mach32 chipset accelerated server
XFree86_P9000	P9000 based accelerated server
XFree86_W32	ET4000/W32 accelerated server
XFree86_AGX	IIT AGX accelerated server
XFree86_Mach64	ATI Mach64 chipset accelerated server

Table 2-2.   *XFree86 Servers*

Network Configuration

When the installation process is finished, you will be asked a series of questions to configure your networking. If you are connected to a network, you will need the information listed in the earlier section, "Network Configuration Information," to configure Linux to interface with that network. If you are using a modem to dial into an Internet service provider, you may need only the DNS information, or, in some cases, the gateway information. OpenLinux also provides NIS network support.

- The hostname for your computer
- Your domain name
- The IP address assigned to your computer
- Your network IP address

■ The netmask

■ The broadcast IP address for your network

■ The gateway router IP address (if your network has a gateway)

■ The IP address of any nameservers your network uses

■ NIS domain and IP address if your network uses an NIS server

It is best not to perform network configuration until you have this information. You can easily use your OpenLinux tools to enter the configuration information later. However, if you do have the information, you can continue with the network configuration steps that follow.

A screen will prompt you for a hostname for your computer. If your computer does not already have a hostname, you can decide on one yourself—they are usually from 4 to 20 characters long—and enter it. (If your computer is already connected to a network, it will probably have a hostname. In that case, check with your network administrator for the hostname, if you do not know it.)

19. Type in the hostname for your system and press ENTER.

20. You are then asked if you have a network card. If you have a network card, choose YES and you will then be asked the following questions. If you are not connected to a network, press N to choose NO and continue with the steps under "Final Configuration." (If you have a stand-alone PC, you are probably not connected to a network.)

   ■ You are asked to confirm that your network device is eth0. This is the default device for an Ethernet setting. Choose the default, or if your network is not Ethernet, choose NO. You are then prompted for your network information.

   ■ Enter your four-part IP address.

   ■ Enter your netmask. A default is shown that works for most configurations.

   ■ Enter the broadcast address for your network.

21. You are then asked if you have a router or gateway system on your network. If so, enter the IP address of that router or gateway. If not, press N to choose NO.

22. Indicate whether you have a DNS nameserver. If so, enter the IP address of that nameserver. (Many Internet service providers have DNS nameservers.)

23. You are then asked if you have an NIS system. Choose YES to configure it. Otherwise, choose NO. To configure NIS, you will need to enter your NIS domain and the IP address of your NIS server.

Your network configuration is now complete.

Final Configuration

The next two screens ask you to choose local or Greenwich mean time and the proper time zone for your system. Local time would be the more common choice for PC users. DOS systems usually operate according to local time. However, Greenwich mean time (GMT) is the standard for Unix computers and will provide better interoperability with other Unix computers on the Internet, worldwide.

24. Choose the type of time and press ENTER. At the next screen, select a time zone and press ENTER. (Most support Microsoft Serial.)

25. The next screen will list a series of mouse types. Choose the type for your mouse and press ENTER.

26. The next screen prompts you to choose the serial port you are using for your mouse. Select the port and press ENTER (usually COM1).

27. You are then prompted to set up your printer. You are first presented with a list of printer drivers each bearing the name of a printer. Use your ARROW keys to select one.

28. Then select the printer port (usually the first parallel port).

29. Choose the default printer resolution (for many printers this is 300 x 300).

30. Choose default paper size (usually letter).

You are then asked to enter a password for the superuser (root user). Make it simple and easy to remember. You will have to log in as the root user many times to configure your system, performing administrative operations such as installing software or configuring applications.

31. At the password prompt, enter the root user password you decide on.

32. Enter it again at the Retype prompt.

33. You are then prompted to enter another password, this one for a normal user account called **co1**. Create a password and enter it, then re-enter it for confirmation. You can add other users as you wish, using administrative tools such as **usercfg**.

Installing LILO

The next screen displays the "Boot Setup Analysis" for LILO, the Linux Loader. LILO will start your Linux system when you boot up. However, if you have more than one operating system on your hard disk, LILO will allow you to choose the one you want to start. LILO will designate one of the operating systems as the default to start up if one is not specified. So, if you have both DOS and Linux on your hard disk, LILO will let you choose the one you want to use.

34. Press ENTER to continue.

35. Choose the partition where you want to install the LILO boot manager. If you are unsure where to install LILO, choose the selected default. This will be the entry already highlighted. The default is chosen based on the system's analysis (usually the Linux root partition).

36. Choose the system you want to start as a default. This is usually Linux or DOS. The Linux system is identified as **/vmlinuz (Linux Kernel Image)**. Your DOS or Windows 95 system will include the term **DOS** with **DOS** or **OS/2** at the end.

37. You are then asked to enter a label for that system. A default term will be displayed for you; **dos** for DOS/Windows 95 and **linux** for Linux. To use the default label, choose OK by pressing ENTER. You can backspace and type in another name if you wish.

38. If you choose the Linux system, then any special hardware boot parameters that you had to specify are displayed. If you had no special hardware configuration problems, this entry will be blank. Choose OK to continue.

39. You can now make additional entries for other operating systems. The screen will list all the systems on your hard drives, DOS as well as Linux. If you have both DOS and Linux on your system, you now need to choose the other operating system. For example, if you choose DOS for your default system, you would now have to choose your Linux system, and vice versa (the Linux system is labeled /**vmlinuz**).

40. Choose the other operating system, DOS or Linux.

41. You are then prompted to enter in a name for this other operating system. If you are now choosing Linux, the term **linux** will be displayed for you and you can just choose OK. Otherwise, enter the label you want to give this other operating system.

42. You can repeat the steps for adding new labels for as many operating systems as you have. Most people would have no more than two, DOS and Linux. If, however, you should have a third operating system on your hard disk, choose its partition and repeat the previous steps.

43. Once you have finished making entries, choose the entry "No further entries to add to LILO," and then press ENTER. Your **lilo.conf** file will then be displayed. This is the file that actually configures LILO. You will see entries for Linux and other operating systems that you entered such as DOS. Press ENTER to confirm installation of LILO. You are then asked to install LILO as configured. Press Y or ENTER to do so. When LILO finishes its installation, press ENTER to continue. Then you are asked to mark the LILO partition as active. Press ENTER to do so.

Finishing Configuration

You will now complete the last steps of configuration.

44. You are then provided with a list of services that will boot up automatically whenever Linux is started. Included is the Apache Web Server. All those

available for OpenLinux Lite are already selected. You can deselect an entry by using the arrow keys to move to that entry and pressing the SPACEBAR. Press ENTER to continue.

45. You are then asked to select your X-Windows server. Use the arrow keys to move to the one you want. Press ENTER to continue.

46. You are then asked whether you want to configure your X-Windows server. It is best to answer NO at this point. Then finish the installation process. Configuring X-Windows can be complicated, and the system could crash if done improperly. This would corrupt the installation, and you would have to start over. Press N or ENTER to choose NO and finish the installation.

You have now completed your installation. A notice to that effect will be displayed.

47. Remove the boot floppy in your disk drive and press ENTER. After a few minutes your system will reboot automatically.

When your system restarts, the login prompt will appear. You can then log in to your Linux system using a login name and a password for any users you have set up. During installation, you already set up a root user and a user named **col**. You can log in to either one of these. If you log in as the root user, you can perform administrative operations such as installing new software or creating more users. To log in as the root user, enter **root** at the prompt and press ENTER. Then enter the root user password at the password prompt and press ENTER. If, at any time, you try to run a program and receive an error such as a notice of a missing file, use Lisa to check if the package is installed. If not, then install it. See Chapter 3 about how to log in and out of your system.

If you are upgrading from a previously installed Linux system and have saved configuration files that you want to use, you can restore them now. Mount the floppy disk where you saved these files and copy the configuration files to your new system. You can also restore any **tar** archived files and packages with the **tar xvMf/dev/fd0** command.

When you are finished, log out of your account using the command **logout**.

```
$ logout
```

You then need to shut down the entire system. Whenever you are ready to shut down the system, hold down the CTRL and ALT keys and press DEL, (CTRL-ALT-DEL). It is very important that you always use CTRL-ALT-DEL to shut down the system; never turn it off as you do with DOS.

Should your Linux system fail to boot at any time, you can use the Install disk that you created to perform an emergency boot. Put the Install disk in your floppy drive and start up your computer. At the boot prompt, enter: **boot ro root=** with the device name of the root Linux partition. For example, if your root Linux partition is **/dev/hda2**, then you would enter **boot ro root=/dev/hda2** as shown here:

```
boot> boot ro root=/dev/hda2
```

Installing and Configuring X-Windows

First you log in as the root user. (At the LILO prompt, enter `linux` and press ENTER to start Linux.)

1. Type **root** at the login prompt and press ENTER.

2. You will be immediately prompted to enter a password for the root user.

3. At the password prompt enter the password you set up for the root user and press ENTER.

Before you can use X-Windows, you have to configure your mouse, keyboard, graphics card, and monitor to support your X-Windows interface. To configure X-Windows, you use the **XF86Setup** program. This is a full-screen graphics user interface in which you simply click on buttons and menu entries to choose options. It can run it at any time should you need to reconfigure your X-Windows interface. With the **XF86Setup** program, this is a very simple process. Configuring your graphics card is a simple matter of choosing it from a list.

Before you configure X-Windows, find the vertical and horizontal frequency of you monitor. (Consult your monitor's hardware documentation. The frequencies could be single numbers or ranges. For example, the synchronization frequencies for an NEC 3V are 31-50 for horizontal and 55-90 for vertical.)

4. Start up the **XF86Setup** program.

To start the **XF86Setup** program enter this command at the shell prompt. The **XF86Setup** program is located in the **/usr/X11R6/bin** directory. It will create an X-Windows configuration file called **/etc/XF86Config** that will be used to run X-Windows on your system.

```
$ /usr/X11R6/bin/XF86Setup
```

If your **XF86Setup** does not start, the reason may be that not all the **XFree86** libraries were loaded during the installation. Use the Lisa utility, described in Chapter 3, to install the **XFree86** package and the **XFree86misc** package if they are not already installed (see installing software in Chapter 3). You should then be able to start **XF86Setup**. If you still can't, try using **XF86Config**.

5. You are then asked to enter graphics mode. Press ENTER.

You are now in the **XF86Setup** program. There are five configuration tasks, each indicated by a button on the top row of the **XF86Setup** window. The buttons are labeled: Mouse, Keyboard, Card, Monitor, and Other. Each button brings up a screen for configuring that task.

At the bottom of the screen are three buttons: Abort, Done, and Help. Abort will cancel the entire **XF86Setup** without making any changes. If you are at all unsure about any of the configuration options, you can simply click on Abort to end the program safely and then start it up later. When you are finished with all the configuration tasks, click the Done button to save your configuration and end the **XF86Setup** program. You will then be ready to start X-Windows with the `startx` command.

> 6. To bring up the Mouse screen, you can press ENTER or ALT-M. When the Mouse screen first appears, a list of keyboard commands are presented. It is advised not to use your mouse until you have configured it. Instead, you can use the keyboard command to select entries on the screen (see Figure 2-1).

The Mouse screen lists a series of mouse brands. These are indicated by a row of buttons at the top of the screen under the label "Select Mouse Protocol." Microsoft is a protocol that most mice are compatible with. Most standard mice are Microsoft serial. Choose the brand for your mouse. You can then set different features such as the number of buttons or the baud rate. Default settings are already entered. For the mouse device path, **/dev/ttyS0** refers to the first serial port, **/dev/ttyS1** to the second,

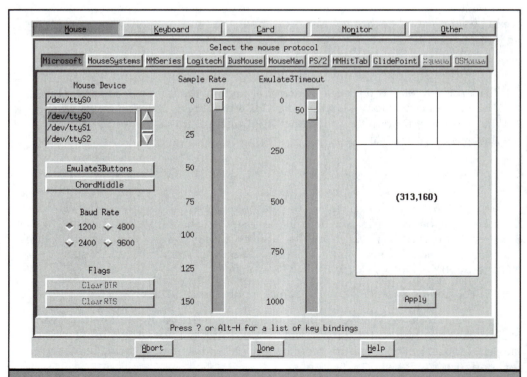

Figure 2-1.   *XF86Setup program depicting the mouse setup*

and so on. **/dev/ttyS0** is already selected, and is usually the port used for a mouse. The B key sets the band rate. The **e** command emulates a middle button on a two-button mouse, and the **c** command enables Chordmiddle, the middle button on a three-button mouse. When finished, press **a** to select the Apply button in the lower-right corner. Your mouse is then configured and ready to use with the rest of the configurations.

7. Click the Keyboard button to bring up the Keyboard screen. There are drop-down menus for selecting the keyboard model and the language you use. You can also set different control key positions or just use the defaults. When finished, select the Apply button located below the picture of the keyboard (see Figure 2-2).

8. There are two screens used for graphics card configurations: A Detailed Setup screen and a CardLlist screen. Ordinarily, you will only have to use the Card List screen. To begin, click on the Card tab. If you have not previously run **XF86Setup**, you will immediately be placed in the Card List screen. If you have previously run the **XF86Setup** program, the Detailed Setup screen will display first. In the lower-right corner of the screen is a button labeled Card List. Choose this button to bring up the Card List screen.

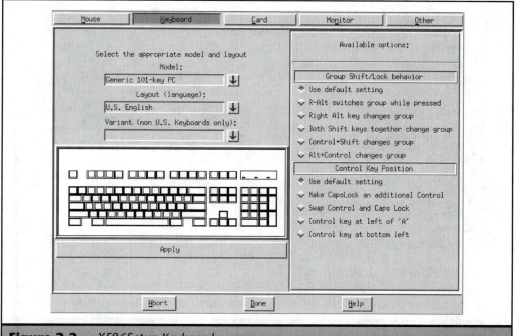

Figure 2-2. *XF86Setup Keyboard screen*

The Card List screen lists most video cards currently available. To the right is a slider bar that you can use to move through the list. Find the video card that your system uses. Select it by clicking on it, then click on the README file button to read information about the server for this card (see Figure 2-3). You can then continue on to the Monitor screen.

If your card is not listed, then choose the Detailed Setup. This brings up the Detailed Setup screen, where you can perform a detailed setup of your card. On the Detailed Setup screen, you will see a row of buttons on the top indicating the different X-Windows servers. Below them are drop-down menus for selecting your chipset, ramdac, and clockchip. There are drop-down menus for selecting the keyboard model and the language you use.

9. Click on the Monitor button to bring up the Monitor screen. To configure your monitor you only need to set the horizontal and vertical frequency ranges. However, it is critically important that these settings be correct. An incorrect frequency can damage your monitor (see Figure 2-4).

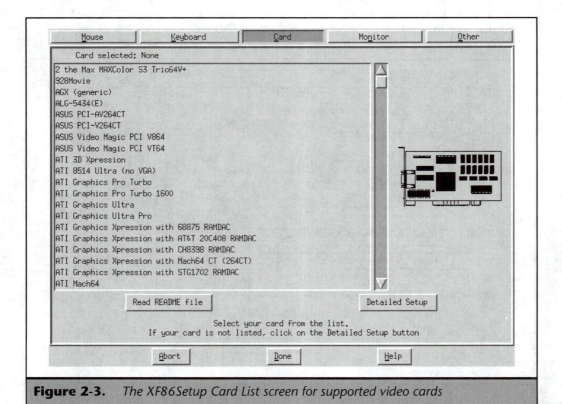

Figure 2-3.   *The XF86Setup Card List screen for supported video cards*

CAUTION: *Before you choose a monitor frequency (Hz), check your hardware documentation. If you set the frequency higher than the one your monitor supports, you can cause serious damage.*

There are boxes at the top of the screen labeled Horizontal and Vertical. Here, you can enter your horizontal and vertical frequencies. After you type in the frequency number, press ENTER to have it entered. You will see the frequency represented on the associated bar. If your monitor supports ranges for each entry, you enter them separated by a dash. For example, an older multisync monitor might have a horizontal frequency of 31–50 and a vertical frequency of 55–90. Below the vertical and horizontal boxes, a vertical and horizontal graph will show the ranges you entered. In a box in the center of the screen is a list of common monitor types. You can click one to select a standard set of frequencies. However, under no condition should you take these frequencies as valid. Always check your monitor documentation for the correct frequencies.

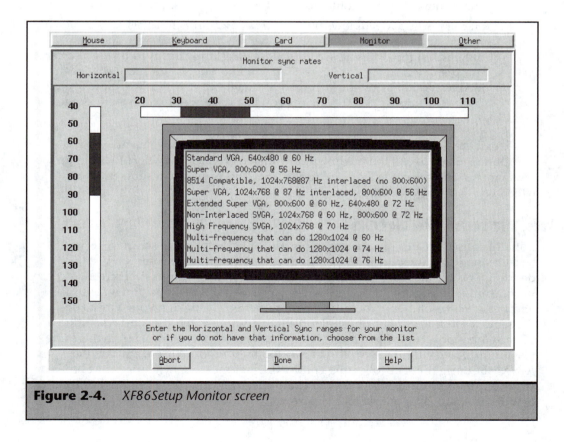

Figure 2-4.   *XF86Setup Monitor screen*

10. Click on the Other button to bring up the Optional Server Settings. This lists a set of five options, the first two of which are already selected. Ordinarily, you will not have to change anything on this screen. The first option allows you to end an X-Windows session from the keyboard with CTRL-ALT-BACKSPACE. The second lets you change video modes with the CTRL-ALT-+ keys (the + key is the one on the keypad). You can easily switch between different resolutions. The third lets you exit the server cleanly and the fourth and fifth allow changes in video, mouse, and keyboard configurations from remote workstations.

11. Upon finishing your X-Windows configuration, choose the Done button at the bottom of the screen. X-Windows starts up, and you are then presented with three buttons: **Run xvidtune**, **save the configuration and exit**, or **Abort**. If X-Windows fails to start, the reason may be that your **XFree86** sever was not installed. Return to the command line and start up Lisa with the Lisa command to install the server you need (see Chapter 3).

12. Choose **save the configuration and exit**. (You can run **xvidtune** later to tune your monitor display should you need to, though most users won't.)

13. You can start up X-Windows with the `startx` command. This command actually starts up the X-Windows, the fvwm window manager, and the Caldera Desktop. You will see the Caldera Desktop displayed on your screen. If the display is smaller or larger than you like, you may want to change the video resolution using the keyboard command CTRL-ALT-+. This places you in a higher resolution. CTRL-ALT-- places you in a lower resolution where images appear larger.

To exit the Caldera desktop, choose Exit Desktop from the File menu.

You then need to exit the fvwm window manager. Click anywhere to bring up the fvwm menu, and select the Exit Desktop option. This brings up a submenu from which you choose Quit Desktop.

The Virtual Desktop

Initially, the screen area of your desktop may not fit the physical screen. This is because the fvwm window manager used for X-Windows implements a Virtual desktop. This means that your desktop can be larger than the physical screen. Moving the cursor to the edge of the screen moves you across the desktop. You will see this effect at lower resolutions. You can turn off this effect by making your Virtual desktop the same resolution as your physical screen. For example, the standard resolution of a 15-inch monitor is 800 x 600. You would need to set the Virtual desktop to this same resolution. You configure your Virtual desktop by placing a Virtual entry in the **/etc/XF86Config** file. The following entry works for most 15-inch monitors. Should you want a larger Virtual desktop you could specify **Virtual 1024 768** for the next size or **Virtual 1152 864** for an even larger size.

```
Virtual 800 600
```

Your **/etc/XF86Config** file is divided into several sections that control all aspects of your X-Windows display. The Virtual setting can be placed in Display subsections of the Screen sections, located toward the end of the file. The Screen section has the heading **Section "Screen"** and its Display sections have the headings **Subsection "Display"**. There will be more than one Screen section, usually one for each of the different drivers your system has installed. If you installed an Accelerated card you would use the Screen section with the entry **Driver "Accel"**. (See Chapataer 21 for more details.)

In the Screen section for Accelerated cards, there will usually be several Display subsections, one for each depth that your video card supports, such as 8, 16, and 24. The default depth is 8. You add the Virtual entry in this Display subsection. If you want to use another depth, use the **DefaultColorDepth** entry to specify it. This will select another Display subsection as the default. Depth determines the number of colors that can be displayed on your screen—8 bit for 256, 16 for 32,000, and 24 for 16 million. Consult information about your card on the **XF86Setup** program for the bit depth it supports (usually either 8, 16, or 24). For example, if you set the DefaultColorDepth to 16, then the Display subsection for depth 16 is used. Be sure there is a Virtual entry there should you want one. The following example shows the Screen section for an Accelerated driver with the Display subsections for the 8 and 16 bit depths. The 8 bit depth uses a Virtual desktop of 1024 x 768, whereas the 16 bit depth uses a Virtual desktop of 800 x 600 and will fit the size of a 15-inch monitor.

```
Section "Screen"
    Driver          "Accel"
    Device          "Primary Card"
    Monitor         "Primary Monitor"
  DefaultColorDepth  16
  SubSection "Display"
      Depth         8
      Modes         "1152x864" "1024x768" "800x600" "640x480"
"640x400" "480x300" "400x300" "320x240" "320x200"
      Virtual 1024 768
    EndSubSection
SubSection "Display"
      Depth         16
      Modes         "1152x864" "1024x768" "800x600" "640x480" "640x400"
      Virtual 800 600
    EndSubSection
```

To edit the file, you can use the Crisplite editor as described in Chapter 4. To edit the file from the command line, use **mcr /etc/XF86Config**. Or you could, instead, use Vi or X (xEmacs). Make a backup copy of this file first, and be sure to change only the Display entries in the Screen section. Be very careful to leave the other sections alone.

Installing Sound Drivers: sound

You have to explicitly install the sound driver for your sound card. It is not done by your OpenLinux installation. Sound drivers are held in a kernel module called **sound.o** kept in the **/lib/modules/2.0.29/misc** directory (2.0.29 is the current version of the Linux kernel used by OpenLinux). The OpenLinux version of the Linux kernel supports modules (older versions may not). The module currently holds standard sound card support using an IRQ of 7 and a DMA of 1 with a base address of 220. You install the module with the **insmod** command as shown here (**insmod sound** will uninstall the sound module):

```
$ insmod sound
```

To have the sound module automatically loaded whenever you start your system, you have to add the term **sound** to the default modules file in the **/etc/modules/2.0.29** directory. On your OpenLinux system, the name of the file begins with the official version name of your Linux system followed by the extension **.defaults**. An easy way to edit it is to use ***.default** or **'uname -v'.default** for the file name. The **uname -v** command displays the official version name. In the **/etc/modules/2.0.29** directory, the following command will easily append the term **sound** to the end of the default modules file. The backquotes around **'uname -v'** and the enclosing double quotes around the entire name as well as the preceding double **>>** are all critical. Currently the name of the default file is **#1 Tue Feb 11 20:36:48 MET 1997.default**.

```
$ echo "sound" >> "'uname -v'.default"
```

You can check the status of your sound card with the following command. If you receive a message saying there is no such device, then your sound card is not installed.

```
$ cat /dev/sndstat
```

You can use a CD player program or use **cat** on sound files to test your sound card. If you hear no sound, your card may not be configured properly. Sound files with the extension **.au** are redirected to the **/dev/audio** device. Those with **.wav** or **.voc** are redirected to the **/dev/dsp** device. The following example plays a sound file:

```
$ cat sample.au  > /dev/audio
```

To run one of the CD player programs, you first have to create a /dev/cdrom link using the device name of your CD-ROM. If your sound card has different IRQ and DMA settings from the default or is not supported in the current configuration, you will have to recompile the **sound.o** module with a new configuration. The sound module source code is in the **/usr/src/linux/drivers/sound** directory. Check the README files for details on how to reconfigure and compile the module, particularly **Readme. modules**. To configure the sound module you enter the command **make config** (or configure) from within that directory. You will be asked a series of questions about your sound card. After configuration, you compile the new sound module with the command **make**. Then use the command **make install** to copy the new **sound.o** file to the **/lib /modules /2.0.29/misc** directory, overwriting the old **sound.o** file. You then install the new sound module with the command **insmod sound**.

Lisa

The installation was carried out by the Linux Installation and System Administration (**lisa**) program. You can use this same program to change any of your configurations. With Lisa you can make any needed modification to your system such as adding new users, mounting new partitions, or installing new printers (see Figure 2-5). You can also add or remove software from your CD-ROM, as well as change your network configuration. Lisa is a simple menu-driven tool that you start from the command line by entering the command **lisa**.

```
# lisa
```

The UP and DOWN arrows move from one menu entry to another. RIGHT ARROW and LEFT ARROW let you select either the Call or Continue buttons. You know you've selected a button if its letters are white. To select a menu entry, move to the entry you want, make sure the Call button is selected, and then press ENTER. The Continue button will move back to the previous menu.

Using Lisa to administer your system and add software is discussed in detail in Chapter 3. Lisa operations to manage your file systems are described in Chapter 7. You can also use Lisa to obtain information about your system, view help files, and to add or remove any kernel modules needed for special hardware configurations.

To obtain information about your system, select the "Verbose system analysis" in the Lisa main menu (see Figure 2-6). From this menu you can find out how your system is currently configured. For example, "Automatic Partition Analysis" will list all the partitions available on your system, and "Automatic Network Analysis" will list all your network information. You can use these entries to check if the information you provided during the installation was correct. If not, you can use Lisa to change them. The "System Configuration" entry in the Lisa main menu brings you into other menus for adding to or changing features of your system configuration.

If your computer has special hardware components and you are having problems with your system, you may need to install Linux drivers or specify certain hardware parameters. You use Lisa to run the Kernel Module Manger to install these drivers or specify hardware parameters. See Appendix A for a list of hardware parameters. From the Lisa main menu, choose System Configuration and then from the next menu,

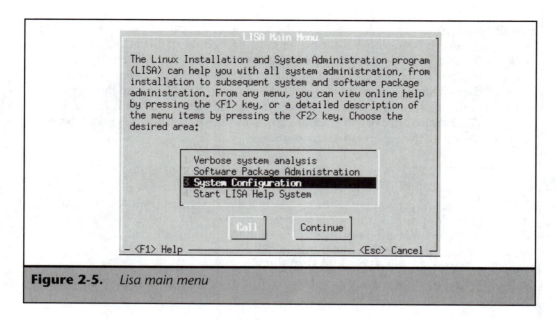

Figure 2-5. Lisa main menu

again choose "System Configuration." Select the "Kernel Module Administration" entry. From this menu you can view lists of loaded and available kernel modules, as well as load or remove modules.

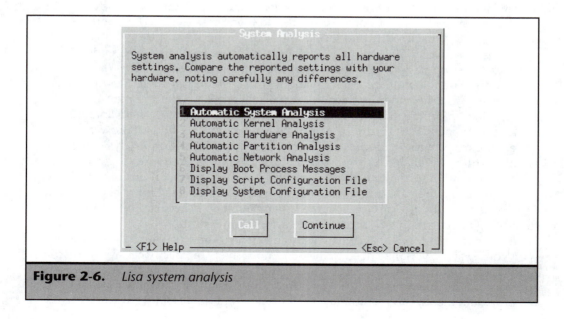

Figure 2-6. Lisa system analysis

Chapter Three

Linux Startup and Setup

To start using Linux, you will need to know how to access your Linux system and, once you are on the system, how to execute commands and run applications. Accessing Linux involves more than just turning on your computer. Once Linux is running, you have to log into the system using a predetermined login name and password. Once on the system, you can start executing commands and running applications. You can then interact with your Linux system using either a command line interface or a graphical user interface (GUI). The Linux systems use the **X-Windows** utility along with window managers and desktops to provide a fully functional GUI, with which you can use windows, menus, and icons to interact with your system.

It is very easy to obtain information quickly about Linux commands and utilities while logged into the system. Linux has several online utilities that provide information and help. You can access an online manual that describes each command, or obtain help that provides more detailed explanations of different Linux features. A complete set of manuals provided by the Linux Documentation Project is on your system and available for you to print or browse through.

This chapter will discuss how to access your Linux system, including logging in and out of user accounts as well as starting the system and shutting it down. Linux commands and utilities are also covered, along with basic operations of the Caldera Desktop. The chapter ends with an explanation of basic system administration operations, such as creating new user accounts and installing software packages.

User Accounts

You never directly access a Linux system. Instead, Linux sets up an interface through which you can interact. A Linux system can actually set up and operate several user interfaces at once, accommodating several users simultaneously. In fact, you can have many users working off the same computer running a Linux system. To a particular user, it appears as if he or she is the only one working on the system. It is as if Linux can set up several virtual computers, and each user can then work on his or her own virtual computer. Such virtual computers are really individually managed interfaces whereby each user interacts with the Linux system.

These user interfaces are frequently referred to as accounts. Unix, which Linux is based on, was first used on large minicomputers and mainframes that could accommodate hundreds of users at the same time. Using one of many terminals connected to the computer, users could log into the Unix system using their login names and passwords. All of this activity was managed by system administrators. To gain access to the system, you needed to have a user interface set up for you. This was commonly known as "opening an account." A system administrator would create the account on the Unix system, assigning a login name and password for it. You then used your account to log in and use the system.

Each account is identified by a login name with access protected by a password. Of course, you can access any account if you know its login name and password. On your

Linux system, you can create several accounts, logging into different ones as you wish. Other people can access your Linux system, making use of login names and passwords you provide for them. In effect, they will have their own accounts on your system.

Recall that in the previous chapter on installing Linux, you created a login name and password for yourself. These are what you will use to access Linux regularly. When you created the login name and password, you were actually creating a new user account for yourself.

You can, in fact, create other new user accounts using special system administration tools. These tools become available to you when you log in as the root user. The root user is a special user account reserved for system administration tasks such as creating users and installing new software. Basic system administration operations are discussed briefly in this chapter, and in detail in Chapters 7, 19, and 20. For now, you will only need your regular login name and password.

Accessing Your Linux System

To access and use your Linux system, you must carefully follow required startup and shutdown procedures. You do not simply turn off and turn on your computer as you do with DOS. You can think of your Linux operating system as operating on three different levels, one running on top of the other. The first level is when you start your Linux system and the system loads and runs. It has control of your computer and all its peripherals. However, you still are not able to interact with it. After Linux starts, it will display a login prompt, waiting for a user to come along and log into the system to start using it. To gain access to Linux, you first have to log in.

You can think of logging in and using Linux as the next level. Now you can issue commands instructing Linux to perform tasks. You can use utilities and programs such as editors or compilers, even games. However, after you initially log in, you will be interacting with the system using a simple command line interface. You type in a command and press ENTER to have the system perform actions. As an alternative to the command line interface, you can use an X-Windows graphical user interface. The Caldera distribution of Linux, OpenLinux, supports a variety of window managers and desktops, including its own desktop metaphor simply called the Caldera Desktop. In Linux, the command **startx** will start the X-Windows GUI that will then allow you to interact with the system using windows, menus, and icons. You can think of the window manager as the third level; the X-Windows window manager runs on top of your command line interface.

The three levels become important in your shutdown procedure. If you are running the X-Windows GUI and you want to shut down, you first need to exit the X-Windows GUI, returning to the command line interface. Then you log out of your shell and return to the system's login prompt. Logging out does *not* shut down the system. It is still running and has control of your machine. You then need to tell the system to shut itself down by issuing a shutdown command: Hold down the CTRL and

ALT keys and press the DEL key (CTRL-ALT-DEL). The system shuts itself down and reboots. When rebooting starts, only then can you turn off your computer.

You can use some shortcuts to move from one level to another. If you are logged in as a root user, you can have Linux both log out and shut down by issuing a shutdown command (see Chapter 19 for a detailed discussion of the shutdown process). There is also a way to have Linux automatically start your X-Windows window manager when you log in (see Chapter 21).

Starting and Shutting Down Linux

When you turn on or reset your computer, the Linux Loader, LILO, will first decide what operating system to load and run. You will see the following prompt enter **linux** to start up the Linux operating system:

```
LILO: linux
```

If, instead, you wait a moment or press the ENTER key, LILO will load the default operating system. (Recall that earlier you designated default operating system.) If you want to run DOS instead, LILO will give you a moment at the prompt to type in the name you gave for DOS, such as **dos**.

As Linux loads, you will see several messages displayed. Then you will be given a login prompt. The system is now running and waiting for a user to log in and use it. You can enter your user name and password to use the system. The login prompt will be preceded by the hostname you gave your system. In this example, the hostname is **turtle.trek.com**:

```
Caldera OpenLinux (TM)
Lite 1
Version 1.1
Copyright (c) 1996-1997 Caldera Inc.

turtle.trek.com login:
```

When you are finished using Linux, you first **logout**. Linux will then display the exact same login prompt, waiting for you or another user to log in again.

Should you want to turn off your computer, you must first shut down Linux. If you don't, you could require Linux to perform a lengthy systems check when it starts up again.

You shut down your system by holding down both the CTRL and ALT keys and pressing the DEL key, CTRL-ALT-DEL. You will see several messages as Linux shuts itself down. Linux will then reboot your computer. During the reboot process, you can turn off your computer. The following describes all the startup and shutdown procedures. Try them to see how they work.

1. Boot your computer.
2. At the LILO prompt type **linux** and press ENTER. (Or just press ENTER if Linux is your default.)
3. After a few messages, the login prompt appears, and you can log into the system and use it.
4. At the login prompt you can also shut down the system. The login prompt will reappear after you log out.
5. You can now turn off your computer.

Logging into and out of Linux: The Command Line

Once you log in, you can enter and execute commands. After you have finished, you need to log out of the system before you shut it down. You do not have to shut down the system if you don't want to. You will be presented with a login prompt, and you could then log in using a different user name, or log in as the root user.

Logging into Linux

Logging into your Linux account involves two steps: entering your user name and then your password. You already know what the login prompt looks like. Type in the login name for your user account. If you make a mistake, you can erase characters with the BACKSPACE key. In the next example, the user enters the user name **richlp**, and is then prompted to enter the password.

```
Caldera OpenLinux (TM)
Lite 1
Version 1.1
Copyright (c) 1996-1997 Caldera Inc.

turtle.trek.com login: richlp
Password:
```

When you type in your password, it will not appear on the screen. This is to protect your password from being seen by others. If you enter either the login or password incorrectly, the system will respond with the error message "Login incorrect" and will ask for your login name again, starting the login process over. You can then re-enter your login name and password.

Once you have entered your user name and password correctly, you are logged into the system. Your command line prompt will be displayed, waiting for you to enter a command. Notice that the command line prompt is a dollar sign, **$**, not a sharp sign, **#**. The **$** is the prompt for regular users, whereas the **#** sign is the prompt solely for the root user. In this version of Linux, your prompt will be preceded by the hostname and the directory you are in. Both will be bounded by a set of brackets.

```
[turtle /home/richlp]$
```

Changing Your Password

Recall that when you first logged in as the root user in the previous chapter, you created a password for your personal user account. Once created, you can change your password for your personal account any time you wish. You can do this while logged into your personal account. You do not have to be logged in as the root user. This is true of any user on the system. Each user can change his or her own password at any time.

Once logged in, you can change your password with the **passwd** command. First decide what your new password should be. It should be easy to remember and at least seven to eight characters. If you are concerned with security, the password should include upper- and lowercase characters as well as some numbers.

When you have chosen your new password, you are ready to change it. Type in the command **passwd** on the command line and press ENTER. The command prompts you for your current password. After entering that and pressing ENTER, you are then prompted for your new password. After entering the new password, you are asked to re-enter it. This is to make sure that you actually entered the password that you intended to enter. Because password characters are not displayed when you type them in, it is easy to make a mistake and press a wrong key.

```
$ passwd
Old password:
New password:
Retype new password:
$
```

If you make a mistake entering the new password, the system displays an error message, and the password will not be changed. The system detects mistakes by matching the two new password entries. If they do not match, an error is detected. If they do match, the entries are considered correct.

The **passwd** command registers your new password with the system immediately. When you log in again, you use the new password.

Logging Out

To end your session, you issue the **logout** command. This returns you to the login prompt, and Linux waits for another user to log in.

 $ **logout**

Starting and Exiting the Window Manager: X-Windows

Once logged into the system, you have the option of starting the X-Windows GUI and using it to interact with your Linux system. You start the X-Windows GUI by entering **startx** on the command line. X-Windows then loads along with the designated window manager. Your Caldera distribution of Linux will also load a desktop metaphor, providing a file and program manager. The X-Windows GUI used with your Caldera distribution of Linux is referred to as the Caldera Desktop. Once it is loaded, you can use your mouse to access menus, open windows, and start programs. Figure 3-1 shows you what the Caldera Desktop looks like.

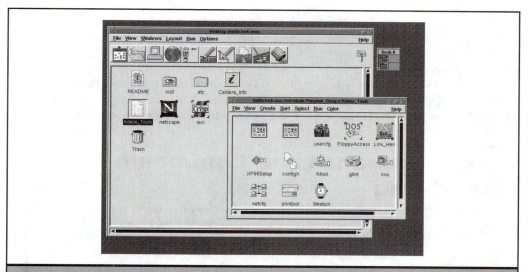

Figure 3-1.   *The Caldera Desktop with Admin_Tools window open*

The features of the Caldera Desktop are just like those in any window environment. You point and click with a mouse to select different icons, menus, and windows. The windows display information, list files, or open applications. As with all window systems, you can have several windows open at the same time. However, only one of those windows will be active. The active window will have purple borders, while all the other inactive windows will have pale gray borders. Moving your mouse pointer to a particular window makes it the active window, rendering all others inactive. The movement of the mouse pointer alone from one window to another will change the active window. There is no need to click the mouse as in other GUIs, such as Microsoft Windows or Mac OS.

One of the more confusing aspects of this design occurs with the overlapping windows. Making a window the active window does not automatically bring it to the front. An active window could still be partially hidden by other overlapping windows. To bring a window to the front, you need to click on that window's title bar, the bar across the top of the window containing the window's name. Clicking anywhere else on the window would only make it the active window, not bring it to the front.

You exit the Caldera Desktop by choosing the Exit Desktop option in the File menu. Across the top of the screen, there is a menu part with several menu entries, one of which is the File menu. Just click on File at the top of the screen to pull down the File menu. Exit Desktop is the last entry. Once you choose Exit Desktop, you will be returned to the window manager which will show up as a blank blue screen. You then need to exit the Window manager. Click anywhere on the screen to pop up the window manager menu, and then select Exit Desktop. This brings up a sub-menu from which you choose Quit Desktop. This will shut down X-Windows.

Linux will shut down X-Windows and return to the command line interface, presenting you with the **$** prompt. You can restart X-Windows anytime by entering **startx** on the command line.

Keep in mind that if you are using the X-Windows GUI (in this case the Caldera Desktop), and you want to log out, you first need to exit the GUI. Then, once you have returned to the command line, you can log out by entering **logout** or **exit**.

Linux Commands and Command Line Editing

Linux has a large set of commands that you can use for such tasks as managing and editing files or communicating with other users. Reflecting its Unix roots, Linux commands are designed to be executed using a command line interface. Even with a GUI, you will often need to execute commands on a command line. Linux commands make extensive use of options and arguments. Be careful to place your arguments and options in their correct order on the command line. The format for a Linux command is the command name followed by options and then by arguments, as shown here:

```
$ command-name   options   arguments
```

An option is a one-letter code preceded by a dash that modifies the type of action the command takes. Options and arguments may or may not be optional, depending on the command. For example, the **ls** command can take an option **-s**. The **ls** command displays a listing of files in your directory, and the **-s** option adds the size of each file in blocks. You would enter the command and its option on the command line as:

```
$ ls -s
```

An argument is data that the command may need to execute its task. In many cases it will be a file name. An argument is entered as a word on the command line after any options. For example, to get information about a particular command, you can use the **man** command with the command's name as its argument. The **man** command used with the command name **ls** would be entered on the command line as:

```
$ man ls
```

The command line is actually a buffer of text that you can edit. Before you press ENTER, you can perform editing commands on the existing text. The editing capabilities provide a way for correcting mistakes you may make when typing in a command and its options. The BACKSPACE and DEL keys allow you to erase the character just typed in. With this character-erasing capability, you can BACKSPACE over the entire line if you wish, erasing what you have entered. CTRL-U erases the whole line and lets you start over again at the prompt.

The shell you will start working in is the BASH shell, your default shell. This shell has special command line editing capabilities that you may find very helpful as you learn Linux. You can easily modify commands you have entered before executing them, moving anywhere on the command line and inserting or deleting characters. This is particularly helpful for very complex commands. You can use CTRL-F or RIGHT ARROW to move forward a character; CTRL-B or the LEFT ARROW to move back a character. CTRL-D or DEL deletes the character the cursor is on, and CTRL-H or

BACKSPACE deletes the character before the cursor. To add text, you just use the ARROW keys to move the cursor to where you want to insert text and type the new characters. At any time, you can press ENTER to execute the command. For example, if you make a spelling mistake when entering a command, rather than re-entering the entire command, you can use the editing operations to correct the mistake.

You can also use UP ARROW to redisplay your previously executed command. You can then re-execute that command or edit it and execute the modified command. You'll find this very helpful when you have to repeat certain operations over and over, such as editing the same file. It is also helpful when you've already executed a command that you had entered incorrectly. In this case you would be presented with an error message and a new, empty command line. By pressing UP ARROW, you can display your previous command, make corrections to it, and then execute it again.

The BASH shell keeps a list, called a *history list*, of your previously entered commands. You can display each command in turn on your command line by pressing UP ARROW. The DOWN ARROW key will move you down the list. You can modify and execute any of these previous commands when you display them on your command line. The history list feature is discussed in more detail in Chapter 15.

Online Manual

Your Linux system also has utilities such as editors, mailers, and manuals. Such utilities are separate programs that have their own interfaces with their own sets of commands. One example is the man online manual that allows you to display information about any Linux command or program. To use the online manual, you just type in the command **man** followed by the name of the command you want information on. In the next example, the user invokes the online manual information for the **ls** command.

```
$ man ls
```

Man documents on a command may be organized into different levels, starting from one. The first level may give basic information about a command, while another level may provide more detailed information. You display a document for a specific level by including the level number as an argument before the command name. For example, to display the man document for crontab at the eighth level, you enter

```
$ man 8 crontab
```

These other level documents will be listed at the end of whatever level document your man operation brings up. Most commands have just one level that is brought up with the **man** command without a level argument.

Upon pressing ENTER, you are placed in the **man** utility, displaying the first page of the **ls** document. **man** has its own set of commands, usually consisting of single keys. Pressing either the SPACEBAR or the F key will advance you to the next page. Pressing the B key will move you back a page. When you are finished, press the Q key to quit the **man** utility and return to the command line.

A manual entry is organized into several segments. Five of the more common segments are the synopsis, description, options, files, and cross-references for the command. The synopsis presents the command's syntax, listing its possible options and arguments. The description of the command tells you exactly what it does on the system. Next, the options are listed and explained. The files segment lists the system files used by the command, and the cross-references list other related commands and manual entries. A shortened version of the manual entry for the **ls** command follows.

```
LS(1L)                                                      LS(1L)


NAME
     ls, dir, vdir - list contents of directories

SYNOPSIS
     ls  [-abcdfgiklmnpqrstuxABCFGLNQRSUX1] [-w cols] [-T cols]
     [-I pattern] [--all] [--directory]  [--inode][--kilobytes]
     [--no-group]  [--hide-control-chars] [--reverse] [--size]
     [--width=cols][--sort={none,time,size,extension}]
DESCRIPTION
     This manual page documents the GNU version of ls.  dir and
     vdir are versions of ls with different default output for-
     mats.   These  programs  list each given file or directory
     name.  Directory contents are sorted alphabetically.   For
     ls,  files are by default listed in columns, sorted verti-
     cally, if the standard output  is  a  terminal;  otherwise
     they  are  listed  one  per  line.   For dir, files are by
     default listed in columns, sorted vertically.   For  vdir,
     files are by default listed in long format.
OPTIONS
     -a, --all
          List  all files in directories, including all files
          that start with '.'.
     -b, --escape
          Quote nongraphic characters  in  file  names  using
          alphabetic and octal backslash sequences like those
          used in C.
     -c, --time=ctime, --time=status
          Sort directory contents  according  to  the  files'
```

```
                      status  change  time  instead  of  the modification
                      time.  If the long listing format  is  being  used,
                      print the status change time instead of the modifi-
                      cation time.
              -d, --directory
                      List directories  like  other  files,  rather  than
                      listing their contents.
              -f      Do  not sort directory contents; list them in what-
                      ever order they are stored on the disk.   The  same
                      as enabling -a and -U and disabling -l, -s, and -t.
              --full-time
                      List times in full, rather than using the  standard
      FSF                        GNU File Utilities                       1
```

The **man** utility has several other helpful features, such as a search capability. You activate a search by pressing either the slash, **/**, or question mark, **?**. A **/** will search forward and the **?** will search backward. Upon pressing the **/**, a line will open at the bottom of your screen, and you then enter a word to search for. Press ENTER to activate the search. The search is actually a pattern search, so you can enter part of a word, or almost any set of characters for that matter. You can repeat the same search by pressing the N key. You don't have to re-enter the pattern.

whatis and apropos

The **whatis** and **apropos** commands will search a database of **man** titles and display any results along with a short description of each. **whatis** will search **man** titles by whole words. For example, if you wanted to see all the manual entries with the letter X in them, you would use the following command (this will give you manual entries dealing with X-Windows topics).

```
$ whatis X
X (3)                    - a portable, network-transparent window
system
X Consortium (3)         - X Consortium information
X Standards (3)          - X Consortium Standards
X security (3)           - X display access control
X (3)                    - a portable, network-transparent window system
X Consortium (3)         - X Consortium information
X Standards (3)          - X Consortium Standards
```

```
X security (3)         - X display access control
(END)
$
```

Both the **whatis** and **apropos** commands place you in a man type of interface. If the results take up more than one page, you can use the F and B keys to move forward or backward. You can also perform pattern searches with the / and ? keys. To quit, you press the Q key. Only then will you return to the command line.

The **apropos** command performs the same task as the **whatis** command, but it searches by pattern instead of whole words. For example, the command **apropos x** will produce a lengthy result of several pages, listing all the man entries beginning with *x*, such as **xwpe** and **xloadimage**. In the next example, the user lists all the manual entries beginning with the pattern **ls**. This will include the **ls** command as well as many others, such as **lseek** or **lsearch**.

```
$ apropos ls
ls, dir, vdir (1)      - list contents of directories
lsattr (1)             - list file attributes on a Linux second
extended file system
lsearch (n)            - See if a list contains a particular element
lseek (2)              - reposition read/write file offset
lsort (n)              - Sort the elements of a list
lsattr (1)             - list file attributes on a Linux second
extended file system
lsearch (n)            - See if a list contains a particular element
lseek (2)              - reposition read/write file offset
lsort (n)              - Sort the elements of a list
(END)
$
```

You can also use the **Helptool** utility to search for keywords in Linux manual documents. **Helptool** can search any information page or text file. Just enter **helptool**, and then choose from the list of topics displayed. (Use Lisa to install it.)

Xman and tkman

If you are working on the desktop, you can use the Xman program to easily search and display manual pages. Xman is an X-Windows-based program. You use mouse clicks on buttons and menus to search and display manual pages. To start Xman, you click on the Xman button on the fvwm toolbar. This opens a small window in the corner with three buttons: Help, Quit, and Manual Page. Click on Manual Page to open the Xman display window. At the top are two menu buttons: Options and Sections. In the Options menu you can select the Search item to open a small search window. Here, enter in a command or topic whose man page you want displayed. You can also use the Section menu to locate commands. This menu lists categories such as User Commands, system administration, devices, and even games. Select one and a panel is displayed with all the man entries for that category; for example, the User Commands item will list all the user commands. Then click on the one you want and the man page for that command will be displayed. You can use a slider bar on the left to move through the man page. Figure 3-2 shows both the man page window and the initial Xman window.

Tkman provides many of the same features as Xman, but with an easier to use interface. There is a box at the top of the window where you enter in the name of a command. Then click on the button labeled "man" to the left of that entry box. For apropos searches, enter the search string in the same entry box and click on the button labeled "apropos". The Volumes menu lets you easily choose topics and the Sections menu lets you set options and provides help. A slider bar lets you move back and forth within a displayed man page. You startup Tkman with the command **tkman** in a terminal window, or by choosing its entry in the fvwm workplace submenu "Other Applications" in the Applications menu.

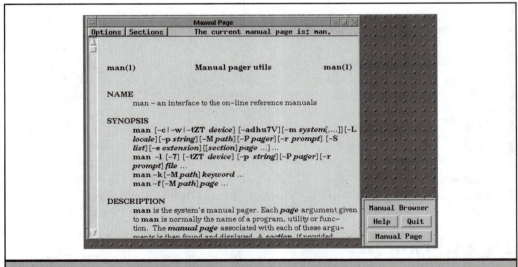

Figure 3-2.   *Xman windows for displaying man pages*

Online Documentation

When start up your Browser, a default Web page lists links for documentation both on your own system and at the Caldera and Redhat Web sites. To use the Caldera and Redhat Web sites, you first have to be connected to the Internet. However, your CD-ROM and your system contain extensive documentation showing you how to use the desktop and take you through a detailed explanation of Linux applications, including the Vi editor and shell operations. The links to this documentation are listed here. Other documentation provides detailed tutorials on different Linux topics.

- *Desktop Interface User's Guide*
- *Linux Installation and Getting Started Guide*
- *Crisplite Editor User's Guide*
- *Linux HOW-TO documents*
- *Known Bugs List*
- *Other Linux documentation*

The **/usr/doc** directory contains the online documentation for many Linux applications. There are subdirectories with the names of installed Linux applications that contain documentation such as README files. You can access the complete set of HOW-TO text files in the **/usr/doc/HOWTO** directory. The HOW-TO series contains detailed documentation on all Linux topics from hardware installation to network configuration. In addition, **/doc/HOWTO/HTML** holds documentation in the form of Web pages that you display with a Web Browser. (Use Lisa to install the HOW-TO html package.

There is also online documentation for GNU applications such as the gcc compiler and the Emacs editor. You can access this documentation by entering the command info. This brings up a special screen listing different GNU applications. The **info** interface has its own set of commands. You can learn more about it by entering **info info**. Typing **m** opens a line at the bottom of the screen where you can enter the first few letters of the application. Pressing ENTER brings up the info file on that application.

Configuring Your System: Easy Setup with Lisa

You are your own system administrator for your Linux system. There are certain administrative tasks you may have to perform, such as creating new user accounts or installing new software. You perform these within a special system administration account called the root. To gain access to this account, you log in as the root user, sometimes called the superuser. As the root user, you will have complete control over your system; you can change it in almost any way you want. You can install software packages, create new accounts, add new devices or disks to your system, or configure X-Windows or your network interfaces.

To perform such administrative tasks, you use the Linux Installation and System Administration program (Lisa) provided with your OpenLinux system and available with many other distributions. It provides an easy-to-use interface for performing basic system administration tasks. As an alternative, there is also a set of Redhat administrative tools available that have more detailed interfaces. These, along with system administration tasks, are described in Chapters 7, 19, and 20. With Lisa, however, you can easily perform many of the essential tasks.

Lisa has a full-screen interface with detailed prompts taking you through steps to perform tasks such as installing a printer or mounting new partitions. There is a detailed online description for Lisa that you can access at the Caldera Web site at **www.caldera.com**. Click on Online Documentation and choose the entries for either OpenLinux Base or OpenLinux Standard. Then select the chapter, Administering OpenLinux.

To use Lisa, you first you have to log in as the root user. Recall that during installation you specified a password for the root user. It is this password that you will use to log in as the root user. If other people are using your Linux system, be careful to keep your root password confidential. Anyone logging in as the root user has superuser capabilities and has the power to destroy any or all of your Linux system.

To log in as the root user, type **root** at the login prompt. (If you are already logged into your regular user account, you need to log out first.) Then, you enter your password for the root user.

```
Caldera OpenLinux (TM)
Lite 1
Version 1.1
Copyright (c) 1996-1997 Caldera Inc.

turtle.trek.com login: root
Password:
```

The easiest way to run Lisa is to enter the **lisa** command on the command line. You can also run it from the desktop, but you will have to first start up the desktop with the **startx** command. Once logged in, you will be given the root user prompt, the **#** symbol. Note how this differs from the user prompt, **$**.

```
# lisa
```

Lisa initially displays a menu with four choices: Verbose system analysis, System Configuration, Software Package Administration, and Help System. You use the System Configuration entry for file management, device configuration, or adding new users. Software Package Administration lets you easily add or remove software packages. The Help System will list the HOW-TO documents available on your system. If you run into problems, you can consult the appropriate HOW-TO document. The Verbose system analysis will provide information on how your system is currently configured. Figure 2-5 in Chapter 2 shows the initial Lisa menu.

Most Lisa screens show buttons at the bottom. A Call button will start up a selection made on the menu. The Continue button will leave the screen, reverting to a previous one, or, in the case of the Main Menu, end the program. If there are two buttons, one will be selected, the other will be de-selected with its name in black. To choose the selected one, you just press ENTER. To access the other one, such as the Continue button, you use the RIGHT or LEFT ARROW keys (you can also use the TAB key). Press the RIGHT ARROW key to select the button on the right, and the LEFT ARROW key for the left button. Then press ENTER. Lisa also provides you with online help. At any point you can press the F1 key to bring up a box with an explanation of the current choice. The Continue button or the ESC key returns you to the prevous screen. To leave Lisa you just have to continually select Continue to go back up to the main menu.

To perform administration tasks you choose the System Configuration entry. This brings up a list of choices for different areas (see Figure 3-3). You can then choose from hardware, system, network, or boot manager configurations. The network entry allows you to perform network configuration such as entering in domain name addresses. Hardware administration allows you to add new devices such as printers. System configuration allows you to perform tasks such as adding new user accounts or mounting partitions.

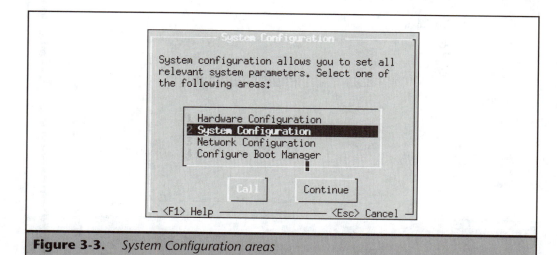

Figure 3-3. *System Configuration areas*

For system administration, select the System Configuration entry in this menu. This brings up a screen with choices shown in Figure 3-4. The "Configure Mount Table" entry allows you to specify partitions or devices that you want mounted automatically when your system starts up. Your main Linux and swap partitions are already entered. See Chapter 7 for a more detailed explanation of partitions and how to mount them.

User Administration brings up a menu with options for managing users and groups (see Figure 3-5). To add a new user, you select the "Add New Users" entry. A series of prompts will ask you to enter a login name, an ID (any number between 100 and 64000), a group, a home directory, a start up shell (usually BASH), and a password. To add a new group you select the "Create a new group" entry.

The Hardware Administration menu will list series of hardware components such as modem, printer, hard disks, and mouse, as well as the XFree86 server. Choose the entry for the item you want to configure. You will be given a list of hardware types that you can choose from. For example, for the CD-ROM, you would choose from a list of different CD-ROM models. The XFree86 server entry allows you to choose different servers. This is helpful if you have changed your graphics card and need to use another server.

From the desktop there are several ways to start up the **Lisa** utility. First, start the desktop by entering the **startx** command. From the desktop, you can click on the Admin button of the fvwm toolbar. This brings up a smaller button bar that has a Lisa button in it. You can also use the fvwm program menu, selecting Lisa under the System administration menu, part of the Applications menu. Finally you can select the System Admin folder on the Caldera Desktop.

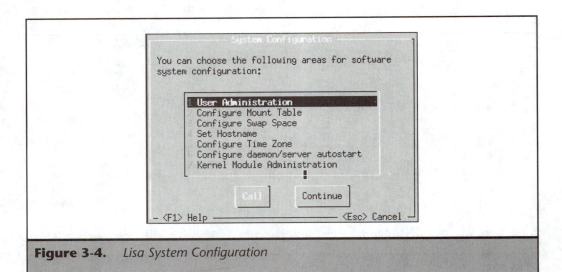

Figure 3-4. *Lisa System Configuration*

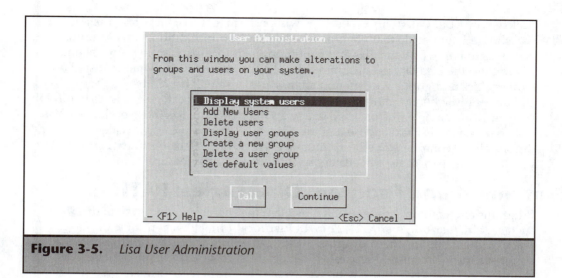

Figure 3-5.   *Lisa User Administration*

Installing Software Packages

Now that you know how to start Linux and access the root user, you can install any other software packages you may want. Installing software is an administrative function performed by the root user. Unless you chose the Complete Install option during your installation, only a few of the many applications and utilities available for users on Linux were installed on your system. Appendix B contains a full listing of all the software packages available on your OpenLinux CD-ROM.

There are several methods of installing software. You can use the graphical interface called *glint* from your desktop. You can also use the Lisa tool from either the desktop or the command line. These are the easiest and most effective ways to install several packages. You can also directly invoke the Redhat Package Manager (RPM) with the **rpm** command from your command line. However, this is a more complex operation. Finally, you can download software from online sources and then use the **rpm** command to install them. This operation is described briefly here, and a detailed explanation is provided in Chapter 7.

Both the Caldera and Redhat distributions of Linux use the Redhat Package Manager (RPM) to organize Linux software into packages that you can automatically install or remove. An RPM software package operates like its own installation program for a software application. A Linux software application will often consist of several files that need to be installed in different directories. The program itself will most likely be placed in a directory called **/usr/bin**, online manual files will go in another directory, and library files in yet another. In addition, the installation may require modification of certain configuration files on your system. The RPM software packages on your OpenLinux CD-ROM will perform all these tasks for you. Also, if you should later decide that you don't want a specific application, you can uninstall packages to remove all the files and configuration information from your system.

You use the Lisa or glint programs to select the packages you want to install or remove. Lisa and glint have different advantages. Lisa will list all the packages alphabetically, whereas glint organizes them into folders by category. Lisa is helpful if you know the name of the package you want (Appendix B lists those packages). You just go down the list and choose it. glint, however, lets you browse by category. You can see all the compilers or editors you have. However, to locate a particular package, you would have to know what category and thereby what folder it is in.

Command and Program Directories: PATH

Programs and commands are usually installed in several standard system directories such as **/bin**, **/usr/bin**, **/usr/X11R6/bin**, or **/usr/local/bin**. However, some packages will place their commands in subdirectories that they create within one of these standard directories or in an entirely separate directory. In such cases, you may not be able to run those commands because your system may not be able to locate them in the new subdirectory. Your system maintains a set of directories that searches for commands each time you execute one. This set of directories is kept in a system variable called PATH that is created when you start your system. If a command is in a directory that is not in this list, then your system will not be able to locate it and run it. To use such commands, you first need to add the new directory to the set of directories in the PATH variable.

On the OpenLinux system, the PATH variable is assigned its set of directories in the **/etc/profile** file. **/etc/profile** is a script that is run when your system starts and is used to configure user's working environments. In this file you will find a line that begins with PATH followed by an = sign and then a list of directories, each separated by a colon. These are the directories that contain commands and programs.

To add a directory, carefully edit the **/etc/profile** file using a text editor such as Crisplite, XEmacs, Emacs, or Vi (you may want to make a backup copy first with the **cp** command). At the end of the list of directories, add the new directory with its full path name before the closing double quote. Be sure there is a colon separating the new directory from the last one. You should also have a colon at the end. For example, if you install the **MH** mail utility, the **MH** commands will be installed in a subdirectory called **mh** in the **/usr/bin** directory. The full path name for this directory is **/usr/bin/mh**. You need to add this directory to the list of directories assigned to PATH in the **/etc/profile** script. (The command **rpm -qpl** *package-name* will list all the directories where commands in an RPM software package are installed.) The following example shows the PATH variable with its list of directories and the **/usr/bin/mh** directory added (shown in bold).

```
PATH="/bin:/usr/bin:/opt/bin:/usr/X11R6/bin:/usr/openwin/bin:/usr/
local/bin:/usr/bin/mh:"
```

The **/etc/profile** script is a system script that is executed for each user when they log in. Individual users can customize their PATH variable by placing a PATH assignment in either their **.bashrc** or **.profile** files. This way a user can access commands and programs, that they create or install for their own use, in their own user directories (see Chapter 15 for more details). The following entry in the **.profile** file would add a user's **mybin** directory to the PATH variable. Use of $PATH keeps all the directories already listed in the **/etc/profile** script. Notice both the colon placed before the new directory, and the use of the $HOME variable to specify the path name for the user's home directory.

```
PATH=$PATH:$HOME/mybin:
```

Lisa: Software Package Management

Choose the Software Package Administration entry on the main Lisa menu. This will give you four choices. The first choice is the Select installation source. To add software from your Linux CD-ROM, you first have to tell Lisa that the software is located there. Choose this entry. A list of devices will be displayed, with the CD-ROM device highlighted. Press ENTER to choose it. Lisa will detect the CD-ROM and ask you to confirm. Press ENTER and you then return to the software packages menu. Move down to the entry Installation of additional software packages (use the ARROW keys), then press ENTER. Lisa displays a list of all the software packages not installed. This may take a few moments.

Each entry will have a small empty set of parentheses to the left. Next to it will be the file name of the software package, displayed in yellow. To the right is a description of the package. To select a package, move to that package using the ARROW keys. The PAGE UP and PAGE DOWN keys will scroll through the list one screen at a time. Once at the package, press SPACEBAR to select it. You will see an *x* appear within the parentheses. You can choose as many packages as you want. If you change your mind and decide you don't want a particular package, you can move to it and press the SPACEBAR on it again. You will see the *x* disappear and the package will be deselected. Once you have selected your packages, press ENTER. All the packages you selected will be installed. Figure 3-6 shows a listing of packages on Lisa. Should you want to cancel the installation, you can use the TAB key to tab to the Cancel button and then press ENTER.

To remove packages, just choose the entry Remove software packages that have already been installed, and a list of installed packages will be displayed. Select the ones you want as you did with the installed list of packages, using the SPACEBAR. When you press ENTER they will be removed from your system.

Linux Installation Manager: glint

The **glint** utility's user-friendly interface makes installing software easy: simply point and click with your mouse. glint automatically copies the software to its appropriate

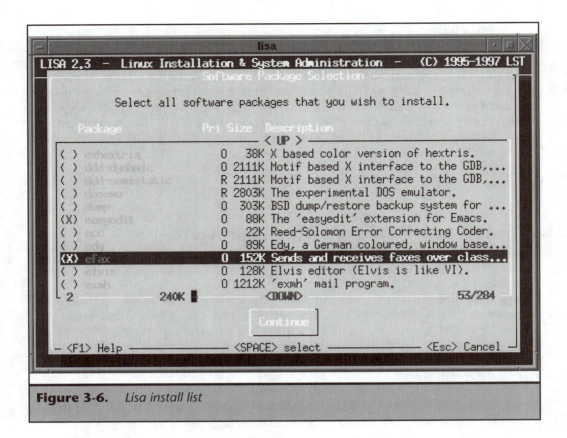

Figure 3-6. *Lisa install list*

directory, including any other special configuration files there may be. Uninstalling is just as simple. glint can locate all the files that make up a software package and remove them.

As with Lisa, you first have to log in as the **root** user. If you want to install software from your CD-ROM, you have to first make the CD-ROM accessible to your system. Unlike Lisa, glint does not do this for you. You need to issue a command that performs an operation called mounting a file system. First place the OpenLinux CD-ROM in your CD-ROM drive and then enter the following command. This makes a disk in your CD-ROM drive accessible to the Linux system. Mounting file systems is discussed in detail in Chapter 7.

```
$ mount /mnt/cdrom
```

glint is an X-Windows program and needs to be run from the desktop. Enter **startx** to start the desktop. You can access glint through the same routes as the Lisa tool: the Admin button on the fvwm toolbar, the fvwm Program menu under System administration in the Applications menu, and the Admin_Tools folder on the Caldera Desktop. Once you start glint, the glint window will be displayed, as shown in Figure 3-7. glint works like a file manager window. It displays application and folder icons. Applications of the same category will be located within the same folder. For example, the Emacs editor will be placed in a folder called Editors, which will in turn be placed in a folder called Applications.

The folders and icons of software packages that you see are the ones already installed on your system (see Figure 3-7). You can use this window to see which software packages you already have and to remove an installed package. Just locate its icon within the appropriate folder, click on it to select it, and then click on the Uninstall button to the right. When you select a package, its icon will have a red border. You can select several icons by just clicking on them, and then uninstall them all at once. To deselect an icon you have already selected, just click on it again. You will see the red border disappear.

When you open and display the contents of a folder, you will notice that one of the icons has the name "Back" with a large black arrow. This is the icon you click on to return to the upper folder that you just came from. For example, if you open the Applications folder by double-clicking on it, the icons for that folder, such as the Games folder, will be displayed along with the Back icon. Clicking on the Games folder opens and displays the icons for the games packages along with a Back icon.

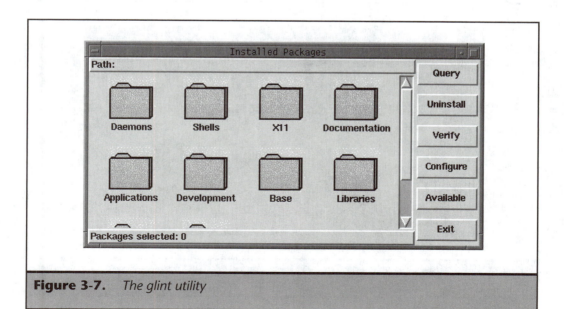

Figure 3-7.   *The glint utility*

To return to the Applications folder, click on the Back icon. Once in the Applications folder, you can click on its Back icon to return to the main folder. By clicking on folders and their Back icons, you can move back and forth through the different collections of software packages.

To install a new software package, first click on the Available button on the right-hand side of the glint window. This opens up a new glint window labeled "Available Packages," which displays folders and icons of uninstalled packages available on your Caldera CD-ROM (see Figure 3-8). The packages are collected within their appropriate folders. Just click on their folders to display them. To install a package, select it by clicking on its icon, and then click on the Install button on the right side of glint's Available Packages window. You can select several packages by clicking on them, and then install them all at once by clicking on the Install button. If you select a package and decide not to install it, you can deselect it by again clicking on its icon. Selected packages will show a red border around their icons. Once you have installed a package, its icon will disappear from the Available Packages window, and it will show up in the Installed window.

To obtain a brief description of any package, select its icon and then click on the Info button in the glint window. If you try to open the Available Packages window and receive an error message to the effect that there are no RPMS packages to install (and you did not choose the Complete Install option), most likely you did not mount the OpenLinux CD-ROM. You can just open a terminal window and enter the mount

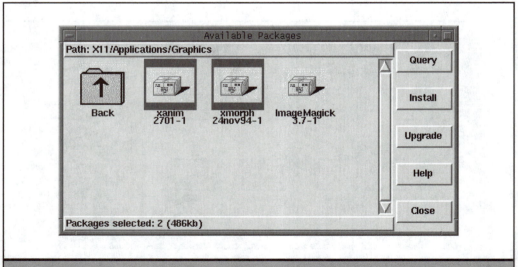

Figure 3-8. *The glint Available Packages window*

command from there. Click on the Xterm button in the fvwm taskbar and then, at the prompt in the terminal window enter the command **mount /mnt/cdrom**.

Command Line Installation: Redhat Package Manager

If you do not have access to the desktop, or would prefer to work from the command line interface, you can use the **rpm** command to manage and install software packages. **rpm** stands for the Redhat Package Manager. It is the command that actually performs installation, removal, and verification of software packages. In fact, both Lisa and glint use the **rpm** command to install and remove packages. Each software package is actually an RPM package, consisting of an archive of software files and information about how to install those files. Each archive resides as a single file with a name that ends with **.rpm**, indicating that it is a software package that can be installed by the Redhat Package Manager.

You can use the **rpm** command to either install or uninstall a package. **rpm** uses a set of options to determine what action to take. Table 3-1 lists the set of **rpm** options. The **-i** option will install the specified software package. With an **-e** option, **rpm** will uninstall the package. A **q** placed before an **i** (**-qi**) will query the system to see if a software package is already installed and display information about the software (**-qpi** will query an uninstalled package file). The **--h** option provides a complete list of **rpm** options. A helpful one is the **--force** option that forces installation. The syntax for the **rpm** command is as follows (*rpm-package-name* is the name of the software package that you want to install):

```
rpm options rpm-package-name
```

The software package name is usually very lengthy, including information about version and release date in its name. All end with **.rpm**. A standard set of Linux applications are in the **Packages/RPMS** directory on your CD-ROM. The packages also reside in the OpenLinux directory, distributed among various subdirectories indicating the type of application such as xapps1 and develop1. The packages will usually be found in a further subdirectory named **RPMS**. Certain special applications such as the Java Development Kit and Xfm are located in the **OpenLinux/contrib** directory. To install a software package from your Caldera CD-ROM, it is easier to move first to the appropriate **RPMS** directory and then install the package you want. If you cannot change to that directory, your CD-ROM may not be mounted on your file system. If so, refer to the previous section on how to mount your CD-ROM (**mount /mnt/cdrom**). For example, to change to the subdirectory that holds the Java Development Kit (JDK) you enter the command:

```
$ cd /mnt/cdrom/OpenLinux/contrib/RPMS
```

An **ls** command will list all the software packages. If you know how the name of a package begins, you should include that with the **ls** command and an attached *****. The list of packages is extensive and will not all fit on one screen. This is helpful for displaying the detailed name of the package. The following example lists X-Windows packages:

```
$ ls x*
```

In the next example, the user installs the JDK package using the **rpm** command. Notice that the full file name is entered. To list the full name, you can use the **ls** command with the first few characters and an asterisk, **ls JDK***.

```
$ rpm  -i JDK_static_1.0.2.p12-3.i386.rpm
```

No distinction is made between installed and uninstalled packages. You have to know the one you want to install and whether or not it is already installed. To find out if a package is already installed, use the **-qi** option with **rpm**. The **-q** stands for query. In the next example, the user checks to see if the JDK is already installed on the system. Notice that the full file name of the **rpm** archive is not needed. If installed, your system has already registered the name of the package and where it is located.

```
$ rpm -qi JDK_static
```

To obtain a list of all the files that the package has installed, as well as the directories it installed to, you use the **-qpl** option. The following example lists all the files in the JDK package.

```
$ rpm -ql JDK_static
```

To remove a software package from your system, first use **rpm -qpi** to make sure it is actually installed. Then, use the **-e** option to uninstall it. As with the **-qpi** option, you do not have to use the full name of the installed file. You only need the name of the application. In the next example, the user removes the JDK_static from the system:

```
$ rpm  -e  JDK_static
```

A complete description of **rpm** and its capabilities is provided in the online manual.

```
$ man rpm
```

Installing Software from Online Sources

Installing software from online sources is complicated by the fact that you first have to access remote sites. To do this, you need to know where the software is located and then use either Netscape or the **ftp** utility to download the package. If you connect to the Internet through a modem you first have to use pppd. Table 3-2 lists several ftp sites for RPM packages. Some packages may not use an RPM format. Instead, they may be compressed archives. To open compressed archives, you use the **gunzip** and **tar** commands. This process is described in detail in Chapter 7. All RPM packages end with an **.rpm** extension. When you download such a package, you must use the **rpm** command to install it. It is preferable to use a package that is in the RPM format. Usually, a software application will be available in both the form of an RPM package and of a tar archive for those who do not have the Redhat Package Manager on their system. Many of the RPM packages for software applications can be found in the **/pub/contrib/i386** directory on the Redhat ftp site, **ftp.redhat.com**, or its mirror sites. You can easily download software in RPM format from this site and use the **rpm** command to install it. Other Linux sites such as Sunsite and tsx-11 have a mix of software available as compressed archives or RPM packages. Versions of Netscape Navigator for Linux in RPM format can be found at the **ftp.caldera.com** site in the **/pub/netscape/navigator** directory, whereas versions as compressed archives are found on the Netscape ftp sites (**ftp5.netscape.com**).

The next example uses ftp to connect to the **ftp.caldera.com** Linux ftp site and downloads the Netscape Navigator Web Browser. The user enters **anonymous** for the login ID and an Internet address for the password. Often a list of mirror sites will be listed. A mirror site holds an exact copy of all the files in that ftp site. If the ftp site is too busy and does not allow you in, or is too slow, it is best to try one of the mirror sites.

Once logged into the ftp site, with the **cd** command, the user changes to the **/pub/netscape/navigator** directory where Linux versions of Netscape Navigator are located. Then the user changes to the **3.01** directory for the 3.01 version of Navigator. To get the current listing of the package you want, enter **ls** with the first few characters of the package name with an asterisk. The user first enters **ls nets*** to display the full name of the package. You will have to use the full name to download with ftp. Most sites will automatically download files in binary format, as indicated for **ftp.caldera.com** when the user first logged in. If the site does not do so automatically, you would have to specify binary format with the **binary** command. The **get** command then downloads the package. Once you are finished downloading all the packages you want, you can leave the ftp site with the **close**. **quit** command.

```
# ftp ftp.caldera.com
Connected to rim.caldera.com.
220 rim.caldera.com FTP server (Version wu-2.4.2-academ[BETA-12](1) Wed Feb
19 03:54:33 MET 1997) ready.
Name (ftp.caldera.com:root): anonymous
331 Guest login ok, send your complete e-mail address as password.
Password: Enter-your-internet-address
230 Guest login ok, access restrictions apply.
Remote system type is UNIX.
Using binary mode to transfer files.
ftp> cd pub/netscape/navigator
250 CWD command successful.
ftp> cd 3.01
250-Please read the file README.license.txt
250-  it was last modified on Tue Aug 19 19:47:00 1997 - 5 days ago
250 CWD command successful.
ftp> ls net*
200 PORT command successful.
150 Opening ASCII mode data connection for /bin/ls.
total 2313
 -r--r--r--    1 root      root       2336089 Aug 17 03:10
netscape-3.01-6.i386.rpm
226 Transfer complete.
ftp> get netscape-3.01-6.i386.rpm
local: netscape-3.01-6.i386.rpm remote: netscape-3.01-6.i386.rpm
200 PORT command successful.
150 Opening BINARY mode data connection for netscape-3.01-6.i386.rpm
(2336089 bytes).
226 Transfer complete.
2336089 bytes received in 711 secs (3.2 Kbytes/sec)
ftp> close
>221 Goodbye.
ftp> quit
#
```

Once downloaded, you install the RPM package with the **rpm -i** command. Downloaded software will usually include README files or other documentation. Be sure to consult them. Students and educators can register Netscape Navigator for free, whereas others can register for a price. Registration entitles you to technical support and upgrade offers. Otherwise, you are free to use Netscape Navigator unregistered.

```
$ rpm -i package-name
```

In the case of the Netscape package, you need to use a special option to force installations. The **/usr/bin/netscape** file already on your OpenLinux system interferes with the RPM installation (the file just tells you that you don't have Netscape). You need to use the **--force** option to overwrite this file with the Netscape program. (Notice there are two dashes in the **--force** option.)

```
$ rpm -i --force netscape-3.01-6.i386.rpm
```

Alternatively, you could use Netscape to access, browse through, and download software without having to bother with all the ftp commands. Be sure to precede an ftp site name with the term **ftp://** instead of the usual **http://**. For **Redhat** you would enter **ftp://ftp.redhat.com**. The Netscape Browser will display a listing of all the files in the directory. You can use the scroll bar to move through the display. To move to a new directory you double-click on its name. Directories will have a yellow folder icon displayed to the left of the name. To reach the **/pub/contrib/i386** directory you first double-click on the **/pub** directory name. This displays that directory's contents. Then click on the contrib folder. From the display of the contrib folder's directories and files, click on the **i386** directory. Figure 3-9 shows a Netscape display of an ftp directory.

To select a package for downloading you first have to hold down the SHIFT key, then click on the package name with the mouse. This brings up a dialog box that displays the package name and indicates the directory it will be downloaded to. Click the OK button to download the file. Figure 3-9 shows such a window. You then use the **rpm -i** command to install it.

Remote Communications

It is very easy to directly connect to a remote system using Linux. After a simple configuration of your modem, you can use any of several telecommunication programs to dial and log in to a remote system. Two of the most popular telecommunication programs are minicom and Seyon. Both provide an easy-to-use interface and advanced features such as automatic logins.

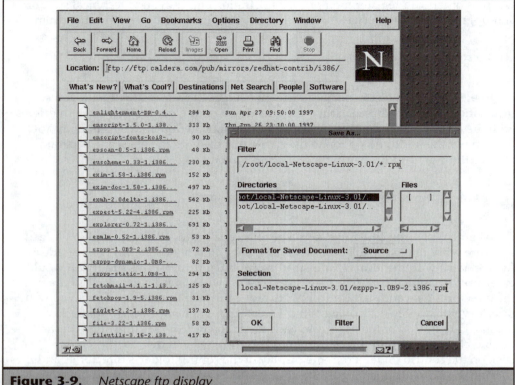

Figure 3-9. *Netscape ftp display*

Modem Setup

If you have a modem connected to your PC, it will be connected to one of four communications ports. The PC names for these ports are COM1, COM2, COM3, and COM4. These ports can also be used for other serial devices such as your mouse. Usually, your mouse is connected to COM1 and your modem is connected to COM2, though in many cases your modem may be connected to COM4. Find out which ports your modem and mouse are connected to; you'll need to know this to access your modem. On the PC, COM1 and COM3 share the same access point to your computer; the same is true of COM2 and COM4. For this reason, you should never have your mouse on COM1 and your modem on COM3. You would find your mouse cutting out whenever you used your modem. If your mouse is on COM1, then your modem should be either on COM2 or COM4.

In Linux, the four communications ports have different names than those used for the PC. Modem ports begin with the name **/dev/cua** with an attached number from 0 to 3. (Notice the numbering begins from 0, not 1.) **/dev/cua0** is the first port, COM1, and **/dev/cua1** are the second ports. The third and fourth ports are **/dev/cua2** and **/dev/cua3**. In many Linux communication programs, you will need to know the port for your modem. This will be either **/dev/cua1** for COM2 or **/dev/cua3** for COM4.

Some communication programs try to access the modem port using just the name **/dev/modem**. Currently, this name does not exist in your system. It is meant to be an alias, another name, for whatever your modem port really is. Once you know what your modem port is, you can easily create this alias using the **ln -s** command. The following would create an alias called modem for the COM2 port, **/dev/cua1**. If your modem port is **/dev/cua3,** you would use that instead. (You have to be logged in as **root** user to execute this command.) The following example sets up the **/dev/modem** alias for the second serial port, **/dev/cua1**.

```
# ln -s /dev/cua1  /dev/modem
```

Your **/dev/mouse** alias should already be set up for the port it uses. This is usually the COM1 port, **/dev/cua0**. If the alias is not set up, or you need to change it, you can use the **ln -s** command. The following example sets up the **/dev/mouse** alias for the first serial port, **/dev/cua0**.

```
# ln -s /dev/cua0  /dev/mouse
```

Telecommunication Programs: minicom and Seyon

minicom is a terminal emulator with which you can dial into and remotely log in to other systems. It is not an X-Windows program. You run it from the command line and it can be run from any user account. To start it up, enter the command **minicom**. This brings up a cursor base screen. You use the CTRL-A character to issue commands. You follow CTRL-A with a character for the operation you want to perform. For example, a CTRL-A followed by a D sequence will bring up the dialing directory. You can quit from any screen by pressing the ESC key. A CTRL-A followed by a Z sequence will display a help screen that lists the different commands. While in this screen you can press the character for that command to execute it. The CTRL-A followed by a P command brings up a screen in which you can enter your modem parameters, specifying baud rate and parity. CTRL-A followed by an O brings up a configuration menu. The Send Port Setup entry brings up a screen for selecting the communications port your modem uses, such as **/dev/cua1**. The Modem entry brings up a screen for entering modem information such as an initialization string. The Filename and Paths entry lets you select directories for downloadin or uploading files.

To make a remote connection, you enter CTRL-A followed by a D to first bring up the dial directory, and then select the number of the system you want to connect to.

The dial directory lets you add or edit entries, with commands for these listed on the bottom of the screen. Use the RIGHT and LEFT ARROW keys to select the one you want. To dial a number, use the UP and DOWN ARROW keys to select the number you want and then select the dial command. On the screen you will see the interactive prompts for login name and password. You can also create a script to automatically perform dial and login operations. Text displayed on your screen from your login session is kept, and you can scroll through it by entering a scroll mode with the CTRL-A followed by a B command. You can scroll forward or backward line by line or page by page.

minicom supports the zmodem, ymodem, xmodem, and kermit transfer protocols. With CTRL-A followed by an S you can send files, and with CTRL-A followed by an R receive them. minicom also lets you add any new protocols you might acquire. CTRL-A followed by an H will hangup the phone line, and CTRL-A followed by an X quits minicom.

Seyon is a telecommunications program that runs from your desktop. It provides terminal emulation and supports transmission protocols for both downloading and uploading files. It includes a dialing directory and a scripting language for automating logins and downloads. The Seyon interface consists of easy-to-use windows, buttons, and menus. Each component supports a variety of features. The dialing directory lets you edit login scripts to select features such as automatic redial and time-outs. Terminal emulation makes use of Xterm windows, giving it Xterm features such as a scroll-back buffer and cut and paste functions. When Seyon starts up, it displays a command center window with different buttons for various tasks. The Transfer button lets you download files. With the Dial button, you dial and log in to a remote system.

Internet Connections with Modems: pppd and ezppp

If you connect to the Internet over a phone line using a modem, then you will have to set up a PPP connection. The Point-to-Point Protocol (PPP) is a protocol used for most connections to the Internet through modems. (If, instead, you are directly connected to an intranet with an Ethernet card, then your network connection should already be configured. If not, you can use Lisa to configure it.)

In Linux, the PPP connection is made with a **pppd** command, described in detail in Chapter 20. You can execute this command directly, as described in the next section, or use an Internet connection utility such a **EzPPP**, also described here. **EzPPP** is not on your CD-ROM. You have to download it from the Redhat contrib directory. To do that, you first have to have a working PPP connection. The following section shows how you would set up a simple PPP connection using the **pppd** command. See Chapter 20 for a more detailed presentation.

pppd

Most Internet service providers use dynamic local and remote addresses in their Internet connections. A simple dynamic connection is described here. For a more detailed discussion of pppd and static addresses, see Chapter 20. pppd makes use of two files to make a connection. The chat script specifies how to connect to the provider with a login name and password. The options file has a set of standard options that pppd uses to configure the connection.

You should first set up the **pppd** options. **pppd** has a great many options. For example, the **noipdefault** option instructs **pppd** to detect and use a dynamic IP address from the ISP remote system. You can list the options after the speed on the command line, but this can make for a very lengthy and complex command line, depending on how many options you need. As an alternative, **pppd** allows you to enter options in the **/etc/ppp/options** file. **pppd** will automatically read and use the options specified in this file each time it is invoked. Listed here are the standard options you will need. Edit the **/etc/ppp/options** file using an editor such as Crisplite, Vi, or XEmacs and enter these options:

/etc/ppp/options

```
crtscts
defaultroute
modem
asyncmap 0
noipdefault
```

You are now ready to set up the connection information. The actual dial-up connection is made by the **chat** command. To make a connection, **chat** has to specify all the connection information: the telephone number, login prompt and user ID, password prompt and password, and any connect strings. A **chat** operation consists of several entries consisting of an expect-reply pair of strings. The first string is what you expect to receive and the second string is what you are sending. If you expect to receive nothing, then you use a null string, **""**. The next segment first expects nothing, as indicated by the empty string, **""**. Then, in response, you are ready to dial the telephone number.

```
""    ATDT5556666
```

Then, the remote system usually sends the login prompt. This is often the word "login" with a colon. You only need the last few characters, **ogin:**. Don't forget the colon. In reply, you send your user ID. Depending on your ISP, you may have to add **\n** to the user ID to enter a newline, as in mylogin\n.

```
ogin:   mylogin
```

After the login, you can expect the password prompt. Again, you only need the last few characters, **word:**. In response, you send your password:

```
word:  mypass
```

These expect-reply pairs are combined into a chat operation using the **chat** command. Usually, you include the **-v** option so that chat will report the actions it takes.

```
'chat -v -f "" ATDT5556666  ogin:  mylogin  word: mypass'
```

You need to incorporate the chat operation into your invocation of the **pppd** command. The entire chat operation will be encased in single quotes and entered on the same line as the **pppd** command. The chat program will use the information in the chat script to initialize your modem, dial up your remote host, and then log in with your user ID and password.

You then only need to enter the **pppd** command with the chat invocation, the device name for your modem, and the modem speed. The standard syntax is shown here. If you are making a static connection to an ISP, you should add the ISP static internet address after the speed.

```
pppd  options  serial-device-name  speed
```

The *serial-device-name* is the device name for your modem. This is likely to be **/dev/cua** with a number attached, usually from 0 to 3, depending on the port you are using for your modem. Port 1 is **cua0**, port 2 is **cua1**, and so on. The *speed* is the baud rate. For a 14.4 modem this is 14400. For a v.28 modem this is 38400, or even 57600. Check with your ISP provider and your modem documentation for the highest speed you can support.

The **connect** option instructs **pppd** to make a connection. It takes as its argument a Linux command that will actually make the connection—usually the **chat** command. You enter **pppd** followed by the **connect** option and the **chat** command with its expect-reply pairs. The entire **chat** operation is encased in single quotes. In the next example, the user invokes **pppd** with the **chat** operation. The modem is connected to port 2, **/dev/cua1**, and the speed is 57600 baud. Notice the single quotes around the entire **chat** operation with its expect-reply pairs.

```
# pppd connect  'chat -v "" ATDT5556666 ogin: mylogin  word:
mypass'  /dev/cua1   57600
```

You are now ready to try **pppd** to connect to your remote system. Any number of things may go wrong. You may not have the right connect string or the modem may be initializing wrong. **pppd** will log descriptions of all the steps it is taking in the **/var/log/messages** file. You can use **more**, **tail**, or **cat** to list these descriptions even as **pppd** is operating. For a successful connection you will see the IP addresses listed as shown here. The following command will display the PPP operations as they take place. When you are finished, you can enter CTRL-C to return to the prompt.

```
$ tail -f /var/log/messages
```

The following is a sample pppd operation, showing the contents of the **/var/log/messages** file as pppd and chat login to a remote system. You have made the connection when you see the local and remote addresses. If you used the **-f** option with tail, you then enter CTRL-C to end the reporting. You could also just use several **tail /var/log/messages** commands without **-f**, to not have to bother with a CTRL-C.

```
# pppd connect 'chat -v "" ATDT5556666 ogin: mylogin word:  mypass'
/dev/cua1 57600
# tail -f  /var/log/messages
Aug 24 17:55:49 turtle chat[294]: send (ATDT8659004^M)
Aug 24 17:55:49 turtle chat[294]: expect (ogin:)
Aug 24 17:56:05 turtle chat[294]: CONNECT 57600^M
Aug 24 17:56:07 turtle chat[294]: ^M
Aug 24 17:56:07 turtle chat[294]: login: -- got it
Aug 24 17:56:07 turtle chat[294]: send (mylogin^M)
Aug 24 17:56:08 turtle chat[294]: expect (word:)
Aug 24 17:56:08 turtle chat[294]: Password: -- got it
Aug 24 17:56:08 turtle chat[294]: send (mypass^M)
Aug 24 17:56:08 turtle pppd[293]: Serial connection established.
Aug 24 17:56:09 turtle pppd[293]: Using interface ppp0
Aug 24 17:56:09 turtle pppd[293]: Connect: ppp0 <--> /dev/cua1
Aug 24 17:56:12 turtle pppd[293]: local  IP address 204.32.168.173
Aug 24 17:56:12 turtle pppd[293]: remote IP address 163.179.4.32
Ctrl-c
#
```

To disconnect your PPP connection, you invoke **pppd** with the **disconnect** option. You must use **chat** to instruct your modem to hang up. For this, you may have to send a modem command such as H0. Be sure to include the modem device name or /dev/modem.

```
# pppd disconnect  'chat  "" +++ ATH0  OK' dev/cua1
```

There are many ways to streamline this process. You can create a chat script to hold the expect-reply pairs. You can also place the entire **pppd** command in a shell script and then use the shell script name alone to execute the entire command. These and other features are described in detail in Chapter 20.

EzPPP

Instead of configuring the connection yourself, it is best to use the EzPPP program described here. EzPPP, written by Jay Painter, makes the process of setting up your PPP connection as simple as the Internet Setup Wizard in Windows 95. You are presented with a series of dialog boxes in which you enter Internet and modem information. Once configured, connecting is simply a matter of clicking on a button labeled CONNECT. EzPPP will run fine from the root user, but needs permission set on certain files to allow use by other users on your system. See the documentation in the **/usr/doc/ezppp*** directory. It also includes a detailed tutorial that you can view with your Web Browser.

EzPPP is not on your OpenLinux CD-ROM, but you can easily download its RPM packages and install them with simple **rpm -i** commands. These packages are located in the Redhat contrib directory at **ftp.redhat.com** in the **/pub/contrib/i386** directory. The program is currently in beta release, but is still very stable. The EzPPP Web page is currently located at **www.serv.net/~cameron/ezppp** (you can link to it through Linux resource pages listed in Table 1-3 in Chapter 1). You can find more information here and an EzPPP HOW-TO document, as well as download the software. This section describes the installation and use of version 1, beta release 9 that requires using QT shared libraries. The QT shared libraries are also in the Redhat contrib directory and will automatically be installed and configured by the **rpm** operation. More recent versions of EzPPP may now be available. There are static and non-static versions. If you download a static version, you will not need the QT libraries.

The following example uses ftp to download EzPPP from the **ftp.redhat.com** site. With the **cd** command, the user changes to the **/pub/contrib/i386** directory where Linux software is located. This directory has a great many packages. To get the current listing of the package you want, enter **ls** with the first few characters of the package name with an asterisk. In this example, the user first enters **ls ezppp*** to display the full name of the EzPPP package. Then the **get** command downloads the **EzPPP RPM** file. Then, another **get** command downloads the QT libraries. The **hash** command is helpful for downloading large files. It displays a hash mark for each data packet received so you know ftp is working.

```
# ftp ftp.redhat.com
 Connected to speedier.redhat.com.
Name (ftp.redhat.com:root): anonymous
331 Guest login ok, send your complete e-mail address as password.
Password:

230 Guest login ok, access restrictions apply.
Remote system type is UNIX.
sUsing binary mode to transfer files.
ftp> cd pub/contrib/i386
>250 CWD command successful.
ftp> ls ezppp*
>200 PORT command successful.
150 Opening ASCII mode data connection for /bin/ls.
-rw-r--r--   1 root     root          74297 May 25 00:55 ezppp-1.0B9-2.i386.rpm
-rw-r--r--   1 root     root          84817 Apr 22 03:38
ezppp-dynamic-1.0B8-1.i386.rpm
-rw-r--r--   1 root     root         301329 Apr 22 03:40 ezppp-static-1.0B8-1.i386.rpm
226 Transfer complete.
ftp> binary
200 Type set to I.
ftp> get ezppp-1.0B9-2.i386.rpm
>local: ezppp-1.0B9-2.i386.rpm remote: ezppp-1.0B9-2.i386.rpm
200 PORT command successful.
150 Opening BINARY mode data connection for ezppp-1.0B9-2.i386.rpm (74297 bytes).
226 Transfer complete.
ftp> hash
>Hash mark printing on (1024 bytes/hash mark).
ftp> ls qt-1*
>200 PORT command successful.
150 Opening ASCII mode data connection for /bin/ls.
-rw-r--r--   1 root     root         419166 Apr  7 20:00 qt-1.31-1.i386.rpm
226 Transfer complete.
ftp> get qt-1.2-1.i386.rpm
>local: qt-1.31-1.i386.rpm remote: qt-1.31-1.i386.rpm
200 PORT command successful.
150 Opening BINARY mode data connection for qt-1.2-1.i386.rpm (419166 bytes).
############################################################################
######################################################################
226 Transfer complete.
```

```
419166 bytes received in 132 secs (3.1 Kbytes/sec)
ftp> close
>221 Goodbye.
ftp> quit
#
```

Once downloaded, you install the RPM packages with the **rpm -i** command.

```
$ rpm -i ezppp-1.0B9-2.i386.rpm
$ rpm -i qt-1.31-1.i386.rpm
```

Once you have installed EzPPP, you then run the program by opening an Xterm window and entering the command **ezppp**. You can also run it through the fvwm Program menu, under the Other Applications menu that is under the Applications menu. The main screen will appear as shown in Figure 3-10.

To set up a connection, you click on the Configure button. This brings up a configuration window that has several panels, much like configuration utilities in Windows 95. One panel will appear in the front, with tabs for the others showing at the top. In the Configuration window there are three panels, one for accounts, another for modem settings, and one for general features. Accounts hold your Internet information. You can have more than one account, depending upon how many different Internet service providers you subscribe to (most users have only one). To create an account you click on the NEW button. This brings up a New Accounts window with a set of panels for Internet information. The Dial panel is where you enter connection information such as the phone number you use to connect to the provider. Be sure to enter a name for the connection. It can be anything you want. The

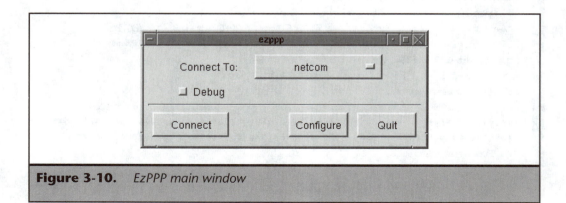

Figure 3-10.   *EzPPP main window*

Arguments button brings up another window for entering PPP arguments. These are options for the PPP daemon and are described in detail in Chapter 20. Usually, you will only need the -detach and defaultroute entries that are already entered, as most standard options are included as defaults. Figure 3-11 shows the Configuration, New Accounts, and Arguments windows.

In the New Account window, the IP panel is where you enter any local and remote IP addresses, as well as a Netmask. Each entry has a Dynamic and Static check button, and the Dynamic ones are already set by default. If your Internet service provider gives you dynamic addresses and a Netmask, as most do these days, you can just leave this panel alone. If, on the other hand, you have a static local or remote address, you will have to bring up the panel and enter them.

Click on the tab labeled DNS to bring up the domain name server panel. Here, you enter in the IP addresses of your Internet service provider's domain name servers. Click on the box labeled IP Address: and type the address. Then click on Add to add it to the list of nameservers. Figure 3-12 shows the panel with some sample IP addresses.

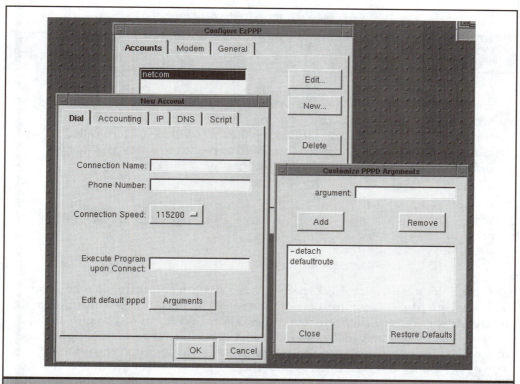

Figure 3-11.   *Configue EzPPP, New Account, and Customize PPPD Arguments windows*

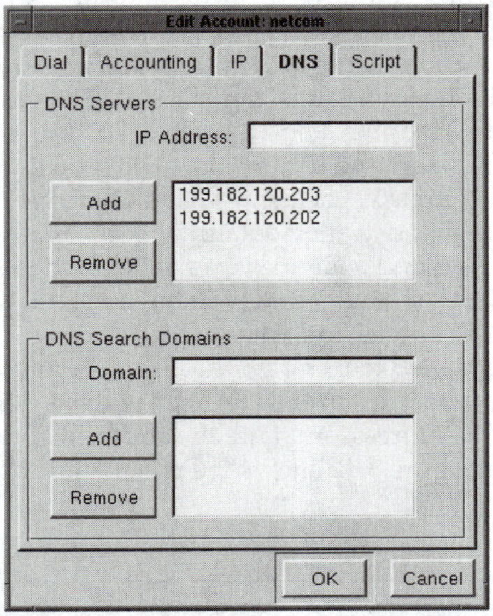

Figure 3-12. *EzPPP domain name server panel*

You then have to create a login script in which you provide the user name and password that you use to connect to your Internet service provider. To do this, you click on the Script tab to bring up the Script panel. You will see a frame called Login Script with several buttons and boxes. You need to create a simple script that will perform the following task using two instructions, send and receive.

```
receive      ogin:
send         username
receive      word:
send         password
```

You will see a button labeled Expect. This is actually a pop-up menu with several entries listing possible login instructions. The entry you select will be shown when the pop-up menu collapses. There are five entries: Expect, Send, Pause, Hangup, and Answer. The instructions usually used to send a string or to expect receiving a string are Send and Expect. If you want a send instruction, select the Send entry; for the receive instruction, select the Expect entry. The box to the right of this button is where you enter text you want that instruction to operate on. For example, for the instruction to receive the text "ogin:", you would select the Expect entry and type **ogin:** into this

box. To place it in the script you click the Add button. You will see both the term
"expect" and the text "ogin:" appear in the script frame below the Add button. If you
make a mistake, you can click on the entry and then click on the Remove button to
delete it. If you need to insert an instruction instead of having it placed at the end, use
the Insert button.

Most login scripts only need two pairs of Send and Expect instructions; one for the
login name and one for the password. The first instruction would Expect the text
"ogin:" and the second would Send text consisting of the login name. The third
instruction would Expect the text "word:", and the fourth would Send the text
consisting of the password. This may vary depending upon how you connect to your
Internet service provider. Figure 3-13 shows a sample login script, where
"my-login-name" would be your user name, and "my-password" would be the
password you use.

You have finished entering in the Internet information. Click OK to close the Script
and New Accounts windows. At the Configure window, click on the Modem tab to
bring up the Modem panel. Make sure the modem port is correct. Modem ports begin
with the name /dev/cua with an attached number from 0 to 3. On your PC, you have
four ports to choose from, 1 through 4. Usually a modem is connected to either 2 or 4.

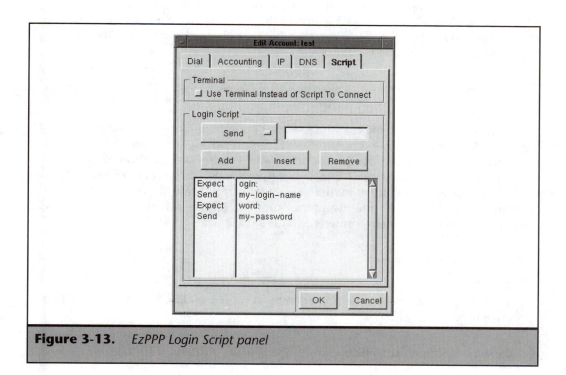

Figure 3-13.   *EzPPP Login Script panel*

The names for these would be /dev/cua1 and /dev/cua3. (The count is from 0, so port 1 is cua0 and port 2 is cua1.)

If you already set up a modem alias for the port, you can just use /dev/modem. You then need to check the dialing prefix as well as any special settings you may need for your modem. You can click on the Edit button to bring up a window with a long list of boxes with settings for your modem. They should already have default settings entered. The first box is where you would enter your modem initialization string, adding such instructions as M0 to turn off the connection sound. The third box, labeled dial string, is where you enter your dialing prefix. ATDT is the default already entered which most people use. Check also the Connect response entry and the Hangup string. The default connect response is CONNECT which is valid for most ISPs. The Hangup string is a standard hangup instruction for most modems.

Once you are finished, close the Configuration window by clicking on the OK button. You are then ready to use EzPPP. Click on the Connect button in the main EzPPP window. If you have problems, click the debug checkbutton. This will bring up a window that will display the connection process and any errors that occur. When EzPPP makes a connection, it will display the amount of time connected, and the Connect button will be changed to Disconnect. To end your session, just click Disconnect. Quit will end the EzPPP program.

You can also set up a button on the fvwm toolbar that will start EzPPP when you click it. Enter the following line at the end of the file **system.fvwmrc.goodstuff** in the **/usr/lib/X11/fvwm** directory. (To display the toolbar, choose Goodstuff in the Desktop menu in the fvwm workplace menu.)

```
*GoodStuff    EzPPP    Game2.xpm      Exec   ""  xlaunch  ezppp
```

EzPPP runs fine if you log into the root user account and operate it from there. However, for normal users to operate EzPPP, certain permissions need to be set for the modem device: the pppd program, and the domain name configuration file to allow access to them by ordinary users. Permissions are discussed in detail in Chapter 7. See the EzPPP HOW-TO document in **/usr/doc/ezppp** directory. To allow access to the modem, use the **chmod** command and the numbers 666. The following example sets the permissions for a modem connected to the COM2 port, /dev/cua1.

```
# chmod 666 /dev/cua1
```

To set the permissions for the **pppd** command you use **chmod** with the **+s** option as shown here:

```
# chmod +s /usr/sbin/pppd
```

Make sure that the **pppd** command is owned by the root user.

```
# chown root.root pppd
```

You can check the permissions and ownership of the **pppd** command with the **ls -l** command (see Chapter 7). They should look like those shown in this example:

```
# ls -l /usr/sbin/pppd
-rwsr-sr-x   1 root        root         84604 Aug 14  1996
/usr/sbin/pppd
```

To allow users to add domain name servers you need to allow access to the **/etc/resovl.conf** file by ordinary users. This is optional. Domain name servers can just as easily be added by the root user.

```
# chmod 666 /etc/resolv.conf
```

Each individual user creates their own EzPPP accounts using the steps described previously. This information is held in a **.ezppprc** file in the user's home directory. In fact, different users could use EzPPP to connect to different Internet service providers.

Email: XFMail

Once you are connected to the Internet, you can use the XFMail program to obtain your mail from your Internet service provider's mail servers. Most ISPs use a POP server to receive mail. First, find out the Internet addresses used for that server. Then, to start the XFMail program just click on the button labeled XFMail on the fvwm Goodstuff toolbar, select it from the fvwm workplace menu, or just type **xfmail** in a terminal window. When you first start XFMail you will be presented with a series of configuration windows for general configuration. Click OK to accept the defaults. To configure access to your POP server, you select the Config item in the Misc menu. This opens a window with several buttons for different configuration tasks. Click on the one labeled POP. A POP window is displayed where you enter the Internet address of your POP server, as well as your user name and password.

In the XFMail window, the buttons on its button bar perform various mail tasks (see Figure 3-14). If you place the mouse over one, a tag will appear explaining the button's function. To check your mail, just click on the appropriate button. Message headers will be displayed and you can double-click on one to display the full message.

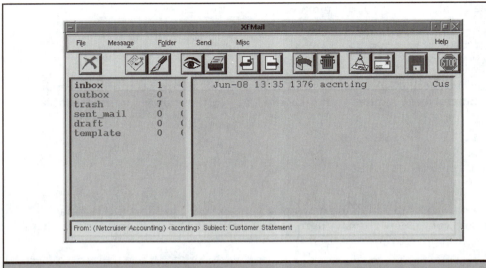

Figure 3-14. *XFMail*

X-Windows and Network Configuration

With the **Network Configuration** utility you can add to and change your network configuration. If you are connected to a network and did not configure it during installation, you can use this utility to perform that configuration. The **Network Configuration** utility is represented by the **netcfg** icon located in the Admin_Tools folder on the root user desktop. To start the utility, double-click the icon, and a small window opens in which you can perform your network configuration. See Chapter 20 for a detailed discussion of the **netcfg** utility.

If you were not able to start X-Windows, you may not have been able to install the correct graphics driver for your system. Though the XF86Setup program provides drivers for most graphics cards, there are a few that it cannot support. See Chapter 21 and Appendix C for more details. There are also other X-Windows configuration programs available such as Xconfigurator or xf86config. These are line-mode configuration tools that do not rely on a full-screen display.

Summary: Getting Started with Linux

To use your Linux system you enter your login name at the login prompt and then your password at the password prompt. Once logged in, you are presented with a command line interface on which you can type commands. Commands can take options and arguments. To execute a command, you type the command with any options and arguments on the command line and then press ENTER. When you are finished using the system, you log out with the **logout** command. The login prompt reappears. If you want to turn off your computer, you first have to shut down the Linux system. You do this by pressing CTRL-ALT-DEL.

Be sure to keep all the necessary startup and shutdown steps in mind when accessing your Linux system. To access the desktop you need to perform three tasks. First you start your Linux system. Once running, you log into the system. You then issue the command **startx** to start the X-Windows with the Caldera Desktop. To shut down the system, you exit the desktop, then log out, and then shut down the system with CTRL-ALT-DEL.

You can also use a window manager to interact with your system using menus, windows, and icons. In the Caldera distribution of Linux, the **startx** command starts the Caldera Desktop, which uses the fvwm window manager and its own file and program managers. You exit the desktop by selecting Exit Desktop from the File menu.

All the steps you need to perform to access Linux are listed here. Keep in mind the login and GUI startup procedures as well as the GUI exit, logout, and shutdown procedures.

1. Boot the computer.

2. At the LILO prompt type **linux** and press ENTER.

   ```
   LILO: linux
   ```

3. At the login prompt, enter your user name, and then at the password prompt enter your password.

   ```
   login: richlp
   Password:
   ```

4. Once logged in, you are presented with the command line prompt, **$**.

   ```
   $
   ```

5. To start the X-Windows GUI, enter the command **startx** at the shell prompt:

   ```
   $ startx
   ```

   This loads the X-Windows GUI that includes X-Windows, the manager, and the Caldera Desktop metaphor. They are collectively referred to as the Caldera Desktop.

6. To exit the X-Windows GUI, select Exit Desktop from the File menu. This returns you to the window manager.

7. Exit the window manager. Click anywhere on the screen to pop up the window manager menu, and then select Exit Desktop. This brings up a submenu from which you choose Quit Desktop. This returns you to the command line prompt.

   ```
   $
   ```

8. To log out enter either **exit** or **logout** on the command line and press ENTER.

   ```
   $ logout
   ```

9. This returns you to the login prompt. You can then log in again, log into another account with another user name, or log in as the root.

   ```
   login:
   ```

10. Now you can shut down Linux by pressing CTRL-ALT-DEL.

11. When the screen goes blank, your computer will start to reboot. At this point you can turn off your computer.

You may need to perform certain system administration tasks, such as creating new user accounts and installing software. You perform such tasks as the root user. You log in as the root user, using the root password. You can then start the desktop and use system administration utilities to perform these tasks. For example, **usercfg** will allow you to create and remove users; **netcfg** will allow you to configure your network connections.

The Caldera distribution of Linux organizes software into packages that you can easily install or uninstall using the **glint** utility or the **rpm** command. The **glint** utility is located on the desktop, and you can use **rpm** tools to perform the same actions on the command line. Table 3-1 lists the **rpm** options.

Mode of Operation	Effect
rpm **-i**options package-file	Installs a package; the complete name of the package file is required
rpm **-u**options package-name	Uninstalls a package; you only need the name of the package, often one word
rpm **-q**options	Queries a package; an option can be a package name or a further option and package name, or an option applied to all packages
rpm **-bO**options package-specifications	Builds your own RPM package
rpm **-verify**options	Verifies that a package is correctly installed; uses same options as query; you can use **-V** or **-y** in place of **-verify**

Table 3-1. *Redhat Package Manager (RPM)*

Mode of Operation	Effect
Install Option (to be used with -i)	
-U	Upgrade; same as install, but any previous version is removed
-p	Displays percentage of package during installation
-t	Tests installation; does not install, just checks for conflicts
-f	Forces installation despite conflicts
-root*directory-path*	Installs at directory
Uninstall Option (to be used with -u)	
-t	Tests uninstall; does not remove, just checks for what will be removed; use with **-v**
Query Option (to be used with -q)	
package-name	Queries package
-a	Queries all packages
-f *filename*	Queries package that owns *filename*
-F	Queries package that owns *filename*; *filename* is read from standard input
-p *package-name*	Queries an uninstalled package
-i	Displays all package information
-l	Lists files in package
-d	Lists only documentation files in package
-c	Lists only configuration files in package
-t	Tests uninstall; does not remove, just checks for what will be removed; use with **-v**

Table 3-1.   *Redhat Package Manager (RPM) (continued)*

Mode of Operation	Effect
General Option (to be used with any option)	
-v	Verbose; displays descriptions of all actions taken
-quit	Displays only error messages
-version	Displays **rpm** version number
-root*directory*	Uses directory as top-level directory for all operations (instead of root)
Other Sources of Information	
RPM-HOWTO on www.redhat.com	More detailed information, particularly on how to build your own RPM packages
man rpm	Detailed list of options

Table 3-1. *Redhat Package Manager (RPM)* (continued)

Linux RPM Software ftp Sites	Directory	Desription
ftp://ftp.redhat.com	/pub/contrib/i386 **/pub/linux/redhat**	RPM packages for applications
ftp://ftp.caldera.com	/pub/mirrors **/redhat-contrib**	RPM packages for applications
ftp://ftp.caldera.com	/pub/netscape /navigator	Netscape navigator RPM package
ftp://sunsite.unc.edu	/pub/linux	RPM and compressed archives
ftp://tsx-11.mit.edu	/pub/linux	RPM and compressed archives
ftp://ftp.x.org	**/contrib**	X-Windows compressed archives

Web Sites	Page Location	Web Page Description
www.ssc.com	/linux/resources /web.html	Linux on the World Wide Web
www.caldera.com	/tech-ref/linux_info .html	Caldera Linux Resources Page
www.redhat.com	/linux-info	Redhat Linux Resources Page
www.cs.washington.edu	/homes/tlau/linux-games	Linux Game Tome
www.xnet.com www.redhat.com	~blatura/linapps.shtml **/linux-info/linux-app-list/linapps.html**	Linux Applications and Utilites Page
www.uk.linux.org	/LxCommercial.html	Linux Commercial Vendors Index
www.m-tech.ab.ca	/linux-biz	Linux Business Applications
www.fokus.gmd.de	/linux/linux-prog.html	Woven Goods list of Linux programs

Table 3-2. *Linux Resources Web Pages (Links) and RPM Software ftp Sites*

Chapter Four

Window Managers and Desktops: X-Windows

Instead of the command line interface, you can use an X-Windows-based GUI to interact with your Linux system. With such an interface you can use icons, windows, and menus to issue commands and run applications. Unlike PC-based GUIs such as Windows or the Mac OS, Linux and Unix systems divide the GUI into three separate components: X-Windows, window managers, and program/file managers. X-Windows is an underlying standardized graphic utility that provides all the basic graphic operations such as opening windows or displaying images. A window manager handles windowing operations such as resizing and moving windows. Window managers vary in the way windows are displayed, using different borders and window menus. All, however, use the same underlying X-Windows graphic utility. A file manager handles file operations using icons and menus, and a program manager runs programs, often allowing you to select commonly used ones from a taskbar. Unlike window managers, file and program managers can differ greatly in their capabilities. The Caldera Desktop is a commercial-level file and program manager. In most cases, different file and program managers can run on the same window manager. Both the Caldera Desktop and the Xfm file manager can run on the fvwm window manager.

All Linux and Unix systems use the same standard underlying X-Windows graphics utility. This means, in most cases, that an X-Windows-based program can run on any of the window managers and desktops. X-Windows-based software is often found at Linux or Unix ftp sites in directories labeled **X11**. You can download these packages and run them on your Caldera Desktop or from fvwm directly. Some may already be in the form of Linux binaries that you can download, install, and run directly. Others will be in the form of source code that can easily be configured, compiled, and installed on your system with a few simple commands. Some applications, such as Motif applications, may require special libraries.

Window, File, and Program Managers

With a window manager you can use your mouse to perform windowing operations such as opening, closing, resizing, and moving windows. There are several window managers available for Linux (see Table 4-1). Some of the more popular ones are the Free Virtual Window Manager (fvwm), fvwm95, LessTif (mwm), Motif (mwm), Xview (olwm), and AfterStep (afterstep). fvwm, written by Robert Nation, is used as the primary window manager on most Linux systems. It is easy to use, powerful, and flexible. fvwm95 is the fvwm window manager with a Windows 95 interface. It uses windows, taskbars, and menus identical to those used by Microsoft's Windows 95 operating system. Future versions will include an explorer file manager, allowing icon-based display and manipulation of files. LessTif is a free clone of Motif. All Motif programs will run with LessTif. Motif is a commercial product that is the same as Motif used for Unix systems. Xview is the Linux version of the Sun System's OpenLook interface (not Solaris). AfterStep is a clone of the NeXTSTEP interface used for the NeXT operating system.

Window managers operate off of the underlying X-Windows graphics utility. X-Windows actually provides the basic operations that allow you to open, move, and close windows as well as display menus and select icons. fvwm and Xview manage these operations each in its own way, providing different interfaces from which to choose. All window managers, no matter how different they may appear, use X-Windows tools. In this sense, Linux is not tied to one type of graphical user interface. On the same Linux system, one user may be using the fvwm window manager, another may be using Xview, and yet another Motif.

Window managers normally provide only very basic window management operations such as opening, closing, and resizing of windows. In addition, file managers and program managers allow you to manage and run programs using icons and menus. With a file manager, you can copy, move, or erase files within different directory windows. With a program manager, you can execute commands and run programs using taskbars and program icons. A desktop program will combine the capabilities of a program manager and a file manager, providing a desktop metaphor with icons and menus to run programs and access files. The Caldera Desktop is one such desktop program. Table 4-1 lists several other desktops, many freely available from Web sites.

Several window managers have been enhanced to include many of the features of a desktop. The fvwm window manager used on most Linux systems has program management capabilities in addition to window handling. It has a taskbar and a workplace menu that you can use to access all your X-Windows programs. With either the menu or the taskbar, you can run any X-Windows program directly from fvwm. Another window manager, fvwm95, provides a Windows 95 desktop interface with the same taskbar and start menu. It is based on fvwm2, but uses the Windows 95 interface. In addition to program management, it plans to eventually support a file manager called explorer. With fvwm95, you can display file and directory icons much as you can in Windows 95.

Starting and Exiting X-Windows Window Managers and File Desktops

As noted in the previous chapter, you start X-Windows by entering **startx** on the command line. Your X-Windows server will then load, followed immediately by the window manager. Your OpenLinux system is currently configured to have the window manager automatically load in the Caldera Desktop. The desktop runs on top of the window manager. The background for the window manager is a slate-blue color. You may see this briefly as the Caldera Desktop is loading. The Caldera Desktop is a brown or gray window with a taskbar across the top and program icons within the window. You can then use your mouse to access menus, open windows, and start programs.

You exit the Caldera Desktop by choosing the Exit Desktop option in the File menu. Like most windows applications, the desktop has a list of menus across the top of the screen. Just click on File to pull down the menu. Exit Desktop is the last entry.

When you choose Exit Desktop, Linux only shuts down the Caldera Desktop. It does not shut down the fvwm window manager. The fvwm window manager shows up on your screen as a dark blue background. You have to exit the window manager in order to shut down X-Windows and return to the Linux command line interface.

To shut down the fvwm window manager, first bring up the fvwm workplace menu. Do this by clicking anywhere on that dark-blue background. You may have to click and drag down a bit to have the menu stay on the screen. Choose the last entry in this menu, Exit Desktop. This brings up a submenu, one of the choices of which is to Quit Desktop. Choose this to exit the window manager and X-Windows. You will then return to the command line interface, which presents you with the $ prompt. You can restart the fvwm anytime you want by entering **startx** on the command line.

You can also start up other window managers or desktops from fvwm, as well as display the fvwm taskbar. In the workplace menu, select the Desktops item. This brings up a window manager's submenu. The Start GoodStuff item in this menu will display the fvwm taskbar, which has icons for accessing frequently used X-Windows programs such as your Web Browser. The Start Looking Glass item starts the Caldera Desktop (Looking Glass is the name of the Caldera Desktop). The window manager's item will bring up a submenu listing some of the other window managers you have installed on your system. To start up a different window manager, you can choose it from this menu. fvwm is already set up to add several of the frequently used window managers to its menu. However, the olwm Xview window manager listed here is not the full Xview window manager. That you would have to first download from online sources and install.

System Configuration Tools

There are a set of easy-to-use configuration tools designed to run in X-Windows that you can use to perform tasks such as installing software, configuring a printer, or adding new users. **XF86Setup**, for configuring X-Windows, is one such tool, as is glint for installing software. Lisa is a menu-driven administration tool that covers all aspects of system administration. There is also a set of window-based tools from the Redhat Linux distribution to provide easy printer, user, and file system configuration. The tools are described in Chapters 3, 7, 19, and 20. These tools can be accessed either from the Caldera Desktop or the fvwm menu as well as the fvwm taskbar. To have access to these tools, you first have to log in as the **root** user. Then start X-Windows with the **startx** command. From the Caldera Desktop, you will see an icon labeled Admin_Tools. Double-click on it to open this window. Icons for each tool will be displayed within it. From the fvwm window manager choose Applications, then System administration. The entry Control_Panel will bring up an icon bar for the Redhat tools. From that submenu, select the tool you want. The fvwm taskbar will have a button labeled Admin that will bring up a button bar for the configuration tools. There will be buttons for the same utilities, such as glint and **XF86Setup**. There will also be buttons labeled RH tools. These will bring up button bars for the Redhat tools such as fstool for managing your file systems, printtool for installing printers, and netcfg for configuring your network. fstool is not designed to work with the auto-mount daemon, amd, and usrcfg is not designed for use with NIS networks.

Windows and Icons

You run applications, display information, or list files in windows. A window is made up of several basic components. The outer border contains resize controls. There are also various buttons with which you can control the size of a window or close the window. Inside the outer border are the main components of the window: the title bar, which displays the name of the window; the menu, through which you can issue commands; and the window pane, which displays the contents of a window.

An fvwm window, as shown in Figure 4-1, allows you to change its shape and size using buttons and resize areas. The resize areas are the corner borders of the window. Click and hold on a resize area and move the mouse to make the window larger or smaller in both height and width.

You can also make the window fill the whole screen by clicking on the Maximize button—the small square within a square—in the upper-right corner of the window. To reduce the window to its original size, just click on the Maximize button again.

If you want to reduce the window to an icon, click on the Minimize button. It's the small square with a dot in the center next to the Maximize button. Once you have reduced the window to an icon, you can reopen it later by double-clicking on that icon.

You can move any window around the desktop by selecting either its title bar or border (not a corner). Move your mouse pointer to the window's title bar; then click and hold on it while you move your mouse pointer. You will see the window move. When you have reached the position you want, release the mouse button. Just clicking on the title bar will move the window to the front of any overlapping windows. The same process holds true for borders. Move the mouse pointer to the edge of the window until you see the pointer transform into a small straight line. Then click and hold on that edge, and move the mouse pointer. You will see the entire window move.

Applications that have been designed as X-Windows programs will have their own menus, buttons, and even icons within their window. You execute commands in such X-Windows applications using menus and icons. If you are running an application such as an editor, the contents of the window will be data that the menus operate on. If you are using the file manager, the contents will be icons representing files and directories. The desktop file manager is discussed in the next chapter on directories and files. Some windows, such as terminal windows, will not have menus.

You can have several windows open at the same time. However, only one of those windows will be active. The active window will have purple borders, and the inactive windows will have pale gray borders. Moving your mouse pointer to a particular window makes it the active window, rendering all others inactive. You don't need to click the mouse, as you do in other GUIs such as Microsoft Windows or Mac OS.

The overlapping windows sometimes cause confusion. Making a window active does not automatically bring it to the front. An active window could still be partially hidden by other overlapping windows. To bring a window to the front, you need to click on that window's title bar. Clicking anywhere else on the window would only make it the active window, not bring it to the front.

Icons represent either applications you can run or data files for those applications. They appear on your desktop window and within file manager windows, with the name of the file or application below them. To run an application, just double-click on its icon.

The Terminal Window: Xterm

From within a Linux window manager you can open a special window called a *terminal* window, which will provide you with a standard command line interface. You can then enter commands on a command line with options and arguments at the prompt displayed in this window. The terminal window is created by a program called Xterm. You can open a terminal window through the fvwm taskbar, the program menu, or from a desktop such as the Caldera Desktop. The terminal window is created by a program called Xterm. The fvwm taskbar has a button labeled Xterm. Just click on that to open an Xterm window. Alternatively, select Shells from the fvwm workplace menu and then Terminals from the submenu, and Xterm from there. To open a terminal window in the Caldera Desktop, double-click on the Terminal icon located on the icon bar at the upper-left corner of your desktop.

Once opened, the window will display a shell prompt, usually the $, and you can enter Linux commands just as you would on the command line. You will see any results of your commands displayed within the terminal window, followed by a shell prompt indicating the beginning of the command line. Keep in mind that your terminal window needs to be your active window for you to use its command line. If it is not the active window, you will need to move the mouse pointer to it to make it active.

An Xterm window supports several text-handling features. To the left of the window is a scroll bar that you can use to scroll back to view previously displayed text. As text moves off the top of the screen, you can scroll back to see it. This is particularly helpful if you are displaying directories with a large number of files that will not fit on one screen. Xterm also lets you copy text and paste it to the command line. You use the left mouse button to copy text and the second mouse button to paste it. You can copy text from any of the text previously displayed, such as previous commands or output from those commands. To copy text, click and hold down the left mouse button while dragging it across the text you want to copy, letting up when you reach the end. Also, double-clicking will select a word and a triple-click will select a line. If you want to extend the selected text, use the third mouse button. Once you have selected text, click the second mouse button. This automatically pastes the text to the end of the command line. Repeating clicks repeats the paste. The copy-and-paste operation is particularly helpful for constructing a complex command from previous ones. You can also copy and paste across different terminal windows.

(The terms *second* and *third mouse button* can be confusing. On a two-button mouse, the second button is the right button, and the third button is the left and right button held down at the same time. On a three-button mouse, the second button is the middle button, and the third button is the right-most button. These three buttons are used to access the Xterm menus. An Xterm window has four menus: the main menu, a VT options menu, a VT font menu, and a Tektronix window options menu. To bring up the main menu, hold down the CTRL key and click the left mouse button. For the VT options menu, hold down the CTRL key and click the second (right or middle) mouse button. To bring up the font menu, use the CTRL key and the third mouse button. You can then set the font and size of characters displayed.)

An Xterm window emulates both a DEC VT 102 terminal and a Tektronix 4014 terminal. There are windows for both, though only the VT window is initially displayed. To display the Tektronix window, select the entry to do this in the VT Options menu (CTRL and second button). This will bring up the Tektronix window that is capable of displaying graphics. Within the Tektronix window you can bring up the Tektronix Options menu with the CTRL key and the second mouse button.

The terminal window has the special capability of being able to run any X-Windows program from its command line. The terminal window operates within the X-Windows environment. To run any X-Windows program, just open an Xterm window and enter the command, pressing ENTER. The X-Windows program will then start up in its own window. For example, to run Netscape you could open a terminal window and type the command **netscape**. A new window will open up running Netscape. You can open as many terminal windows as you want and then start an X-Windows program from each. However, closing a terminal window will also close the program started from it.

You will notice that the terminal window in which you entered the X-Windows command appears to suspend itself. There is no following prompt after you press ENTER to run the program. That is because the terminal window is currently busy running the X-Windows program you just executed. You can have the terminal window free itself to execute other commands while that program is running by invoking the program with an ampersand (&). Technically, this places it in the background as far as the terminal window is concerned (see Chapter 5). But you are free to move to that X-Windows program's window and run it there. The following example would run Netscape, freeing the terminal window to run other commands. Notice the prompt:

```
$ netscape  &
$
```

When you are finished using the terminal window, close it by typing the command **exit** on the command line. Each terminal window is its own shell, and **exit** is the command to end a shell. (Shells are discussed in detail in Chapter 5.) Figure 4-1 shows the terminal window. The user has entered several commands, and the output is

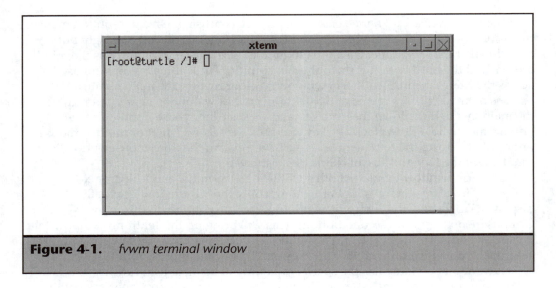

Figure 4-1. *fvwm terminal window*

displayed in the window. As you reach the bottom of the window, the text displayed will scroll up, line by line, just as a normal terminal screen would.

You can, of course, use the window controls to make the terminal window larger or smaller. You can even minimize it to an icon and later reopen it.

X-Windows Multitasking

One of the most useful features of your Linux X-Windows interface is its ability to open several operations at the same time, each with its own window. Notice that in the command line interface you can only work on one task at a time (there is an exception discussed in Chapter 5 dealing with what are called *background processes*). You issue a command and after it executes, you can execute another. In X-Windows you can have several different applications running at once. Moving your mouse pointer from one window to another effectively moves you from one application to another. This feature of X-Windows illustrates one of the most useful capabilities of Linux: Concurrency, the ability to have several processes operating at the same time. In your X-Windows interface, you can have several applications running at the same time, each with its own window.

This feature can be easily illustrated using terminal windows. You can have several terminal windows open at the same time, each with its own command line. To open a terminal window from the Caldera Desktop, double-click on the Terminal icon in the icon bar; from fvwm, use either the workplace menu or the Xterm button on the fvwm icon bar. To open a second terminal window, double-click on the Terminal icon again. To open yet another terminal window, just double-click on the icon yet again, and so on. Each terminal window will have its own command line, and moving your mouse pointer from one window to another moves you from one command line to another.

You can type a command in the active window and execute it. You can then move to another terminal window and type in another command. Each terminal window operates independently of the other. If you issue a command that takes a while to execute, and you move to another window, you will notice that the command in the window you just left is still executing.

The fvwm Window Manager and Desktop

Although there are many window managers available for use on Linux, this chapter only covers the basic features of fvwm. The fvwm window manager provides not only the basic window, taskbar, and menu tools, but also several advanced features such as virtual desktops. In fact, with fvwm you can have several desktops, each with different windows and programs open on them. Figure 4-2 shows the fvwm workplace menu and taskbar, as well as an Xterm window and the Netscape Browser running directly from fvwm.

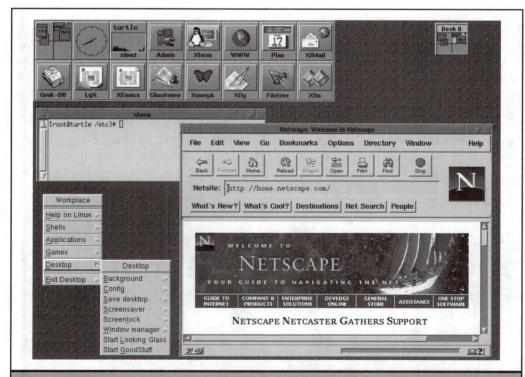

Figure 4-2.   *The fvwm desktop including taskbar and workplace menu with terminal window and Netscape running*

The fvwm Workplace Menu

To bring up the fvwm workplace menu, click and slightly drag downward with your mouse. The workplace menu will pop up. The entries on this main menu lead to submenus. Selecting an item will also bring up a submenu. Some of these submenus themselves list other submenus. For example, applications will bring up a submenu listing categories for all your X-Windows programs. Selecting the graphics item will bring up a list of all the X-Windows graphic programs on your system. If you choose Xpaint, the Xpaint program will then start up.

When you install or remove an X-Windows program, fvwm will automatically update the workplace menu. Entries have already been set up for frequently used X-Windows programs. New programs may be added to the Other Applications submenu found in the Applications menu. Currently, fvwm is configured to check for any new programs in the **/usr/X11R6/bin** and **/usr/openwin/bin** directories. These will be added to the workplace menu.

To quit fvwm, select the Exit Desktop entry from this menu. This brings up a submenu that includes the item Quit Desktop. When you select this, fvwm will exit and X-Windows along with it.

The GoodStuff Taskbar

The recent version of fvwm includes the GoodStuff taskbar which displays buttons for frequently used X-Windows commands (see Figure 4-3). The GoodStuff taskbar should be displayed when you start up the fvwm window manager; if not, you can bring it up by selecting Start GoodStuff from the Desktops menu in the workplace menu. Each button will display the name of a program. Just click on the button to start that program. For example, to open an Xterm window, just click on the button labeled Xterm. The button WWW will start up your Internet Browser (Netscape if you have it; Arena otherwise). The Xfm button starts up the Xfm file manager, with menus and

Figure 4-3. *fvwm GoodStuff taskbar*

icons for accessing your directories and files. If you selected a standard install, you may not have all these programs installed. If not, you will be asked if you want to install them.

To have the GoodStuff taskbar permanently displayed on your fvwm desktop, select a position entry in the GoodStuff menu located within the Config menu within Desktops on the fvwm workplace menu. You can choose to position it on the top, bottom, left, or right of your screen. You can move or resize the taskbar as you wish. To move the taskbar, click on its edge with the right button, and then drag it to where you want it. To resize, click and drag on its edge or corner with the left button. If you no longer want the taskbar displayed, choose the disable entry in the GoodStuff menu located within the Config menu within Desktops on the fvwm workplace menu.

The configuration file for the taskbar is called **system.fvwmrc.goodstuff** and is located in the **/usr/lib/X11/fvwm** directory. The bottom of the file has entries for the buttons in the taskbar. You can remove a button by placing a # at the beginning of its line. You can also add other lines for new buttons. A button entry begins with the keyword ***GoodStuff**, followed by the text you want displayed in the button and then the picture you want for the button. The line ends with the command to execute, usually beginning with the **Exec** command, followed by an empty string and the **xlaunch** command and then the program's name. The following example adds a button for the Crisplite editor. The command to invoke the Crisplite editor is **mcr**.

```
*GoodStuff  Crisplite  dtp.xpm    Exec   ""  xlaunch  mcr
```

The **.xpm** file is the picture to be displayed. You can find many more such files in the **/usr/share/data/pixmaps** and **/usr/openwin/lib/pixmaps** directories.

Virtual Desktops: fvwm

Initially, you may find the virtual desktop disconcerting—it is a kind of built-in enlargement feature. You will discover that the area displayed on your screen may be only part of the desktop. Moving your mouse pointer to the edge of your screen moves the screen over the hidden portions of the desktop. You will also notice a small square in the upper-right corner of your desktop display. This is called the *pager,* and you use it to view different areas of your virtual desktop. The pager is divided into four smaller squares. You can think of each square as a separate extension of your desktop. It's as if you have a very large desk, only part of which is shown on the screen. The active part of the desk is a highlighted square, usually in white. This is the area of the desktop currently displayed by your screen. By moving this highlighted square you can move to different parts of the desk. You use the right mouse button to click and drag this highlighted square. You can also click on one of the four sections in the pager to move to that part of your desk. You could place different windows in different parts of your desk and then move to that part when you want to use them. This way, everything you want on your desktop does not have to be displayed on your screen at once, cluttering it up. If you are working on the desktop and everything suddenly disappears, it may be that you accidentally clicked on one of the other squares. Just click on the upper-left square again to return to your original display. You should see your original windows reappear.

Certain items will always be displayed on your screen, no matter what part of the virtual desktop you display. These are called "sticky" items. The fvwm pager is one, as is the fvwm taskbar. For example, the fvwm pager will always show up in the upper-right corner of your screen no matter what part of the virtual desktop you are viewing. Windows, on the other hand, are not sticky. They stay wherever you placed them on the virtual desktop.

The Caldera Desktop can be either sticky and stay with the screen display or a window and remain on just one window on the virtual desktop. The left-most icon on the Caldera taskbar toggles between sticky and a window. If it is a window, you will see the desktop bordered by a standard fvwm window that you can move or resize as you wish. As a sticky image, the window border is absent. No matter where the screen moves across the virtual desktop, the Caldera Desktop is displayed in place on the screen with its taskbar, menus, and icons. Icons that you have placed on your desktop will appear in the same position in every section. That way, you always have access to an icon on the desktop.

Initially, the screen area of your virtual desktop may not even cover one of the sections on your pager. You can make it cover the entire section by setting the Virtual entry in the **/etc/XF86Config** file to the resolution of your monitor as described in Chapter 2. In most 15-inch monitors, this would be 800 x 600.

Most window managers, including fvwm, also support multiple desktops. The desktop, in this sense, is the screen along with the items displayed on it such as icons, menus, and windows. Window managers such as fvwm allow you to use many different desktops. fvwm can support about four billion desktops.

The Caldera Desktop

The Caldera Desktop is an integrated program and file manager, providing you with menus and icons with which you can manage your files, run programs, and configure your system. The Caldera Desktop provides easy access to Internet tools as well as the many Linux software programs available. It is a commercial product offered with Caldera's commercial packages. This Looking Glass desktop is provided with Caldera Lite on a 90-day trial basis. (In the fvwm workplace menu, the Caldera Desktop is referred to as Looking Glass.) You will be able to take full advantage of all Caldera Desktop features, such as toolbars, configuration utilities, file management windows, and automatic history lists.

When you start the Caldera Desktop, you will notice an icon bar displayed across the top. It initially contains icons that represent common Linux operations such as opening a terminal window or locating files. This is a configurable icon bar. You can add your own icons for specific operations. The desktop also has a versatile file manager. For each directory, you can open a window that shows all the files in that directory, displayed as icons. You can then run applications by double-clicking on their icons, or you can move the icons out of the file manager window and onto the desktop for easier access.

The desktop is a window on which you can place icons. Scroll bars on the right side and bottom let you move across those icons should there be too many to fit on your screen (see Figure 4-4). You will notice that several icons are already on your desktop window. For example, one icon represents the Crisplite editor and another the Netscape Browser. You can remove any of these icons and add others as you wish.

The icon bar across the top of the desktop contains frequently used Linux operations, such as the file manager or terminal window. You can add icons of your own to the icon bar, or remove any of the ones already there. To the right of the icon bar are your clock and an icon for obtaining help. The desktop help feature will display balloon help text for any part of the desktop you point to.

Above the icon bar is a standard menu bar. The different entries cover operations to configure the desktop or issue Linux commands. You have already seen the Exit

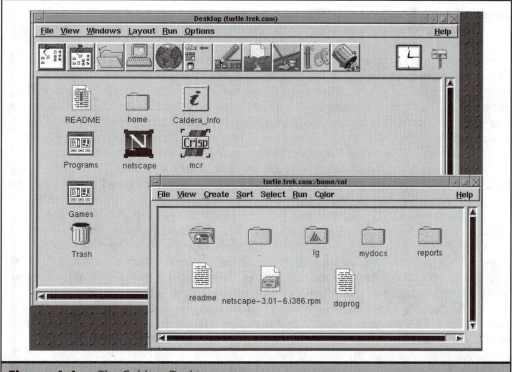

Figure 4-4.   *The Caldera Desktop*

Desktop entry in the File menu. Notice the underlined letter in each menu name. This represents a keyboard shortcut that you can use to execute a command. To open the File menu, for example, you can press F instead of moving your mouse up to the menu bar to click on the File entry.

By selecting different windows, menus, and icons on your screen using a mouse, you can run the application associated with the icon, opening a new window for it.

The right mouse button opens a File drop-down menu. Instead of moving the mouse up to the menu bar, you can click on the right mouse button to open the File menu on your screen at that position. You can then select an option, such as Exit Desktop.

Directory Windows

Instead of a command line on which you enter commands and file name arguments, the directory windows on the Caldera Desktop allow you to use menus, icons, and windows to manage files and directories. In the desktop, a directory is displayed as a window. Instead of using an **ls** command to display the files in your directory, the files are already displayed for you as icons. The directories are represented by icons that look like folders. The idea is that directories operate like folders that hold documents—that is to say, files. You open a directory and examine the files in it, just as you would open a folder and examine its contents.

All directory windows have the same set of menus for performing file and directory operations: File, View, Create, Sort, Select, Run, and Color. The File menu allows you to perform basic file operations. The View menu allows you to display your files in different ways, either as icons, names, or names with their full set of file information. The Create menu allows you to create new directories. The Sort menu lets you sort your files either by name, size, type, or any other file feature. With the Select menu, you can select a set of files by pattern matches on file names, or just select all the files in the directory. The Run menu lets you open a command line for entering commands, and the Color menu lets you color code your file names. To open a directory window, move your mouse pointer to the folder icon located on the icon bar.

When you double-click on a folder icon, the Open Directory window appears; there you can specify the name of the directory you want to open. A box labeled "Directory:" is at the top of the window. In the box, the last directory that you accessed will be highlighted. To access your home directory, leave this box empty. Press the DEL or BACKSPACE key to erase the highlighted path name already there. Then, just click on the OK button at the bottom of the window. A file manager window will open for your home directory, displaying all the files and directories in it.

You can use the Open Directory window to access any directory you wish. All you need to do is enter the path name of that directory in the Directory box. As an aid to entering path names, the Open Directory window includes a History box that lists the path names of all the previous directories you have accessed. If you see one listed that you want to access, just click on it and its path name appears in a box labeled "Directory:".

By deselecting the positionable item in the View menu, you can divide the directory window into a top and bottom pane. The folder icons for the directories appear in the top pane, and in the bottom the file icons bear different pictures depending on the application they are used for. To the right of each pane is a scroll bar that you can use to scroll through the display of either your directories or the files in a particular directory. You can also change the size of each pane. Between the two panes, next to their scroll bars, is a small bar that you can use to make one pane larger and the other smaller. Moving the bar up makes the directory pane smaller while increasing the size of the file pane. Moving down does the opposite.

Once an icon is selected, you can perform an operation on it. For example, to copy a file, select the file's icon and then choose the Copy option in the File menu. A special window will open, prompting you for the name of the copy. To erase a file, select the file's icon and then choose the Remove option in the File menu. The file will be deleted and its icon removed from the directory window.

One of the basic operations on an icon is the Open operation. You can open an icon either by moving the mouse to it and double-clicking, or by clicking on the icon and then selecting the Open option in the File menu. Depending on whether the icon is a file, directory, or application, different actions take place. If you open an application, the application's window opens and the application begins execution. On the other hand, if you open a directory, another directory window opens up, displaying the icons in that directory. If, however, you open a file icon, the application associated with that file is executed using that file. For example, if the **mydata** file is a Vi editor data file, then when you double-click on the file's icon, the Vi editor application window opens with the **mydata** file as the text to be edited.

You can create your own directories in a directory window just as, in the command line interface, you can use **mkdir** to create directories. To create a directory, first choose the Directory option in the Create menu. This creates a new directory icon with the default name Dir1 highlighted below it. Simply type in the name you want for the new directory. Once you have finished typing the new name, you can deselect it by clicking anywhere else on the window.

A directory will reside as an icon in a window until you open a window for it. There are two ways of opening a directory window. You can either open a separate window for the directory, or you can change the current window to that directory. To change the window to display a new directory, simply double-click on the icon for that directory. In effect, opening a directory is the same as changing your working directory with the **cd** command. Your menu options will then operate on the files and icons in this newly displayed directory.

You will notice that among the directory icons displayed in your file manager window is a directory with a name consisting of two periods, ... The two periods represent the parent directory. If you want to move to the parent directory for the current directory, just double-click on this directory icon. Doing so is equivalent to using the **cd..** command.

You use the Move option in the File menu either to rename or move a file. To rename a file, select the file's icon and choose the Move option. This opens a dialog window with a box at the top labeled "Move to:". You just enter the new name for the file. Alternatively, with the mouse alone, you can use the click-and-drag method to move a file from one directory to another. First, open a separate window for the directory that you want to move the file to. Then move the mouse to the icon of the file you want to move. Press and hold down your left mouse button while you drag the icon over to the window of the directory you want to move the file to. Then lift up on the mouse button. The file's icon will appear in the new directory.

As with the Move operation, there are two ways to copy a file: Either click and drag with the mouse, or use the Copy option in the File menu. Using the File menu, first select the file's icon and then choose the Copy option. This opens the Copy Items to Directory dialog window. Type the name of the copy in the box toward the top of the window labeled "Copy to:". Then click on the OK button at the bottom of the dialog window.

With the mouse and the CTRL key, you can use the click-and-drag method to copy a file from one directory to another. The click-and-drag method for copying differs from the one for moving because you must hold down the CTRL key during the whole operation. As in moving a file, you first open the window of the directory that you want to copy the file to. Then move the mouse to the icon of the file you want to copy and select it. Holding down the CTRL key, press and hold down your left mouse button as you drag the icon over to the new window. Lift up on the mouse button and the CTRL key, and the file's icon will appear in the other directory.

You can erase files either by dragging the file's icon to the Trash Can icon, or by choosing the Remove entry in the File menu. If you drag a file to the trash can, it remains there until you empty the trash. You can also remove whole directories, if you wish, by dragging their directory icons to the trash can.

You can set any of the permissions for a file or directory by selecting the Information item in the File menu. This opens a window with three selections: Access, Ownership, and Dates. Click on the button for Access to open a window listing the access permissions. Here, you can click on buttons to specify read, write, and execute permissions for owner, group, or other. (Permissions are explained in detail in Chapter 7.) The Ownership selection allows you to change a file's owner.

Managing the Caldera Desktop

The desktop is an interface that you can customize for your own needs. You can place file, program, and directory icons on your desktop for easy access. You can create layouts of your desktop, saving snapshots of a certain set of open windows and icons on your desktop. You can then select a layout that automatically opens those windows and displays those icons. You can also configure your desktop by specifying items for your icon bar or setting preferences for how files are created, displayed, or removed.

As you work on your desktop, you may need to have different icons, windows, or programs open for different tasks. For example, if you are working with a database, you might have a database program window open and the directory window for the database files open. For graphics work, you might have icons for graphics programs on your desktop and directory windows for graphics files. Instead of opening and closing windows when you move from one task to another, you can save your entire desktop as a layout. Then, to work on a particular task, just open that layout. For the database work, a user could create a layout for it called something like "datawork" and then open that layout whenever he or she needed to work on the database.

There are several layouts already provided. The root and admin layouts are helpful for administrative operations when you have logged in as the root user. They include an Admin_Tools icon for accessing configuration tools. Figure 3-1 in Chapter 3 shows a root layout. The user default layout includes a clock and several commonly used buttons in the icon bar. The left-most button will expand the desktop to the full size of the screen and make it sticky, moving with you around the virtual desktop. Clicking it again reduces it to a window. The next button over in the icon bar is used to give a smaller desktop window or sticky image. Figure 4-4 shows the Caldera Desktop with the user default layout.

To create a layout, set your desktop the way you want the layout to look, opening the windows you want and placing icons you want on the desktop. Then select the Layouts item in the Layout menu. This opens a Layout window. In the box labeled "Layouts," click on the Current entry (the first entry). Below the Layouts box is a Name field. Click on it and type in the name you want to give the layout. Then, from among the buttons at the bottom of this window, click on the Save button. Click on the Close button to close the Layout window. The new layout will be listed in the Layout menu. To restore it, just select its entry in the menu.

Installing Window Managers and File Managers

Your OpenLinux Lite system uses the fvwm window manager and a proprietary file and program manager called Looking Glass, simply referred to as the Caldera Desktop. The name of the Caldera Desktop program is **lg**. With OpenLinux Lite, you are granted three free months' use of the Caldera Desktop, after which it will become inoperable. You can continue to use the fvwm window manager with its own program manager and any one of several public-licensed file managers. There are also GNU file managers available. With such a file manager, you will be able to use icons and menus, instead of just the windows provided by fvwm. The Xfm file manager is available on your OpenLinux Lite CD-ROM. You can easily install it using glint or Lisa. There are also many different file managers available online that you can download and install. You can download file managers from Linux ftp mirror sites, usually located in the **/pub/Linux/X11/** directory. The Linux Applications and Utilities Page lists several file managers whose sites you can link to and download the software (see Table 3-2 in Chapter 3). If you know the package name of the file manager you want, it is best to download its RPM version from the Redhat contrib directory, **ftp.redhat.com/pub/ contrib/i386**.

As an alternative to fvwm window manager, you can use other window managers such as Xview, fvwm2, fvwm95, LessTif, AfterStep, and Motif. Some of these also have associated file managers that give you a complete desktop interface. You can download the RPM versions of any of these window managers from the contrib directory on the Redhat ftp site. If you are using ftp, use the **ls** command with the first few characters of the window manager's name with an asterisk to list its RPM file. It is, of course, easier to download using a Web Browser such as Netscape. Most of these window managers also have their own Web sites from which you can download the original source code.

Starting Window Managers

Normally, you should be able to start most window managers by first starting fvwm and then choosing the name of the window manager in the Window manager menu in the Desktop entry of the fvwm workplace menu. There will be entries for fvwm95, olvwm, and others (but not AfterStep). If you want to start the window manager directly, you have to place an entry for it in an **.xinitrc** file. Chapter 21 discusses in detail how to set up an **.xinitrc** file and place window manager invocations in it. Your home directory initially does not have an **.xinitrc** file. A simple way to create one is to copy the system's **.xinitrc** file. When you start X-Windows, the **.xinitrc** file will be used to configure your X-Windows session, instead of the system's **.xinitrc** file. The system's **.xinitrc** file is located at **/usr/X11R6/lib/X11/xinit/xinitrc**. The following command makes a copy of it. Be sure you are in your home directory. Notice that the **.xinitrc** file has a preceding dot as part of its name, whereas the system's **.xinitrc** file does not.

```
$ cp /usr/X11R6/lib/X11/xinit/xinitrc  .xinitrc
```

You just have to place the command to start the window manager you want at the end of your **.xinitrc** file. Be sure to comment out any other window managers by placing a # at the beginning of the lines that hold their commands. Leave the rest of the file alone. The following example shows instructions for commenting out fvwm and running fvwm95 instead.

```
# start the window-manager and redirect output to xconsole
#  some applications are started by the window manager itself
# exec fvwm > /dev/console 2>&1
exec fvwm95
```

To go back to fvwm, just remove its comment symbol, the #, and place one in front of the line for fvwm95.

Should you also want to automatically load other programs such as a file manager, you can place their commands before the command for the window manager. Put an ampersand (&) after the command. Chapter 21 discusses this in more detail. The following example starts the Xfm file manager when the AfterStep window manager starts up.

```
xfm &
exec afterstep
```

fvwm and fvwm2

You can easily download and install new versions of fvwm as they become available. The OpenLinux Lite CD-ROM attached with this book uses version 1.24r of fvwm. This current version supports features such as the taskbar, workplace menu, and modules. Modules are small programs that can be loaded and run dynamically much like extensions are in the Mac.

A new version of fvwm called fvwm2 for fvwm version 2.0 is currently under development. Version 2.0.46 is now in beta release. fvwm2 extends the capabilities of fvwm to provide better configuration files, allows customization of individual windows, and provides better module support. For example, the Panel module deploys a CDE-like taskbar under fvwm2. (CDE stands for Common Desktop Environment, the new standard for Unix GUIs.) fvwm2 is the current fvwm development project and will replace fvwm 1.24. You can obtain newer versions of fvwm2 as they come out, from the fvwm Web page currently located at **www.hpc.uh.edu/fvwm.html**. RPM packages of the new fvwm versions are also available at the Redhat contrib directory at the Redhat ftp site, **fvwm2-2.0.46-4. i386.rpm**. The first full release of fvwm2 is nearing completion.

Xview: olwm and olvwm

An alternative to the fvwm window manager is Xview. Xview is the implementation of Sun System's OpenLook interface. Those familiar with OpenLook will find that the Linux version runs much the same way. You can download Xview from **sunsite.unc.edu** ftp site, in the **/pub/Linux/libs/X/xview** directory, **xview-3.2p1.4. bin.tar.gz**. This Xview package includes both the olwm and olvwm window managers as well as several utilities such as a clock and text editor. The olvwm version of Xview supports a virtual desktop.

The Xview package on your OpenLinux CD-ROM contains a set of shared libraries that provide OpenLook menus, buttons, and other widgets. These are used in many Linux applications. Though applications that use these Xview widgets do not have to use the Xview window manager, they do use the Xview libraries. So you can run applications like the textedit Xview editor in the fvwm window manager. The buttons and menus that textedit uses are Xview widgets, though it can operate in an fvwm window. Your OpenLinux Xview package is not the full Xview window manager. It is a subset of libraries with a few popular applications.

To install the full Xview window manager, first download its tar archive from **sunsite.unc.edu**. You then have to remove the installation of the OpenLinux Xview package (use Lisa). Check to make sure that the directory **/usr/openwin** is completely removed. If not, change to the **/usr** directory (**cd /usr**) and remove it with the **rm-r openwin** command. Then unpack the Xview package you downloaded with the **tar xvf** command. This creates a subdirectory named **usr** in your current directory. In this **usr** directory is a subdirectory named **openwin**, which you move into the **/usr** directory (notice the forward slash).

```
# mv usr/openwin  /usr
```

Then run the **ldconfig** command on the **/usr/openwin/lib** directory. This sets up the Xview libraries.

```
# ldconfig /usr/openwin/lib
```

Make sure a **/usr/openwin/lib** entry is in the **/etc/ld.so.config** file. Because the Xview archive is not an RPM package, you had to perform the installation tasks yourself, such as moving files to the right directory and running **ldconfig**. Other window managers can be obtained in RPM format that will automatically install and configure their files for you.

You can start up olwm from fvwm by choosing Switch to olvwm from the window manager menu in the Desktop entry in the fvwm workplace menu, or use a modified **.xinitrc** file with a call to olwm or olvwm instead of fvwm. It is best to use olvwm started from an **.xinitrc** file. olvwm provides a Virtual desktop, like fvwm. When you first bring up the olvwm window manager, you will be presented with a blank screen and a pager with six squares displayed in the upper-left corner. Double-click on any square to move to that screen. To bring up the Xview workspace menu, click anywhere on the screen with the right mouse button. The workspace menu is a pinnable menu. You will see a picture of a push-pin at the top. If you click on it, the workplace menu will remain displayed at that place on the screen. Click on the pin again to be able to remove the workplace menu. The "X11 Progs" entry in the workspace menu automatically lists installed X11 programs, and the "Xview Progs" entry lists all Xview programs (those installed in **/usr/openwin/bin**).

Window components are slightly different from those in fvwm, though they serve much the same function. Menus are displayed with the right mouse button. On the workspace menu, you bring up submenus by right-clicking on the small triangle to the right of a menu item. To move window and pinned menus you click and drag with the left mouse button on the very edge of the window (not the right mouse button as in fvwm). See Figure 4-5.

Xview components are installed in the **/usr/openwin** directory. Here you will find subdirectories such as **/usr/openwin/bin** that hold Xview programs and **/usr/openwin /lib** that hold Xview libraries. When X-Windows starts up, it has to have a shell variable called OPENWINHOME set to the Xview directory, **/usr/openwin**. If you

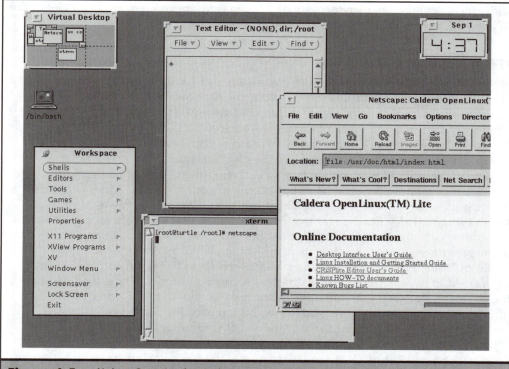

Figure 4-5. *Xview OpenLook window manager*

examine your **.xinitrc** file discussed in the previous section, you will see an entry that makes such an assignment.

The **/usr/openwin/lib** directory contains the menu files used to display the Xview workspace menu and its submenus. You can add entries to these menus if you wish. An entry consists of the label to be displayed followed by the action to take. For example, to add an entry to the workspace menu for Netscape you would place the following entry in the **openwin-menu** file. The xview man pages has a detailed explanation of Xview menus and the kind of entries you can make.

```
"Netscape"      exec /usr/bin/netscape.
```

Your CD-ROM includes a very good Xview file manager called treebrowser that is invoked with the command **tb**. There is also a Linux version of the XVfilemanager available that you can download from the XVfilemanager Web site (see Table 4-1). Follow the INSTALL file instructions to install it. With either file manager installed, you now have a complete desktop. You can also use XVfilemanager or treebrowser with any other window managers such as fvwm or AfterStep, as long as you leave the Xview libraries installed.

fvwm95 and qvwm

fvwm95 and qvwm are Linux window managers that have a Windows 95 user interface, complete with taskbar and start menu. Window components are the same. You can even minimize windows to the taskbar. fvwm95 is based on the fvwm2 window manager, using much of the same source code, and like fvwm2, it supports modules. Currently, it does not have a file manager, but one is under development. It is called explorer and will operate like the file manager in Windows 95.

The fvwm95 window manager has several window modules that provide capabilities similar to fvwm. It has a button bar, in addition to the Windows 95 taskbar, that operates like the fvwm taskbar. There are buttons for frequently used programs such as Xterm. It also has a pager that operates like the fvwm pager, giving you a six-section virtual desktop. A mini-button bar brings up a small taskbar with just a few of the programs. A pager module displays a much larger pager depicting four desktops labeled for different tasks such as Internet and development. You can move from desktop to desktop as well as different sections in each. Clicking anywhere on the screen background will pop up a menu that provides entries for frequently used utilities, as well as the modules such as the button bars. See Figure 4-6.

The fvwm95 Web page is currently located at **ftp://mitac11.uia.ac.be/html-test/ fvwm95.html** with an official mirror site at **www.terraware.net/ftp/pub/Mirrors/ FVWM95/fvwm95.html**. (You can link to it from the fvwm Web page, which you can link to from the Linux Resources page at the **www.caldera.com** Web site.) For your OpenLinux system, it is best to download the RPM version of the software from the Redhat ftp site, **ftp.redhat.com/put/contrib/i386**, though you can also download it from the fvwm95 Web sites. There are also several icon packages you should install. Also, if you performed a standard install of OpenLinux Lite, you will have to first install the X-Windows development libraries from your CD-ROM. The current fvwm95 packages are listed here. Check for newer versions. Use the **rpm-i** command to install them.

```
fvwm95-2.0.43a-2.i386.rpm
fvwm95-icons-2.0.43a-2.i386.rpm
fvwm95-mini-icons-2.0.42a-1.i386.rpm
fvwm95-modules-2.0.42a-1.i386.rpm
fvwm95-utils-2.0.42a-1.i386.rpm
```

Qvwm is a very stable Windows 95-like window manager that was developed with original code. It is a fully-functional virtual window manager with a nine-pane pager. Qvwm provides standard Windows 95 features such as a Start menu and shortcuts. Shortcuts are moveable to any part of the desktop. However, it is a work in

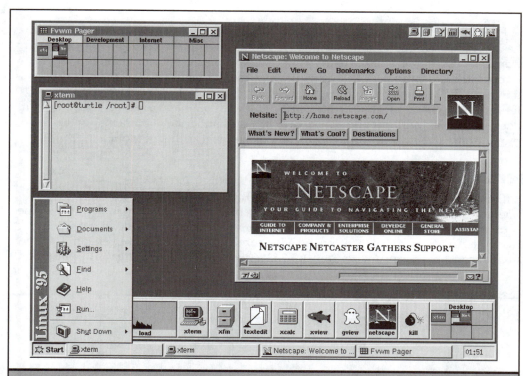

Figure 4-6. *The fvwm95 window manager with start menu, button bar, pager, Xterm window, and Netscape running*

progress currently in beta release. An RPM package with qvwm Linux binaries is available in the Redhat contrib directory, and you can obtain the most recent version of the source code downloaded from the qvwm mirror site at **qv.myth.co.uk**, or from the home page listed in Table 4-1. Using simple **xmkmf** and **make** commands you can easily compile and install qvwm. Qvwm requires the libg++ and xpm libraries, so be sure they are installed before you try to run this window manager.

The qvwm configuration file is **qvwm.system**, located in the **/usr/X11R6/lib/ X11/qvwm** directory. Users can also create their own configuration file called **.qvwmrc**. The qvwm man page details how to make Start menu entries and shortcuts. Start menu entries in the configuration file consist of an item, icon, and command, each encased in quotes. For a shortcut entry, enter the shortcut name, the icon you want for the shortcut, and the command to be executed. The icon can be any pixmap. Be sure to place the pixmap in Qvwm's pixmaps directory. The following is a shortcut entry for netscape.

```
"Netscape"   "netscape.xpm"   "netscape"
```

LessTif: mwm

LessTif is an OSF/Motif clone designed to run any Motif program. It is free of charge from the LessTif Web site, currently at **www.lesstif.org/lesstif.html**. You can link to it through the Caldera Linux Resources page on the Caldera Web site. You can also download RPM versions from the Redhat contrib directory at the Redhat ftp site, **lesstif-0.87-2.i386.rpm**. You invoke LessTif with the command **mwm**. Currently, LessTif does not run all Motif programs. The project is still under development, but it provides the same window management look and feel as that of Motif.

AfterStep

AfterStep originated as a clone of the NeXTSTEP interface used on the NeXT operating system, but has since added features of its own, as shown in Figure 4-7. The source code is based on the fvwm window manager. You can download AfterStep from the AfterStep Web site (**afterstep.edoc.com**), or obtain the RPM version from the Redhat contrib directory, **AfterStep-1.0-3.i386.rpm**. AfterStep features an applications

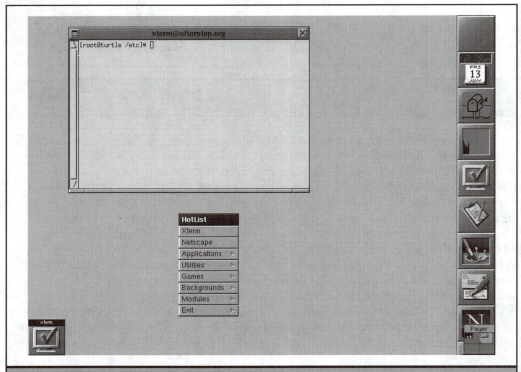

Figure 4-7. *The AfterStep window manager*

loader called Wharf that can contain folders of other applications. There are also pop-up menus and NeXTSTEP-style icons. The AfterStep Web site contains a number of screen shots describing different ways the interface can be configured. Sample **.steprc** configuration files are provided.

Motif

Motif is proprietary software that you have to purchase from a vendor for about $150. Motif and Xview are the two major competing window interfaces provided for Unix, representing two different window standards. These two standards have been recently integrated into a new GUI standard for Unix called the Common Desktop Environment (CDE). Commercial desktops with CDE interfaces are currently available for Linux.

The Crisplite and XEmacs Editors

Two very easy to use and full-featured text editors called Crisplites and XEmacs are provided for you by OpenLinux Lite. These editors incorporate many of the features found in the Vi and Emacs editors (see Chapters 17 and 18). At the same time, you have the ease of use provided by window-based editors. You can select commands using menus and toolbars, scroll through text with scroll bars, resize your window, and use your mouse to select text and easily move, copy, or delete it (see Figure 4-8).

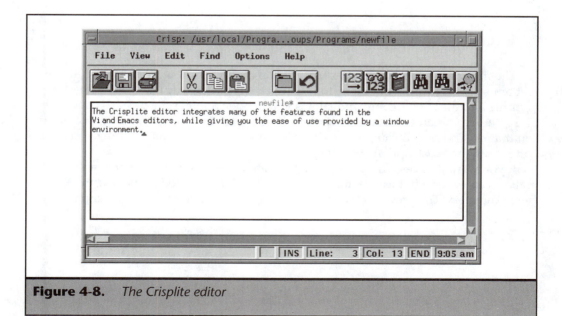

Figure 4-8.   *The Crisplite editor*

Through the Help menu on the main window, you can open the online manual, which provides a detailed explanation of all Crisplite features.

The Crisplite editor is already installed on your OpenLinux system. On the Caldera Desktop, you will see an icon for the Crisplite editor. Just double-click on it to start it up. Currently, Crisplite is not on the fvwm workplace menu. An easy way to add it is to create a link from the **/usr/bin/mcr** program to **/usr/X11R6/bin/mcr**. It will show up in Other Applications with the title mcr. To start XEmacs, you can click on its button on the fvwn GoodStuff task bar, or enter the **xemacs** command in an Xterm window.

The Crisplite and XEmacs editors open a window with menus and a toolbar. Within the window, you can enter text. With your mouse, you can click and drag to select text. The toolbar buttons provide easy access to standard editing functions such as opening and saving files, and copying and pasting text. Crisplite is designed to let you work on many different files at the same time. You can have several windows open, each operating on a separate file. Using your mouse, you can click from one to the other. You can also open up buffers to compose text that you can later move into a file. See Chapter 18 for a more detailed discussion of XEmacs.

You can also use a simple screen-based version of Crisplite with your command line interface. You do not have to start up X-Windows and the desktop. This command line version of Crisplite uses only arrow keys to move the cursor and control and function keys to issue commands. But it does provide a full-screen view, allowing you to work on your text screen by screen. You start up the command line version of Crisplite with the **cr** command, usually followed by the name of the file you want to edit.

```
$ cr myfile
```

The file you are editing will be displayed on the screen. You can then type in new text or use the arrow keys to move to different parts of the text. The CTRL-W key saves your file and the CTRL-E command allows you to open another file or start a new one. The CTRL-X command quits the editor. See the Crisplite manual for a listing of editing commands. Those who want to use Crisplite with the Vi command set can invoke the editor with the **-mvi** option, **cr-mvi**.

If you want to access Crisplite through a button on the fvwm toolbar, you have to make an entry for it in the **system.fvwmrc.goodstuff** file located in the **/usr/lib/X11/ fvwm** directory. The previous section on the fvwm toolbar shows such an entry.

Summary: X-Windows

With Linux X-Windows window managers and desktops, you can interact with your system using menus, windows, and icons as well as set up efficient and easy access to Linux programs and Internet tools. To start X-Windows, enter the command **startx** on the command line. X-Windows supports a variety of window managers and desktops. Several of these are listed in Table 4-1, along with Web sites that you can download them from.

The fvwm window manager supports virtual and multiple desktops. It also has its own workplace menu and taskbar from which you can start the X-Windows program. A virtual desktop extends the desktop area to include several screen views. A pager lets you move to each view. Each part of the desktop can have windows open. The fvwm virtual desktop supports four screen views and fvwm95 supports six. Certain items such as taskbars are considered sticky, and will be displayed on all views of the virtual desktop.

The desktop programs such as Looking Glass integrate file and program management capabilities. With directory windows, you can use icons and menus to manage files and directories. The menus of a directory window contain commands that you can use to copy, move, print, erase, or perform other operations on files.

You can download most of the window and file managers in the form of RPM packages from the Redhat contrib directory, **ftp.redhat.com/pub/contrib/i386**. It is, however, difficult to tell what a particular software package is. Linux Resource Web Pages will organize software by category with descriptions. See, for example, the Linux Applications and Utilities page at **www.chariott.com/linapps.html**.

Window Managers	Command	Description	Web Site
TWM	twm	Tom's window manager	
FVWM	fvwm	The free virtual window manager (v. 1.24)	www.hpc.uh.edu/fvwm
FVWM2	fvwm2	Version 2.0 of fvwm (currently beta)	www.hpc.uh.edu/fvwm
FVWM95	fvwm95	Windows 95 interface based on fvwm2	www.terraware.net/ftp/pub/Mirrors/FVWM95/fvwm95.html
Q Virtual Window Manager	qvwm	Windows 95 interface using original programming	www-masuda.is.s.u-tokyo.ac.jp/~kourai/qvwm/qvwm-e.html
Xview	olwm olvwm	The Xview window manager (OpenLook). olvwm supports a virtual desktop	sunsite.unc.edu/pub/Linux/libs/X/xview
AfterStep	afterstep	Based on the NeXTSTEP interface	afterstep.edoc.com
LessTif	mwm	A clone of Motif	www.lesstif.org
Motif	mwm	Motif window manager and desktop (commercial product)	
Macintosh-like Virtual Window Manager	mlvwm	A clone of the Macintosh interface, window manager with menus	www.iaseste.or.at/linux
amiwn	amiwn	An Amiga window manager interface	www.lysator.liu.se/~marcus/amiwn

Table 4-1. *Window and File Managers (for most software, install using RPNI located in the Redhat Contrib directory, ftp//ftp.redhat.com/pub/contrib/i386)*

Window Managers	Command	Description	Web Site
Generic Window Manager	`gwm`	A GNU window manager	ftp.x.org/contrib/window _managers/gwm
WindowMaker	`wmaker`	A NeXTSTEP clone	www.myth.co.uk/ ~ximenes
Enlightenment		An original window manager	www.rasterman.com
The K desktop	`kwm` `kde`	The K Desktop Environment Window, file manager, and tools	www.kde.org
Freedom Lite		Window manager for Freedom interface	fsw.com
File Managers			
Caldera Desktop (Looking Glass)	`lg`	Commercial desktop from Caldera	www.caldera.com
Xfm	`xfm`	File manager	col/contrib/RPMS (open Linux CD-ROM)
treebrowser	`tb`	File manager using Xview widgets	
XVfilemanager	`xvfilemgr`	File manager using Xview widgets and icons	www.info.polymtl.ca/ ada2/coyote/www
TKDesk	`tkdesk`	A TK-based file manager	www.people.mainz. netsurf.de/~bolik/ tkdesk
Midnight Commander		Clone of Norton Commander	mc.blackdown.org/mc
Filerunner		File manager	www-c.informatik. uni-hanover.de/ ~kaiser/dfm
DFM	`dfm`	File manager	www.cd.chalmers.se/ ~hch/filerunner.html

Table 4-1.   *Window and File Managers (continued)*

PART TWO

Linux Operations

Chapter Five

Shell Operations

T he shell is a command interpreter that provides a line-oriented interactive interface between the user and the operating system. You enter commands on a command line, and they are then interpreted by the shell and sent as instructions to the operating system. This interpretive capability of the shell provides for many sophisticated features. For example, the shell has a set of special characters that can generate file names. It can redirect input and output. It can also run operations in the background, freeing you to perform other tasks.

Three different types of shells have been developed for Linux: the Bourne Again shell (BASH), the Public Domain Korn shell (PDKSH), and the TCSH shell. All three shells are available for your use, although the BASH shell is the default. All examples so far in this book have used the BASH shell. You only need one type of shell to do your work. This chapter discusses features common to all shells, whereas Chapters 15 and 16 cover distinguishing features of the BASH, PDKSH, and TCSH shells. You will see how you can configure shells using aliases, history events, and system variables. The shells even have their own programming languages. This chapter focuses on common features of command execution; specifically, command line editing, special characters, redirection, pipes, variables, scripts, and job control.

The Command Line

When you log into Linux, you are presented with a command line interface. This consists of a single line into which you enter commands with any of their options and arguments. A shell *prompt*, such as the one shown here, marks the beginning of the command line:

```
$
```

Linux installs with the Bourne Again Shell, commonly referred to as the BASH shell. The BASH shell has a dollar sign prompt; but Linux has several other types of shells, each with its own prompt. The different types of shells are discussed at length beginning with Chapter 15.

When the system prompt appears, you are logged into the system. The prompt designates the beginning of the command line. You are now ready to enter a command and its arguments at the prompt. In the next example, the user enters the **date** command, which displays the date. The user types the command on the first line and then presses ENTER to execute the command.

```
$ date
Sun July 7 10:30:21 PST 1996
```

When you log in, you are actually placed into the shell, which interprets the commands you enter and sends them to the system. The shell follows a special *syntax* for interpreting the command line. The first word entered on a command line must be the name of a command. The next words are options and arguments for the command. Each word on the command line must be separated by one or more spaces or tabs.

```
$ Command    Options    Arguments
```

When you enter a Linux command, the shell first reads the command name and then checks to see if there is an actual command by that name. If there is no such command, the shell issues an error message.

Options and Arguments

An *option* is a one-letter code preceded by a dash that modifies the type of action that the command takes. One example of a command that has options is the **ls** command. The **ls** command, with no options, displays a list of all the files in your current directory. It merely lists the name of each file with no other information.

With a **-l** option, the **ls** command will modify its task by displaying a line of information about each file, listing such data as its size and the date and time it was last modified. In the next example, the user enters the **ls** command followed by a **-l** option. The dash before the **-l** option is required. Linux uses it to distinguish an option from an argument.

```
$ ls -l
```

Another option, **-a**, lists all the files in your directory, including what are known as hidden files. *Hidden files* are often configuration files and always have names beginning with a period. For this reason they are often referred to as *dot files*. In most cases, you can also combine options. You do so by preceding the options with an initial dash and then listing the options you want. The options **-al**, for example, will list information about all the files in your directory, including any hidden files.

```
$ ls -al
```

Another option for the **ls** command is **-F**. With this option, the **ls** command displays directory names with a preceding slash so that you can easily identify them.

Most commands are designed to take arguments. An *argument* is a word that you type in on the command line after any options. Many file management commands take file names as their arguments. For example, if you only wanted the information displayed for a particular file, you could add that file's name after the **-l** option:

```
$ ls -l mydata
```

Depending on the command, you may or may not have to enter arguments. Some commands, such as **ls**, do not require any arguments. Other commands may require a minimum number of arguments. For example, the **cp** command requires at least two arguments. If the number of arguments does not match the number required by the command, then the shell issues an error message.

Remember that options are entered on the command line before the arguments. In the case of the **cp** command, the **-i** option for checking the overwrite condition is entered before the file name arguments. Here are some examples of entering commands:

```
$ ls                        Command without options
$ ls -F                     Command with option
$ cp -i mydata newdata      Command with option and arguments
```

Command Line Features

The command line is actually a buffer of text that you can edit. Before you press ENTER, you can perform editing commands on the text you have entered. The editing capabilities are limited, but they do provide a way for correcting mistakes. The BACKSPACE and DEL keys allow you to erase the character just typed in. With this character-erasing capability, you can backspace over the entire line if you wish, erasing what you have entered. The CTRL-U key combination erases the whole line and lets you start over again at the prompt. In the next example, the user types **dat1** instead of **date**. Using BACKSPACE, the user erases the **1** and then enters an **e**.

```
$ dat1
$ dat
$ date
```

The shell you will start working in is the BASH shell, your default shell. This shell has special command line editing capabilities that you may find very helpful as you learn Linux. You can easily modify commands you have entered before executing them, moving anywhere on the command line and inserting or deleting characters. This is particularly helpful for very complex commands. You can use CTRL-F or RIGHT ARROW key to move forward a character, the CTRL-B or the LEFT ARROW key to move back a character. CTRL-D or DEL deletes the character the cursor is on, and CTRL-H or BACKSPACE deletes the character before the cursor. To add text, you just use the arrow keys to move the cursor to where you want to insert text and type in the new characters. At any time, you can press ENTER to execute the command. For example, if you make a spelling mistake when entering a command, rather than re-entering the entire command, you can use the editing operations to correct the mistake.

You can also use the UP ARROW key to redisplay your previously executed command. You can then re-execute that command or edit it and execute the modified command. You can then re-execute that command or edit it and execute the modified version. You'll find this very helpful when you have to repeat certain operations over and over, such as editing the same file. It is also helpful when you've already executed a command that you had entered incorrectly. In this case you would be presented with an error message and a new, empty command line. By pressing the UP ARROW key you can redisplay your previous command, make corrections to it, and then execute it again. This way, you would not have to enter the whole command over again.

The BASH shell keeps a list, called a *history list*, of your previously entered commands. You can display each command in turn on your command line by pressing the UP ARROW key. The DOWN ARROW key will move you down the list. You can modify and execute any of these previous commands when you display them on your command line. This history feature is discussed in more detail in Chapter 15.

Some commands can be very complex and take some time to execute. When you mistakenly execute the wrong command, you can interrupt and stop such commands with the interrupt keys—CTRL-C or DEL.

You can place more than one command on the same line, or you can use several lines to enter a single command. To enter more than one command on the same line, separate the commands with a semicolon. The next example shows the **ls** command and the **cp** command entered on the same line.

```
$ ls -F ; cp -i mydata newdata
```

You can enter a command on several lines by typing a backslash just before you press ENTER. The backslash "escapes" the ENTER key, effectively continuing the same command line to the next line. In the next example, the **cp** command is entered on three lines. The first two lines end in a backslash, effectively making all three lines one command line.

```
$ cp -i \
mydata \
newdata
```

Special Characters and File Name Arguments: *, ?, [ ]

File names are the most common arguments used in a command. Often you may know only part of the file name, or you may want to reference several file names that have the same extension or begin with the same characters. The shell provides a set of special characters that search out, match, and generate a list of file names. These special characters are the asterisk, question mark, and brackets (*****, **?**, **[]**). Given a partial file name, the shell uses these matching operators to search for files and generate a list of file names found. The shell replaces the partial file name argument with the list of matched file names. This list of file names can then become the arguments for commands such as **ls** that can operate on many files. Table 5-1 (found at the end of this chapter) lists the shell's special characters.

You can use the asterisk, *****, to reference files beginning or ending with a specific set of characters. You place the asterisk before or after a set of characters that form a pattern to be searched for in file names. If the asterisk is placed before the pattern, file names that end in that pattern are searched for. If the asterisk is placed after the pattern, file names that begin with that pattern are searched for. Any matching file name is copied into a list of file names generated by this operation. In the next example, all file names beginning with the pattern "doc" are searched for and a list generated. Then all file names ending with the pattern "day" are searched for and a list generated.

```
$ ls
doc1 doc2 document docs mydoc monday tuesday
$ ls doc*
doc1 doc2 document docs
$ ls *day
monday tuesday
$
```

File names often include an extension specified with a period and followed by a single character. The extension has no special status. It is only part of the characters making up the file name. Using the asterisk makes it easy to select files with a given extension. In the next example, the asterisk is used to list only those files with a **.c** extension. The asterisk placed before the **.c** constitutes the argument for **ls**.

```
$ ls *.c
calc.c main.c
```

You can use the special character, *****, with the **rm** command to erase several files at once. The asterisk first selects a list of files with a given extension, or beginning or ending with a given set of characters, and then presents this list of files to the **rm** command to be erased. In the next example, the **rm** command erases all files beginning with the pattern "doc".

```
$ rm doc*
```

The asterisk by itself matches all files. If you use a single asterisk as the argument for an **rm** command, all your files will be erased. In the next example, the **ls *** command lists all files, and the **rm *** command erases all files.

```
$ ls *
doc1 doc2 document docs mydoc myletter yourletter
$ rm *
$ ls
$
```

Use the ***** special character carefully and sparingly with the **rm** command. The combination can be very dangerous. A misplaced ***** in an **rm** command without the **-i** option could easily erase all your files. The first command in the next example erases only those files with a **.c** extension. The second command, however, erases all files. Notice the space between the asterisk and the period in the second command. A space in a command line functions as a *delimiter*, separating arguments. The asterisk is considered one argument and the **.c** another. The asterisk by itself matches all files and, when used as an argument with the **rm** command, instructs **rm** to erase all your files.

```
$ rm *.c
$ rm * .c
```

The question mark, **?**, matches only a single incomplete character in file names. Suppose you want to match the files **doc1** and **docA**, but not document. Whereas the asterisk will match file names of any length, the question mark limits the match to just one extra character. The next example matches files that begin with the word "doc" followed by a single differing letter.

```
$ ls
doc1 docA document
$ ls doc?
doc1 docA
```

You can use more than one question mark in a pattern if you wish, and you can place the question marks anywhere in the pattern. The next example searches for a pattern with three possible differing characters.

```
$ ls ?y?oc?
mydocs mylock Sydoc1
```

You can combine the **?** with other special characters to construct very powerful matching operations. Suppose you want to find all files that have a single character extension. You could use the asterisk to match the file name proper, and the **?** to match the single character extension: ***.?**. In the next example, the user displays all files that have a single character extension.

```
$ ls *.?
calc.c  lib.a
```

Whereas the ***** and **?** special characters specify incomplete portions of a file name, the brackets, **[]**, allow you to specify a set of valid characters to search for. Any character placed within the brackets will be matched in the file name. Suppose you want to list files beginning with "doc" but only ending in 1 or A. You are not interested in file names ending in 2, or B, or any other character. Here is how it's done:

```
$ ls
doc1 doc2 doc3 docA docB docD document
$ ls doc[1A]
doc1 docA
```

You can also specify a set of characters as a range, rather than listing them one by one. A dash placed between the upper and lower bound of a set of characters selects all characters within that range. The range is usually determined by the character set in use. In an ASCII character set, the range a-g will select all lowercase alphabetic characters from *a* through *g* inclusive. In the next example, files beginning with the pattern "doc" and ending in characters 1 through 3 are selected. Then those ending in characters B through E are matched.

```
$ ls doc[1-3]
doc1 doc2 doc3
$ ls doc[B-E]
docB docD
```

You can combine the brackets with other special characters to form very flexible matching operators. Suppose you only want to list file names ending in either a **.c** or **.o** extension, but no other extension. You can use a combination of the asterisk and brackets: ***[co]**. The asterisk matches all file names, and the brackets match only file names with extension **.c** or **.o**.

```
$ ls *.[co]
main.c   main.o   calc.c
```

There may be times when a special character is part of a file name. In these cases, you need to quote the special character by preceding it with a backslash in order to reference the file. In the next example, the user needs to reference a file that ends with the **?** character, **answers?**. The **?** is, however, a special character and would match any file name beginning with "answers" that has one more characters. In this case, the user quotes the **?** with a preceding backslash in order to reference the file name.

```
$ ls answers\?
answers?
```

You can combine a quoted character with special characters in your file name. In the next example, the user lists all files beginning with "answers?" that have an extension.

```
$ ls answers\?.*
answers?.quiz   answers?.mid   answers?.final
```

Standard Input/Output and Redirection

When Unix was designed, a decision was made to distinguish between the physical implementation and logical organization of a file. Physically, Unix files are accessed in randomly arranged blocks. Logically, all files are organized as a continuous stream of bytes. Linux, as a version of Unix, has this same organization. Aside from special system calls, the user never references the physical structure of a file. To the user, all files have the same organization—a byte stream. Any file can be easily copied or appended to another because all files are organized in the same way. In this sense, there is only one standard type of file in Linux, the byte-stream file. Linux makes no implementational distinction between a character file and a record file, or a text file and a binary file.

This logical file organization extends to input and output operations. The data in input and output operations is organized like a file. Data input at the keyboard is placed in a data stream arranged as a continuous set of bytes. Data output from a command or program is also placed in a data stream and arranged as a continuous set of bytes. This input data stream is referred to in Linux as the *standard input*, and the output data stream is called the *standard output*.

Because the standard input and standard output have the same organization as that of a file, they can easily interact with files. Linux has a redirection capability that lets you easily move data in and out of files. You can redirect the standard output so that, instead of displaying the output on a screen, you can save it in a file. You can also redirect the standard input away from the keyboard to a file, so that input is read from a file instead of from your keyboard.

When a Linux command is executed that produces output, this output is placed in the standard output data stream. The default destination for the standard output data stream is a device, in this case, the screen. *Devices*, such as the keyboard and screen, are treated as files. They receive and send out streams of bytes with the same organization as that of a byte-stream file. The screen is a device that displays a continuous stream of bytes. By default, the standard output will send its data to the screen device, which will then display the data.

For example, the **ls** command generates a list of all file names and outputs this list to the standard output. This stream of bytes in the standard output is then directed to the screen device. The list of file names is then printed on the screen. The **cat** command also sends output to the standard output. The contents of a file are copied to the standard output whose default destination is the screen. The contents of the file are then displayed on the screen. Figure 5-1 shows the basic relationship between the standard input and the keyboard device, and between the standard output and the screen device.

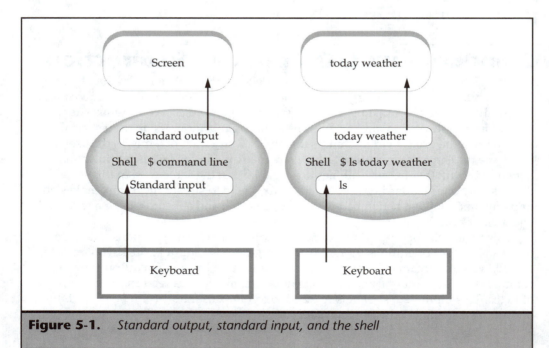

Figure 5-1. *Standard output, standard input, and the shell*

Redirecting the Standard Output: > and >>

Suppose that instead of displaying a list of files on the screen, you would like to save this list in a file. In other words, you would like to direct the standard output to a file rather than the screen. To do this, you place the output redirection operator, **>** (greater-than sign), and the name of a file on the command line after the Linux command. Table 5-2 (found at the end of this chapter) lists the different ways you can use the redirection operators. In the next example, the output of the **cat** command is redirected from the screen device to a file. As shown in Figure 5-2, instead of the contents of the file **myletter** being printed to the screen, they are redirected to the file **newletter**.

```
$ cat myletter > newletter
```

The redirection operation creates the new destination file. If the file already exists, it will be overwritten with the data in the standard output. You can set the **noclobber** feature to prevent overwriting an existing file with the redirection operation. In this case, the redirection operation on an existing file will fail. You can overcome the **noclobber** feature by placing an exclamation point after the

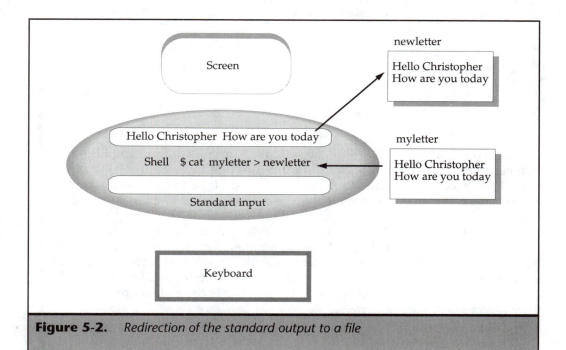

Figure 5-2. *Redirection of the standard output to a file*

redirection operator. The next example sets the **noclobber** feature for the BASH shell and then forces the overwriting of the **oldletter** file if it already exists.

```
$ set -o noclobber
$ cat myletter >! oldletter
```

Redirection File Creation

Though the redirection operator and file name are placed after the command, the redirection operation is not executed after the command. In fact, it is executed before the command. The redirection operation creates the file and sets up the redirection before it receives any data from the standard output. If the file already exists, it will be destroyed and replaced by a file of the same name. In effect, the command generating the output is executed only after the redirected file has been created.

In the next example, the output of the **ls** command is redirected from the screen device to a file. First the **ls** command lists files, and in the next command, **ls** redirects its file list to the **listf** file. Then the **cat** command displays the list of files saved in **listf**. Notice that the list of files in **listf** includes the **listf** file name. The list of file names generated by the **ls** command will include the name of the file created by the redirection operation, in this case, **listf**. The **listf** file is first created by the redirection operation, and then the **ls** command lists it along with other files. This file list output by **ls** is then redirected to the **listf** file, instead of being printed on the screen.

```
$ ls
mydata intro preface
$ ls > listf
$ cat listf
mydata intro listf preface
```

Errors occur when you try to use the same file name for both an input file for the command and the redirected destination file. In this case, since the redirection operation is executed first, the input file, since it exists, is destroyed and replaced by a file of the same name. When the command is executed, it finds an input file that is empty.

In the **cat** command shown next, the file **myletter** is the name for both the destination file for redirected output and the input file for the **cat** operation. As shown in the next example, the redirection operation is executed first, destroying the **myletter** file and replacing it with a new and empty **myletter** file. Then the **cat** operation is executed and attempts to read all the data in the **myletter** file. However, there is now nothing in the **myletter** file.

```
$ cat myletter > myletter
```

Appending the Standard Output: >>

You can also *append* the standard output to an existing file using the **>>** redirection operator. Instead of overwriting the file, the data in the standard output is added at the end of the file. In the next example, the **myletter** and **oldletter** files are appended to the **alletters** file. The **alletters** file will then contain the contents of both **myletter** and **oldletter**.

```
$ cat myletter >> alletters
$ cat oldletter >> alletters
```

The Standard Input

Many Linux commands can receive data from the standard input. The standard input itself receives data from a device or a file. The default device for the standard input is the keyboard. Characters typed into the keyboard are placed in the standard input, which is then directed to the Linux command.

The **cat** command without a file name argument reads data from standard input. When you type in data on the keyboard, each character will be placed in the standard input and directed to the **cat** command. The **cat** command will then send the character to the standard output—the screen device—which displays the character on the screen.

When you try this, you will find that as you enter a line, that line will immediately be displayed on the screen. This is due to the line buffering method used in many Linux systems. *Line buffering* requires that a user type in an entire line before any input is sent to the standard input. The **cat** command receives a whole line at a time from the standard input, and it will immediately display the line. In the next example, the user executes the **cat** command without any arguments. As the user types in a line, it is sent to the standard input, which the **cat** command reads and sends to the standard output:

```
$ cat
This is a new line
This is a new line
for the cat
for the cat
command
command
^D
$
```

The **cat** operation will continue until a CTRL-D character (**^D**) is entered on a line by itself. The CTRL-D character is the end-of-file character for any Linux file. In a sense, the user is actually creating a file at the keyboard and ending it with the end-of-file character. Remember, the standard input, as well as the standard output, have the same format as any Linux file.

If you combine the **cat** command with redirection, you have an easy way of saving what you have typed to a file. As shown in the next example, the output of the **cat** operation is redirected to the **mydat** file. The **mydat** file will now contain all the data typed in at the keyboard. The **cat** command, in this case, still has no file arguments. It will receive its data from the standard input, the keyboard device. The redirection operator redirects the output of the **cat** command to the file **mydat**. The **cat** command has no direct contact with any files. It is simply receiving input from the standard input and sending output to the standard output.

```
$ cat > mydat
This is a new line
for the cat
command
^D
$
```

Redirecting the Standard Input: <

Just as with the standard output, you can also redirect the standard input. The standard input may be received from a file rather than the keyboard. The operator for redirecting the standard input is the less-than sign, **<**. In the next example, the standard input is redirected to receive input from the **myletter** file rather than the keyboard device. The contents of **myletter** are read into the standard input by the redirection operation. Then the **cat** command reads the standard input and displays the contents of **myletter**.

```
$ cat < myletter
hello Christopher
How are you today
$
```

You can combine the redirection operations for both standard input and standard output. In the next example, the **cat** command has no file name arguments. Without file name arguments, the **cat** command receives input from the standard input and sends output to the standard output. However, the standard input has been redirected to receive its data from a file, and the standard output has been redirected to place its data in a file.

```
$ cat < myletter > newletter
```

Pipes: |

You will find yourself in situations in which you need to send data from one command to another. In other words, you will want to send the standard output of a command to another command, not to a destination file. Suppose you want to send a list of your file names to the printer to be printed. You need two commands to do this: the **ls** command to generate a list of file names and the **lpr** command to send the list to the printer. In effect, you need to take the output of the **ls** command and use it as input for the **lpr** command. You can think of the data as flowing from one command to another. To form such a connection in Linux, you use what is called a pipe. The *pipe operator*, |, (vertical bar character) placed between two commands forms a connection between them. The standard output of one command becomes the standard input for the other. The pipe operation receives output from the command placed before the pipe and sends this data as input to the command placed after the pipe. As shown in the next example, you can connect the **ls** command and the **lpr** command with a pipe. The list of file names output by the **ls** command is piped into the **lpr** command.

```
$ ls | lpr
```

You can combine the pipe operation with other shell features such as special characters to perform specialized operations. The next example prints only files with a .c extension. The **ls** command is used with the asterisk and ".c" to generate a list of file names with the .c extension. Then this list is piped to the **lpr** command.

```
$ ls *.c | lpr
```

Whereas redirection simply places output in a file, pipes send output to another Linux command. You may wonder why this cannot be accomplished with redirection. You need to keep in mind the difference between a file and a command: A file is a storage medium that holds data. You can save data on it or read data from it. A command is a program that executes instructions. A command may read or save data in a file, but a command is not in itself a file. For this reason, a redirection operation operates on files, not on commands. Redirection can send data from a program to a file, but it cannot send data from a program to another program. Only files can be the destination of a redirection operation, not other programs.

You can, however, simulate the piping process through a series of redirection operations. You could send the output of one command to a file. Then, on the next line, you could execute a command using that file as redirected input. The next example uses two redirection operations in two separate commands to print a list of file names. This same task was performed in the previous examples using a single pipe operation. The pipe operation literally takes the standard output of one command and uses it as standard input for another command.

```
$ ls *.c > tempfile
$ lpr < tempfile
```

Up to this point we have been using a list of file names as input, but it is important to note that pipes operate on the standard output of a command, whatever that might be. The contents of whole files or even several files can be piped from one command to another. In the next example, the **cat** command reads and outputs the contents of the **mydata** file, which are then piped to the **lpr** command.

```
$ cat mydata | lpr
```

Suppose you want to print out data you are typing in from the keyboard instead of data from a file. Remember that the **cat** command without any arguments reads data from the standard input. In the next example, **cat** takes input from the keyboard instead of a file and pipes the output to the **lpr** command. The **cat** command is executed before the **lpr** command, so you first enter your data for the **cat** command on the keyboard, ending with the end-of-file, CTRL-D. The input for a piped byte stream may come from any source.

```
$ cat | lpr
This text will
be printed
^D
$
```

Linux provides **cat** with a **-n** option that outputs the contents of a file, adding line numbers. If you want to print your file with line numbers, you must first use the **cat** command with the **-n** option to output the contents of the file with line numbers added. You then pipe this output to the **lpr** command for printing, for example:

```
$ cat -n  mydata | lpr
```

You do much the same thing for displaying a file with line numbers. In this case, the numbered output is usually piped to the **more** command for screen-by-screen examination. You can even specify several files at once and pipe their output to the **more** command, examining all the files. In the next example, both **mydata** and **preface** are numbered and piped to the **more** command for screen-by-screen examination.

```
$ cat -n mydata preface | more
```

Linux has many commands that generate modified output; the **cat** command with the **-n** option is only one. Another is the **sort** command. The **sort** command takes the contents of a file and generates a version with each line sorted in alphabetic order. It works best with files that are lists of items. Commands like **sort** that output a modified version of its input are referred to as filters. Filters are discussed in detail in Chapter 14. They are often used with pipes. In the next example, a sorted version of **mylist** is generated and piped into the **more** command for display on the screen. Note that the original file, **mylist**, has not been changed and is not itself sorted. Only the output of **sort** in the standard output is sorted.

```
$ sort mylist | more
```

You can, of course, combine several commands, connecting each pair with a pipe. The output of one command can be piped into another command, which, in turn, can pipe its output into still another command. Suppose you have a file with a list of items that you want to print out both numbered and in alphabetic order. To print the numbered and sorted list, you can first generate a sorted version with the **sort** command and then pipe that output to the **cat** command. The **cat** command with the **-n** option then takes as its input the sorted list and generates as its output a numbered, sorted list, which can then be piped to the **lpr** command for printing. The next example shows the command, and in Figure 5-3 a sorted and numbered version of the **mylist** file is printed.

```
$ sort mylist | cat -n | lpr
```

You can accomplish the same task in a more cumbersome way, using redirection and a series of separate commands. In this case, two new temporary files (**sfile** and **nfile**) are needed to hold the output of each operation.

```
$ sort mylist > sfile
$ cat -n < sfile > nfile
$ lpr < nfile
```

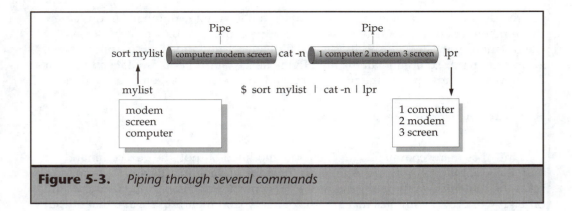

Figure 5-3. *Piping through several commands*

The standard input piped into a command can be more carefully controlled with the standard input argument, **-**. When you use the dash as an argument for a command, it represents the standard input. Suppose you would like to print a file with the name of its directory at the top. The **pwd** command outputs a directory name, and the **cat** command outputs the contents of a file. In this case, the **cat** command needs to take as its input both the file and the standard input piped in from the **pwd** command. The **cat** command will have two arguments: the standard input as represented by the dash and the file name of the file to be printed.

In the next example, the **pwd** command generates the directory name and pipes it into the **cat** command. For the **cat** command, this piped-in standard input now contains the directory name. As represented by the dash, the standard input is the first argument to the **cat** command. The **cat** command copies the directory name and the contents of the **mylist** file to the standard output, which is then piped to the **lpr** command for printing. If you want to print the directory name at the end of the file instead, simply make the dash the last argument and the file name the first argument, as in **cat mylist -** .

```
$ pwd | cat - mylist | lpr
```

Pipes and Redirection: tee

Suppose you want to redirect the standard output to a file and, at the same time, display the contents of that output on the screen so that you can see what you are saving. You can do this with the **tee** command. The **tee** command copies the standard output to a file. It takes as its argument the name of the new file to which the standard output is copied. The standard output continues on its way, but as it passes through the **tee** command, its contents are copied to a file. It is as if the standard output were split into two copies, one being redirected to a file and the other continuing on its way, often to the screen. The next example copies the contents of the file **mylist** to the file **newlist** and displays the contents on the screen.

```
$ cat mylist | tee newlist
```

The **tee** command is handy when you are modifying output and you would like to save the modified output in a file and also see what the modifications look like. In the next example, the file **mylist** is again sorted and the sorted output is piped to the **tee** command. The **tee** command then both saves the sorted output in a file called **sfile** and displays it on the screen.

```
$ sort mylist | tee sfile
computer
modem
screen
$
```

You could use redirection to save the output in a file first and then later print out the file:

```
$ sort mylist > sfile
$ cat sfile
computer
modem
screen
$
```

Suppose, however, you need to save your output in a file as well as print it. In this case, the standard output needs to continue to another command. You need to use **tee** to copy the output to another file while allowing the standard output to be piped into the next command. In the next example, the output of the **sort** command is first piped to **tee**, which copies the output to the file **sfile**. The output itself is then piped into the **lpr** command to be printed.

```
$ sort mylist | tee sfile | lpr
```

Be careful when you use redirection with pipes. A standard output redirection specifies a destination for the standard output. The standard output is saved and stored in that destination file. Once saved, there is no output to be piped into another command. Though redirection can take place at the end of a series of pipe operations, it cannot take place *within* pipe operations. The next example is a valid use of pipes and redirection. The output of the **sort** command is piped to the **cat** command with the **-n** option to number lines, and then the result is saved in the **nfile** file.

```
$ sort mylist | cat -n > nfile
```

What if you need to save the result in **nfile** and print it out? You cannot do something like this:

```
sort mylist | cat -n > nfile | lpr      ERROR
```

The only way to save the output in a file and print it is to use the **tee** command:

```
$ sort mylist | cat -n | tee nfile | lpr
```

You can use **tee** anywhere in the piping sequence. The next example saves a sorted version of the list while printing the numbered version.

```
$ sort mylist | tee sfile | cat -n | lpr
```

Redirecting and Piping the Standard Error: >&, 2>

When you execute commands, it is possible that an error could occur. You may give the wrong number of arguments, or some kind of system error could take place. When an error occurs, the system will issue an error message. Usually such error messages are displayed on the screen, along with the standard output. However, Linux distinguishes between standard output and error messages. Error messages are placed in yet another standard byte stream called the *standard error*. In the next example, the **cat** command is given as its argument the name of a file that does not exist, **myintro**. In this case, the **cat** command will simply issue an error:

```
$ cat myintro
cat : myintro not found
$
```

Because error messages are in a separate data stream than the standard output, error messages will still appear on the screen for you to see even if you have redirected the standard output to a file. In the next example, the standard output of the **cat** command is redirected to the file **mydata**. However, the standard error, containing the error messages, is still directed to the screen.

```
$ cat myintro > mydata
cat : myintro not found
$
```

Like the standard output, you can also redirect the standard error. This means that you can save your error messages in a file for future reference. This is helpful if you need a record of the error messages. Like the standard output, the standard error's default destination is the screen device, but you can redirect the standard error to any file or device that you choose using special redirection operators. In this case, the error messages will not be displayed on the screen.

Redirection of the standard error relies on a special feature of shell redirection. You can reference all the standard byte streams in redirection operations with numbers. The numbers 0, 1, and 2 reference the standard input, standard output, and standard error, respectively. By default, an output redirection, **>**, operates on the standard output, 1. However, you can modify the output redirection to operate on the standard error by preceding the output redirection operator with the number 2. In the next example, the **cat** command again will generate an error. The error message is redirected to the standard byte stream represented by number 2, the standard error.

```
$ cat nodata 2> myerrors
$ cat myerrors
cat : nodata not found
$
```

You can also append the standard error to a file by using the number 2 and the redirection append operator, **>>**. In the next example, the user appends the standard error to the **myerrors** file, which then functions as a log of errors.

```
$ cat nodata 2>> myerrors
$ cat compls 2>> myerrors
$ cat myerrors
cat : nodata not found
cat : compls not found
$
```

To redirect both the standard output and the standard error, you need a separate redirection operation and file for each. In the next example, the standard output is redirected to the file **mydata**, whereas the standard error is redirected to **myerrors**. If **nodata** actually exists, **mydata** will hold a copy of its contents.

```
$ cat nodata 1> mydata 2> myerrors
$ cat myerrors
cat : nodata not found
$
```

If, however, you want to save your errors in the same file as that used for the redirected standard output, you need to redirect the standard error into the standard output. In the BASH shell, you can reference a standard byte stream by preceding its number with an ampersand: **&1** references the standard output. You can use such a reference in a redirection operation to make a standard byte stream a destination file. The redirection operation **2>&1** redirects the standard error into the standard output. In effect, the standard output becomes the destination file for the standard error. Conversely, the redirection operation **1>&2** redirects the standard input into the standard error.

In the next example, the **cat** command has as its argument the name of a file that does not exist, **nodata**. The resulting error message is redirected to the file **mydata**. Both the contents of the standard error and the standard output will be saved in the same file, **mydata**. The message is not displayed on the screen but, instead, saved in a file. To see the error message, simply display the contents of the **mydata** file. If the **nodata** file actually existed, then **mydata** would hold the contents of that file instead of error messages.

```
$ cat nodata 1> mydata 2>&1
$ cat mydata
cat : nodata not found
```

The default output stream for a **>&** operation is the standard output, and the default input stream is the standard error. If the preceding operation is written without using numbers, as shown in the next example, any error messages will be redirected into the standard output and saved in the same destination file for the standard output.

```
$ cat nodata >& mydata
```

Shell Variables

You define variables within a shell, and such variables are known—logically enough—as *shell variables*. There are many different shells. Some utilities, such as the mailx utility, have their own shells with their own shell variables. You can also create your own shell using what are called shell scripts. You have a user shell that becomes active as soon as you log in. This is often referred to as the login shell. Special system variables are defined within this login shell. Shell variables exist as long as your shell is active, that is, until you exit the shell. For example, logging out will exit the login shell. When you log in again, any variables that you may need in your login shell will have to be defined once again.

Definition and Evaluation of Variables: =, $, set, unset

You define a variable in a shell when you first use the variable's name. A variable's name may be any set of alphabetic characters, including the underscore. The name may also include a number, but the number cannot be the first character in the name. A name may not have any other type of character, such as an exclamation point, an ampersand, or even a space. Such symbols are reserved by the shell for its own use. Also, a name may not include more than one word. The shell uses spaces on the command line to distinguish different components of a command such as options, arguments, and the name of the command.

You assign a value to a variable with the assignment operator, **=**. You type in the variable name, the assignment operator, and then the value assigned. Do not place any spaces around the assignment operator. The assignment **operation poet = Virgil**, for example, will fail. (The C-shell has a slightly different type of assignment operation that is described in the section on C-shell variables later in this chapter.) You can assign any set of characters to a variable. In the next example, the variable **poet** is assigned the string **Virgil**.

```
$ poet=Virgil
```

Once you have assigned a value to a variable, you can then use the variable name to reference the value. Often you use the values of variables as arguments for a command. You can reference the value of a variable using the variable name preceded by the **$** operator. The dollar sign is a special operator that uses the variable name to reference a variable's value, in effect, evaluating the variable. Evaluation retrieves a variable's value, usually a set of characters. This set of characters then replaces the variable name on the command line. Wherever a **$** is placed before the variable name, the variable name is replaced with the value of the variable. In the next example, the shell variable **poet** is evaluated and its contents, **Virgil**, are then used as the argument for an **echo** command. The **echo** command simply echoes or prints a set of characters to the screen.

```
$ echo $poet
Virgil
```

You must be careful to distinguish between the evaluation of a variable and its name alone. If you leave out the **$** operator before the variable name, all you have is the variable name itself. In the next example, the **$** operator is absent from the variable name. In this case, the **echo** command has as its argument the word "poet", and so prints out "poet".

```
$ echo poet
poet
```

The contents of a variable are often used as command arguments. A common command argument is a directory path name. It can be tedious to retype a directory path that is being used over and over again. If you assign the directory path name to a variable, you can simply use the evaluated variable in its place. The directory path you assign to the variable is retrieved when the variable is evaluated with the **$** operator. The next example assigns a directory path name to a variable and then uses the evaluated variable in a copy command. The evaluation of **ldir** (which is **$ldir**) results in the path name **/home/chris/letters**. The copy command evaluates to **cp myletter /home/chris/letters**.

```
$ ldir=/home/chris/letters
$ cp myletter $ldir
```

You can obtain a list of all the defined variables with the **set** command. The next example uses the **set** command to display a list of all defined variables and their values.

```
$ set
poet   Virgil
ldir   /home/chris/letters/old
$
```

If you decide that you do not want a certain variable, you can remove it with the **unset** command. The **unset** command "undefines" a variable. The next example undefines the variable **poet**. Then the user executes the **set** command to list all defined variables. Notice that **poet** is missing.

```
$ unset poet
$ set
ldir   /home/chris/letters/old
$
```

TCSH Shell Variables

There is only a slight difference between variables in the TCSH shell and those in the BASH shell. In the TCSH shell, you assign a value to a variable with the **set** command and the assignment operator. To assign a value to a variable, first type **set**, then the variable name, the assignment operator, and the value assigned. The assignment operator must have either a space on both sides or no spaces. It cannot have a space on one side and not the other. For example, > **set poet =Virgil** is an error. Here, the variable **poet** is assigned the string **Virgil**:

```
> set poet=Virgil
```

Like the BASH shell, the TCSH shell also uses the dollar sign to evaluate variables. Evaluation retrieves a variable's value, usually a set of characters. This set of characters then replaces the variable name in the shell command. In the next example, the shell variable **poet** is evaluated, and its contents, **Virgil**, are then used as the argument for an **echo** command.

```
> echo $poet
Virgil
```

As with the BASH shell, double quotes, single quotes, and a backslash will suppress the evaluation of special characters. Also, back quotes can be used to assign the results of commands to variables. In the next example, the double quotes suppress the **?** special character.

```
> set notice = "Is the meeting tomorrow?."
> echo $notice
Is the meeting tomorrow?
>
```

Shell Scripts: User-Defined Commands

You can place shell commands within a file and then have the shell read and execute the commands in the file. In this sense, the file functions as a shell program, executing shell commands as if they were statements in a program. A file that contains shell commands is called a *shell script*.

You enter shell commands into a script file using a standard text editor such as the Vi editor. The **sh** or **.** command used with the script's file name will read the script file and execute the commands. In the next example, the text file called **lsc** contains an **ls** command that displays only files with the extension **.c**.

lsc

```
ls *.c
```

```
$ sh lsc
main.c calc.c
$ . lsc
main.c calc.c
```

You can dispense with the **sh** and **.** commands by setting the executable permission of a script file. When the script file is first created by your text editor, it is only given read and write permission. The **chmod** command with the **+x** option will give the script file executable permission. (Permissions are discussed in Chapter 7.) Once it is executable, entering the name of the script file at the shell prompt and pressing ENTER will execute the script file and the shell commands in it. In effect, the script's file name becomes a new shell command. In this way, you can use shell scripts to design and create your own Linux commands. You only need to set the permission once. In the next example, the **lsc** file's executable permission for the owner is set to on. Then the **lsc** shell script is directly executed like any Linux command.

```
$ chmod u+x lsc
$ lsc
main.c calc.c
```

Just as any Linux command can take arguments, so also can a shell script. Arguments on the command line are referenced sequentially starting with **1**. An argument is referenced using the **$** operator and the number of its position. The first argument is referenced with **$1**, the second with **$2**, and so on. In the next example, the **lsext** script prints out files with a specified extension. The first argument is the extension. The script is then executed with the argument **c** (of course, the executable permission must have been set).

lsext

```
ls *.$1
```

```
$ lsext c
main.c calc.c
```

In the next example, the commands to print out a file with line numbers have been placed in an executable file called **lpnum**, which takes a file name as its argument. The command to print out the line numbers is executed in the background.

lpnum

```
pr -t -n $1 | lp &
```

```
$ lpnum mydata
```

You may need to reference more than one argument at a time. The number of arguments used may vary. In **lpnum** you may want to print out three files at one time and five files at some other time. The **$** operator with the asterisk, **$***, references all the arguments on the command line. Using **$*** allows you to create scripts that take a varying number of arguments. In the next example, **lpnum** is rewritten using **$*** so that it can take a different number of arguments each time you use it.

lpnum

```
pr -t -n $* | lp &
```

```
$ lpnum mydata preface
```

Using a shell script is another way to create an alias for a command. In the next example, the **rmi** shell script contains an **rm** command that has the **-i** option. The **rm** command will first ask for approval from the user before erasing a file.

rmi

```
rm -i $*
```

$ **rmi mydata doc1**

Jobs: Background, Kills, and Interruptions

In Linux, you not only have control over a command's input and output but also over its execution. You can run a job in the background while you execute other commands. You can also cancel commands before they have finished executing. You can even interrupt a command, starting it up again later from where you left off. Background operations are particularly useful for long jobs. Instead of waiting at the terminal until a command has finished execution, you can place it in the background. You can then continue executing other Linux commands. You can, for example, edit a file while other files are printing.

Canceling a background command can often save you a lot of unnecessary expense. If, say, you execute a command to print out all your files and then realize you have some very large files you do not want to print out, you can reference that execution of the print command and cancel it. Interrupting commands is rarely used, and sometimes, it is unintentionally executed. You can, if you want, interrupt an editing session to send mail, and then return to your editing session, continuing from where you left off. The background commands as well as commands to cancel and interrupt jobs are listed in Table 5-2.

In Linux, a command is considered a *process*—a task to be performed. A Linux system can execute several processes at the same time, just as Linux can handle several users at the same time. There are commands to examine and control processes, though they are often reserved for system administration operations. Processes actually include not only the commands a user executes but also all the tasks the system must perform to keep Linux running.

The commands that users execute are often called jobs in order to distinguish them from system processes. When the user executes a command, it becomes a job to be performed by the system. The shell provides a set of job control operations that allow the user to control the execution of these jobs. You can place a job in the background, cancel a job, or interrupt one.

Background and Foreground: &, fg, bg

You execute a command in the background by placing an ampersand on the command line at the end of the command. When you do so, a user job number and a system process number are displayed. The user job number, placed in brackets, is the number by which the user references the job. The system process number is the number by which the system identifies the job. In the next example, the command to print the file **mydata** is placed in the background.

```
$ lpr mydata &
[1]  534
$
```

You can place more than one command in the background. Each is classified as a job and given a name and a job number. The command **jobs** will list the jobs being run in the background. Each entry in the list will consist of the job number in brackets, whether it is stopped or running, and the name of the job. The **+** sign indicates the job currently being processed, and the **−** sign indicates the next job to be executed. In the next example, two commands have been placed in the background. The **jobs** command then lists those jobs, showing which one is currently being executed.

```
$ lpr intro &
[1]  547
$ cat *.c > myprogs &
[2]  548
$ jobs
[1]  +  Running  lpr intro
[2]  -  Running  cat *.c > myprogs
$
```

If you wish, you can place several commands at once in the background by entering the commands on the command line, separated by an ampersand, **&**. In this case, the **&** both separates commands on the command line and executes them in the background. In the next example, the first command to **sort** and redirect all files with a **.l** extension, is placed in the background. On the same command line, the second command, to print all files with a **.c** extension, is also placed in the background. Notice that the two commands each end with **&**. The **jobs** command then lists the **sort** and **lpr** commands as separate operations.

```
$ sort *.l > ldocs & lpr *.c &
[1]  534
```

```
[2]   567
$ jobs
[1]   +   Running   sort *.1 > ldocs
[2]   -   Running   lpr
$
```

After you execute any command in Linux, the system will tell you what background jobs, if you have any running, have been completed so far. The system will not interrupt any operation, such as editing, to notify you about a completed job. If you want to be notified immediately when a certain job ends, no matter what you are doing on the system, you can use the **notify** command to instruct the system to tell you. The **notify** command takes as its argument a job number. When that job is finished, the system will interrupt what you are doing to notify you that the job has ended. The next example tells the system to notify the user when job 2 has finished.

```
$ notify %2
```

You can bring a job out of the background with the foreground command, **fg**. If there is only one job in the background, the **fg** command alone will bring it to the foreground. If there is more than one job in the background, you must use the job's number with the command. You place the job number after the **fg** command, preceded with a percent sign. In the next example, the second job is brought back into the foreground. You may not immediately receive a prompt again because the second command is now in the foreground and executing. When the command is finished executing, the prompt will appear, and you can execute another command.

```
$ fg %2
cat *.c > myprogs
$
```

There is also a **bg** command that places a job in the background. This command is usually used for interrupted jobs and is discussed shortly, under "Interruptions: CTRL-Z."

Canceling Jobs: kill

If you want to stop a job that is running in the background, you can force it to end with the **kill** command. The **kill** command takes as its argument either the user job number or the system process number. The user job number must be preceded by a percent sign, **%**. You can find out the job number from the **jobs** command. In the next example, the **jobs** command lists the background jobs; then job 2 is canceled.

```
$ jobs
[1]   +   Running   lpr intro
[2]   -   Running   cat *.c > myprogs
$ kill %2
$
```

You can also cancel a job using the system process number, which you can obtain with the **ps** command. The **ps** command displays a great deal more information than the **jobs** command does. It is discussed in detail in the chapter on systems administration. The next example lists the processes a user is running. The PID is the system process number, also known as the process ID. TTY is the terminal identifier. The time is how long the process has taken so far. COMMAND is the name of the process.

```
$ ps
PID     TTY     TIME     COMMAND
523     tty24   0:05       sh
567     tty24   0:01       lpr
570     tty24   0:00       ps
```

You can then reference the system process number in a **kill** command. Use the process number without any preceding percent sign. The next example kills process 567.

```
$ kill 567
```

Interruptions: CTRL-Z

You can interrupt a job and stop it with the CTRL-Z command. This places the job to the side until it is restarted. The job is not ended; it merely remains suspended until you wish to continue. When you're ready, you can continue with the job in either the foreground or the background using the **fg** or **bg** command. The **fg** command will restart an interrupted job in the foreground. The **bg** command will place the interrupted job in the background.

There will be times when you need to place a job that is currently running in the foreground into the background. However, you cannot move a currently running job directly into the background. You first need to interrupt it with CTRL-Z, and then place it in the background with the **bg** command. In the next example, the current command to list and redirect .c files is first interrupted with a CTRL-Z. Then that job is placed in the background.

```
$ cat *.c > myprogs
^Z
$ bg
```

Often, while in the Vi editor, you may make the mistake of entering a CTRL-Z instead of a SHIFT-ZZ to end your session. The CTRL-Z will interrupt the Vi editor and return you to the Linux prompt. The editing session has not ended; it has only been interrupted. You may not detect such a mistake until you try to log out. The system will not allow you to log out while an interrupted job remains. To log out, you must first restart the interrupted job with the **fg** command. In the case of the Vi editor interruption, the **fg** command will place you back in the Vi editor. Then a ZZ editor command will end the Vi editor job and you can log out. In the next example, the **jobs** command shows that there are stopped jobs. The **fg** command then brings the job to the foreground.

```
$ jobs
[1]  +  Stopped  vi mydata
$ fg %1
```

Delayed Execution: at

With the **at** command, you can execute commands at a specified time. Instead of placing a job immediately in the background, you can specify a time when you want it executed. You can then log out and the system will keep track of what commands to execute and when to execute them.

The **at** command takes as its argument a time when you want commands executed. The time is a number specifying the hour followed by the keywords a.m. or p.m. You can also add a date. If no date is specified, today's date is assumed. The **at** command will then read in Linux commands from the standard input. You can enter these commands at the keyboard, ending the standard input with a CTRL-D. You can also enter the commands into a file, which you can then redirect through the standard input to the **at** command. In the next example, the user decides to execute a command at 4:00 a.m.

```
$ at 4am
lpr intro
^D
$
```

In the next example, the user places several commands in a file called **latecmds** and then redirects the contents of this file as input to an **at** command. The **at** command will execute the commands at 6:00 p.m.

latecmds

```
lpr intro

cat *.c > myprogs
```

```
$ at 6pm < latecmds
```

You have a great deal of leeway in specifying the time and date. The **at** command assumes a 24-hour sequence for the time unless modified by the keywords a.m. or p.m. You can specify minutes in an hour by separating the hour and minutes with a colon, for example, 6:30. The **at** command also recognizes a series of keywords that specify certain dates and times. The keyword noon specifies 12 p.m. You can use the keyword midnight instead of 12 a.m. In the next examples, the user executes commands using a minute specification and then the keyword noon.

```
$ at 8:15pm < latecmds
$ at noon < latecmds
```

The date can be specified as a day of the month or a day of the week. The day of the month consists of the number of the day and a keyword representing the month. Months can be represented by three-letter abbreviations, for example, January is written as Jan. The day of the month follows the month's name. If there is no name, then the current month is assumed. Feb 14 specifies the fourteenth of February; 21 by itself specifies the twenty-first day of the current month. In the next example, the user first executes commands on the 15th of this month and then on the 29th of October.

```
$ at 8:15pm  15 < latecmds
$ at noon Oct 29 < latecmds
```

If you only want to run a job within your current week, you need only specify the day of the week instead of the day of the month. Each day of the week is represented by its name. Thus, entering tuesday as your date will run your commands on Tuesday. You can also use the keywords today and tomorrow for your date. In the next examples, the user executes commands on Friday and then tomorrow.

```
$ at 8:15pm  friday < latecmds
$ at noon tomorrow < latecmds
```

With either the time or date, you can specify an increment. For example, you could have commands executed one week from today or two months from Friday. You specify an increment using the **+** operator followed by a keyword denoting a segment of time. Segments of time keywords are: minutes, hours, days, weeks, months, or years. The plural *s* can be left off to denote one segment, for example, week is one week. The increment is added to the time or date that you specify. For example, to run commands one month from the 19th, you would enter **19 + month** for the date. One week from tomorrow is tomorrow + week. Two weeks from today is **today +2 weeks**. In the next example, the user executes commands 6 weeks from Monday and then 3 months from today.

```
$ at 8:15pm  monday +6 weeks < latecmds
$ at noon today +3 months < latecmds
```

The **at** command has options that allow you to list the **at** jobs you have waiting, and to cancel any of those **at** jobs. Each time you execute an **at** command, the Linux commands you specify for late execution are queued and listed as an **at** job. You can obtain a list of your **at** jobs by entering the **at** command with the **-1** option. Each job will have a number with which you can reference it.

```
$ at -1
732893802.a     Fri Sept 27 20:15:00  1996
732893803.a     Tue Sept 24 12:00:00  1996
```

You can cancel your **at** jobs using the **-r** option. To cancel a specific job, you need to enter the job's number after the **-r** option. In the next example, the user cancels **at** job 732893802.a.

```
$ at -r 732893802.a
$ at -l
732893802.a      Tue Sept 24 12:00:00  1996
```

Ordinarily, the **at** command will not notify you when a job has been executed. However, with the **-m** option, you can request that you be notified by mail when an **at** job finishes execution. You can specify a particular job number to receive mail just for that job. In the next example, you will be notified by mail when **at** job 732893803.a has executed.

```
$ at -m 732893803.a
```

Summary: Shell Operations

The shell is a command interpreter that provides an interface between the user and the operating system. You enter commands on a command line that are then interpreted by the shell and sent as instructions to the operating system. The shell has sophisticated features, such as special characters, redirection, pipes, scripts, and job control.

The shell has three special characters, *****, **?**, **[]**, which allow you to generate a list of file names for use as arguments on the command line. The ***** will match any possible sequence of characters, the **?** matches any one character, and the **[]** matches a specified set of characters. You can even combine the special characters to compose complex matches.

In Linux, files and devices, as well as input and output from commands, all have the same structure—a byte stream. All input for a command is placed in a data stream called the standard input, and all output is placed in a data stream called the standard output. Because the standard input and standard output have the same structure as that of files, they can easily interface with files. Using redirection operators, you can redirect the standard input or the standard output from and to a file. With the **>** redirection operator, you can redirect the standard output from a command to a file. With the **<** redirection operator, you can redirect the standard input to be read from a file. You can also use the redirection append operator, **>>**, to append standard output to a file that already exists.

Since the input and output for commands has the same standard format, you can easily use the output of one command as input for another. Pipes allow you to take the standard output of one command and pipe it to another command as standard input. On the same command line, you can string together several commands, each receiving their input from the output of another command.

Using an editor, you can create files that contain shell commands and variable definitions. Such files are known as shell scripts. A shell script can even have argument variables that will receive arguments typed in at the command line. By setting the executable permission of the shell script, you can treat the name of the shell script file as if it were another command.

You can also define variables in the shell and assign them values. You evaluate a variable by placing a **$** before the variable name. You can use variables as arguments in commands. They can hold directory path names, or even commands to be executed.

When you execute a command, it is treated by Linux as a job to be performed. You can instruct Linux to execute a job in the background, allowing you to continue executing other commands. Placing the **&** background operator at the end of the command line instructs the system to run this command in the background. You can list the jobs that you have in the background using the **jobs** command. With the **fg** command, you can bring a job in the background into the foreground. You can also cancel background jobs using the **kill** command, or interrupt jobs using the CTRL-Z command.

Standard Error Redirection Symbols	Execution
ENTER	Executes a command line
;	Separates commands on the same command line
`command`	Executes a command
*	Matches on any set of characters in file names
?	Matches on any single character in file names
[ ]	Matches on a class of possible characters in file names
\	Quotes the following character. Used to quote special characters
>	Redirects the standard output to a file or device, creating the file if it does not exist and overwriting the file if it does exist
>!	Forces the overwriting of a file if it already exists. This overrides the **noclobber** option
<	Redirects the standard input from a file or device to a program
>>	Redirects the standard output to a file or device, appending the output to the end of the file
|	Pipes the standard output of one command as input for another command
&	Executes a command in the background
!	History command

Standard Error Redirection Symbols	Execution
2>	Redirects the standard error to a file or device
2>>	Redirects and appends the standard error to a file or device
2>&1	Redirects the standard error to the standard output

Table 5-1.   *Shell Symbols*

Standard Error Redirection Symbols	Execution
>&	Redirects the standard error to a file or device
|&	Pipes the standard error as input to another command

Table 5-1. *Shell Symbols* (continued)

Command	Execution
ENTER	Executes a command line
;	Separates commands on the same command line
command *opts args*	Enters backslash before carriage return in order to continue entering a command on the next line
`command`	Executes a command
BACKSPACE CTRL-H	Erases the previous character
CTRL-U	Erases the command line and starts over
CTRL-C	Interrupts and stops a command execution

Special Characters for Filename Generation	Execution
*	Matches on any set of characters
?	Matches on any single characters
[]	Matches on a class of possible characters
\	Quotes the following character. Used to quote special characters

Redirection	Execution
command > *filename*	Redirects the standard output to a file or device, creating the file if it does not exist and overwriting the file if it does exist

Table 5-2. *The Shell Operations*

Redirection	Execution
command **<** *filename*	Redirects the standard input from a file or device to a program
command **>>** *filename*	Redirects the standard output to a file or device, appending the output to the end of the file
command **>!** *filename*	In the C-shell and Korn shell, the exclamation point forces the overwriting of a file if it already exists. This overrides the **noclobber** option
command **2>** *filename*	Redirects the standard error to a file or device in the Bourne shell
command **2>>** *filename*	Redirects and appends the standard error to a file or device in the Bourne shell
command **2>&1**	Redirects the standard error to the standard output in the Bourne shell
command **>&** *filename*	Redirects the standard error to a file or device in the C-shell

Pipes	Execution
command **|** *command*	Pipes the standard output of one command as input for another command
command **|&** *command*	Pipes the standard error as input to another command in the TCSH-shell

Background Jobs	Execution
&	Executes a command in the background
fg %*jobnum*	Brings a command in the background to the foreground or resumes an interrupted program
bg	Places a command in the foreground into the background
CTRL-Z	Interrupts and stops the currently running program. The program remains stopped and waiting in the background for you to resume
notify %*jobnum*	Notifies you when a job ends

Table 5-2. *The Shell Operations* (continued)

Background Jobs	Execution
kill *%jobnum* **kill** *processnum*	Cancels and ends a job running in the background
jobs	Lists all background jobs. Not available in the Bourne shell, unless it is using the jsh shell
ps	Lists all currently running processes including background jobs

at *time date*	Executes commands at a specified time and date; *time* can be entered with hours and minutes and qualified as am or pm
	    hour:minutes am pm
	date is specified as a day of the month or day of the week
	
	    month day
	month can be represented by a three-letter abbreviation
	Jan, **Feb**, etc.
	day is specified by a name
	monday tuesday wednesday, etc.
	
	Keywords can be used to specify the date and time
	am, **pm**, **now**, **noon**, **midnight**, **today**, **tomorrow**
	
	You can increment from a date or time by a time segment using the **+** operator. A number after the **+** operator specifies how many time segments
	
	    date **+***num time-segment*
	time-segment can be
	hours minutes days weeks months years
	
	The **next** keyword increments by a time segment from the current date or time
	next *time-segment*
	next week

Table 5-2. *The Shell Operations* (continued)

Background Jobs

`options`

    l *jobnum* (lists current **at** jobs)
    r *jobnum* (cancels a job)
    m *jobnum* (notification by mail when job finishes)

Table 5-2. *The Shell Operations (continued)*

Chapter Six

The Linux File Structure

In Linux, all files are organized into directories that, in turn, are hierarchically connected to each other in one overall file structure. A file is referenced not just according to its name but also to its place in this file structure. You can create as many new directories as you want, adding more directories to the file structure. The Linux file commands can perform sophisticated operations such as moving or copying whole directories along with their subdirectories. You can use file operations such as **find**, **cp**, **mv**, and **ln** to locate files and copy, move, or link them from one directory to another.

Together, these features make up the Linux file structure. This chapter will first examine different types of files as well as file classes. Then the chapter examines the overall Linux file structure and how directories and files can be referenced using path names and the working directory. The last part of the chapter discusses the different file operations such as copying, moving, and linking files.

Linux Files

You can name a file using any alphabetic characters, underscores, and numbers. You can also include periods and commas. However, a number cannot begin a file name, and except in certain special cases, you should never begin a file name with a period. Other characters, such as slashes, question marks, or asterisks, are reserved for use as special characters by the system and cannot be part of a file name. File names can be as long as 256 characters.

You can include an extension as part of a file name. A period is used to distinguish the file name proper from the extension. Extensions can be useful for categorizing your files. You are probably familiar with certain standard extensions that have been adopted by convention. For example, C source code files always have an extension of **.c**. Files that contain compiled object code have a **.o** extension. You can, of course, make up your own file extensions. The next examples are all valid Linux file names.

```
preface
chapter2
New_Revisions
calc.c
intro.bk1
```

There are also special initialization files that are used to hold shell configuration commands. These are the hidden, or dot files, referred to in Chapter 5 that begin with a period. Dot files have predetermined names. Recall that when you use **ls** to display your file names, the dot files will not be displayed. To include the dot files, you need to use **ls** with the **-a** option. Dot files are discussed in more detail in Chapter 14.

File Types

As you know from Chapter 5, all files in Linux have one physical format—a byte stream. A byte stream is just a sequence of bytes. This allows Linux to apply the file concept to every data component in the system. Directories are classified as files, and so are devices. Treating everything as a file allows Linux to organize and exchange data more easily. The data in a file can be sent directly to a device such as a screen, because a device interfaces with the system using the same byte-stream file format as regular files.

This same file format is used to implement other operating system components. The interface to a device such as the screen or keyboard is designated as a file. Other components, such as directories, are themselves byte-stream files, but they have a special internal organization. A directory file contains information about a directory, organized in a special directory format. Since these different components are treated as files, they can be said to constitute different *file types*. A character device is one file type. A directory is another file type. The number of these file types may vary according to your specific implementation of Linux. However, there are four common types of files: ordinary files, directory files, character device files, and block device files. Though you may rarely reference a file's type, it can be useful when searching for directories or devices. Later in the chapter, you will see how to use the file type in a search criteria with the **find** command to specifically search for directory or device names.

File Classifications: the file and od Commands

Though all ordinary files have a byte-stream format, they may be used in different ways. The most significant difference is between binary and text files. Compiled programs are examples of binary files. However, even text files can be classified according to their different uses. You can have files that contain C programming source code or shell commands, or even a file that is empty. The file could be an executable program or a directory file. The Linux **file** command helps you determine what a file is used for. It examines the first few lines of a file and tries to determine a classification for it. The **file** command looks for special keywords or special numbers in those first few lines, but it is not always accurate. In the next example, the **file** command examines the contents of two files and determines a classification for them.

```
$ file monday reports
monday:     text
reports:    directory
```

To illustrate the variety of classifications, the **file** command, in the next example, examines a C source code file, an executable file, and an empty file.

```
$ file calc.c proj newdata
calc.c:      C program text
proj:        executable
newdata:     empty
```

The **file** command also takes a **-f** option that allows you to read file names from a file rather than entering them on the command line. In the next example, the file names are read from the file **myfiles**.

```
$ cat myfiles
calc.c proj newdata

$ file -f myfiles
calc.c:      C program text
proj:        executable
newdata:     empty
```

If you need to examine the entire file byte-by-byte, you can do so with the **od** command. The **od** command performs a dump of a file. By default, it prints out every byte in its octal representation. However, you can also specify a character, decimal, or hexadecimal representation. The **od** command is helpful when you need to detect any special character in your file, or if you want to display a binary file. If you perform a character dump, then certain nonprinting characters will be represented in a character notation. For example, the carriage return will be represented by a **\n**. Both the **file** and **od** commands with their options are listed in Table 6-1 at the end of the chapter.

The File Structure

Linux organizes files into a hierarchically connected set of directories. Each directory may contain either files or other directories. In this respect, directories perform two important functions. A directory holds files, much like files held in a file drawer, and a directory connects to other directories, much like a branch in a tree is connected to other branches. With respect to files, directories appear to operate like file drawers, with each drawer holding several files. To access files, you open a file drawer. However, unlike file drawers, directories can contain not just files, but other directories. In this way, a directory can connect to another directory.

Because of the similarities to a tree, such a structure is often referred to in computer terminology as a *tree structure*. However, it could more accurately be thought of as an upside-down bush, rather than a tree. There is no trunk. The tree is represented upside down, with the root at the top. Extending down from the root are the branches. Each branch grows out of only one branch, but it can have many lower branches. In this respect, it can be said to have a *parent-child structure*. In the same way, each directory is itself a subdirectory of one other directory. Each directory may contain many subdirectories, but is itself the child of only one parent directory.

Figure 6-1 illustrates the hierarchical file structure. Beginning with the *root* directory at the top, other directories branch out. Each directory has several other directories or files, but a directory can only have one parent directory. The directory **chris**, for example, has two subdirectories: **reports** and **programs**. However, **chris** itself is connected to only one parent directory, the directory called **home**.

The Linux file structure branches into several directories beginning with a root directory, **/**. Within the root directory there are several system directories that contain files and programs that are features of the Linux system. The root directory also contains a directory called **home** that may contain the home directories of all the users in the system. Each user's home directory, in turn, will contain the directories the user has made for his or her own use. Each of these could also contain directories. Such nested directories would branch out from the user's home directory; see Figure 6-2.

Home Directories

When you log into the system, you are placed within your home directory. The name given to this directory by the system is the same as your login name. Any files you create when you first log in will be organized within your home directory. However, within your home directory, you can create more directories. You can then change to these directories and store files in them. The same is true for other users on the system. Each user has his or her own home directory identified by the appropriate login name. They, in turn, can create their own directories.

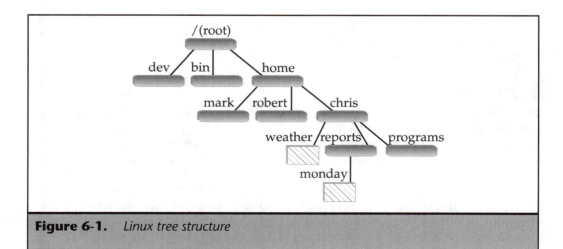

Figure 6-1.   *Linux tree structure*

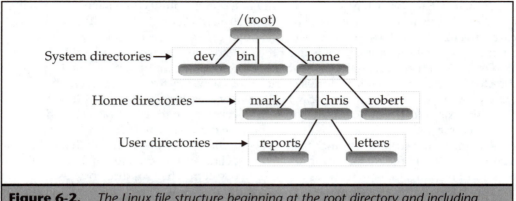

Figure 6-2. *The Linux file structure beginning at the root directory and including system, home, and user directories*

You can access a directory either through its name or by making it the default directory. Each directory is given a name when it is created. You can use this name in file operations to access files in that directory. You can also make the directory your default directory. If you do not use any directory names in a file operation, then the default directory will be accessed. The default directory is referred to as the *working directory*. In this sense, the working directory is the one you are currently working from.

When you log in, the working directory is your home directory, usually having the same name as your login name. You can change the working directory by using the **cd** command to designate another directory as the working directory. As the working directory is changed, you can move from one directory to another. Another way to think of a directory is as a corridor. In such a corridor, there are doors with names on them. Some doors lead to rooms; others lead to other corridors. The doors that open to rooms are like files in a directory. The doors that lead to other corridors are like other directories. Moving from one corridor to the next corridor is like changing the working directory. Moving through several corridors is like moving through several directories.

Path Names

The name that you give to a directory or file when you create it is not its full name. The full name of a directory is its *path name*. The hierarchically nested relationship among directories forms paths, and these paths can be used to unambiguously identify and reference any directory or file. In Figure 6-3, there is a path from the root directory, /, through the **home** directory to the **robert** directory. There is another path from the root directory through the **home** and **chris** directories to the **reports** directory. Though parts of each path may at first be shared, at some point they differ. Both the directories **robert** and **reports** share the two directories, root and **home**. Then they differ. In the **home** directory, **robert** ends with **robert**, but the directory **chris** then

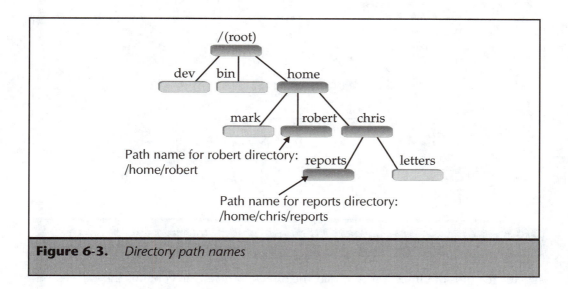

Figure 6-3. *Directory path names*

leads to **reports**. In this way, each directory in the file structure can be said to have its own unique path. The actual name by which the system identifies a directory will always begin with the root directory and consist of all directories nested above that directory.

In Linux, you write a path name by listing each directory in the path separated by a forward slash. A slash preceding the first directory in the path represents the root. The path name for the **robert** directory is **/home/robert**. The path name for the **reports** directory is **/home/chris/reports**.

Path names also apply to files. When you create a file within a directory, you give the file a name. However, the actual name by which the system identifies the file is the file name combined with the path of directories from the root to the file's directory. In Figure 6-4, the path for the **weather** file consists of the root, **home**, and **chris** directories and the file name **weather**. The path name for **weather** is **/home/chris /weather** (the root directory is represented by the first slash).

Path names may be absolute or relative. An *absolute path name* is the complete path name of a file or directory beginning with the root directory. A *relative path name* begins from your working directory; it is the path of a file relative to your working directory. Using the directory structure described in Figure 6-4, if **chris** is your working directory, the relative path name for the file **monday** is **/reports/monday**. The absolute path name for **monday** is **/home/chris/reports/monday**.

System Directories

The root directory that begins the Linux file structure contains several system directories. The system directories contain files and programs used to run and maintain the system. Many contain other subdirectories with programs for executing

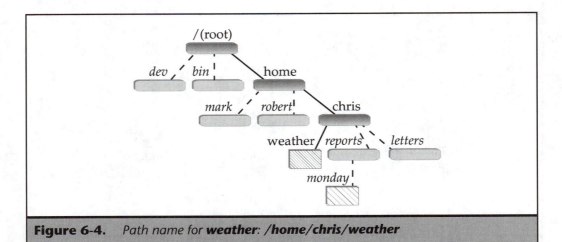

Figure 6-4. *Path name for **weather**: **/home/chris/weather***

specific features of Linux. For example, the directory **/user/bin** contains the various Linux commands that users execute, such as **cp** and **mv**. The directory **/bin** holds interfaces with different system devices, such as the printer or the terminal. Table 6-2 lists the basic system directories, and Figure 6-5 shows how they are organized in the tree structure.

Listing, Displaying, and Printing Files: ls, cat, more, and lpr

One of the primary functions of an operating system is the management of files. You may need to perform certain basic output operations on your files, such as displaying

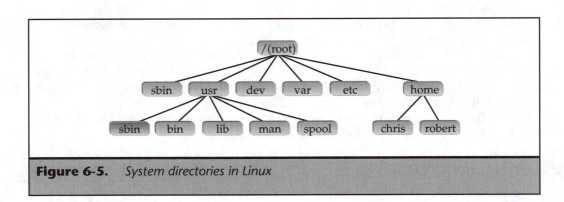

Figure 6-5. *System directories in Linux*

them on your screen or printing them out. The Linux system provides a set of commands that perform basic file management operations such as listing, displaying, and printing files, as well as copying, renaming, and erasing files. These commands are usually made up of abbreviated versions of words. For example, the **ls** command is a shortened form of "list" and lists the files in your directory. The **lpr** command is an abbreviated form of "line print" and will print a file. The **cat** and **more** commands display the contents of a file on the screen. Table 6-3 lists these commands with their different options.

When you log into your Linux system, you may want a list of the files in your **home** directory. The **ls** command, which outputs a list of your file and directory names, is useful for this. The **ls** command has many possible options for displaying file names according to specific features. These are discussed in detail in Chapter 5.

Displaying Files: cat and more

You may also need to look at the contents of a file. The **cat** and **more** commands display the contents of a file on the screen. **cat** stands for "concatenate." It is actually a very complex and versatile command, as described in Chapter 7. Here it is used in a very limited way, displaying the text of a file on the screen:

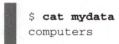

```
$ cat mydata
computers
```

The **cat** command outputs the entire text of a file to the screen at once. This presents a problem when the file is large because its text quickly speeds past on the screen. The **more** command is designed to overcome this limitation by displaying one screen of text at a time. You can then move forward or backward in the text at your leisure. You invoke the **more** command by entering the command name followed by the name of the file that you want to view.

```
$ more mydata
```

When **more** invokes a file, the first screen of text is displayed. To continue to the next screen, you press the **f** key or the SPACEBAR. To move back in the text, you press the **b** key. You can quit at any time by pressing **q**.

Printing Files: lpr, lpq, and lprm

When you need to print files, use the **lpr** command to send files to the printer connected to your system. In the next example, the user prints the **mydata** file.

```
$ lpr mydata
```

If you want to print out several files at once, you can specify more than one file on the command line after the **lpr** command. In the next example, the user prints out both the **mydata** and **preface** files.

```
$ lpr mydata preface
```

Printing jobs are placed in a queue and printed one at a time in the background. You can continue with other work as your files print. You can see the position of a particular printing job at any given time with the **lpq** command. **lpq** gives the owner of the printing job (the login name of the user who sent the job), the print job ID, the size in bytes, and the temporary file in which it is currently held. In this example, the owner is **chris** and the print ID is 00015.

```
$ lpq
Owner      ID      Chars      Filename
chris      00015    360       /usr/lpd/cfa00015
```

Should you need to cancel an unwanted printing job, you can do so with the **lprm** command. **lprm** takes as its argument either the ID number of the printing job or the owner's name. **lprm** will then remove the print job from the print queue. For this task, **lpq** is very helpful, for it will provide you with the ID number and owner of the printing job that you need to use with **lprm**. In the next example, the print job 15 is canceled.

```
$ lprm  00015
```

You can have several printers connected to your Linux system. One of these will be designated the default printer, and it is to this printer that **lpr** will print, unless another printer is specified. With **lpr** you can specify the particular printer you want your file printed on. Each printer on your system will have its own name. You can specify which printer to use with the **-P** option followed by that printer's name. In the next example, the file **mydata** is printed on the evans1 printer.

```
$ lpr -Pevans1 mydata
```

Managing Directories: mkdir, rmdir, ls, cd, and pwd

As described in Chapter 4, you can create and remove your own directories, as well as change your working directory, with the **mkdir**, **rmdir**, and **cd** commands. Each of these commands can take as their argument the path name for a directory. The **pwd** command will display the absolute path name of your working directory. In addition to these commands, the special characters represented by a single dot, a double dot, and a tilde can be used to reference the working directory, the parent of the working directory, and the **home** directory. Taken together, these commands allow you to manage your directories. You can create nested directories, move from one directory to another, and use path names to reference any of your directories. Those commands commonly used to manage directories are listed in Table 6-4.

Creating and Removing Directories: mkdir and rmdir

You create and remove directories with the **mkdir** and **rmdir** commands. In either case, you can also use path names for the directories. In the next example, the user creates the directory **reports**. Then the user creates the directory **letters** using a path name.

```
$ mkdir reports
$ mkdir /home/chris/letters
```

You can remove a directory with the **rmdir** command followed by the directory name. In the next example, the user removes the directory **reports** with the **rmdir** command. Then the directory **letters** is removed using its path name.

```
$ rmdir reports
$ rmdir /home/chris/letters
```

Listing Directories: ls

You have seen how to use the **ls** command to list the files and directories within your working directory. However, to distinguish between file and directory names, you need to use the **ls** command with the **-F** option. A slash is then placed after each directory name in the list.

```
$ ls
weather reports letters
```

```
$ ls -F
weather reports/ letters/
```

The **ls** command will also take as an argument any directory name or directory path name. This allows you to list the files in any directory without having to first change to that directory. In the next example, the **ls** command takes as its argument the name of a directory, **reports**. Then the **ls** command is executed again, only this time the absolute path name of **reports** is used.

```
$ ls reports
monday tuesday
$ ls /home/chris/reports
monday tuesday
$
```

Path Names: the pwd Command

Within each directory, you can create still other directories, in effect, nesting directories. Using the **cd** command, you can change from one directory to another. However, there is no indicator that tells you what directory you are currently in. To find out what directory you have changed to, use the **pwd** command to display the name of your current working directory. The **pwd** command displays more than just the name of the directory—it displays the full path name, as shown in the next example. The path name displayed here consists of the **home** directory, **dylan**, and the directory it is a part of, **home**. Each directory name is separated by a slash. The root directory is represented by a beginning slash.

```
$ pwd
/home/dylan
```

Change Directory: the cd Command

As you already know, you can change directories with the **cd** command. Changing to a directory makes that directory the working directory, which is your default directory. File commands such as **ls** and **cp**, unless specifically told otherwise, will operate on files in your working directory.

When you log into the system, your working directory is your **home** directory. When a user account is created, the system also creates a **home** directory for that user. When you log in, you are always placed in your **home** directory. The **cd** command allows you to make another directory the working directory. In a sense, you can move from your **home** directory into another directory. This other directory then becomes the default directory for any commands and any new files created. For example, the **ls** command will now list files in this new working directory.

The **cd** command takes as its argument the name of the directory you want to change to.

```
$ cd directory-name
```

In the next example, the user changes from the **home** directory to the **props** directory. The user issues a **pwd** command to display the working directory.

```
$ pwd
/home/dylan
$ cd props
$ pwd
/home/dylan/props
$
```

You can also change to another directory by using its full path name. In the next example, the **cd** command takes as its argument the path name for the **letters** directory.

```
$ cd /home/chris/letters
$ pwd
/home/chris/letters
$
```

Notice that when you create a new directory, you are already in a working directory. Any directories that you then create are nested within that working directory. The working directory within which you create a new directory and the new directory itself take on a parent-child relationship. The working directory is the parent of the newly created directory. If, within the **home** directory, the user creates a **props** directory, then the **home** directory is the parent of the **props** directory, and **props** is the child of the **home** directory.

You can use a double dot symbol, **..**, to represent a directory's parent. It literally represents the path name of the parent directory. You can use the double dot symbol with the **cd** command to move back up to the parent directory, making the parent directory the current directory. In the next example, the user moves to the **props** directory and then changes back to the **home** directory.

```
$ cd props
$ pwd
/home/dylan/props
$ cd ..

$ pwd
/home/dylan
```

If you want to change back to your **home** directory, you only need to enter the **cd** command by itself, without a file name argument. You will change directly back to the **home** directory, making it once again the working directory. In the next example, the user changes back to the **home** directory.

```
$ cd
```

In the next example, the **cd** command returns to the user's **home** directory, **chris**, and **pwd** displays the path name for that **home** directory.

```
$ pwd
/home/chris/letters
$ cd
$ pwd
/home/chris
```

You will find yourself changing from your **home** directory to another directory and back again frequently. In the next example, the user changes from his **home** directory, **dylan**, to the **props** directory. The user then changes back to his **home** directory with the **cd** command alone. Before each change, the user issues a **pwd** command to display the working directory.

```
$ pwd
/home/dylan
$ cd props
$ pwd
/home/dylan/props
$ cd
$ pwd
/home/dylan
```

Nested Directories

Let's see how the **cd** command can be used to progress through a series of nested directories. In the next example, the **cd** command changes to the **letters** directory. The **mkdir** command then makes a new subdirectory for **letters** called **thankyou**. Using the **cd** command again, the user changes to the **thankyou** directory. Within that directory, yet another subdirectory is created called **birthday**. The user then changes to that directory. Each time, the **pwd** command displays the path name. At the end, the **cd** command with no arguments returns to the **home** directory. The **ls** command with the **-R** option will print out all nested subdirectories below the working directory.

```
$ pwd
/home/chris
$ cd letters
$ pwd
/home/chris/letters
$ mkdir thankyou
$ cd thankyou
$ pwd
/home/chris/letters/thankyou
$ mkdir birthday
$ cd birthday
$ pwd
/home/chris/letters/thankyou/birthday
$ cd
$ pwd
/home/chris
$ ls -R
letters:
thankyou
letters/thankyou
birthday
letters/thankyou/birthday
$
```

Referencing the Working and Parent Directories: . and . .

A directory will always have a parent (except, of course, for the root). For example, in the last listing, the parent for **thankyou** is the **letters** directory. When a directory is created, two entries are made: one represented with a dot, **.**, and the other represented by a double dot, **. .** . The dot represents the path names of the directory, and the double dot represents the path name of its parent directory. The double dot, used as an argument in a command, references a parent directory. The single dot references the directory itself. In the next example, the user changes to the **letters** directory. The **ls** command is used with the **.** argument to list the files in the **letters** directory. Then the **ls** command is used with the **..** argument to list the files in the parent directory of **letters**, the **chris** directory.

```
$ cd letters
$ ls .
thankyou
$ ls ..
weather letters
$
```

Figure 6-6 illustrates the use of the dot and double dot representations for the parent and working directories. As in the previous example, the parent is the **home** directory, **chris**, and the working directory is **letters**.

You can use the single dot to reference your working directory, instead of using its path name. For example, to copy a file to the working directory retaining the same name, the dot can be used in place of the working directory's path name. In this sense, the dot is another name for the working directory. In the next example, the user copies the **weather** file from the **chris** directory to the **reports** directory. The **reports** directory is the working directory and can be represented with the single dot.

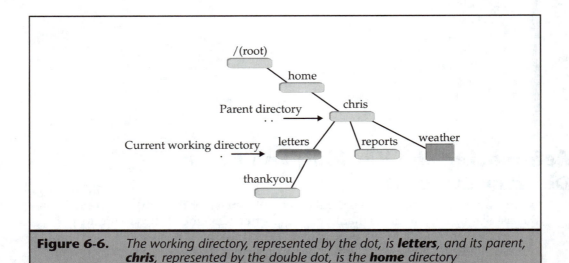

Figure 6-6. *The working directory, represented by the dot, is **letters**, and its parent, **chris**, represented by the double dot, is the **home** directory*

```
$ cd reports
$ cp /home/chris/weather  .
```

The **..** symbol is often used to reference files in the parent directory. In the next example, the **cat** command displays the **weather** file in the parent directory. The path name for the file is the **..** symbol followed by a slash and the file name.

```
$ cat ../weather
raining and warm
```

You can use the **cd** command with the **..** symbol to step back through successive parent directories of the directory tree from a lower directory. In the next example, the user is placed in the **thankyou** directory. Then the user steps back up to the **chris** directory by continually using the command **cd ..** .

```
$ pwd
/home/chris/letters/thankyou
$ cd ..
$ pwd
/home/chris/letters
$ cd ..
$ pwd
/home/chris
```

There are many times when you will use both the **..** and **.** as arguments to a command. For example, with **letters** as the working directory, **weather** can be copied down to **letters** referencing the **chris** directory with **..** and the **letters** directory with **.** .

```
$ cp ../weather .
```

Using Absolute and Relative Path Names: ~

As mentioned earlier, you can reference files and directories using absolute and relative path names. However, each has its limitations. Though an absolute path name can reference any file or directory, it is usually lengthy and complex, making it difficult to use. A relative path name is often simpler and easier to use, but it is limited in the number of files it can reference. Usually, you will use relative path names whenever possible and absolute path names only when necessary. Some shells provide a way to abbreviate part of an absolute path name.

The relative path name starts from the working directory. In the next example, the **ls** command is used first with the relative path name and then with the absolute path name of **thankyou**. The working directory is the user's **home** directory, **chris**, and the relative path name of the **thankyou** directory is **letters/thankyou**. The absolute path name of the **thankyou** directory is **/home/chris/letters/thankyou**.

```
$ ls letters/thankyou
larisa
$ ls /home/chris/letters/thankyou
larisa
$
```

Relative path names can only reference files in subdirectories of the working directory. The subdirectories can be nested to any depth, but their paths must branch from the working directory. Suppose you need to reference a directory that is higher up in the directory tree or off in another branch from the working directory. For example, given **letters** as the working directory, suppose you want to display a file in a directory that is not a subdirectory of **letters**, say, the **reports** directory. In this case, you have to use the absolute path name for **reports**. In the next example, the user references the file **monday** in the **reports** directory using its absolute path name.

```
$ cat /home/chris/reports/monday
```

You also need to use an absolute path name when referencing directories higher in the directory tree than the working directory. Given **thankyou** as the working directory, suppose the user wants to display a file in your **home** directory, **/home/chris**. The **chris** directory is not a subdirectory of **thankyou** and cannot be referenced with a relative path name. In this case, the user would have to use the absolute path name to reference a file in his **home** directory. In the next example, the user is in the **thankyou** directory and wants to display a file **weather** in the **home** directory, **/home/chris**. To do so, the user needs to use an absolute path name for **weather**.

```
$ pwd
/home/chris/letters/thankyou
$ cat /home/chris/weather
raining and warm
$
```

The absolute path name from the root to your **home** directory could be especially complex and, at times, even subject to change by the system administrator. To make it easier to reference, you can use a special character, the tilde ~, which represents the absolute path name of your **home** directory. In the next example, the user references the **weather** file in the **home** directory by placing a tilde and slash before **weather**.

```
$ pwd
/home/chris/letters/thankyou
$ cat ~/weather
raining and warm
$
```

You must specify the rest of the path from your **home** directory. In the next example, the user references the **monday** file in the **reports** directory. The tilde represents the path to the user's **home** directory, **/home/chris**, and then the rest of the path to the **monday** file is specified.

```
$ cat ~/reports/monday
```

File and Directory Operations: find, cp, mv, rm, and ln

As you create more and more files, you may want to back them up, change their names, erase some of them, or even give them added names. Linux provides you with several file commands that allow you to search for files, copy files, rename them, or remove files. If you have a large number of files, you can also search them to locate a specific one. The commands are shortened forms of full words, consisting of just two characters. The **cp** command stands for "copy" and copies a file, **mv** stands for "move" and will rename or move a file, **rm** stands for "remove" and will erase a file, and **ln** stands for "link" and will add another name for a file. One exception to this rule is the **find** command, which performs searches of your file names to find a file. Table 6-5 lists these different operations, including their options.

Searching Directories: find

Once you have a large number of files in many different directories, you may need to search them to locate a specific file or files of a certain type. The **find** command allows you to perform such a search. The **find** command takes as its arguments directory names followed by several possible options that specify the type of search and the criteria for the search. **find** then searches within the directories listed and their subdirectories for files that meet this criteria. The **find** command can search for a file based on its name, type, owner, and even the time of the last update.

```
$ find directory-list -option  criteria
```

The **-name** option has as its criteria a pattern and instructs **find** to search for the file name that matches that pattern. To search for a file by name, you use the **find** command with the directory name followed by the **-name** option and the name of the file.

```
$ find directory-list -name filename
```

The **find** command also has options that merely perform actions, such as outputting the results of a search. If you want **find** to display the file names it has found, you simply include the **-print** option on the command line along with any other options. The **-print** option instructs **find** to output to the standard output the names of all the files it locates. In the next example, the user searches for all the files in the **reports** directory with the name **monday**. Once located, the file, with its relative path name, is printed out.

```
$ find reports -name monday -print
reports/monday
```

The **find** command will print out the file names using the directory name specified in the directory list. If you specify an absolute path name, the absolute path of the found directories will be output. If you specify a relative path name, only the relative path name is output. In the previous example, the user specified a relative path name, **reports**, in the directory list. Located file names were output beginning with this relative path name. In the next example, the user specifies an absolute path name in the directory list. Located file names are then output using this absolute path name.

```
$ find /home/chris -name monday -print
/home/chris/reports/monday
```

If you want to search your working directory, you can use the dot in the directory path name to represent your working directory. The double dot would represent the parent directory. The next example searches all files and subdirectories in the working directory, using the dot to represent the working directory. If you are located in your **home** directory, this is a convenient way to search through all of your own directories. Notice that the located file names are output beginning with a dot.

```
$ find . -name weather -print
./weather
```

You can use shell special characters as part of the pattern criteria for searching files. However, the special character must be quoted in order to avoid evaluation by the shell. In the next example, all files with the **.c** extension in the **programs** directory are searched for.

```
$ find programs -name '*.c' -print
```

Search Criteria

You can also use the **find** command to locate other directories. In Linux, a directory is officially classified as a special type of file. Though all files have a byte-stream format, some files, such as directories, are used in special ways. In this sense, a file can be said to have a file type. The **find** command has an option called **-type** that searches for a file of a given type. The **-type** option takes a one-character modifier that represents the file type. The modifier that represents a directory is a **d**. In the next example, both the directory name and the directory file type are used to search for the directory called **thankyou**.

```
$ find /home/chris -name thankyou -type d -print
/home/chris/letters/thankyou
$
```

As noted previously, file types are not really so much different types of files as they are the file format applied to other components of the operating system, such as devices. In this sense, a device is treated as a type of file, and you can use **find** to search for devices, directories, as well as ordinary files. Table 6-6 lists the different types available for the **find** command's **-type** option.

The **find** command includes many different types of search criteria. You can search for a file by size, the time it was last accessed, the number of links it has, or the group it belongs to, as well as many other criteria. The different search criteria are listed in Table 6-6. Two of the more commonly used options are the **-size** and **-mtime** options. Each takes a number as its argument. By default, the **-size** option measures in blocks, but if you place a **c** after the number, it will measure in characters (bytes). You can modify the number with a **+** or **-** to look for a file greater than or less than the given size. For example, **+100c** will select files greater than 100 characters.

The **-mtime** option searches for files by how many days ago they were last modified. For example, using this option, you could locate all the files you worked on two days ago. In the next example, the **find** command uses the **-size** option to locate all files whose size is greater than 10 bytes. In the second example, **find** uses the **-mtime** option to search for those files modified three days ago.

```
$ find . -size +10c -print
.weather
./reports/monday

$ find . -mtime +3 -print
./weather
```

Complex Searches

When options are listed on the command line, they form an implied AND operation. Only files that meet all the criteria for the search have their names listed. However, using quoted parentheses and logical OR and NOT operators, you can construct complex search queries. The **find** command's NOT operator is an exclamation mark, **!**. A **!** placed before any search criteria negates the criteria. If the criteria is false, then the file is a match. For example, the following command prints out all files that do not have a **.c** extension.

```
$ ls
main.c lib.o today
$ find . ! -name "*.c" -print
lib.o today
```

The **find** command's logical OR operator is a **-o** . A **-o** placed between two search criteria treats the search criteria as part of an OR expression. If a file meets one or the other of the criteria, it is considered a match. You need to place the **-o** operation with its search criteria operands within quoted parentheses. Parentheses are quoted by putting a backslash before them and placing a space before and after them. The next command searches for files that have the name **weather**, as well as any directories. Notice the spaces around the quoted parentheses.

```
$ find . \( -name weather -o -type d \) -print
./weather
./reports
./letters
./letters/thankyou
```

You can form complex logical operations by combining search criteria using quoted parentheses. The next example searches for a directory named **reports** and any files that have a file size greater than 10 bytes. Quoted parentheses are placed around the **-name** and **-type** AND operation as well as the **-size** OR operation. The logical operations in the command can be formulated as:

```
((name = reports) AND (file = directory type)) OR (size > 10)

$ find . \( \( -name reports -type d \) -o -size+10 \) -print
./reports
./weather
```

Copying Files

To make a copy of a file, you simply give **cp** two file names as its arguments. The first file name is the name of the file to be copied—the one that already exists. This is often referred to as the source file. The second file name is the name you want for the copy. This will be a new file containing a copy of all the data in the source file. This second argument is often referred to as the destination file. The syntax for the **cp** command follows:

```
$ cp source-file destination-file
```

In the next example, the user copies a file called **proposal** to a new file called **oldprop**.

```
$ cp proposal oldprop
```

When the user lists the files in that directory, the new copy will be among them.

```
$ ls
proposal   oldprop
```

It is possible that you could unintentionally destroy another file with the **cp** command. The **cp** command generates a copy by first creating a file and then copying data into it. If another file has the same name as the destination file, then that file is destroyed and a new file with that name is created. In a sense, the original file is overwritten with the new copy. In the next example, the **proposal** file is overwritten by the **newprop** file. The **proposal** file already exists.

```
$ cp newprop  proposal
```

In Chapter 15 you will learn how you can configure your system to detect this overwrite condition. Until then, it may be safer to use the **cp** command with the **-i** option. With this option, **cp** will first check to see if the file already exists. If it does, you will then be asked if you wish to overwrite the existing file. If you enter **y**, the existing file will be destroyed and a new one created as the copy. If you enter anything else, it will be taken as a negative answer, and the **cp** command will be interrupted, preserving the original file.

```
$ cp -i  newprop  proposal
Overwrite proposal?  n
$
```

Copying Files to Directories

To copy a file from your working directory to another directory, you only need to use that directory name as the second argument in the **cp** command. The name of the new copy will be the same as the original, but the copy will be placed in a different directory. Files in different directories can have the same names. Because they are in different directories they are registered as different files.

```
$ cp filenames directory-name
```

To copy a file from the **home** directory to a subdirectory, simply specify the directory's name. In the next example, the file **newprop** is copied from the working directory to the **props** directory.

```
$ cp newprop props
```

The **cp** command can take a list of several file names for its arguments, so you can copy more than one file at a time to a directory. Simply specify the file names on the command line, entering the directory name as the last argument. All the files are then copied to the specified directory. In the next example, the user copies both the files **preface** and **doc1** to the **props** directory. Notice that **props** is the last argument.

```
$ cp preface doc1 props
```

You can use any of the special characters described in Chapter 5 to generate a list of file names to use with **cp** or **mv**. For example, suppose you need to copy all your C source code files to a given directory. Instead of listing each one individually on the command line, you could use a ***** special character with the **.c** extension to match on and generate a list of C source code files (all files with a **.c** extension). In the next example, the user copies all source code files in the current directory to the **sourcebks** directory.

```
$ cp *.c sourcebks
```

If you want to copy all the files in a given directory to another directory, you could use ***.*** to match on and generate a list of all those files in a **cp** command. In the next example, the user copies all the files in the **props** directory to the **oldprop** directory. Notice the use of a **props** path name preceding the ***.*** special characters. In this context, **props** is a path name that will be appended before each file in the list that ***.*** generates.

```
$ cp props/*.* oldprop
```

You can, of course, use any of the other special characters, such as **.**, **?**, or **[]**. In the next example, the user copies both source code and object code files (**.c** and **.o**) to the **projbk** directory.

```
$ cp *.[oc] projbk
```

When you copy a file, you may want to give the copy a different name than the original. To do so, place the new file name after the directory name, separated by a slash.

```
$ cp filename directory-name/new-filename
```

In the next example, the file **newprop** is copied to the directory **props** and the copy is given the name **version1**. The user then changes to the **props** directory and lists the files. There is only one file and it is called **version1**.

```
$ cp newprop props/version1
$ cd props
$ ls
version1
```

When you want to copy a file from a child directory such as **props** to a parent directory, you need to specify the name of the child directory. The first argument to **cp** is the file name to be copied. This file name must be preceded by the name of the child directory and separated by a slash. The second argument is the name the file will have in the parent directory.

```
$ cp child-directory-name/filename   new-filename
```

In the next example, the file **version1** is copied from the directory **props** up to the **home** directory.

```
$ cp props/version1   version1
```

Suppose, however, you have changed your working directory to that of a child directory and then want to copy a file from the child directory up to the parent. You need some way to reference the parent. You can do so using the double dot symbol, which represents the path name of the parent directory.

```
$ cp filename ..
$ cp filename ../new-filename
```

For example, if **props** is your current working directory and you want to copy the file **version1** from **props** up to its parent (in this case, the user's **home** directory), you need to use the double dot symbol in the second argument of the **cp** command.

```
$ cp version1 ..
```

If you want to give the copy of **version1** a new name, add the new name in the second argument, preceding it with a slash.

```
$ cp version1   ../newversion
```

Moving Files

You can use the **mv** command either to change the name of a file or to move a file from one directory to another. When using **mv** to rename a file, you simply use the new file name as the second argument. The first argument is the current name of the file that you are renaming.

```
$ mv original-filename   new-filename
```

In the next example, the **proposal** file is renamed with the name **version1**.

```
$ mv proposal version1
```

As with **cp**, it is very easy for **mv** to accidentally erase a file. When renaming a file, you might accidentally choose a file name that is already used by another file. In this case, that other file will be erased. The **mv** command also has a **-i** option that will check first to see if a file by that name already exists. If it does, then you will be asked first if you want to overwrite it. In the next example, a file already exists with the name **version1**. The overwrite condition is detected and you are asked whether or not you want to overwrite that file.

```
$ ls
proposal version1
$ mv -i  version1  proposal
Overwrite proposal?  n
$
```

You can move a file from one directory to another by using the directory name as the second argument in the **mv** command. In this case, you can think of the **mv** command as simply moving a file from one directory to another, rather than renaming the file. After you move the file, it will have the same name as it had in its original directory, unless you specify otherwise.

```
$ mv filename directory-name
```

In the next example, the file **newprop** is moved from the **home** directory to the **props** directory.

```
$ mv newprop props
```

Should you want to rename a file when you move it, you can specify the new name of the file after the directory name. The directory name and the new file name are separated by a forward slash. In the next example, the file **newprop** is moved to the directory **props** and renamed as **version1**.

```
$ mv newprops props/version1
$ cd props
$ ls
version1
```

A file can just as easily be moved from a child directory back up to the parent directory by specifying the child directory's name before the file name.

```
$ mv props/version1   version1
```

Suppose, however, you have changed your working directory to that of a child directory and then want to move a file from the child directory up to the parent. As with the **cp** command, you can use the double dot symbol to reference the parent directory.

```
$ mv filename ..
$ mv filename ../new-filename
```

If **props** is your current working directory and you want to move **version1** from **props** up to its parent, the **home** directory, then you can use the double dot symbol as the second argument of the **mv** command.

```
$ mv version1 ..
```

If you want to give the **version1** file a new name in the parent directory, you need to add the new name in the second argument, preceding it with a slash.

```
$ mv version1 ../oldprop
```

The actual name of a file is its file name preceded by its directory path. When **tuesday** was moved to the **reports** directory, its path name was actually changed. The full name of the **monday** file changed from **/home/chris/tuesday** to **/home/chris /reports/tuesday**. Its path name now includes the directory **reports**. In this sense, renaming a file is more like moving it.

You could just as easily use an absolute path name. In the next example, **today** is moved to the **reports** directory and given a new name, **tuesday**. Notice that the absolute path name is used for the file name argument in both the **mv** and **ls** commands.

```
$ mv today /home/chris/reports/tuesday
$ ls /home/chris/reports
monday tuesday
$
```

As with the **cp** command, the **mv** command can also move several files at once from one directory to another. You only need to enter the file names on the command line. The destination directory is always the last name you enter. In the next example, the user moves both the files **wednesday** and **friday** to the **lastweek** directory.

```
$ cp wednesday friday lastweek
```

You can also use any of the special characters described in Chapter 5 to generate a list of file names to use with **mv**. In the next example, the user moves all source code files in the current directory to the **newproj** directory.

```
$ mv *.c newproj
```

If you want to move all the files in a given directory to another directory, you can use ***.*** to match on and generate a list of all those files. In the next example, the user moves all the files in the **reports** directory to the **repbks** directory.

```
$ mv reports/*.*  repbks
```

Moving and Copying Directories

You can also copy or move whole directories at once. Both **cp** and **mv** can take as their first argument a directory name, allowing you to copy or move subdirectories from one directory into another. The first argument is the name of the directory to be moved or copied, and the second argument is the name of the directory within which it is to be placed. The same path name structure that is used for files applies to moving or copying directories.

You can just as easily copy subdirectories from one directory to another. To copy a directory, the **cp** command requires that you use the **-r** option. The **-r** option stands for "recursive." It directs the **cp** command to copy a directory as well as any subdirectories it may contain. In other words, the entire directory sub-tree, from that directory on, will be copied. In the next example, the **thankyou** directory is copied to the **oldletters** directory. There are now two **thankyou** subdirectories, one in **letters** and one in **oldletters**.

```
$ cp -r letters/thankyou oldletters
$ ls -F letters
/thankyou
$ ls -F oldletters
/thankyou
```

Suppose that, instead of copying a directory, making it a subdirectory of another directory, you just want to copy its files over. To copy all the files in one directory to another, you need to specify their file names. The asterisk special character will match all the file and directory names within a directory. To copy all the files in the **letters** directory to **oldletters**, you use the asterisk as your first argument in order to generate a list of all the file names in **letters**. If you need to specify a path name for the first argument, you can do so and place the asterisk at the end. In the next example, all the files in the **letters** directory are copied to the **oldletters** directory. A path name is specified for **letters**, and the asterisk at the end of the path name matches all files in the **letters** directory.

```
$ cp letters/* oldletters
```

In order to include the subdirectories in **letters** in the copy operation, you need to use the **-r** option with **cp**.

```
$ cp -r letters/* oldletters
```

The ~ Special Character

You have already seen how you can use the tilde to represent the absolute path name of the **home** directory. For example, to copy a file from a lower directory back to the **home** directory, you can use the tilde in place of the **home** directory's absolute path name. In the next example, the user changes to the **reports** directory and then copies the file **monday** from the **reports** directory up to the **home** directory.

```
$ cd reports
$ cp monday ~
```

To give a new name to the copied file when copying up to the **home** directory, place the new name after a **~/**. In the next example, the file **monday** is copied back up to the **home** directory and the copy is given the name **today**.

```
$ cp monday ~/today
```

The tilde is used in the same way for arguments in the **mv** command. In the next example, the file **monday** is moved from the **reports** directory back up to the **home** directory.

```
$ mv monday ~
```

If you are renaming a file while moving it to the **home** directory from a lower directory, the new name of the file is preceded by a tilde and a slash, **~/**. In the next example, there is a change to the **reports** directory, and then the file **monday** is moved back up to the **home** directory and renamed as **today**.

```
$ cd reports
$ mv monday ~/today
```

The tilde can be used wherever you would use the path name for the **home** directory. In the next example, a previously described **mv** and **ls** command are executed with the tilde.

```
$ mv weather ~/reports/monday
$ ls ~/reports
monday
$
```

Erasing a File: the rm Command

As you use Linux, you will find that the number of files you use increases rapidly. It is easy to generate files in Linux. Applications such as editors, and commands such as **cp**, easily create files. Eventually, many of these files may become outdated and useless. You can then remove them with the **rm** command. In the next example, the user erases the file **oldprop**.

```
$ rm oldprop
```

The **rm** command can take any number of arguments, allowing you to list several file names and erase them all at the same time. You just list them on the command line after you type **rm**.

```
$ rm proposal version1 version2
```

Be careful when using the **rm** command. It is irrevocable. Once a file is removed, it cannot be restored. Suppose, for example, you enter the **rm** command by accident while meaning to enter some other command, such as **cp** or **mv**. By the time you press ENTER and realize your mistake, it is too late. The files are gone. To protect against this kind of situation, you can use the **rm** command's **-i** option to confirm that you want to erase a file. With the **-i** option, you are prompted separately for each file and asked whether or not to remove it. If you enter **y**, the file will be removed. If you enter anything else, the file is not removed. In the next example, the **rm** command is instructed to erase the files **proposal** and **oldprop**. It then asks for confirmation for each file. The user decides to remove **oldprop** but not **proposal**.

```
$ rm -i proposal oldprop
Remove proposal? n
Remove oldprop? y
$
```

Links: the ln Command

You can give a file more than one name using the **ln** command. You might want to reference a file using different file names to access it from different directories. The added names are often referred to as links.

The **ln** command takes two arguments: the name of the original file and the new, added file name. The **ls** operation will list both file names, but there will be only one physical file.

```
$ ln original-file-name added-file-name
```

In the next example, the **today** file is given the additional name **weather**. It is just another name for the **today** file.

```
$ ls
today
$ ln today weather
$ ls
today weather
```

You can give the same file several names by using the **ln** command on the same file many times. In the next example, the file **today** is given both the names **weather** and **weekend**.

```
$ ln today weather
$ ln today weekend
$ ls
today weather weekend
```

You can use the **ls** command with the **-l** option to find out if a file has several links. **ls** with **-l** lists several pieces of information, such as permissions (described in the next chapter), as well as the number of links a file has, its size, and the date it was last modified. In this line of information, the first number, which precedes the user's login name, specifies the number of links a file has. The number before the date is the size of the file. The date is the last time a file was modified. In the next example, the user lists the full information for both **today** and **weather**. Notice that the number of links in both files is 2. Furthermore, the size and date are the same. This suggests that both files are really different names for the same file.

```
$ ls -l today weather
-rw-rw-r-- 2  chris  group 563  Feb  14   10:30  today
-rw-rw-r-- 2  chris  group 563  Feb  14   10:30  weather
```

This still does not tell you specifically what file names are linked. You can be somewhat sure if two files have exactly the same number of links, sizes, and modification dates, as in the case of the files **today** and **weather**. However, to be certain, you can use the **ls** command with the **-i** option. With the **-i** option, the **ls** command lists the file name and its *inode* number. An inode number is a unique number used by the system to identify a specific file. If two file names have the same inode number, they reference the exact same file. They are two names for the same file. In the next example, the user lists **today**, **weather**, and **larisa**. Notice that **today** and **weather** have the same inode number.

```
$ ls -i today weather larisa
1234 today    1234 weather    3976 larisa
```

The added names, or links, created with **ln** are often used to reference the same file from different directories. A file in one directory can be linked to and accessed from another directory. Suppose you need to reference a file that is in the **home** directory from within another directory. You can set up a link from that directory to the file in the **home** directory. This link is actually another name for the file. Because the link is in another directory, it can have the same name as the original file.

To link a file in the **home** directory to another directory, use the name of that directory as the second argument in the **ln** command.

```
$ ln filename directory-name
```

In the next example, the file **today** in the **chris** directory is linked to the **reports** directory. The **ls** command will list the **today** file in both the **chris** directory and the **reports** directory. In fact, there is only one copy of the **today** file, the original file in the **home** directory.

```
$ ln today reports
$ ls
today reports
$ ls reports
today
$
```

Just as with the **cp** and **mv** commands, you can give another name to the link. Simply place the new name after the directory name, separated by a slash. In the next example, the file **today** is linked to the **reports** directory with the name **wednesday**. There is still only one actual file, the original file called **today** in the **chris** directory. However, **today** is now linked to the directory **reports** with the name **wednesday**. In this sense, **today** has been given another name. In the **reports** directory, the **today** file goes by the name **wednesday**.

```
$ ln today reports/wednesday
$ ls
today reports
$ ls reports
wednesday
$
```

You can easily link a file in any directory to a file in another directory by referencing the files with their path names. In the next example, the file **monday** in the **reports** directory is linked to the directory, **chris**. Notice that the second argument is an absolute path name.

```
$ ln monday /home/chris
```

To erase a file, you need to remove all of its links. The name of a file is actually considered a link to that file. Hence the command **rm** that removes the link to the file. If you have several links to the file and remove just one of them, the others stay in place and you can reference the file through them. The same is true even if you remove the original link—the original name of the file. Any added links will work just as well. In the next example, the **today** file is removed with the **rm** command. However, there is a link to that same file called **weather**. The file can then be referenced under the name **weather**. See Figure 6-7.

```
$ ln today weather
$ rm today
$ cat weather
The storm broke today
and the sun came out.
$
```

Symbolic Links and Hard Links

Linux supports what are known as symbolic links. Links, as they have been described so far, are called *hard links*. Though hard links will suffice for most of your needs, they suffer from one major limitation. A hard link may fail when you try to link to a file on some other user's directory. This is because the Linux file structure can be physically segmented into what are called file systems. A file system can be made up of any physical memory device or devices, from a floppy disk to a bank of hard disks. Though the files and directories in all file systems are attached to the same overall directory tree, each file system will physically manage its own files and directories. This means that a file in one file system cannot be linked by a hard link to a file in another file system. If you try to link to a file on another user's directory that is located on another file system, your hard link will fail.

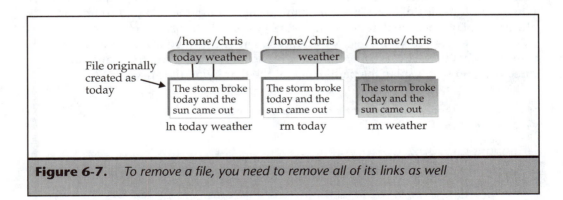

Figure 6-7.   *To remove a file, you need to remove all of its links as well*

To overcome this restriction, you use symbolic links. A *symbolic link* holds the path name of the file it is linking to. It is not a direct hard link, but rather information on how to locate a specific file. Instead of registering another name for the same file as a hard link does, a symbolic link can be thought of as another symbol that represents the file's path name. It is another way of writing the file's path name.

You create a symbolic link using the **ln** command with the **-s** option. In the next example, the user creates a link called **lunch** to the file **/home/george/veglist**.

```
$ ln -s lunch /home/george/veglist
```

If you list the full information about a symbolic link and its file, you will find that the information displayed is different. In the next example, the user lists the full information for both **lunch** and **/home/george/veglist** using the **ls** command with the **-l** option. The first character in the line specifies the file type. Symbolic links have their own file type represented by a **l**. The file type for **lunch** is **l**, indicating that it is a symbolic link, not an ordinary file. The number after the term "group" is the size of the file. Notice that the sizes differ. The size of the **lunch** file is only 4 bytes. This is because **lunch** is only a symbolic link—a file that holds the path name of another file—and a path name takes up only a few bytes. It is not a direct hard link to the **veglist** file.

```
$ ls lunch /home/george/veglist
lrw-rw-r-- 1  chris   group 4    Feb  14   10:30   lunch
-rw-rw-r-- 1  george  group 793  Feb  14   10:30   veglist
```

To erase a file, you need to remove only its hard links. If there are any symbolic links left over, they will not be able to access the file. In this case, a symbolic link would hold the path name of a file that no longer exists.

Unlike hard links, you can use symbolic links to create links to directories. In effect, you can create another name with which you can reference a directory. However, if you use a symbolic link for a directory name, bear in mind that the **pwd** command always displays the actual directory name, not the symbolic name. In the next example, the user links the directory **thankyou** with the symbolic link **gifts**. When the user uses **gifts** in the **cd** command, the user is actually changed to the **thankyou** directory. **pwd** will display the path name for the **thankyou** directory.

```
$ ln -s /home/chris/letters/thankyou  gifts
$ cd gifts
$ pwd
/home/chris/letters/thankyou
$
```

If you want to display the name of the symbolic link, you can access it in the **cwd** variable. The **cwd** variable is a special system variable that holds the name of a directory's symbolic link, if there is one. Variables such as **cwd** are discussed in Chapter 15. You display the contents of **cwd** with the command: **echo $cwd**.

```
$ pwd
/home/chris/letters/thankyou
$ echo $cwd
/home/chris/gifts
```

Summary: The Linux File Structure

In Linux, files are organized into directories. Directories themselves are connected hierarchically to each other, forming a treelike structure. Each directory contains files and other directories. At the top of the hierarchy is the root directory, which branches out into system directories and users' home directories. System directories contain utilities used to run the Linux system, and home directories are the users' login directories.

The nesting of directories forms a path from a higher directory to a lower one and vice versa. The set of directories from the root to a given directory is the directory's path name. In fact, each file has a path name consisting of the set of directories from the root to the file's directory. This path name together with the file's name constitutes the absolute path name of the file.

You can easily manage directories—creating new ones, removing old ones, and changing from one directory to another. Within a directory you can create other directories, nesting them to any depth. While logged into the system, you are always working within a default directory. This default directory is known as your working directory. Any files you create will be placed in this directory, unless otherwise specified. You can change your default directory with the **cd** command. In this sense, you can move from one directory to another. When you first log into the system, your default directory is your **home** directory.

You can perform file operations between directories or on the directories themselves. You can move files from one directory to another, as well as copy files to other directories. You can even move or copy entire directories. You can also create links for files. A link is another name for a file. You can have a link in one directory that references a file in another directory.

Command	Execution
file	Examines the first few lines of a file to determine a classification
-f *filename*	Reads the list of file names to be examined from a file
od	Prints out the contents of a file byte-by-byte in either octal, character, decimal, or hexadecimal; octal is the default
-c	Outputs character form of byte values; nonprinting characters have a corresponding character representation
-d	Outputs decimal form of bytes values
-x	Outputs hexadecimal form of bytes values
-o	Outputs octal form of bytes values

Table 6-1. *The **file** and **od** Commands*

Directory	Function
/	Begins the file system structure—called the root
/home	Contains users' **home** directories
/bin	Holds all the standard commands and utility programs
/usr	Holds those files and commands used by the system; this directory breaks down into several subdirectories
/usr/bin	Holds user-oriented commands and utility programs
/usr/sbin	Holds system administration commands
/usr/lib	Holds libraries for programming languages
/usr/doc	Holds Linux documentation
/usr/man	Holds the online manual **man** files
/usr/spool	Holds spooled files, such as those generated for printing jobs and network transfers
/sbin	Holds system administration commands for booting the system
/var	Holds files that vary, such as mailbox files
/dev	Holds file interfaces for devices such as the terminal and printer
/etc	Holds system configuration files and any other system files

Table 6-2.   *Standard System Directories in Linux*

Command or Option	Execution
`ls`	This command lists file and directory names `$ ls`
`cat`	This filter can be used to display a file. It can take file names for its arguments. It outputs the contents of those files directly to the standard output, which, by default, is directed to the screen `$ cat` filenames
`more`	This utility displays a file screen-by-screen. It can take file names for its arguments. It outputs the contents of those files to the screen, one screen at a time `$ more` filenames
`+`*num*	Begins displaying the file at page *num*
`numf`	Skips forward *num* number of screens
`numb`	Skips backward *num* number of screens
`d`	Displays half a screen
`h`	Lists all **more** commands
`q`	Quits **more** utility
`lpr`	Sends a file to the line printer to be printed; a list of files may be used as arguments
`-P` *printer-name*	Selects a specific printer
`lpq`	Lists the print queue for printing jobs
`lprm`	Removes a printing job from the printing queue

Table 6-3.   *Listing, Displaying, and Printing Files*

Command	Execution
mkdir	Creates a directory **$ mkdir reports**
rmdir	Erases a directory **$ rmdir letters**
ls -F	Lists directory name with a preceding slash **$ ls -F** **today reports/letters/**
ls -R	Lists working directory as well as all subdirectories
cd *directory name*	Changes to the specified directory, making it the working directory; **cd** without a directory name changes back to the home directory **$ cd reports** **$ cd**
pwd	Displays the path name of the working directory **$ pwd** **/home/chris/reports**
directory name/filename	A slash is used in path names to separate each directory name. In the case of path names for files, a slash separates the preceding directory names from the file name **$ cd /home/chris/reports** **$ cat /home/chris/reports/mydata**
..	References the parent directory. You can use it as an argument or as part of a path name **$ cd ..** **$ mv ../larisa oldletters**
.	References the working directory. You can use it as an argument or as part of a path name **$ ls .** **$ mv ../aleina .**
~/*pathname*	The tilde is a special character that represents the path name for the **home** directory. It is useful when you need to use an absolute path name for a file or directory **$ cp monday ~/today** **$ mv tuesday ~/weather**

Table 6-4. *Directory Commands*

Command	Execution
cp *filename filename*	Copies a file. **cp** takes two arguments: the original file and the name of the new copy. You can use path names for the files in order to copy across directories `$ cp today reports/monday`
cp -r *dirname dirname*	Copies a subdirectory from one directory to another. The copied directory will include all its own subdirectories `$ cp -r letters/thankyou oldletters`
mv *filename filename*	Moves (renames) a file. **mv** takes two arguments: the first is the file to be moved. The second argument can be the new file name or the path name of a directory. If it is the name of a directory, then the file is literally moved to that directory, changing the file's path name. `$ mv today /home/chris/reports`
mv *dirname dirname*	Moves directories. In this case, the first and last arguments are directories. `$ mv letters/thankyou oldletters`
ln *filename filename*	Creates added names for files referred to as links. A link can be created in one directory that references a file in another directory `$ ln today reports/monday`
rm *filenames*	Removes (erases) a file. Can take any number of file names as its arguments. Literally removes links to a file. If a file has more than one link, you need to remove all of them in order to finally erase a file `$ rm today weather weekend`

Table 6-5. *File Operations*

Command or Option	Execution
find	Searches directories for files based on a search criteria. This command has several options that specify the type of criteria and actions to be taken
-name *pattern*	Searches for files with the *pattern* in the name
-group *name*	Searches for files belonging to this group *name*
-size *numc*	Searches for files with the size *num* in blocks. If **c** is added after *num*, then the size in bytes (characters) is searched for
-mtime *num*	Searches for files last modified *num* days ago
-newer *pattern*	Searches for files that were modified after the one matched by *pattern*
-print	Outputs the result of the search to the standard output. The result is usually a list of file names, including their full path names
-type *filetype*	Searches for files with the specified file type
b	Block device file
c	Character device file
d	Directory file
f	Ordinary (regular) file
p	Named pipes (fifo)
l	Symbolic links

Table 6-6.   *The* **find** *Command*

Chapter Seven

File Management Operations

Linux provides several features for managing your files and directories. You can find out detailed information about files, such as when they were last updated and how many links they have. You can also control access to your files. Each file in Linux has permissions that determine who has access to it, as well as what kind of access they can have. You can allow other users to access given files or restrict access to just yourself.

Files reside on physical devices such as hard drives, CD-ROMs, or floppy disks. The files on each device are organized into a file system. To access files on a device, you attach its file system to a specified directory. This is called mounting the file system. For example, to access files on a floppy disk, you first mount its file system to a particular directory. This chapter discusses how you can access CD-ROMs, floppy disks, and hard disk partitions. You can even access an MS-DOS hard drive partition or floppy disk, as well as file systems on a remote server.

You can also back up your files into an archive, storing them for later retrieval, or you can combine them into an archive file for transfer across a network to another system. You can also compress your files, preparing them for more efficient transfer or just to take up less space for backups. Archiving and compression are used extensively for online software packages. You can download a compressed and archived software package, and then decompress it and expand the archive. You are then ready to install the new software package on your system. This is a very common way to obtain new Linux software.

This chapter will first examine the different file and directory permissions. Then will discuss accessing file systems, followed by archiving and compression methods.

Displaying File Information: ls -l

As shown in Figure 7-1, the **ls -l** command displays detailed information about a file. First the permissions are displayed, followed by the number of links, the owner of the file, the name of the group the user belongs to, the file size in bytes, the date and time the file was last modified, and the name of the file. The group name indicates the group that is being given group permission. In Figure 7-1, the file type for **mydata** is that of an ordinary file. There is only one link, indicating that the file has no other names, no other links. The owner name is **chris**, the same as the login name, and the group name is **weather**. There are probably other users who also belong to the weather group. The size of the file is 207 bytes. It was last modified on February 20, at 11:55 a.m. The name of the file is **mydata**.

If you want to display this detailed information for all the files in a directory, simply use the **ls -l** command without an argu ment.

```
$ ls -l
-rw-r--r--  1  chris weather 207  Feb 20  11:55  mydata
-rw-rw-r--  1  chris weather 568  Feb 14  10:30  today
-rw-rw-r--  1  chris weather 308  Feb 17  12:40  monday
```

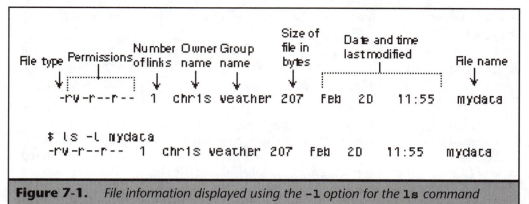

Figure 7-1. *File information displayed using the* **-l** *option for the* **ls** *command*

File and Directory Permissions: chmod

Each file and directory in Linux contains a set of permissions that determines who can access them and how. You set these permissions to limit access in one of three ways: you can restrict access to yourself alone; you can allow users in a predesignated group to have access, or you can permit anyone on your system to have access; and you can control how a given file or directory is accessed. A file and directory may have read, write, and execute permission. When a file is created, it is automatically given read and write permissions for the owner, allowing you to display and modify the file. You may change these permissions to any combination you want. A file could have read-only permission, preventing any modifications. It could also have execute permission, allowing it to be executed as a program.

There are three different categories of users that can have access to a file or directory: the owner, the group, or others. The owner is the user who created the file. Any file that you create, you own. You can also permit your group to have access to a file. Often, users are collected into groups. For example, all the users for a given class or project could be formed into a group by the system administrator. It is possible for a user to give access to a file to other members of the group. Finally, you can also open up access to a file to all other users on the system. In this case, every user on your system could have access to one of your files or directories. In this sense, every other user on the system makes up the "others" category.

Each category has its own set of read, write, and execute permissions. The first set controls the user's own access to his or her files—the owner access. The second set controls the access of the group to a user's files. The third controls the access of all other users to the user's files. The three sets of read, write, and execute permissions for the three categories—owner, group, and other—make a total of nine types of permissions.

As you saw in the previous section, the **ls** command with the **-l** option displays detailed information about the file, including the permissions. In the next example, the first set of characters on the left is a list of the permissions that have been set for the **mydata** file.

```
$ ls -l mydata
-rw-r--r--  1  chris weather 207 Feb  20  11:55   mydata
```

An empty permission is represented by a dash, **-**. The read permission is represented by *r*, write by *w*, and execute by *x*. Notice that there are ten positions. The first character indicates the file type. In a general sense, a directory can be considered a type of file. If the first character is a dash, a file is being listed. If it is *d*, information about a directory is being displayed.

The next nine characters are arranged according to the different user categories. The first set of three characters is the owner's set of permissions for the file. The second set of three characters is the group's set of permissions for the file. The last set of three characters is the other users' set of permissions for the file. In Figure 7-2, the **mydata** file has the read and write permissions set for the owner category, the read permission only set for the group category, and the read permission set for the other users category. This means that, though anyone in the group or any other user on the system can read the file, only the owner can modify it.

You use the **chmod** command to create different permission configurations. **chmod** takes two lists as its arguments: permission changes and file names. You can specify the list of permissions in two different ways. One way uses permission symbols and is referred to as the *symbolic method*. The other uses what is known as a binary mask and is referred to as either the *absolute* or the *relative method*. Of the two, the symbolic method is the more intuitive and will be presented first. Table 7-1, at the end of the chapter, lists options for the **chmod** command.

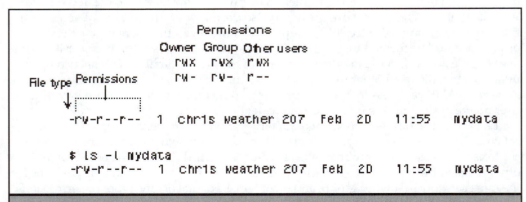

Figure 7-2.   *Owner, group, and other file permissions: r stands for read permission, w for write, and x for execute; a dash is a permission that is off*

Setting Permissions: Permission Symbols

As you might have guessed, the symbolic method of setting permissions uses the characters *r*, *w*, and *x* for read, write, and execute, respectively. Any of these permissions can be added or removed. The symbol to add a permission is the plus sign, **+**. The symbol to remove a permission is the minus sign, **-**. In the next example, the **chmod** command adds the execute permission and removes the write permission for the **mydata** file. The read permission is not changed.

```
$ chmod +x-w mydata
```

There are also permission symbols that specify each user category. The owner, group, and others categories are represented by the *u*, *g*, and *o* characters, respectively. Notice that the owner category is represented by a *u* and can be thought of as the user. The symbol for a category is placed before the read, write, and execute permissions. If no category symbol is used, all categories are assumed, and the permissions specified are set for the user, group, and others. In the next example, and in Figure 7-3, the first **chmod** command sets the permissions for the group to read and write. The second **chmod** command sets permissions for other users to read. Notice that there are

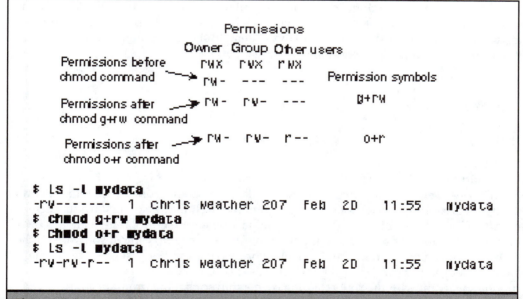

Figure 7-3. *Using permission symbols to set permissions*

no spaces between the permission specifications and the category. The permissions list is simply one long phrase, with no spaces.

```
$ chmod g+rw mydata
$ chmod o+r mydata
```

A user may remove permissions as well as add them. In the next example, the read permission is set for other users, but the write and execute permissions are removed.

```
$ chmod o+r-wx mydata
```

There is another permission symbol, *a*, that represents all the categories. The *a* symbol is the default. In the next example, both commands are equivalent. The read permission is explicitly set with the *a* symbol denoting all types of users: other, group, and user.

```
$ chmod a+r mydata
$ chmod +r mydata
```

One of the most common permission operations is setting a file's executable permission. This is often done in the case of shell program files, which are discussed in Chapters 8 and 16. The executable permission indicates that a file contains executable instructions and can be directly run by the system. In the next example, the file **lsc** has its executable permission set and then executed.

```
$ chmod u+x lsc
$ lsc
main.c lib.c
$
```

In addition to the read/write/execute permissions, you can also set ownership permissions for executable programs. Normally, the user that runs a program will own it while it is running, even though the program file itself may be owned by another user. The User ID permission allows the original owner of the program to always own it, even while another user is running the program. For example, most software on the system is owned by the root user but run by ordinary users. Some such software may have to modify files owned by the root. In this case, the ordinary user would need to run that program with the root retaining ownership so that the program could have the permissions to change those root-owned files. The Group ID permission works the same way except for groups. Programs owned by a group will retain ownership, even when run by users from another group. The program can then change the owner group's files.

To add both the User ID and Group ID permissions to a file, you use the **s** option. The following example adds the User ID permission to the pppd program, which is owned by the root user. When an ordinary user runs pppd, the root user will retain ownership, allowing the pppd program to change root-owned files.

```
#  chmod +s /usr/sbin/pppd
```

The User ID and Group ID permissions show up as an *s* in the execute position of the owner and group segments. User ID and Group ID are essentially variations of the execute permission, *x*. Read, write, and User ID permission would be *rws* instead of just *rwx*.

```
# ls -l /usr/sbin/pppd
-rwsr-sr-x   1 root      root        84604 Aug 14  1996 /usr/sbin/pppd
```

One other special permission provides efficient use of programs. The sticky bit will instruct the system to keep a program in memory after it finishes execution. This is useful for small programs that are used frequently by many users. The sticky bit permission is *t*. The sticky bit shows up as a *t* in the execute position of the other permissions. A program with read and execute permission with the sticky bit would have its permissions displayed as *r-t*.

```
# chmod +t  /usr/X11R6/bin/xtetris
# ls -l /usr/X11R6/bin/xtetris
-rwxr-xr-t   1 root      root        27428 Nov 19  1996
/usr/X11R6/bin/xtetris
```

Absolute Permissions: Binary Masks

Instead of permission symbols, many users find it more convenient to use the absolute method. The absolute method changes all the permissions at once, instead of specifying one or the other. It uses a binary mask that references all the permissions in each category. The three categories, each with three permissions, conform to an octal binary format. Octal numbers have a base eight structure. When translated into a binary number, each octal digit becomes three binary digits. A binary number is a set of 1 and 0 digits. Three octal digits in a number translate into three sets of three binary digits, which is nine altogether and the exact number of permissions for a file.

You can use the octal digits as a mask to set the different file permissions. Each octal digit applies to one of the user categories. You can think of the digits matching up with the permission categories from left to right, beginning with the owner category. The first octal digit applies to the owner category, the second to the group, and the third to the others category.

The actual octal digit that you choose will determine the read, write, and execute permissions for each category. At this point, you need to know how octal digits translate into their binary equivalents. The following table shows how the different octal digits, 0 to 7, translate into their three-digit binary equivalents. You can think of the octal digit first being translated into its binary form, and then each of those three binary digits being used to set the read, write, and execute permissions. Each binary digit is then matched up with a corresponding permission, again moving from left to right. If a binary digit is 0, the permission is turned off. If the binary digit is 1, the permission is turned on. The first binary digit sets the read permission on or off, the second sets the write permission, and the third sets the execute permission. For example, an octal digit 6 translates into the binary digits 110. This would set the read and write permission on, but set the execute permission off.

Octal	Binary
0	000
1	001
2	010
3	011
4	100
5	101
6	110
7	111

When dealing with a binary mask, you need to specify three digits for all three categories as well as their permissions. This makes it less versatile than the permission symbols. To set the owner execute permission on and the write permission off for the **mydata** file, as well as retain the read permission, you need to use the octal digit 5 (101). At the same time, you need to specify the digits for group and other users access. If these categories are to retain read access, you need the octal number 4 for each (100). This gives you three octal digits, 544, which translate into the binary digits 101 100 100. In Figure 7-4, these permissions are set for the **mydata** file.

```
$ chmod 544 mydata
```

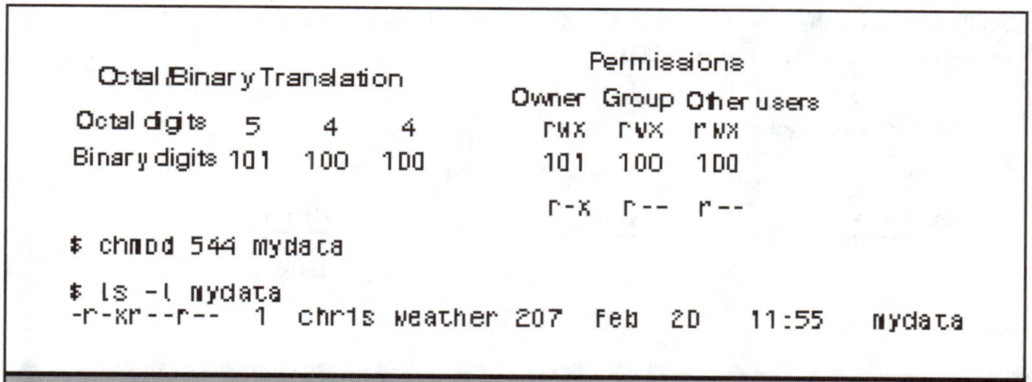

```
        Octal /Binary Translation              Permissions
                                        Owner  Group  Other users
        Octal digits   5     4     4     rwx    rwx    rwx
        Binary digits 101   100   100     101    100    100

                                          r-x    r--    r--

    $ chmod 544 mydata

    $ ls -l mydata
    -r-xr--r--   1  chris weather 207  Feb  20  11:55   mydata
```

Figure 7-4.   *Using octal digits to set permissions*

Instead of painstakingly working out the octal-to-binary conversion in order to figure out what numbers you should use, there is a simple alternative. The read, write, and execute permissions can be associated with the numbers 4, 2, and 1, respectively (see the next table). To find out what octal number you need to specify for a certain category, just add the associated numbers for the permission you want turned on. If you want to give a category a read and write permission, simply add 4 (read) and 2 (write) to give you 6. This is your octal number. To give a category read and execute permission, just add 4 (read) and 1 (execute) to give you 5. To set all the permissions, you would add 4 (read), 2 (write), and 1 (execute) to get 7, which is the equivalent of a binary 111. The next example uses this method to calculate the permissions used in the previous example. The owner is given read and execute permission, and the group and other users are given only read permission.

```
owner       rx        4 + 1 = 5
group       r     4         4
others      r     4         4
                          544          101 100 100
$ chmod 544 mydata
```

For example, to give members of your group both read and write permission to a given file and deny access to any other users on the system, you need the octal digit 6 (110) for the group and 0 for the other users. Using 6 also for the owner retains read and write permission for the owner. You could also calculate the read and write permissions by adding 4 (read) and 2 (write) to get 6. Since you do not want any permissions for other users, you give them 0. This gives you the octal digits 660, which translate into the binary digits 110 110 000. Notice that an octal 0 will set all permissions off, using a binary 000.

```
$ chmod 660 mydata
```

Permission	Number	Binary
r	4	100
w	2	010
x	1	001

One of the most common uses of the binary mask is to set the execute permission. As Chapter 8 will describe, you can create files that contain Linux commands. Such files are called shell scripts. To have the commands in a shell script executed, you must first indicate that the file is executable—that it contains commands that the system can execute. There are several ways to do this, one of which is to set the executable permission on the shell script file. Suppose you just completed a shell script file and need to give it executable permission in order to run it. You also want to retain read and write permission, but deny any access by the group or other users. The octal digit 7 (111) will set all three permissions, including execute (you can also add 4-read, 2-write, and 1-execute to get 7). Using 0 for the group and other users denies them access. This gives you the digits 700, which are equivalent to the binary digits 111 000 000. In the next example, the owner permission for the **myprog** file is set to include execute permission.

```
$ chmod 700 myprog
```

If you want others to be able to execute and read the file but not change it, you can set the read and execute permissions and turn off the write permission with the digit 5 (101). In this case, you would use the octal digits 755, having the binary equivalent of 111 101 101.

```
$ chmod 755 myprog
```

For the ownership and sticky bit permissions, you add another octal number to the beginning of the octal digits. The octal digit for User ID permission is 4 (100); for Group ID, it is 2 (010); and for the sticky bit, it is 1 (001). The following example sets the User ID permission to the pppd program, along with read and execute permissions for the owner, group, and others.

```
# chmod 4555 /usr/sbin/pppd
```

The following example sets the sticky bit for the xtetris program.

```
# chmod 1755  /usr/X11R6/bin/xtetris
```

The next example would set both the sticky bit and the User ID permission on the XMan program. The permission 5755 has the binary equivalent of 101 111 101 101.

```
# chmod 5755 /usr/X11R6/bin/xman
# ls -l /usr/X11R6/bin/xman
-rwsr-xr-t   1 root     root         44364 Mar 26 04:28 /usr/X11R6/bin/xman
```

Directory Permissions

You can also set permissions on directories. The read permission set on a directory allows the list of files in a directory to be displayed. The execute permission allows a user to change to that directory. The write permission allows a user to create and remove his or her own files in that directory. If you allow other users to have write permission on a directory, they can add their own files to it. When you create a directory, it is automatically given read, write, and execute permission for the owner. You may list the files in that directory, change to it, and create files in it.

Like files, directories have sets of permissions for the owner, the group, and all other users. Often, you may want to allow other users to change to and list the files in one of your directories, but not let them add their own files to it. In this case, you would set read and execute permissions on the directory, but not write permission. This would allow other users to change to the directory and list the files in it, but not create new files or copy any of their files into it. The next example sets read and execute permission for the group for the **thankyou** directory but removes the write permission. Members of the group may enter the **thankyou** directory and list the files there, but they may not create new ones.

```
$ chmod g+rx-w letters/thankyou
```

Just as with files, you can also use octal digits to set a directory permission. To set the same permissions as in the previous example, you would use the octal digits 750, which has the binary equivalent of 111 101 000.

```
$ chmod 750 letters/thankyou
```

As you know, the **ls** command with the **-1** option will list all files in a directory. To list only the information about the directory itself, add a **d** modifier. In the next example, **ls -ld** displays information about the **thankyou** directory. Notice that the first character in the permissions list is *d*, indicating that it is a directory.

```
$ ls -ld thankyou
drwxr-x---  2  chris 512 Feb 10 04:30   thankyou
```

If you have files that you want other users to have access to, you need to not only set permissions for that file, but also to make sure that the permissions are set for the directory that the file is in. Another user, in order to access your file, must first access the file's directory. The same applies to parents of directories. Though a directory may give permission to others to access it, if its parent directory denies access, the directory cannot be reached. In this respect, you have to pay close attention to your directory tree. To provide access to a directory, all other directories above it in the directory tree must also be accessible to other users.

In Figure 7-5, the user wants to open up the **thankyou** directory to all other users. To do so, other users need access to the **chris** and **letters** directories. This is done by setting the execute permission on in the other category for each directory. Notice that

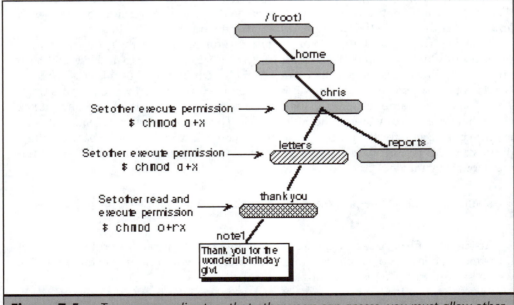

Figure 7-5.   *To open up a directory that other users can access, you must allow other users access to any of its parent directories as well*

only the execute permission needs to be set, not the read or write. Other users will not be allowed to list files or add files to either **chris** or **letters**. They can only change to those directories or reference their subdirectories.

Changing a File's Owner or Group: chown and chgrp

Though other users may be able to access a file, only the owner can change its permissions. If, however, you want to give some other user control over one of your file's permissions, you can change the owner of the file from yourself to the other user. The **chown** command transfers control over a file to another user. This command takes as its first argument the name of the other user. Following the user name, you can list the files you are giving up. In the next example, the user gives control of the **mydata** file to Robert.

```
$ chown robert mydata
$ ls -l mydata
-rw-r--r--  1  robert weather 207  Feb  20 11:55  mydata
```

You can also, if you wish, change the group for a file, using the **chgrp** command. **chgrp** takes as its first argument the name of the new group for a file or files. Following the new group name, you then list the files that you want changed to that group. In the next example, the user changes the group name for today and weekend to the forecast group. The **ls -l** command then reflects the group change.

```
$ chgrp forecast today weekend
$ ls -l
-rw-r--r--  1  chris weather 207  Feb  20 11:55  mydata
-rw-rw-r--  1  chris forecast 568  Feb  14 10:30  today
-rw-rw-r--  1  chris forecast 308  Feb  17 12:40  weekend
```

File Systems: mount and umount

Although all the files in your Linux system are connected into one overall directory tree, the files themselves reside on storage devices such as hard drives or CD-ROMs. The Linux files on a particular storage device are organized into what is referred to as a *file system*. Your Linux directory tree may encompass several file systems, each on different storage devices. The files themselves are organized into one seamless tree of directories beginning from the root directory. Although the root may be located in a file system on your hard drive partition, there will be a path name directly to files located on the file system for your CD-ROM.

The files in a file system remain separate from your directory tree until you specifically connect them to it. A file system has its files organized into its own directory tree. You can think of this as a subtree that must be attached to the main directory tree. For example, a floppy disk with Linux files will have its own tree of directories. You need to attach this subtree to the main tree on your hard drive partition. Until they are attached, you will not be able to access the files on your floppy disk.

Attaching a file system on a storage device to your main directory tree is called *mounting the device.* This is done with the **mount** command. To access files on a CD-ROM, first you have to mount the CD-ROM. The mount operation will attach the directory tree on the storage device to a directory that you specify. You can then change to that directory and access those files. Mounting file systems can only be done as the root user. It is a systems administration task and cannot be performed by a regular user. To mount a file system, be sure to log in as the root user. Table 7-2 list the different options for the **mount** command.

The mount command takes two arguments: the storage device through which Linux accesses the file system, and the directory in the file structure to which the new file system is attached. *mountpoint* is the directory on your main directory tree where you want the files on the storage device attached. *device* is a special device file that connects your system to the hardware device. The syntax for the **mount** command follows:

```
# mount device mountpoint
```

Device files are located in the **/dev** directories and usually have abbreviated names ending with the number of device. For example, **fd0** may reference the first floppy drive attached to your system. On Linux systems operating on PCs, the hard disk partitions have a prefix of **hd** followed by an alphabetic character that labels the hard drive and then a number for the partition. For example, **hda2** references the second partition on the first hard drive. In most cases, you can use the **man** command with a prefix to obtain more detailed information about that kind of device. For example, **man sd** displays the man pages for SCSI devices.

For a file system to be accessible, it must be mounted. Even the file system on your hard disk partition has to be mounted with a **mount** command. However, when you install your Linux system and create the Linux partition on your hard drive, your system is automatically configured to mount your main file system whenever it starts. Floppy disks and CD-ROMs, however, have to be explicitly mounted. The following example mounts a floppy disk in the first floppy drive device (fd0) to the **/mydir** directory.

```
# mount /dev/fd0   /mydir
```

Before you can shut down your system, all your mounted file systems have to be unmounted. Your main file system is automatically unmounted for you. However, should you want to replace a mounted file system with another, you must first explicitly unmount the one already mounted. Say that you have mounted a floppy disk and now you want to take it out and put in a new one. You must unmount that floppy disk before you can put in and mount the new one. You unmount a file system with the **umount** command. **umount** can take as its argument either a device name or the directory where it was mounted. Here is the syntax:

```
# umount device-or-mountpoint
```

The following example unmounts the floppy disk mounted to the **/mydir** directory:

```
# umount /dev/fd0
```

Using the example where the device was mounted on the **/mydir** directory, you could just use that directory to unmount the file system.

```
# umount /mydir
```

There is one important constraint on the **umount** command. You can never unmount a file system that you are currently working in. If you change to a directory within a file system that you then try to unmount, you will receive an error message saying that the file system is busy. For example, suppose you mount the OpenLinux CD-ROM on the **/mnt/cdrom** directory, and then change to that **/mnt/cdrom** directory. If you decide to change CD-ROMs, you first have to unmount the current one with the **umount** command. This will fail because you are currently in the directory it is mounted to. You first have to leave that directory before you can unmount the CD-ROM.

```
# mount /dev/hdc /mnt/cdrom
# cd /mnt/cdrom
# umount /mnt/cdrom
umount: /dev/hdd: device is busy
# cd /root
# umount /mnt/cdrom
```

The file systems on each storage device are formatted to take up a specified amount of space. For example, you may have formatted your hard drive partition to take up 300MB. Files installed or created on that file system will take up part of the space, and the remainder will be available for new files and directories. To find out how much space you have free on a file system, you can use the **df** command. It will list all your file systems by their device names, how much memory they take up, and the percentage of the memory used, as well as where they are mounted. **df** is also a very safe way to obtain a listing of all your partitions, instead of using **fdisk**.

```
$ df
Filesystem      1024-blocks  Used Available Capacity Mounted on
/dev/hda3          297635   169499   112764     60%    /
/dev/hda1          205380   182320    23060     89%    /mnt/dos
/dev/hdc           637986   637986        0    100%    /mnt/cdrom
```

You can also use **df** to tell you what file system a given directory belongs to. Just enter **df** with the directory name, or **df .** for the current directory.

```
$ df .
Filesystem      1024-blocks  Used Available Capacity Mounted on
/dev/hda3          297635   169499   112764     60%    /
```

To make sure nothing is wrong with a given file system, you can use the **fsck** command to check it. Enter **fsck** and the device name that references the file system. Table 7-3 lists the **fsck** options. The following examples check the disk in the floppy drive and the primary hard drive:

```
# fsck   /dev/fd0
# fsck   /dev/hda1
```

Mounting and Formatting Floppy Disks

To access a file on a floppy disk, you first have to mount that disk onto your Linux system. The device name for your floppy drive is **fd0**, and it is located in the directory **/dev**. **/dev/fd0** references your floppy drive. Notice the number **0** after **fd**. If you have more than one floppy drive, they will be represented by **fd1**, **fd2**, and so on. You can mount to any directory you want. However, your OpenLinux installation already created a convenient directory to use for floppy disks, **/mnt/floppy**. The following example mounts the floppy disk in your floppy drive to the **/mnt/floppy** directory:

```
# mount /dev/fd0   /mnt/floppy
```

Bear in mind that you are mounting a particular floppy disk, not the floppy drive. You cannot just remove the floppy disk and put in another one. The **mount** command has attached those files to your main directory tree, and your system expects to find those files on a floppy disk in your floppy drive. If you take out the disk and put another one in, you will get an error when you try to access it.

To change disks, you must first unmount the floppy disk already in your disk drive; then, after putting in the new disk, you must explicitly mount that new disk. To do this, use the **umount** command. Notice that there is no *n* in the **umount** command.

```
# umount    /dev/fd0
```

For the unmount operation, you can specify either the directory it is mounted on or the **/dev/fd0** device.

```
# umount   /mnt/floppy
```

You can now remove the floppy disk, put in the new one and then mount it.

```
# mount    /mnt/floppy
```

When you shut down your system, any disk you have mounted will be automatically unmounted. You do not have to explicitly unmount it.

To format a floppy disk, use the **mkfs** command. This creates a Linux file system on that disk. Be sure to specify the **ext2** file system type with the **-t ext2** option. Once formatted, you can then mount that file system. **mkfs** takes as its arguments the device name and the number of memory blocks on the disk (see Table 7-4). At 1000 bytes per block, 1400 formats a 1.44MB disk. You do not first mount the blank disk; you simply put it in your floppy drive and enter the **mkfs** command with its arguments. The next example formats a 1.44MB floppy disk.

```
# mkfs -t ext2 /dev/fd0  1400
```

Mounting CD-ROMs

You can also mount CD-ROM disks to your Linux system. On the OpenLinux system, the directory **/mnt/cdrom** has been reserved for CD-ROM file systems. You will see an entry for this in the **/etc/fstab** file. To mount a CD-ROM, all you have to do is enter the command **mount** and the directory **/mnt/cdrom**. You do not need to specify the device name. Once mounted, you can access the CD-ROM through the **/mnt/cdrom** directory.

```
# mount /mnt/cdrom
```

As with floppy disks, keep in mind that you are mounting a particular CD-ROM, not the CD-ROM drive. You cannot just remove the CD-ROM and put in a new one. The **mount** command has attached those files to your main directory tree, and your system expects to find them on a disc in your CD-ROM drive.

To change discs, you have to first unmount the CD-ROM that is already in your CD-ROM drive with the **umount** command. Your CD-ROM drive will not open until you issue this command. Then, after putting in the new disc, you must explicitly mount that new CD-ROM.

```
# umount   /mnt/cdrom
```

You can now remove the CD-ROM and put in the new one. Then issue a **mount** command to mount it.

```
# mount    /mnt/cdrom
```

If you want to mount a CD-ROM to another directory, you have to include the device name in the **mount** command. The following example mounts the disc in your CD-ROM drive to the **/mydir** directory. The particular device name for the CD-ROM in this example is **/dev/hdc**.

```
# mount /dev/hdc   /mydir
```

The device name for your CD-ROM drive will vary depending upon the type of CD-ROM you have. The device name for an IDE CD-ROM has the same prefix as an IDE hard disk partition, **hd**. It is identified by a following character that distinguishes it from other IDE devices. For example, an IDE CD-ROM connected to your secondary IDE port may have the name **hdc**. An IDE CD-ROM connected as a slave to the secondary port may have the name **hdd**. The actual name will be determined when the CD-ROM is installed, as happened when you installed your Linux system. SCSI CD-ROM drives use a different nomenclature for their device names. They begin with **sd** for SCSI drive and are followed by a distinguishing character. For example, the name of a SCSI CD-ROM could be **sdb** or **sda**. The name of your CD-ROM was determined when you installed your system. You can find out what it is by either examining the **/etc/fstab** file or using **fstool** on your root user desktop.

To change discs, you have to unmount the CD-ROM that is already in your CD-ROM drive; then, after putting in the new disc, you must explicitly mount that new CD-ROM.

```
# umount /mydir
```

You can now remove the CD-ROM and put in the new one. Then issue a **mount** command to mount it.

```
# mount   /dev/hdc   /mydir
```

Mounting Hard Drive Partitions: Linux and MS-DOS

You can mount either Linux or MS-DOS hard drive partitions with the **mount** command. However, it is much more practical to have them mounted automatically using the **/etc/fstab** file as described in the next section. The Linux hard disk partitions you created during installation are already automatically mounted for you. To mount a Linux hard disk partition, enter the mount command with the device name of the partition and the directory you want to mount it to. IDE hard drives use the prefix **hd**, and SCSI hard drives use the prefix *sd*. The prefix for a hard disk is followed by an alphabetic character that labels the hard drive and then a number for the partition. For example, **hda2** references the second partition on the first IDE hard drive, and **sdb3** refers to the third partition on the second SCSI hard drive. To find the device name, you can use **df** to display your hard partitions or examine the **/etc/fstab** file. The next example mounts the Linux hard disk partition on **/dev/hda4** to the directory **/mnt/mydata**.

```
# mount -t ext2  /dev/hda4  /mnt/mydata
```

You can also mount an MS-DOS partition and directly access the files on them. As with a Linux partition, you use the mount command, but you also have to specify the file system type as MS-DOS. For that, use the **-t** option and the type **msdos**. In the next example, the user mounts the MS-DOS hard disk partition **/dev/hda1** to the Linux file structure at directory **/mnt/dos**. **/mnt/dos** is a common designation for MS-DOS file systems, though you can mount it in any directory. Be sure that you have already created the directory.

```
# mount -t msdos  /dev/hda1  /mnt/dos
```

If you want to mount a new partition from either a new hard drive or your current drive, you must first create that partition using either the Linux **fdisk** or **cfdisk** and format it with **mkfs**. Once created and formatted, you can then mount it on your system. To start **cfdisk**, enter **fdisk** on the command line. This will bring up an interactive program that you can use to create your Linux partition. Be very careful using Linux **fdisk**. It can literally erase your entire hard disk if you are not careful.

fdisk operates much as described in the installation process discussed in Chapter 2. The command **n** will create a new partition, and the command **t** will allow you to set its type to that of a Linux type, 83. Table 7-5 lists the **fdisk** commands.

Hard disk partitions are named with **hd** (IDE drive) or **sd** (SCSI drives), followed by an alphabetic letter indicating the hard drive and then a number for the partition on the hard drive. They can belong to any operating system such as MS-DOS, OS/2, or Windows NT, as well as Linux. The first partition created is called **hda1**—the first partition on the first IDE hard drive, *a*. If you add another partition, it will have the name **hda2**. If you add a new IDE hard drive, its first partition will have the name **hdb1**.

Once you have created your partition, you have to format it. For this, use the **mkfs** command and the name of the hard disk partition. A hard disk partition is a device with its own device name in the **/dev** directory. You have to specify its full path name with the **mkfs** command. For example, the second partition on the first hard drive will have the device name **/dev/hda5**. The next example formats that partition.

```
# mkfs -t ext2   /dev/hda5
```

You can now mount your new hard disk partition, attaching it to your file structure.

Automatically Mounting File Systems: the fstab file

When adding a new hard disk partition to your Linux system, you will most likely want to have it automatically mounted on startup, and unmounted when you shut down. Otherwise, you will have to mount and unmount the partition explicitly each time you boot up and shut down your system. To have Linux automatically mount the file system on your new hard disk partition, you only need to add its name to the **fstab** file. You can do this by directly and carefully editing the **fstab** file to type in a new entry, or you can use the **fstool** command as described in the next section. The **fstab** file is located in the **/etc** directory. It lists the file systems that are mounted by the **mount** command with the **-a** option. This **mount -a** command is in your **/etc/rc.d /rc.boot** file. The commands perform system initialization operations. They are executed every time you boot your system. When you shut down your system, a **umount -a** command is executed that unmounts all the file systems listed in **fstab**. The **umount -a** command is found in your **/etc/rc.d/init/halt** file, which contains commands to be executed whenever you shut down your system. In this way, any file system you specify in your **/etc/fstab** file is automatically mounted when the system starts, and automatically unmounted when it shuts down. Other systems such as Redhat may put the **mount -a** command in a file named **/etc/rc.d/rc.sysinit**.

An entry in a **fstab** file contains several fields, each separated by a space or tab. The first field is the name of the file system to be mounted. This usually begins with **/dev**, such as **/dev/hda3** for the third hard disk partition. The next field is the directory in your file structure where you want the file system on this device to be attached. The third field is the type of file system being mounted. Table 7-6 provides a list of all the different types you can mount. The type for a standard Linux hard disk partition is **ext2**. The next example shows an entry for the main Linux hard disk partition. It is mounted at the root directory, **/**, and has a file type of **ext2**.

```
/dev/hda3  /  ext2  defaults  0  1
```

The field after the file system type lists the different options for mounting the file system. There is a default set of options that you can specify by simply entering **defaults**. You can list specific options next to each other separated by a comma (no spaces). The defaults option specifies that a device is read/write, asynchronous, block, that ordinary users cannot mount on it, and programs can be executed on it. By contrast, a CD-ROM only has a few options listed for it, **ro** and **noauto**. **ro** specifies that this is read only, and **noauto** that it is not automatically mounted. The **noauto** option is used with both CD-ROMs and floppy drives so they won't automatically mount, since you do not know if you will have anything in them when you start up. At the same time, the entries for both the CD-ROM and the floppy drive specify where they are to be mounted when you do decide to mount them. Table 7-7 lists the options for mounting a file system. An example of CD-ROM and floppy drive entries follows. Notice that the type for a CD-ROM file system is different from a hard disk partition, **iso9660**. The floppy drive also has all the default options of the hard disk partitions.

```
/dev/fd0    /mnt/floppy  ext2     defaults,noauto  0  0
/dev/hdc    /mnt/cdrom   iso9660  ro,noauto        0  0
```

The last two fields consist of an integer value. The first one is used by the **dump** command to determine if a file system needs to be dumped, backing up the file system. The last one is used by **fsck** to see if a file system should be checked and in what order. If the field has a value of 1, it indicates a boot partition. The 0 value means that the **fsck** does not have to check the file system.

A copy of an **/etc/fstab** file is shown here. Notice that the first line is comment. All comment lines begin with a **#**. The entry for the **/proc** file system is a special entry used by your Linux operating system for managing its processes. It is not an actual device.

/etc/fstab

# <device>	<mountpoint>	<filesystemtype>	<options>	<dump>	<fsckorder>
/dev/hda3	/	ext2	defaults	0	1
/dev/hdc	/mnt/cdrom	iso9660	ro,noauto	0	0
/dev/fd0	/mnt/floppy	ext2	defaults,noauto	0	
/proc	/proc	proc	defaults		
/dev/hda2	none	swap	sw		
/dev/hda1	/mnt/dos	msdos	defaults	0	0

To make an entry in the **/etc/fstab** file, you can either edit the **/etc/fstab** file directly or use the utility **fstool** that will prompt you for information and then make the correct entries into your **/etc/fstab** file.

As noted earlier, you can mount MS-DOS partitions used by your MS-DOS operating system onto your Linux file structure, just as you would mount any Linux file system. You only have to specify the file type of **msdos**. You may find it convenient to have your MS-DOS partitions automatically mounted when you start up your Linux system. To do this, you just have to put an entry for your MS-DOS partitions in your **/etc/fstab** file. You make an entry for each MS-DOS partition you want to mount, and specify the device name for that partition followed by the directory that you want to mount it in. **/mnt/dos** would be a logical choice (be sure that the **dos** directory has already been created in **/mnt**). For the file system type, enter **msdos**. The next example shows a standard MS-DOS partition entry for an **/etc/fstab** file. Notice that the last entry in the **/etc/fstab** file example was an entry for mounting an MS-DOS partition.

```
/dev/hda1 /mnt/dos  msdos  defaults  0  0
```

For any partition with an entry in the **/etc/fstab** file, you can mount it using only the mount directory specified in its **fstab** entry. You do not have to enter the device file name. The **mount** command will look up the entry for it in the **fstab** file, using the directory to identify the entry, and in that way, find the device name. For example, to unmount the **/dev/hda1** DOS partition in the previous example, the **mount** command only needs to know the directory it is mounted to, in this case, **/mnt/dos**.

```
# mount /mnt/dos
```

If your **/etc/fstab** file ever becomes corrupted—say a line gets deleted accidentally or changed—then your system will boot into a maintenance mode, giving you read-only access to your partitions. To gain read/write access so you can fix your **/etc/fstab** file, you have to remount your main partition. The following command performs such an operation:

```
# mount -n -o remount,ro  /
```

You can use the **/etc/fstab** example here as a guide to show how your entries should look. The **/proc** and **swap** partition entries are particularly critical.

Linux File System Manager: Lisa and fstool

You can use the Lisa tool to administer your **fstab** file, instead of editing it directly. Lisa is equipped to work with the amd daemon and is thus preferable. In the System Configuration menu, you will see an entry for "Mount Table Configuration." This entry brings up the menu shown in Figure 7-6, listing options to display, add, or delete entries in your mount table, the **/etc/fstab** file.

To add an entry, choose "Add a new entry to the mount table." The next screen prompts you to enter the name of the partition or NFS path you want to mount (see Figure 7-7). It will validate the entry, making sure it is an actual partition or accessible path. You are then asked to enter the path for the directory where you want to mount that partition's file system. You are then asked whether you want to make the file system read-write or read-only.

The "Delete an entry" option allows you to remove entries from the file system. Be very careful not to accidentally delete your root file system, the one mounted at /, as well as the /proc and swap partitions.

Instead of Lisa, you can use the Redhat **fstool** utility to manage your **/etc/fstab** file. **fstool** is easier to use and provides you with much more information. However, **fstool** is currently not designed to work with the amd daemon. You can access

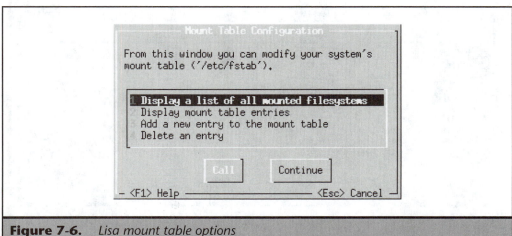

Figure 7-6.   *Lisa mount table options*

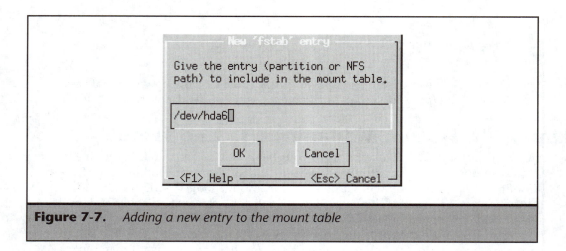

Figure 7-7. Adding a new entry to the mount table

fstool from the fvwm taskbar or menu, as well as from the Caldera root desktop in the Admin_Tools folder. When you start up **fstool**, a window opens that lists the contents of your **/etc/fstab** file. Using buttons and menus, you can mount and unmount file systems, add new file systems to your **/etc/fstab** file, and change any options for your file system. You can also easily add NFS file systems. Figure 7-8 shows the **fstool** window.

The entries for the file systems listed in the **fstab** file are displayed in the center window pane. The top row provides a heading for each field. Five buttons across the

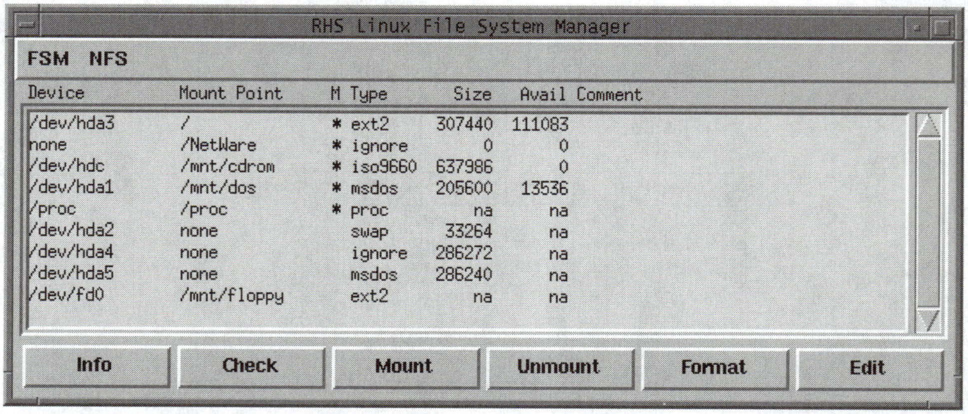

Figure 7-8. The **fstool** window

bottom describe various operations you can carry out on each file system. Just click on the file system entry and it will highlight. Then click on the button. Clicking on the Info button will open a window that displays detailed information about the file system, including the number of bytes still unused. The Check button checks the file system for errors. The Mount and Unmount buttons both mount and unmount selection file systems. The Format button formats a file system, and the Edit button allows you to change certain fields such as file system options. Be very careful when using **fstool**. You don't want to unmount a system that you need access to, nor do you want to unintentionally format a file system, thereby losing all your data on it.

The upper left-hand corner of the window holds two menus, one configuring your File System Manager (FSM), and one for Network File System (NFS). NFS file systems are described in the next section. You can configure the file system manager to display more information in the window, such as the percentage of unused memory on your file systems. You also use the FSM menu to add and remove file systems from your **/etc/fstab** file. The Add entry will let you add a file system and the Delete entry will remove it. For example, to add an MS-DOS file system on a hard disk partition to the **/etc/fstab** file, you would select Add from the FSM menu and then enter the device name for the file system.

Network File Systems: NFS and /etc/exports

The Network File System (NFS) allows you to mount a file system on a remote computer as if it were local to your own system. You can then directly access any of the files on that remote file system. This has the advantage of allowing different systems on a network to directly access the same files, without each having to keep their own copies. There would be just one copy on a remote file system that each computer could then access.

NFS operates over a TCP/IP network. The remote computer that holds the file system makes it available to other computers on the network. It does so by exporting the file system, which entails making entries in an NFS configuration file called **/etc/exports**, as well as running two daemons to support access by other systems, **rpc.mountd** and **rpc.nfsd**. An entry in the **/etc/exports** file specifies the file system to be exported and the computers on the network that can access it. For the file system, enter its mount point, the directory it was mounted to. This is followed by a list of computers that can access this file system. A comma-separated list of mount options placed within a set of parentheses may follow each computer. For example, you might want to give one computer read-only access and another read and write access. If only the options are listed, they are applied to anyone. A list of mount options are provided in Table 7-8. Examples of entries in an **/etc/exports** file are shown here. Read-only access with no security check is given to all computers to the file system mounted on the **/pub** directory, a common name used for public access. Read and write access is given to the **ant.trek.com** computer for the file system mounted on the **/home/foodstuff** directory. The next entry would allow access

by **butterfly.trek.com** to your CD-ROM. The last entry denies anyone access to
/home/richlp.

/etc/exports

```
/pub             (ro,insecure,all_squash)
/home/foodstuff  ant.trek.com(rw)
/mnt/cdrom       butterfly.trek.com(ro)
/home/richlp     (noaccess)
```

Once an NFS file system is made available, different computers on the network
have to first mount it before they can use it. You can mount an NFS file system either
by an entry in the **/etc/fstab** file or by an explicit mount command. An NFS entry in
the **/etc/fstab** file has a mount type of NFS. An NFS file system name consists of the
hostname of the computer it is located on, followed by the path name of the
directory where it is mounted. The two are separated by a colon. For example,
rose.berkeley.edu:/home/project specifies a file system mounted at **/home/project**
on the **rose.berkeley.edu** computer.

There are also several NFS-specific mount options that you can include with your
NFS entry. You can specify the size of datagrams sent back and forth, and the amount
of time your computer will wait for a response from the host system. You can also
specify whether a file system is to be hard mounted or soft mounted. For a
hard-mounted file system, your computer will continually try to make contact if for
some reason the remote system fails to respond. A soft mount, after a specified
interval, will give up trying to make contact and issue an error message. A hard mount
is the default. Table 7-9 and the man pages for **mount** contain a listing of these NFS
client options. They differ from the NFS server options indicated previously.

An example of an NFS entry follows. The remote system is **ant.trek.com** and the
file system is mounted on **/home/projects**. This file system is to be mounted on the
local system's **/home/richlp** directory. The type of system is NFS and the **timeo** option
specifies that the local system will wait up to 20 one-tenths of a second for a response,
two seconds.

```
ant.trek.com:/home/projects   /home/richlp      nfs   timeo=20
```

You can also use the mount command with the **-t nfs** option to explicitly mount an
NFS file system. To explicitly mount the previous entry, use the following command:

```
# mount -t nfs -o timeo=20   ant.trek.com:/home/projects
/home/richlp
```

NIS

On networks supporting NFS many resources and devices are shared by the same systems. Normally, each system would have to have their own configuration files for each device or resource. Changes would entail updating each system individually. However, NFS provides a special service called Network Information Services (NIS) that will maintain such configuration files for the entire network. For changes, you would only need to update the NIS files. NIS works for information required for most administrative tasks, such as those relating to users, network access, or devices. For example, you can maintain password information with an NIS service, having only to update those NIS password files.

NIS was developed by Sun Microsystems and was originally known as Sun's Yellow Pages (YP). NIS files are kept on an NIS server (NIS servers are still sometimes referred to as YP servers). Individual systems on a network use NIS clients to make requests from the NIS server. The NIS server maintains its information on special database files called *maps*. There are Linux versions for both NIS clients and servers. Linux NIS clients will easily connect to any network using NIS.

Your Caldera CD-ROM contains both the Linux NIS client and server software in RPM packages that install with default configurations. The NIS client is installed as part of the initial OpenLinux installation, and you can use Lisa to configure your NIS client at any time. NIS client programs are ypbind (the NIS client daemon), ypwhich, ypcat, yppoll, ypmatch, yppasswd and ypset. Each has its own man page with details of their use. The NIS server programs are ypserv, ypinit, yppasswdd, yppush, ypxfr, and netgroup—each also with its own man page. A detailed NIS-HOWTO document is available in the **/usr/doc/HOWTO** directory.

Archive Files and Devices: tar

The tar utility creates archives for files and directories. With tar, you can archive specific files, update them in the archive, and add new files, as you wish, to that archive. You can even archive entire directories with all their files and subdirectories, all of which can be restored from the archive. tar was originally designed to create archives on tapes. The term "tar" stands for tape archive. You can create archives on any device, such as a floppy disk, or you can create an archive file to hold the archive. tar is an ideal utility for making backups of your files or combining several files into a single file for transmission across a network.

On Linux, tar is often used to create archives on devices or files. You can direct tar to archive files to a specific device or a file by using the **f** option with the name of the device or file. The syntax for the **tar** command using the **f** option is shown in the next example. The device or file name is often referred to as the archive name. When creating a file for a tar archive, the file name is usually given the extension **.tar**. This is a convention only and is not required. You can list as many file names as you wish. If a directory name is specified, then all of its subdirectories will be included in the archive.

```
$ tar optionsf archive-name.tar directory-and-file-names
```

To create an archive, use the **c** option. Combined with the **f** option, **c** will create an archive on a file or device. You enter this option before and right next to the **f** option. Notice that there is no preceding dash before a **tar** option. Table 7-10 lists the different options you can use with tar. In the next example, the directory **mydir** and all of its subdirectories are saved in the file **myarch.tar**.

```
$ tar cf myarch.tar mydir
```

The user can later extract the directories from the tape using the **x** option. The **xf** option extracts files from an archive file or device. The **tar** extraction operation will generate all subdirectories. In the next example, the **xf** option directs **tar** to extract all the files and subdirectories from the tar file **myarch.tar**.

```
$ tar xf myarch.tar
```

You use the **r** option to add files to an archive that has already been created. The **r** option appends the files to the archive. In the next example, the user appends the files in the **letters** directory to the **myarch.tar** archive.

```
$ tar rf myarch.tar letters
```

Should you change any of the files in your directories that you have previously archived, you can use the **u** option to instruct **tar** to update the archive with any modified files. **tar** compares the time of the last update for each archived file with those in the user's directory and copies into the archive any files that have been changed since they were last archived. Any newly created files in these directories will be added to the archive as well. In the next example, the user updates the **myarch.tar** file with any recently modified or newly created files in the **mydir** directory.

```
tar uf myarch.tar mydir
```

If you need to see what files are stored in an archive, you can use the **tar** command with the **t** option. The next example will list all the files stored in the **myarch.tar** archive.

```
tar tf myarch.tar
```

To back up the files to a specific device, specify the device as the archive. In the next example, the user creates an archive on the floppy disk in the **/dev/fd0** device and copies into it all the files in the **mydir** directory.

```
$ tar cf /dev/fd0 mydir
```

To extract the backed-up files on the disk in the device, use the **xf** option:

```
$ tar xf /dev/fd0
```

If the files you are archiving take up more space than would be available on a device such as a floppy disk, you can create a tar archive that uses multiple labels. The **M** option instructs tar to prompt you for a new storage component when the current one is filled. When archiving to a floppy drive with the **M** option, tar will prompt you to put in a new floppy disk when one becomes full. You can then save your tar archive on several floppy disks.

```
$ tar cMf /dev/fd0 mydir
```

To unpack the multiple-disk archive, place the first one in the floppy drive and then issue the following **tar** command using both the **x** and **M** options. You will be prompted to put in the other floppy disks as they are needed.

```
$ tar xMf /dev/fd0
```

The tar operation will not perform compression on archived files. If you want to compress the archived files, you can instruct tar to invoke the gzip utility to compress them. With the lowercase **z** option, tar will first use gzip to compress files before archiving them. The same **z** option will invoke gzip to decompress them when extracting files.

```
$ tar czf  myarch.tar mydir
```

Bear in mind that there is a difference between compressing individual files in an archive and compressing the entire archive as a whole. Often, an archive is created for transferring several files at once as one tar file. To shorten transmission time, the archive should be as small as possible. You can use the compression utility gzip on the archive tar file to compress it, reducing its size, and then send the compressed version. The person receiving it can decompress it, restoring the tar file. Using gzip on a tar file often results in a file with the extension **.tar.gz**. The extension **.gz** is added to a compressed gzip file. The next example creates a compressed version of **myarch.tar** using the same name with the extension **.gz**.

```
$ gzip myarch.tar
$ ls
$ myarch.tar.gz
```

If you have a default device specified, such as a tape, and you want to create an archive on it, you can simply use **tar** without the **f** option and a device or file name. This can be helpful for making backups of your files. The name of the default device is held in a file called **/etc/default/tar**. The syntax for the **tar** command using the default tape device is shown in the following example. If a directory name is specified, all of its subdirectories will be included in the archive.

```
$ tar option directory-and-file-names
```

In the next example, the directory **mydir** and all of its subdirectories are saved on a tape in the default tape device.

```
$ tar c mydir
```

In this example, the **mydir** directory and all of its files and subdirectories are extracted from the default tape device and placed in the user's working directory:

```
$ tar x  mydir
```

XTar

The XTar X-Windows application lets you use windows and menus to select a tar archive file and unpack it. You start it up either by entering the command **xtar** in an Xterm window or selecting its entry from the fvwm workplace menu. XTar has three menus: XTar, Options, and Attributes. You first select a tar archive file using the Open item on the XTar menu. This opens a file selection box where files in a directory are displayed and you can move from one directory to another. Once you select the tar archive you want, all the files making up the tar archive are then listed in the main window. With XTar you have the option of either unpacking the entire tar archive or just a few files within it. To unpack the entire archive, select the Unpack All item in the XTar menu. The Unpack All As item lets you unpack to a directory of your choosing. To unpack a particular file, first select it (you can use the Search function in the XTar menu to find it), then select the Extract item in the Options menu. Options also has a View item for just displaying short text files such as a README file. Figure 7-9 shows the XTar program displaying a **tar.gz** file. XTar can work equally with a compressed archive (you do not have to decompress it first).

File Compression: gzip

There are several reasons for reducing the size of a file. The two most common are to save space or, if you are transferring the file across a network, to save transmission time. The gzip utility is the GNU compression utility used to compress and decompress files. To compress a file, enter the command **gzip** and the file name. This will replace the file with a compressed version of it with the extension **.gz**.

```
$ gzip mydata
$ ls
mydata.gz
```

```
                          XTar V1.4
  XTar   Options   Set Attributes                        Help

  Filename: SpecTcl1.1.tar.gz
  File Size: 761 K                    Unpacked Size: 1.46 MB
  -r--r--r--    26746/10        1015  Sep 25 11:47 1997  SpecT
  -r--r--r--    26746/10       26576  Sep 22 12:53 1997  SpecT
  -r--r--r--    26746/10        1842  Sep 22 12:49 1997  SpecT
  -r--r--r--    26746/10         888  Sep 25 11:47 1997  SpecT
  -r--r--r--    26746/10         975  Jun 26 20:49 1997  SpecT
  -r--r--r--    26746/10       13362  May 12 11:50 1997  SpecT
  -r--r--r--    26746/10       10478  Jul 30 12:51 1997  SpecT
  -r--r--r--    26746/10       19189  Sep 22 12:42 1997  SpecT
  -r--r--r--    26746/10        5046  Jun 25 17:31 1997  SpecT
  -r--r--r--    26746/10        9698  Jul 30 12:51 1997  SpecT
  -r--r--r--    26746/10        7377  Jul 30 12:51 1997  SpecT
```

Figure 7-9.   *XTar tar archive utility*

To decompress a gzip file, use either **gzip** with the **-d** option or the command **gunzip**. These commands will decompress a compressed file with the **.gz** extension and replace it with a decompressed version with the same root name, but without the **.gz** extension. When you use **gunzip**, you do not even have to type in the **.gz** extension. **gunzip** and **gzip -d** will assume it. Table 7-11 lists the different **gzip** options.

```
$ gunzip mydata.gz
$ ls
mydata
```

Suppose you want to display or print the contents of a compressed file without first having to decompress it. The command **zcat** will generate a decompressed version of a file and send it to the standard output. You can then redirect this output to a printer or display a utility such as **more**. The original file will remain in its compressed state.

```
$ zcat mydata.gz | more
```

You can also compress archived tar files. This will result in files with extensions **.tar.gz**. Compressed archived files are often used for transmitting very large files across networks.

```
$ gzip myarch.tar
$ ls
myarch.tar.gz
```

You can compress tar file members individually using the **tar z** option that invokes **gzip**. With the **z** option, tar will invoke **gzip** to compress a file before placing it in an archive. However, archives with members compressed with the **z** option cannot be updated, nor can they be added to. All members have to be compressed and all have to be added at the same time.

You can also use the **compress** and **uncompress** commands to create compressed files. They generate a file that has a **.Z** extension and use a different compression format than **gzip**. **compress** and **uncompress** are not that widely used, but you may run across **.Z** files from time to time. You can use the **uncompress** command to decompress a **.Z** file. **gzip** is the standard GNU compression utility and should be used instead of **compress**.

Installing Software from Compressed Archives: .tar.gz

Linux software programs are available at different sites on the Internet. You can download any of this software and install it on your system. You download software using the ftp program described in Chapter 10. The software is usually downloaded in the form of a compressed archive file. This is an archive file that was created with **tar** and then compressed with **gzip**. To install such a file, you have to first decompress it with the **gunzip** utility and then use **tar** to extract the files and directories making up the software package. Instead of **gunzip**, you could also use **gzip -d**. The next example decompresses the **SpecTel1.1.tar.gz** file, replacing it with a decompressed version called **SpecTel1.1.tar**.

```
$ ls
 SpecTel1.1.tar.gz
$ gunzip SpecTel1.1.tar.gz
$ ls
SpecTel1.1.tar
```

First use **tar** with the **t** option to check the contents of the archive. If the first entry is a directory, that directory will be created and the extracted files placed in it. If the first entry is not a directory, you should first create one and then copy the archive file to it. Then extract the archive within that directory. If there is no directory as the first entry, files will be extracted to the current directory. You have to create a directory yourself to hold these files.

```
$ tar tf SpecTel1.1.tar
```

Now you are ready to extract the files from the tar archive. You use **tar** with the **x** option to extract files, the **v** option to display the path names of files as they are extracted, and the **f** option followed by the name of the archive file:

```
$ tar xvf SpecTel1.1.tar
```

You can combine the decompressing and unpacking operation into one **tar** command by adding a **z** option to the option list, **xzvf**. The following command both decompresses and unpacks the archive:

```
$ tar xzvf SpecTel1.1.tar.gz
```

Installation of your software may differ for each package. Instructions are usually provided along with an installation program.

Downloading Compressed Archives from Online Sites

Many software packages under development or designed for cross-platform implementation may not be in an RPM format. Instead, they may be archived and compressed. These file names for these files will end with the extensions **.tar.gz** or **.tar.Z**. In fact, most software with an RPM format also has a corresponding **.tar.gz** format. After you download one, you will first have to decompress it with **gunzip** and then unpack it with the **tar** command. Many RPM packages only contain binary versions of software applications. If you want the source code for the application, you would have to download and unpack the compressed archive for that application.

In the next example, the user uses ftp to connect to the **sunsite.unc.edu** Linux ftp site. For the login id, the user enters **anonymous**, and for the password, the user enters his or her Internet address. The download mode can be set to binary by entering in the keyword **binary**. With the **cd** command, the user changes to the **pub/Linux/libs/X/xview** directory where the Xview window manager software is located (see Chapter 3). The **get** command then downloads the package. The **close** command cuts the connection and **quit** leaves the **ftp** utility.

```
# ftp sunsite.unc.edu
Connected to sunsite.unc.edu.
220-                  Welcome to the SunSITE USA ftp archives!
1997) ready.
Name (sunsite.unc.edu:root): anonymous
331 Guest login ok, send your complete email address as password.
Password: your-email-address
230 Guest login ok, access restrictions apply.
Remote system type is Unix.
Using binary mode to transfer files.
ftp> cd pub/Linux/libs/X/xview
>250-README for libs/X/xview
250-What you'll find here: various Xview and OpenLook libraries
250 CWD command successful.
ftp> ls xv*
>200 PORT command successful.
150 Opening ASCII mode data connection for /bin/ls.
-rw-rw-r--  1 67       1002         6100 Jun 27 11:16 xview-3.2p1.4.README
-rw-rw-r--  1 67       1002      2192197 Jun 27 11:17 xview-
```

```
3.2p1.4.bin.tar.gz
226 Transfer complete.
ftp> get xview-3.2p1.4.bin.tar.gz
>local: xview-3.2p1.4.bin.tar.gz remote: xview-3.2p1.4.bin.tar.gz
200 PORT command successful.
150 Opening BINARY mode data connection for
xview-3.2p1.4.bin.tar.gz (2192197 bytes).
226 Transfer complete.
2192197 bytes received in 728 secs (2.9 Kbytes/sec)
ftp> close
221 Goodbye.
ftp> quit
#
```

Alternatively, you could just use Netscape or another Web Browser to access, browse through, and download software without having to bother with all the **ftp** commands. Be sure to precede an ftp site name with the term **ftp://** instead of the usual **http://**. For Sunsite you would enter: **ftp://sunsite.unc.edu**. Once you have selected the software you want, hold down the SHIFT key and click on it to download it.

Once downloaded, any file that ends with a **.Z** or **.gz** is a compressed file that has to be decompressed. You would use the **gunzip** command followed by the name of the file.

```
# gunzip xview-3.2p1.4.bin.tar.gz
```

If the file then ends with **.tar**, it is an archived file that has to be unpacked using the **tar** command. Before you unpack the archive, you should move it to the directory you want it in. Source code that you intend to compile is usually placed in the **/usr/src** directory. Most archives will unpack to a subdirectory that they create, placing all those files or directories making up the software package into that subdirectory. For example, the **xview-3.2p1.4.bin.tar** will unpack to a subdirectory called **usr**. To check if an archive will unpack to a directory, use **tar** with the **t** option to list its contents and see if the names are prefixed by a directory. If so, that directory will be created and the extracted files placed in it. If there is no directory name, you should first create one and then copy the archive file to it. Then extract the archive within that directory.

```
# tar tf xview-3.2p1.4.bin.tar
```

Now you are ready to extract the files from the tar archive. You use **tar** with the **x** option to extract files, the **v** option to display the path names of files as they are extracted, and the **f** option followed by the name of the archive file:

```
# tar xvf xview-3.2p1.4.bin.tar
```

Installation of your software may differ for each package. Instructions are usually provided along with an installation program. Downloaded software will usually include README files or other documentation. Be sure to consult them.

Compiling Software

Some software may be in the form of source code that you will need to compile before you can install it. This is particularly true of programs designed for cross-platform implementations. Programs designed to run on various Unix systems such as Sun, as well as on Linux, may be distributed as source code that is downloaded and compiled in those different systems. Compiling such software has been greatly simplified in recent years by the use of configuration scripts that will automatically detect a given system's configuration and compile the program accordingly. For example, the name of the C compiler on a system could be **gcc** or **cc**. Configurations scripts will detect which is present and use it to compile the program.

Before you compile software, you should first read the README or INSTALL files included with it. These will give you detailed instructions on how to compile and install this particular program. If the software used configuration scripts, then compiling and installing usually involves only the following three simple commands:

```
# ./configure
# make
# make install
```

The **./configure** command performs configuration detection. The **make** command performs the actual compiling, using a makefile script generated by the **./configure** operation. The make install will install the program on your system, placing the executable program in a directory like **/usr/local/bin** and any configuration files in **/etc**. Any shared libraries it created may go into **/usr/lib**.

If you are compiling an X-Windows-based program, be sure that the X11 development libraries have been installed. If you choose a standard install when you installed your OpenLinux systems, these will not be installed. You will have to install them using either Lisa or glint. Be sure that the xmkmf program is also installed. See Chapter 21 for more information about X-Windows programs. Many X-Windows applications may need special shared libraries. For example, some applications may need the xforms library or the qt library. Some of these you will have to obtain from online sites. For example, the qt libraries are located at **www.troll.no**, though RPM versions of both the qt and xforms libraries are in the Redhat contrib directory.

Many X-Windows programs use **xmkmf** instead of a configure script to generate the needed **makefile**. In this case, you would enter the command **xmkmf** in place of **./configure**. Be sure to consult the INSTALL and README files for the software. Usually, you only need to issue the following commands within the directory that contains the source code files for the software.

```
xmkmf
make
make install
```

If there is no configure script and the program does not use **xmkmf**, you may just have to enter the **make** command, followed by a make install operation. Check the README or INSTALL files for details.

```
make
make install
```

Be sure to check the documentation for such software to see if there are any changes for you to make to the makefile. There may be only a few, but more detailed changes require an understanding of C programming and how **make** works with it. If you successfully configure the makefile, you may just have to enter the make and make install operations. For example, many of the games located at **sunsite.unc.edu** in the **/pub/Linux/games** directory may require some changes for their makefile. One possible problem is locating the development libraries for C and X-Windows. X-Windows libraries are in the **/usr/X11R6/lib** directory. Standard C libraries are located in the **/usr/lib** directory.

The mtools Utilities: msdos

Your Linux system provides a set of utilities known as mtools that let you easily access a floppy disk formatted for MS-DOS. The **mcopy** command allows you to copy files to and from an MS-DOS floppy disk in your floppy drive. No special operations, such as mounting, are required. With mtools, you do not have to mount an MS-DOS partition to access it. For an MS-DOS floppy disk, just place the disk in your floppy drive, and you can then use **mtool** commands to access those files. For example, to copy a file from an MS-DOS floppy disk to your Linux system, use the **mcopy** command. You specify the MS-DOS disk with **a:** for the A drive. Unlike normal DOS path names, path names used with **mtool** commands use forward slashes instead of back slashes. The

directory **docs** on the A drive would be referenced by the path name **a:/docs**, not
a:\docs. The next example copies the file **mydata** to the MS-DOS disk and then copies
the **preface** file from the disk to the current Linux directory. Notice that, unlike DOS,
mtools uses forward slashes instead of backward slashes.

```
$ mcopy mydata a:
$ mcopy a:/preface   .
```

You can use the **mdir** command to list files on your MS-DOS disk, and you can use
the **mcd** command to change directories on it. The next example lists the files on the
MS-DOS disk in your floppy drive and then changes to the **docs** directory on that drive.

```
$ mdir a:
$ mcd a:/docs
```

Most of the standard MS-DOS commands are available as **mtool** operations. You
can create MS-DOS directories with **mmd** and erase MS-DOS files with **mdel**. A list of
mtool commands is provided in Table 7-12. For example, to display a file on drive **b:**
on an MS-DOS 5 1/4-inch floppy drive, use **mtype** and the name of the file preceded
by **b:/**.

```
$ mtype b:/readme
```

Access to MS-DOS partitions is configured by the **/etc/mtools.conf** file. This file
lists several different default MS-DOS partitions and disk drives. Each drive or
partition is identified with a particular device name. Entries for your floppy drives are
already entered, using the device names **/dev/fd0** and **/dev/fd1** for the first and second
floppy drives. An entry in the **/etc/mtools.conf** file takes the form of the drive label
followed by the term file and the equal sign, and then the device name of the drive or
partition that you want identified with this label. The device name is encased in
quotes. For example, assuming that the first hard disk partition is an MS-DOS
partition and has the device name of **/dev/hda1**, then the following entry would
identify this as the **c:** drive on an MS-DOS system:

```
drive c: file="/dev/hda1"
```

It is important that you have the correct device name for your partition. These are
listed in the **/etc/fstab** file and can also be viewed with the fstool utility on your root
user desktop. If you have a SCSI hard disk, the hard disk partitions will have the form
of **sd** followed by a character for the hard drive and a number for the partition in it.

sda1 refers to the first partition on the SCSI hard drive. IDE hard drives have the form of **hd**, also followed by a character and a partition number. **hda1** refers to the first partition on an IDE hard drive.

When you first install your OpenLinux system, your **/etc/mtools.conf** file will configure the **c:** drive to refer to a SCSI hard disk partition. There is also one for the IDE hard disk partition, but it is commented out with a preceding #. If you have an IDE hard drive (as most users will), you need to remove the preceding # symbol from the entry for the IDE hard disks partition and place a preceding # symbol in front of the entry for the SCSI partition. Also, if your MS-DOS partition on your IDE hard drive is not the first partition, you will have to change the device name. For example, if the MS-DOS partition is the second partition, the device name will be **/dev/hda2**. If you have several MS-DOS partitions, you can add entries for each one, assigning a different label to each. The following example assigns the **d:** label to the fourth hard disk partition on an IDE drive:

```
drive d: file="/dev/hda4"
```

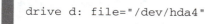

/etc/mtools.conf

```
drive a: file="/dev/fd0" exclusive
drive b: file="/dev/fd1" exclusive

# First SCSI hard disk partition
#drive c: file="/dev/sda1"

# First IDE hard disk partition
drive c: file="/dev/hda1"
drive d: file="/dev/hda4"

#dosemu floppy image
drive m: file="/var/lib/dosemu/diskimage"

#dosemu hdimage
drive n: file="/var/lib/dosemu/diskimage" offset=3840

#Atari ramdisk image
drive o: file="/tmp/atari_rd" offset=136

mtools_lower_case=1
```

Once the DOS hard disk partitions are referenced, you can then use their drive letters to copy files to and from them to your Linux partitions. The following command copies the file **mydoc.html** to the C partition in the directory **webstuff** and renames it **mydoc.htm**. Notice the use of forward slashes instead of backward ones.

```
$ mcopy mypage.html c:/webstuff/mypag.htm
```

Because of the differences in the way DOS and Linux handle newlines in text files, you should use the **-t** option whenever copying a DOS text file to a Linux partition. The following command copies the **mydoc.txt** file from the **c:/project** directory to the **/newdocs** directory.

```
$ mcopy -t c:/project/mydoc.txt   /newdocs
```

DOS and Windows Emulators: DOSemu, Wine, and Willow

Emulators are available for Linux that let you run DOS and Windows programs. These are projects still in development and their success is only partial, to date. As emulators, they run programs slower than DOS or Windows would. The DOS emulator is DOSemu. You can install it from your OpenLinux CD-ROM. It includes sample configuration files called **config.dist** located in the examples directory. This contains a long list of configuration options. All are commented out with a preceding **#** symbol. You need to copy this file to **dosemu.conf**. Edit the **dosemu.conf** file, removing the **#** from the entries that apply to your system. Explanations are given for each section in the file.

To create a bootable floppy DOS disk, use **mcopy** to copy the **command.com**, **sys.com**, **emufs.sys**, **ems.sy.cdrom.sys**, and **exitemu.com** files to that disk. To run the DOS emulator, enter **dos** on the command line. To exit the emulator, enter **exitemu**. **dos -?** gives you a list of **dos** command options.

The Wine emulator is designed to run Windows programs. It is still in development, with new versions continually being released. At this point it is considered very experimental. You can download a version from the **/pub/Linux /ALPHA/wine/development** directory at **sunsite.unc.edu**. The Windows FAQ provides detailed information.

The Willow Toolkit provides a Windows API for cross-platform development. It includes the Willow Twin Libraries and Tools. Applications can be written using the Windows API and then implemented on different systems using the Willow Twin Libraries. There is support for both Win 32 and Windows applications. The Willow Twin Libraries are made available under the GNU public license. See the Willow Web site for more information (**www.willow.com**).

Summary: File Management

You can set permissions on a file or directory to control access by other users. A file or directory can be set for read, write, and execute permissions. Either the owner, the group, or all other users can have access. The command **chmod** sets these permissions, and the **ls** command with the **-l** option lists files and directories with their current permissions.

Different storage devices each contain their own file system that you can mount and access. You can access CD-ROMs, floppy disks, and hard disk partitions. You can also mount MS-DOS hard drive partitions and access them directly from your Linux system. By placing an entry for a file system in the **/etc/fstab** file, you can have a file system mounted automatically when you boot. If you are on a network, mount and access file systems on a remote server.

To transmit files or to back them up, you can archive and compress them. The **tar** command archives files, and the **gzip** command compresses them. Most software packages available online are both archived and compressed. They usually have file names that end with **tar.gz**. You can download them, use **gunzip** to decompress them, and then use **tar xf** to expand the archive. You can then install the software using **rpm**.

Command or Option	Execution
chmod	Changes the permission of a file or directory
Options	
+	Adds a permission
-	Removes a permission
=	Assigns entire set of permissions
r	Sets read permission for a file or directory. A file can be displayed or printed. A directory can have the list of its files displayed
w	Sets write permission for a file or directory. A file can be edited or erased. A directory can be removed

Table 7-1.   **chmod** *Command Options*

Command or Option	Execution
Options	
x	Sets execute permission for a file or directory. If the file is a shell script, it can be executed as a program. A directory can be changed to and entered
u	Sets permissions for the user who created and owns the file or directory
g	Sets permissions for group access to a file or directory
o	Sets permissions for access to a file or directory by all other users on the system
a	Sets permissions for access by the user, group, and all other users
s	Sets User ID and Group ID permission, program owned by owner and group
t	Sets sticky bit permission; program remains in memory
chgrp *groupname filenames*	Changes the group for a file or files
chown *user name filenames*	Changes the owner of a file or files
ls -l *filename*	Lists a file name with its permissions displayed
ls -ld *directory*	Lists a directory name with its permissions displayed
ls -l	Lists all files in a directory with its permissions displayed

Table 7-1. **chmod** *Command Options (continued)*

Mount Option	Description
-f	Fakes the mounting of a file system. Use it to check if a file system can be mounted
-v	Verbose mode. **mount** displays descriptions of the actions it is taking. Use with **-f** to check for any problems mounting a file system, **-fv**
-w	Mounts the file system with read and write permission
-r	Mounts the file system with only read permission
-n	Mounts the file system without placing an entry for it in the **mstab** file
-t *type*	Specifies the type of file system to be mounted. See Table 7-6 for valid file system types
-a	Mounts all file systems listed in **/etc/fstab**
-o *option-list*	Mounts file system using a list of options. This is a comma-separated list of options following **-o**. See Table 7-7 for a list of the options and the man pages for **mount** for a complete listing

Table 7-2.   *The* **mount** *Command*

Option	Description
file-system	Specifies the file system to be checked. Uses file system's device name, such as **/dev/hda3**
-A	Checks all file systems listed in the **/etc/fstab** file
-V	Verbose mode. Lists actions that **fsck** takes
-t *file-system-type*	Specifies the type of file system to be checked
-a	Automatically repairs any problems
-l	Lists the names of all files in the file system
-r	Asks for confirmation before repairing file system
-s	Lists superblock before checking file system

Table 7-3.   **fsck** *Options for Checking and Repairing File Systems*

Option	Description
blocks	Number of blocks for the file system. 1440 blocks for 1.44MB floppy disk
-t *file-system-type*	Specifies the type of file system to format. The default is the standard Linux file system type, **ext2**
fs *–options*	Options for the type of file system specified
-V	Verbose mode. Displays description of each action **mkvfs** takes
-v	Instructs the file system builder program that **mkvfs** invokes to show actions it takes
-c	Checks a partition for bad blocks before formatting it
-l *file-name*	Reads list of bad blocks

Table 7-4.   **mkfs** *Options*

Command	Description
a	Sets and unsets the bootable flag for a partition
c	Sets and unsets the DOS compatibility flag
d	Deletes a partition
l	Lists partition types
m	Displays a listing of **fdisk** commands
n	Creates a new partition
p	Prints the partition table, listing all the partitions on your disk
q	Quits without saving changes. Use this to abort an **fdisk** session if you made a mistake
t	Selects the file system type for a partition
v	Verifies the partition table
w	Writes partition table to disk and exits. At this point the changes are made, irrevocably
x	Displays a listing of advanced **fdisk** commands. With these, you can set the number of cylinders, sectors, and heads, print raw data, and change the location of data in the partition table

Table 7-5.   **fdisk** *Commands*

Types	Description
minux	Minux file systems. File names limited to 30 characters
ext	Earlier version of Linux file system, no longer in use
ext2	Standard Linux file system supporting large file names and file sizes
xiaf	Xiaf file system
msdos	File system for MS-DOS partitions
hpfs	File system for OS/2 high-performance partitions
proc	Used by operating system for processes
nfs	NFS file system for mounting partitions from remote systems
umsdos	UMS-DOS file system
swap	Linux swap partition or swap file
sysv	Unix System V file systems
iso9660	File systems for mounting CD-ROMs

Table 7-6.   *File System Types*

Option	Description
async	All I/O to the file system should be done asynchronously
auto	Can be mounted with the **-a** option
defaults	Use default options: **rw**, **suid**, **dev**, **exec**, **auto**, **nouser**, and **async**
dev	Interprets character or block special devices on the file system
noauto	Can only be mounted explicitly. The **-a** option will not cause the file system to be mounted
exec	Permits execution of binaries
nouser	Forbids an ordinary (i.e., non-root) user to mount the file system
remount	Attempts to remount an already-mounted file system. This is commonly used to change the mount flags for a file system, especially to make a read-only file system writable
ro	Mounts the file system read-only
rw	Mounts the file system read-write
suid	Allows set-user-identifier or set-group-identifier bits to take effect
sync	All I/O to the file system should be done synchronously
user	Allows an ordinary user to mount the file system. Ordinary users always have the following options activated: **noexec**, **nosuid**, and **nodev**
nodev	Does not interpret character or block special devices on the file system
nosuid	Does not allow set-user-identifier or set-group-identifier bits to take effect

Table 7-7. *Options for File Sytems:* **-o** *and* **/etc/fstab**

General Option	Description
`secure`	Requires authentication. This is on by default
`ro`	Allows only read-only access
`rw`	Allows read-write access. This is the default
`noaccess`	This makes everything below the directory inaccessible for the named client
`link_absolute`	Leaves all symbolic links as they are. This is the default operation
`link_relative`	Converts absolute symbolic links (where the link contents start with a slash) into relative links by prepending the necessary number of forward slashes to get from the directory containing the link to the root on the server
User ID Mapping	
`squash_uids` `squash_gids`	Specifies a list of uids and gids that should be subject to anonymous mapping
`all_squash`	Maps all uids and gids to the anonymous user. Useful for NFS-exported public ftp directories, news spool directories, etc.
`no_all_squash`	This is the opposite option to **no_all_squash**, and is the default setting
`root_squash`	Maps requests from uid/gid 0 to the anonymous uid/gid
`no_root_squash`	Turns off root squashing. Does not map requests from uid/gid 0. This is the default
`anonuid` `anongid`	These options explicitly set the uid and gid of the anonymous account. This option is primarily useful for PC/NFS clients, where you might want all requests to appear to be from one user
`map_daemon`	Turns on dynamic uid/gid mapping. uids in NFS requests are translated to the equivalent server uids. uids in NFS replies are mapped the other way. The default setting is map identity, which leaves all uids untouched

Table 7-8.   **/etc/exports** Options

Option	Description
rsize=n	The number of bytes NFS uses when reading files from an NFS server. The default is 1024 bytes
wsize=n	The number of bytes NFS uses when writing files to an NFS server. The default is 1024 bytes
timeo=n	The value in tenths of a second before sending the first retransmission after a timeout. The default value is seven-tenths of a second
retry=n	The number of times to retry a backgrounded NFS mount operation before giving up. The default is 10,000 times
soft	Mounts system using soft mount
hard	Mounts system using hard mount. This is the default
intr	Allows NFS to interrupt the file operation and return to the calling program. The default is to not allow file operations to be interrupted
bg	If the first mount attempt times out, continue trying the mount in the background. The default is to fail without backgrounding
tcp	Mounts the NFS file system using the TCP protocol instead of the default UDP protocol

Table 7-9.   *NFS Options*

Command	Execution
tar *options files*	Backs up files to tape, device, or archive file
tar *options* **f** *archive_name filelist*	Backs up files to specific file or device specified as *archive_name filelist*. Can be file names or directories

Options

c	Creates a new archive
t	Lists the names of files in an archive
r	Appends files to an archive
u	Updates an archive with new and changed files; adds only those files that have been modified since they were archived or files that are not already present in the archive
w	Waits for a confirmation from the user before archiving each file; allows you to update an archive selectively
x	Extracts files from an archive
m	When extracting a file from an archive, no new time stamp is assigned
M	Creates multiple-volume archive that may be stored on several floppy disks
f *archive-name*	Saves the tape archive to the file archive-name instead of to the default tape device; when given an archive-name, the **f** option saves the tar archive in a file of that name
f *device-name*	Saves a tar archive to a device such as a floppy disk or tape. **/dev/fd0** is the device name for your floppy disk; the default device is held in **/etc/default/tar-file**
v	Displays each file name as it is archived
z	Compresses or decompresses archived files using **gzip**

Table 7-10.   *File Backups: tar*

Option	Execution
-c	Sends compressed version of file to standard output; each file listed is separately compressed **$ gzip -c mydata preface > myfiles.gz**
-d	Decompresses a compressed file; alternatively, you can use **gunzip** **$ gzip -d myfiles.gz** **$ gunzip myfiles.gz**
-h	Displays help listing
-l *file-list*	Displays compressed and uncompressed size of each file listed **$ gzip -l myfiles.gz**
-r *directory-name*	Recursively searches for specified directories and compresses all the files in them; the search begins from the current working directory; when used with **gunzip**, compressed files of a specified directory will be uncompressed
-v *file-list*	For each compressed or decompressed file, displays its name and the percentage of its reduction in size
-num	Determines the speed and size of the compression; the range is from -1 to -9. A lower number gives greater speed but less compression, resulting in a larger file that compresses and decompresses quickly; -1 gives the quickest compression, but with the largest size; -9 results in a very small file that takes longer to compress and decompress. The default is -6

Table 7-11. gzip *Options*

Command	Execution
mcopy *filename filename*	Copies a file to and from an MS-DOS disk and your Linux system. The following copies a file from an MS-DOS diskette to your Linux system **mcopy a:**/filename directory-or-filename The following copies a file from Linux for an MS-DOS diskette in your floppy drive **mcopy** *filename* **a:**/*filename*
mcd *directory-name*	Changes directory on your MS-DOS file system. The following lists files on an MS-DOS disk in your floppy drive **mdir a:**
mdir	Lists the files on an MS-DOS disk in your floppy drive
mattrib	Changes the attribute of an MS-DOS file
mdel *filename*	Deletes an MS-DOS file
mformat	Adds an MS-DOS file system to a diskette
mlabel	Makes a volume label
mmd *directory-name*	Makes an MS-DOS directory
mrd *directory-name*	Removes an MS-DOS directory
mread *filename filename*	Low-level reads (copies) an MS-DOS file to Unix
mren *filename filename*	Renames an MS-DOS file
mtype *filename*	Displays contents of an MS-DOS file
mwrite *filename filename*	Low-level writes (copies) a Unix file to MS-DOS

Table 7-12.   *Mtools Access Commands*

PART THREE

Networking

Chapter Eight

Electronic Mail

279

Your Linux system has electronic mail utilities that allow you to send messages to other users on your system or other systems, such as those on the Internet. You can send and receive messages in a variety of ways, depending on the electronic mail utility you use. This book presents two of the most popular electronic mail utilities available on Linux: Mail and Elm. Each of these defines a different type of interface. Though all electronic mail utilities perform the same basic tasks of receiving and sending messages, they tend to have very different interfaces. The Mail utility employs a basic command line interface, operating within its own shell. It is found on most Linux systems and is considered a standard. The Elm utility uses a full screen interface and employs single key commands much like those used for the Vi editor. Both are provided by your OpenLinux system enclosed with this book.

In addition to sending messages by electronic mail, you can also use the Write and Talk utilities to communicate directly with other users who are currently logged in. These utilities set up a direct connection with another user, allowing you to communicate as you would over a radio or telephone.

Local and Internet Addresses

Each user on a Linux system has a mail address, and whenever you send mail, you will be required to provide the address of the user to whom you are sending the message. For users on your local Linux system, addresses can consist of only the user's login name. However, when sending messages to users on other systems, you need to know not only the login name but also the address of the system they are on. Internet addresses require that the system address be uniquely identified.

Most systems have Internet addresses that you can use to send mail. Internet addresses use a form of addressing called domain addressing. A system is assigned a domain name, which, when combined with the system name, gives the system a unique address. This domain name is separated from the system name by a period and may be further qualified by additional domain names. Here is the syntax for domain addresses:

```
login-name@system-name.domain-name
```

Systems that are part of a local network are often given the same domain name. The domain name for both the **garnet** and **violet** systems at U.C. Berkeley is **berkeley.edu**. To send a message to **chris** on the **garnet** system, you simply include the domain name:

chris@garnet.berkeley.edu.

In the next example, a message is sent to **chris**, located on the **garnet** system, using domain addressing.

```
$ mail chris@garnet.berkeley.edu < mydata
```

Early domain names reflect the fact that the Internet was first developed in the United States. They qualify Internet addresses by category such as commercial, military, or educational systems. The domain name **.com** indicates a commercial organization, whereas **.edu** is used for educational institutions. As the Internet developed into a global network, a set of international domain names were established. These domain names indicate the country in which a system is located, for example, **.fr** represents France, **.jp** represents japan, and **.us** represents the United States. Table 8-1 lists several common international domain names.

Mail Transport Agents: deliver, sendmail, smail

Mail is transported to and from destinations using mail transport agents. The **deliver** agent handles mail exchanged between users on your own local system. **sendmail** and **smail** send and receive mail from destinations on the Internet or at other sites on a network. To send mail over the Intenet they use the Simple Mail Transport Protocol (SMTP). For the more direct UUCP connections they use the UUCP protocols. **sendmail** is a smaller agent that is easy to configure, whereas **smail** is more complex as well as more powerful. Your Caldera Network Desktop automatically installs and configures **sendmail** for you. Upon starting up your Caldera system you can send and receive messages over the Internet. If you are using a different Linux distribution, you may have to install and configure the Mail Transport Agents yourself. You can also download updated versions of these agents from Linux ftp sites and install them yourself.

Before users on your system can send and receive mail locally you have to configure a loopback interface. This will enable your system to address itself, allowing it to send and receive mail to and from itself. A loopback interface uses the host name **localhost** and a special IP address that is reserved for use by local systems, **127.0.0.1**. The Caldera Network Desktop package already has such a loopback interface installed.

You can examine your **/etc/hosts** file to see if your loopback interface has been configured as the local host. You will see **localhost 127.0.0.1** listed as the first entry. If there is no entry for "localhost", you may have to create a loopback interface yourself using the **ifconfig** and **route** commands as shown here. **lo** is the term for loopback.

```
ifconfig lo 127.0.0.1
route add -net 127.0.0.0
```

Check to see if these commands are in your network initialization file, **rc.inet1**, in the **/etc/rc.d/** directory. If not, you should add them. Once added, the loopback interface will automatically be created every time you start up your system. For the Redhat version of Linux the initialization file is **inet** in the **/etc/rc.d/init/** directory. See Chapter 20 on Network Administration for a detailed discussion of these commands and files.

Accessing Mail on Remote POP Mail Servers: popclient

Your Linux system is equipped to send any messages through the Internet, whether you are directly connected through a network or dialing into an Internet Service Provider (ISP). However, if you are using an ISP, most likely you will be using that ISP's mail server to receive mail. The user name you use to login to the ISP, is usually also used as your email name on the ISP's mail server. For example, if you logged into an ISP using the login name Larisa, your email name would also be Larisa. Mail sent to you using that email name is placed in the ISP's mail server, where you can pick it up when you login. The type of mail server used to receive mail is usually a POP server. POP stands for Post Office Protocol. To access your mail you access your ISP's POP server.

Programs such as **mail** and **elm** will read mail sent to and received by your Linux system. These programs currently do not have the ability to access mail on your ISP's POP server, as that is a separate remote system. However, you can use the **popclient** program to download mail from your ISP's POP server to your own system, and then read it using **mail** or **elm**.

To use **popclient** you have to know the Internet address of your ISP's POP server. This usually begins with popd, for example, **popd.ix.netcom.com** for the Netcom POP server. Check with your ISP for the correct name. You also have to determine if the POP server uses a pop2 protocol or a pop3 protocol. Most systems use pop3. You indicate a pop3 protocol with a **-3** option and pop2 with a **-2**. You also have to provide the email name that you use on the ISP's POP server. For this you use the **-u** option followed by the email name. The syntax for the popclient command for a pop3 server follows:

```
popclient -3 -u username pop-server
```

Once you have executed the command you will be prompted for a password. This is the password to your email account on the POP server. Usually this is the same as the password you use to login to the ISP, though, some ISPs allow you to have a different one. If you want to skip the password prompt you can include with the **-p** option with the password when you invoke **popclient**.

```
popclient -3 -u username -p password pop-server
```

To use **popclient** just connect to your ISP and then enter the **popclient** commands with the options and the POP server name on the command line. You will see messages telling you if there is mail and, if so, how many messages are being downloaded. You can then use **mail**, **elm**, or any other mail program to read the messages.

```
# popclient -3 -u mylogin  -p mypass  popd.ix.netcom.com
NETCOM (Version: 1.6 Rel (SB)) at ix10 starting : built on Jun 25
1997 16:07:34.
2 messages in folder
reading message 1.
reading message 2.
[root@turtle /root]# mail
Mail version 5.5-kw 5/30/95.  Type ? for help.
"/var/spool/mail/root": 2 messages 2 new
>N  1 root@turtle.trek.com  Fri Aug 29 00:05   15/555    "birthday"
 N  2 root@turtle.trek.com  Fri Aug 29 00:05   15/552    "party"
& q
Held 2 messages in /var/spool/mail/root
```

The messages downloaded are placed in the mailbox of the user executing the **popclient** command. If you login to your Linux system as Chris, then the messages are placed in the Chris mailbox. If you login as Larisa, they are placed in the Larisa mailbox. You can specify a specific mailbox with the **-o** option, adding the messages to that mailbox file, instead of to the one's the system maintains.

It may be convenient to integrate both **popclient** and mail program commands into one script. That way you just have to execute one command to have **popclient** download messages and have a mail program start up and read them. **popclient** has return values that you can use to check if there were messages or not (the popclient mail pages). **popclient** returns a 0 if there were messages, 1 if there were none, and other values if an error occurred. The following script, called **popelm**, used **popclient** to check for messages and download them. If there are messages, then **elm** is called to display them. If there were no messages, then the "No Mail" message is displayed (remember to use **chmod 755** *script-name* to make the script executable).

popelm

```
#!/usr/bin/bash
if popclient -3  -u mylogin -p
mypass  my-ISP-POP-server
    then
        elm
    else
        echo "No mail"
fi
```

The Mail Utility

With the Mail utility, you can easily send and receive messages to and from other users. Sending a message is as simple as typing in a login name followed by the text of the message. Receiving messages is merely a matter of selecting a message from a list of received messages. When sending messages in Mail, there are commands for modifying the message text and what is known as the message header. When receiving messages, you can reply to them, save them in files, or simply delete them. There is a special initialization file, **.mailrc**, that configures your Mail utility with special features such as aliases.

What is known now as the Mail utility was originally created for BSD Unix and called, simply, **mail**. Later versions of Unix System V adopted the BSD **mail** utility and renamed it **mailx**. Most Linux systems, including Redhat Linux, use this **mailx** utility and simply refer to it as Mail.

Sending Messages

The message you send in Mail can be something you type in at the keyboard, or it can be the contents of a file. While you are entering a message at the keyboard, you can edit it using special tilde commands. These commands allow you to save a message, redisplay what you have written, or invoke an editor with which to edit the message.

To send a message, type **mail** along with the address of the person to whom you are sending the message. Press ENTER and you will be prompted for a subject. Enter the subject of the message and press ENTER again. At this point, you are placed in input mode. Anything typed in is taken as the contents of the message. Pressing ENTER adds a new line to the text. When you have finished typing your message, press CTRL-**d** on a line of its own to end the message and send it. You will see EOT (end-of-transmission) displayed after you press CTRL-**d**.

In the next example, the user sends a message to another user whose address is **robert**. The subject of the message is "Birthday." After typing in the text of the message, the user presses CTRL-**d**.

```
$ mail robert
Subject: Birthday
    Your present is in the mail
    really.

^D
EOT
$
```

Standard Input and Redirection

The Mail utility receives input from the standard input. By default, the standard input is taken from what the user enters on the keyboard. However, with redirection, standard input can be taken from a file. Therefore, with redirection, you can use the contents of a file as the message for the Mail program. You can create and edit a text file with the Vi editor and then use that text file as redirected input for the Mail utility. In the next example, the file **mydata** is redirected as input for the Mail utility and sent to **robert**.

```
$ mail robert < mydata
```

Notice that when you mail a file through redirection, you do not have a chance to enter a subject for the actual mail message. However, the **mail** command has a **-s** option that allows you to specify the subject of a message on the command line. This subject will then show up in the header list of the person who receives the file. Table 8-2 lists several other Mail options that are discussed later in the chapter. In the next example, Robert sends the file **mydata** and specifies the subject as "party."

```
$ mail -s party chris < mydata
```

Sending Mail to Several Users

You can send a message to several users at the same time by listing those users' addresses as arguments on the command line following the **mail** command. In the next example, the user sends the same message to both **chris** and **aleina**.

```
$ mail chris aleina
Subject: Birthday
   Your present is in the mail
   really.
^D
EOT
$
```

You can also use redirection to send the contents of a file to several users at once. In the next example, the contents of the **mydata** file is sent to both **robert** and **aleina**.

```
$ mail robert aleina < mydata
```

Copying a Message to a File

You may also want to save a copy of the message you are sending for yourself. You can copy a mail message to a file in your account by specifying a file name on the command line after the addresses. The file name must be a relative or full path name, containing a slash. A path name identifies an argument as a file name to which mail will save a copy of the message being sent. In the next example, the user saves a copy of the message to a file called **birthnote**. A relative path name is used, with the period denoting the current working directory: **./birthnote**.

```
$ mail robert ./birthnote
Subject: Birthday
Your present is in the mail
really.
^D
EOT
$ cat birthnote
Subject: Birthday
   Your present is in the mail
   really.
$
```

The technique works equally as well when using redirection and multiple addresses:

```
$ mail robert aleina < mydata ./birthnote
```

Editing Mail Messages: The Tilde Commands

There are two components to a message: the header and the text. The header contains information about the message, such as the addresses of people to whom the message is to be sent and the subject. The addresses are specified as arguments of the **mail** command. The Mail utility then prompts the user to enter the subject of the message. After entering the subject, the user enters the text of the message.

A set of message commands known as tilde commands allow you to perform editing operations both on the header and the text. A tilde command consists of a one-character command preceded by a tilde that is entered on a line of its own. The tilde (which functions as a special character) and the command are not taken as part of the message. Should you need to enter the tilde as a character in the message, you can do so by entering two tildes next to each other, **~~**. The set of commonly used tilde commands are listed in Table 8-2. You can also obtain a listing of the tilde commands with the **~?** tilde command.

There are then three basic kinds of operations you perform in sending a message: you enter header information, you enter the text of the message, and you enter tilde commands to perform operations on either the header or the text. Tilde commands for the header allow you to change address and subject information. The tilde commands for the text allow you to redisplay, save, and use an editor to modify the text.

Tilde Commands for the Message Text

Unlike an editor, there is no command mode when entering the text of a mail message. Once you have entered the subject and pressed ENTER, you are placed into an input mode in which you enter the text of the message. The input mode for the Mail utility is subject to all the same restrictions of the input mode in the Vi editor. You are simply typing in a stream of characters. The only kind of correction you may perform is BACKSPACE, which will erase the character to the immediate left of the cursor on that line. No other type of correction is allowed. You may not move the cursor or perform any other type of editing operation.

You can overcome all the restrictions of the Mail input mode by invoking the Vi editor with the **~v** command. You enter the **~v** command on a line by itself, followed by ENTER. Once you have accessed the Vi editor, your message can be edited like any other text. In effect, you are using the Vi editor to compose your message instead of relying on the Mail input mode. In the Vi editor, the message you have typed in so far will be displayed as text to be edited.

The Vi editor's save commands will save to the Mail message, not to a file. When you exit the Vi editor with the **zz** command, you save to the Mail message and return to the input mode of the Mail utility. However, the text of the message will not be redisplayed. Instead, the word "continue" in parentheses is displayed on the screen.

You can then enter more text, execute other tilde commands, or end and send the message with CTRL-**d**.

Though the invocation of the Vi editor is one of the most useful tilde commands, you may also want to perform basic operations on the text such as redisplaying it, saving the text to a file, or reading in text from another file.

You can redisplay your message at any time with the **~p** tilde command, which prints out the message entered so far. When you enter the **~p** command on a line by itself and press ENTER, everything you have typed in will be displayed. It is sometimes reassuring to enter the **~p** command after returning from the Vi editor. If you do so, you will notice that all the text edited and entered while in the Vi editor is displayed as the message.

```
$ mail aleina
Subject: Files
    This is a list of all the
    students in my class.
~p
_____
Message contains:
To: aleina
Subject: Files
    This is a list of all the
    students in my class.
(continue)
^D
EOT
$
```

There are also tilde commands that allow you to save your message to a file, or to read the contents of a file into your message. The **~w** tilde command will save your message, and **~r** will read in text from another file, making it part of the message. You enter the **~w** command with the name of the file the message is to be written to. The **~r** command is entered with the name of the file to be read. In the next example, **~w mydata** saves the input message to the file **mydata**. The **~r** command then reads the contents of the file **mynames** and inserts it into the Mail message.

```
$ mail aleina
Subject: Files
    This is a list of all the
    students in my class.
~w mydata
"mydata" 2/48
```

```
~r mynames
"mynames" 3/15
~p
_____
Message contains:
To: aleina
Subject: Files
    This is a list of all the
    students in my class.
mary
joe
harold
(continue)
^D
EOT
$
```

Should you change your mind and decide that you do not want to send the message, you can quit Mail with either the **~x** or the **~q** tilde command. The message is abandoned and you are returned to the shell. If you use the **~q** command, the text is saved in a file called **dead.letter**.

```
$ mail aleina
Subject: Files
    This is a list of all the
    students in my class.
~x
$
```

You can also process the text of your message through filters. You can use the current text of your message as input to a filter whose output will then replace the text of your message. For example, if your message consists of a list, you can pipe the list to the **sort** filter, and then have the contents of the message replaced by the sorted output. The ~| tilde command allows you to pipe your text through a filter. ~| takes as its argument a filter. The text of the message becomes the standard input that is piped into the filter. The output of the filter then replaces the message. In the next example, the user makes use of the ~| sort command to sort the list in the message.

```
$ mail george
Subject: Names
```

```
      mary
      joe
      harold
~| sort
~p
_____
Message contains:
To: george
Subject: Names
      harold
      joe
      mary
(continue)
^D
EOT
```

One very helpful filter, **fmt**, was designed especially to format Mail messages. Often, when you are entering a message, the lines of text are not of an even length, as they are in a word processor. The **fmt** filter will format your lines so that they all have a standard length of approximately 72 characters. Lines beginning with spaces or tabs are taken as the beginning of paragraphs. In the next example, the user makes use of **fmt** to format the message.

```
$ mail george
Subject: Title
George,
    Have you thought of a new
title for the
project we were discussing
last month?
It should have a new theme based on
the realistic expectations of
our target audience.
~| fmt
(continue)
~p
_____
Message contains:
To: george
Subject: Title
George,
```

```
    Have you thought of a new title for the project we were
discussing last month?  It should have a new theme based on the
realistic expectations of our target audience.
(continue)
^D
EOT
$
```

Tilde Commands for the Message Header

Other tilde commands allow you to change components of the message header. There are four possible components of a message header: the address list, the subject, the carbon copy list, and the blind carbon copy list. The two carbon copy components are optional. You must always have an address list and, though you may leave the subject empty, you will usually be prompted to type in something for it.

The list of addresses to whom the message is being sent is initially entered on the command line when Mail is invoked. If, while you are entering your message, you want to add more addresses, you can do so with the **~t** tilde command.

The **~s** command allows you to enter a new subject for your message. To change your subject entry, type the **~s** command followed by the new subject. In the next example, both the subject and the address list are changed. The addressee **larisa** is added to the address list. Now the message will be sent to both **larisa** and **aleina**. Then the subject is changed from "Files" to "Class Roster."

```
$ mail aleina
Subject: Files
This is a list of all the
students in my class.
~t larisa
~s Class Roster
_____

Message contains:
To: aleina larisa
Subject: Class Roster
    This is a list of all the
    students in my class.
(continue)
^D
EOT
$
```

You may want to send an associate a copy of a message you sent to someone else. That copy would contain the address of the person it was sent to. In effect, you are giving someone a carbon copy of a message you sent out, including the header, not just the text. To do this, you create a carbon copy list of addresses with the **~c** command. Enter **~c** and the list of addresses that will receive a copy of the message.

Everyone receiving the copy and those receiving the original message will have this carbon copy list printed at the end of the message. If you do not wish to have a person's address printed in this list, and yet still have that person receive a copy of the message, you can send the carbon copy using a blind carbon copy list. Enter the **~b** command followed by the addresses that you do not want printed at the end of the message. Only those addresses on the normal carbon copy list will appear on the message. In the next example, **larisa** and **marylou** will receive carbon copies and have their addresses listed at the end of each copy of the message. **valerie**, on the other hand, will also receive a carbon copy, but will not have her address listed in any of the copies.

```
$ mail aleina
Subject: Files
This is a list of all the
students in my class.
~c larisa marylou
~b valerie
~p
_____
Message contains:
To: aleina
Subject: Files
Cc: larisa marylou
Bcc: valerie
    This is a list of all the
    students in my class.
(continue)
^D
EOT
$
```

If you should need to change all the header components, you can use the **~h** command to change them all at once. You will first be prompted for a new address list, then a new subject, and finally, a new carbon copy list.

Receiving Mail: The Mail Shell

As messages are sent to you, they are placed in your mailbox. A mailbox is really a file filled with recently received messages that remain there until you retrieve them. To retrieve messages, you invoke the Mail utility by typing **mail** by itself on the command line. The Mail utility is a complex program for managing messages with its own shell and its own set of commands and prompt. Upon invoking the Mail utility, you enter the Mail shell, where you can receive messages, reply to messages, and even send new messages. The commonly used Mail commands are listed in Table 8-3.

If there is no mail waiting in the mailbox, a notice saying that there is no mail will be displayed. You only enter the Mail shell if messages are waiting. In the next example, the user attempts to enter the Mail shell. However, since there are no messages waiting, a simple notice is displayed, and the user remains in his login shell.

```
$ mail
Sorry, no mail
$
```

When you first enter the Mail shell, a list of header summaries for each message is displayed. Summary information is arranged into fields beginning with the status of the message and the message number. The status of a message is indicated by a single uppercase letter, usually **N**, for "new," or **U**, for "unread." A message number, used for easy reference to your messages, follows the status field. The next field is the address of the sender, followed by the date and time it was received, and then the number of lines and characters in the message. The last field contains the subject the sender gave for the message. After the header summaries, the Mail shell displays its prompt, a question mark, **?**. At the Mail prompt, you enter commands that operate on the messages. Here is an example of a Mail header summary:

```
$ mail
Mail version 5.5-kw 5/30/95. Type ? for help.
"/var/spool/mail/chris": 3 messages 3 new
>N  1 valerie    Tue Feb 11 10:14:32 5/44    "Budget"
 N  2 aleina     Wed Feb 12 12:30:17 28/537 "Birthday"
 N  3 robert     Fri Feb 14  8:15:24 16/293 "Homework"
?
```

Message Lists and the Current Message Marker

Mail references messages either through a message list or through the current message marker (>). The greater-than sign is placed before a message that is considered the current message. The current message is referenced by default when no message number is included with a Mail command. For example, in the preceding header summaries, if no message number is given in the command, then message 1 will be referenced, since it is the current message. When a message is referenced in a command, it automatically becomes the current message, and the current message marker moves to its header. If you were to display message 2, then message 2 would become the new current message.

You can also reference a message using a message list. Many Mail commands can operate on several messages. You reference several messages in a Mail command using a message list consisting of several message numbers. You can also specify a range of messages by entering the number of the first message in the range followed by a dash and then the message number of the last message in the range. Given the messages in the previous example, you can reference all three messages with **1-3**.

You can also use special characters to reference certain messages. The **^** references the first message; for example, **^-3** specifies the range of messages from the first message to the third message. The **$** references the last message; so **4-$** would reference messages from 4 to the last message. **$** by itself just references the last message. The period, **.**, references the current message. And the asterisk, *****, references all messages. For example, to display all messages, you could use the command **p ***.

You can also select a group of messages based on the addresses of senders or the subject. An address by itself constitutes a message list that references all messages sent by the user with that address. **robert** is a message list referencing all messages sent by Robert. A slash followed by a pattern references all messages whose subject field contains that pattern. For example, **/birthday** is a message list referencing all messages with the subject "birthday."

You can also reference messages according to their status by entering a colon followed by a character representing the status of the messages you want. The characters are lowercase versions of the uppercase status codes used in the header summaries. For example, **n** represents new messages that are indicated with a status code **N** in header summaries. **:n** is a message list that references all new messages. The command **p :n** would display all new messages; **:u** would reference all unread messages—those with a status code of **U**.

Displaying Messages

Another set of commands is used to display messages. Simply entering the number of the message by itself will display that message. The message will then be output, screen by screen. Press the SPACEBAR or the ENTER key to continue to the next screen. If you enter the number 1 at the Mail prompt, the first message will be displayed for you.

If you want to look at several messages, one after the other, you need only enter their message numbers at the Mail prompt. Other commands allow you to reference and display messages according to their position with respect to the current message. You can display the message before the current message with the **-** command. If you use a number with the **-** command, you can reference a message positioned several messages before the current message. If message 6 were the current message, **-4** would reference message 2. You can also reference messages after the current message. The **+** and **n** commands and the ENTER key all display the next message after the current message.

If you want to display a range of messages, you need to use the **p** and **t** commands. These commands, like most other commands in Mail, take as their argument a message list. In a message list you can specify a set of messages to be referenced or a range of messages, as well as a single message. You specify a set of messages by listing their numbers one after the other, separated by a space, for example, **1 3** will reference messages 1 and 3. **p 1 3** will display messages 1 and 3. You specify a range using a dash; for example, **1-3** will reference messages 1, 2, and 3, and **p 1-3** will display all three messages.

The **p** or **t** command without a message list will display the current message, **>**. You can also use **+** or **-** with either command to display the messages before or after the current message. In the next example, the **p** command without a message number prints out the current message, message 1. Then the second message is displayed using the **p** command and the message number.

```
Mail version 5.5-kw 5/30/95. Type ? for help.
"/var/spool/mail/chris": 3 messages 3 new
>N 1 valerie    Tue Feb 11 10:14:32 5/44    "Budget"
 N 2 aleina     Wed Feb 12 12:30:17 28/537 "Birthday"
 N 3 robert     Fri Feb 14  8:15:24 16/293 "Homework"
& p
From valerie Wed Feb 11 10:14:17 PST 1996
To: chris
Subject: Budget
Status: R

You are way under budget
so far.
Congratulations

        Val

& p 2
From aleina Wed Feb 11 10:14:17 PST 1996
To: chris
Subject: Birthday
Status: R

Yes, I did remember your present

        Aleina


&
```

The following table lists several examples of the **p** command using differently composed message lists. Remember the use of special characters **^**, **$**, and ***** to reference the first, last, and all messages, as well as the **:** to reference special types of messages. You can also reference by addresses or subjects.

Command	Function
p $	Displays the last message
p *	Displays all messages
p ^-3	Displays from the first to the third message
p .-$	Displays from the current message to the last message
p n	Displays the next message, not the current one
p +2	Displays second message down from the current message
p /budget	Displays messages with the pattern "budget" in their subject field
p dylan	Displays messages sent by the user with the address "dylan"
p :n	Displays newly received messages
p :u	Displays previously unread messages
p :r	Redisplays the messages you have already read

After a message has been displayed, you are again given the Mail prompt, **&**. However, the header summaries are not automatically redisplayed. Using the **h** command (for "headers"), you can redisplay the header summaries at any time. In the next example, the user enters the **h** command to redisplay the list of message headers.

```
& h
>N 1 valerie    Tue Feb 11 10:14:32 5/44    "Budget"
 N 2 aleina     Wed Feb 12 12:30:17 28/537 "Birthday"
 N 3 robert     Fri Feb 14  8:15:24 16/293 "Homework"
&
```

Sometimes the list of headers will be so long that it will take up more than one screen. In that case, the **h** command will only display the first screen of headers. The command **z+** and **z-** move forward and backward to the next and previous screen of headers. If you know the number of the particular message header you want, you can use the **h** command with that number to display the header. **h12** will display the header for message 12, as well as the headers before and after it.

Deleting and Undeleting Messages

Unless you instruct Mail to erase a message, any messages you have read will be automatically saved when you leave the Mail shell. You can erase a message using the delete command, **d**. Entering the **d** command with a message number deletes that message. The command **d2** deletes message 2. You can delete several messages at once by listing a set or a range of message numbers: **d 2-4** deletes messages 2, 3, and 4. If you enter the **d** command without a message number, then the current message, **>**, is deleted. In the next example, the user deletes the third message.

```
Mail version 5.5-kw 5/30/95. Type ? for help.
"/var/spool/mail/chris": 3 messages 3 new
>N 1 valerie     Tue Feb 11 10:14:32 5/44     "Budget"
 N 2 aleina      Wed Feb 12 12:30:17 28/537  "Birthday"
 N 3 robert      Fri Feb 14  8:15:24 16/293  "Homework"
& d 3
& h
>N 1 valerie     Tue Feb 11 10:14:32 5/44     "Budget"
 N 2 aleina      Wed Feb 12 12:30:17 28/537  "Birthday"
&
```

Before leaving the Mail shell, if you change your mind and want some of the deleted messages to be saved, you can do so using the **u** command. The **u** command lets you restore a message that has been deleted within a given Mail session. The delete command does not immediately erase a message. All messages are held until you quit the Mail shell. Again, you can specify several messages or a range of messages. The command **u3** restores message 3; **u 2-4** restores messages 2, 3, and 4. For example:

```
& h
>N 1 valerie     Tue Feb 11 10:14:32 5/44     "Budget"
 N 2 aleina      Wed Feb 12 12:30:17 28/537  "Birthday"
& u 3
& h
>N 1 valerie     Tue Feb 11 10:14:32 5/44     "Budget"
 N 2 aleina      Wed Feb 12 12:30:17 28/537  "Birthday"
 N 3 robert      Fri Feb 14  8:15:24 16/293  "Homework"
&
```

Replying to Messages and Sending New Messages: R, r, m, and v

While receiving messages, you can also send your own messages. You can either reply to messages that you have just received or send entirely new messages, just as you would using the **mail** command and an address. In replying to a message, Mail allows you to automatically make use of the header information in a received message. You need only specify the message that you are replying to and then type in your reply.

You use the **R** and **r** commands to reply to a message you have received. The **R** command entered with a message number will generate a header for sending a message and then place you into the input mode to type in the message. The header will consist of the address of the sender and the subject specified by the sender. The subject header will also have the added title **Re:**, to indicate a reply. Simply type in your reply and end with CTRL-**d** on a line of its own. The reply will be immediately sent to the sender.

```
Mail version 5.5-kw 5/30/95. Type ? for help.
"/var/spool/mail/chris": 3 messages 3 new
>N 1 valerie     Tue Feb 11 10:14:32 5/44    "Budget"
 N 2 aleina      Wed Feb 12 12:30:17 28/537 "Birthday"
 N 3 robert      Fri Feb 14  8:15:24 16/293 "Homework"

& R 2
To: aleina
Subject: RE: Birthday
Is it a really big present?
^D
EOT
&
```

Suppose the sender has sent the message you received to several users. You can use the **r** command to send your reply not only to the sender, but also to all the users the message was sent to. Be careful of the **r** command. You may not want your reply sent to all the people who received the message. If you only want your reply sent to the sender alone, you need to use the **R** command.

You can also create and send a new message using the **m** command. Messages are sent just as they are sent from your login shell, except that the **m** command is used instead of **mail**. In the next example, the user sends a new message to **cecelia**.

```
Mail version 5.5-kw 5/30/95. Type ? for help.
"/var/spool/mail/chris": 3 messages 3 new
```

```
>N 1 valerie     Tue Feb 11 10:14:32 5/44    "Budget"
 N 2 aleina      Wed Feb 12 12:30:17 28/537  "Birthday"
 N 3 robert      Fri Feb 14  8:15:24 16/293  "Homework"


& m cecelia
Subject: Birthday
Did you remember my present?
oops


^D
EOT
&
```

As with any Mail message, you can use the tilde commands for both message replies and new messages sent from the Mail shell. With the **~v** tilde command, you can edit a message reply in the Vi editor and then return to the input mode of the message reply. Upon sending the reply with a CTRL-**d**, you return to the Mail shell prompt.

Suppose that in sending a message, you wish to include the contents of one of the messages that you have received. For example, in composing a reply to someone, you may want to include the text of the message that the user sent you. Or you may want to include a message you received from one person in a reply to another, in effect, forwarding the message. With the **~m** and **~f** tilde commands, you can read the contents of a message into the message you are sending. The **~m** and **~f** tilde commands take as their argument a message list, usually a message number. For example, the tilde command **~m 2** reads the contents of the second message into the new message you are currently composing. The **~m** and **~f** commands differ in that the **~m** command will indent each line of the message it reads in, distinguishing it from the rest of your message. The **~f** command performs no indentation, inserting the message as is.

You can also use the **v** command to directly edit a message that you received. For example, you might want to annotate a message with your own comments before you save it. Or you might want to add your comments directly to the message and then use **~m** to use it in a reply or to send to someone else. To edit a specific message, you simply specify the message number after the **v** command: **v 3** will edit the third message.

Quitting the Mail Shell

The **q** command quits the Mail utility and returns you to the login shell command line. Messages that you have read are placed in a file called **mbox** in your home directory. The Mail utility notifies you of how many messages were saved in your **mbox** file. By default, these messages are removed from your incoming mailbox. If for some reason you do not want a message removed, use the command **pre** with the message number before you quit. The message will remain in your incoming mailbox file.

If you quit before reading a message, the message remains in your incoming mailbox file, waiting for the next time you enter the Mail utility to read messages. The next time you enter the Mail shell, these messages are displayed in the message list with the letter **U** placed before them. This indicates that they are previously received messages that are as yet unread.

```
Mail version 5.5-kw 5/30/95. Type ? for help.
"/var/spool/mail/chris": 3 messages 2 new
>N 1 valerie    Tue Feb 11 10:14:32 5/44    "Budget"
 N 2 cecelia    Wed Feb 12 12:30:17 28/537 "Birthday"
& q
Saved 1 message in mbox
$
```

You can also exit the Mail shell with the **x** command. The **x** command is like a generalized undo command. Any messages that you have deleted during this Mail session will be undeleted.

Saving and Accessing Messages in Mailbox Files: s and S

Instead of saving messages in the **mbox** file, you can use the **s** command to explicitly save a message to a file of your choice. However, the **s** command saves a message with its header, in effect, creating another mailbox file. You can then later access this mailbox file using the Mail utility, much the same way that **mail** accesses waiting messages.

You save a message with the **s** command by typing **s** with the message number, followed by the name of the file to which the message is to be saved. If the file already exists, the message will simply be appended to the end of the file. In the next example, the command **s2 family_msgs** saves the second message to the **family_msgs** file. More than one message can be saved to the same file by specifying a set or range of message numbers: **s1-3 family_msgs** saves messages 1, 2, and 3 to the file **family_msgs**.

```
Mail version 5.5-kw 5/30/95. Type ? for help.
"/var/spool/mail/chris": 3 messages 3 new
>N 1 valerie    Tue Feb 11 10:14:32 5/44    "Budget"
 N 2 aleina     Wed Feb 12 12:30:17 28/537 "Birthday"
 N 3 robert     Fri Feb 14  8:15:24 16/293 "Homework"
& s 2 family_msgs
```

You can save messages to whatever files that you specify. Often it helps to organize messages from a specific sender into one file and name that file with the sender's address. For example, all messages from **robert** could be saved in a file called **robert**. Instead of the **s** command, you can use the **S** command to do this automatically for you. The **S** command followed by a message list will save that message to a file that has the name of the message's sender. If the file does not exist, **S** will create it. In the next example, the user saves message 3 to a file named after the message's sender, in this case **robert**.

```
Mail version 5.5-kw 5/30/95. Type ? for help.
"/var/spool/mail/chris": 3 messages 3 new
>N 1 valerie    Tue Feb 11 10:14:32 5/44    "Budget"
 N 2 aleina     Wed Feb 12 12:30:17 28/537 "Birthday"
 N 3 robert     Fri Feb 14  8:15:24 16/293 "Homework"
& S 3
& q
$ ls
mbox robert
$
```

Saving messages to a file with their message headers creates a mailbox file that you can read and manage using the Mail utility. The headers provide the Mail utility with information it needs to reference messages by a message number, display a header list, delete messages, and execute any other Mail commands. You can access a mailbox file either by invoking the Mail utility with the **-f** option and the mailbox file name, or, if you are already using Mail, by executing the **folder** command that switches to a specified mailbox file. For example, the command **mail -f family_msgs** accesses the mailbox file **family_msgs**. Each message in the **family_msgs** mailbox file will then be displayed in a message list. The Mail commands such as **d** and **p** will work on these messages.

```
$ mail -f family_msgs
Mail version 5.5. Type ? for help.
"family_msgs": 1 message
 >  1 aleina     Wed Feb 12 12:30:17 28/537 "Birthday"
&
```

Mail is designed to operate on any mailbox file that you specify. By default, when you invoke Mail, you automatically begin to operate on your incoming mailbox where the system places newly received mail. You can, however, switch to another mailbox file at any time and operate on the messages there. You can switch to yet another mailbox file, and so on, as you wish, or switch back to your incoming mailbox. To switch to another mailbox file, you enter the **folder** command followed by the name of the mailbox file. The header summaries for this mailbox file will then be displayed, and you can perform operations on messages. To switch back to your incoming mailbox, you enter **folder** followed by the symbol **%**, which represents the name of your incoming mailbox. You can also switch back and forth between two mailboxes using the **#** symbol for the mailbox file name. **#** represents the previous mailbox file accessed.

In the next example, the user begins Mail with the incoming mailbox and then uses the **folder** command to switch to the **family_msgs** mailbox file. The user then switches back to the incoming mailbox with the **folder %** command.

```
$ mail
Mail version 5.5-kw 5/30/95. Type ? for help.
"/var/spool/mail/chris": 2 messages 2 new
>N 1 valerie    Tue Feb 11 10:14:32 5/44    "Budget"
 N 2 robert     Fri Feb 14  8:15:24 16/293 "Homework"
& folder family_msgs
Held 2 messages in /var/spool/mail/chris
"family_msgs": 1 message
>  1 aleina     Wed Feb 12 12:30:17 28/537 "Birthday"
& folder %
"/var/spool/mail/chris": 2 messages 2 new
>N 1 valerie    Tue Feb 11 10:14:32 5/44    "Budget"
 N 2 robert     Fri Feb 14  8:15:24 16/293 "Homework"
```

As mentioned previously, when you quit the Mail utility, the messages that you have read are saved with their headers in the **mbox** file. If the **mbox** file already exists, the new messages are appended to the end. You may want to go back and access a previously read message saved in **mbox**. Since the **mbox** file contains the message headers, it is a mailbox file that you can access with the Mail utility. You can access the **mbox** file either by invoking Mail with a **-f** option followed by the name **mbox**, (**mail -f mbox**), or by switching to **mbox** using the **folder** command and the symbol **&**, which represents the name of the file used to save your read messages (**folder &**). A list of header summaries for all your previously read messages is displayed with the headers. Mail commands such as **p** and **d** can display or delete them. You can even send replies to messages using the **R** or **r** commands. In the next example, the user invokes Mail to access previously read messages.

```
$ mail -f mbox
Mail version 5.5-kw 5/30/95. Type ? for help.
"/var/spool/mail/chris": 2 messages
>  1 marylou   Mon Feb 10 09:24:22 24/976   "Trip"
```

```
    2 dylan      Fri Feb  8 11:15:12 17/834   "Food"
&
```

Saving Message Text in Files: Sending and Receiving Files

Suppose you want to save only the text of a message without the header information. In this case, you use the **w** command to save a message to a file without the header. Its syntax is the same as that of the **s** command. **w1 newbudget** writes message 1 without its header to the file **newbudget**. The file **newbudget** is a standard text file, not a mailbox file. It cannot be accessed by the Mail utility.

```
Mail version 5.5-kw 5/30/95. Type ? for help.
"/var/spool/mail/chris": 3 messages 3 new
>N 1 valerie    Tue Feb 11 10:14:32 5/44    "Budget"
 N 2 aleina     Wed Feb 12 12:30:17 28/537 "List"
 N 3 robert     Fri Feb 14  8:15:24 16/293 "Homework"
& w 1 newbudget
```

You can make use of this feature to receive full documents from other users, instead of just messages. Any user can send you a text file through the Mail utility using redirection. Then you can use the **w** command to receive and save that text file. In turn, you can send a text file to another user who can then use the **w** command to receive that file.

To send a text file through the Mail utility, you must use redirection. The Mail utility's input mode accepts standard input. Standard input, in turn, can be redirected to receive input from a text file. In the next example, the user sends the file **complist** to **chris**.

```
$ mail chris < complist
```

When you receive the text file, a Mail header is attached to the file. To save the file without the Mail header, you use the **w** command. If the **complist** file was received as message 1, then the command **w1 complist** saves the message as a text file without the Mail header:

```
$ mail
Mail version 5.5-kw 5/30/95. Type ? for help.
"/var/spool/mail/chris": 1 message 1 new
>N 1 aleina     Tue Feb 11 10:14:32 5/44
& w 1 complist
```

Sending files through Mail has one major limitation. You can only send character files, not binary files. The Mail utility will corrupt a binary file in the transmission process as well as insert a header. However, there are special file transfer utilities such as ftp that you can use to send binary files. These are discussed in Chapter 11. Such utilities are far more reliable than Mail for transferring very large files as well as binary files.

Mail Aliases, Options, and the Mail Shell Initialization File: .mailrc

The Mail utility has its own initialization file, called **.mailrc**, that is executed each time Mail is invoked, either for sending or receiving messages. Within it you can define Mail options and create Mail aliases. You can set options that add different features to mail, such as changing the prompt or saving copies of messages that you send. With a Mail alias, you can easily send a message to several users. You will find this very useful for broadcasting different messages to the same group of users.

Mail Aliases

You may often need to send—or broadcast—messages to the same group of users. For example, suppose you are part of a study group. You will want to send the same messages, such as when you are meeting next, to every person in the group. Ordinarily, each time you send a message to this group of users, you would have to type in all their addresses. However, it is possible to define an alias for a set of addresses so that, instead of listing all the addresses each time you broadcast, you could use the alias. The alias replaces the list of addresses on the command line.

To define an alias, you enter the keyword **alias**, followed by the alias you have chosen, and then the list of addresses it represents. There's one catch: to alias addresses for use in Mail commands, you need to define the alias within the Mail shell. Each time you leave and then reenter the Mail shell, you need to redefine the alias. This can be done automatically by placing the alias definition in the Mail shell initialization file, **.mailrc**. To enter an alias into the **.mailrc** file, first edit the **.mailrc** file with a text editor such as Vi. Then enter the **alias** command, followed by the alias and the list of addresses. Be sure there is no new line character splitting up the list of addresses. In the next example, the alias **myclass** is defined in the **.mailrc** file.

.mailrc

```
alias myclass  chris dylan aleina justin larisa
```

When the Mail utility is invoked, the **.mailrc** file is automatically executed, defining the alias. When you use Mail to send a message, you can use the alias in place of the list of addresses on the command line. You could also use the alias when sending messages within the Mail shell. In either case, the **.mailrc** file is executed, defining the alias. In the following example, the **myclass** alias is used in place of the addresses. The contents of the file **homework** are sent to all the users whose addresses are aliased by **myclass**.

```
$ mail myclass < homework
```

Mail Options

Mail also provides a set of options that you can define in the **.mailrc** file that will be active each time you use Mail. For example, you could define the Mail prompt to be something other than the **&**. Table 8-4 lists several of the more common Mail options. You set a Mail option using the keyword **set** followed by the option name and then, if called for, an equal sign and a string. For example, **set prompt="*"** will set the Mail prompt to an asterisk. When **.mailrc** is executed, it will then set all the options that you have specified in it.

One useful option is **sign**, which specifies a signature that you can insert into your message using the **~a** tilde command. Often the **sign** option is set to your name and can include other information, such as your phone number or network address. The next example sets the signature to "Robert and Valerie."

```
set sign="Robert and Valerie"
```

You can then use the **~a** tilde command to insert your signature in any message:

```
$ mail aleina
Subject: Dinner
Lets have ice cream for dessert
OK?
~a
Robert and Valerie
^D
EOT
$
```

Another useful option is the **record** option. This option instructs Mail to automatically save any messages that you create and send. In setting the **record** option, you need to specify what file Mail will save your sent messages to. In the next example, the user sets the **record** option and has sent messages saved in a file called **outbox**. If no absolute path name is specified, the file is placed in your home directory.

```
set record="outbox"
```

Organizing Your Mailbox Files: folder, MBOX, and outfolder

You will notice that mailbox files that you create with your **s** and **S** commands, as well as your **mbox** file, can often end up scattered throughout different directories on your system. Mailbox files that you create with the **s** command are placed in your current working directory, whatever that may be at the time you invoke Mail. Mailbox files that you create with the **S** command, as well as your **mbox** file, are placed in your home directory. Instead of your home directory or working directory, you could place all your mailbox files in one specified directory. To do so, you need to make use of three special options: **folder**, **MBOX**, and **outfolder**.

First you need to create the directory that you want to hold your mailbox files. Then you set the **folder** option in your **.mailrc** file, assigning to it the path name of that directory. This directory is often referred to as the **folder** directory. The **folder** option performs two tasks. First, any mailbox files that you create using the **S** command will be placed in the directory assigned to **folder**. Second, setting the **folder** option activates the **+** symbol as a special character in Mail file names that represents the **folder** directory. When using the **s** command, you can precede a mailbox file name with the **+** symbol to save it to the **folder** directory, along with the other mailboxes. When using the **folder** command to switch to another mailbox file, you can precede the file name with a **+** symbol so that Mail will search for the file in the **folder** directory.

In the next example, the user has created a directory called **/home/chris/mail** and has assigned this path name to the variable **folder**. Now any mailbox files that the user creates using the **S** command are placed in that directory. You can give the directory any name you wish. In this case, it is simply called **mail**.

```
set folder="/home/chris/mail"
```

In the following example, the user saves message 2 to a mailbox file called **family_msgs**. The file name is preceded by a **+** symbol, which represents the directory held by the **folder** option. Given the setting of the **folder** option in the preceding example, the file name **+family_msgs** will save the **family_msgs** mailbox file to the directory **/home/chris/mail**, along with any other mailbox files. Then the user switches to another mailbox file in the **folder** directory, making sure to precede the mailbox file name with a **+** symbol so that Mail will search for it in the **folder** directory, and not the current working directory.

```
Mail version 5.5-kw 5/30/95. Type ? for help.
"/var/spool/mail/chris": 3 messages 3 new
>N 1 valerie    Tue Feb 11 10:14:32 5/44    "Budget"
 N 2 aleina     Wed Feb 12 12:30:17 28/537 "Birthday"
 N 3 robert     Fri Feb 14  8:15:24 16/293 "Homework"
& s 2 +family_msgs
"/usr/mail/chris/mail/family_msgs" [Appended]
& folder +family_msgs
Held 2 messages in /usr/mail/chris
"+family_msgs": 1 message 1 new
>  1 aleina     Wed Feb 12 12:30:17 28/537 "Birthday"
```

Your **mbox** file will not, however, be automatically placed in the **folder** directory. The name for the **mbox** file is held in a special variable called **MBOX**. You can have **mbox** placed in your **folder** directory by assigning the name **mbox** preceded by a **+** sign to the **MBOX** variable: **+mbox**. As in the case of the **folder** option, you would normally make the **MBOX** assignment in your **.mailrc** file.

```
set MBOX=+mbox
```

You can also specify that the file you have designated for saving outgoing messages be placed in your **folder** directory. You need to have already defined your **record** option, assigning the name of the file for your outgoing messages. Then to have this file placed in your **folder** directory, you set the **outfolder** option, as shown here:

```
set outfolder
```

You could also simply assign to the **record** option, the file name for your outgoing messages preceded by a **+** symbol:

```
set record=+outbox
```

Having set these three options, all your mailbox files will be kept in one designated directory. All settings should be placed in your **.mailrc** file. A sample **.mailrc** file follows, incorporating Mail aliases as well as many of the variable and option assignments.

.mailrc

```
alias myclass  chris dylan aleina justin larisa
set sign="Robert and Valerie"
set folder="/home/chris/mail"
set MBOX=+mbox
set record=outbox
set outfolder
set prompt="*"
```

The Elm Utility

Another popular mail utility, Elm, was developed by Dave Taylor. Though it is not an official standard mail utility, it has become widely used. Unlike Mail, which is command line oriented, Elm has a screen-oriented, user-friendly interface that makes mail tasks easy to execute. Messages are displayed one screen at a time, and you can move back and forth through the message, screen by screen. Instead of entering commands on a command line, the keys on your keyboard become single-letter commands that execute mail operations, just as single-letter Vi commands execute editing operations. Many of the commands used in Elm bear a similarity to commands used in utilities such as **more** and Vi. Table 8-5 lists the different Elm commands.

Sending Mail with Elm

With Elm, you send a message to any user by using the **elm** command. The message can be something you type in at the keyboard, or it can be the contents of a file. When you are entering a message at the keyboard, you are actually using a standard editor, such as Vi.

To send a message, type **elm** along with the address of the person to whom you are sending the message. When you press ENTER, Elm will display the name of the person to whom you are sending the message, and then prompt you for the subject. Elm displays the actual name of the person, not the address. It obtains the user's name from online information much the same way that the **finger** command can obtain the name of a user.

```
$ elm robert


Send only mode [ELM 2.4 PL20]
```

```
To: Robert Petersen
Subject of message: Birthday
Copies to:



Invoking editor...
```

At the subject prompt, you enter a subject. Then Elm prompts you for a carbon copy list. You can then enter the addresses of other users whom you want to have a copy of the message, or you can simply press ENTER if you do not want any carbon copies sent. Upon pressing ENTER at this point, you are placed in the standard editor, usually Vi, and you can use the editor to enter your message. Remember that you are in the Vi editor—to actually enter text, you first have to enter the Vi input mode with either the **a** or **i** command. Then, after entering your text, you press ESC to return to the Vi command mode. When you have finished entering your message, you save and exit Vi with the **ZZ** command.

```
Your present is in the mail
really
~
~
~
~
~
~
```

After editing the message, Elm will prompt you for an action, at which time you can send it, quit without sending, edit the message again, or edit its headers. Each option is listed with a single-letter command. Simply press the key, just as you would press a Vi editor command key. There is no command line in which you enter the letter and press ENTER.

```
Please choose one of the following options by parenthesized
letter:
e)dit message, edit h)eaders, s)end it, or f)orget it
```

When you invoke the Elm utility, you can specify the subject on the command line using the **-s** option. In the next example, the subject "Tonight's celebration" is specified on the command line. The user will then not be prompted for the subject by Elm.

```
$ elm george -s "Tonight\'s celebration"
```

The **h** option displayed in the Elm message menu is for editing the header. With this option, you can change any of the entries in your message header, and you can enter other header values, such as addresses for blind carbon copies. When you press **h**, a message header edit screen is displayed, listing a prompt for each header field. To edit or add values to a header field, simply enter the first character of the header prompt. At the bottom of the screen you will be prompted with the name of the field, and you can then enter a new value. Press ENTER and the new value is displayed in the header field.

For example, to change the subject, press **s**, and you will be prompted to enter a new subject. After entering the new subject and pressing ENTER, the new value for the subject field is displayed in the header. You can then edit another header field. To add addresses to the blind carbon copy, press **b**, type in the addresses, and press ENTER. You leave the Message Header Edit Screen by pressing ENTER, instead of the first character of a header prompt. This places you back at the message menu. Figure 8-1 shows a sample of the Message Header Edit Screen.

Receiving Mail Using Elm

To receive mail using Elm, you invoke the Elm utility the same way you do to send mail—you enter **elm** by itself on the command line. The Elm utility then displays a list of message headers representing messages you have received. The headers are displayed from the top of the screen. At the bottom of the screen is an information menu listing the different commands you can perform on the screen of message headers. This list of headers is referred to in Elm as the *index*. The message headers are displayed on the screen much like text in a Vi editor. If you have more than one screen of message headers, you can move to the next screen with the + key. You can also move back a screen with the - key.

The Elm message headers look just like the headers in Mail. An Elm header displays the status, message number, date, name of the sender, number of lines in the message, and the subject. As in Mail, the message status is represented by a letter code. An **N** indicates a newly received message, and **O** indicates an old message, one that is still unread. The message number can be used to reference the message in Elm commands. Figure 8-2 shows an example of an Elm message header. All the messages are newly received. The first message is from Gabriel Matoza and was sent on Feb 11. It contains 5 lines, and its subject is "Budget." Notice that the full name of the sender is displayed, not simply the address.

The current header is either preceded by an arrow, **->**, or highlighted by the background. To perform an operation on a message, you must make that message's

```
                    Message Header Edit Screen

T)o: robert (Robert Petersen)
C)c:
B)cc:
S)ubject Birthday

R)eply to:
A)ction:                              E)xpires:
P)riority:                            Precede(n)ce:
I)n-reply to:

Choose header, u)ser defined header, d)omainize
!)shell, or {enter}

Choice:
```

Figure 8-1. *Elm's message editing screen*

```
Mailbox is '/var/spool/mail/chris' with 3 messages
N1 Gabriel Matoza        Feb 11      (5)        "Budget"
N2 Aleina Petersen       Feb 12      (28)       "Birthday"
N3 Marylou Carrion       Feb 14      (16)       "Homework"

You can use any of the following commands by pressing the first character:
d)elete or u)ndelete mail, m)ail a message, r)eply or f)orward mail, q)uit
To read a message, press {enter}. j = move down, k = move up, ? = help

Command:
```

Figure 8-2. *Elm headers*

header the current header. You can do this in several ways. You can enter its message number and press ENTER. You can also make a header the current header by moving to it on the screen using the movement commands, **j** and **k**. **j** moves up to the previous header, and **k** moves down to the next header. You can also use the UP and DOWN ARROW keys. The arrow or highlight indicating the current header will move as you press the **j** or **k** commands, moving to the next or previous message header. If the first header is the current header, then pressing the **j** key twice will make the third header the current header.

To display the current message, you simply press ENTER. To display a specific message, either move to that message with the **k** or **j** keys or enter the message number, and then press ENTER. A new screen will appear in which the message is displayed. If the message is larger than a screen, you can move through it, screen by screen, using the same commands as those in the **more** utility. Pressing the SPACEBAR moves you to the next screen, and pressing **b** moves you back a screen. You can even search for particular patterns in the message.

```
Message 1/3 From Aleina Petersen          Feb 11, 96 04:13:56 am -0300


Subject: Birthday
To: robert (Robert Petersen)
Date: Mon, 12 Feb 1996 10:14:17 -0700 (PDT)


Yes, I did remember your present

        Aleina



Command ('i' to return to index):
```

Once you have examined your message, you can use the **i** command to return to the header screen. Simply press the **i** key. The **i** stands for index, which is the term Elm uses to refer to the list of headers.

You can print messages by pressing the **p** key. Press **p** alone to print the message for the current message header, or type a message number followed by **p** to print a particular message.

If you want to perform an operation on several messages at once, you can first tag them using the **t** command, and then the next Elm command that you enter will operate on all of them. To tag a message, you move to that message header and press **t**. A **+** sign will appear before that message header. Suppose you want to print several messages. You could tag the headers for those messages using the **t** command and then press **p** to print them. In the next example, the user has tagged the first two messages. If the user then presses **p**, messages 1 and 2 will both be printed.

```
+N 1  Gabriel Matoza      Feb 11  (5)    "Budget"
+N 2  Aleina Petersen     Feb 12  (28)   "Birthday"
 N 3  Marylou Carrion     Feb 14  (16)   "Homework"
```

   Elm also allows you to select a current header by using pattern searches. There are several Elm commands that search different parts of a message for a specified pattern. The **/** command searches the address and subject fields of a header for a particular pattern. A double slash command, **//**, searches the text of a message for a pattern. If you enter a **/** command, you are then prompted to enter a pattern. Upon pressing ENTER, Elm searches address and subject fields in each message for that pattern. It stops at the first occurrence it finds and makes that header the current header. Using the previous example, if you searched for a header that has the pattern "birth", you would locate and make message 2 the current header.

   A **//** command will search the text of your messages for a pattern. You enter a **//** command, and then Elm prompts you to enter a pattern. Elm searches the text of all your messages and makes the header of the first message with that pattern in its text the current header. For example, if the user enters a **//** and the pattern **congratulations**, then Elm will match on the pattern "congratulations" in the text of the first message, making that the current header:

```
->N 1  Gabriel Matoza      Feb 11  (5)    "Budget"
  N 2  Aleina Petersen     Feb 12  (28)   "Birthday"
  N 3  Marylou Carrion     Feb 14  (16)   "Homework"
```

   Other search commands perform specific operations, such as the CTRL-**t** command that tags headers with a certain pattern, or the CTRL-**d** command that deletes headers with a pattern. You can use the CTRL-**t** command to tag all messages from a certain user or messages that deal with a certain topic. You could then perform an operation on those messages, such as printing them out. For example, to print all messages that deal with the subject "birthday," you first enter CTRL-**t** and the pattern **birthday** to tag all messages that deal with birthdays, and then press the **p** command to print those messages.

Quitting the Elm Utility

You can quit the Elm utility by pressing the **q** key. Before you leave Elm, you will be asked whether or not you wish to save your read messages in your received mailbox file. The name of the received mailbox file is contained in the Elm variable called

received. You will also be asked whether you want to keep unread messages in your incoming mailbox so that you can read them later. If not, they will be deleted. Also, if you have deleted any messages during this session, you will be asked to confirm the delete. In the next example, the user confirms deleted messages, saves read messages in the received mailbox, and keeps unread messages for later access.

```
Delete message? (y/n) n
Move read messages to "received" folder? (y/n) y
Keep unread messages in incoming mailbox? (y/n) y
Keeping 2 messages and storing 1
```

There are several other commands that you can use to quit Elm. A **Q** command will quit without any prompts for received and unread messages. Preset defaults will be used to determine whether messages are to be saved or not. The **x** and CTRL-**q** commands will quit the Elm utility, leaving the incoming mailbox as you found it. Any deletions, read or unread messages, will be ignored.

Deleting and Undeleting Messages: d and u

To delete the message whose header is the current header, simply press **d**. This will mark the status of the message with a **D** and will delete it when you exit the Elm utility. To delete a message whose header is not the current header, use either the **j** or **k** key to move to that header or enter the message number, and then press the **d** key. To delete message 5 press **5** and then d. To delete several messages at once, first tag them with the **t** command, and then press the **d** key. In the next example, the user has deleted the second message. Its status is now marked with a **D**.

```
   N 1   Gabriel Matoza      Feb 11   (5)    "Budget"
 ->D 2   Aleina Petersen     Feb 12   (28)   "Birthday"
   N 3   Marylou Carrion     Feb 14   (16)   "Homework"
```

You can also use the CTRL-**d** command to select a set of headers to be deleted that contain a specified pattern in their addresses or subjects. You can use this feature to select and delete messages from a certain user or messages that deal with a specific topic. In the next example, the user decides to delete all messages from Aleina. The user presses CTRL-**d** and is prompted for a pattern, in this case "Aleina." The second and fourth messages are matched in their address field and marked for deletion.

```
   N 1   Gabriel Matoza      Feb 11   (5)    "Budget"
   D 2   Aleina Petersen     Feb 12   (28)   "Birthday"
```

```
   N 3   Marylou Carrion      Feb 14   (16)   "Homework"
 ->D 4   Aleina Petersen      Feb 16   (32)   "Party"
```

To undelete a message, move to its header or enter its message number, and then press the **u** key. The status of the message will change from **D** to **U**, indicating an undelete. Whereas the **u** key undeletes the current message or tagged messages, the CTRL-**u** command will undelete any messages with a certain pattern in their address or subject fields. CTRL-**u** works the same way as CTRL-**d**.

Replying to Messages

While in the Elm utility, you can send a reply to any messages that you receive. Elm will use the header information in a message to determine the address of the sender. The **r** command sends a reply to a message. You reply to a message by first making its header the current header or by entering the message number, and then pressing the **r** key. Upon pressing **r**, Elm first asks if you want to include a copy of the message in your reply. You enter **y** or **n**. Elm then opens up a screen with the sender's name and subject displayed at the top. The cursor is positioned at the subject so that you can modify it if you wish. Press ENTER to continue. You are then prompted for any carbon copies that you want to send. Upon pressing ENTER, you then enter a standard editor such as Vi in which you type the text of your reply. Just as with a regular message, to enter text, you must first enter the input mode with an **a** command. You exit the input mode with ESC. Then the **ZZ** command saves the text and returns you to Elm. The menu for sending messages is displayed. You then press the **s** key to send the message.

Sending Messages from Elm

You send messages while in the Elm utility with the **m** command. Upon pressing the **m** key, you are prompted for the address of the user to whom you want to send the message. You enter the address and are then prompted for the subject. After the subject, you are asked if you want to send any carbon copies. If not, press ENTER. You are then in the Vi editor and can edit and input your message. Upon exiting the editor, you can send the message with the **s** command.

Saving Messages in Elm

You can save a message to a mailbox file using the **s** command. Either make the message you want to save the current header or enter the message number, and then press the **s** key. At the bottom of the screen, Elm gives you a save prompt with a default mailbox file name. This name is the name of the sender of the message. Elm assumes that you may want to organize the messages that you save into different mailbox files according to the person who sent them. To save your message in the mailbox file for the sender displayed at the save prompt, just press ENTER. If, instead, you want to save the message to a file of your own choosing, at the save prompt, enter an **=** sign followed immediately by the name of the file. For example, to save your message in the file **birthdays**, enter **=birthdays**.

If you want to save several messages to the same mailbox file, you could first tag the message headers and then press the **s** key. The mailbox file that you then specify will have all the tagged messages saved in it.

Elm also provides two special mailbox files whose names are referenced in the Elm variables **received** and **sent**. The **received** mailbox file operates like the **mbox** file in Mail. Messages that you read are automatically saved in this file when you exit Elm. The **sent** file usually holds messages you have sent. You can specifically save your message in the **received** mailbox file by entering a **>** at the save prompt. A **<** will save the message in the **sent** mailbox.

Reading Mailbox Files with Elm

While in Elm, you can switch over to reading a specific mailbox file instead of incoming messages. The **c** command will prompt you for the name of a mailbox file. Simply press the **c** key and the prompt appears. The prompt will display the name of the mailbox file used to hold received messages from the sender in the current message header. You can specify your own mailbox file by entering the name of the file preceded by an **=** sign. **=birthdays** will specify the **birthdays** mailbox file. In the next example, the current header is a message sent by the user called **aleina**. When the user presses the **c** command, the "Change folder" notice is displayed at the Command prompt, and, as a default, the name of the user who sent the current message is displayed at the "Change to which folder" prompt. In this case, the user's name is **aleina**.

```
Command: Change folder
Change to which folder: =aleina
The user then enters the new folder name at the prompt,
overwriting =aleina:

Command: Change folder
Change to which folder: =birthdays
```

Once you have changed to the other folder, the headers for all the messages in this mailbox file will be displayed, and you can display the messages, delete them from the file, or send replies. The folder's name will be displayed at the top of the screen.

You can change to any other folder you wish by entering a name at the folder prompt. Entering a **!** will change back to the incoming mailbox. Pressing **>** will change to the **received** files folder, and **<** to the **sent** files folder.

Elm Aliases: Alias Menu and aliases.text

You can create an alias using either the Elm alias menu within the utility, or by entering aliases into a special Elm initialization file called **aliases.text**. The alias menu is by far the easiest and most efficient way to manage your Elm aliases. However, if you wish to create group aliases, such as those used by Mail, you will need to know how to enter an alias directly into the **aliases.text** file.

Elm Aliases: Alias Menu

To create an alias within the Elm utility, you use the **a** command, which displays an alias menu. You can enter commands in the menu to create an alias, delete an alias, or list all aliases or particular aliases. To create a new alias, you select the new alias option by pressing the **n** key. Elm then prompts you for the alias, the user's name, and the user's address. It then automatically installs and adds the alias to the **aliases.text** file.

```
Aliases [ELM 2.4 PL20]




You can use any of the following commands by pressing the first
    character;
a)lias current message, n)ew alias, d)elete or u)ndelete an alias,
    m)ail to alias, or r)eturn to main menu.  To view an alias,
    press <enter>.
j = move down, k = move up, ? = help

Alias: n
Add a new alias to database..
Enter alias name: mark
```

The following prompts will all be displayed on the same line, one after the other. After entering the name of the alias, that prompt and name are replaced by a prompt for the last name of the person for whom you are making the alias. The prompt for the first name then replaces the one for the last name, and so on, for the address. Finally, you are asked if you want to accept the new prompt. You can enter either **y** or **n**.

```
Enter last name for mark: Petersen
Enter first name for mark: Mark
Enter optional comment for mark:
Enter address for mark: mark@violet.berkeley.edu
```

```
Messages addressed as: mark@violet.berkeley.edu (mark petersen)
New alias: mark is 'Mark Petersen'. Accept new alias? (y/n) y
```

You can also create an alias for the sender of the message referenced by the current message header. In this case, you press the **a** command at the Elm alias menu. Elm will then prompt you for an alias name but take the user's name and the user's address from the message header. The alias will be automatically installed and added to **aliases.text**. This is perhaps the easiest way to create an alias.

You can delete an alias by pressing the **d** key. Elm prompts you for the alias name and then deletes the alias from the **aliases.text** file. You can also list aliases with the **l** command or list a particular alias with its name and address using the **p** command.

Elm Aliases: .elm and aliases.text

Elm maintains a **.elm** directory in your own home directory with which it will configure your use of Elm. Each time you invoke Elm, it generates a shell for your own use, within which you can define your own aliases and configuration variables. The **.elm** directory contains special initialization files in which you can place alias or variable definitions. These initialization files operate like the **.mailrc** file, configuring your Elm utility just as **.mailrc** configures Mail.

You can define Elm aliases in the **aliases.text** file in the **.elm** directory. The syntax for an Elm alias is the alias followed by an **=** sign and the user's name followed by another **=** sign and the user's address.

```
alias = user name = user address
```

In the next example, the user creates an alias for Gabriel Matoza whose address is **gabriel@garnet.berkeley.edu**.

```
gabe = Gabriel Matoza = gabriel@garnet.berkeley.edu
```

You can have more than one alias for the same person. You just list the aliases, separated by a colon. In the next example, the user creates two aliases for Robert Petersen at **robert@violet.fallon.edu**.

```
robert, bob = Robert Petersen = robert@violet.fallon.edu
```

Once you have created individual aliases, you can use them to create group aliases. A group alias operates in the same way as aliases used in Mail's **.mailrc** file. When you send a message to a group alias, the message is sent to every user in that group. You define a group alias with the following syntax. The *alias-list* contains the previously defined aliases that reference individual users, separated by commas.

```
group alias = group name = alias-list
```

In the next example, the user creates a group alias using "gabe" and "robert," defined previously. The alias group is called **myclass** and the group name is "photography class". If the user sends a message to **myclass**, it will go to **robert@violet.fallon.edu** and to **gabriel@garnet.berkeley.edu**.

```
myclass = photography class = robert, gabe
```

An example of the **alias.text** file follows. Notice that the individual aliases are defined first, followed by the group aliases that make use of them.

```
alias.text
gabe = gabriel matoza = valerie@garnet.berkeley.edu
robert, bob = robert petersen = robert@violet.eugene.edu
myclass = photography class = robert, val
```

Whenever you add new aliases to the **alias.text** file, you must install them in the Elm utility by executing the command **newalias**.

Elm Options: .elmrc

Elm has a number of different options with which to configure your Elm shell. These options are variables that you can turn on or off, or assign values to. Some Elm options are simple switches that you turn on or off using the special values **YES** and **NO**. For example, the assignment **alwaysstore = YES** will set the option to always store received mail in the **received** mailbox file. Other Elm options hold string values. For example, the assignment **receivedmail = mybox** assigns the string "mybox" to the **receivedmail** option. This option holds the file name of the file used as the received mail file. In this case, received mail will be saved to the **mybox** file.

You set options either by entering assignments to the **.elmrc** file in your **.elm** directory, or by using the options menu within the Elm utility. Within Elm, the command **o** brings up the options menu. The options menu only displays the more commonly used options. To change an option, you press the first character of one of the options displayed, and then you are prompted to enter a new value.

Pine

Pine is a Mail program that also functions as a newsreader. Pine stands for Program for Internet News and Email. With Pine email functions you can easily send messages, documents, and pictures. It has an extensive list of options, and has flexible Internet connection capabilities, letting you receive both mail and Usenet news. Pine also lets you maintain an address book where you can place frequently used email addresses. Pine runs from the command line using a simple cursor based interface. Enter the **pine** command to start up Pine.

Pine supports full screen cursor controls. It displays a menu whose items you can select by moving the cursor with the arrow keys to the entry and pressing ENTER as shown in Figure 18-3. Each item is labeled with a capital letter; you can also select the item by entering this letter. The O command brings up a list of other Pine commands you can use.

To send a message, select the Compose Message item. This brings up a screen where you can enter your message. You are first taken through the different entries for the header, which prompts you for an email address and subject. You can even attach files. Then you type in the text of the message. A set of commands listed at the bottom of the screen are used for different tasks. You can read a file with CTRL-R and cancel the message with CTRL-C. Use CTRL-X to send the message as shown in Figure 18-4.

```
PINE 3.95   MAIN MENU                          Folder: INBOX   0 Messages


        ?      HELP            -  Get help using Pine

        C      COMPOSE MESSAGE  -  Compose and send a message

        I      FOLDER INDEX    -  View messages in current folder

        L      FOLDER LIST     -  Select a folder to view

        A      ADDRESS BOOK    -  Update address book

        S      SETUP           -  Configure or update Pine

        Q      QUIT            -  Exit the Pine program



     Copyright 1989-1996.  PINE is a trademark of the University of Washington.

  ? Help                    P PrevCmd                  R RelNotes
  O OTHER CMDS ? [Help]     N NextCmd                  K KBLock
```

Figure 8-3.   *Pine main menu*

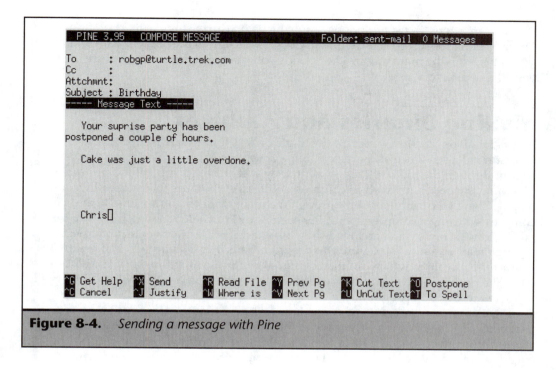

Figure 8-4. *Sending a message with Pine*

Pine organizes both sent and received messages into folders that you select using the Folder List entry on the main menu. The different available folders will be listed from left to right. Three folders are automatically set up for you; INBOX, sent-mail, and saved-messages. The INBOX folder holds mail that you have received, but not yet read. Sent-mail is for messages you have sent to others, and saved-messages are messages you have read and want to keep. Use the LEFT and RIGHT ARROW keys to select the one you want and press ENTER. Selecting the INBOX folder will list the messages you have received. Headers for received messages will be displayed, and you can choose a specific header to view your message. The folder you select becomes your default folder. You can go back to it by selecting the Folder Index entry in the main menu.

Pine is designed to work with the Internet and is capable of reading Internet newsgroups. The Config entry listed on the Setup screen will open an options list in which you can place entries for your Internet mail server or news server. If you are using an Internet service, you can enter the domain names for the new server or mail server. Your mail will be sent out over the Internet.

Newgroups are treated by Pine as just another mail folder. To list a newsgroup, select the Folder List entry and use the A command to add the name of the newsgroup. It will then be listed as another folder. When you select it, the newsgroup headers are listed instead of mail headers. You can also post news using Pine, just as you would send a message.

Pine has an extensive list of options with which you can customize its operations. These options are accessed through the Config selection in the Setup screen that is accessible from the main menu. The options you change are saved in a **.pinrc** file in your home directory.

Mailing Binaries and Archives

Internet mail operations are set up to handle only text messages; that is, those consisting of a sequence of characters. Binary files such as compiled programs cannot be sent through the mail utilities—if sent, they will arrive corrupted and unusable. The same is true for archived or compressed files. A set of files that you archive into one file using **tar** cannot be sent through the mail. Nor can you send a file that you compressed using a compression utility such as **gzip**. There is a way, however, for you to convert binary and archived files into character files that you can then send through mail utilities. The **uuencode** program translates a binary file into one that is character equivalent, which can then be sent through a mail utility such as **mail** or **elm**. The person receiving such an encoded file can then convert it back to a binary file using the **uudecode** program.

The **uuencode** program is designed to work on either the standard input or on a particular file. In either case you have to provide a name for the file that will be created when the encoded data is converted back to binary. **uuencode** outputs the encoded binary data to the standard output. **uuencode** has the following syntax:

```
uuencode file name
```

where *name* is the name to be given to the decoded binary data and *file* is the name of a binary file to be encoded. Keep in mind that since **uuencode** sends the encoded data to the standard output, you should redirect this output to a file; then you can send that file.

The **uudecode** program takes as its argument the file that holds the encoded data. It will generate a binary file using the name you provided in the **uuencode** operation. The basic steps are shown here:

```
uuencode file name > datafile
mail address < datafile
& s msg-num datafile
uudecode datafile
```

The file is encoded and mailed as a message. When that message is received, it is saved as a file that is then decoded, generating a binary file called *name*.

In the next example, the user encodes the picture file called **dylan.gif**. Picture files such as gif and jpeg files are binary files and have to be translated to character format before they can be mailed. In this case, the name of the binary file and the name to be used for the decoded version of the file are the same. The encoded output is redirected to a file called **dylanpic**:

```
$ uuencode dylan.gif  dylan.gif  > dylanpic
```

dylanpic is the file that contains only character data, although this character data is encoded binary data. The user can then send **dylanpic** through the mail system:

```
$ mail larisa@ix.com < dylanpic
```

Once received, you simply use **uudecode** to convert the encoded data back to its binary form. **uudecode** will create a binary file, giving it the name specified for **uuencode**. In the following example, the data from **dylanpic** file has been received as a message. The receiver then saves this message as **dylanpic**. **uudecode** then converts this message to the original binary format and places it in a file called **dylan.gif**. The name that the receiver saves the message as does not have to be the same as the one the sender used. You can use any name, but you must use that same name with **uudecode**.

```
$ mail
Mail version 5.5-kw 5/30/95.  Type ? for help.
"/var/spool/mail/chris": 1 message 1 unread
>U  1 robert                Mon Apr  8 00:06 236/14104
& s 1 dylanpic
"dylanpic" [New file]
& q
$ uudecode dylanpic
$ ls
dylan.gif
```

You can do the same for archived and compressed files. For example, you could send several gif picture files in the same message by first combining them into one archived file and then compressing it. Then, you could encode the compressed archived file with **uuencode** and mail it as a message. The person receiving it can decode the message to a compressed archived file that can then be decompressed in order to extract the gif pictures. You can do this for entire directories and their subdirectories as well. In the following two examples, the entire **birthday** directory is archived by **tar** and compressed with **gzip**. The compressed archive is then encoded into character data and saved in a file called **birthdaydir**. The name given to the binary data is **birthday.tar.gz**. The file is sent as a message through **mail**. The receiver saves this message in a file called **birthd**. **uudecode** then decodes the **birthd** file, generating the **birthday.tar.gz** file that can then be decompressed and extracted to create the **birthday** directory in its entirety.

```
$ tar cvf birthday.tar  birthday
$ gzip birthday.tar
$ uuencode birthday.tar.gz birthday.tar.gz > birthdaydir
$ mail aleina@pango1.com  < birthdaydir
$ mail
Mail version 5.5-kw 5/30/95.  Type ? for help.
"/var/spool/mail/chris": 1 message 1 new
>N  1 robert               Mon Apr  8 00:10 236/14162
& s 1 birthd
"birthd" [New file]
& q
$ uudecode birthd
```

Since the **uuencode** program can receive binary data from the standard input, you could combine the archive, compression, encoding, and mailing operations into one pipe sequence as shown here:

```
$ tar cf - birthday | gzip | uuencode birthday.tar.gz | mail
    aleina@pango1.com
```

The **-** in the **tar** operation represents the standard output and will instruct **tar** to send its output to the standard output instead of a file. Notice that the name to be used for the decoded binary file is still included as an argument to **uuencode**. **uudecode**, when applied to this message, will generate a binary file called **birthday.tar.gz**.

The **uudecode** and **uuencode** programs are in the **sharutils.4.1-2** software package on your Caldera CD-ROM. If you choose a minimum install for your Linux system, they will not be installed. You will have to use **glint** or **rpi -i** to install the package. Table 8-6 shows some mail and communication utilities.

Notifications of Received Mail: From and biff

As your mail messages are received, they are automatically placed in your mailbox file, but you are not automatically notified when you receive a message. To find out if you have any messages waiting, you can either use the Mail utility to retrieve the messages, or you can use the From and biff utilities simply to tell you if you have any mail waiting.

The From utility tells what messages you have received and are waiting to be read. For each waiting message, it lists the senders' addresses and times that each message was received. To use From, you enter the keyword **from** and press ENTER.

```
$ from
1 From valerie Sun Feb 11 10:14:32 1996
   Subject: Budget
2 From aleina Mon Feb 12 12:30:17 1996
   Subject: Birthday
3 From robert Wed Feb 14  8:15:24 1996
   Subject: Homework
$
```

The biff utility notifies you immediately when a message is received. It is helpful when you are expecting a message and want to know as soon as it arrives. Biff automatically displays the header and beginning lines of messages as they are received. To turn on biff, you enter **biff y** on the command line. To turn it off, you enter **biff n**. To find out if biff is on or not, enter **biff** alone. It displays a message notification whenever a message arrives, no matter what you may be doing at the time. You could be in the middle of an editing session and biff will interrupt it to display the notification on your screen. You can then return to your editing session. In the next example, the user first sets biff on. Then biff notifies the user that a message has been received. The user then checks to see if biff is still on.

```
$ biff y
$
New mail for chris has arrived:
--Date: Sun Feb 11 12:30:21
From: dylan
To: chris
Subject: Food
    Chris,
        Have you tried the chocolate
...more...
```

```
$
$ biff
is y
$
```

You can temporarily block biff by using the **mesg n** command to prevent any message displays on your screen. **mesg n** will not only stop any Write and Talk messages, it will also stop biff and Notify messages. Later you can unblock biff with a **mesg y** command. A **mseg n** command comes in handy should you not want to be disturbed while working on some project.

Communications with Other Logged-in Users: Write and Talk

You may, at times, want to communicate immediately with other users on your Linux system and not wait for them to read their mail. You can do so with the Write and Talk utilities, provided that the other user is also logged into your Linux system. The Write utility operates like radio communication, allowing you to contact someone already logged in and display a message on their screen. The Talk utility operates like a telephone, allowing you to have a direct two-way conversation with another user.

Direct Connections: The Write Utility

The Write utility lets you send real-time messages to another user. The message the sender types is immediately displayed on the receiver's screen. In this sense, Write is guaranteed to get someone's immediate attention. However, Write has one important limitation. It can only connect to users who are already logged in. If you are not sure if someone is logged in, you can use the **who** command to find out.

Write is not like the standard mail operation. It does not send messages that are placed in a mailbox file; it displays a message directly on another user's screen. When you enter the **write** command followed by a user's login name, a connection to that user is opened. You can then enter text that is displayed on the receiver's screen. To end the connection, enter CTRL-**d** on a line of its own. The receiver, meanwhile, will first have a notice displayed on his or her screen saying that a message was sent by you and giving the date and time. Immediately after this, the message itself will be displayed.

In the next example, a user writes a message to **cecelia**. After entering the message, the user presses CTRL-**d** to cut the connection.

```
$ write cecelia
How are you today?
^D
```

cecelia receives a message header followed by the message. The CTRL-**d** entered by the sender shows up as EOT.

```
Message from gabriel [Tues July 5 10:31]
How are you today?
EOT
```

You can also use Write to establish two-way communication between you and another user. You issue the **write** command followed by a login name. The user receiving the Write notice responds with a **write** command of his or her own, with the sender's login name. The messages sent back and forth by you and the other user are displayed on both terminal screens.

Interactive Write communication should be handled as if you were talking over a radio. First one user sends a message and then indicates that the message is finished, and then the other user responds. A common convention adopted by many Linux and Unix users is to indicate the end of a message by pressing **o**, for "over." Press **oo**, "over and out," to indicate that you are finished communicating and wish to sign off. You physically end the connection with CTRL-**d**. However, both users must enter CTRL-**d**. Your CTRL-**d** cuts your connection with the other user, and the other user's CTRL-**d** ends that user's connection with you.

A Write communication will be displayed on your screen no matter what you are doing. If you do not want to be interrupted by Write messages suddenly being displayed on your screen, you can suppress them with the **mesg** command. The **mesg** command takes two possible options, **y** or **n**. **mesg -n** suppresses reception of a Write message; **mesg -y** restores reception of write messages.

Interactive Communication: The Talk Utility

You can use the Talk utility to set up an interactive two-way communication between you and another user. Unlike Write, Talk operates more like a phone call—both you and the other user can type in messages simultaneously. The **talk** utility operates more like a phone call where two people are constantly talking back and forth to each other.

You initiate the communication by entering the **talk** command followed by the other user's address, usually the login name. This displays a message on the other user's screen asking if he or she wants to **talk** and giving your address. The user then responds with a **talk** command of his or her own using your address. Both your screen and the other user's screen then split into two segments. The top segment displays what you type, and the bottom segment displays what the other user types. Either user can end the session with an interrupt character, usually CTRL-**c**.

Summary: Mail

With electronic mail utilities, you can send messages to other users on your system. A user's login name constitutes his or her address. Two commonly used electronic mail utilities with very different interfaces are described in this chapter: Mail and Elm.

Mail is the standard electronic mail utility found on most Linux and Unix systems. It has a simple command line interface with its own set of commands that operate within a special Mail shell. The different Mail commands for sending and receiving messages can be thought of as defining the basic mail operations found in all electronic mail utilities. When sending a message with Mail, you can perform operations such as redisplaying the message, saving the message to a file, or invoking the Vi editor to edit the message. You can also create a message in an editor, save it in a file, and then send the contents of the file as a message. For Mail, this involves using redirection to use the contents of a file as input for the **mail** command.

To receive messages, you invoke the Mail utility with the command **mail**. You are first given a list of message headers. Each header provides information about a message, including the person who sent it and the subject of the message. Different Mail commands allow you to read, print, save, or delete a message. You can even reply to a message, sending a response immediately.

You can send a message to more than one user at a time by listing the user addresses on the command line next to the **mail** command. Instead of listing all the addresses, you can create an alias for them in the **.mailrc** file. The **.mailrc** file contains commands executed whenever the **mail** command is executed. When you send a message to those users, you can use the alias instead of the list of their addresses.

The Elm utility uses a full screen interface with single key commands to perform much the same operations for sending, receiving, and saving messages, as well as creating aliases for addresses. The full screen interface often makes Elm much easier to use than Mail.

The **write** and **talk** commands establish direct communications with another user who is currently logged in. No messages are actually sent. Instead, whatever you type is displayed immediately on another user's terminal. The **write** command is like a radio communication in which one user talks and then waits for the other's reply. The **talk** command is like a phone call in which both users can talk simultaneously.

Internet Addresses	Description
login-name@*system*.*domain*	Internet mail addresses
	`chris@garnet.rose.edu`

Standard Domains

`com`	Commercial organization
`edu`	Educational institution
`gov`	Government organization
`int`	International organization
`mil`	Military
`net`	Networking organization
`org`	Non-profit organization

International Domains

`at`	Austria
`au`	Australia
`ca`	Canada
`ch`	Switzerland
`de`	Germany
`dk`	Denmark
`es`	Spain
`fr`	France
`gr`	Greece
`ie`	Ireland
`jp`	Japan
`nz`	New Zealand
`uk`	United Kingdom (Britain)
`us`	United States

Table 8-1.   *Internet Domains*

Mail Command Options	Description
-f *mailbox-filename*	Invokes the Mail utility to read messages in a mailbox file in your directory rather than your mailbox of waiting messages
-H	Displays only the list of message headers
-s *subject*	When sending messages, specifies the subject
-v	Displays the sequence of Mail operations used to send a message
Tilde Commands for Message Header	
~h	Prompts the user to enter addresses, subject, and carbon copy list
~s *subject*	Enters a new subject
~t *addresses*	Adds addresses to the address list
~c *addresses*	Adds addresses to the carbon copy list
~b *addresses*	Adds addresses to the blind carbon copy list
Tilde Commands for Message Text	
~v	Invokes the Vi editor; changes are saved to the message text
~p	Redisplays the text of the message
~q	Quits the message and leaves the Mail utility
~w *filename*	Saves the message in a file
~r *filename*	Reads the contents of a file into the message text
~e	Invokes the default text editor
~ | *filter*	Pipes the contents of a message to a filter and replaces the message with the output of that filter

Table 8-2. *Mail Commands for Sending Messages*

Tilde Commands for Message Text	Description
~m *message-list*	When sending messages or replying to received mail, inserts the contents of a received message; the contents are indented; used when receiving messages
~f *message-list*	When sending messages or replying to received mail, inserts the contents of a received message; unlike ~m, there is no indentation; used when receiving messages
General Tilde Commands	
~?	Displays a list of all the tilde commands
~~	Enters a tilde as a character into the text
~! *command*	Executes a shell command while entering a message

Table 8-2. *Mail Commands for Sending Messages (continued)*

Status Codes	Description
N	Newly received messages
U	Previously unread messages
R	Reads messages in the current session
P	Preserved messages, read in previous session and kept in incoming mailbox
D	Deleted messages; messages marked for deletion
O	Old messages
*	Messages that you have saved to another mailbox file

Table 8-3. *Mail Commands for Receiving Messages*

Display Messages	Description
h	Redisplay the message headers
z+ z-	If header list takes up more than one screen, scrolls header list forward and backward
t *message-list*	Displays a message referenced by the message list; if no message list is used, the current message is displayed
p *message-list*	Displays a message referenced by the message list; if no message list is used, the current message is displayed
n or **+**	Displays next message
-	Displays previous message
top *message-list*	Displays the top few lines of a message referenced by the message list; if no message list is used, the current message is displayed
Message Lists	
message-number	References message with message number
num1–num2	References a range of messages beginning with *num1* and ending with *num2*
.	Current message
^	First message
$	Last message
*****	All the messages waiting in the mailbox
/*pattern*	All messages with pattern in the subject field
address	All messages sent from user with address

Table 8-3. *Mail Commands for Receiving Messages* (continued)

Message Lists	Description
: *c*	All messages of the type indicated by *c*; message types are as follows: **n** newly received messages **o** old messages previously received **r** read messages **u** unread messages **d** deleted messages
Deleting and Restoring Messages	
d *message-list*	Deletes a message referenced by the indicated message list from your mailbox
u *message-list*	Undeletes a message referenced by the indicated message list that has been previously deleted
q	Quits the Mail utility and saves any read messages in the **mbox** file
x	Quits the Mail utility and does *not* erase any messages you deleted; this is equivalent to executing a **u** command on all deleted messages before quitting
pre *message-list*	Preserves messages in your waiting mailbox even if you have already read them
Sending and Editing Messages	
r	Sends a reply to all persons who received a message
R	Sends a reply to the person who sent you a message
m *address*	Sends a message to someone while in the Mail utility
v *message-list*	Edits a message with the Vi editor
Saving Messages	
s *message-list filename*	Saves a message referenced by the message list in a file, including the header of the message
S *message-list*	Saves a message referenced by the message list in a file named for the sender of the message

Table 8-3.   *Mail Commands for Receiving Messages* (continued)

Saving Messages	Description
w *message-list filename*	Saves a message referenced by the message list in a file without the header; only the text of the message is saved
folder *mailbox-filename*	Switches to another mailbox file
%	Represents the name of incoming mailbox file **folder %** switches to incoming mailbox file
#	Represents name of previously accessed mailbox file **folder #** switches to previous mailbox file
&	Represents name of mailbox file used to save your read messages automatically; usually called **mbox** **folder &** switches to **mbox** file
General Commands	
?	Displays a list of all the Mail commands
! *command*	Executes a user shell command from within the Mail shell

Table 8-3. *Mail Commands for Receiving Messages* (continued)

Options	Description

alias *name address-list*	Creates an alias for a list of addresses
	    alias myclass chris aleina larisa
	    $ mail myclass

asksub	Prompts for subject **set asksub**
askcc	Prompts for carbon copy addresses **set askcc**
prompt=*string*	Redefines Mail prompt **set prompt="&"**

Table 8-4. *Mail Options*

Options	Description
sign=*string*	Defines string to be inserted by the **~a** tilde command into a message that you are inputting **set sign=**"Robert and Valerie"
folder=*directory*	Saves any mailbox files created by the **s** or **S** command to the directory assigned to it **set folder=$HOME/mail**
record=*filename*	Automatically saves a copy of any message that you create and send; messages are saved in a file specified when you set the **record** option **set record=$HOME/outbox**
outfolder	Places record file in folder directory; in the following example, outbox will be a file in the directory defined by **folder** **set record=outbox** **set outfolder**
MBOX=*filename*	Holds the name of the **mbox** file to which read messages are automatically saved; by default, **mbox** is placed in your home directory; to put it in the **folder** directory, place a + sign before the **mbox** name **set MBOX=+mbox**

Table 8-4. *Mail Options (continued)*

Sending Messages	Description
elm *address*	Sends a message using Elm
s	Sends the message
e	Edits the message
f	Forgets the message, quits, and does not send
h	Edits the header of the message

Table 8-5. *Elm Commands*

Receiving Messages	Description
elm	Invokes the Elm utility

?	Invokes help; press key used for a command to display information about that command
	   ? Displays a list of all commands
	   . Returns to Elm index

q	Quits the Elm utility with prompts for saving read and unread messages, and deleting messages marked for deletion
Q	Quits the Elm utility with no prompts
x and CTRL-q	Quits the Elm utility leaving your mail as you found it; no deletions are made or messages saved; messages remain as you found them
+	Displays next index screen if headers take up more than one screen
–	Displays previous index screen if headers take up more than one screen
Selecting a Message	
j	Moves down to the next message header, making it the current message
k	Moves up to the previous message header, making it the current message
message-number	Makes the header whose message number is *message-number* the current message
/*pattern*	Searches for the pattern in the subject or address headers, making the first header with a match the current message
//*pattern*	Searches for the pattern in the text of messages, making the first message with a match the current message
t	Tags the current message; a + sign appears before the message; you can tag several messages and then perform an operation on them all at once

Table 8-5. *Elm Commands* (continued)

Selecting a Message	Description
CTRL-**t**	Searches address and subject headers for a pattern and tags all messages that match

Operations on Messages

ENTER	Displays the current message
i	Returns to headers (index)
p	Prints the current message
d	Deletes the current message; the header is marked with a D and deleted when you exit Elm
CTRL-**d**	Searches address and subject headers for a pattern and deletes all messages that match
u	Undeletes the current message
CTRL-**u**	Searches address and subject headers for a pattern and undeletes all messages that match
r	Replies to the current message; the address and subject are taken from the current message's header; you then compose and send your reply as you would any other message

s	Saves the current message or tagged messages in a mailbox file; by default, the message is saved to a mailbox file using the address of the user who sent the message; you can specify your own mailbox file by entering the name of the file preceded by an = sign
	    =*mailbox-filename*
	You can also save the message to received or sent mailbox files using the following commands:
	   > Saves message to received mailbox file
	   < Saves message to sent mailbox file

Operations

m	Sends a message from the Elm utility; you compose and send a message

Table 8-5.   *Elm Commands* (continued)

Operations	Description
c	Uses Elm to operate on a specific mailbox file; the command switches from incoming mail to any other mailbox file with messages
a	Manages Elm aliases; upon pressing the **a** command, the alias menu is displayed with the following options:
	a Creates an alias using the name and address of the current message
	m Creates an alias using a name and address that you enter
	d Deletes an alias
	l Lists aliases
	p Displays the name and address of particular aliases
	s Displays any system aliases
	r Returns to Elm main menu

Table 8-5. *Elm Commands* (continued)

Utility	Description
mail	Mail utility for sending and receiving mail
elm	Mail utility for sending and receiving mail
uuencode *filename*	Encodes a binary file into a character format allowing it to be sent through a mail system; redirects to a file and sends that file **uuencode** *filename* **>** *datafile*
uudecode *file*	Decodes a uuencoded file, generating a binary file with the name designated by **uuencode**
from	Tells you what messages you have received
biff	Notifies you of received mail
write *address*	Displays a message on a logged-on user's terminal
talk *address*	Sets up two-way communication with a logged-on user

Table 8-6. *Mail and Communication Utilities*

Chapter Nine

Usenet and Newsreaders

Usenet is an open mail system on which users post news and opinions. It operates like a systemwide mailbox that any user on your Linux system can read or send messages to. Users' messages are incorporated into Usenet files, which are distributed to any system signed up to receive them. Each system that receives Usenet files is referred to as a site. Certain sites perform organizational and distribution operations for Usenet, receiving messages from other sites and organizing them into Usenet files that are then broadcast to many other sites. Such sites are called backbone sites and they operate like publishers, receiving articles and organizing them into different groups.

To access Usenet news, you need access to a news server. A news server receives the daily Usenet newsfeeds and makes them accessible to other systems. Your network may have a system that operates as a news server. If you are using an Internet Service Provider, a news server is probably maintained for your use. To read Usenet articles, you use a newsreader, a client program that connects to a news server and accesses the articles. On the Internet and in TCP/IP networks, news servers communicate with newsreaders using the Network News Transport Protocol (NNTP) and are often referred to as nntp news servers.

Alternatively, you could also create your own news server on your Linux system to run a local Usenet news service or to download and maintain the full set of Usenet articles. Several Linux programs, called News Transport Agents, can be used to create such a server.

Usenet News

Usenet files were originally designed to function like journals. Messages contained in the files are referred to as articles. A user could write an article, post it in Usenet, and have it immediately distributed to other systems around the world. Someone could then read the article on Usenet instead of waiting for a journal publication. Usenet files themselves were organized as journal publications. Since journals are designed to address specific groups, Usenet files were organized according to groups called newsgroups. When a user posts an article, it is assigned to a specific newsgroup. If another user wants to read that article, he or she looks at the articles in that newsgroup. You can think of each newsgroup as a constantly updated magazine. For example, to read articles on computer science, you would access the Usenet newsgroup on computer science.

More recently, Usenet files have also been used as bulletin boards on which people carry on debates. Again, such files are classified into newsgroups, though their articles read more like conversations than journal articles.

Each newsgroup has its own name, which is often segmented in order to classify newsgroups. Usually the names are divided into three segments: a general topic, subtopic, and specific topic. The segments are delimited by periods. For example, you may have several newsgroups that deal with the general topic **rec**, which stands for recreation. Of those, some newsgroups may deal with only the subtopic **food**. Again, of those, there may be a group that only discusses a specific topic, such as **recipes**. In this case, the newsgroup name would be **rec.food.recipes**.

Many of the bulletin board groups are designed for discussion only, lacking any journal-like articles. Many of these begin with either **alt** or **talk** as their general topic. For example, **talk.food.chocolate** may contain conversations about how wonderful or awful chocolate is thought to be, and **alt.food.chocolate** may contain informal speculations about the importance of chocolate to the basic structure of civilization as we know it. Here are some examples of Usenet newsgroup names:

```
comp.ai.neural-nets
comp.lang.pascal
sci.physics.fusion
rec.arts.movies
rec.food.recipes
talk.politics.theory
```

Linux has newsgroups on various topics. Some are for discussion, others are sources of information about recent developments. On some you can ask for help for specific problems. A current list of some of the popular Linux newsgroups is provided here. For a more compete list see Chapter 1.

comp.os.linux.announce	Announcements of Linux developments
comp.os.linux.admin	System adimination questions
comp.os.linux.misc	Special questions and issues
comp.os.linux.setup	Installation problems
comp.os.linux.help	Questions and answers for particular problems

You read Usenet articles with a newsreader, such as **trn** or **tin**, which allows you first to select a specific newsgroup and then read the articles in it. A newsreader operates like a user interface, allowing you to browse through and select available articles for reading, saving, or printing. **trn**, perhaps the most widely used newsreader today, is a more recent and powerful version of an earlier newsreader called **rn**. It employs a sophisticated retrieval feature called threads that pulls together articles on the same discussion or topic.

You can create articles of your own that you can then add to a newsgroup for others to read. Adding an article to a newsgroup is called posting the article. You post an article using a separate utility called Pnews.

Installing trn and tin

Before you can use **trn** and **tin**, you may have to install them. **tin** is not automatically installed by the Caldera Express Install procedure. You first have to log in as the root user. Before you install, make sure you have mounted your Linux CD-ROM with the following command:

```
$ mount /mnt/cdrom
```

To install **trn** and **tin**, you can either use the **glint** installation program available on your Caldera Desktop, or issue an **rpm** command on the command line. With **glint**, first open the window for your available packages. Then locate and click on the Applications icon. Locate the News icon and click on it. You will then see the **trn** and **tin** packages displayed. Click to select them, and then choose Install.

Alternatively, from the command line, you can change to the **/mnt/cdrom/ packages/RPMS** directory. Then issue the commands:

```
$ rpm -i trn-3.6.1.i386.rpm
$ rpm -i tin-1.22-1.i386.rpm
```

Both **tin** and **trn** can read Usenet news provided on remote news servers that use the Network News Transport Protocol (NNTP). Many such remote news servers are available through the Internet. To connect to a remote news server, first assign the Internet address of the news sever to a shell variable called **NNTPSERVER**, and then export that variable. The assignment and export of **NNTPSERVER** can be done in a login initialization file such as **.bash_profile**.

```
$ NNTPSERVER=news.servername.com
$ export NNTPSERVER
```

To connect to the remote news server using **tin**, either invoke **tin** with the **-r** option, or use the **rtin** command.

```
$ tin -r
```

News Transport Agents

Usenet news is provided over the Internet as a daily newsfeed of articles for over 10,000 newsgroups. This newsfeed is sent to sites that can then provide access to the news for other systems through newsreaders. These sites operate as news servers, and the newsreaders used to access them are their clients. The news server software, called News Transport Agents, is what provides newsreaders with news, allowing you to read newsgroups and post articles. For Linux, three of the popular News Transport Agents are INN, nntp, and Cnews. Both Cnews and nntp are smaller, simpler, and useful for small networks. INN is more powerful and complex, and was designed with large systems in mind.

Daily newsfeeds on Usenet are often very large and consume much of a news server's resources in both time and memory. For this reason, you may not want to set up your own Linux system to receive such newsfeeds. If you are operating in a network of Linux systems, you can designate one of them as the news server and install the News Transport Agent on it to receive and manage the Usenet newsfeeds. Users on other systems on your network can then access that news server with their own newsreaders.

If your network already has a news server, you do not need to install a news transport agent at all. You just have to use your newsreaders to remotely access that server (see **NNTPSERVER** in the previous section). In the case of an Internet Service Provider, such providers will often operate their own news servers, which you can also remotely access using your own newsreaders, such as **trn** and **tin**. Bear in mind though that **trn** and **tin** will have to take the time to download all the articles for selected newsgroups as well as updated information on all the newsgroups.

You can also use News Transport Agents to run local versions of news for just the users on your system or your local network. To do this, you would install nntp or Cnews and configure them just to manage local newsgroups. Users on your system could then post articles and read local news. You could also use INN, though the other agents would be adequate for local networks.

INN

The InterNetNews (INN) News Transport Agent, which is on your Caldera CD-ROM, provides full news server capabilities. Use **glint** or **rpm** to install it from your Caldera CD-ROM, or you can download it from any Linux ftp site, such as **sunsite.unc.edu**. Be sure to select the Redhat version of the INN package so you can use **rpm** to install it. The next example uses **rpm** to install INN.

```
$ rpm -i inn-3.6.1.i386.rpm
```

This will install the INN programs as well as configuration files in the appropriate directories.

In your **/usr/doc** directory, you will find a directory of HOW-TO documents. INN is configured to start automatically whenever you start your system. The primary program for INN is **innd**. The **d** stands for daemon, a program that is loaded at system startup and continues running in the background as you do your work. Various INN configuration files can be found in **/etc/news**. Among these are **inn.conf**, which sets options for INN, and **host.nntp**, which controls access to your system's news. You can edit any of these configuration files should you need to. **man** pages will be installed for all the INN programs and many of the configuration files, such as **innd**, **inn.conf**, **rnews**, and **host.nntp**. Correct configuration of INN can be a complex and time-consuming process. Be sure to consult reference and online resources such as the HOW-TO documents on your CD-ROM in **/docs/HTML/news.html**.

The trn Newsreader

With the popular **trn** newsreader, you can scroll through a list of newsgroups, select one, and then read the articles in it. The **trn** interface has several powerful features, such as pattern searches for groups of articles. The **trn** newsreader is an enhancement of **rn** that allows you to display and search articles by subject, article, or threads. The *t* in **trn** stands for "threaded." A thread is any connection between articles, such as articles that share the same subject or follow-up articles to a previously posted article. You can still use the standard **rn** commands to move from one article to the next. However, **trn**'s special interface, called a selector, allows you to move through a threaded set of articles. For example, if you are reading an article on a particular subject and you give an **n** command to go to the next article, you go to the next article on that subject (in the thread), not to the next sequentially posted article as you would normally do. Instead of moving through a newsgroup's articles according to their posted order, you can move through them using different threads, examining articles according to different subjects. The same is true for an article and its follow-up articles. An article and its follow-ups are threaded so that upon reading an article, pressing the **n** command will move you to the first follow-up to that article, not to the next sequentially posted article. Using threads, you can use the **n** command to read an article with all of its follow-ups, instead of searching separately for each one. The **trn** newsreader commands are listed in Table 9-1.

    trn operates on two levels: the newsgroup list and the article list. When you first execute **trn**, you select a newsgroup from a list of newsgroups. Commands move you from one newsgroup to another in the list. Once you have found the one you want, you can then select articles to read in that newsgroup. When you have finished reading, you can leave that newsgroup and select another in the newsgroup list. You use the **trn** selector to display, organize, and move through the article list, though you can also use the standard **rn** commands to manage the article list.

    The **trn** newsreader distinguishes between those newsgroups with unread news and those with no unread news. You can use certain **trn** commands to search for and select only those newsgroups with unread news. The term "unread news" refers to articles that you personally have not read in a newsgroup. **trn** keeps track of what a user has read or not read by means of a **.newsrc** file placed in the user's account. Each user has his or her own **.newsrc** file, which consists of a list of all the newsgroups provided by the Usenet server. Each entry is used to keep track of whether there is read or unread news in it.

The **trn** newsreader also allows you to subscribe or unsubscribe to a newsgroup. When you first use **trn**, you will be given access to all newsgroups provided by your Usenet server, automatically subscribing you to all newsgroups. However, there may be many newsgroups that you have no interest in. Instead of having them clutter up your **trn** interface, you can unsubscribe to them. You can subscribe to them again later, if you change your mind. The **.newsrc** file keeps track of those newsgroups that you subscribe to.

Newsgroup List

You enter the **rn** newsreader by typing the command **rn** at your Linux prompt. **rn** will initially display a short list of newsgroup headers. However, before doing so, **trn** will first check an official list of new newsgroups with those listed in your **.newsrc** file. If there are any new newsgroups not yet listed in your **.newsrc** file, then **trn** will ask, one by one, if you want to subscribe to them. At each prompt, you can enter **y** to add the newsgroup and **n** not to add it.

There can, at times, be a great many new newsgroups to decide on. Should you want to skip this initial subscription phase, you can do so by invoking **trn** with the **-q** option. With **-q**, **trn** will go directly to displaying the newsgroup headers, skipping any new newsgroup queries.

```
$ trn -q
```

After the subscription phase, **trn** checks to see if there are any newsgroups listed in your **.newsrc** file that have unread news in them. If so, the newsgroup headers for the first few of these are displayed. Each newsgroup header tells how many unread articles remain in a given newsgroup. **trn** then prompts you as to whether you want to read articles in the first newsgroup. If not, you can enter the **n** command to move to the next newsgroup. The **p** command moves you back to the previous newsgroup.

To list articles in a newsgroup, you enter **+** at the prompt. This displays the **trn** selector from which you can select the article you want to display. If you enter **y**, you will skip the list of articles and display the first article in the newsgroup. You will then be prompted to read the next article or quit and return to the newsgroup list. You can leave the newsgroup and return to the newsgroup list by entering **q** at the prompt.

In the next example, the user enters the **trn** interface, and a list of newsgroup headers is displayed. The user is then prompted for the first header, which the user skips with the **n** command. At the next header, the user enters a **+** command to list articles in the **comp.os.linux.misc** newsgroup.

```
$ trn
comp.ai.language                        3 articles
```

```
comp.os.linux.misc                    1   article
rec.arts.movies                       7   articles
rec.food.recipes                      245 articles
sci.physics.fusion                    32  articles
talk.politics.theory                  126 articles
 etc.


====== 3 unread articles in comp.ai.language -- read now? [+ynq] n
====== 1 unread articles in comp.os.linux.misc -- read now? [ynq] +
```

trn has a variety of commands for moving through the list of newsgroups. You can move to the first or last newsgroup, the next or previous newsgroup, or the newsgroup whose name has a specific pattern. For example, a **$** will place you at the end of the newsgroup list. Many commands are designed to distinguish between read and unread newsgroups. The **^** places you at the first newsgroup with unread news, whereas the number 1 places you at the first newsgroup in the list, whether it is read or not. The lowercase **n** and **p** commands place you at the next and previous unread newsgroups. To move to the next or previous newsgroup regardless of whether it is read or not, you use the uppercase **N** and **P** commands.

When you first start using **trn**, many of your newsgroups will have a vast number of unread articles in them. Instead of reading each one, you could simply start with a clean slate by marking them all as read. The **c** command entered at the newsgroup prompt will mark all articles in the newsgroup as read. Then, unread-sensitive commands such as **n** and **p** cannot select the newsgroup until new articles are posted for it.

Often, you will know the name of a newsgroup that you want to access. Instead of stepping through newsgroups one at a time with **n** and **p** commands to get to the one you want, you can use pattern searches to move directly to it. The pattern searching commands give **trn** great versatility in locating newsgroups. To perform a pattern search for a newsgroup, at the prompt you enter a **/** followed by the pattern. The **/** performs a forward search through the list of newsgroups. The **?** performs a backward search. In the next example, the user searches for the newsgroup on food recipes.

```
$ trn
comp.ai.language                      3   articles
comp.os.linux.misc                    1   article
rec.arts.movies                       7   articles
rec.food.recipes                      245 articles
sci.physics.fusion                    32  articles
```

```
talk.politics.theory                        126 articles
 etc.


====== 3 unread articles in comp.ai.language -- read now? [+ynq]
/food.recipes
 Searching...
====== 245 unread articles in rec.food.recipes -- read now?
[+ynq] +
```

You can also locate a newsgroup by its full name. The **g** command followed by a newsgroup's name will locate that newsgroup.

```
====== 3 unread articles in comp.ai.language -- read now? [+ynq]
g rec.food.recipes
Searching...
====== 245 unread articles in rec.food.recipes -- read now? [+ynq]
```

The **trn** list and search commands reference only those newsgroups that you have subscribed to. With the **l** command you can list or search for unsubscribed newsgroups. The **l** command by itself lists all newsgroups that you have not subscribed to. Followed by a pattern, the **l** command searches unsubscribed newsgroups for that pattern, listing those matched. For example, **ltrek** searches for unsubscribed newsgroups with the pattern "trek" in their names.

You can subscribe to a newsgroup with the **a** command. Enter **a** followed by the name of the newsgroup you want. You can unsubscribe from a newsgroup with the **u** command. For example, **u rec.foods.recipes** will unsubscribe that newsgroup. If you tried to select it with search commands such as **/** or **g**, you would not find it. Of course, the **l** command would locate it: **l rec.foods.recipes**. To once again subscribe to this newsgroup, you would use the command **a rec.foods.recipes**.

The trn Selector

As mentioned earlier, typing **+** at the **trn** prompt enters the selector, which allows you to use threads. The selector consists of a screen that lists each article's author, thread count, and subject. Any follow-up articles are preceded by a **>** symbol. Articles are grouped according to the threads they belong to. The first article in each thread is preceded by an ID consisting of a lowercase alphabetic character or a single digit, starting from *a*. A sample **trn** selector screen is shown here:

```
rec.food.recipes      258 articles (moderated)

a    Dylan Chris        1    Fruit Salad
b    Cecelia Petersen   1    Fudge Cake
d    Richard Leland     2    Chocolate News
     Larisa@atlash
     Aleina Petersen    1    >White chocolate
     Maryann Price      1    >Chocolate Fudge
     mark@pacific       1    >
     Justin G.          1    >Chocolate
e    George Petersen    1    Apple Muffins
f    Marylou Carrion    1    REQUEST: romantic dinners
g    Valerie Fuller     1    REQUEST: Dehydrated Goodies
i    Carolyn Blacklock  1    REQUEST: Devonshire Cream
     Bill Bode          1    >
j    Bonnie Matoza      1    Sauces
l    Gabriel Matoza     1    Passion Fruit
o    Ken Blacklock      1    REQUEST: blackened (red)fish
     augie@napa         3    >blackened (red)fish
     John Carrion
     Anntoinnete

-- Select threads (date order) -- 24%
```

Upon entering the selector, the first screen of articles is displayed, and the first thread is preceded with an *a*. To display the next screen of articles, you press either the SPACEBAR or the > key. You can display the previous screen by pressing the < key. Upon displaying the next screen, threads will again be listed beginning from *a*. The ID preceding a thread is unique to that thread only for that screen; they are simply a screen device for referencing threads displayed on the screen at that time.

To read an article, you first select the thread for that article, and then instruct the selector to display it. You select a thread by pressing the key corresponding to its ID. For example, pressing **d** selects the thread that has a *d* at the beginning of its first line. You will notice that upon selecting a thread, a **+** symbol appears before its ID. Once you have selected the thread, you can then display its articles by pressing either the ENTER key or uppercase **z**. The first article in the thread will be displayed. Pressing the **n** key moves you to the next article in the thread. Once you have found the article you want, you can read it using any of the standard **trn** commands for displaying articles. If the article takes up more than one screen, you can display the next screen by pressing the SPACEBAR.

You can return to the selector any time by pressing the **+** key. Should you no longer want to read articles in a given thread, you need to deselect the thread. You do so by again pressing the key that corresponds to its ID. You will notice that a **+** symbol appears before the ID of a selected thread. Upon deselecting the thread, this **+** symbol will disappear.

You can also use cursor commands to select a thread. When the selector screen first appears, the cursor is placed at the *a* before the first thread. Using the cursor **n** and **p** commands or arrow keys, you can move to the next thread or back to the previous thread. The **n** command moves down to the next thread, and the **p** command moves back to the previous thread. You can also use the UP and DOWN ARROW keys. To start displaying articles in a particular thread, you can simply move the cursor to that thread's ID and press ENTER or **z**.

If you want to examine several threads, you can mark each one by pressing the key corresponding to the ID displayed before the thread. To select the thread preceded by *b*, just press the **b** key. Then move on to the next thread you want, and do the same. A **+** symbol will appear after each thread that you have selected. You can move from one screen to another, selecting the threads you want, and then begin displaying articles based on those threads.

Selector Display Modes: Article, Subject, and Thread

The selector has three display modes: article, subject, and thread, which correspond to how the selector displays articles. You can easily choose the mode you want by pressing the **s** command and entering **a** for article, **s** for subject, or **t** for thread. You can also switch back and forth between the different modes by pressing the **=** key.

Each mode can be thought of as a kind of thread. When using the subject mode, articles are grouped according to their subject entries. A subject is whatever a user enters into the subject field of an article's header. Articles with the same subject entry are threaded together. Subject groupings are limited to those articles that share exactly the same subject entries in their header. Articles that have even slightly different subject entries will not be grouped together.

When using the thread mode, articles are grouped with any posted follow-ups, as well as with articles of the same subject. The follow-up articles are preceded by a **>** symbol. The thread mode differs from the subject mode in that it will include all follow-up articles, even though such articles may have different subject entries. The article mode does not display threads. Articles are listed individually, each preceded by its own ID, in posted sequence.

The selector screen will appear differently depending on the display mode you are using. In the subject mode, the selector displays the author of each article, grouping them into subject categories. With the first author in a subject category, the number of articles in the category is displayed, followed by the category's subject. The subject is listed only once, followed by a list of authors, each representing an article. An ID is placed only before the first article in the subject category. In the subject mode, an ID references a subject, not a particular article. On the screen, IDs are placed only at the beginning of different subject groupings. To select a subject, press the key corresponding to its ID. The subject mode provides easy access to articles on different topics, and the list of subject headings also provides a quick summary of topics being discussed in the newsgroup.

In the next example, the selector is in the subject mode. Notice that item **d** specifies the subject Chocolate News. There are two articles in this subject category, one with the author Richard Leland and another with the author Larisa@atlash. The article count specifies two articles. The same is true for item **i**, except that the second article is a follow-up article, as indicated with a **>** symbol. Item **u** specifies a subject category of three articles, all of which are follow-ups. Notice that these are actually follow-ups to item **o**, though item **o** has a slightly different subject title.

```
rec.food.recipes                 258 articles (moderated)

a      Dylan Chris          1    Fruit Salad
b      Cecelia Petersen     1    Fudge Cake
d      Richard Leland       2    Chocolate News
       Larisa@atlash
e      George Petersen      1    Apple Muffins
f      Marylou Carrion      1    REQUEST: romantic dinners
g      Valerie Fuller        1    REQUEST: Dehydrated Goodies
i      Carolyn Blacklock    1    REQUEST: Devonshire Cream
       Bill Bode            1    >
j      Bonnie Matoza        1    Sauces
l      Gabriel Matoza       1    Passion Fruit
o      Ken Blacklock        1    REQUEST: blackened (red)fish
r      dylan@sf             1    REQUEST: Cheese Toast
s      Penny Bode           1    REQUEST: Sausage Recipes
t      gloria@stlake        1    Biscuit Recipe
u      augie@napa           3    >blackened (red)fish entree
       John Carrion
       Anntoinnete
v      John Gunther         1    Oatmeal Cookies

-- Select subjects (date order) -- 24%
Selector mode:  Threads, Subjects, Articles? [tsa] s
```

In the thread mode, the selector displays articles that are connected either by follow-up or by subject. In other words, the thread mode groups articles that are in any way connected to each other. Follow-up articles are listed below the original article and preceded by a **>** sign. A grouping of this sort is often referred to as a thread. Using the thread mode, you can easily access an article and all follow-ups posted on it to check out any discussion or comments. Articles related by subject will be in the same thread, along with their own follow-ups. Each thread will have its own ID. To select a thread, just press the corresponding key for its ID.

In the next example, the **trn** selector is in the thread mode. Notice how the screen differs from the subject mode. Item **d** now includes follow-up articles as well as articles on the same subject. Item **d** represents a thread consisting of six articles. The first two share the same subject, and the remaining four are follow-up articles to them, as indicated by the **>** symbol. Many of these follow-up articles have different subject titles, while two of them, Maryann Price and mark@pacific, are two follow-up articles that have the same subject. Notice that the **o** item represents a thread beginning with the Ken Blacklock article and includes its three follow-ups, augie@napa, John Carrion, and Anntoinette. The three follow-ups all have the same subject, though it is different from the initial article in the thread.

```
rec.food.recipes     258 articles (moderated)

a    Dylan Chris        1    Fruit Salad
b    Cecelia Petersen   1    Fudge Cake
d    Richard Leland     2    Chocolate News
     Larisa@atlash
     Aleina Petersen    1    >White chocolate
     Maryann Price      2    >Chocolate Fudge
     mark@pacific
     Justin G.          1    >Chocolate
e    George Petersen    1    Apple Muffins
f    Marylou Carrion    1    REQUEST: romantic dinners
g    Valerie Fuller     1    REQUEST: Dehydrated Goodies
i    Carolyn Blacklock  1    REQUEST: Devonshire Cream
     Bill Bode          1    >
j    Bonnie Matoza      1    Sauces
l    Gabriel Matoza     1    Passion Fruit
o    Ken Blacklock      1    REQUEST: blackened (red)fish
     augie@napa         3    >blackened (red)fish entree
     John Carrion
     Anntoinete

-- Select threads (date order) -- 24%
Selector mode:  Threads, Subjects, Articles? [tsa] t
```

In the next example, the articles are simply arranged by posted order, each article having its own ID. Notice how items **d** and **e** have the same subject. No threads are active in the article mode. Articles and their follow-ups are scattered throughout the display. For example, though the article augie@napa is a follow-up to Ken Blacklock, each has its own ID in different parts of the display, **r** and **v**.

```
rec.food.recipes              258 articles (moderated)

a    Dylan Chris          Fruit Salad
b    Cecelia Petersen     Fudge Cake
d    Richard Leland       Chocolate News
e    Larisa@atlash        Chocolate News
f    George Petersen      Apple Muffins
g    Marylou Carrion      REQUEST: romantic dinners
i    Valerie Fuller       REQUEST: Dehydrated Goodies
j    Carolyn Blacklock    REQUEST: Devonshire Cream
l    Bonnie Matoza        Sauces
o    Gabriel Matoza       Passion Fruit
r    Ken Blacklock        REQUEST: blackened (red)fish
s    dylan@sf             REQUEST: Cheese Toast
t    Penny Bode           REQUEST: Sausage Recipes
u    gloria@stlake        Biscuit Recipe
v    augie@napa           >blackened (red)fish
w    John Gunther         Oatmeal Cookies
x    Margaret             REQUEST: Potato Salad
y    Frank Moitoza        REQUEST: Sesame Chicken
z    maryann@sebast       >Summer desserts

-- Select subjects (date order) -- 24%
Selector mode:  Threads, Subjects, Articles? [tsa] a
```

Displaying Articles: trn Thread Trees

When you select an article, its header is displayed followed by a **(more)** prompt and
the first page of the text. The article will be displayed screen by screen, just as files are
displayed screen by screen with the More utility. To continue to the next screen, you
press the SPACEBAR. You can move backward one page at a time by pressing the **b** key.
The **q** command allows you to quit before reading the whole article. You can also
search the text of the article for a pattern. The **g** command followed by a pattern will
locate the first occurrence of that pattern in the text. You can repeat the search with the
G command.

```
rec.food.recipes (moderated) #7155 (229 more)                           (1)
From: richpete@garnet.berkeley.edu (Richard Petersen)
[1] Spelling Cookies
```

```
Followup-To: poster
Date: Mon Dec 20 04:48:01 PST 1995
Organization: University of California, Berkeley
Lines: 43

Spelling Cookies
                    INGREDIENTS
        1 cup flour
        2 teaspoons single acting baking powder, or 1 teaspoon double
               acting baking powder, or 1 teaspoon baking soda
        1/2 teaspoon nutmeg
        1/4 teaspoon cinnamon
        3/4 cup butter   (or 1 1/2 sticks)
        1 cup brown or dark brown sugar
        1/2 cup regular sugar
        1 egg
        1 teaspoon vanilla extract
        1/4 cup milk
--MORE--(44%)
```

Upon pressing the SPACEBAR the next screen of the message is displayed.

```
rec.food.recipes (moderated) #7155 (229 more)
[1] Spelling Cookies


    12 ounces semisweet chocolate chips
    pecan or walnut bits
    3/4 cup wheat germ
    2 3/4 cups rolled oats (Old Fashioned Quaker Oats)


                    STEPS
    1. Mix brown and regular sugars together.
    2. Cream butter, then mix in sugars. Then mix in egg, vanilla
extract, and milk until creamy.
    3. Separately mix flower, cinnamon, nutmeg, baking powder (or
baking soda), salt (if wanted).
    4. Mix in flower concoction into butter/sugar concoction
until creamy.
    5. With spatula add in wheat germ, then nuts, then chocolate
chips, then oats.
```

```
     6. Preheat oven to about 300 degrees.  Spoon out onto cookie
sheets. Cook for about 20 minutes or so.  Watch carefully.  When
top of cookies begin to brown they are done.
     7.  Eat immediately or refrigerate.  Aging only improves
taste.
     8.  These are called spelling cookies because when I gave the
recipe to a friend in my class her daughter found so many
spelling mistakes that she called them spelling cookies.
     9.  Eat at your own risk.   Good luck.

End of article 7155 (of 7158) -- what next? [npq] +
```

At the end of the article you will be presented with a prompt asking what you want to do next. The choices **n**, **p**, and **q** will be displayed in brackets. Pressing **n** will display the next article in the newsgroup, and **p** will display the previous article. To return to your selector screen of newsgroup articles, you press **+**, as shown in the next example. Pressing **q** will return to the newsgroup list.

```
End of article 7155 (of 7158) -- what next? [npq] +
```

When you display the first article in a thread, a thread tree will appear in the upper-right corner of the screen. A thread tree represents the connections between articles in a thread. Each unread article is represented by a number starting from 1, with each enclosed in brackets. Lines connect the different article numbers. The number representing the article you are currently displaying is highlighted in the thread tree. Once you read an article and move on to another, the read article's number is enclosed in parentheses, and the next article's number is highlighted.

A thread tree illustrates the relationship between articles. The first article in a thread is located in the upper-left corner of the tree. Branching to the right and down, the next column, are any follow-up articles to that article. Follow-up articles are connected to each other by lines. For example, the follow-up articles for the first article in the thread are arranged as a column of bracketed numbers set to the right of the first article's number. A line connects the article's number to its first follow-up. Any other follow-up articles are arranged in a column below this first follow-up, each connected by a line. The last follow-up article will be connected by a slanted line. Figure 9-1 shows such a thread tree.

A follow-up article may, in turn, have its own follow-ups. People may respond to another person's response, carrying on a conversation or debate on a particular point. The number of a second follow-up is positioned to the right of the follow-up's number. That second follow-up may also have its own follow-up, and the number will be positioned to the right of that follow-up's number. You could have a whole string of sequential follow-ups, arranged in a horizontal line, as shown in Figure 9-2.

Any given follow-up could have more than one follow-up of its own. These follow-ups are arranged in a column below the first follow-up. Thus, a thread tree can

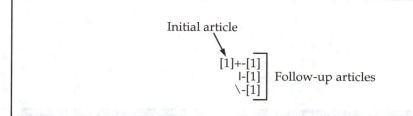

Figure 9-1.   *Thread tree showing initial article and follow-up articles*

extend horizontally and vertically. Horizontally the thread lists a follow-up that responds to previous follow-ups and that may, in turn, have a follow-up responding to it. Vertically the thread lists several follow-ups that are all responses to one particular follow-up.

Articles related by subject are listed below the first article. These are not connected by lines. Looking at the thread tree, the left-most column of article numbers indicates subject groupings, and any articles branching to the right are follow-up articles. As shown in Figure 9-3, articles that share the same subject are arranged in the outer column.

The numbers that represent articles in the thread tree indicate whether articles share the same subject. The first article, represented by the number 1, indicates the initial subject of the thread. Articles that share the same subject will have the same number. Other articles with the number 1 share the same subject as the first article. Many times, however, articles in the same thread may have different subjects, and these will be represented with a different number. Any subsequent articles with that same subject will share that same number. The first article with a different subject will be represented by a number 2, and any other articles with a number 2 will share that same subject. As different subjects in the thread are encountered, they are incrementally given a new number. Such a numbering system allows you to identify different subtopics in the thread. It is like detecting different parts of a conversation

```
                  Follow-ups to follow-ups
                            |
  [1]+-[1]       _____
   |-[1]--[1]--[1]
   \-[1]
```

Figure 9-2.   *Thread tree showing articles that are follow-ups to follow-ups*

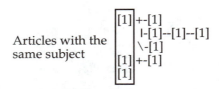

Figure 9-3. `trn` *thread tree showing subject articles*

that veer off into different topics. Also, should part of a thread contain a subject you are not interested in, you can easily identify what articles in the thread to avoid. Figure 9-4 shows a thread tree with different subjects. The first follow-up article is represented by a number 2, indicating that this article has a different subject from that of the first article. Again, the article below it is represented by a number 3, indicating that it has yet another subject.

You can use the thread tree to move from one article to another in the thread, going directly to any article without having to display any intervening articles. You can even move backward in the thread. Thread trees are a very easy way to move back and forth to different articles in a thread. You use the arrow keys to move up and down and across the thread tree, highlighting different article numbers as you go. For example, if you press a DOWN ARROW key, you move from the current article number to the one below it, highlighting it. Pressing the RIGHT ARROW key moves you to the article number on the right. Repeatedly pressing the RIGHT ARROW key moves you to article numbers farther on the right. The LEFT ARROW key will move you back to the left, and the UP ARROW will move you up. The article for the number you have currently highlighted will be displayed. As you move through the thread tree, different articles are displayed.

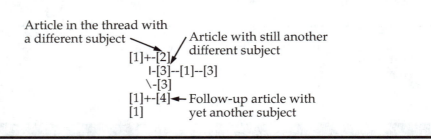

Figure 9-4. `trn` *thread tree showing articles with different subjects*

Saving Articles

You can save any article that you have read. After displaying the article, enter the **s** command with a file name. If the file does not yet exist, you will be asked if you want to use a mailbox file format for it. If you enter **y**, the file will be a mailbox file, and the article will be saved as one message in that mailbox. You can then use the **mailx** command with the **-f** option to read the articles saved in that file. If, however, you simply press ENTER, the file will have a standard text file format.

```
rec.food.recipes (moderated) #7155 (229 more)                    (1)
From: richpete@garnet.berkeley.edu (Richard Petersen)
Subject: Spelling Cookies
Followup-To: poster
Date: Mon Dec 20 04:48:01 PST 1995
Organization: University of California, Berkeley
Lines: 43


Spelling Cookies
                    INGREDIENTS
        1 cup flour
        2 teaspoons single acting baking powder, or 1 teaspoon double
              acting baking powder, or 1 teaspoon baking soda
        1/2 teaspoon nutmeg
        1/4 teaspoon cinnamon
        3/4 cup butter  (or 1 1/2 sticks)
        1 cup brown or dark brown sugar
        1/2 cup regular sugar
        1 egg
        1 teaspoon vanilla extract
        1/4 cup milk
End of article 7155 (of 7158) -- what next? [npq] s spellcookies

File /h/garnet_d/richpete/News/spellcookies doesn't exist--
        use mailbox format? [ynq] y
Saved to mailbox /h/garnet_d/richpete/News/spellcookies

End of article 7155 (of 7158) -- what next? [npq]
```

Other articles that you save to an already existing file will simply be appended to it. In the case of mailbox files, the added articles will become new messages. When saving more than one article in the same file, the mailbox format has several advantages. You can easily access particular articles using Mail. You can also mail replies to authors of articles using the **R** command, and you can easily incorporate an article in messages to other users.

Replying to Articles in trn: Follow-ups and Messages

You can reply to a specific article either by posting a follow-up article of your own or by sending the author a message by mail. A follow-up article is an article that you post on Usenet in response to another article you have read, and anyone on Usenet can read it. A mail message, on the other hand, is a private message that you send using Linux mail. The **f** and **F** commands will post a follow-up article, and the **r** and **R** commands send a reply message.

Posting Follow-ups

You post a follow-up article from within the **trn** newsreader. While you are reading an article, you can post a follow-up to it by entering the **f** or **F** commands. These commands invoke Pnews, which actually enters and posts your follow-up article. The **F** command will include the text of the article you are responding to in your follow-up. The text will be displayed indented with each line preceded by a > sign.

You can also post a follow-up by locating the article you want to respond to and pressing the **f** command. You are then placed in the editor with the header for your follow-up. You can enter the text of your article and edit the header fields if you want. Upon exiting the editor, you are prompted to either send, abort, edit, or list the follow-up article. The **send** command posts the article for you.

You can see how follow-ups allow you to carry on discussions about an article in your newsgroup. You can not only read an article, you can also read what other people think of it in follow-up articles. As described earlier, you can even post follow-ups to the follow-ups, carrying on discussions with other users about an article. You post a follow-up of a follow-up by locating the follow-up article and then pressing **f** and posting your response.

When responding to an article, it is often helpful to include the original text in your follow-up. You can do so using the **F** command. Each included line of article text is preceded by a > sign. You do not have to keep the entire text of the article in your follow-up. Suppose you only want to respond to one part of the article. While in the editor, you can delete all but that part of the article, and your follow-up article will then list only that part of the original article and any comments that you decide to add. You can even use the editor to insert your own comments throughout the included text of the original article, providing a kind of annotated version of it. Use the **F** command to make your follow-ups clearer and avoid having to retype others' comments.

The **F** command is very useful when posting follow-ups to follow-ups. It is often clearer to include those comments a user has made that you are responding to. Instead of painstakingly typing them in yourself, the **F** command will include the follow-up article text automatically for your own follow-up.

Mailing Replies to Authors

Instead of posting a follow-up for everyone to read, you can simply mail a reply directly to the author of an article. You do so with either the **r** and **R** commands. First locate the article you want to send a reply to, and then press **r**. The article header is displayed, and the mail program is invoked. You are placed in your editor, and you can then enter your message. The header will also be included so that you can change your subject entry or summary line if you want. When you leave the editor, you are asked if you want to send, abort, edit, or list the message. The **send** command will mail the message to the author of the article.

Should you want to include a copy of the article's text in your message, you use the **R** command. As with the **F** command, the **R** command will include the text of the article with each line preceded by a **>** sign. In the editor, you can then delete, copy, or move the text as you wish.

Marking Articles

Once you have read an article, **trn** will no longer display its header in the article list, and you will no longer be able to access it at a later date through **trn**. If you want to be able to come back to the article at a later date, you can mark the article as unread so that **trn** will continue to display its header in the article list. To mark an article as unread, enter the **m** command when you read it. If you only want to read it during the next session, use the **M** command.

Article Selections

You can select a group of articles based on pattern searches or number references. A pattern search followed by a colon and one of the **trn** commands will apply that command to every article with that pattern, not just to the next article. In effect, a pattern search followed by a colon will select a group of articles upon which you can perform operations. For example, if you want to save all articles dealing with the subject "cookies" you could issue the command **/cookies/:s cookfile**, as shown in the next example.

```
End of article 6914 (of 7158) -- what next? [npq] /cookies/:s
cookfile
Searching...7094
File /h/garnet_d/richpete/News/cookfile doesn't exist--
        use mailbox format? [ynq] y
Saved to mailbox /h/garnet_d/richpete/News/cookfile
7128    Appended to mailbox /h/garnet_d/richpete/News/cookfile
```

```
7155    Appended to mailbox /h/garnet_d/richpete/News/cookfile
done
End of article 6914 (of 7158) -- what next? [npq]
```

The ^ symbol is a special pattern that represents all articles. To save all articles to a file, you use the command:

```
/^/:s myfile
```

When used with the = command, a pattern can provide you with a listing of articles on a certain topic. The = command lists the number and subject of each article. When qualified by a pattern, it only lists those articles on that subject. The next example lists the numbers and subjects of all unread articles on cookies.

```
/cookies/:=
```

If you want to include all read articles in your list, you need to qualify the pattern with **r**. The next example provides a listing of all articles on cookies, including read ones:

```
/cookies/r:=
```

By default, a pattern only searches the subject field of an article. When used with the **a** qualifier, a pattern searches throughout the entire text of an article. The next example provides a list of all recipes that use chocolate. The results of this particular query is often too long to print out.

```
/chocolate/a:=
```

You can also reference a group of articles by listing their numbers separated by commas. End the list with a colon followed by a command applied to those articles. Since articles are consecutively numbered, you can include number ranges in your list, for example, **3-5** references articles 3, 4, and 5. To save articles 34, 17, and 9-12, you would use the command:

```
34,17,9-12:s myfile
```

In the next example, the user saves articles 7155 and 7128 to the file **goodcook**:
7155, 7128:s goodcook.

```
End of article 6919 (of 7158) -- what next? [npq] 7155,7128:s
goodcook
7155    Appended to mailbox /h/garnet_d/richpete/News/goodcook
7128    Appended to mailbox /h/garnet_d/richpete/News/goodcook

End of article 6919 (of 7158) -- what next? [npq]
```

In both pattern and number references, you can append other commands to be applied to the group of articles. Just separate each command with a colon. In the next example, articles 34, 17, and 9-12, are both saved and printed.

```
34,17,9-12:s myfile: | lp
```

trn Options

You can use a number of options with **trn**. With the **-n** option you can specify a newsgroup or type of newsgroup that you want to read. With the **-l** option you can list just newsgroup headers. In the next example, the user lists the newsgroup headers for the **rec.food.recipes** newsgroups.

```
$ trn -l -n rec.food.recipes
```

With the **-q** option you can skip the subscription phase and move directly to reading your newsgroups.

```
$ trn -q rec.food.recipes
```

Article List : the rn Newsreader

As an alternative to the **trn** selector, you can use **rn** commands to display and select items in your article list. The **rn** commands for moving through the newsgroup list and the article list are often the same. Depending on what type of list you are operating on, you will either move through newsgroups or articles. For example, the **n** command for the newsgroup list moves you to the next newsgroup, whereas the **n** command for the article list moves you to the next article. The **rn** newsreader commands are listed in Table 9-2.

Once you have located the newsgroup you want, you enter the article level and select the article in that newsgroup that you want to read. Upon pressing **y** at the newsgroup prompt, you enter the article level, and the header of the first article in the newsgroup is displayed. You can then read the first article or use article-level commands to move to another article in the newsgroup. The article-level commands are the same as those described earlier for moving through the newsgroup list. To move to the next article, you use the **n** command. The **p** command moves you back an article. The **^** command moves to the first unread article, and the **$** command moves to the last article.

You can also move to a particular article by entering its number. Articles in a newsgroup are numbered consecutively. You can obtain a list of unread article titles and their numbers by pressing the **=** sign. Each line will list the number of the article, its title, and its subject. Entering the number of the article will move you to it.

```
End of article 7155 (of 7158) -- what next? [npq] 7155
rec.food.recipes (moderated) #7155 (229 more)                    (1)
From: richpete@garnet.berkeley.edu (Richard Petersen)
```

With **rn** you can also use pattern searches at the article level to locate an article. The **/** command, followed by a pattern, searches forward in the article list for an article with that pattern in the subject field of its header. The **?** command will search backward. In the next example, the user searches the subject field of articles for the pattern "cookies."

```
End of article 7050 (of 7158) -- what next? [npq] /cookies
Searching...
```

Using qualifiers with the pattern search, you can specify whether you want to search the text of articles, the entire header, or articles you have already read. The **a** qualifier searches the entire text of articles for a pattern. The **h** qualifier searches the entire header, and the **r** qualifier includes read articles in the search. In the next example, the user searches the headers of articles for the pattern "richpete," including any articles that have already been read.

```
End of article 6914 (of 7158) -- what next? [^Nnpq] /richpete/hr
Searching...
```

You can also search for articles that have the same subject. To do so, you first locate an article with the subject you are looking for. To locate the next article with that same subject, you press CTRL-**n**. You then move to that article. Consecutive CTRL-**n**'s will find the next articles with the same subject. CTRL-**p** searches backward for the previous article with the same subject.

Posting Articles: Pnews

You can post your own articles for a newsgroup of your choice. Perhaps the most commonly used utility for posting articles is Pnews. It prompts you for certain header information, places you in an editor in which you can type in your article, and then prompts you either to send, edit, save, or quit the article.

To begin, enter the **Pnews** command at your Linux prompt. You are then prompted to enter the newsgroup for the article. To see the full list of newsgroups, enter a **?** at the newsgroups prompt. It is, however, a good idea to have already decided on what newsgroups you want. You can obtain a listing of newsgroups at any time from the newsgroups file located in the **news** directory on your system.

After selecting your newsgroups, you are asked to specify distribution. Distribution can be made at ever widening areas. You can post your article for local viewing for users on your own system, or you can post it for worldwide viewing. There are various intermediate levels of distribution, such as North America, the United States, or a specific state or city. Pnews will first list possible prefixes, and then you enter the one you want at the distribution prompt. For the United States you would enter **usa**.

Next you are asked to enter a title or subject of the article. This will be used to classify the article and will be searched in pattern searches. You are then asked if you really want to post the article. To continue, enter **y**. You are then asked if you have a prepared file to include in your article. Often it is easier to write your article and save it to a file first, using a standard editor. Once it is ready, you can post the contents of that file. The contents of the file you specify are then read into the article that is being posted. If you do not enter a file name at this point, Pnews will automatically place you in an editor where you can type in your article.

Finally, Pnews prompts you either to send, abort, edit, or list the article. You need enter only the first character of a command to execute it. For example, if you change your mind and decide not to post the article, you just enter **a** at this prompt, quitting Pnews without sending the article. On the other hand, you can enter **e** at the prompt to edit the article, in case you notice any mistakes or want to add something. You would then be placed in the standard editor with the contents of the article displayed. Here, you can make the changes you want and return to the Pnews prompt upon exiting the standard editor (**zz** for Vi). To post the article, enter **s**, for send, at this prompt. The article is sent to the Usenet manager and posted in the appropriate newsgroup.

If you want to use the standard editor to type the text of the article, you simply press ENTER when asked for a prepared file to include. You are then asked to enter an editor. Within brackets, Pnews will display the default standard editor it uses—often Vi—and you can simply press ENTER to use it. Pnews then places you in the default editor and displays the header information. You are free to change fields in the header if you want. You can change your subject or even your newsgroup. You then use standard editing commands to type the text of your article. When finished, exit the editor (if you are using Vi, press **ZZ**). Pnews prompts you to send, abort, edit, or list your article. You can, of course, edit your article again by typing **e** at this prompt. To finally post the article, you enter **s** at the prompt.

Pnews Signatures: The .signature File

You usually end an article with the same standard signature information, such as your name, Internet address or addresses, and a polite sign-off. As you write more articles, it is helpful to have your signature information automatically added to your articles. To do so, you need to create a file called **.signature** in your home directory and enter your signature information in it. Pnews will read the contents of the **.signature** file and place them at the end of your article. You can use any standard editor to create your **.signature** file.

The tin Newsreader

The **tin** newsreader operates using a selector that is much like the one used in the **trn** newsreader. However, **tin** has a screen selector for both newsgroups and articles. When you enter **tin**, the selector displays the screen listing your newsgroups. You can then select the newsgroup you want and display a screen for its articles.

One set of screen movement commands are used for all screens, whether for newsgroups, article lists, or article text. CTRL-**d**, CTRL-**f**, and SPACEBAR all move you forward to the next screen. CTRL-**u**, CTRL-**b**, and **b** all move you backward to the previous screen. The UP ARROW and the **k** key move you up a line on the screen, and the DOWN ARROW and **j** key move you down a line. The **q** command will move you back from one selector to another. For example, if you are in the article selector, pressing **q** will move you back to the newsgroup selector. **Q** will quit the **tin** newsreader entirely.

tin also has a set of editing and history commands that you can use to edit any commands that you enter. ESC will always erase a command you have entered and let you start over. The editing commands are a subset of the Emacs commands. CTRL-**d** deletes a character, CTRL-**f** and the RIGHT ARROW key move right one character. CTRL-**b** and the LEFT ARROW key move back one character. To insert new text, move your cursor to the position you want and start typing. **tin** also keeps a history of the commands you enter. You can recall the previous commands with CTRL-**p**, moving back, one by one, through a list of your previously entered commands. CTRL-**n** moves you forward through the list. You can find a complete listing of all **tin** commands in the **tin** manual pages, which you can invoke by typing **man tin**. The **tin** newsreader commands are listed in Table 9-3.

When you start **tin**, it first displays a screen of newsgroups. The term "Group Selection" will be shown at the top of the screen. To its right will be "h=help." Pressing the **h** key will bring up a help menu. The newsgroups are listed with a selection number that identifies the newsgroup, followed by the number of unread articles, and then the name of the newsgroup.

To select a newsgroup, you must first move to it. You can do this in a variety of ways. If you see your newsgroup displayed on the screen, you can just use your UP and DOWN ARROW keys to move to it. CTRL-**d** will move you to the next screen, and CTRL-**u** will move you back. Instead of using the arrow keys, you can move directly to a newsgroup by entering its index number. You can also locate a newsgroup by using pattern searches. You enter the **/** followed by a pattern. **?** performs a backward search.

Once you have located the newsgroup you want, press ENTER to display a list of its articles. A list of commonly used commands are displayed at the bottom of the screen. The **s** command will subscribe to a new newsgroup, and the **u** command will unsubscribe.

```
Group Selection (agate.berkeley.edu 3230)         h=help

    1    3      comp.ai.language
    2    1      comp.os.linux.misc
    3    7      rec.arts.movies
    4    24     rec.food.recipes
    5    32     sci.physics.fusion
    6    126    talk.politics.theory

    <n>=set current to n, TAB=next unread, /=search pattern,
c)atchup,
  g)oto, j=line down, k=line up, h)elp, m)ove, q)uit, r=toggle
all/unread,
    s)ubscribe, S)ub pattern, u)nsubscribe, U)nsub pattern,
y)ank in/out

search forwards > rec.food
```

The **tin** newsreader displays the subject and author of each article in the newsgroup preceded by an index number and, if unread, a **+**. The **+** sign indicates all unread articles. Working from the selector, you can choose articles you want to display. You select an article by moving the cursor to that article and pressing ENTER. Both the newsgroup and article selector screens use many of the same commands. The UP and DOWN ARROW keys will move you from one article to the next. If there is more than one screen of articles, you can move back and forth through them using CTRL-**u** or

CTRL-**d**. You can also move to an article by typing its index number. An example of the **tin** article selector screen follows.

```
rec.food.recipes (119T 124A 0K 0H R)          h=help

65    +    Fruit Salad                   Dylan Chris
66    +    Fudge Cake                    Cecelia Petersen
67    +    Chocolate News                Richard Leland
68    +    Chocolate News                Larisa@atlash
69    +    Apple Muffins                 George Petersen
70    +    REQUEST: romantic dinners     Marylou Carrion
71    +    REQUEST: Dehydrated Goodies   Valerie Fuller
72    +    REQUEST: Devonshire Cream     Carolyn Blacklock
73    +    Sauces                        Bonnie Matoza
74    +    Passion Fruit                 Gabriel Matoza
75    +    REQUEST: blackened (red)fish  Ken Blacklock
76    +    REQUEST: Cheese Toast         dylan@sf
77    +    REQUEST: Sausage Recipes      Penny Bode
78    +    Biscuit Recipe                gloria@stlake
79    +    >blackened (red)fish          augie@napa
80    +    Oatmeal Cookies               John Gunther
81    +    REQUEST: Potato Salad         Margaret
82    +    REQUEST: Sesame Chicken       Frank Moitoza
83    +    >Summer desserts              maryann@sebast

    <n>=set current to n, TAB=next unread, /=search pattern,
^K)ill/select,
  a)uthor search, c)atchup, j=line down, k=line up, K=mark read,
l)ist thread,
    |=pipe, m)ail, o=print, q)uit, r=toggle all/unread, s)ave,
t)ag, w=post
```

The commonly used commands for accessing articles are displayed at the bottom of the screen. You can search articles for a specified pattern with the **/** command. The **a** command allows you to search for articles by a specified author. The **s** command will save an article. You can post an article of your own to the newsgroup by pressing the **w** command. You will be prompted for header information, and then you enter the text of your message. Once you have selected and displayed an article, you will also be able to post follow-ups and send replies.

Once you have selected an article, it is displayed. If the article takes up more than one screen, you can move forward by pressing the SPACEBAR and backward by pressing the **b** key. With the **B** command you can search the article for a specified pattern, and with the **s** command you can save it. With the **f** command you can post a follow-up to the article, and with the **r** command you can send a message to the author.

```
Mon, 20 Dec 1995 04:48:o1   rec.food.recipes   Thread   33 of  119
Lines 43                    Spelling Cookies   No responses
richpete@garnet.berkeley.edu. Richard Petersen at University of
California


Spelling Cookies
                    INGREDIENTS
        1 cup flour
        2 teaspoons single acting baking powder, or 1 teaspoon
          double acting baking powder, or 1 teaspoon baking soda
        1/2 teaspoon nutmeg
        1/4 teaspoon cinnamon
        3/4 cup butter  (or 1 1/2 sticks)
        1 cup brown or dark brown sugar
        1/2 cup regular sugar
        1 egg
        1 teaspoon vanilla extract
        1/4 cup milk

  <n>=set current to n, TAB=next unread, /=search pattern,
^K)ill/select,
      a)uthor search, B)ody search, c)atchup, f)ollowup, K=mark
read,
        |=pipe, m)ail, o=print, q)uit, r)eply mail, s)ave, t)ag,
w=post


    --More--(44%)  [46/100]
```

You can also automatically select articles and newsgroups by moving to their entries and pressing **+**. A ***** will appear before the automatically selected entries. These are known as *hot items*. You can reference these automatically selected items in the various **tin** commands such as the **same** or **mail** commands.

Encoded Binaries: uuencode and uudecode

Certain newsgroups specialize in encoded binary files. In these newsgroups, articles consist of encoded binary files such as **jpeg** pictures. Newsgroups as well as mail utilities cannot handle binary files. They can only handle character files. However, you can translate a binary file into a character format and then post or send that version. To do so, you need to use the **uuencode** and **uudecode** programs. **uuencode** translates a binary file into a character file. You can then post that character file to a newsgroup or send it to another user through email. **uudecode** will decode a file that has been encoded with **uuencode**. You can save a uuencoded file from a newsgroup and then translate it back into a binary file using **uudecode**. See Chapter 8 for a discussion of these two programs.

Newsgroups that specialize in binary files usually have the word "binaries" in their names. For example, **alt.binaries.pictures** holds articles consisting of uuencoded **jpeg** or **gif** pictures. **alt.binaries.multimedia** has uuencoded **mpeg** or **mov** files. Many times binary files will be posted in several parts, one per article. You would need to download all the articles making up the binary file, and then use **uudecode** to decode and combine them back into one binary file.

Summary: Usenet and Newsreaders

Usenet can be thought of as an online electronic news service containing journal articles, recent bulletins, and discussions on different topics. Usenet is divided by topic into different newsgroups. You can access a newsgroup and read the articles in it. You can also compose and post articles of your own to a particular newsgroup. You can respond to an article either by posting your response in the same newsgroup for everyone to read or by sending your response as a message directly to the article's author.

To access Usenet articles, you can use one of several available newsreader programs. Two of the more popular programs are **trn** and **tin**. **trn** allows you to search newsgroups and articles using pattern searches, as well as copy articles and post articles of your own. **trn** also distinguishes between read and unread articles, giving you easy access to newly posted articles in a newsgroup. **trn** makes use of an interface called a selector that lists articles grouped according to threads, allowing you to reference articles by subject or by related follow-up articles. You can select the group of articles you want to examine and then move through these related articles. When displaying articles in a thread, you can make use of a thread tree that delineates the relationship of follow-up articles. Using the tree, you can move from one article to any other article in the thread.

The **tin** newsreader uses selectors for both newsgroups and for articles within a newsgroup. It shares many of the same features of **trn**. Newsgroups are accessed through a selector, allowing easy reference.

Option	Function/Description
`-c`	Checks for any unread newsgroups
`-r`	Restarts in previous newsgroup
`-q`	Skips new newsgroup selection when starting
`-0`*mode sort-order*	

Mode

`a`	Article mode
`s`	Subject mode
`t`	Thread mode

Sort-order

`d`	Date
`s`	Subject
`a`	Author
`c`	Article count
`g`	Subject-date groups

Selecting Newsgroups

`y`	Selects the current newsgroup
`n`	Moves to the next newsgroup with unread articles
`N`	Moves to the next newsgroup
`p`	Moves to the previous newsgroup with unread articles
`P`	Moves to the previous newsgroup
`-`	Moves to the previously selected newsgroup
`^`	Moves to the first newsgroup with unread articles
num	Moves to newsgroup with that number
`$`	Moves to the last newsgroup

Table 9-1. `trn` *Commands*

Option	Function/Description
g_newsgroup-name_	Moves to newsgroup with that name
/_pattern_	Searches forward to the newsgroup with that pattern
?_pattern_	Searches backward to the newsgroup with that pattern
L	Lists subscribed newsgroups
l_pattern_	Lists unsubscribed newsgroups
u _newsgroup-name_	Unsubscribed newsgroups
a _newsgroup-name_	Subscribed to a newsgroup
c	Marks articles in a newsgroup as read

Displaying Selector

+	Enters the selector from the **trn** line prompt, or leaves the selector and returns to the **trn** line prompt
S	Selects selector mode: subject, thread, or article **Selector Mode: Threads, Subjects, Articles? [tsa]** **s** Subject mode, displays articles by subject **a** Article mode, displays individual articles **t** Thread mode, displays articles by threads
=	Switches between article and subject/thread selector
O	Sorts selector items by date, author, thread count, or subject. User is prompted to enter **d**, **a**, **n**, or **s**. (Note that this command is an uppercase O.) The options differ depending on whether you are in the subject or thread modes **Subject Order by Date, Subject, or Count? [dscDSC]** **Thread Order by Date, Subject, Author, subject-date Groups?**
L	Sets selector item display to short, medium, or long forms
E	Exclusive mode; displays only selected articles
k	Removes an article or subject from the selector display

Table 9-1.   **trn** _Commands_ (continued)

Option	Function/Description
U	Displays unread articles
Moving Through Selector	
SPACEBAR	Displays the next screen of articles
>	Displays the next screen of threads
<	Displays the previous screen of articles
$	Displays the last screen of articles
^	Displays the first screen of articles
Selecting Articles in the Selector	
id	Selects/deselects an article thread
id*	Selects/deselects articles with the same subject as ID
n	Moves to the next thread ID
p	Moves to the previous thread ID
z	Begins displaying selected articles; returns to newsgroup screen when finished
x	Begins displaying selected articles, but moves to the next newsgroup when finished

/*pattern*	Searches forward to the article with that pattern in each article's subject field
	Modifiers
	h Searches forward to the article with that pattern in the header
	   /*pattern*/**h**
	a Searches forward to the article with that pattern in either the header or the text
	   /*pattern*/**a**
	r Includes read articles in your search
	   /*pattern*/**r**
	c Makes search case sensitive
	   /*pattern*/**c**

Table 9-1. `trn` *Commands* (continued)

Option	Function/Description
?_pattern_**?**	Searches backward to the article with that pattern in each article's subject field **Modifiers** **h** Searches backward to the article with that pattern in the header **?**_pattern_**?h** **a** Searches forward to the article with that pattern in either the header or the text **r** Includes read articles in your search **c** Makes search case sensitive
/	Repeats previous forward search
?	Repeats previous backward search
/_pattern_**:**_command_	Selects a group of articles matching the pattern and applies the **trn** command to all
_id,id_**:**_command_	Selects a group of articles referenced by the numbers and applies the **trn** command to all

Displaying Articles

SPACEBAR	Displays the next screen of the article
ENTER	Scrolls to the next line of the article
d	Scrolls to the next half screen of the article
b	Displays the previous screen of the article
v	Redisplays article from the beginning
q	Displays last screen of the article
g _pattern_	Searches for pattern in the text
G	Repeats pattern search in the text

Saving Articles

:w	Saves selected article

Table 9-1.   **trn** _Commands_ (continued)

Option	Function/Description
`:s`	Saves selected article to a mailbox file
Replying to Articles	
`r`	Replies to current article
`R`	Replies to current article and includes article text in the reply
`f`	Posts a follow-up to the current article
`F`	Posts a follow-up including the text of the current article
Marking Articles	
`m`	Marks current article as read
`n`	Marks current article as read and moves to next article
`j`	Marks current article as read and displays end of article
`c`	Marks all articles as read in the current newsgroup
`trn` Option Variables	
`EDITOR`	Editor for composing replies
`MAILPOSTER`	Mail utility for sending replies
`PAGER`	Page utility for reading articles
`SAVEDIR`	Directory in which to save articles
`NAME`	Your full name to be used for article headers that you post
`ORGANIZATION`	Your organization name for article headers that you post
`NNTPSERVER`	NNTP remote news server address

Table 9-1. `trn` *Commands* (continued)

Selecting Articles	Function
y	Displays the current article
n	Moves to the next article with unread articles
N	Moves to the next article
p	Moves to the previous article with unread articles
P	Moves to the previous article
-	Moves to the previously selected article
^	Moves to the first article with unread articles
num	Moves to article with that number
$	Moves to the last article
CTRL-n	Moves to the next article with the same subject as the current one
CTRL-p	Moves to the previous article with the same subject as the current one

Table 9-2. rn *Article List Commands for* **trn**

Screen Movement Commands	Effect/Description
DOWN ARROW, **j**	Moves down a line
UP ARROW, **k**	Moves up a line
$	Goes to last line
CTRL-**U**, CTRL-**B**, **b**, PAGE UP	Goes to previous screen
CTRL-**D**, CTRL-**F**, SPACEBAR, PAGE DOWN	Goes to next screen
CTRL-**L**	Redraws screen
q	Returns to previous level
Q	Quits **tin**

Command Editing and History	
CTRL-**f**, RIGHT ARROW	Moves to next character
CTRL-**b**, LEFT ARROW	Moves to previous character
CTRL-**d**, BACKSPACE, DEL	Deletes character
CTRL-**p**	Previously entered command in history list
CTRL-**n**	Next entered command in history list
ESC	Erases command entered

Newsgroup Selector	
num	Goes to newsgroup with that index number
ENTER	Selects current newsgroup
TAB	Goes to next unread newsgroup
/	Searches forward
?	Searches backward
g	Chooses a new group by name

Table 9-3. **tin** *Newsreader Commands*

Newsgroup Selector	Effect/Description
K	Marks article/thread as read and goes to next unread
l	Lists articles within current thread
C	Marks all articles as read and goes to next unread group
c	Marks all articles as read and goes to group selection menu
s	Subscribes to a newsgroup
u	Unsubscribes to a newsgroup
S *pattern*	Subscribes to newsgroups with *pattern*
U *pattern*	Unsubscribes to newsgroups with *pattern*
M	Displays menu of configurable options
v	Shows version information
h	Help command
CTRL-K	Kill/Auto select current newsgroup
H	Toggles mini-help menu
I	Toggles inverse video
Article Selector	
num	Goes to article with that index number
$	Goes to last article
ENTER	Selects current article
TAB	Goes to next unread article
a	Author forward search
A	Author backward search
/	Subject forward search
?	Subject backward search

Table 9-3. `tin` *Newsreader Commands* (continued)

Article Selector	Effect/Description
n	Goes to next group
p	Goes to previous group
N	Goes to next unread article
P	Goes to previous unread article
d	Toggles display of subject or subject and author
r	Toggles display to show all/only unread articles
u	Toggles display of unthreaded and threaded articles
z	Marks article as unread
Z	Marks thread as unread
X	Marks all unread articles that have not been selected as read
t	Tags current article for cross-posting/mailing /piping/printing/saving
U	Untags all tagged articles
s	Saves article/thread/hot/pattern/tagged articles to file
m	Mails article/thread/hot/pattern/tagged articles to someone
o	Outputs article/thread/hot/pattern/tagged articles to printer
w	Posts an article to current group
W	Lists articles posted by user
x	Cross-posts current article to another group
*	Selects thread
.	Toggles selection of thread
@	Reverses all selections (all articles)
~	Undoes all selections (all articles)

Table 9-3. `tin` *Newsreader Commands* (continued)

Article Selector	Effect/Description
+	Performs auto-selection on groups or articles creating hot items; these items will have a * displayed before them
=	Marks threads selected if at least one unread article is selected
!	Escapes shell
–	Shows last message
|	Pipes article/thread/hot/pattern/tagged articles into command

Displaying Article

b	Moves back a page
SPACEBAR	Moves forward a page
B	Article body search
;	Marks threads selected if at least one unread article is selected
s	Saves article/thread/hot/pattern/tagged articles to file
m	Mails article/thread/hot/pattern/tagged articles to someone
o	Outputs article/thread/hot/pattern/tagged articles to printer
w	Posts an article to current group
f	Posts follow-up for current article
r	Sends reply to author of article

tin Option Variables

VISUAL	Editor for composing replies
NNTPSERVER	NNTP remote news server address

Table 9-3. tin *Newsreader Commands (continued)*

Chapter Ten

Internet Tools

The Internet is a network of computers around the world that you can access with an Internet address and a set of Internet tools. Many computers on the Internet are configured to operate as servers, providing information to anyone who requests it. The information is contained in files that you can access and copy. Each server, often referred to as a site, has its own Internet address by which it can be located. Linux provides a set of Internet tools that you can use to access sites on the Internet and then locate and download information from them.

To access Internet sites, your computer must be connected to the Internet. You may be part of a network that is already connected to the Internet. If you have a stand-alone computer, such as a personal computer, you can obtain an Internet connection from an Internet Service Provider (ISP). Once you have an Internet address of your own, you can configure your Linux system to connect to the Internet and use various Internet tools to access different sites. Chapter 12 describes how to configure your Linux system to make such a connection.

The Internet tools telnet and ftp allow you to connect to another Internet site. telnet performs a remote login to another computer connected on the Internet. You could use it to search the Library of Congress online catalogue, for example. ftp connects to a site and allows you to perform file transfers both from and to it. You can connect to a site that has Linux software and download software directly to your computer using ftp.

Finding out what information is available and on what system it is located, as well as where on the system it is stored, can be an overwhelming task. Ordinarily you would need to know the location of the file ahead of time. However, two Internet tools, Archie and Gopher, allow you to search for files on the network. Using Archie is like searching on an online catalogue; just as you can use keywords to search for a title of a book, with Archie you can use patterns to search for the name of a file. Gopher operates more like a reference librarian. It provides you with a series of menus listing different topics. You move from one menu to the other, narrowing your topic until you find the information you want. Using Gopher, you can then directly transfer your information without having to resort to ftp.

In the last few years, the Web Browsers have become the primary tool for accessing information on the Internet. However, Web Browsers rely on underlying Internet tools that actually retrieve and transfer information. telnet, ftp, Archie, and Gopher are all tools developed to locate and access Internet sites and to retrieve information from them. Web Browsers make use of these tools to obtain information on the Internet, but they often hide their use from the user, making for smoother interaction. Most of the tasks you perform on the Internet may be done easily with a Web Browser. You may only need to use the Internet tools described in this chapter for more specialized tasks, such as downloading files from a specific ftp site. For example, you would use ftp if you wanted to download a new Linux software program from a Linux ftp site.

Internet Addresses

The Internet uses a set of network protocols called TCP/IP, which stands for Transmission Control Protocol/Internet Protocol. In a TCP/IP network, messages are broken into small components called datagrams that are then transmitted through various interlocking routes and delivered to their destination computers. Once received, the datagrams are reassembled into the original message. Datagrams are also referred to as packets. Sending messages as small components has proven to be far more reliable and faster than sending them as one large bulky transmission. With small components, if one is lost or damaged, only that component has to be re-sent, whereas if any part of a large transmission is corrupted or lost, the entire message has to be re-sent.

On a TCP/IP network such as the Internet, each computer is given a unique address called an IP address. The IP address is used to identify and locate a particular host—a computer connected to the network. An IP address consists of a set of four segments, each separated by a period. The segments consist of numbers that range from 0 to 255, with certain values reserved for special use. The IP address is divided into two parts, one that identifies the network and the other that identifies a particular host. The number of segments used for each is determined by the class of the network. On the Internet, networks are organized into three classes depending on their size—classes A, B, and C. A class A network will use only the first segment for the IP address and the remaining three for the host, allowing a great many computers to be connected to the same network. Most IP addresses reference smaller, class C, networks. For a class C network, the first three segments are used to identify the network, and only the last segment identifies the host. The syntax looks like this:

```
net.net.net.host
```

In a class C network, the first three numbers identify the network part of the IP address. This part is divided into three network numbers, each identifying a subnet. Networks on the Internet are organized into subnets beginning with the largest and narrowing to small subnetworks. The last number is used to identify a particular computer that is referred to as a host. You can think of the Internet as a series of networks with subnetworks, and these subnetworks have their own subnetworks. The rightmost number identifies the host computer, and the number preceding it identifies the subnetwork that the computer is a part of. The number to the left of that identifies the network that the subnetwork is part of, and so on. The Internet address 192.18.187.4 references the fourth computer connected to the network identified by the number 187. Network 187 is a subnet to a larger network identified as 18. This larger network is itself a subnet of the network identified as 192. Here's how it breaks down:

`192.18.187.4`	IP address
`192.18.187`	Network identification
4	Host identification

An IP address is officially provided by the Network Information Center (NIC) that administers the Internet. You can obtain your own Internet address from the NIC, or if you are on a network already connected to the Internet, your network administrator can assign you one. If you are using an Internet Service Provider, the ISP may obtain one for you or, each time you connect, may temporarily assign one from a pool they have on hand.

Certain numbers are reserved. The numbers 127, 0, or 255 cannot be part of an official IP address. The address 127.0.0.0 is the loopback address that allows users on your computer to communicate with each other. The number 255 is a special broadcast identifier that you can use to broadcast messages to all sites on a network. Using 225 for any part of the IP address references all nodes connected at that level. For example, 192.18.255.255 broadcasts a message to all computers on network 192.18, all its subnetworks, and their hosts. The address 192.18.187.255 broadcasts to every computer on the local network. If you use 0 for the network part of the address, the host number will reference a computer within your local network. For example, 0.0.0.6 references the sixth computer in your local network. If you want to broadcast to all computers on your local network, you can use the number 0.0.0.255.

All hosts on the Internet are identified by their IP addresses. When you send a message to a host on the Internet, you must provide its IP address. However, using a sequence of four numbers of an IP address can be very difficult. They are hard to remember, and it's easy to make mistakes when typing them. To make it easier to identify a computer on the Internet, the Domain Name Service (DNS) was implemented. The DNS establishes a domain name address for each IP address. The domain name address is a series of names separated by periods. Whenever you use a domain name address it is automatically converted to an IP address that is then used to identify that Internet host. The domain name address is far easier to use than its corresponding IP address.

A domain name address needs to be registered with the NIC so that each computer on the Internet will have a unique name. Creating a name follows specified naming conventions, as discussed earlier in Chapter 8. The domain name address consists of the hostname, the name you gave to your computer, a domain name, the name that identifies your network, and an extension that identifies the type of network you are on. Here is the syntax for domain addresses:

```
host-name.domain-name.extension
```

In the following example, the domain address references a computer called sunsite on a network referred to as unc, and it is part of an educational institution, as indicated by the extension edu.

```
sunsite.unc.edu
```

The conversion of domain addresses to IP addresses used to be performed by each individual host. And for a few frequently used addresses for which you know the IP address, this can still be done. However, there are now so many computers connected to the Internet that domain name conversion has to be performed by special servers known as Domain Name Servers or simply nameservers. A nameserver holds a database of domain name addresses and their IP addresses. Local networks will sometimes have their own nameservers. If a nameserver does not have the address, then it may call on other nameservers to perform the conversion. A program on your computer called a resolver will obtain the IP address from a nameserver and then use it in the application where you specified the domain name address.

With the **whois** and **nslookup** commands, you can obtain information for domain nameservers about different networks and hosts connected to the Internet. Enter **whois** and the domain name address of the host or network, and **whois** will display information about the host, such as the street address and phone number as well as contact persons.

```
$ whois   domain-address
```

The **nslookup** command takes a domain address and finds its corresponding IP address.

```
$ nslookup   domain-address
```

nslookup has an interactive mode that you enter by not specifying any domain name. You can then use **nslookup** to search for other kinds of information about a host. For example, the HINFO option will find out what type of operating system a host uses. The **nslookup** man page specifies a list of different options and how to use them.

Remote Login: telnet

You use the **telnet** command to log in remotely to another system on your network. The system can be on your local area network or available through an Internet connection. telnet operates as if you were logging into another system from a remote terminal. You will be asked for a login name and, in some cases, a password. In effect, you are logging into another account on another system. In fact, if you have an account on another system, you could use telnet to log into it.

Usually, telnet is used to connect to hosts on the Internet that provide certain public services, such as the Library of Congress and its online catalogue, or sites that provide you with Archie indexes. Such sites allow guest logins, meaning that they do not require any specific login name or password. Anyone can log in. However, such sites are specially designed to handle public access, presenting you with menus of options that control your access to the system.

You invoke the telnet utility with the keyword **telnet**. If you know the name of the site you want to connect with, you can just enter **telnet** and the name of the site on the Linux command line. In the next example, the user specifies the garnet system.

```
$ telnet garnet.berkeley.edu
Connected to garnet
login:
```

telnet also has a command mode with a series of commands that you can use to configure your connection. You can enter the telnet command mode either by invoking telnet with the keyword **telnet** or by pressing CTRL-] during a session. The telnet **help** command will list all the telnet commands that you can use. Table 10-1 provides a list of commonly used telnet commands, and a comprehensive list is available on the man pages (**man telnet**). In the next example, the user first invokes the telnet utility. Then a prompt is displayed, indicating the command mode, **telnet>**. The telnet command **open** then connects to another system.

```
$ telnet
telnet> open garnet.berkeley.edu
Connected to garnet.berkeley.edu
login:
```

Once connected, you follow the login procedure for that system. If you are logging into a regular system, you will have to provide a login name and password. Once logged in, you will be provided with the operating system prompt that, in the case of Linux or Unix, will either be **$** or **%**. You are then directly connected to an account on that system and can issue any commands you want.

When you have finished your work, you log out. This will break the connection and return you to the telnet prompt on your own system. You can then quit telnet with the **quit** command.

```
telnet> quit
```

When using telnet to connect to a site that provides public access, you will not need to provide a login name or password. Access is usually controlled by a series of menus that restricts what you can do on that system. Figure 10-1 shows a telnet session accessing the online catalog of the Library of Congress at **locis.loc.gov**.

```
$ telnet locis.loc.gov
```

If you are logging into a specific account on another system, you can use the **-1** option to specify the login name of that account. This allows you to skip the login prompt. You can use the **-1** option with either the telnet invocation on the command line or with the **open** command, as shown in the next examples. Here the user is logging into a specific account called richpete on the **rose.berkeley.edu** system.

```
$ telnet rose.berkeley.edu -1 richpete
telnet> open rose.berkeley.edu -1 richpete
```

```
        L O C I S :   LIBRARY OF CONGRESS INFORMATION SYSTEM

           To make a choice: type a number, then press ENTER


    1   Library of Congress Catalog      4   Braille and Audio

    2   Federal Legislation              5   Organizations

    3   Copyright Information            6   Foreign Law

    *   *   *   *   *   *   *   *   *   *   *   *

    7   Searching Hours and Basic Search Commands
    8   Documentation and Classes
    9   Library of Congress General Information
   10   Library of Congress Fast Facts
   11   * * Announcements * *



   12   Comments and Logoff
        Choice:
```

Figure 10-1. *Library of Congress telnet connection*

Certain online software, such as Gopher or Web Browsers, will, when called for, make telnet connections to public sites automatically. In such cases, you may suddenly find yourself presented with a simple menu of options rather than the detailed graphics interface of a Web Browser or page display of a Gopher. At this point, you are remotely logged into another site with telnet, using that site's interface to obtain controlled access to its resources. Simply follow the menu options, and when you leave the site, you will be returned to your Web Browser or Gopher page.

Network File Transfer: ftp

One of the most widely used Internet tools is ftp. You can use ftp to directly transfer very large files from one site to another. It can handle both text and binary files. ftp stands for File Transfer Protocol. It operates on systems connected to networks that use the TCP/IP protocols, such as the Internet. ftp has its own set of commands, listed in Table 10-2, that you can use to manage your file transfers.

ftp performs a remote login to another account on another system connected to you on a network such as the Internet. Once logged into that other system, you can transfer files to and from it. To log in you will need to know the login name and password for the account on the remote system. For example, if you have accounts at two different sites on the Internet, you can use ftp to transfer files from one to the other. However, there are also many sites on the Internet that allow public access using ftp. Many sites serve as depositories for very large files that anyone can access and download. Such sites are often referred to as ftp sites, and in many cases their Internet address will begin with the word "ftp". One such site is **sunsite.unc.edu**, which specializes in Linux files. These public sites allow anonymous ftp login from any user. For the login name you use the word "anonymous," and for the password you use your Internet address. You can then transfer files from that site to your own system.

You invoke the ftp utility with the command **ftp**. If there is one specific site that you want to connect to, you can include the name of that site on the command line after the **ftp** keyword. Otherwise, you will need to connect to the remote system with the ftp command **open**. You are then prompted for the name of the remote system with the prompt (to). Upon entering the remote system name, ftp connects you to the system and then prompts you for a login name. The prompt for the login name will consist of the word "Name" and, in parentheses, the system name and your local login name. Sometimes the login name on the remote system is the same as the login name on your own system. If they are the same, just press ENTER at the prompt. If they are different, enter the remote system's login name. After entering the login name, you are prompted for the password. In the next example, the user connects to the remote system garnet and logs into the robert account.

```
$ ftp
ftp> open
(to) garnet
Connected to garnet.berkeley.edu.
220 garnet.berkeley.edu FTP server (ULTRIX Version 4.1 Sun May 16
10:23:46 EDT 1996) ready.
Name (garnet.berkeley.edu:root): robert
password required
Password:
user robert logged in
ftp>
```

To save a step, you can directly specify the remote system on the command line when you invoke ftp. This connects you to that system without the need of the **open** command. The login procedure then begins.

```
$ ftp garnet.berkeley.edu
Connected to garnet.berkeley.edu.
220 garnet.berkeley.edu FTP server (ULTRIX Version 4.1 Sun May 16
10:23:46 EDT 1996) ready.
Name (garnet.berkeley.edu:root):
```

To access a public ftp site, you have to perform an anonymous login. Instead of a login name, you enter the keyword **anonymous**. Then, for the password, you enter your Internet address. Once the ftp prompt is displayed, you are ready to transfer files. You may need to change to the appropriate directory first or set the transfer mode to binary. The following example is a complete ftp session in which the user performs an anonymous login and then downloads the Archie software package. The site access is the **sunsite.unc.edu** ftp site. After changing to the **/pub/Linux/system /Network/info-systems** directory, the user downloads the Archie software with the **get** command.

```
$ ftp sunsite.unc.edu
Connected to fddisunsite.oit.unc.edu.
220 helios FTP server (Version wu-2.4(39) Tue May 16 01:34:21 EDT
1996) ready.
```

```
Name (sunsite.unc.edu:root): anonymous
331 Guest login ok, send your complete e-mail address as password.
Password:
230 Guest login ok, access restrictions apply.
Remote system type is UNIX.
Using binary mode to transfer files.
ftp> cd /pub/Linux/system/network/info-systems
250 CWD command successful.
ftp> ls
200 PORT command successful.
150 Opening ASCII mode data connection for /bin/ls.
total 1130
drwxrwxr-x    4 67        1002          512 Jan 16 02:54 .
drwxr-xr-x   20 67        1002         1024 Sep  5  1995 ..
drwxr-xr-x    2 67        1002          512 Jul 21  1994 .cap
-rw-r--r--    1 67        1002          570 Jan 16 02:55 INDEX
-rw-r--r--    1 67        1002          586 Apr  8  1995
 archie-1.4.1.linux.lsm
-rw-r--r--    1 67        1002        24335 Apr  9  1995
 archie-1.4.1.linux.tar.gz
-rw-r--r--    1 67        1002       109147 Sep 25  1995
 archie-1.4.1.src.tar.gz
226 Transfer complete.
ftp> binary
200 Type set to I.
ftp> get archie-1.4.1.linux.tar.gz
200 PORT command successful.
150 Opening BINARY mode data connection for
 archie-1.4.1.linux.tar.gz (24335 bytes).
226 Transfer complete.
24335 bytes received in 7.87 secs (3 Kbytes/sec)
ftp> close
221 Good-bye.
ftp> quit
```

Once logged in, you can execute Linux commands on either the remote system or your local system. You execute a command on your local system in ftp by preceding the command with an exclamation point. Any Linux commands without an exclamation point are executed on the remote system. In the next example, the first command lists files in the remote system, and the second command lists files in the local system.

```
ftp> ls
ftp> !ls
```

There is one exception to this rule. Whereas you can change directories on the remote system with the **cd** command, to change directories on your local system, you need to use a special ftp command called **lcd** (local **cd**). In the next example, the first command changes directories on the remote system, and the second command changes directories on the local system.

```
ftp> cd
ftp> lcd
```

You close your connection to a system with the **close** command. You can then open another connection if you wish. To end the ftp session, use the **quit** or **bye** command.

```
ftp> close
ftp> bye
Good-bye
$
```

To transfer files to and from the remote system, use the **get** and **put** commands. The **get** command will receive files from the remote system to your local system, and the **put** command will send files from your local system to the remote system. In a sense, your local system **get**s files *from* the remote and **put**s files *to* the remote. In the next example, the file **weather** is sent from the local system to the remote system using the **put** command.

```
ftp> put weather
PORT command successful.
ASCII data connection
ASCII Transfer complete.
ftp>
```

You can transfer files in character mode or binary mode. The character mode is the default. The command **ascii** sets the character mode, and the command **binary** sets the binary mode. If you are transferring either programs or compressed files, be sure to set the binary mode first. A program is a binary file and must be transferred in

binary mode. Most software packages available at Internet sites are archived and
compressed files. These you will also have to download in binary mode. In the next
example, the transfer mode is set to binary, and the archived software package
life.tar.gz is sent from the remote system to your local system using the **get** command.

```
ftp> binary
ftp> get life.tar.gz
PORT command successful.
Binary data connection
Binary Transfer complete.
ftp>
```

Often you may want to send several files, specifying their names with special
characters. **put** and **get**, however, operate only on a single file and do not work with
special characters. To transfer several files at a time, you have to use two other
commands, **mput** and **mget**. When you use **mput** or **mget**, you will be prompted for a
file list. You can then either enter the list of files or a file-list specification using special
characters. For example, ***.c** would specify all the files with a .c extension, and *****
would specify all files in the current directory. In the case of **mget**, each file will be
sent, one by one, from the remote system to your local system. Each time, you will be
prompted with the name of the file being sent. You can type **y** to send the file or **n** to
cancel the transmission. You will then be prompted for the next file. The **mput**
command works in the same way but sends files from your local system to the remote
system. In the next example, all files with a .c extension are sent to your local system
using **mget**.

```
ftp> mget
(remote-files) *.c
mget calc.c? y
PORT command successful
ASCII data connection
ASCII transfer complete
mget main.c? y
PORT command successful
ASCII data connection
ASCII transfer complete
ftp>
```

Archie

On the Internet there are a great many sites that are open to public access. They
contain files that anyone can obtain using file transfer programs such as ftp. However,

unless you already know where a file is located, it can be very difficult finding it. There are so many sites to check out. Archie is designed to search for files and tell you where they can be found. Once you know the site, you can use ftp to access it and download the file. You can think of Archie as an online index of all the files available at different Internet sites.

Archie has a database of all the file names and their sites that is updated monthly. Copies of this database are located at different Archie sites that operate as Archie servers. You can query these sites, searching for specific file names, and the Archie server will give you the results, listing different files and the sites where they reside.

You can access an Archie server either through an interactive telnet session or by using an Archie client installed on your own system. An Archie client will automatically access an Archie server for you, perform your query, and retrieve the results. Because of the potential demand on Archie, users are encouraged to use an Archie client if available, instead of interactively logging in. However, if you do not have an Archie client, you will have to telnet to an Archie server and perform your queries directly on that server. Because of demand, many Archie servers may limit the number of users that can access it at any one time, as well as the time a user can take making queries. Table 10-3 lists the options for an Archie client and the commands used for Archie servers.

Archie client software is not included with your Caldera Network Desktop. However, you can download it from the **ftp.mcgill.ca** ftp site or from **sunsite.unc.edu** and its mirror sites. At **sunsite.unc.edu**, Archie is currenly located in the directory **/pub/Linux/system/Network/info-systems**. The current Archie software package is named **archie-1.4.1.linux.tar.gz**. Once downloaded you unzip and extract it with **gunzip** and **tar xvf**. This creates a directory called **/archie-1.4.1** that holds the source code files (the previous ftp example shows an actual download of the Archie client software). You compile your Archie client by changing to that directory and entering the command **make**. This will create an Archie client program called **archie**. You then copy this Archie program to the **/bin** or **/usr/local/bin** directories. The **INSTALL** file holds more detailed instructions on how to create your Archie client program.

Archie Client

If your system has an Archie client, you can execute an Archie by entering the keyword **archie** followed by an option and a pattern. The pattern is then used to search for matching file names. Here is the syntax for an Archie command:

```
$ archie -option pattern
```

If you enter a pattern without an option, Archie treats the pattern as a full file name. In the next example, the user searches for a file with the file name **recipe**.

```
$ archie recipe
```

Different Archie options allow you to create more powerful queries. The options cannot be combined. Should you do so, only the last one will be used. The **-c** option will treat the pattern as an incomplete pattern and search for its occurrence anywhere in a file name. In the next example, the user searches for any file name with the pattern **recipe** in it. It will match on **recipe**, **cookie_recipe**, and **oldrecipes**.

```
$ archie -c recipe
```

The **-s** option performs the same kind of pattern search as a **-c** option but ignores case. It will match either upper- or lowercase versions of a pattern. In the next example, the user will match on file names such as **recipe**, **Recipe**, and **oldRecipes**.

```
$ archie -s recipe
```

The **-r** option allows you to use regular expressions. This means that you can use special characters to match on variations of a file name. Suppose, for example, that you want to make an exact search for a file name in which only the first character may or may not be capitalized. The regular expression **[Rr]ecipe** searches for file names beginning with either upper- or lowercase *r*: **recipe** or **Recipe**. Also, an **s*** placed at the end will search for file names with or without an ending *s*: **recipes** or **recipe**.

```
$ archie -r [Rr]ecipes*
```

Other options control Archie's output. The **-m** option followed by a number limits the number of matched items that are output. If you want to see only the first ten items, you can use **-m10**. The **-t** option will output items sorted by date, beginning with the most recent.

```
$ archie -m10 -t java

Host sun.rediris.es
    Location: /docs/faq/comp/lang
      DIRECTORY drwxr-xr-x        512  Mar 30 02:18  java

Host sunsite.rediris.es
```

```
     Location:/software/linux/distributions/jurix/source/networking/www
        DIRECTORY drwxr-xr-x          512  Mar  4 02:52  java
     Location: /software/linux/networking/net-sources/www
        DIRECTORY drwxr-xr-x          512  Mar  3 08:13  java

Host kobra.efd.lth.se
     Location: /pub/languages
        DIRECTORY drwxr-xr-x          512  Jan 24 13:51  java

Host sunsite.rediris.es
     Location: /software
        DIRECTORY drwxr-xr-x          512  Dec 13 17:36  java
```

To save your results you can redirect them to a file using the **-o** option with a file name. In the following example, the results of the Archie search are placed in a file named **javares**.

```
$ archie -m50 -t java -o javares
```

Archie Servers

Several Archie public servers are available on the Internet. Their addresses usually begin with the word "archie". For example, **archie.sura.net**, **archie.internic.net**, and **archie.doc.ic.ac.uk** are all popular Archie servers. Archie servers are located around the world, with several in the United States. You should only use an Archie server if, for some reason, you do not have access to an Archie client. On your own system you should install and use your Archie client. Archie servers are helpful if you have to perform a search, but you are using a system that has no Archie client.

To use an Archie server, you need to log into it first using telnet. When you are prompted for a login name, you enter the keyword **archie**. Once logged in, you will receive an Archie prompt: **archie>**. At the prompt you can execute searches or set parameters. You execute searches with the command **prog** followed by the string to search for. The following example searches for files with the file name **Linux**.

```
archie> prog Linux
```

As with the Archie client, you can qualify your search using regular expressions or a partial pattern match. To do so, you set the feature search to a specific option using the **set** command.

```
archie> set search option
```

The **rgex** option searches using a regular expression, and the **sub** option searches with a partial pattern. In the next example, the user searches for file names that contain the pattern "Linux".

```
archie> set search sub
archie> prog Linux
```

The following example uses a regular expression to perform a search. The regular expression **[Rr]ecipes*** searches for file names beginning with either upper- or lowercase *r* and ending with or without an *s*: **recipes** or **Recipe**.

```
archie> set search regex
archie> prog [Rr]ecipes*
```

In addition, you can set options that control your output. For example, you can limit the number of retrieved items by setting **maxhits**. The variable **sortby** is used to output items sorted on a specified field. You set a variable using the keyword **set** followed by the variable name and then the variable value. In the next example, the user limits the items output to ten and **sorts** the output by the name of the host.

```
archie> set maxhits 10
archie> set sortby hostname
```

Once you have finished your session, you can log out using the **quit** command.

```
archie> quit
```

Xarchie

Xarchie is an X-Windows program that lets you use menus and listboxes to perform an Archie search and display its results. You can even use Xarchie to perform an ftp operation for a file you select, downloading it to your system. Xarchie has three menus, File, Settings, and Query. The fourth item on the menu bar is an Abort button that you can use to stop an Archie search. The last item is a Help button that starts a window displaying various Xarchie help files. Click the one you want displayed. Xarchie operates by accessing an Archie server to perform a search and then displays the results. The list of Archie servers is displayed by selecting the Archie Host item in the Settings menu. The Settings menu also contains items for configuring your search, letting you determine the sorting sequence or the pattern-matching method.

To perform a search, enter the search term in the box labeled Search Term, and then select the Item entry in the Query menu. The display window is separated into several listboxes, the first of which lists the Internet sites found. When you click a particular site, the pathname for the file you are looking for is displayed in the second listbox (there can be more than one). The third listbox shows the item found, and can be either a file or a directory. If it is a directory you can double-click on it and the list of files in it will be displayed. To download a file, click on the filename and select the Get item from the File menu. Complete information for an Archie entry is shown in the boxes below the listboxes. Figure 10-2 shows the Xarchie program displaying a result from a search on the term "java".

An Internet User Interface: Gopher

Gopher is a user-friendly, menu-driven catalogue of Internet services and resources. It operates as a user interface for Internet services. Gopher combines the capabilities of telnet, ftp, and Archie, allowing you to browse through and select different available

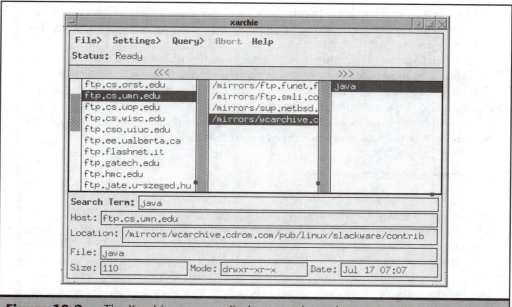

Figure 10-2. *The Xarchie program displays search results*

databases, files, and online information services. The Gopher interface uses a top-down menu system that moves from more general to more specific topics. You work your way down from one menu to another until you locate the item you want.

Gopher is designed to place at your fingertips information distributed throughout a network. It was originally created at the University of Minnesota to provide a campuswide distributed information service connecting different university departments. Each department maintained its own Gopher information server that anyone using a Gopher client could access. This distributed model was quickly adopted for use across the Internet to provide easy access to the numerous information services available there. Many universities maintain Gopher servers that can be used both within their campuses and across the Internet.

To access Gopher servers, you need to use a Gopher client program. The Gopher client provides a menu interface through which you make your requests and then carries out your requests, whether it be to connect to another service or transfer a file. There are several Gopher clients commonly available. Your Caldera CD-ROM has a copy of **xgopher**, an X-Windows-based Gopher client with buttons and drop-down menus that allow you to move through Gopher menus. You can also download the University of Minnesota line-based Gopher client from **boombox.micro.umn.edu** in the **/pub/gopher** directory ftp site. You can also obtain it as well from the Linux ftp site and its mirror sites in the **/pub/packages/info-systems/gopher /boombox/unix** directory. The current software package is named **gopher2_3.tar.gz**. You do not need X-Windows to run it and consequently it tends to be very fast. This client is part of a larger Gopher software package that includes a Gopher server, described in Chapter 12. When you decompress and extract this package, a directory called **gopher2_3** will be created. To create your Gopher client, change to this directory and execute the command **configure**. This detects your system configurations and creates makefiles tailored to it. You then enter the command **make client**. This will create your Gopher client program. The **INSTALL** file in the **/doc** directory has more detailed information about the installation procedure.

When you invoke the Gopher client, you can specify the Gopher server to access. The following example accesses the **gopher.tc.umn.edu** Gopher server.

```
$ gopher gopher.tc.umn.edu
```

The names of many Gopher servers begin with the word "gopher". If you do not specify a Gopher server, then the default server will be accessed. In this case you just enter the term **gopher** on the command line. You can determine the default server by pressing the **O** command once you have started your Gopher program. This will bring up an options menu from which you can configure your Gopher client. The options menu saves its information in a configuration file called **.gopherrc** that is kept in your home directory.

It is also possible to use telnet to access one of several available Gopher public clients such as **gopher.uiuc.edu**. Use telnet to access the server's address and log in using the first name of the address, usually **gopher**. As with Archie, it is strongly recommended that you use your own Linux system's Gopher client if possible.

Gopher Menus

A Gopher menu consists of a list of menu items that can represent files, other menus, databases, or telnet connections. Each type of item is indicated by a qualifier placed at the end of the entry. Items that are files end with a period qualifier. Items that are other menus end with a slash. Database items end with the symbols **<?>**. The qualifier **<CSO>** indicates a CSO nameserver used to search for user addresses and information. The **<TEL>** qualifier indicates a telnet connection. The **<Picture>**, **<Movie>**, and **<)** qualifiers reference images, video, and sound files, respectively. Figure 10-3 shows a Gopher menu.

When a Gopher menu is first displayed, an arrow will appear before the first menu item. You use the arrow to select the menu item you want. You move the arrow from one menu item to another by using the arrow keys on your keyboard. The UP ARROW moves the arrow up to the previous item, and the DOWN ARROW moves the arrow to the next item. The next example shows the top Gopher menu. The first three items have a / qualifier, indicating that these are other menus. The first item ends in a period, indicating that it is a text file. Notice the arrow placed before the first menu item.

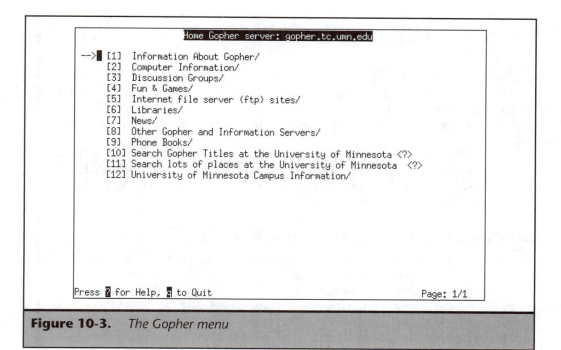

Figure 10-3. *The Gopher menu*

Once you have positioned the arrow at the menu item you want, you can select and display the item by pressing ENTER. Alternatively, you could enter the number of the menu item followed by pressing ENTER. You can continue moving from one menu to another until you find the item you want. Should you want to move back to a previous menu, you can press the **u** key. You can quit Gopher at any time by pressing the **q** key. Table 10-4 lists the Gopher commands.

A Gopher menu can be very lengthy, often consisting of many pages. To move to the next screen, you simply press the SPACEBAR. The **b** command moves you back to the previous screen in the menu. The number of the screen you are currently on, as well as the total number of screens in the menu, are displayed in the lower-right corner.

To locate an item, you could page through all the screens one by one, or you could use Gopher's menu item search capability. Gopher can perform a pattern search on the text of each menu item. To perform a search, you press the slash key, **/**. A box will open in the middle of the screen, prompting you to enter a search pattern. After you enter the pattern, you press ENTER to execute the search. The text of each menu item will be searched for the pattern. You can cancel the search at any time by pressing CTRL-**g**. Upon pressing ENTER, a search is made and the results displayed. You can continue searching through menus until you reach the item you want. To display the item, select it and press ENTER. Once you have displayed an item, Gopher will prompt you as to whether you want to save, mail, or print the information, or simply return to your last Gopher menu.

```
Press <RETURN> to continue, <m> to mail, <s> to save, or <p> to print:
```

The save option is the equivalent of an ftp operation. The file containing the information just displayed is transferred to your own account. Alternatively, you can simply mail information to yourself or to some other user who can then retrieve the information as a mail message. You could also simply print the information without saving it.

The xgopher client works much the same way with just a few differences. Instead of positioning an arrow, you can use your mouse to click on a menu item. A double-click will select an item. Buttons and drop-down menus move you back and forth through the Gopher menus. Figure 10-4 shows the xgopher client.

Using Gopher to Access Services

You can just as easily use Gopher to access information services such as online library catalogues. Such a service will be represented by a menu item qualified by a `<TEL>` at the end. When you choose the item, Gopher will telnet to the service for you. For example, you can use Gopher to log into the Library of Congress. First you select the Libraries menu from the Gopher menu. This brings up another Gopher menu listing possible online libraries that you can access. Select the item that brings up a Gopher

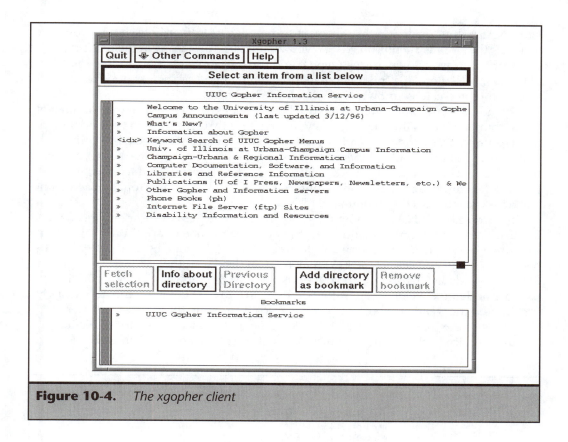

Figure 10-4. *The xgopher client*

menu for the Library of Congress. From this menu you can select the item that displays another Gopher menu listing online systems. Notice that some of these items are files, others are yet more Gopher menus, and two are online information services as indicated with the **<TEL>** qualifier. You then select the item to connect to the Library of Congress online catalogue. The Gopher client then makes the telnet connection, warning you that you are now leaving Internet and Gopher and entering an online service.

Once logged into an online information service, you are operating according to whatever interface and commands that service provides. In the case of the Library of Congress, you are given a menu and asked to qualify your search. You can then perform searches using keywords and display the results. To end the session, you simply log off.

Gopher Bookmark Menu

As you search through Gopher for different items, you may want to save certain menus or menu items for later access. Say, for example, you follow the progress of the latest NASA shuttle mission over the next several days. Ordinarily, each time you need to access the Gopher menus on NASA, you would have to start from the top menu and work your way down. Instead, you could use the Gopher bookmark capability to place the NASA item in a special bookmark menu that you can access directly. In a sense, you can create your own customized Gopher menu.

You add a menu or menu item to your bookmark list using the **A** and **a** commands. The **A** command adds the whole menu you are currently displaying to your bookmark list. The lowercase **a** command adds a menu item that you have selected to your bookmark list. Having added the menu or menu item to your bookmark list, you can then access them in your bookmark menu. The bookmark list is used to generate a bookmark menu whose items consist of those in the bookmark list. You then access the bookmark menu with the **v** command.

In the case of the NASA example, as shown in Figure 10-5, the user only needs to locate it once in the Gopher menus and then add it to the bookmark list using the **A** or **a** command. Whenever the user wants to access the NASA item, he or she displays the bookmark menu and selects the NASA menu item displayed there.

You can add as many items to your bookmark list as you wish. In Figure 10-6, the user has added the weather report for San Francisco to the bookmark menu. The user first located the weather report for San Francisco by moving through several menus, starting with the News menu. From the News menu, the user moved to the National Weather Service Forecasts menu, which lists states. The user chose California and

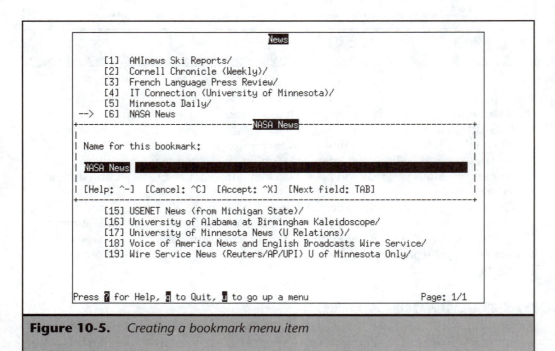

Figure 10-5.   *Creating a bookmark menu item*

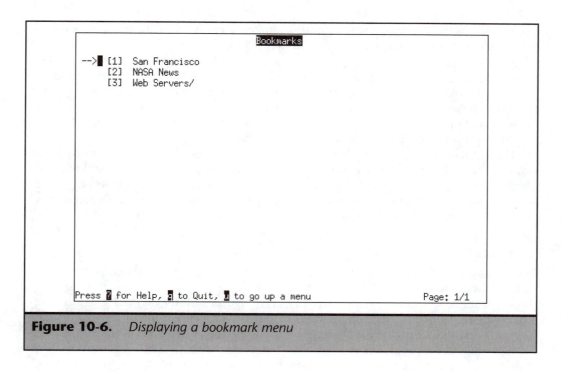

Figure 10-6. *Displaying a bookmark menu*

moved to the California menu, which lists the cities in California. Finally, the user moved the arrow to the item for San Francisco. The user then pressed the **a** key to add the San Francisco menu item to his or her bookmark menu. A box opened up in the middle of the screen with a prompt for the name this menu item will have in the bookmark menu. The name of the selected menu item is already displayed as the default name, in this case, San Francisco. The user then added the word "Weather," making the name of this new menu item in the bookmark menu "San Francisco Weather." Now, to find the weather for San Francisco, the user only needs to press the **v** key to bring up the bookmark menu and select the menu item San Francisco Weather. The user no longer needs to move through the long series of menus from News, to Forecasts, to State, and finally to City.

When you no longer need to access an item or menu in your bookmark list directly, use the **d** command to remove it. For example, once the user no longer needs to access the NASA menu item, he or she can simply delete it from the bookmark menu by selecting it and pressing the **d** key.

Just as you can save items, you can also save entire menus in your bookmark list. You add a menu to your bookmark list using the **A** command. The **A** command adds the whole menu you are currently displaying to your bookmark menu. Say, for example, you are going to be referencing weather reports for cities in California over the next several weeks. You could use the Gopher bookmark capability to place the California weather report menu as an item in your bookmark menu. Whenever you need to access the California weather report menu, you display your bookmark menu and select the California weather menu item displayed there.

Such a feature is particularly useful in saving the results of Archie searches made through Gopher. In the main Gopher menu, the item for ftp searches allows you to perform an Archie search for files that you can then have downloaded to your account. The result of the search is listed as another Gopher menu. Each menu item is a file located on an anonymous ftp server. Selecting such a menu item will instruct Gopher to access the ftp server and transfer the file to your system.

The Gopher menu that results from such Archie searches is temporary. Should you want to save it for further use and reference, you need to place it in your bookmark menu. Simply give the **A** command when displaying this Gopher menu, and it will be added to your bookmark menu. You can then use your bookmark menu to access this menu containing your Archie search results.

Veronica

Resources on a given topic can be widely dispersed through the Internet. You could end up having to search, one by one, for each resource on a given topic, working through different Gopher menus each time. The Veronica utility was designed to streamline this process. Veronica will search all Gopher menus for menu items, using keywords provided by the user. Veronica will then generate a customized menu consisting of all the menu items it has found. In effect, with Veronica, you can create temporary Gopher menus on specialized topics. You can then select the menu item you want, just as you would on any standard Gopher menu.

To use Veronica, you first need to access the Veronica menu on Gopher. The Veronica menu lists different Veronica servers that you can use to search Gopher menus. The second and third menu items provide more information about Veronica. The first menu item is always empty. There is a **<?>** qualifier at the end of each server menu item, indicating a database to be queried by keywords. Select a server and press ENTER. A box will open up in the middle of the screen, prompting you to enter keywords for the search. Upon pressing ENTER, Veronica performs the search. The result is a customized Gopher menu consisting of all the menu items Veronica was able to locate. You can then move to the menu item you want and select it. If you want to know where exactly a menu item comes from, you can simply move to the menu item and press = to display information about it.

Though the menus generated by Veronica are temporary, you can save a menu by adding it as an item to your bookmark list. While displaying your Veronica-generated menu, give the **A** command to add it to your bookmark list. You can then later access the menu through your bookmark menu, which you display with the **v** command. You can save as many Veronica searches as you want, making them items in your bookmark menu. You can also save particular items in your Veronica-generated menu by selecting the items one by one and giving the lowercase **a** command.

WAIS

WAIS (Wide Area Information Servers) is an information service designed to search available databases on the Internet. Throughout the Internet there are many WAIS databases, which consist of articles covering such diverse topics as movies and programming. A WAIS database is any collection of documents that have been indexed using WAIS indexing software. WAIS servers set up indexes that can be used to search documents.

To search WAIS databases, you use either a WAIS client utility such as **waisq**, **swais,** or **xwais**, or a Web Browser such as Netscape. **waisq** uses a simple command line interface. **swais** provides a full-screen interface. **xwais** is designed for X-Windows interfaces. The **swais** commands and options are listed in Table 10-5. A WAIS client allows you to select a WAIS database and perform searches using complex Boolean queries. The results are then listed and numbered. You then choose the number of the article in this list that you want. This will display the article, and you can save or print it. You can also use your Web browser to access WAIS sites such as **www.wais.com**. There, you can perform searches on many different topics or move to other WAIS sites.

Unlike searches in other information services, WAIS both performs full text searches of database articles and ranks its results. WAIS searches the entire text of each article, not just the article title or a predetermined list of index words. In this respect, the content of each article is examined, providing a more comprehensive search. The results of a WAIS search are ranked from 0 to 1,000, beginning with those articles that best respond to the search having the highest scores. You can use these results to further expand or narrow your search.

If you want to use a WAIS client, you will have to first download it and install it. These are complete packages that include the WAIS server, an indexer, as well as both **swais** and **xwais** clients. A free version of WAIS called freeWAIS has been made available by the Clearinghouse for Network Information Discovery and Retrieval (CNIDR). Their Web site at **ftp.cnidr.org** has a Linux version of freeWAIS already compiled and ready to use. You can also download the source code and compile it yourself. freeWAIS is also available at **sunsite.unc.edu** and its mirror sites in the **/pub/packages/info-systems/wais** directory.

To directly access WAIS databases, you need to install WAIS source files onto your system. A WAIS source file contains the Internet address of a WAIS database as well as information about it. A source file has the extension **.src** and should be placed in your **/usr/lib/wais-sources** directory. You may have to create this directory. You can obtain a set of WAIS source files for commonly accessed WAIS databases from **sunsite.unc.edu**.

In the **/pub/packages/info-systems/wais** directory, first locate and download the file **wais-servers.tar.Z.**, then place this file in the **/usr/lib/wais-sources** directory. Decompress and extract the file with **gunzip** and **tar**. A large number of WAIS source files will be extracted. One in particular, called the **directory-of-servers.src**, references the WAIS server at **quake.think.com**, which holds the main directory of WAIS servers. The next time you start up **swais** you will be presented with a long list of databases to choose from. Each of these databases has its own WAIS source file in **/usr/lib/wais-sources**. Press the / key to search the database names or use the arrow keys to move from one to another. Once you have found the one you want, press ENTER to select it. You can choose everything from artworks in the Smithsonian to kitchen recipes.

You can also create your own WAIS database using the freeWAIS server software. You can then set up a collection of documents, index them, and make them available for searching by other users on the Internet. The freeWAIS server software is described in Chapter 12.

Summary: Accessing the Internet

Linux has a set of Internet tools that you can use to locate and access information sites on the Internet. With telnet you can remotely log into another computer connected on the Internet. For example, you could directly connect to the online catalogue for the Library of Congress and perform queries on it. With ftp you can download files from an ftp site to your own computer. With Archie you can find out where certain files may be located. Gopher combines all these features into a powerful and easy-to-use interface for browsing the Internet. Information is organized into a series of menus that you can move through until you find the information you want. Finally, you can use WAIS for comprehensive searches on a variety of databases.

telnet Command mode	Effect
-d	Sets the debug toggle to TRUE
-a	Attempts automatic login using USER variable as set by ENVIRON option
-n *tracefile*	Opens *tracefile* for recording trace information
-l *user*	Connects to a remote system with user as the login name
-e escape char	Sets telnet escape character
telnet Command Mode	
close	Closes a telnet session and returns to command mode
open *host* [[-l] *user*][-*port*]	Opens a connection to the specified host

Table 10-1. *telnet Options and Commands*

telnet Command mode	Effect
quit	Closes any open telnet session and exits telnet
! *command*	Executes a Linux command
status	Shows the current status of telnet
? *command*	With no arguments, displays a help summary; if a command is specified, displays the information for that command
set *variable value* **unset** *variable value*	Sets different telnet variables; see **man** pages for a complete list
toggle arguments ...	Toggles different flags between true and false; see **man** pages for complete list of flags

Table 10-1. *telnet Options and Commands* (continued)

Command	Effect
ftp	Invokes ftp program
open	Opens a connection to another system
close	Closes connection to a system
quit or **bye**	Ends ftp session
get *filename*	Sends file from remote system to local system
put *filename*	Sends file from local system to remote system
mget *regular-expression*	Allows you to download several files at once from a remote system; you can use special characters to specify the files; you will be prompted one by one for each file transfer in turn
mput *regular-expression*	Allows you to send several files at once to a remote system; you can use special characters to specify the files; you will be prompted one by one for each file to be transferred

Table 10-2. *ftp Commands*

Command	Effect
`binary`	Transfers files in binary mode
`ascii`	Transfers files in ascii mode
`cd` *directory*	Changes directories on the remote system
`lcd` *directory*	Changes directories on the local system
`help` or `?`	Lists ftp commands

Table 10-2. *ftp Commands* (continued)

Archie Client Option	Description/Effect
`archie` *options* *search-string*	
`-e`	Exact pattern match (default)
`-c`	Searches file names for occurrence of pattern
`-s`	Searches file names ignoring case
`-r`	Pattern is a regular expression
`-t`	Sorts the results by date
`-l`	Outputs results as a record that can be parsed by programs
`-o` *filename*	Places result of search in *filename*
`-h` *hostname*	Queries the hostname Archie server
`-m`*num*	Limits the maximum number of results (matches)
`-N`*num*	Estimates number of results of a query (default 0)
`-L`	Lists the known Archie servers
`-V`	Verbose option; Archie notifies user of progress in long searches

Table 10-3. *Archie Commands*

Public Server Commands	**Description/Effect**
`prog`	Searches file names for occurrence of pattern
`list`	Lists the known Archie servers
`site`	Lists files at a particular host
`mail`	Mails results of search
`quit`	Logs out of Archie server
`help`	Displays help
`set` *variable value*	Sets Archie variables
`show`	Displays current values of Archie variables
`unset`	Removes variables
Server Variables	
`autologout` *num*	Number of minutes that Archie waits idle before automatically logging you out of the Archie server; the default is usually 15 minutes **set `autologout`** 10
`mailto` *address*	Mail address to which results are sent **set `mailto` richpete@garnet.berkeley.edu**
`maxhits` *num*	Limits the maximum number of results (matches) **set `maxhits`** 10
`pager`	Uses the default pager utility, such as More, to display your results **set `pager`** **unset `pager`**

`search` *option*	Type of search
	set `search` `subcase`
	  `search` options
	    `sub` Pattern search within file names
	    `subcase` Pattern search that distinguishes between upper- and lowercase
	    `exact` Exact pattern match
	    `regex` Uses regular expressions

Table 10-3. *Archie Commands* (continued)

Server Variables	Description/Effect

sortby *option*	Type of sort for output
	set sortby *filename*
	  sortby options
	    none No sort
	    filename Sorts the results alphabetically by file name
	    hostname Sorts the results by hostname
	    time Sorts the results from most recent date
	    size Sorts the results from largest size
	    rfilename Reverses alphabetical file name sort
	    rhostname Reverses alphabetical hostname sort
	    rtime Sorts the results from oldest date
	    rsize Sorts the results from smallest size

status	Issues status reports on searches as they are performed **set status** **unset status**
term *terminal-id*	Type of terminal you are using **set term** vt100

Table 10-3. *Archie Commands* (continued)

Option	Effect
gopher [**-sb**] [**-t** *title*] [**-p** *path*] [*hostname port*]	
-p *string*	Specifies a selector string to send to the root-level server on startup
-t *string*	Sets the title of the initial screen for the Gopher client
Menu Item Qualifiers	
.	File
/	Menu
<CSO>	CSO nameserver

Table 10-4. *Gopher Commands*

Menu Item Qualifiers	**Effect**
`<TEL>`	telnet connection
`<Picture>`	Graphic, such as gif or jpeg
`<)`	Sound file
`<Move>`	Video, such as mov or avi
`<HTML>`	Hypertext document
`<Bin>`	Binary file
`<HCX>`	Macintosh BinHexed file
`<PC Bin>`	DOS binary file
`<MIME>`	Multipurpose Internet Mail extensions file
`<?>`	Database with keyword search
Moving to and Selecting Menu Items	
k and UP ARROW	Moves up to previous menu item
j and DOWN ARROW	Moves down to next menu item
num	Moves to *num* item in menu
l, RIGHT ARROW, ENTER	Press one of these to select the current menu item
Searching a Menu for an Item	
/*pattern*	Searches menu items for pattern and moves to first item with that pattern
n	Repeats previous search of menu items
Operations Performed on Menu Items	
=	Displays information about a menu item
s	Saves the current item to a file
m	Mails the current item to a user
p	Prints the current item

Table 10-4.   *Gopher Commands* (continued)

Moving Through Menu Screens	Effect
>, +, SPACEBAR	Moves to next menu screen
<, -, b	Moves back to previous menu screen
Return to Previous Menus	
u, .	Moves back to previous menu
m	Returns to top main menu
Bookmark Commands	
a	Adds selected item to bookmark list
A	Adds current menu to bookmark list
d	Removes a bookmark from the bookmark list
v	Displays bookmark list
Options, Quit, and Help Commands	
q	Quits Gopher
Q	Quits Gopher without prompt
?	Help
O	Displays and changes options for Gopher
Environment Variables	
PAGER	Client will use that to display files to the user
GOPHER_MAIL	Program to send mail (must understand **-s** option)
GOPHER_PLAY	Program to play sound
GOPHER_TELNET	Program to contact telnet services
GOPHER_HTML	Program to display HTML documents
GOPHER_PRINTER	Program to print from a pipe

Table 10-4. *Gopher Commands* (continued)

Option	Description/Effect
-s *sourcename*	Selects *sourcename* for search; sources are discussed in Chapter 12
-S *sourcedir*	Specifies a source directory; default is **~/wais-sources**
-C *sourcedir*	Specifies a common source directory; default is **/usr/lib/wais-sources**
-h	Help message
Command	
j, DOWN ARROW, **^N**	Moves down one source
k, UP ARROW, **^P**	Moves up one source
J, **^V**, **^D**	Moves down one screen
K, ESC **v**, **^U**	Moves up one screen
###	Position to source number ###
/sss	Searches for source *sss*
SPACEBAR, **.** (period)	Selects current source
=	Deselects all sources
v, **,** (comma)	Views current source info
<ret>	Performs search
s	Selects new sources (refresh sources list)
w	Selects new keywords
X, **-**	Removes current source permanently
o	Sets and shows **swais** options
h, **?**	Shows this help display
H	Displays program history
q	Leaves this program

Table 10-5. *WAIS Client Commands*

Chapter Eleven

The World Wide Web

413

The World Wide Web (WWW) is a hypertext database of different types of information distributed across many different sites on the Internet. A hypertext database consists of items that are linked to other items, that in turn may be linked to yet other items, and so on. Upon retrieving an item, you can then use that item to retrieve any related items. For example, you could retrieve an article on the Amazon rain forest and then use it to retrieve a map of the rain forest or a picture of the rain forest. In this respect, a hypertext database is like a web of interconnected data that you can trace from one data item to another. Information is displayed in pages known as Web pages. On a Web page certain keywords are highlighted that form links to other Web pages or to items such as pictures, articles, or files.

The World Wide Web links data across different sites on the Internet throughout the world. It is often referred to as WWW or simply as the Web. The World Wide Web originated in Europe at CERN research laboratories. CERN remains the original WWW server. An Internet site that operates as a Web server is known as a Web site. Such Web sites are often dedicated to specialized topics or institutions, for example, the Smithsonian Web site or the NASA Web site. These Web sites usually have an Internet address that begins with www, as in **www.caldera.com**, the Web site for Caldera. Once connected to a Web site, you can use hypertext links to move from one Web page to another.

To access the Web you use a client program called a Browser. There are many different Web Browsers to choose from. There are Browsers available for use on Unix, Windows, the Mac, and for Linux. Certain Browsers, such as Netscape and Mosaic, have versions that operate on all such systems. On your Linux system you can choose from several Web Browsers. Your OpenLinux system comes with Arena Browser. In addition to Arena, you have the Lynx Browser. This is a line-mode Browser that displays only lines of text. You can download several other Browsers to your system at no charge. For example, Mosaic and Netscape are X-Windows-based Browsers that provide full picture, sound, and video display capabilities. Mosaic is available under a free public license. You can download a trial version of Netscape from the Netscape Web site.

URL Addresses

An Internet resource is accessed using a Universal Resource Locator (URL), shown in Figure 11-1. A URL is composed of three elements: the transfer protocol, the hostname, and the path name. The transfer protocol and hostname are separated by a colon and two slashes, **://**. The path name always begins with a single slash.

```
transfer-protocol://host-name/path-name
```

The transfer protocol is usually **http** (HyperText Transfer Protocol), indicating a Web page. Other possible transfer protocols are **gopher**, **ftp**, and **file**. As their

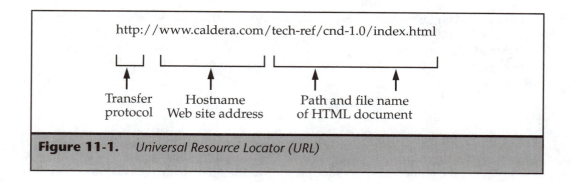

Figure 11-1.   *Universal Resource Locator (URL)*

names suggest, **gopher** and **ftp** initiate Gopher and ftp sessions. **file** displays a text or a directory file, as well as an HTML file. Table 11-1 lists the various transfer protocols.

The hostname is the computer that a particular Web site is located on. You can think of this as the address of the Web site. By convention most hostnames begin with www. In the next example, the URL locates a Web page called **toc.html** on the **home.netscape.com** Web site.

```
http://home.netscape.com/toc.html
```

If you do not want to access a particular Web page, you can leave it out, and you will automatically access the Web site's home page. To access a Web site directly, you can just use its hostname. The default name for a Web site's home page is **index.html**, located in the site's top directory. A Web site can override the default and specify a particular file as the home page. However, if no file is specified, the **index.html** file is taken to be the home page. In the next example, the user brings up the Caldera home page.

```
http://www.caldera.com/
```

The path name specifies the directory where the resource can be found on the host system, as well as the name of the resource's file. For example, **/pub/Linux/newdat.html** references an HTML document called **newdat** located in the **/pub/Linux** directory. As you move to other Web pages on a site you may move more deeply into the directory tree. In the following example, the user accesses the **faq.html** document in the directory **/tech-ref/cnd-1.0/faq**.

```
http://www.caldera.com/tech-ref/cnd-1.0/faq/faq.html
```

As just explained, should you specify a directory path name without a particular Web page file, your Web Browser will look for a file called **index.html** in that directory. An **index.html** file in a directory operates as the default Web page for that directory. In the next example, the **index.html** Web page in the **/tech-ref/cnd-1.0** directory is displayed.

```
http://www.caldera.com/tech-ref/cnd-1.0/index.html
```

You can use this technique to access local Web pages on your system. For example, once installed, the demo Web pages for Java are located in **/usr/local/java/**. Since it is on your local system you do not need to include a hostname. There is an **index.html** page in the **/usr/local/java/** directory that will be automatically displayed when you specify the directory path. You can do the same for your system documentation, which is in Web-page format located in the **/usr/doc/HTML/ldp** directory.

```
file:/usr/local/java
file:/usr/doc/HTML/ldp
```

If you reference a directory that has no **index.html** file, the Web server will create one for you, and your Browser will then display it. This index will simply list the different files and directories in that directory. You can click on an entry to display a file or move to another directory. The first entry will be a special entry for the parent directory.

The resource file's extension indicates the type of action to be taken on it. A picture will have a **.gif** or **.jpeg** extension and will be converted for display. A sound file will have a **.au** or **.wav** extension and will be played. The following URL references a **gif** file. Instead of displaying a Web page, your Browser will invoke a graphics viewer to display the picture. Table 11-2 provides a list of the different file extensions.

```
http://www.train.com/engine/engine1.gif
```

Web Pages

A Web page is a specially formatted document that can be displayed by any Web Browser. You can think of a Web page as a word processing document that can display both text and graphics. Within the Web page, links can be embedded that call up other Internet resources. An Internet resource can be a graphic, a file, a telnet connection, or even another Web page. The Web page acts as an interface for accessing different Internet tools, such as ftp, to download files, or telnet, to connect to an online catalog or other remote service.

When you first start your desktop, you will notice the Caldera Info icon displayed, as shown here. This is the icon that your desktop uses to display HTML pages.

Caldera_Info

Web pages display both text and graphics. Text is formatted with paragraphs and can be organized with different headings. Graphics of various sizes may be placed anywhere in the page. Throughout the page there will usually be anchor points that you can use to call up other Internet resources. Each anchor point is associated with a particular Internet resource. One anchor point may reference a picture, another a file; others may reference other Web pages or even other Web sites. These anchor points are specially highlighted text or graphics that usually appear in a different color from the rest of the text. Whereas ordinary text may be black, text used for anchor points may be green, blue, or red. You select a particular anchor point by moving your mouse pointer to that text or picture and then clicking on it. The Internet resource associated with that anchor point will then be called up. If it is a picture, the picture will be displayed. If it is another Web page, that Web page is displayed. If the Internet resource is on another Web site, that site will be accessed. The color of an anchor point indicates its status and the particular Web Browser you are using. Both Mosaic and Netscape use blue for anchors that you have not yet accessed. Netscape uses purple for anchors you have already accessed, and Mosaic uses red. All these colors can be overridden by a particular Web page.

Your Web Browser will keep a list of the different Web pages that you accessed for each session. You will be able to move back and forth easily in that list. Having called up another Web page, you can use your Browser to move back to the previous one. Web Browsers construct their lists according to the sequence in which you displayed your Web pages. They keep track of the Web pages you are accessing, whatever they may be. However, on many Web sites, several Web pages are meant to be connected in a particular order, like chapters in a book. Such pages usually have buttons displayed at the bottom of the page that reference the next and previous pages in the sequence. Clicking on the Next button will display the next Web page for this site. The Home button will return you to the first page for this sequence.

Web Browsers

Most Web Browsers are designed to access several different kinds of information. They can access a Web page on a remote Web site or a file on your own system. Some Browsers can also access a remote news server or an ftp site. The type of information for a site is specified by the keyword **http** for Web sites, **nntp** for news servers, **ftp** for ftp sites, and **file** for files on your own system.

To access a Web site you enter **http://** followed by the Internet address of the Web site. If you know a particular Web page you want to access on that Web site, you can add the path name for that page, attaching it to the Internet address. Then simply press ENTER. The Browser will connect you to that Web site and display its home page or the page you specified.

You can just as easily use a Web Browser to display Web pages on your own system by entering the term **file** followed by a colon, **file:**, with the path name of the Web page you want to display. You do not specify an Internet site. Remember, all Web pages have the extension **.html**. Links within a Web page on your own system can connect you to other Web pages on your system or to Web pages on remote systems. When you first start a Web Browser on your Caldera Network Desktop, your Browser displays a local Web page on your own system that has links to the Caldera Web site where you can obtain online support. If you wish, you can create your own Web pages, with their own links, and make one of them your default Web page.

Web pages on a Web site will often contain links to other Web pages, some on the same site and others at other Web sites. Through these links you can move from one page to another. As you move from Web page to Web page, using the anchor points or buttons, your Browser will display the URL for the current page. Your Browser keeps a list of the different Web pages you have accessed in a given session. Most Browsers have buttons that allow you to move back and forth through this list. You can move to the Web page you displayed before the current one, and then move back further to the one before that. You can move forward again to the next page and so on.

To get to a particular page you may have moved through a series of pages, using links in each to finally reach the Web page you want. To access any Web page, all you need is its URL address. If you want to access a particular page again, you can enter in its URL address and move directly to it, without moving through the intervening pages as you did the first time. Instead of writing down the URL addresses and entering them yourself, most Web Browsers can keep a hotlist—a list of favorite Web pages you want to access directly. When you are displaying a Web page you want to access later, just instruct your Browser to place it on the hotlist. The Web page will usually be listed in the hotlist by its title, not its URL. To access that Web page later, select the entry in the hotlist.

Most Web Browsers can also access ftp and Gopher sites. You may find that using a Web Browser to access an ftp site is easier than using the ftp utility. Directories and files are automatically listed, and selecting a file or directory is just a matter of clicking on its name. First enter **ftp://** and the Internet address of the ftp site. The contents of a directory will be displayed, listing files and subdirectories. To move to another directory, just click on it. To download a file, click on its name. You will see an entry listed as **..**, representing the parent directory. You can move down the file structure from one subdirectory to another and move back up one directory at a time by selecting **..**. To leave the ftp site, just return to your own home page. You can also use your Browser to access Gopher sites. Enter **gopher://** followed by the Internet address of the Gopher site. Your Web Browser will display the main Gopher menu for that site. You can then move from one Gopher menu to the next.

Most Browsers can connect to your news server to access specified newsgroups or articles. This is a local operation, accessing the news server you are already connected to. You enter **nntp** followed by a colon and the newsgroup or news article. Some Browsers, such as Netscape, have an added Newsreader Browser that allows them to access any remote news servers.

As noted previously, there are several popular Browsers available for Linux. Four distinctive ones are described here; the Netscape Navigator, Mosaic, Arena, and Lynx. Netscape and Mosaic are X-Windows-based Web Browsers capable of displaying graphics, video, and sound, as well as operating as newsreaders and mailers. Arena is a Browser designed to support the development of new features of HTML 3, the Markup language that Web pages are written in. Lynx is a command line-based Browser with no graphics capabilities. But in every other respect it is a fully functional Web Browser. Arena and Lynx are both provided with your Caldera Lite Network Desktop. You can easily download and install versions of Netscape and Mosaic. You can also download more recent versions of Arena and Lynx. Netscape is a commercial product available for a 90-day free trial. Mosaic, Arena, and Lynx are all free of charge.

Netscape Navigator

Hypertext databases are designed to access any kind of data, whether it is text, graphics, sound, or even video. Whether you can actually access such data depends to a large extent on the type of Browser you use. One of the more popular Web Browsers is the Netscape Navigator. Versions of Netscape operate on different graphical user interfaces such as X-Windows, Microsoft Windows, and the Macintosh. Using X-Windows, the Netscape Browser can display graphics, sound, video, and Java-based programs (you will learn about Java a little later in the chapter). You can obtain more information about Netscape on its Web site: **www.netscape.com**.

You can obtain a copy of Netscape Navigator from the Caldera ftp site at **ftp.caldera.com**. Chapter 3 shows you how to download and install an RPM package of the Netscape Navigator Browser. You could also obtain compressed archive versions (.tar.gz) from the Netscape ftp sites such as **ftp8.netscape.com**. A compressed archive version has to be decompressed and unpacked with the gunzip and tar xvf commands, once the archive has been placed in an install directory such as **/usr/local**.

Once you have generated your Netscape Browser, you are ready to use it. Netscape Navigator is an X-Windows application that you have operated from your desktop. If you haven't done so already, start your desktop with the **startx** command. Then use a directory window to open the directory you placed Netscape Navigator in. Find the Netscape icon and double-click on it. You may want to move the Netscape icon onto the desktop for easy access. The Netscape Navigator icon looks like this:

Netscape Navigator displays an area at the top of the screen for entering a URL address and a series of buttons for various Web page operations (see Figure 11-2). Drop-down menus provide access to Netscape features. To access a Web site, you enter its address in the URL area and press ENTER.

The icon bar, shown in Figure 11-3, across the top of the Browser, holds buttons for moving from one page to another and performing other operations. The Back-arrow and Forward-arrow buttons move you back and forth through the list of Web pages you have already accessed in a given session. The Home button (picture of house) exits a Web site and places you back in your own system. There is also a Stop button, in the form of a stop sign, that becomes active when you are linking to and displaying a new Web page. If the Web page is taking too long to display, you may want to click on the Stop button to stop the process.

Netscape refers to the URLs of Web pages you want to keep in a hotlist as bookmarks, marking pages you want to access directly. The Bookmarks menu lets you

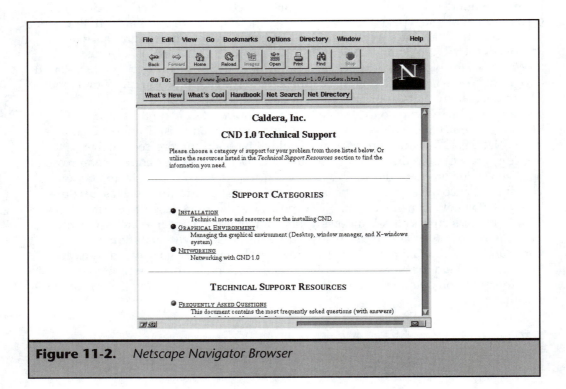

Figure 11-2. *Netscape Navigator Browser*

Figure 11-3. *Netscape Navigator icon bar*

add your favorite Web pages to a hotlist. You can then view your bookmarks and select one to move to.

Through the Mail item in the Windows menu you can open a fully functional mail client with which you can send and receive messages over the Internet. The News item, also in the Windows menu, opens a fully functional newsreader with which you can read and post articles in Usenet newsgroups. In this respect, your Netscape Navigator is more than just a Web Browser. It is also a Mail program and a newsreader.

Other items in the Windows menu enhance your Web Browser operations. In the address book you can keep a list of Web site URLs. The Bookmark item lets you edit your list of bookmarks, adding new ones or removing old ones. The History item is a list of previous URLs you have accessed. If you want to go back to a Web page that you did not save as a bookmark, you can find it in the history list. You can then use Netscape to receive and send mail as well as access Usenet newsgroups.

The Options menu in the Netscape Navigator lets you set several different kinds of preferences for your Browser. You can set preferences for mail and news, the network, and security, as well as general preferences. In general preferences you can determine your home page and how you want the toolbar displayed. For mail and news you can enter the mail and news servers you use on the Internet. Netscape can be set to access any number of news servers that you subscribe to and that use the NNTP transfer protocols. You can switch from one news server to another if you wish.

If you are on a network that connects to the Internet through a firewall, you will have to use the Proxies screen to enter the address of your network's firewall gateway computer. A *firewall* is a computer that operates as a controlled gateway to the Internet for your network. There are several types of firewalls. One of the most restrictive uses programs called *proxies* that receive Internet requests from users and then makes those requests on their behalf. There is no direct connection to the Internet. From the Options menu select Network, then choose the Proxies screen. Here, enter the IP address of your network's firewall gateway computer.

To save a Web page, select the Save As entry in the File menu. This opens a dialog box with a default directory specified. There are three boxes. The top box is for a filter. The bottom box is the name of the file. The middle box lists different directories in the current directory. You can enter a path and file name of your own, or you can click on the .. entry in the middle box to move back through the directory tree, and then click on directory names to move into those directories. When you have reached the directory you want, you can save your Web page.

Mosaic

Mosaic, which can display graphics, sound, and video data, was the first graphics-based Browser developed for the Web. Unlike Netscape, it is available free to anyone. There are versions of Mosaic for different graphical user interfaces such as X-Windows, Microsoft Windows, and the Macintosh. It was developed by the National Center for Supercomputing Applications (NCSA) at the University of Illinois at Urbana-Champaign. More information about Mosaic is available at the NCSA Web site: **www.ncsa.uiuc.edu**. You can download a copy of Mosaic from the Mosaic ftp site at **ftp.ncsa.uiuc.edu** in the directory **/Web/Mosaic/Unix/binaries**. This directory will display directories for different version numbers. Those with a **b** in the directory name are new beta versions currently being tested. The current version of Mosaic is 2.6, located in directory **2.6**. There is also a beta version of 2.7 available in directory **2.7b**. Change to a directory and use the **get** command to download the Linux version.

```
# ftp ftp.ncsa.uiuc.edu
Connected to ftp.ncsa.uiuc.edu.
220 curley FTP server (Version wu-2.4(25) Thu Aug 25 13:14:21 CDT 1994) ready.
Name (ftp.ncsa.uiuc.edu:root): anonymous
331 Guest login ok, send your complete e-mail address as password.
Password:
230-
230-Welcome to NCSA's new anonymous FTP server! I hope you find what you are
230-  looking for. If you have any technical problems with the server,
230-  please e-mail to ftpadmin@ncsa.uiuc.edu. For other questions regarding
230-  NCSA software tools, please e-mail softdev@ncsa.uiuc.edu.
230 Guest login ok, access restrictions apply.
Remote system type is UNIX.
Using binary mode to transfer files.
ftp> cd /Web/Mosaic/Unix/binaries
250 CWD command successful.
ftp> cd 2.6
250-Please read the file README-2.6
250-  it was last modified on Fri Jul  7 14:31:14 1995 - 267 days ago
250 CWD command successful.
ftp> ls
200 PORT command successful.
150 Opening ASCII mode data connection for /bin/ls.
total 22596
drwx------    2 101      10            2048 Jul  7  1995 .
drwxr-xr-x    6 12873    wheel         2048 Oct 25 17:51 ..
-rw-r--r--    1 101      10          797705 Jul  7  1995 Mosaic-ibm-2.6.Z
```

```
rw-r--r--   1 101      10         915718 Jul  7  1995 Mosaic-indy-2.6.Z
-rw-r--r--   1 101      10         903973 Jul  7  1995 Mosaic-linux-2.6.Z
-rw-r--r--   1 101      10         648431 Jul  7  1995 Mosaic-sgi-2.6.Z
-rw-r--r--   1 101      10        1708074 Jul  7  1995
    Mosaic-solaris-23-2.6.Z
-rw-r--r--   1 101      10           1835 Jul  7  1995 README-2.6
ftp> binary
200 Type set to I.
ftp> get Mosaic-linux-2.6.Z
200 PORT command successful.
150 Opening BINARY mode data connection for Mosaic-linux-2.6.Z (903973 bytes).
226 Transfer complete.
903973 bytes received in 276 secs (3.2 Kbytes/sec)
ftp> get README-2.6
200 PORT command successful.
150 Opening BINARY mode data connection for README-2.6 (1835 bytes).
226 Transfer complete.
1835 bytes received in 0.74 secs (2.4 Kbytes/sec)
ftp> close
221 Good-bye.
ftp> quit
# exit
```

The file will be a **.Z** compressed file, not an archived and gzip compressed file
(**.tar.gz**) as the Netscape file was. To decompress it you just use **gunzip**, not **tar**. This
will result in a file called **Mosaic-linux-2.6**. Use **chmod** to change the permissions on
the file to be executable, 755. Then place this file in the directory you want to access it
from. In the next example, the user decompresses the file, makes it executable, and
moves the Mosaic Browser to the **/usr/local** directory.

```
$ gunzip Mosaic-linux-2.6.Z
$ chmod 755 Mosaic-linux-2.6.Z
$ mv Mosaic-linux-2.6.Z /usr/local
```

Like Netscape, Mosaic is an X-Windows application. You must have your desktop
running before you can use it. Within your desktop, open the directory where you
placed your Mosaic Browser, find its icon, and click on it. For easier access you can
drag the Mosaic icon onto your desktop. The Mosaic window will open, displaying
your home Web page (see Figure 11-4).

The Mosaic window has two boxes at the top. The first displays the title of the
current Web page. The second is for entering URLs. The contents of the Web page are
then displayed. At the bottom of the window are a series of buttons for navigating the
Web pages you access. The Back and Forward buttons move you back and forth

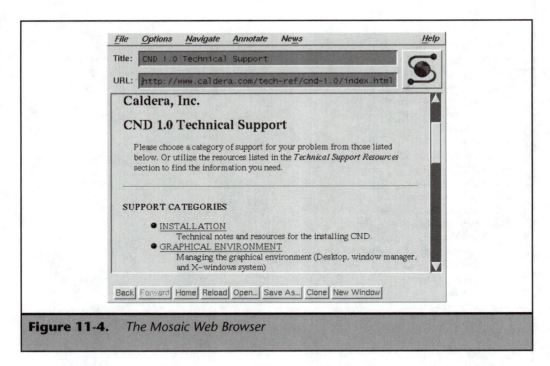

Figure 11-4. *The Mosaic Web Browser*

through a list of Web pages you have accessed. The Home button returns you to your own home page. The Save As button saves the current Web page on your own system.

When you attempt to access a Web page, the globe image in the upper-right corner will spin. Once the Web page is displayed, the globe will stop spinning. Should you decide not to access the Web page while the globe is spinning, you can stop the access by clicking on the globe. In this respect, the globe functions as a stop button. Sometimes, attempts to access a Web page may take a great deal of time. You can simply cancel your request by clicking on the spinning globe.

The menus across the top of the Mosaic window allow you to manage your Web searches. With the Navigate menu, you maintain a hotlist of favored Web sites. The Options menu has several entries for configuring your Mosaic Browser. You can set your home page or specify mail or news servers. You can also set default colors used for the background and for URL links. The News menu lets you use your Mosaic Browser to access Usenet newsgroups, displaying and saving articles. Mosaic also has built-in security features that can protect your system.

Arena

Arena is an experimental Browser designed as a testbed for the new HTML 3 language and the WC3 libraries. Arena supports tables, mathematical formulas, and style sheets. It is not meant to be a full-featured Web Browser; rather, it is intended as a tool for the development of HTML 3 Web pages. Arena is installed on your Caldera Lite Desktop as your default Web Browser. It presents a screen with buttons at the top for commands, followed by a URL entry area, and then the Web page display area.

A series of buttons across the top of the Arena Browser controls movement and executes commands (see Figure 11-5). To enter a new URL in the URL area, you first click on the Open button. This will clear the area and you can then enter your new URL. Use CTRL-**h** to backspace. The Abort button to the left of the URL entry area will cancel a Web access operation. The Forward button moves you forward a page and the Back button moves you back to a previously displayed page. The Home button returns you to your Home page. The other buttons function exactly as they do in other Windows applications.

One helpful command for those developing HTML 3 pages is the View button. When you click on the View button, the Web page is displayed as an HTML document, an ASCII text with HTML tags embedded in it. This way you can see how your Web pages are constructed. If you want to see how a particular effect was done, you can click on view to see the HTML tags used.

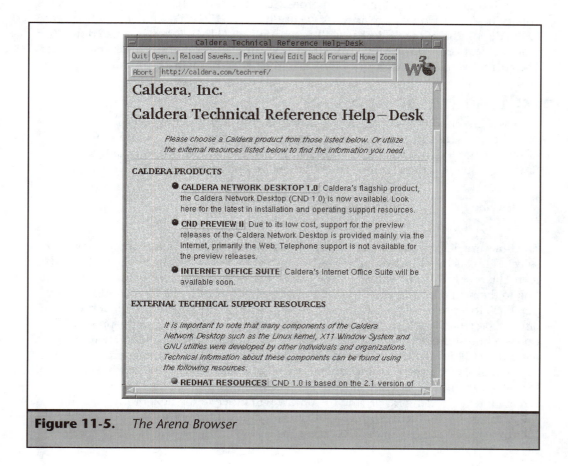

Figure 11-5. *The Arena Browser*

You can set your Home Web page, the default editor, and any proxies, by corresponding shell environment variables. To change your Home page, you set the **WWW_HOME** variable to the URL of that Web page. To set the default editor, you set the **EDITOR** variable to the name of the editor you want to use. If you need to specify a proxy, you can set the **http_proxy** variable to the URL of the proxy. Shell environment variables are usually set in your **.bash_profile** or **.bschrc file**. In the BASH shell you also have to export the variables. The following shows several examples. If you are using the C-shell, you have to use the **setenv** command.

```
WWW_HOME=file://home/httpd/html/myfile.html
EDITOR=vi
http_proxy=pango1.train.com
export WWW_HOME  EDITOR  http_proxy
```

To find out more about the Arena project, click on the Help button. This connects you to the Arena Home page at **www.w3.org/hypertext/WWW/Arena/**. Here you can find a discussion of the project as well as tutorials on HTML 3. You can also download more current versions of Arena from the **ftp.w3.org** ftp site in the **/pub/arena** directory. The current version of Arena for Linux is in the file **arena-beta-2b-linux.tar.gz**.

Lynx: Line-Mode Browser

Lynx is a line-mode Browser that you can use without X-Windows (see Figure 11-6). A Web page is displayed as text only. A text page can contain links to other Internet resources, but will not display any graphics, video, or sound. To start the Lynx Browser, you enter **lynx** on the command line and press ENTER.

```
$ lynx
```

The links are displayed in bold and dispersed throughout the text of the Web page. A selected link is highlighted in reverse video with a shaded rectangle around the link text. The first link is automatically selected. You can then move sequentially from one link to the next on a page by pressing the DOWN ARROW key. The UP ARROW key moves you back to a previous link. To choose a link, you first highlight it and then press either ENTER or the RIGHT ARROW key. If you want to go to a specific site, press **g**. This opens a line at the bottom of the screen with the prompt **URL to open:**. There, you can enter the URL for the site you want. Pressing **m** will return you to your Home page. The text of a Web page is displayed one screen at a time. To move to the next screen of text, you can either press SPACEBAR or PAGE DOWN. PAGE UP displays the previous screen of text. Pressing DOWN and UP ARROW will move to the next or previous links in the text, displaying the full screen of text around the link. To display a description of the current Web page with its URL, press the = key.

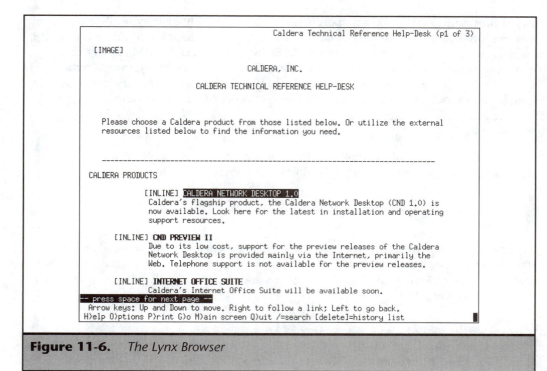

Figure 11-6.   *The Lynx Browser*

Lynx keeps a list of all the Web pages you access in a session. LEFT ARROW moves you back to a previously displayed page. RIGHT ARROW moves you forward to the next page in the list. Lynx refers to this list of Web pages as a *history list*. You can directly display this history list by pressing DEL. You can then use your UP and DOWN ARROW, keys to select a particular Web page link and use RIGHT ARROW or ENTER to access it. Lynx also supports bookmarks. By pressing **a**, you automatically add the current Web page to a bookmark file. Press **v** to display the list of bookmarks. As with a history list, you can use the UP and DOWN ARROW to select a bookmark link. Pressing either RIGHT ARROW or ENTER will move to and display that Web page.

Lynx uses a set of one letter commands to perform various Browser functions. By pressing the **?** key at any time, you can display a list of these commands. For example, pressing the **d** key will download a file. The **h** key will bring up a help menu. To search the text of your current Web page, you press the **/** key. This opens up a line at the bottom of the screen where you enter your search pattern. Lynx will then highlight the next instance of that pattern in the text. By pressing **n**, Lynx will display the next instance. The **** key will toggle you between a source and rendered version of the current Web page, showing you the HTML tags or the formatted text.

Except for the display limitations, Lynx is a fully functional Web Browser. You can use Lynx to download files or make telnet connections. All information on the Web is still accessible to you. Since it does not require much of the overhead that graphics-based Browsers need, Lynx can operate much faster, quickly displaying Web page text. This feature makes it ideal for public Web clients. You can telnet to a public Web client, such as **info.cern.ch**, and use its line-mode Browser to access the Web, rather than accessing from your own system. Of course, since you are operating from a remote system, you will not be able to download any files. This is a simple way to access the Web if you do not have access to a Web Browser on your current system.

HotJava

The Linux version of the HotJava Browser is currently available. You can download a copy through links in the Blackdown Web site.

```
http://www.blackdown.org/java-linux.html
```

Select and click the Java Products option. The Browser is a compressed archive, **.tar.gz**. First move that archive to the directory where you want the HotJava program installed, such as **/usr/local**. Then decompress and unpack it with gunzip and tar, or just **tar xvzf** as shown here:

```
# mv hjbl_0sd-linux-nort.tar.gz   /usr/local
# cd /usr/local
# tar xvzf hjbl_0sd-linux-nort.tar.gz
```

This creates a directory called HotJava1.0 within which are bin and lib sub directories. The command for starting the HotJava Browser is in the **HotJava1.0/bin** directory and is called **hotjava**. You should place the path name for that bin directory in your **PATH** in the **/etc/profile** or **.profile** scripts, **/usr/local/HotJava1.0/bin**. You can then start the HotJava Browser with the command.

```
# hotjava
```

The HotJava 1.0 version uses JDK 1.1.1. You should first have JDK 1.1.1 installed and set the **JDK_HOME** variable to whatever the location of JDK 1.1.1 is on your system, for example, **/usr/local/jdk1.1.1**.

The HotJava Browser is shown in Figure 11-7. The HotJava Browser can be easily customized to your particular needs. Its Places menu allows you to collect Web page addresses or use Netscape bookmarks. It can also display both frames and tables. HotJava includes support for security features such as signed applets. It is more flexible in its reading of HTML code, allowing the Browser to recover successfully from errors. HotJava also supports the Unicode 2.0 character set, which allows it to display both Latin and non-Latin characters such as Chinese, Japanese, and Korean.

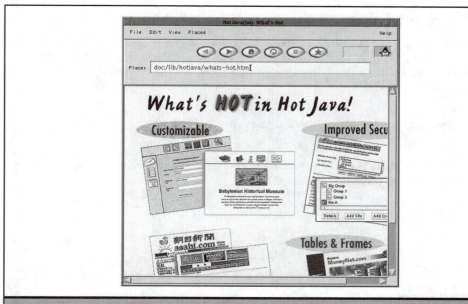

Figure 11-7. *The HotJava Web Browser*

Web Search Utilities

Finding the particular Web page on the Internet that you want can be a very slow process. Often, you have to move from one link to another with your Browser until you track down a Web page on a particular topic. Web page links are very restrictive in this respect. To search for a Web page, you can either use an index or a program that will search the Web for you. An index acts as a kind of yellow pages for the Internet, allowing you to search for Web pages using complex queries. One of the most popular indexes is located at the Yahoo site, http://www.yahoo.com. Here you can search for pages on any given topic.

You can also use programs known as *spiders* that are designed to search the Web directly, site by site. Some popular spiders are the WebCrawler and the World Wide Web Worm (WWWW). A spider not only lists pages on a given topic, but also lists the links from those pages to others with associated topics. In addition, a spider can show you not only a page you are looking for, but its links to other pages on the Web. You can obtain the WWWW spider from: **www.cs.colorado.edu/home/mcbryan/ WWWW.html**. The WebCrawler is available from: **www.biotech.washington.edu/ WebCrawler/WebCrawler.html**

JAVA for Linux

Numerous Java-based products are currently adaptable for Linux. There are Linux versions of the Java Development Kit (JDK), the HotJava Browser, and the Java Web server. You can download most of these products through links in the Blackdown Web page located at

```
http://www.blackdown.org/java-linux.html
```

Select the Java Products entry for a list of links to available Java products. A few of the currently available products are listed here:

JDK 1.0.2	Java Development Kit 1.0
JDK 1.1.3	Java Development Kit 1.1.3
JDBC	JDBC Database Access API
BDK	JavaBeans Development Kit (requires JDK 1.1.1)
Java Web Server	
JSDK	The Java Servlet Development Kit
JWS20	The Workshop 2.0 Build 125
HotJava	HotJava 1.0 Web browser (requires JDK 1.1.1)
BISS-AWT Java Framework	A free Framework/AWT replacement
Castanet Tuner 1.1	

Java Development Kit: JDK

The Java Development Kit provides tools for creating and debugging your own Java applets and provides support for Java applications such as the HotJava Browser. The kit includes demonstration applets with source code. You can obtain detailed documentation about the JDK from the Sun Web site at

```
http://java.sun.com/products/jdk/
```

There are two releases of the JDK available, 1.0 and 1.1. 1.0 is the older release supported by most Browsers. 1.1 is a newer release that is not supported by some older versions of Browsers. JDK 1.1 includes advanced features such as JavaBeans and database connectivity. Both JDK releases are available for Linux. You can download them from a Java-Linux mirror site that you can link to through the Blackdown web page (**www.blackdown.org**) mentioned earlier. Select the "Getting the JDK" entry. JDK 1.0 is also available on the OpenLinux CD-ROM. Many Java applications such as HotJava browser requires JDK 1.1. For these you will have to download and install JDK 1.1. There are currently two versions of JDK 1.1 available: JDK 1.1.1 and the more recent JDK 1.1.3.

JDK 1.0.2

Version 1.0.2 of the Java Development Kit is also located on your OpenLinux CD-ROM in the **contrib** directory as an RPM package. This is the final version of JDK 1.0. To install it, you first mount the CD-ROM and then change to the **RPMS** subdirectory in the OpenLinux **contrib** directory. There you will find both a static and shared version of the JDK. The shared version is for those who have the Motif shared libraries. For OpenLinux Lite, use the static version. With the **rpm -i** command you then install that JDK package. (You cannot use Lisa to install packages in the contrib directory.)

```
# mount /mnt/cdrom
# cd /mnt/cdrom/OpenLinux/contrib/RPMS
# ls JDK*
JDK_shared-1.0.2.pl2-3.i386.rpm    JDK_static-1.0.2.pl2-3.i386.rpm
# rpm -i  JDK_static-1.0.2.pl2-3.i386.rpm
```

The JDK package installs the Java applications, libraries, and demos in the **/usr/local/java** directory. Java applications include a Java compiler, **javac**, a Java debugger, **jdb**, and an applet viewer, **appletviewer**. To use these applications you have to add the **/usr/local/java/bin** directory to your **PATH** in either the **/etc/profile** or **.profile** initialization files (see Chapter 15). The **appletviewer** is located in the **/usr/local/java** directory and you should add this directory also to your **PATH**. The applications included are listed in Table 11-1.

JDK 1.1.1

JDK 1.1 offers new capabilities over JDK 1.0. JDK 1.1 supports Internationalization, signed applets, JAR file format, AWT (window toolkit) enhancements, JavaBeans component model, networking enhancements, Math package for large numbers, Remote Method Invocation (RMI), Reflection, database connectivity (JDBC), new Java Native Interface, Object Serialization, Inner Classes, and performance enhancements. Detailed descriptions of these features can be found in the JDK documentation.

There are currently two versions of the JDK 1.1: JDK 1.1.1 and the newer JDK 1.1.3. The following discussion explains how to install JDK 1.1.1. You can follow a similar procedure for JDK 1.1.3. The Linux version of JDK 1.1.1 is currently packaged as compressed archives. You need to download, decompress, and unpack the **.tar.gz** file. Once you download the archive, place it in the directory want the JDK 1.1.1 installed in, usually a directory like **/usr/local**. You then decompress it with gunzip and unpack it with **tar xvf**, or combine both operations with **tar xvzf** as shown here:

```
# mv jdk.1.1.1-linux-v3.tar.gz  /usr/local
# cd /usr/local
#  tar xvzf jdk.1.1.1-linux-v3.tar.gz
```

A directory will be created called **jdk1.1.1** where you'll find the **bin** and **lib** subdirectories holding the Java applications and libraries. You should add the **/usr/local/jdk1.1.1/bin** directory to your **PATH** in the **/etc/profile** or **.profile** script (**.login** for the TCSH shell). Also, in either the **/etc/profile** or **.profile** you should add an entry that assigns the respective directory to the JDK_HOME variable, as shown here. This variable is used by various Java application such as HotJava to locate the Java interpreter.

```
JDK_HOME=/usr/local/jdk1.1.1/bin
```

JDK 1.0 and 1.1 Tools	Description
java	The Java interpreter
javac	The Java compiler
jdb	The Java debugger
javadoc	Generates API documentation in HTML format
javah	Creates C header files and C stub files for a Java class
javap	Disassembles compiled Java files
appletviewer	Allows you to run applets without a World Wide Web browser
JDK 1.1 Added Tools	
jar	Java Archive Tool

Table 11-1. *JDK Tools and Directories*

JDK 1.0 and 1.1Tools	Description
`javakey`	Digital Signing Tool
`native2ascii`	Native-To-ASCII Converter
`rmic`	Java RMI Stub Converter
`rmiregistry`	Java Remote Object Registry
`serialver`	Serial Version Command
`updateAWT`	AWT 1.1 Conversion Tool
Java Directories	
`bin`	Java applications
`lib`	Java class libraries
`include`	Java include files
`demo`	Java example applets

Table 11-1.   *JDK Tools and Directories (continued)*

Java Applets

You create a Java applet much as you would create a program using a standard programming language. You first use a text editor to create the source code. The source code is saved in a file with a **.java** extension. Then you can use the **javac** compiler to compile the source code file, generating a Java applet. This applet file will have the extension **.class**. For example, in the **/usr/local/java/demo/Blink** directory is a Java source code file named **Blink.java**. You can go to that directory and then compile the **Blink.java** file, generating a **Blink.class** file.

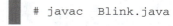

```
# javac  Blink.java
```

The **example1.html** file in that directory runs the **Blink.class** applet. Start up your Browser and access this file to run the Blink applet.

An applet is called within a Web page using the **<applet>** HTML tag. This tag can contain several attributes, one of which is required: **code**. You assign to **code** the name of the compiled applet. There are several optional attributes you can use to set features such as the region used to display the applet and its alignment. You can even access applets on a remote Web site. A complete listing of the different applet features can be found in the **/usr/local/java/README.jdk** file. In the following example, the applet called **Blink.class** will be displayed in a box on the Web Browser that has a height of 140 pixels and a width of 100 pixels and is aligned in the center.

```
<applet code="Blink.class" width=100 height=140
align=center></applet>
```

To invoke the debugger you use the **appletviewer** command with the **-debug** option and the name of the HTML file that runs the applet.

```
appletviewer -debug  mypage.html
```

Using Linux as a Web Server

Linux systems are ideal for creating your own Web site. To do this you have to configure your Linux system as a server (described in Chapter 12). You will also need to create the Web pages and resources that you want to make up your Web site. Web pages are not difficult to create. Links from one page to another will move users through your Web site. You can even create links to Web pages or resources on other sites.

Network Configuration as a Web Server

Your Caldera Network Desktop is already configured to operate as a Web server. The httpd software for managing a Web server is already installed and running. All you need to do is perform the necessary network server configurations and then designate the files and directories open to remote users. If you are using another version of Linux, you may need to obtain and install a Web server. Table 11-3 lists several popular Web servers.

Creating Your Own Web Site

To create your own Web site you will first have to obtain an Internet address and connect your system to the Internet. Having done this, all you have to do is start your Web server daemons and have the correct directories set up for use by your Web site users. Your Caldera Network Desktop has already installed the Web server daemon and has set up the appropriate directories. All you have to do to have a working Web site is to connect to the Internet and create your Web pages. The directory set up by your Caldera Web server for your Web site pages is **/home/httpd/html**. Place the Web pages that you create in that directory. You can make other subdirectories with their own Web pages to which these can link. There are many excellent texts on Web page creation and management, in particular, *The World Wide Web: The Complete Reference* by Rick Stout. A brief description of Web page construction is provided here. You can obtain up-to-date information on current developments in HTML at the following Web page.

```
http://www.w3.org/hypertext/WWW/MarkUp/MarkUp.html
```

Creating Web Pages with HTML

Web pages are created using HTML, the HyperText Markup Language that is a subset of SGML (the Standard Generalized Markup Language). Creating an HTML document is a matter of inserting HTML tags in a text file. In this respect, creating a Web page is as simple as using a tag-based word processor. You use the HTML tags to format text for display as a Web page. The Web page itself is a text file that you can create using any text editor, such as Vi. For those familiar with tag-based word processing on Unix systems you will find it conceptually similar to nroff. There are HTML tags to indicate headings, lists, and paragraphs, as well as to reference Web resources. Table 11-4 lists many of the commonly used HTML tags.

There are alternatives to manually creating a Web page. The Linux version of WordPerfect can automatically generate a Web page from a WordPerfect document. You could create your Web page using all the word processing features of WordPerfect. There are also special Web page creation programs such as **tkWWW**, that easily help you create very complex Web pages without ever having to explicitly type any HTML tags. Everything is done with objects in a window interface (see Table 11-3). Keep in mind though that no matter what tool you use to create your Web page, the Web page itself will be an HTML document.

Page and Text Format

An HTML tag consists of a keyword enclosed in angle brackets, for example, the tag for paragraph is <P>. Tags are usually used in pairs, with the end tag the same as the beginning but with a preceding slash. So you would begin a paragraph with the <P> tag and end the paragraph with the corresponding </P> tag. All Web pages are enclosed with the <HTML> tag. The first entry in your Web page should be <HTML>, and the last </HTML>. You can divide your Web page into sections for the heading and the body. The heading contains the title for your Web page. The body contains the contents.

Formatting Text

In the body of your Web page you can use formatting tags to organize your text headings, paragraphs, or lists. You enter a heading with the tag <Hn>, where n refers to the level of the heading. <H1> is a top-level heading, <H2> is the next level, and so on. Depending on the Browser used, the subheading may be indented or portrayed in a smaller or different font. Each head has to be terminated with its own ending tag—<H1> with </H1>, and <H2> with </H2>.

You use the UL and LI tags to display a list of items. At the beginning and end of the list, you insert <UL> and </UL>. Each item within the list is entered with it own <LI> and </LI> tags. UL displays a bulleted list. For a numbered list you can use OL.

You can position components such as pictures or paragraphs at either the top, bottom, or middle of your Web page using the TOP, BOT, and MID tags.

Referencing Internet Resources: HREF

You can designate certain text or pictures in your Web page as links to other Web pages or to items such as pictures or documents. The items can be on your system or at other Web sites. When the user chooses the text referencing a link, that item or Web page will be retrieved. To create a link, you associate certain text or pictures in your Web page with a URL of an Internet resource. This resource can be another Web page, an item such as a picture or file, or even another Internet tool, such as ftp or telnet. You use an HREF anchor tag to create such a link. The HREF anchor tag begins with <A HREF=. The URL is entered following the = sign and is enclosed within double quotes. A closing > ends the opening HREF anchor tag. After opening HREF tag, you enter the text that is displayed on your Web page to reference this URL. The closing </A> anchor tag ends the text. When the Web page is displayed on a Browser, you will see this text set to a special color to indicate that it references a URL. You can also include an image reference, in which case the user can click on the image to reference the URL. Its syntax is as follows:

```
<A HREF="URL">text</A>
```

In the following example, the HREF anchor tag will connect to a Web page on the www.caldera.com system. The text "Caldera's documentation on the Internet" will be displayed in color, usually blue. When the user clicks on that text, the URL **www.caldera.com/doc** will be accessed. As the transfer protocol is http, this resource will be displayed as a Web page.

```
<A HREF="http://www.caldera.com/doc/"> Caldera's documentation on
the Internet</A>
```

If you include an image reference in the text portion, users can click on the image to reference the URL. Image references are discussed in the next section. In the next example, an image reference to the **books.gif** image file will display that image on the Web page. The user can then click on the books image to reference the URL. The image reference is **<IMG SRC="book2.gif">**.

```
<H3><A HREF="http://www.caldera.com/doc/gs/gs.html"><IMG
SRC="book2.gif">
Getting Started with the Network Desktop (Internet)</A></H3>
```

To access a Web page on your own system you do not need the transfer protocol or the hostname. You only have to specify the path name. The path name can be a relative path name from the directory in which the current Web page is located. In the next example, the Web page **desktop.html** is located in the subdirectory **lg** on your own system.

```
<H3><A HREF="lg/desktop.html">Desktop User's Guide</A></H3>
```

Instead of referencing a separate Web page, you can reference certain labeled text on the same page that you have identified by a specific name. This is referred to as a hypertext target or named element. An HREF anchor can then access this target, jumping to that text. To reference such a target in an HREF anchor, you precede its name with a # sign. In the following HREF anchor, the text "The newest engine" will be displayed on the Web page. When the user clicks on this text, the target on the Web page labeled with the name engine1 will be displayed. The target can be a heading, a picture, or any text segment.

```
<A HREF="#engine1">The newest engine</A>
```

There are currently several ways you can create a hypertext target. You can simply use the NAME anchor tag with a target name followed by the text of the target. In the next example, the target name is engine1 and the target text is "This is the newest engine on the block". The name can be used in HREF anchors to identify the particular hypertext target.

```
<A NAME="engine1"> This is the newest engine on the block</A>
```

Given both the HREF anchor and the NAME anchor, you can use the HREF anchor to reference the text specified in the NAME anchor. When the user clicks on the text, "The newest engine", specified by the HREF anchor, he or she will be moved to the part of the Web page beginning with the text "This is the newest engine on the block", as specified by the NAME anchor. This technique is often used to move users to different headings, with each heading starting a different segment of the page's topic. To name a heading, you need to enclose the entire heading within NAME anchor tags.

```
<A NAME="Heading-name">
<Hn>Heading text<\Hn>
</A>
```

You can then jump to the text using the name you gave to the heading.

```
<A HREF="#Heading-name">some text</A>
```

In the next example, engine1 now references a heading, not just text.

```
<A NAME="engine1">
<H2>This is the newest engine on the block<\H2>
</A>
```

With the most recent version of HTML, called HTML 3, you can use the ID tag to create targets. You can make anything a target, including pictures.

```
<Hn ID="name"> Heading text<\Hn>
```

Images and Sounds

You can also use HTML commands to display pictures on your Web page. The picture is either a gif or jpeg file, usually in the same directory as the Web page. The <IMG SRC=*filename*> tag will display a specified picture. For example, to display a picture called **books.gif,** you place it within the IMG tag.

```
<IMG SRC="books.gif">
```

The IMG tag displays the picture as part of the Web page. You can, however, display an image externally using a separate image display program. To do so you reference the graphics file with an HREF tag. In effect you are linking to the picture file and the application that displays it.

```
<HREF="engine.gif">The greatest engine in the world<\A>
```

You use the same method to play sound and video files. These files rely on outside applications to run them. An HREF tag will link to the sound or video file and run its associated application.

```
<HREF="whistle.au">Steam melody<\A>
```

Web Page Example

The **cald1.html** file shown here is a shortened form of the **/usr/doc/HTML/calderadoc /caldera.html** file on your system. It illustrates many of the features discussed concerning Web page construction. The entire page is enclosed in <HTML> and </HTML> tags. The title of the page is defined within the <TITLE> tags, which are placed within the <HEAD> tags. The <BODY> tags mark the text that will be displayed on the Web page. The <H1> tag prints a heading in very large text. <P> tags format the following text into paragraphs. <H2> and <H3> tags display progressively smaller headings. The <HR> tag draws a line across the page. Anchor tags with URL references, <A HREF>, are embedded within both paragraphs and headings. The anchor tags within headings include images that can be used to reference the URL. Many of the URLs reference local files and others reference Web pages on remote sites. For example, <A HREF="crisp/crisp.html"> references a local Web page called **crisp.html** in the subdirectory **crisp**. <A HREF="http://home.netscape.com/eng /mozilla/2.0/handbook/"> references the **handbook** directory on the home.netscape.com Web site. Figure 11-8 shows how the **cald1.html** will be displayed.

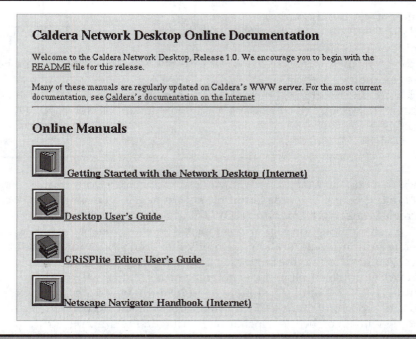

Figure 11-8. *The **cald1.html** Web page for Online Documentation*

cald1.html

```
<HTML>
<HEAD>
<TITLE>Caldera Network Desktop Online Documentation</TITLE>
</HEAD>
<BODY>
<H1>Caldera Network Desktop Online Documentation</H1>
<P>
Welcome to the Caldera Network Desktop, Release 1.0. We encourage you to
begin with the <A HREF="file:/etc/README">README</A> file for this
release.
<P>
Many of these manuals are regularly updated on Caldera's WWW server.
For the most current documentation, see <A HREF="http://www.caldera
.com/doc/"> Caldera's documentation on the Internet</A>
<HR>
<H2>Online Manuals</H2>
<H3><A HREF="http://www.caldera.com/doc/gs/gs.html">
<IMG SRC="book2.gif"> Getting Started with the Network Desktop
(Internet)</A></H3>
<H3><A HREF="lg/desktop.html"><IMG SRC="books.gif">Desktop User's
Guide</A></H3>
<H3><A HREF="crisp/crisp.html"><IMG SRC="books.gif">CRiSPlite Editor
User's Guide </A></H3>
<H3><A HREF="http://home.netscape.com/eng/mozilla/2.0/handbook/">
<IMG SRC="book2.gif">Netscape Navigator Handbook (Internet)</A></H3>
</BODY>
</HTML>
```

Taking what you have learned so far, you can easily create your own Web page. All
you need is a text editor. The **index.html** file shown next is an example of a Web page
you can create yourself. The **/usr/doc/HOWTO/ldp** directory holds numerous Web
pages that are documentation for various topics. There are Web pages for the PPP
protocols and printing configuration. Currently there is no index for these different
Web pages. You have to find the beginning page for each group. For example, the file
Sound-HOWTO.html is itself an index referencing a set of HTML files beginning
with **Sound-HOWTO-1.html**. The following **index.html** file creates an index that
you can use to access any of these HTML files directly. Each HOWTO Web page
has a heading with an embedded anchor referencing it. For example, <H2><A
HREF="PPP-HOWTO.html">PPP HOWTO </A></H2> references the file

PPP-HOWTO.html. The text PPP HOWTO is displayed on the Web page. When you click on this text, the PPP-HOWTO Web page will be displayed.

/usr/doc/HOWTO/ldp/index.html

```
<HTML>
<HEAD>
<TITLE>Index of HOWTO Documents</TITLE>
</HEAD>
<BODY>
<H1>List of HOWTO Documents</H1>
<H2>by Dylan Petersen</H2>
<P>
v.1.0, 5 April 1996
<P>
<H2><A HREF="Printing-Usage-HOWTO.html">Printing
HOWTO</A></H2>
<H2><A HREF="Sound-HOWTO.html">Sound HOWTO</A></H2>
<H2><A HREF="NET-2-HOWTO.html">Network HOWTO</A></H2>
<H2><A HREF="PPP-HOWTO.html">PPP HOWTO</A></H2>
<H2><A HREF="News-HOWTO.html">News HOWTO</A></H2>
<H2><A HREF="Mail-HOWTO.html">Mail HOWTO</A></H2>
<H2><A HREF="UUCP-HOWTO.html">UUCP HOWTO</A></H2>
<H2><A HREF="Hardware-HOWTO.html">Hardware HOWTO </A></H2>
<H2><A HREF="Ethernet-HOWTO.html">Ethernet HOWTO</A></H2>
</BODY>
</HTML>
```

Once you have created this Web page you can display it using your Web Browser. First make sure you have placed the **index.html** file in the **/usr/doc/HTML/ldp** directory. Then enter the URL, **file:/usr/doc/HTML/ldp/index.html**, in your Web Browser. You will see your Web page displayed. Click on a HOWTO heading to bring up its Web page. Figure 11-9 shows you what the **index.html** page looks like.

There is currently no way to return to the index page once you have accessed a HOWTO page. You could, of course, just click on the Back button on your Web Browser until you come to it. However, you can place an HREF anchor within a Web HOWTO page that will return you to the index page. A possible anchor is shown here:

```
<A HREF="index.html">Return to Main Index</A>
```

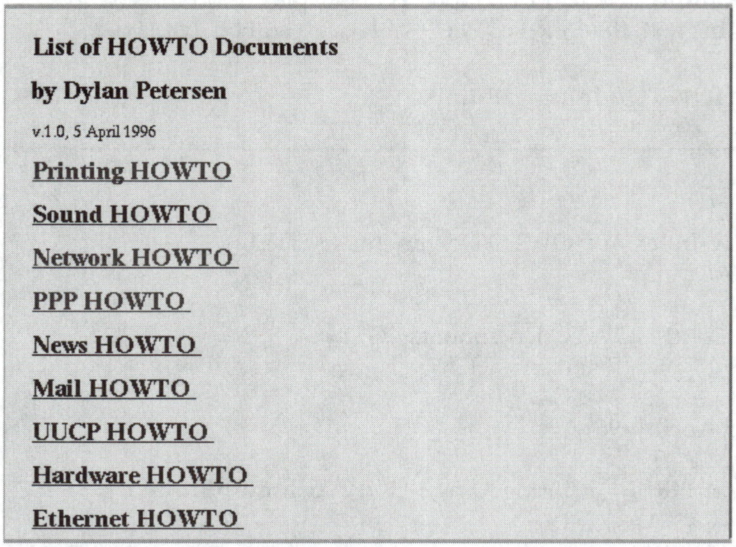

List of HOWTO Documents

by Dylan Petersen

v.1.0, 5 April 1996

<u>**Printing HOWTO**</u>

<u>**Sound HOWTO**</u>

<u>**Network HOWTO**</u>

<u>**PPP HOWTO**</u>

<u>**News HOWTO**</u>

<u>**Mail HOWTO**</u>

<u>**UUCP HOWTO**</u>

<u>**Hardware HOWTO**</u>

<u>**Ethernet HOWTO**</u>

Figure 11-9. *The index.html Web page for HOWTO pages*

Common Gateway Interfaces

A Common Gateway Interface (CGI) is a program that a Web server at a Web site can use to interact with Web Browsers. When using a Browser to display a Web page at a particular Web site, the Web page may call up CGI programs to provide you with certain real-time information or to receive information from you. For example, a Web page may execute the server's **date** command to display the current date whenever the Web page is accessed.

A CGI script can be a Linux shell script or a program. For the shell script you can use the BASH or TCSH shell commands described in Chapters 15 and 16. Programs can be developed using a programming language such as C. There are also two special HTML operations that are considered CGI scripts: query text and forms. Both receive and process interactive responses from particular users.

You have seen how a user can use a Browser to display Web pages at a given Web site. In effect the user is receiving information in the form of Web pages from the Web site. A user can also, to a limited extent, send information back to the Web site. This is usually information specifically prompted for in a Web page displayed by your Browser. The Web server then receives and processes that information using the CGI programs.

On a Web page you can use a single field to prompt for a one-line response from the user, or use a form that has a collection of fields. The <ISINDEX> tag displays a single edit box in which a user can type text. This is usually used to obtain keywords for a search and is referred to as a document-based query.

A form is a Web page that holds several input fields of various types. These can be input boxes for entering text or check boxes and radio boxes that users simply click on. The text boxes can be structured, allowing a certain number of characters to be entered, as in a phone number. It can also be unstructured, allowing users to type in sentences as they would for a comment. Forms are referred to as form-based queries.

After entering information into a form, the user sends it back to the server by clicking on a Submit button. The server receives the form and, along with it, instructions to run a specific CGI program to process the form.

Summary: WWW

The World Wide Web (WWW) links different types of information distributed worldwide across the Internet, and presents that information in an easy-to-use format known as Web pages. These are documents written in the HyperText Markup Language (HTML). A single Web page can link to another Web page, that in turn can link to yet another. These pages can be at the same site or at different sites. More importantly, each Web page can display a variety of information that you can access such as text, pictures, video, and sound. Information resources on the Internet are identified by Universal Resource Locators (URL), which are made up of three components: the transfer protocol, the Web site hostname, and the file name of the resource. The transfer protocol determines how a resource is accessed: http accesses a Web page, whereas ftp initiates a file transfer. URLs can be used to access Web pages or resources at other sites.

You use Web Browsers to display Web pages at Web sites throughout the Internet. Web Browsers will keep track of the different Web pages that you access in a session, allowing you to move back and forth among these pages. You can also keep a hotlist of Web pages you like and use the Browser to directly access them. Many Web Browsers also have the capability to operate as newsreaders and mailers. There are several popular Web Browsers available for Linux such as the Netscape Navigator and Mosaic.

Your Linux system can also operate as a Web server, and the details of configuring a Web server are discussed in Chapter 12 (the Caldera Network Desktop already has a Web server installed and configured). Using Web server software, you can set up your own Web site. Once you have your Web server software, you then need to create the Web pages for your site. Since a Web page is a text file that contains HTML tags that are used to format the page, composing a Web page is a matter of entering text with the appropriate HTML tags. HREF anchor tags are used to reference Internet resources with URLs. You can have several Web pages distributed in different subdirectories, each having links to Web pages on your system or at other Web sites. Within directories, a Web page (usually named **index.html**) operates as a table of contents with links to other pages in the directory.

Protocol	Description
`http`	Hypertext Transfer Protocol for Web site access
`gopher`	Access Gopher site
`ftp`	File Transfer Protocol for anonymous ftp connections
`telnet`	Makes a telnet connection
`wais`	Access WAIS site
`news`	Reading Usenet news; uses Net News Transfer Protocol (NNTP)

Table 11-2. *Web Transfer Protocols*

File Type	Description
.html	Web page document formatted using HTML, the HyperText Markup Language
Graphics Files	
.gif	Graphics, using gif compression
.jpeg	Graphics, using jpeg compression
Sound Files	
.au	Sun (Unix) sound file
.wav	Microsoft Windows sound file
.aiff	Macintosh sound file
Video Files	
.QT	Quicktime video file, multiplatform
.mpeg	Video file
.avi	Microsoft Windows video file

Table 11-3. *Web Resource File Types*

Web Browsers	Location
Netscape Navigator	ftp3.netscape.com/pub/navigator/*n.n*/unix ftp3.netscape.com through ftp8.netscape.com are available as well as many mirror sites
NCSA Mosaic	ftp.ncsa.uiuc.edu/Web/Mosaic/unix/
Arena	http://www.w3.org/hypertext/WWW/Arena/Status.html ftp.w3.org/pub/arena
Lynx	ftp://ftp2.cc.ukans.edu/pub/lynx (included with most distributions)
HTML Editors	
Phoenix	http://www.bsd/uchicago.edu/ftp/pub/phoenix
tkWWW	http://www.w3.org/hypertext/WWW/tkWWW ftp.aud.alcatel.com/pub/tcl/extensions
Web Servers	
Apache	http://www.apache.org
CERN httpd	ftp://info.cern.ch/pub/www.bin
NCSA httpd	ftp.ncsa.uiuc.edu http://boohoo.ncsa.uiuc.edu
Plexus	http://www.bsdi.com/2.2.1/dist/Plexus.html
Netscape Server	ftp3.netscape.com/pub/server/*n.n*/unix
Web Utilities	
Java	ftp.blackdown.org/pub/Java/linux
WebCrawler	http://www.biotech.washington.edu/WebCrawler/WebCrawler.html
World Wide Web Worm	http://www.cs.colorado.edu/home/mcbryan/WWWW.html http://info.cern.ch/WWW/Tools

Table 11-4. *Tools for Using the Web*

Basic Tags	Description
<HTML>_Web page_**</HTML>**	Place <HTML> as the first entry in your Web page and </HTML> as the last
<HEAD> _Head of Web page_ **</HEAD>**	The head segment of a Web page; includes any configuration entries and the title entry
<TITLE>_title text_**</TITLE>**	The title of the Web page; this will be used in hotlists to identify the page easily
<BODY> _Text of Web page_ **</BODY>**	The body of the Web page; this is the material that is displayed as the Web page
<ADDRESS> _Address of creator_ **<\ADDRESS>**	Internet address of Web page creator
<BASE=Href" _Web page path name_**">**	Path name of Web page that serves as base path name for any relative path names on that page

Format

<H_n_**>**_Heading title_**<\H**_n_**>**	Headers; _n_ is sequential subhead level, as in <H1> for top level, <H2> for subheads, etc.
<P>_paragraph text_**</P>**	Paragraphs
<CENTER>	Center text
<BLINK>	
** **	Line break
<PRE> _Preformatted text_ **</PRE>**	Displays the following text as it appears with no formatting
<HR>_Horizontal rule_**</HR>**	Displays a line across the page
<CLEAR>	Forces break in text

Images

<IMAGE SRC="_file.gif_"	Image to be displayed in Web page

Table 11-5.   _HTML Codes for Web Pages_

Images	Description
ALIGN="*position*"	Positions images or text on the Web page; *position* can be **Bottom**, **Top**, **Left**, or **Right**
WIDTH=	Sets width for display of image
HEIGHT=	Sets height

Anchors

<A*Anchor tag* **/A>**	Anchor tag, such as URL reference
HREF="*URL address*"> *reference text*	URL reference; ties the specified text to the URL address
<A NAME="*text*">*Anchor text*< **/A>**	Creates an anchor reference for text in the Web page
<A NAME="*Heading text*"> **<H***n*>*Heading text*<**\H***n*> **</A>**	Makes a heading an anchor reference in the Web page
ID="*Anchor text*"	Uses ID instead of NAME to create anchor text in the Web page
<H*n* **ID=**"*Anchor text*" >*Heading text*<**\H***n*>	Uses ID to make a heading an anchor text
<A HREF="**#***Anchor text*" >*Text displayed in page*</**A**>	A reference to anchor text in the Web page
<LINK REL=*Relationship* **HREF=**"*URL reference*">	Creates a link to other Web pages making up the Web site; displays buttons at top and bottom of Web page with relationship described by **REL** **REL=**Relationship Relationship of current Web page to others: **Previous** HRL for previous Web page **Next** HRL for next Web Page **Home** HRL for home Page **Banner** HRL for banner displayed for all Web pages

Table 11-4. *HTML Codes for Web Pages* (continued)

Lists	**Description**
`<LH>`*List header*`</LH>`	Name for the list
`<LI>`*List item text*`</LI>`	List item
`<UL>`*List item entries*`</UL>`	Unordered list
`<OL>`*Ordered list entries*`</OL>`	Ordered list, usually numbered
`<DL>`*List entries*`</DL>`	Definition list; a list of terms and an explanation of each called a definition; a *term* is a word that you specify
`<DT>`*Definition term*`</DT>`	Term for a definition list entry
`<DD>`*Definition*`</DD>`	Text associated with a definition term

Tables

`<TABLE>`*Table entries*`</TABLE>`	Displays a table
`<TC>`*Table caption*`</TC>`	
`<TR>`*Table row*`</TR>`	
`<TH>`*Table head*`</TH>`	
`<TD>`*Table cell*`</TD>`	

Configuration

BGCOLOR=rrggbb	Background color; hexadecimal number representing color; rr = red, gg = green, bb = blue; all 0s = no color (black); all 1s = white, FFFFFF; it is set in the **BODY** tag `<BODY BGCOLOR=`*137HF2*`>`
TEXT=rrggbb	Color of text; it is set in the **BODY** tag
BACKGOUND=*file.gif*	Picture to use as background for Web page; it is set in the **BODY** tag

Table 11-4. *HTML Codes for Web Pages* (continued)

Entities	Description
&lt	<
&gt	>
&amp	&
&quot	"

Table 11-4.   *HTML Codes for Web Pages* (continued)

Chapter Twelve

Internet Servers

Reflecting the close relationship between Unix and the development of the Internet, Linux is particularly good at providing Internet services such as Web, WAIS, ftp, and Gopher. But instead of just accessing other sites, you can set up your own Linux system to be a Web site or an ftp site. Other people can then access your system using Web pages you created or download files you provide for them. A system that operates this way is called a server and is known by the service it provides. You can set up your system to be a Web server or an ftp server, connecting it to the Internet and turning it into a site that others can access. A single Linux system can provide several different services. Your Linux system can be a Web server and an ftp server as well as a Gopher and WAIS server, all at the same time. One user could download files using your ftp services while another reads your Web pages. All you have to do is install and run the appropriate server software for each service. Each one operates as a continually running daemon looking for requests for its particular services from remote users.

The OpenLinux system is already a Web, ftp, and Gopher server. It was designed with Internet servers in mind. Normally you would have to obtain and install server software yourself, but when you install OpenLinux, the server software for these services is automatically installed and configured for you. Every time you start the Caldera Network Desktop you also start the Web and ftp server daemons. To turn your Linux system into a Web server, all you have to do is create Web pages. For an ftp server, you only have to place the files you want to make available in the ftp directories. A Gopher server is also automatically installed.

To operate your Linux system as an Internet server, you must obtain a connection to the Internet and provide access to your system for remote users. Access is usually a matter of allowing anonymous logins to directories reserved for server resources. Your OpenLinux system is already configured to allow such access for Web and ftp users. Connections to the Internet that can accommodate server activity can be difficult to come by. You may need a dedicated connection, or you may need to use a connection set up by an Internet Service Provider. You are no longer connecting only yourself to the Internet, but you are allowing many other users to make what could be a great many connections to you through the Internet.

If you only want to provide the services to a local area network, you will not need a special connection. Also, you can provide these services to users by allowing them to connect over a modem and log in directly. Users could dial into your system and use your Web pages or use ftp to download files. In whatever situation you want to use these services, you will need the appropriate server software installed and running.

This chapter examines Internet servers for the four different services: Web, ftp, WAIS, and Gopher. As the Web, ftp, and GN Gopher servers are already installed, you will not have to perform the installation procedures described. However, these sections will tell you in what directories the services are set up and how to place files such as Web pages in them. WAIS is not set up on your Caldera Network Desktop, so you will have to obtain the server software and install it as described in this chapter.

Starting Servers

A server is a daemon that runs concurrently with your other programs, continuously looking for a request for its services either from other users on your system or from remote users connecting to your system through a network. When it receives a request from a user, it starts up a session to provide its services. For example, if users want to download a file from your system, they can use their own ftp client to request that your ftp server start a session for them. In the session, they can access and download files from your system.

Your server needs to be running for a user to access its services. If you set up a Web site on your system with HTML files, you must have the httpd Web server program running before users can access your Web site and display those files.

There are several ways to start a server. One way is to do it manually from the command line by entering the name of the server program and its arguments. Upon pressing enter, the server will start although your command line prompt will reappear. The server will run concurrently as you go complete other tasks. To see if your server is running, you can enter the following command to list all currently running processes. You should see a process for the server program you started up.

```
# ps -ax
```

Instead of manually executing all the server programs each time you boot your system, your system can automatically start the servers. There are two ways to do this, depending on how you want to use a server. You can have a server running continuously from the time you start your system until you shut it down, or you can have the server start only when it receives a request from a user for its services. If a server is being used frequently, you may want to have it running all the time. If it is used rarely, you may just want it to start when a request comes in. For example, if you are running a Web site, your Web server will be receiving requests all the time from remote hosts on the Internet. However, for an ftp site, you may receive requests infrequently, in which case you may want to have the ftp server start only when it receives a request. Of course certain ftp sites receive frequent requests, which would warrant a continually running ftp server.

To automatically start a server with the system, use a startup script in the **/etc/rc.d/init.d** directory. To start the server only when a request for its services is received, you configure it by the **inetd** daemon. **inetd** looks for server requests and then starts up the server when a request comes through. Your OpenLinux system has already configured the Web server to start automatically and run continuously. There is a script for it in the **/etc/rc.d/init.d** directory called **httpd.init**. The ftp server is configured to run under **inetd**. It will start only when someone initiates an ftp session with your system. You will find an entry for the ftp server in the **inetd.conf** configuration file, but there is no script for it in **/etc/rc.d/init.d** as there is for the Web server.

Server init Scripts

OpenLinux uses a method of implementing startup files that may not be found on other distributions. For other distributions you may have to place the server command in a system initialization file such as **rc.local**. For your OpenLinux, you can use special startup scripts in the **/etc/rc.d/init.d** directory.

The **/etc/rc.d/init.d** directory holds shell scripts that are executed automatically whenever you boot your system. These shell scripts have commands to execute particular programs such as servers. You will find one there for the Web server called **httpd**. Be careful never to touch or modify any of the other scripts. These start essential programs such as your network interface and your printer daemon. A sample startup script, called the **skeleton** script, is provided in this directory. To create a new startup script for a server, you can begin by copying the **skeleton** script. Then edit this new script and place the server path name and the server command in the appropriate places. As an example, the **httpd** script is shown here. The name of the Web server program is **httpd**, **$NAME=httpd**. Notice the line for checking the existence of this program, [**-f $DAEMON**], where **$DAEMON** is set to the **/usr/sbin/httpd** program.

/etc/rc.d/init.d/httpd

```
#!/bin/sh
# httpd        This shell script takes care of starting and stopping httpd.
PATH=/bin:/usr/bin:/sbin:/usr/sbin
NAME=httpd
DAEMON=/usr/sbin/$NAME

# Source function library.
. /etc/rc.d/init.d/functions
# Source networking configuration.
. /etc/sysconfig/network
# Check that networking is up.
[ ${NETWORKING} = "no" ] && exit 0
[ ! -r /etc/sysconfig/daemons/$NAME ] && exit 0
. /etc/sysconfig/daemons/$NAME
[ "$ONBOOT" = "no" -a "$PROBABLY" = "booting" ] && exit 0
DAEMON=$DAEMON.$VARIANT
[ -f $DAEMON ] || exit 0
# See how we were called.
```

```
case "$1" in
 start)
  # Start daemons.
  if [ -f /etc/httpd/$VARIANT/conf/httpd.conf ]; then
    echo -n "Starting $IDENT services ($VARIANT): "
    start-stop-daemon -S -n $NAME -x $DAEMON — -f
/etc/httpd/$VARIANT/conf/httpd.conf
    touch /var/lock/subsys/httpd
    echo "."
  elif [ "$PROBABLY" = "goofing" ]; then
    echo "$VARIANT httpd not configured: Skipped!"
  fi
  ;;
 stop)
  # Stop daemons.
  [ -f /var/lock/subsys/httpd ] || exit 0
  if [ -f /var/run/$NAME.pid ]; then
    echo -n "Shutting down $VARIANT httpd: "
    start-stop-daemon -K -p /var/run/$NAME.pid -n $NAME
    echo "."
  fi
  rm -f /var/lock/subsys/httpd
  ;;
 *)
  echo "Usage: httpd {start | stop}"
  exit 1
esac

exit 0
```

The **httpd** script first executes the a script to define functions used in these startup scripts and then executes a networks script to determine the network configuration. It then checks for the existence of a configuration file for this daemon, and if it exists, it executes the file. For the httpd daemon, the configuration file is called **/set/ssyconfig.daemons/httpd**. This file sets the value of the **$VARIANT** variable used in later commands, in this case, Apache.

```
. /etc/rc.d/init.d/functions
. /etc/sysconfig/network
[ ! -r /etc/sysconfig/daemons/$NAME ] && exit 0
        . /etc/sysconfig/daemons/$NAME
```

The Web server is executed with the following line found in this script. The **$NAME** variable has been set to httpd and the **$DAEMON** to the Web server program, **/usr/sbin/httpd**. The **-f** option specifies this Web server's configuration file, where **$VARIANT** is the particular Web server used, in this case, Apache. The **start-stop-daemon** function with the **-S** option will start up the daemon.

```
start-stop-daemon -S -n $NAME -x $DAEMON -- -f
/etc/httpd/$VARIANT/conf/httpd.conf
```

The **start-stop-daemon** function with the **-K** option will shut down the daemon, using the **-p** option to specify the process id and the **-n** option for the name.

```
start-stop-daemon -K -p /var/run/$NAME.pid -n $NAME
```

These init scripts are accessed from links in subdirectories setup for each possible run-level. In the **/etc/rc.d** directory, there is a set of subdirectories whose names have the format **rc***N***.d**, where *N* is a number referring to a runlevel. The **rc** script will detect the runlevel that the system was started in and then execute only the startup scripts specified in the subdirectory for that runlevel. The default runlevel is 3, the multiuser level. When you start your system, the **rc** script will execute the startup scripts specified in the **rc3.d** directory. The **rc3.d** directory holds symbolic links to certain startup scripts in the **/etc/rc.d/init.d** directory (see Chapter 6 for a discussion on symbolic links). So the **httpd** script in the **/etc/rc.d/init.d** directory is actually called through a symbolic link in the **rc3.d** directory. The symbolic link for the **/etc/rc.d/httpd** script in the **rc3.d** directory is **S85httpd**. To have a server automatically start, you would first create a startup script for it in the **/etc/rc.d/init.d** directory and then create a symbolic link to that script in the **/etc/rc.d/rc3.d** directory.

Suppose you have installed the Gopher server on your system and now want to have it start automatically. The easiest way to create a startup script for the **gopherd**, the University of Minnesota's Gopher server program, is to first make a copy of the **httpd** script, naming the copy **gopherd**. Both **httpd** and **gopherd** are network servers and use much of the same script.

```
# cp httpd gopherd
```

You then edit the **gopherd** script and replace all references to **httpd** with **gopherd**. For the **$DAEMON** variable you should assign the path name for the **gopherd** server program, probably **/usr/sbin/gopherd**.

```
$NAME=gopherd

$DAEMON=/usr/sbin/gopherd
```

The following line executes the **gopherd** server. Notice that the command includes arguments such as the directory for Gopher files. Argument requirements vary from server to server. The **httpd** Web server program has no arguments. You can remove references to the $**VARIANT** variable.

```
start-stop-daemon -S -n $NAME -x $DAEMON /usr/lib/gopher-data
```

Now you change to the **/etc/rc.d/rc3.d** directory and make a symbolic link to that **/etc/rc.d/init.d/gopherd** script. The **ln** command with the **-s** option creates a symbolic link.

```
# ln -s /etc/rc.d/init.d/gopherd S94gopherd
```

Now when you start your system, the **gopherd** server is automatically started up, running concurrently and waiting for requests.

Instead of copying the **httpd** script, you could also have copied the **skeleton** script. This would require you to replace lines referencing **skeleton** with the lines to check, start, and shut down the **gopherd** server. You would also have to add lines to execute the **/etc/sysconfig/network** script and to check that networking is operating.

You will notice that there is no script for the ftp server. As implemented by OpenLinux, the ftp server is managed by the **inetd** program, described in the next section. If you should want to have the ftp server running all the time, you could make an **init** script for it and a symbolic link, just as described for the **gopherd** server. The name of the ftp server program is **in.ftpd**. You would also have to disable **inetd** management of the ftp server by commenting out its entry in the **inetd.conf** file.

netd Server Management

If your system averages only a few requests for a specific service, you do not need the server for that service running all the time. You only need it when a remote user is accessing its service. The **inetd** daemon manages Internet servers, invoking them only when your system receives a request for their services. **inetd** checks continuously for any requests by remote users for a particular Internet service, and when it receives a request it then starts the appropriate server daemon. For example, when **inetd** receives a request from a user to access ftp, it starts **ftpd**, the ftp daemon. **ftpd** then handles the request, allowing the remote user to download files.

For **inetd** to call the appropriate server daemon, it must be configured for that service. You place entries for that server in the **/etc/services** and the **/etc/inetd.conf** files. The **/etc/services** file lists services available on your system. An entry in

/etc/services consists of the name of the service followed by its port and protocol separated by a slash. Entries for ftp as they appear in your Redhat **/etc/service** file are shown here. Other distributions may require only one entry for ftp.

```
ftp-data        20/tcp
ftp             21/tcp
```

The **/etc/inetd.conf** file is the **inetd** configuration file. For this entry you specify the service, its protocol, and the server program to invoke. An entry for ftp is shown here. Server paths and arguments may vary according to different Linux distributions.

```
# <service> <sock_type> <proto> <flags> <user>  <server_path>    <args>
ftp          stream      tcp     nowait  root    /usr/sbin/ftpd   ftpd
```

On other Linux distributions, the configuration lines may be there, but they may be commented out with a preceding **#** symbol. Just remove the **#**. If there are no configuration entries, you will have to add them.

tcpd

You can use the **tcpd** daemon to add another level of security to **inetd** managed servers. You can set up **tcpd** to monitor a server connection made through **inetd**. **tcpd** will verify remote user identities and check to make sure they are making valid requests. With **tcpd** you can also restrict access to your system by remote hosts. Lists of hosts are kept in the **hosts.allow** and **hosts.deny** files. Entries in these files have the format **service:hostname:domain**. The domain is optional. For the service you can specify a particular service such as ftp or you can enter **ALL** for all services. For the hostname you can specify a particular host, or **ALL** for all hosts. In the following example, the first entry allows access by all hosts to the Web service, **http**. The second entry allows access to all services by the **pango1.train.com** host. The third and fourth entries allow **rose.berkeley.edu** and **caldera.com** ftp access.

```
http:ALL
ALL:pango1.train.com
ftp:rose.berkeley.edu
ftp:caldera.com
```

The **hosts.allow** file holds hosts that you allow access to. If you want to allow access to all but just a few specific hosts, you can specify **ALL** for a service in the **hosts.allow** file, but list the one you are denying access in the **hosts.deny** file. The **tcpd** man pages (**man tcpd**) provide more detailed information about **tcpd**.

To have **tcpd** monitor a server, you have to place the path name for **tcpd** in the path name field of a server's entry for the **inetd.conf** file. This is what your Caldera Network Desktop has already done for the **ftpd** server entry. Instead of the path name for the **ftpd** program, **/usr/sbin/in.ftpd**, there is the path name for the **tcpd** daemon, **/usr/sbin/tcpd**. The argument field that follows then lists the **in.ftpd** server program.

```
# <service>  <sock_type>  <proto>  <flags>  <user>  <server_path>   <args>
ftp          stream       tcp      nowait   root    /usr/sbin/tcpd  in.ftpd
```

When **inetd** receives a request for an ftp service, it calls the **tcpd** daemon which then takes over and monitors the connection. Then it starts up the **in.ftpd** server program. By default, **tcpd** will allow all requests. To allow all requests specifically for the ftp service you would enter in the following in your **/etc/hosts.allow** file. The entry **ALL:ALL** opens up your system to all hosts for all services.

```
ftp:ALL
```

ftp Server

OpenLinux has already installed an ftp server and has created the directories where you can place files for ftp access. The directories have already been configured to control access by remote users, restricting use to just the ftp directories and any subdirectories. The directory reserved for your ftp files is **/home/ftp**. You just have to place the files you want to allow access to in the **/home/ftp/pub** directory. You can also create subdirectories and place files there. Once connected to a network, a remote user can ftp to your system and download files you have placed in **/home/ftp/pub** or any of its subdirectories.

Although OpenLinux has already been configured as an ftp site, it may be helpful to understand how it is set up. Also, if you are using another system, you will need to know the following procedures to install an ftp server and create its data directories. However, for OpenLinux, it has all been done for you already. You do not need to do any of this.

Ftp server software is available at different Linux ftp sites. At **sunsite.unc.edu** and its mirror site, ftp server software is located in the **/pub/Linux/systems/Network/file-transfer** directory. The Washington University ftp server is a file called **wu-ftpd-2.4-fixed.tar.gz**. In the future you may want to download a new version of your ftp server software from such a site and use it to upgrade your server. If you download an ftp server from an ftp site, you will have to decompress the file and extract the archive. Several directories will be created for documentation and source code. The server package will include installation instructions for creating your server directories and compiling your software.

The ftp server, **ftpd**, must be running to allow ftp access by remote users. (**ftpd** options are shown in Table 12-1.) As with other servers, you can start the ftp server at boot time, through **inetd** when a request is received, or directly from the command line. The use of **inetd** for the ftp server is described in detail in the previous section, "Starting Servers." To start the ftp server when you boot your system, you have to set up an **init** script for it in the **/etc/rc.d/init.d** directory, as was described for the Web server. To start the ftp server from the command line, you enter the **ftpd** command with any options or arguments. The **ftpd** server can be called with several options. Usually it is called with the **-1** option that allows logins. The **-t** and **-T** options set timeouts for users, cutting off those that have no activity after a certain period of time. The **-d** option displays debugging information, and **-u** sets the umask value for uploaded files. The command name for the ftp server installed on your Caldera Desktop is **in.ftpd**—use it to invoke the ftp server directly.

The Ftp Server Configuration Files

There are a set of configuration files that you can use to manage your ftp site. On your OpenLinux system, these files are located in the **/etc** directory and begin with the characters "ftp." The **ftpaccess** file determines capabilities that users will have when they gain access to your ftp site. Access, information, permissions, logging, and several miscellaneous capabilities can be designated. For example, you can create aliases for

Option	Effect
-d	Writes debugging information to the syslog
-1	Logs each ftp session in the syslog
-t_seconds_	Sets the inactivity timeout period to specified seconds (default is 15 minutes)
-T_seconds_	The maximum timeout period allowed when timeout is set by user (default is two hours)
-a	Enables use of the ftpaccess(5) configuration file
-A	Disables use of the ftpaccess(5) configuration file
-L	Logs commands sent to the **ftpd** server to the syslog
-i	Logs files received by **ftpd** to xferlog
-o	Logs files transmitted by **ftpd** to the syslog

Table 12-1. *Web server Directories and http Options*

certain directories, display a message when ftp users login, or prevent anonymous users from deleting files. A **loginfails** entry determines the number of login tries a user can make before being cut off, and the **email** entry specifies the email address of the ftp administrator. The man page for **ftpaccess** lists the possible entries. When you installed your OpenLinux system, the ftp server was automatically installed and configured. The **ftpaccess** file with its current configuration is shown in this section.

Capabilities are set for three different types of users, anonymous, guest, and real. Anonymous users are any users using the anonymous login name. Guest users can be those with special guest accounts or access. A real user is one who has an account on the system and is using an ftp connection to access it. You can define your own class using the class option. In the **ftpaccess** file shown here, a class called **all** is created that consists of all users of the anonymous, guest, and real types.

The message entry specifies a file with the message to be displayed and when that message is to appear. You can have one message appear when users login and other messages displayed when users enter certain directories. For example, the following entry will display the message in the **/welcome.msg** file when a user logs in.

```
message /welcome.msg        login
```

To set permissions you use the command followed by a yes or no and then a list of the user types or classes. In the **ftpaccess** file shown here, all users can perform tar and compress operations, but anonymous and guest users are prohibited from using chmod, delete, overwrite, and rename operations. They cannot erase files, modify them, or change their names or permissions.

/etc/ftpaccess

```
class  all  real,guest,anonymous  *
email root@localhost
loginfails 5
readme  README*   login
readme  README*   cwd=*
message /welcome.msg    login
message .message        cwd=*

compress  yes    all
tar       yes    all
chmod     no     guest,anonymous
delete    no     guest,anonymous
overwrite no     guest,anonymous
rename    no     guest,anonymous
```

```
log transfers anonymous,real inbound,outbound
shutdown /etc/shutmsg
passwd-check rfc822 warn
```

You use the **ftphosts** file to allow or deny access by other host computers to your ftp site. The **ftpusers** files lists users that cannot be accessed through ftp. For example, the root user should not be accessible through an ftp connection even if you knew the password. **ftpgroups** is a group access file that allows ftp users to become members of specified groups on your system. This file lists special group passwords. The private entry must be set to yes in the **ftpaccess** file. See Table 12-2 for a listing of possible **ftpconversions** such as compression and archive operations. For **ftpaccess** entries, see Table 12-3.

The ftp User Account

To allow anonymous ftp access by other users to your system you must create a user account named ftp. You can then place restrictions on the ftp account to keep any remote ftp users from accessing any other part of your system. You must also modify the entry for this account in your **/etc/passwd** file to prevent normal user access to it. The following is the entry that you will find in your **/etc/passwd** file on your Caldera Network Desktop that sets up an ftp login as an anonymous user.

ftpaccess	Access, information, permission, logging, and other capabilities for ftp users
ftpconversions	Ftp conversion table for compression and archive operations
ftpusers	List of users that cannot be accessed through ftp such as *root*
ftpgroups	Groups accessible to ftp users with specified password. The format is: *access-group:encrypted:real-group* *access-group* is an arbitrary string. *real-group* is the name of a valid group listed in /etc/group
ftphosts	Allow or deny access by different hosts to your Ftp site. **allow** *username addrglob* [*addrglob...*] Only allow host(s) matching *addrglob* to log in as *username*. **deny** *username addrglob* [*addrglob...*] Always deny host(s) matching *addrglob* to log in as *username*.

Table 12-2. *Ftp Configuration Files*

Access Capabilities	Description
autogroup *group classglob* [*classglob*...]	This allows access to a groups read only files and directories by particular classes of anonymous users. *group* is a valid group from **/etc/group**
class *class typelist addrglob* [*addrglob*...]	Define *class* of users, with source addresses of the form *addrglob*. *typelist* is comma-separated list of the user types; "anonymous," "guest," and "real"
deny *host-addrglob message_file*	Always deny access to host(s) matching host-addrglob. message_file is displayed
guestgroup *groupname* [*groupname*...]	Allow guest access by a real user, where the user is a member of the specified group. A password entry for the guest user will specify a home directory within the ftp site directories
limit *class n times message_file*	Limit class to n users at times *times*, displaying *message_file* if access is denied
noretrieve *file-list*	Deny retrieval of these
loginfails *number*	After *number* login failures, terminate the ftp connection. Default value is 5
private *yes* | *no*	The user becomes a member of the group specified in the group access file **ftpgroups**
Informational Capabilities	
banner *file*	The banner is displayed before login. File requires full path name
email *email-address*	Defines the email address of the ftp manager

Table 12-3. *Ftpaccess Entries (Terms Ending in "glob" Can Use Filename Matching Operators; *, ?, and [ ]); Typelist is a Comma-Separated List of Any of the Keywords "anonymous," "guest," and "real"*

message *file* { *when* { *class* ...}}	ftp displays the contents of the *file* at login time or upon changing directories. The when parameter may be "LOGIN" or "CWD=*dir*"; *dir* specifies the directory which will display the message when entered There can be "magic cookies" in the message file which cause the ftp server to replace the cookie with a specified text string such as the date or the user name
readme *file* { *when* { *class*}}	The user is notified at login time or upon using the change working directory command that *file* exists and was modified on such-and-such date.
Logging Capabilities	
log commands *typelist*	Enables logging of individual commands by users
log transfers *typelist directions*	Enables logging fo file transfers. directions is a comma-separated list of the terms "inbound" and "outbound," and will log transfers for files sent to the server and sent from the server
Miscellaneous Capabilities	
alias *string dir*	Defines an alias, string, for a directory
cdpath *dir*	Defines an entry in the cdpath. This defines a search path that is used when changing directories
compress yes | no *classglob* [*classglob* **tar** yes | no *classglob* [*classglob*...]...]	Enables compress or tar capabilities for any class matching of *classglob*. The actual conversions are defined in the external file **ftconversion**
shutdown *path*	If the file pointed to by *path* exists, the server will check the file regularly to see if the server is going to be shut down
virtual *address* root | banner | logfile *path*	Enables the virtual ftp server capabilities

Table 12-3. *Ftpaccess Entries (Terms Ending in "glob" Can Use Filename Matching Operators; *, ?, and [ ]); Typelist is a Comma-Separated List of Any of the Keywords "anonymous," "guest," and "real" (continued)*

Permission Capabilities	Allows or disallows the ability to perform the specified function. By default, all users are allowed
chmod yes|no *typelist*	Allow or disallow changing file permissions
delete yes|no *typelist*	Allow or disallow deleting files, rm
overwrite yes|no *typelist*	Allow or disallow modifying files
rename yes|no *typelist*	Allow or disallow re-naming files, mv
umask yes|no *typelist*	Allow or disallowfile creation permissions
passwd-check none|trivial|rfc822 (enforce|warn)	Define the level and enforement of password checking done by the server for anonymous ftp
path-filter *typelist mesg allowed_charset { disallowed regexp...}*	For users in *typelist*, path-filter defines regular expressions that control what a filename can or can not be. There may be multiple disallowed regexps
upload *root-dir dirglob* yes|no *owner group mode* ["dirs"|"nodirs"]	Define a directory with dirglob that permits or denies uploads

Table 12-3. *Ftpaccess Entries (Terms Ending in "glob" Can Use Filename Matching Operators; *, ?, and [ ]); Typelist is a Comma-Separated List of Any of the Keywords "anonymous," "guest," and "real" (continued)*

```
ftp:*:14:50:FTP User:/home/ftp:
```

The asterisk in the password field blocks the account, which prevents any other users from gaining access to it and thereby gaining control over its files or access to other parts of your system. The user ID, 14, is a unique ID. The comment field is "FTP User". The login directory is **/home/ftp**. When ftp users log into your system, this is the directory they will be placed in. If a home directory has not been set up, create one and then change its ownership to the ftp user with the **chown** command.

The group ID is the ID of the **ftp** group, which is set up just for anonymous ftp users. You can set up restrictions on the **ftp** group, thereby restricting any anonymous ftp users. Here is the entry for the **ftp** group that you will find in the **/etc/group** file. For other Linux distributions, if you do not have one, you should add it.

```
ftp::50:
```

The permissions for the **/home/ftp** directory should deny write access. You do not want ftp users creating and deleting directories. You use the **chmod** command with the permission 555 to turn off write access: **chmod 555 /home/ftp**.

The **/home/ftp** directory and its permission, password, and group entries have already been set up on your Caldera Network Desktop. If you are setting up an ftp server on another distribution, you will have to set up **/home/ftp** yourself.

ftp Server Directories

To protect your system from any unwanted access by ftp users, you should create a restricted set of directories attached to the ftp directory, in this case, **/home/ftp**. A list of directories is provided in Table 12-4. An important part of protecting your system is preventing remote users from using any commands or programs that are not in the restricted directories. For example, you would not let a user use your **ls** command to list file names since **ls** is located in your **/bin** directory. At the same time, you want to let the ftp user list file names using an **ls** command. To do this you make a new bin directory in the **/home/ftp** directory and then make a copy of the **ls** command and place it in **/home/ftp/bin**. This bin directory would be restricted to use by ftp users,

/home/ftp	ftp server directory; owned by root (on some distributions this may be **/usr/local/ftp**); all directories and subdirectories would have permissions of 555 or 755 to restrict other and group access to read and execute only
/home/ftp/bin	ftp bin directory to hold commands that ftp remote users can execute, such as **ls** and **cd**
/home/ftp/etc	ftp etc directory to hold configuration files such as its own **passwd** file
/home/ftp/pub	ftp directory where the files you are making available for downloading are placed; you can set up any subdirectories you wish
/home/ftp/lib	ftp lib directory used if the **ls** command needs the **ld.so.1** file

Table 12-4. *ftp Directories*

and whenever they use the **ls** command, they are using the one in **/home/ftp/bin**, not the one you use in **/bin**. Do this for any commands you want to make available to ftp users. Other commands you will need are **cd** to allow users to change directories and **more** to let them display text files. Your Caldera Network Desktop has already created the **/home/ftp/bin** directory and installed a basic set of commands in it. You can add others if you wish.

You will also need a **/home/ftp/etc** directory, which holds a copy of your **passwd** and **group** files. Again the idea is to prevent any access to the original files in the **/etc** directory by ftp users. The **/home/ftp/etc/passwd** file should be edited to remove any entries for regular users on your system. All other entries should have their passwords set to * to block access. For the **group** file remove all user groups and set all passwords to *.

```
# cat /home/ftp/etc/passwd
root:*:0:0:::
bin:*:1:1:::
operator:*:11:0:::
ftp:*:14:50:::
nobody:*:99:99:::

# cat /home/ftp/etc/group
root::0:
bin::1:
daemon::2:
sys::3:
adm::4:
ftp::50:
```

A directory called **/home/ftp/pub** holds the files you are making available for downloading by remote ftp users. When ftp users log in, they will be placed in the **/home/ftp** directory and can then change to the **/home/ftp/pub** directory to start accessing those files. Within **/home/ftp/pub** you can add as many files and directories as you wish. You can even designate some directories as upload directories, allowing ftp users to transfer files to your system.

Some Linux systems require that the **ls** command have access to the **libc.so.1** and **rld** files in order to work. These are usually located in your **/lib** directory. Since you do not want to provide even indirect access to your system by ftp users, you have to create a **/home/ftp/lib** directory and then make a copy of these files and place the copies in there. In addition, since **rld** uses the **/dev/zero** file, you also have to create a **/home/ftp/dev** directory and use **mknod** to make a copy of the **/dev/zero** device file and place it in this directory.

Permissions

To restrict ftp users to the **/home/ftp** directory and its subdirectories, you have to hide the rest of the file structure from it. In effect, you have to make the **/home/ftp** directory appear to be the root directory as far as ftp users are concerned. The real root directory, **/**, and the rest of the directory structure remain hidden. You use the `chroot` command to make the **/home/ftp** directory appear as a root directory, with the ftp user as the argument.

```
# chroot ftp
```

Now when ftp users issue a `cd /` command to change to the root, they will always change to the **/home/ftp** directory.

As a further restriction, all the directories that hold commands in **/home/ftp**, as well as the commands themselves, should be owned by the root, not by the ftp user. In other words, no ftp user should have any control over these directories. You change the ownership of a directory using the `chown` command. The following example changes the ownership of the **/home/ftp/bin** directory and the **/home/ftp/bin/ls** command to the root. The root has to own **/home/ftp/bin**, **/home/ftp/etc**, and all the files they contain. The Caldera Network Desktop has already done this for you. For other distributions you may have to set the ownership yourself.

```
# chown root  /home/ftp/bin
```

Permissions for the ftp directories should be set to allow access for ftp users. Recall that there are three sets of permissions—read, write, and execute for the owner, the group, and others. To allow access by ftp users, the group and other permissions for directories should be set to both read and execute. The execute permission allows ftp users to access that directory, and the read permission allows listing the contents of the directory. Directories should not allow write permission by ftp users. You don't want them to be able to delete your directories or make new ones. For example, the **/home/ftp/bin** directory needs both read and execute permissions since ftp users have to access and execute its commands. This is particularly true for directories such as **/home/ftp/pub**, which holds the files for downloading. It must have both read and execute permissions set.

You as the owner of the directories will need write permission to be able to add new files or subdirectories. Of course, you only need this when you are making changes. To add further security, you could set these directories at just read and execute even for the owner when you are not making changes. You can set all permissions to read and execute with the `chmod` command and the number 555 followed by the directory name. This sets the owner, group, and other permissions to read and execute. The permissions currently in place for the ftp directories on your

Caldera Network Desktop are designated by the number 755, giving the owner write permission.

```
# chmod 555 /home/ftp/bin
```

Permissions for files within the **/home/ftp/bin** and other special ftp directories can be more restrictive. Some files only need to be read, while others have to be executed. Files such as **ls** and **rld** in the **/home/ftp/bin** or **/home/ftp/lib** directories only have to be executed. These could have their permissions set to 555. Files in the **/home/ftp/etc** directory such as **passwd** and **group** could have their permissions set to 111. They only have to be read. You always use the **chmod** command to set permissions for files, as shown in the following example. These permissions are already set on your Caldera Network Desktop. For other distributions you may have to set them yourself.

```
# chmod 111 /home/ftp/etc/passwd
```

ftp Files

In each directory set up under **/home/ftp/pub** to hold ftp files, you should create a **readme** file and an **index** file as a courtesy to ftp users. The **readme** file contains a brief description of the kind of files held in this directory. The **index** file should contain a listing of the files and a description of what each one holds.

Web Server

OpenLinux automatically installs the Apache Web server on your system during installation, with all the necessary directories and configuration files. Your OpenLinux system is already a fully functional Web site. Every time you start your system, the Web server starts up also, running continuously. The directory reserved for your Web site data files is **/home/httpd/html**. Place your Web pages in this directory or in any subdirectories. Apache provides online support and tutorials for its Web server at **http://www.apache.org**. There is also online support available from Caldera at **http://www.caldera.com**. You can obtain more detailed information there on developing your Web site and any problems you may encounter.

There is nothing more you have to do. Once connected to a network, remote users will be able to access your Web site. It may be helpful to understand how a Web site is set up. Also, if you are using another system, you will need to know the following procedures to install a Web server and create its supporting directories.

The Web server installed on your OpenLinux sets up your Web site in the **/home/httpd** directory. It also sets up several directories for managing the site, as listed in Table 12-5. **cgi-bin** holds the gateway interfaces, and the **icons** file holds

Web Server Directories	Description
/home/httpd	Location of your Web server directories
/home/httpd/cgi-bin	Common gateway interfaces and scripts
/home/httpd/icons	Icons for home pages
/home/httpd/html	The Web pages for your Web site
/etc/httpd/variant/conf	Holds your Web server configuration files where *variant* is the particular Web server; for example, **/etc/httpd/apache/conf** for the Apache Web server installed on OpenLinux
httpd Option	
−d *directory*	Allows you to specify a directory for the httpd program if it is different from the default directory
−f *config-file*	Allows you to specify a configuration file different from **httpd.conf**
−v	Displays the version

Table 12-5. *Web Server Directories and httpd Options*

the icons used for your home page. Your Web pages are to be placed in the **/home/httpd/html** directory. Place the **index.html** file for your home page there. Your configuration files are located in a different directory, **/etc/httpd/conf**.

There are also other Web servers freely available that you could also use if you wish. The NCSA httpd Web server was one of the first servers developed. Apache is very similar and corrects some of the problems with the NCSA httpd server. You can download server software from most Linux ftp sites. At Linux ftp sites and mirror site, Web server software is located in the **/pub/Linux/systems/Network/info-systems /www/server** directory. You can use ftp or Netscape to access this directory. In the future you may want to download a new version of your Web server software from such a site and use it to upgrade your server.

If you download a Web server from an ftp site, you will have to decompress the file and extract the archive. Many of the same directories will be created, with added ones for documentation and source code. The server package will include installation instructions for creating your server directories and compiling your software.

Configuring Your Web Server

You configure your Web server software using several configuration files in the **/etc/httpd/conf** directory. Configuration varies depending on whether you want to run the Web server continuously as a daemon, or have it called when needed by **inetd**. If you are expecting a great deal of use, you should just run it directly as a daemon.

The **httpd.conf** file configures the Web server daemon. It lists a set of variables and their values. Each entry consists solely of a variable name followed by a value, separated by a space. These variables set different features of your Web server. Some require path names, whereas others just need to be turned on or off with the keywords **on** and **off**. These variables are already set for the Caldera Network Desktop. You can, however, add to the list or change the ones already there. Table 12-6 provides a complete listing of the different variables you can place in the **httpd.conf** file. Many of the entries are preceded by comments explaining their purpose. The following is an example of the ServerAdmin variable used to set the address where users can send mail for administrative issues. You replace the you@your.address entry with the address you want to use to receive system administration mail.

```
# ServerAdmin: Your address, where problems should be e-mailed.
ServerAdmin you@your.address
```

Only a few of the variables are set in this file. You do not need to set all of them. Some require specific information about your system. For example, ServerName specifies a separate hostname for your Web server. It must be a valid hostname in its own right. Suppose the hostname of your system was **richlp.ix.com**. You could have a separate hostname for your server called **www.ix.com**. Notice that the entry is commented with a preceding **#**. Just remove the **#** and type your Web server's hostname in place of **new.host.name**.

```
# ServerName allows you to set a hostname which is sent back to clients for
# your server if it's different than the one the program would get (i.e. use
# "www" instead of the host's real name).

#ServerName new.host.name
```

The **srm.conf** file configures the Web server's resources. It lists a set of variables and their values. Entries are usually preceded by commented explanations. Some already have values assigned, others you may need to enter yourself. You can change entries using a standard text editor. A list of these variables is provided in Table 12-7. The next example shows the entry for DocumentRoot. A commented explanation precedes the entry. The entry itself consists of the variable name followed by the value—in this case a directory path name.

Variable	Description
AccessConfig	Location of **access.conf** file (default is **conf/access.conf**)
AgentLog	Log file for actions (default is **logs/agent_log**)
ErrorLog	The location of the error log file; if this does not start with /, ServerRoot is prepended to it (default is **logs/error_log**)
Group	Group ID server runs when operating as a daemon
IdentityCheck	Checks identity of remote users
MaxClients	Limits total number of servers running, i.e., limits the number of clients who can simultaneously connect; if this limit is ever reached, clients will be locked out (default is 150)
MaxRequestsPerChild	Number of requests each child process is allowed to process before the child dies (default is 30)
PidFile	The file the server should log its pid to (default is **/logs/httpd.pid**)
Port	Port to wait for requests
ResourceConfig	Location of **srm.conf** file (default is **conf/srm.conf**)
ServerAdmin	Administrator's email address
ServerName	Separate hostname for the server
ServerRoot	The root directory for users of the Web server; also the directory where the server's config, error, and log files are kept (default is **/usr/local/etc/httpd**)
ServerType	Either stand-alone or **inetd**
StartServers	Number of servers to start with (default is 5)
TimeOut	Number of seconds to wait for a user request; if none is received in that time period, the user is logged out (default is 400)
TransferLog	Path to logs (default is **logs/access_log**)
TypesConfig	Location of MIME configuration file (default is **conf/mime.conf**)
User	User ID of the server

Table 12-6.   *Variables for **httpd.conf***

Variable	Description
AccessFileName	File in each directory that holds access control information (**.htaccess** is the default)
AddDescription	Short description of file placed in server-generated indexes
AddEncoding *extensions-list*	Allows certain browsers with the capability to decompress files as they retrieve them; the extensions list contains extensions used to designate different types of compressions, such as **.gz** for **gzip** **AddEncoding x-gzip gz**
AddIcon *image file file-extensions*	Icons to use for particular file types; you specify the image file followed by a list of file name extensions, such as **.mpg**, **.bin**, or **.ps** **AddIcon /icons/movie.gif .mpg .qt**
AddIconByEncoding	Specifies icon and adds encoding information
AddIconByType	Uses MIME type to determine icon use
AddLanguage *language extension*	Allows you to specify the language of a document; you can then use content negotiation to give a browser a file in a language it can understand, then specify the language and an extension **AddLanguage en .en**
AddType *type/subtype extension*	Allows you to override MIME types without actually editing them, and designate specified files as certain types; commented entries are listed in the Apache **srm.conf-dist** file for enabling use of files such as map files
Alias *alias-name path-name*	Creates aliases for different path names **Alias /icons/ /usr/local/etc/httpd/icons/**
DefaultType	The default MIME type used for documents that the server cannot find the type of from file name extensions (default is **text/html**)
DefaultIcon	Which icon to show for files that do not have an icon

Table 12-7.   *Variables for* **srm.conf**

Variable	Description
DirectoryIndex	File names for your Web site indexes; these are files to use as a prewritten HTML directory index; separate multiple entries with spaces (default is **index.html**)
DocumentRoot	The directory out of which you will serve your documents; by default, all requests are taken from this directory, but symbolic links and aliases may be used to point to other locations (default is **/usr/local/etc/httpd/htdocs**)
FancyIndexing	Adds icons and file name information to file list for indexing; set on or off
HeaderName	File that should be appended to directory indexes (default is HEADER)
IndexIgnore *file-list*	Set of file names that directory indexing should ignore; these are files such as README or HEADER
IndexOptions	Indexing options
LanguagePriority *language-list*	Allows you to give precedence to some languages; content negotiation is ambiguous **LanguagePriority en fr de**
OldScriptAlias	Same as **Alias**
ReadmeName	The name of the README file the server will look for by default (default is README)
Redirect	Tells users where to find documents that are no longer on your server
ScriptAlias *alias-name path-name*	Controls which directories contain server scripts **ScriptAlias /cgi-bin/ /usr/local/etc/httpd/cgi-bin/**
UserDir	The name of the directory that is appended to a user's home directory if a ~user request is received (default is **public_html**)

Table 12-7. *Variables for **srm.conf** (continued)*

```
DocumentRoot /usr/local/etc/httpd/htdocs
```

The **access.conf** file determines the services that will be made available to users in the directories your server has access to. This file consists of a series of directives, each encased in a set of directory tags. The beginning tag is the word "Directory" with a directory path name, encased within less-than and greater-than symbols, <Directory *pathname*>. The ending tag uses the same <> symbols but with a slash preceding the term "Directory", </Directory>. Within the tags you can have several directives.

With the Options directive you can enable certain features such as use of symbolic links. With AllowOverride you can determine to what extent an **.htaccess** file in the directory can override the features set by a directive.

With the Limit directive, you can modify the **access.conf** file to control access to your system by Web users. The Limit directive uses a set of tags just like the Directory tags. <Limit> begins a Limit directive and </Limit> ends it. The Limit directive specifies who can have access to your Web server. There are several options you can use. For example, the **allow** option followed by a list of hostnames restricts access to just those users. The **deny** option with a list of hostnames denies access by those systems. Table 12-8 lists the different directives and their options.

You will find two Directory entries already in your **access.conf** file. The first Directory is meant to apply to the Directory that is your Web site root. This is where your Web pages are located. Check to see that the path name used in this first Directory entry is in fact the path name of your Web site root directory. If not, be sure to change it. An example of a Directory entry follows.

```
# This should be changed to whatever you set DocumentRoot to.
<Directory /home/httpd/htdocs>
Options Indexes FollowSymLinks
AllowOverride All
# Controls who can get stuff from this server.
<Limit GET>
order allow,deny
allow from all
</Limit>
</Directory>
# Place any directories you want access information for after this one.
```

Directory Tag	Description
`<Directory` *path-name>* `</Directory>`	Specifies directory to set controls for; ends with `</Directory>`

Directives

`Options` *feature-list*	Server options for specified directories; placed within Directory or Limit directives	
	All	Enables all features
	ExecCGI	CGI scripts executable
	FollowSymLinks	Enables symbolic links
	Includes	Allows use of include files
	IncludeNoExec	Allows include files but disables exec option
	Indexes	Allows users to retrieve indexes
	None	All features are disabled
	SymLinksIfOwnerMatch	Checks user ID before using symbolic links
`AllowOverride` *feature-list*	Controls options that the **.htaccess** files in directories can override	
	All Unrestricted access	
	AuthConfig	
	AuthName Authorization name of directory	
	AuthType Authorization type of directory	
	AuthUserFile File containing user names and passwords	
	AuthGroupFile File containing allowable group names	
	FileInfo Enables AddType and AddEncoding directives	
	Limit Enables Limit directive	
	None No access allowed	
	Options Enables Options directive	
`<Limit>` `</Limit>`	Controls access to your Web server using the following designations; the term **all** refers to all hosts	
	allows *host-list* **-host-list**	Permits specified hosts in the host-list access
	denies *host-list* **host-list**	Denies specified hosts in host-list from access
	orders *options*	Order in which deny and allow list are evaluated, as in: **order deny,allow**
	requires *host-list* **host-list**	Requires authentication using the AuthUserFile file

Table 12-8. *Directives for access.conf*

Starting the Web Server

You can start your Web server manually with the command **httpd**. This command has several options. The **-d** option allows you to specify a directory for the **httpd** program if it is different from the default directory. With the **-f** option you can specify a configuration file different from **httpd.conf**. The **-v** option displays the version.

As noted previously in the discussion of **init** scripts, your OpenLinux system automatically starts up the Web server daemon, invoking it whenever you start your system. A startup script for the Web server called **httpd** is in the **/etc/rc.d/init.d** directory. A symbolic link through which the **rc** program runs is in the **/etc/rc.d/rc3.d** directory and is called **S85httpd**. For systems using other Linux distributions, you can place the Web server command in a system startup script such as **rc.local** or **rc.sysinit**.

If you want to have **httpd** called by the **inetd** daemon, place an entry for **httpd** in the **/etc/services** and **/etc/inetd.conf** files. **/etc/services** lists the different services available on your system. For a Web server you enter **http** with a *port*/tcp specification.

```
http    80/tcp
```

The Web server entry in the **/etc/inetd.conf** file is similar to the entry for the ftp server. The path name for the Web server installed on your Caldera Network Desktop is **/usr/sbin/httpd**. **httpd** takes no arguments.

```
http stream tcp nowait nobody /usr/sbin/httpd  httpd
```

To have Web server requests monitored and controlled by **tcpd**, you place the **/usr/sbin/tcpd** path name in place of the **/usr/sbin/httpd** path name.

```
http stream tcp nowait nobody /usr/sbin/tcpd  httpd
```

You also have to specify the **inetd** value for the ServerType variable in your **httpd.config-dist** file.

```
# ServerType is either inetd, or standalone.
ServerType inetd
```

OpenLinux is not configured to run your Web server from **inetd**. If you want this done, you will have to place the appropriate entries in **/etc/services** and **/etc/inetd.conf** as well as remove your Web server from the list of startup daemons in the autostart list. To configure the autostart list, choose "System Configuration" from the Lisa main menu, then "System Configuration" again from the next menu. Then choose the "Configure daemon/server autostart" entry. A list of daemons and servers appears. The items with an 'x' next to them are the ones that will start up when you start your system. Move to the Web Server entry and press the SPACEBAR to deselect it, removing the 'x'. Then press ENTER. (See Chapter 19 for a discussion of the Startup Daemon menu.)

If you install another Web server, you have to make sure that the configuration files are set up and installed. If you are using another distribution and are installing Apache yourself, you will notice that versions of the configuration files ending with the extension **.conf-dist** are provided. You have to make copies of these with the same prefix but with just the extension **.conf**. The Web server reads configuration information only from files with a **.conf** extension. You can then go ahead and make your configuration entries.

To check your Web server, just start your Web Browser and enter the Internet domain name address of your system. For the system **turtle.trek.com** the user enters **http://turtle.trek.com**. This should display the home page you placed in your Web root directory. A simple way to do this is to use **lynx**, the command line Web Browser. Just start **lynx** and then press **g** to open a line where you can enter a URL for your own system. Then **lynx** will display your Web site's home page. Be sure to first place an **index.html** file in the **/home/httpd/html** directory.

You can also use telnet to check if your Web server is operating. Use telnet, the hostname of your system, and the port that your Web server is operating off of.

```
telnet  turtle.trek.com 80
```

Gopher Server

A Gopher server presents a highly organized way to access Internet resources such as data files or graphics. Unlike ftp, with Gopher you can present users with a menu of items from which they can choose. One menu can lead to another menu or to another Gopher site. In this respect, Gopher is like the Web, allowing you to move from one site to another in search of resources, but it is like ftp in that only the resources are listed. There is no text or graphics to give you explanations.

Gopher uses a TCP/IP protocol called the Gopher protocol. It provides for the very fast transmission of Gopher menu files. Gopher information is held in these files, which contain lists of items accessible at certain sites. Each item is organized into five fields specifying the information about the item and where it can be found. The fields are separated by tabs: type, display name, selector string, hostname, and port.

The type can be one of several possible Gopher codes, as listed in Table 12-9. The display name is a description of the item as it will appear on the Gopher menu. The selector string is the item's unique identifier. The hostname is the hostname of the system where the item is located, and the port is the port to use when accessing this host system (usually 70).

Gopher was developed at the University of Minnesota where it is currently supported, with new versions continually being developed. You can obtain a copy of Gopher from the University of Minnesota Gopher ftp site at **boombox.micro.umn.edu** in the directory **/pub/gopher/unix**. You can also obtain the Gopher server software from most Linux ftp sites. A copy is available at **sunsite.unc.edu** and its mirror sites in the **/pub/Linux/systems/Network/info-systems/gopher** directory or in **/pub/packages/info-systems/gopher/boombox-mirror/unix**. There is also a GNU Public Licensed Gopher server available called GN Gopher. It is already on your Caldera CD-ROM as the **gn-2.22-1.i386.rpm** package. Use rpm or glint to install and configure your GN Gopher server. The University of Minnesota provides the

File Type	Description
0	Text file
1	Gopher directory
2	CSO phone book server
3	Error
4	BinHex Macintosh file, HQX
5	Binary DOS file
6	Unix UUencoded file
7	Full text index (Gopher menu file)
8	Telnet session, includes the remote host's address
9	Binary file
g	GIF image file
h	HTML file
I	Graphic image file (other than GIF)
M	MIME multipart mixed message
P	Adobe PDF file
s	Sound file
T	TN3270 telnet session

Table 12-9. *Gopher File Types*

Gopher software free to any educational institution and for noncommercial uses. It does ask a license fee for commercial users or anyone charging a fee for information accessed through a version of their Gopher server. The GN Gopher server is provided free to anyone, commercial or not. The University of Minnesota also has a more advanced version of Gopher called Gopher+ that it is currently provided as a commercial product.

The procedures for creating GN and the University of Minnesota Gopher servers are different. Examples in this chapter use the 2.3 version of the University of Minnesota Gopher and the 2.20 version of GN Gopher, currently available at most Linux ftp sites. You will probably be able to obtain more recent versions. The University of Minnesota Gopher software package includes Gopher clients in addition to the sever. The GN Gopher software package includes only the server.

The **gopher** client is a very fast line-mode client. There are, however, many other Gopher clients available from other sources, such as the **xgopher** client, a package on your Caldera CD-ROM that runs on your desktop.

The Gopher User Account and Data Directory

You will have to have a data directory for your Gopher data files as well as a user account and group specifically for Gopher access. Although the Caldera Network Desktop has already created the Gopher user, it has not created the data directory. If you are using another distribution you will also have to create the Gopher user.

Gopher User Account

To better control access by other Gopher users to your system, you should have an account named **gopher**. Your Caldera Network Desktop has already created the Gopher account and has fully configured it. The following is the entry that you will find in your **/etc/passwd** file on your Caldera Network Desktop for the Gopher user.

```
gopher:*:13:30:gopher:/home/gopher
```

The asterisk in the password field blocks the account, which prevents any other users from gaining access to it and thereby gaining control over its files or access to other parts of your system. The user ID, 13, is a unique ID. The comment field is "gopher". The login directory is **/home/gopher**. When Gopher users log into your system, this is the directory they will be placed in.

For other distributions you will have to create the Gopher account. You can then place restrictions on it to keep any remote Gopher users from accessing any other part of your system. You would also have to modify the entry for this account in your **/etc/passwd** file to prevent normal user access to it by placing an asterisk in the password entry field of the Gopher password.

The group ID is the ID of the **gopher** group, which is set up just for Gopher users. You can set up restrictions on the **gopher** group, thereby restricting any Gopher users. Here is the entry for the **gopher** group that you will find in the **/etc/group** file. For other Linux distributions, if you do not have one, you should add it.

```
gopher::30:
```

Gopher Data Directory

The Caldera Network Desktop has specified that **/home/gopher** is to be used as the Gopher data directory, for its gn Gopher server. The data directory for your Gopher files should be the same as the home directory for the Gopher user account. Should you want to use a different directory directory, change its ownership to that of the

Gopher user with the **chown** command. When you configure your Gopher server software, be sure to specify that directory as your Gopher data directory. Otherwise, your server will not be able to find your Gopher files.

The University of Minnesota Gopher

In the following examples, the user has downloaded the University of Minnesota Gopher software package for Linux, which is called **gopher2_3.tar.gz**. The package is first unzipped with **gunzip** and then the files and directories are extracted using **tar**. This creates a directory called **gopher2_3**. Within this directory are different subdirectories for documentation and the applications. The **gopherd** directory holds your source code for the Gopher server, and the **gopher** directory holds the source code for your Gopher client. The **doc** directory has the documentation, including your man documents.

```
# gunzip gopher2_3.tar.gz
# ls
gopher2_3.tar
# tar xvf gopher2_3.tar
# ls
gopher2_3    gopher2_3.tar
# cd gopher2_3
# ls -F
Copyright MANIFEST Makefile.config.in Makefile.in README conf.h
config.guess config.h.in config.sub configure configure.in
copyright doc/ gopher/ gopherd/ gophfilt/ install-sh make.com
object/ patchlevel.h
```

To install the Gopher server, you first specify options in certain configuration files located in the **gopherd** directory. You have to provide information such as the directory where you want to place your Gopher menu files. You then compile the Gopher software. Compiling the software is merely a matter of entering the command **make** in your Gopher source code directory. **make** uses a Makefile to correctly compile the Gopher program for you. With version 2.3, University of Minnesota Gopher has a **configure** utility that automatically detects how your system is configured and creates Makefiles tailored to your specific system. Any system specific information has to be explicitly set in configuration files.

Configuring the University of Minnesota Gopher Server

Before you create your Gopher server, you have to configure it using entries in the **gopherd.conf** and **gopherdlocal.conf** file. In the University of Minnesota Gopher version these are found in the **gopherd** subdirectory. **gopherd.conf** is designed to configure system specific features such as the number of connections permitted. **gopherdlocal.conf** customizes your Gopher server providing information like the name of the administrator and controlling access by specified remote systems.

gopherd.conf   The **gopherd.conf** and **gopherdlocal.conf** files contain the configuration specifications for your Gopher server. A set of commented default specifications are already listed in the file. You just need to uncomment the ones you want by deleting the **#** at the beginning of the line, and then change any values if you wish.

You can set options such as the maximum number of users allowed or the compression method for transmitting files. Options are entered with the option's specification and a colon followed by a space and the option's value. The following example sets the maximum number of users.

```
MaxConnections: 15
```

You have to specify an alias for the Gopher service on your system. You do this with the **hostalias:** entry. Usually this is just the full hostname of your system, though some systems may identify it with the host part of the name as **gopher**. In the next example, the **hostalias** is the full hostname, **garnet.train.com**.

```
hostalias: garnet.train.com
```

You may also have to set the full path name for the **gopherdlocal.conf** file. There is an entry that begins with the **include** command and specifies the location of the gopherdlocal.conf file. On your Caldera Network Desktop, your **gopherd** server along with the **gopherd.conf** and **gopherdlocal.conf** files should be installed in the **/usr/sbin** directory. When the **gopherd** server is run, it reads the **gopherd.conf** file for configuration information, which in turn reads the **gopherdlocal.conf** file for specific configuration information. The **include** operation in **gopherd.conf** may need to have the full path name for **gopherdlocal.conf**, which in this case would be **/usr/sbin/gopherdlocal.conf**.

```
include: /usr/sbin/gopherdlocal.conf
```

With the **ignore** and **ignore_patt** options you can restrict the files that are accessible to Gopher users. **ignore** will deny access to any file with a specified extension, for example, **ignore: conf** denies access to any file with a .conf extension. **ignore_patt** restricts any file with the specified pattern, for example, **ignore_patt bin** denies access to any file whose file name contains the pattern "bin".

gopherdlocal.conf The **gopherdlocal.conf** file is designed to hold local customizations. Its entries will override comparable entries in the **gopherd.conf** file. In the **gopherdlocal.conf** file you specify management information such as the name of the system administrator and the description of your Gopher service. There are two entries in the **gopherdlocal.conf** file for the system administrator: Admin: and AdminEmail:. Use the Admin: entry to add the system administrator's name. You can also add other information, such as a phone number. Use the AdminEmail: entry for the system administrator's email address.

```
Admin: Richard Petersen
AdminEmail:  rp@richlp.com
```

A series of entries provide information about your Gopher server. The Abstract: entry is a notice displayed to any user who uses your system. It briefly describes what your Gopher server provides. The Language: entry is used to tell users what language most of your files are in. These are both entries you should make. Other informational entries are options. For the Org: entry you can enter your organization, and for Loc: you can enter your address. The BummerMsg: entry specifies the message that is displayed when users make an error or cannot get onto your site because it is already in use by the maximum number of users.

With the access: option you can restrict access by other systems. An access: entry has the following format:

```
access: hostname permission-list num
```

The hostname is the domain name or IP address of either a network or a remote system. The num setting specifies how many users from that network or system can have access at any one time. The permission list sets the permissions for users from that network or system. There are four possible permissions: browse, ftp, read, and search. To turn off a permission you precede it with an exclamation point (!). The browse permission allows users to list files in directories, ftp allows your system to be used as an ftp gateway, read allows access to files, and search allows access to indexes.

For the hostname you can specify a network address, the address of a particular system, or a default entry that allows access by any system. The default entry uses the keyword **default** for the hostname. In the next example, the Gopher server is open to any user with the read and search permissions enabled, but with the browse and ftp permissions denied. No single network or system can have more than 15 of their users on your Gopher server at one time.

```
access: default  !ftp read search !browse  15
```

To control access from a particular network you can use an access: entry with the network's domain name. In the next example, up to 5 users from the network **train.com** can access your Gopher server, but they have no browse capability.

```
access: train.com   ftp read search !browse  5
```

Instead of a domain name you can use an IP address for a network or system. For the network you specify only the network portion of an IP address. Don't forget to end the address with a period. In the next example, the network with the address 199.189. is denied use of your system as an ftp gateway. Only 7 users are allowed on at one time.

```
access: 199.189.   !ftp read search browse  7
```

To provide access by a particular system you enter that system name for the host. In the next example, the system with the IP address of 204.166.189.21 has full access to your Gopher system. If the system is a stand-alone PC used by one person, you could specify that only one user from that system can have access.

```
access: 204.166.189.21 ftp read search browse  1
```

Makefile.config and conf.h   Before you compile your Gopher server, you should check your **Makefile.config** and **conf.h** files for certain configurations. In the **Makefile.config** file first check the directory path that the Gopher program expects to operate from. This is assigned to a variable called PREFIX. If you want to operate Gopher out of a different directory, modify the default path name that is assigned to the PREFIX variable. The Caldera Network Desktop expects to find server programs in the **/usr/sbin** directory. You should move PREFIX to this directory. You can also modify other directory variables if you wish.

```
PREFIX=/usr/sbin
```

You should also check the entries for the DOMAIN, SERVERPORT, SERVERDATA, and SERVEROPTS variables. The DOMAIN variable specifies the network portion of your hostname. For **richlp.ix.com** the network portion would be **.ix.com**. Be sure to include the preceding period. If your hostname command displays your fully qualified domain name, then you can just leave this blank.

```
DOMAIN=.ix.com
```

The SERVERPORT variable is set to 70, and you should leave it at this for general access. The SERVERDATA variable holds the path name for the directory where your Gopher data files are kept. By default this is **/gopher-data**. If you want to use another directory, you have to assign it to SERVERDATA. For the Caldera Network Desktop you should set this to **/home/gopher**. The SERVEROPTS variable is assigned a list of options used to control your Gopher service. You can add the date and time to titles or set the maximum number of users. A list of these options can be found in Table 12-10.

```
SERVERDATA=/home/gopher
```

In the **conf.h** file you can set values for features such as the length of timeouts and the programs to use for certain operations such as viewing a graphics file. The **conf.h** file contains a list of define entries familiar to those with C programming experience. An entry begins with **#define** followed by an uppercase term and then a value. To change a value for a specific term, carefully use your text editor to delete the value and type the new one in its place. Default values are already entered. The next example sets the print operations to the **lpr** command.

```
#define PRINTER_COMMAND "lpr"
```

For the Gopher client you use the CLIENT1_HOST entry to specify the Gopher server to which it will be connected by default. The next example connects to **gopher.tc.umn.edu**, the original Gopher Internet site.

```
#define CLIENT1_HOST  "gopher.tc.umn.edu"
```

The **conf.h** file can be confusing. This is a C program file, not a shell script file. It looks different from other configuration files. In most configuration files, a **#** is a comment, but in the **conf.h** file it is the beginning of a define directive. In **conf.h** a comment is anything encased by an opening **/*** and a closing ***/**. Such entries are commented out, disabling them. To enable them you remove the **/*** and ***/** symbols around them.

Though the default entries for the **conf.h** file should work fine, you can change them if you wish. However, be careful to change entries used for Linux systems. Linux uses any entries not reserved for other systems. If you see an entry preceded by a **#if**

Makefile.config	Description
PREFIX	The base path name for installing software (default is **/usr/local**)
CLIENTDIR	Directory where Gopher client is installed (default is **/usr/local/bin**)
CLIENTLIB	Gopher client help files
MAN1DIR	Directory where the man pages for the Gopher client are installed
MAN8DIR	Directory where the man pages for **gopherd** server are installed
SERVERDIR	Directory where Gopher server and configuration files are installed (**gopherd** and **gopherd.conf**— default is **/usr/local/etc**)
CLIENTOPTS	Options for the Gopher client program -DONOMAIL Remote users cannot mail files -DAUTOEXITONU Treat q and u as the same, and automatically exit from the top menu (useful if Gopher called from another application)
DOMAIN	If your system does not return the fully qualified domain name, you have to specify the network address of your system; otherwise, leave null
SERVERPORT=*num*	Sets port that Gopher server uses to wait for requests, usually 70
SERVERDATA=*pathname*	Location of the Gopher data files to be made available by the Gopher server; for the Caldera Network Desktop this directory is **/usr/lib/gopher-data**

Table 12-10. *University of Minnesota Gopher **Makefile.config** and **conf.h***

Makefile.config	Description	
SERVEROPTS=*options-list*		
Options for Gopher Server	-DADD_DATE_AND_TIME	Adds date and time to
		Gopher titles
	-DDL dl	Sets up support for
		database utility
	-DCAPFILES compatibility	Provides
		with **.cap**
	directories	
	-DLOADRESTRICT	Restricts user access
	-DSETPROCTITLE	Sets process title displayed by ps
DLPATH	Path to dl database	
conf.h		
CLIENT1_HOST	Host to contact first (default host listed here) **#define CLIENT1_HOST "gopher.tc.umn.edu"**	
CLIENT2_HOST	Host to contact **#define CLIENT2_HOST "gopher2.tc.umn.edu"**	
CLIENT1_PORT	Port to contact first (default is 70) **#define CLIENT1_PORT 70**	
CLIENT2_PORT	Port to contact (default is 70)	
PAGER_COMMAND	Command to page through text	
MAIL_COMMAND	Command for Gopher users to send mail (default is **/bin/mail**)	
TELNET_COMMAND	Command to use for telnet sessions (default is telnet)	
PRINTER_COMMAND	Command to use for printing (default is **lpr**)	
PLAY_COMMAND	Command to use for playing sounds (default is **/bin/false**)	
IMAGE_COMMAND	Command to use for viewing graphics (default is **xloadimage**)	
HTML_COMMAND	Command to use for viewing Web pages (no default, but can specify **lynx**)	

Table 12-10. *University of Minnesota Gopher **Makefile.config** and **conf.h** (continued)*

Makefile.config	Description
MAXLOAD	Load average at which to restrict connections (default is 10.0)
READTIMEOUT	Timeout in seconds for network reads (default is 1 * 60)
WAISMAXHITS	Maximum number of retrieved items to return from a WAIS query (default is 40)
NOMAIL	If defined, restricts users from mailing or downloading files (currently commented out with enclosing /* */, remove comments to enable)
GOPHERHELP	Online Gopher help file
TN3270_COMMAND	Command for TN3270 sessions
conf.h	
MIME_COMMAND	Command for MIME operations (default is metamail -P)
AFTP_HOST	Sets ftp gateway (currently set to **gopher-gw.micro.umn.edu**)
CONF_FILE	Sets the location of the **gopherd.conf** file; the default is **/usr/local/etc/gopherd.conf**; for the Caldera Network Desktop you have to change this to **/usr/sbin** **#define CONF_FILE /usr/sbin**
DELETE_BOOKMARKS_ONLY	Restricts **delete** command to deleting bookmarks (currently commented out)

Table 12-10.   *University of Minnesota Gopher **Makefile.config** and **conf.h** (continued)*

defined(*system***)**, where system is the name of an operating system, then the following entries only apply to that operating system, until the next **#endif**. Thus, **#if defined(sun)** applies only to Sun systems. There is a large section devoted entirely to the VMS operating system. Most entries that apply to Linux are at the end of the **conf.h** file, with a few at the beginning.

You are now ready to compile your Gopher software. You can compile both the Gopher client and the Gopher server with the following command.

```
# make install
```

To compile just one or the other, use the **make** command with either the term "client" or "server".

```
# make client
# make server
```

This creates a server program called **gopherd**. You can then invoke **gopherd** directly or from **inetd**.

Starting the University of Minnesota Gopher

Before you start your Gopher server, you should first create some Gopher menu files as described in the next section. As noted in a prior section, "Starting Servers," you can start the Gopher server from the command line, or at boot time automatically using an **init** script, or through **inetd** when a request for the Gopher service is received. The University of Minnesota Gopher Server options are listed in Table 12-11.

Option	Description
-C	Disables caching of directory requests
-c	Runs without **chroot** restrictions; allows access to files outside Gopher data root through symbolic links, such as system man files; potential security risk, should use with **-u** *username* option
-D	Enables debugging
-I	Uses **inetd** to invoke Gopher
-L *num*	Specifies maximum load average
-l *logfile*	Logs connections to log file
-o *conf-file*	Specifies alternate **gopherd.conf** configuration file
-u *username*	Runs **gopherd** under username; provides added restrictions for security purposes
-U *userid*	Runs **gopherd** under userid; provides added restrictions for security purposes (same as **-u**)

Table 12-11. *University of Minnesota Gopher Server Option*

The Caldera Network Desktop has already configured your system to run Gopher through **inetd**. This configuration expects to locate the Gopher data directory in **/home/gopher**. In the **/etc/services** file you will find an entry for Gopher as shown here. It specifies the name of the service with the port number and the protocol. On other distributions you may have to enter it.

```
gopher  70/tcp
```

There is already an entry for Gopher in the **/etc/inetd.conf** file. The entry currently references the GN Gopher server, **gn**. You will have to modify it for the **gopherd** server. In place of the entry for **gn** you enter **gopherd** with the **-I** option and the path name for the Gopher data directory. The **-I** option specifies that **gopherd** is to be called with **inetd**. You can also add the port number, in this case, 70. This entry is also set up to use the **tcpd** to monitor and control access by remote users. Your entry should look like the following example. The Gopher data files are in **/home/gopher**, and the port is 70. The arguments, including the name of the **gopherd** program are **gopherd -I /home/gopher 70**.

```
gopher stream tcp nowait root  /usr/sbin/tcpd  gopherd -I
/home/gopher 70
```

Should you not want to use **tcpd**, you can replace it with the path name for the **gopherd** server program.

```
gopher stream tcp nowait root  /usr/sbin/gopherd gopherd -I
/home/gopher 70
```

If you want to start the **gopherd** server on the command line, you enter **gopherd** and as its arguments the path name of the directory for the Gopher data files and the port number. **gopherd** has several possible options, as listed in Table 12-12. As a precaution you can use the **-u** option to specify an owner other than root to run **gopherd**. You have to first create the user and enter a ***** in the password field of its **passwd** entry. The user's home directory will be the gopher data directory. The Caldera Network Desktop has already created a user called gopher. In the following example, the full path name for the **gopherd** server program is **/usr/sbin/gopherd**, the Gopher data files are in **/home/gopher**, and the port is 70.

```
/usr/sbin/gopherd -u gopher /home/gopher 70
```

gopherd.conf	**Description**
hostalias: *DNS-alias-name*	Uses this hostname instead of the system's; hostname must be a valid DNS name; used to reference Gopher servers on a system such as **gopher.ix.com** **hostalias: gopher.turnip.com**
cachetime: *seconds*	Seconds that a cache file used to cache Gopher directories remains valid
viewext: *extension Gophertype Prefix Gopher+Type [Language]*	Maps a file name extension onto a particular Gopher type; most of these are already set for you in the **gopherd.conf file**. The first argument is an extension such **.gif**; the second argument is the single character Gopher type (1, 0, I, etc.); the third argument is a prefix that will be appended to the normal file name path; the fourth argument is the Gopher+ view attribute or Internet Media Type (formerly called MIME Content Types), such as image/gif; the optional fifth argument is a language to use for the file instead of the default language **viewext: .jpg I 9 image/JPEG** **viewext: .html h 0 text/html**
ignore: *extension*	Ignores files with specified extension; these files are not presented to Gopher users **ignore: bin**
ignore_patt: *regular-expression*	Ignores files that match the regular expression; these files are not presented to Gopher users
blockext: *extension*	Maps files with specified extension to attribute blocks
decoder: *extension program*	The specified program will be run on files with the indicated extension when the file is retrieved; used with compressed files **decoder: .gz /usr/gnu/bin/zcat**
pids_directory: *path-name*	A scratch directory to store pid files in

Table 12-12. *gopherd.conf* and *gopherdlocal.conf Entries*

gopherd.conf	Description
`maxconnections:` *num*	The number of concurrent connections that the Gopher server can handle at the same time
gopherdlocal.conf	
`admin:` *administrator-name-and-info*	The administrator's name and added information such as a phone number
`adminemail:` *email-address*	Email address of Gopher server administrator
`site:` *site-description*	Descriptive name of the site
`loc:` *address*	Address of site—street, city, etc.
`geog:`	Longitude and latitude for site
`language:` *default-language*	Default language used by the site
`secureusers:` *filename*	Specifies file listing authorized hosts and networks
`bummermsg:`	Message displayed when a client is denied access
`access:` *domain name access-list*	Allows you to determine who can browse directories, read files, and search your system. The first argument is a domain name, IP address, or default; the second argument is a list of comma-separated words determining access; the words are: browse, read, search, and ftp. Each can be preceded by a ! to deny access; `default !browse, read, search, !ftp` sets the default to deny browsing and ftp, but allow reading and searching. If you set the default first, it will be inherited by following entries and you only need to specify the access that differs. Optionally, you can base the access on the number of concurrent transactions in an added argument `access: default browse,read,search,ftp 5`

Table 12-12. *gopherd.conf* and *gopherdlocal.conf* Entries (continued)

To have the Gopher server start automatically whenever you boot, you can create an **init** script for it in the **/etc/rc.d/init.d** directory. The section on **init** scripts at the beginning of this chapter provides a detailed description on how to do this for the **gopherd** server.

GN Gopher Server

Your Caldera Linux system is already configured for your GN Gopher server. The GN Gopher server is automatically installed if you choose the Complete Install option, but with the Recommended Install option, you have to use rpm or glint to install the **gn-2.22-1.i386.rpm** package. In either case, your Gopher server is ready to use. You can start adding Gopher files and menus to the **/home/gopher** directory. Be sure to run **mkcache** to make your gopher files accessible to gopher clients. However, if you are using another version of Linux, you will have to download the standard GN Gopher server package, gn-2.20.tar.gz, from a Linux ftp site, and then configure and install it. Unzipping and extracting this file will create a directory called **gn-2.20** that holds the GN Gopher server sources and documentation.

The GN Gopher package contains source code that you need to configure for Linux before you compile it. There is one configuration file, **config.h**, and a Makefile that holds compiler directives. The **INSTALL** file in the **docs** subdirectory has detailed instructions on how to create your GN server, as well as setting up a Gopher site. The **docs/examples** directory has numerous examples of GN Gopher menus.

Configuring the GN Gopher Server

To configure the GN Gopher server, you modify entries in the **config.h** file and the Makefile. There are certain entries that are compulsory, that you have to specify. These are clearly indicated at the beginning of the file with the heading "Compulsory items to fill in". You have to enter your hostname and the path name of the Gopher data directory, as well as specify that you are using a Linux system. You can make any other customizations you want. An entry in the **config.h** file has the format of a **#define** term followed by the item and then the value you want for it. You can change the value, not the item. The following entries are valid for the Caldera Network Desktop distribution of Linux. In place of the hostname **garnet.train.com** you should have your own system's hostname.

```
#define GN_HOSTNAME    "garnet.train.com"
#define ROOT_DIR  "/home/gopher"
#define LINUX
#define MAINTAINER    "mailto:justin@garnet.train.com"
#define ROOT_MENU_NAME  "GN -- A Gopher/HTTP Server"
#define GN_LOGFILE  "/var/log/gn.log"    /* "/path/to/gn.log" */
```

```
#define MIME_TYPE_FILE  "/usr/local/gn_mime.types"
#define WAISGN  "/usr/sbin/waisgn"
```

Following the compulsory items there are several other items that you also change if you wish, though the defaults should work fine. Should you want to use a different port you can specify it in the DEFAULTPORT entry. You can set the time out with the TIMEOUT entry and set the maximum depth of menu searches in the MAXDEPTH entry. In the Makefile you have to specify the type of C compiler you are using and the directories where you want your server program placed. You will find two entries for the CC which designates the type of C compiler to use. The one specifying **gcc** will be commented out with a preceding #. The one for **cc** will not. You have to comment the **cc** entry by placing a # before it and remove the # from the **gcc** entry. This sets the CC entry to the **gcc** compiler. Also, in the Makefile you can set SERVERBINDIR, which holds the directory path where you want to place the server program. BINDIR is the directory for the **mkcache** an **uncache** programs. Set these to the directories where you want those programs placed such as **/usr/sbin**. On your Caldera Network Desktop using the Redhat distribution, the SERVERFINDER directory should be set to **/usr/sbin**, the directory that holds daemons. Though the **mkcache** and **uncache** programs can go anywhere, it may be best to also place them together with the GN server by also setting BINDIR to **/usr/sbin**.

Just below these variables, you will find the following entry for **include** directories. Uncomment the one for Linux by removing the preceding # so that it reads

```
# INCLUDES= -I.. -I../gn
# For Linux use
INCLUDES= -I.. -I../gn -I/usr/include/bsd
```

Further down in the Makefile you will find an empty entry for the Libraries as shown here.

```
#    Libraries to be included.
LIBS   =
```

Following this entry will be comments specifying libraries for different systems. The Linux specification will look like this:

```
#For Linux use
#LIBS = -lbsd
```

You can either uncomment this LIBS entry by removing the preceding #, or type in the -lbsd value in the prior empty LIBS entry.

```
LIBS = -lbsd
```

Once configured, you can then create the server by entering **make**. This creates two executable server programs called **sgn** and **gn**. **gn** is for use with **inetd**, while **sgn** is the stand-alone daemon that you can run directly. It also creates two utility programs, **mkcache** and **uncache**. Then enter **make install** to install these programs on your system.

Starting the GN Gopher Server

You are now ready to start the server. However, before you start your Gopher server, you should first create some Gopher menu files as described in the next section. You can either run the server as a stand-alone daemon or through **inetd**. See Tables 12-13 and 12-14.

The Caldera Network Desktop has already configured your system to run the GN Gopher server through **inetd**. After creating and installing the GN Gopher server, all you have to do to have a fully functioning Gopher server is to create your Gopher data files and place them in the **/home/gopher** directory.

To use **inetd**, there have to be entries for the Gopher server in the **/etc/services** and **/etc/inetd.conf** files. The Caldera Network Desktop has already placed those entries. You will find the following entry in the **/etc/services** file.

```
gopher 70/tcp
```

In the **/etc/inetd.conf** file, you will find the following entry for the GN Gopher server. Notice that the GN Gopher server is invoked with **gn**. This is the version of the GN server that works through **inetd**. Also, **tcpd** is used to monitor and control Gopher access.

```
gopher stream tcp nowait root /usr/sbin/tcpd  gn
```

You can also start the GN Gopher at boot time with an **init** script or directly from the command line. In both cases, the server has to be run as a stand-alone daemon using the **sgn** version of the GN Gopher. If you want to start Gopher at boot time, you have to create an **init** script for it in the **/etc/rc.d/init.d** directory as described in a previous section, "Starting Servers." You enter **sgn** with arguments specifying the path name of the directory for the Gopher data files and the port number (usually 70). The port number is specified with the **-p** option. As a precaution **sgn** will automatically run as the user specified in the USERID entry in the **config.h** file.

```
sgn -p 70 /home/gopher
```

GN_HOSTNAME	Sets the hostname for your server; this is the hostname of your system
ROOT_DIR	Sets the Gopher data directory; for the Caldera Network Desktop this is **/home/gopher**
LINUX	Defines Linux as your operating system; the default here will be SUN_OS; you have to replace it with LINUX
MAINTAINER	Mail address of administrator
ROOT_MENU_NAME	Name you want displayed as the title of your Gopher menu; default is "GN — A Gopher/HTTP Server"
GN_LOGFILE	Location for a GN log file
MIME_TYPE_FILE	Location of MIME configuration file; default is **/usr/local/gn_mime.types**; you place this file anywhere, but be sure to set this path name accordingly
WAISGN	Path name of the **waisgn** program that handles WAIS indexes **/usr/sbin/waisgn**
DEFAULTPORT	Sets the default port for Gopher access, currently 70
TIMEOUT	Sets the timeout waiting for requests
MAXDEPTH	Sets the maximum depth of menu searches
USERID	The user ID that the GN server will be run as for security purposes
GROUPID	The group ID that the GN server will be run as for security purposes
DECOMPRESS	Program used to decompress files; default is **/usr/local/bin/zcat**
MENUFNAME	Sets the name used for menu files; the default is **menu**
TEMPDIR	Sets the temporary directory; default is **/tmp**

Table 12-13.   *The GN Server config File*

CC	Sets the C compiler; default setting is cc; you have to change it to gcc; CC = gcc
INCLUDE	Sets Include directories; should be set to use **/usr/include/bsd**
SERVBINDIR	Directory for your GN and SGN server programs; default is **../bin**; should be set to **/usr/sbin**
BINDIR	Directory for cache support programs; default is **../b**; should be set to **/usr/sbin**
LIBS=	Sets the library used; uncomment the one for Linux by removing #; should be set to **-lbsd**

Table 12-14.   *The GN Server Makefile*

Testing the Gopher Server

Once your Gopher server is running, you can test it using either telnet or a Gopher client. With telnet, you telnet into your own system specifying the port used for Gopher. The following command tests a Gopher server on the **garnet.train.com** system. Startup messages will be displayed.

```
telnet garnet.train.com 70
```

If you then press ENTER, the menu items for the main Gopher directory on your server will be displayed, output in the following format:

```
type display-name   selector   hostname   port
```

Here is an example of a test of a Gopher server:

```
# telnet garnet.train.com 70
Trying 127.0.0.1...
Connected to garnet.train.com.
Escape character is '^]'.

0About My Weather Site  0/intro     garnet.train.com    70     +
1California Weather Information  1/calif    garnet.train.com    70     +
1New York Weather this week   1/newyork    garnet.train.com    70     +
1The Weather in Hawaii    1/weather/hawaii/
garnet.train.com    70
.
```

You can also use your Gopher client to access your own Gopher server. In the next example, the Gopher client on **garnet.train.com** is used to access the Gopher server on the same system. The main Gopher menu for the Gopher server will be displayed and the user can then select and access items.

```
gopher garnet.train.com
```

Gopher Directories

A Gopher menu that you see displayed when you access a Gopher site, is generated using special files contained within a Gopher directory. Gopher menus are designed to operate by directory, listing the different files available within a directory or referencing another directory. Special Gopher menu configuration files within each directory provide information about the different data files available and how to access them. The University of Minnesota Gopher server uses **.cap** directories and link files to organize Gopher menus. The GN Gopher server uses a **menu** and **.cache** file. However, the entries for the link and GN menu files are much the same.

Gopher Cap and Link Files

By default any files and subdirectories in a Gopher directory are automatically displayed in a Gopher menu in alphabetical order. Data files are given a type 0, and directories a type 1. The name used for each menu item is the name of the file or directory. You can override this listing by using cap files.

Your Gopher data files can have any name you wish to give them. However, Gopher files are usually described in a Gopher menu using a descriptive sentence. By selecting that menu item, the file associated with that sentence is selected. The association between this descriptive sentence and the Gopher data file is carried out either by special files in a **.cap** directory or by entries in an extended link file.

Each directory of Gopher data files can have its own **.cap** directory, which holds files of the same name as those in the Gopher data directory. If you have a Gopher data file called **engine.1**, there will be a file in the **.cap** directory also called **engine.1**. A file in the **.cap** directory contains three entries: Name, Type, and Numb. Name is assigned the descriptive sentence used for the menu item that references the Gopher data file. The Type entry specifies the type of Gopher resource. 1 is a directory and 0 is a text file. The Numb entry is assigned the number of your Gopher entry in the Gopher menu; for example, Numb=3 indicates that this is the third item in the Gopher menu.

.cap/engine.1

```
Name=The best engine in the world
Type=0
Numb=1
```

When displayed on the Gopher menu this entry will appear as the first entry. Selecting it will select the **engine.1** Gopher data file.

```
1. The best engine in the world.
```

Although **.cap** files can be used to reference data files in your directory, they do not reference files in other directories or at other Gopher sites. For this you use a link entry in a link file. There is one link file in a directory that has several link entries to different Gopher resources. A link file is any file beginning with a period. A common name for a link file is **.links**.

Each entry for a link has five variables set: Name, Type, Port, Path, and Host. You can also add an entry for the menu order, NUMB. The Name entry is the descriptive sentence used in the menu item. The Port is the port used for connection to a remote system and is usually set to 70. The Type is the type of resource that the menu item references. A resource could be a file, but it can also be a telnet session or a graphics file. Gopher can reference files other than data files. The Path variable holds the path name for the resource that the menu item references. The path name here is the path starting from the Gopher data directory. The directory **/home/gopher/calif** would have a path name of **/calif**, where **/home/gopher** is the Gopher data directory. The path name can also be preceded by the Type. The **calif** directory could be entered as **1/calif**, 1 being the type for a directory. Host holds the hostname where the resource is to be found. For your own system this will be your own hostname. If the resource is located on another system, it will have that system's hostname. A **+** sign for the Port and Host entries will indicate the current port and hostname. For files and directories on your own system, it is best to leave out the Port and Hostname entries.

.links

```
Name=The best engine in the world
Type=1
Port=70
Path=1/engines
Host=richlp.ix.com
```

You may also use links to set up ftp or WAIS connections to other systems to access files or information from them. In this case the service you are using and its arguments are specified in the Path entry. Both Host and Port have a + entry. The format for an ftp link is shown here:

```
Name=ftp-file-or-directory
Type=1
Path=ftp:hostname/path/
Host=+
Port=+
```

For example, to set up an ftp link to access the file **caboose1** on **chris.train.com**, you would set the path as shown in the following example. The current port and hostname are indicated by + for their entries.

```
Name=The last caboose
Type=0
Port=+
Path=ftp:pango1.train.com/usr/lib/gopher-data/caboose1
Host=+
```

For a WAIS link you can access WAIS resources on your own system or on a remote system. For your own system you use **waisrc:** followed by the path to the WAIS resource. For a remote system you include the hostname after **waisrc:**, for example:

```
waisrc:pango1.train.com/usr/wais/data.
```

You can also set up a link to execute shell scripts, rather than just accessing a resource. In this case the Path variable is set to **exec:** followed by the script arguments and name. The arguments are enclosed in double quotes, and if there are none you just use an empty set of quotes. The argument and script are separated by a colon.

```
Path=exec:"arguments":script
```

Instead of maintaining separate **.cap** files in each directory along with a separate link file, you can use an extended link file to hold both the local file entries and the link entries. A common name for a link file is **.names**. The **.names** would list each Name and Numb entry along with a Path entry to specify the location of the file. The

.**names** file also has an Abstract entry that allows you to enter a brief description of the file's contents. In the .**names** file shown here the first entry references a local file in the directory whereas the second entry references a remote Gopher site.

.**names**

```
Path=/engines
Name=The best engine in the world
Numb=1
Abstract=A discussion of the best steam engine ever built.

Name=The oldest train running
Type=1
Port=70
Path=1/museums
Host=pango1.train.com
```

GN Gopher Directories

GN Gopher directories place their menu entries in a file called **menu**. Each Gopher directory will have its own **menu** file with the entries for each menu item. GN Gopher uses the same set of entries as described for the University of Minnesota Gopher with a few exceptions. Within the **menu** file you list the Path, Name, Numb, and Abstract for each menu item. However, before the path name in the Path entry you have to specify the Gopher type. This is usually a one digit number such as 0 for text files and 1 for directories.

```
Name=About My Weather Site
Path=0/intro
Type=0
Numb=1
Abstract=Important Weather Information.
```

GN Gopher requires the creation of a .**cache** file for each directory. You make a .**cache** file by executing the **mkcache** program within that directory. You can do this to each **gopher** directory, or just execute **mkcache** with the **-r** option from the main **gopher-data** directory. The **mkcache -r** command will make the .**cache** files for the current directory and any of its nested subdirectories. On your Caldera Network Desktop, you can run **mkcache -r** from your **/home/gopher** directory to create .**cache** files for all your Gopher directories.

GN Gopher also fully supports Web pages. It can display Web pages and use Web page HREF references in its menu items. See the GN documentation for a detailed discussion on these capabilities.

Gopher Indexes: gopherindex

With the **gopherindex** command you can create full text indexes of your Gopher data documents. **gopherindex** is provided as part of the University of Minnesota Gopher software package, and uses **waisindex** to perform its indexing, so you must have WAIS installed to use it. It takes as its arguments several possible options and a Gopher data directory. All the documents in the data directory will be indexed. The **-N** option specifies a description of the index file to be used in a Gopher menu. The following example indexes all the files in **/home/gopher/baseball**.

```
/usr/sbin/gopherindex -v -N "Search CIS Services Short Courses"
/home/gopher/baseball
```

Instead of using **gopherindex** you can use **waisindex** directly and then create a link for the index file.

```
waisindex -r /home/gopher/baseball
```

You create the link entry for the index file in that directory's link or menu file. Type 7 is a WAIS index type of document.

```
Type=7
Name=Baseball Index
Host=+
Port=+
Path=7/.index/index
```

A Gopher Example

Here is a simple Gopher example. It is a Gopher site with files that hold weather information for several states. The files for each state are placed in their own directories. You begin with a Gopher menu in the Gopher data directory. The items in this menu are defined in the **.names** file (for GN Gopher this would be named the menu file). Most of the menu items are references to other Gopher directories. One is a file with general introductory information about the Gopher site. In the main Gopher directory there is only this intro file and the **.names** file. The next two items link to local Gopher directories, **calif** and **newyork**. The last item links to another Gopher site located at **garnet.train.com**.

.names

```
Path=/intro
Name=About My Weather Site
Numb=1
Type=0
Abstract=Important Weather Information.

Name=California Weather Information
Numb=2
Type=1
Path=/calif

Name=New York Weather this week
Numb=3
Type=1
Path=/newyork

Name=The Weather in Hawaii
Numb=4
Type=1
Port=70
Path=/usr/lib/weather/hawaii/
Host= garnet.train.com
```

The California menu item references the **calif** subdirectory. Here are located the files with information on California weather. The **calif** directory lists two data files, a link file, and a **.caps** directory. In the **.caps** directory there are two files, each having the name of a data file in the **calif** directory. For the **surf.data** and **storm.data** files in the **calif** directory, there is also a **surf.data** and **storm.data** file in the **.caps** directory. These **.caps** directory files are shown here.

surf.data

```
Name=Surfing Conditions
Numb=1
Type=0
```

storm.data

```
Name=Storm Advisory
Numb=2
Type=0
```

In the **calif** directory, the **.links** file lists an entry to access a file on a remote system.

.links

```
Name=The Weekend Snowpack
Numb=3
Type=0
Port=+
Path=ftp:rose.net.com/usr/lib/weather/snow/current.txt
Host=+
```

For the GN gopher, the menu file looks very similar with the exception that each path name must be preceded by the type of the file (0 for text files and 1 for directories).

menu

```
Name=About My Weather Site
Path=0/intro

Name=California Weather Information
Path=1/calif

Name=New York Weather this week
Path=1/newyork

Name=The Weather in Hawaii
Path=0/usr/lib/weather/hawaii/
```

WAIS Server

WAIS (Wide Area Information Service) searches a database of documents using keywords and displays the documents it finds with a ranking of their importance. It is a very effective way to make information available throughout a network. WAIS was developed by Thinking Machines and is now managed by WAIS Inc. A free version of WAIS, called freeWAIS, is available through the Clearinghouse for Networking Information Discovery and Retrieval (CNIDR). You can obtain a Linux version of freeWAIS from CNIDR and Linux ftp sites.

The freeWAIS package includes clients, a server, and an indexer program. (See Tables 12-15 and 12-16.) The clients are called **swais**, **xwais**, and **waissearch**. They are used to enter requests and display results. The indexer is called **waisindex**. You use it to create indexes of keywords for your WAIS documents, providing fast and effective search capabilities. The server is called **waisserver**. With it you can create your own WAIS site and allow other users to perform searches on your WAIS documents.

You can obtain freeWAIS from the **ftp.cnidr.org** site or most Linux ftp sites. The ftp site at **ftp.cnidr.org** has a Linux version of freeWAIS already compiled and ready to use. For Linux the current package is **freeWAIS–0.5–linux.tar.gz** located in the **/pub/CNDIR.tools/freewais** directory. You can also download the source code and compile it yourself. This package is called simply **freeWAIS–0.5.,tar.Z**. This is one

Option	Description
-p *portnum*	Listens to the port; if the *portnum* is supplied, then that port number is used
-s	Listens to standard I/O for queries
-d *directory*	Uses this directory as the default location of the indexes
-e *path-name*	Redirects error output to *path-name*, if supplied, or to **/dev/null**

-1 *log_level*	Sets logging level 0, 1, 5 and 10
	   0 logs nothing (silent)
	   1 logs only errors and warnings
	   5 logs messages of MEDIUM priority
	  10 logs everything

-u *user*	Runs the server as the user specified
-v	Displays current version and date of server

Table 12-15. *The WAIS Server: z3950*

waisindex Files	Description
index-name.doc	Information about the document, including the size and name
index-name.dct	Dictionary file with list of each unique word cross-indexed to inverted file
index-name.fn	List of all files created for the index
index-name.hl	Table of all headlines; headlines are the titles and are displayed when in retrieved results
index-name.inv	The inverted file containing a table of words, a ranking of their importance, and their connection to the indexed documents
index-name.src	A source description file that contains information about the index, what system it is located on, the topic it deals with, who maintains it, etc.
index-name.status	Contains user-defined information
waisindex Options	
-a	Appends index to an existing one
-contents	Indexes the contents of a file (default)
-d *path-name*	Specifies a path name for index files; the path name will be appended to the front of the index's file name
-e *logfile*	Redirects error messages to *logfile*
-export	Adds hostname and TCP port to source description files to allow Internet access; otherwise, no connection information will be included and the files will be accessed locally

-l *num*	Sets logging level 0, 1, 5 and 10
	  0 logs nothing (silent)
	  1 logs only errors and warnings
	  5 logs messages of MEDIUM priority
	  10 logs everything

-mem	The amount of memory to use during indexing
-M	Links different types of files

Table 12-16.   *waisindex*: Options and File Types

`waisindex` **Options**	**Description**
`-contents` `-nocontents`	Determines whether to index the contents of a document; `-contents` indexes the entire document; `-nocontents` indexes only the header and file name, not the contents
`-pairs` `-nopairs`	How to treat consecutive capitalized words; `-pairs` (the default) treats capitalized words as one term; `-nopairs` treats them as separate terms
`-pos` `-nopos`	Whether to include word's position information in the index; `-pos` includes this information allowing proximity searches, but increasing the size of the index; `-nopos` does not include this information
`-r`	Recursively indexes subdirectories
`-register`	Registers indexes with WAIS Directory of Services
`-t`	Specifies the type of document file
`-T`	Sets the type of document
Document File Types	
`filename`	The text type that uses the file name as the headline
`first_line`	The text type that uses the first line in the file as the headline
`one_line`	The text type that indexes each sentence
`text`	The text type that indexes the document; headline is the path name
`ftp`	Contains ftp code for accessing other systems
`GIF`	GIF image file
`PICT`	PICT image file
`TIFF`	TIFF image file
`MPEG`	MPEG file
`MIDI`	MIDI file
`HTML`	HTML file used for Web pages

Table 12-16. `waisindex`: *Options and File Types* (continued)

waisindex Options	Description
mail_or_rmail	Indexes the mbox mailbox file
mail_digest	Indexes email using the subject as the headline
netnews	Indexes USENET news
ps	Postscript file

Table 12-16. *waisindex*: Options and File Types (continued)

source code package that can be configured for different systems. freeWAIS is also available at **sunsite.unc.edu** and its mirror sites in the **/pub/packages/info-systems/wais** directory. Several versions will be listed.

Create a directory where you want to place freeWAIS, usually **/home/wais**. It is recommended that you download the package of precompiled binaries for Linux, freeWAIS–0.5–linux.tar.gz. You then unzip the file with **gunzip** and extract the archive with **tar xvf**. This will create a directory called **freeWAIS-0.5–linux**. This directory will hold those binaries. All you have to do is install them in an appropriate directory such as **/usr/bin**. The source code, however, has to first be configured before you can create its binaries, and if you downloaded the source code and want to compile freeWAIS yourself, you must first configure the software.

Configuring and Installing freeWAIS Source Code: Makefile and ir.h

If you downloaded the source code, this directory will hold several subdirectories: **doc** for documentation and **src** for source code. One in particular, **wais-test**, holds test files for your server.

You will first have to set the TOP variable in the Makefile. TOP is assigned the path name of the directory where the freeWAIS source code is located. Enter the full path name of the directory that your WAIS source is located in.

Besides the Makefile, there are several specialized Makefiles each with an extension for a particular operating system. The **Makefile.linux** file holds the **make** commands for creating a Linux version of freeWAIS. This file is already configured for Linux. There are, however, several options you can specify or remove, and there are detailed descriptions of each option. These options are assigned to the CFLAGS variable. A set of default options are already included. Here is a sample of the CFLAGS entry. This is the only line you should ever change.

```
CFLAGS = -Wall -m486 -fwritable-strings -Who-unused -I$(INCLUDE)
-DTELL_USER -DUSG -DSECURE_SERVER -DRELEVANCE_FEEDBACK -DBOOLEANS
-DPARTIALWORD -DLITERAL -DSOUND -DBIBDB -DLINUX
```

Here is a list of other useful options:

Makefile Option	Description
-DBIO	Allows indexing on biological symbols
-DBOOLEANS	Enables Boolean searches using AND, OR, and NOT
-DBINGINDER	Used for indexing large sets of documents
-DLITERAL	Literal string search
-DPARTIALWORD	Enables the use of the * in pattern matches to match on any variation of a pattern, for example, **hum*** matches human, hummingbird
-DRELEVANCE_FEEDBACK	Allows you to select relevant documents from a search and use them as the basis for new searches
-DSECURE_SERVER	Provides better server security
-DTELL_USER	Tells the server who is connecting
-DUSE_SYSLOG	Logs in using syslog

You can, if you wish, restrict access to your WAIS service by only certain selected networks or systems. To do this, create a **SERV_SEC** file and enter the domain names and IP addresses of allowable networks and systems. The **SERV_SEC** file is defined in an entry for the **ir.h** file in the **include** directory, as shown here:

```
#define SERVSECURITYFILE  "SERV_SEC"
```

An entry in the **SERV_SEC** file consists of the domain name followed by the IP address. The IP address is optional, for example:

```
pango1.train.com   204.166.189.21
```

You can further refine access to specific databases, allowing only specified networks and systems access to certain databases. To do this you set up a **DATA_SEC** file. This file is defined in an entry for the **ir.h** file in the include directory, as shown here:

```
#define DATASECURITYFILE  "DATA_SEC"
```

Each entry in the **DATA_SEC** file first lists the database followed by the domain name and an optional IP address. To allow access by all users to a certain database you use a ***** for the domain name. The next example shows entries in the **DATA_SEC** file. The second entry opens the **oldata** database to all users.

```
mydata    pango1.train.com    204.166.189.21
oldata         *                    *
```

Once you are ready to compile freeWAIS, you issue the following **make** command with the term "linux". This will create your WAIS clients, indexer, and server programs for your Linux system. First, run **xmkmf** in the **src/x** directory to create the Makefile for **xwais**.

```
#  make linux
```

Creating Indexes

To use WAIS, you have to create indexes for the documents you want to make available. This indexing process is carried out by the **waisindex** command that creates a particular WAIS database. You can index a single file, a group of files, or whole directories and subdirectories of files. The data files together with their index form a WAIS data base. You can separately index different files or groups of files, setting up several different WAIS databases on your server. The WAIS databases should be located in the WAIS data directory that was specified when the WAIS server was invoked.

waisindex creates an inverted file index, referencing every word in the designated files. This allows keyword searching on the full text of documents. **waisindex** takes several options followed by the name of the file, group of files, or directory to be indexed as the last argument. With the **-d** option you can specify a name for the index. **waisindex** creates several index files for a document that are used to manage the index. Each will have its own extension indicating its function, but all will have the index name specified by the **-d** option as the prefix. If you do not specify a name, the term "index" will be used as the prefix. Also, if you want to have your database accessible to other users on the Internet, you have to add the **-export**

option. Without this option, your database is accessible only to other users on your system. The **-export** option is discussed in the next section. The **waisindex** options and the index files are listed in Table 12-14.

```
waisindex -d index-file -export file-list
```

If you list more than one file to be indexed, all those files will be referenced by the single index. If you want to index all the files in a subdirectory, you use the **-r** option followed by the directory name.

```
waisindex -d index-file -export -r directory-name
```

To add a file or directory to an existing database, you index it with the **-a** option. You also have to use the **-d** option and the database name to add the indexing of this file to that database. You can add several files by listing them on the command line. If you want to add a directory of files, you have to use the **-r** option followed by the directory name.

```
waisindex -d index-file -a -export file-list
```

In the next examples, the user first indexes the files **cookies** and **cakes**, creating an index called **recipes** for that group of files. Queries on **recipes** will search both **cookies** and **cakes**. In the next example, the user indexes the **pies** file and adds it to the **recipes** index. The WAIS **recipes** database now includes the files **cookies**, **cakes**, and **pies**. Now the user indexes the **snacks** directory, including all its files as well as files in any of its subdirectories. The name of the index is **junkfood**. In the final example, indexing is carried out again on the **snacks** array, but this time the indexing is added to the **recipes** database. The **junkfood** database still exists and references the **snacks** directory.

```
# waisindex -d recipes -export cookies cakes
# waisindex -d recipes -export -a pies
# waisindex -d junkfood -export -r snacks
# waisindex -d recipes -export -a -r snacks
```

With the **-t** option you are able to index different types of files. You can index images, mailbox files, and even HTML pages, as well as standard text documents. The different document types are listed in Table 12-14. For text documents, you can refine your indexing by specifying the one_line type. If you index by line, WAIS will indicate the line in the document where a keyword is found. In the next example, the user indexes each line of the document **breads** and creates the index, called **cereals**.

```
#  waisindex -d cereals -t one_line breads
```

The **waisindex** command can also associate different types of files with a specified document. For example, if you have image, video, or sound files that you want to associate with a specific text document, you can have **waisindex** link those files together. When a user retrieves the text document, the associated image, video, or sound files will also be retrieved. As the user reads the text she or he can also display a picture or play a sound. Associated files must have the same prefix as the document they are linked to. For example, if you have a document called **train.txt**, you can have a picture of a train in a file called **train.gif** and the sound of a train in **train.midi**. You use the **-M** option and a list of file types with the **-export** option to link a set of files to an index.

```
# waisindex -d train -M text, tiff, mpeg, midi  -export
/user/waisdata/train/*
```

To integrate WAIS with your Web resources, you need to create WAIS indexes for your Web pages. You use **waisindex** with the **-T HTML** option, specifying that the type of document being indexed is an HTML document. The name of the index could be something like **myweb**. This allows WAIS to search Web HTML documents. In the next example, the user indexes Web pages located in the **/home/httpd/html** directory. The name of the index is **myweb** and the type is HTML. The full contents of each Web page are indexed as specified by the **-contents** option. The **-export** option will include hostname information for easy Internet access.

```
# waisindex -d myweb -T HTML  -contents -export -r
/home/httpd/html/*.html
```

Your WAIS Sources

When you index files to make a database accessible, **waisindex** will create a source file for the database—the source file is the means by which other users can reach your database; it provides information such as the name of the database. Some WAIS databases will charge for access, specifying a cost, and the source file will show this information. You will see the address of the maintainer where you can send comments. The source file ends with a short description of the WAIS database.

If you specified the **-export** option when the database was created with **waisindex**, several fields will be added to allow users on other systems access to your database. Two fields for Internet address information are added, one for the IP name and the other for the IP address of your host system. Another field is added to specify the port (usually 210) to be used to access the WAIS database on your computer (the host computer). If you did not use the **-export** option, these fields will be absent. In this case, only users on your system will be able to access the database.

If necessary, you can modify any of the fields in a source file. The entire source is enclosed in parentheses, with each field on a line of its own beginning with a colon and the field name. You can edit the source file and add more to the description. Notice that the description is enclosed in double quotes, with the first quote following the term "description" and the closing quote on a line by itself after the descriptive text. The following example is a source for zipcodes in a file called **zipcodes.src**.

```
(:source
   :version  3
   :ip-address "192.31.181.1"
   :ip-name "quake.think.com"
   :tcp-port 210
   :database-name "/proj/wais/db/sources/zipcodes"
   :cost 0.00
   :cost-unit :free
   :maintainer "wais@quake.think.com"
   :description "
 WAIS index of USA Zip Code database.
 The full Zipcodes file may be obtained via FTP using the URL:
 <ftp://obi.std.com/obi/ZIPCODES/zipcode.txt>
 "
 )
```

Other users use the source file to access its WAIS database. The source file tells a user which host it is located on and what it is called. You can think of it as a URL for WAIS databases. The remote user has to first have the source file in order to access the database. You can either send the source file to a user who then can insert their host's wais-sources directory, or register the source file with a WAIS server that maintains a directory of servers such as **quake.think.com** and **cnidr.org**. Your source will be placed there with other sources. Using a WAIS client such as **swais**, users can access this directory of servers and find your WAIS database listed there. Then they can select and query your database.

You register a database when you create it by including the **-register** option when indexing the files with **waisindex**. You can also wait and register it later, perhaps after you've tested it. Use the **waisindex** command with the **-d** option and the index name, followed by the **-register** option.

```
waisindex -d recipes -register
```

Testing Your WAIS Server

In the freeWAIS-0.5 source code package, there is a directory called **test-wais** that holds a set of test files you can use to test indexing and server access. Within the directory you will find a shell script called **test.waisindex**. If you examine this shell script, you will find several **waisindex** commands, creating several different databases using test files. This creates four test indexes. The test-Bool index tests Boolean search capabilities. The test-Comp index tests the handling of compressed files. The test-Docs index tests recursive searches using the documentation in the **docs** directory, and test-Multi checks the handling of different types of files such as GIF graphics files. (The commands have a preceding **../bin/** path before their name. If you have downloaded WAIS binaries and already installed them, you should remove the preceding **../bin/**.)

You will notice that a source file is created for each test database: a **boolean.src** and a **doc.src**. To locally test your server, copy these source files to the directory that your WAIS clients use for their WAIS sources. For example, if **swais** uses **/usr/lib/wais-sources** as its sources directory, then copy the **test-boolean.src** (source) file to it. Now start your WAIS server either through **inetd** or directly (if you start it up directly, be sure to place an ampersand at the end). Use the path of the **test-wais** directory as your WAIS data directory. When you start up **swais**, it will list all the sources in its source directory, including the test-boolean source and the other test sources. You can then select and query your test sources which will then access your WAIS server and return the results. Try searching on the keyword "boolean". You can also simply move the wais-test directory to your WAIS data directory. To make one overall database you can index wais-test with the **-r** option.

Starting freeWAIS

You can have WAIS run continuously or have it called by **inetd** when needed. To start the WAIS server you use the command **waisserver** with several possible options. You can use the **-d** option to specify the default location of your WAIS indexes. You can also set the port with **-p** or the user name with **-u**. Be sure to add an ampersand at the end of the command. When called directly, **waisserver** has to be run in the background. To run WAIS as a continuous daemon, you should enter the **waisserver** command in an **rc.d/init** initialization file, such as **wais.init**. The following is an example of the **waisserver** command.

```
waisserver -d /usr/wais/wais_index &
```

To provide your WAIS service with more security, it's a good idea to run **waisserver** as a user other then root. Create a user and place a * in its **passwd** entry. Then use the **-u** option with that user name when you start **waisserver**. In the following example, **waisserver** runs as the user **sports**.

```
waisserver -u sports -d /usr/wais/wais_index &
```

To have **inetd** start the WAIS server you must place the appropriate entries in the **/etc/services** and **/etc/inetd.conf** files. For the **/etc/services** file you place the following entry.

```
z3590        210/tcp      # Z39_50 protocol for WAIS
```

Then in the **inetd.conf** file you place the entry to invoke the WAIS server. When **waisserver** is called as **waisserver.d**, it knows it is being run under **inetd**. For this reason, the first argument in the argument list is **waisserver.d**.

```
z3590   stream  tcp  nowait  root  /usr/sbin/waisserver
waisserver.d  /home/wais -e server.log
```

Summary: Internet Servers

You can set up your Linux system to operate as a server for various Internet services. All you need is the appropriate server software and securely organized directories. Server software is freely available for setting up your Linux system as an ftp server, a Web server, a Gopher server, or a WAIS server. OpenLinux automatically installs the Web and ftp server software during installation. With the desktop, you are immediately ready to operate your Linux system as a Web site or an ftp site.

You can have all the different Internet servers running at the same time. They operate as daemons, waiting for requests from remote users. When a request for a particular service is received, the appropriate server processes the request. One remote user could connect to your ftp server and download files, while another could connect to your Web server and view your Web pages. Depending on how often a server is used, you can have it running continuously, or use the **inetd** daemon to call it only when it is needed. To run a server continuously you simply invoke its server program. With **inetd**, you have to place entries in the **/etc/services** and **/etc/inet.conf** files and then run the **inetd** daemon.

The Internet server software is freely available online at different Linux sites. See Chapter 1 for some of these sites. At **sunsite.unc.edu** and its mirror sites, most server software is currently kept in directories located in **/pub/Linux/systems/info-systems**. You should keep this in mind for downloading and installing more current versions in the future. The Caldera Network Desktop currently has installed the Apache Web server and the wa-ftpd ftp server.

Chapter Thirteen

Remote Access

517

Linux provides the ability to access other Linux or Unix systems remotely. You can copy files or execute Linux commands, as well as log in remotely to accounts on those systems. Instead of working through an interface, such as ftp or Gopher, you can execute remote access commands within your own shell that will then perform actions on a remote system.

Remote access commands operate across network connections. There are two different types of network connections that Unix and Linux systems can use, each with its own protocols. The TCP/IP protocols used with the Internet (see Chapter 10) can also be used for local networks. Networks using TCP/IP often have dedicated connections, such as Ethernet connections. The UUCP protocols are an alternative set of protocols that provide network communication between Linux and Unix systems. However, UUCP is an older protocol that was designed to operate between systems that were not already connected on a network. With UUCP, one system can connect to another across phone lines at a predetermined time, sending a batched set of communications all at once. UUCP is very helpful for making a direct connection to a particular system, transferring data, and then cutting the connection. UUCP allows you to set up direct modem-to-modem communication with another system.

TCP/IP and UUCP each has its own set of remote access commands, reflecting the strengths and weaknesses of each. The remote access commands for TCP/IP are referred to as remote or simply **r** commands. Common command names are preceded by an *r* to indicate that their operations are remote. For example, **rcp** is the command to copy a file remotely from one system to another. The **r** commands have the advantage of performing real-time operations. For systems on your network that allow you access, you can copy files and execute commands, and the operations will be carried out immediately. It is very easy, with **r** commands, to copy whole directories from one system to another. However, you can only access systems with connections that support TCP/IP, such as Ethernet, CSLIP, or PPP.

With UUCP you can dial across regular phone lines into any system that will permit you access. UUCP operates in batches. Users on a system submit their requests for copying files or executing commands on a remote system. Those requests are then gathered together and sent all at once when a connection is made to the remote system. The remote system receives the requests, executes them, and then makes another connection to your system to send back responses. Some requests may be to copy files from the remote system to your own. In this case, those files will be sent by the remote system to yours when it responds. Needless to say, execution of remote operations can be very time-consuming with UUCP. A user has to wait for the system to send the request, and then for the remote system to respond.

TCP/IP Remote Access Operations: rwho, rlogin, rcp, and rsh

The TCP/IP network communications package makes use of remote access commands first developed at UC Berkeley for Arpanet. They allow you to log in remotely to another account on another system and to copy files from one system to another. You can also obtain information about another system, such as who is currently logged on. When a system address is called for, these remote access commands use domain name or IP addressing. Domain addressing was originally designed for use on Arpanet, as were the TCP/IP remote access commands. The TCP/IP remote access commands are listed in Table 13-1.

Many of the TCP/IP commands have comparable network communication utilities used for the Internet. For example, the TCP/IP command **rlogin**, which remotely logs into a system, is similar to telnet. The **rcp** command, which remotely copies files, performs much the same function as ftp. The TCP/IP commands differ in the ease of use and control they provide to users. You easily access other accounts you may have on different Unix or Linux systems, and you can control access by other users to your account without having to give out your password. In effect, you can provide a kind of group permissions to your account for different users.

TCP/IP Network System Information: rwho, ruptime, and ping

There are several TCP/IP commands that you can use to obtain information about different systems on your network. You can find out who is logged in, get information about a user on another system, or find out if a system is up and running. For example, the **rwho** command functions in the same way as the **who** command. It displays all the users currently logged into each system in your network.

```
$ rwho
violet      robert:tty1     Sept 10 10:34
garnet      chris:tty2      Sept 10 09:22
```

The **ruptime** command displays information about each system on your network. The information shows how each system has been performing. **ruptime** shows whether a system is up or down, how long it has been up or down, the number of users on the system, and the average load on the system for the last 5, 10, and 15 minutes.

```
$ ruptime
violet      up      11+04:10,     8 users,   load 1.20 1.10    1.00
garnet      up      11+04:10,    20 users,   load 1.50 1.40    1.30
```

The **ping** command detects whether or not a system is up and running. The **ping** command takes as its argument the name of the system you want to check. The next example checks to see if violet is up and connected to the network.

```
$ ping violet
violet is alive
$
```

If the system you want to check is down, you will get a response like that in the next example. In this case, garnet is down and disconnected from the network.

```
$ ping garnet
no answer from garnet
$
```

Remote Access Permission: .rhosts

You use a **.rhosts** file to control access to your account by users using TCP/IP commands. Users create the **.rhosts** file on their own accounts using a standard editor such as Vi. It must be located in the user's home directory. In the next example, the user displays the contents of a **.rhosts** file.

```
$ cat .rhosts
garnet chris
violet robert
```

The **.rhosts** file is a simple way to allow other people access to your account without giving out your password. To deny access to a user, simply delete the system's name and the user's login name from your **.rhosts** file. If a user's login name and system are in a **.rhosts** file, then that user can directly access that account without knowing the password. This type of access is not necessary for remote login operations to work (you could use a password instead); the **.rhosts** file is required for other remote commands, such as remotely copying files or remotely executing Linux commands. If you want to execute such commands on an account in a remote system, that account must have your login name and system name in its **.rhosts** file.

The type of access **.rhosts** provides allows you to use TCP/IP commands to access other accounts directly that you may have on other systems. You do not have to log into them first. In effect, you can treat your accounts on other systems as extensions of the one you are currently logged into. Using the **rcp** command, you can copy any files from one directory to another no matter what account they are on. With the **rsh** command, you can execute any Linux command you wish on any of your other accounts.

Remote Login: rlogin

It is possible that you could have accounts on different systems in your network, or be permitted to access someone else's account on another system. You could access an account on another system by first logging into your own and then remotely logging in across your network to the account on the other system. You can perform such a remote login using the **rlogin** command. The **rlogin** command takes as its argument a system name. The command will connect you to the other system and begin login procedures.

Login procedures using **rlogin** differ from regular login procedures in that the user is not prompted for a login name. **rlogin** assumes that the login name on your local system is the same as the login name on the remote system. Upon executing the **rlogin** command, you are immediately prompted for a password. After entering the password, you are logged into the account on the remote system.

rlogin assumes the login name is the same because most people use **rlogin** to access accounts they have on other systems with their own login name. However, when the login name on the remote system is different from the one on the local system, the option, **-l** allows you to enter a different login name for the account on the remote system. The syntax is shown here:

```
$ rlogin system-name -l login-name
```

In the next example, the user logs into a system called violet using the login name robert.

```
$ rlogin violet -l robert
password
$
```

Once logged into a remote system, you can execute any command you wish. You can end the connection with either **exit**, CTRL-**d**, **~.**, or **logout** (TCSH or C-shell).

Remote File Copy: rcp

You can use the **rcp** command to copy files to and from remote and local systems. **rcp** is a file transfer utility that operates like the **cp** command, but across a network connection to a remote system. The **rcp** command requires that the remote system have your local system and login name in its **.rhosts** file. The **rcp** command begins with the keyword **rcp** and has as its arguments the source file and copy file names. To specify the file on the remote system, you need to place the system name before the file name, separated by a colon, as shown here:

```
$ rcp system-name:source-file   system-name:copy-file
```

When copying to a remote system, the copy file will be a remote file and require the remote system's name. The source file is one on your own system and does not require a system name:

```
$ rcp source-file   remote-system-name:copy-file
```

In the next example, the user copies the file **weather** from his own system to the remote system violet and renames the file **monday**.

```
$ rcp weather violet:monday
```

When copying a file on the remote system to your own, the source file is a remote file and will require the remote system's name. The copy file will be a file on your own system and does not require a system name:

```
$ rcp remote-system-name:source-file   copy-file
```

In the next example, the user copies the file **wednesday** from the remote system violet to his own system and renames the file **today**.

```
$ rcp violet:wednesday today
```

You can also use **rcp** to copy whole directories to or from a remote system. The **rcp** command with the **-r** option will copy a directory and all its subdirectories from one system to another. Like the **cp** command, **rcp** requires a source and copy directory. The directory on the remote system requires the system name and colon placed before the directory name. When you copy a directory from your own system to a remote system, the copy directory will be on the remote system and requires the remote system's name.

```
$ rcp -r source-directory   remote-system-name:copy-directory
```

In the next example, the user copies the directory **letters** to the directory **oldnotes** on the remote system violet.

```
$ rcp -r letters violet:oldnotes
```

When you copy a directory on a remote system to one on your own system, the source directory is on the remote system and requires the remote system name:

```
$ rcp -r remote-system-name:source-directory  copy-directory
```

In the next example, the user copies the directory **birthdays** on the remote system violet to the directory **party** on his own system.

```
$ rcp -r violet:birthdays party
```

You may, at times, want to use special characters such as asterisks for file name generation, or the dot to reference the current directory. Shell special characters are evaluated by your local system, not by the remote system. If you want a special character to be evaluated by the remote system, you must quote it. To copy all the files with a **.c** extension in the remote system to your own, you will need to use the asterisk special character: ***.c**. You must be careful to quote the asterisk special character. In the next example, the files with a **.c** extension on the violet system are copied to the user's own system. Notice that the asterisk is quoted with a backslash. The dot, indicating the current directory, is not quoted. It will be evaluated to the current directory by the local system.

```
$ rcp violet:\*.c .
```

The next example copies the directory **reports** from the user's own system to the current directory on the remote system. Notice that the dot is quoted. It will be evaluated by the remote system.

```
$ rcp -r reports violet:\.
```

Remote Execution: rsh

At times, you may need to execute a single command on a remote system. The **rsh** command will execute a Linux command on another system and display the results on your own. Your system name and login name must, of course, be in the remote system's **.rhosts** file. The **rsh** command takes two general arguments, a system name and a Linux command. The syntax is as follows:

```
$ rsh remote-system-name  Linux-command
```

In the next example, the **rsh** command executes an **ls** command on the remote system violet to list the files in the **/home/robert** directory on violet.

```
$ rsh violet ls /home/robert
```

Special characters are evaluated by the local system unless quoted. This is particularly true of special characters that control the standard output, such as redirection operators or pipes. The next example lists the files on the remote system and sends them to the standard output on the local system. The redirection operator is evaluated by the local system and redirects the output to **myfiles**, which is a file on the local system.

```
$ rsh violet ls /home/robert > myfiles
```

If you quote a special character, it becomes part of the Linux command evaluated on the remote system. Quoting redirection operators will allow you to perform redirection operations on the remote system. In the next example, the redirection operator is quoted. It becomes part of the Linux command, including its argument, the file name **myfiles**. The **ls** command then generates a list of file names that is redirected on the remote system to a file called **myfiles**, also located on the remote system.

```
$ rsh violet ls /home/robert '>' myfiles
```

The same is true for pipes. The first command shown next prints out the list of files on the local system's printer. The standard output is piped to your own line printer. In the second command, the list of files is printed on the remote system's printer. The pipe is quoted and evaluated by the remote system, piping the standard output to the printer on the remote system.

```
$ rsh violet ls /home/robert | lpr
$ rsh violet ls /home/robert '|' lpr
```

Unix to Unix CoPy: uucp

There are a set of remote commands that you can use with the UUCP to perform operations on other systems. For example, the **uucp** command will copy a file from one system to another. Just as you can access files on your own system, you can also access files on other systems. UUCP commands, however, are subject to the same permission restrictions as your own local commands. Protected files and directories cannot be accessed. Only files and directories with the other user permission set can be accessed.

You can think of UUCP commands as referencing files on other Linux systems through a mail system. These commands are designed to operate using point-to-point communication. It is as if you were using the mail capability of different systems to implement a network. When you issue a UUCP command for a given system, the command is queued and collected with other commands for that same system. The commands are then mailed to that system for execution. Once that system receives the commands and executes them, it mails back any results. Several systems can arrange to receive and send commands to each other, forming a UUCP network. The entire process then depends on each system in the network sending and receiving commands to and from other systems. In this respect, the network is only as strong as its weakest link. On the other hand, it requires no special structure, only the sending and receiving of what are essentially messages.

There are four major UUCP commands: **uuto**, **uupick**, **uucp**, and **uux**. The **uuto** command mails files to other systems, and **uupick** receives those files. These commands are used for sending and receiving large files. The **uucp** command copies files from one system to another. The **uux** command remotely executes a Linux command on another system. Many of the UUCP commands correspond to the TCP/IP remote access commands. **uucp** operates much like **rcp** and **uux** like **rsh**.

Installing and Configuring UUCP

The UUCP package is not automatically installed on your Linux system. For the Caldera Network Desktop you need to mount your Caldera CD-ROM and then either use glint from the root user's desktop or the **rpm** command to install the UUCP package. Alternatively, you can download the package from Linux ftp sites, using **gunzip** to decompress it and then **tar** to install the files. Several versions of Linux UUCP are available. Configuration formats may vary in the different versions, so be sure to consult any included installation instructions. Two of the more popular are Taylor UUCP and HDP UUCP. Taylor UUCP is the version included here.

Once installed, you must configure UUCP. This can be a very complex process. Be sure to consult the documentation on UUCP, such as HOW-TO documents, and even texts on the subject. A simple configuration involves setting the configuration files located in **/usr/lib/uucp**. There are three configuration files: **Permissions**, **Devices**, and **Systems**. The **Permissions** file lists the different systems and the type of access they have to your system, as well as the systems you can access. The **Devices** file lists the modems you use for UUCP communications along with initialization information, such as speed. The **Systems** file lists dial-in and login information for the different Linux or Unix systems you can access, including phone numbers, login names, and passwords.

In the **Permissions** file you list a system you want to interact with along with permissions for that system. That system, in turn, must have a similar entry in its **Permissions** file permitting you access. Permissions are set by assigning values to certain variables. There is a set of variables set for each system, and they are all entered on the same line (you can use \ to escape the newline character if you want to enter them on separate lines). The variables are listed here.

MACHINE	Remote system you wish to access and that allows access from **MACHINE=rose**
LOGNAME	Permissions specified for this login name will apply to the remote system when it accesses yours **LOGNAME=uucp**
COMMANDS	Command that the remote system can execute on your system **COMMANDS=uucp:uux**
READ	Spool directories for holding transmission to be sent on to the remote system **READ=/usr/spool/uucppublic**
WRITE	Spool directories for holding transmissions received from remote system **WRITE=/usr/spool/uucppublic**
SENDFILES	Specifies whether you can send files to the remote system **SENDFILES=yes**
REQUEST	Specifies whether the remote system can request files from your system **SENDFILES=no**

A sample **Permissions** file is shown here. The remote system is called rose. The login name my system uses when accessing rose is uucp. The commands that rose can execute on my system are **uucp** and **uux**. Any transmissions that my system sends to rose are held in the **/usr/spool/uucppublic** directory. Any transmissions that rose sends my system are also placed in **/usr/spool/uucppublic**. My system can send files to rose, but rose cannot ask for files.

/usr/lib/uucp/Permissions

```
LOGNAME=uucp MACHINE=rose \
  READ=/usr/tmp:/usr/spool/uucp/uucppublic \
  WRITE=/usr/tmp:/usr/spool/uucp/uucppublic \
  SENDFILES=yes REQUEST=yes \
  COMMANDS=rmail:rnews:uucp
```

In the **Systems** file there is a separate line for each system's dial-in and login information. The line begins with the remote system name. Then you specify the modem to use. You can enter **Any** to let UUCP choose any available modem. You then specify the modem type, usually **ACU**, which stands for Automatic Calling Unit. Then you enter the modem speed. You can specify a range if you want. The telephone number follows. Then you specify the last few characters of the login prompt, such as **ogin:** followed by the login name. Do the same for the password, **word:** and then the password. A sample entry for the **/usr/lib/uucp/Systems** file is shown here.

```
rose Any  ACU 19200  5555555 "" \r ogin:  richlp word: mypass
```

The **Devices** file lists your modem type, the port it uses, its speed, and a driver file. You can have multiple entries for the same modem specifying different speeds and drivers. The modem type is usually ACU (Automatic Calling Unit), the type for modems that can dial numbers themselves. All modems currentlly made have this type. A sample entry for the **Devices** file follows. The port is cua4, the 4th serial port; the speed is 38400.

```
ACU cua4 - 38400 dialfast
```

UUCP Addressing

A UUCP network usually uses the path form of addressing, which reflects the UUCP point-to-point form of communications. Systems may be connected to other systems at different locations across the country, which in turn may be connected to other systems in other parts of the world. All these systems are not directly connected to each other—one system is connected to another system, which in turn is connected to yet another system, and so on. You can reach a system on the far end of a network by sending a message that is then passed along by intermediately connected systems. If the garnet system is connected to the stan system, for example, which in turn is connected to the bell system, then a user on garnet can reach a user on bell through stan. However, the communication is not made in real-time. A message is actually sent as part of a batched collection of messages that are sent from one system to another, being delivered as they reach their addressed systems.

In a path form of addressing, the system address is placed before the user's login name and separated by an exclamation point. Here is the syntax for path addressing:

```
system!login-name
```

In the next example, the mailx utility sends a message to the user chris on the Linux system called garnet. Chris's address is represented using a path format.

```
$ mailx garnet!chris < mydata
```

Within the C-shell, the path form of addressing requires that a backslash be placed before the exclamation point. The exclamation point by itself in the C-shell denotes the **history** command. The backslash will escape the exclamation point, treating it as an exclamation point character, not as a **history** command. The syntax for a C-shell path address, as well as an example of the C-shell path used in a **mailx** command, are shown here:

```
system\!login-name
> mailx garnet\!chris < mydata
```

In a path form of addressing, the address of a user on another system consists of the intermediate systems you have to go through to get to that user's system. Each intermediate system is written in the address sequentially before the user's system and separated by an exclamation point. If you are on garnet and want to send a message to robert on the bell system, then you have to specify any intermediate systems through which the message is to be sent. In the following example, the intermediate system is stan, giving an address of **stan!bell!robert**. There may be any number of intermediate systems. If, to send a message to aleina at rose, you have to go through three intermediate systems, you must specify those three intermediate systems in the address. In the next examples, messages are sent through intermediate systems to reach a final destination. In the first command, a message is sent to the stan system, which then passes it on to bell where robert is located. In the second command, the message is first sent to lilac, which passes it on to sf. sf then passes it on to rose where aleina is located.

```
$ mailx stan!bell!robert < mydata
$ mailx lilac!sf!rose!aleina < mydata
```

There are often several different intermediate paths of connected systems that you can specify. A network is connected together in many different ways. Some are shorter than others. Finding a correct sequence of systems with which to address a user can become very complicated very fast. The next two commands show two different paths to the same system. The first example travels through three systems before it arrives at rose: lilac, mac, and violet. The second example only travels through one system, sf.

```
$ mailx lilac!mac!violet!rose!aleina < mydata
$ mailx sf!rose!aleina < mydata
```

Connected Systems: uname

In a UUCP network you may be connected to many systems. The command **uname** will list the systems to which a user can remotely connect and perform remote commands such as **uucp** on. In the next example, the **uname** command lists all connected systems.

```
$ uname
garnet
rose
lilac
$
```

The **uname** command with the **-l** option will display the name of your own system.

```
$ uname -l
violet
$
```

The **uname** command generates a list of system names that are sent to the standard output. The list of names may be large, so you may want to save it in a file or print it out, instead of just displaying it on the screen. You can redirect this list of system names to a file to save it, pipe it to a printer to print it out, or filter it through a search filter to detect a specific system name. In the next example, the first command saves the list of system names in a file, the next command prints the list, and the last command uses **grep** to see if a specific system name is in the list.

```
$ uname > syslist
$ uname | lpr
$ uname | grep garnet
garnet
$
```

Making UUCP Connections: uucico and uuxqt

On your Linux system the uucico program handles all your UUCP communications. uucico stands for UUCP Call-In Call-Out. It is a daemon that waits for any incoming UUCP transmission, saving it in the directory **/usr/lib/uucp/uucppublic**. A follow-up program called uuxqt then interprets and executes the operations specified in the transmission. Both uucico and uuxqt are system administration operations that are performed only by the root user.

The uucico program also sends transmissions to other systems. UUCP requests are batched together and then sent by uucico to the next system on its UUCP network. Operations for a specified system will continue to be transmitted from one system to another in the UUCP network, until they reach their intended system.

As the root user, you can use uucico to dial into another system that is waiting for your connection. The program will then make the connection, transmit any **uucp** command requests, and then receive responses and other **uucp** requests from the other system. The syntax for using uucico is as follows:

```
uucico    -options   remote-name
```

Two helpful options are **-r** to suppress an automatic wait time for redialing, and **-x** with the number 9, which sets debugging so you can see the actions uucico is taking. In the next example, the root user makes a connection to the rose system.

```
$ uucico   -r -x 9   rose
```

Mail File Transfer: uuto and uupick

UUCP provides a mail facility for sending large files. The command **uuto** sends files, and the command **uupick** receives files. Together these commands operate much like the **mailx** command. The **uuto** command operates in a batch mode. Your request is queued along with other uuto requests on your system. When your request reaches the top of the queue, your file is sent. If, in the meantime, you change your file, then that changed file will be sent. The **uuto** command has an option that allows you to avoid such a conflict. The **-p** option will immediately copy your file to the system's spool directory and, when the time comes, send that copy. You can then modify the original as much as you wish. The **uuto** command also has a **-m** option that notifies you when the file has been sent. The options for **uuto** are listed in Table 13-2. The syntax for the **uuto** command and its options is shown here:

```
$ uuto filename address
$ uuto -m -p filename address
```

In the next example, the file **mydata** is sent to address marylou at violet.

```
$ uuto mydata violet!marylou
```

You receive files sent to you by the **uuto** command with the **uupick** command. To receive your files, you first enter **uupick** on the command line without arguments. The files received from other systems sent with the **uuto** command are then sequentially displayed. You are first prompted with the name of the first file received. The prompt ends with a question mark waiting for you to reply. You then enter a reply that specifies how you want to dispose of the received file. One common response is **m**, which moves the file into your current directory. To move the file to a specific directory, you can specify a directory path after **m**. Upon pressing ENTER, you are then prompted with the name of the next file received. You then enter a response and, upon pressing ENTER, are prompted with the name of the next file. This continues until you have processed the entire list of files sent to you with the **uuto** command. If you should just press ENTER with no response, then the file remains unreceived and will be prompted for again the next time you execute the **uupick** command. The different **uupick** commands are listed in Table 13-2.

In the next example, the **uupick** command prompts the user for three files received. The first file, **mydata**, is moved to the current directory. The size of the file in blocks is then displayed. The second file, **party**, is moved to the directory **birthdays**. The file **project** is not disposed of. It will be prompted for again the next time the user executes **uupick**.

```
$ uupick
from system violet: file mydata ? m
10 blocks
from system garnet: file party ? m /home/chris/birthdays
2 blocks
from system violet: file project ?
$
```

You may want to check on whether you received any files from someone on a specific system. The **uupick -s** option followed by a system name will prompt you only for files received from that system. In the next example, **uupick** will prompt only for those files received from violet.

```
$ uupick -s violet
```

Direct File Copy: uucp and uustat

Whereas the **uuto** command sends files from one account to another, the **uucp** command copies a file directly from one user's directory to another user's directory. With **uucp** it is as if the different accounts are only different directories on other systems, directories to which you have access. Like **cp**, **uucp** takes two arguments: the name of the source file and the name of the copy.

```
$ uucp source-file copy-file
```

You can use **uucp** to copy files from your directory to one on another system, or to copy a file on another system to your own directory. In either instance the copy name or the source name will include the name of the other system as well as the full path name of the file. In the next example, the file **mydata** is copied to the directory **george** on the violet system.

```
$ uucp mydata violet!/home/george/mydata
```

The **uucp** command operates in a batch mode in the background. Your **uucp** request is queued, and when it reaches the top of the queue, your file is copied. If you change your file in the meantime, then the current changed version is copied. You can overcome this conflict with the **-C** option. With the **-C** option, the file is copied to the system spool directory when you issue the **uucp** command. Then when it is time to actually perform the copy, the system uses the version in the spool directory. The different **uucp** options are listed in Table 13-2. In the next example, the **mydata** file will be copied to the spool directory and that version used in the **uucp** operation.

```
$ uucp -C mydata violet!/home/george/mydata
```

If the directory that you may designate in your **uucp** command does not actually exist in the remote user's file system, the **uucp** command will create it. However, the remote user may not want you creating such a directory in his or her system. In that case you can use the **-f** option, which will instruct **uucp** not to create a directory if it does not already exist. In the next example, the user copies a file to the **birthday** directory in george's home directory. In the first **uucp** command, the **birthday** directory will be created if it does not already exist. In the second **uucp** command, the **birthday** directory will not be created.

```
$ uucp party violet!/home/george/birthday/party
```

```
$ uucp -f party violet!/home/ george /birthday/party
```

There may be times when you only know the user's name, not the user's full path name beginning from the root. Yet, you need to specify the full path name of the file on the other system in order to reference it in a **uucp** command. You can use the UUCP tilde operator to find the full path name of that user. The tilde, **~**, takes as its argument a user name and evaluates to the full path name of that user's home directory. For example, **~george** evaluates to **/home/george**. You can then use the tilde and the user name as part of a path name, to provide you with a full path name for a file. In the next example, the tilde is used to specify a full path name, first for **mydata** and then for **party**. The second command copies the file **party** on the violet system to the user's own directory.

```
$ uucp mydata violet!~george/mydata
$ uucp violet!~george/party party
```

With **uucp**, you can also copy files from one remote system to another remote system. The next example copies **mydata** from a directory on violet to a directory on garnet.

```
$ uucp violet!~george/mydata  garnet!~robert/mydata
```

Remember that **uucp** commands are executed in batch mode. They may take some time to perform their task. The command **uustat** lists information about current **uucp** operations. With the **-u** option, you can display **uucp** jobs for a specific user. With the **-s** option, you can display jobs for a specific system. The next example displays the **uucp** jobs for robert that were directed to the system garnet.

```
$ uustat -urobert -sgarnet
```

You can also use **uustat** to kill **uucp** jobs. **uustat** will list the job number of each **uucp** job in progress. Add a **-k** option and the job ID to kill the **uucp** job.

```
$ uustat -k 795
```

Remote Execution: uux

With the **uux** command, you can remotely execute a command on files on other systems. In a **uux** command, files and commands are referenced using their paths. For example, **violet!~robert/filmdata** refers to the **filmdata** file in robert's home directory on the violet system. Commands and files on your own system are referenced with a preceding exclamation point, **!**, with no system name. **!mydata** refers to the **mydata** file on your own system. The same rule is applied to the command to be executed. To execute a command on your own system, you precede it with a single exclamation point. In the next example, the file **filmdata** in robert's home directory is displayed on the user's own terminal.

```
$ uux !cat violet!~robert/filmdata
```

In a **uux** command, you need to quote special characters, such as those used for redirection and pipes (**>**, **<**, **|**), in order to avoid their evaluation by your shell. You can quote them individually or place the entire command within quotes. In the next example, the **cat** command copies files and then pipes them to the printer.

```
$ uux '!cat violet!~george/party garnet!~robert/food | lpr'
```

If you want to use a command on a remote system, you need to precede it with its system path. For example, suppose you want to print a file on a remote system's printer instead of your own. You then precede the **lpr** command with the system's path. In the next example, the user prints the file **filmdata** on the remote system's printer.

```
$ uux "!cat violet!~robert/filmdata | violet!lpr"
```

Like **uucp** commands, **uux** commands are not executed right away. They are placed on a queue and executed when they reach the head of the queue. In the meantime, you may have changed some of the files your **uux** command operates on. In that case the changed files are operated on. As in the **uucp** command, you can avoid this conflict by using the **uux** command with the **-C** option. This option makes an immediate copy of the files involved and then operates on those copies when it is time to execute. A list of **uux** options is provided in Table 13-2.

Each particular Linux system will often restrict the commands that can be executed with **uux**. Commands such as **rm**, which erases files, are usually not allowed. The commands that can be executed with **uux** on a given system are listed in the permissions file, **/usr/lib/uucp/Permissions**.

Summary: Remote Access

You can access remote systems across a network using the remote commands for either the TCP/IP or UUCP network protocols. The TCP/IP remote commands allow you to log in remotely to accounts on other systems. You can also copy files and execute Linux commands on those systems. However, for your remote commands to work on a remote system, you must first be given access by that remote system. To provide such access, the remote system needs to have a **.rhosts** file that lists your system name and login name.

The UUCP protocol is an alternative to TCP/IP. It is simpler in design and use. It lacks some of the powerful features of a TCP/IP network, but is easier to implement. UUCP networks use a path form of addressing. One system may be connected to another system through several intervening systems. There are UUCP remote commands for sending files, copying files to and from remote systems, remotely executing commands, and remotely logging into other systems.

Command	Effect
rwho	Displays all users logged into systems in your network
ruptime	Displays information about each system on your network
ping	Detects whether a system is up and running
Remote Commands	
rlogin *system-name*	Allows you to log in remotely to an account on another system $ **rlogin violet**
-l	Allows you to specify the login name of the account $ **rlogin violet -l robert**

Table 13-1. *TCP/IP Remote Access Commands and Their Options*

Command	Effect
-x	Turns on DES encryption for all data transmitted
-d	Turns on socket debugging
-e	Sets escape character for **rlogin** session; by default escape is ~ character
-E	Prevents any character from being interpreted as an escape character
-8	Allows for 8-bit data path to permit special codes to be transmitted
-k *realm*	Obtains Kerberos tickets for the remote host in the specified realm instead of the remote host's realm
Remote Commands	
rcp *sys-name:file1* *sys-name:file2*	Allows you to copy a file from an account on one system to an account on another system; if no system name is given, the current system is assumed $ **rcp mydata violet:newdata**
-r	With the **-r** option, allows you to copy directories instead of just files $ **rcp -r newdocs violet:edition**
-p	Preserves the modification times and modes of source files
-d	Turns on socket debugging
-x	Turns on DES encryption for all data transmitted
-k *realm*	Obtains Kerberos tickets for the remote host in the specified realm instead of the remote host's realm
-K	Turns off Kerberos authentication

Table 13-1. *TCP/IP Remote Access Commands and Their Options* (continued)

Command	Effect/Description
uucico *options remote-system*	Dials into and connects to a remote system; this is a systems administration action performed only as the root user $ **uucico -r -x rose**
-r	Starts in master mode (calls out to a system); implied
-s *system*	If no system is specified, calls any system for which work is waiting to be done
-r0 -s slave	Starts in slave mode; this is the default
-f	Ignores any required wait for any systems to be called
-l, -p	Prompts for login name and password using "login: " and "password:"
-p *port*	Specifies port to call out on or listen to
-c	Calls named system only if there is work for that system
-x *type*	Turns on debugging type; the number 9 turns on all types. Types are: abnormal, chat, handshake, uucp-proto, proto, port, config, spooldir, execute, incoming, outgoing. Debug information is placed in **/usr/spool/uucp/Debug**
uuxqt	Program called by uucico to execute **uux** requests
uname	Lists the systems to which yours is connected
uuto *filename address*	Mail command for sending large files to another system $ **uuto mydata violet!aleina**
-m	Notifies sender when file was sent
-p	Copies file to spool directory and sends the copy
uupick	Mail command that receives files sent to you using **uuto**; you are sequentially prompted for each file
uupick	
m *dir*	Moves file received to your directory

Table 13-2.   *UUCP Commands and Options*

Command	Effect/Description
a *dir*	Moves all files received to your directory
d	Deletes the file received
p	Displays the file received
ENTER	Leaves file waiting
q	Quits **uupick**
*	Lists **uupick** commands
! *cmd*	Executes a Linux command, escaping to your shell
uucp *sys-name* **!** *filename* *sys-name* **!** *filename*	Copies files from one system to another $ **uucp mydata violet!robert/newdata**
-m	Notifies the user when a **uucp** job is completed
-n *user*	Notifies the remote user when a **uucp** job is performed
-C	Copies file to spool directory and sends that copy
-c	Does not copy file to spool directory (default)
-f	Does not create destination directories
-g	Specifies grade of service (high, medium, low)
uustat	Lists current **uucp** jobs; with the **-k** option and the job number, you can delete a **uucp** job
-a	Lists all jobs for all users
-u *user*	Lists all jobs for specific user
-s *system*	Lists all jobs for specific system
-k *jobid*	Kills a **uucp** job
-c	The queue time for a job
uux	Remotely executes a command on another system; file names and command name must be preceded with an exclamation point
-z	Notifies user the job is successful
-n	Suppresses notification of job's success

Table 13-2. *UUCP Commands and Options (continued)*

Command	Effect/Description
-C	Copies file to spool directory and sends that copy
-c	Does not copy file to spool directory (default)
-g	Specifies grade of service (high, medium, low)
cu	Remotely logs into an account on another system (call Unix)
-s	Specifies baud rate (transmission speed), such as 1200, 2400, 4800, 9600, 38400, etc.
-c	Selects local area network to be used
-l	Selects communications line to be used
-e	Sets even parity
-o	Sets odd parity
-h	Sets half-duplex
-n	Prompts for telephone number instead of entering it on the command line
~!	Temporarily returns to local system $ **~[garnet]!**
exit	Ends use of local system and returns to remote
~%	A one-command escape to local system $ **~[garnet]% cd newdocs**
~% take *remote-file*	Copies a file from remote system to local system $ **~[garnet]% take mydata**
~% put *remote-file*	Copies a file from local system to remote system $ **~[garnet]% put party**
ct	Remotely connects from your system to a terminal through an auto-answer modem (connect terminal); takes as an argument a telephone number of the terminal; has several options for specifying transmission features, such as baud rate and parity $ **ct 6427400**

Table 13-2. *UUCP Commands and Options* (continued)

Command	Effect/Description
-s	Baud rate $ **ct -s1200 6427400**

Table 13-2. *UUCP Commands and Options* (continued)

PART FOUR

Shells

Chapter Fourteen

Filters and Regular Expressions

One of the more popular innovations of Unix that was carried over to Linux is the filter. Filters are commands that read data, perform operations on that data, and then send the results to the standard output. Filters generate different kinds of output, depending on their task. Some filters only generate information about the input, other filters output selected parts of the input, and still other filters output an entire version of the input, but in a modified way. Some filters are limited to one of these, while others have options that specify one or the other. You can think of a filter as operating on a stream of data, receiving data and generating modified output. As data is passed through the filter, it is analyzed, screened, or modified.

The data stream input to a filter consists of a sequence of bytes that can be received from files, devices, or the output of other commands or filters. The filter operates on the data stream but does not modify the source of the data. If a filter receives input from a file, the file itself is not modified. Only its data is read and fed into the filter.

The output of a filter is usually sent to the standard output. It can then be redirected to another file or device, or piped as input to another utility or filter. All the features of redirection and pipes apply to filters. Often data will be read by one filter and its modified output piped into another filter. Data could easily undergo several modifications as it is passed from one filter to another. However, it is always important to realize that the original source of the data is never changed.

Many utilities and filters use patterns to locate and select specific text in your file. Sometimes, you may need to use patterns in a more flexible and powerful way, searching for several different variations on a given pattern. There is a set of special characters that you can include in your pattern to enable a flexible search. A pattern that contains such special characters is called a *regular expression*. Regular expressions can be used in most filters and utilities that employ pattern searches such as Ed, **sed**, **awk**, **grep**, and **egrep**. Though many of the special characters used for regular expressions are similar to the shell special characters, they are used in a different way. Shell special characters operate on file names. Regular expressions search text.

This book organizes filters into three general categories: file filters, editing filters, and data filters. This chapter presents file and editing filters. You can find discussions of data filters in most Unix books. Detailed tables of all filters are provided at the end of this chapter that include the data filters. First you will see how filters operate using redirection and pipes and look at different types of output that filters generate. Then the editing filters will be discussed, followed by an examination of regular expressions.

Using Redirection and Pipes with Filters: cat, tee, head, and tail

Filters send their output to the standard output and so, by default, display their output on the screen. The simplest filters merely output the contents of files. You have already seen the **cat** and **tee** commands. What you may not have realized is that **cat** and **tee** are filters. They receive lines of data and output a version of that data. The **cat** filter receives input and copies it out to the standard output, which, by default, is displayed on the screen. The **tee** filter receives input and copies the output both to the standard output and to a specified file. In addition to **cat** and **tee**, two other filters output files: **head** and **tail**. The **head** filter outputs part of the beginning of a file, and **tail** outputs the end of the file.

You can save the output of a filter in a file or send it to a printer. To do so, you need to use redirection or pipes. To save the output of a filter to a file, you redirect it to a file using the redirection operation, >. To send output to the printer, you pipe the output to the **lpr** utility, which will then print it. In the next command, the **cat** command pipes its output to the **lpr** command, which then prints it.

```
$ cat complist | lpr
```

Other commands for displaying files, such as **more**, may seem to operate like a filter, but they are not filters. You need to distinguish between a filter and device-oriented utilities such as **lpr** and **more**. Filters send their output to the standard output. A device-oriented utility such as **lpr**, though it receives input from the standard input, sends its output to a device. In the case of **lpr**, the device is a printer; for **more**, the device is the terminal. Such device-oriented utilities may receive their input from a filter, but they can only output to their device.

All filters accept input from the standard input. In fact, the output of one filter can be piped as the input for another filter. However, many filters also accept input directly from files. Such filters can take file names as their arguments and read data directly from those files. The **cat** and **sort** filters operate in this way. They can receive input from the standard input or use file name arguments to read data directly from files.

If you do not specify a file name when you use **cat**, the **cat** command will take its input from the standard input. Thus, the **cat** command will wait for you to type something in and then read what you have typed as input. You end the standard input with a CTRL-D, the end of file character. **cat** will read this standard input and then output it to the standard output. In the next example, the **cat** command reads input from the standard input, in this case the keyboard, and redirects the output to a file called **mydata**.

```
$ cat > mydata
Hello Marylou
     How are you
today
^D
$
```

One of the more powerful features of **cat** is that it can combine the contents of several files into one output stream. This output can then be piped into a utility or even another filter, allowing the utility or filter to operate on the combined contents of files as one data stream. For example, if you want to view the contents of several files at once, screen by screen, you must first combine them with the **cat** filter and then pipe the combined data into the **more** filter. The **more** command is, then, receiving its input from the standard input. In the following set of examples, the **cat** filter copies the contents of **preface** and **intro** into a combined output. In the first example this output is piped into the **more** command. The **more** filter then allows you to view the combined text, screen by screen. In the second, the output is piped to the printer using the **lpr** command, and in the third, the output is redirected to a file called **frontdata**.

```
$ cat preface intro | more
$ cat preface intro | lpr
$ cat preface intro > frontdata
```

A filter can receive input from a pipe, as well as send output to one. You can pipe the output of a filter or utility into a given filter, which can then pipe output to still another filter. You can even set up a sequence of filters that pipe the output of one as input into another. You could pipe the output of the **cat** filter as input to another filter, instead of a utility. Notice that such a filter would then receive its input from the piped standard input, not from files. For example, suppose you want both to print the output of **cat** and save the output to another file. You can first save the output to a file by using the **tee** filter and then pipe it into the **lpr** utility for printing. **tee** is a filter that copies the standard input to a file and also sends it on to the standard output. Notice that **tee** receives its input from the piped output of the **cat** filter. In the next example, the **tee** filter first saves the output in the **frontcopy** file and then pipes it on to the **lpr** utility.

```
$ cat preface intro | tee frontcopy | lpr
```

Outputting the Beginning and End of a File: head and tail

Suppose that, instead of displaying the entire file, you only want to check the first few lines to see what the file is about. For this you can use another filter, the **head** filter. **head** displays the first few lines of either a file or the standard input. Like many filters, the **head** filter has different options that allow you to control the output. By default, the **head** filter displays the first ten lines of a file. You can specify the number of lines you want displayed as an option on the command line. Enter a dash followed by the number of lines that you want displayed. In the next example, first **cat** is used to output the **preface** file, and then the first three lines of the file are displayed, using **head**.

```
$ cat preface
A text file in Unix
consists of a stream of
characters.  An editor can
be used to create such
text files, changing or
adding to the character
data in the file.
$ head -3 preface
A text file in Unix
consists of a stream of
characters.  An editor can
```

If, instead, you want to see just the end of a file, you can use yet another filter—the **tail** filter. By default, **tail** displays the last ten lines of a file. As with the **head** filter, using a dash followed by a number specifies how many lines you want displayed. In the next example, the last three lines of the **preface** file are displayed.

```
$ tail -3 preface
text files, changing or
adding to the character
data in the file.
```

tail reads in data and outputs a filtered version of it, in this case, the last few lines of the data. Just as with **cat**, you can pipe the output of **tail** or **head** to the printer or redirect it to a file. In the next example, the **tail** filter pipes the last five lines of the **preface** file to the printer.

```
$ tail -5 preface | lpr
```

Types of Filter Output: wc, spell, and sort

The output of a filter may be a modified copy of the input, selected parts of the input, or simply some information about the input. Some filters are limited to one of these, while others have options that specify one or the other. The **wc**, **spell**, and **sort** filters illustrate all three kinds of output. The **wc** filter merely prints out counts of the number of lines, words, and characters in a file. The **spell** filter selects misspelled words and outputs only those words. The **sort** command outputs a complete version of the input, but in sorted order. These three filters are listed in Table 14-1 with their more commonly used options.

Counting Words: wc

The **wc** filter takes as its input a data stream, which is usually data read from a file. It then counts the number of lines, words, and characters (including the newline character, found at the end of a line) in the file and simply outputs these counts. In the next example, the **wc** command is used to find the number of lines, words, and characters in the **preface** file.

```
$ wc preface
6      27     142    preface
```

The **wc** command has three options that allow you to output any one of these specific counts: the line count, word count, or character count. With the **-1** option, **wc** counts only the number of lines. The **-w** option allows **wc** to count only words. And with the **-c** option, **wc** counts only characters.

Spell Checking: spell

The **spell** filter checks the spelling of words in its input and outputs only those words that are misspelled.

```
$ spell foodlistsp
soop
vegetebels
```

Using redirection, you can save those words in a file. With a pipe, you can print them out. In the next example, the user saves the misspelled words to a file called **misspell**.

```
$ spell foodlistsp > misspell
```

Remember that you can pipe the output of one filter into another filter, in effect applying the capabilities of several filters to your data. For example, suppose you only want to know how many words are misspelled. You could pipe the output of the **spell** filter into the **wc** filter, which would count the number of misspelled words. In the next example, the words in the **foodlistsp** file are spell-checked, and the list of misspelled words is piped to the **wc** filter. The **wc** filter, with its **-w** option, then counts those words and outputs the count.

```
$ spell preface | wc -w
2
```

Sorting Files: sort

The **sort** filter outputs a sorted version of a file. **sort** is a very useful utility with many different sorting options. These options are primarily designed to operate on files arranged in a database format. In fact, **sort** can be thought of as a powerful data manipulation tool, arranging records in a database-like file. This chapter examines how **sort** can be used to alphabetize a simple list of words.

The **sort** filter sorts, character by character, on a line. If the first character in two lines is the same, then **sort** will sort on the next character in each line. In the next example, the **sort** filter outputs a sorted version of **foodlist**. Notice in the second and third lines that the characters are the same up to the second word. **sort** will then sort starting with the characters in the second words, "vegetables" and "fruit".

```
$ cat foodlist
vegetable soup
fresh vegetables
fresh fruit
lowfat milk

$ sort foodlist
fresh fruit
fresh vegetables
lowfat milk
vegetable soup
```

You can, of course, save the sorted version in a file or send it to the printer. In the next example, the user saves the sorted output in a file called **slist**.

```
$ sort foodlist > slist
```

The **sort** filter can also operate on the standard input. Suppose you want to combine the lines in several files and sort them all as one group. You can use the **cat** filter to combine the lines from files and then pipe these combined lines into the **sort** filter. **sort** will then output a sorted version that includes all the lines. In the next example, the sorted output of **veglist** and **fruitlist** is saved to a file called **clist**.

```
$ cat veglist fruitlist | sort > clist
```

Searching Files: grep and fgrep

The **grep** and **fgrep** filters search the contents of files for a pattern. They then inform you of what file the pattern was found in and print out the lines in which it occurred in each file. Preceding each line is the name of the file the line is in. **grep** can search for only one pattern, whereas **fgrep** can search for more than one pattern at a time. The **grep** and **fgrep** filters, along with their options, are described in Table 14-1.

The **grep** and **fgrep** filters are useful for locating files about certain topics. The patterns can be thought of as keywords that you use to search for files that contain those terms. In the case of **grep**, the searching capabilities are further enhanced by what are called regular expressions (**fgrep** does not allow regular expressions). These are expressions used in the Ed line editor and are discussed later in this chapter.

grep

The **grep** filter takes two types of arguments. The first argument is the pattern to be searched for; the second argument is a list of file names, which are the files to be searched. You enter the file names on the command line after the pattern. You can also use special characters, such as the asterisk, to generate a file list.

```
$ grep pattern filenames-list
```

In the next example, the **grep** command searches the lines in the **preface** file for the pattern "stream".

```
$ grep stream preface
 consists of a stream of
```

If you want to include more than one word in the pattern search, you enclose the words within single quotation marks. This is to quote the spaces between the words in the pattern. Otherwise, the shell would interpret the space as a delimiter or argument on the command line, and **grep** would try to interpret words in the pattern as part of the file list. In the next example, **grep** searches for the pattern "text file".

```
$ grep 'text file' preface
A text file in Unix
text files, changing or
```

If you use more than one file in the file list, **grep** will output the name of the file before the matching line. In the next example, two files, **preface** and **intro**, are searched for the pattern "data". Before each occurrence, the file name is output.

```
$ grep data preface intro
preface: data in the file.
intro: new data
```

As mentioned earlier, you can also use shell special characters to generate a list of files to be searched. In the next example, the asterisk special character is used to generate a list of all files in your directory. This is a simple way of searching all of a directory's files for a pattern.

```
$ grep data *
```

The special characters are often useful for searching a selected set of files. For example, if you want to search all your C program source code files for a particular pattern, you can specify the set of source code files with a ***.c**. Suppose you have an unintended infinite loop in your program and need to locate all instances of iterations. The next example searches only those files with a **.c** extension for the pattern "while" and displays the lines of code that perform iterations.

```
$ grep while *.c
```

The **grep** filter has a set of options that vary its output. You can add line numbers, output just the count of lines with pattern matches, output all the lines that do not have matches instead of those that do, or simply output the names of files in which a match has been made. You can also instruct **grep** to ignore upper and lowercase. These options are listed in Table 14-1.

fgrep

fgrep is faster than **grep** and can quickly search files for more than one pattern at a time. However, unlike **grep**, **fgrep** cannot search for regular expressions. **fgrep** will not evaluate special characters. It can only search explicit patterns.

You can enter the patterns on the command line or, with the **-f** option, you can read them in from a file. On the command line, as in a file, each pattern must be separated by a newline character. The entire pattern list is enclosed in double quotation marks, and each newline character separating each pattern is itself quoted by a backslash. In the next example, the user searches the **preface** file for lines that have either the pattern "editor" or "create". Notice that "editor" and "create" are separated by a newline character, and that the newline character is quoted by a preceding backslash.

```
$ fgrep "editor\
create" perishables
characters. An editor can
be used to create such
```

With the **-f** option, **fgrep** reads the pattern list from a file. The file contains a list of patterns, each on its own line. **fgrep** will search for those patterns in parallel. This strategy is helpful when you have a set of commonly used words that you often need to search for. In the next example, the user has placed the patterns to be searched in the **mypats** file. Then, **fgrep** reads the patterns from **mypats**.

```
$ cat mypats
editor
create

$ fgrep -f mypats preface
```

Editing Filters

In Linux, as in Unix, text files are organized into a series of lines. For this reason, many editors and filters are designed to operate on a text file line by line. The very first Unix editor, Ed, is a line editor whose commands reference and operate on a text file one line at a time. Other editing utilities and filters operate on text much the same way as the Ed line editor. In fact, the Ed editor and other editing filters use the same set of core line editing commands. The editing filters such as **sed** and **diff** use those same line editing commands to edit filter input.

Editing filters perform edit operations on filter input that is read from files or received from the standard input. Like the filters described previously, edit filters receive input, perform operations on it, and generate as output a modified version of the input. In a sense, the data is filtered. An edit filter receives lines of text as its input and performs line editing operations on them, outputting a modified version of the text.

There are three major edit filters: **tr**, which translates characters; **diff**, which outputs editing information about two files; and **sed**, which performs line editing operations on the input. As a filter, **sed** makes no modifications to any file. Instead, it generates an edited version of the file. The **diff** filter provides editing information in the form of line editing operations. It shows what line editing commands need to be performed in order to make one file the same as the other. The line editing operations themselves show how the two files are different.

The Stream Editor: sed

The **sed** filter performs line editing operations on input that is either read from files or received from the standard input. The name **sed** stands for stream editor. A **sed** command takes as its arguments a line editing operation and a file list. The **sed** command generates an edited version of the files in the file list and sends it to the standard output. The files are not themselves changed. All lines in the files are output whether they have been edited or not. In this sense, **sed** generates a complete, though edited, copy of the input files.

```
$ sed 'edit-command' file-list
```

The **sed** editor has a set of editing commands that are the same as those in the Ed line editor. The line editing command is placed within single quotes to prevent any special characters from being evaluated by the shell. The **sed** editing commands are listed in Table 14-2. In the next example, an edited version of **preface** is generated by the **sed** command. The editing command **3 d** is the same as the Ed line editing command to delete line 3. The **sed** line editor command will modify the output by deleting the third line.

```
$ sed '3 d' preface
A text file in Unix
consists of a stream of
be used to create such
text files, changing or
adding to the character
data in the file.
```

As in Ed, a **sed** editing command is a single letter. The **sed** command for deleting a line is the letter **d**. The **a** command appends text after a selected line. The **n** command outputs lines with line numbers. The **i** command inserts text before the line. The **c** command replaces the selected line or lines with new text. And the **s** command replaces the selected text on a line. All of these operate in the same way as their counterparts in the Ed line editor.

One of the more common line editing operations is pattern substitution. Like the Ed substitution command, the **sed** substitution command consists of an **s** followed by a pattern and replacement text. The substitution command substitutes the matched pattern in a line with replacement text.

```
$ sed 's/create/generate/' preface
A text file in Unix
```

> consists of a stream of
> characters. An editor can
> be used to **generate** such
> text files, changing or
> adding to the character
> data in the file.

The **sed** command can execute several editor commands at the same time. You can either enter the editing commands on the command line or place them in a file to be read by **sed**. The **-e** option allows you to enter more than one editing command on the command line. Each editing command must have the **-e** option placed before it. The **-f** option allows a set of editing commands to be read from a file. The **-f** option is followed by the name of the file that contains the editing command. **sed** will then read a set of Ed line editor commands from that file. In the next example, the editing commands are read from the file **myed**.

```
$ sed -f myed preface

$ cat myed
1d
s/create/generate/g
```

Though many of the **sed** editing commands are the same as those found in the Ed line editor, those commands that require more than one line to execute need to be read in from a file. Commands such as the **a** command, which appends text after a selected line, require that you enter more than one line. The first line is the **a** command and the following lines are the text to be added. When you do so, you need to quote the newline character at the end of each line. Doing so prevents the shell from interpreting that particular character as the end of a Linux command.

The **sed** command receives input as a stream of data. It can read this input stream either from the standard input or from files. If no files are specified for the **sed** command, then input is taken from the standard input. Line numbers will reference the place of a line in the input stream, whether the input comes from a file or the standard input. Through the standard input, **sed** can receive data piped in from the output of another Linux operation, or data typed in from the keyboard. Data may also be redirected from a file or a device. In all cases, the **sed** editor is editing a stream of data, and this is where it gets its name.

You could think of the **sed** command as the **cat** command with editing capability. Like **cat**, **sed** can receive input either from the standard input or a file list. If files are listed as arguments to the **sed** command, then input is taken from those files. If no files are listed, then input is taken from the standard input. Like the **cat** command,

sed then outputs a copy of the input to the standard output. However, unlike **cat**, editing operations are first performed on the output. The editing operations are line editing commands specified in the first argument to **sed**. These line editing operations are applied to the output, generating an edited version of the input. The original input, including files listed as arguments to **sed**, are left untouched. Only the standard output has been modified. The standard output may then be redirected by the redirection operation to a file, creating an edited version of the original input. In the next example, the modified output of **sed** is redirected to a file. The file **pfile** then contains an edited version of the **preface** file.

```
$ sed '3 d' preface > pfile
```

Differences and Changes: diff

The **diff** filter compares two files and outputs those lines that are different. **diff** shows you not only what is different in two files, but also how they are different. The **diff** filter outputs line editing information that shows you how the first file can be changed to make it the same as the second. The editing changes that the first file would have to undergo define how it is different from the second file. In this sense, the output of the **diff** command is editing information.

This editing information can be useful to you when you are working on a document and you want to keep track of how the document has changed. You can keep an original version of the document and make changes to a copy of it. To see how your document has changed, use **diff** to compare the original with the current working copy.

diff compares a line in the first file to a line in the second file, one line at a time. It outputs only those lines that are different—in other words, lines that are unique to each file. Those lines unique to the first file are listed with a less-than sign placed before each line. Those lines unique to the second file are listed with a greater-than sign placed before each line. Lines that are the same in both files are not listed.

```
$ diff file1 file2
file1-linenums edit-command file2-linenums
< Differing line in file1
> Differing line in file2
```

Before the lines, **diff** outputs editing information that specifies how the first file must be changed to make it the same as the second file. The first file may need several different types of editing changes at different places in the file. Each change will begin with an editing directive and be followed by the differing lines from one or both of the files. Lines may need to be deleted, added, or changed in order to make the first file the same as the second. The editing directive takes the form of line numbers and three possible editing directives: **a**, **d**, and **c**. An **a** specifies lines that must be added from the second file to the first file. It is the same as the Ed line editing command **a**, which appends input. After the **a** command, **diff** lists the lines from **file2** that need to be added to **file1**.

The **d** command specifies lines that must be deleted from the first file to make it like the second file. It functions in the same way as the Ed line editing command **d**. After the **d** command, **diff** lists the lines in **file1** that need to be deleted. The **c** command indicates lines in the first file that need to be changed to lines in the second file. It is the same as the Ed line editing command **c**, which changes lines. In **diff**, the **c** command reads more like a replacement operation. It indicates the lines in the first file that must be replaced by lines in the second file. After the **c** command, **diff** will list both the lines in the first file that are to be replaced and the lines in the second file that will replace those lines in the first file. Both sets of lines are separated by a dashed line. The following examples list the syntax for each editing directive and the type of output that follows each.

```
f1-linenum a f2-line1, f2-line2          Append lines from
     file2 to after f1-linenum in file1.
> file2 lines


f1-line1, f1-line2 d f1-linenum          Delete the lines in
     file1.
< file1 lines


f1-line1, f1-line2 c f2-line1, f2-line2  Replace lines in file1
     with lines in file2.
< file1 lines
-----------
> file2 lines
```

A line number or a range of line numbers is placed both before and after the editing directive. The line numbers placed before the editing directive reference lines in the first file. Line numbers placed after the editing directive reference lines in the second file. The editing directive is read from left to right and specifies how the first file must be changed to make it like the second file. For example, reading from left to right, the editing directive **5a10,14** specifies that after line 5 in the first file, you need to add lines 10 through 14 from the second file. This modification will make the first file the same as the second file. The editing directive **3d** specifies that line 3 must be deleted from the first file to make it like the second. The command **4,6c9** specifies that lines 4 through 6 in the first file need to be changed to (replaced by) line 9 from the second file.

You could, if you want, save the output of **diff** by redirecting it to a file. In the next example, the user saves the differences between **doc.v1** and **doc.v5** to the file

changes5. If you are dealing with changes to an original document, such a file can constitute a record of changes that you have made so far. In this example, you can think of **doc.v1** as the original document and **doc.v5** as the latest version of the original. **changes5**, then, contains all the changes to the original that were made to obtain the **doc.v5** version. As you make more changes, you can use **diff** to record them. Together, those files containing these changes will show you how you are developing your document.

```
$ diff -b doc.v1 doc.v5 > changes5
```

Regular Expressions

Regular expressions allow you to match possible variations on a pattern, as well as patterns located at different points in the text. You can search for patterns in your text that have different ending or beginning letters, or you can match text that is at the beginning or end of a line. The regular expression special characters are the circumflex, dollar sign, asterisk, period, and brackets: ^, $, *, ., []. The circumflex and dollar sign match on the beginning and end of a line. The asterisk matches repeated characters, the period matches single characters, and the brackets match on classes of characters.

Matching the Beginning and End of a Line: ^, $

To match on patterns at the beginning of a line, you enter the ^ followed immediately by a pattern. The ^ special character makes the beginning of the line an actual part of the pattern to be searched. In the next example, **^consists** matches on the line beginning with the pattern "consists".

```
^consists
consists of a stream of
```

The next example uses the $ special character to match patterns at the end of a line.

```
such$
 be used to create such
```

Matching Any Character: .

The period is a special character that matches any one character. Any character will match a period in your pattern. The pattern **b.d** will find a pattern consisting of three letters. The first letter will be *b*, the third letter will be *d*, and the second letter can be any character. It will match on "bid", "bad", "bed", "b+d", "b d", for example. Notice that the space is a valid character (so is a tab).

For the period special character to have much effect, you should provide it with a context—a beginning and ending pattern. The pattern **b.d** provides a context consisting of the preceding *b* and the following *d*. If you specified **b.** without a *d*, then any pattern beginning with *b* and having at least one more character would match. The pattern would match on "bid", "bath", "bedroom", "bump", as well as "submit", "habit", and "harbor".

You can use as many period special characters in a regular expression as you want. Using several periods side by side allows you to match on a pattern with the same prefixes or suffixes. For example, the pattern **box..** matches on text beginning with "box" and ending with any two characters. It will match on "boxes" and "boxer" as well as "boxed".

You can also combine the period special character with the ^ and **$** to match on the beginning and end of a line. Suppose you have a file whose lines end with file names and you want to match on files that begin with "week" and have only one more character, such as **week1**, **week2**, **weeka**, but not **weekend**. You can use the pattern **week.$** to match on any of those file names.

```
week.$
    reports on week4
    reports on week15      no match
    week1 weather          no match
```

Matching Repeated Characters: *

The asterisk special character, *****, matches on zero or more consecutive instances of a character. The character matched is the one placed before the asterisk in the pattern. You can think of the asterisk as an operator that takes the preceding character as its operand. The asterisk will search for any repeated instances of this character. Here is the syntax of the asterisk special character:

```
c*    matches on zero or more repeated occurrences of whatever
      the character c is:
c cc ccc cccc  and so on.
```

The asterisk comes in handy when you need to replace several consecutive instances of the same character. The next example matches on a pattern beginning with *b* and followed by consecutive instances of the character *o*. This regular expression will match on "boooo", "bo", "boo", and "b".

```
bo*
    book
    born
    booom
    zoom      no match
```

It is necessary to provide a context for the * special character. The * matches zero or more instances of a character. Suppose you want to locate one or more instances of the character *b*. You are looking for the patterns "b", or "bb", or "bbb", and so on, in the text. You may think that the pattern **b*** will do the job. It will not. The * also matches on the zero occurrence of the character. Any other character in the line is preceded by a zero occurrence of the character you are matching on. **b*** matches on *b's* as well as the zero instance that precedes any other character in the line. In effect, the pattern will match on every character in every line. In the next example, the pattern *b** matches on every character. The characters in each line that are not *b* are each preceded by a zero instance of the character *b*. For example, the character *a* is preceded by a zero instance of *b*.

```
b*
    aaaa
    abb
    aabbb
```

To avoid this problem you need to provide a context for the * special character. In this case, the context you need is another *b*. The pattern **bb*** matches on one or more instances of the *b* character. First it matches on "b" and then zero or more consecutive instances of "b". Using the same example, the pattern **bb*** matches only on the sequence of *b's* in the second and third lines:

```
bb*
    aaaa
    abb
    aabbb
```

The **.*** pattern used by itself will match on any character in the line; in fact, it selects the entire line. If you have a context for **.***, you can match different segments of the line. A pattern placed before the **.*** special characters will match the remainder of the line from the occurrence of the pattern. A pattern placed after the **.*** will match the beginning of the line up until the pattern. The **.*** placed between patterns will match any intervening text between those patterns on the line. In the next example, the pattern **.*and** matches everything in the line from the beginning up to and including the letters "and". Then the pattern **and.*** matches everything in the line from and including the letters "and" to the end of the line. Finally, the pattern **/o.*F/** matches all the text between and including the letters *o* and *F*.

```
.*and     Hello to you and to them Farewell

and.*     Hello to you and to them Farewell

o.*F      Hello to you and to them Farewell
```

Because the ***** special character matches zero or more instances of the character, you can provide a context with zero intervening characters. For example, the pattern **I.*t** matches on "It" as well as "Intelligent".

Classes of Characters: [ ]

Suppose that instead of matching on a specific character or allowing a match on any character, you need to match only on a selected set of characters. For example, you might want to match on words ending with an *A* or *H*, as in "seriesA" and "seriesH", but not "seriesB" or "seriesK". If you used a period, you would match on all instances. Instead, you need to specify that *A* and *H* are the only possible matches. You can do so with the brackets special characters.

You use the brackets special characters to match on a set of possible characters. The characters in the set are placed within brackets and listed next to each other. Their order of listing does not matter. You can think of this set of possible characters as defining a class of characters, and characters that fall into this class are matched. You may notice that the brackets operate much like the shell brackets. In the next example, the user searches for a pattern beginning with "doc" and ending with either the letters *a*, *g*, or *N*. It will match on "doca", "docg", or "docN", but not on "docP".

```
doc[agN]
    List of documents
    doca docb
    docg docN docP
```

The brackets special characters are particularly useful for matching on various suffixes or prefixes for a pattern. For example, suppose you need to match on file names that begin with the pattern "week" and have several different suffixes, as in **week1**, **week2**, and so on. To match on just those files with suffixes 2, 4, and 5, you enclose those characters within brackets. In the next example, notice that the pattern **week[245]** matches on **week2** and **week4**, but not on **week1**.

```
week[245]
    week2 weather
    reports on week4
    week1 reports          no match
```

The brackets special characters are also useful for matching on a pattern that begins in either upper or lowercase. Linux distinguishes between upper and lowercase characters. The pattern "computer" is different from the pattern "Computer"; "computer" would not match on the version beginning with an uppercase C. To match on both patterns, you need to use the brackets special characters to specify both c and C as possible first characters in the pattern. Place the uppercase and lowercase versions of the same character within brackets at the beginning of the pattern. For example, the pattern **[Cc]omputer** searches for the pattern "computer" beginning with either an uppercase C or a lowercase c.

Sometimes, you may want to match most instances of a pattern but avoid certain exceptions. These exceptions can be thought of as forming an exclusive class of characters. To match on all characters except an exclusive class of characters, you use the brackets with a circumflex, ^. The circumflex is placed within the brackets and before the characters. Instead of matching on the characters, any characters other than these will be matched. For example, to match on all file names beginning with the pattern "week", except those ending with 5 and 7, you use the following pattern:

```
week[^57]
    week7 weather          no match
    reports on week4
    week5 reports          no match
```

You can specify a range of characters within the brackets with the dash. Characters are ranged according to the character set that is being used. In the ASCII character set, lowercase letters are grouped together. Specifying a range with [a-z] selects all the lowercase letters. In the first example shown next, any lowercase letter will match the pattern. More than one range can be specified by separating the ranges with a comma. The ranges [A-Za-z] selects all alphabetic letters, both upper and lowercase.

```
doc[a-z]        doca docg docN docP
doc[A-Za-z]     doca docg docN docP
```

Using ranges, the pattern **week[14][^12]** can be more accurately rewritten as **week[14][3-9]**. The previous pattern matches on any characters other than 1 or 2, including alphabetic characters. By using the range **[3-9]**, only the numeric characters from 3 to 9 are matched.

```
week[14][3-9]
    week43 weather
reports on week15
    week41 reports           no match
    week4g reports           no match
```

You can combine brackets with other special characters to create highly effective matching patterns. If you combine the brackets with the asterisk, you can match on multiple instances of a specific set of characters. For example, the pattern **doc[123]*** searches for any pattern beginning with "doc" and ending with any combination of the characters 1, 2, or 3. The pattern would search for **doc221** as well as **doc3321311**. To search for any number, use the dash to specify the range 0-9 to select all numbers. The pattern **doc[0-9]*** matches any pattern beginning with "doc" and ending with a number. The pattern will locate **doc582** and **doc7834103**. You can also use the brackets and the asterisk to specify numbers beginning or ending with certain integers. The pattern **23[0-9]*** matches on all numbers beginning with 23, such as 235 or 2378945. The pattern **[0-9]*\.50** matches on any number ending with .50, such as 7.50 or 1000.50.

Using both ranges and the asterisk, you can specify patterns that have certain features. For example, you can match on patterns that are only in uppercase, or patterns that only contain numbers. In such cases, you need to be sure to provide a context for the asterisk special character. Remember that the ***** matches on zero or more instances of a character. To provide a context for a range of characters, simply specify the range again before the one used with the *****. The pattern **[0-9][0-9]*** will match on one or more instances of a numeric character. The pattern **[A-Z][A-Z]*** will match on one or more instances of an uppercase character.

```
[A-Z][A-Z]*     we sold 9645 IBM and DEC components

[0-9][0-9]*     we bought 9645 oranges today
```

Sometimes you may need to combine several special characters in a pattern (see the table here). For example, the pattern **^[^0-9]*** selects all text from the beginning of a line up to the first number. The pattern **[^0-9]*$** selects all text from the end of a line up to the first number.

```
^[^0-9]*        We bought 9645 oranges today

[^0-9]*$        We bought 9645 oranges today
```

Character	Match	Operation
^	Start of a line	References the beginning of a line
$	End of a line	References the end of a line
.	Any character	Matches on any one possible character in a pattern
*	Repeated characters	Matches on repeated characters in a pattern
[ ]	Classses	Matches on classes of characters (a set of characters) in the pattern

grep and Regular Expressions

Though shell special characters allow you to match on file names, regular expressions allow you to match on data within files. Using **grep** with regular expressions, you can locate files and the lines in them that match a specified pattern. You can use special characters in a **grep** pattern, making the pattern a regular expression. **grep** regular expressions use the *, ., and [ ], as well as the ^ and $ special characters.

Suppose that you want to use the long form output of **ls** to display just your directories. One way to do this is to generate a list of all directories in the long form and pipe this list to **grep**, which can then pick out the directory entries. You can do this by using the ^ special character to specify the beginning of a line. Remember that in the long form output of **ls**, the first character indicates the file type. A **d** represents a directory, an **l** represents a symbolic link, and **a** represents a regular file. Using the pattern ^**d**, **grep** will match only on those lines beginning with a *d*.

```
$ ls -l | grep '^d'
drwxr-x---  2  chris 512 Feb 10  04:30  reports
drwxr-x---  2  chris 512 Jan 6  01:20  letters
```

If you only want to list those files that have symbolic links, you can use the pattern ^l:

```
$ ls -l | grep '^l'
lrw-rw-r-- 1  chris  group 4   Feb 14   10:30  lunch
```

Be sure to distinguish between the shell special character and special characters used in the pattern. When you include special characters in your **grep** pattern, you need to quote the pattern. Notice that regular-expression special characters and shell special characters use the same symbols: the asterisk, period, and brackets. If you do not, then any special characters in the pattern will be interpreted by the shell as shell special characters. Without quotes, an asterisk would be used to generate file names rather than being evaluated by **grep** to search for repeated characters. Quoting the pattern guarantees that **grep** will evaluate the special characters as part of a regular expression. In the next example, the asterisk special character is used in the pattern as a regular expression and in the file name list as a shell special character to generate file names. In this case, all files in the current directory will be searched for patterns with zero or more *s*'s after "report".

```
$ grep 'reports*' *
mydata: The report was sitting on his desk.
weather: The weather reports were totally accurate.
```

The brackets match on either a set of characters, a range of characters, or a non-match of those characters. For example, the pattern **doc[abc]** matches on the patterns "doca", "docb", and "docc", but not on "docd". The same pattern can be specified with a range: **doc[a-c]**. However, the pattern **doc[^ab]** will match on any pattern beginning with "doc", but not ending in *a* or *b*. Thus, "docc" will be retrieved but not "doca" or "docb". In the next example, the user finds all lines that reference "doca", "docb", or "docc".

```
$ grep 'doc[abc]' myletter
File letter doca and docb.
We need to redo docc.
```

Full Regular Expressions and Extended Special Characters: |, ( ), +, and ?

Certain Linux utilities such as **egrep** and awk can make use of an extended set of special characters in their patterns. These special characters are |, ( ), +, and ?, and are listed here:

Character	Execution
pattern | *pattern*	Logical OR for searching for alternative patterns
(*pattern*)	Parentheses for grouping patterns
char +	Searches for one or more repetitions of the previous character
char ?	Searches for zero or one instance of the previous character

The **+** and **?** are variations on the ***** special character, whereas **|** and **( )** provide new capabilities. Patterns that can use such special characters are referred to as full regular expressions. The Ed and Ex standard line editors do not have these extended special characters. Only **egrep**, which is discussed here, and awk have extended special characters.

The **+** sign matches one or more instances of a character. For example, **t+** matches at least one or more *t*'s, just as **tt*** does. It will match on "sitting" or "biting", but not "ziing". The **?** matches zero or one instance of a character. For example, **t?** matches on one *t* or no *t*'s, but not "tt". The expression **it?i** will match on "ziing" and "biting" but not "sitting". In the next examples, repeated *n* characters followed by an *e* is searched for. With the **+** special character, the regular expression **an+e** will match on one or more instances of *n* preceded by *a* and followed by *e*. The "ane" is matched in "anew", and "anne" is matched on "canned". In the second example, the regular expression **an?e** searches for zero or one instance of *n* preceded by *a* followed by *e*. Thus "ane" in "anew" is matched, but not the "anne" in "canned".

```
an+e
    anew
    canned

an?e
    anew
    canned      no match
```

The **|** and **( )** special characters operate on pattern segments, rather than just characters. The **|** is a logical OR special character that specifies alternative search patterns within a single regular expression. Though part of the same regular expression, the patterns are searched for as separate patterns. The search pattern **create|stream** will search for either the pattern "create" or "stream".

```
create|stream
  consists of a stream of
  be used to create such
```

egrep combines the capabilities of **grep** and **fgrep**. Like **fgrep**, it can search for several patterns at the same time. Like **grep**, it can evaluate special characters in its patterns and it can search for regular expressions. However, unlike **grep**, it can evaluate extended special characters such as the logical OR operator, **|**. In this respect, **egrep** is the most powerful of the three search filters.

To search for several patterns at once, you can either enter them on the command line separated by a newline character as **fgrep** does, or you can use the logical OR special character in a pattern to specify alternative patterns to be searched for in a file. The patterns are actually part of the same regular expression, but they are searched for as separate patterns. The pattern **create | stream egrep** will search for either the pattern "create" or the pattern "stream".

```
$ egrep 'create|stream' preface
consists of a stream of
 be used to create such
```

Groupings can help you refine the selection of patterns. Suppose you want to list those files that were updated from the hours of 6:00 a.m. to 12:00 p.m. If you only used the classes special characters **[01][6-90-2]**, you would match not only 12 but also 02; not only 06 but also 16. Grouping with the | special character can help you overcome such a problem. The regular expression **(0[6-9] | 1[0-2])** will successfully match only the hours from 6 to 12, as shown in the next example.

```
$ ls -l | egrep '(0[6-9]|1[0-2]):.*$'
-rw-r--r--  1  chris weather 207  Jan 27  10:55  forecast
-rw-rw-r--  1  chris weather 308  Feb 17  12:40  monday
-rw-r--r-x  1  chris medical 789  Feb 06  06:45  roster
-rw-rw-r-x  1  chris weather 942  Feb 12  08:20  storm
```

Summary: Filters

A filter takes, as its input, data from the standard input, examines it, and generates a filtered output. The original data is not affected. There are three general categories of filters: file filters, editing filters, and data filters. File filters perform basic operations such as displaying files and searching files for patterns. Editing filters perform editing operations, and data filters manipulate data fields in files. All can enhance their capabilities by using regular expressions to form powerful pattern matching operations.

Though many filters take file names as their arguments, all can receive data from the standard input. This allows you to pipe data from one filter to another. On a command line, you can specify a series of filters in which the output of one is piped as input to another. In this sense, the same data can be passed through several filters, the output being modified as it is passed along.

Filters generate different kinds of output, depending on their task. Some filters only generate reports, such as the **wc** filter that outputs the number of words in a file. Other filters output selected parts of a file. The **spell** filter outputs only misspelled words. The **head** and **tail** filters output only the beginning and ending lines in a file. The **diff** filter outputs differing lines in a file. Still other filters output an entire version of the input, but in a modified way. The **pr** filter outputs files in a paginated format with headers and page numbers, and the **sort** filter outputs a sorted version of a file.

Most filters have a set of options that allow you to further modify the output. For example, the **pr** filter with the **-n** option outputs text with line numbers. The **tail** filter with a **-** and a number allows you to determine how many lines you want to display.

File Filters

The file filters perform basic operations on files, such as displaying files, comparing files, searching for patterns, generating a formatted version of a file, and backing up files. The **cat**, **head**, and **tail** filters display a file. **cat** displays the entire file, whereas **head** displays the beginning lines of a file, and **tail** displays the last lines of a file. The **tail** filter has several options that allow you to reverse lines or designate how much of the file is displayed.

The **cmp** and **comm** filters compare files. The **cmp** filter performs a character-by-character comparison and outputs the line number and first differing character. The **comm** filter performs more of a line-by-line comparison, outputting lines that are unique to each file and those that are the same.

The **grep** filter searches a file for a particular pattern. You can search several files at a time if you want. **grep** will output the file name and the line number in the file where the pattern is located. **grep** has several different options, one of which, **-n**, will output the line number along with any matched lines.

The **pr** filter outputs a file or files in a paginated format. **pr** has many options, such as designating a header with the **-h** option or setting the page width using the **-w** option. Of particular interest is the ability of **pr** to output line numbers using the **-n** option. Combined with the **-t** option to suppress headers, you can use **-n** to generate a simple text version of your file that has line numbers.

The **cpio** filter allows you to manage backups of your files. With **cpio**, you can copy your files to an archive file and then later extract copies. **cpio** does not directly access and archive files but makes use of redirection to read from and save to an archive file. The **cpio** filter has two major options: the **-i** option for archiving files and the **-o** option for extracting files. You can also back up directories to an archive file. But if you do so, you need to use the **find** command to first generate full path names of all the files in your directories.

Edit Filters

Linux text files are organized and referenced as a series of lines by many editing utilities such as line editors and edit filters. A core set of line editing commands are used in all these utilities to perform editing operations on lines of text. Text is referenced line by line, and then line editing commands operate on those lines. A line can be referenced with a line number or a pattern search. A pattern search locates and references the line that contains the pattern. Certain lines can also be referenced using special line references. The **$** references the last line in the file, and the period references the current line. In a line editor, such as Ed, the **+** symbol references the next line and the **-** symbol references the previous line. You can mark a line using the **k** command followed by a single letter, and then reference the marked line using that letter preceded by a single quote.

Having referenced a line or lines, you can execute line editing commands to input lines, delete and replace lines, as well as copy and move lines. If you want to modify specific text within a line, you need to use the substitution command. The substitution command allows you to replace a pattern in a line with other specified text. Notice that a pattern is used both in searches to locate a line and in the substitution command to match text within a line.

The **tr**, **diff**, and **sed** filters perform editing operations on input read from files of the standard input. They are useful for generating a modified version of a text file. The edit filters receive input from files or standard input, and then output an edited form of that input. This output can then be directed to a file or a device such as a printer.

The **sed** filter is actually a stream editor that performs Ed line editing operations on the input, generating an edited form of the input. However, unlike other editors, the **sed** editing commands are, by default, global. You can restrict the application of **sed** editing commands by using line numbers and patterns. A pattern placed before a **sed** editing command restricts it to only those lines with that pattern.

The **diff** filter compares two files and outputs the lines that are different. It specifically outputs editing information, showing how the first file can be changed to become a copy of the second file. The **diff** filter with its **-e** option allows you to output line editing commands that you can then use to make the first file an exact copy of the second.

The **tr** filter will translate characters in the input stream. It can perform several translations at the same time using two character lists. A character from the first list is translated into a corresponding character in the second list. The **tr** filter also has options that allow you to delete characters or replace multiple instances of characters. One common use of **tr** is the simple encryption of files.

Regular Expressions

Searching text sometimes requires a more powerful and flexible pattern matching capability. Many of the utilities that have editing capabilities use a standard set of special characters designed for use in patterns that search text. A pattern that contains such special characters is called a regular expression. Though some of the special characters are similar to shell special characters, they do not do the same thing. Regular-expression special characters are designed for text searches, whereas shell special characters match and generate file names.

With a regular-expression special character, you can reference the end or beginning of a line (**$** and **^**), repeated instances of a character (*****), or any possible character and any possible class of characters (**.** and **[]**). You will find regular expressions used in many utilities that have editing capabilities. The **sed** and awk utilities make extensive use of regular expressions.

A special character is only special within a pattern. Outside of a pattern it may have a different meaning or simply be a character. For example, the dollar sign, **$**, in the line editor references the last line in a file. Within a pattern, the **$** is a special character referencing the end of a line, **/$/**. In the replacement text of the substitution command, the **$** is simply the dollar sign character.

The replacement text in a substitution command has its own separate set of special characters. They are used to construct the replacement text. If you want to use the character equivalent of a special character in either a pattern search or replacement text, you can quote the special character with a backslash. For example, searching for a pattern that contains a period requires that you quote the period with a backslash: **\.**.

The **grep** filter will perform pattern searches on files and output the lines where a specified pattern occurs. **grep** has numerous options with which you can output line numbers or file names as well as non-matches. There are two variations on the **grep** filter: **fgrep** and **egrep**. As noted in Chapter 8, **fgrep** can search for several matches at once but does not allow special characters in its patterns. **egrep** can also search for several patterns at once but does allow the use of special characters in its patterns. In fact, **egrep** also allows the use of extended special characters such as **|**, **+**, and **?**.

Data Filters

There is a set of filters that perform data operations on an input stream. These data filters, like other filters, operate on a stream of input, receiving data and generating modified output. The data filters are designed to operate on files whose text is organized into fields of data much like a single file database. Each line in the file is a record, and each word in the line constitutes a field in that record. The data filter takes as its input a file containing such records, and it outputs records selected on the basis of a given criteria.

There are five data filters: **sort**, **cut**, **paste**, **join**, and **uniq** (see Table 14-3). The **sort** filter generates a sorted version of the file in which all records are sorted alphabetically according to a specified field. **sort** is also a more general purpose filter that you can use to sort lines in any text file. The **cut** filter outputs all entries for a selected field in a data file. The **paste** filter generates output that combines the records of several data files. The **join** filter generates output that combines the records in two files by comparing the values of specified fields. The **uniq** filter detects fields that have the same values. It allows you to count how many fields have the same values as well as eliminating any repetitions from its output.

Though the data filters cannot perform many of the complex operations found in professional database management software, you will find that they can perform many of the more common operations. You can sort data and selectively display fields. You can also selectively retrieve matching records in different files. You can even combine data filters to form complex queries. For example, you could use the **join** filter to combine selected records from different files and then pipe the output to the **sort** filter to sort the results.

Command	Execution
cat *filenames*	Displays a file. It can take file names for its arguments. It outputs the contents of those files directly to the standard output, which, by default, is the screen
tee *filename*	Copies the standard input to a file while sending it on to the standard output. It is usually used with another filter and allows you to save output to a file while sending the output on to another filter or utility
head *filename*	Displays the first few lines of a file. The default is ten lines, but you can specify the number of lines
tail *filename*	Displays the last lines in a file. The default is ten lines, but you can specify the number of lines **$ tail** *filenames*

Options

−*num*	Displays the number of lines specified by *num* and starting from the end of the file
+*num*	Displays the rest of the text, starting from page *num*

Options

−*c*	Displays by characters. This option is used with either *num* or +*num*, where *num* refers to a number of characters to be displayed
−*l*	Displays by line. This option is used with either *num* or +*num*, where *num* refers to a number of lines to be displayed. This is the default option
−*r*	Displays lines in reverse order. This option is used with either *num* or +*num*, where *num* refers to a number of lines to be displayed in reverse. **+1r** displays the entire file in reverse order
wc *filename*	Counts the number of lines, words, and characters in a file and outputs only that number

Options

c	Counts the number of characters in a file
l	Counts the number of lines in a file

Table 14-1. *File Filters*

Command	Execution
w	Counts the number of words in a file
spell *filename*	Checks the spelling of each word in a file and outputs only the misspelled words
+*filename*	Use this option with **spell** to specify your own user-defined dictionary of words to be searched
sort *filename*	Outputs a sorted version of a file
cmp *filename filename*	Compares two files, character by character, checking for differences. It stops at the first difference it finds and outputs the character position and line number
comm *filename filename*	Compares two files, line by line, and outputs both files according to lines that are similar and different for each
grep *pattern filenames*	Searches files for a pattern and lists any matched lines
Options	
i	Ignores upper and lowercase differences
c	Only outputs a number—the count of the lines with the pattern
Options	
l	Displays the names of the files that contain the matching pattern
n	Outputs the line number along with the text of those lines with the matching pattern
v	Outputs all those lines that do not contain the matching pattern
fgrep *patterns file-list*	Searches files in the file list for several patterns at the same time. It executes much faster than either **grep** or **egrep**; however, **fgrep** cannot interpret special characters. It cannot search for regular expressions
f *filename*	With this option, **fgrep** reads its pattern list from a file called *filename*

Table 14-1.   *File Filters* (continued)

Command	Execution
egrep *pattern file-list*	Searches files in the file list for the occurrence of a pattern. Like **fgrep**, it can read patterns from a file. Like **grep**, it can use regular expressions, interpreting special characters. However, unlike **grep**, it can also interpret extended special characters such as **?**, **|**, and **+**
-f *filename*	With this option, **egrep** reads its pattern list from *filename*
pr	Outputs a paginated version of the input, adding headers, page numbers, and any other specified format
cpio *generated-filenames*	**cpio -o >** *archive-file* **cpio -i** *filenames* < *archive-file*	Copies files to an archive and extracts files from an archive. It has two modes of operation: one using the **-o** option to copy files to an archive, and the other using the **-i** option to extract files from an archive. When copying files to an archive, you need to first generate the list of file names using a command such as **ls** or **find**

Table 14-1. *File Filters (continued)*

Command	Execution
sed *editing-command file-list*	Outputs an edited form of its input. **sed** takes as an argument an editing command and a file list. The editing command is executed on input read from files in the file list. **sed** then outputs an edited version of the files. The editing commands are line editing commands similar to those used for the Ed line editor
Options	
n	With this option, **sed** does not output lines automatically. This option is usually used with the **p** command to output only selected lines
f *filename*	With this option, **sed** reads editing commands *filename*

Table 14-2. *Edit Filters*

Command	Execution
Line Commands	You need to quote any new line characters if you are entering more than one line
Options	
a	Appends text after a line
i	Inserts text before a line
c	Changes text
d	Deletes lines
p	Prints lines
w	Writes lines to a file
r	Reads lines from a file
q	Quits the sed editor before all lines are processed
n	Skips processing to next line
s/*pattern*/*replacement*/	Substitutes matched pattern with replacement text
g **s/***pat*/*rep*/**g**	Global substitution on a line
p **s/***pat*/*rep*/**p**	Outputs the modified line
w **s/***pat*/*rep*/**w** *fname*	Writes the modified line to a file
/*pattern*/	A line can be located and referenced by a pattern
diff *filename filename*	Compares two files and outputs the lines that are different as well as the editing changes needed to make the first file the same as the second file
f1-linenum **a** *f2-line1, f2-line2*	Appends lines from file2 to after f1-linenum in file1
f1-line1, f1-line2 **d** *f1-linenum*	Deletes the lines in file1
f1-line1, f1-line2 **c** *f2-line1, f2-line2*	Replaces lines in file1 with lines in file2
Options	
b	Ignores any trailing or duplicate blanks

Table 14-2.   *Edit Filters (continued)*

Command	Execution
c	Outputs a context for differing lines. Three lines above and below are displayed
e	Outputs a list of Ed editing commands that, when executed, change the first file into an exact copy of the second file
tr *first-character-list* *second-character-list*	Outputs a version of the input in which characters in the first character list that occur in the input are replaced in the output by corresponding characters in the second character list
Options	
[ ]	Specifies a range of characters
d	With this option, tr deletes any charaacter in the character list
c	Replaces those characters not in the character list
s	Replaces multiple instances of characters in the character list with only one corresponding replacement character

Table 14-2.   *Edit Filters* (continued)

Command	Execution
sort *-option file-list*	Sorts the lines it receives as input. You use it to generate a sorted version of a file. You can perform alphabetic sorts, reverse sorts, and numeric sorts
Options	
-o *filename*	Saves the output of **sort** in *filename*. You can use this option to safely overwrite the original input file, giving you a sorted file

Table 14-3.   *Data Filters*

Command	Execution
c	Checks only to see if the file is sorted. If the file is not sorted, **sort** displays an error message; otherwise, it displays nothing
m	Merges previously sorted files
u	Outputs repeated line only once
Sorting Data	
d	Dictionary sort ignores any characters in the character set that are not alphabetic, numbers, or blanks
f	Ignores case
i	Ignores nonprinting characters
M	Sorts months. Fields whose values are the names of the month are sorted
n	Sorts according to the numeric value of a field, not its character value
r	Sorts in reverse order
Sorting Fields	
b	Ignores any leading blanks before a field
+*num*	The number of fields to skip on a line. Sorting begins from the next field. **+2** skips the first two fields and begins sorting on the third field
−*num*	The number of the field where sorting on a line ends. **−3** will stop a sort on a line at the third field
-tc	Specifies a new field delimiter, c. The default is a space
paste -*option file-list*	Joins lines from different files into a new combined output
-ddelimiter-list	Allows you to specify your own delimiter for separating joined lines
cut -*option file-list*	Copies out specified fields or columns in a file. You must always use either the **-f** option or the **-c** option with cut

Table 14-3.   *Data Filters* (continued)

Command	Execution
Options	
-f*num*	Specifies what fields you want copied out of a file. Fields are numbered from 1
-f*num1 , num2*	Specifies fields to be cut out
-f*num1 – num2*	Specifies a range of fields beginning with *num1* and ending with *num2*
-c*num – num*	Allows you to specify columns of characters to be cut out
-d*delimiter-list*	Allows you to specify your own delimiter to look for in a file
join *-option file-list*	Joins the lines of different files if the values of a specified field in each file match
uniq *options input-file output-file*	Eliminates repeated lines from its input. You can also compare lines based on selected fields. Lines whose selected fields have the same values are considered repetitions and can be eliminated from the output
Options	
c	Allows uniq to output each line preceded by the number of times the line occurs in the input
d	With this option, uniq only outputs repeated lines
u	Only outputs lines that are not repeated
-*num*	The number of fields to be skipped for comparison. Only the remaining fields are compared
+*num*	The number of characters to be skipped for comparison

Table 14-3. *Data Filters* (continued)

Chapter Fifteen

The Bourne Again Shell (BASH)

Three different major shells have been developed for Linux: the Bourne Again shell (BASH), the Public Domain Korn shell (PDKSH), and the TCSH shell. Both the BASH and TCSH shells are enhanced versions of their corresponding Unix shells. The BASH shell is an advanced version of the Bourne shell, which includes most of the advanced features developed for the Korn shell and C-shell. TCSH is an enhanced version of the C-shell that was originally developed for BSD versions of Unix. PDKSH is a subset of the Unix Korn shell. Though their Unix counterparts differ greatly, the Linux shells share many of the same features. In Unix, the Bourne shell lacks many capabilities found in the other Unix shells. However, in Linux, the BASH shell incorporates all the advanced features of the Korn shell and C-shell, as well as the TCSH shell.

All three shells are available for your use, though the BASH shell is the default. All examples so far in this book have used the BASH shell. You log into your default shell, but you can change to another shell by entering its name. **tcsh** invokes the TCSH shell, **bash** the BASH shell, and **ksh** the PDKSH shell. You can leave a shell with the CTRL-**d** or **exit** command.

You only need one type of shell to do your work. Chapter 5 discussed features common to all shells, while this chapter and the next discuss the BASH and TCSH shells. This book does not cover the PDKSH shell. PDKSH is a subset of the Korn shell, and most of the advanced features of the Korn shell have already been incorporated into the BASH shell.

Command and File Name Completion

The BASH command line has a built-in feature very similar to the TCSH shell's feature that performs command and file name completion. If you enter an incomplete pattern as a command or file name argument, you can then press TAB to activate the command and file name completion feature, which will complete the pattern. If there is more than one command or file with the same prefix, the shell will simply beep and wait for you to add enough characters to select a unique command or file name. In the next example, the user issues a **cat** command with an incomplete file name. Upon pressing TAB, the system searches for a match and, when it finds one, fills in the file name. The user can then press ENTER to execute the command.

```
$ cat pre tab
$ cat preface
```

The shell can also perform file name completion to list the partially matching files in your current directory. If you press ESC followed by a question mark, ESC **?**, the shell will list all the file names matching the incomplete pattern. In the next example, the ESC **?** after the incomplete file name generates a list of possible file names. The shell then redraws the command line, and you can type in the complete name of the file you want, or type in distinguishing characters and press TAB to have the file name completed.

```
$ ls
document docudrama
$ cat doc escape ?
document
docudrama
$ cat docudrama
```

Command Line Editing

The BASH shell has built-in command line editing capabilities that let you easily modify commands you have entered before executing them. If you make a spelling mistake when entering a command, rather than reentering the entire command, you can use the editing operations to correct the mistake before executing the command. This is particularly helpful for commands that use arguments with lengthy path names.

The command line editing operations are a subset of the Emacs editing commands. You can use CTRL-**f** or the RIGHT ARROW key to move forward a character, the CTRL-**b** or the LEFT ARROW key to move back a character. CTRL-**d** or DEL will delete the character the cursor is on. To add text, you just move the cursor to where you want to insert text and type in the new characters. At any time, you can press ENTER to execute the command. As described in the next section, you can also use the command line editing operations to modify history events—previous commands that you have entered.

History

In the BASH shell, the history utility keeps a record of the most recent commands you have executed. The commands are numbered starting at 1, and there is a limit to the number of commands remembered—the default is 500. The history utility is a kind of short-term memory, keeping track of the most recent commands you have executed. To see the set of your most recent commands, type **history** on the command line and press ENTER. A list of your most recent commands is then displayed, preceded by a number.

```
$ history
1 cp mydata today
2 vi mydata
3 mv mydata reports
```

```
4 cd reports
5 ls
```

Each of these commands is technically referred to as an event. An event describes an action that has been taken—a command that has been executed. The events are numbered according to their sequence of execution. The most recent event has the highest number. Each of these events can be identified by its number or beginning characters in the command.

The history utility lets you reference a former event, placing it on your command line and allowing you to execute it. The easiest way to do this is to use UP ARROW and DOWN ARROW to place history events on your command line one at a time. You do not need to display the list first with **history**. Pressing UP ARROW once will place the last history event on your command line. Pressing it again places the next history event on your command. Pressing DOWN ARROW will place the previous event on the command line.

The BASH shell also has a history event completion operation invoked by the ESC TAB command. Much like standard command line completion, you enter part of the history event that you want. Then you press ESC, followed by TAB. The event that matches the text you have entered will be located and used to complete your command line entry. If more than one history event matches what you have entered, you will hear a beep, and you can then enter more characters to help uniquely identify the event you want.

You can then edit the event displayed on your command line using the command line editing operations. The LEFT ARROW and RIGHT ARROW keys move you along the command line. You can insert text wherever you stop your cursor. With BACKSPACE and DEL, you can delete characters. Once the event is displayed on your command line, you can press ENTER to execute it.

You can also reference and execute history events using the **!** history command. The **!** is followed by a reference that identifies the command. The reference can be either the number of the event or a beginning set of characters in the event. In the next example, the third command in the history list is referenced first by number and then by the beginning characters.

```
$ !3
mv mydata reports
$ !mv
mv mydata reports
```

You can also reference an event using an offset from the end of the list. A negative number will offset from the end of the list to that event, thereby referencing it. In the next example, the fourth command, **cd mydata**, is referenced using a negative offset, and then executed. Remember that you are offsetting from the end of the list, in this case event 5, up toward the beginning of the list, event 1. An offset of 4 beginning from event 5 places you at event 2.

```
$ !-4
vi mydata
```

If no event reference is used, then the last event is assumed. In the next example, the command **!** by itself executes the last command the user executed, in this case, **ls**.

```
$ !
ls
mydata today reports
```

You can also use a pattern to reference an event. The pattern is enclosed with question marks. In the next example, the pattern **?myd?** references the third event, **vi mydata**.

```
> !?myd?
vi mydata
```

History Event Editing

You can also edit any event in the history list before you execute it. In the BASH shell there are two ways to do this. You can use the command line editor capability to reference and edit any event in the history list. You can also use a history **fc** command option to reference an event and edit it with the full Vi editor. Each approach involves two very different editing capabilities. The first is limited to the commands in the command line editor, which edits only a single line with a subset of Emacs commands. However, at the same time, it allows you to reference events easily in the history list. The second approach invokes the standard Vi editor with all of its features, but only for a specified history event.

With the command line editor, not only can you edit the current command, but you can also move to a previous event in the history list to edit and execute it. The CTRL-**p** command then moves you up to the prior event in the list. The CTRL-**n** command will move you down the list. The ESC **<** command moves you to the top of the list, and the ESC **>** command moves you to the bottom. You can even use a pattern to search for a given event. The slash followed by a pattern searches backward in the list, and the question mark followed by a pattern searches forward in the list. The **n** command repeats the search.

Once you have located the event you want to edit, you use the Emacs command line editing commands to edit the line. CTRL-**d** will delete a character. CTRL-**f** and the RIGHT ARROW move you forward a character, and CTRL-**b** or the LEFT ARROW move you back a character. To add text, you position your cursor and type in the characters you want. Table 15-1 lists the different commands for referencing the history list.

If, instead, you want to edit an event using a standard editor, you need to reference the event using the **fc** command and a specific event reference, such as an event number. The editor used is the one specified by the shell as the default editor for the **fc** command. The next example will edit the fourth event, **cd reports**, with the standard editor and then execute the edited event.

```
$ fc 4
```

You can select more than one command at a time to be edited and executed by referencing a range of commands. You select a range of commands by indicating an identifier for the first command followed by an identifier for the last command in the range. An identifier can be the command number or the beginning characters in the command. In the next example, the range of commands 2 through 4 are edited and executed, first using event numbers and then using beginning characters in those events.

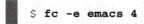

```
$ fc 2 4
$ fc vi c
```

fc uses the default editor specified in the **FCEDIT** special variable. Usually, this is the Vi editor. If you want to use the Emacs editor instead, you use the **-e** option and the term **emacs** when you invoke **fc**. The next example will edit the fourth event, **cd reports**, with the Emacs editor and then execute the edited event.

```
$ fc -e emacs 4
```

Configuring History: HISTFILE and HISTSAVE

The number of events saved by your system is kept in a special system variable called **HISTSIZE**. By default this is usually set to 500. You can change this to another number by simply assigning a new value to **HISTSIZE**. In the next example, the user changes the number of history events saved to 10 by resetting the **HISTSIZE** variable.

```
$ HISTSIZE=10
```

The actual history events are saved in a file whose name is held in a special variable called **HISTFILE**. By default this file is the **.bash_history** file. However, you can change the file in which history events are saved by assigning its name to the **HISTFILE** variable. In the next example, the value of **HISTFILE** is displayed. Then a new file name is assigned to it, **newhist**. History events will then be saved in the **newhist** file.

```
$ echo $HISTFILE
.bash_history
$ HISTFILE="newhist"
$ echo $HISTFILE
newhist
```

Aliases

You use the **alias** command to create another name for a command. The **alias** command operates like a macro that expands to the command it represents. The alias does not literally replace the name of the command; it simply gives another name to that command.

An **alias** command begins with the keyword **alias** and the new name for the command, followed by an equal sign and the command that the alias will reference. There can be no spaces around the equal sign. In the next example, **list** becomes another name for the **ls** command.

```
$ alias list=ls
$ ls
mydata today
$ list
mydata today
$
```

You can also use an alias to substitute for a command and its option. However, you need to enclose both the command and the option within single quotes. Any command that you alias that contains spaces must be enclosed in single quotes. In the next example, the alias **lss** references the **ls** command with its **-s** option, and the alias **lsa** references the **ls** command with the **-F** option. **ls** with the **-s** option lists files and their sizes in blocks, and the **ls** with the **-F** option places a slash before directory names. Notice that single quotes enclose the command and its option.

```
$ alias lss='ls -s'
$ lss
```

```
mydata 14    today  6    reports  1
$ alias lsa='ls -F'
$ lsa
mydata today /reports
$
```

You may often use an alias to include a command name with an argument. If you find yourself executing a command that has an argument with a complex combination of special characters on a regular basis, you may want to alias it. For example, suppose you often list just your source code and object code files—those files ending in either a **.c** or **.o**. You would need to use as an argument for **ls**, a combination of special characters — ***.[co]**. Instead, you could alias **ls** with the ***.[co]** argument, giving it a simple name. In the next example, the user creates an alias called **lsc** for the command **ls*.[co]**.

```
$ alias lsc='ls *.[co]'
$ lsc
main.c main.o lib.c lib.o
```

You can also use the name of a command as an alias. This can be helpful in cases where you should only use a command with a specific option. In the case of the **rm**, **cp**, and **mv** commands, the **-i** option should always be used to ensure that an existing file is not overwritten. Instead of constantly being careful to use the **-i** option each time you use one of these commands, the command name can be aliased to include the option. In the next example, the **rm**, **cp**, and **mv** commands have been aliased to include the **-i** option.

```
$ alias rm='rm -i'
$ alias mv='mv -i'
$ alias cp='cp -i'
```

The **alias** command by itself provides a list of all aliases in effect and their commands. You can remove an alias by using the **unalias** command. In the next example, the user lists the current aliases and then removes the **lsa** alias.

```
$ alias
lsa=ls -F
list=ls
```

```
rm=rm -i
$ unalias lsa
```

Controlling Shell Operations

The BASH shell has several features that allow you to control the way different shell operations work. For example, setting the **noclobber** feature prevents redirection from overwriting files. You can turn these features on and off like a toggle, using the **set** command. The **set** command takes two arguments: an option specifying on or off and the name of the feature. To set a feature on, you use the **-o** option, and to set it off, you use the **+o** option. Here is the basic form:

```
$ set -o feature          turn the feature on
$ set +o feature          turn the feature off
```

Three of the most common features are described here: **ignoreeof**, **noclobber**, and **noglob**. Table 15-2 lists these different features as well as the **set** command.

ignoreeof

Setting **ignoreeof** enables a feature that prevents you from logging out of the user shell with a CTRL-**d**. CTRL-**d** is not only used to log out of the user shell, but also to end user input that is entered directly into the standard input. It is used often for the Mailx program or for utilities such as **cat**. You could easily enter an extra CTRL-**d** in such circumstances and accidentally log yourself out. The **ignoreeof** feature prevents such accidental logouts. In the next example, the **ignoreeof** feature is turned on using the **set** command with the **-o** option. The user can now only log out by entering the **logout** command

```
$ set -o ignoreeof
$ ctrl-d
Use exit to logout
$
```

noclobber

Setting **noclobber** enables a feature that safeguards existing files from redirected output. With the **noclobber** feature, if you redirect output to a file that already exists, the file will not be overwritten with the standard output. The original file will be preserved. There may be situations in which you use, as the name for a file to hold the

redirected output, a name that you have already given to an existing file. The
noclobber feature prevents you from accidentally overwriting your original file. In
the next example, the user sets the **noclobber** feature on and then tries to overwrite
an existing file, **myfile**, using redirection. The system returns an error message.

```
$ set -o noclobber
$ cat preface > myfile
myfile: file exists
$
```

There may be times when you want to overwrite a file with redirected output.
In this case, you can place an exclamation point after the redirection operator. This
will override the **noclobber** feature, replacing the contents of the file with the
standard output.

```
$ cat preface >! myfile
```

noglob

Setting **noglob** enables a feature that disables special characters in the user shell. The
characters *****, **?**, **[]**, and **~** will no longer expand to matched file names. This feature is
helpful if you have special characters as part of the name of a file. In the next example,
the user needs to reference a file that ends with the **?** character, **answers?**. First the
user turns off special characters using the **noglob** feature. Now the question mark on
the command line is taken as part of the file name, not as a special character, and the
user can reference the **answers?** file.

```
$ set -o noglob
$ ls answers?
answers?
```

Environment Variables and Subshells: export

When you log into your account, Linux generates your user shell. Within this shell,
you can issue commands and declare variables. You can also create and execute shell
scripts. However, when you execute a shell script, the system generates a subshell. You
then have two shells, the one you logged into and the one generated for the script.
Within the script shell, you could execute another shell script, which would have its
own shell. When a script has finished execution, its shell terminates and you return to

the shell it was executed from. In this sense you can have many shells, each nested within the other.

Variables that you define within a shell are local to it. If you define a variable in a shell script, then, when the script is run, the variable is defined with that script's shell and is local to it. No other shell can reference it. In a sense, the variable is hidden within its shell.

You can define environment variables in all three major types of shells: BASH, PDKSH, and TCSH shells. However, the strategy used to implement environment variables in the BASH shell is very different from that of the TCSH shell. In the BASH shell, environment variables are exported. That is to say, a copy of an environment variable is made in each subshell. For example, if the myfile variable is exported, a copy is automatically defined in each subshell for you. In the TCSH shell, on the other hand, an environment variable is defined only once and can be directly referenced by any subshell.

In the BASH shell an environment variable can be thought of as a regular variable with added capabilities. To make an environment variable, you apply the **export** command to a variable you have already defined. The **export** command instructs the system to define a copy of that variable for each new shell generated. Each new shell will have its own copy of the environment variable. This process is called exporting variables.

In the next example, the variable myfile is defined in the **dispfile** script. It is then turned into an environment variable using the **export** command. The myfile variable will now be exported to any subshells, such as that generated when **printfile** is executed.

dispfile

```
myfile="List"
export myfile

echo "Displaying $myfile"
pr -t -n $myfile

printfile
```

printfile

```
echo "Printing $myfile"
lpr $myfile &
```

```
$ dispfile
Displaying List
1 screen
2 modem
3 paper
Printing List
$
```

It is a mistake to think of exported environment variables as global variables. A new shell can never reference a variable outside of itself. Instead, a copy of the variable with its value is generated for the new shell. You can think of exported variables as exporting their values to a shell, not themselves. For those familiar with programming structures, exported variables can be thought of as a form of call-by-value.

Configuring Your Login Shell with Special Shell Variables

As noted earlier, when you log into your account, the system generates a shell for you. This shell is referred to as either your login shell or your user shell. When you execute scripts, you are generating subshells of your user shell. You can define variables within your user shell, and you can also define environment variables that can be referenced by any subshells that you generate.

Linux sets up special shell variables that you can use to configure your user shell. Many of these special shell variables are defined by the system when you log in, but you define others yourself.

A reserved set of keywords are used for the names of these special variables. You should not use these keywords as the names of any of your own variable names. The special shell variables are all specified in uppercase letters, making them easy to identify. Special local variables are in lowercase. For example, the keyword **HOME** is used by the system to define the **HOME** variable. **HOME** is a special environment variable that holds the path name of the user's home directory. On the other hand, the keyword **noclobber**, covered earlier in the chapter, is used to define the **noclobber** variable. This special local variable prevents redirection from overwriting files.

Many of the special variables that are automatically defined and assigned initial values by the system when you log in can be changed, if you wish. However, there are some special variables whose values should not be changed. For example, the **HOME** variable holds the path name for your home directory. Commands such as **cd** reference the path name in the **HOME** special variable in order to locate your home directory. Some of the more common of these special variables are described in this section.

Other special variables are defined by the system and given an initial value that you are free to change. To do this, you redefine them and assign a new value. For example, the **PATH** variable is defined by the system and given an initial value; it contains the path names of directories where commands are located. Whenever you execute a command, the shell searches for it in these directories. You can add a new directory to be searched by redefining the **PATH** variable yourself so that it will include the new directory's path name.

There are still other special variables that the system does not define. These are usually optional features, such as the **EXINIT** variable that allows you to set options for the Vi editor. You must define and assign a value to such variables each time you log in. In this sense they can be described as user-defined special variables. These user-defined special variables are further broken down into environment and local variables.

There is no official classification for the three different types of special variables. This text applies a classification of its own, referring to the special variables you should not change as *system-determined* special variables, those you can change as *redefinable* special variables, and those you need to define yourself as *user-defined* special variables.

You can obtain a listing of the currently defined special variables using the **env** command. The **env** command operates like the **set** command, but only lists special variables.

```
$ env
USERNAME=chris
ENV=/home/chris/.bashrc
HISTSIZE=1000
HISTFILE=/home/chris/.bash_history
HISTFILESIZE=1000
HOSTNAME=garnet
LOGNAME=chris
HISTFILESIZE=1000
CDPATH=:$HOME/letters:$HOME/oldletters
MAIL=/var/spool/mail/chris
WWW_HOME=file:/usr/doc/calderadoc-0.80-1/Caldera_Info
TERM=linux
HOSTTYPE=i386
PATH=/sbin:/bin:/usr/sbin:/usr/bin:/usr/X11R6/bin:/home/chris/bin:
HOME=/home/chris
SHELL=/bin/bash
PS1=[\u@\h \W]\$
PS2=>
MAILCHECK=10000
```

```
MAILPATH=/home/mail/chris:/home/chris/projmsgs
CRPATH=/usr/lib/CRiSPlite/macros
OSTYPE=Linux
NNTPSERVER=nntp.ix.netcom.com
EXINIT='set nu ai'
TZ=PST5PDT
SHLVL=1
_=/usr/bin/env
```

You can automatically define redefinable and user-defined special variables using special shell scripts called initialization files. An initialization file is a specially named shell script executed whenever you enter a certain shell. You can edit the initialization file and place in it definitions and assignments for special variables. When you enter the shell, the initialization file will execute these definitions and assignments, effectively initializing special variables with your own values. For example, the BASH shell's **.profile** file is an initialization file that is executed every time you log in. It contains definitions and assignments of special variables. However, the **.profile** file is basically only a shell script, which you can edit with any text editor such as the Vi editor; changing, if you wish, the values assigned to special variables.

In the BASH shell, all the redefinable and user-defined special variables are designed to be environment variables. When you define or redefine a special variable, you also need to export it in order to make it an environment variable. This means that any change you make to a special variable must be accompanied by an **export** command. You shall see that at the end of the login initialization file, **.profile**, there is usually an **export** command for all the special variables defined in it.

System-determined Special Variables

Three of the commonly used system-determined special variables, **HOME**, **LOGNAME**, and **TZ**, are described here. They are defined by the system and available for your use as soon as you log in, and should not be changed. All are environment variables, accessible to any subshells.

HOME

The **HOME** variable contains the path name of your home directory. Your home directory is determined by the system administrator when your account is created. The path name for your home directory is automatically read into your **HOME** variable when you log in. In the next example, the **echo** command displays the contents of the **HOME** variable.

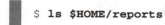

```
$ echo $HOME
/home/chris
```

The **HOME** variable is often used when you need to specify the absolute path name of your home directory. In the next example, the absolute path name of **reports** is specified using **HOME** for the home directory's path.

```
$ ls $HOME/reports
```

LOGNAME

The **LOGNAME** variable holds only your login name, not a path name. A user with the login name chris would have chris as the value of his **LOGNAME** variable. You can use **LOGNAME** in certain situations in which you need to use just your login name. In the next example, the user knows that his mailbox directory will have the same name as his login name. He can either use his login name directly or simply reference it in the **LOGNAME** variable. The **LOGNAME** variable would be preferable if the user should decide to change his or her login name.

```
$ ls /usr/mail/$LOGNAME
```

TZ

The **TZ** variable specifies the time zone that your system is using. It is set by the system when you log in. **TZ** displays its value in three different fields. The first three letters represent the local time zone, the next letter is the number of hours the local time differs from Greenwich mean time, and the last three letters represent the local daylight saving time zone. In the next example, the **TZ** variable holds the value for Pacific standard time, which differs eight hours from Greenwich mean time, and uses Pacific daylight saving time.

```
$ echo $TZ
PST8PDT
```

BASH Shell Redefinable Special Variables

The redefinable special variables hold such information as the location of Linux commands, the location of your mailbox file, and even the symbol used for your prompt. You may modify any one of these variables through simple assignment operations.

Some of the more common of the redefinable special variables are **SHELL**, **PATH**, **PS1**, **PS2**, and **MAIL**. The **SHELL** variable holds the path name of the program for the type of shell that you log into. The **PATH** variable lists the different directories to be searched for a Linux command. The **PS1** and **PS2** variables hold the prompt symbols. The **MAIL** variable holds the path name of your mailbox file.

SHELL

In Linux, any one of the three shells—BASH, PDKSH, or TCSH—can be the type of shell you use when you log in. The **SHELL** variable holds the path name of this shell; in a sense, it is your default shell. The shell programs are held in the **/bin** directory. Here is a listing of the path names for the different shell programs:

BASH shell: /bin/bash
PDKSH shell: /bin/pdksh
TCSH shell: /bin/tcsh

In the next example, the contents of the **SHELL** variable are displayed.

```
$ echo $SHELL
 /bin/sh
```

PATH

The **PATH** variable contains a series of directory paths separated by colons. Each time a command is executed, the paths listed in the **PATH** variable are searched one by one for that command. For example, the **cp** command resides on the system in the directory **/usr/bin**. This directory path is one of the directories listed in the **PATH** variable. Each time you execute the **cp** command, this path is searched and the **cp** command located. The system defines and assigns **PATH** an initial set of path names. In Linux the initial path names are **/usr/bin** and **usr/sbin**.

The shell can execute any executable file, including programs and scripts that you have created. For this reason, the **PATH** variable can also reference your working directory; so if you want to execute one of your own scripts or programs in your working directory, the shell can locate it.

There can be no spaces between the path names in the string. A colon with no path name specified references your working directory. Usually a single colon is placed at the end of the path names as an empty entry specifying your working directory. For example, the path name **/usr/bin:/usr/sbin:** references three directories: **/usr/bin**, **/usr/sbin**, and your current working directory.

```
$ echo $PATH
/usr/bin:/usr/sbin:
```

You can add any new directory path you wish to the **PATH** variable. This can be very useful if you have created several of your own Linux commands using shell scripts. You could place these new shell script commands in a directory you created and then add that directory to the **PATH** list. Then, no matter what directory you are in, you can execute one of your shell scripts. The **PATH** variable will contain the directory for that script, so that directory will be searched each time you issue a command.

You add a directory to the **PATH** variable with a variable assignment. You can execute this assignment directly in your shell. In the next example, the user chris adds a new directory called **mybin** to the **PATH**. Though you could carefully type in the complete path names listed in **PATH** for the assignment, you can also use an evaluation of **PATH**, **$PATH**, in their place. In this example, an evaluation of **HOME** is also used to designate the user's home directory in the new directory's path name. Notice the empty entry between two colons, which specifies the working directory.

```
$ PATH=$PATH:$HOME/mybin
$ export PATH
$ echo $PATH
/usr/bin:/usr/sbin::/home/chris/mybin
```

If you add a directory to **PATH** yourself while you are logged in, the directory would be added only for the duration of your login session. When you log back in, the login initialization file, **.bash_profile**, would again initialize your **PATH** with its original set of directories. The **.bash_profile** file is described in detail a bit later in the chapter. To permanently add a new directory to your **PATH**, you need to edit your **.bash_profile** file and find the assignment for the **PATH** variable. Then you simply insert the directory, preceded by a colon, into the set of path names assigned to **PATH**.

PS1 and PS2

The **PS1** and **PS2** variables contain the primary and secondary prompt symbols, respectively. The primary prompt symbol for the BASH shell is a dollar sign, **$**. You can change the prompt symbol by assigning a new set of characters to the **PS1** variable. In the next example, the shell prompt is changed to the **->** symbol.

```
$ PS1="->"
-> export PS1
->
```

You can change the prompt to be any set of characters, including a string, as shown in the next example.

```
$ PS1="Please enter a command: "
Please enter a command: export PS1
Please enter a command: ls
mydata /reports
Please enter a command:
```

The **PS2** variable holds the secondary prompt symbol, which is used for commands that take several lines to complete. The default secondary prompt is **>**. The added command lines will begin with the secondary prompt instead of the primary prompt. You can change the secondary prompt just as easily as the primary prompt, as shown here:

```
$ PS2="@"
```

Like the TCSH shell, the BASH shell provides you with a predefined set of codes that you can use to configure your prompt. With them you can make the time, your user name, or your directory path name a part of your prompt. You can even have your prompt display the history event number of the current command you are about to enter. Each code is preceded by a \ symbol. **\w** represents the current working directory, **\t** the time, and **\u** your user name. **\!** will display the next history event number. In the next example, the user adds the current working directory to the prompt.

```
$ PS1="\w $"
/home/dylan $
```

The codes must be included within a quoted string. If there are no quotes, the code characters are not evaluated and are themselves used as the prompt. **PS1=\w** will set the prompt to the characters **\w**, not the working directory. The next example incorporates both the time and the history event number with a new prompt.

```
$ PS1="\t \! ->"
```

The following table lists the codes for configuring your prompt.

\!	Current history number
\$	Use **$** as prompt for all users except the root user, which has the **#** as its prompt.
\d	Current date
\s	Shell currently active
\t	Time of day
\u	User name
\w	Current working directory

MAIL, MAILCHECK, and MAILPATH

The **MAIL** variable has the path name for your mailbox file in which the system places messages that are sent to you. The waiting messages that you read when you invoke Mailx are taken from this file. The mailbox files and the Mailx utility are described in Chapter 8. Though you can change the value of **MAIL**, you would rarely, if ever, do so. The system needs this path name in order to locate your mailbox file.

```
$ echo $MAIL
/var/mail/chris
```

The **MAILCHECK** variable sets the time interval in which you will be notified of new mail. If you are expecting mail and want to be notified as soon as possible when it arrives, you can shorten this time interval. If you do not want to be bothered, you can lengthen it. The default is 10 minutes, or 600 seconds. In the next example, the time interval is set to 1200 seconds (20 minutes).

```
$ MAILCHECK=1200
$ export MAILCHECK
```

The **MAILPATH** variable contains path names of other mailbox files that you may want checked for incoming mail. Unlike **MAIL** and **MAILCHECK**, **MAILPATH** is a user-defined special variable. To use it, you need to define it and assign a value. You would assign **MAILPATH** the path names of any other mailbox files you want checked. In the next example, the user specifies a mailbox file other than the one specified in **MAIL** to be checked for incoming mail.

```
$ MAILPATH=/home/mail/$1OGNAME
$ export MAILPATH
```

BASH Shell User-defined Special Variables

The user-defined special variables in the BASH shell hold information such as your current terminal type or the default configuration for your Vi editor. Many variables such as **TERM** and **CDPATH** enhance shell operations. Others are designed to work with special utilities. For example, the **EXINIT** variable configures the Vi and Ex editors. Both the redefinable and user-defined special variables for the BASH shell are listed in Table 15-2.

User-defined special variables are not defined by the system. If you want to use them, you need to define and assign values to them yourself. Three of the more common user-defined special variables are **CDPATH**, **TERM**, and **EXINIT**. The **CDPATH** variable holds the path names of the directories that the **cd** command can easily locate. The **TERM** variable holds the terminal name of the terminal that you are currently using. **EXINIT** holds configuration commands for the Vi and Ex editors.

CDPATH

If **CDPATH** is undefined, then when the **cd** command is given a directory name as its argument, it searches only the current working directory for that name. However, if **CDPATH** is defined, **cd** will also search the directories listed in **CDPATH** for that directory name. If the directory name is found, **cd** changes to that directory. This is helpful if you are working on a project in which you constantly have to change to directories in another part of the file system. To change to a directory that has a path name very different from the one you are in, you would need to know the full path name of that directory. Instead, you could simply place the path name of that directory's parent in **CDPATH**. Then **cd** will automatically search the parent directory, finding the name of the directory you want. Notice that you assign to **CDPATH** the path name of the parent of the directory you want to change to, not the path name of the directory itself.

In the next example, **CDPATH** is modified to include **/home/chris/letters**. **letters** is the parent for the **thankyou** directory. Whenever the **cd** command is entered with the argument **thankyou**, the directories in **CDPATH** will be automatically searched, including **letters**, and **thankyou** will be located.

```
$ CDPATH=$CDPATH:/home/chris/letters
$ export CDPATH
$ echo $CDPATH
:/home/chris/letters
$ cd thankyou
$ pwd
/home/chris/letters/thankyou
$
```

You can, of course, edit the **.bash_profile** file and permanently add a directory name to the **CDPATH** variable.

It is advisable to use the **HOME** variable to specify the home directory part of the path in any new path name added to **CDPATH**. This is because it is possible that your home directory path name could be changed by the system administrator in any reorganization of the file system. **HOME** will always hold the current path name of the home directory. In the next example, the path name **/home/chris/letters** is specified with **$HOME/letters**.

```
$ CDPATH=$CDPATH:$HOME/letters
$ export CDPATH
$ echo $CDPATH
:/home/chris/letters
```

TERM

The **TERM** variable holds the name of the terminal you are currently using. If you log in from a terminal, you are asked for your terminal's name, and the name you enter is placed in the **TERM** variable. Utilities such as the standard editors will use **TERM** to find out what your terminal type is. This allows them to map commands to your keyboard and screen. The following command will display your terminal type:

```
$ echo $TERM
tvi925
```

If you want to change your terminal type, you can do so by assigning another terminal name to the **TERM** variable. In the next example, the **TERM** variable is assigned the terminal type vt100. You then need to export the **TERM** variable to make it accessible throughout your shell.

```
$ TERM=vt100
$ export TERM
$
```

EXINIT

The **EXINIT** variable holds editor commands with which to configure the Ex and Vi editors. When you invoke these editors, the commands in the **EXINIT** variable are executed. These commands usually set other commands that specify such features as line numbering or indentation. They are discussed in detail in Chapter 17.

In the next example, the **EXINIT** variable is assigned an editor **set** command to execute. This **set** command sets line numbering and automatic indent. Notice that the two commands can be abbreviated and combined into one string.

```
$ EXINIT='set nu ai'
$ export EXINIT
```

BASH Shell Login Initialization File: .profile

The **.profile** file is the BASH shell's login initialization file, which can also be named **.bash_profile**. It is a script file that is automatically executed whenever a user logs in. The file contains shell commands that define special environment variables used to manage your shell. They may be either redefinitions of system-defined special variables or definitions of user-defined special variables. For example, when you log in, your user shell needs to know what directories hold Linux commands. It will reference the **PATH** variable in order to find the path names for these directories. However, first, the **PATH** variable must be assigned those path names. In the **.bash_profile** file there is an assignment operation that does just this. Since it is in the **.bash_profile** file, the assignment is executed automatically when the user logs in.

Special variables also need to be exported, using the **export** command, in order to make them accessible to any subshells you may enter. You can export several variables in one **export** command by listing them as arguments. Usually at the end of the **.bash_profile** file there is an **export** command with a list of all the variables defined in the file. If a variable is missing from this list, you may not be able to access it. Notice the **export** command at the end of the **.profile** file in the example described next.

A copy of the standard **.bash_profile** file provided for you when your account is created is listed in the next example. Notice how **PATH** is assigned as is the value of **$HOME**. Both **PATH** and **HOME** are system special variables that the system has already defined. **PATH** holds the path names of directories searched for any command that you enter, and **HOME** holds the path name of your home directory. The assignment **PATH=$PATH:$HOME/bin** has the effect of redefining **PATH** to include your **bin** directory within your home directory. So your **bin** directory will also be searched for any commands, including ones you create yourself, such as scripts or programs. Notice that **PATH** is then exported so that it can be accessed by any subshells. Should you want to have your home directory searched also, you can use the Vi or Emacs editor to modify this line in your **.bash_profile** file to **PATH=$PATH:$HOME\bin:$HOME**, adding **:$HOME** at the end. In fact, you can change this entry to add as many directories as you want searched.

.profile

```
# .bash_profile

# Get the aliases and functions
if [ -f ~/.bashrc ]; then
   . ~/.bashrc
fi

# User-specific environment and startup programs

PATH=$PATH:$HOME/bin
ENV=$HOME/.bashrc
USERNAME=""

export USERNAME ENV PATH
```

Your Linux system also has its own profile file that it executes whenever any user logs in. This system initialization file is simply called **profile** and is found in the **/etc** directory, **/etc/profile**. It contains special variable definitions that the system needs to provide for each user. A copy of the system **.profile** file follows. Notice how **PATH** is redefined to include the **/usr/X11R6/bin** directory. This is the directory that holds the X-Windows commands that you execute when using the Caldera Desktop. **HISTFILE** is also redefined to include a larger number of history events.

/etc/profile

```
# /etc/profile

# Systemwide environment and startup programs
# Functions and aliases go in /etc/bashrc

PATH="$PATH:/usr/X11R6/bin"
PS1="[\u@\h \W]\\$ "

ulimit -c 1000000
umask 002

HOSTNAME='/bin/hostname'
HISTSIZE=1000
HISTFILESIZE=1000
# Default page for the arena browser
WWW_HOME=file:/usr/doc/calderadoc-0.80-1/Caldera_Info
# Default path for CRiSPlite
CRPATH=/usr/lib/CRiSPlite/macros

export PATH PS1 HOSTNAME HISTSIZE HISTFILESIZE WWW_HOME CRPATH
if [ "$TERM" = console ]
then
    MINICOM="-l -m -con -tmc" ; export MINICOM
fi
```

Your **.profile** initialization file is a text file that can be edited by a text editor like any other text file. You can easily add new directories to your **PATH** by editing **.bash_profile** and using editing commands to insert a new directory path name in the list of directory path names assigned to the **PATH** variable. You can even add new variable definitions. If you do so, be sure, however, to include the new variable's name in the **export** command's argument list. For example, if your **.bash_profile** file does not have any definition of the **EXINIT** variable, you can edit the file and add a new line that assigns a value to **EXINIT**. The definition **EXINIT='set nu ai'** will configure the Vi editor with line numbering and indentation. You then need to add **EXINIT** to the **export** command's argument list. When the **.bash_profile** file executes again, the **EXINIT** variable will be set to the command **set nu ai**. When the Vi editor is invoked, the command in the **EXINIT** variable will be executed, setting the line number and auto-indent options automatically.

In the following example, the user's **.bash_profile** has been modified to include definitions of **EXINIT** and redefinitions of **CDPATH**, **PS1**, and **HISTSIZE**. The redefinition of **HISTSIZE** reduces the number of history events saved, from 1000 defined in the system **.profile** file, to 30. The redefinition of the **PS1** special variable changes the prompt to include the path name of the current working directory. Any changes that you make to special variables within your **.bash_profile** file will override those made earlier by the system's **.profile** file. All these special variables are then exported with the **export** command.

.profile

```
# .bash_profile

# Get the aliases and functions
if [ -f ~/.bashrc ]; then
   . ~/.bashrc
fi

# User-specific environment and startup programs

PATH=$PATH:$HOME/bin:$HOME
ENV=$HOME/.bashrc
USERNAME=""
CDPATH=$CDPATH:$HOME/bin:$HOME
HISTSIZE=30
EXINIT='set nu ai'
PS1="\w \$"

export USERNAME ENV PATH CDPATH HISTSIZE EXINIT PS1
```

Though .profile is executed each time you log in, it is not automatically reexecuted after you make changes to it. The **.profile** file is an initialization file that is *only* executed whenever you log in. If you want to take advantage of any changes you make to it without having to log out and log in again, you can reexecute **.profile** with the dot (**.**) command. **.profile** is a shell script and, like any shell script, can be executed with the **.** command.

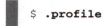

```
$ .profile
```

The BASH Shell Initialization File: .bashrc

The **.bashrc** file is an initialization file that is executed each time you enter the BASH shell or generate any subshells. If the BASH shell is your login shell, **.bashrc** is executed along with your **.bash_login** file when you log in. If you enter the BASH shell from another shell, the **.bashrc** file is automatically executed, and the variable and alias definitions it contains will be defined.

The **.bashrc** shell initialization file is actually executed each time you generate a shell, such as when you run a shell script. In other words, each time a subshell is created, the **.bashrc** file is executed. This has the effect of exporting any local variables or aliases that you have defined in the **.bashrc** shell initialization file. The **.bashrc** file usually contains the definition of aliases and any feature variables used to turn on shell features. Aliases and feature variables are locally defined within the shell. But the **.bashrc** file will define them in every shell. For this reason, the **.bashrc** file usually holds such aliases as those defined for the **rm**, **cp**, and **mv** commands. The next example is a **.bashrc** file with many of the standard definitions.

.bashrc

```
# Source global definitions
if [ -f /etc/bashrc ]; then
    . /etc/bashrc
fi
set -o ignoreeof
set -o noclobber

alias rm 'rm -i'
alias mv 'mv -i'
alias cp 'cp -i'
```

Linux systems usually contain a system **.bashrc** file that is executed for all users. This may contain certain global aliases and features needed by all users whenever they enter a BASH shell. This is located in the **/etc** directory, **/etc/.bashrc**. A user's own **.bashrc** file, located in the home directory, will contain commands to execute this system **.bashrc** file. The **. /etc/bashrc** command in the previous example of **.bashrc** does just that.

You can add any commands or definitions of your own to your **.bashrc** file. If you have made changes to **.bashrc** and you want them to take effect during your current login session, you need to reexecute the file with either the **.** or the **source** command:

```
$ source .bashrc
```

The BASH Shell Logout Initialization File: .bash_logout

The **.bash_logout** file is also an initialization file, which is executed when the user logs out. It is designed to perform any operations you want done whenever you log out. Instead of variable definitions, the **.bash_logout** file usually contains shell commands that form a kind of shutdown procedure—actions you always want taken before you log out. One common logout command is to clear the screen and then issue a farewell message.

As with **.bash_profile**, you can add your own shell commands to **.bash_logout**. In fact, the **.bash_logout** file is not automatically set up for you when your account is first created. You need to create it yourself, using the Vi or Emacs editor. You could then add a farewell message or other operations. In the next example, the user has a **clear** and an **echo** command in the **.bash_logout** file. When the user logs out, the **clear** command will clear the screen, and then the **echo** command will display the message "Good-bye for now".

.bash_logout

```
clear
echo "Good-bye for now"
```

BASH Shell Programming

The BASH shell has programming-languagelike capabilities that allow you to create complex shell programs. A shell program combines Linux commands in such a way as to perform a specific task. The Linux shell provides you with many programming tools with which to create shell programs. You can define variables and assign values to them. You can also define variables in a script file and have a user interactively enter values for them when the script is executed. There are loop and conditional control structures that repeat Linux commands or make decisions on which commands you want to execute. You can also construct expressions that perform arithmetic or comparison operations. All these programming tools operate like those found in other programming languages.

You can combine shell variables, control structures, expressions, and Linux commands to form a shell program. Usually, the instructions making up a shell program are entered into a script file that can then be executed. You can create this script file using any standard editor. To run the shell program, you then execute its script file. You can even distribute your program among several script files, one of which will contain instructions to execute others. You can think of variables, expressions, and control structures as tools you use to bring together several Linux commands into one operation. In this sense, a shell program is a new, complex Linux command that you have created.

Shell Scripts: Commands and Comments

A shell script is a text file that contains Linux commands, which you enter using any standard editor. You can then execute the commands in the file by using the file name as an argument to any **sh** or dot command (**.**). They read the commands in shell scripts and execute them. You can also make the script file itself executable and use its name directly on the command line as you would use the name of any command.

You make a script file executable by setting its execute permission using the **chmod** command. The executable permission for the **chmod** command can be set using either symbolic or absolute references. The symbolic reference **u+x** sets the execute permission of a file. The command **chmod u+x hello** will set the execute permission of the **hello** script file. You can now use the script file name **hello** as if it were a Linux command. You only need to set the executable permission once. Once set, it remains set until you explicitly change it.

hello

```
echo "Hello, how are you"
```

```
$ chmod u+x hello
$ hello
Hello, how are you
$
```

An absolute reference will set read and write permission at the same time that it sets the execute permission. See Chapter 7 for a more detailed explanation of absolute and symbolic permission references. In brief, a 700 will set execute as well as read and write permission for the user; 500 will set only execute and read permission; 300 only execute and write permission; and 400 only execute permission. Users most often set 700 or 500. In the next example, the user sets the execute permission using an absolute reference.

```
$ chmod 750 hello
$ hello
Hello, how are you
$
```

It is often helpful to include in a script file short explanations describing what the file's task is as well as describing the purpose of certain commands and variables. You can enter such explanations using comments. A comment is any line or part of a line preceded by a sharp sign, #, with the exception of the first line. The end of the comment is the next new line character, the end of the line. Any characters entered on a line after a sharp sign will be ignored by the shell. The first line is reserved for identification of the shell, as noted in the following discussion. In the next example, a comment describing the name and function of the script is placed at the head of the file.

hello

```
# The hello script says hello

echo "Hello, how are you"
```

You may want to be able to execute a script that is written for one of the Linux shells while you are working in another. Suppose you are currently in the TCSH shell and want to execute a script you wrote in the BASH shell that contains BASH shell commands. First you would have to change to the BASH shell with the **sh** command, execute the script, and then change back to the TCSH shell. You can, however, automate this process by placing as the first characters in your script, **#!**, followed by the path name for the shell program on your system.

Your shell always examines the first character of a script to find out what type of script it is—BASH, PDKSH, or TCSH shell script. If the first character is a space, the script is assumed to be either a BASH or PDKSH shell script. If there is a **#** alone, the script is a TCSH shell script. If, however, the **#** is followed by a **!** character, then your shell reads the path name of a shell program that follows. A **#!** should always be followed by the path name of a shell program identifying the type of shell the script works in. If you are currently in a different shell, that shell will read the path name of the shell program, change to that shell, and execute your script. If you are in a different shell, the space or **#** alone is not enough to identify a BASH or TCSH shell script. Such identification works only in their own shells. To identify a script from a different shell, you need to include the **#!** characters followed by a path name.

For example, if you put **#!/bin/sh** at the beginning of the first line of the **hello** script, you could execute it directly from the TCSH shell. The script will first change to the BASH shell, execute its commands, and then return to the TCSH shell (or whatever type of shell it was executed from). In the next example, the **hello** script includes the **#!/bin/sh** command. The user then executes the script while in the TCSH shell.

hello

```
#!/bin/sh

# The hello script says hello

echo "Hello, how are you"
```

```
> hello
Hello, how are you
```

Variables and Scripts

In the shell, you can create shell programs using variables and scripts. Within a shell program, you can define variables and assign values to them. Variable definitions were discussed in detail in Chapter 5. A brief discussion is presented here since variable definitions are used in shell programs for many purposes.

Variables are used extensively in script input and output operations. The **read** command allows the user to interactively enter a value for a variable. Often **read** is combined with a prompt notifying the user when to enter a response. Another form of script input, called the Here document, allows you to use lines in a script as input to a command. This overcomes the need to always read input from an outside source such as a file.

Definition and Evaluation of Variables: =, $, set, unset

A variable is defined in a shell when you first use the variable's name. A variable name may be any set of alphabetic characters, including the underscore. The name may also include a number, but the number cannot be the first character in the name. A name may not have any other type of character, such as an exclamation point, ampersand, or even a space. Such symbols are reserved by a shell for its own use. A name may not include more than one word, because a shell uses spaces to parse commands, delimiting command names and arguments.

You assign a value to a variable with the assignment operator. You type the variable name, the assignment operator, =, and then the value assigned. Note that you cannot place any spaces around the assignment operator. Any set of characters can be assigned to a variable. In the next example, the greeting variable is assigned the string "Hello".

```
$ greeting="Hello"
```

Once you have assigned a value to a variable, you can then use that variable to reference the value. Often you use the values of variables as arguments for a command. You can reference the value of a variable using the variable name preceded by the **$** operator. The dollar sign is a special operator that uses a variable name to reference a variable's value, in effect, evaluating the variable. Evaluation retrieves a variable's value—a set of characters. This set of characters then replaces the variable name on the command line. Thus, wherever a **$** is placed before the variable name, the variable name is replaced with the value of the variable.

In the next example, the shell variable greeting is evaluated and its contents, "Hello", are then used as the argument for an **echo** command. The **echo** command simply echoes or prints a set of characters to the screen.

```
$ echo $greeting
Hello
```

You can obtain a list of all the defined variables with the **set** command. If you decide that you do not want a certain variable, you can remove it with the **unset** command.

NOTE: Table 15-3 is a general collection of commands used in different places like **echo**, **read**, *and* **break**.

Variable Values: Strings

The values that you assign to variables may consist of any set of characters. These characters may be a character string that you explicitly type in, or the result obtained from executing a Linux command. In most cases, you will need to quote your values using either single quotes, double quotes, backslashes, or back quotes. Single quotes, double quotes, and backslashes allow you to quote strings in different ways. Back quotes have the special function of executing a Linux command and using the results as arguments on the command line.

Quoting Strings: Double Quotes, Single Quotes, and Backslashes

Although variable values can be made up of any characters, problems occur when you want to include characters that are also used by the shell as operators. Your shell has certain special characters that it uses in evaluating the command line. As mentioned earlier, a space is used to parse arguments on the command line. The asterisk, question mark, and brackets are special characters used to generate lists of file names. The period represents the current directory. The dollar sign is used to evaluate variables, and the greater-than and less-than characters are redirection operators. The ampersand is used to execute background commands, and the vertical bar pipes execute output. If you want to use any of these characters as part of the value of a variable, you must first quote them. Quoting a special character on a command line makes it just another character. It is not evaluated by the shell.

Double and single quotes allow you to quote several special characters at a time. Any special characters within double or single quotes are quoted. A backslash quotes a single character—the one that it precedes. If you want to assign more than one word to a variable, you need to quote the spaces separating the words. You can do so by enclosing the words within double quotes. You can think of this as creating a character string to be assigned to the variable. Of course, any other special characters enclosed within the double quotes will also be quoted.

The following examples show three ways of quoting strings. In the first example, the double quotes enclose words separated by spaces. Because the spaces are enclosed within double quotes, they are treated as characters, not as delimiters used to parse command line arguments. In the second example, single quotes also enclose a period, treating it as just a character. In the third example, an asterisk is also enclosed within the double quotes. The asterisk is considered just another character in the string and is not evaluated.

```
$ notice="The meeting will be tomorrow"
$ echo $notice
"The meeting will be tomorrow"

$ message='The project is on time.'
$ echo $message
The project is on time

$ notice="You can get a list of files with ls *.c"
$ echo $notice
You can get a list of files with ls *.c
```

Double quotes, however, do not quote the dollar sign—the operator that evaluates variables. A **$** next to a variable name enclosed within double quotes will still be evaluated, replacing the variable name with its value. The value of the variable will then become part of the string, not the variable name. There may be times when you want a variable within quotes to be evaluated. In the next example, the double quotes are used so that the winner's name will be included in the notice.

```
$ winner=dylan
$ notice="The person who won is $winner"
```

```
$ echo $notice
The person who won is dylan
```

On the other hand, there may be times when you do not want a variable within quotes to be evaluated. In that case, you would have to use the single quotes. Single quotes suppress any variable evaluation and treat the dollar sign as just another character. In the next example, single quotes prevent the evaluation of the winner variable.

```
$ winner=dylan
$ result='The name is in the $winner variable'
$ echo $result
The name is in the $winner variable
```

If, in this case, the double quotes were used instead, an unintended variable evaluation would take place. In the next example, the characters "$winner" are interpreted as a variable evaluation.

```
$ winner=dylan
$ result="The name is in the $winner variable"
$ echo $result
The name is in the dylan variable
```

You can always quote any special character, including the **$** operator, by preceding it with a backslash. The backslash is useful when you want to evaluate variables within a string and also include **$** characters. In the next example, the backslash is placed before the dollar sign in order to treat it as a dollar sign character, **\$**. At the same time, the variable **$winner** is evaluated since double quotes do not themselves quote the **$** operator.

```
$ winner=dylan
$ result="$winner won \$100.00""
$ echo $result
dylan won $100.00
```

Values from Linux Commands: Back Quotes

Though you can create variable values by typing in characters or character strings, you can also obtain values from other Linux commands. However, to assign the result of a Linux command to a variable, you first need to execute the command. If you place a Linux command within back quotes on the command line, that command is first executed and its result becomes an argument on the command line. In the case of assignments, the result of a command can be assigned to a variable by placing the command within back quotes to first execute it. Think of back quotes as a kind of expression that contains both a command to be executed and its result, which is then assigned to the variable. The characters making up the command itself are not assigned.

In the next example, the command **ls *.c** is executed and its result is then assigned to the variable **listc**. The command **ls *.c** generates a list of all files with a **.c** extension, and this list of files will then be assigned to the **listc** variable.

```
$ listc=`ls *.c`
$ echo $listc
main.c prog.c lib.c
```

Keep in mind the difference between single quotes and back quotes. Single quotes treat a Linux command as a set of characters. Back quotes force execution of the Linux command. There may be times when you accidentally enter single quotes when you mean to use back quotes. The following examples illustrate the difference. In the first example, the assignment for the **lscc** variable has single quotes, not back quotes, placed around the **ls *.c** command. In this case, **ls *.c** are just characters to be assigned to the variable **lscc**. In the second example, back quotes are placed around the **ls *.c** command, forcing evaluation of the command. A list of file names ending in **.c** is generated and assigned as the value of **lscc**.

```
$ lscc='ls *.c'
$ echo $lscc
ls *.c
$ lscc=`ls *.c`
$ echo $lscc
main.c  prog.c
```

Quoting Commands: Single Quotes

There are times when you may want to use single quotes around a Linux command. Single quotes allow you to assign the written command to a variable. If you do so, you can then use that variable name as another name for the Linux command. Entering the variable name preceded by the **$** operator on the command line will execute the command. In the next example, a shell variable is assigned the characters that make up a Linux command to list files, **'ls -F'**. Notice the single quotes around the command. When the shell variable is evaluated on the command line, the Linux command that it contains will become a command line argument and will be executed by the shell.

```
$ lsf='ls -F'
$ $lsf
mydata /reports /letters
$
```

In effect, you are creating another name for a command, like an alias. You will see in later chapters on the specific shells that you can use a special alias command to do this for you.

Script Input and Output: echo, read, and <<

Within a script you can use the **echo** command to output data and the **read** command to read input into variables. In addition, you can use a Here document to specify data within the script and redirect it to a command.

Within a script, the **echo** command will send data to the standard output. The data is in the form of a string of characters. As you have seen, the **echo** command can output variable values as well as string constants.

The **read** command reads in a value for a variable. It is used to allow a user to interactively input a value for a variable. The **read** command literally reads the next line in the standard input. Everything in the standard input up to the new line character is read in and assigned to a variable. In shell programs, you can combine the **echo** command with the **read** command to prompt the user to enter a value and then read that value into a variable. In the **greetvar** script in the next example, the user is prompted to enter a value for the greeting variable. The **read** command then reads the value the user typed and assigns it to the greeting variable.

greetvar

```
echo Please enter a greeting:
read greeting

echo "The greeting you entered was $greeting"
```

```
$ greetvar
Please enter a greeting:
hi
The greeting you entered was hi
$
```

When dealing with user input, you must consider the possibility that the user may enter shell special characters. Any special characters in a Linux command, whether within a script or not, will be evaluated unless quoted. If the value of a variable is a special character and the variable's value is referenced with a **$**, then the special character will be evaluated by the shell. However, placing the evaluated variable within quotes prevents any evaluation of special characters such as **$**. In the **greetvar** script, **$greeting** was placed within a quoted string, preventing evaluation of any special characters. However, if **$greeting** is not quoted, then any special characters it contains will be evaluated.

There are times when you want special characters evaluated. Suppose you want to retrieve the list of files beginning with characters the user enters. In this case, any special characters entered by the user need to be evaluated. In the **listfiles** script that follows, any special characters for generating file lists will be expanded. Notice that **$fref** is not quoted.

listfiles

```
echo Please enter a file reference:
read fref

echo The files you requested are: $fref
```

```
$ listfiles
Please enter a file reference:
*.c
The files you requested are: calc.c lib.c main.c
```

Normally, a shell script contains a series of commands. However, there may be times when you need to enter data as well as commands. You may want to type lines of data into the shell script and use the data as input for one of the commands. The Here operation allows you to do this. It is a redirection operation, redirecting data within a shell script into a command. It is called Here because the redirected data is here in the shell script, not somewhere else in another file. The Here operation is represented by two less-than signs, **<<**. The **<<** operator can be thought of as a kind of redirection operator, redirecting lines in a shell script as input to a command. The **<<** operator is placed after the command to which input is being redirected. Lines following the **<<** operator are then taken as input to the command. The end of the input can be specified by an end-of-file character, CTRL-**d**. Instead of using an end-of-file character, you can specify your own delimiter. A word following the **<<** operator on the same line is taken to be the ending delimiter for the input lines. The delimiter can be any set of symbols. All lines up to the delimiter are read as input to the command.

In the next example, a message is sent to the user mark. The input for the message is obtained from a Here operation. The delimiter for the Here operation is the word **myend**.

mailmark

```
mail mark << myend
Did you remember
the meeting
    robert
myend
```

Script Command Line Arguments

Like Linux commands, a shell script can take arguments. When you invoke a script, you can enter arguments on the command line after the script name. These arguments can then be referenced within the script using the **$** operator and the number of its position on the command line. Arguments on the command line are sequentially numbered from 1. The first argument is referenced with **$1**, the second argument with **$2**, and so on. The argument **$0** will contain the name of the shell script, the first word on the command line.

These argument references can be thought of as referencing read-only variables. For those familiar with programming terminology, you can think of words on the command line as arguments that are passed into argument variables, **$1** through **$9**. The argument variables are read-only variables. You cannot assign values to them. Once given the initial values, they cannot be altered. In this sense, argument variables function more as constants—constants determined by the command line arguments. Each word on the command line is parsed into an argument unless it is quoted. If you enter more than one argument, you can reference them with each corresponding argument number. In the next example, four arguments are entered on the command line.

greetargs

```
echo "The first argument is: $1"
echo "The second argument is: $2"
echo "The third argument is: $3"
echo "The fourth argument is: $4"
```

```
$ greetargs Hello Hi Salutations "How are you"
The first argument is: Hello
The second argument is: Hi
The third argument is: Salutations
The fourth argument is: How are you
$
```

A set of special arguments allows you to reference different aspects of command line arguments, such as the number of arguments or all the arguments together: **$***, **$@**, **$#**. The **$#** argument contains the number of arguments entered on the command line. This is useful when you need to specify a fixed number of arguments for a script. The argument **$*** references all the arguments in the command line. A command line may have more than nine arguments. The **$@** also references all the arguments on the command line, but allows you to separately quote each one. The difference between **$*** and **$@** is not clear until you use them to reference arguments using the **for-in** control structure. For this reason, they are discussed only briefly here and more extensively in the section on control structures later in the chapter.

In the next example, the command line arguments are displayed first using the **$*** special variable and then **$@**. The number of arguments is displayed using the **$#** special variable.

sargs

```
echo $*
echo $@
echo "There are $# arguments"
```

```
$ sargs Hello Hi Welcome
Hello Hi Welcome
Hello Hi Welcome
There are 3 arguments
```

Export Variables and Script Shells

When you execute a script file, you initiate a new process that has its own shell. Within this shell you can define variables, execute Linux commands, and even execute other scripts. If you execute another script from within the script currently running, the current script suspends execution, and control is transferred to the other script. All the commands in this other script are first executed before returning to continue with the suspended script. The process of executing one script from another operates much like a function or procedure call in programming languages. You can think of a script calling another script. The calling script waits until the called script finishes execution before continuing with its next command.

Any variable definitions that you place in a script will be defined within the script's shell and only known within that script's shell. Variable definitions are local to their own shells. In a sense, the variable is hidden within its shell. Suppose, however, you want to be able to define a variable within a script and use it in any scripts it may call. You cannot do this directly, but you can export a variable definition from one shell to another using the **export** command. When the **export** command is applied to a variable, it will instruct the system to define a copy of that variable for each new subshell generated. Each new subshell will have its own copy of the exported variable. In the next example, the myname variable is defined and exported.

```
$ myname="Charles"
$ export myname
```

It is a mistake to think of exported variables as global variables. A shell can never reference a variable outside of itself. Instead, a copy of the variable with its value is generated for the new shell. Exported variables export their values to a shell, not themselves. An exported variable operates to some extent like a scoped global parameter. It is copied to any shell derived from its own shell. Any shell script called directly or indirectly after the exported variable's shell will be given a copy of the exported variable with the initial value.

Arithmetic Shell Operations: let

The **let** command is the BASH shell command for performing operations on arithmetic values. With **let** you can compare two values or perform arithmetic operations such as addition or multiplication on them. Such operations are used often in shell programs to manage control structures or perform necessary calculations. The **let** command can be indicated either with the keyword **let** or with a set of double parentheses. The syntax consists of the keyword **let** followed by two numeric values separated by an arithmetic or relational operator, as shown here:

```
$ let value1 operator value2
```

You can use as your operator any of those listed in Table 15-4. The **let** command automatically assumes that operators are arithmetic or relational. You do not have to quote shell-like operators. **let** also automatically evaluates any variables and converts their values to arithmetic values. This means that you can write your arithmetic operations as simple arithmetic expressions. In the next example, the **let** command multiplies the values 2 and 7. The result is output to the standard output and displayed.

```
$ let 2*7
14
```

If you want to have spaces between operands in the arithmetic expression, you must quote the expression. The **let** command expects one string.

```
$ let "2 * 7"
```

You can also include assignment operations in your **let** expression. In the next example, the result of the multiplication is assigned to **res**.

```
$ let "res = 2 * 7"
$ echo $res
14
$
```

You can also use any of the relational operators to perform comparisons between numeric values, such as checking to see whether one value is less than another. Relational operations are often used to manage control structures such as loops and conditions. In the next example, **helloprg** displays the word "hello" three times. It makes use of a **let** less-than-or-equal operation to manage the loop, **let "again <= 3 "**, and to increment the again variable, **let "again = again + 1"**. Notice that when again is incremented, it does not need to be evaluated. No preceding **$** is needed. **let** will automatically evaluate variables used in expressions.

helloprg

```
again=1
while let "again <= 3"
        do
        echo $again Hello
        let "again = again + 1"
        done
```

```
$ helloprg
1 Hello
2 Hello
3 Hello
```

Control Structures

You can control the execution of Linux commands in a shell program with control structures. Control structures allow you to repeat commands and to select certain commands over others. A control structure consists of two major components: a test and commands. If the test is successful, then the commands are executed. In this way, you can use control structures to make decisions as to whether commands should be executed.

There are two different kinds of control structures: loops and conditions. A loop repeats commands, whereas a condition executes a command when certain conditions are met. The BASH shell has three loop control structures: **while**, **for**, and **for-in**. There are two condition structures: **if** and **case**.

The **while** and **if** control structures are more for general purposes, such as performing iterations and making decisions using a variety of different tests. The **case** and **for** control structures are more specialized. The **case** structure is a restricted form of the **if** condition and is often used to implement menus. The **for** structure is a limited type of loop. It runs through a list of values, assigning a new value to a variable with each iteration.

The **if** and **while** control structures have as their test the execution of a Linux command. All Linux commands return an exit status after they have finished executing. If a command is successful, its exit status will be 0. If the command fails for any reason, its exit status will be a positive value referencing the type of failure that occurred. The **if** and **while** control structures check to see if the exit status of a Linux command is 0 or some other value. In the case of the **if** and **while** structures, if the exit status is a zero value, then the command was successful and the structure continues.

The test Command

Often you may need to perform a test that compares two values. Yet the test used in control structures is a Linux command, not a relational expression. There is, however, a Linux command called **test** that can perform such a comparison of values. The **test** command will compare two values and return as its exit status a 0 if the comparison is successful.

With the **test** command, you can compare integers, strings, and even perform logical operations. The command consists of the keyword **test** followed by the values being compared, separated by an option that specifies what kind of comparison is taking place. The option can be thought of as the operator, but is written, like other options, with a minus sign and letter codes. For example, **-eq** is the option that represents the equality comparison. However, there are two string operations that actually use an operator instead of an option. When you compare two strings for equality you use the equal sign, **=**. For inequality you use **!=**. Table 15-5 lists all the options and operators used by **test**. The syntax for the **test** command is shown here:

```
test value -option value
test string = string
```

In the next example, the user compares two integer values to see if they are equal. In this case, you need to use the equality option, **-eq**. The exit status of the **test** command is examined to find out the result of the test operation. The shell special variable **$?** holds the exit status of the most recently executed Linux command.

```
$ num=5
$ test $num -eq 10
$ echo $?
1
```

Instead of using the keyword **test** for the **test** command, you can use enclosing brackets. The command **test $greeting = "hi"** can be written as

```
$ [ $greeting = "hi" ]
```

Similarly, the test command **test $num -eq 10** can be written as

```
$ [ $num -eq 10 ]
```

The brackets themselves must be surrounded by white spaces: a space, TAB, or ENTER. Without the spaces it would be invalid.

The **test** command is used extensively as the Linux command in the test component of control structures. Be sure to keep in mind the different options used for strings and integers. Do not confuse string comparisons and integer comparisons. To compare two strings for equality, you use **=**; to compare two integers, you use the option **-eq**.

Conditions: if, if-else, elif, case

The BASH shell has a set of conditional control structures that allow you to choose what Linux commands to execute. Many of these are similar to conditional control structures found in programming languages, but there are some differences. The **if** condition tests the success of a Linux command, not an expression. Furthermore, the end of an **if-then** command must be indicated with the keyword **fi**, and the end of a **case** command is indicated with the keyword **esac**. The condition control structures are listed in Table 15-6.

if-then

The **if** structure places a condition on commands. That condition is the exit status of a specific Linux command. If a command is successful, returning an exit status of 0, then the commands within the **if** structure are executed. If the exit status is anything other than 0, then the command has failed and the commands within the **if** structure are not executed.

The **if** command begins with the keyword **if** and is followed by a Linux command whose exit condition will be evaluated. This command is always executed. After the command, the keyword **then** goes on a line by itself. Any set of commands may then follow. The keyword **fi** ends the command. Often, you need to choose between two alternatives based on whether or not a Linux command is successful. The **else** keyword allows an **if** structure to choose between two alternatives. If the Linux command is successful, then those commands following the **then** keyword are executed. If the Linux command fails, then those commands following the **else** keyword are executed. The syntax for the **if-then-else** command is shown here:

```
if Linux Command
    then
        Commands
    else
        Commands
fi
```

The **elsels** script in the next example executes the **ls** command to list files with two different possible options, either by size or with all file information. If the user enters an **s**, files are listed by size, otherwise, all file information is listed.

elsels

```
echo Enter s to list file sizes,
echo otherwise all file information is listed.
echo –n "Please enter option: "
read choice

if [ "$choice" = s ]
  then
     ls -s
  else
        ls -l
fi
echo Good-bye
```

```
$ elsels
Enter s to list file sizes,
otherwise all file information is listed.
Please enter option: s
total 2
     1 monday     2 today
$
```

The **if** structure is often used to check whether the user entered the appropriate number of arguments for a shell script. The special shell variable **#** contains the number of arguments the user entered. Using **$#** in a test operation allows you to check whether the user entered the correct number of arguments.

If an incorrect number of arguments has been entered, you may need to end the shell script. You can do this with the **exit** command, which ends the shell script and returns an exit condition. **exit** takes a number argument. An argument of 0 indicates that the shell script ended successfully. Any other argument, such as 1, indicates that an error occurred. In the next example, the **ifarg** script takes only one argument. If the user fails to enter an argument, or enters more than one argument, then the **if** test will be true, and the error message will be printed out and the script exited with an error value.

ifarg

```
if [ $# -ne 1 ]
   then
   echo Invalid number of arguments
   exit 1
fi

echo $1
```

```
$ ifarg

Invalid number of arguments
```

The **elif** structure allows you to nest **if-then-else** operations. The **elif** structure stands for "else if." With **elif**, you can choose between several alternatives. The first alternative is specified with the **if** structure, followed by other alternatives, each specified by its own **elif** structure. The alternative to the last **elif** structure is specified with an **else**. If the test for the first **if** structure fails, control will be passed to the next **elif** structure, and its test will be executed. If it fails, control is passed to the next **elif** and its test checked. This continues until a test is true. Then that **elif** has its commands executed and control passes out of the **if** structure to the next command after the **fi** keyword.

The Logical Commands: && and ||

The logical commands perform logical operations on two Linux commands. The syntax is as follows:

```
command && command
```

```
command || command
```

In the case of the logical AND, **&&**, if both commands are successful, then the logical command is successful. For the logical OR, **||**, if either command is successful, then the OR is successful and returns an exit status of 0. The logical commands allow you to use logical operations as your test command in control structures.

case

The **case** structure chooses among several possible alternatives. The choice is made by comparing a value with several possible patterns. Each possible value is associated with a set of operations. If a match is found, the associated operations are performed. The **case** structure begins with the keyword **case**, an evaluation of a variable, and the keyword **in**. A set of patterns then follows. Each pattern is a regular expression terminated with a closing parenthesis. After the closing parenthesis, commands associated with this pattern are listed, followed by a double semicolon on a separate line, designating the end of those commands. After all the listed patterns, the keyword **esac** ends the **case** command. The syntax looks like this:

```
case string in
    pattern)
        commands
        ;;
    pattern)
        commands
        ;;
    *)
        default commands
        ;;
    esac
```

A pattern can include any shell special characters. The shell special characters are the *, [ ], ?, and |. You can specify a default pattern with a single * special character. The * special character matches on any pattern and so performs as an effective default option. If all other patterns do not match, the * will. In this way, the default option is executed if no other options are chosen. The default is optional. You do not have to put it in.

A **case** structure is often used to implement menus. In the program **lschoice**, in the next example, the user is asked to enter a choice for listing files in different ways. Notice the default option that warns of invalid input.

lschoice

```
# Program to allow the user to select different ways of
#   listing files

echo  s. List Sizes
echo  l. List All File Information
echo  c. List C Files

echo -n "Please enter choice: "
read choice

case $choice in
   s)
      ls -s
      ;;
   l)
      ls -l
      ;;
   c)
      ls *.c
      ;;
   *)
      echo Invalid Option
esac
```

```
$ lschoice
s. List Sizes
l. List All File Information
c. List C Files
Please enter choice: c
main.c   lib.c   file.c
$
```

Loops: while, for-in, for

The BASH shell has a set of loop control structures that allow you to repeat Linux commands. They are the **while**, **for-in**, and **for** structures. Like the BASH **if** structure, **while** and **until** test the result of a Linux command. However, the **for** and **for-in** structures do not perform any test. They simply progress through a list of values, assigning each value in turn to a specified variable. Furthermore, the **while** and **until** structures operate like corresponding structures found in programming languages, whereas the **for** and **for-in** structures are very different. The loop control structures are listed in Table 15-6.

while

The **while** loop repeats commands. A **while** loop begins with the keyword **while** and is followed by a Linux command. The keyword **do** follows on the next line. The end of the loop is specified by the keyword **done**. Here is the syntax for the **while** command:

```
while Linux command
    do
        commands
    done
```

The Linux command used in **while** structures is often a test command indicated by enclosing brackets. In the **myname** script, in the next example, you are asked to enter a name. The name is then printed out. The loop is controlled by testing the value of the variable again using the bracket form of the **test** command.

myname

```
again=yes

while [ "$again" = yes ]
do
    echo -n "Please enter a name: "
    read name
    echo "The name you entered is $name"

    echo -n "Do you wish to continue? "
    read again
done

echo Good-bye
```

```
$ myname
Please enter a name: George
The name you entered is George
Do you wish to continue? yes
Please enter a name: Robert
The name you entered is Robert
Do you wish to continue? no
Good-bye
```

for-in

The **for-in** structure is designed to reference a list of values sequentially. It takes two operands—a variable and a list of values. Each value in the list is assigned, one by one, to the variable in the **for-in** structure. Like the **while** command, the **for-in** structure is a loop. Each time through the loop, the next value in the list is assigned to the variable. When the end of the list is reached, the loop stops. Like the **while** loop, the body of a **for-in** loop begins with the keyword **do** and ends with the keyword **done**. The syntax for the **for-in** loop is shown here:

```
for variable in list of values
    do
    commands
    done
```

In the **mylistfor** script, the user simply outputs a list of each item with today's date. The list of items makes up the list of values read by the **for-in** loop. Each item is consecutively assigned to the grocery variable.

mylistfor

```
tdate='date +%D'

for grocery in milk cookies apples cheese
do
    echo "$grocery     $tdate"
done
```

```
$ mylistfor
milk        12/23/93
cookies     12/23/93
apples      12/23/93
cheese      12/23/93
$
```

The **for-in** loop is handy for managing files. You can use special characters to generate file names for use as a list of values in the **for-in** loop. For example, the ***** special character, by itself, generates a list of all files and directories, and ***.c** lists files with the **.c** extension. The special character ***** placed in the **for-in** loop's value list will generate a list of values consisting of all the file names in your current directory.

```
for myfiles in *
    do
```

The **cbackup** script makes a backup of each file and places it in a directory called **sourcebak**. Notice the use of the ***** special character to generate a list of all file names with a **.c** extension.

cbackup

```
for backfile in *.c
do
    cp $backfile sourcebak/$backfile
```

```
        echo $backfile
    done
```

```
$ cbackup
io.c
lib.c
main.c
$
```

for

The **for** structure without a specified list of values takes as its list of values the command line arguments. The arguments specified on the command line when the shell file is invoked become a list of values referenced by the **for** command. The variable used in the **for** command is set automatically to each argument value in sequence. The first time through the loop, the variable is set to the value of the first argument. The second time, it is set to the value of the second argument.

The **for** structure without a specified list is equivalent to the list **$@**. **$@** is a special argument variable whose value is the list of command line arguments. In the next example, a list of C program files is entered on the command line when the shell file **cbackuparg** is invoked. In **cbackuparg**, each argument is automatically referenced by a **for** loop. **backfile** is the variable used in the **for** loop. The first time through the loop, **$backfile** holds the value of the first argument, **$1**. The second time through, it holds the value of the second argument, **$2**.

cbackuparg

```
for backfile
do
    cp $backfile sourcebak/$backfile
    echo "$backfile"
done
```

```
$ cbackuparg  main.c  lib.c  io.c
main.c
lib.c
io.c
```

Summary: BASH Shell

Three different types of shells have been developed for Linux: the BASH shell, the PDKSH shell, and the TCSH shell. The BASH shell incorporates most of the commands found in the PDKSH and TCSH shells, including features such as command line editing, the history utility, and aliasing. With history you can list and reference previous commands that you have executed. You can even edit those commands, executing the edited versions. The BASH shell **alias** command allows you to give another name to a command. The alias can reference a command or a command with its arguments.

The BASH shell also has a set of shell features that you can turn on and off. Three common features are **ignoreeof**, **noclobber**, and **noglob**. **ignoreeof** prevents accidental logouts. **noclobber** prevents the redirection operation from overwriting existing files. The **noglob** feature treats special characters as ordinary characters.

There is also a set of special variables used to configure your user shell. Some are defined by the system and can be redefined by you. Others are user-defined, and you must explicitly define them. Various special variables govern the configuration of different aspects of your environment. For example, the **PATH** special variable specifies what directories hold Linux commands. The **EXINIT** variable holds the default configuration for the Ex and Vi editors.

Special variables are assigned values in initialization files. Initialization files are shell scripts invoked automatically when a shell is entered. In the BASH shell, the login initialization file is called **.bash_profile**. In the C-shell it is called **.login**. The BASH shell also has a **.bash_logout** file that is automatically executed when you log out. All shells have shell initialization files. These are files that are executed each time you enter a shell. In the BASH shell this file is called the **.bashrc** file.

The BASH shell has a programming capability that operates like a programming language. You can define variables and assign values to them. You can also interactively read values into a variable. There are control structures that you can use to implement loops and conditions. You can enter shell programming statements into a script file and execute the script, just as you would do with a program.

You can define variables in the shell and assign them values. You evaluate a variable by placing a **$** before the variable name. You can use variables as arguments in commands. They can hold directory path names, or even commands to be executed.

Using an editor, you can create files that contain shell commands and variable definitions. Such files are known as shell scripts. A shell script can even have argument variables that will receive arguments typed in at the command line. By setting the executable permission of the shell script, you can treat the name of the shell script file as if it were another command.

Script input and output is controlled with the **echo** and **read** commands as well as the Here document. **echo** outputs data to the standard output. The **read** command allows you to read input into a variable interactively. The input is taken from the standard input, whether it is entered at the keyboard or redirected from a file. The Here document allows you to use text directly typed in the script as input to a Linux command. The Here operator is **<<** followed by a user-defined delimiter. The delimiter is placed at the end of text to be input to a command.

Variables are text variables. They take as their values strings. Aside from equality, there are no operators that perform operations on variables. If you want to perform arithmetic or relational operations on variables, you need to use the **let** command. In the BASH shell, the **let** command allows you to use variables as if they were numeric. You can perform such operations as addition, subtraction, and multiplication.

The loop and condition control structures correspond to similar structures in programming languages. The loop structures are the **while**, **for-in**, and **for** loops. The condition structures are the **if** and **case** conditions. The **while** loop operates much like those in other languages. The loop continues until a test is false. However, in BASH shell control structures, the test is a Linux command. All commands in Linux return an exit status upon completing execution, denoting whether the command was successful or not. If the Linux command has an exit status of 0, the command was successful. If the exit status is any non-zero value, the command was unsuccessful. In the case of a **while** loop, a Linux command is the test. If the Linux command was successful, then the loop continues. If it fails, the loop stops.

A special Linux command called **test** can be used to implement programming-languagelike tests. The **test** command can compare two values, performing relational operations on them. If the relational operation is true, the exit status of the **test** command will be a 0—a success. If false, its exit status will be some other value. With the **test** command, you can control a loop using a relational operation that compares two operands.

The **if** control structure conditions the execution of commands upon a test. Like the **while** structure, this test is itself a Linux command. If the Linux command is successful, then the commands within the **if** are executed. The **if** structure can use the **test** command to implement programminglike conditional operations. The **test** command can perform relational operations between two variables, allowing the **if** to succeed if the relational operation is true. The **elif** and **else** structures allow you to construct nested **if** conditions. **elif**, like **if**, has as its test a Linux command.

The **case** structure works like a restricted version of the **if** structure—it compares a single value with a set of possible values. If a match is found, then operations associated with that matched value are executed. **case** is very useful for implementing menus, in which users make choices among several possible options.

The **for-in** structure runs through a list of values, assigning each value in turn to a specified variable. There is no test. The list of values can be generated by any of several Linux commands. For example, **ls** will generate a list of file names. A list of values can also be specified by a list of words. Each word is then a value assigned in turn to the **for** variable. The loop will always continue until all values have been assigned. The **for** structure uses as its list the command line arguments. There is no explicit list of values.

Command Line Editing	Effect
CTRL-**b** or LEFT ARROW	Moves left one character (backward to the previous character)
CTRL-**f** or RIGHT ARROW	Moves right one character (forward to the next character)
CTRL-**a**	Moves to beginning of a line
CTRL-**e**	Moves to end of a line
ESC **f**	Moves forward one word
ESC **b**	Moves backward one word
DEL	Deletes the character the cursor is on
BACKSPACE or CTRL-**h**	Deletes the character before the cursor
CTRL-**d**	Deletes the character after the cursor
CTRL-**k**	Removes (kills) the remainder of a line

History Commands	Effect
CTRL-**n** or DOWN ARROW	Moves down to the next event in the history list
CTRL-**p** or UP ARROW	Moves up to the previous event in the history list
ESC **<**	Moves to beginning of the history event list
ESC **>**	Moves to end of the history event list
ESC TAB	History event matching and completion
fc *event-reference*	Edits an event with the standard editor and then executes it **options** -l List recent history events; same as **history** command -e *editor event-reference* Invokes a specified editor to edit a specific event

Table 15-1.   *Command Line Editing, History Commands, and History Event References*

Command Line Editing	Effect
!*event num*	References an event with event number
!*characters*	References an event with beginning characters
!?*pattern*?	References an event with a pattern in the event
!–*event num*	References an event with an offset from the first event
!*num*–*num*	References a range of events

Table 15-1. *Command Line Editing, History Commands, and History Event References (continued)*

Shell Special Variables	Function
System-determined	
HOME	Path name for user's home directory
LOGNAME	Login name
USER	Login name
TZ	Time zone used by system
Redefinable Special Variables	
SHELL	Path name of program for type of shell you are using
PATH	List of path names for directories searched for executable commands
PS1	Primary shell prompt
PS2	Secondary shell prompt
IFS	Interfield delimiter symbol
MAIL	Name of mail file checked by mail utility for received messages
MAILCHECK	Interval for checking for received mail

Table 15-2. *BASH Shell Special Variables and Features*

Shell Special Variables	Function
User-defined Special Variables	
MAILPATH	List of mail files to be checked by mail for received messages
TERM	Terminal name
CDPATH	Path names for directories searched by **cd** command for subdirectories
EXINIT	Initialization commands for Ex/Vi editor
BASH Shell Features	
$ set -+o *feature*	Korn shell features are turned on and off with the **set** command; **-o** sets a feature on and **+o** turns it off **$ set -o noclobber** *set noclobber on* **$ set +o noclobber** *set noclobber off*
ignoreeof	Disabled CTRL-**d** logout
noclobber	Does not overwrite files through redirection
noglob	Disables special characters used for file name expansion: *****, **?**, **~**, and **[]**

Table 15-2. *BASH Shell Special Variables and Features* (continued)

BASH Shell Commands	Effect
break	Exits from **for**, **while**, or **until** loop
continue	Skips remaining commands in loop and continues with next iteration
echo	Displays values **-n** Eliminates output of new line
eval	Executes the command line

Table 15-3. *BASH Shell Commands and Arguments*

BASH Shell Commands	Effect
exec	Executes command in place of current process; does not generate a new subshell, uses the current one
exit	Exits from the current shell
export *var*	Generates a copy of *var* variable for each new subshell (call-by-value)
history	Lists recent history events
let *"expression"*	Evaluates an arithmetic, relational, or assignment expression using operators listed in Table 15-4. The expression must be quoted
read	Reads a line from the standard input
return	Exits from a function
set	Assigns new values for these arguments (when used with command line arguments); lists all defined variables (when used alone)
shift	Moves each command line argument to the left so that the number used to reference it is one less than before; argument 3$ would then be referenced by $2, and so on; $1 is lost
test *value option value* [*value option value*]	Compares two arguments; used as the Linux command tested in control structures **test 2 -eq $count** **[2 -eq $count]**
unset	Undefines a variable
Command Line Arguments	
$0	Name of Linux command
$n	The *n*th command line argument beginning from 1, $1-$n; you can use **set** to change them
$*	All the command line arguments beginning from 1; you can use **set** to change them
$@	The command line arguments individually quoted
$#	The count of the command line arguments

Table 15-3.   *BASH Shell Commands and Arguments* (continued)

BASH Shell Commands	Effect
Process Variables	
$$	The PID number, process ID, of the current process
$!	The PID number of the most recent background job
$?	The exit status of the last Linux command executed

Table 15-3. *BASH Shell Commands and Arguments* (continued)

Arithmetic Operators	Function
*	multiplication
/	division
+	addition
–	subtraction
%	modulo—results in the remainder of a division
Relational Operators	
>	greater-than
<	less-than
>=	greater-than-or-equal-to
<=	less-than-or-equal-to
=	equal in expr
==	equal in let
!=	not-equal
&	logical AND
|	logical OR
!	logical NOT

Table 15-4. *Expression Operators: **let***

Integer Comparisons	Function
`-gt`	greater-than
`-lt`	less-than
`-ge`	greater-than-or-equal-to
`-le`	less-than-or-equal-to
`-eq`	equal
`-ne`	not-equal
String Comparisons	
`-z`	Tests for empty string
`-n`	Tests for string value
`=`	equal strings
`!=`	not-equal strings
`str`	Tests to see if string is not a null string
Logical Operations	
`-a`	Logical AND
`-o`	Logical OR
`!`	Logical NOT
File Tests	
`-f`	File exists and is a regular file
`-s`	File is not empty
`-r`	File is readable
`-w`	File can be written to, modified
`-x`	File is executable
`-d`	File name is a directory name
`-h`	File name is a symbolic link
`-c`	File name references a character device
`-b`	File name references a block file

Table 15-5.   *Test Command Operations*

Condition Control Structures: if, else, elif, case	Function
if *command* **then** *command* **fi**	**if** executes an action if its test command is true

if *command* **then**
  command
else
  command
fi
	if-else executes an action if the exit status of its test command is true; if false, then the **else** action is executed

if *command* **then**
  command
elif *command* **then**
  command
else
  command
fi
	elif allows you to nest **if** structures, enabling selection among several alternatives; at the first true **if** structure, its commands are executed and control leaves the entire **elif** structure

case *string* **in** *pattern*) *command***;;** **esac**	**case** matches the string value to any of several patterns; if a pattern is matched, its associated commands are executed
command **&&** *command*	The logical AND condition returns a true 0 value if both commands return a true 0 value; if one returns a non-zero value, then the AND condition is false and also returns a non-zero value
command **||** *command*	The logical OR condition returns a true 0 value if one or the other command returns a true 0 value; if both commands return a non-zero value, then the OR condition is false and also returns a non-zero value
! *command*	The logical NOT condition inverts the return value of the command

Table 15-6.   *BASH Shell Conditions and Loops*

Condition Control Structures: if, else, elif, case	Function
Loop Control Structures: while, until, for, for-in, select	
while *command* **do** *command* **done**	**while** executes an action as long as its test command is true
until *command* **do** *command* **done**	**until** executes an action as long as its test command is false
for *variable* **in** *list-values* **do** *command* **done**	**for-in** is designed for use with lists of values; the variable operand is consecutively assigned the values in the list
for *variable* **do** *command* **done**	**for** is designed for reference script arguments; the variable operand is consecutively assigned each argument value
select *string* **in** *item-list* **do** *command* **done**	**select** creates a menu based on the items in the *item-list*; then it executes the command; the command is usually a **case**

Table 15-6.   *BASH Shell Conditions and Loops* (continued)

Chapter Sixteen

The TCSH Shell

The TCSH shell is essentially a version of the C-shell with added features. It is fully compatible with the standard C-shell and incorporates all of its capabilities, including the shell language and the history utility. The C-shell, itself, was originally developed for use with BSD Unix. It incorporates all the core commands used in the original Bourne shell, but differs significantly in more complex features such as shell programming. The C-shell was developed after the Bourne shell and was the first to introduce new features such as command line editing, the history utility, and aliasing. The Korn shell later incorporated many of these same features, adding to them with more versatile command line and history editing. Similar improvements were then incorporated into the BASH and TCSH shells. TCSH has more advanced command line and history editing features than those found in the original C-shell.

The TCSH, BASH, and PDKSH shells all share the same set of basic shell operations, as described in Chapter 5. One notable difference for the TCSH shell is that it uses a different default prompt, the **>** instead of the **$**. This chapter focuses on the TCSH shell operations that differ from the other shells, namely, command line editing, history, and shell environment variables and initialization scripts. TCSH shell programming is also covered in this chapter. See Table 16-1 for the TCSH shell history commands.

Command Line Completion

The command line has a built-in feature that performs command and file name completion. If you enter an incomplete pattern as a file name argument, you can press TAB to activate this feature, which will then complete the pattern with a file name. If you press CTRL-D, it will expand to all file names matching a pattern. To use this feature, you type the partial name of the file on the command line and then press TAB. The shell will automatically look for the file with that partial prefix and complete it for you on the command line. In the next example, the user issues a **cat** command with an incomplete file name. When the user presses TAB, the system searches for a match and, upon finding one, fills in the file name.

```
> cat pre tab
 > cat preface
```

If more than one file has the same prefix, the shell will match the name as far as the file names agree and then beep. You can then add more characters to select one or the other. For example:

```
> ls
document docudrama
> cat doc tab
 > cat docu beep
```

If, instead, you want a list of all the names that your incomplete file name matches, you can press CTRL-D on the command line. In the next example, the CTRL-D after the incomplete file name generates a list of possible file names.

```
> cat doc Ctrl-d
document
docudrama
> cat docu
```

The shell redraws the command line, and you can then type in the remainder of the file name, or type in distinguishing characters, and press TAB to have the file name completed.

```
    > cat docudrama
```

History

As in the BASH and PDKSH shells, the TCSH shell's history utility keeps a record of the most recent commands you have executed. The history utility is a kind of short-term memory, keeping track of a limited number of the most recent commands. If the history utility is not automatically turned on, you first have to define it with a **set** command and assign to it the number of commands you want recorded. This is often done as part of your shell configuration, which is discussed in Chapter 14. In the next example, the history utility is defined and set to remember the last 5 commands.

```
> set history=5
```

The commands remembered are technically referred to as *events*. To see the set of your most recent events, enter **history** on the command line and press ENTER. A list of your most recent commands is displayed, preceded by an event number.

```
> history
1 ls
2 vi mydata
3 mv mydata reports
4 cd reports
5 ls -F
>
```

The history utility lets you reference a former event by placing it on your command line and allowing you to execute it. However, you do not need to display the list first with history. The easiest way to do this is to use your UP ARROW and DOWN ARROW keys to place history events on your command line one at a time. Pressing the UP ARROW key once will place the last history event on your command line. Pressing it again places the next history event on your command line. The DOWN ARROW key will place the previous command on the command line.

You can also edit the command line. The LEFT ARROW and RIGHT ARROW keys move you along the command line. You can then insert text wherever you stop your cursor. With the BACKSPACE and DEL keys, you can delete characters. CTRL-A moves your cursor to the beginning of the command line, and CTRL-E moves it to the end. CTRL-K deletes the remainder of a line from the position of the cursor, and CTRL-U erases the entire line.

Displaying the history list provides you with a more powerful interface for referencing history events. Each of these events can be referenced by either its event number, the beginning characters of the event, or a pattern of characters in the event. A pattern reference is enclosed in question marks, **?**. You can reexecute any event using the history command, **!**. The exclamation point is followed by an event reference such as an event number, beginning characters, or a pattern. In the next examples, the second command in the history list is referenced first by an event number, then by the beginning characters of the event, and then by a pattern in the event.

```
> !2
vi mydata
> !vi
vi mydata
> !?myd?
vi mydata
```

You can also reference a command using an offset from the end of the list. Preceding a number with a minus sign will offset from the end of the list to that command. In the next example, the second command, **vi mydata**, is referenced using an offset.

```
> !-4
vi mydata
```

An exclamation point is also used to identify the last command executed. It is equivalent to an offset of -1. In the next examples, both the offset of 1 and the exclamation point reference the last command, **ls -F**.

```
> !!
ls -F
mydata /reports

> !-1
ls -F
mydata /reports
```

History Event Substitutions

An event reference should be thought of as a representation of the characters making up the event. The event reference **!1** actually represents the characters "ls". As such, you can use an event reference as part of another command. The history operation is basically a substitution. The characters making up the event replace the exclamation point and event reference entered on the command line. In the next example, the list of events is first displayed. Then a reference to the first event is used as part of a new command. The event reference **!1** evaluates to **ls**, becoming part of the command **ls > myfiles**.

```
> history
1 ls
2 vi mydata
3 mv mydata reports
4 cd reports
5 ls -F

> !1 > myfiles
ls > myfiles
```

You can also reference particular words in an event. An event is parsed into separate words, each identified sequentially by a number starting from 0. An event reference followed by a colon and a number references only a word in the event. Using the preceding example, the event reference **!3:2** first references the third event, **mv mydata reports**, and the second word in that event, **mydata**. You can use such word references as part of a command. In the next example, **2:0** references only the first word in the second event, **vi**. The command evaluates to **vi preface**.

```
> !2:0 preface
vi preface
```

Using a range of numbers, you can reference several words in an event. The number of the first and last word in the range are separated by a dash. In the next example, **3:0-1** references the first two words of the third event, **mv mydata**.

```
> !3:0-1 oldletters
```

The special characters **^** and **$** represent the second word and the last word in an event. They are used to reference arguments of the event. If you needed just the first argument of an event, then **^** would reference it. The **$** references the last argument. The range **^-$** references all the arguments (the first word, the command name, is not included). In the next examples, the arguments used in previous events are referenced and used as arguments in the current command. First, the first argument (the second word) in the second event, **mydata**, is used as an argument in an **lp** command, printing the file. Then the last argument in the third event, **reports**, is used as an argument in the **ls** command, listing out the file names in **reports**. Then the arguments used in the third event, **mydata** and **reports**, are used as arguments in a **copy** command.

```
> lpr !2:^
lpr mydata
> ls !3:$
ls reports
> cp !3:^-$
cp mydata reports
```

The asterisk is a special symbol that represents all the arguments in a former command. It is equivalent to the range **^-$**. The last example just shown can be rewritten using the asterisk:

```
> cp !3*
cp mydata reports
```

In the C-shell as well as the TCSH shell, whenever the exclamation point is used in a command, it is interpreted as a history command reference. If you need to use the exclamation point for other reasons, such as an electronic mail address symbol, you have to escape the exclamation point by placing a backslash in front of it:

```
> mail garnet\!chris < mydata
```

Aliases

You use the **alias** command to create another name for a command. The alias operates like a macro that expands to the command it represents. The alias does not literally replace the name of the command; it simply gives another name to that command.

An **alias** command begins with the keyword alias and the new name for the command, followed by the command that the alias will reference. In the next example, the **ls** command is aliased with the name **list**. **list** becomes another name for the **ls** command.

```
> alias list ls
> ls
mydata intro
> list
mydata intro
>
```

Should the command you are aliasing have options, you will need to enclose the command and the option within single quotes. An aliased command that has spaces will need quotation marks as well. In the next example, **ls** with the **-l** option is given the alias **longl**:

```
> alias longl 'ls -l'
> ls -l
-rw-r--r--  1  chris weather 207 Feb  20  11:55    mydata
> longl
-rw-r--r--  1  chris weather 207 Feb  20  11:55    mydata
>
```

You can also use the name of a command as an alias. In the case of the **rm**, **cp**, and **mv** commands, the **-i** option should always be used to ensure that an existing file is not overwritten. Instead of constantly being careful to use the **-i** option each time you use one of these commands, you can alias the command name to include the option. In the next examples, the **rm**, **cp**, and **mv** commands have been aliased to include the **-i** option.

```
> alias rm 'rm -i'
> alias mv 'mv -i'
> alias cp 'cm -i'
```

The alias command by itself provides a list of all aliases in effect and their commands. An alias can be removed with the **unalias** command.

```
> alias
lss    ls -s
list   ls
rm     rm -i
> unalias lss
```

TCSH Shell Feature Variables: Shell Features

The TCSH shell has several features that allow you to control how different shell operations work. The TCSH shell's features include those in the PDKSH shell as well as many of its own. For example, the TCSH shell has a **noclobber** option to prevent redirection from overwriting files. Some of the more commonly used features are **echo, noclobber, ignoreeof**, and **noglob**. (See Table 16-2.) The TCSH shell features are turned on and off by defining and undefining a variable associated with that feature. A variable is named for each feature, for example, the **noclobber** feature is turned on by defining the **noclobber** variable. You use the **set** command to define a variable and the **unset** command to undefine a variable. To turn on the **noclobber** feature you issue the command: **set noclobber**. To turn it off you use the command: **unset noclobber**.

```
$ set   feature-variable
$ unset feature-variable
```

These variables are also sometimes referred to as toggles since they are used to turn features on and off.

echo

Setting echo enables a feature that displays a command before it is executed. The command **set echo** turns the echo feature on, and the command **unset echo** turns it off.

ignoreeof

Setting **ignoreeof** enables a feature that prevents users from logging out of the user shell with a CTRL-D. It is designed to prevent accidental logouts. With this feature turned off, you can log out by pressing CTRL-D. However, CTRL-D is also used to end user input entered directly into the standard input. It is used often for the mail program or for utilities such as **cat**. You could easily enter an extra CTRL-D in such circumstances and accidentally log yourself out. The **ignoreeof** feature prevents such accidental logouts. When it is set, you have to explicitly log out, using the **logout** command:

```
$ set ignoreeof
$ ctrl-d
Use logout to logout
$
```

noclobber

Setting **noclobber** enables a feature that safeguards existing files from redirected output. With the **noclobber** feature, if you redirect output to a file that already exists, the file will not be overwritten with the standard output. The original file will be preserved. There may be situations in which you use a name that you have already given to an existing file as the name for the file to hold the redirected output. The **noclobber** feature prevents you from accidentally overwriting your original file:

```
> set noclobber
> cat preface > myfile
myfile: file exists
$
```

There may be times when you want to overwrite a file with redirected output. In this case, you can place an exclamation point after the redirection operator. This will override the **noclobber** feature, replacing the contents of the file with the standard output:

```
> cat preface >! myfile
```

noglob

Setting **noglob** enables a feature that disables special characters in the user shell. The characters *****, **?**, **[]**, and **~** will no longer expand to matched file names. This feature is helpful if, for some reason, you have special characters as part of a file name. In the next example, the user needs to reference a file that ends with the **?** character, **answers?**. First the user turns off special characters, using the **noglob** option. Now the question mark on the command line is taken as part of the file name, not as a special character, and the user can reference the **answers?** file.

```
$ set noglob
$ ls answers?
answers?
```

TCSH Special Shell Variables for Configuring Your System

As in the BASH shell, you can use special shell variables in the TCSH shell to configure your system. Some are defined initially by your system, and you can later redefine them with a new value. There are others that you must initially define yourself. One of the more commonly used special variables is the **prompt** variable that allows you to create your own command line prompts. Another is the **history** variable with which you determine how many history events you want to keep track of.

In the TCSH shell, many special variables have names and functions similar to those in the BASH or PDKSH shells. Some are in uppercase, but most are written in lowercase. The **EXINIT** and **TERM** variables retain their uppercase form. However, **history** and **cdpath** are written in lowercase. Other special variables may perform similar functions, but have very different implementations. For example, the **mail** variable holds the same information as BASH **MAIL**, **MAILPATH**, and **MAILCHECK** variables together. See Table 16-3 for a list of these variables.

prompt, prompt2, prompt3

The **prompt**, **prompt2**, and **prompt3** variables hold the prompts for your command line. You can configure your prompt to be any symbol or string that you want. To have your command line display a different symbol as a prompt, you simply use the **set** command to assign that symbol to the **prompt** variable. In the next example, the user assigns a **+** sign to the **prompt** variable, making it the new prompt.

```
> set prompt = "+"
+
```

You can use a predefined set of codes to make configuring your prompt easier. With them, you can make the time, your user name, or your directory path name a part of your prompt. You can even have your prompt display the history event number of the current command you are about to enter. Each code is preceded by a **%** symbol, for example, **%/** represents the current working directory, **%t** the time, and **%n** your user name. **%!** will display the next history event number. In the next example, the user adds the current working directory to the prompt.

```
> set prompt = "%/ >"
/home/dylan >
```

The next example incorporates both the time and the history event number with a new prompt.

```
> set prompt = "%t %! $"
```

Here is a list of the codes:

Code	Function
%/	Current working directory
%h, %!, !	Current history number
%t	Time of day
%n	User name
%d	Day of the week
%w	Current month
%y	Current year

The **prompt2** variable is used in special cases when a command may take several lines to input. **prompt2** is displayed for the added lines needed for entering the command. **prompt3** is the prompt used if the spell check feature is activated.

cdpath

The **cdpath** variable holds the path names of directories to be searched for specified subdirectories referenced with the **cd** command. These path names form an array just like the array of path names assigned to the TCSH shell **path** variable. Notice the space between the path names.

```
> set cdpath=(/usr/chris/reports /usr/chris/letters)
```

history and savehist

As you learned earlier, the **history** variable can be used to determine the number of history events you want saved. You simply assign to it the maximum number of events that **history** will record. When the maximum is reached, the count starts over again from 1. The **savehist** variable, however, holds the number of events that will be saved in the file **.history** when you log out. When you log in again, these events will become the initial history list.

In the next example, up to 20 events will be recorded in your history list while you are logged in. However, only the last 5 will be saved in the **.history** file when you log out. Upon logging in again, your history list will consist of your last 5 commands from the previous session.

```
> set history=20
> set savehist=5
```

mail

In the TCSH shell, the **mail** variable combines the features of the **MAIL**, **MAILCHECK**, and **MAILPATH** variables in the BASH and PDKSH shells. The TCSH shell **mail** variable is assigned as its value an array whose elements contain both the time interval for checking for mail and the directory path names for mailbox files to be checked. To assign values to these elements, you assign an array of values to the **mail** variable. The array of new values is specified with a list of words separated by spaces and enclosed in parentheses. The first value is a number that sets the number of seconds to wait before checking for mail again. This value is comparable to that held by the BASH shell's **MAILCHECK** variable. The remaining values consist of the directory path names of mailbox files that are to be checked for your mail. Notice that these values combine the functions of the BASH and Korn shells' **MAIL** and **MAILPATH** variables.

In the next example, the **mail** variable is set to check for mail every 20 minutes (1200 seconds), and the mailbox file checked is in **usr/mail/chris**. The first value in the array assigned to mail is 1200, and the second value in the array is the path name of the mailbox file to be checked.

```
> set mail ( 1200 /usr/mail/chris )
```

You can, just as easily, add more mailbox file path names to the **mail** array. In the next example, two mailboxes are designated. Notice the spaces surrounding each element.

```
> set mail ( 1200 /usr/mail/chris /home/mail/chris )
```

TCSH Shell Initialization Files: .login, .tcshrc, .logout

The TCSH shell has three initialization files: **.login**, **.logout**, and **.tcshrc**. The files are named for the operation they execute. The **.login** file is a login initialization file that executes each time you log in. The **.logout** file executes each time you log out. The **.tcshrc** file is a shell initialization file that executes each time you enter the TCSH shell, either from logging in or by explicitly changing to the TCSH shell from another shell with the **tcsh** command.

.login

The TCSH shell has its own login initialization file called the **.login** file that contains shell commands and special variable definitions used to configure your shell. The **.login** file corresponds to the **.profile** file used in the BASH and PDKSH shells.

A **.login** file contains **setenv** commands that assign values to special environment variables, such as **TERM**. You can change these assigned values by editing the **.login** file with any of the standard editors. You can also add new values. Remember, however, that in the TCSH shell, the command for assigning a value to an environment variable is **setenv**. In the next example, the **EXINIT** variable is defined and assigned the Vi editor's line numbering and auto-indent options.

> `setenv EXINIT 'set nu ai'`

Be careful when editing your **.login** file. Inadvertent editing changes could cause variables to be set incorrectly or not at all. It is wise to make a backup of your **.login** file before editing it.

If you have made changes to your **.login** file and you want the changes to take effect during your current login session, you will need to reexecute the file. You do so using the **source** command. The **source** command will actually execute any initialization file, including the **.tcshrc** and **.logout** files. In the next example, the user reexecutes the **.login** file.

> `source .login`

If you are also planning to use the PDKSH shell on your Linux system, you need to define a variable called **ENV** within your **.login** file and assign it the name of the PDKSH shell's initialization file. If you should later decide to enter the PDKSH shell from your TCSH shell, the PDKSH shell's initialization file can be located and executed for you. In the example of the **.login** file shown next, you will see that the last command sets the PDKSH shell's initialization file to **.kshrc** to the **ENV** variable: `setenv ENV $HOME/.kshrc`.

.login

```
setenv term vt100
setenv EXINIT 'set nu ai'

setenv ENV $HOME/.kshrc
```

.tcshrc

The **.tcshrc** initialization file is executed each time you enter the TCSH shell or generate any subshells. If the TCSH shell is your login shell, then the **.tcshrc** file is executed along with your **.login** file when you log in. If you enter the TCSH shell from another shell, the **.tcshrc** file is automatically executed, and the variable and alias definitions it contains will be defined.

The **.tcshrc** shell initialization file is actually executed each time you generate a shell, such as when you run a shell script. In other words, each time a subshell is created, the **.tcshrc** file is executed. This allows you to define local variables in the **.tcshrc** initialization file and have them, in a sense, exported to any subshells. Even though such user-defined special variables such as **history** are local, they will be defined for each subshell generated. In this way, **history** is set for each subshell. However, each subshell has its own local **history** variable. You could even change the local **history** variable in one subshell without affecting any of those in other subshells. Defining special variables in the shell initialization file allows you to treat them like BASH shell exported variables. As discussed in Chapter 15, an exported variable in a BASH or PDKSH shell only passes a copy of itself to any subshell. Changing the copy does not affect the original definition.

The **.tcshrc** file also contains the definition of aliases and any feature variables used to turn on shell features. Aliases and feature variables are locally defined within the shell. But the **.tcshrc** file will define them in every shell. For this reason, **.tcshrc** usually holds such aliases as those defined for the **rm**, **cp**, and **mv** commands. The next example is a **.tcshrc** file with many of the standard definitions.

.tcshrc

```
set shell=/usr/bin/csh
set path= $PATH (/bin /usr/bin . )
set cdpath=( /home/chris/reports /home/chris/letters )

set prompt="! $cwd >"
set history=20

set ignoreeof
set noclobber

alias rm  'rm -i'
alias mv  'mv -i'
alias cp  'cp -i'
```

Local variables, unlike environment variables, are defined with the **set** command. Any local variables that you define in **.tcshrc** should use the **set** command. Any variables defined with **setenv** as environment variables, such as **TERM**, should be placed in the **.login** file. The next example shows the kinds of definitions found in the **.tcshrc** file. Notice that the **history** and **noclobber** variables are defined using the **set** command.

```
set history=20
set noclobber
```

You can edit any of the values assigned to these variables. However, when editing the path names assigned to **path** or **cdpath**, bear in mind that these path names are contained in an array. Each element in an array is separated by a space. If you add a new path name, you need to be sure that there is a space separating it from the other path names.

If you have made changes to **.tcshrc** and you want them to take effect during your current login session, remember to reexecute the **.tcshrc** file with the **source** command:

```
> source .tcshrc
```

.logout

The **.logout** file is also an initialization file, but it is executed when the user logs out. It is designed to perform any operations you want done whenever you log out. Instead of variable definitions, the **.logout** file usually contains shell commands that form a shutdown procedure. For example, one common logout command is the one to check for any active background jobs; another is to clear the screen and then issue a farewell message.

As with **.login**, you can add your own shell commands to the **.logout** file. Using the Vi editor, you could change the farewell message or add other operations. In the next example, the user has a **clear** and an **echo** command in the .logout file. When the user logs out, the **clear** command will clear the screen, and **echo** will display the message "Good-bye for now".

.logout

```
clear
echo "Good-bye for now"
```

TCSH Shell Programming

The TCSH shell, like the BASH and PDKSH shells, also has programming languagelike capabilities. You can define variables and assign values to them. You can place variable definitions and Linux commands in a script file and then execute that script. There are also loop and conditional control structures with which you can repeat Linux commands or make decisions on which commands you want to execute. You can also place traps in your program to handle interrupts.

The TCSH shell differs from other shells in that its control structures conform more to a programming language format. For example, the test condition for a TCSH shell's control structure is an expression that evaluates to true or false, not to a Linux command. A TCSH shell expression uses the same operators as those found in the C programming language. You can perform a variety of assignment, arithmetic, relational, and bitwise operations. The TCSH shell also allows you to declare numeric variables that can easily be used in such operations.

TCSH Shell Variables, Scripts, and Arguments

As you've already seen, the TCSH shell uses shell variables much the same way as the BASH and PDKSH shells do. You can define variables in a shell and assign values to them, as well as reference script arguments. You can also define environment variables that operate much like BASH shell exported variables. The TCSH shell differs in the way it defines variables and the type of variables you can define. The TCSH shell defines its variables using the TCSH shell commands **set**, **@**, and **setenv**. The TCSH shell also allows you to define numeric variables and arrays. The **@** command defines a numeric variable on which you perform arithmetic operations. Parentheses and brackets allow you to define and reference arrays.

Scripts also operate in much the same way, but with several crucial differences. A TCSH shell script must begin with a sharp (or pound) sign (**#**) in the first column of the first line. Also, though prompts can be output using the **echo** command, there is no **read** command to handle input. Instead, you need to redirect the standard input to a variable.

TCSH Shell Variables

In the TCSH shell, you need to first declare a variable before you can use it. You declare a variable with the **set** command followed by the variable's name. A variable name may be any set of alphabetic characters, including the underscore. The name may also include a number, but the number cannot be the first character in the name. A name may not have any other type of character, such as an exclamation point, ampersand, or even a space. Such symbols are reserved by the shell for its own use. A name may not include more than one word since the shell parses its command line on the space. The space is a delimiter between the different elements of the command line. The next example declares the variable **greeting**. You can later undefine the variable with the **unset** command.

```
> set greeting
```

You also use the **set** command to assign a value to a variable. You type in the keyword **set**, the variable name, the assignment operator, **=**, and then the value assigned. Any set of characters can be assigned to a variable. In the next example, the variable **greeting** is assigned the string "hello".

```
> set greeting="hello"
```

In the TCSH shell assignment operation, you either need to place spaces on both sides of the assignment operator or have no spaces at all. The assignment operation

```
> set greeting ="hello"
```

will fail because there is a space before the assignment operator, but not after.

You can obtain a list of all the defined variables by using the **set** command without any arguments. The next example uses **set** to display a list of all defined variables and their values.

```
> set
greeting hello
poet   Virgil
```

As in the BASH shell, the dollar sign, **$**, is a special operator that evaluates a shell variable. Evaluation retrieves a variable's value—usually a set of characters. This set of characters then replaces the variable name. In effect, wherever a **$** is placed before a variable name, the shell replaces the variable name with the value of the variable. In the next example, the shell variable **greeting** is evaluated and its contents, "hello", are then used as the argument for an **echo** command. The **echo** command prints a set of characters on the screen.

```
> echo $greeting
hello
```

TCSH Shell Scripts: Input and Output

You can easily define and use variables within a shell script. As in the example coming up, you can place Linux commands, such as the assignment operation and **echo**, in a file using a text editor. You can then make the file executable and invoke it on the command line as another command. Remember that to add the execute permission, you use the **chmod** command with a u+x permission or the 700 absolute permission. Within a script, you can use the **echo** command to output data. However, input is read into a variable by redirecting the standard input. There is no comparable version of the **read** command in the TCSH shell.

The TCSH shell examines the first character of a file to determine whether or not it is a TCSH shell script. Remember that all TCSH shell scripts must have as the first character on the first line, a **#** character. This identifies the file as a TCSH shell script. Notice the **#** character at the beginning of the **greet** script. The **#** character placed anywhere in the file other than the first character of the first line, operates as a common character.

greet

```
#
# Script to output hello greeting

set greeting="hello"
echo The value of greeting is $greeting
```

```
> chmod u+x greet
> greet
The value of greeting is hello
```

The **set** command combined with the redirection operation, **$<**, will read whatever the user enters into the standard input. The next example reads user input into the **greeting** variable.

```
> set greeting = $<
```

You can place the prompt on the same line as the input using the **echo** command. The TCSH shell uses a special option for **echo**, the **-n** option, which eliminates the new line character at the end of the output string. The cursor remains on the same line at the end of the output string:

```
> echo -n Please enter a greeting:
```

If you wish to include a space at the end of your prompt, you need to place the output string within double quotes, including the space:

```
> echo -n "Please enter a greeting: "
```

The **greetpt** script, shown next, contains a TCSH shell version of a prompt remaining on the same line as the input.

greetpt

```
#

echo -n "Please enter a greeting: "
set greeting = $<

echo "The greeting you entered was $greeting"
```

```
> greetpt
Please enter a greeting: hello
The greeting you entered was hello
>
```

Argument Array: argv

When a shell script is invoked, all the words on the command line are parsed and placed in elements of an array called **argv**. **argv[0]** will hold the command name. Beginning with **argv[1]** and on, each element will hold an argument entered on the command line. In the case of shell scripts, **argv[0]** will always contain the name of the shell script. Just as with any array element, you can access the contents of an argument array element by preceding it with a **$** operator. **$argv[1]** accesses the contents of the first element in the **argv** array—the first argument. If more than one argument is entered, they can be referenced with each corresponding element in the **argv** array. In the next example, the **myargs** script prints out four arguments. Four arguments are then entered on the command line

myargs

```
#

echo "The first argument is: $argv[1]"
echo "The second argument is: $argv[2]"
echo "The third argument is: $argv[3]"
echo "The fourth argument is: $argv[4]"
```

```
> myargs Hello Hi yo "How are you"
The first argument is: Hello
The second argument is: Hi
The third argument is: yo
The fourth argument is: How are you
>
```

An **argv** element can be abbreviated to the number of the element preceded by a **$** sign. **$argv[1]** can be written as **$1**. This makes for shell scripts whose argument references are very similar to BASH and PDKSH shell argument references. A special argument variable **argv[*]** references all the arguments in the command line. **$argv[*]** can be abbreviated as **$***. Notice that this is the same name used in the BASH shell to reference all arguments.

The **#argv** argument variable contains the number of arguments entered on the command line. This is useful for specifying a fixed number of arguments for a script. The number can be checked to see if the user has entered the correct amount.

The **arglist** script in the next example shows the use of both the **argv[*]** and **#argv** special argument variables. The user first displays the number of arguments, using **#argv**, and then uses **argv[*]** to display the list of arguments entered.

arglist

```
#

echo "The number of arguments entered is $#argv"
echo "The list of arguments is: $argv[*]"
```

```
> arglist Hello hi yo
The number of arguments entered is 3
The list of arguments is: Hello hi yo
```

Numeric Variables: @

In the TCSH shell, you can declare numeric variables using the **@** command instead of the **set** command. You can then perform arithmetic, relational, and bitwise operations on such variables. In this respect, the TCSH shell is similar to programming languages. Numeric and string variables are two very different types of objects managed in very different ways. You cannot use the **set** command on a numeric variable. The **@** command consists of the keyword **@**, the variable name, an assignment operator, and an expression. The next example declares the numeric variable **num** and assigns the value 10 to it.

```
> @ num = 10
```

Many different assignment operators are available for you to use, such as increments and arithmetic assignment operators. They are the same as those used in awk and in the C programming language. The expression can be any arithmetic, relational, or bitwise expression. You can create complex expressions using parentheses. The operands in an expression should be separated from the operator by spaces, for example, 10*5 is not a valid expression and should be written with spaces, 10 * 5. You can also use a numeric variable as an operand in an expression. In the next example, the variable **count** is declared as numeric and used in an arithmetic expression. Notice that count is evaluated with a **$** operator so that the value of count, 3, is used in the expression. See Table 16-4 for a list of numeric operators.

```
> @ count = 3
> @ num = 2 * ($count + 10)
> echo $num
26
```

Environment Variables: setenv

The TCSH shell has two types of variables: local variables and environment variables. A local variable is local to the shell it was declared in; an environment variable operates like a scoped global variable. It is known to any subshells, but not to any parent shells. An environment variable is defined with the **setenv** command. You assign a value to an environment variable using the **setenv** command, the variable name, and the value assigned. There is no assignment operator. In the next example, the greeting environment variable is assigned the value "hello".

```
> setenv greeting hello
```

Whenever a shell script is called, it generates its own shell. If a shell script is executed from another shell script, it will have its own shell separate from that of the first script. There are now two shells, the parent shell belonging to the first script and a subshell, which is the new shell generated when the second script was executed. When a script is executed from within another script, its shell is a subshell of the first script's shell. The original script's shell is a parent shell.

Each shell has its own set of variables. The subshell cannot reference local variables in the parent shell, but it can reference environment variables. Any environment variables declared in the parent shell can be referenced by any subshells.

Control Structures

As in other shells, the TCSH shell has a set of control structures that let you control the execution of commands in a script. There are loop and conditional control structures with which you can repeat Linux commands or make decisions on which commands you want to execute. The **while** and **if** control structures are more general purpose control structures, performing iterations and making decisions using a variety of different tests. The **switch** and **foreach** control structures are more specialized operations. The **switch** structure is a restricted form of the **if** condition that checks to see if a value is equal to one of a set of possible values. The **foreach** structure is a limited type of loop that runs through a list of values, assigning a new value to a variable with each iteration.

The TCSH shell differs from other shells in that its control structures conform more to a programming language format. The test condition for a TCSH shell control structure is an expression that evaluates to true or false, not a Linux command. One key difference between BASH shell and TCSH shell control structures is that TCSH shell structures cannot redirect or pipe their output. They are strictly control structures, controlling the execution of commands.

Test Expressions

The **if** and **while** control structures use an expression as their test. A true test is any expression that results in a non-zero value. A false test is any expression that results in a 0 value. In the TCSH shell, relational and equality expressions can be easily used as test expressions, because they result in 1 if true and 0 if false. There are many possible operators that you can use in an expression. The test expression can also be arithmetic or a string comparison, but strings can only be compared for equality or inequality.

Unlike the BASH and PDKSH shells, you must enclose the TCSH shell **if** and **while** test expressions within parentheses. The next example shows a simple test expression testing to see if two strings are equal.

```
if ( $greeting == "hi" ) then
    echo Informal Greeting
endif
```

The TCSH shell has a separate set of operators for testing strings against other strings or against regular expressions. The **==** and **!=** test for the equality and inequality of strings. The **=~** and **!~** operators test a string against a regular expression and test to see if a pattern match is successful or not. The regular expression can contain any of the shell special characters. In the next example, any value of greeting that begins with an upper- or lowercase *h* will match the regular expression, **[Hh]***.

```
if ( $greeting =~ [Hh]* ) then
    echo Informal Greeting
endif
```

Like the BASH shell, the TCSH shell also has several special operators that test the status of files. Many of these operators are the same. In the next example, the **if** command tests to see if the file **mydata** is readable. Table 16-5 lists these operators, and Table 16-6 lists TCSH shell commands and variables.

```
if ( -r mydata ) then
    echo Informal Greeting
endif
```

Shell Conditions: if-then, if-then-else, switch

The TCSH shell has a set of conditional control structures with which you make decisions about what Linux commands to execute. Many of these conditional control structures are similar to conditional control structures found in the BASH shell. There are, however, some key differences. The TCSH shell **if** structure ends with the keyword **endif**. The **switch** structure uses the keyword **case** differently. It ends with the keyword **endsw** and uses the keyword **breaksw** instead of two semicolons. Furthermore, there are two **if** control structures: a simple version that executes only one command,

and a more complex version that can execute several commands as well as alternative commands. The simple version of **if** consists of the keyword **if** followed by a test and a single Linux command. The complex version ends with the keyword **endif**. The TCSH shell's conditional control structures are listed in Table 16-7.

if-then　The **if-then** structure places a condition on several Linux commands. That condition is an expression. If the expression results in a value other than 0, then the expression is true, and the commands within the **if** structure are executed. If the expression results in a 0 value, then the expression is false, and the commands within the **if** structure are not executed.

The **if-then** structure begins with the keyword **if** and is followed by an expression enclosed in parentheses. The keyword **then** follows right after the expression. You can then specify any number of Linux commands on the following lines. The keyword **endif** ends the **if** command. Notice that, whereas in the BASH shell the **then** keyword is on a line of its own, in the TCSH shell, **then** is on the same line as the test expression. The syntax for the **if-then** structure is shown here:

```
if ( Expression ) then
        Commands
    endif
```

The **ifls** script shown next allows you to list files by size. If you enter an **s** at the prompt, each file in the current directory is listed, followed by the number of blocks it uses. If the user enters anything else, the **if** test fails and the script does nothing.

ifls

```
#
echo -n "Please enter option: "
set option = $<

if ($option == "s") then
        echo Listing files by size
        ls -s
    endif
```

```
> ifls
Please enter option: s
Listing files by size
total 2
    1 monday     2 today
>
```

if-then-else   Often, you need to choose between two alternatives based on whether or not an expression is true. The **else** keyword allows an **if** structure to choose between two alternatives. If the expression is true, then those commands immediately following the test expression are executed. If the expression is false, those commands following the **else** keyword are executed. The syntax for the **if-else** command is shown here:

```
if ( Expression ) then
        Commands
    else
        Commands
endif
```

The **elsels** script in the next example executes the **ls** command to list files with two different possible options, either by size or with all file information. If the user enters an **s**, files are listed by size; otherwise, all file information is listed. Notice how the syntax differs from the BASH shell version of the **elsels** script described in the previous chapter.

elsels

```
#
echo Enter s to list file sizes,
echo otherwise all file information is listed.
echo -n "Please enter option: "
set option = $<

if ($option == "s") then
     ls -s
     else
     ls -l
endif
echo Good-bye
```

```
> elsels
Enter s to list file sizes,
otherwise all file information is listed.
Please enter option: s
total 2
     1 monday      2 today
Good-bye
>
```

switch   The **switch** structure chooses among several possible alternatives. It is very similar to the BASH shell's **case** structure. A choice is made by comparing a string with several possible patterns. Each possible pattern is associated with a set of commands. If a match is found, the associated commands are performed. The **switch** structure begins with the keyword **switch** and a test string within parentheses. The string is often derived from a variable evaluation. A set of patterns then follows. Each pattern is preceded with the keyword **case** and terminated with a colon. Commands associated with this choice are listed after the colon. The commands are terminated with the keyword **breaksw**. After all the listed patterns, the keyword **endsw** ends the **switch** structure. The syntax for the **switch** structure is shown here:

```
switch (test-string)
    case pattern:
            commands
            breaksw
    case pattern:
            commands
            breaksw
    default:
            commands
            breaksw
    endsw
```

Each pattern will be matched against the test string until a match is found. If no match is found, the default option is executed. The default choice is represented with the keyword **default**. The **default** is optional. You do not have to put it in. However, it is helpful for notifying the user of test strings with no match.

A **switch** structure is often used to implement menus. In the program **lschoice**, in the next example, the user is asked to enter an option for listing files in different ways. Notice the **default** option that warns of invalid input.

lschoice

```
#
echo s. List Sizes
echo l. List All File Information
echo c. List C Files

echo -n "Please enter choice: "
set choice = $<
```

```
switch ($choice)
   case s:
      ls -s
      breaksw
   case l:
      ls -l
      breaksw
   case c:
      ls *.c
      breaksw
   default:
      echo Invalid Option
      breaksw
   endsw
```

```
> lschoice
s. List Sizes
l. List All File Information
c. List C Files
Please enter choice: c
io.c    lib.c    main.c
>
```

Loops: while and foreach

The TCSH shell has a set of loop control structures that allow you to repeat Linux commands: **while**, **foreach**, and **repeat**. The TCSH shell's loop control structures are listed in Table 16-7. The **while** structure operates like corresponding structures found in programming languages. Like the TCSH shell's **if** structure, the **while** structure tests the result of an expression. The TCSH shell's **foreach** structure, like the **for** and **for-in** structures in the BASH shell, does not perform any tests. It simply progresses through a list of values, assigning each value in turn to a specified variable. In this respect, the **foreach** structure is very different from corresponding structures found in programming languages.

while   The **while** loop repeats commands. A **while** loop begins with the keyword **while** and is followed by an expression enclosed in parentheses. The end of the loop is specified by the keyword **end**. The syntax for the **while** loop is shown here:

```
while ( expression )
        commands
    end
```

The **while** can easily be combined with a **switch** structure to drive a menu. In the next example, notice that the menu contains a **quit** option that will set the value of **again** to **no** and stop the loop.

lschoicew

```
#
set again=yes

while ($again == yes)
echo "1. List Sizes"
echo "2. List All File Information"
echo "3. List C Files"
echo "4. Quit"
echo -n "Please enter choice: "
set choice = $<

switch ($choice)
   case 1:
      ls -s
      breaksw
   case 2:
      ls -l
      breaksw
   case 3:
      ls *.c
      breaksw
   case 4:
      set again = no
      echo Good-bye
      breaksw
   default
      echo Invalid Option
   endsw

end
```

```
> lschoicew
1. List Sizes
2. List All File Information
3. List C Files
4. Quit
Please enter choice: 3
```

```
main.c    lib.c    file.c
1. List Sizes
2. List All File Information
3. List C Files
4. Quit
Please enter choice: 4
Good-bye
>
```

foreach   The **foreach** structure is designed to sequentially reference a list of values. It is very similar to the BASH shell's **for-in** structure. The **foreach** structure takes two operands—a variable and a list of values enclosed in parentheses. Each value in the list is assigned to the variable in the **foreach** structure. Like the **while** structure, the **foreach** structure is a loop. Each time through the loop, the next value in the list is assigned to the variable. When the end of the list is reached, the loop stops. Like the **while** loop, the body of a **foreach** loop ends with the keyword **end**. The syntax for the **foreach** loop is shown here:

```
foreach variable ( list of values )
    commands
end
```

In the **mylist** script, in the next example, the user simply outputs a list of each item with today's date. The list of items makes up the list of values read by the **foreach** loop. Each item is consecutively assigned to the variable grocery.

mylist

```
#
set tdate='date '+%D''

foreach grocery ( milk cookies apples cheese )
    echo "$grocery    $tdate"
end
```

```
$ mylist
milk        12/23/96
cookies     12/23/96
apples      12/23/96
cheese      12/23/96
$
```

The **foreach** loop is useful for managing files. In the **foreach** structure, you can use shell special characters in a pattern to generate a list of file names for use as your list of values. This generated list of file names then becomes the list referenced by the **foreach** structure. An asterisk by itself generates a list of all files and directories. ***.c** lists files with the **.c** extension. These are usually C source code files. The next example makes a backup of each file and places the backup in a directory called **sourcebak**. The pattern ***.c** generates a list of file names that the **foreach** structure can operate on.

cbackup

```
#

foreach backfile ( *.c )
    cp $backfile sourcebak/$backfile
    echo $backfile
end
```

```
> cbackup
io.c
lib.c
main.c
```

The **foreach** structure without a specified list of values takes as its list of values the command line arguments. The arguments specified on the command line when the shell file was invoked become a list of values referenced by the **foreach** structure. The variable used in the **foreach** structure is set automatically to each argument value in sequence. The first time through the loop, the variable is set to the value of the first argument. The second time, it is set to the value of the second argument, and so on.

In the **mylistarg** script in the next example, there is no list of values specified in the **foreach** loop. Instead, the **foreach** loop consecutively reads the values of command line arguments into the grocery variable. When all the arguments have been read, the loop ends.

mylistarg

```
#
set tdate='date '+%D"

foreach grocery ( $argv[*] )
    echo "$grocery    $tdate"
end
```

```
$ mylistarg milk cookies apples cheese
milk        12/23/96
cookies     12/23/96
apples      12/23/96
cheese      12/23/96
$
```

You can explicitly reference the command line argument by using the argv[*] special argument variable. In the next example, a list of C program files is entered on the command line when the shell file **cbackuparg** is invoked. In the **foreach** loop, argv[*] references all the arguments on the command line. Each argument will be consecutively assigned to the variable backfile in the **foreach** loop. The first time through the loop, $backfile is the same as $argv[1]. The second time through, it is the same as $argv[2]. The variable argnum is used to reference each argument. Both the argument and the value of backfile are displayed to show that they are the same.

cbackuparg

```
#

@ argnum = 1
foreach backfile ($argv[*])
    cp $backfile sourcebak/$backfile
    echo "$backfile $argv[$argnum]"
    @ argnum = $argnum + 1
end
```

```
> cbackuparg  main.c  lib.c  io.c
main.c main.c
lib.c lib.c
io.c io.c
```

Summary

You can use the TCSH shell's **history** utility to list and reference previous commands that you have executed. You can even edit those commands and execute the edited versions. With the TCSH shell's **alias** command, you can give another name to a command. The alias can reference a command or a command with its arguments.

The TCSH shell has a set of features that you can turn on and off. Some commonly used features are **ignoreeof**, **noclobber**, and **noglob**. The **ignoreeof** feature prevents accidental logouts, and **noclobber** prevents the redirection operation from overwriting existing files. The **noglob** feature treats special characters as merely ordinary characters.

Like the BASH and PDKSH shells, the TCSH shell also has a shell programming capability that operates like a programming language. You can define variables and assign values to them. You can use control structures to implement loops and conditions. You place variable definitions, shell commands, and control structures in a shell script and execute the script, just as you would do with a program.

Variables can be either strings or numeric variables. String variables are declared and assigned values with the **set** command. Numeric variables are declared and assigned values with the **@** command. The **@** command allows you to use complex arithmetic, relational, and bitwise expressions whose results can be assigned to a numeric variable. You can also declare environment variables. An environment variable is known to any subshells of the shell it was defined in. Environment variables are defined and assigned values with the **setenv** command. They are most often used for shell special variables.

The loop and condition structures correspond to similar structures in programming languages. The loop structures are the **while** and the **foreach** loops. The condition structures are the **if** and **switch** conditions. The **while** loop and **if** condition operate much as they do in programming languages. The loop continues until a test expression is false. The **if** condition executes its commands if its test expression is true. The test expression is a TCSH shell expression. The operators used in a TCSH shell expression are similar to those found in the C programming language. There is a wide range of assignment, arithmetic, relational, and bitwise operators, many of which are not available in the BASH or PDKSH shell. Like C program expressions, a TCSH shell expression is true if it results in a non-zero value; it is false if it results in a 0 value.

The **switch** structure works like a restricted version of the **if** structure. The **switch** structure compares a string with a set of possible patterns. If a match is found, then operations associated with that matched pattern are executed. **switch** is useful for implementing menus, from which a user makes a choice among several possible options.

The **foreach** structure runs through a list of values, assigning each value in turn to a specified variable. There is no test. The list of values can be generated by a pattern and shell special characters. For example, the asterisk, *****, will generate a list of your file names. A list of values can also be specified by a set of words. Each word is then a value assigned in turn to the **for** variable. The loop will always continue until all values have been assigned.

Event References	**Function**
!*event num*	References an event with event number
!*characters*	References an event with beginning characters
!**?***pattern***?**	References an event with a pattern in the event
!**–***event num*	References an event with an offset from the first event
!*num–num*	References a range of events

Event Word References	
!*event num:word num*	References a particular word in an event
!*event num***:^**	References first argument (second word) in an event
!*event num***:$**	References last argument in an event
!*event num***:^–$**	References all arguments in an event
!*event num***:***	References all arguments in an event

Event Editing Substitutions	
!*event num***:s/***pattern***/***newtext***/**	Edits an event with a pattern substitution. References a particular word in an event.
!*event num***:sg/***pattern***/***newtext***/**	Performs a global substitution on all instances of a pattern in the event
!*event num***:s/***pattern***/***newtext***/p**	Suppresses execution of the edited event

Table 16-1. *TCSH Shell History Commands*

Shell Features	Function
set and **unset**	Shell features are turned on and off with the **set** and **unset** commands $ **set** *feature-variable* $ **set noclobber** *set noclobber on* $ **unset noclobber** *set noclobber off*
echo	Displays each command before executing it
ignoreeof	Disables CTRL-D logout
noclobber	Does not overwrite files through redirection
noglob	Disables special characters used for file name expansion: *****, **?**, **~**, and **[]**
notify	Notifies user immediately when background job is completed
verbose	Displays command after a history command reference

Table 16-2.   *TCSH Shell Features*

System Determined		Description
home	HOME	Path name for user's home directory
	LOGNAME	Login name
cwd		Path name of current working directory
Redefinable Special Variables		
shell	SHELL	Path name of program for login shell
path	PATH	List of path names for directories searched for executable commands
prompt		Primary shell prompt

Table 16-3.   *TCSH Shell Special Variables*

Redefinable Special Variables	Description
`mail`	Name of mail file checked by mail utility for received messages
User-Defined Special Variables	
`cdpath`	Path names for directories searched by **cd** command for subdirectories
`history`	Number of commands in your history list
`savehist`	Number of commands in your history list that you save for the next login session. Commands are saved in a file named **.history**
`EXINIT`	Initialization commands for Ex/Vi editor
`TERM`	Terminal name

Table 16-3. *TCSH Shell Special Variables* (continued)

Assignment Operators	Function/Description
`=`	Assignment
`+=`	Adds to expression and then assigns
`-=`	Subtracts from expression and then assigns
`*=`	Multiplies with expression and then assigns
`/=`	Divides into expression and then assigns
`%=`	Modulo operation with expression and then assigns
`++`	Increment variable
`--`	Decrement variable

Table 16-4. *Numeric Operators*

Arithmetic Operators	Function/Description
–	Minus unary operator
+	Addition
–	Subtraction
*	Multiplication
/	Division
%	Modulo
Relational Operators	
>	Greater-than
<	Less-than
>=	Greater-than-or-equal
<=	Less-than-or-equal
!=	Not-equal
==	Equal

Table 16-4. *Numeric Operators (continued)*

String Comparisons	Function/Description
==	Equal strings
!=	Not-equal strings
=~	Compares string to a pattern to test if equal. The pattern can be any regular expression
!~	Compares string to a pattern to test if not equal. The pattern can be any regular expression

Table 16-5. *Expression Operators*

Logical Operations	Function/Description
&&	Logical AND
||	Logical OR
!	Logical NOT
File Tests	
-e	File exists
-r	File is readable
-w	File can be written to, modified
-x	File is executable
-d	File name is a directory name
-f	File is an ordinary file
-o	File is owned by user
-z	File is empty

Table 16-5.   *Expression Operators (continued)*

Shell Commands	Function
echo	Displays values **-n** eliminates output newline
eval	Executes the command line
exec	Executes command in place of current process. Does not generate a new subshell; uses the current one
exit	Exits from the current shell
setenv *var*	Makes variable available for reference by each new subshell (call-by-reference)

Table 16-6.   *TCSH Shell Commands and Variables*

Shell Commands	Function
`printenv`	Displays values of environment variables
`set`	Assigns new values to variables. Used alone, lists all defined variables
`@`	Assigns numeric expressions
`shift`	Moves each command line argument to the left so the number used to reference it is one less than before—argument $3 would then be referenced by $2, and so on; $1 is lost
`unset`	Undefines a variable
`unsetenv`	Undefines an environment variable
Command Line Arguments	
`$argv[0]` `$0`	Name of Linux command
`$argv[n]` `$n`	The *n*th command line argument beginning from 1, `$1-$n` You can use **set** to change them
`$argv[*]` `$*`	All the command line arguments beginning from 1. You can use **set** to change them
`$#argv` `$#`	The count of the command line arguments

Table 16-6.   *TCSH Shell Commands and Variables* (continued)

Conditional Control Structures:
if-then, else, switch

`if`(*expression*) **then** *commands* `endif`	If the expression is true, the following commands are executed. You can specify more than one Unix command

`if`(*expression*) **then**
 command
 `else`
 command
 `endif`
	If the expression is true, the command after **then** is executed. If the expression is false, the command following **else** is executed

Table 16-7.   *TCSH Shell Control Structures*

Conditional Control Structures:
`if-then, else, switch`

`switch`(*string*)
`case pattern:`
command
`breaksw`
`default:`
command
`endsw`
	Allows you to choose among several alternative commands

Loop Control Structures:
`while` **and** `foreach`

`while`(*expression*) *command* `end`	Executes commands as long as the expression is true

`foreach` *variable* `(arg-list)`
command
`end`
	Iterates the loop for as many arguments as there are in the argument list. Each time through the loop, the variable is set to the next argument in the list; operates like `for-in` in the Bourne shell

Table 16-7.   *TCSH Shell Control Structures* (continued)

PART FIVE

Editors and Utilities

Chapter Seventeen

The Vi Editor

Although many different kinds of editors may be available on any given Linux system, all systems have the two standard editors: Ed and Vi. Ed and Vi are standard applications that were originally developed for Unix systems along with the Ex editor. Vi, which stands for "visual," remains one of the most widely used editors in Linux. The line editor, Ed, is rarely used. As a line editor, it displays and edits only one line at a time, making it difficult to use. The Vi editor displays a whole screen of data at a time and allows you to edit any data shown on the screen.

When Unix was first developed, the Vi editor represented a significant advancement over other text editors of the time. Since then, more powerful and easy-to-use editors, such as WordPerfect, have become available on many Unix and Linux systems. Your particular Linux system may have a text editor or word processor that you are more familiar with. If so, you do not need to study the Vi editor. OpenLinux contains the Crisplite editor, which is much easier to use than Vi. Still, it is helpful to know Vi, since it is standard on all Unix and Linux systems. If you ever have to work on another system with a different word processor than the one you use, you know that you can always use Vi. The Vi editor is the same on all systems and in all versions of Linux and Unix.

Because of its visual interface, Vi is easier than the Ed line editor for beginners to learn. However, Vi is also a very sophisticated editor with a variety of complex commands. It is easy to become confused and lost when first attempting to learn the features of this editor. There are often several ways to do the same operation with slightly different effects. This chapter will focus first on a central core of commands needed to perform basic editing operations. Once these core commands are mastered, you can consider the more complex operations described in sections that follow.

Vi Command, Input, and Line Editing Modes

Editors use a keyboard for two very different operations: to specify editing commands and to receive character input. As editing commands, certain keys will perform deletions, some will execute changes, and others will perform cursor movement. As character input, keys will represent characters that can be entered into the file that is being edited. In many common PC editors these two different functions are divided among different keys on the keyboard. Alphabetic keys are reserved for character input. Function keys and control keys specify editing commands such as deleting text or moving the cursor.

Such PC-style editors can rely on the existence of an extended keyboard that includes function and control keys. Unix, however, was designed to be independent of any specific type of keyboard. Any type of terminal or personal computer can be mapped into a Unix system. Editors in Unix were designed to assume a minimal keyboard with alphabetic characters, some control characters, as well as the ESC and ENTER keys. Instead of dividing the command and input functions among different keys, the Vi editor has two separate modes of operation for the keyboard: command mode and input mode. In command mode, all the keys on the keyboard become editing commands. In the input mode, the keys on the keyboard become input characters.

When you change modes, the functionality of the keyboard changes. When you invoke the Vi editor, you are placed in command mode. Each key now becomes an editing command. Pressing a key executes a certain command. For example, pressing the **x** key deletes a character from your text. Pressing the **l** key moves the cursor right one character. Some of these editing commands, such as **a** or **i**, enter the input mode. Upon pressing the **i** key, you leave the command mode and enter the input mode.

Once in the input mode, the keyboard again changes functionality. Each key now represents a character to be input to the text. The keyboard becomes like a typewriter. When you press a key, its corresponding character is added to the text. For example, pressing the **x** key simply adds an *x* to the text. Pressing the TAB key enters a tab character into the file. The one exception is ESC. Pressing ESC automatically returns you to the command mode, and the keys once again become editor commands. You can then easily re-enter the input mode with any of the input editing commands. As you edit text, you will find yourself constantly moving from the command mode to the input mode and back again.

Though the Vi command mode handles most editing operations, there are some, such as file saving and global substitutions, that it cannot perform. For such operations you need to execute line editing commands. You enter the line editing mode using the Vi colon command, **:**. The colon is a special command that allows you to perform one line editing operation. Upon pressing the colon, a line opens up at the bottom of the screen with the cursor placed at the beginning of the line. You are now in the line editing mode. In this mode, you enter an editing command on a line, press ENTER, and the command is executed. Entry into this mode is only temporary. Upon pressing ENTER, you are automatically returned to the Vi command mode, and the cursor returns to its previous position on the screen. Figure 17-1 illustrates the three different modes of operation in Vi.

The command and input operations constitute two very separate modes. Add to this the line editing mode, and you are faced with three very different modes of operation in Vi. The line editing mode operates on a line: you type in a command with its arguments and terminate the command by pressing ENTER. The Vi command mode, however, operates by single keys. Simply pressing a key or sequence of keys executes an editor command. The Vi input mode inputs characters into a text file. Any key is a valid character except for ESC. The ESC key returns you to the command mode.

Creating, Saving, and Quitting a File in Vi

With the Vi editor you can create, save, close, and quit files. The commands for each are not all that similar. Saving and quitting a file involves the use of special line editing commands, whereas closing a file is a Vi editing command. Creation of a file is usually specified on the same shell command line that invokes the Vi editor.

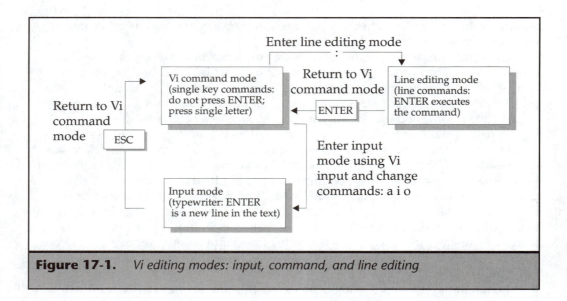

Figure 17-1. *Vi editing modes: input, command, and line editing*

To edit a file, type **vi** and the name of a file on the shell command line. If a file by that name does not exist, the system will create it. In effect, giving the name of a file that does not yet exist instructs the Vi editor to create that file. The following command invokes the Vi editor, working on the file **booklist**. If **booklist** does not yet exist, the Vi editor will create it.

```
$ vi booklist
```

After executing the **vi** command, you enter Vi's command mode. Each key becomes a Vi editing command, and the screen becomes a window onto the text file. Text is displayed screen by screen. The first screen of text is displayed, and the cursor is positioned in the upper-left corner. With a newly created file, there is no text to display. This fact is indicated by a column of tildes at the left-hand side of the screen. The tildes represent that part of a screen that is not part of the file.

Remember that when you first enter the Vi editor you are in the command mode. To enter text, you need to enter the input mode. In the command mode, the **a** key is the editor command for appending text. Pressing this key places you in the input mode. Now, the keyboard operates like a typewriter and you can input text to the file. If you press ENTER, you will merely start a new line of text. After entering text, you can leave the input mode and return to the command mode by pressing ESC.

Once finished with the editing session, you exit Vi by typing two capital Z's, **ZZ**. You hold down the SHIFT key and press Z twice. This sequence first saves the file and then exits the Vi editor, returning you to the Linux shell.

When you edit a file, it is first read into a work buffer. Any changes or additions of text are made to the copy of the file in the work buffer. The original file remains on the disk. Only by executing a save command is the original file overwritten by the work buffer version. At the end of each session, the **ZZ** command will save the file before quitting, overwriting the original file with the work buffer version.

However, you may want to save a file several times throughout your editing session. Saving a file is performed by the line editing command **w**, which writes a file to the disk. It is equivalent to the Save command found in other word processors. To save a file in Vi, you first press the colon key to access the line editing mode, then type in a **w** and press ENTER. The file is saved, and you automatically return to the Vi command mode.

A mistake that beginners often make in attempting to save a file is to forget to press ESC first when in the input mode. The colon command is an editing command. It can only be executed within the command mode. If you are in the input mode and press the colon key, it will simply be taken as a colon character and input into the text. If you are in the input mode and you want to save your file, you must first press ESC to exit the input mode and enter the command mode. Then a **:w** command will save the file. Notice that the **:w** command with a file name also functions like the Save As operation in other word processors. The file currently being worked on is saved as another file.

You will find that you also need to use the **:w** command whenever you edit an unnamed file. When you invoke the Vi editor without a file name argument, you will automatically be editing an unnamed file. In the next example, the user invokes the Vi editor on the shell command line but does not specify any filename. In this case the user will edit an unnamed file.

    $ **vi**

You can input text and perform editing operations on an unnamed file, but no actual file has yet been created. If you are editing an unnamed file, the Vi editor will not allow you to use **ZZ** to exit an editing session—you must first create the file. You do this using the **:w** save command followed by the new file's name. After you press the colon key, a line appears at the bottom of the screen. Next you enter the letter **w**, a space, the name of the file, and then press ENTER.

    :w booklist

After pressing ENTER, you will return to the Vi command mode, and the cursor will return to its previous location on the screen. The new file name will be displayed at the bottom of the screen, and the **ZZ** command will now work. Note that if there already is a file with the name you selected, the save operation will fail. In this event, simply repeat the **:w** command with another file name.

You can quit the Vi editor using the :**q** command. Unlike the **ZZ** command, the :**q** command does not perform any save operation before it quits. In this respect, it has one major constraint. If there have been any modifications to your file since the last save operation, then the :**q** command will fail and you will not leave the editor. However, you can override this restriction by placing a **!** qualifier after the :**q** command. The command :**q!** will quit the Vi editor without saving any modifications made to the file in that session since the last save.

Many of the line editing commands correspond to Vi commands. A case in point is the **ZZ** Vi command. You can combine the commands **w** and **q** to perform the same operations as the **ZZ** Vi command. The command :**wq** will save a file and leave the Vi editor. :**wq** is equivalent to **ZZ**.

Managing Editing Modes in Vi

Saving, quitting, and adding text to a file involve all the editing modes available in Vi. Upon invoking Vi, you are placed into the command mode. The **a** command places you in the input mode so that you can add text. The ESC key returns you from the input mode to the command mode. To save or quit a file, you must enter the line editing mode with the colon command. The line editing commands **w** and **q** will save and quit the file. Pressing ENTER after entering the line editing command both executes the command and returns you to the Vi command mode.

Much of the difficulty in managing the Vi editor is keeping track of which mode you are in. During a Vi editing session, the keyboard is constantly changing state between the command and input modes. The two modes are exclusive. While in the input mode no editing commands may be executed, and while in the command mode nothing may be input. There is usually no alert telling you whether you are in the command or input mode. This can be devastating if you think you are in the input mode but actually are in the command mode. If, while in the command mode, you press keys thinking you are entering text, you are in fact executing a series of editing commands. Unintended editing operations could suddenly take place on the text.

If you lose track of which mode you are in, you can use ESC to indirectly determine the mode. Pressing ESC while in input mode returns you to command mode. However, pressing ESC while in command mode simply makes the computer beep. If you press ESC and hear a beep, you were already in command mode. If nothing happens, you were in input mode and have now returned to command mode.

A common error occurs if you attempt to end the editing session while in input mode. You can only end an editing session in command mode. Remember that entering **ZZ** while in input mode simply adds the characters to the text. Two Z's will appear on the screen, and Vi will remain in the input mode waiting for further input. To end an editing session when in input mode, you must first exit input mode by pressing ESC, and then type **ZZ**. Once in the command mode the keys become editing commands and two capital Z's, **ZZ**, are the command for ending the editing session and saving the text.

Vi Editing Commands: Common Operations

This section presents a subset of Vi's many editing commands. Basic cursor movement, input, search, and editing operations are discussed. The Vi editor is designed to operate on many different text components, including lines, characters, words, sentences, and even paragraphs. This section will limit discussion to single characters and lines. Commands for operating on textual components such as words and sentences are discussed in the section on advanced commands later in the chapter. Figure 17-2 lists this basic set of Vi commands that you need to get started in Vi, and Table 17-1 lists the commands commonly used to move through the text.

Moving Through the Text in Vi

You can move through the text by moving the cursor, scrolling screen by screen, or moving to a specific line. Vi has the basic cursor movements for moving up and down, left and right, across the text displayed on the screen. You can also move forward and backward through the text a screen at a time. Sometimes you may need to move to a specific line in the text. You can do so in Vi using a line number.

Cursor Movement

While in command mode, you can move the cursor across the text by using the keys for movement commands. The **h**, **j**, **k**, and **l** commands perform the basic cursor movement operations. The **h** and **l** keys move the cursor horizontally across characters in a line. The **h** key moves the cursor one character to the left, and the **l** key moves it one character to the right. The **j** and **k** keys move the cursor up and down lines. The **j** key moves down one line and the **k** key moves up one line. Notice that if you hold a cursor command key down, the command will be repeated. Holding down the **l** key will move you to the end of a line.

Notice also, that to make moving the cursor easy, these keys are positioned near or under the fingertips of your right hand. When editing, you frequently need to move the cursor across characters in a line and from one line to another. Many keyboards also have a set of arrow keys that you can use instead of the **h**, **j**, **k**, and **l** keys. In addition, you can use ENTER in place of the **j** key to move the cursor down a line. The SPACEBAR can be used in place of the **l** key to move the cursor left one character.

Each text line begins at the left column of the screen and ends when you press ENTER. If the cursor is at the end of the line and you press the **l** key to move right, the computer will beep and the cursor will not move. The same is true if the cursor is on the first character of a line and you press the **h** key to move left. The beep indicates that the cursor has reached a text boundary.

The end of the line is not necessarily the right side of the screen; it is wherever you pressed ENTER. When moving to the right on a line with the **l** key, the cursor will stop where the text for that line ends. You can only move across text that actually exists in

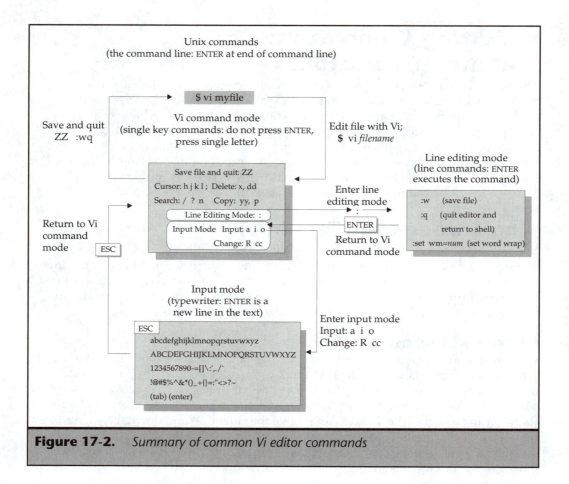

Figure 17-2. *Summary of common Vi editor commands*

the file. The space between the end of a line and the right side of the screen is dead space on the screen; it is not part of the text file. If the cursor is positioned at the end of a line and you then move the cursor to the next line, you will notice that the cursor moves to the end of the next line.

The screen operates like a window on your text file, showing only one screen of text at a time. You can move this window forward or backward across your text using various commands. If you position the cursor at the top or bottom line on the screen, the **j** and **k** keys will cause the screen to scroll vertically throughout the text file, line by line. The **j** key moves the cursor down the screen one line at a time. Once the cursor is on the last line of the screen, pressing the **j** key will move the screen down one line, losing one line off the top of the screen and including a new line at the bottom of the screen. Continually pressing the **j** key while the cursor is positioned at the last line

Cursor Movement	Effect	Delete	Effect
h	Left	x	Deletes character
l	Right	dd	Deletes a line
k	Up		
j	Down	**Change**	**Effect**
CTRL-F	Next screen	r	Replaces a character
CTRL-B	Previous screen	cc	Changes a line
g	Last line specific line	R	Overwrites
Input		**Move**	
a	Appends	p	Inserts deleted/copied text
i	Inserts	dd p	Moves a line
o	Opens a line		
Search		**Copy**	
/	Searches pattern	yy p	Copies a line
?	Searches pattern		
n	Repeats search		

Table 17-1.   *Common Vi Editor Commands*

on the screen moves the screen down the text file, line by line. The reverse is true for the **k** key.

You also can move through the text a whole screen at a time using the CTRL-F and CTRL-B keys. The CTRL-F key moves forward one screen of text, and CTRL-B moves backward one screen of text. Once you have moved forward in your file, you may want to move back toward the beginning of your text. You can do so, screen by screen, by pressing CTRL-B.

Line Numbers: G

You can move to a particular line using the **G** command and a line number. Vi sequentially numbers each line of text. The **G** command (it must be uppercase *G*) moves the cursor to a particular line. You first enter the line number and then press the **G** key. The cursor then moves to that line. You can also use the **G** command to move quickly to the end of your file. If no line number is entered before you press the **G** key, then the cursor moves directly to the end of the file. The **G** key by itself is a quick way to locate the end of a very large file.

Modifying Text in Vi: Input, Deletions, and Changes

Editing your text usually involves modifying it in some way. You can add more text at different places in your file. You may decide to delete text that you have already entered. Or you may need to change part of your text. Vi has an extensive set of commands for inputting text in different ways as well as deleting or changing different text segments, such as characters, lines, sentences, words, and paragraphs. Vi also allows you to undo any changes you make to your file, even text that you have input. The undo command, **u**, will undo the previous Vi command. Be sure to keep this in mind as you make changes to your file. It is very easy, at times, to make unintentional changes to your file. You can easily undo such changes with the **u** command.

Input

You already know that when the Vi editor is invoked and a new file is created, you are placed in command mode. To enter text, you need to execute an input command, such as **a**, that will place you in the input mode. Once in the input mode, the keyboard becomes like a typewriter and any character you press is entered into the text.

Once in the input mode, you may enter as much text as you wish until you press ESC. You can also delete the most recently entered character by pressing BACKSPACE. Use of the BACKSPACE key is restricted to input mode and erases only characters to the left. By continually pressing BACKSPACE, you can erase all the characters keyed in since entering input mode.

Most PC-style word processors automatically wrap text for you when you reach the right margin, but Vi does not do so automatically. In Vi a new line is created in the text only when you press ENTER while in the input mode. Though Vi does not automatically insert new lines when the cursor reaches the end of the screen, it may appear that way on the screen display. Lines longer than the length of the screen are wrapped around to appear as two lines on the screen. However, the editor treats them as one. You can, if you wish, set a Vi option that will automatically insert new lines at a specified margin. This is the word-wrap margin, and you set it with the line editing command **:set wm=***col*. In this case, *col* is the column for the right margin. The command **:set wm=70** will set the word-wrap margin to the 70th column. Whenever you reach the 70th column when entering text, a new line is automatically inserted.

There are several input commands, each of which enters the input mode at a different point in the text relative to the cursor. The most common input commands are **a** (append), **i** (insert), and **o** (open). The **a** key places the user into input after the character the cursor is on. The **i** key places the user into input before the character the cursor is on. The **o** key opens a new line below the line the cursor is on and places the user into input at the beginning of that new line. Because the **i** command inserts before the character the cursor is on, it is often used to insert text before a word. If the cursor is on the first character of a word, the **i** command will enter the insert mode before the word. The **a** command can be used to add text after a word. If the cursor is on the last character of a word, the **a** command will enter the input mode after the word.

The difference between the **i** and **a** commands becomes significant when you want to add text to either the beginning or end of a line. You use the **i** command to insert text at the beginning of a line, and the **a** command to add text to the end of a line. To insert text at the beginning of a line, you should place the cursor on the first character in the line. The **i** command will then insert text before that character. To add text at the end of a line, you should position the cursor on the last character in the line. The **a** command will then add text after that character. Be careful not to confuse the two commands. If the cursor is positioned on the last character in a line and you press the **i** key, the new text will be inserted before that last character. The same kind of error occurs if you use the **a** command to insert characters at the beginning of a line. When the cursor is positioned at the first character in a line and you press the **a** key, the new text is added after that first character, not at the beginning of the line.

Instead of just adding text on a given line, you may want to insert a whole new line. For this you use the **o** command. It can be thought of as inserting a line between two lines. You are not limited to input on that line. The new line is only a starting point for entering the input mode. Once in the input mode, pressing ENTER will add as many lines as you wish. In fact, the **o** command is equivalent to first placing the cursor at the end of a line, and pressing the **a** command and then ENTER. The **a** command places you into input and ENTER inserts a new line. The **o** command is often used to add text to the end of a file. The cursor is positioned on the last line of the file and the **o** command then opens up a new line below the end of the file. You then enter into the input mode and can add as much text as you want.

Deletions

The simplest deletion operations are those to delete single characters or whole lines of text. Pressing the **x** key deletes a single character. Whatever character the cursor is on will be deleted. The **dd** sequence of keys deletes the line that the cursor is on.

Changes

You can change any text by first deleting it with deletion commands and then entering the input mode to enter new text. To change a word, you could first repeatedly use the **x** command to delete the word and then use the **i** or **a** command to enter input and type in the new word. The Vi editor has a set of change commands that streamlines this process, automatically deleting words, lines, sentences, and paragraphs and placing you into the input mode. These are covered at length in the advanced section later in the chapter. Here, we will cover changing lines and characters, as those are the simplest operations.

The **cc** sequence of keys changes an entire line. First, **cc** deletes the text on the line, and then it enters input mode. You can then type in new text, until you press ESC to leave input mode. The **cc** command operates like a combination of the **dd** and **o** commands. **dd** deletes the line and **o** opens up a new line.

You use the **r** command to change a single character. The **r** command deletes whatever character the cursor is on and then waits for you to enter a replacement character. The character the cursor is on will be replaced by whatever character you enter. The **r** command, unlike other change commands, does not place you in the input mode. After typing in the replacement character, you remain in command mode.

The **R** key is a replacement command that overwrites text until you press ESC. You are placed in the input mode, but for every character you type in, a corresponding character is deleted from the text. This command may appear similar to an overwrite mode used in other types of word processors, but it is not. Like the **cc** command, you are actually placed in the input mode and must exit that mode with ESC before you can edit any further. Be careful not to confuse **r** and **R**. The command **r** will change only a single character. However, the command **R** will overwrite text until you press ESC. If you accidentally press **R** instead of **r**, you could unintentionally overwrite text. In this case, you need to press ESC and press the **u** command to undo the damage.

Undo

As you delete and change text, you may accidentally delete or change the wrong text and want to restore the text to its original condition. The undo command, **u**, lets you restore the text to its condition before the most recent editing command was executed. The **u** command will undo any modifications made by the input, deletion, and change commands. You may need to use this command a great deal as you learn Vi. It is easy to execute a command accidentally. If you accidentally delete a line, you can press the **u** key to restore the deleted text. If you change a line and decide you don't want the change, you can undo it with the **u** command.

Repeat Factor

You can delete or change more than one line at a time by typing in a number before the delete or change command. In those cases, the number does not represent a line number as it does with the **G** command. Instead, the number functions as a repeat factor. Any number entered before a command repeats that command (with the exception of the **G** command). For example, **3x** will delete three characters instead of one; **2dd** will delete the next two lines.

Again, be sure not to confuse the two uses for the numbers. For example, suppose you intend to use the **G** command to move to a line, then change your mind after entering a line number but before pressing **G**. Entering a line number such as 200 and then changing your mind and entering an **x** instead of a **G** will delete 200 characters. The repeat factor also applies to input and change commands. Let's say you enter the line number 50 and then execute an **i** command, instead of **G**, and input some text. Upon pressing ESC to end the input, the editor will insert 50 copies of the input into the file. Suddenly your file will contain 50 repetitions of the input just entered. If you do change your mind and decide to execute another editing command after entering a line number, you can erase the number by pressing ESC.

Should the mistake occur despite your best efforts, you can correct it with the undo command, **u**. A repeated editing command is taken as one editing operation and can be undone by pressing the **u** key. In the case of the 200 repeated **x** character deletions, all 200 deletions can be undone by pressing the **u** key immediately after the deletions occur.

Breaking and Joining Lines

The process of breaking or joining lines using Vi is more complex than that of PC-style editors. In a PC-style editor you simply press ENTER to break a line, or use BACKSPACE to join lines. In Vi, breaking a line requires the use of an input command to first enter the input mode in which you can then press ENTER. Joining a line requires a whole new Vi command, the uppercase **J** key. You cannot use BACKSPACE to join lines.

To break a line into two lines, place the cursor at the point in the line where you want it to be broken. Then enter the input command **i** or **a**. Remember that **i** inserts before the cursor and **a** appends after the cursor. Once in the input mode, press ENTER. Pressing ESC returns you to command mode. There are now two lines, the first terminated when you press ENTER. To join two lines, press **J**, and the line below the cursor is joined to the line that the cursor is on. It is as if you never pressed ENTER. However, in Vi, the new line character alone cannot be deleted by any of the deletion commands; the **dd** command deletes the new line character along with all the text on the line.

Copying, Moving, and Searching Text in Vi

You can copy and move text from one location to another in your file. Though it is possible to move and copy any text segment, such as words and sentences, this section discusses only the movement and copying of lines. You can also search your text for specific words or patterns. With the Vi editor, you can search forward or backward in your text as well as repeat searches.

Moving and Copying Lines: dd, yy, and p

To move text, you must first delete the text that you want to move. The **dd** command will delete a line. A number entered before the **dd** command will delete that many lines from and including the line that the cursor is on. These deleted lines are placed in the temporary buffer. Next, you move the cursor to the line where you want text inserted. Finally, press the **p** command, and the editor inserts the deleted lines after the line on which the cursor rests.

You can copy lines of text with the **yy** command. Preceding the **yy** command with a number will copy that many lines, including the line that the cursor is on. To copy lines of text, place the cursor on the first line to be copied. Enter the number of lines you want copied, followed immediately with the **yy** command. This command copies the lines to the temporary buffer. Then move the cursor to the line where the copied lines are to be inserted, and press the **p** command. The copied lines are inserted after the line the cursor is on. An uppercase **Y** is the same as the **yy** command and will also copy lines.

Searches

As you work on your text, you may need to search for and locate certain words or parts of words. The Vi editor has the ability to search forward and backward in a file for a given pattern. The slash key (**/**) is the Vi editing command for pattern searches. Pressing the slash key opens up a line at the bottom of the screen. A slash appears at the beginning of the line, and the cursor is positioned after the slash. You then enter the pattern you want to search for. When you press ENTER, the editor will search for the pattern, starting where the cursor was when the slash command was executed, and continuing toward the end of the file. The slash command is a forward search. If the pattern is found, the cursor is positioned at that instance of the pattern.

The question mark key (**?**) performs a pattern search, moving backward in a file. Pressing the question mark key also opens up a line at the bottom of the screen. After you type in a pattern, the search is conducted from the position of the cursor back toward the beginning of the file.

The **n** key is a command to repeat a search. A pattern is first entered and searched with the slash or question mark key. Pressing the **n** key initiates a search for the next instance of the pattern in the file. If the pattern was entered with a slash, the search will be carried out forward in the file. If the pattern was entered with a question mark, the search will be carried out backward toward the beginning of the file. If either the end or beginning of the file is reached, the search will wrap around. You can repeatedly press the **n** key to find more instances of the pattern throughout the file.

Advanced Vi Editing Commands

So far, only the basic Vi editing commands have been discussed, but there are, in fact, many more. Most lowercase editing commands have a corresponding uppercase command that performs the same action with some variation. For example, the lowercase **o**, which opens a line below the current line, has the counterpart **O**, which opens a line above the current line. This section examines different screen movement commands and then the different modifying commands, such as those that perform input, change, and delete operations.

You can also reference your text according to different text segments, such as a word, sentence, or paragraph. In the previous section, you only learned how to reference single characters or whole lines. For example, the **1** command moves the cursor left a character, and the **j** command moves the cursor down a line. However, you can also move across text segments using the **w**, **)**, and **}** commands. A **w** command moves left one word; the right parenthesis, **)**, moves one sentence; and the right brace, **}**, moves one paragraph. You can use these commands to qualify other Vi commands to operate on these text segments. For example, you can qualify the change command, **c**, with a word command, **w**, to change a word, **cw**. You can qualify a **d** command with a **)** command, **d)**, to delete a sentence. The qualifier is entered after the primary command.

Advanced Cursor Movement

Vi has many commands designed to let you move throughout your text any way you wish. You can move to different characters on a line and move across text segments such as words, sentences, and paragraphs. You can also move to different lines of text displayed on your screen: the top, bottom, or middle lines. You can even move to different lines using references such as line numbers, patterns, or marks. For example, you can mark a line with a special code letter and then later return to that line using just the code letter.

Many of these movement commands can be thought of as positional references. For example, a line number or pattern can reference a particular line. A word or sentence command can reference a particular word or sentence. Such commands can be combined with modifying commands to change different text segments. You can combine a word reference with a change command to change a word. You can also combine a pattern with a delete command to delete text up to the line referenced by that pattern. You could combine the reference to the bottom line on the screen with the copy command to copy lines from the cursor to the bottom line. Keep the positional referencing aspect of these movement commands in mind as you examine them in this section. You can use them with commands in the next section to modify your text.

Vi organizes text into lines that you can then reference using line numbers, patterns, or marks. As noted in the previous section, you can use the **G** command to locate a line with its number. The **G** command takes a preceding line number and positions the cursor at that line. If no line number is given, **G** goes to the end of the file by default. You can also use **G** with the change and delete commands. **dG** deletes the rest of the file from the current line. **cG** deletes the rest of the file and places the user into input mode.

A pattern search, indicated with a beginning slash, will locate the next line with that pattern and position the cursor on that line. The slash opens a line at the bottom of the screen and allows you to enter a pattern. Upon pressing ENTER, the next line with that pattern will be located and the cursor positioned on it. The question mark also performs a search for a pattern but toward the beginning of the file. The **?** searches backward, and the **/** searches forward.

The **n** command repeats the previous search, either forward or backward in the file. The uppercase **N** command also repeats the previous pattern search, but in the reverse direction. If a forward pattern search was effected using the **/** command, the **N** command will perform a backward search. If a backward search was performed using the **?** command, then **N** will perform a forward search.

The pattern search can be considered a text boundary. Delete and change commands can use patterns to reference lines. The delete command followed by a pattern search deletes all text between the current line and the line with the pattern. **d/hello/** deletes all lines from the current line to the line with "hello". **c/hello/** changes those lines.

Vi contains two special characters for designating the beginning and end of a word in a pattern. The beginning of a word is represented with a **\<**, and the end of a word is represented with a **\>**. The pattern **/\<make\>/** only searches for the line with the word "make." The pattern **/\<make/** searches for lines with a word beginning with "make," such as "makeup."

As a variation on the pattern command, the **%** command will locate a corresponding opening or closing parenthesis, bracket, or brace. If the cursor is positioned on an opening parenthesis, the **%** command will locate the next closing parenthesis no matter where that may be in the file. If the cursor is on a closing parenthesis, using **%** will search backwards for the next opening parenthesis. The same is true for braces and brackets. This command is especially helpful for programming language source code files that make extensive use of nested parentheses, brackets, and braces.

You can mark lines and use the marks as line references in other commands. The command **m** followed by a letter marks that line with the letter. A single quote placed before the letter references the line. You can use a mark in any command in place of a line number. **mb** marks a line with the letter *b*. The command **'bG** then goes to that line. The mark alone will also move to that line. **'b** moves to the line marked with a *b*. You can use a mark to reference lines to be deleted or changed. **'bd** deletes all lines from the current line to the line marked *b*.

The single quote is also used to reference your previous position in the text. You can move the cursor back to its previous location using two single quotes, **''**. In a sense, the second single quote is a mark that references the previous position to the cursor. Repeatedly pressing two single quotes moves you back and forth from your previous position to your current position.

Line Editing Commands

The Vi line editing commands include the same commands as those listed for the Sed editor, as described in Chapter 14. Most editing tasks are more easily executed with Vi commands. However, if you want to reference text using their line numbers, you will need to use the line editing commands. For example, suppose you want to delete lines 9 through 17. With Vi screen commands you can locate line 9 and then figure out that you need to delete the next 8 lines. With the line editing commands, you simply reference the range of lines 9,17 in a delete command, **d: 9,17 d**. The line referencing capability of the line editing commands is especially helpful when you want to make global operations. You can reference the entire text with the range **1,$**. The **$** is a special character that references the last line in a file.

As previously noted, the colon, **:**, is a Vi editing command that opens up a line at the bottom of the screen and allows you to enter a line editing command. After entering the line editing command, the cursor returns to its Vi position on the screen, and you continue working in the Vi editing mode. The line editing mode in Vi is most often used for global operations. These are usually entered within Vi as one line editing command using the colon.

You perform a global substitution by referencing all lines in the file and executing a substitution command on each one. The **$** references the last line in the file, and the range **1,$** references all lines in the file. A substitution command will substitute a matched pattern with a replacement pattern, and, when modified with a **g**, will replace text throughout the entire line. All instances of the pattern on the line will be replaced. The global line reference combined with the substitution command will perform a global substitution. Here is the format for such a command:

```
: 1,$ s/pattern/text/g
```

The next command replaces all instances of the pattern "milk" with the pattern "yogurt".

```
: 1,$ s/milk/yogurt/g
```

As with Sed, all special characters are operative in Vi line editing operations. In the next example, the first word in each line is replaced by a minus sign. The circumflex, ^, when used in a pattern, is a special character indicating the beginning of a line. The brackets indicate a range of possible characters. **[a-z]** matches on any lowercase characters. The ***** is a special character that matches on repeated instances of the preceding character. **[a-z]*** will match on any sequence of alphabetic characters. A space follows. The pattern searches for any set of alphabetic characters at the beginning of a line and ending with a space. The replacement text of the substitution command consists only of a minus sign and a space.

```
: 1,$ s/^[a-z]* /- /
```

Options in Vi: set and .exrc

Vi has a set of options with which to configure your editor. You set an option with the **set** line editing command. You can set options within Vi using the Vi line editing mode. The **set** command followed by the option name sets the option on. If the characters "no" are attached to the beginning of the option name, then the option is set off. For example, the command **set number** sets the number option, which numbers your lines; whereas the command **set nonumber** turns off the number option. The command **set** by itself provides a list of all options the user has set. If an option is already set, the command **set** followed by that option's name will display the value of the option. The command **set all** will display the settings of all the options.

The Vi Initialization File: .exrc

You may want to set certain options for every file you edit. Instead of setting these options manually for each file each time you edit them, you can place these options in your **EXINIT** shell variable, or in editor initialization files, and have them automatically set for you. To use the **EXINIT** variable to set your options automatically, you need to assign the **EXINIT** variable a quoted **set** command specifying what options you want set. Whenever you invoke Vi, the **set** command stored in **EXINIT** is automatically executed. In the next example, the user assigns to the **EXINIT** variable, the quoted **set** command to set both the **nu** option for numbering lines and the **ic** option for ignoring case in searches.

```
$ EXINIT='set nu ic'
```

Though you can assign the **set** command to the **EXINIT** variable in your shell, you would normally assign it in your login or shell initialization files. Then, whenever you log in, the **EXINIT** variable is automatically assigned its **set** command. In the next example, the quoted **set** command is assigned to **EXINIT** in the user's **.bash_profile** initialization file.

.bash_profile

```
EXINIT='set nu ic'
```

Options set in this way will be set for every file you edit. However, there are options that you may need for only a selected set of files. For example, you may want to number lines in only your C source code files, and word-wrap your lines only in your document files. You can tailor your options for a selected set of files by using an editor initialization file called **.exrc**. The **.exrc** file contains commands to configure your editor. When Vi is invoked, the shell first searches for an **.exrc** file in the current working directory. If there is one, the shell runs it, executing the commands. These are usually **set** commands setting the options for the editor. In the next example, the **.exrc** file contains the **set** commands to set the number and ignore case options.

.exrc

```
set nu
set ic
```

If there is no **.exrc** file in your working directory, the shell searches your home directory for an **.exrc** file. You can have a separate **.exrc** file in as many directories as you wish. This allows you to customize the editor according to the files you have in a given directory. For example, a directory with your source code files may require that line numbers be displayed. The **.exrc** file in this directory would have a **set** command that sets the **number** option. When you invoke the editor in this directory, the **.exrc** file in this directory will be read and its commands executed, automatically setting the **number** option. In yet another directory, you may need to have your lines word wrapped. The **.exrc** file in that directory would have the **set** command for setting the **wordwrap** option. When you invoke the editor in that directory, your lines will be automatically wrapped.

There are options that you can set that control aspects of the search operation. You can ignore case, quote special characters, or wrap the search around the end or beginning of the file. If you set the **ignorecase** option, then searches will ignore upper- or lowercase characters in making matches. A search for **/There** will retrieve both "there" and "There." You can abbreviate the **ignorecase** option with **ic**. The commands **set ignorecase** and **set ic** turn the option on, whereas **set noignorecase** and **set noic** turn it off. The **wrapscan** option allows a search to wrap around the file. A forward search, once the search has reached the end of the file, will wrap around to the beginning and continue searching until the current cursor position. A backward search, once the beginning of the file has been reached, will wrap around to the end and continue.

There are several options that you can set to control how your text is displayed. You can display text with line numbers, display nonprinting characters, limit the number of lines displayed on the screen, or affect tab positions in the text. You have already seen the command **set number**, which sets the line numbering option. It can be abbreviated to **set nu**. You can use the **nonumber** option to turn the line numbering option off: **set nonumber**.

You set the amount of spaces displayed for tabs with the **tabstop** option. The command **set tabstop=5** sets the number of spaces between tabs to 5. The **tabstop** option can be abbreviated to **ts**. **set ts=3** sets the tab stops to 3 spaces. The **tabstop** option is only a display option. It does not affect the tab spacing in the actual text file. Though the tab stops may be set to 5 in the editor, the tabs may still print out on a printer at the standard 8 spaces.

There are several options that affect the way you input text. These options take effect when you are in the Vi input mode and are typing in text. While in the input mode, you can automatically start a new line at a specified margin, you can automatically indent a new line, you can check for an opening parenthesis when entering a closing parenthesis, and you can determine the number of spaces you can backtab when in input.

The **wrapmargin** option, which can be abbreviated to **wm**, determines the position of the right margin of the text. When inputting text with **wrapmargin** on, a line is wrapped at the margin to the next line by automatically inserting a new line character. The command **set wrapmargin=30** will create an input margin of 30 characters. When you type in the 30th character of a line, a new line will automatically be inserted, and you begin at that new line. You can cancel the right margin by setting the **wrapmargin** option to 0: **set wm=0**. If the **wrapmargin** option is off, a new line will not be automatically inserted; you must press ENTER or you will continue on the same line.

The **autoindent** option, abbreviated **ai**, implements automatic indenting. The **autoindent** option works in the input mode while you are entering text. When you enter tabs to indent with the autoindent on, the next line will automatically be indented by the same amount of tabs. If the current line is further indented, the next line will also be indented to the same extent. Though the **autoindent** option allows you to increase the indent, you may also need to lessen the extent of the indentation at some point. You might want the next line to start farther to the left. Each tab in an autoindent can be canceled on an input line, one by one, with CTRL-D. The first CTRL-D shifts the cursor back by one tab; the second CTRL-D shifts the cursor back by another tab. You can always turn off the autoindent with the **set noai** command.

Summary: the Vi Editor

The Vi editor is a text editor used to create text files. Vi has three modes: command mode, input mode, and line editing mode. In each mode, the nature of the keyboard changes. In command mode, each key is an editor command. In the input mode, the keyboard becomes a typewriter, with each key inputting a character into the text file. In line editing mode, a line opens up at the bottom of the screen and allows you to enter a line editing command.

You edit a file by specifying its name on the shell command line that invokes the Vi editor. You save and quit a file with the commands **w** and **q!**. These are entered in line editing mode. The colon is the command to enter line editing mode. The **ZZ** command will end the session, saving the file and quitting Vi.

When using the Vi editor, you are constantly changing between input and command modes. Input commands such as **a** and **i** will place you directly into the input mode. The change commands such as **cc** will first delete text and then place you in the input mode. Though there are many ways to enter the input mode, there is only one way to leave it—with ESC. Once in the input mode, pressing ESC will return you to the command mode.

Vi is a sophisticated editor with an extensive number of commands for full screen text manipulation. You can move across words, sentences, and paragraphs. Most lowercase commands have an uppercase counterpart. A lowercase **i** for input has an uppercase **I** for input at the beginning of a line. The first section of this chapter focuses on a core set of commands needed to perform basic editing operations. The later sections focus on the advanced features of Vi.

Editing commands in the Vi editor deal with text as characters, lines, words, sentences, and paragraphs. There are change, copy, and deletion operations that operate on all of these text segments. (See Tables 17-2 through 17-4.) You can move and copy text, undo text, and search forward and backward through the text for patterns.

Often these commands contain similar components with some differences. The deletion command for deleting a character is **x** whereas the deletion command for deleting a line is **dd**. Sometimes you may accidentally delete or change text. The **u** command undoes the previous editing operation. If you unintentionally delete or change text, you can undo the operation by pressing the **u** key.

The Vi editor also has an extensive set of options that are set with the **set** command. These options can set such features as line numbering and word wrap. You can set options manually within the editor or you can assign a quoted **set** command to the **EXINIT** variable in your login or shell initialization files. The options specified in that **set** command will be automatically set when you invoke the editor. You can also create an editor initialization file, *.exrc*, and place **set** commands in it. Whenever you invoke the Vi editor, the commands in the *.exrc* file in the current directory are executed.

Key	Cursor Movement
h	Moves cursor left one character
l	Moves cursor right one character
k	Moves cursor up one line
j	Moves cursor down one line
w	Moves cursor forward one word
W	Moves cursor forward one space delimited word
b	Moves cursor back one word
B	Moves cursor back one space delimited word
e	Moves cursor to the end of the next word
E	Moves cursor to the end of the next space delimited word
0	Moves cursor to the beginning of the line
$	Moves cursor to the end of the line
ENTER	Moves cursor to beginning of next line
−	Moves cursor to beginning of previous line
(	Moves cursor to beginning of sentence
)	Moves cursor to end of sentence; successive command moves to beginning of next sentence
{	Moves cursor to beginning of paragraph
}	Moves cursor to end of paragraph
CTRL-F	Moves forward by a screen of text; the next screen of text is displayed
CTRL-B	Moves backward by a screen of text; the previous screen of text is displayed
CTRL-D	Moves forward by one-half screen of text
CTRL-U	Moves backward by one-half screen of text
G	Moves cursor to last line in the text

Table 17-2. *Vi Editor Commands*

Key	Cursor Movement
*num*G	Moves cursor to specific line number **45G** will place the cursor on line 45
H	Moves cursor to line displayed on screen
M	Moves cursor to middle line displayed on screen
L	Moves cursor to bottom line displayed on screen
' '	Moves the cursor to its previous location in the text
m*mark*	Places a mark on a line of text; the mark can be any alphabetic character
' *mark*	Moves the cursor to the line with the mark
Input	All input commands place the user in input; the user leaves input with ESC
a	Enters input after the cursor
A	Enters input at the end of a line
i	Enters input before the cursor
I	Enters input at the beginning of a line
o	Enters input below the line the cursor is on; inserts a new empty line below the one the cursor is currently on
O	Enters input above the line the cursor is on; inserts a new empty line above the one the cursor is currently on
Delete	
x	Deletes the character the cursor is on
X	Deletes the character before the character the cursor is on
dw	Deletes the word the cursor is on
db	Deletes to beginning of a word
dW	Deletes space delimited word
dB	Deletes to beginning of a space delimited word
dd	Deletes the line the cursor is on

Table 17-2.   *Vi Editor Commands* (continued)

Delete

D	Deletes the rest of the line the cursor is on
d0	Deletes text from cursor to beginning of line
d	Deletes following text specified
d)	Deletes the rest of a sentence
d}	Deletes the rest of a paragraph
dG	Deletes the rest of the file
dm	Followed by a mark, deletes everything to mark
dL	Deletes the rest of the screen
dH	Deletes to the top of the screen
J	Joins the line below the cursor to the end of the current line; in effect, deleting the new line character of the line the cursor is on
Change	Except for the replace command, **r**, all change commands place the user into input after deleting text
s	Deletes the character the cursor is on and places the user into the input mode
cw	Deletes the word the cursor is on and places the user into the input mode
cb	Changes to beginning of a word
cW	Changes space delimited word
cB	Changes to beginning of a space delimited word
cc	Deletes the line the cursor is on and places the user into input
C	Deletes the rest of the line the cursor is on and places the user into input
c0	Changes text from cursor to beginning of line
c	Changes following text specified
c)	Changes the rest of a sentence
c}	Changes the rest of a paragraph

Table 17-2.   *Vi Editor Commands* (continued)

Change

cG	Changes the rest of the file
cm	Followed by a mark, changes everything to mark
cL	Changes the rest of the screen
cH	Changes to the top of the screen
r	Replaces the character the cursor is on; after pressing **r** the user enters the replacement character; the change is made without entering input; the user remains in the Vi command mode
R	First places into the input mode, then overwrites character by character; appears as an overwrite mode on the screen but actually is in input mode
Move	Moves text by first deleting it, moving the cursor to desired place of insertion, and then pressing the **p** command. (When text is deleted, it is automatically held in a special buffer.)
p	Inserts deleted or copied text after the character or line the cursor is on
P	Inserts deleted or copied text before the character or line the cursor is on
dw p	Deletes a word, then moves it to the place you indicate with the cursor (press **p** to insert the word *after* the word the cursor is on)
dw P	Deletes a word, then moves it to the place you indicate with the cursor (press **P** to insert the word *before* the word the cursor is on)
dd p	Deletes a line, then moves it to the place you indicate with the cursor (press **p** to insert the word *after* the line the cursor is on)
d p	Deletes following text specified, then moves it to the place you indicate with the cursor (press **p** or **P**)
d) p	Moves the rest of a sentence
d} p	Moves the rest of a paragraph
dG p	Moves the rest of the file
dm p	Followed by a mark, moves everything to mark
dL p	Moves the rest of the screen

Table 17-2.   *Vi Editor Commands (continued)*

Move	
dH p	Moves to the top of the screen
Copy	Copy commands are meant to be used in conjunction with the **p** command. Upon copying text, the user moves the cursor to the place where the copy is to be inserted; the **p** command then inserts the text after the character or line the cursor is on
yw	Copies the word the cursor is on, then moves the word to the place you indicate with the cursor (press **p** to insert after the word the cursor is on)
yb	Copies to beginning of a word
yW	Copies space delimited word
yB	Copies to beginning of a space delimited word
yy or **Y**	Copies the line the cursor is on, then moves the line to the place you indicate with the cursor (press **p** to insert after the line the cursor is on)
y	Copies following text specified
y)	Copies the rest of a sentence
y}	Copies the rest of a paragraph
yG	Copies the rest of the file
ym	Followed by a mark, copies everything to mark
yL	Copies the rest of the screen
yH	Copies to the top of the screen
Search	The two search commands open up a line at the bottom of the screen and allow the user to enter a pattern to be searched for; press ENTER after typing in the pattern
/_pattern_	Searches forward in the text for a pattern
?_pattern_	Searches backward in the text for a pattern
n	Repeats the previous search, whether it was forward or backward
N	Repeats the previous search in opposite direction

Table 17-2. *Vi Editor Commands (continued)*

Search	
/	Repeats the previous search in forward direction
?	Repeats the previous search in backward direction
Buffers	There are 9 numbered buffers and 26 named buffers; named buffers are named with each lowercase letter in the alphabet, *a-z*. You use the double quote to reference a specific buffer
"*buf-letter*	Named buffer—references a specific named buffer, **a**, **b**, etc.
"*num*	Numbered buffer—references a numbered buffer with a number *1-9*

Table 17-2. *Vi Editor Commands* (continued)

File Operation		Effect
w	Write	Saves file
r *filename*	Read	Inserts file text
q	Quit	Quits editor
Delete, Move, and Copy		
d	Delete	Deletes a line or set of lines
m*Num*	Move	Moves a line or set of lines by deleting them and then inserting them after line *Num*
co*Num*	Copy	Copies a line or set of lines by copying them and then inserting the copied text after line *Num*
Line Reference		**Description**
Num	Line number	A number references that line number
*Num***,** *Num*	Set of lines	Two numbers separated by a comma references a set of lines

Table 17-3. *Vi Line Editing Commands*

Line Reference		Description
Num–Num	Range of lines	Two numbers separated by a dash references a range of lines
–Num	Offset reference	The minus sign preceding a number offsets to a line before the current line
+Num	Offset reference	The plus sign preceding a number offsets to a line after the current line
$	Last line in file	The dollar sign symbol references the last line in the file
/*Pattern*/	Pattern ref	A line can be located and referenced by a pattern; the slash searches forward
?*Pattern*?	Pattern ref	A line can be located and referenced by a pattern; the question mark searches backward
g/*Pattern*/	Global pattern	A set of lines can be located and referenced by a repeated pattern reference; all lines with a pattern in it are referenced
Special Character		
.	Any character	Matches on any one possible character in a pattern
*	Repeated chars	Matches on repeated characters in a pattern
[]	Classes	Matches on classes of characters, a set of characters, in the pattern
^	Start of a line	References the beginning of a line
$	End of a line	References the end of a line
/<	Start of a word	References the start of a word
>/	End of a word	References the end of a word

Table 17-3. *Vi Line Editing Commands* (continued)

Substitution Command		Description
s/*pattern*/ *replacement*/	Substitution	Locates pattern on a line and substitutes pattern with replacement pattern
s/*pattern*/ *replacement*/**g**	Global substitution on a line	Substitutes all instances of a pattern on a line with the replacement pattern
Num–Num **s**/*pattern*/ *replacement*/	Substitution	Performs substitutions on the range of lines specified
1,$ s/*pattern*/ *replacement*/**g**	Global substitution on the file	Substitutes all instances of a pattern in the file with the replacement pattern

Table 17-3.   *Vi Line Editing Commands (continued)*

Search Option	Abbreviation	Default	Description
ignorecase	ic	**noic**	Ignores upper- and lowercase in searches
magic		magic	Makes special characters effective
wrapscan	ws	**nows**	Wraps search around to beginning of file
Display Option			
number	nu	**nonm**	Displays line numbers
list		nolist	Tabs, and displays new line with **^I** and **$**
window		window=23	Sets number of lines displayed on screen
tabstop	ts	**ts=8**	Sets tab spacing for editor display only

Table 17-4.   *Vi Search, Display, and Input Options*

Input Option	Abbreviation	Default	Description
wrapmargin	wm	wm=0	Inserts new line at right margin while inputting
autoindent	ai	noai	Automatically indents; CTRL-D back indents
shiftwidth	sw	sw=8	Backtab and line shift spacing
showmatch	sm	nosm	Shows opening (, {, [shows closing), },]
beautify	bf	nobt	Prevents input of control characters

Table 17-4. *Vi Search, Display, and Input Options* (continued)

Chapter Eighteen

The Emacs Editor

The Emacs editor operates much like a standard word processor. The keys on your keyboard are input characters. Commands are implemented with special keys such as control (CTRL) keys and alternate (ALT) keys. There is no special input mode, as there is in Vi or Ed. You type in your text, and if you need to execute an editing command, such as moving the cursor or saving text, you use a CTRL key.

Such an organization makes the Emacs editor easy to use. However, Emacs is anything but simple—it is a sophisticated and flexible editor with several hundred commands. Emacs also has special features, such as multiple windows. You can display two windows for text at the same time. You can also open and work on more than one file at a time, and display each on the screen in its own window.

A GNU version of Linux was developed by Richard Stallman and is available on your Caldera CD-ROM. It is a standard feature on most Linux systems. The Emacs editor, however, is not installed as part of your Express Install. To use Emacs, you will first have to use glint to install the Emacs software package. Be sure to log in as the root user and mount your Caldera CD-ROM first.

Emacs derives much of its power and flexibility from its ability to manipulate buffers. Emacs can be described as a buffer-oriented editor. Whenever you edit a file in any editor, the file is copied into a work buffer, and editing operations are made on the work buffer. In many editors, there is only one work buffer, allowing you to open only one file. Emacs can manage many work buffers at once, allowing you to edit several files at the same time. You can edit buffers that hold deleted or copied text. You can even create buffers of your own, fill them with text, and later save them to a file.

Creating a File Using Emacs

You invoke the Emacs editor with the command **emacs**. You can enter the name of the file you want to edit, or if the file does not exist, it will be created. In the next example, the user prepares to edit the file **mydata** with Emacs.

```
$ emacs mydata
```

Like Vi, Emacs is a full screen editor. In the case of a newly created file, the screen will be empty except for the bottom two lines. The cursor will be positioned in the upper-left corner. The bottom line is called the echo area, and it functions as a kind of Emacs command line. It is also used to display Emacs messages. The line above it is called the mode line and is used to display status information about the text being edited. The mode line will be highlighted in reverse video. The different features displayed on an Emacs screen are illustrated in Figure 18-1.

To enter text, you simply start typing—you are always in the input mode. Editing commands, such as movement commands, are implemented with CTRL keys. For example, to move the cursor right, use CTRL-**f**, and to move the cursor left, use CTRL-**b**. To move up one line, use CTRL-**p**, and to move down one line, use CTRL-**n**.

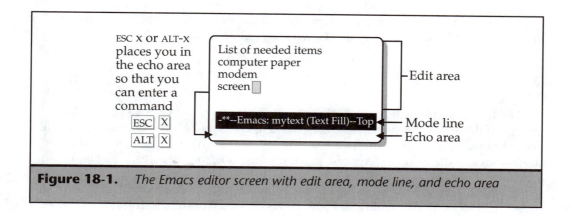

Figure 18-1. *The Emacs editor screen with edit area, mode line, and echo area*

You can save your text at any time with the CTRL-**x** CTRL-**s** command sequence. Many Emacs commands are made up of CTRL key combinations. The command sequence to quit the editor is CTRL-**x** CTRL-**c**. When you have finished editing the file, you should first save the file with CTRL-**x** CTRL-**s** before quitting the editor with CTRL-**x** CTRL-**c**.

Meta-Keys, Line Commands, and Modes

The Emacs editor operates much like any normal word processor. There is only one mode, the input mode. If you hit any character key you are entering data into the file. All character keys are input characters, not commands. A character key can be thought of as any key you type in directly, as opposed to CTRL keys or ALT keys. Character keys are any keys you could type in at a typewriter.

Commands are assigned to CTRL keys as well as meta-keys. In this version of Emacs, a meta-key may be either an ALT key sequence or escape (ESC) key sequence. On other systems, they may be one or the other. ALT key sequences operate like CTRL keys. While you hold down ALT, you press another key, and then let up on both. The ESC key sequence is slightly different. First, you press ESC and let up on it. Then you press another key. ESC key sequences have been in use far longer than ALT keys because many older keyboards do not have ALT keys. For this reason, this chapter will describe meta-keys as ESC key sequences, bearing in mind that meta-keys could also be implemented as ALT keys on your terminal.

CTRL keys and meta-keys constitute only a part of the many commands available in Emacs. All commands can be entered using command words typed in the echo area. (Think of the echo area as the Vi line editing mode.) The meta-key commands ALT-**x** or ESC **x** will place you in the echo area. Once in the echo area, you execute a command by typing in the command and any of its arguments and pressing ENTER. Table 18-1 lists the Emacs editing commands.

The mode line displays status information about the text being edited. The mode line is made up of several components, with the following form:

```
-ST-Emacs: BufferName  (major minor)------Place--
```

The first field, ST, indicates whether the file has been saved or not since the last change to the text. If the field displays two asterisks, **, the text has been changed, but not yet saved. If the field displays two dashes, --, the text has not been changed since the last save. If the field displays two percent signs, %%, the file is read-only and cannot be modified.

The NAME field is the name of the buffer. In the case of files, this will be the name of the file. The PLACE field indicates how far you are positioned in the file. For example, if the PLACE field is 40%, the text being displayed is 40 percent of the way through the file. In the next example, the mode line indicates that the file has not been saved since the last change, the name of the buffer is **mytext**, and the cursor is positioned at the top of the file.

```
-**-Emacs: mytext       (text fill)----  --Top--
```

The MAJOR/MINOR field indicates the major and minor modes for editing the file. Emacs recognizes several major modes, the most common of which is the text mode. Different types of files require special editing configurations. A C program file, for example, may need special indentation features. For this reason, there is a special editing mode for C programs. Emacs recognizes other standard modes, such as nroff and Lisp. Emacs determines the mode by examining the extension used in the file name. A .c extension indicates a C program file. In that case, Emacs will use the C mode. If there is no extension, Emacs will use the text mode. If, for some reason, Emacs cannot determine the mode for the file, it will use the fundamental mode, which offers no special features.

Emacs has three minor modes: fill, overwrite, and abbrev. The fill mode is usually the default. It automatically wraps long lines in the file. The overwrite mode allows you to overwrite text, and the abbrev mode allows you to use abbreviations when entering text.

Emacs Editing Commands

The Emacs editing commands perform many of the same operations found in other editors. All the commands are implemented with CTRL keys, ALT keys, or an ESC key sequence. Many also have a command name that you can enter in the echo area. This section describes many of the most useful commands.

Movement Commands

As in Vi, Emacs has a set of basic cursor movement commands. CTRL-**f** moves the cursor forward one character, and CTRL-**b** moves the cursor back one character. The CTRL-**f** and CTRL-**b** commands can be thought of as right and left cursor movement on a line. However, whereas in Vi, right and left cursor movement is limited to a line, the back and forward cursor movement of Emacs is not. Emacs views the file as a stream of characters, not a set of lines. A backward cursor movement moves back across characters in the file and may continue back across lines. The same is true for the forward movement.

There are also commands that move you forward and backward in the text by lines and by screens. The CTRL-**n** and CTRL-**p** commands move the cursor up and down lines. CTRL-**n** moves the cursor down to the next line. If the line is the last line on the screen, the screen will scroll to display the next line. CTRL-**p** moves the cursor up to the previous line. If the cursor is on the top line, the screen will scroll to display the previous line. The CTRL-**v** and CTRL-**z** commands move you through the text, screen by screen. CTRL-**v** moves you forward to the next screen of text. CTRL-**z** moves you backward to the previous screen of text.

You can also move according to text segments, such as words and paragraphs. The meta-key commands ESC **f** and ESC **b** move the cursor forward and backward by a whole word. ESC **]** moves you to the beginning of the next paragraph. ESC **[** moves you to the previous paragraph. Any of these commands let you quickly move through the text in either direction. There are also movement commands that position you in particular places in the text. The CTRL-**a** command positions you at the beginning of a line. The CTRL-**e** command positions you at the end of a line. CTRL-**l** moves you to the center of the screen. ESC **<** moves you to the beginning of the file, and ESC **>** moves you to the end of the file.

You can repeat a command by preceding it with the Emacs repeat command, ESC *num*, where *num* is the number of times the next command you enter will be repeated. For example, to move the cursor five characters to the right, first enter the repeat command with the number 5 followed by the CTRL-**f** command:

```
Esc 5 Ctrl-f
```

You can use the repeat command in the same way for input. The ESC key and a number followed by any character inputs the character that number of times into the text. ESC **3 T** enters three *T*'s into the text.

Deletions

Deleting text permanently removes the text from the file. There are two basic deletion operations: one to delete the character before the cursor and one to delete the character after the cursor. CTRL-**d** deletes the character after the cursor. The DEL key deletes the character before the cursor. They are comparable to pressing BACKSPACE.

Kill Buffers and Moving Text

Emacs makes a distinction between deleting and killing text. Deleting text permanently removes the text from the file. Killing text removes the text from the file buffer, but copies it into what is called a kill buffer from which it can later be retrieved. Killing text works much like the deletion process in Vi. Killed text is placed in one of a set of kill buffers set up by the editor. As you kill text, each kill buffer is filled in turn. The kill buffers are circularly linked. When all are filled, the first one used is overwritten with the next text that is killed.

At any time, you can insert the contents of any kill buffer back into the text. In this sense, the kill commands are meant to be one part of a text movement operation. You kill and thereby remove text from one place in your file. Then you can move to a different location and insert the removed text.

You can remove (kill) different segments of text, such as words or lines. The ESC DEL command removes the word before the cursor, and the ESC **d** command removes a word after the cursor. You can precede these kill commands with the repeat command, ESC *num*, to delete several words. For example, ESC **3** ESC **d** will delete three words.

The CTRL-**k** command removes the remainder of a line. To remove a whole line, first place the cursor at the beginning of the line with the CTRL-**a** command, and then issue a CTRL-**k** command. However, a CTRL-**k** does not remove the new line character at the end of the line. The line is still there, it is merely empty. To remove the new line character as well, enter another kill command: CTRL-**k** CTRL-**k**. The second CTRL-**k** deletes the new line character. To remove an empty line, you only need to enter one CTRL-**k**, since there is no text, just the new line character. As in the case of removing words, you can precede the CTRL-**k** command with the repeat command in order to remove several lines. For example, ESC **10** CTRL-**k** CTRL-**k** will delete ten lines.

Once you have removed text to a kill buffer, you can reinsert it in the file with the CTRL-**y** command. CTRL-**y** is often referred to as the yank command. Whatever text has been placed in the kill buffer will be inserted into the text. If the kill buffer contains words, CTRL-**y** will insert words. If the kill buffer contains lines, CTRL-**y** will insert lines.

Moving text involves first removing text to a kill buffer with a kill command and then inserting the text with the yank command, CTRL-**y**. In the next example, the command sequence moves the current line of text up five lines. Notice the use of the repeat command before the cursor movement command.

```
Ctrl-k Ctrl-k
Esc 5 Ctrl-p
Ctrl-y
```

If you accidentally remove too many lines or insert text in the wrong place, you can undo it with CTRL-**x u**. Emacs even allows you to undo all changes to the text since the editing session began with the ESC **x** command.

Regions: Point and Mark

You can select a block of text by creating a region relative to the cursor. A region is any text between the character the cursor is on and any previously marked text. You mark a place in the text with the CTRL-**@** command. That marked place is the end of your region. Then move the cursor to any other point in the file. The text between the marked character and the cursor is your region. Technically, the cursor position is referred to as the point and the marked character is referred to as the mark.

There are commands that perform operations on regions. For example, you can copy or remove regions. CTRL-**w** kills a region, removing it to a kill buffer. The ESC **w** command copies a region to a kill buffer. You could remove a region with CTRL-**w**, and then use CTRL-**y** to reinsert the region in the file—in effect, moving the region.

Emacs does not display a mark in the file. If you forget where you placed the mark, you can use the CTRL-**x** CTRL-**x** command sequence to locate the mark. The CTRL-**x** CTRL-**x** command interchanges the point and the mark, moving the cursor to the position where you placed the mark. You can move the cursor back to its original position with another CTRL-**x** CTRL-**x** sequence.

You can also define different text segments as regions. The mark-paragraph command, ESC **h**, selects a paragraph the cursor is on as a region. The point is the beginning of the paragraph and the mark is placed at the end of the paragraph. CTRL-**x** CTRL-**p** selects the page the cursor is on, making the page a region. The mark-whole-buffer command, CTRL-**x h**, selects the entire buffer, making the whole text a region. Here are examples of these region commands:

```
Esc h  Ctrl-w             Delete a paragraph
Esc h  Esc w              Copy a paragraph
Ctrl-x Ctrl-p  Esc w      Copy a page
Ctrl-x h  Esc g           Justify entire text
```

Incremental Searches

You enter searches with the CTRL-**s** command. The CTRL-**s** command places you in the echo area where you type in the pattern to be searched for. The CTRL-**s** command performs an incremental search. Emacs begins the search as soon as you enter the first character. As you enter more characters in the pattern, Emacs locates text that matches the growing pattern. For example, if you are typing in the word "preface," upon typing **p**, the cursor moves to the next p in the text. Upon typing **r**, the cursor moves to "pr". You end the input by pressing ESC. Here is the basic form to search forward in a file for a pattern:

```
Ctrl-s pattern
```

The CTRL-**r** command searches backward in a file. Neither command will wrap around. The CTRL-**s** command stops at the end of the file, and the CTRL-**r** command stops at the beginning of the file. Emacs remembers the last pattern searched. A CTRL-**s** or CTRL-**r** command entered without a pattern will search for the previous pattern.

Regular Expression Searches

The Emacs editor allows you to use any of the regular expression special characters used in the Vi, Ex, and Ed editors. To use a regular expression in a search, you precede CTRL-**s** or CTRL-**r** search commands with ESC. Thus, ESC CTRL-**s** or ESC CTRL-**r** allow you to use regular expressions in your search string.

Substitutions: Replace and Query-Replace

You perform substitutions in Emacs using either a replace or query-replace operation. The replace operation performs global substitutions. For this reason it is rarely used. The query-replace operation allows you to perform single substitutions. In fact, it will search for an instance of a pattern and then query you as to whether you want to replace it, skip it, or quit the query-replace operation. This gives you more control over the substitutions. Both operations have special commands for searching regular expressions.

Global Substitutions: Replace

You perform straightforward global substitutions using the **replace-string** command. You enter this command in the echo area. It is not bound to any key. You access the echo area with ESC **x**, and then type in the command **replace-string**. You are then prompted for a pattern and its replacement text. This command has the same effect as the global substitution operations in Ex. The **replace-string** command cannot operate on any regular expressions. If you want to use regular expressions in a replace operation, you need to use the **replace-regexp** command.

Query-Replace

The ESC **%** command is the **query-replace** command. It searches for and then replaces text. It operates somewhat like the substitution command in the Ex editor. First you enter ESC **%** followed by the pattern to be replaced, and then press ENTER. On the same line, enter the replacement text and again press ENTER. The first instance of the pattern is located. You then have several possible options, each represented by a key. If you enter **y**, for example, you will replace the text and move on to the next instance. An **n** will skip replacement of this instance and move on to the next.

```
Esc %  pattern  Enter replacement-text  Enter
query-replace option
```

The options for the **query-replace** command are listed in the following table:

y or SPACEBAR	Changes and advances to next instance of pattern
n or DEL	Skips the change and advances
^	Goes back to previous instance of pattern
!	Replaces all remaining instances
.	Replaces and exits
ESC	Exits **query-replace**

The following sequence replaces the next instance of the pattern "milk" with "yogurt" and then advances to the next instance. The user would exit the query-replace operation by pressing ESC.

```
Esc % milk      .
yogurt

y
```

Like the search commands, the **query-replace** command does not allow special characters in the search pattern. If want to use special characters, you need to use the command **query-replace-regexp**. You enter this command in the echo area by first pressing ESC **x**.

Using Windows in Emacs

Windows allow you to view different parts of the same file, or to view different files at the same time. A window command is usually a CTRL-**x** followed by a specified number. For example, CTRL-**x 2** opens up a new window on the text. CTRL-**x 0** closes the current window. The Emacs window commands are listed in Table 18-2.

When you have more than one window open, the one with the cursor is known as the current window. This is the one that is active. Any editing commands will operate on the text displayed in this window. You can move to another window with the CTRL-**x o** and CTRL-**x p** commands. CTRL-**x o** will move from one window to the next, sequentially, in the order they were opened. CTRL-**x p** moves to the previous window.

You can close a window with CTRL-**x 0** and close all but the current window with CTRL-**x 1**.

When you open a new window, you can display it either next to or below the current window. The CTRL-**x 5** command splits the screen horizontally into two windows displayed side by side. The CTRL-**x 2** command splits the screen vertically, with one window above the other.

Once you have opened your window, you can change its size with the CTRL-**x ^** and CTRL-**x }** commands. CTRL-**x ^** extends the current window vertically, increasing its height. CTRL-**x }** extends the current window horizontally, increasing its width.

Windows are very helpful for moving text in your file. When you first open a new window on the same text, the new window shows the same text as the old one. In the new window, you can then move to other parts of the text. You can remove text in one window to a kill buffer, change to another window, and then insert the removed text using the other window.

Windows are also helpful for displaying what you have already written. You can easily check what you have written in another part of your document by displaying it in another window as you write.

Buffers and Files

As mentioned earlier, when you edit a file with any editor, the file's contents are read from the disk into a buffer in memory. A buffer is a segment of memory used to hold characters. You can think of it as an array of characters. You then perform editing operations on the buffer. When you have finished editing the buffer, you save the contents of the buffer to the file.

Emacs focuses on the fact that editors actually operate on buffers. You can edit buffers used for files or buffers used for other purposes. You can even create your own buffers, enter text into them; and, if you want, you can later save the contents to a file. The Vi editor, by contrast, allows you to edit only one file buffer.

File Buffers

Buffers used for files are created when you open a file. You can also simply open a buffer and then later save it to a file. In either case, the buffer becomes tied to that file. Such buffers are called file buffers. The command sequence CTRL-**x** CTRL-**f** *filename* opens a file with its own buffer. The command sequence CTRL-**x** CTRL-**s** saves the contents of the buffer to the file, and the command sequence CTRL-**x** CTRL-**c** quits the file. The different file buffer commands are listed in Table 18-3.

You can have more than one file open at the same time, each with its own buffer. To display two file buffers at the same time on the screen, you need to use the window commands discussed in the previous section. CTRL-**x 2** first creates a new window. Then CTRL-**x** CTRL-**f** *filename* displays that file buffer in the new window. The command CTRL-**x 4f** *filename* performs both operations, creating a new window and displaying another file buffer in it.

Emacs has a special utility called dired that interfaces with your directory and allows you to select files in your directory for editing, saving, and even deletion. You enter the dired utility with the command CTRL-**x d**. A list of files in your directory is then displayed. The list is more like a menu. Each file name is really an item on the menu. You move from one item to the next and perform operations on it.

The dired utility has its own set of commands for moving from one item to the next and for selecting items. The **n** command moves to the next file name. The **p** command moves to the previous file name. The **e** command opens the file for editing. If the name selected is a directory, then dired changes directories and displays the file names in the new directory. The name .. is the directory name for the parent directory. Selecting it moves you up the directory tree to the parent directory, displaying its file names.

You can also save and delete files. Moving to a file and pressing **s** marks the file for saving. Moving to a file and pressing **d** marks the file for deletion. The file is not actually deleted until you leave the dired utility. Should you change your mind, the **u** command will remove any marks for saving or deletion. You leave the dired utility by changing back to your previous buffer with the CTRL-**x b** command.

Unattached Buffers

With the command CTRL-**x b**, you can create buffers not associated with any files. When you press CTRL-**x b**, Emacs prompts you for the name of the buffer. If the buffer does not already exist, a new one will be created. You can also use CTRL-**x b** to change to a specific buffer. After the CTRL-**x b**, simply enter the name of the buffer at the prompt. The buffer that you select will be displayed in the current window. In this way, you can use CTRL-**x b** to change from one buffer to another. CTRL-**x** CTRL-**b** displays a list of all buffers.

If you want to open up a new buffer in its own new window, you must first open the new window, change to the new window, and then open the new buffer with the CTRL-**x b** command. You can open a new window and a new buffer at the same time with the CTRL-**x 4b** command. Upon entering the command, a new window will be opened up, and you will be prompted for the name of the buffer.

Figure 18-2 shows three windows, each used to edit a buffer. Of the three buffers, one is a file buffer, **mytext**, and the two others are unattached buffers: **topics** and **preface**. As the user works in **mytext**, he or she can switch to the other windows, adding new topics in the **topics** buffer, or composing more text for the **preface**. When the user quits Emacs, the contents of the unattached buffers are lost. However, the user could copy the contents of an unattached buffer into a file buffer, or simply save the unattached buffer directly to a file of its own.

You do not necessarily need to have a separate window for each buffer. The CTRL-**x b** command will actually switch your window from editing one buffer to another buffer. CTRL-**x b topics** switches the user to the **topics** buffer. Buffers are sequentially ordered according to when you created them. CTRL-**x b** by itself switches to the next buffer in that order.

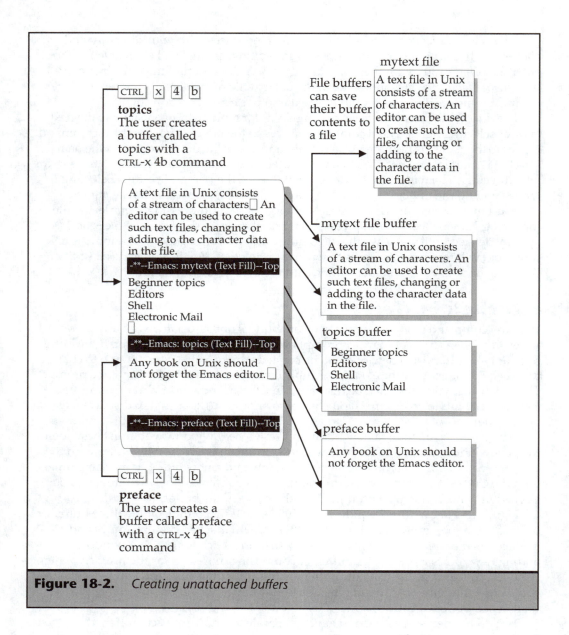

Figure 18-2. *Creating unattached buffers*

Like dired, there is a special utility for managing buffers. The command **buffer-menu** places you into an interactive utility that displays all buffer names. Using the same commands as in dired, you can change to buffers, delete buffers, or save buffers. You enter the **buffer-menu** command in the echo area, which you access with ESC-**x**.

Help

Emacs provides several help utilities, such as an online manual and a tutorial. You access the help utilities through a CTRL-**h** sequence. CTRL-**h** followed by another CTRL-**h** lists the many possible options. An option of special note is the tutorial. CTRL-**h t** places you into an online tutorial that provides you with special lessons on Emacs. Table 18-4 lists the Emacs help commands.

XEmacs

XEmacs is the complete Emacs editor with a graphical user interface and Internet applications. The Internet applications, which you can easily access from the main XEmacs button bar, includes a Web Browser, a mail utility, and a newsreader. You can start XEmacs by clicking its icon on the Goodstuff toolbar, or from the fvwm Workplace menu (Applications/Software Development), or by entering in the command xemacs in an Xterm window. The main XEmacs window is displayed with a button bar across the top for basic editing operations and for Internet applications. XEmacs supports the basic GUI editing operations: Selection of text with click and drag mouse operations: cut, copy, and paste; and a scrollbar for moving through text. At the bottom of the XEmacs window the Mode line and Echo areas are displayed as on the standard Emacs editor. You can enter keyboard commands in the Echo area just as you would in the Emacs editor. From the XEmacs menus at the top of the window, you can execute most file, edit, and buffer operations. The File menu manages buffers, windows, and frames. The Edit menu handles edit operations like cut, copy, and paste, as well as search and replace. An Options menu lets you set options for editing and printing. From the Apps menu you can access other applications like mail, the newsreader, and the Web Browser. The Buffers menu lists your active buffers. The Help menu lists several help documents including FAQs and Web pages. The XEmacs menus are very helpful for more complicated Emacs operations such as opening multiple frames or windows on a text, as well as managing buffers and file buffers. When you an execute operation through a menu item, its equivalent keyboard command will appear in the Echo area. Figure 18-3 shows the XEmacs window.

Clicking the Mail button will bring up another XEmacs window that will list received messages and also let you compose new ones. You can compose, reply, or print messages using buttons on the side of the window. To display a message click on its header and press SPACEBAR. You can display the headers by choosing the "Display Summary" item in the Folder menu. When composing a message, you have full use of the XEmacs editor with all its features including spell checking and search/replace. A new window is opened up that prompts you for the address and subject. This window also has all the XEmacs editing buttons and menus. When you

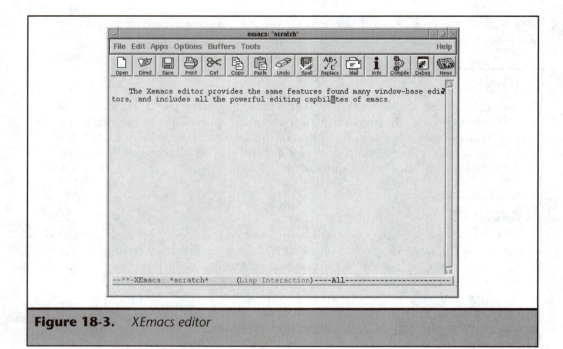

Figure 18-3.   *XEmacs editor*

are finished editing your message, choose the "Send and Exit" item in the Mail menu located at the end of the menubar.

Clicking the News button brings up another window that displays the XEmacs newsreader, listing your Usenet new groups. If you are using an ISP, it will use the name of the news server in the NNTPSERVER variable. An easy way to start the Web Browser is to choose the "XEmacs WWW Page" from the Help menu. The Web Browser supports standard Browser features like bookmarks. However, you can choose to use any Web Browser you want. The "Open URLs with" item in the Options menu lets you choose from Browsers available on your system like Netscape or Lynx.

Summary: Emacs

Emacs is a buffer-oriented text editor that you can use like a word processor. All keys are input keys. Commands are bound to CTRL keys and meta-keys. A meta-key may be either an ESC sequence or an ALT key. An Emacs text file is character oriented, not line oriented. You can move character by character, word by word, or paragraph by paragraph throughout the file.

Emacs makes a distinction between deleting text and removing text. Deletions are permanent, whereas removing text places the text in a buffer that you can later access. These buffers are called kill buffers, and the commands that remove text are called kill commands. Emacs terminology often refers to killing a word or killing a line. This means that a word or line has been removed from the text and placed in a kill buffer. You can insert the contents of a kill buffer at a later point in the file. You move text by first removing text to a kill buffer and then inserting it at another point in the file.

Emacs allows you to open several windows on the screen in which you can display either the same file or different files. You can split the screen into windows horizontally or vertically. The windows can display different parts of the same file. You can move text by removing it in one window and then inserting it in the text displayed in another window.

You can open several files at once, each with its own buffer. You can also create your own buffers that are unattached to any file. You can then easily change from one buffer to another, editing each in turn. You can even access the kill buffers and edit them. The buffer-menu utility provides a menu interface for all your buffers, making it easier to select the one you want.

You can display several buffers at the same time, each in its own window. A buffer used for a file is a file buffer. When you display more than one file buffer on the screen, you are displaying the contents of two files on the screen at the same time. The dired utility provides a menu interface for all files in your directory, allowing you to open, save, or delete specific ones.

Cursor Movement	Effect
CTRL-**b**	Moves left one character (backward to the previous character)
CTRL-**f**	Moves right one character (forward to the next character)
CTRL-**n**	Moves down one line (the next line)
CTRL-**p**	Moves up one line (the previous line)
CTRL-**v**	Moves forward one screen
CTRL-**z**	Moves backward one screen
CTRL-**l**	Moves to center of screen
ESC **f**	Moves forward one word
ESC **b**	Moves backward one word
ESC **]**	Moves to next paragraph
ESC **[**	Moves back to previous paragraph

Table 18-1. *Emacs Editor Commands*

Cursor Movement	Effect
CTRL-**a**	Moves to beginning of a line
CTRL-**e**	Moves to end of a line
ESC **<**	Moves to beginning of buffer, usually beginning of file
ESC **>**	Moves to end of buffer, usually end of file
ESC *num*	Repeats the following command *num* number of times
ESC **x**	Moves to echo area to enter a command

Deletions

DEL	Deletes the character before the cursor
CTRL-**d**	Deletes the character after the cursor

Kills and Yanks

CTRL-**k**	Removes the remainder of a line (kills the rest of the line)
CTRL-**k** CTRL-**k**	Removes the remainder of a line and the new line character at the end
ESC **d**	Removes a word after the cursor
ESC DEL	Removes the word before the cursor
ESC **k**	Removes the remainder of a sentence
CTRL-**w**	Removes a region (deletes a block)
CTRL-**y**	Inserts (yanks) the contents of a kill buffer into the text
CTRL-**x u**	Undoes the previous command

Search and Replace

CTRL-**s**	Searches for a pattern forward in the text
CTRL-**r**	Searches for a pattern backward in the text (reverse)
ESC CTRL-**s**	Searches for a regular expression forward in the text

Table 18-1. *Emacs Editor Commands (continued)*

Search and Replace	Effect
ESC CTRL-**r**	Searches for a regular expression backward in the text
replace string	Performs a global substitution
replace regexp	Performs a global substitution using regular expression
query-replace-regexp	Searches for a regular expression in query and replace operation
ESC **%** *pattern* ENTER *replacement* ENTER	Queries and replaces a pattern

	Key	
	SPACEBAR	Replaces and moves to next instance
	DEL	Does not replace and moves to next instance
	ESC	Quits search-replace operation
	.	Replaces and exits
	!	Replaces all remaining instances
	^	Moves back to previous replacement

Regions

CTRL-**@** or CTRL-SPACEBAR	Marks a region (block)
CTRL-**x** CTRL-**x**	Exchanges cursor (point) and marks
ESC **H**	Marks a paragraph as a region
CTRL-**x** CTRL-**p**	Marks a page as a region
CTRL-**x h**	Marks the entire text in buffer as a region

Text Format

auto-fill-mode	Sets fill mode option
ESC *num* CTRL-**x f**	Sets position of right margin
ESC **q**	Justifies a paragraph
ESC **q**	Justifies a region

Table 18-1. *Emacs Editor Commands* (continued)

Command	Effect
CTRL-**x** 2	Splits to new window vertically
CTRL-**x** 5	Splits to new window horizontally
CTRL-**x** o	Selects other window
CTRL-**x** p	Selects previous window
ESC CTRL-**v**	Scrolls the other window
CTRL-**x** 0	Closes current window
CTRL-**x** 1	Closes all but the current window
CTRL-**x** ^	Extends the current window vertically
CTRL-**x** }	Extends the current window horizontally

Table 18-2. *Emacs Window Commands*

File Buffer Command	Effect
CTRL-**x** CTRL-**f**	Opens and reads a file into a buffer
CTRL-**x** CTRL-**s**	Saves the contents of a buffer to a file
CTRL-**x** CTRL-**c**	Quits editor
CTRL-**x** CTRL-**v**	Closes the current file and opens a new one (visiting a new file)
CTRL-**x** i	Inserts contents of a file to a buffer
CTRL-**x** CTRL-**q**	Opens a file as read-only; you cannot change it

Table 18-3. *Emacs File Buffer and Buffer Commands*

File Buffer Command	Effect
CTRL-**x d**	Enters the dired buffer that has a listing of your current directories; moves to different file and directory names; displays other directories; selects and opens files
	n Moves to next file or directory name
	p Moves to previous file or directory name
	e If the cursor is on a directory, enters that directory; if the cursor is on a file, opens that file
	s Marks a file for saving
	d Marks a file for deletion
	u Unmarks a file for deletion
	x Executes marked files
Buffer Command	
CTRL-**x b**	Changes to another buffer; you are prompted for the name of the buffer to change to (to create a new buffer, enter a new name)
CTRL-**x k**	Deletes (kills) a buffer
CTRL-**x** CTRL-**b**	Displays a list of all buffers
ESC **x buffer-menu**	Selects different buffers from a list of buffers
	d or k Marks a buffer for deletion
	u Unmarks a buffer
	s Marks a buffer for saving
	x Executes marked buffers

Table 18-3.   *Emacs File Buffer and Buffer Commands*

Help Command	Effect
CTRL-**h** CTRL-**h**	Lists possible help options
CTRL-**h i**	Accesses the Emacs manual
CTRL-**h t**	Runs the Emacs tutorial
CTRL-**h b**	Displays keys and the commands they represent

Table 18-4.   *Emacs Help Commands*

PART SIX

Administration

Chapter Nineteen

Systems Administration

731

As a version of Unix, Linux is designed to serve many users at the same time. As an operating system, Linux provides an interface between the users and the computer with its storage media, such as hard disks and tapes. Users have their own shells through which they interact with the operating system. However, you may need to configure the operating system itself in different ways. You may need to add new users, printers, or terminals. You have already seen in Chapter 7 how to add new file systems. Such operations come under the heading of system administration. The person who performs such actions is referred to as either a system administrator or a superuser. In this sense there are two types of interaction with Linux: regular users' interaction and the superuser, performing system administration tasks. This chapter will cover only the basic operations in system administration. You will learn about system states, managing users, and configuring printers and terminals. The chapter is meant to be an introduction to the complex tasks of system administration. Tables 19-1 through 19-7 are found at the end of the chapter for your reference.

System Management: Superuser

To perform system administration operations you must first have the correct password that allows you to log in as the root user, or superuser. Since a superuser has the power to change almost anything on the system, such a password is usually a carefully guarded secret given only to those whose job it is to manage the system. With the correct password you can log into the system as a system administrator and configure the system in different ways. You can start up and shut down the system as well as change to a different operating mode, such as a single-user mode. You can also add or remove users, add or remove whole file systems, back up and restore files, and even designate the system's name. The different commands that you use in system management are listed in Table 19-1.

When you log into the system as a superuser you are placed in a shell from which you can issue administrative Linux commands. The prompt for this shell is a sharp sign, **#**. In the next example, the user logs into the system as a superuser. The password is, of course, not displayed.

```
login: root
password:
#
```

As the root user you can use the **passwd** command to change the password for the root login as well as for any other user on the system.

```
# passwd root
New password:
Re-enter new password:
#
```

While logged into a regular user account, it may be necessary for you to log into the root and become a superuser. Ordinarily you would have to log out of your user account first and then log into the root. Instead, you can use the **su** command to log in directly to the root while remaining logged into your user account. A CTRL-**d** will return you to your own login. In the next example, the user is already logged in. The **su** command then logs the user into the root, making the user a superuser.

```
$ pwd
/home/chris
$su
login: root
password:
# pwd
/
# ^D
$
```

The Root User Desktop

OpenLinux provides you with several Redhat system configuration tools that simplify many system administration tasks. These tools are only available on your root user desktop. You first have to log in as the **root** user and provide the password. Once logged in, you can issue the **startx** command to start your root user desktop. Unlike a regular user's desktop, the root user desktop displays numerous icons for system configuration tools. Table 19-1 lists these tools, and Figure 19-1 shows the root user desktop icons.

The usercfg utility allows you to manage users and groups—adding, modifying, or deleting user accounts (discussed later in this chapter). The netcfg utility allows you to configure your network interfaces (see Chapter 20). With the fstool utility you can configure your file systems—mounting, unmounting, and formatting them (see Chapter 7). With timetool you can set the system time and date (discussed in this chapter). Using printtool, you can configure new printers, interfacing them with your system (discussed in this chapter). Finally, you use the glint utility to install software packages from your Caldera CD-ROM (see Chapter 3). You can also use glint to uninstall them. Instead of these specialized tools, you can use Lisa, which performs all of these functions.

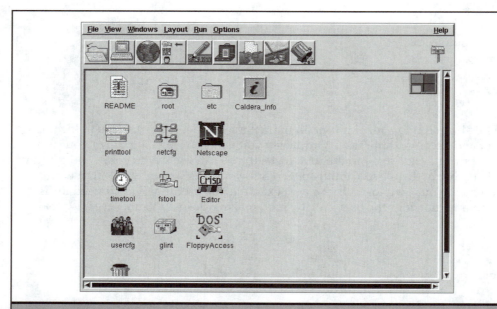

Figure 19-1. *The root user desktop: usercfg, netcfg, timetool, printtool, fstool, glint*

System Time and Date

You can easily set the system time and date using the time configuration utility on your root user desktop. This is represented on the desktop by the icon labeled "timetool." Recall that you set the time and date when you first installed your system. You should not need to do so again. However, if you entered the time incorrectly or moved to a different time zone, you could use this utility to change your time without having to reinstall your system.

Double-click on the timetool icon to open the Time Configuration window. You can make changes to any part of the time you wish (see Figure 19-2). Move your mouse pointer to the hour, for example, and then click. The hour will be highlighted. You use the two triangles below the time and date display to increase or decrease the time or date entry. If you select the hour, then clicking on the upper triangle will set the time forward to the next hour. The bottom inverted triangle will move the hour backward. The same is true for the date.

Once you have set the new time and date, click on the Set System Clock button at the bottom of the window. Then click on the Exit Time Machine button to exit the Time Configuration window.

You can also use the **date** command on your root user command line to set the date and time for the system. As an argument to **date**, you list (with no delimiters)

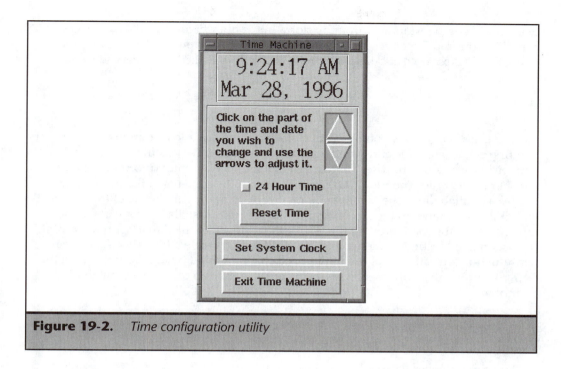

Figure 19-2. *Time configuration utility*

the month, day, time, and year. In the next example the date is set to September 18 at 2:30 p.m., 1996 (09 for September, 18 for the day, 1430 for the time, and 96 for the year):

```
# date 0918143096
Sat Sept 18 14:30:00 EDT 1996
```

Scheduling Tasks: crontab

Though not a system file, you will find a crontab file very helpful in maintaining your system. A crontab file lists actions to take at a certain time. The cron daemon constantly checks the user's crontab file to see if it is time to take these actions. Any user can set up a crontab file of his or her own. The root user can set up a crontab file to take system administrative actions, such as backing up files at a certain time each week or month.

A crontab entry has six fields: the first five are used to specify the time for an action and the last field is the action itself. The first field specifies minutes (0-59), the second field the hour (0-23), the third field is the day of the month (1-31), the fourth field is the month of the year (1-12), and the fifth field is the day of the week (0-6), starting with 0 as Sunday. In each of the time fields you can specify a range, a set of values, or use the asterisk to indicate all values. For example, 1-5 for the day-of-week field would specify Monday through Friday. In the hour field, 8, 12, 17 would specify 8 a.m., 12 noon, and 5 p.m. An * in the month-of-year field would indicate every month. The following example backs up the **projects** directory at 2:00 a.m. every weekday.

```
0 2 1-5 * * tar cf  /home/chris/backp  /home/chris/projects
```

You use the **crontab** command to install your entries into a crontab file. To do this you first create a text file and type your crontab entries. Save this file with any name you wish, such as **mycronfile**. Then to install these entries, enter **crontab** and the name of the text file. The **crontab** command takes the contents of the text file and creates a crontab file in the **/usr/spool/cron** directory, adding the name of the user that issued the command. In the next example, the root user installs the contents of the **mycronfile** as the root's crontab file. This will create a file called **/usr/spool/cron/root**. If a user named justin installed a crontab file, it would create a file called **/usr/spool /cron/justin**. You can control use of the **crontab** command by regular users with the **/etc/cron.allow** file. Only users with their names in this file can create crontab files of their own.

```
# crontab mycronfile
```

You should never try to edit your crontab file directly. Instead, use the **crontab** command with the **-e** option. This will open your crontab file in the **/usr/spool/cron** directory with the standard text editor, such as Vi. **crontab** with the **-l** option will display the contents of your crontab file, and the **-r** option will delete the entire file. Invoking **crontab** with another text file of crontab entries will overwrite your current crontab file, replacing it with the contents of the text file.

System States: init and shutdown

Your Linux system has several states, numbered from 0 to 6, and a single-user state represented by the letters **s** and **S**. When you power up your system, you enter the default state. You can then change to other states with the **init** command. For example, state 0 is the power down state. The command **init 0** will shut down your system. State 6 stops the system and reboots. Other states reflect how you want the system to be used. State 1 is the administrative state, allowing access only to the superuser. This allows you as administrator to perform administrative actions without interference from others. State **s** is a single-user state that allows use of the system by only one user. State 2 is a partial multiuser state, allowing access by many users, but with no remote file sharing. State 3, the default state, is the multiuser state that implements full remote file sharing. You can change the default state by editing the **/etc/inittab** file and changing the **init** default entry. The states are listed in Table 19-3.

No matter what state you start in, you can change from one state to another with the **init** command. If your default state is 2, you will power up in state 2, but you can change to, say, state 3 with **init 3**. In the next example, the **init** command changes to state **s**, the single-user state.

```
# init s
```

Though you can power down the system with the **init** command and the 0 state, you can also use the **shutdown** command. This command has a time argument that gives users on the system a warning before you power down. You can specify an exact time to shut down or a period of minutes from the current time. The exact time is specified by *hh*:*mm* for the hour and minutes. The period of time is indicated by a + and the number of minutes. The **shutdown** command takes several options with which you can specify how you want your system shut down. The **-h** option simply shuts down the system, whereas the **-r** option shuts down the system and then reboots it. In the next example, the system is shut down after ten minutes. The shutdown options are listed in Table 19-4.

```
# shutdown -h +10
```

To shut down the system immediately, you can use **+0** or the word **now**. The following example has the same effect as the CTRL-ALT-DEL method of shutting down your system, as described in Chapter 3. It shuts down the system immediately and then reboots.

```
# shutdown -r now
```

With the **shutdown** command you can include a warning message to be sent to all users currently logged in, giving them time to finish what they are doing before you shut them down.

```
# shutdown -h +5  "System needs a rest"
```

If you do not specify either the **-h** or the **-r** options, the **shutdown** command will shut down the multiuser mode and shift you to an administrative single-user mode. In effect, your system state changes from 3 (multiuser state) to 1 (administrative single-user state). Only the root user is active, allowing the root user to perform any necessary system administrative operations that other users might interfere with.

You use the **runlevel** command to see what state you are currently running in. In the next example the system is running in state 3. The word "runlevel" is another term for state.

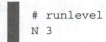

```
# runlevel
N 3
```

System Initialization Files: /etc/rc.d

Each time you start your system, it reads a series of startup commands from system initialization files located in your **/etc/rc.d** directory. These initialization files are organized according to different tasks. Some are located in the **/etc/rc.d** directory itself and others are located in a subdirectory called **init.d**. You should not have to change any of these files. Configuration tools such as netcfg and fstool will make changes for you. The organization of system initialization files varies among Linux distributions. The Redhat organization is described here. Some of the files you will find in **/etc/rc.d** are listed in Table 19-2.

The **/etc/rc.d/rc.sysinit** file holds the commands for initializing your system, including the mounting of your file systems. The **/etc/rc.d/rc.local** file is the last initialization file executed. Here you can place commands of your own. If you look at this file, you will see the message that is displayed for you every time you start the system. You can change that message if you wish.

The **/etc/rc.d/init.d** directory is designed primarily to hold files that both start up and shut down different specialized daemons. It is here that network and printer daemons are started up. You will also find files to start font servers and Web site daemons. These files perform double duty, starting up a daemon when the system starts up and shutting down the daemon when the system shuts down. The type of files in **init.d** are designed in a way to make it easy to write scripts for starting up and shutting down specialized applications. The **skeleton** file is a sample file for how to write scripts for this directory. It uses functions defined in the **functions** file, as do many of the other **init.d** files. Many of these files are set up for you automatically. You will not need to change them. If you do, be sure to do your homework on how they work first.

When you shut down your system, the **halt** file, which contains the commands to do this, is called. The files in **init.d** will be called to shut down daemons, and the file systems will be unmounted. In the current distribution of Redhat, **halt** is located in the **init.d** directory. For other distributions, it may be called **rc.halt** and located in the **/etc/rc.d** directory.

Managing Users

As a superuser you can manage user logins on your system. You can add or remove users as well as add and remove groups. You also have access to system initialization

files that you can use to configure all user shells. And you have control over the
default initialization files that are copied into an account when it is first created. With
them, you can decide how accounts are to be initially configured.

You can obtain information about users on your system with the **who** command.
Add the **-u** option to display a list of those users currently on the system. The
command displays the login name, the login port, the date and time of login, the
length of inactivity (if still active), and the process ID for the login shell. For example:

```
# who -u
root        console      Oct 12 10:34       .       1219
valerie     tty1         Oct 12 22:18      10       1492
```

Adding and Removing Users with usercfg

You can add as many new user accounts as you wish, or remove existing ones. You
add a new user account with the user configuration utility. This is represented on the
desktop by the icon labeled "usercfg." (Or you can use the Lisa tool.)

Double-clicking on the icon starts the utility, which opens the main User
Configuration window. This window, labeled "UserCfg," lists all current user accounts
on your system. Notice that your own personal user account is listed (see Figure 19-3).

To add a user, click on the Add button on the bottom left of the UserCfg window.
This will open a new window with fields for user account information (see Figure
19-4). In the Name field, enter the login name you want to give for this account.
"Name" is not a person's name, it is the name for the account, such as root or richlp.
This login name must be eight characters or less and cannot have any spaces or
punctuation.

Upon entering the login name, the other fields will be filled with default values,
except for the Full Name field. Move to this field and type in the user's real name, first
and last. You can then enter a password for this account. The user can change it later
from within this account using the **passwd** command. The system will generate a
default password for you. However, you can change it at this point. Notice that before
the Password field, there is a small inverted triangle indicating a drop-down menu.
Click and hold on this to open a menu with password options. One of these options is
to edit the password. Upon selecting this, you can type in a password of your own
choosing. Click OK to enter the password. The password will appear in the Password

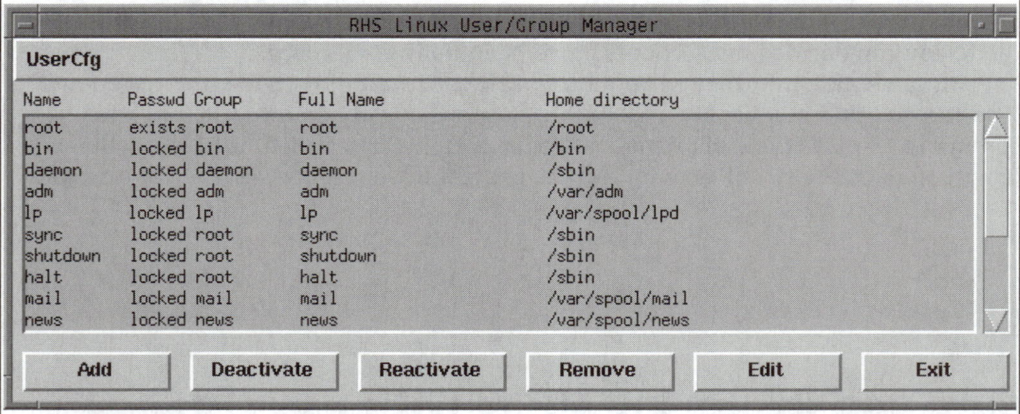

Figure 19-3. *User configuration utility*

field. Other options are to have no password (none) or to lock the account until you choose a password at a later date (locked).

Other fields allow you to select the login shell, the user's home directory, or the user groups. You will not need to change any of these. When you are finished with all

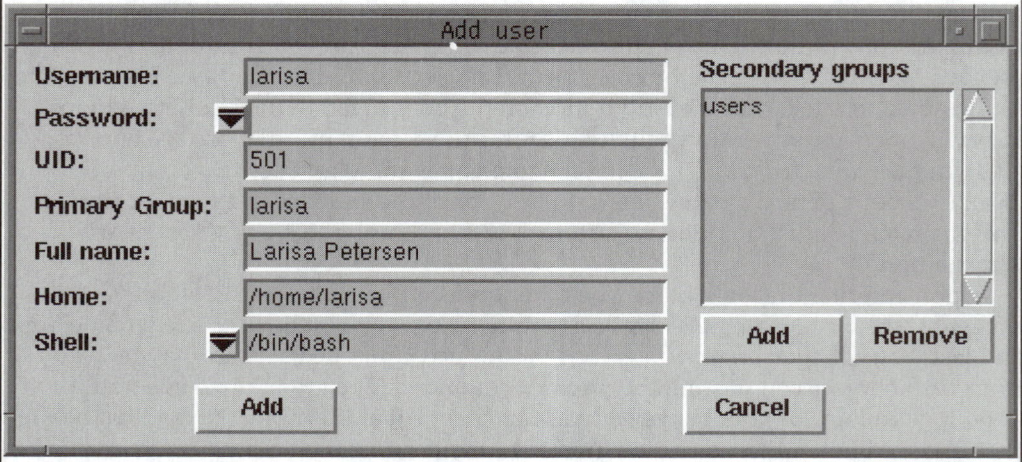

Figure 19-4. *Adding a new user*

the fields, click on the Add button at the bottom of this window. You will then be asked if you want to set up a home directory for this user. Choose OK. The new user will be displayed on the UserCfg window.

To remove a particular user, first click on that user's name in the UserCfg window. Then click on the Remove button. You will be asked to confirm that you want to remove the user. Choose YES. Now you will be asked if you want to remove the user's home directory and email information. Again choose YES. You are then asked if you want to modify the owner of orphaned files. Removing the user does not automatically erase that user's files. Such files are known as orphaned files. By modifying ownership, you can access and remove them. The owner of such files will be designated by the term "nobody."

You may at times want to lock an account, denying all access to it and its files. You can do this by deactivating the account—in effect, turning it off. The files for this account remain intact, and when you decide to reactivate the account, the files can then be accessed.

To deactivate an account, click on that account's name in the UserCfg window. Then click on the Deactivate button. You are given the option to compress the account's files, which will save disk space. (You are actually asked if you want to compress the user's home directory.) Choose YES to compress the user's files.

To reactivate the account, just click on the user's name in the UserCfg window, and then click on the Reactivate button. If the files were compressed on deactivation, they will now be decompressed.

Any utility to add a user, such as usercfg, makes use of certain default files and directories to set up the new account. There are a set of path names that usercfg uses to locate these default files or to know where to create certain user directories. For example, **/etc/skel** holds initialization files for a new user. A new user's home directory is placed in the **/home** directory. You can change these path names, if you wish, by selecting the **set paths** item in the UserCfg menu located in the upper-left corner of this window. A window will open, listing entries for all the path names. You can then change the ones you want. A list of the path names follows:

/home	Location of the user's own home directory
/mail	Location of the user's mail directory
/etc/skel	Holds the default initialization files for the login shell, such as **.bash_profile** and **.cshrc**
/etc/shell	Holds the login shells, such as BASH or TCSH

The /etc/passwd File

When you add a user, an entry for that user is made in the **/etc/passwd** file, commonly known as the password file. Each entry takes up one line that has several fields separated by colons. The fields are

username	Login name of the user
password	Encrypted password for the user's account
user id	Unique number assigned by the system
group id	Number used to identify the group the user belongs to
comment	Any user information, such as the user's full name
home directory	The user's home directory
login shell	Shell to run when the user logs in; this is the default shell, usually **/bin/bash**

The following is an example of a **/etc/passwd** entry. The entry for Mark has a * in its password field, indicating that a password has not yet been created for this user. For such entries you have to use **passwd** to create a password. Notice also that user IDs, in this particular system, start at 500 and increment by one.

```
richp:YOTPd3Pyy9hAc:500:500:Caldera Desktop
    User:/home/richp:/bin/bash
mark:*:501:501:Caldera Desktop User:/home/mark:/bin/bash
```

The **/etc/passwd** file is a text file that you can edit using a text editor. You can change fields in entries and even add new entries. The only field you cannot effectively change is the password. This has to be encrypted. To change the password field, you should always use the **passwd** command.

Though you can make entries directly to the **/etc/passwd** file, it is easier and safer to use usercfg or the adduser and useradd utilities. These programs will not only make entries in the **/etc/passwd** file, but also create the home and mail directories for the user as well as install initialization files in the user's home directory.

Managing User Environments: /etc/skel

Each time a user logs in, two profile scripts are executed. There is a system profile script that is the same for every user, and there is the **.bash_profile** script that each user has in his or her home directory. The system profile script is located in the **/etc** directory and named **profile** with no preceding period. As superuser, you can edit the profile script and put in any commands that you want executed for each user when he or she logs in. For example, you may want to define a default path for commands in case the user has not done so. Or you may wish to notify the user of recent system news or account charges.

When you first add a user to the system, you must provide the user with a skeleton **.bash_profile** file. The **useradd** command will do this automatically by searching for a **.bash_profile** file in the directory **/etc/skel** and copying it to the user's new home directory. The **/etc/skel** directory contains a skeleton initialization file for **.bash_profile** files or, if you are using the C-shell as your login shell, **.login** and **.logout** files. It also provides initialization files for BASH and C-shell: **.bshrc** and **.cshrc**.

As superuser, you can configure the **.profile** file in the **/etc/skel** any way you wish. Usually, basic system variable assignments are included that define path names for commands, system prompts, mail path names, and terminal default definitions. In short, the **PATH**, **TERM**, **MAIL**, and **PS1** variables are defined. Once users have their own **.bash_profile** files, they can redefine variables or add new commands as they wish.

Adding Users with adduser

You can also add a new user to the system with the **adduser** command. This command is entered on your command line and is very easy to use. There are different versions of adduser. The one on Redhat Linux comes from the Debian Linux distribution. It operates somewhat differently from other distributions, such as Slackware. This version of adduser takes as its argument the user name for the account you are creating. Upon pressing ENTER, it then creates the new account using default values. You can use **passwd** to create a password for the new account. This adduser program is a shell script located in the **/usr/sbin** directory. If you are familiar with shell programming, you can edit this script to change its default values.

```
# adduser robert
Looking for first available UID... 503
Looking for first available GID... 503
Adding login: robert...done.
Creating home directory: /home/robert...done.
Creating mailbox: /var/spool/mail/robert...done.
Don't forget to set the password.
 # passwd robert
Changing password for robert
Enter an empty password to quit.
New password (? for help):
New password (again):
Password changed for robert
#
```

With different versions of adduser found on other Linux distributions, you simply enter the word **adduser** without any arguments. You are then prompted for each piece of information needed to set up a new user. At the end of each prompt, within brackets, adduser will display a default value. To accept this default value as your entry, just press ENTER. After you have typed all your entries, adduser will create the new account. Once you have added a new user login, you need to give the new login a password. The login is inaccessible until you do.

Adding and Removing Users with useradd, usermod, and userdel

Other distributions of Linux may use useradd, usermod, and userdel to manage user accounts. All these commands take in all their information as options on the command line. If an option is not specified, they use predetermined default values. With the **useradd** command you enter values as options on the command line, such as the name of a user to create a user account. It will then create a new login and directory of that name using all the default features for a new account.

```
# useradd chris
```

The useradd utility has a set of predefined default values for creating a new account. The default values are the group name, the user ID, the home directory, the **skel** directory, and the login shell. The group name is the name of the group the new account is placed in. By default, this is "other," which means that the new account belongs to no group. The user ID is a number identifying the user account. This starts at 1 with the first account and increments automatically for each new account. The **skel** directory is the system directory that holds copies of initialization files. These initialization files are copied into the user's new home directory when it is created. The login shell is the path name for the particular shell the user will use. You can display these defaults using the **useradd** command with the **-D** option. The **useradd** command has options that correspond to each default value. Table 19-5 holds a list of all the options that you can use with **useradd**. You can use specific values in place of any of these defaults when creating a particular account. Once you have added a new user login, you need to give the new login a password. The login is inaccessible until you do. In the next example, the group name for the chris account is set to intro1 and the user ID is set to 578.

```
# useradd chris -g intro1 -u 578
```

The **usermod** command allows you to change the values for any of these features. You can change the home directory or user ID. You can even change the user name for the account.

When you want to remove a user from the system, you can use the **userdel** command to delete the user's login. In the next example the user chris is removed from the system.

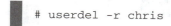

```
# userdel -r chris
```

Adding and Deleting Groups

Redhat distributions of Linux use the usercfg utility to manage groups. On other Linux distributions you can manage groups with the **groupadd**, **groupmod**, and **groupdel** commands. Groups are listed in the **/etc/group** file with one entry per file and several fields separated with colons. The fields for the group entries are as follows:

group name	Name of the group; must be unique
password	Usually an asterisk to allow anyone to join the group; a password can be added to control access
group id	Number assigned by the system to identify this group
users	List of users that belong to the group

Here is an example of an entry in an **/etc/group** file. The group is called engines, there is no password, the group ID is 100, and the users that are part of this group are chris, robert, valerie, and aleina.

```
engines::100:chris,robert,valerie,aleina
```

As in the case of the **/etc/passwd** file, you can edit the **/etc/group** file directly using a text editor. Instead of using either usercfg or groupdel, you could just delete the entry for that group in the **/etc/group** file. However, this can be risky should you make accidental changes.

Managing Groups Using usercfg

You can add, remove, and modify any groups easily with the usercfg utility on your root user desktop. To manage groups using usercfg, first open the UserCfg menu in the upper-left corner of the UserCfg window. This menu lists several options, one of which is Edit Groups. Another is Edit Users. To work on groups choose the Edit Groups item. When you are finished working on groups and want to return to working on users, choose the Edit Users item on this menu.

A Group window will be displayed, listing all your groups (see Figure 19-5). Each entry will have three fields: the group name, the group ID, and the number of users that are part of this group. You can use the scroll bar on the side to move through the list of groups. At the bottom of the window are three buttons: to add a group, just click on the Add button; to delete or change a group, first click on a group entry in the list

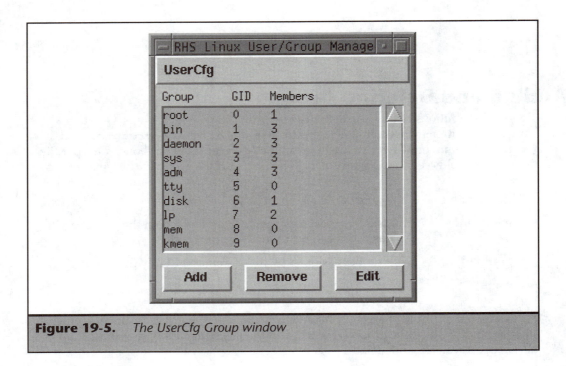

Figure 19-5. *The UserCfg Group window*

to select it, and then click on the Remove button to remove a group or the Edit button to modify a group.

Upon choosing the Add button, another window opens that prompts you for the various fields making up a group entry (see Figure 19-6). In the box labeled Name you enter the name of the group. A group ID will already be entered for you in the GID box, but you can enter one of your own if you wish. The lower half of the window contains a list of users that belong to this group. You can scroll through the list using the scroll bar. Initially this list will be empty. To add users to this list, you click on the Add button to the left of the list. This opens yet another window where you can select the users you want in your group. This window displays a list of all users, again with a scroll bar that you can use to see all the names. To add a user to the group, first click on the user in the list and then click on the Add button located at the bottom left of this window. You can add as many users as you want. Once you have added all the users you want to a group, click on the Done button located in the lower-right corner of the window. This returns you to the Group window where the list of users for the group now includes all the users you just added. You can also use this window to remove users from a group. Below the Add button is a Remove button. From the list, select the user you want to remove, and then click on the Remove button.

Once you have finished making all your entries, you click on another button labeled Add located in the lower-left corner of the window. This window will close,

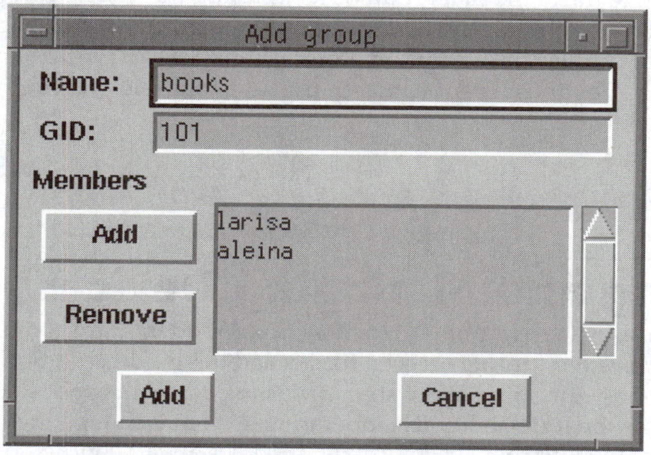

Figure 19-6.   *New Group window*

and you will return to the Group window. You will see the new group added to the list of groups.

The Edit operation works much the same way as the Add operation. You are presented with a window listing the Name and GID entries as well as the list of users for the group. You can then change the name or group ID, and remove users from the group or add new ones.

Managing Groups Using groupadd, groupmod, and groupdel

With the **groupadd** command you can create new groups. When you add a group to the system, the system will place the group's name in the **/etc/group** file and give it a group ID number. **groupadd** only creates the group category. Users are individually added to the group. In the next example, the **groupadd** command creates the engines group.

```
# groupadd engines
```

You can delete a group with the **groupdel** command. In the next example, the **engines** group is deleted.

```
# groupdel engines
```

You can change the name of a group or its ID using the **groupmod** command. Just enter **groupmod -g** with the new ID number and the group name. To change the name of a group, you use the **-n** option. Enter **groupmod -n** with the new name of the group followed by the current name. In the next example, the engines group has its name changed to caboose.

```
# groupmod -n caboose engines
```

Installing and Managing Devices

All the peripherals, such as printers, terminals, and modems, are connected to your Linux operating system through special files called device drivers. Such a file contains all the information your operating system needs to control the specified device. This design introduces great flexibility. The operating system is independent of the specific details for managing a particular device; the specifics are all handled by the device file. The operating system simply informs the device what task it is to perform, and the device file tells it how. If you change devices, you only have to change the device file, not the whole system.

The name of a device file is designed to reflect the task of the device. Printer device files begin with **lp** for "line print." Since you could have more than one printer connected to your system, the particular printer device files are distinguished by two or more numbers or letters following the prefix **lp**, such as **lp0**, **lp1**, **lp2**. The same is true for terminal device files. They begin with the prefix **tty**, for "teletype," and are further distinguished by numbers or letters such as **tty0**, **tty1**, **ttyS0**, and so on.

In Linux there are two types of devices: block and character. A block device, such as a hard disk, transmits data a block at a time. A character device, such as a printer or modem, transmits data one character at a time, or rather as a continuous stream of data, not as separate blocks. Device driver files for character devices will have a **c** as the first character in the permissions segment displayed by the **ls** command. Device driver files for block devices will have a **b**. In the next example, **lp0** (the printer) is a character device and **hda1** (the hard disk) is a block device.

```
# ls -l hda1 lp0
brw-rw----    1 root       disk       3,    1 Sep  7  1994 hda1
crw-r-----    1 root       daemon     6,    0 Dec 31  1979 lp0
```

Installing and maintaining new devices such as printers and terminals is a task for system administration. To install a new printer, you have to be logged into the system as the root user, the superuser. You can then modify files in key directories such as those for devices in the **/dev** directory.

The numbers that follow a device file prefix are unique identifiers for the device. As such, they can only be created by the operating system. You cannot create them yourself.

Creating Device Files: mknod

You use the **mknod** command to create a device file, either a character or block type. The **mknod** command has the following syntax:

```
mknod   options   device   device-type   major-num   minor-num
```

The device type can be either **b**, **c**, **p**, or **u**. As already mentioned, the **b** indicates a block device, and **c** is for a character device. The **u** is for an unbuffered character device, and **p** is for a FIFO device. Devices of the same type often have the same name, for example, Ethernet cards will all have the name **eth**. Devices of the same type are then uniquely identified by a number that is attached to the name. This number has two components, the major number and the minor number. Devices may further have the same major number, but if so, the minor number will always be different. This major and minor structure is designed to deal with situations in which several devices may be dependent on one larger device, such as several modems connected to the same I/O card. They would all have the same major number that would reference the card, but each modem would have a unique minor number. Both the minor and major numbers are required for block and character devices (**b**, **c**, and **u**). However, they are not used for FIFO devices.

Installing and Managing Printers

Your Linux system can easily access printers connected to your PC. Setting up a printer interface is fairly simple. It is a matter of determining a device file to use and placing printer configuration entries in your **printcap** file. You may also have to set up printing filters. The PrintTool utility on your root user desktop can provide a very easy interface for setting up and managing your printers (its icon is shown here).

printtool

Using just PrintTool, you can easily install a printer on your Linux system. Follow these steps:

1. In the PrintTool window, select the Add button. This opens up an Edit window that displays several fields in which you enter printer configuration information.

2. In the Names field, you enter in the names you want to use for the printer. Each name is separated by a |. You should include **lp** as one of your names. **lpr** used without a specified printer name will use the printer named **lp**.

3. In the Spool directory fields, the default spool directory will already be entered for you. You can change it to another directory if you wish.

4. For the Device field, it's customary to enter **/dev/lp1**. This is the parallel printer device for computers that use an AT bus which most computers today use. If you have a serial device you will have to use a different device name.

5. For the Input Filter you can click on the Select button to display a window with three fields. Each field has a Select button by it that will display a set of currently available options. The Select button for the PrinterType field opens a menu of printers that you can choose from. The Select button for the Resolution field lists several possible resolutions. The Select button for the PaperSize field lists paper sizes such as letter and legal.

6. When you are finished, click on the OK button to close the window and do the same for the Edit window. You will see your printer listed in the PrintTool window, as shown in Figure 19-7.

7. Choose the Quit item from the PrintTool menu to quit PrintTool. You are now ready to print.

For a detailed explanation of printer installation, see the **Printing-HOWTO** file in **/usr/doc/HOWTO**.

The Redhat distribution of Linux creates three device names for parallel printers automatically during installation. They are **lp0**, **lp1**, and **lp2**. (Most systems these days use **lp1**.) The number used in these names corresponds to a parallel port on your PC. **lp0** references the LPT1 parallel port usually located at address 0x03bc. **lp1** references the LPT2 parallel port located at 0x0378, and **lp2** references LPT3 at address 0x0278. If you are not sure at what address your parallel port is located, you can use the **msd.exe** command on your DOS system to find out. **lp0** connects to an XT bus and **lp1** connects to an AT bus.

You use **mknod** to make a printer device. Printer devices are character devices and must be owned by the root and daemon. The permissions for printer devices are write and execute for the owner and read for the group, 620 (see Chapter 7 for a discussion of file permissions). The major device number is set to 6, and the minor device number is set to the port number of the printer, such as 0 for LPT1 and 1 for LPT2. Once the device is created, you use **chown** to change its ownership to **root.daemon**. In the next example, a parallel printer device is made on the first parallel port, **/dev/lp0**. The **-m** option specifies the permissions, in this case, 620. The device is a character device, as indicated by the **c** argument following the device name. The major number is 6, and

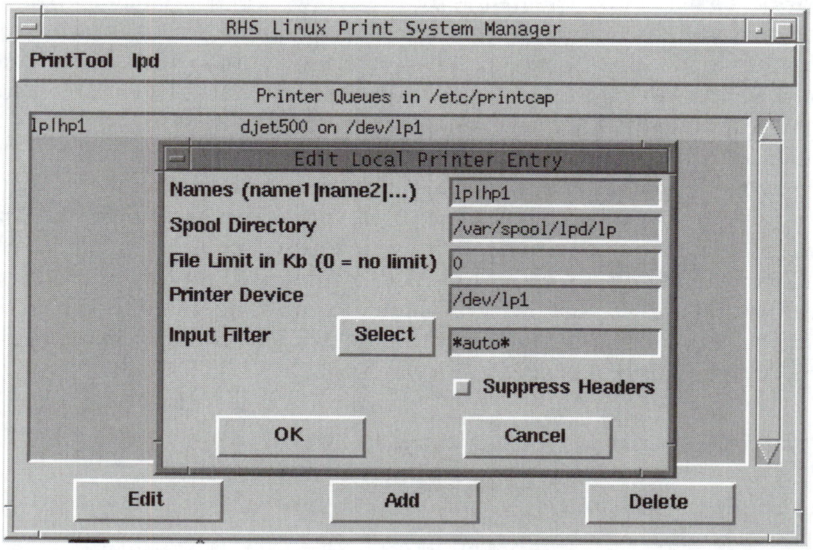

Figure 19-7.   *Using Printtool to install a new printer*

the minor number is 0. If you were making a device at **/dev/lp2**, the major number would still be 6 but the minor number would be 2. Once made, the **chown** command then changes the ownership of the parallel printer device to **root.daemon**.

```
# mknod -m 620 /dev/lp0 c 6 0
# chown root.daemon /dev/lp0
```

Be sure to check that a spool directory has been created for your device. If not, you will have to make one.

When your system prints a file, it makes use of special directories called spool directories. A print job is a file to be printed. When you print a file to a printer, a copy of it is made and placed in a spool directory set up for that printer. The location of the spool directory is obtained from the printer's entry in the **/etc/printcap** file. In the spool directory two files are made for each print job. One begins with **df** and is the data file containing the copy of the file to be printed. The other begins with **cf** and is the control file for the print job. It contains information about the print job, such as the user it belongs to.

The **/etc/printcap** file holds entries for each printer connected to your system. A printcap entry holds information such as the path name for a printer's spool directory and the device name of the printer port that the printer uses. The first field in a printcap entry is a list of possible names for the printer. These are names you can make up yourself, and you can add others if you wish. Each name is separated by a |. You use these names to identify the printer when entering various printer commands or options, such as the **-P** option. They are also used for special shell variables, such as the **PRINTER** variable, used in many initialization scripts.

The fields following the list of names set different fields for your printer. The fields have two letter names and are usually assigned a value using the **=**. These assignments are separated by colons. Three of the more important fields are **lp**, **sd**, and **of**. **lp** is set to the device name that the printer uses. **sd** is set to the path name of the spool directory, and **of** is set to the particular filter used for this printer. Some have Boolean values and will just list the field name with no assignment for a true value. You can find a complete listing of the printcap fields in the printcap man pages: **man 8 printcap**. An example of a printcap entry follows.

```
##PRINTTOOL## LOCAL djet500c 600x600 letter {}
hp1|lp:\
    :sd=/var/spool/lpd/lp:\
    :mx#0:\
    :lp=/dev/lp1:\
    :if=/var/spool/lpd/lp/filter:
```

Instead of making your own entries in the **/etc/printcap** file, you can use the Redhat printtool utility, located on your root user desktop, to make them for you automatically.

Printing on your system is handled by a print daemon called **lpd**. **lpd** is constantly running, waiting for print jobs and then managing their printing procedures. **lpd** takes its print jobs from a print queue that you can list using the **lpq** command. The **lpr** command will place a job on the print queue, and **lpd** will then take it in turn and print it. As noted in Chapter 5, **lpr** takes as its argument the name of a file. You can also feed data to **lpr** through the standard input, piping in the data to be printed from another operation. The **-P** option allows you to specify a particular printer. In the next example, the user first prints the file **preface**. Then she uses the **cat** command to generate combined output of the files **intro** and **digest**. This is piped to the **lpr** command, which will then print it. Finally, the user prints the file **report** to the printer with the name **hp1**.

```
$ lpr preface
$ cat intro digest | lpr
$ lpr -Php1 report
```

You can also print directly to the printer by simply redirecting output to the printer's device file. This does not place anything on the print queue. The print operation becomes a command to be immediately executed. However, your system is occupied until the file completes printing. The following example uses this technique to print the **report** file to a printer connected to device **lp1**.

```
$ cat report > /dev/lp1
```

To manage the printing jobs on your printer or printers, enter the command **lpc** and press ENTER. You are then given an LPC> prompt at which you can enter **lpc** commands to manage your printers and their jobs. The **status** command with the name of the printer displays whether the printer is ready, how many print jobs it has, and so on. The **stop** and **start** commands can stop a printer and start it back up. See Table 19-6 for a listing of **lpc** commands.

```
# lpc
lpc> status hp1
hp1|lp1:
    queuing is enabled
    printing is enabled
    1 entry in spool area
```

You can manage the print queue using the **lpq** and **lprm** commands. **lpq** lists the printing jobs currently on the print queue. With the **-P** option and the printer name you can list the jobs for a particular printer. If you specify a user name, you can list the print jobs for that user. With the **-l** option, **lpq** displays detailed information about each job. If you want information on a specific job, you can just use that job's ID number with **lpq**.

With the **lprm** command you can remove a printing job from the queue, erasing it before it can be printed. **lprm** takes many of the same options as **lpq**. To remove a specific job, just use **lprm** with the job number. To remove all printing jobs for a particular user, enter **lprm** with the user name. To remove all printing jobs for a particular printer, you use the **-P** option with the printer name.

lprm has a special argument indicated by a dash, **-**, that references all print jobs for the user who issues the command. For example, to remove all your own print jobs, you can just enter **lprm -**. If you logged in as the root user, then **lprm -** will remove all print jobs for all printers and users from the print queue, emptying it completely.

You should not use **lprm** to kill a printing job that has already started printing. Instead, you may have to use the **kill** command on the print job process. You can display processes using the **ps -ax command**, then use **kill** and the number of the process to end it. For a job that is already printing, you will see a process for its filter. This is the process to kill.

Installing and Managing Terminals and Modems

With a multiuser system such as Linux, you will probably have several users logged in at the same time. Each user, would, of course, need his or her own terminal through which to access the Linux system. The monitor on your PC acts as a special terminal called the console, but you can add other terminals through either the serial ports on your PC or through a special multiport card installed on your PC. The other terminals can be stand-alone terminals or PCs using terminal emulation programs. For a detailed explanation of terminal installation, see the **Term-HOWTO** file in **/usr/doc/HOWTO**. A brief explanation is provided here.

For each terminal you add, you must create a character device on your Linux system. As with printers, you use the **mknod** command to create terminal devices. The permissions for a terminal device are 660. Terminal devices are character devices with a major number of 4 and minor numbers usually beginning at 64. The serial ports on your PC are referred to as COM1, on up to COM4. They correspond to the terminal devices **/dev/ttyS0** through **/dev/ttyS3**. Note that several of these serial devices may already be used for other input devices such as your mouse and for communications devices such as your modem. If you have a serial printer, then one will already be used for that. Before you create a terminal device, first determine the serial port it is connected to. If you've installed a multiport card, you will have many more ports to choose from. Once you have created the terminal device you then change its ownership to that of **root.tty**. In the next example, the user creates a terminal device for the COM3 port, **/dev/ttyS2**.

```
#   mknod  -m 660 /dev/ttyS2  c 4 66
#   chown root.tty  /dev/ttyS2
```

Terminal devices are managed by your system using the **getty** program and a set of configuration files. When your system starts, it reads a list of connected terminals in the **inittab** file and then executes a **/etc/getty** program for each one. The **getty** program sets up the communication between your Linux system and a specified terminal. It obtains from the **/etc/gettydefs** file certain parameters such as speed and the login prompt as well as any special instructions.

```
# Format: <speed># <init flags> # <final flags> #<login
    string>#<next-speed>
# 38400 fixed baud Dumb Terminal entry
DT38400# B38400 CS8 CLOCAL # B38400 SANE -ISTRIP CLOCAL #@S login:
    #DT38400
```

The **/etc/inittab** file holds instructions for your system on how to manage terminal devices. A line in the **/etc/inittab** file has four basic components: an ID, runlevel, action, and process. Terminal devices are identified by ID numbers, beginning with 1 for the first device. The runlevel at which the terminal operates is usually 1. The action is usually "respawn," which says to continually run the process. The process is a call to **/etc/getty** with the baud rate and terminal device name.

The **/etc/ttys** file associates the type of terminal used with a certain device. It consists of two columns, the first for the type of terminal and the second for the terminal device names. A terminal type is a special term as defined in the **termcap** file. For example, **vt100** refers to a VT100 terminal, and **tvi920c** refers to a TeleVideo 920c. **console** refers to the monitor on your system. The terminal type is assigned to a user's **TERM** shell variable when logging in through the corresponding device.

/etc/termcap holds the specifications for different terminal types. These are the different types of terminals users could use to log into your system. Your **/etc/termcap** file is already filled with specifications for most of the terminals currently produced. An entry in the **/etc/termcap** file consists of various names that can be used for a terminal separated by a | and then a series of parameter specifications, each ending in a colon. It is here that you find the name used for a specific terminal type. You can use **more** to display your **/etc/termcap** file and then use a search, **/**, to locate your terminal type.

```
tvi925|925|televideo model 925:\
    :hs:xn:am:bs:co#80:li#24:cm=\E=%+ %+
        :cl=\E*:cd=\Ey:ce=\Et:is=\El\E":\
    :al=\EE:dl=\ER:im=:ei=:ic=\EQ:dc=\EW:if=/usr/lib/tabset
        /stdcrt:\
    :ho=^^:nd=^L:bt=\EI:pt:so=\EG4:se=\EG0:sg#1:us=\EG8:ue=
        \EG0:ug#1:\
    :up=^K:do=^V:kb=^H:ku=^K:kd=^V:kl=^H:kr=^L:kh=^^:ma=^V^J^L :\
    :k1=^A@\r:k2=^AA\r:k3=^AB\r:k4=^AC\r:k5=^AD\r:k6=^AE\r:k7=^AF
        \r:\
    :k8=^AG\r:k9=^AH\r:k0=^AI\r:ko=ic,dc,al,dl,cl,ce,cd,bt:\
    :ts=\Ef:fs=^M\Eg:ds=\Eh:sr=\Ej:
```

There are many options that you can set for a terminal device. To change these options you can use the **stty** command instead of changing configuration files directly. **stty** with no arguments lists the current setting of the terminal.

When a user logs in, it is helpful to have the terminal device initialized using the **tset** command. Usually the **tset** command is placed in the user's **.bash_profile** file and is automatically executed whenever he or she logs into the system. You use the **tset** command to set the terminal type and any other options the terminal device requires. A common entry of **tset** for a **.bash_profile** file follows. The **-m dialup:** option prompts the user to enter a terminal type. The type specified here is a default type that will be displayed in parentheses. The user just presses ENTER to choose the default. The prompt will look like this: **TERM=(vt100)?**

```
eval `tset -s -Q -m dialup:?vt00`
```

LILO

You can configure your Linux Loader (LILO) using the **/etc/lilo.conf** file and the command **lilo**. If you examine your **/etc/lilo.conf** file, you will find it organized into different segments called stanzas, one for each operating system that LILO is to start up. If your Linux system shares your computer with a DOS system, you should see two stanzas listed in your **/etc/lilo.conf** file, one for Linux and one for DOS. Each stanza will indicate the hard disk partition that the respective operating system is located on. It will also include an entry for the label. This is the name you enter at the LILO prompt to start that operating system.

You can, if you wish, make changes directly to the **/etc/lilo.conf** file using a text editor. Whenever you make a change, you have to execute the **lilo** command to have it take effect. Type **lilo** and press ENTER.

/etc/lilo.conf

```
# general section
boot = /dev/hda
install = /boot/boot.b
message = /boot/message
prompt
# wait 20 seconds (200 10ths) for user to select the entry to load
timeout = 200
# default entry
default = dos
image = /vmlinuz.gen
    label = linux
    root = /dev/hda3
    read-only
other = /dev/hda1
    label = dos
    table = /dev/hda
    loader = /boot/chain.b
```

Unless specified by the default entry, the default operating system that LILO boots is the one whose segment is the first listed in the **lilo.conf** file. Because the Linux stanza is the first listed, this is the one that LILO will boot if you do not enter anything at the LILO prompt. If you would like to have your DOS system be the default, you can use **lilo** with the **-D** option to reset the default, or edit the **lilo.conf** file to assign a value to **default**. You could also use a text editor to place the DOS stanza first, before the Linux stanza. Be sure to execute **lilo** to have the change take effect. The next time you start your system, you could just press ENTER at the LILO prompt to have DOS loaded, instead of typing **dos**.

```
# lilo -D dos
```

There are a number of LILO options that you can set using either command line options or by setting options in the **lilo.conf** file. These are listed in Table 19-7.

Summary: System Administration

You may need to perform basic system administration operations such as adding or deleting users, adding file systems to your file structure, and configuring different devices such as printers and terminals. To have the permission to perform such tasks you need to log into the system as a superuser. To become the superuser you have to log in as the root user. The root login gives you total control, allowing you to change any feature of the system.

You can determine in what mode the system will run. There is a single-user mode, a multiuser mode, an administrative mode, as well as a shutdown mode. The multiuser mode is usually the default. You use the shutdown mode to turn the system off or to change to another mode.

As a superuser, you can manage other users on the system, adding user logins and passwords as well as deleting user logins. You can create groups or delete groups and add or remove users from groups. You can also add devices such as printers, modems, and terminals. To add a device, you use the **mknod** command to create a device file for it. You may also have to make entries in various configuration files, depending on the type of device you are adding.

Your root user desktop holds many useful utilities for managing the various system administration tasks. The usercfg program lets you easily add, remove, and modify both users and groups. The timetool utility lets you set the system date and time. The printtool utility will automatically configure your printer for you, placing the appropriate entry in your **/etc/printcap** file. The netcfg program lets you configure network interfaces (as discussed in Chapter 20), and the fstool program lets you manage your file systems, mounting and unmounting them as you wish (see Chapter 7).

Root User Desktop Utility	Description
usercfg	Manages your users and groups, allowing you to add, remove, or modify users as well as add, remove, and modify groups
timetool	Sets the system date and time
printtool	Configures a printer, creating a printer device and printcap entry for the printer
netcfg	Configures your network interfaces (see Chapter 20)
fstool	Configures your file systems, allowing you to mount, unmount, add, remove, or format file systems using your **/etc/fstab** file (see Chapter 7)
Basic System Adminstration	
su root	Logs a superuser into the root from a user login; the superuser returns to the original login with a CTRL-**d**
passwd *login-name*	Sets a new password for the login name
crontab *options file-name*	With *file-name* as an argument, installs **crontab** entries in the file to a crontab file; these entries are operations executed at specified times **-e** Edits the crontab file **-l** Lists the contents of the crontab file **-r** Deletes the crontab file
init *state*	Changes the system state (see Table 19-3)
lilo *options Config-file*	Reconfigure the Linux Loader (LILO)
shutdown *options time*	Shuts down the system; similar to CTRL-ALT-DEL
date	Sets the date and time for the system
mknod	Creates a device such as a printer or terminal device

Table 19-1. *System Administration Commands*

Basic System Administration	Description
adduser *username*	Adds a new user, creating a password file entry and home and mail directories with initialization files; uses **passwd** command to create a password for the user

Printer Management

lpr *options file-list*	Prints a file; copies the file to the printer's spool directory and places it on the print queue to be printed in turn **-P***printer* Prints the file on the specified printer
lpq *options*	Displays the print jobs in the print queue **-P***printer* Prints queue for the specified printer **-l** Prints a detailed listing
lprm *options Printjob-id* or *User-id*	Removes a print job from the print queue; you identify a particular print job by its number as listed by **lpq**; if you use *User-id*, it will remove all print jobs for that user **-** Refers to all print jobs for the logged-in user; if the logged-in user is the root, it refers to all print jobs **-P***printer* Removes all print jobs for the specified printer
lpc	Manages your printers; at the LPC> prompt you can enter commands to check the status of your printers and take other actions (see Table 19-6 for a list of **lpc** commands)

Terminal Management

stty	Allows you to set different options for a terminal device
tset *options*	Initializes your terminal device with a specific terminal type

Table 19-1.   *System Administration Commands* (continued)

File	Description
/etc/inittab	Sets the default state as well as terminal connections
/etc/passwd	Contains user password and login configurations
/etc/group	Contains a list of groups with configurations for each
/etc/fstab	Automatically mounts file systems when you start your system
/etc/lilo.conf	The LILO configuration file for your system
/etc/printcap	Contains a list of each printer and its specifications
/etc/termcap	Contains a list of terminal type specifications for terminals that could be connected to the system
/etc/gettydefs	Contains configuration information on terminals connected to the system
/etc/skel	Directory that holds the versions of initialization files such as **.bash_profile** that are copied to new users' home directories
/etc/ttys	List of terminal types and the terminal devices with which they correspond
System Initialization Files	
/etc/rc.d	Directory that holds system startup and shut down files
/etc/rc.d/rc.sysinit	Initialization file for your system
/etc/rc.d/rc.local	Initialization file for your own commands; you can freely edit this file to add your own startup commands; it is the last startup file executed
/etc/rc.d/init.d	Directory that holds many of the initialization files to start up and shut down various daemons

Table 19-2. *System Administration Configuration Files*

System Initialization Files	Description
/etc/rc.d/init.d/halt	Operations performed each time you shut down the system, such as unmounting file systems; called **rc.halt** in other distributions
/etc/rc.d/init.d/lpd.init	Start up and shut down the **lpd** daemon
/etc/rc.d/init.d/inet	Operations to set up network interfaces and the **inet** daemon; calls the **networks** file
/etc/rc.d/init.d/httpd.init	Operations to start up and shut down your Web server daemon, **httpd**
/etc/rc.d/init.d/cfs.init	Operations to start up and shut down your Caldera font server
/etc/rc.d/init.d/ipx	Operations to start up and shut down your NetWare IPX daemon

Table 19-2.   *System Administration Configuration Files* (continued)

State	Description
init *state*	Changes the system state; you can use it to power up or power down a system, allow multiuser or single-user access; the **init** command takes as its argument a number representing a system state
System States	
0	Halt (do *not* set the default to this); shuts down system completely
1	Administrative single-user mode; denies other users access to the system but allows root access to entire multiuser file system
2	Multiuser, without NFS (the same as 3, if you do not have networking)

Table 19-3.   *Redhat's Runlevel States for System*

System States	Description
s or **S**	Single user; only one user has access to system; used when you want all other users off the system or you have a single-user personal system
3	Full multiuser mode; allows remote file sharing with other systems on your network
4	Unused
5	X11 only
6	Reboots; shuts down and restarts the system (do *not* set the default to this)

Table 19-3. *Redhat's Runlevel States for System* (continued)

Option	Description
shutdown **[-rkhncft]** *time* [*warning-message*]	Shuts the system down after the specified time period, issuing warnings to users; you can specify a warning message of your own after the time argument; if neither **-h** or **-r** are specified to shut down the system, the system sets to the administrative mode, runlevel state 1
Argument	
time	Has two possible formats—it can be an absolute time in the format *hh:mm*, with *hh* the hour (one or two digits) and *mm* the minute (in two digits); it can also be in the format **+***m*, with *m* the number of minutes to wait; the word **now** is an alias for **+0**
Option	
-t *sec*	Tells **init** to wait *sec* seconds between sending processes the warning and the kill signal, before changing to another runlevel

Table 19-4. *System Shutdown Options*

Option	Description
-k	Doesn't really shut down; only sends the warning messages to everybody
-r	Reboots after shutdown, runlevel state 6
-h	Halts after shutdown, runlevel state 0
-n	Doesn't call **init** to do the shutdown—you do it yourself
-f	Does a *fast* reboot
-c	Cancels an already running shutdown; no time argument

Table 19-4. *System Shutdown Options* (continued)

Command	Description
useradd *username options*	Adds new users to the system
usermod *username options*	Modifies a user's features
userdel -r *username*	Removes a user from the system
useradd, usermod Options	
-u *userid*	Sets the user ID of the new user; the default is the increment of the highest number used so far
-g *group*	Sets a group or name
-d *dir*	Sets the home directory of the new user
-s *shell*	Sets the login shell directory of the new user
-c *str*	Adds a comment to the user's entry in the system password file: **/etc/passwd**
-k *skl-dir*	Sets the skeleton directory that holds skeleton files, such as **.profile** files, that are copied to the user's home directory automatically when it is created; the default is **/etc/skel**

Table 19-5. *User and Group Management Commands (for Redhat use* **usercfg** *or* **adduser** *instead)*

useradd, usermod Options	Description
-D	Displays defaults for all settings
Group Management Commands	
groupadd	Creates a new group
groupdel	Removes a group
groupmod *option*	Modifies a group **-g** Changes a group ID **-n** Changes a group name

Table 19-5. *User and Group Management Commands (for Redhat use* **usercfg** *or* **adduser** *instead)* (continued)

Command	Operation
help [*command ...*]	Prints a short description of each command
abort *printers*	Terminates an active spooling daemon on the local host immediately and then disables printing for the specified printers; use **all** to indicate all printers
clean *printers*	Removes any temporary files, data files, and control files that cannot be printed
disable *printers*	Turns the specified printer queues off; new jobs will not be accepted
down *printers message*	Turns the specified printer queue off, disables printing and puts message in the printer status file
enable *printers*	Enables spooling for the listed printers; allows new jobs into the spool queue
quit or **exit**	Exits from **lpc**

Table 19-6. **lpc** *Commands*

Command	Operation
restart *printers*	Starts a new printer daemon; used if the printer daemon, **lpd**, dies, leaving jobs yet to be printed
start *printers*	Enables printing and starts a spooling daemon for the listed printers
status *printers*	Displays the status of daemons and queues on the local machine
stop *printers*	Stops a spooling daemon after the current job completes and disables printing
topq *printer* [*jobnum* ...] [*user* ...]	Places the jobs in the order listed at the top of the printer queue
up *printers*	Enables everything and starts a new printer daemon; undoes the effects of **down**

Table 19-6.   **lpc** *Commands* (continued)

Command Line Option	lilo.conf option	Description
-b *bootdev*	**boot=***bootdev*	Boot device
-c	**compact**	Enables map compaction; speeds up booting
-d *dsec*	**delay=***dsec*	Timeout delay to wait for you to enter the label of an operating system at the LILO prompt when you boot up
-D *label*	**default=***label*	Uses the kernel with the specified label, instead of the first one in the list, as the default kernel to boot
-i *bootsector*	**install=***bootsector*	File to be used as the new boot sector

Table 19-7.   *LILO Options for Command Line and* **lilo.conf**

Command Line Option	lilo.conf option	Description
-f *file*	**disktab=***file*	Disk geometry parameter file
-l	**linear**	Generates linear sector addresses instead of sector/head/cylinder addresses
-m *mapfile*	**map=***mapfile*	Uses specified map file instead of the default
-P fix	**fix-table**	Fixes corrupt partition tables
-P ignore	**ignore-table**	Ignores corrupt partition tables
-s *file*	**backup=***file*	Alternates save file for the boot sector
-S *file*	**force-backup=***file*	Allows overwriting of existing save file
-v	**verbose=***level*	Increases verbosity
-u		Uninstalls LILO by copying the saved boot sector back
-V		Prints version number
-t		Test only; does not really write a new boot sector or map file; uses together with **-v** to find out what LILO is about to do
-I		Displays label and path name of running kernel; label is held in BOOT_IMAGE shell variable

Table 19-7. *LILO Options for Command Line and **lilo.conf** (continued)*

Chapter Twenty

Network Administration

Linux systems are configured to connect into networks that use the TCP/IP protocols. These are the same protocols that the Internet, as well as many local networks, use. In Chapter 10 you were introduced to TCP/IP, a robust set of protocols that are designed to provide communications between systems with different operating systems and hardware. The protocols were developed in the 1970s as a special DARPA project to enhance communications between universities and research centers. The protocols were originally developed on Unix systems, with much of the research carried out at the University of California, Berkeley. Linux, as a version of Unix, benefits from much of this original focus on Unix.

The TCP/IP protocols actually consist of different protocols, each designed for a specific task in a TCP/IP network. The two basic protocols are the Transmission Control Protocol (TCP), which handles receiving and sending communications, and the Internet Protocol (IP), which handles transmitting communications. Other protocols provide various network services. The Domain Name Service (DNS) provides address resolution. The File Transfer Protocol (ftp) provides file transmission, and Network File Systems (NFS) provides access to remote file systems. Table 20-1 lists the different TCP/IP protocols.

Administering and configuring a TCP/IP network on your Linux system is not particularly complicated. There are a set of configuration files that your system uses to set up and maintain your network. Table 20-2 provides a complete listing. Many of these can be managed using administrative programs such as **netcfg** on your root user desktop. You can also use the more specialized programs, such as **netstat**, **ifconfig**, and **route**. Some configuration files are easy to modify yourself using a text editor. Table 20-3 lists the commonly used network administration programs.

If, during your installation, you entered the configuration information for your network, your system is ready to go. If your Linux system is already connected to a network, say an Ethernet network, then you do not need anything from this chapter, unless you want to understand how Linux is setting up your network connections. If you dial into a network through a modem, say to an Internet service provider (ISP), you will find the SLIP and PPP sections of this chapter useful. These tell you how to have your Linux system dial up an ISP and make the correct network connection. If you are having difficulty connecting to a network, or you are setting one up yourself, then all the information in this chapter will be helpful.

TCP/IP Network Addresses

As explained in Chapter 10, a TCP/IP address is organized into four segments consisting of numbers separated by periods. This is called the IP address. Part of this address is used for the network address, and the other part is used to identify a particular host in that network. The network address identifies the network that a particular host is a part of. Usually, the network part of the address takes up the first three segments and the host takes the last segment. Altogether, this forms a unique address with which to identify any computer on a TCP/IP network. For example, in the IP address 199.35.209.72, the network part is 199.35.209 and the host part is 72. The host is a part of a network whose own address is 199.35.209.0.

The IP address of the host, or host address, is only one of several addresses you will need in order to connect the host to a network. In addition, you will need the network address, broadcast address, gateway address (if there is one), nameserver address, and a network mask, or netmask. All of these are asked for during installation. If you provided them at that time, they will all be automatically entered into the appropriate configuration files. Also, any entries that you make through the **netcfg** utility on your root user desktop will be entered. (Table 20-2 lists these network configuration addresses.)

Network Address

You can easily figure out the network address using your host address. It is the network part of your host address, with the host part set to 0. So the network address for the host address 199.35.209.72 is 199.35.209.0.

Systems derive the network address from the host address using the netmask. For those familiar with computer programming, a bitwise AND operation on the netmask and the host address results in zeroing the host part, leaving you with the network part of the host address.

Broadcast Address

The broadcast address allows a system to send the same message to all systems on your network at once. As with the network address, you can easily figure it out using your host address; it has the host part of your address set to 255. The network part remains untouched. So the broadcast address for the host address 199.35.209.72 is 199.35.209.255 (you combine the network part with 255 in the host part).

Gateway Address

Some networks will have a computer designated as the gateway to other networks. Every connection to and from the network to other networks passes through this gateway computer. If you are on this type of network, you will have to provide the gateway address. If your network does not have a gateway, or you use a stand-alone system or dial into an Internet service provider, you do not need a gateway address.

Usually a gateway address has the same network part of a hostname, with the host part set to 1. The gateway address for the host address 199.35.209.72 may be 199.35.209.1. However, this is just a convention. To be sure of your gateway address, ask your network administrator for it.

Nameserver Addresses

Many networks, including the Internet, have computers that operate as domain nameservers to translate the domain names of networks and hosts into IP addresses.

This makes your computer identifiable on a network, using just your domain name rather than your IP address. You can also use the domain names of other systems to reference them, so you don't have to know their IP addresses. You do, however, have to know the IP addresses of any domain nameservers for your network. You can obtain the addresses from your system administrator (there is often more than one). Even if you are using an Internet service provider, you will have to know the address of the domain nameservers that your ISP operates for the Internet.

Netmask

The netmask is used to derive the address of the network you are connected to. The netmask is determined using your host address as a template. All the numbers in the network part of your host address are set to 255, and the host part is set to 0. This, then, is your netmask. So the netmask for the host address 199.35.209.72 is 255.255.255.0. The network part, 199.35.209, has been set to 255.255.255, and the host part, 72, has been set to 0. Systems can then use your netmask to derive your network address from your host address. They can determine what part of your host address makes up your network address and what those numbers are.

TCP/IP Configuration Files

A set of configuration files in the **/etc** directory, shown in the following table, are used to set up and manage your TCP/IP network. They specify such network information as host and domain names, IP addresses, and interface options. It is in these files that the IP addresses and domain names of other Internet hosts that you want to access are entered. If you configured your network during installation, you will already find that information in these files. The **netcfg** program on your desktop and the **netconfig** program on your command line both provide an easy interface for entering the configuration data for these files.

File	Function
/etc/hosts'	Associates hostnames with IP addresses
/etc/networks	Associates domain names with network addresses
/etc/rc.d/init.d/inet	Contains commands to configure your network interface when you boot up
/etc/HOSTNAME	Holds the hostname of your system
/etc/host.conf	Resolves options
/etc/resolv.conf	Contains list of domain nameservers

Identifying Hostnames: /etc/hosts

Without the unique IP address that the TCP/IP network uses to identify computers, a particular computer could not be located. Since IP addresses are difficult to use or remember, domain names are used instead. For each IP address there is a domain name. When you use a domain name to reference a computer on the network, your system translates it into its associated IP address. This address can then be used by your network to locate that computer.

Originally, it was the responsibility of every computer on the network to maintain a list of the hostnames and their IP addresses. This list is still kept in the **/etc/hosts** file. When you use a domain name, your system looks up its IP address in the **hosts** file. It is the responsibility of the system administrator to maintain this list. Because of the explosive growth of the Internet and the development of more and more very large networks, the responsibility for associating domain names and IP addresses has been taken over by domain nameservers. However, the **hosts** file is still used to hold the domain names and IP addresses of frequently accessed hosts. Your system will always check your **hosts** file for the IP address of a domain name before taking the added step of accessing a nameserver.

The format of a domain name entry in the **hosts** file is the IP address followed by the domain name, separated by a space. You can then add aliases for the hostname. After the entry, on the same line, you can enter a comment. A comment is always preceded by a **#** symbol. You will already find an entry in your **hosts** file for "localhost" with the IP address 127.0.0.1. Localhost is a special identification used by your computer to enable users on your system to communicate locally with each other. The IP address 127.0.0.1 is a special reserved address used by every computer for this purpose. It identifies what is technically referred to as a loopback device.

/etc/hosts

```
127.0.0.1       turtle.trek.com        localhost
199.35.209.72   turtle.trek.com
204.32.168.56   pango1.train.com
202.211.234.1   rose.berkeley.edu
```

Network Name: /etc/networks

The **/etc/networks** file holds the domain names and IP addresses of networks that you are connected to, not the domain names of particular computers. Networks have shortened IP addresses. Depending on the type of network, they will use one, two, or three numbers for their IP addresses. You will also have your localhost network IP address 127.0.0.0. This is the network address used for the loopback device.

The IP addresses are entered, followed by the network domain names. Recall that an IP address consists of a network part and a host part. The network part is the network address you will find in the **networks** file. You will always have an entry in this file for the network portion of your computer's IP address. This is the network address of the network your computer is connected to.

/etc/networks

```
loopback 127.0.0.0
trek.com 199.35.209.0
```

Network Initialization: /etc/rc.d/init.d/inet

The **/etc/rc.d/init.d/inet** file holds the startup commands for configuring your network. Many of the entries are automatically made for you when you use **netcfg** or configure your network during installation. You will find the **ifconfig** and **route** commands, for example, as described in the next section. You will also find your hostname, network address, and the other required addresses. You should never attempt to modify this file directly unless you are sure of what you are doing and know something about Linux shell programming. If you are using another Linux distribution such as Slackware, the initialization file may be called **/etc/rec.d/rc.inet1** or simply **/etc/rc.inet1**.

/etc/HOSTNAME

The **/etc/HOSTNAME** file holds your system's hostname. To change your hostname, you change this entry. The **netcfg** program allows you to change your hostname and will place the new name in **/etc/HOSTNAME**. Instead of displaying this file to find your hostname, you can use the **hostname** command.

```
$ hostname
turtle.trek.com
```

Network Interfaces and Routes: ifconfig and route

Your connection to a network is made by your system through a particular hardware interface such as an Ethernet card or a modem. Data passing through this interface is then routed to your network. The **ifconfig** command configures your network interfaces, and the **route** command will route them accordingly. The **netcfg** window on your Caldera Network Desktop performs the same configuration of network interfaces as **ifconfig** and **route**. If you configure an interface with **netcfg**, you do not have to use **ifconfig** or **route**. If you are using another Linux system, the **netconfig** utility also performs the same configuration as **netcfg**. However, you can directly configure interfaces using **ifconfig** and **route**, if you wish.

Every time you start your system, the network interfaces and their routes have to be established. You can have this done automatically for you when you boot up by placing the **ifconfig** and **route** commands for each interface in the **/etc/rc.d/init.d/inet** initialization file, which is executed whenever you start your system. If you use **netcfg** on your Caldera Network Desktop to configure your network interfaces, then the appropriate **ifconfig** and **route** commands are automatically added to the **/etc/rc.d/init.d/inet** file. You do not have to add them. If you did not use the **netcfg** command, you have to enter them yourself.

Netcfg and Lisa

The easiest way to create a network interface is to use one of the configuration tools, Lisa or **netcfg**. To use Lisa, just enter the command **lisa** at the command line and move to the Network Configuration menu from the System Configuration entry. You can then choose to Configure General Network Services to enter your Domain Name Server addresses, or choose to enter a Hostname.

You can also use the **netcfg** program on your root user desktop to set up a network interface. Just log into the root account and use **startx** to start the desktop. You will see an icon labeled "**netcfg**." Double-click on it, and it will display a window showing all your network interfaces. As shown in Figure 20-1, with **netcfg** you can change and add to your network configuration.

The **netcfg** window displays interfaces, nameservers, and hosts. Each is displayed and managed in its own window, with its own buttons. The Interface window lists your current interfaces. You can use the buttons at the bottom of this window to add, configure, activate, or deactivate an interface. When adding a new interface, another window will open up, listing entry boxes for required information. Here, you enter such information as the interface's name and IP address. Upon closing this window, you will see an entry for this interface appear in the Interface window.

The Nameserver window to the right lists all current nameservers. You can use its buttons to add or remove nameservers. Any entries you make here are automatically entered into the **/etc/resolv.conf** file. The bottom window lists the hosts with their IP numbers and hostnames. These are other computers that you are connected to. With the window's buttons, you can add or remove hosts or edit the current hosts. Changes and new entries will be saved to your **/etc/hosts** file.

You can also change your hostname. Select the hostname item on the **netcfg** menu in the upper-left corner. You will then be prompted for a new hostname. Your entry will be placed in the **/etc/hostname** file, replacing the previous one.

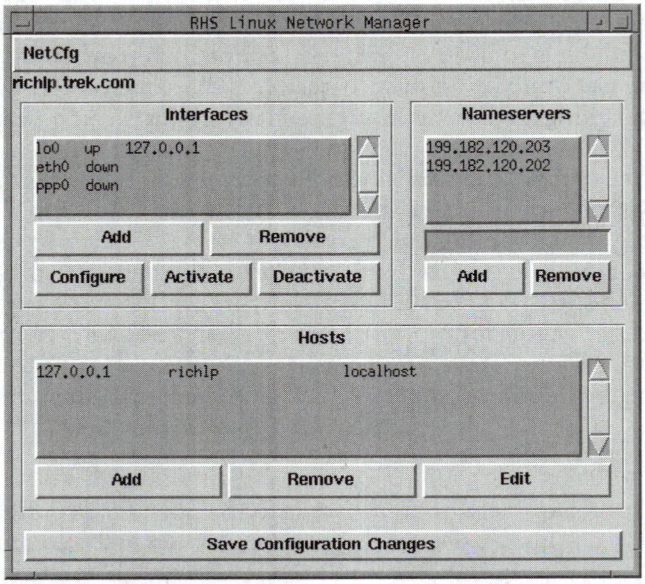

Figure 20-1. *The* `netcfg` *utility*

Once you have made all your changes, click on the Save Configuration button to make them permanent. The new information you entered will be added to the appropriate network configuration files.

ifconfig

The **ifconfig** command takes as its arguments the name of an interface and an IP address, as well as options. **ifconfig** then assigns the IP address to the interface. Your system now knows that there is such an interface and that it references a particular IP address. In addition, you can specify whether the IP address is a host or network address. You can use a domain name for the IP address, provided the domain name is listed along with its IP address in the **/etc/hosts** file. The syntax for the **ifconfig** command follows:

```
# ifconfig  interface  -host_net_flag  address  options
```

The *host_net_flag* can be either **-host** or **-net** to indicate a host or network IP address. The **-host** flag is the default. The **ifconfig** command can have several options, which set different features of the interface, such as the maximum number of bytes it can transfer (**mtu**) or the broadcast address. The **up** and **down** options activate and deactivate the interface. In the next example, the **ifconfig** command configures an Ethernet interface.

```
# ifconfig eth0  204.32.168.56
```

For a simple configuration such as this, **ifconfig** automatically generates a standard broadcast address and netmask. The standard broadcast address is the network address with the number 255 for the host address. Remember that the standard netmask is 255.255.255.0. However, if you are connected to a network with a particular netmask and broadcast address, you will have to specify them when you use **ifconfig**. The option for specifying the broadcast address is **broadcast**; for the network mask, it is **netmask**. Table 20-4 lists the different **ifconfig** options. In the next example, **ifconfig** includes the netmask and broadcast address.

```
# ifconfig eth0 204.32.168.56    broadcast 204.128.244.127
netmask 255.255.255.0
```

Point-to-point interfaces such as Parallel IP (PLIP), Serial Line IP (SLIP), and Point-to-Point Protocol (PPP) require that you include the **pointopoint** option. A PLIP interface name is identified with the name **plip** with an attached number; for example, **plip0** is the first PLIP interface. SLIP interfaces use **slip0**, and PPP interfaces start with **ppp0**. Point-to-point interfaces are those that usually operate between only two hosts, such as two computers connected over a modem. When you specify the **pointopoint** option, you need to include the IP address of the host. Later in the chapter, you will see how you can use SLIP and PPP interfaces to dial up and connect your system to an Internet service provider.

In the next example, a PLIP interface is configured that connects the computer at IP address 199.35.209.72 with one at 204.166.254.14. If there were domain addresses listed for these systems in **/etc/hosts**, those domain names could be used in place of the IP addresses.

```
# ifconfig  plip0  199.35.209.72  pointopoint 204.166.254.14
```

Should you need to, you can also use **ifconfig** to configure your loopback device. The name of the loopback device is **lo**, and its IP address is the special address 127.0.0.1. The following example shows the configuration:

```
# ifconfig lo 127.0.0.1
```

The **ifconfig** command is very useful for checking on the status of an interface. If you enter the **ifconfig** command alone with the name of the interface, information about that interface is displayed.

```
# ifconfig eth0
```

To see if your loopback interface is configured, you can use **ifconfig** with the loopback interface name, **lo**.

```
# ifconfig lo

lo          Link encap:Local Loopback
            inet addr:127.0.0.1  Bcast:127.255.255.255  Mask:255.0.0.0
            UP BROADCAST LOOPBACK RUNNING  MTU:2000  Metric:1
            RX packets:0 errors:0 dropped:0 overruns:0
            TX packets:12 errors:0 dropped:0 overruns:0
```

Routing

A packet that is part of a transmission takes a certain *route* to reach its destination. On a large network, packets are transmitted from one computer to another until the destination computer is reached. The route determines where the process starts and what computer your system needs to send the packet to in order for it to reach its destination. On small networks, routing may be static; that is, the route from one system to another is fixed. One system knows how to reach another, moving through fixed paths. However, on larger networks and on the Internet, routing is dynamic. Your system knows the first computer to send its packet off to, and then that computer takes it from there, passing it on to another that then determines where to pass it on to. For dynamic routing, your system needs to know very little. Static routing, however, can become very complex, since you have to keep track of all the network connections. Your routes are listed in your routing table in the **/proc/net/route** file. To display the routing table, enter **route** with no arguments.

```
# route
Kernel routing table
Destination      Gateway        Genmask         Flags Metric  Ref   Use Iface
loopback         *              255.0.0.0        U     0       0      12 lo
pango1.train.com *              255.255.255.0    U     0       0       0 eth0
```

Each entry in the routing table has several fields, providing information such as the route destination and the type of interface used. The different fields are listed in the following table.

Field	Description
Destination	Destination IP address of the route
Gateway	IP address or hostname of the gateway the route uses; * indicates no gateway is used
Genmask	The netmask for the route
Flags	Type of route: U=up, H=host, G=gateway, D=dynamic, M=modified
Metric	Metric cost of route
Ref	Number of routes that depend on this one
Window	TCP window for AX.25 networks
Use	Number of times used
Iface	Type of interface this route uses

You should have at least one entry in the routing table for the loopback interface. If not, you will have to route the loopback interface using the **route** command. The IP address for an interface has to be added to the routing table before you can use that interface. You add an address with the **route** command and the **add** option.

```
route  add  address
```

The next example adds the IP address for the loopback interface to the routing table.

```
route add 127.0.0.1
```

The **add** argument has several options, as specified in the man pages for **route**. If you are adding a specific static route, you will need to use these options to specify such features as the netmask, gateway, interface device, or destination address. However, if an interface has already been brought up by **ifconfig**, then **ifconfig** can draw much of its information from the interface configuration. For example, to set a route for an Ethernet connection that has already been configured by **ifconfig**, you only need to enter the **-net** option and the IP address of the destination. **ifconfig** uses the IP address to locate the interface configured for it and then uses that information to establish the route. The following example is the routing of an Ethernet interface.

```
# route add -net  204.32.168.0
```

If your system is connected to a network, there should be at least one entry in your routing table that specifies the default route. This is the route taken by a message packet when no other route entry leads to its destination. The destination for a default route is the keyword **default**.

You can delete any route you've established by invoking **ifconfig** with the **del** argument and the IP address of that route, as in this example:

```
# route del -net  204.32.168.0
```

Monitoring Your Network: ping and netstat

With the **ping** program, you can check to see if you can actually access another host on your network. **ping** will send a request to the host for a reply. The host then sends a reply back, and it is displayed on your screen. **ping** will continually send such a request until you stop it with a break command, a CTRL-**c**. You will see one reply after another scroll by on your screen until you stop the program. If **ping** cannot access a host, it will issue a message saying that the host is unreachable. If **ping** fails, it is an indication that your network connection is not working. It may just be the particular interface, a basic configuration problem, or a bad physical connection. To use **ping**, enter **ping** and the name of the host.

```
$ ping pang01.train.com
```

The **netstat** program provides real-time information on the status of your network connections, as well as network statistics and the routing table. **netstat** has several options you can use to bring up different information about your network (see Table 20-5).

```
# netstat
Active Internet connections
Proto Recv-Q Send-Q Local Address      Foreign Address      (State)       User
tcp      0      0 turtle.trek.com:01  pang01.train.com.:ftp ESTABLISHED  dylan
Active UNIX domain sockets
Proto RefCnt Flags      Type          State         Path
unix  1      [ ACC ]    SOCK_STREAM   LISTENING     /dev/printer
unix  2      [ ]        SOCK_STREAM   CONNECTED     /dev/log
unix  1      [ ACC ]    SOCK_STREAM   LISTENING     /dev/nwapi
unix  2      [ ]        SOCK_STREAM   CONNECTED     /dev/log
unix  2      [ ]        SOCK_STREAM   CONNECTED
unix  1      [ ACC ]    SOCK_STREAM   LISTENING     /dev/log
```

The **netstat** command with no options will list the network connections on your system. First, active TCP connections are listed and then the active domain sockets. The domain sockets contain processes used to set up communications between your system and other systems. The various fields are described in the following table.

Field	Description
Proto	Protocol used for the connection: TCP, UDP
Recv-Q	Bytes received but not yet used by the system
Send-Q	Bytes sent to remote system, but not yet confirmed as received
Local Address	Local hostname and port number
Foreign Address	Remote hostname and port number assigned to a connection; port number can be connection type, such as telnet or ftp
(State)	State of connection to remote host ESTABLISHD, connection established SYN_SENT, trying to make connection SYN_REC, connection being created FIN_WAIT1, connection shutting down CLOSED, connection closed LISTEN, listening for remote connection UNKNOWN, unknown state

Domain Socket

Proto	Protocol for socket, usually **unix**
RefCnt	Number of processes currently in socket
Flag	
Type	Mode socket is accessed
State	State of the socket FREE, socket is not used LISTENING, waiting for connection UNCONNECTED, no current connection CONNECTING, trying to make connection CONNECTED, currently connected DISCONNECTING, closing a connection
Path	Path name used by processes to access socket

You can use **netstat** with the **-r** option to display the routing table, and **netstat** with the **-i** option displays the usage for the different network interfaces. The following table explains the coded information.

```
# netstat -i
Kernel Interface table
Iface   MTU Met  RX-OK RX-ERR RX-DRP RX-OVR   TX-OK TX-ERR TX-DRP TX-OVR Flags
lo     2000   0      0      0      0      0      58      0      0      0 BLRU
```

MTU	Maximum number of bytes for one transmission
RX-OK	Packets received with no errors
RX-ERR	Packets received with errors
RX-DRP	Packets dropped
RX-OVR	Packet overrun errors
TX-OK	Packets sent with no errors
TX-ERR	Packets sent with errors
TX-DRP	Packets dropped in transmission
TX-OVR	Packets dropped in transmission with overrun errors
Flags	Interface characteristics:
	A, receives packets for Multicast addresses
	B, receives broadcasts
	D, debugging is on
	L, loopback interface
	M, promiscuous mode
	N, no trailers processed on packets
	O, address resolution protocol is off
	P, point-to-point interface
	R, interface is running
	U, interface is activated, up

Domain Name Service (DNS)

Each computer connected to a TCP/IP network such as the Internet is identified by its own IP address. An IP address is a set of four numbers specifying the location of a network and of a host (a computer) within that network. IP addresses are difficult to remember, so a domain name version of each IP address is also used to identify a host. As described in Chapter 10, a domain name consists of two parts, the hostname and the domain. The hostname is the computer's specific name, and the domain identifies the network that the computer is a part of. The domains used for the United States usually have extensions that identify the type of host. For example, **.edu** is used for educational institutions and **.com** is used for businesses. International domains usually have extensions that indicate the country they are located in, such as **.du** for Germany or **.au** for Australia. The combination of a hostname, domain, and extension forms a unique name by which a computer can be referenced. The domain can, in turn, be split into further subdomains.

As you know, a computer on a network can still only be identified by its IP address, even if it has a domain name. You can use a domain name to reference a computer on a network, but this involves using the domain name to look up the corresponding IP address in a database. The network then uses the IP address, not the domain name, to access the computer. Before the advent of very large TCP/IP networks such as the Internet, it was feasible for each computer on a network to maintain a file with a list of all the domain names and IP addresses of the computers connected on its network. Whenever a domain name was used, it was looked up in this file and the corresponding IP address located. You can still do this on your own system for remote systems that you access frequently.

As networks became larger, it became impractical and, in the case of the Internet, impossible for each computer to maintain its own list of all the domain names and IP addresses. To provide the service of translating domain addresses to IP addresses, databases of domain names were developed and placed on their own servers. To find the IP address of a domain name, a query is sent to a nameserver that then looks up the IP address for you and sends it back. In a large network, there can be several nameservers covering different parts of the network. If a nameserver cannot find a particular IP address, it will send the query on to another nameserver that is more likely to have it. Nameservers can also provide information such as the company name and street address of a computer, or even the person maintaining it.

Nameservers are queried by resolvers. These are programs specially designed to obtain addresses from nameservers. To use domain names on your system, you will have to configure your own resolver. Your local resolver is configured by your **/etc/host.conf** and **/etc/resolv.conf** files.

host.conf

Your **host.conf** file lists resolver options (shown in the following table). Each option can have several fields, separated by spaces or tabs. You can use a **#** at the beginning of a line to enter a comment. The options tell the resolver what services to use. The order of the list is important. The resolver will begin with the first option listed and move on to the next ones in turn. You will find the **host.conf** file in your **/etc** directory along with other configuration files.

order	Specifies sequence of name resolution methods
	hosts Checks for name in the local **/etc/host** file
	bind Queries a DNS nameserver for address
	nis Uses Network Information Service protocol to obtain address

alert	Checks addresses of remote sites attempting to access your system; you turn it on or off with the **on** and **off** options
nospoof	Confirms addresses of remote sites attempting to access your system
trim	For checking your local host's file, removes the domain name and checks only for the hostname; allows you to use just a hostname in your host file for an IP address instead of the complete **host.domain.ext name**
multi	For checking your local hosts file, allows a host to have several IP addresses; you turn it on or off with the **on** and **off** options

In the next example of a **host.conf** file, the **order** option instructs your resolver first to look up names in your local **/etc/hosts** file and then, if that fails, to query domain nameservers. The system does not have multiple addresses.

/etc/host.conf

```
# host.conf file
# Lookup names in host file and then check DNS
order bind host
# There are no multiple addresses
multi off
```

/etc/resolv.conf

For the resolver to do its job, it must have access to domain nameservers. In the **resolv.conf** file, you provide the resolver with the addresses of the domain nameservers that your system has access to. There are three different types of entries that you can make in your **resolv.conf** file, each preceded by one of three keywords: domain, nameserver, and search. For the domain entry, you list the domain name of your system. You can, if you wish, add search entries. A search entry provides a list of domains to try if only a hostname is given. If there is a system that you access frequently, you could enter its domain name in a search entry and then just use its hostname as the address. Your resolver will then try to find the hostname using the domain name listed in the search entry.

Following the search entries, if there are any, you place your nameserver entries. For each nameserver your system has access to, you enter **nameserver** and the nameserver's IP address. There may be several nameservers that you can access. The order is important. Often, networks will have a primary nameserver, followed by several secondary ones. The primary one is expected to be queried first. To do this, you must have its IP address entered in the first nameserver entry.

The following is an example of a **resolv.conf** file. The domain of the host computer is **berkeley.edu**. The IP addresses of the nameservers for this domain are listed in the nameserver entries. The search entry will allow just the hostname for a computer in the **unc.edu** domain to be used as an address. For example, to access **sunsite.unc.edu**, a user would only have to enter the hostname as an address, **sunsite**.

/etc/resolv.conf

```
# resolv.conf file
domain berkeley.edu
search unc.edu
nameserver  204.199.87.2
nameserver  204.199.77.2
```

Setting Up Your Own Nameserver: named

If you are administering a network and you need to set up a nameserver for it, you can configure a Linux system to operate as a nameserver. To do so, you have to start up the **named** daemon. **named** is designed to start with the system and then wait for domain name queries. It makes use of several configuration files that enable it to answer requests. The **named.boot** file specifies the domain that the server supports as well as the directory for its working files. The **named.hosts** file holds information about that domain. It consists of resource records that list information about the different hosts in the domain. The records use a very specific format with codes placed in appropriate fields. The **named.rev** file maps IP addresses to hostnames. The **named.ca** file sets up caching for the nameserver. The process of setting up your own nameserver can be complicated. Refer to HOW-TO documentation, the man entry for **named**, and to Linux texts specializing in network administration.

SLIP and PPP

As an alternative to hardwired network connections such as Ethernet, you can use a modem with telephone lines. There are two protocols that can transmit IP communications across the telephone lines. These are the Serial Line Internet Protocol (SLIP) and the Point-to-Point Protocol (PPP). SLIP is an older protocol, whereas PPP is more recent, though very stable. Many high-speed connections used by current Internet service providers (ISP) use PPP. The SLIP and PPP protocols are especially designed for users who connect their systems to the Internet over a modem and telephone line. Usually, a connection is made to an ISP that then connects the system to the Internet through its own systems.

An Internet service provider will support either SLIP or PPP on a given line. Find out which protocol your ISP supports. You need to use one or the other.

Setting up a SLIP or PPP connection can be a complicated process. For more detailed explanations, see the PPP-HOWTO and the Net-2-HOWTO documents in **/usr/doc/HOWTO**. There are also Web page instructions in **/usr/doc/HTML**.

Preparations for Connecting to SLIP or PPP

To make a SLIP or PPP connection, you must have TCP/IP networking enabled and a loopback interface configured. The Caldera Network Desktop does this automatically. Internet service providers usually maintain domain nameservers that you can use. You have to find the IP address of these nameservers and enter them into your **/etc/resolv** file. You can also use Lisa or **netcfg** on the desktop to enter the address, and they will place them in the **/etc/resolv** file for you. In any event, use **more** or **cat** to display the contents of **/etc/resolv** to make sure the domain name addresses are there. Without them, none of the Internet addresses you enter will be recognized.

PPP

The Point-to-Point Protocol (PPP) is a more recent and more versatile protocol that is quickly becoming popular. It provides a much more stable connection and can support a variety of network protocols, not just the Internet protocols. PPP performs much of its work automatically. It does not need a set of commands for each specific step as SLIP does. PPP will automatically determine remote IP addresses, static or dynamic.

A PPP connection is set up using the **pppd** program. **pppd** will configure your connection, setting MTU limits and obtaining IP addresses. However, unlike **dip**, **pppd** does not make the initial connection. It does not dial up through your modem and provide login and password information. To use **pppd**, you first have to establish the connection to the remote host. You can make such a connection using the **chat** program, which has its own options and format. The **chat** program first makes the connection, and then **pppd** configures it. However, you do not have to call chat first and then **pppd**. **pppd** is designed to take as its argument a program that will make the connection—in this case, **chat**. You simply specify chat along with its options on the command line with **pppd**. In **fact**, the entire **pppd** operation takes place on one command line, unlike the **dip** script.

Static and dynamic IP addresses are distinguished by **pppd** by whether you include a set of IP addresses as an argument on the command line and the use of the **noipdefault** option. If you do include the IP addresses, then **pppd** assumes you have a static connection and these are the remote and local addresses to use to establish that connection. If you do not specify any addresses as arguments, then **pppd** assumes a default remote and local address. The default local address is the IP address of your systems as specified in your **/etc/hostname** file. A default remote address will try to be determined from remote addresses in your **/etc/hosts** file. **pppd** assumes you use dynamic addresses and will look for them when a connection is made. To have **pppd** assume dynamic addresses, you use the **noipdefault** option, as well as not specifying any addresses. **noipdefault** instructs **pppd** not to use default addresses. With no addresses specified, **pppd** then assumes that dynamic addresses will be received from the remote host.

The local and remote static addresses are entered next to each other, separated by a colon. The local address is entered first. The following example specifies a local address of 199.35.209.72 and remote address of 163.179.4.22.

```
199.35.209.72:163.179.4.22
```

Should you use a dynamic remote address, but your own local address, you can specify just your local address followed by the colon. **pppd** will then use your local address and dynamically receive your remote address.

```
199.35.209.72:
```

Since your local address as specified in your **/etc/hostname** file is your default local address, you do not even have to enter it on the command line. You could just enter the **pppd** command with no addresses. **pppd** will use your hostname address as your local address and receive a remote address from the remote host.

Most Internet service providers that use dynamic addresses will provide you with both the local and remote address. In this case, you do not enter any addresses at all and you have to specify the **noipdefault** option. **noipdefault** will prevent the use of the **hostname** address as the default local address. Lacking any addresses, **pppd** will obtain both from the remote host.

Chat Scripts

The best way to use chat is to invoke a chat script. To make a connection, chat has to specify all the connection information: the telephone number, login prompt and user ID, password prompt and password, and any connect strings. You could enter this as a string after the **chat** command on the command line, but this makes for a very long and complex command line. Instead, you can create a file with the chat information in it and then use the **-f** option and the file name with the **chat** command. Such files are called chat scripts.

A chat script consists of one line organized into different segments for the parts of the connection procedure. Each segment consists of an expect-reply pair of strings. The first string is what you expect to receive and the second string is what you are sending. If you expect to receive nothing, then you use a null string, **" "**. Each expect-reply pair performs a specific task in the login process. You can start with an initialization of your modem, should you need to do this. Many users can just use the default settings. Then, the number is dialed to make the connection. You can then check to see if the connection was made. A login name is provided at the login prompt. And finally, a password is sent at the password prompt.

If you decide to initialize your modem, you need to start with an expect-reply entry to perform this task. You expect nothing at first, so the expect string is only an empty string, two double quotes, **" "**. For the reply string, you specify the codes for your modem initialization. When entering the codes for your initialization string, you will have to escape any code beginning with **&**. For chat, the **&** is a break and will stop the process. As shown here, **&F2** is preceded by a backslash to quote the **&**.

```
""   AT\F2V1L0
```

The next expect-reply entry dials the phone number. If you have an initialization string before it, then its expect string will be the word OK. This is the response from your modem of "OK," indicating that there was no problem initializing your modem. If, however, you did not enter an expect-reply entry for initializing your modem, then the expect string would just be a null string, **" "**. In either case, the reply string is the modem command to dial the number, ATDT, combined with the phone number.

```
OK   ATDT5558888
```

You will usually receive a connect string indicating that you have connected to the remote system. This can vary from system to system. There may not even be a connect string at all. On many systems, the connect string is the word CONNECT; on others, it is the baud rate, or speed. In this example, the user receives the speed as the connect string. The response to a connect string is usually nothing, though it can also be a newline. Recall that you represent no response with an empty string—two double quotes, **" "**. The newline is represented in a chat script with a **\n**. (Some remote systems expect an MS-DOS newline, which is actually a carriage return character, **\r**, followed by a newline character, **\n**.) See Table 20-6 for a listing of chat script special characters. In the next example, a newline is sent in response.

```
57600 \n
```

After the connect string, the remote system usually sends the login prompt. This is often the word "login" with a colon. You only need the last few characters, **ogin:**. Don't forget the colon. In reply, you send your user ID. Depending on your ISP, you may have to add **\n** to the user ID to enter a newline, as in *mylogin*\n. Some ISPs may require you to include other characters.

```
ogin:  mylogin
```

After the login, you can expect the password prompt. Again, you only need the last few characters, **word:**. In response, you send your password. If needed, be sure to add the **\n** to enter the newline.

```
word:  mypass
```

All this fits together on just one line. You have a sequence of words indicating alternating received and sent text.

```
" "   AT\&F2V1L0 OK  ATDT8888888 CONNECT  \n  ogin: mylogin   word:  mypass
```

If you did not initialize your modem, it would look slightly different.

```
" " ATDT8888888 CONNECT  \n  ogin:  mylogin  word:  mypass
```

If your ISP does not require you to send a return character on receiving the CONNECT string, you can leave that out, reducing the chat script as shown here:

```
" " ATDT8888888 ogin:  mylogin  word:  mypass
```

In a chat script, you can break the expect and reply pairs into separate lines, one pair to a line, with the strings for each pair separated by a space or tab. You could also put it all on the very first line if you wish. The file name for the script has the extension **.chat**. The next example shows the **mycon.chat** script with pairs entered on separate lines.

mycon.chat

```
" "     AT\&F2V1L0
OK     ATDT4448888
CONNECT  \n
ogin:  mylogin
word:  mypass
```

You can then call the chat script with the **chat** command and the **-f** option, as shown here. The chat program will use the information in the chat script to initialize your modem, dial up your remote host, and then log in with your user ID and password.

```
chat -f  mycon.chat
```

Many remote systems and modes will send error messages if something should go wrong in the connection process. You can use the special expect string, **ABORT**, followed by a key term to detect such an error message. If such a term is received, chat cancels the connection procedure. If you are using a command line only, you can enter abort strings either where you would expect them to occur in the connection process or at the very beginning. Within a chat script, as shown here, the abort strings are placed at the beginning. The next example would expect a NO CARRIER or a BUSY response before the login prompt. In either case, an initial connection failed, and chat will cancel the remaining steps. Notice the quotes around NO CARRIER. If a string has a space in it, you have to quote it.

mycon.chat

```
ABORT   'NO CARRIER'
ABORT   BUSY
" "     AT\&F2V1L0
OK      ATDT5558888
CONNECT \n
ogin:   mylogin
word:   mypass
```

You need to incorporate the chat operation into your invocation of the **pppd** command. The entire chat operations will be encased in single quotes and entered on the same line as the **pppd** command. The chat program will use the information in the chat script to initialize your modem, dial up your remote host, and then log in with your user ID and password. **chat** will make the connection and then **pppd** will configure it.

The Point-to-Point Protocol daemon (**pppd**) is invoked with several possible options. Its standard syntax is

```
pppd options serial-device-name speed local:remote-addresses ppp-options
```

The *serial-device-name* is the device name for your modem. This is likely to be **/dev/cua** with a number attached, usually from 0 to 3, depending on the port you are using for your modem. Port 1 is **cua0**, port 2 is **cua2**, and so on. The *speed* is the baud rate. For a 14.4 modem, this is 14400. For a v.28 modem, this is 38400, or even 56700. Check with your ISP and your modem documentation for the highest speed you can support.

The options specify configuration features such as your MTU size and whether you are receiving a dynamic IP address. The **connect** option instructs **pppd** to make a connection. It takes as its argument a Linux command that will actually make the connection—usually the **chat** command. You enter **pppd** followed by the **connect** option and the **chat** command with its **-f** option and chat script file name. The **chat** command and its **-f** option with the chat file name are all enclosed in quotes to distinguish them from other **pppd** options. In the next example, the user invokes **pppd** with the **chat** command using the **mycon.chat** chat script. The modem is connected to port 4, **/dev/cua1**, and the speed is 57600 baud.

```
# pppd connect 'chat -f mycon.chat' /dev/cua1 57600
```

To disconnect your PPP connection, you invoke **pppd** with the **disconnect** option. You must use chat to instruct your modem to hang up. For this, you may have to send a modem command such as H0. You will probably find it more convenient to place the **chat** commands in a chat file, as shown here:

```
# pppd disconnect 'chat -f turnoff.chat'
```

turnoff.chat

```
-- \d+++\d\c OK
ATH0 OK
```

To make the disconnect process easier, you can place the **pppd** commands within a shell script, just as can be done for the connect process.

PPP Options

pppd has a great many options. The more commonly used ones are listed in Table 20-7. See the **pppd** man pages for a complete list. For example, the **mru** option sets the "maximum receive unit" size. **pppd** instructs the remote system to send packets no larger than this size. The default is 1500, and 296 or 542 is recommended for slower modems. The **defaultroute** option instructs **pppd** to set up the PPP connection as the default route. The lack of any addresses combined with the **noipdefault** option instructs **pppd** to detect and use a dynamic IP address from the ISP remote system. You have to specify this option if you have an ISP that supplies dynamic IP addresses. The **crtscts** option uses hardware flow control, and the **modem** option uses the modem control lines. You can list the options after the speed on the command line, as shown here:

```
# pppd connect 'chat -f mycon.chat' /dev/cua1  57600  mru 1500
defaultroute noipdefault crtscts modem
```

In the following command, the presence of addresses instructs **pppd** to use these addresses to establish a static connection. The local address is 199.35.209.72 and the remote address is 163.179.4.22.

```
# pppd connect 'chat -f mycon.chat' /dev/cua1  57600
199.35.209.72:163.179.4.22 mru 1500 defaultroute crtscts modem
```

This can make for a very lengthy and complex command line, depending on how many options you need. As an alternative, **pppd** allows you to enter options in the file **/etc/ppp/options** as well as in a **.ppprc** file. **pppd** will automatically read and use the options specified in these files each time it is invoked. You can specify as many options as you wish, entering each on a separate line. With the **#** symbol, you can also enter comments, explaining the options and their settings. The **/etc/ppp/options** file contains system default options for **pppd**. You create this file as the root user, and it is the first options file called when **pppd** is invoked. Each user can have a **.ppprc** file in his or her own home directory. These options are specified by a particular user and are read after the system's **/etc/ppp/options** file. A brief example of an options file is shown here.

/etc/ppp/options

```
# /etc/ppp/options -*- sh -*- general options for pppd
crtscts
defaultroute
modem
mru 542
asyncmap 0
netmask 255.255.255.0
noipdefault
```

To make this process easier, the Redhat implementation of Linux includes a file in the **/etc/ppp** directory called **options.tpl**, an options template. This already lists all the options with default values and includes extensive explanations of each option. However, all the options are commented out with a preceding **#** at the beginning of each line. Instead of creating your own options file from scratch, you could copy the **options.tpl** to **options**, making it the options file. Then, with an editor such as Vi, you could remove the **#** symbol from the beginning of the line for the options you want to use. For example, to enable **noipdefault**, use your editor to locate that line and delete the preceding **#**. To turn an option back off, use your editor to reinsert a **#** at the beginning of that option's line. With this approach, you can quickly specify all the options you need. Now when you invoke **pppd,** you do not have to enter any of these options on the command line.

With your options specified in the **/etc/ppp/options** file, you then only need to enter the **pppd** command with the **chat** invocation, the device name for your modem, and the modem speed.

```
$ pppd connect 'chat -f mycon.chat' /dev/cua1 57600
```

You can reduce your entry even further by placing the **pppd** invocation in a shell script and then just executing the shell script. Recall that a shell script is a text file that you create with any text editor. You type the command invocation with all its arguments as you would on the command line. Be sure to precede the **pppd** command with an **exec** command. **exec** runs **pppd** from your command line shell, not the script's shell. You then make the script executable with the command **chmod 755** *script-name*. Now to execute your **pppd** operation, just enter the script name on the command line and press ENTER. In the next example, the **pppd** connect operation is placed in a shell script called **pppcon**, and the user simply enters **pppcon** to invoke **pppd**.

pppcon

```
exec pppd connect 'chat -f mycon.chat' /dev/cua1 57600
```

```
$ pppcon
```

You are now ready to try **pppd** to connect to your remote system. Any number of things may go wrong. You may not have the right connect string or the modem may be initializing wrong. **pppd** will log descriptions of all the steps it is taking in the **/var/log/messages** file. You can use **tail** to list these descriptions even as **pppd** is operating. For a successful connection, you will see the local and remote IP addresses listed at the end as shown here.

```
$ tail /var/log/messages
```

To receive an ongoing display of messages as they are entered in the **/var/log/messages** file, use the **tail** command with the **-f** option, as shown here. Use a CTRL-**c** to end the process.

```
$ tail -f /var/log/messages
Mar 23 20:01:03 richlp pppd[208]: Connected...
Mar 23 20:01:04 richlp pppd[208]: Using interface ppp0
Mar 23 20:01:04 richlp kernel: ppp: channel ppp0 mtu = 1500, mru = 1500
Mar 23 20:01:04 richlp kernel: ppp: channel ppp0 open
Mar 23 20:01:04 richlp pppd[208]: Connect: ppp0  /dev/cua3
Mar 23 20:01:09 richlp pppd[208]: local  IP address 204.32.168.68
Mar 23 20:01:09 richlp pppd[208]: remote IP address 163.179.4.23
```

The Redhat distribution of Linux provides you with a sample login PPP script called **ppp-on** in the **/usr/sbin** directory. You can use a text editor to set the correct values to certain variables such as Phone and Password. You also must be careful to set the correct arguments and options for both the **chat** and the **pppd** commands. If you have already set options in the **/etc/ppp/options** file, you can remove most of the options that you would normally specify on the command line. Also, be sure to set the correct speed and device name for the modem. Once working, all you then have to enter is **ppp-on** to establish your PPP connection. If you have trouble disconnecting, try the **ppp-off** command. This is a shell script located in **/usr/sbin** that kills the PPP process directly.

It is also possible to use **dip** to invoke **pppd** and set up a PPP connection. When you set the mode to PPP in a **dip** script, you are in fact executing the **pppd** program. In this case, you would not need a **chat** script to make the connection, since **dip** has already done this. However, there are several options that **pppd** needs to have set when it is invoked. These options cannot be specified in the **dip** script. Instead, you have to set them up in the **/etc/ppp/options** file that **pppd** automatically reads whenever it is executed.

Providing Incoming PPP Connections from Other Systems

As with SLIP, you can also configure your system to be a PPP server, allowing remote systems to dial into yours and make PPP connections. You only need to create one special account and a script to invoke **pppd** with the **-detach** and **silent** options. The script is usually called **ppplogin**—here is an example:

/etc/ppp/ppplogin

```
exec pppd -detach silent modem crtscts
```

With the **-detach** option, **pppd** won't detach itself from the line it is on. The **silent** option makes **pppd** wait for a remote system to make a link to your system.

The **modem** option monitors the modem lines, and **crtscts** uses hardware flow control.

The special account has the name **ppp**. The **/etc/passwd** entry for the **ppp** account would appear as follows:

```
ppp:*:501:300:PPP Account:/tmp:etc/ppp/ppplogin
```

PPP Security: CHAP

To ensure security for PPP connections you have to use additional protocols. Two have been developed for PPP, the Password Authentication Protocol (PAP) and the Challenge Handshake Authentication Protocol (CHAP). CHAP is considered a more secure protocol. It uses an encrypted challenge system that requires the two connected systems to continually authenticate each other. The keys for the encryption are kept in the **/etc/ppp/chap-secrets** file. To use CHAP in your PPP connections, you include the **auth** option when you invoke **pppd**. Also, you must enter the required information for the remote host into the **/etc/ppp/chap-secrets** file. The following is an example of a **/etc/ppp/chap-secrets** entry. Entries for the PAP in **/etc/ppp/pap-secrets** have the same format.

etc/ppp/chap-secrets

pango1.train.com	turtle.trek.com	"my new hat"
*	turtle.trek.com	"confirmed tickets"
turtle.trek.com	pango1.train.com	"trek on again"

A CHAP secrets entry has up to four fields: the client's hostname, the server's hostname, a secret key, and a list of IP possible addresses. For a particular computer trying to make a connection to your system, you can specify that it supply the indicated secret key. Instead of specifying a particular computer, you can use a * to indicate any computer. Any system that knows the designated secret key can connect to your system. In the first entry in the following example, the server is the user's own system, **turtle.trek.com**, and it allows **pango1.train.com** to connect to it if it provides the secret key specified. In the next entry, any remote system can connect to **turtle.trek.com** if they know the secret key "confirmed tickets".

```
pango1.train.com     turtle.trek.com    "my new hat"
   *                 turtle.trek.com    "confirmed tickets"
```

You also have to make entries for remote systems that you want to access. In that case, the remote system is the PPP server and you are the client. In the next example, **turtle** can connect to **pango1** with the secret key "trek on again."

```
turtle.trek.com pango1.train.com "trek on again"
```

SLIP and CSLIP: dip

There are two types of SLIP connections, the standard one referred to as just SLIP, and the newer Compress SLIP, referred to as CSLIP. Be sure you know which type of connection your Internet service provider is giving you. You will have to specify one or the other as your protocol mode when you connect. Except for specifying the mode, the connection procedure is the same for both. References to SLIP will apply to both SLIP and CSLIP unless specifically noted.

You use the **dip** program to manage and set up your SLIP connection. Given the appropriate information, **dip** will make a connection for you to your ISP. You can then use all the Internet applications on your system, such as Netscape or ftp.

The **dip** program operates like an interpreter. In a file called a **dip** script, you specify certain commands needed to log into the ISP and make the connection. The **dip** program then reads the commands in this file, executing them one by one. For example, the command **dial** will use your modem to dial up your ISP. A **dip** script has an extension **.dip**. Once your **dip** script is ready, you can then invoke **dip** with the name of the script. You may also want to add the **-v** option to display each command as it executes to see if any problems arise. The following shows the basic syntax for invoking **dip**.

```
$ dip -v  scriptfile.dip
```

Table 20-8 lists the different commands for a **dip** script. Several of the key commands are **port**, **speed**, **dial**, **get**, **modem**, **mode**, and **default**. **dip** also uses several special variables that hold connection information, such as $rmtip that holds the IP address of the remote system.

Scripts will vary slightly, depending on the different login procedures of Internet service providers. The login prompt, phone number, and connect string vary from one ISP to another. However, there are two significantly different formats, depending on whether your ISP provides you with a static or dynamic IP address. To set up a SLIP connection, determine what type of IP address your ISP is giving you.

If you have difficulty connecting to your system with a **dip** script, you might want to run **dip** in the interactive mode, **-t**. In this mode, **dip** generates its own shell with the prompt DIP>. You can then enter **dip** commands one at a time at the prompt. If you also use the **-v** option, **dip** will display a detailed description of all the actions it takes. For the login process, you could also use the **term** command at the **dip** prompt.

This places you in a terminal mode, in which you will be prompted directly by your ISP system for your user ID and password. Once connected, a CTRL-] returns you to the **dip** shell prompt. You can then continue, setting the route and mode. **term** is a way for you to see exactly what login and password prompts the remote ISP system is sending you. Once you have worked out the connection procedure, it is, of course, much easier to use a **dip** script.

```
#  dip -t -v
 DIP>
```

If you need to cut a **dip** connection, you use the **dip** command with the **-k** option. You can also add the **-l** option and a line to cut a specific connection. The **dip** command with just **-k** will cut the most recent connection. The **-k** option is helpful if you succeed in making a connection but for some reason are unable to log in or establish your line mode. The connection will remain active until you specifically cut it by entering **dip** with the **-k** option.

```
$ dip -k
```

Static IP Addresses in dip Scripts

A static IP address is an address that your ISP gives you to keep. Your computer is always identified by this address. When you initiate a SLIP connection to the ISP's remote host, you use your static IP address to identify your system. For connections using a static IP address, you assign your static IP address to the variable **$local** and the ISP remote host's address to the variable **$remote**. You use the **get** command to assign a value to a variable. These assignments take place at the very beginning of your **dip** script. **dip** will look for the respective IP addresses in these variables. Once the IP addresses are set, you can continue with the commands for the login procedure. A listing of the different **dip** variables is provided in Table 20-9.

```
get $local   static-IP-address
get $remote  remote-IP-address
```

The dip Script

The following is an example of a **dip** script using a static address. An example of this script can be found in the man page for **dip**. The script begins with a series of commands to set up the modem. First, the device the modem is on is determined. The COM1, COM2, COM3, and COM4 ports correspond to **/dev/cua0**, **/dev/cua1**, **/dev/cua2**, and **/dev/cua3**. Notice that the device counts from 0, so that **com4** corresponds to **cua3**. The speed is then set to 57600, the standard setting for a v.28

modem. The **init** command specifies the initialization string for the modem. Here, you enter any special codes for your particular modem. The **reset** command takes that string and uses it to initialize the modem.

mystatic.dip

```
# For a static IP address assign your system's IP address to the variable $local
get $local 199.35.209.72
# For a static IP address assign the remote system's IP address to the variable
$remote
get $remote 163.179.4.22
# Set the netmask to 255.255.255.0
netmask 255.255.255.0
# Set port and speed.
port cua3
speed 57600
init AT&F2V1M0
reset
# The Standard errlvl values:
#   0 - OK
#   1 - CONNECT
#   2 - ERROR
#   3 - BUSY
#   4 - NO CARRIER
#   5 - NO DIALTONE
wait OK 2
if $errlvl != 0 goto modem_trouble
dial 555-8888
if $errlvl != 1 goto modem_trouble
# Connection made, now login to the system.
wait ogin: 20
if $errlvl != 0 goto error
send mylogin\n
wait ord: 20
if $errlvl != 0 goto error
send mypass\n
# We are now logged in.
wait CONNECT 15
if $errlvl != 0 goto error
# Set up the SLIP operating parameters.
get $mtu 296
# Sets up SLIP connection as default route.
```

```
default
mode CSLIP
print You are now connected to $locip as  $rmtip
goto exit
modem_trouble:
print Trouble occurred with the modem...
error:
print CONNECT FAILED to $remote
quit 1
exit:
exit
```

Next, the static and remote IP addresses are assigned to the **$local** and **$remote** variables. The actual login can now proceed. The **dial** command dials the indicated number. If the dial-in fails to make a connection, it will return an error value to the **$errlvl** variable. This value is checked right after the **dial** command to see if there was a problem and to skip the rest of the script, printing out an error message, if there was. The **wait** command then waits for a connect string. This may vary by ISP. For some, it may be the word CONNECT; for others, it may be the baud rate, such as 57600. **wait** will continually look for the connect string in transmissions that the remote host is sending you. The number after the connect string is the number of seconds to wait for it to come through. After this period, **wait** will time-out instead of just waiting indefinitely. Again **$errlvl** is checked to see if this failed. Be sure you know what the connect string is. If you don't, check with your ISP or try using the terminal mode to interactively log in and see what the remote system is sending you. In response to the connect string, you can then send a return. The symbol for a return is **\n**. For some remote hosts, you may have to use the DOS version of a return, which is represented by two symbols, **\r\n**.

The next **wait** command waits for the remote host to send you the login prompt. You only need the last part of the prompt, not the whole word. Usually, the prompt is **login:**, and you only have to specify **ogin:**. If this does not work, check with your ISP to find out what your login prompt is. After the login prompt is received, the **send** command sends the user's login name. You will have to enter a return at the end of the login name, as in: **mylogin\n**. Some ISPs require that you qualify your login name in some way. The next **wait** command waits for the password prompts to be sent. This is usually "password:" and you only need the last few characters, **word:**. Then, you use the **send** command to send your password. You will have to include the return, **\n**.

A **print** command then tells you that you were able to connect and displays the remote host's address. You now have to configure the connection, setting the route and the type. The **default** command makes this connection your default route. The

mode command determines the type of connection. This depends on the type of connection your ISP is giving you. You can have a standard SLIP connection, as indicated by SLIP, or you could have a compressed SLIP connection, as indicated by CSLIP. Use the appropriate one with the **mode** command to establish your TCP/IP connection.

Dynamic IP Addresses with dip

A dynamic IP address is an address that your ISP gives you when you connect to the system. Your ISP keeps a pool of IP addresses that it hands out to users as they connect. This means that your IP address may be different each time you connect— you will not know ahead of time what your IP address will be. As part of the connect procedure, your ISP will send your system the IP address it has assigned you for this session. You then need to detect this address and use it as your system's IP address on the Internet.

Your ISP will send your system the IP address after you connect and log in. You then have to grab this address and assign it to the **$local** variable. The **get** command with the option **remote** will assign a value that is received from the remote host; in this case, the ISP's remote system you are connecting to. After you send your password, but before you set the default route and the mode, you enter the following **get** commands. You first receive the local IP address for your system and then the remote system's IP address. There is no earlier assignment of a value to either the **$local** or **$remote** variable.

```
get $local remote
 get $remote remote
```

You can add a time-out number at the end of these commands in case the remote system fails to send them. The following example shows where the remote and local **get** commands would go in the **dip** script.

```
# We are now logged in.
wait CONNECT 15
if $errlvl != 0 goto error
# get the dynamically provided IP address for the remote system
get $remote remote
# get the dynamically provided IP address assigned for the local
system, your system
get $local remote
# Set up the SLIP operating parameters.
get $mtu 1500
# Sets up SLIP connection as default route.
default
```

With the **Netcfgnetcfg** program, you can more easily configure your **dip** scripts. The upper-left box of the **netcfg** window displays your different network interfaces. For a SLIP connection, you can choose to add a new interface and then select the SLIP type. You are offered three different options: Ethernet, SLIP, and PPP. You are also asked to name the interface. A SLIP interface name consists of **sl** followed by a number, beginning with 0, as in **sl0**. It is possible to use **dip** to configure a PPP connection, but it is far more reliable to use the **pppd** program described earlier in the chapter.

Having named your interface, you are then presented with a window listing the different values used by a **dip** script, including your phone number, IP address, password, and login name. Enter the values in the appropriate fields. Then click OK. These values are used in a specially designed **dip** script called **/etc/dip-script**. When you activate this SLIP interface, this script executes and the **dip** values you entered are inserted in the appropriate places. You can edit the **/etc/dip-script** file if you need to. You can also copy it, make changes to the copy, and use that instead of **/etc/dip-script**. There is a place in your SLIP interface configuration for entering your own **dip** script to use instead of the default, **/etc/dip-script**.

The **/etc/dip-script** file as provided is designed for static IP addresses. If your ISP provides dynamic IP addresses, you will have to change the **/etc/dip-script** file or make a copy and change that, designating the copy as your **dip** script in the **netcfg** interface configuration. You will have to delete the two **get local** and **get remote** entries at the top of the file and enter the **get $local remote** and **get $remote remote** entries right before the **get mtu** command, as shown here.

```
wait @@@connect-string@@@ 30
  if $errlvl != 0 goto error
loggedin:
# Lines for dynamic addressing
get   $local   remote
get   $remote   remote
get $mtu @@@mtu@@@
  default
done:
  print CONNECTED to $remote with address $rmtip
```

Providing Incoming SLIP Connections from Other Systems: diplogin

With Linux, not only can you make a SLIP connection to a remote system, but other systems can make their own SLIP connections to your system. Another system can dial into your system and make a SLIP connection. If you have provided an account for a user on that remote system, then the user could dial in a SLIP connection and log into that account. Such remote dial-up SLIP connections are managed by **dip** with the **-i** option. This places **dip** in a dial-in mode to receive incoming connections. This invocation of **dip** can also be made by **diplogin**, which is a symbolic link to **dip**. In the dial-in mode, **dip** will prompt a remote user for a user ID and a password, and then make the SLIP connection.

You first have to create an account for the remote user on your system. You can use Lisa, **usercfg**, or **adduser** to create the account. If you are concerned with security, you might want to place the user's home directory in a special directory that you can more easily control, such as **/tmp**. Creating a user account places an entry for that user in the **/etc/passwd** file. In the following entry, the user's name is **robert**, the password is **starq**, and the home directory is **/tmp**.

```
robert:starq:204:12:UUNET:/tmp:/usr/sbin/diplogin
```

The last field in the password entry specifies the type of login shell the user will have. Here, the login shell is **diplogin**, which is a symbolic link to the **dip** program. **dip** will search for the user name in the **/etc/diphosts** file to obtain login and configuration information.

Once you have created the account, you have to configure its SLIP connection. These configurations are placed in the **/etc/diphosts** file. There are seven fields to each entry, separated by colons. The first is the user ID, followed by a secondary password. The third field is the hostname or IP address of the remote system, followed by the hostname or IP address of your local system. The fifth field is the network mask, followed by an informational field for comments. The last field specifies the connection parameters for the account, such as the protocol (CSLIP or SLIP) and the MTU value.

If you specified a secondary password, **diplogin** will prompt for this password before the standard user login procedure.

/etc/diphosts

```
# user : password : remote host : local host : netmask : comments :
protocol,MTU
robert:starq:rose.berkeley.edu:richlp.ix.com:255.255.255.0::SLIP,1500
valerie::pango1.train.com: richlp.ix.com: 255.255.255.0::CSLIP,296
```

Summary: Network Administration

TCP/IP networks are configured and managed with a set of utilities such as **netcfg**, **ifconfig**, **route**, and **netstat**. **ifconfig** operates from your root user desktop and allows you to fully configure your network interfaces, adding new ones and modifying others. Entries are made automatically to the respective configuration files. Your system uses a variety of network configuration files as shown in Table 20-2. **ifconfig** and **route** are lower-level programs that require more specific knowledge of your network to use effectively. **netstat** provides you with information about the status of your network connections.

If your system does not have a direct hardware connection to a network, such as an Ethernet connection, and you dial into a network through a modem, you will probably have to set up a SLIP or PPP connection. If you are using an Internet service provider, you have to set up such a connection. SLIP connections are easily set up using the **dip** program with **dip** scripts. PPP connections use **chat** scripts and an options file. PPP is a new protocol that is becoming much more widely used.

Protocol	Description
Transport	
TCP	Transmission Control Protocol; places systems in direct communication
UDP	User Datagram Protocol
Routing	
IP	Internet Protocol; transmits data
ICMP	Internet Control Message Protocol; status messages for IP
RIP	Routing Information Protocol; determines routing
OSPF	Open Shortest Path First; determines routing
Network Addresses	
ARP	Address Resolution Protocol; determines unique IP address of systems
DNS	Domain Name Service; translates hostnames into IP addresses
RARP	Reverse Address Resolution Protocol; determines addresses of systems
User Services	

Table 20-1.   *TCP/IP Protocols*

Protocol	Description
FTP	File Transfer Protocol; transmits files from one system to another using TCP
TFTP	Trivial File Transfer Protocol; transfers files using UDP
TELNET	Remote login to another system on the network
SMTP	Simple Mail Transfer Protocol; transfers email between systems
Gateway	
EGP	Exterior Gateway Protocol; provides routing for external networks
GGP	Gateway-to-Gateway Protocol; provides routing between Internet gateways
IGP	Interior Gateway Protocol; provides routing for internal networks
Network Services	
NFS	Network File Systems; allows mounting of file systems on remote machines
NIS	Network Information Service; maintains user accounts across a network
RPC	Remote Procedure Call; allows programs on remote systems to communicate
BOOTP	Boot Protocol; starts system using boot information on server for network
SNMP	Single Network Management Protocol; provides status messages on TCP/IP configuration

Table 20-1. *TCP/IP Protocols (continued)*

Address	Description
Host address	IP address of your system; it has a network part to identify the network you are on and a host part to identify your own system
Network address	IP address of your network (network part of your host IP address with host part set to 0)
Broadcast address	IP address for sending messages to all hosts on your network at once (network part of your host IP address with host part set to 255)
Gateway address	IP address of your gateway system if you have one (usually the network part of your host IP address with host part set to 1)
Domain nameserver addresses	IP addresses of domain nameservers that your network uses
Netmask	Network part of your host IP address set to 255s with host part set to 0 (255.255.255.0)
File	
/etc/hosts	Associates hostnames with IP addresses
/etc/networks	Associates domain names with network addresses
/etc/rc.d/init.d/inet	Script to configure your Ethernet interface when you boot up
/etc/host.conf	Lists resolver options
/etc/hosts	Lists domain names for remote hosts with their IP addresses
/etc/resolv.conf	Lists domain nameserver names, IP addresses (Nameserver), and domain names where remote hosts may be located (Search)

Table 20-2.   *TCP/IP Configuration Addresses and Files*

File	
/etc/protocols	Lists protocols available on your system
/etc/services	Lists available network services such as ftp and telnet
/etc/hostname	Holds the name of your system

Table 20-2. *TCP/IP Configuration Addresses and Files (continued)*

Program	Description
netcfg	The root user desktop program for configuring and managing your network interfaces
ifconfig *-hostflag IP-address options*	Configuration of a network interface
route *action IP-address*	Routes a network interface; **route** by itself lists the routing table
ping *hostname*	Checks to see if a remote host is reachable. Use CTRL-**c** to stop
netstat	Issues reports on state of network connections
hostname	Displays your current hostname
dip *options dip-script*	For modem connections, creates a SLIP connection
pppd *chat-script dev speed options*	For modem connections, creates a PPP connection

Table 20-3. *Network Administration Programs*

Option	Description
interface	Name of the network interface; these are usually located in the **/dev** directory—for example, **/dev/eth0**
aftype	Address family for decoding protocol addresses; default is **inet**, currently used by Linux
up	Activates an interface
down	Deactivates an interface
-arp	Turns ARP on or off; preceding – turns it off
-trailers	Turns on or off trailers in Ethernet frames; preceding – turns it off
-allmulti	Turns on or off the promiscuous mode; preceding – turns it off. This allows network monitoring
metric *n*	Cost for interface routing (not currently supported)
mtu *n*	Maximum number of bytes that can be sent on this interface per transmission
dstaddr *address*	Destination IP address on a point-to-point connection
netmask *address*	IP network mask; preceding – turns it off
broadcast *address*	Broadcast address; preceding – turns it off
point-to-point *address*	Point-to-point mode for interface; if address is included, it is assigned to remote system
hw	Sets hardware address of interface
address	Hostname or IP address assigned to interface

Table 20-4. `ifconfig` *Options*

Option	Description
-a	Display information about all Internet sockets, including those sockets that are just listening
-i	Display statistics for all network devices
-c	Continually displays network status every second until the program is interrupted
-n	Display remote and local address as IP addresses
-o	Display timer states, expiration times, and backoff state for network connections
-r	Display the kernel routing table
-t	Display information about TCP sockets only, including those that are listening
-u	Display information about UDP sockets only
-v	Display version information
-w	Display information about raw sockets only
-x	Display information about Unix domain sockets

Table 20-5. `netstat` *Options*

Option	Description
-f *filename*	Executes **chat** commands in the chat script with name *filename*
-l *lockfile*	Makes UUCP style like file using *lockfile*
-t *num*	Timeout set to *num* seconds
-v	A description of all **chat** actions are output to the **/log/messages** file; use **tail**, **cat**, or **more** on this file to display the descriptions **tail /log/messages**
Special Character	
BREAK	Sends break to modem
' '	Sends null string with single newline character
\b	BACKSPACE
\c	Suppresses new line sent after reply string
\d	Makes **chat** wait for one second
\K	Sends break; when specifying string for modem initialization, and codes beginning with K may have to be escaped
\n	Sends newline characters
\N	Sends null character
\p	Pauses for 1/10 of a second
\q	String does not appear in **syslog** file
\r	Sends or expects a new line
\s	Sends or expects a space
\t	Sends or expects a tab
****	Sends or expects a backslash
nnn	Specifies a character in octal
^*C*	Specifies a control character

Table 20-6. **Chat** *Options and Special Characters*

Option	Description
device-name	Uses the specified device; if the device name does not have **/dev** preceding it, **pppd** will add it for you
speed *num*	Sets the modem speed (baud rate)
asyncmap *map*	Sets the async character map that specifies what control characters cannot be sent and should be escaped
auth	Requires the remote host to authenticate itself
connect *Connection-operation*	Uses the Connection operations to set up the connection; the Linux command here is usually **chat**, which makes the actual connection
crtscts	Uses hardware flow control
xonxoff	Uses software flow control
defaultroute	pppd sets a default route to the remote host
disconnect *Linux-command*	Runs the specified command after **pppd** cuts its connection. This is usually a **chat** operation
escape *c,c,...*	Causes the specified characters to be escaped when transmitted
file *filename*	Reads **pppd** options from the specified file
lock	Uses UUCP-style locking on the serial device
mru *num*	Sets the maximum receive units to *num*
netmask *mask*	Sets the PPP network interface mask

Table 20-7. **pppd** *Options*

Option	Description
`noipdefault`	For dynamic IP addresses provided by ISP; searches the incoming data stream from the remote host for both the local and remote IP addresses assigned to your system for that Internet session; you must have this option to connect with a dynamic IP address
`passive`	Makes **pppd** wait for a valid connection instead of failing when it can't make the connection immediately
`silent`	**pppd** waits for a connection to be made by a remote host

Table 20-7.   `pppd` *Options (continued)*

Option	Description
`-v`	Verbose mode; displays descriptions of all actions taken
`-t`	Test mode; places you in an interactive shell with the prompt DIP>
`-p` *mode*	Sets mode, line protocol, to either CSLIP or SLIP
`-a`	Prompts for user name and password
`-i`	Acts as a dial-in server
`-k`	Kills the **dip** process that runs (has locked) the specified tty device (see **-1** option), or else the most recent invocation of **dip** (a process started by somebody else is not killed)

Table 20-8.   `dip` *Options and Commands*

Option	Description
-l *tty_line*	Indicates the line to be killed (requires **-k** option)
-m *mtu*	Sets the maximum transfer unit (MTU) (default is 296)
chatkey *keyword code*	Adds a keyword and error-level code to error codes returned by dial
config *args*	Directly configures SLIP interface
databits *bits*	Number of bits in connection (default is 8)
default	Sets default route
dial *telephone-number*	Dials the telephone number
echo *on /off*	The arguments **on** or **off** turn echo on or off; with echo on, **dip** will display what it sends and receives from the modem
flush	Eliminates unread responses from the modem
get *$var value*	Sets the variable *$var* to the value
get *$var*	Sets the variable *$var* to the next value received across the line connection
get *$var* **ask**	Prompts the user to enter a value for the variable
goto *label*	Jumps to *label* in **dip** script
help	Lists **dip** commands
if *$var operator number*	Tests the value of a variable; the number must be an integer
init *string*	Initialization string for modem
mode SLIP/CSLIP	Sets the protocol mode for the connection and places **dip** in daemon mode

Table 20-8. **dip** *Options and Commands (continued)*

Option	Description
modem *type*	Sets the modem type: HAYES
netmask	Sets the netmask for the route **dip** takes
parity E/O/N	Sets the parity to even, odd, or none
password	Prompts the user to enter a password
print	Displays text to your screen
port *dev*	Sets the port that **dip** will use
quit	Exits **dip**
reset	Sends the **init** string to the modem
send *text*	Sends *text* to remote host
sleep *number*	Delays processing for number of seconds
speed *number*	Sets the baud rate for the connection: 2400, 9600, 38400, 56700
stopbits *bits*	Sets the number of stop bits
timeout *number*	Default time-out set to number of seconds
term	Places **dip** in terminal emulation mode so it operates like a terminal; you can then interact with the remote system directly for login and password prompts (press CTRL-] to return to **dip**)
wait *word number*	**dip** waits for the specified word to be received for the number of seconds

Table 20-8. **dip** *Options and Commands (continued)*

Variable	Description
`$local`	Hostname of the local system; your hostname
`$locip`	IP address for the local system; your own IP address
`$remote`	Hostname of remote system that you are connected to
`$rmtip`	IP address of remote system
`$mtu`	Maximum transfer unit; the maximum number of bytes transferred at one time
`$modem`	Type of modem used (read-only)
`$port`	Name of the serial device **dip** uses (read-only)
`$speed`	Speed for the serial device (read- only)
`$errlvl`	Holds the result code returned by the last command executed; you can use it to test for errors; 0 indicates success (read-only)

Table 20-9.   `dip` *Variables*

Chapter Twenty-One

Configuring the
X-Windows System

X-Windows is designed for flexibility—there are various ways you can configure it. You can run it on most of the different video cards available, even accelerated graphics cards. X-Windows is not tied to any specific desktop interface. It provides an underlying set of graphical operations that user interface applications such as window managers and file managers make use of. A window manager uses these operations to construct widgets for manipulating windows, such as scroll bars, resize boxes, and close boxes. Different window managers can construct them to appear differently, providing interfaces with very different appearances. All will work on X-Windows. There are a variety of different window managers for you to choose from. Each user on your system could run a different window manager, each using the same underlying X-Windows graphic operations. You can even run X-Windows programs without any window or file managers.

To run X-Windows, the XFree86 server appropriate for the system's video card has to be installed, and configuration information provided about your monitor, mouse, and keyboard. This information resides in a configuration file called **/etc/XF86Config**. The file uses technical information that is best generated by an X-Windows configuration program such as XF86Setup. When you configured X-Windows when you installed your system (see Chapter 2), this file was automatically generated.

You can configure your own X-Windows interface using the **.xinitrc** and **/usr/X11R6/lib/X11/xinit/xinitrc** configuration files where window managers, file managers, and initial X-Windows applications can be selected and started up. (In OpenLinux, the **/usr/X11R6/lib/X11/xinit/** directory is a link to the **/etc/X11/xinit/** directory where the files are actually held.) There is also a set of specialized X-Windows commands that you can use to configure your root window, load fonts, or configure X-Windows resources such as setting the color of window borders. You can also download X-Windows utilities from online sources that serve as Linux mirror sites, usually in their **/pub/Linux/X11** directory. If you have to compile an X-Windows application, there are special procedures you may have to use as well as support packages that should be installed.

In addition to configuring X-Windows, you can also configure your window manager. The fvwm window manager has its own set of configuration files that you can use to add buttons to its taskbar or entries to its menus, even setup of keyboard bindings.

XFree86 Servers

The XFree86 servers support a wide range of video cards and monitors. There are servers for Monochrome, VGA, and Super VGA video cards. In addition, there are a series of servers designed for accelerated video cards, a server for each chipset. Table 21-1 lists the current XFree86 servers. For more detailed information, consult the XFree86 documentation in the **/usr/X11R6/lib/X11/doc** directory. There you will find files for the specific servers available as well as types of cards supported. The **AccelCards** file lists all the hardware currently supported, including chipsets, and the

Monitors file lists monitor configurations. Also, consult the man pages for the different driver types. The driver types and the associated man pages are listed here.

Video Cards	Man Pages
Accelerated Cards	XF86_Accel
Monochrome Cards	XF86_Mono
VGA Cards	XF86_VGA16
SVGA Cards	XF86_SVGA

The XFree86 servers that you specified when you installed your system are automatically installed. You will have to explicitly install other servers using Lisa, glint, or rpm. They are located on the CD-ROM in the directory **OpenLinux/install/ xbasis1**. Each package that contains an XFree server starts with the term "XFree86". You have to install the package appropriate for your graphics card. Most standard cards will work with the SVGA server, XF86_SVGA. If you are using a simple Monochrome or VGA card, you install just the XF86_Mono or XF86_VGA generic server. However, if you have an accelerated graphics card, you first have to find out what chipset is used on it. Consult the manual or documentation that comes with the card. If you can't find out the chipset, you can use a utility called Superprobe that will analyze your card to determine this information. First, read the man pages for Superprobe to determine the correct arguments to use when invoking it. The name of a particular server usually includes the type of chipset it supports. For example, if you have an S3 chipset on your graphics video card, you would use the XFree86_S3 package. If you have a ViRGE chip (Diamond Stealth 3D 2000), you would use the S3V server. In some cases the same chipset is used by different graphic card brands. If you do not find the server package you need on the CD-ROM, you can check for more recent versions at any Linux mirror site usually in the directory **/pub/Linux/X11/servers**.

```
rpm -i XFree86_S3-3.2-1.i386.rpm
```

/etc/XF86Config file

Once you have installed your XFree86 server, the next step is to configure your X-Windows interface. This involves generating a configuration file called **XF86Config**, located in the **/etc** directory, that contains all the specifications for your graphics card, monitor, keyboard, and mouse. Although you could create the file directly, it is better to use a configuration utility such as XF86Setup or XF86Config. With these, you just answer questions about your hardware and the program will generate the appropriate **/etc/XF86Config** file.

You will need specific information on hand about your hardware. For your monitor, you will have to know the horizontal and vertical sync frequency ranges and bandwidth. For your graphics card, you have to know the chipset and you may even need to know the clocks. For your mouse, you should know whether it is Microsoft compatible or some other brand such as Logitech. Also, know the port that your mouse is connected to.

XF86Setup provides you with a full-screen interface where you can very easily select features for your mouse, keyboard, graphics card, and monitor. XF86Setup is described in detail in Chapter 2. However, if you have problems configuring with XF86Setup, you can use XF86Config, which presents you with line mode prompts where you type in responses or enter a menu selection. It provides explanations of each step.

The **/etc/XF86Config** file is organized into several parts as shown here. You can find a detailed discussion of all these sections and their entries in the XF86Config man page. All of these are set by the XF86Setup program. For example, the Monitor Screen generates the Monitor section in the **XF86Config** file, the Mouse screen generates the Pointer section, and so on. A section in the file begins with the keyword **Section** followed by the name of the section in quotes. The section ends with the term **EndSection**. Comments have a **#** sign at the beginning of the line. Entries for each section begin with a data specification followed by a list of values. For example, in the Files section where the **rgb** color data is listed, a line begins with the data specification **RgbPath** followed by the path name for that **rgb** color data file.

Files	Directories for font and **rgb** files
Module	Dynamic module loading
ServerFlags	Miscellaneous options
Keyboard	Keyboard specifications
Pointer	Mouse configuration
Monitor	Monitor configuration (set horizontal and vertical frequency)
Device	Video card configuration
Screen	Configures display, setting virtual screen, display colors, screen size, and other features

Although you can directly edit the file using a standard text editor, it's always best to rely on the setup programs such as XF86Setup to make changes. Most of the sections you will never have to touch. However, you may have to make changes to the Screen section, located at the end of the file. To do so you would edit the file and add or change entries in the Screen section. As noted in Chapter 2, you have to make changes to the Screen section to configure your virtual screen display and set the number of colors supported. Since the Screen section is the one you would most likely change, it will be discussed first, even though it comes last, at the end of the file.

Screen

A Screen section begins with a Driver entry that specifies the driver name. There are five driver names, one for each type of XFree86 server: Accel, Mono, SVGA, VGA2, and VGA16. The Accel driver name is used for all accelerated X servers such as S3_XFree86. Mono is for non-VGA mono drivers supported by the XF86_Mono server. VGA2 and VGA16 are used for the VGA server, and SVGA is used for the XF86_SVGA server. If you are using the XFree86_SVGA server, the Driver entry would have "svga". If you are using any of the accelerated servers, this entry would be "Accel". Setup programs such as XF86Setup will generate Screen sections for each of these. If you have an accelerated card and were able to install a server for it, then X-Windows will use the Accel screen section. That is where you would make any changes. If you are instead using the SVGA server, you would use the SVGA screen section.

After the Driver entry, the Device and Monitor entries specify the monitor and video card you are using. The name given in the Identifier entry in these sections is used to reference those components. A monitor given the Identifier name Nec3v will have the entry **Monitor Nec3v** in the Screen section.

```
Section "Screen"
    Driver          "Accel"
    Device          "Primary Card"
    Monitor         "Primary Monitor"
    DefaultColorDepth  16
    SubSection "Display"
        Depth       8
        Modes       "1152x864" "1024x768" "800x600" "640x480"
"640x400" "480x300" "400x300" "320x240" "320x200"
        Virtual 800 600
    EndSubSection
    SubSection "Display"
```

The Screen section has Display subsections, one for each depth supported. Whereas the previous sections were configuring hardware, the Display subsection configures display features such as the number of colors displayed and the virtual screen size. There are three main entries: Depth, Modes, and Virtual. The Depth entry is the screen resolution: 8, 16, and 24. You can add the DefaultColorDepth entry to set the default color depth to whatever your X server will support: 8 for 256K, 16 for 32K, and 24 for 16M. Modes are the modes allowed given the resolution. Virtual is the size of the virtual screen. You can have a virtual screen larger than your display area. When you move your mouse to the edge of the displayed screen, it will scroll to that hidden part of the screen. This way you can have a working screen much larger than the physical size of your monitor. The usual setting for a virtual screen is 1024 x 768, a 17-inch monitor size. You could also set it to 1152 x 864, a 21-inch monitor size. For a 15-inch monitor, the virtual screen is usually set to 1024 x 768. If you want to disable the virtual screen, you can set the Virtual entry to 800 x 600, making the display the same size as the physical screen.

Virtual 1024 768	17-inch virtual screen
Virtual 1152 864	21-inch virtual screen
Virtual 800 600	15-inch screen (disable virtual screen)

Any of these features in this section can be safely changed. In fact, to change the virtual screen size you will have to modify this section. However, other sections in the **XF86Config** file should be left alone, unless you are certain of what you are doing.

Files, Modules, ServerFlags, and Keyboard

The Files section lists different directories for resources that XFree86 needs. These are mostly the fonts available on your system. A font entry begins with the data specification **FontPath** and is followed by the path name for that font. A sample of these entries is shown here:

```
RgbPath     "/usr/X11R6/lib/X11/rgb"
FontPath    "/usr/X11R6/lib/X11/fonts/misc:unscaled"
```

The Module section specifies modules to be dynamically loaded. Dynamic modules are supported on Linux ELF systems. The **Load** entry will load a module. See the XF86Config man page for more details.

There are several flags that can be set for the XFree86 server. You can find a complete listing in the XF86Config man page. For example, the **NoTrapSignals** enables the core to be dumped for debugging purposes. **DontZap** disables the use of CTRL-ALT-BACKSPACE to shut down the server. **DontZoom** disables switching between graphic modes.

The keyboard section determines your keyboard type and sets the layout, model, and protocol used. For example, the following entry sets the layout. There are a large number of options for this section. Consult the XF86Config man pages for a complete listing.

```
XkbLayout      "us"
```

Pointer

The pointer section configures your mouse and any other pointer devices. This section has only a few entries, with some tailored for specific types of mice. The Protocol entry specifies the protocol your mouse uses such as Microsoft or Logitech. The Device entry is the path name for the mouse device. The following example shows a standard Pointer section for a Microsoft mouse at 1200 baud. The device file is **/dev/mouse**.

```
Section "Pointer"
   Protocol        "Microsoft"
   Device          "/dev/mouse"
   BaudRate        1200
EndSection
```

The following is a listing of the Pointer section entries.

Protocol	Mouse protocol (do man XF86Config for complete listing)
Device	Device path such as **/dev/mouse** or **/dev/cua0**
BaudRate	Baud rate for serial mouse
Emulate3Buttons	Enables two-button mouse to emulate third button by pressing both left and right buttons at once
ChordMiddle	Three-button mouse configuration on some Logitech mice
ClearDTR and ClearRTS	Clear DTR and RTS lines, valid only for Mouse Systems mice
SampleRate	Set the sampling rate (logitech)

Monitor

There should be a Monitor section for each monitor used on your system. As noted in Chapter 2, the vertical and horizontal frequencies have to be accurate, or you can damage your monitor. A monitor section begins with entries that identify the monitor such as vendor and model names. The HorizSync and VerRefresh entries are where the vertical and horizontal frequencies are specified. Most monitors can support a variety of resolutions. Those resolutions are specified in the Monitor section by ModeLine entries. There is a ModeLine entry for each resolution. The entry has five values, the name of the resolution, its dot clock value, and then two sets of four values, one for the horizontal timing and one for the vertical timing, ending with flags. The flags specify different characteristics of the mode such as Interlace to indicate that the mode is interlaced, and +hsync and +vsync to select the polarity of the signal.

```
ModeLine "name"  dotclock  horizontal-freq  vertical-freq  flags
```

A sample of a ModeLine is shown here. It is best to leave the entire Monitor section alone, relying on the entries generated by XF86Setup.

```
Modeline  "800x600"   50.00 800 856 976 1040 600 637 643 666 +hsync +vsync
```

Commonly used entries for the Monitor section are listed here.

Identifier	A name to identify the monitor
VendorName	Manufacturer
ModelName	The make and model
HorizSync	The horizontal frequency; can be a range or series of values
VerRefresh	Vertical refresh frequency; can be a range or series of values
Gamma	Gamma correction
ModeLine	Specifies a resolution with dotclock, horizontal timing, and vertical timing for that resolution

Device

The Device section specifies your video card. It begins with entries that identify the card such as VendorName, BoardName, and Chipset. The amount of video ram is indicated in the VideoRam entry. The Clocks entry lists your clock values. There are many different entries that can be made in this section such as Ramdac for a Ramdac chip, should the board have one, and MemBase for the base address of a frame buffer, should it be accessible. See the XF86Config man pages for a detailed list and descriptions.

Though you could safely change the VideoRam entry—for example, if you added more memory to your card—it is not safe to change the Clocks entry. If you get the clock values wrong, you could easily destroy your monitor. Rely on the clock values generated by XF86Setup or other XFree86 setup programs. If the clock values are missing, the server is able to automatically determine them. This may be the case for newer cards.

X-Windows and Window Managers

As noted in Chapter 3, instead of the command line interface, you can use an X-Windows window manager and file manager, allowing you to interact with your Linux system using windows, buttons, and menus. Window managers provide basic window management operations such as the opening, closing, and resizing of windows, and file managers allow you to manage and run programs using icons and menus. In addition, a file manager allows you to copy, move, or erase files, as well as open up windows for different directories.

There are several window managers available for Linux. Several of the more popular Linux window managers are the Free Virtual Window Manager (fvwm) and Xview (olwm), twm, fvwm95 (fvwm95), LessTif (mwm), AfterStep (afterstep), and Motif (mwm). All except Motif are free. Xview is the Linux version of the Sun System's OpenLook interface. fvwm95 is a variation of fvwm that provides a Windows 95 interface, including the taskbar. LessTif is a free Motif clone that provides a Motif interface and will run Motif applications. twm is an older window manager that provides basic windowing capabilities. fvwm, twm, and Xview have already been installed on your OpenLinux system. The other window managers you can download from their Web sites or the Redhat contrib directory. (You can consult Linux resources pages as noted in Table 3-2 in Chapter 3.) You can download and install recent versions of any window manager as they become available.

Your OpenLinux system currently uses fvwm, as do most Linux systems. With a window manager, you can think of a window as taking the place of a command line. Operations you perform through the window are interpreted and sent to the Linux system for execution. Window managers operate off the underlying X-Windows system that actually provides the basic window operations that allow you to open, move, and close windows as well as display menus and select icons. fvwm and Xview manage these operations, each in their own way, providing their own unique interfaces. The advantage of such a design is that you can have different window managers that can operate on the same Linux system. In this sense, Linux is not tied to one type of graphical user interface (GUI). On the same Linux system, one user may be using the fvwm window manager, another may be using the Xview window manager, and still another the fvwm95, all at the same time.

fvwm is GNU public-licensed software—it is yours free of cost, and if you use fvwm by itself, you can still run any X-Windows program. As noted in Chapter 4, fvwm has its own workplace menu and taskbar. You can also run any X-Windows program from an Xterm terminal window. From fvwm, start up with an Xterm window. There you can type the name of an X-Windows application and upon pressing ENTER, the X-Windows application will start up with its own window. It is best to invoke an X-Windows application as a background process by adding an ampersand after the command. A separate window will open up for the X-Windows application that you can work in. You can run any of the X-Windows software included on your Caldera CD-ROM this way. Often the name of an X-Windows applications begins with an *x*, although there are exceptions such as Netscape and Mosaic. You can also download a wide variety of X-Windows software from Linux ftp sites. They are usually in a directory named **X11** such as **/pub/Linux/X11**.

Very rarely is an X-Windows application tied to a particular window manager. You can run the same X application such as Netscape on fvwm, Xview, fvwm95, and any other window manager. It is even possible to run X-Windows applications without any window managers at all. You can still open a very simple Xterm window and start up X applications from there. An X application really only needs X-Windows to operate. The window would not have any window manipulation widgets such as those for changing its size or ionizing it, not even a close box. The only way to close it is to enter the exit command. The X-Windows programs you run will have their own menus and buttons, but will operate in bare static windows.

fvwm Configuration Files

When the fvwm window manager starts up, it will execute its own configuration files. These files perform tasks such as displaying buttons on the fvwm taskbar, setting up entries in the workplace menu, and determining what programs to initially start up, if any. These configuration files are located in the **/usr/X11R6/lib/X11/fvwm** directory. Each begins with the term *system*. The primary configuration file is **system.fvwmrc**. This file in turn calls the others such as **system.fvwmdesk** and **system.fvwmrc.goodstuff**. You can modify any of these files to configure your fvwm window manager as you wish. For example, if you want to add buttons in the taskbar, you can add entries in the **system.fvwmrc.goodstuff** file. Table 21-2 lists the different fvwm configuration files.

Changes to the **system.fvwmrc** file would set the systemwide default for all the users on your system. However, each user can set up an individual **.fvwmrc** configuration file in his or her own home directory that would apply only to that user. This file would then be used to configure fvwm each time the user executes the **startx** command.

The Taskbar: system.fvwmrc.goodstuff

To add buttons to the taskbar, make new entries in the **system.fvwmrc.goodstuff** file. Entries begin with the keyword ***GoodStuff**. This is followed by the text that you want to appear under the picture displayed in the button. Then enter a picture that you want displayed. A picture is a pixmap figure having the file name extension **.xpm**. You can find pictures in the **/usr/openwin/lib/pixmaps** and **/usr/share/data/pixmaps** directories. Following the picture is the fvwm operation. This operation can be any one of several fvwm commands, though it is usually the **Exec** command. **Exec** will execute a Linux command or program. Following the **Exec** command is a name that can be used for a menu entry. For button bars, the name is just an empty string, **" "**. The **xlaunch** command and the name of the program follow. **xlaunch** is used to execute the program. The following example adds a button for the Crisplite editor. The command to invoke the Crisplite editor is **mcr**.

```
*GoodStuff  Crisplite  dtp.xpm     Exec  ""  xlaunch  mcr
```

To remove an entry from the taskbar, you can either delete that line or just comment it out by inserting a **#** symbol at the beginning of the line. Other window managers that also support taskbars will have similar configuration files.

The Workplace Menu: system.fvwmrc.menu

The **system.fwmrc.menu** file holds the configurations for the workplace menus. The main workplace menu is at the end of the file with submenus defined above it. The workplace menu along with other major submenus are defined with the **PopupSMenu** command. Entries are made on separate lines and often an entry is another menu, indicated by a Popup entry. A **Popup** entry will be followed by the entry title to be displayed in the menu, and then the name of the associated menu. Characters in the entry title that have a preceding **&** are underlined and used as keyboard shortcuts. Pressing that character selects the menu entry. Part of the menu is shown here.

```
PopupSMenu('Workplace','
    Title      "Workplace"
    Nop        ""
    Popup      "&Help on Linux"     Help
    Nop        ""
    Popup      "&Shells"                Shells
)
```

Many of the submenus are defined with the **PopupMenu** command. It is followed by a list of entry titles and commands, separated by commas with the whole list encased in parentheses. The first entry is usually the title of the submenu; then a title followed by a command is entered, followed by another title and command pair. The **&** symbol can be used to specify keyboard shortcuts. The "Text and Publishing" submenu is one such **Popup** menu, part of which is shown here.

```
PopupMenu('Text and Publishing', 'MenuItem',
    'L&yX (WYSIWIM TeX)', 'lyx',
    'X&wpick (Screen shot)', 'xwpick HOME/xwpick.gif',
    'X&fig (Vector graphic)',  'xfig'
)
```

To add an entry to a menu, find the menu and insert a line with the entry title and the command you want. For example, to insert an entry for the Crisplite editor in the Text and Publishing menu, you would insert the following line. The & before the *c* means that a keyboard shortcut for the *c* key is set up. Be sure to include the commas.

```
"Crisplite",       m&cr,
```

Be sure that you do not modify a file called **system.fvwmrc.menu.prep.** This is a file generated by fvwm to actually create the workplace menu. It is based on the information in the **.menu** file.

X-Windows programs that are installed in the **/usr/X11R6/bin** directory are automatically added for you to the Other Applications submenu in the Applications menu. So you can still access any X-Windows program from the workplace menu. Adding an entry in the menu file will place it in a particular submenu, instead of the catch-all Other Applications menu.

Icon Styles and Device Bindings: .styles and .bindings

The **system.fvwmrc.styles** file holds entries that specify styles for particular program windows. For example, the StaysOnTop style shown here for the pager will keep the pager on top of any other window. Style entries are also used to specify the picture to use when a program window is iconified. You can change these entries to have different pixmap figures displayed, or add new entries for new programs.

```
Style "FvwmPager"    StaysOnTop
Style "xgraph"       Icon graphs.xpm
```

The **system.fvwmrc.bindings** file holds bindings for all the mouse buttons and keyboard keys. Here the mouse buttons for the workplace menu are defined, as well as the keyboard keys. ALT-F1 will bring up the workplace menu, as will clicking on the left mouse button (button 1). The following is an entry for binding the ALT-F1 key to the workplace menu. The Context is the window the key will be active in; *A* stands for any and *R* for the root window. The modifier is any extra key that has to be held down like the ALT key. *M* stands for the meta key (ALT key) and *S* stands for the SHIFT key.

```
# Key         Context  Modifi  Function
Key F1        A    M    Popup "Workplace"
```

Startup Applications: system.fvwmdesk

The **startx** command on your OpenLinux system is initially configured to start X-Windows, then the fvwm window manager, followed by the Caldera Desktop Looking Glass. This automatic startup of the Caldera Desktop is actually carried out by fvwm's configuration scripts. These configuration files can be used to specify programs you want automatically started when fvwm starts up.

Currently, the **startx** command calls the **xinit** command with the **/etc/X11/init /xinitrc** configuration file. This **xinitrc** file performs basic X-Windows configuration operations, and, as its last command, executes the fvwm window manager. The fvwm window manager has its own startup files located in the **/usr/X11R6/lib/X11/fvwm** directory. The primary configuration file is **system.fwmrc**, which executes a command called **StartupFunction** that is defined in the **system.fvwmdesk** file. In this file **StartupFunction** is defined as executing the **lg** command, which starts the Caldera Desktop (**lg** stands for Looking Glass, the actual name of the Caldera Desktop). If you don't want the Caldera Desktop to automatically start up with **startx**, you can simply comment out the line with the **lg** command by inserting a **#** at the beginning of the line. If you want another file manager or desktop automatically started by fvwm, you could insert that command into the **system.fvwmdesk** file. You can just as easily comment out the entire **StartupFunction** in the **system.fvwmrc** file, as shown here:

```
#    Function "I" StartupFunction
```

If you remove the automatic startup of the Caldera Desktop from fvwm, you can still use the fvwm workplace menu to start it. In the Desktop submenu you will find an entry for Looking Glass (the Caldera Desktop). Choosing this option will start up the Caldera Desktop. You could also start up another file manager or desktop instead.

X-Windows Command Line Arguments

You can start up any X-Windows application either within a **.xinitrc** script or on the command line in an Xterm window. Most X-Windows applications take a set of standard X-Windows arguments used to configure the window and display that the application will use. You can set the color of the window bars, give the window a specific title, specify the color and font for text, as well as position the window at a specific location on the screen. Table 21-3 lists these X-Windows arguments. They are discussed in detail in the X man pages, man X.

One commonly used argument is **-geometry**. This takes an additional argument that specifies the location on the screen where you want an application's window displayed. In the next example, the xclock X-Windows application is called with a geometry argument. A set of up to four numbers specifies the position. +0+0 references the upper-left-hand corner. There, you will see the clock displayed when you start up X-Windows. -0-0 references the upper-right-hand corner.

```
& xclock -geometry +0+0 &
```

With the **-title** option, you can set the title displayed on the application window. Notice the use of quotes for titles with more than one word. You set the font with the **-fn** argument and the text and graphics color with the **-fg** argument. **-bg** sets the background color. The following example starts up an Xterm window with the title "My New Window" in the title bar. The text and graphics color is green and the background color is gray. The font is Helvetica.

```
$ xterm -title "My New Window"  -fg green -bg gray  -fn
/usr/fonts/helvetica  &
```

X-Windows Configuration Files

X-Windows uses several configuration files as well as X-Windows commands to configure your X-Windows system. Some of the configuration files belong to the system and should not be modified. However, each user can have his or her own set of configuration files such as **.xinitrc** and **.Xresources** that can be used to configure a personalized X-Windows interface. These configuration files are automatically read and executed when X-Windows is started up with the **startx** command. Within these configuration files you can execute X-Windows commands used to configure your system. With commands such as **xset** and **setroot**, you can add fonts or control the display of your root window. Table 21-3 provides a list of X-Windows configuration files and commands. You can obtain a complete description of your current X-Windows configuration using xdypinfo. The XMan pages provide a detailed introduction to the X-Windows commands and configuration files.

```
$ man X
```

X-Windows is started up using the **xinit** command. However, you do not invoke this command directly, but through the **startx** command that you always use to start X-Windows. Both of these commands are found in the **/usr/X11R6/bin** directory, along with many other X-Windows-based programs. The **startx** command is a shell script that executes the **xinit** command. The **xinit** command, in turn, will first look for an X-Windows initialization script called **.xinitrc**, in the user's home directory. If there is no **.xinitrc** script in the home directory, then **xinit** will use **/usr/X11R6/lib/X11/xinit/xinitrc** as its initialization script. Both **.xinitrc** and **/usr/X11R6/lib/X11/xinit/xinitrc** have commands to configure your X-Windows server and execute any initial X-Windows commands such as starting up the window manager. You can think of the **/usr/X11R6/lib /X11/xinit/xinitrc** script as a default script. On your OpenLinux system, the **/usr/X11R6/lib /X11/xinit** directory is actually a symbolic link to the **/etc/X11/xinit** directory where these default initialization files reside.

The OpenLinux system does not initially set up any **.xinitrc** scripts in any of the home directories. These would have to be created by a particular user who wants one. Each user can create a personalized **.xinitrc** script in his or her home directory, configuring and starting up X-Windows as desired. This also applies to the root user. Until a user sets up a **.xinitrc** script, the **/usr/X11R6/lib/X11/xinit/xinitrc** script is used. You can examine this script to see how X-Windows starts up. There are certain configuration operations required for X-Windows that must be in the **.xinitrc** file. For a user to create his or her own **.xinitrc** script, it is best to first copy the **/usr/X11R6/lib/X11/xinit/xinitrc** to his or her home directory and name it **.xinitrc**. Then each user can modify the particular **.xinitrc** file as desired. (Notice that the system **xinitrc** file has no preceding period in its name, whereas the home directory **.xinitrc** file set up by a user does have a preceding period.) You can consult the man pages on **xinit** and **startx** for more information.

In addition to **xinit**, there are also commands such as **xrdb** and **xmodmap** that configure your X-Windows interface. X-Windows graphic configurations are listed in a resource file called **.Xresources**. Each user can have a customized **.Xresources** file in his or her home directory, configuring X-Windows to particular specifications. The **.Xresources** file contains entries for configuring specific programs such as the color of certain widgets. There is also a systemwide version called **/usr/X11R6/lib/X11/xinit/.Xresources**. (Notice that, unlike **/usr/X11R6/lib/X11/xinit/xinitrc**, there is a period before Xresources in the **/usr/X11R6/lib/X11/xinit/.Xresources** file name.) The **.Xdefaults** file contains the same kind of entries for configuring resources as .Xresources. An **.Xdefaults** file is accessible by programs on your system, but not by those running on other systems.

OpenLinux installs only with a system **.Xresources** file. You can create an **.Xresources** file of your own in your home directory, and add resource entries to it. You could also copy the **/usr/X11R6/lib/X11/xinit/.Xresources** file and edit the entries there or add new ones of your own. The configuration is carried out by the **xrdb** command, which reads both the system's **.Xresources** file and any .Xresources or .Xdefaults file in the user's home directory. **xrdb** is currently executed in the **/usr/X11R6/lib/X11/xinit/xinitrc** script. If you create your own **.xinitrc** script in your home directory, be sure it executes the **xrdb** command with at least your own **.Xresources** file or the **/usr/X11R6/lib/X11/xinit/.Xresources** file (preferably both). You can ensure this by simply using a copy of the system's **.xinitrc** script as your own **.xinitrc** file and then modifying that copy as you wish. See the man pages on **xrdb** for more details on resources. Also, you can find a more detailed discussion of Xresources as well as other X-Windows commands in the man pages for X.

An entry in the **.Xresources** file consists of a value assigned to a resource, class, or resources for an application. Usually, these are resources used for widgets or classes of widgets in an application. The resource designation typically consists of three elements separated by a period: the application, an object in the application, and the resource. The entire designation is terminated by a colon and the value follows. For example, suppose you want to change the color of the hour hand to blue in the oclock application. The application is oclock, the object is clock, and the resource is hour: oclock.clock.hour. The entry would look like this:

```
oclock.clock.hour: blue
```

The object element is actually a list of objects denoting the hierarchy leading to a particular object. In the oclock example there is only one object, but in many applications the object hierarchy can be very complex. This would require a lengthy set of objects listed to specify the one you want. To avoid this complexity you can use the asterisk notation to reference the object you want directly, using an asterisk in place of the period. You just need to know the name of the resource you want to change. The following example sets the oclock minute and hour hands to green.

```
oclock*hour: green
oclock*minute: green
```

You can also use the asterisk to apply a value to whole classes of objects. Many individual resources are grouped into classes. You can reference all the resources in a class by their class name. Class names begin with an uppercase character. For example, in the Xterm application, the background and pointer color resources are both part of the Background class. The reference **XTerm*Background** would change all of these resources in an Xterm window. However, any specific references will always override the more general ones.

You can also use the asterisk to change the values of a resource in objects for all of your applications. In this case, you place an asterisk before the resource. For example, to change the foreground color to red for all the objects in every application, you would enter

```
*foreground: red
```

If you just wanted to change the foreground color of the scroll bars in all your applications you would use:

```
*scrollbar*foreground: blue
```

The **showrgb** command will list the different colors available on your system. You can use the descriptive name or a hexadecimal form. Values can also be fonts, bitmaps, and pixmaps. You could change the font displayed by certain objects in, or for graphic applications, change background or border graphics. Resources vary with each application. Applications may support very different kinds of objects and the resources for them. Check the man pages and documentation for an application to learn what resources it supports and the values accepted for them. Some resources take boolean values that can turn features on or off. Others can specify options. Some applications will have a default set of resource values that will be automatically placed in your system's **.Xresources** or **.Xdefaults** files.

The **/usr/X11R6/lib/X11/xinit/.Xmodmap** file holds configurations for your input devices such as your mouse and keyboard (for example, you can bind keys such as BACKSPACE or reverse the click operations of your right and left mouse buttons). Each user can create a custom **.Xmodmap** file in his or her home directory to configure the system's input devices. This is helpful if users connect through their own terminals to your Linux system. The **.Xmodmap** file is read by the **xmodmap** command, which performs the configuration. **xmodmap** will first look for an **.Xmodmap** file in the user's home directory and use that. If there is no **.Xmodmap** in the home directory, it will use the **/usr/X11R6/lib/X11/xinit/.Xmodmap** file. The **xmodmap** command is currently executed in the **/usr/X11R6/lib/X11/xinit/xinitrc** file. If you have your own **.xinitrc** script in your home directory, it should execute the **xmodmap** command with either your own **.Xmodmap** file or the **/usr/X11R6/lib/X11/xinit/.Xmodmap** file. See the man pages on **xmodmap** for more details.

Usually, a **.xinitrc** script will have X-Windows commands like **xset** and **xsetroot** used to configure different features of your X-Windows session. The **xset** command sets different options such as turning on the screen saver or setting the volume for the bell and speaker. You can also use **xset** to load fonts. See the **xset** man pages for specific details. With the **b** option and the on or off argument, **xset** will turn your speaker on or off. The following example turns the speaker on.

```
xset b on
```

You use **xset** with the **-s** option to set the screen saver. With the on and off arguments you can turn the screen saver on or off. Two numbers entered as arguments will specify the length and period in seconds. The length is the number of seconds the screen saver waits before activating. The period is how long it waits before regenerating the pattern.

The **xsetroot** command lets you set the features of your root window (setting the color or displaying a bitmap pattern—you can even use a cursor of your own design). Table 21-3 lists the different **xsetroot** options. See the man pages for **xsetroot** for options and details. The following **xsetroot** command uses the **-solid** option to set the background color of the root window to blue.

```
xsetroot -solid blue
```

The **/usr/X11R6/lib/X11/xinit/xinitrc** also contains commands and variables for configuring the Looking Glass desktop and the Xview window manager, as well as the fvwm window manager.

The invocation of the window manager is always the last command in the **.xinitrc** script. X-Windows will exit after finishing the execution of whatever the last command in the **.xinitrc** script is. By making the window manager the last command, exiting the window manager will shut down your X-Windows session. Any other programs that you want to initially start up should be placed before the window manager command. If you want to start up Netscape or the Xfm file managers automatically whenever you execute **startx**, you could place the commands for these applications before the window manager command. Applications should be followed by an **&** to allow them to run in the background. The following example runs both the Xfm file manager and Netscape when fvwm starts up.

```
xfm &
netscape &
exec fvwm
```

A simple version of an **.xinitrc** file follows. It is designed to start up the fvwm window manager with the Xfm file manager. The OPENWINHOME and HELPPATH variables specify the directories where Xview libraries are located, for those applications that need them. If placed in your home directory, this **.xinitrc** file will instruct **xinit** to start up fvwm with Xfm (note the preceding period in the **.xinitrc** file name). When fvwm starts up, the taskbar and pager will be displayed along with a window for Xfm. Click anywhere on the screen with the left mouse button to bring up the workplace menu.

.xinitrc

```
#!/bin/sh
# $XConsortium: xinitrc.cpp,v 1.4 91/08/22 11:41:34 rws Exp $

userresources=$HOME/.Xresources
usermodmap=$HOME/.Xmodmap
sysresources=/usr/X11R6/lib/X11/xinit/.Xresources
sysmodmap=/usr/X11R6/lib/X11/xinit/.Xmodmap

export OPENWINHOME=/usr/openwin
export HELPPATH=$OPENWINHOME/help

# merge in defaults and keymaps
if [ -f $sysresources ]; then
    xrdb -merge $sysresources
```

```
fi

if [ -f $sysmodmap ]; then
    xmodmap $sysmodmap
fi

if [ -f $userresources ]; then
    xrdb -merge $userresources
fi

if [ -f $usermodmap ]; then
    xmodmap $usermodmap
fi

# start some nice programs
xfm &

exec fvwm
```

A sample of a bare bones **.xinitrc** file called **xinitrc.before.fvwm** is located in the **/etc/X11/xinit** directory. It lacks the configuration commands used for fvwm, Xview, and the Looking Glass (Caldera) desktops. However, it is a good example of the basic cofiguration operations needed to run X-Windows. The script will open three Xterm windows and run the twm window manager. You can copy this script to your home directory as your **.xinitrc** file if you want (making sure to make a backup copy of your current **.xinitrc** file if you have one). You can then add configuration operation and commands as you wish. For example, you could remove some of the **xterm** commands, start up a different window manager (adding in any needed configuration variables), or start up a specific application such as Netscape. If you don't want **xclock** started up, you can comment out its commands by entering a preceding **#**.

Fonts

Your X-Windows fonts are located in a directory called **/usr/X11R6/.lib/X11/fonts**. X-Windows fonts are loaded using the **xfs** command. **xfs** reads the **/etc/X11/fs/config** configuration file that lists the font directories in an entry for the term **catalogue**. The XMan pages provides a detailed discussion on fonts. To install a set of fonts, place them in a directory whose path you can add to the catalogue entry to have them automatically installed. You can also separately install a particular font with the **xset** command and its **+fp** option. Fonts for your system are specified in a font path. The font path is a set of file names, each holding a font. The file names include their complete path. An example of the catalogue entry in the **/etc/X11/config** file follows.

This is a comma-delimited list of directories. These are directories where X-Windows will first look for fonts.

```
catalogue =
/usr/X11R6/lib/X11/fonts/misc/,,/usr/X11R6/lib/X11/fonts/Speedo/,,/usr
/X11R6/lib/X11/fonts/Type1/,,/usr/X11R6/lib/X11/fonts/75dpi/,,/usr/X11
R6/lib/X11/fonts/100dpi/
```

Before you can access newly installed fonts, you have to first index them with the **mkfontdir** command. From within the directory with the new fonts, enter the **mkfontdir** command. You can also use the directory path as an argument to **mkfontdir**. After indexing the fonts, you can then load them using the **xset** command with the **fp rehash** option. To have the fonts automatically loaded, add the directory with full path name to the catalogue entry in the **xfs** configuration file. The following shows how to install a new font and then load it:

```
$ cp newfont.pcf  ~/myfonts
$ mkfontdir ~/myfonts
$ xset fp rehash
```

Within a font directory, there are several special files that hold information about the fonts. The **fonts.dir** file lists all the fonts in that directory. In addition, you can set up a **fonts.alias** file to give other names to a font. Font names tend to be very long and complex. A **fonts.scale** file holds the names of scalable fonts. See the man pages for **xfs** and **mkfontdir** for more details.

With the **xset +fp** and **-fp** options, you can specifically add or remove particular fonts. **fn** with the **rehash** argument will then load the fonts. With the default argument, the default set of fonts are restored. The **+fp** adds a font to this font path. For your own fonts, you can place them in any directory and specify their file name, including their complete path. The next example adds the **myfont** font in the **/usr/local/fonts** directory to the font path. Then the **fp** option with the **rehash** argument loads the font.

```
xset +fp  /usr/local/fonts/myfont
xset fp rehash
```

To remove this font you would use **xset -fp** /usr/home/myfont and follow it with the **xset fp rehash** command. If you want to reset your system back to the set of default fonts, enter the following:

```
xset fp default
xset fp rehash
```

With **xlsfonts**, you can list the fonts currently installed on your system. To display an installed font to see what it looks like, use **xselfonts**. You can browse through your fonts, selecting the ones you like.

Compiling X-Windows Applications

To compile X-Windows applications, you should first make sure that the XFree86 development package is installed along with any other development package you may need. These will contain header files and libraries used by X-Windows programs. The name of such packages will contain the term **devel**, for example, **XFree86-devel-3.1.2-2.i386.rpm**. Also, many X-Windows applications may need special shared libraries. For example, some applications may need the **xforms** library or the **qt** library. Some of these you will have to obtain from online sites, though most are available in the Redhat contrib directory in RPM form.

Many X-Windows applications require that a Makefile be generated that is configured to your system. This is done using an Imakefile provided with the application source code. The **xmkmf** command installed on your system can take an Imakefile and generate the appropriate Makefile. Once you have the Makefile, you can use the **make** command to compile the application. The **xmkmf** command actually uses a program called **imake** to generate the Makefile from the Imakefile; however, you should never use **imake** directly. Consult the man pages for **xmkmf** and **make** for more details (see Chapter 7 for examples). Recently many programs use configuration scripts to generate a Makefile. In that case you only need to enter the **./configure** command, instead of **xmkmf**.

Summary: Configuring X-Windows

The XFree86 servers provide a wide range of hardware support but can be challenging to configure. If you have installed the correct XFree86 server (see Table 21-1), you can configure it by running the **XF86setup** program in the **/usr/X11R6/bin** directory. There are also other configuration utilities available such as **xf86config** or **Xconfigurator**. All these utilities ask you questions about your hardware and create an **/etc/XF86Config** file. When X-Windows starts up, it reads the configuration information in the **/etc/XF86Config** file.

Each user can also create his or her own commands for starting up the window manager and desktop using a **.xinitrc** file in his or her home directory. In this file you can place the command for starting up the window manager, desktop, and whatever X applications you may want. You could also just specify the window manager alone, or a window manager and a desktop. It is best to create a **.xinitrc** file by copying the **/usr/X11R6/lib/X11/xinit/xinitrc** file.

The fvwm window manager has its own set of configuration files. You can use them to add buttons to the taskbar and entries to the workplace menu, and to specify what programs you want started up.

Server	Type
XFree86_SVGA	Color SVGA server. Includes drivers for most video cards
XFree86_VGA16	16-color SVGA and VGA non-accelerated server
XFree86_Mono	Monochrome non-accelerated server
XFree86_S3	S3 accelerated server
XFree86_S3V	S3 ViRGE and ViRGE/VX accelerated server (many 3D cards)
XFree86_I128	Number 9 Imagine 128 accelerated server
XFree86_8514	8514/A accelerated server
XFree86_Mach8	ATI Mach8 accelerated server
XFree86_Mach32	ATI Mach32 chipset accelerated server
XFree86_P9000	Weitek accelerated server
XFree86_W32	ET4000/W32 accelerated server
XFree86_agx	IIT AGX accelerated server
XFree86_Mach64	ATI Mach64 chipset accelerated server

Table 21-1. *XFree86 Servers*

Configuration File	Description
system.fvwmdesk	Desktop startup
system.fvwmrc	Main configuration file
system.fvwmrc.bindings	Mouse and Key bindings
system.fvwmrc.config	Configuration variables
system.fvwmrc.functions	Defined functions
system.fvwmrc.goodstuff	Taskbar entries
system.fvwmrc.menus	Menu entries
system.fvwmrc.menus.exclude	Excluded menu entries
system.fvwmrc.menus.prep	fvwm-generated menu
system.fvwmrc.modules	Modules
system.fvwmrc.options	Options
system.fvwmrc.styles	Program window styles

Function Key Keyboard Binding	Description
ALT-F1	Workplace menu
ALT-SHIFT-H	Help menu
ALT-SHIFT-S	Shells menu
ALT-SHIFT-A	Applications menu
ALT-SHIFT-G	Games menu
ALT-SHIFT-D	Desktop menu
ALT-SHIFT-T	Terminals menu
ALT-SHIFT-C	Config menu
ALT-SHIFT-P	Productivity Tools menu
ALT-SHIFT-F	Graphics menu
ALT-SHIFT-X	Text and Publishing menu
ALT-SHIFT-V	Software Development menu
ALT-SHIFT-I	Internet Connectivity menu
ALT-SHIFT-R	Amusement menu
ALT-SHIFT-Y	System administration menu

Table 21-2. *fvwm Configuration Files and Keyboard Bindings*

X-Windows Command	Explanation	
xterm	Opens up a new terminal window	
xset	Sets X-Windows options; see man pages for complete listing	
	-b	Configures bell
	-c	Configures key click
	+fp *fontlist*	Adds fonts
	-fp *fontlist*	Removes fonts
	led	Turns on or off keyboard LEDs
	m	Configures mouse
	p	Sets pixel color values
	s	Sets the screen saver
	q	Lists current settings
xsetroot	Configures the root window	
	-cursor *cursorfile maskfile*	Sets pointer to bitmap pictures when pointer is outside any window
	-bitmap *filename*	Sets root window pattern to bitmap
	-gray	Sets background to gray
	-fg *color*	Sets color of foreground bitmap
	-bg *color*	Sets color of background bitmap
	-solid *color*	Sets background color
	-name *string*	Sets name of root window to string
xmodmap	Configures input devices; reads the **.Xmodmap** file	
	-pk	Displays current keymap
	-e *expression*	Sets key binding
	keycode NUMBER = KEYSYMNAME	Sets key to specified key symbol
	keysym KEYSYMNAME = KEYSYMNAME	Sets key to operate the same as specified key
	pointer = NUMBER	Sets mouse button codes
xrdb	Configures X-Windows resources; reads the **.Xresources** file	

Table 21-3. *X-Windows Commands, Configuration Files, and Arguments*

X-Windows Command	Explanation
xdm	X-Windows Display Manager; runs the XFree86 server for your system; usually called by **.xinitrc**
startx	Starts up X-Windows by executing **xinit** and instructing it to read the **.Xclients** file
xfs *config-file*	The X-Windows font server
mkfontdir *font-directory*	Index new fonts, making them accessible by the font server
xlsfonts	Lists fonts on your system
xfontsel	Displays installed fonts
xdpyinfo	Lists detailed information about your X-Windows configuration
xinit	Starts up X-Windows, first reading the system's **.xinitrc** file; when invoked from **startx**, it also reads the user's **.Xclients** file; **xinit** is not called directly, but through **startx**
xmkmf	Creates a Makefile for an X-Windows application using the application's Imakefile; invokes **imake** to generate the Makefile (never invoke **imake** directly)
Configuration Files	
.Xmodmap	User's X-Windows input devices configuration file
.Xresources	User's X-Windows resource configuration file
.Xdefaults	User's X-Windows resource configuration file
.xinitrc	User's X-Windows configuration file read automatically by **xinit**, if it exists
.Xclients	User's X-Windows configuration file (used on Redhat and other Linux distributions)
/usr/X11R6/lib /X11/xinit/xinitrc	System X-Windows initialization file; automatically read by **xinit**

Table 21-3.   *X-Windows Commands, Configuration Files, and Arguments* (continued)

X-Windows Command	Explanation
Configuration Files	
/usr/X11R6/lib /X11/xinit/.Xresources	System X-Windows resources file; read by **.xinitrc**
/usr/X11R6/lib /X11/xinit/.Xmodmap	System X-Windows input devices file; read by **.xinitrc**
/usr/lib/X11/rgb.txt	X-Windows colors; each entry has four fields; the first three fields are numbers for red, green, and blue; the last field is the name given to the color
/usr/X11R6/lib/X11 /xinit/xinitrc.before.fvwm	An X-Windows **.xinitrc** sample file without fvwm or Caldera Desktop (on the OpenLinux system)
X-Windows Application Configuration Arguments	See XMan pages for detailed explanations
–bw *num*	Borderwidth of pixels in frame
–bd *color*	Border color
–fg *color*	Foreground color (for text or graphics)
–bg *color*	Background color
–display *display-name*	Displays client to run on; displays name consisting of hostname, display number, and screen number (see XMan pages)
–fn *font*	Font to use for text display
–geometry *offsets*	Location on screen where X-Windows application window is placed; offsets are measured relative to screen display

Table 21-3. *X-Windows Commands, Configuration Files, and Arguments* (continued)

X-Windows Command	Explanation
X-Windows Application Configuration Arguments	
`-iconic`	Starts application with icon, not with open window
`-rv`	Switches background and foreground colors
`-title` *string*	Title for the window's title bar
`-name` *string*	Name for the application
`xrm` resource-*string*	Specifies resource value
Desktops, Window and File Managers	
`lg`	The Caldera Desktop
`fvwm`	The fvwm window manager
`olvwm`	The Xview window manager (OpenLook)
`fvwm95`	The fvwm95 (Windows 95) window manager
`qvwm`	The qvwm (Windows 95) window manager
`mwm`	LessTif window manager
`xfm`	The Xfm file manager
`aftersetp`	The AfterStep window manager
`mlvwm`	A Macintosh window manager
`mfm`	The Motif window manager

Table 21-3. *X-Windows Commands, Configuration Files, and Arguments* (continued)

Chapter Twenty-Two

Typesetting: TeX, LaTeX, and Ghostscript

From its early inception, Unix has had document processing tools that allow the user to perform sophisticated word processing operations. They are used to create the online manual pages that you display with the **man** command. You can easily use these tools to create your own online manual pages for whatever projects or software you may develop. These tools operate like filters, reading an input file and generating output that is usually meant to be printed. The input file holds special instructions that direct the filter on how to format the output. The major document processing tools in Unix are called nroff, troff, tbl, eqn, and pic. Linux has GNU versions of all these tools that can be accessed either with the same names or those names with an initial 'g'. There are GNU versions of troff, tbl, eqn, and pic that also have the alternative names of gtroff, gtbl, geqn, and gpic. nroff performs basic text processing, and troff performs more sophisticated typesetting. tbl, eqn, and pic are preprocessors for troff that allow you to create tables, display mathematical equations, and draw simple objects. Each has its own set of instructions that you enter into your input file along with troff instructions. The GNU version of troff is compatible with Unix troff. You can use the same troff commands for both. However, the output of the GNU versions of tbl, eqn, and pic can only be processed by GNU troff, not Unix troff.

Word processing operations using nroff and troff instructions can become very complex. To simplify the process, nroff and troff have two macro packages: **ms** and **mm**. A macro represents a set of nroff instructions. You can use the macro instead of the instructions. For example, instead of using a set of nroff instructions to start a new paragraph, you can use a single macro. The **ms** macros are geared toward standard word processing operations, whereas the **mm** macros perform specialized tasks such as formatting letters, memos, and lists.

The document processing tools in Linux may seem somewhat primitive when compared to the currently available word processing programs. You cannot see how the document is formatted until after you have entered the text and instructions, and then have had the text processed. You need to keep in mind that in the 1970s, when these tools were developed, there were very few powerful word processors that could provide the same easy access as the Unix document processors. Even today, nroff and troff remain powerful word processing tools. However, they do lack the ease of use currently found in WYSIWYG (what you see is what you get) word processors. Today, popular word processors such as Corel WordPerfect and Microsoft Word are available for Unix and Linux systems. Several current commercial word processors for Linux are included in Redhat's Applixware Office Suite, Caldera's StarOffice, and Corel's WordPerfect 7 (**www.redhat.com**, **www.caldera.com**, and **www.sdcorp.com/ wplinux.htm**).

Still, nroff and troff are standard on all Unix systems as well as on Linux systems. You can easily and quickly use them to processes simple documents. They are also inexpensive and efficient to use. Most of the work is done on a simple standard editor. nroff and troff jobs can then be placed in the background to be processed when the system can get to them. All the Unix and Linux document processing tools contain a complex set of instructions.

There is also a special command called **groff** that you can use to access the other tools. **groff** is designed to help you invoke these tools and to easily generate printable output, particularly, PostScript output. Output is not limited to PostScript. When invoked, **groff** will process output through gtroff and then take gtroff's output and process it for a specified device. The default device is PostScript, ps. You can change this with either the **-T** option or by setting the GROFF_TYPESETTER configuration variable. To send output to the printer you use the **-l** option. The following example prints the file **myfile** on the printer using the **-ms** macros.

```
groff -ms -l myfile
```

You could also pipe the output to the **lpr** command.

```
groff -ms myfile | lpr
```

Should you want to save the PostScript output in a file, you could redirect the output of groff to a file instead of using the **-l** option to print it.

```
groff -ms myfile > myfileps
```

With groff, you can easily invoke the other tools using specified options. Normally, when you need to use eqn or tbl, you would have to take care to invoke eqn first, then tbl, and finally troff, all tied together in a sequence of pipes. However, with groff, instead of a complicated sequence of piped operations, you only need one invocation of groff with the required options. With the **-t** option, groff invokes gtbl to process tables, with **-e** the geqn processor, and with **-p** the pic processor. In this chapter, examples will invoke each tool separately in order to show how each operation works with the other. At the same time, the groff alternative will also be portrayed. The following example will first invoke geqn and gtbl.

```
groff -e -t -l myfile
```

Though nroff output can be displayed on your screen, gtroff, geqn, gtbl, and gpic output is meant to be printed. When working with these tools, it is best to use an X-Windows viewer so that you do not have to print out a document each time you make a change. This is particularly true when working with gtbl, geqn, or gpic to format tables, equations, and figures. groff comes with a viewer called **gxditview** that is invoked when you use the **groff** command with the **-X** option. A window will open up on your X-Windows desktop displaying the output. Clicking inside the window opens a menu for paging and quitting. The **-X** option overrides any previous postprocessor setting. In the next example, the user displays the output of a file that is formatting equations and tables on the groff X-Windows viewer, instead of printing it out.

```
groff -e -t -X myfile
```

To use groff, you first create an input file using any of the standard editors. In the input file, you enter in nroff or troff instructions and your text. After you are finished, you then invoke the **groff** command using the input file name as an argument. groff is different from other filters in that it reads format commands embedded in the input file. Depending upon the format instruction, groff will format a word, line, paragraph, or the whole text. The instruction is placed on a line of its own and preceded by a period.

Formatting is complicated by the fact that there are no paragraphs in the input file. A line in the input file can be thought of as a basic formatting field. Instructions operate on lines, sets of lines, and the text as a whole. Other instructions may set page offset as well as headers and footers for the entire text. Such instructions can be thought of as operating on all the lines in the text.

By default, nroff fills lines in the formatted output. The input line will usually end in a carriage return before the right margin. The **fill** option takes words from the next input line and uses them to fill up the current line in the formatted version of the text. In a sense, the **fill** option deletes the carriage return at the end of the input line and inserts its own when the line has been filled up to the right margin. With the **fill** option, input lines will not correspond to output lines. This means that you may enter in as many carriage returns as you like into the input file. This is very different from other word processors in which the carriage return is taken as a formatting instruction that specifies the end of a paragraph. You can combine format instructions to form compact formatting effects. Many such sets of instructions have been combined into macros. Instead of specifying a complex set of instructions, you can use a corresponding macro instead. There are two macro packages, the ms (manuscript) and mm (memorandum) packages. Each is invoked as an option to groff. The **-ms** option invokes the **ms** macros. The **-mm** option invokes the **mm** macros.

For example, to center, underline, and indent text as well as entering hard returns and empty lines, requires only simple instructions. The **.ce** instruction centers the input line entered below it. You can insert a carriage return of your own into the output with the **.br** instruction. The **.br** instruction literally breaks the formatting, causing nroff to start a new line. It overrides the filling of text and forces a carriage return to be inserted in the output. The **.sp** instruction enters an empty line into the output. The **.ls** command determines the line spacing of your document. **.ls 2** sets the line spacing to two, effectively double-spacing your text. The text following this instruction will be double-spaced until another **.ls** instruction is reached.

Macros are especially useful for complex formatting operations. A macro represents a set of nroff instructions. For example, a paragraph can be specified by an **.sp** followed by a **.ti**, a new line, and an indentation. The **ms** macro **.PP** represents both instructions and is used to format a paragraph. Like regular nroff instructions, macros are placed on a line of their own, preceded by a period. Macros are in uppercase. This distinguishes them from the lowercase nroff instructions. For example, the **.B**, **.I**, and **.R** macros set the style of the current font. The style stays in effect until the style is changed with another macro. The **.I** macro underlines text. It stands for italics and some printers may be able to italicize text instead of underlining it. The **.B** macro displays text in boldface. The **.R** macro displays text in its normal style. You use this macro to change back from either the **.I** or **.B** macro. In the next example, the user makes use of the **.B** macro to print the title in boldface. Then, the name is underlined using the **.I** macro. The **.R** macro changes back to the normal style. Within the text, **.I** summer underlines just the word "summer," and **.B** beach boldfaces the word "beach."

input file

```
.B
.ce
My Summer Vacation
.I
.ce
Larisa Petersen
.R
.PP
I spent my
.I summer
 vacation
at the
.B beach.
One day I went
swimming.
```

output

My Summer Vacation
Larisa Petersen

I spent my *summer* vacation at the **beach**. One day I went swimming.

Typesetting

TeX is a professional-level typesetting application for formatting text. Like troff, it reads a standard character file of text with tags that instruct TeX how to format that text. TeX generates a device-independent file (dvi) that can then be converted to various forms of output such as a PostScript file or an X-Windows display. Like troff, there are basic lower level TeX commands that can be combined by macros to perform more complex tasks such as formatting headings and paragraphs. You can design your own TeX macros for any given document. TeX has been popularly used to typeset technical documents that have complex mathematical formulas. It is also portable across any Unix or Linux system.

TeX is designed to be easily extensible. You can extend the capabilities of TeX beyond the standard set of macros by defining your own macros. This capability has been used to develop TeX-based programs with macros defined for certain tasks. Such a program, LaTeX, provides macros that simplify desktop publishing tasks. LaTeX itself is extensible, able to load and use any number of macro packages. Another TeX-based program, MuTeX, allows you to typeset music. BibTeX is used to generate bibliographies. Printer drivers as well as detailed documentation are also available. Most of these have been combined into the TeTeX software package. TeTeX includes TeX, LaTeX, dvi drivers, several popular macro packages, support programs, and detailed documentation. It is designed for installation on Unix and Linux systems, and is included on the OpenLinux CD-ROM.

You can obtain current TeX software, including macro packages and support programs, from Internet sites that are part of the Comprehensive TeX Archive Network (CTAN). CTAN is maintained as a cooperative work among members of the TeX Users Group (TUG), German-speaking TeX Users Group (DANTE), and the UK TeX Users Group (UKTUG). Each CTAN Internet site has an extensive collection of TeX programs, macros, and tools that are continually updated and added to. All sites have identical collections. Check the README files in various directories for information on their contents. Some popular CTAN sites are

> **ftp.cdrom.com**   **/pub/tex/ctan**
> **ftp.tex.ac.uk**   **/tex-archive**
> **ftp.dante.de**   **/tex-archive**

From the various TeX User Group Web sites such as **www.tug.org**, you can access TeX Internet resources such as online tutorials, TeX- and LaTeX-related software, and printed manuals. You can also link to helpful Web sites such as Don Knuth's home page. Corresponding ftp sites such as **ftp.tug.org** hold the complete CTAN collection. The TUG user group also publishes a newsletter on TeX topics called TUGboat.

Your TeTeX package already includes extensive documentation. Once TeTeX is installed, you can find the documentation in the **/usr/TeX/texmf/doc** directory and its subdirectories. The TeX FAQ is located in the **help** subdirectory. The **fontname** subdirectory contains a list of fonts available for TeX. The **/usr/TeX/info** directory contains detailed documentation on LaTeX, fonts, and other topics. The documentation is in the form of textinfo files, a special format. To access these files you use the **info** command and the topic name. The command **info info** brings up a tutorial on texinfo. The following examples access the LaTeX and font name manuals.

```
$ info latex
$ info fontname
```

You can also access the TeTeX HOWTO Web pages provided by the Linux Documentation Project at **http://sunsite.unc.edu/LDP/HOWTO**.

TeX Files

As with troff, you create a TeX file with any standard text editor such as Vi, Emacs, or Crisplite. A TeX file should have the extension **.tex** in its name. Once you have a TeX file, you process it with the **tex** command as shown here:

```
$ tex myfile.tex
```

If your file uses LaTeX macros as described in later sections, then you need to use the **latex** command.

```
$ latex myfile.tex
```

Both the **tex** and **latex** commands will generate a dvi file that you can then convert to different forms of output. The dvi file will have the same prefix as the original TeX file but with a **.dvi** extension. The previous command generates a dvi file called **myfile.dvi**. Any messages, warning, or errors resulting in processing the TeX file are placed in a file with the extension **.log**. Any errors from processing the **myfile.tex** would be found in a file called **myfile.log**.

You use one of the dvi drivers to generate the type of output you want. The dvi driver for generating PostScript files is dvips. It takes as its argument the dvi file and outputs to the standard output. If you have a PostScript printer, you can send the output of dvips directly to it. Otherwise, you need to use Ghostscript to process the PostScript data for use on your printer. The following commands generate PostScript output and sends it to the printer; the second example uses Ghostscript (gs).

```
$ dvips myfile.dvi | lpr
$ dvips myfile.dvi | gs | lpr
```

To send output to a file you use the **-o***filename* option. The following example generates a PostScript file called **myfile.ps**. You can view such a file on your desktop with the **ghostview** command, as shown here.

```
$ dvips -omyfile.ps myfile.dvi
$ ghostview myfile.ps
```

Whereas nroff allows you to output to the screen and troff requires printing for detailed output, you can display TeX output on an X-Windows window. The **xdvi** command, executed from within your window manager, will display the formatted output of a dvi file in a desktop window. This way you do not have to print the file to see its output.

```
$ xdvi myfile.dvi &
```

xdvi uses several single-letter commands to move through the displayed file. **n** will move to the next page, and **b** or **p** will move to the previous page. **g***pagenum* moves to a particular page, and **q** will quit the program. The **u**, **d**, **l**, and **r** keys move the display up, down, left, and right two-thirds of a window. **c** will center the display on the cursor.

TeX commands

Unlike troff, TeX recognizes word processing components such as sentences, words, and paragraphs. A word is a group of characters separated by any number of spaces. The number of spaces are ignored. TeX only sees one. A sentence is any word ending with a period, question mark, exclamation, or colon. The end of a paragraph is designated with a blank line. Repeated blank lines are treated as one. TeX commands are listed in Table 22-1.

TeX commands are placed in the text preceded by a special character. The character used depends on the type of operations. Standard TeX commands are prefixed with a backslash or escape character. TeX comments are preceded by a percent sign. The special characters that TeX uses are ****, **{**, **}**, **#**, **$**, **%**, **-**, **^**, **&**, and the space. Spaces separate words, **%** precedes comments, and **** precedes a TeX command. For example, all TeX files need to end with the **\bye** command. This will end TeX processing. Should you need to use any of these characters, including the space, as part of your text, you can just precede them with a backslash (with the exception of the backslash itself). **\%** outputs the "%" character, and **** followed by a space is the space character. The **** is a special command for inserting a new line, a line break. To print a backslash character, you have to use the **\backslash** command. The TeX special characters are listed in Table 22-2. The following example is a TeX file with two paragraphs. You can enter in the text any way you want on any number of lines. TeX will format it all into the appropriate paragraphs, ignoring multiple spaces and any TeX comments.

myfile.tex

```
hello there
\bye
hello there
```

TeX also allows you to apply any command to a specified grouping of text. Text can be grouped with opening and closing braces as well as **\begingroup** and **\endgroup** commands. The TeX command or commands are placed just after the opening brace. These commands are applied to the entire group. This is helpful if you want to apply a font change to just a title or several words without having to explicitly change the font back for the rest of the text. The following example italicizes just the title:

```
{\it my title}
```

Paragraphs

The **\par** command creates a new paragraph. You can use it instead of an empty line. You can embed **\par** commands anywhere in the text and they will generate paragraphs at those points. **\noindent** will not indent a paragraph on the first line. It is similar to the nroff **LP** command. You can control paragraph indentation with the **\parindent** *value* command. A positive value moves it in, and a negative value moves it out.

With the **\break** command, you can insert line breaks or page breaks. **\break** within a paragraph inserts a line break, and between paragraphs it inserts a page break. The **\nobreak** command allows you to keep text together that would otherwise be broken across pages. For example, to keep a line on the same page or a paragraph, you could precede it with the **\nobreak** command.

Paragraph margins are specified with the **\leftskip** and **\rightskip** commands. A positive number will move the margins in, and a negative number will move them out. **\leftskip 1 in** moves the left margin in one inch. **\rightskip -.5 in** moves the right margin out half an inch.

Spacing

TeX has several horizontal and vertical spacing operations. You can measure the spacing according to character width (**em**), inches (**in**), point size (**pt**), or millimeters (**mm**). The **\hskip** and **\hfill** commands operate on a line, allowing you to add spacing or specify sizes or to flush text. For example, **\hskip 1 in** will insert one inch of empty space in a line. **\hskip 4 em** will insert empty space equivalent to the size of four characters.

The **\hfill** command fills space on a line, should there be any available. This is useful for flushing small lines to the left or right. The **\hfill** command placed before the text will flush it to the right, placed after flushes it to the left. **\hfill** commands on both sides of the text will center it.

Vertical spacing is controlled by the **\vfill** and **\vskip** commands. **\vskip** with the specified size will leave that much space in the output. **\smallskip**, **\medskip**, and **\bigskip** are easy-to-use versions of **\vskip**, not requiring a size. **\vfill** will distribute available space between following paragraphs. For example, to fill up a half-empty page at the end of a document, you could use **\vfill** to distribute that space among all the paragraphs.

The **\baslineskip** command controls the spacing between lines. You can use it to do effective double-spacing. **\parskip** controls spacing between paragraphs. You can make the spacing more or less as you wish.

Headers and Footers

Headers and footers are specified by the **\headline** and **\footline** commands. These take a list of TeX commands enclosed in braces. A useful command is the **\pageno** command to display the page number. An **\hfill** command to the right or left will place any text to the left or right margin. The following places the page number and the title "Chapter One" in the right margin of the header. The page number is also placed in the footer in the right margin.

```
\headline={\hfil Chapter One}
\footline={\hfil \the\pageno}
```

Fonts

TeX has several built-in fonts with their own TeX commands. You can easily change from one to the other. Once changed, that font remains in effect until another font is specified. The built-in fonts are **\rm** for Roman, **\tt** for typewriter, **\bf** for bold, **\sl** for slanted, and **\it** for italic.

TeX has available a large number of fonts that you can define and use in your file. You can either redefine a font definition already in place or create a new one. For example, say you want to use Helvetica Bold instead of the standard bold font, and you want to reference it with the **\bf** definition. You can redefine **\bf** to reference the Helvetica Bold font. The **\font** command allows you to redefine a font or define a new one.

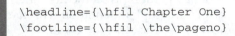

```
\font\font-definition=font-name
```

The font name for an Adobe PostScript Helvetica Bold font is phvb8r. To redefine
\bf to reference this font you would use the following font definition:

```
\font\bf=phvb8r
```

If you wanted to create a new definition with which to reference a font, you make
a new font definition name of your own, one not already in use by other commands.
The following example creates a font definition called agbf for Adobe PostScript Avant
Garde Bold font:

```
\font\agbf=pagb8r
```

A font name is made up of several components: the supplier, the general name of
the font, its weight, and any variants. A supplier is usually a company such as Adobe
or Apple. A supplier is represented by a single character. For example, **p** refers to an
Adobe PostScript font. The general name of a font is usually a two character code. **ag**
stands for Avant Garde, and **hv** stands for Helvetica. The weight of the font refers to
its style, such as bold or italic. This is represented by a single letter, for example, **b** for
bold, **i** for italic, and **r** for regular. Variants have to do with implementation details.
The variant of many Adobe fonts is 8r for 8-bit encoding. A complete listing of font
names can be found in **/usr/TeX/texmf/doc/fontname** in the **.map** files. Here are some
samples of font names:

```
phvr8r              Adobe PostScript Helvetica Normal
phvb8r              Adobe PostScript Helvetica Bold
pagb8r              Adobe PostScript AvantGarde Bold
```

To specify a particular keyboard character, you can use the **\char** command
followed by the character number of that character. This is helpful for fonts that use a
special character set, such as a symbol font or Zaph Dingbats. For example, if you wanted
to display the check mark in the Zaph Dingbats font, you would use the **\char** command
to specify the character with its keyboard number, in this case, **\char 52**.

The following example shows the use of TeX commands to format text and define
fonts. Use is made of both forms of grouping commands and text, the {} and the
\begingroup and **\endgroup** pair. Both empty lines and **\par** are used to start
paragraphs. The output is displayed in Figure 22-1, with the exception that there is no
number for the Section.

```
\font\cbf=pcrb
\font\hbf=phvb
\headline{Chapter 21 \hfill}
\footline={ \hfill Page  \the\pageno}
```

```
\def\beginmylines{ \begingroup \medskip \noindent \cbf  }
\def\endmylines{\medskip \endgroup }
\noindent {\hbf TeX Files}

As with troff, you create a TeX file with any standard text editor
such as Vi, Emacs, or Crisplite.  A TeX file should have the
extension \bf .tex \rm in its name.  Once you have a TeX file you
process it with the {\cbf tex} {\it filename}  command as shown here.
\medskip
\noindent {\cbf \$ tex myfile.tex}
\medskip

If your file uses LaTeX macros as described in later sections
then you need to use the {\cbf latex} command.
\beginmylines
\$ latex myfile.tex
\endmylines
\par Both the tex and latex commands will generate a dvi file
that you can then convert to different forms of output. The dvi
file will have the same prefix as the original TeX file but
with a {\bf .dvi} extension.  The previous command generates a
dvi file called {\bf myfile.dvi}.
\bye
```

1   TeX Files

As with troff, you create a TeX file with any standard text editor such as Vi, Emacs, or Crisplite. A TeX file should have the extension **.tex** in its name. Once you have a TeX file you process it with the `tex` *filename* command as shown here.

```
$ tex myfile.tex
```

If your file uses LaTeX macros as described in later sections then you need to use the **latex** command.

```
$ latex myfile.tex
```

Both the **tex** and **latex** commands will generate a dvi file that you can then convert to different forms of output. The dvi file will have the same prefix as the original TeX file but with a **.dvi** extension. The previous command generates a dvi file called **myfile.dvi**.

Figure 22-1. *LaTeX and TeX text formatting*

Mathematical Formulas

Like eqn, you can embed mathematical formulas within the text or place them between paragraphs. A beginning and ending **$** symbol is used to designate a mathematical formula. Special TeX commands format mathematical symbols such as **\pi** for pi and **\int** for integral (see Table 22-3). To embed a formula within text, you encase it within two single **$** symbols. To display the formula between paragraphs, you use a double set of **$** symbols, **$$** and **$$**. In the following example, 2+3 will be placed within the text and x*y will be centered in its own space, breaking up the line. These next sentences will have the following output: **This is the $2+3$ embedded formula. This is the display $$x*y $$ shown here**.

```
This is the 2+3 embedded formula.   This is the display


                        x * y


shown here.
```

Subscripts and superscripts are represented by the ^ and _ commands. The syntax for the subscript command is **text_{subtext}**, where subtext will become a subscript of text. **a_{i}** makes **i** a subscript of **a**, **a$_i$**. The superscript command has the same syntax. **text^{suptext}**. **x^{b}** makes **b** a superscript of **x**, **x^b**. The superscript or subscript can be any TeX or LaTeX commands, including complex equations.

There are numerous commands for displaying mathematical symbols. Two of the more common are **\sum** for the summation symbol and **\int** for the integral symbol. Both take two arguments, the beginning value prefixed with a ^ and the ending value prefixed with a _.

```
n \sum ^{1} _{a _{i}
```

The element $res = \dfrac{b}{a^i}$ has nothing to do with the following equation.

$$ave = \dfrac{\sum_{n}^{l} a_i}{n}$$

Figure 22-2. *Embedded and separate equations*

Output for the following example is shown in Figure 22-2. It shows the use of embedded fractions and a complex formula displayed on its own line.

```
\par The element $ res = { b \atop \overline{a ^{i}}}$ has nothing
to do with the following equation.
$$ave = {\underline{ {\sum ^{1} _{n}} \; {a ^{i}}} \atop  n} $$
\bye
```

Macros are commonly used to define your own customized TeX operations. Instead of text, you can specify any sequence of TeX commands. You define TeX macros using the **\def** command. The format is as follows:

```
\def macro-name { text }
```

The macro operation is a simple text substitution. It substitutes the instances of the macro name with the specified text. This text can be regular text or TeX commands. You could use a macro as a way to abbreviate a large title or name. For example, the following macro will replace "myed" with "The New Vi Editor" throughout the text.

```
\def\myed{The New Vi Editor}
```

The text can even include TeX commands for that text.

```
\def\myed{The \tt New \rm Vi Editor}
```

TeX macros can take parameters, letting you specify different arguments each time you use them. You define parameters with the **#** and a number for each parameter. **\agegp#1#2** defines two parameters referenced by **#1** and **#2** for the macro named **agegp**. To reference the parameter in the macro's text, you use the **#** and the number of the parameter. **#1** references the first parameter. The following example defines a macro with two parameters.

```
\def\agegp#1#2{This is a #1 movie for #2}
```

When using a macro that has parameters, you specify each argument enclosed within its own set of braces. A macro with parameters must always have the same corresponding number of arguments when it is used. For example, the **agegp** macro always has to have two arguments, no more and no less.

```
\agegp{terrible}{teenagers}
\agegp{great}{adults}
```

The output for these macros is

```
This is a terrible movie for teenagers
The is a great movie for adults.
```

LaTeX

LaTeX is a set of TeX macros that provide easy-to-use formatting capabilities. Instead of detailing a complex set of TeX commands you can use a corresponding LaTeX macro instead. In many respects, LaTeX is like the **mm** macros used for nroff and troff, allowing you to generate different types of documents. The LaTeX macros allow you to focus on formatting the general layout of the text. The current version of LaTeX is LaTeX2e, and is included in the TeTeX package with OpenLinux. LaTeX3 is currently under development.

Documentation for LaTeX can be found in the **/usr/TeX/texmf/doc/latex** directory. The **general** subdirectory contains dvi versions of the LaTeX manual. You can generate a PostScript version using **dvips** and then use **Ghostview** to view it. Documentation for different packages are found in various subdirectories such as **generic**, **latex**, and **tools**. **fonts** contains lists of available fonts. Much of the documentation is only in the form of dvi files. The easiest way to view them is to first generate them as PostScript files using **dvips** with the **-o**_filename_ option, and then use Ghostview to display them (you can use **xdvi** but it can be time consuming). The following commands generate a PostScript file and then use Ghostview to view it.

```
dvips -omyman.ps manual.dvi
ghostview myman.ps
```

LaTeX operates in one of three basic modes: paragraph, math, and LR (left to right). In paragraph mode, it automatically fills paragraphs, aligning text with the margins. In math mode, it creates mathematical formulas, displaying them. In LR mode, it operates like a drawing program, drawing figures and repeating text as is. The **\tabular** environment that you use to create tables does not operate in paragraph mode and will require explicit line breaks at the end of the line you enter for the table data. A line break can be entered with double backslashes, ****.

Document Classes

With LaTeX, you can format different types of documents. LaTeX defines several document types, called classes. The article class is used for documents such as journal articles. The book class is for complete volumes. The report class is used for lengthy reports. To create a LaTeX document, you first have to define the class of document you want using the **\documentclass** macro. This macro takes as its argument the name of the class. Text for a LaTeX document is organized into a preamble and a body. The body is defined by the **\begin{document}** and **\end{document}** macros. You place the body of your text within these two macros. Any text entered before the **\begin{document}** macro is taken to be the preamble. The following example defines a document with the article class and establishes the body of the document:

```
\documentclass{article}
\begin{document}
This is my text
\end{document
```

Once you have created your LaTeX file, you then use the `latex` command to perform TeX processing with the LaTeX macros. A dvi file is generated just as with the `tex` command. You can then use TeX conversion commands to generate output.

```
$ latex myfile.tex
```

There are four standard document classes that you can use: article, letter, report, and book. There are commands tailored for particular classes. For example, the **\closing** command is used in the letter class to specify a signoff greeting such as "Sincerely." The article class was originally designed for journal articles and is used for short documents. The book class is used for large documents containing separate chapters that can even be organized into parts. The report class is for medium-size documents that may have chapters but are not as large as a book document. The letter class has two alternative formats, business and personal. It will organize a letter, placing address and date in the appropriate position. In addition there is a special document class called slides for preparing slides. The different document classes and their options are listed in Table 22-4.

To set general layout features for the entire document, you can specify options for the **\documentclass** macro. The options are encased with brackets and placed after the **\documentclass** name. You can specify features such as the default font size, the sides of a page used, the size of the paper, and the positioning of formulas. Table 24-4 lists some of those options. The following example will print on two sides of a page (**twoside**) and sets the font size to 12 point (12 pt). Multiple options are separated by commas.

```
\documentclass[twoside,12pt]{article}
```

Packages

LaTeX is inherently extensible. You can create new definitions of macros and use them as commands in your LaTeX document. This extensibility has allowed people to develop packages of LaTeX macros designed for specialized tasks. For example, the graphicx package defines macros for importing epsf files, and the rotating package allows you to rotate text on the page. There are a great many such packages available to you, both as part of the TeTeX installation and at different Internet sites. Packages currently available are located in the **texmf/tex** subdirectories. They have the extension **.sty**. Documentation is in the **/doc** subdirectories.

To load a package into your document, you use the **\usepackage** command in the preamble. The following example adds the makeidx package that enables the creation of indexes:

    \usepackage{makeidx}

You can also use the **\import** command to insert the contents of any file into your LaTeX file. **\import** is used for files that contain LaTeX macros you want defined for your document. You can define your own macros, place them in a file, and then import that file whenever you want to use them in a document.

    \import *myfile.tex*

Page Format

The **\pagestyle** macro sets the layout for your pages. There are four standard formats for headers and footers, specified by different arguments for the **\pagestyle** macro: **empty**, **plain**, **headings**, and **myheadings**. **empty** will print no headers and footers, whereas **plain** will print only a footer consisting of a centered page number. **headings** places a running heading on each page that is determined by the document style. **myheadings** allows you to use the mark commands to specify your own headings for either odd and even pages or just single pages.

For **myheadings** document style, you can use the mark commands to set the text of the heading. The **\markboth**{*left-head*}{*right-head*} is used for documents with odd and even headers. To generate odd/even pages, your document style must have the **twoside** option; for example, **\documentstyle[twoside]{article}**. **\markright** {*right-head*} is used for just single headers in a **oneside** document.

There are also commands for particular features. You can create double columns with the **\twocolumn** command and switch back to one column with the **\onecolumn** command. **\pagenumbering**{*num-style*} allows you to set the page numbering style. The possible styles are arabic, roman, and alph (alphabetic). The **\thispagestyle** macro will let you set the page layout for just the current page.

Fonts

LaTeX supports a standard set of font definitions that are listed in Table 22-5. It also has font size commands that allow you to easily change a font's size. You can choose type sizes such as **\tiny**, **\small**, and **\large** as well as **\LARGE** for all caps. **\normalsize** is the default.

Definitions of new fonts are placed in the preamble before the body of the text. You use the **\font**\def-name=fontname command. The following example creates a definition for the PostScript Helvetica font and calls it helf. The font can then be referenced with the font title **\helf**.

```
\documentclass(article)
\font\helf=phvr
\begin(document)
\helf This text is in helvetica, \bf but this is in normal bold face.
\end(document)
```

You can also redefine any of the standard fonts with the **\font** command. You could define a different font for **\it** and **\bf**.

Sectioning

LaTeX is particularly useful for setting up different components of your document such as section headings, a title, and a table of contents. The article class uses the macros **\section**, **\subsection**, **\subsubsection**, **\paragraph**, **\subparagraph**, and **\appendix**. Except for **\appendix**, they all can take a heading name as their argument.

```
\section{C compiler}
\subsection{Libraries}
```

The report and book classes have two other macros: **\part** and **\chapter**. **\chapter** defines a chapter title, and **\part** defines a set of chapters in the book or report.

These sectioning macros are used to generate the table of contents. The **\tableofcontents** macro will generate the table of contents. If you do not want a particular heading displayed in the table of contents, you can suppress it with an asterisk placed after the macro name. **\section*{computers}** will not be displayed in the table of contents. Table 22-6 lists the sectioning macros.

To create a title, you use the **\maketitle** macro placed at the beginning of the body of the text. However, the information for the title is placed in the preamble, before the body begins. The **\title**{My title} sets up the title "My title". Other information placed here is the author, specified by the **\author**{name} macro. The following set of macros sets up the title and then creates it.

```
\title{Hockey}
\author{Christopher}
\begin{document}
\maketitle
```

Footnotes and Cross-References

LaTeX also supports footnotes and cross-references. The commands you use to create footnotes depend on whether the footnote references text in outer paragraph mode or inner paragraph mode. Outer paragraph mode is the paragraph mode for normal text, whereas inner paragraph mode is for text contained within some other environment such as the box of a figure or a cell of a table. Table 22-6 lists the footnote and cross-reference commands.

For outer paragraph mode, you use the **\footnote[**_number_**]** {_text_} command. A numbered footnote text is placed at the bottom of the page. With the optional argument, number, you can specify your own number for the footnote. To footnote text in inner paragraph mode, you use the **\footnotemark** macro to create the reference in the text. Then, in outer paragraph mode, you can use **\footnotetext[**_number_**]** {_text_} to set up the text of that footnote at the bottom of the page.

You use the **\label** and **\ref** macros to set up cross-references. The **label** command takes as its argument a key with which to reference that point in the text. The key can be any name you make up. You can then use the **\ref** macro with that key to reference that point in the text. **\ref** will generate the section number for that point in the text. **\pageref** can be used to reference a page number instead.

```
\label{myplace}
\ref{myplace}
\pageref{myplace}
```

Environments

LaTeX has a set of environments in which different tasks can be performed, some with their own set of commands. You can use the **tabular** environment to create a table using table commands. The **figure** environment will position and number a figure on a page and let you use the **\caption** command to enter a caption for it. Table 22-7 lists several commonly used LaTeX environments.

Environments start with a **\begin**{_env-name_} macro and end with a corresponding **\end**{_env-name_} macro. Some environments have specialized commands that you use, such as **\circle** for drawing a circle in a picture environment. Other environments, such as the tabular environment, also look for specially formatted text. Still others format any included text. For example, **begin{quote}** followed by lines of text and then an **end{quote}** macro will indent and quote any included text.

Certain environments operate in paragraph mode, whereas others operate in LR or math mode. Those that operate in LR mode need to have line breaks entered at the end of each line using the **\\ line break** command. If you do not, then LR mode will read all the lines in the environment as all one line, instead of separate ones. The tabular, picture, and eqnarray are all LR mode environments. When creating tables and figures, you have to enter in a \\ at the end of each line. Other LR mode environments are **center**, **flushright**, and **flushleft**. These environments are designed to operate on separate lines, centering them on top of each other or flushing them right or left. Each line must end with a line break, ****.

```
\begin{center}
This is centered text\\
And so is this\\
\end{center}
```

To center or flush text in paragraph mode, you would use the **\centering**, **\raggedleft**, and **\raggedright** commands within an environment or the main text. **\raggedright** will left-justify paragraphs, leaving the right side ragged, and **\raggedleft** will right-justify paragraphs. These are designed to operate on whole paragraphs. Table 22-6 lists the LaTeX commands for formatting paragraphs.

The following example illustrates the use of LaTeX environments for formatting text. Fonts are defined and grouped with text much as they are in TeX. The **twoside** option in the **\documentstyle** command permits the use of **\markboth** to set both even and odd headers. The output is the same as shown in Figure 22-1.

```
\documentstyle[twoside]{article}
\font\cbf=pcrb
\font\crf=pcrr
\pagestyle{myheadings}
\markboth{\ Chapter 21 \hfill }{ \hfill Linux: The Complete
Reference\ }
\begin{document}
\section{TeX Files}

As with troff, you create a TeX file with any standard text editor
such as Vi, Emacs, or Crisplite.  A TeX file should have the
extension \bf .tex \rm in its name.  Once you have a TeX file you
process it with the \cbf tex \it filename \rm command as shown
here.
```

```
\begin{flushleft}
\crf \$ tex myfile.tex \\
\end{flushleft}

If your file uses LaTeX macros as described in later sections
then you need to use the {\cbf latex} command.
\begin{flushleft}
\crf \$ latex myfile.tex \\
\end{flushleft}

Both the {\cbf tex} and {\cbf latex} commands will generate a dvi
file that you can then convert to different forms of output. The
dvi file will have the same prefix as the original TeX file but
with a {\bf .dvi} extension.  The previous command generates a
dvi file called {\bf myfile.dvi}.
\end{document}
```

Counters

LaTeX maintains counter variables for those environments that perform numbering of objects such as the figure, equation, and table environments. The name of the counter is the same as the environment. In addition, counters are kept for the different sectioning commands, keeping a count of sections such as chapters, subsections, and paragraphs (see Table 22-6). Counters are also kept for footnotes and pages. You can access the value of a given counter with the **\value**{*count-name*} command.

The **\addcounter**{*name*}{*increment*} command will force an increment of the named counter, and **\addcounter**{*name*}{*value*} resets the named counter to the specified value. **\newcounter**{*name*} creates a new counter called *name*. You can change the display of a counter to alphabetic, Roman numeral, or Arabic with the **\alph**, **\roman**, and **\arabic** commands.

Lists

LaTeX has several list environments for creating numbered, bulleted, or labeled lists. The **enumerate** environment creates numbered lists, description labeled lists, and itemized bulleted lists. Entries for a list are made with the **\list** command. Depending upon the environment, list takes certain options. For example, in the **description** environment, list takes as its option the label for that entry, a descriptive name. The following example generates a number list of items.

```
\begin{enumerate}
\item{ Clean house }
```

```
\item{ Mow lawn }
\item{ Get gas }
\end{enumerate}
```

The following **description** environment creates a descriptive list of items. The label for each item is enclosed within brackets. This label will be displayed to the left of the item, right-flushed and boldfaced.

```
\begin{description}
\item[Aleina]{ Book on drawing with pens and paints.}
\item[Larisa]{ A new library card for all the books that she wants
to read over again.}
\item[Cecelia]{ A new word processor.}
\end{description}
```

The **itemize** environment creates a bulleted list. The following example places a bullet before each item in the list:

```
\begin{itemize}
\item{milk}
\item{ yogurt }
\item{ vegetables }
\end{itemize}
```

With the **list**{*label*}{*spacing*} environment, you have more control over how your list is printed. The **list** environment takes two arguments, a label and a spacing argument. The label argument is usually a set of LaTeX commands that determine how the list is to be labeled. Spacing is the amount of space you want to leave between the label and its item. You can use this command to set up lists that have figures or pictures as their labels, rather than the standard bullets, words, or numbers. The label argument can be LaTeX figure or picture commands to create a graphic. In the following example, a check mark picture from the Zaph Dingbats font is used as the label for a list. First, the Zaph Dingbats font (**pzdr**) is defined as the **\zdf** command. The **\char** command is used to reference a particular character in that font. **\zdf\char 52** is the check mark figure. This command is used in the label argument of the **list** command, making the checkmark the label used for the list items. See Figure 22-3.

```
\documentclass{article}
\newfont{\zdf} {pzdr}
```

```
\begin{document}
\begin{list}{\zdf\char 52}{Gift List}
\item{ Book on drawing with pens and paints.}
\item{ A new library card.}
\item{ A new word processor.}
\end{list}
\end{document}
```

There is also a package called dingbats that defines a **dingbat** environment with commands you can use to easily reference and use Zaph Dingbat characters. Documentation is available in the **doc/tools** directory.

Tables

There are two standard LaTeX environments used for tables: table and tabular. The **tabular** environment creates a table, and the **table** environment will position the table on the page as well as number and label it. Another external environment called **supertabular** is also available for tables that take up more than one page.

The **table** environment allows you to position and number a table. It has an option permitting you to control placement of the table (see Table 22-6). The **h** option will position it where the table occurs in the text, **t** will position it at the top of the page, **b** at the bottom of the page, and **p** on a page with itself or other objects. Within the **table** environment, you can use the **\caption** command to create a table title. The number of the table is automatically generated. The table itself is usually a table created by the **tabular** environment. In this case, a **tabular** environment with its table-making commands is placed within the **table** environment. However, the table could just as easily be an external epsf picture that you load in. (See the "The picture Environment" section later in the chapter.)

```
\begin{table}[placement]
The table
\caption{table title}
 \end{table}
```

With the **tabular** environment you can create your own tables. It has one mandatory argument for column alignment. The *column-align* argument specifies how you want columns aligned: left, right, or center. Like **gtbl**, you use a single letter code for each column. **l** stands for left-aligned, **r** for right, and **c** for center. The | will place a line between columns. {|l|r|r|c|} will left-align the first column, right-align the next two, and center the last. Vertical lines are drawn between each, as well as one on each end to draw an outside border (sides of a box). **tabular**'s **position** option allows you to vertically align the table on the top or bottom rows (default is the center).

```
\begin{tabular}[position]{column-align}
entry & entry ... & entry \\
\end{tabular}
```

You enter the data for each row of the table on separate lines. Each line needs to be terminated with a line break, ****. Each entry in the row is separated by an ampersand, **&**, cutting the row into separate fields, one for each column. The ampersands need to be borders with spaces. The following example shows the data for one row of a three-column table.

```
War and Peace & Tolstoy & 15.75 \\
```

The **\cline** and **\hline** commands draw lines along rows of the table across its columns. **\cline** will draw a line across a specified number of columns, whereas **\hline** draws a line across the entire width of the table. Two **\hline** commands together will draw a double line. **\vline** draws a vertical line within a row. Should you want a line between rows, you can place an **\hline** command at the end of the line, after the line break. **\multicolumn{**numcols**}{**align**}{**text**}** makes an entry in a table that spans several columns. *num-cols* is the number of columns to span and *align* is the alignment as indicated by **l**, **r**, or **c**. The following example creates a table of four rows and three columns, all left-aligned. A title spanning all the columns is created and centered using the **\multicolumn** command. **\multicolumn** is also used to create individual headings for each column.

```
\documentclass{article}
\begin{document}
\begin{tabular}{|l|l|r|}
\hline
\multicolumn{3}{|c|}{Book List} \\
\multicolumn{1}{|c|}{Title} & \multicolumn{1}{c}{Author} &
    [c|}{Price} \\ \hline \hline
War and Peace & Tolstoy & 15.75 \\ \hline
Christmas Carol & Dickens & 3.50 \\ \hline
Iliad & Homer & 10.25 \\ \hline
Raven & Poe & 2.50 \\ \hline
\end{tabular}
\end{document}
```

Book List		
Title	**Author**	**Price**
War and Peace	Tolstoy	15.75
Christmas Carol	Dickens	3.50
Iliad	Homer	10.25
Raven	Poe	2.50

Figure 22-3. *A LaTeX list*

One of the shortcomings of the **tabular** environment is that it does not support tables that span more than one page. For such tables, you can use the **supertabular** package. This package defines the **supertabular** environment that has all the commands of the **tabular** environment, but with added commands for formatting a table across several pages. Heading and subheadings can be redisplayed at the top of each page. See **doc/latex/styles** for documentation.

Mathematical Formulas: math Mode

LaTeX, of course, supports the same Math environments as TeX, as well as several other Math environments. LaTeX supports both the use of the set of single **$** symbols for inline mathematical formulas and the set of double **$$** symbols for formulas to be positioned on their own line. LaTeX defines these as the **math** and **displaymath** environments. You can just as easily use the **\begin(math)** and **\begin(displaymath)** environments for such formulas. In environments are LaTeX environments that add other features such as number of equations and organizing them into arrays.

In addition to the **math** and **displaymath** environments, LaTeX adds several environments that add other features such as numbering of equations and organizing them into arrays (equation, array, and eqnarray). The **equation** environment will center an equation and place an equation number on the right side.

```
\begin{equation}
math formula
\end{equation}
```

The **array** environment is a tabular environment for equation. As in the **tabular** environment, match formulas are arranged in rows and columns. Each line is a row with different columns separated by the **&**. Each line must end with a ****. **array** takes an argument that specifies the justification of each column, just like **tabular** (**l** for left, **r** for right, and **c** for center).

```
\begin{array}{justification}
 entry & entry ... & entry \\
\end{array}
```

The **eqnarray** operates like **array**, but labels each row with an equation number. It is helpful for listing several equations vertically, each with their own number.

```
\begin{eqnarray}
 formula \\
 formula \\
\end{eqnarray}
```

LaTeX also adds several new commands for formatting equations. The **\frac{***num***}{***dem***}** command creates a fraction, where *num* is the numerator and *dem* is the denominator. The following example creates a fraction of 3/5. The numerator and denominator can also be any complex mathematical formula.

```
\frac{3}{5}
```

There are numerous commands for displaying mathematical symbols. Some of the more commonly used symbols are described here. A more complete listing can be found in Table 22-8. Two of the more common are **\sum** for the summation symbol and **\int** for the integral symbol. Both take two arguments, the beginning value prefixed with a ^ and the ending value prefixed with a _.

```
n \sum ^{1} _{a _{i}
```

The **\overbrace{***text***}** and **\underbrace{***text***}** commands place text either above or below a horizontal brace. The **\overline{***text***}** and **\underline{***text***}** commands place text either above or below a horizontal line.

Various forms of ellipses are supported. **\ldots** produces a normal ellipsis. **\cdots** places an ellipsis in the center of a line, **\vdots** displays a vertical ellipsis, and **\ddots** displays a diagonal ellipsis.

There are symbols for mathematical functions such as square root. **\sqrt[***root-value***]{***number***}** displays a root symbol of *number* for the root-value. The *root-value* is optional, and, if left out, no *root-value* is displayed, presenting the square root. The following examples display the square root of 16 and the cubed root of 9.

```
\sqrt{16}
\sqrt[3]{9}
```

The next example uses LaTeX commands to format the same mathematical formulas used in the TeX example in the previous section. The output is the same as shown in Figure 22-2. The equation environment is used to number the equation.

```
\documentclass{article}
\pagestyle{empty}
\begin{document}
The element $ res = \frac{b}{a ^{i}}$ has nothing to do with the
following equation.
\begin{equation}
ave = \frac {\sum ^{1} _{n} \; {a _{i}}} { n}
\end{equation}
\end{document}
```

Graphics

With LaTeX, you can display pictures in your text. The pictures can be either drawings or photographs. There are several ways to generate drawings for a LaTeX document. You can do them with **drawing** environments that have commands to draw objects such as lines and circles, or you can create the drawings with a drawing program such as xfig and then import the drawing as you would a photograph.

figure

You use the **figure** environment to position, number, and label a picture or graphic. The picture can be a drawing created by a **drawing** environment or an imported graphic such as a PostScript epsf file. You can include these commands and their **picture** environment within a **figure** environment. You can place any of these within a **\begin{figure} \end{figure}** pair. Within this pair, you can then create a caption for the figure with the **\caption** macro. The following example creates a simple box:

```
\begin{figure}
picture
\caption{mybox}
\end{figure}
```

Importing Photographs and Drawings: Encapsulated PostScript Files (epsf)

You can import photographs and drawings into your TeX documents as encapsulated PostScript files. If the photograph or drawing you want to import is not already in this format, you will have to convert it. For example, if you have a photograph in a jpeg or gif format, you first have to convert it to an epsf file. **xv**, a program available on your OpenLinux system, will easily perform such a conversion. After opening **xv** (enter **xv & ** from an Xterm window), press the right button to bring up the command buttons. Choose load and load in your picture. Then choose save and change the file type at the top of the menu to PostScript. This epsf file will have an extension of **.ps**. You can then import it to your LaTeX document.

To import an encapsulated PostScript file to your LaTeX document, you have to first include a package that defines commands to perform that operation. There are several packages available, each with different commands. Some of those available with your TeTeX package are **epsf**, **graphics**, **graphicx**, and **epsfig**. The **epsf** package is the simplest, can be loaded using the **input** command in the preamble. This defines a command called **epsffile** that you can then use to import an epsf file. The following example imports an epsf file called **mypic.ps**.

```
\documentclass{article}
\begin{document}
\input epsf
\epsffile{temp.ps}
\end{document}
```

Other packages, such as **graphicx**, include commands with more capabilities. For example, with **graphicx** you can import compressed epsf files. The **graphicx** and **epsfig** command are loaded with the **usepackage** command. **graphicx** uses a command called **includegraphics** to import the epsf file. You can find documentation for **graphicx** in the **doc/latex/graphics** directory. The following example imports an epsf file with the **graphicx** package as well as using the **figure** environment to center, number, and label the imported graphic. The **caption** command is used to make a label.

```
\documentclass{article}
\usepackage{graphicx}
\begin{document}
\begin{figure}
\includegraphics{mypic.ps}
\caption{This is my picture}
\end{figure}
\end{document}
```

Drawing Environments

LaTeX has a standard drawing environment called **picture** with which you can generate very simple objects such as circles and lines. More powerful drawing packages such as **eepic**, **pictex**, **texdraw**, **pstricks**, and **xypic** are also available with your TeTeX installation. You have to load these packages first before you can use them. The documentation for **texdraw**, **pstricks**, and **xypic** can be found in the **doc/generic** directory. The commands for the drawing environments are similar to the **gpic** utility described in the previous chapter. You can also use **gpic** to generate TeX commands for drawing objects.

For any complicated drawings, it is always preferable to use a separate drawing program such as **xfig** to first create the drawing. **xfig** is set up to generate LaTeX commands for the various drawing packages. You can choose from epic, eepic, pictex, and picture. A TeX file with these commands will be generated that you can then insert into a standard LaTeX file. Be sure to load the drawing package you need with \usepackage.

Alternatively, you can convert the drawing file to an encapsulated PostScript (epsf) file. With defined **epsf** commands, a TeX file can import any epsf (PostScript) file. Many drawing programs will allow saving files as epsf files. You can also use the **xv** program to convert such files. The method for importing epsf files is described in the next section.

The picture Environment

With the **picture** environment, you can create simple lines, circles and rectangles. **picture** takes two arguments specifying its position. The first is its size in terms of width and height, and the second is its position on the page as referenced by x and y coordinates. The measurements are in millimeters. **picture** operates in LR mode, so each line must end with a line break, \\. The **picture** environment has its own set of commands (see Table 22-6). \circle creates a circle. The following example creates a circle 100 mm in diameter.

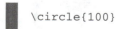

```
\circle{100}
```

\line draws a line of a specified length and slope. \vector draws a line with an arrow. These commands take as their first argument an x and y slope. These values range between -4 and +4. The second argument is the length of the line or vector. \makebox creates a box of specified width and height. With the \oval command, you can create an oval, also specifying width and height. \framebox places a frame around an object. \makebox, \framebox, and \oval let you position text in a specified quadrant. You use a two-character combination of the following codes as options to these commands: **t** for top, **b** for bottom, **r** for right, and **l** for left. The following example will draw a square box 2 inches in length with text starting from the left side.

```
\framebox[2 in][l]{Input File}
```

You can position an object at a particular coordinate using the **\put** command. Otherwise, objects will be placed next to each other. **\put** takes as its first argument the x and y coordinates, where you want to place the object. Then the object is listed. The following draws a circle 50 mm up and 20 mm to the right from the lower corner of the picture.

```
\puts{50,20}{\circle{100}} \\
```

The following example creates a box with the words "Input File", a circle above the box, and a line with an arrow between them.

```
\begin{picture}(300,300)(10,10) \\
\framebox[1 in][l]{Input File} \\
\put(-20,10){\vector(0,0){50}} \\
\put(-20,80){\circle{100}} \\
\end{picture}
```

Letters

The **letter** environment operates within the letter document style. You can set up several **letter** environments with a TeX file that has a letter document style, letting you write several letters in the same document. Within the **letter** environment you can use several letter LaTeX commands for different components of a letter, such as the signature and return address (see Table 22-9). The **letter** environment takes as its arguments the name and address of the recipient. The following example sets up a **letter** environment within a letter document class.

```
\documentstyle{letter}
 \begin{document}
\begin{letter}{name \\ address \\ city, state zip}
\end{letter}
 \end{document}
```

The letter begins with the **\opening{***text***}** command, followed by the text of the letter. The text argument for **\opening** is the salutation you want in the opening greeting, such as Dear Sirs.

```
\opening{Dear Sirs}
```

The text of the letter is treated as verbatim material, no LaTeX commands work within it. You then end the text of the letter with the **\closing{***text***}** command. The text argument for **\closing{***text***}** is the signoff you want displayed. For example:

```
\closing{Sincerely yours}
```

Following the **\closing** command, you can then specify other letter features such as carbon copies and list enclosure: **\cc** carbon copy and **\encl** list enclosure.

If you want the letter formatted as a personal letter with a return address in the upper-right corner, you need to define the return address with the **\address** command. Without the **\address** command, the letter will assume the paper has a letterhead already on it. The return address for your letter is specified with the **\address{***Return address***}** command. The return address should be entered as one line with **** separating the name, address, and city lines.

```
\address{name \\ address \\ city,state zip }
```

Your name is specified with the **\signature{***your-name***}** operation. The is your name as it will appear at the bottom of the letter. You can add other lines, using **** to separate them.

```
\documentstyle{letter}
\begin{document}
\begin{letter}{Mrs. Barbie Ken \\ Beanie Inc. \\ 5321 East St. \\ Inland, MA 55555}
\address{ Larisa Petersen \\ 7777 Book Drive \\ Ourtown, CA 90000 }
\signature{Larisa Petersen}
\opening{Dear Sir}
I can say that after extensive real world testing of your new
products, that some do not quite stand up to the everyday
pressure that consumers may impose on them. Most, however, survive
even the most reckless care.
\closing{Sincerely yours}
\cc{Aleina, Christopher, and Dylan}
\encl{Durability Report, Half-life Estimates}
\end{letter}
\end{document}
```

With the **firstpagestyle**, you can specify a telephone number and a location. **\telephone**{*number*} will display your telephone number and **\location**{*address*} will designate an address other than your standard one.

Defining New Commands, Environments, and Fonts

You can create a new command of your own with **\newcommand**. The **\renewcommand** allows you to redefine a current macro. These operations take as their arguments the command's name, followed by the number of arguments encased in brackets and then the definition itself within braces.

```
\newcommand{cmd-name}[number-args]{definition}
 \renewcommand{cmd-name}[number-args]{definition}
```

You can define your own environments with the **\newenvironment** command. **\renewenvironment** redefines a current one. For these operations, you need to define beginning commands for the begin macro and terminating commands for the end macro that will encase the environment. The first argument for these operations is the environment name followed by the number of arguments and then a definition of commands for the begin macro followed by a definition for the end macro.

```
\newenvironment{name}[number-args]{begin-definition}{end-definition}
\renewenvironment{name}[number-args]{begin-definition}{end-definition}
```

The **newfont** command performs much the same operation as **\font**, allowing you to define new fonts for your document.

```
\newfont{def-name} {fontname}
```

Table 22-10 lists the different LaTeX commands you can use to create new commands, environments, and fonts.

TeX Applications

There are several popular TeX applications included with your TeTeX installation that extend the capabilities of Tex. There are man pages for each, a list of which is located in the **/usr/TeX/man/whatis** file. VirTeX and IniTeX are programs designed to allow quick processing of a TeX document. IniTeX will generate a specially formatted binary file with a **.fmt** extension that will replace fonts and macro commands with their component commands, cutting down on processing time. VirTeX can then read the **.fmt** file and quickly generate a dvi file. Both VirTeX and IniTeX are included with your TeTeX installation.

The BibTeX is a TeX application for generating a bibliography. You use the **bibtex** command on a LaTeX file that has BibTeX-supported macros. Documentation for BibTeX is located in **doc/bibtex**. ps2frag allows you to generate TeX-formatted labels for an imported graphic. This is helpful for images on which you need to display complex mathematical formulas. slitex is a utility to generate slides from TeX files. MetaFont (mt) is program that allows you to design your own fonts and logos.

AmSTeX is a set of macros that provides very powerful mathematical typesetting capabilities. They can be included into LaTeX with the AmSLaTeX package. LamsTeX is a TeX application that uses its own command set designed for content-oriented formatting. It also includes the AmSTeX macros. It has its own command, **lamstex**, with which to process its files.

There are many other packages and applications available at the CTAN Internet sites. One particularly useful one is the **LaTeX2HTML** application that allows you to use TeX and LaTeX to generate Web pages. Another application is LyX, an X-Windows LaTeX editor included on your OpenLinux CD-ROM.

Ghostscript and Ghostview

Ghostscript is a program to interpret PostScript files and print them on devices that do not support PostScript. Much of the documentation available online these days is in the form of PostScript files. To print such files, you would ordinarily need a printer with PostScript. Ghostscript allows you to still print these files on printers that do not have PostScript.

You invoke the Ghostscript interpreter with the command **gs**. It takes as arguments the names of PostScript files that you want to print. The Ghostscript interpreter will issue messages as it processes files. When finished, you exit the interpreter by entering **quit**.

```
$ gs myfile.ps
```

The following is an example of a Ghostscript session that saves its output to a file called **myd**. The Ghostscript output is displayed page by page as the user presses RETURN to display the next one. After displaying all the pages, the Ghostscript prompt, **GS>**, is displayed, waiting for the user to enter a command. The **quit** command then quits the Ghostscript interpreter. You can suppress these messages with the **-q** option.

```
$ gs -sOutputFile=myd  mydoc.ps
Aladdin Ghostscript 3.33 (4/10/1995)
Copyright (C) 1995 Aladdin Enterprises, Menlo Park, CA.  All rights
reserved.

This software comes with NO WARRANTY: see the file COPYING for details.
Loading NimbusMonL-Regu font from
/usr/lib/ghostscript/fonts/n0220031.pfb... 1689900 381057 1320152 28093 0
done.
Loading NimbusMonL-Bold font from
/usr/lib/ghostscript/fonts/n0220041.pfb... 1730052 410797 1320152 33311 0
done.
>>showpage, press <return> to continue<<

GS>quit
$
```

The **gs** command has a great many options. Table 22-11 lists the Ghostscript
options. One of the more important ones is the **-sDEVICE** option that allows you to
set the device for output. By default, Ghostscript will output to the standard printer.
Should you have other printers connected, you could designate one of them as the
output device for Ghostscript. The following example sets the output device to the
Deskjet printer.

```
-sDEVICE=deskjet
```

Instead of the command line, you can change devices while in the interpreter.
The **selectdevice** command preceded with the device name in parentheses will
select the device.

```
(deskjet) selectdevice
```

You can also use the environment variable **GS_DEVICE** to reset the default output
device for Ghostscript (see Table 22-11 for other variables).

```
GS_DEVICE=deskjet
```

With the **-sOutputFile** option, you can redirect output to a file. The following
command outputs to a file called **myfile.ot**.

```
-sOutputFile=myfile.ot
```

If you want to generate a separate file for each page, you use the *name*%d.*ext* for the name. For the %d, a number will be generated. For the option **-sOutputFile= myfile%d.ot** the files **myfile1.ot**, **myfile2.ot**, etc. will be generated.

You can set the paper size with the **-sPAPERSIZE** options to specify a known paper size such as a4, legal, ledger, or 11×17. You can also configure Ghostscript for X-Windows using special Ghostscript entries in the **.Xdefaults** files. You can configure features of the window display and also font use.

Ghostview and GV

With Ghostview, you can display the output of Ghostscript on X-Windows. This way, you can display the output of any PostScript file on your desktop, instead of printing it out. With it you can display any documentation in the form of PostScript files, or display PostScript documents you are working on. To start up Ghostview, you use the **ghostview** command with a file name in an Xterm window, as shown here (you can also access it through the fvwm Workplace menu):

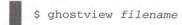

```
$ ghostview filename
```

A Ghostview window will display the formatted PostScript text on the right side. Clicking on the text in the window will open a zoom window with enlarged text. A left-click displays the text in low resolution, center-click in medium resolution, and right-click in high resolution.

To the immediate left of the text is a vertical window listing the table of contents. For most text, this will be a list of page numbers. A **>** symbol will identify the page currently being displayed. You can move from page to page by selecting the number you want with the Center-Click button. A left-click will select a page and the right-click will extend the selection. You can perform many of the screen operations with keyboard commands. The SPACEBAR displays the next page and the **b** key displays the previous page. + will increase magnification and - will decrease it. Table 22-12 lists the Ghostview keyboard commands.

On the left side of the Ghostview window is a menu box with five menu buttons. The **File** menus allows you to open and print files as well as quit the application. **Page** lets you easily move from page to page as well as mark pages. **Magstep** lets you change the display magnification. **Orientation** allows you to rotate, flip, and choose landscape views of the file. **Media** lets you select the page size.

Johannes Plass's GV is a more recent application for displaying the output of Ghostscript on X-Windows. It is based on the original Ghostview program by Jim Theisen. GV adds new features and also functions as an Adobe PDF viewer, letting you display Adobe PDF files. You can obtain a copy of GV in an rpm package from the Redhat ftp site's **contrib** directory (**ftp.redhat.com**). A source code version is available from the GV home page currently located at **wwwthep.physik.uni-mainz.de/ ~plass/gv/**. The GV Web page includes documentation and current information about GV.

Command	Action
\bye	End a TeX document
Paragraphs	
\par or *empty-line*	Start a new paragraph with first line indented
\noindent	New paragraph with no first line indent
Pre-defined Fonts	
\rm	Roman
\tt	Typewriter
\bf	Bold
\it	Italic
\sl	Slanted
Font Definition	
\font *fontname=font*	Define a font. *fontname* is the TeX name you give to the font. *font* is the font's actual name
Spacing Measures	
em	Width of a character; font-dependent
in	Inches
pt	Points
mm	Millimeters

Table 22-1. *TeX Commands*

Command	Action
Spacing Commands	
\hskip *num-measure*	Insert space of the specified size into a line
\vskip *num-measure*	Insert a line of the specified size between lines
\smallskip	Insert a small empty line between lines
\medskip	Insert a medium empty line between lines
\bigskip	Insert a large empty line between lines
\hfill	Fill empty space on a line. Used to flush text left or right on a line **\hfill** *text* flush right *text* **\hfill** flush left **\hfill** *text* **\hfill** center
\vfill	Fill empty space between lines
Page Layout	
\headline={ *text* **}**	Header
\footline={ *text* **}**	Footer
\hsize=*num-measure*	Paragraph text box size
\baselineskip= *num-measure*	Regular spacing between lines
\parskip=*num-measure*	Regular spacing between paragraphs
Groups	
\begingroup	Begin a grouping
\endgroup	End a grouping
{*text*} {*command text*}	Grouping (same effect as **\begingroup** and **\endgroup**). Commands in group apply only to text in group

Table 22-1. *TeX Commands (continued)*

Command	Action
Positioning Objects	
\topinsert *object* **\endinsert**	Position an object such as a figure at the top of the page
\pageinsert *object* **\endinsert**	Position an object on a page of its own
Macros	
\def*macro-name***{***text***}**	Define a new macro
\def*macro-name* *parameter-list***{***text***}**	Define a new macro with parameter
# *num*	Define a parameter for a macro. Used in the parameter list `\def\myn#1#2{My name is #1 #2}`

Table 22-1. *TeX Commands* (continued)

Command	Description
c	Quote the following single character
tex-command	Commands
%*tex-comment*	Comments
{*text*}	Groupings
#*num*	Parameter
$*formula*$	Embedded mathematical formula within text
$$*formula*$$	Mathematical formula displayed on a line of its own
^	Superscript
_	Subscript
&	
\\	Newline
space	Separates words
empty-line	Separates paragraphs

Table 22-2. *TeX Special Characters*

Command	Symbol	Description
`^{expr}`	x^i	Superscripts
`\alpha`	α	Alpha
`\delta`	δ	Delta
`\beta`	β	Beta
`\epsilon`	ϵ	Epsilon
`\sigma`	σ	Sigma
`\mu`	μ	Mu
`\theta`	θ	Theta
`\prod`	Π	Product symbol
`\pi`	π	Pi
`\sum`	Σ	Summation symbol
`\int`	$\int$	Integral symbol
`\subset`	$\subset$	Subset
`\supset`	$\supset$	Superset
`\Delta`	Δ	Delta
`\equiv`	$\equiv$	equivalent
`\neq`	$\neq$	Not equal
`\leq`	$\leq$	Less than or equal
`\geq`	$\geq$	Greater than or equal
`\div`	$\div$	Division
`\bullet`	$\bullet$	Bullet
`\times`	$\times$	Times
`\ast`	$\ast$	Asterisk
`\ldots`	$\ldots$	Horizontal ellipses

Table 22-3. *TeX and LaTeX Mathematical Symbols*

Classes	Action
`\documentclass{`*classname*`}`	Define the document class for this file
`\begin{`*document*`}`	Begin the body of a document
`\end{`*document*`}`	End the body of a document
Document Classes	
`article`	Short documents such as journal articles
`book`	Book-length documents with chapters
`letter`	A letter, business or personal
`report`	Long reports with several chapters
`slides`	Generates slides
Document Class Options	
`11pt`	11 point size
`12pt`	12 point size
`twoside`	Two-sided page printing (not letter)
`oneside`	One-side page printing (not letter)
`openright`	Start chapters on odd pages
`openany`	Start chapters on either odd or even pages
`leqno`	Number formulas on left side
`draft`	Draft output
`fleqn`	Flush equation to the left
`leqno`	Place equation number to the bottom left
`acm`	(not for letter or book)
`letterpaper, a4, paper`	Paper sizes

Table 22-4. *Document Classes*

Font Style	Function
\rm	Roman
\it	Italics
\em	Emphasis (toggles between \it and \rm)
\bf	Boldface
\sl	Slanted
\sf	Sans serif
\sc	Small caps
\tt	Typewriter

Font Sizes	
\tiny	Very small font size
\scriptsize	Size for script font
\footnotesize	Size for footnotes
\small	Small font size
\normalsize	Default font size
\large	Large font size
\Large	Initial caps
\LARGE	All caps
\huge	Huge font size
\Huge	Initial caps

Character Operations	
_{*text*}	Subscript (use math mode for expressions)
^{*text*}	Superscript (use math mode for expressions)
\symbol{*number*}	Display the symbol for that number in the characters set
\underline{text}	Underlines text
\ldots	Ellipsis (works in all modes)

Table 22-5. *LaTeX Font Styles and Character Operations*

Command	Function
\addtocounter{*counter*} {*value*}	Add a value to a counter
\alph{*counter*}	Print value of a counter using alphabetic characters
\arabic{*counter*}	Print value of a counter using numbers
\roman{*counter*}	Print value of a counter using Roman numerals
\newcounter{*name*}	Define a new counter
\setcounter{*counter*} {*value*}	Assign new value to a counter
\stepcounter{*counter*}	Increment counter
\usecounter{*counter*}	Use a counter in a list environment
\value{*counter*}	Use the value of a counter in an expression
Page Style and Headers	
\pagestyle{*style*}	Define placement of headers and footers for entire document:
	`empty` no header or footer
	`plain` print only page number in footer
	`headings` print even and odd headers
	`myheadings` define your own headers
\thispagestyle{*style*}	Define placement of headers and footers for this page only
\markboth{*even-header*} {*odd-header*}	Set your own even and odd headers
\markright{*single-header*}	Set your own header
\twocolumn	Start a new page with two columns
\onecolumn	Start a new page with one column
\item [*label*]	Define a list item within a **list** environment such as enumerate, itemize, or description

Table 22-6.   *LaTeX Commands*

Command	Function
Paragraphs and Lines	
`empty-line , \par`	Starts and indents a new paragraph
`\indent`	Indent this paragraph
`\noindent`	Do not indent this paragraph
`\centering`	Center paragraphs
`\raggedright`	Left-justification
`\raggedleft`	Right-justification
`\linebreak`	Break the line
`\newline`	Break the line prematurely
`\nolinebreak`	Don't break the current line
`\newpage`	Start a new page
`\nopagebreak`	Don't make a page break here
`\pagebreak`	Make a page break here
`\verb`	For verbatim text, printed exactly as typed
Section Headings	
`\section{`*heading-text*`}`	A section heading
`\subsection{`*heading-text*`}`	A subsection heading
`\subsubsection{`*heading-text*`}`	A sub-subsection heading
`\paragraph{`*heading-text*`}`	A paragraph heading
`\subparagraph{`*heading-text*`}`	A subparagraph heading
`\appendix`	The appendix
`\part{`*part-title*`}`	A part heading
`\chapter{`*chapter-title*`}`	A chapter title
`\tableofcontents`	Use headings to create table of contents

Table 22-6.   *LaTeX Commands* (continued*)*

Command	Function
Titles	
\maketitle	Make a title for the document
\title{*title-text*}	Define the title
\author{*author-name*}	Define the author
\date	Generate the date
Footnotes	
\footnote[*number*] {*footnote-text*}	Create a footnote. As an option, you can specify your own number for the footnote
\footnotemark	Place a footnote reference within a paragraph (uses footnotetext)
\footnotetext{*text*}	Footnote text. Used for footnote mark within a paragraph
\label{*label-name*}	Mark point to text for a cross-reference using label name
\ref{*label-name*}	Create a cross-reference specifying a section
\pageref{*label-name*}	Create a cross-reference specifying a page
Environments	
\caption{*text*}	Insert a caption (use with **figure** and **table** environments)
\begin{*environment-name*}	Begin an environment and label it *environment-name*. Apply environment's formatting to following text
\end{*environment-name*}	Close environment

Table 22-6. *LaTeX Commands* (continued)

Command	Function
Table Commands (tabular environment)	
`\cline{`*coli-colj*`}`	Draw a horizontal line spanning columns indicated by range starting from *coli* to *colj*
`\hline`	Draw a horizontal line spanning all columns
`\multicolumn{`*cols*`}{`*align*`}{`*text*`}`	Create an entry that spans the specified number of columns, or create a customized entry. *align* is the alignment (l, r, or c)
`\vline`	Draw a vertical line
Picture Commands (picture environment)	
`\put(`*x coord,y coord*`){`*objects*`}`	**put** performs the actual drawing of objects. Places the objects at the given coordinates
`\circle[*]{`*diameter*`}`	Create a circle of size diameter
`\oval(`*width,height*`)[`*position*`]`	Create an oval of size width and height and place any text within it. Text can be positioned at different quadrants using combinations of **t**, **b**, **l**, **r** for position option
`\line(`*x slope,y slope*`){`*length*`}`	Draw a line of specified length and slope
`\vector(`*x slope,y slope*`){`*length*`}`	Draw a line with an arrow at the end of specified length and slope
`\makebox(`*width,height*`)[`*position*`]{`*text*`}`	Create a box of size width and height and place any text within it. Text can be positioned at different quadrants using combinations of **t**, **b**, **l**, **r** for position option
`\framebox(`*width,height*`)[`*position*`]{`*objects*`}`	Create a box of size width and height and place it around specified objects. Text can be positioned at different quadrants using combinations of **t**, **b**, **l**, **r** for position option
`\dashbox{`*dash length*`}(`*width,height*`){`*text*`}`	Create a dashed box of size width and height and place any text within it. Length of dashes can be specified

Table 22-6. *LaTeX Commands* (continued)

Command	Function
Picture Commands (picture environment)	
`\frame{...}`	Place a frame directly around an object with no space in between
`\multiput`(*x coord*,*y coord*) (*delta x*,*delta y*) {*number of copies*}{*object*}	Draw multiple copies of an object
Bibliography	
`\bibitem`[*label*]{*cite_key*}	Create a bibliographic entry using label. If label is missing, use enumerated labels. *cite_key* is used to create a list of citations
`\cite`[*text*]{*key_list*}	Refer to a bibliography item. *key_list* is list of citation keys
`\nocite`{*key_list*}	Add *key_list*

Table 22-6. *LaTeX Commands* (continued)

Environment	Action
`figure`	Number and position a figure or picture (use `\caption` to label)
`table`	Number and position a table (use `\caption` to label).
`tabular`	Create tables
`picture`	Create drawing
Math Environments	
`equation`	Number and position equation
`math`	Embed math formula within text
`displaymath`	Display math formula on line of its own
`array`	Math array
`eqnarray`	Sequence of aligned equations
`theorems`	Label and number a theorem

Table 22-7. *LaTeX Environments*

Environment	Action
Line Format	
`center`	Center lines
`flushleft`	Left-align lines
`flushright`	Right-align lines
`tabbing`	Reset tabs within environment
`minipage`	Set up mini-page
`titlepage`	Set up special title page
Lists	
`enumerate`	Numbered lists. Use **\item** for entries
`itemize`	Bulleted lists. Use **\item** for entries
`description`	Labeled lists. Use **\item** for entries
`list`{*label*}{*spacing*}	Create list with specified label and spacing. Label can be LaTeX commands. Use **\item** for entries
Specialized Environments	
`letter`	Create a letter (used within letter document class)
`quote`	Quote a paragraph
`quotation`	Quote several paragraphs
`verbatim`	Display text exactly as entered
`verse`	Poetry
`theBibliograph`	Bibliography items

Table 22-7. *LaTeX Environments* (continued)

Math Environment Symbol	Action
$	Embedded math formulas
$$	Display math formulas, displayed on their own line
Math spacing	
\;	Thick space
\:	Medium space
\,	Thin space
\!	Negative thin space
LaTeX Math Operations	
\cdots	Horizontal ellipsis placed at the center of the line
\ddots	Diagonal ellipsis
\vdots	Vertical ellipsis
\ldots	Ellipsis (works in all modes)
\frac{*num*}{*den*}	Generates a fraction with *num* divided by *den*
\overbrace{*text*}	Generates a brace over text
\underbrace{*text*}	Generates text with a brace underneath
\overline{*text*}	Overlines text
\underline{*text*}	Underlines text (works in all modes)
\sqrt[*root*]{*arg*}	Generates square root of its argument (the optional argument, *root*, determines the root)

Table 22-8.   *LaTeX Mathematical Operations*

Command	Action
\begin{letter} {*name* \\ *address* \\ *city, state zip*}	Begin a letter environment, starting a new letter. Address components are separated by \\
\address{*Return address*}	Your return address
\cc{*name* \\ *name* \\ *etc*}	Cc list. Entries separated by \\
\closing{*text*}	End letter text and specify farewell text such as 'Sincerely'
\encl{*enclosure-list*}	List of enclosed material. Entries separated by \\
\location{*address*}	The organization's address. Appears only if **firstpage** page style is used
\makelabels{*number*}	Making address labels. Entered in preamble
\name{*name*}	Name to be included for the return address
\opening{*text*}	Start the letter text and specify an opening salutation such as 'Dear Sir'
\ps	Adding a PostScript
\signature{*name*}	Printed name for signature
\startbreaks	Allow page breaks
\stopbreaks	Disallow page breaks
\telephone{*number*}	Telephone number. Appears only if **firstpage** page style is used

Table 22-9. `letter` *Environment Commands*

Command	Action
\newcommand{*cmd*} [*args*] [*default*] {*definition*}	Define a new command
\renewcommand{*cmd*} [*args*] [*default*] {*definition*}	Change the definition of an existing command
\newenvironment{*env_name*} [*args*] [*default*] {*begdef*} {*enddef*}	Define a new environment
\renewenvironment{*env_name*} [*args*] {*begdef*} {*enddef*}	Change the definition of an existing environment
\newtheorem{*env_name*} [*numbered_like*] {*caption*}	Define a new environment that handles theorems
\newfont{*cmd*} {*font_name*}	Create a new command to reference a font
Using Packages and Including Files	
\usepackage{*package*}	Load in a LaTeX package
\include{*file*}	Conditionally include a file
\includeonly{*file-list*}	Determine which files are included
\input{*file*}	Unconditionally include a file

Table 22-10. *LaTeX Definition Commands*

Command Line Option	Action
-h or **-?**	Help display with list of available devices on your system
@_filename_	The list of file names that Ghostscript will process are held in the file _filename_
-f_filename_	Process file name that begins with period
-I_directories_	Add directories to library file search path
-S_name=str_	Define a string
-q	Suppress standard startup messages
-g_num1**x**num2_	The height and width of the display device
-r_num**x**num_	Set the x and y resolution for the printer
-	Read data from standard input instead of file
-dDISKFONTS	Specify character outlines for fonts
-dNODISPLAY	Suppress initialization of output device
-dNOPAUSE	Disable prompt and pause at end of each page
-dNOPLATFONTS	Disable fonts on your system
-dSAFER	Allow read-only of files
-sDEVICE=_device_	Select an output device
-sOutputFile=_filename_	Select an output file

Environment Variables

GS_DEVICE	Default device to print to
GS_LIB	Directories to search for fonts and files
GS_LIB_DEFAULT	Directories to search after those specified in GS_LIB
GS_FONTPATH	List of directories for PostScript fonts

Table 22-11. _Ghostscript Options and Variables_

Key	Action
Q	Quit
O	Open a file
R	Reopen a file
S	Save marked pages
P	Print marked pages
SHIFT-P	Print all pages
BACKSPACE, B	Display the previous page
SPACE, RETURN, F	Display the next page
PERIOD, CTRL-L	Redisplay the page
M	Mark the page
N	Unmark the page
0-5	Select magnification of the displayed file
+	Increase magnification
-	Decrease magnification
U	Scroll up
D	Scroll down
H	Scroll left
L	Scroll right

Table 22-12. *Ghostview Keyboard Commands*

Chapter Twenty-Three

Compilers and Libraries: gcc, g++, and gdb

A n application is an executable program created by a programmer using one of several programming languages. Linux provides several utilities with which a programmer can control development of an application. Foremost among these is the **gcc** utility, which invokes the compiler for the C and C++ programming languages, generating an executable version of a program. Most Linux applications are written in the C or C++ programming languages.

Application development often makes extensive use of libraries. You can create your own libraries or choose from specialized libraries. You can use libraries such as the X-Windows library to program X-Windows displays, or the gdbm library with which you can have database access to files. Libraries have become more flexible, and can now be shared or loaded dynamically.

Other utilities allow you to better manage the development of your applications. The **gdb** symbol debuggers help you to locate run-time errors. **indent** and **cproto** help you prepare your source code. Autoconf and RPM help you package your software for distribution. There are also compilers for all the major programming languages. There are compilers for Pascal, Lisp, Ada, Fortran, Basic, and Modula-2.

Getting Information: info

Though there are man pages for all the compilers and their tools, much more detailed information is available through the GNU info system. These are files located in the **/usr/info** directory that contain detailed descriptions and examples for various GNU tools. They are the equivalent of compact online manuals. There are info documents for the gcc compiler, the C and C++ libraries, the **Autoconf** utility, and even Indent. Other applications may have their own local directories with info files such as the **/usr/TeX/info** directory that holds info files for LaTeX. You invoke the main menu of info documents by entering the command **info**.

```
$ info
```

You then use the SPACEBAR to page down the menu. When you find a topic you want, you press the M key. This opens up a line at the bottom of the screen where you can type in the name of the menu item. Upon pressing ENTER, that document comes up. Pressing B pages you back to the beginning, and U puts you up to the previous menu. The command **info info** will bring up a tutorial on how to use **info**.

The C Compiler: gcc

There is a special relationship between the Unix operating system and the C programming language. The C programming language was developed specifically as a tool for programming the Unix operating system. The code for the Unix operating system is actually written in C. Linux has the same kind of special relationship. Most

Linux systems include the GNU version of the C compiler, **gcc**. The C programming language is a very complex language with many different features. This section briefly describes the basic components of the C programming language and uses them to construct a useful programming example. With an example program, we can then examine the different ways you can compile C programs.

You invoke the GNU C compiler on your Linux system with the **gcc** command. The **gcc** command, in turn, calls four other components. The first is the preprocessor. A C program contains special preprocessor commands that modify the code before it is sent to the compiler. The second component is the compiler itself. The compiler will process the code and generate an assembly code version of the program. The third component is the assembler. The assembler will use the assembly code version of the program to generate an object code version. The fourth component is the linker. The linker uses the program's object code to generate an executable file. The default name of this executable file is **a.out**. Normally, you should give the executable file a name of your own choosing. The **-o** option takes a file name as its argument. This file name will be the name of the executable file instead of the default, **a.out**. A list of **gcc** options is provided in Table 23-1. In the next example, the **gcc** command compiles the program **greet.c**. The user names the executable file "**greet**". The executable file is run by entering it at the Linux prompt as if it were a command.

```
$ gcc greet.c -o greet
$ greet
Hello, how are you
```

With multiple file programs, you need to keep in mind the difference between the C compiler and the linker. The purpose of a C compiler is to generate object code, whereas the purpose of a linker is to build an executable file using object code files. The C compiler will individually compile each source code file, generating a separate object code file for each one. These object code files will have the extension **.o** instead of **.c**. You compile and link multiple file programs using the same **gcc** command. Simply list the source code file names as arguments on the command line. In the next example, the user compiles the bookrecs program by invoking **gcc** with the source code files that make it up. The **-o** option specifies that the executable file will be called **bookrecs**.

```
$ gcc main.c io.c -o bookrecs
```

You can use the **gcc** utility to perform just a link operation by only listing object code files as its arguments. An object code file has a **.o** extension. In the next example, the user just performs a link operation. No compiling takes place. Of course, this operation assumes that the object code files have been previously generated.

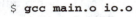

```
$ gcc main.o io.o
```

As you develop and debug your program, you will be making changes to source code files and then recompiling your program to see how it runs. If you have a very large program made up of many source code files, it would be very inefficient to recompile all of them if you only made changes to just a few of them. Those to which you made no changes do not need to be recompiled, just linked. You can direct the **gcc** utility to do just that, by mixing source code files and object code files as arguments on the command line. Source code files have a **.c** extension, and object code files have a **.o** extension. **gcc** will compile the source code files you specified on the command line, but will only use the object code files with the linker. This has the advantage of being able to compile only those files where changes have been made. If changes were made in **main.c**, but not in **io.c**, **io.c** would not have to be compiled. You would then specify the source code file **main.c** and the object code file **io.o** on the command line. In the next example, **io.o** will not be compiled, whereas **main.c** will be compiled.

```
$ gcc main.c io.o -o bookrecs
```

ELF and a.out Binary Formats

There are two possible formats for binary files such as executable programs. The first is the a.out format that is the original format used on Unix systems as well as early Linux systems. The term a.out comes from the default name given to an executable file by the Unix C compiler. As shared libraries came into use, difficulties arose with the a.out format. Adapting an a.out format for use as a shared library is a very complex operation. For this reason, a new format was introduced for Unix System 5 release 4 and for Solaris. It is called the Executable and Linking Format (ELF). Its design allowed for the easy implementation of shared libraries.

The ELF format has been adopted as the standard format for Linux systems. All binaries generated by the gcc compiler are in ELF format (even though the default name for the executable file is still a.out). Older programs that may still be in the a.out format will still run on a system supporting ELF.

C++ and Objective C: g++

The **gcc** utility is also a C++ compiler. It can read and compile any C++ program. However, it will not automatically link with the C++ Class library. You would have to invoke it on the command line. Alternatively, you can use the command **g++**, which invokes the gcc compiler with the C++ Class library.

C++ source code files have a different extension than regular C files. Several different extensions are recognized for C++: C, cc, cxx, or cpp. Other than this difference, you compile C++ programs just as you would C programs. Instead of **gcc**, it is preferable to use the **g++** command. The following example compiles a C++ program **myprog.cpp**.

```
$ g++  myprog.cpp  -o myprog
```

The gcc compiler also supports Objective-C programs. Objective-C is an object-oriented version of C originally developed for NeXt systems. To compile a program in Objective-C, you use the **gcc** command with the **-lobjc** option. **-lobjc** links to the Objective-C library, **libobjc.so**.

Other Compilers: Pascal, ADA, Lisp, and Fortran

A great many programming languages are supported on your Linux system. Many are available on your OpenLinux CD-ROM. In addition to C and C++, you can compile Pascal, ADA, Lisp, Basic, and Fortran programs. In several cases, the compiling is handled by the gcc compiler, which is designed to recognize source code files for other programming languages. For example, G77 is the GNU Fortran compiler. This compiler is integrated with the gcc compiler. The command **g77** will compile a Fortran program by invoking the gcc compiler with options to recognize Fortran code, using the G77 features of gcc. The ADA 95 compiler is called **gnat**. The info file on ADA provides detailed information on **gnat**. You can compile an ADA program using the command **gnatmake** with the file name.

Creating and Using Libraries: Static, Shared, and Dynamic

There are usually functions in a C program that rarely need to be compiled. There may also be functions that you may want to use in different programs. Often, such functions perform standardized tasks such as database input/output operations or screen manipulation. You can precompile such functions and place them together in a special type of object code file called a library. The functions in such a library file can be combined with a program by the linker. They save you the trouble of having to recompile these functions for each program you develop.

Different types of applications make use of specialized libraries that are placed in system directories and made available for use in developing programs. For example, there is a library, libdbm, that contains dbm functions for implementing database access to files. You can use these functions in your own programs by linking to that library. Mathematical applications would use the math library, libm, and X-Windows applications would use the Xlib library, libX11. All programs make use of the standard C library, libc, that contains functions to perform tasks such as memory management and I/O operations (A new version of the GNU libc library, 2.0, will soon be available.)

These libraries are placed within system directories such as **/usr/lib**, where they can be accessed by anyone on the system. You can also create your own library just for use with your own particular program, or make one that you would want accessed by others.

Libraries can be either static, shared, or dynamic. A static library is one whose code is incorporated into the program when it is compiled. A shared library, however, has its code loaded for access whenever the program is run. When compiled, such a program simply notes the libraries it needs. Then, when run, that library is loaded and the program can access its functions. A dynamic library is a variation on a shared library. Like a shared library, it can be loaded when the program is run. However, it does not actually load until instructions in the program tell it to. It can also be unloaded as the program runs, and another could be loaded in its place. Shared and dynamic libraries make for much smaller code. Instead of a program including the library as part of its executable file, it only needs a reference to it.

Most libraries currently developed are shared libraries. Shared libraries were made feasible by the implementation of the ELF binary format, though there is an older a.out format for shared (tagged) libraries. ELF is currently the standard format used for all binary files in Linux.

The GNU libraries are made available under a Library GNU Public License (LGPL). The conditions of this license differ from the standard GNU license in that you are free to charge for programs developed using these libraries. However, you do have to make available the source code for those libraries you used.

Libraries made available on your system reside in the **/usr/lib** and **/lib** directories. The names of these libraries always begin with the prefix **lib** followed by the library name and a suffix. The suffix differs, depending on whether it is a static or shared library. A shared library has the suffix **.so** followed by major and minor version numbers. A static library simply has an **.a** extension. A further distinction is made for shared libraries in the old a.out format. These have the extension **.sa**.

```
libname.so.major.minor
libname.a
```

The *name* can be any string, and uniquely identifies a library. It can be a word, a few characters, or even a single letter. The name of the shared math library is **libm.so.5**, where the math library is uniquely identified by the letter **m** and the major version is 5. **libm.a** is the static math library. The name of the X-Windows library is **libX11.so.6**, where the X-Windows library is uniquely identified with the letters **X11** and its major version is 6.

You can link libraries to your programs using the gcc compiler. For example, the libc.so.5 library contains the standard I/O functions. This library is automatically searched and linked whenever the linker generates an executable file. The standard I/O library contains numerous functions that include input/output operations such as **printf**. There are other system libraries that you can access, such as the math library.

Though the libc.so.5 library is automatically linked, most other system libraries need to be explicitly referenced on the command line.

Most shared libraries are found in the **/usr/lib** and **/lib** directories. These will always be searched first. Some shared libraries are located in special directories of their own. A listing of these are placed in the **/etc/ld.conf** configuration file. These directories will be searched also for a given library. By default, Linux will first look for shared libraries, then static ones. Whenever a shared library is updated or a new one installed, you need to run the **ldconfig** command to update its entries in the **/etc/ld.conf** file as well as links to it (if you install from an RPM package, this is usually done for you, though not always).

To reference a library file in one of these searchable directories when you invoke the **gcc** compiler, you use the **-l** option followed by the unique part of a system library's name: **-l***name*. To instruct the linker to use the standard math library, you enter **-lm** on the **gcc** command line. **-l** will look first for the **lib***name*.**so** file, in this case, **libm.so**. This is a link to the actual library file. In the next example, the bookrecs program is created and linked to the math library. Notice the **-lm** option.

```
$ gcc main.c io.c -o bookrecs -lm
```

There are many different libraries currently available for your use. One of the more popular is the **libncurses.a** library, which contains simple cursor movement routines. You would reference the **libncurses.so** library on the command line with **-lncurses**. In the next example, the user invokes both the math and curses libraries.

```
$ gcc main.c io.c -o bookrecs -lm -lncurses
```

To reference a library in another directory, you have to specify that directory using the **-L***dir* option. This option adds the specified directory to the list of directories that will be searched with the **-l** option. In the following example, the user links to a library in the **mydir** directory called **myio.so**. For a shared library, you will first have to have the dl and ld link names set up, such as **libmyio.so** and **libmyio.so.1** for a **libmyio.so.1.0** file (see the next section).

```
$ gcc main.c -o bookrecs -Lmydir -lmyio
```

The gdb Symbolic Debugger

gdb is the symbolic debugger available on your Linux system. If you run your program and it crashes for some reason, you can use a symbolic debugger to track down the error. A symbolic debugger allows you to step through your program line by line, displaying the source code for each line as you execute it. You can decide to stop in specific functions and display the contents of active variables. You can even check specific addresses and the contents of the stack.

To be able to use an executable file with a symbolic debugger, you need to compile and link your program using the **-g** option. In the next example, a program is compiled and prepared for the symbolic debuggers. Once you have a prepared executable file, you can then use it with the symbolic debugger.

```
$ gcc -g main.c io.c
```

You invoke the gdb debugger with the keyword **gdb** and the name of the executable file. In the next example, the name of the executable file is **a.out**.

```
$ gdb a.out
```

The **gdb** command will place you in the debugger, replacing the Linux prompt ($), with the gdb prompt (gdb). You run your program in the debugger by typing at the prompt the command **run**:

```
(gdb) run
```

If your program has in it an **fopen** or **open** statement, it means it will be using a data file at some point in the program. If this is so, then gdb needs to also know the name of such a data file. When you type **run in gdb** to run your program, you must also supply the actual name of such data files.

```
(gdb) run filename
```

When you are finished, leave the debugger with the quit command, **q** or **quit**.

```
(gdb) quit
```

Most **gdb** commands have a single-letter equivalent consisting of the first letter of the command. Instead of entering the command **run**, you can enter just **r**. For **quit**, you can enter the letter **q**, for **print** just **p**, and for **next** the letter **n**. The gdb commands are listed in Table 23-2.

You display the contents of a variable using the **print** command. Enter the word **print** followed by the variable name. In the next example, the user displays the contents of the count variable.

```
(gdb) print count
10
```

With the **where** command, you can display the function names and arguments of the functions that have been called at any point in your program. In the next example, the user is currently in the calc function. Entering the **where** command displays the functions main, as well as calc and its arguments.

```
(gdb) where
#3   calc(newcost = 2.0) at calc.c:25
#1   main () at main.c:19
#2   0x8000455 in ___crt_dummy__ ()
```

You can obtain a listing of all the variables and arguments defined in a function. The **info locals** command will display variable and argument values currently defined. In the next example, the user displays the defined variables.

```
(gdb) info locals
cost = 2
name = "Richard\000\000"
count = 10
count2 = 10
nameptr = 0x8000570 "petersen"
countptr = (int *) 0xbffffde8
```

You can set breakpoints in your program using the **break** command. When you reach a breakpoint your program will stop. You can then step through your program line by line using the **next** or **step** commands. When you wish, you can advance to the next breakpoint by using the **cont** command.

xxgdb

xxgdb provides an easy-to-use X-Windows access to the gdb debugger. xxgdb is organized into a set of vertically positioned subwindows. Initially five subwindows are displayed. A top subwindow, called the file window, has the name of the file currently being displayed. The next subwindow displays the program's source code file and is called the source window. A scroll bar to the left allows you to scroll through the text. Below that is the message window for displaying gdb status and error messages. The bottom subwindow, called the dialog window, is used for entering gdb commands and displaying their results. A scroll bar to the left allows you to view previous commands and their results. Above it is the command window. This is a subwindow that lists a series of buttons for different gdb commands. To execute a command such as **run** or **step**, just click on that button. You can horizontally change the size of any window using the small squares located to the right on the dividers between subwindows.

Programming Tools

There are many tools available that help you prepare and organize your source code. The **indent** utility will indent the braces used for blocks in a consistent format, making the code easier to read. **cproto** generates a list of function declarations for all your defined functions for use in header files. **f2c** and **p2c** can translate Fortran and Pascal programs into C programs. **xwpe** is an X-Windows programming environment similar to Turbo C. Many more tools are available. You can find links to them on the Linux Applications and Utilities page under Development (see the Linux Resources Web Pages table at the end of Chapter 3).

Once you have finished developing your software, you may then want to distribute it to others. Ordinarily, you would pack your program into a tar archive file. People would then download the file and unpack it. You would have to have included detailed instructions on how to install it and where to place any supporting documentation and libraries. If you were distributing the source code, users would have to figure out how to adapt the source code to their systems. There are any number of variations that may stop compilation of a program.

The Redhat Package Manager (RPM) and Autoconf are designed to automate these tasks. Autoconf is used to automatically configure source code to a given system. The Redhat Package Manager will automatically install software on a system in the designated directories, along with any documentation, libraries, or support programs. Both have very complex and powerful capabilities, able to handle the most complex programs. Several Linux distributions like Redhat and Caldera support RPM packages.

Development Tools

An application is an executable program created by a programmer using one of several programming languages. Linux provides several utilities with which a programmer can control development of an application. Foremost among these is the **make** utility. The **make** utility interfaces with the Linux operating system to provide an easy way to maintain and compile programs. The **RCS** utility allows you to better control program changes. It organizes changes into different versions that can be stored and later accessed. You can even use the **man** utility to create your own online documentation for your applications. All of these utilities are complex and powerful tools.

The make Utility

You will often be working with a program that has many source code files. As you develop the program, making modifications, you will need to compile the program over and over again. However, you need only compile those source code files in which you made changes. The linker then links the newly generated object code files with previously compiled object code files, creating a new executable file. The fact that only a few of your source files are actually compiled drastically cuts down on the work of the compiler. Each time you need a new executable program, you do not need to recompile each source code file.

It can be very difficult in large programs with many source code files to keep track of which files have been changed and need to be compiled, and which files need only to be linked. The **make** utility will do this for you. **make** was designed for a development environment in which different source code files in a program are constantly being modified. **make** keeps track of which source files have been changed and which have not. It then recompiles only those that have been changed, linking them with the rest of the object code files to create a new executable file. In the next example, the user enters the command **make** on the command line to invoke the **make** utility. **make** then compiles those files that have recently been modified and creates a new executable file. **make** displays each Linux command it executes.

```
$ make
cc -c main.c
cc -c io.c
cc main.o io.o
```

To understand how the **make** utility works, you need to realize that it uses a source code file's time stamp to determine whether or not it should be compiled. Whenever a file is created, re-created, or modified in any way, a new time stamp is placed on it by the Linux operating system. If you create a file at 1:00, that file is stamped with the time 1:00. If you then change the file at 6:00, the file is re-stamped with the time 6:00. When compiling a program, only those source code files that have been changed need to be recompiled. Since the change of any file changes the time stamp, the time stamp can be used to determine which files need to be compiled. In this way, **make** knows which files need to be compiled and actually selects the files to be compiled for the programmer.

A dependency line specifies a dependency relationship between files. **make** operates in terms of dependencies. A source code file is used to create an object code file, which in turn is used to create a runnable program. The program can be said to be dependent on the object code file, which in turn is dependent on the source code file. You need to specify the dependency relationship between a source code file and an object code file in a dependency line. In another dependency line, you need to specify the dependency relationship between an executable file and all its object code files.

A dependency line can be thought of as a kind of conditional statement. The dependency relationship is its test condition. If an object code file depends on a source code file and the source code file has been recently modified, then the test condition is true and the file is then recompiled. However, the syntax for a dependency line is a bit more complex than a standard conditional statement. A dependency line consists of three components: a target file, a list of dependency files, and a Linux command. If any of the dependency files has been modified more recently than the target file, then the Linux command is executed. The target file and the dependent files are written on the same line, separated by a colon. You can either place the Linux command on the same line, separated from the dependent files by a semicolon, or you can place the Linux command on the next line preceded by a tab. You can list more than one Linux command if you wish. When entered on the same line you separate Linux commands with semicolons. On separate lines, each Linux command has to be preceded by a tab. The dependency line ends with a following empty line. In these examples, the Linux command is an invocation of the cc compiler, compiling a source code file or linking object code files. The syntax for a dependency line is as follows:

```
target file : dependent files ; Linux command
empty line

target file : dependent files
tab     Linux command
empty line
```

In the following **makefile**, we construct the dependency lines for a C program consisting of two source code files: **main.c** and **io.c**. In such a two-file program, there are really five files to manage. For each **.c** file there is a corresponding **.o** file. There is the executable file, **bookrecs**. You need to set up your **makefile** with dependency lines to manage all of these files, specifying dependencies for each. An object code file (**.o**) is dependent on a source code (**.c**) file. An executable file, **bookrecs**, is dependent on several object code files. In this example, **bookrecs** is dependent on (made up of) the two object code files **main.o** and **io.o**. Each object code file is, in turn, dependent on their respective source code files; **main.o** on **main.c** , and **io.o** on **io.c**.

In the **makefile**, three dependency lines are needed for the **bookrecs**, **main.o**, and **io.o** files, respectively. Notice that the linking and compilation of the program are split up among the different dependency lines. The Linux command for the **bookrecs** target only links the two object code files, creating a new executable file. It invokes **gcc** with only object code files, causing only the linker to be invoked. The Linux commands for the **main.o** and **io.o** targets only compile, creating **.o** object files. The **–c** option used with **gcc** means that no linking is done, only compilation, generating the object code file for this source code file.

makefile

```
bookrecs : main.o io.o
gcc main.o io.o-o bookrecs

main.o : main.c
gcc -c main.c

io.o : io.c
gcc -c io.c
```

The Revision Control System: RCS

When you work on a major project, you are continually changing source code. You may detect bugs or you may add other features. Sometimes changes may unintentionally result in new bugs. A record of all the changes to your program may help you track down bugs and any possible design errors. The Revision Control System (RCS) is a Linux utility that keeps track of all changes that you have made to a program. In effect, RCS provides you with a set of prior versions for your program. You can view each version and examine the changes made for each.

RCS is very helpful in a situation in which a team of programmers is working on the same program. Each programmer may make changes to the program at different times. RCS can record each change a programmer makes and when it was made. It can even include notes about a change.

RCS stores an original version of a file and then records all changes to the file. Using this information it can generate any one of several possible versions of a file. RCS does not actually store separate full versions of a file. Instead, it uses the change information and the original file to create a full version of the file. The commands that manage RCS files are listed in Table 23-3.

A set of recorded changes to a file is called a version. Each version is assigned a version number that has several components, the first two of which are the release and level numbers. By default, the first version is assigned a release number of 1 and a level number of 1. A version is often referred to by its release and level numbers. The first version is called version 1.1 or delta 1.1. Subsequent versions will have the same release number with an incremented level number. The next version will be 1.2, then 1.3, etc. You can also change the release number manually.

To create an RCS file, you first create an RCS directory. Within this directory are placed the RCS files for your programs. You can then create an RCS file with the **ci** command. The **ci** command takes one argument, the name of the original file. The RCS file will be created in the RCS directory with the extension **,v**. A **main.c** file will have an RCS file called **main.c,v** in the RCS directory. If your program is initially made up of several source code files, you need to create an RCS file for each one, including its source code suffix. In the next example, the user creates an RCS file for the **main.c** program.

```
$ ci main.c
RCS/main.c,v  <-- main.c
enter description, terminated with single '.' or end of file:
NOTE: This is NOT the log message!
>> Bookrecs main program
>> .
initial revision: 1.1
done
```

To edit your source code file using RCS, you must first have RCS generate a copy of the source code file. This copy will have the same name as the RCS file, but without the **,v** suffix. For the **main.c,v** file, RCS will generate a file called **main.c**. To save the copy once you have made changes, you simply register any changes you make to the RCS file.

The RCS **co** command generates a copy of the source code file. The **co** command has several options. The **co** command with no options simply generates a read-only copy of the source code file. The **–l** option generates a copy of the source code file that you can edit. **–l** stands for lock, and when you use this option, the main.c program in the **RCS main.c,v** file is locked. No other programmers with access can access it. This means that only one programmer at a time can change a given file. When finished, you check in the program, registering your changes and unlocking it for use by others. In the next example, the **co** command generates an editable copy of the source code file **main.c,v**.

```
$ co -l main.c
RCS/main.c,v  -->  main.c
revision 1.1 (locked)
done
```

Once you have finished editing your source code file, you then register your changes in the RCS file with the **ci** command. You enter the keyword **ci** followed by the name of the RCS file. You are then prompted to enter comments. In effect, editing a copy of the file generated with **co** creates a new version of the source code file, a new set of changes constituting a new version. The new version number (1.2) is displayed. In the next example, the user saves the changes to **main.c** by generating a new version, 1.2.

```
$ ci main.c
RCS/main.c,v  <--  main.c
new revision: 1.2; previous revision: 1.1
enter log message, terminated with single '.' or end of file:
>> Added prompts
>> .
done
```

Online Manuals for Applications: man

As you develop a program for use on Linux, you may need to document it. If it is a large application worked on by several programmers at once, documentation may become essential. Documentation often takes the form of a manual describing different commands and features of a program. Many times an application is broken down into separate programs. It is very helpful to both users and program developers to be able to retrieve and display appropriate sections of an application's manual. Such an online manual provides instant access to documentation by all users and developers. In Chapter 3, you have already seen how you can use the **man** command to display information about Linux commands. The **man** command provides access to an online manual for Linux commands. You can also use the **man** command to manage your own online manual for your own applications. You can create **man** documents using special **man** text processing macros. You can then instruct the **man** command to read these documents.

One of the more common uses today of gnroff is the creation of online manual documents. The online manual that you find on your Linux system is actually a gnroff document. You use a set of macros called the **man** macros to create your own online manual entries. If you create a new command and want to document it, you can create a manual document for it and read this document with the **man** command.

When you call the **man** command with the name of a document, the **man** command uses gnroff to format the document and then display it. The actual document that you create is an unformatted text file with the appropriate **man** macros. The **man** macros are very similar to the **ms** macros. You can actually format and display a manual document directly by using the **gnroff** command with the **-man** option. In the next example, both commands display the manual document for the **ls** command.

```
$ man ls
$ gnroff -man /usr/man/man1/ls | more
```

man Document Files

You can create a **man** document file using any standard text editor. The name that you give to the text file is the name of the command or topic it is about with a section number as an extension. The name of a document about the **who** command would be called **who.1**. In the example described here, the document is about the **bookrec** command and has a section number **1**. Its name is **bookrec.1**. Section numbers are discussed in the nest section on **man** directories.

A man document is organized into sections with a running title at the top. The sections may be named anything you wish. By convention, a man document for Linux commands is organized into several predetermined sections such as NAME, SYNOPSIS, and DESCRIPTION. You are, however, free to have as many sections as you want and to give them names of your own choosing. The actual document that you create is an unformatted text file with the appropriate **man** macros. A manual document requires at least two different **man** macros: **TH** and **SH**. **TH** provides a running title that will be displayed at the top of each page displayed for the document as well as the document's section number. You use the **SH** macro for each section heading. You can add other macros as you need them, such as a **PP** macro for paragraph formatting or an **IP** macro for indented paragraphs. The **man** macros are listed in Table 23-4.

You enter a macro in your document at the beginning of a line and preceded by a period. Any text that you enter in the lines after the macro will be formatted by it. A macro stays in effect until another macro is reached. Some macros, like **SH** and **TH**, take arguments. You enter in arguments after the macro on the same line. The **SH** macro takes as its argument the name of a section. You enter the section name on the same line as the **SH** macro. The body of the section then follows. The body of the section text is entered in as a series of short lines. These lines will later be formatted by man into a justified paragraph. In the next example, the user enters in the **SH** macro and follows it with the section name DESCRIPTION. In the following lines, the user enters in the text of the section.

```
.SH DESCRIPTION
mylistopt provides alternative ways
of displaying your grocery list.
You can display it with numbers
the list in a file.
```

Your man document is organized into a series of section heading macros with their names and text. The following template gives you an idea of how to organize your man document. It is the organization usually followed by the online manual for Linux commands.

```
.TH COMMAND    Section -number

.SH NAME
command and brief description of function
.SH SYNOPSIS
command and options.  Each option is encased in brackets.  This
section is sometimes called the SYNTAX.
.SH DESCRIPTION
 Detailed description of command and options.  Use paragraph
macros for new paragraphs: PP, LP, and IP
.SH OPTIONS
 Options used for the command
.SH EXAMPLES
 Examples of how a command is used
.SH FILE
 File used by the command
.SH "SEE ALSO"
 References to other documentation or manual documents
.SH DIAGNOSTICS
 Description of any unusual output.
.SH WARNINGS
 Warning about possible dangerous uses of the command
.SH BUGS
 Surprising features and bugs.
```

Within the text of a section, you can add other macros to perform specific text processing operations. You enter in these macros on a line by themselves. Some will also take arguments. The **.PP** macro starts a new paragraph. The **.IP** macro starts an indented paragraph and is usually used to display options. You enter in the option as an argument to the **.IP** macro and then the following text is indented from it. The **.I** macro underlines text. The **.B** macro will boldface text. Both the **.B** macro and **.I** macro take as their argument the word you want to boldface or underline. By convention, the command name and options in the NAME section are set in boldface with the **.B** macro. Any other use of command names is usually underlined with the **.I** macro. One final note. If you use any hyphens, you need to quote them with a backslash.

In the next example, the user creates an online document for the bookrec program described earlier. Notice how the text is formatted into justified paragraphs. The options are displayed using indented paragraphs specified by the **.IP** macro.

bookrec.1—man document file   man output

```
.TH  BOOKREC  1
.SH NAME
bookrec  \-Input and display a book record
.SH SYNOPSIS
.B bookrec
[ \-t ] [ \-p] [ \-f]
.SH DESCRIPTION
.I  bookrec
allows the user to input a title and price
for a book.  Then both elements
of the record are displayed
.SH  OPTIONS
.IP t
Display only the title
.IP p
Display only the price.
.IP f
Save the record to a file
.SH DIAGNOSTICS
 Date output has the form of m/d/y.
.SH BUGS
 The program can only read and display one record.
.br
 It does not as yet allow you to read records from a file.
.SH FILES
 The command uses no special files.
.SH "SEE ALSO"
```

The **man** utility looks for a particular manual document in a system directory set aside for manual documents such as **/usr/man**. The **/usr/man** directory itself does not contain manual documents. Rather, it contains subdirectories called section directories, which in turn contain the documents. The name of a section directory begins with the word **man** and ends with the section number. **man1** is the name of the first section directory in a manual. There are usually about seven section directories, beginning with **man1** and ending with **man7**. In your own manual directory, you can have as many or as few section directories as you want, though you always have to have a **man1** directory.

Section directories allow you to create several documents of varying complexity and subject matter for the same command or topic. For example, the document in section 1 for the **man** command gives only a general description, whereas the document in section 7 for the **man** command lists all the **man** macros. These documents are identified by section numbers and reside in the appropriate section directory. The section number of a document, as noted previously, is entered in as an argument to the **.TH** macro. To retrieve an online document from a particular section, enter in the section number before the command name. The next example displays the document on the **bookrec** command that is in the third section directory. If you enter no section number, the first section is assumed.

```
$ man 3 bookrec
```

gcc	The **gcc** utility creates an executable program using a preprocessor, compiler, assembler, and a linker. The preprocessor executes preprocessing commands found in the source code file. Such commands perform simple text substitutions. The compiler compiles a source code file into assembly code. The assembler then compiles assembly code files into object code files. The linker then links object code files into an executable file. **gcc** takes as possible arguments source code, object code, and assembly code files as well as several options. **gcc** recognizes a file by its extension: .c C source code files .o Object code files .s Assembly code files .C C++ files .cpp C++ files
Options	
-S	Output only assembly code. Assembly code versions of compiled files have the extension **.s**; the example will generate a file called **greet.s**
-P	Output result of preprocessor
-c	Create object code file only; object code versions of compiled files have the extension **.o**
-g	Prepare compiled program for use with symbolic debugger
-o filename	Name executable file name; default is **a.out**

Table 23-1.   *The gcc Utility For The C Compiler*

-O	Optimize compilation
-lfilename	Link system library by name of file name; the file name is preceded by lib and has an extension of **.a**; neither is included on the **cc** command line; the **-l** options must always be placed after source code and object code file names on the command line

Table 23-1. *The gcc Utility For The C Compiler* (continued)

Running Programs in gdb

r	**run**	Run the program
q	**quit**	Quit gdb

Displaying Variables and Arguments

p *var*	**print** *var*	Display the contents of a variable
p &*var*	**print &***var*	Display the address of a variable
set var = *value*		Assign a value to a variable during the gdb session
where		Display a stack trace showing sequence of function calls with function names and their arguments
	info locals	Display defined variables and arguments

Displaying Lines

1 *linenum*	**list** *linenum*	Display lines beginning with the specified line number

Table 23-2. *The gdb Symbolic Debugger*

1 *func*	**list** *func*	Display lines in a function
1 *num*, *num*	**list** *num*, *num*	Display a range of lines
Stepping and Continuing Execution		
n	**next**	Single-step execution line by line, executing the current line and displaying the next line to be executed
s	**step**	Single-step execution line by line, executing the current line and displaying the next line to be executed
c	**cont**	Continue execution of the program
Setting and Deleting Breakpoints		
b	**break**	Set breakpoint at current line
	break *line*	Set breakpoint at specified line
	break *func*	Set breakpoint at first line in the specified function
	info break	List all breakpoints
d *num*	**delete** *num*	Delete breakpoints. You need to specify the number of the breakpoint
	delete	Delete all breakpoints

Table 23-2. *The gdb Symbolic Debugger* (continued)

RCS	The Revision Control System (RCS) allows you to control the development of a program; with RCS, you can establish different versions of your program as you make changes; you can later retrieve different versions or obtain a record of how your program developed; an RCS file is created with the **ci** command and managed with the **rcs** command; versions are retrieved with the **co** command, and versions are erased with the **rcs -o** command
ci	The **ci** command updates an RCS file, creating new versions; if the RCS file does not already exist, **ci** will create it using the extension **,v**; you usually use **ci** to save an edited copy of a file that you previously retrieved using **co** with the **-1** option; saving this edited copy will create a new version for the file within the RCS file $ **ci main.c**

Options

-r*version*	This option will allow you to specify the release and version number you want to begin with when creating a new version $ **ci -r5.2 main.c**
co	The **co** command retrieves a version of an RCS file; with no option, it retrieves a read-only version; if no version number is specified, then the most recent version is retrieved

Options

-1	This option will retrieve an editable version of an RCS file, locking the file to prevent others from changing it; the file remains locked until you use **ci** to check it back in $ **co -e main.c**
rcs	The **rcs** command manages RCS files and can be used to control access to an RCS file by other users

Options

-a*user-name*	This option will add user-name to the list of users that can access a specified RCS file $ **res -arobert main.c**

Table 23-3.   *The RCS Utility*

	-e*user-name*	This option will remove user-name from the list of users that can access a specified RCS file $ res -erobert main.c
	-l*release*	This option will lock a specific release for everyone but the creator of the file $ res -12 main.c
	-u*release*	This option will unlock a specific release $ res -u2 main.c
	-L*release*	This option will lock a specific release for everyone, including the creator of the file $ res -L2 main.c
	-U*release*	This option will unlock a specific release for everyone, including the creator of the file $ res -U2 main.c
	-o*release*	This option will delete a version from an RCS file $ res -o2.3 main.c
rlog		The **rlog** command outputs information about the different releases and versions in a RCS file; without an argument, it outputs summary information for each version
	Options	
	-r*version*	This option will output information about a specific version $ rlog -r2 main.c
	-d*date*	This option will output information about versions created on a specified date; the format for the date is year, month, day separated by slashes, and hour, minute, second separated by colons; all except the year are optional $ rlog -d93/04/12 main.c
	-d<	Followed by a less-than sign, this option will output information that is earlier than a specified date $ rlog -d>93/04/12 main.c

Table 23-3.   *The RCS Utility (continued)*

-d<	Preceded by a greater-than sign, this option will output information that is later than a specified date **$ rlog ->d93/04/12 main.c**

Table 23-3. *The RCS Utility (continued)*

`man`	The manual command can search and display online manual documents; you can create your own online manual documents and instruct man to search for them; the **man** command searches for documents in section directories specified by the word man followed by a section number, man1; when you create your own manual directories, be sure to include section directories
`man` *command-name*	Search for and display online manual documents **$ man who**
MANPATH	Shell special variable that holds the directory path name the **man** command automatically searches; you can add new path names with an assignment operation **$ MANPATH=$MANPATH:/$HOME/man**
Options	
num	Search only specified section for a manual document **$ man 3 bookrec**
-M *directory-name*	Search only specified directory for manual documents **$ man -M $HOME/man bookrec**
The man Macros	
.TH *title sec-num*	Used to enter running title of the online document
.SH *section-name*	Used to enter section headings
.B *word*	Used to boldface words such as command names
.I *word*	Used to underline word
.IP *option*	Formats indented paragraph. Used to enter in options in the OPTIONS section
.PP	Formats paragraph. Starts a new paragraph

Table 23-4. `man` *Command and Macros for Creating Online Documents*

Chapter Twenty-Four

Perl

917

The Practical Extraction and Report Language (Perl) is a scripting language that has all the capabilities of awk and sed, but with many more features. Perl was originally designed to operate on files like awk and sed do, generating reports and handling very large files. However, Perl was designed as a core program to which features could be easily added. Over the years, Perl's capabilities have been greatly enhanced. It can now control network connections, process interaction, and even support a variety of database management files. At the same time, Perl remains completely portable. A Perl script will run on any Unix system, as well as most other operating systems such as Windows and Mac. Perl is also used extensively for implementing CGI scripts on Web sites.

Your CD-ROM contains both Perl5 and Perl4 versions of Perl. Perl4 is included for computability with older Perl programs. There are extensive and detailed man pages on Perl, discussing all aspects of the language with a great many examples. The man pages begin with the term perl; for example, perlfunc discusses the built-in Perl functions and perlsyn describes the different control structures.

There are extensive Internet resources for Perl. On the Perl Web site at **www.perl.com**, you can access documentation, software, newsgroups, and support. Specialized Perl Web sites focus on programming, conferences, and reference resources. The Comprehensive Perl Archive Network (CPAN) maintains ftp sites that hold an extensive collection of utilities, modules, documentation, and current Perl distributions. You can also link to a CPAN site through the Perl Web site. Several of the Perl Web sites are listed here:

- **www.perl.com**
- **language.perl.com**
- **reference.perl.com**
- **conference.perl.com**
- **republic.perl.com**
- **www.perl.com/CPAN/CPAN.html**
- **www.cis.ufl.edu/Perl**

The **language.perl.com** site focuses on programming. Through it, you can access detailed FAQ's on topics such as CGI, modules, and security. You can also access software archives and more detailed documentation. The **reference.perl.com** site lets you access resources by topic, such as networking, CGI, and graphics. The **conference.perl.com** provides interactive conferences as well as text of previous conferences. The **republic.perl.com** lets you join the Programming Republic of Perl.

There are several Usenet newsgroups that discuss different Perl issues. You can use them to post questions and check out current issues. Here is a listing of the current newsgroups:

- comp.lang.perl.announce
- comp.lang.perl.misc
- comp.lang.perl.modules
- comp.lang.perl.tk
- comp.infosystems.www.authoring.cgi

Perl Command Line Operations

You can execute any Perl command from the shell command line by using the command **perl** with the **-e** option. The Perl command you want to execute should then be entered and quoted within single quotes. The following Perl operation prints the string "hello" using the Perl **print** command. The command ends with a semicolon.

```
perl -e  'print "hello";'
```

You can use Perl this way for simple operations, much as you would single-line gawk commands. Perl will not read input from the standard input unless you explicitly instruct it to with a while loop. Unlike gawk, it does not read the standard input by default. The following example searches for the pattern "Dickens." The file **books** is first read by the **cat** command and piped to the **perl** command as standard input.

```
cat books | perl -e 'while(<STDIN>){ if(/Dickens/){ print; }}'
```

The following **gawk** command is equivalent:

```
cat books | gawk '/Dickens/ {print}'
```

This command line use of Perl is rarely used. Normally, Perl commands are placed in script files that are then executed, much like shell scripts.

Perl Scripts

Usually, Perl commands are placed in a file that is then read and executed by the **perl** command. In effect, you are creating a shell in which your Perl commands are executed. Files containing Perl commands must have the extension **.pl**. This identifies that file as Perl script that can be read by the **perl** command. There are two ways that you can use the **perl** command to read Perl scripts. You can enter the **perl** command on the shell command line, followed by the name of the Perl script. Perl will read and execute the commands. The following example executes a Perl script called **hello.pl**:

```
$ perl hello.pl
```

You can also include the invocation of the **perl** command within the Perl script file, much as you would for a shell script. Place the following shell instruction on the first line of your file. This automatically invokes the Perl shell and will execute the following Perl commands in the script. **/usr/bin/perl** is the location of the **perl** command on the OpenLinux system. On other systems, it could be located in the **/usr/local/bin** directory. The command **which perl** will return the location of Perl on your system.

```
#!/usr/bin/perl
```

Then, to make the script executable, you would have to set its permissions to be executable. The **chmod** command with the **755** option sets executable permissions for a file, turning it into a program that can be run on the command line. You only have to do this once per script. You do not have to do this if you use the **perl** command on the command line, as noted previously. The following example sets the executable permissions for the **hello.pl script**.

```
$ chmod 755 hello.pl
```

Perl has many similarities to gawk and to the C programming language. Like C, Perl commands end with a semicolon. As in gawk, there is a **print** command for outputting text. Perl also uses the same escape sequence character to output newlines, **\n**, and tabs, **\t** (see Table 24-1). Comments, as in the shell and gawk, are lines that begin with a **#**. The following is an example of a Perl script. It prints out the word "hello" and a newline. Notice the invocation of the **perl** command on the first line.

helloprg

```
#!/usr/bin/perl

print "hello \n";
```

```
$ helloprg
hello
```

Though Perl is an interpreted language, the entire Perl script is first validated before it is executed, checking for errors ahead of time. Should there be any, they will be displayed on your screen, specifying line numbers and error messages. Many of the error messages can be obscure. The following are some of the more common errors.

- One of the more common errors is failing to enter semicolons at the end of a line. Perl commands look a lot like shell and gawk commands, which do not take semicolons, so it is easy to forget them.

- Control structures must have blocks; they cannot have just a single command, as is the case in C.

- Variables must always be prefixed with a **$** symbol. This is very different from gawk and C.

Parts of a Perl program can be split into separate files and then read into a main file with the **use** command. Such files end with the extension **.pm** and are referred to as either packages or modules. Often, they contain enhanced operations for tasks such as file handling or text searches. A standard set of Perl modules and packages are located in the **/usr/lib/perl5** directory. The perlmod man page has a detailed discussion of Perl packages and modules, including dynamically loaded modules. The following command reads in the **find.pm** package that provides a Perl version of the shell **find** command for searching directories:

```
use /usr/lib/perl5/File/find.pm ;
```

Perl Input and Output: <> and print

A Perl script can accept input from many different sources. It can read input from different files, from the standard input, and even from pipes. Because of this, you have to identify the source of your input within the program. This means that, unlike gawk but like a shell program, you have to explicitly instruct a Perl script to read input. A particular source of input is identified by a file handle, a name used by programs to reference an input source such as a particular file. Perl already sets up a file handle for the standard input and the standard output, as well as the standard error. The file handle for the standard input is **STDIN**.

The same situation applies to output. Perl can output to many different destinations, whether they be files, pipes, or the standard output. File handles are used to identify files and pipes when used for either input or output. The file handle

STDOUT identifies the standard output, and **STDERR** is the file handle for the standard error. We shall first examine how Perl uses the standard input and output, and later discuss how particular files are operated on.

Perl can read input from the standard input or from any specified file. The command for reading input consists of the less-than, **<**, and greater-than symbols, **>**. To read from a file, a file handle name is placed between them, **<MYFILE>**. To read from the standard input, you can simply use the **STDIN** file handle, **<STDIN>**. **<STDIN>** is similar to the **read** command in the Bourne shell programming language.

```
<STDIN>
```

Whatever the **<STDIN>** command reads is placed in a special variable named **$_**. You can then use this variable to manipulate whatever has been read. For example, you can use **$_** in a **print** command to display what was input. **$_** is a special variable, much like **$0** in gawk. It is the default for many commands. If the line read by **<STDIN>** is not assigned, it is automatically placed in **$_**. If the **print** command has no argument, it will print the value of **$_**. If the **chomp** command has no argument, it operates on **$_**, cutting off the newline.

myread

```
#!/usr/bin/perl
# Program to read input from the keyboard and then display it.

$_ = <STDIN>;                      #Read data from the standard input
print "This is what I entered: $_";   #Output read data as part of a string
```

```
$ myread
larisa and aleina
This is what I entered: larisa and aleina
```

You can use the **print** command to write data to any file or to the standard output. File handle names are placed after the **print** command and before any data such as strings or variables. If no file handle is specified, then **print** outputs to the standard output. The following examples both write the "hello\n" string to the standard output. The explicit file handle for the standard output is **STDOUT**. If you do not specify an argument, then **print** will output whatever was read from the standard input.

```
print STDOUT "hello\n";
print "hello\n";
```

A null file handle, **<>**, is a special input operation that will read input from a file listed on the command line when the Perl script is invoked. Perl will automatically set up a file handle for it and read. If you list several files on the command line, then Perl will read the contents of all of them using the null file handle. You can think of this as a cat operation in which the contents of the listed files are concatenated and then read into the Perl script.

Perl File Handles

You use the **open** command to create a file handle for a file or pipe. The **open** command takes two arguments, the name of the file handle and the file name string. The name of the file handle is a name you make up. By convention, it is in uppercase. The file name string can be the name of the file or a variable that holds the name of the file. This string can also include different modes for opening a file. By default, a file is opened for reading. But you can also open a file for writing, or for appending, or for both reading a writing. The syntax for **open** follows:

```
open ( file-handle, filename-string);
```

In the next example, the user opens the file reports, calling the file handle for it **REPS**:

```
open (REPS, "reports");
```

Often the file name will be held in a variable. You then use the **$** with the variable name to reference the file name. In this example, the file name "reports" is held in the variable **filen**:

```
filen = "reports";
open (REPS, $filen );
```

To open a file in a specific mode such as writing or appending, you include the appropriate mode symbols in the file name string before the file name, separated by a space. The different mode symbols are listed in Table 24-2. **>** opens a file for writing and **+>** opens a file for both reading and writing. In the next example, the **reports** file is opened for both reading and writing.

```
open (REPS, "+> reports");
```

If you are using a variable to hold the file name, you can include the evaluated variable within the file name string, as shown here:

```
open (REPS, "+> $filen");
```

To read from a file using that file's file handle, you simply place the file handle within the **<** and **>** symbols. **<REPS>** reads a line of input from the **reports** file. In the myreport program, the **reports** file is opened and its contents are displayed.

myreport.pl

```
#!/usr/bin/perl
# Program to read lines from the reports file and display them

    open(REPS, "< reports");        # Open reports file for reading only
    while ( $ldat = <REPS> )        # Read a line from the reports file
      {
      print $ldat;                  # Display recently read line
      }
    close REPS;                     # Close file
```

Perl Variables and Expressions

Perl variables can be numeric or string variables. Their type is determined by context, the way they are used. You do not have to declare them. A variable that is assigned a numeric value and is used in arithmetic operations is a numeric variable. All others are treated as strings. To reference a variable in your program, you precede it with a **$** symbol, just as you would for a shell variable.

You can use the same set of operators with Perl variables as with C variables, with the exception of strings. Strings use the same special comparison terms as used in the Bourne shell, not the standard comparison operators. Those are reserved for numeric variables. However, other operators such as assignment operators work on both string and numeric variables. In the next example, the variable **myname** is assigned the string "Larisa". The assignment operator is the **=** symbol.

```
$myname = "Larisa";
```

For a numeric variable, you can assign a number. This can be either an integer or a floating point value. Perl treats all floating point values as double precision.

```
$mynum = 45;
$price = 54.72;
```

Perl also supports arithmetic expressions. All the standard arithmetic operators found in other programming languages are used in Perl. Expressions can be nested using parentheses. Operands can be numeric constants, numeric variables, or other numeric expressions. In the following examples, **$mynum** is assigned the result of an addition expression. Its value is then used in a complex arithmetic expression whose result is assigned to **$price**.

```
$mynum = 3 + 6;
$price = ( 5 * ($num / 3);
```

Perl supports the full range of assignment operators found in gawk and C. The **++** and **--** operators will increment or decrement a variable. The **+=** and **-=** and their variations will perform the equivalent of updating a variable. For example, **i++** is the same as i = i + 1, and i += 5 is the same as i= i + 5. Increment operations such as **i++** are used extensively with loops.

You can easily include the value of a variable within a string by simply placing the variable within it. In the following example, the value of **$nameinfo** would be the string "My name is Larisa \n":

```
print "The number of items is $mynum \n"
$nameinfo = "My name is $myname \n"
```

To assign data read from a file to a variable, just assign the result of the read operation to the variable. In the next example, data read from the standard input is assigned to the variable **$mydata**:

```
$mydata = <STDIN>;
```

When reading data from the keyboard into a variable, the carriage return character will be included with the input string. You may not want to have this carriage return remain a part of the value of the variable. To remove it, you can use the **chomp** command. **chomp** removes the last character of any string. With data input from the keyboard, this happens to be the carriage return.

```
chomp $myinput;
```

In the next example, the user inputs his or her name. It is assigned to the myname variable. The contents of **myname** is then output as part of a string. **chomp** is used to remove the carriage return from the end of the **$myname** string before it is used as part of another string.

readname.pl

```
#!/usr/bin/perl
$myname = <STDIN>;
chomp $myname;

print "$myname just ran this program\n";
```

```
$ myread.pl
larisa Petersen
larisa Petersen just ran this program
```

Arrays and Lists

In Perl, you create an array by assigning it a list of values. A list in Perl consists of a set of values encased in parentheses and separated by colons. The following example is a list of four values:

```
( 23, 41, 92, 7)
```

You assign this list to the array you wish to create, preceding the array name with an **@** sign. This assignment will initialize the array, sequentially beginning with the first value in the list.

```
@mynums = (23, 41, 92, 7);
```

Once the array has been created, you can reference its individual elements. The elements start from 0, not 1. The mynums array has four elements, numbered from 0 to 3. You can reference individual elements using an index number encased within brackets. **[0]** references the first element, and **[2]** references the third element. The following example prints out the first element and then the fourth element. Notice that the array name is prefixed with a **$**.

```
print $mynums[0] ;
print $mynums[2] ;
```

You can change the value of any element in the array by assigning it a new value. Notice that you use a **$**, not an **@** sign, preceding an individual array element. The **@** sign is used to reference the entire array and is used when you are assigning whole lists of values to it. The **$** sign references a particular element, which is essentially a variable.

```
$mynums[2] = 40;
```

There is no limit to the number of elements in the array. You can add more by simply referencing a new element and assigning it a value. The following assignment will add a fifth element to the mynums array:

```
$mynums[4] = 63;
```

Each array will have a special variable that consists of a **#** and the name of the array. This variable is the number of elements currently in the array. For example, **#mynums** holds the number of elements in the mynums array. The following example prints out the number of elements. Notice the preceding **$**.

```
print   "$#mynums";
```

When assigning a list to an array, the values in a list do not have to be of the same type. You can have numbers, strings, and even variables in a list. Similarly, elements of the array do not have to be of the same type. One element could be numeric, and another a string. In the next example, a list with varied elements is assigned to the myvar array.

```
@myvar = ( "aleina", 11, 4.5, "a new car");
```

You can reference the entire set of elements in an array as just one list of values. To do this, you use the array name prefixed by the **@** sign. The following example will output all the values in the mynums array:

```
print @mynums;
```

The **@** is used here instead of the **$**, because the array name is not itself a variable. It is considered a list of values. Only the individual elements are variables. This means that to just reference all the values in an array, you use the **@** sign, not the **$**. This is even true when you want to assign one array to another. In the next example, the values of each element in mynums are assigned to corresponding elements in newnums. Notice the **@** used for mynums. You can think of **@mynums** as evaluating to a list of the values in the mynums array, and this list being then assigned to newnums.

```
@newnums = @mynums;
```

The list of values referenced by an array name can be used in a string, just as the value of a variable can. In the next example, the values of the elements in the mynums array are incorporated into a string. This string is then assigned to the myreport variable. Notice the use of the **@** as a prefix to the array name, **@mynums**.

```
$myreport = "Here are the numbers I have: @mynums \n";
print $myreport;
```

However, individual elements of an array are variables and need to be referenced using an index and the $ sign. The following example uses the value of the third element in the mynums array:

```
$myelement= "This is the value of the third element: $mynums[2] \n";
print $myelement;
```

Array Management Functions: List Operations

Perl has a set of functions designed to help you to easily manage arrays. With simple commands you can perform common array operations such as listing the contents of an array, sorting an array, or sequentially referencing each element one by one. In this respect, you can think of an array as a list, and these functions as performing list operations. Table 24-3 lists the array and list functions.

Both **push** and **pop** operate on the end of an array, adding or removing the last element. You can think of them as adding or removing an element at the end of a list. **push** adds a new element to the end of the array. **push** takes as its arguments the array, followed by a list of values that you want added as elements to the array. It can add several new elements at a time. **pop** removes the last element from an array. **pop** will return as its value that last element. The **shift** and **unshift** operators work on the beginning of a list. **shift** will remove the first element in a list, making the next element the first one. The **unshift** operation adds a new element to the beginning of the list. **shift** takes as its argument an array and returns the value of the first element it removes. **unshift** takes as its argument an array followed by the value of the element you want to add. It then returns the total number of elements now in the array. The **sort** operation will sort the elements in an array according to the system's character set, usually the ASCII character set. **sort** will arrange elements in ascending order. The sort operation returns the list of sorted values. The **split** operation is used to create an array and assign it values derived from a string. The values are determined by a specified delimiter that is used to segment the string, forming the different values that will be assigned to elements in the array. **split** is often used with lines of input data that are already arranged into fields that are separated by a delimiter such as a comma or colon. You can use the grep function to search an array or any list. **grep** operates much like the Unix utility grep. It takes as its arguments a pattern and a list, usually an array. **grep** returns the value of the element matched.

Associative Arrays

An associative array uses strings to index elements in an array, instead of numbers. You can think of the index string as a keyword that you can use to find an element. In Perl, an associative array is defined with a **%** prefixing the array name. The list of values that it is assigned consists of an index string and element value pairs. An index string is followed by the elements value, which is then followed by the next index string and element value, and so on. In the next example, the associative array **city** is defined with four elements, each having an integer value and each indexed with the name of a city.

```
% city = ('Sacramento', 4,
    'Fallon', 86,
    'Napa', 7,
    'Alameda', 53 ) ;
```

You reference an element in an associative array using its index string. The index string is encased in single quotes and braces (not brackets).

```
print  $city{'Fallon'};
```

To add a new element in an associative array, you need to provide both the string to be used as the index for this element as well as the element's value.

```
$city{'LA'} = 45;
```

To reference the list of values for an associative array you use the **%** sign with the array name. The following example prints out all values of the city array:

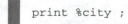

```
print %city ;
```

Perl also has a set of list operations designed to work on associative arrays. With these operations, you can generate lists of keys or values. They are helpful for easily iterating through an associative array. The keys operation takes as its argument an associative array and returns a list of all the index strings used to reference the elements in that array. Having obtained the index strings, you can then use them for referencing each element in the array. For example, with the operation you can generate a list of index strings that you can then use in a foreach loop to reference and print out each element of an associative array in turn.

Control Structures

Perl has a set of control structures similar to those used in the gawk, C-shell, and C programming languages. Perl has loops with which you can repeat commands, and conditions that allow you to choose among specified commands. For the test expressions, there are two different sets of operators for use with strings and numeric values. Table 24-4 lists the numeric operators and Table 24-5 lists the string operators. You can also use pattern operations that allow the use of regular expressions. Table 24-6 lists the Perl control structures with their syntax.

Loops

Perl loops are the **while, do-until, for**, and **foreach** loops. The **while** loop is the more general purpose loop, whereas the **for** and **foreach** loops provide special capabilities. The **foreach** is particularly helpful in processing lists and arrays. The **while, do-until**, and **for** loops operate much like their counterparts in the C programming language. The **for** loop, in particular, has the same three expression formats as the C for loop. The **foreach** loop is similar to its counterpart in the C-shell, able to easily handle lists of items.

You can easily adapt the while loop for use with arrays. The variable used to control a loop can also be used, inside the loop, to index an array. In the next example, the elements of the **title** array are assigned the value of each title. Then, the contents of each element are printed out using a **for** loop. Notice that the **$#num** holds the count of elements in the array. **$#num** is used as the upper bound in the **for** loop test expression in order to check when the loop should stop.

titlearr.pl

```
#!/usr/bin/perl
# Program to define and print out a scalar array

@title = ( "Tempest", "Iliad", "Raven");      # define array with 3 elements

for($i = 0; $i <= $#title; $i++)              # Loop through array, $#title is size

            {
            print "$title[$i] \n";   # Print an element of the title array
            }
```

```
$ titlearr.pl
Tempest
Iliad
Raven
```

The **foreach** loop is useful for managing arrays. In the **foreach** loop, you can use the array name to generate a list of all the element values in the array. This generated list of values then becomes the list referenced by the **foreach** loop. You can also specify a range of array elements, using only those values for the list, or a set of individual elements. In the next example, the array name **@mylist** is used to generate a list of its values that the **foreach** loop can operate on, assigning each one to **$myname** in turn.

mynumlist.pl

```
#!/usr/bin/perl
# Program to use foreach to print out an array

@mylist = ( 34, 21, 96, 85);           # define array of 4 elements

foreach $mynum ( @mylist )             # Assign value of each element to $mynum
    {
    print "$mynum \n";
    }
```

Using the **@ARGV** array, you can specify the command line arguments as a list of values. The arguments specified on the command line when the program was invoked become a list of values referenced by the foreach loop. The variable used in the foreach loop is set automatically to each argument value in sequence. The first time through the loop, the variable is set to the value of the first argument. The second time, it is set to the value of the second argument, etc.

The number of arguments that a user actually enters on the command line can vary. The **#ARGV** variable will always hold the number of arguments that a user enters. This is the number of elements that are in the **ARGV** array. If you want to reference all the elements in the **ARGV** array using their indexes, you will need to know the number of elements, **#ARGV**. For example, to use the **foreach** loop to reference each element in the **ARGV** array, you would use the .. operator to generate a list of indexes. **0..$#ARGV** generates a list of numbers beginning with 0 through to the value of **$#ARGV**.

Perl has a set of special commands designed to give you more refined control over loops and blocks. They correspond to similar commands used in the C programming language. These commands need to make use of labels. If you use them within a loop, you need to label that loop; then when one of these commands is used, it references that loop.

The **last** command corresponds to the C **break** command. It stops execution of a loop. It can also be used to break out of a block. **last** is used with blocks to simulate switch structures. The **next** command skips over the remaining statements in the loop. It is similar to the C **continue** command. It is designed to work with the continue block. A continue block consists of the command **continue** followed by a block. This block is executed at the end of the loop. Even if a **next** command skips over the remaining statements, the continue block is always executed. You can use it to ensure that operations like increments are performed. The **redo** command will re-execute a loop, even if its test proves false. It has no corresponding C command. Both the **redo** and the **last** commands will ignore any continue block.

Conditions: if, elsif, unless, and switch

Perl supports if-else operations much as they are used in other programming languages. The **if** structure with its **else** and **elsif** components allows you to select alternative actions. You can use just the **if** command to choose one alternative, or combine that with **else** and **elsif** components to choose among several alternatives. The **if** structure has a test expression encased in parentheses followed by a block of statements. If the test is true, the statements in the block are performed. If not, the block is skipped. Unlike other programming languages, only a block can follow the test, and any statements, even just one, has to be encased with it. The following example tests to see if an open operation on a file was successful. If not, then it will execute a **die** command to end the program. The NOT operator, **!**, will make the test true if open fails, thereby executing the **die** command.

```
if (!(open (REPS, "< $filen"))) {
    die "Can't open $filen";
}
else  {
        print "Opened $filen successfully";
        }
```

String Functions

Perl provides several functions and operators for manipulating strings (see Table 24-7). The **length**, **index**, and **substr** perform standard string operations such as obtaining the length of a string or copying a substring from a string. **split** performs a special task. It generates an array from a string, cutting the string into array element values. It is similar to the **split** function used in gawk. **split** was discussed previously with the array list operations. The dot operator concatenates strings and the x operator generates strings consisting of repeated characters.

You use the dot operator, **.**, to concatenate two strings. The following example adds a ".dat" suffix to the root file name. If the contents of **$curfile** is myaddress, then **$newfile** would be "myaddress.dat". With the repetition operator, x, you can repeat a string any number of times. You precede the **x** operator with the string to be repeated and then follow the **x** operator with the number of times you want to repeat the string. The string can be single characters or any number of characters. You can also use the **x** operator to generate a list whose members all have the same value, and then use that list to initialize an array. In the next example, an array is assigned a list of five zeros (0, 0, 0, 0, 0). But instead of typing out the list, the list is generated by an **x** operator, (0) x 5.

```
@myarray = (0) x 5 ;
```

Pattern Matching

Like Sed and gawk, Perl can search for a pattern on a given line. Such a search pattern is indicated by enclosing slashes. **/Dickens/** searches for the pattern Dickens in a line. By default, a pattern search operates on the contents of the _$ special variable. This variable usually holds the contents of the recently read line of input, wherever that may come from. If the recent input command was **<STDIN>**, then _$ will hold a line read from the standard input, and a following pattern search will search that line. In the next example, the user reads a line from the standard input, then searches for the pattern **/Dickens/** in it.

```
<STDIN>;
/Dickens/;
```

To search the contents of a variable for a pattern, you use the **=~** operator with the pattern search operation. You use the variable name as the left-hand operand, and the pattern search operation as the right-hand operand. Table 24-8 lists Perl pattern matching operators and options. The following example looks for the pattern "Christmas" in the **$title** variable.

```
$title =~ /Christmas/
```

Perl supports the full range of regular expressions in its pattern matching, including extended special characters. The *, +, ?, {}, ., ^, $, and [] special characters can all be used to construct complex search operations. Chapter 14 discusses regular expressions in depth. In addition, Perl has a set of escape characters used in regular expressions that operate as a shorthand for many of the commonly used patterns. For example, **\w** matches on any alphanumeric character and is equivalent to the regular expression [A-Ba-b0-9]+. **\d** matches on numbers and **\s** on whitespaces. **\b** prefixing a word lets you search for a word, rather than any pattern. Uppercase versions perform negative matches. **\W** matches on anything other than alphanumeric characters and **\D** on anything other than numbers. Table 24-9 lists the special characters available for use in Perl regular expressions.

Functions: sub

In your Perl script you can define subroutines, permitting you to better organize your program. Instead of one long series of statements, you can define separate subroutines for specific tasks. Tasks you wish to perform more than once do not have to have their code repeated in the program. You can just define a subroutine for it and call that subroutine as many times as you need to. Subroutines are defined with the **sub** command followed by the subroutine name and a block of statements. Within the block of statements you can have any Perl statements you wish. Subroutines operate like functions do in C programs and procedures in other programs. They can take arguments and have parameters with predetermined names. Table 24-10 lists the different components that can make up a Perl subroutine. The following example defines a subroutine called **dispfile**.

```
sub dispfile
    {
    print "Please enter in name of file to be displayed: ";
    chomp($filename = <STDIN>);
    system("cat $filename");
}
```

Subroutines can have arguments passed to them and return values back to the calling statement. Arguments and return values are passed as lists. Arguments specified in a subroutine call are placed in a list and assigned to the @_ array that is then passed to the subroutine. The @_ array will hold the arguments for the subroutine currently being called. To access a particular argument, you use array or list operations to reference elements of the @_ array. @_ is used in every subroutine to access that subroutine's arguments.

Arguments are arranged in the @_ array, counting from 0, and are referenced as you would elements of any scalar array. The first argument would be referenced with $_[0] and the second with $_[1], and so on. The following example, dispfilearg, is designed to receive as its argument the name of a file. It uses $_[0] to access a file name passed to it using the @_ array.

```
sub dispfilearg
    {
    system("cat $_[0]");
}
```

The subroutine calls would be any of the following:

```
dispfilearg ("myfile");
&dispfilearg  "myfile";
```

For constants, the @_ list holds only values. However, if you use a variable or array as an argument, then @_ will reference those objects. In effect, with variables and arrays, call by reference is implemented. This means that references to elements of the @_ array, reference the original objects. Changes made by referencing these objects through the @_ array will change the original object in the calling function. So, if a string variable is used as an argument to a function, and then that argument is referenced through @_ and used in the assignment operation, then the value of that variable is changed.

Escape Character	Description
\a	Bell
\b	Backspace
\cC	Control character C. **\cD** is CTRL-D
\f	Form feed
\e	Escape character
\n	Newline
\r	Return
\t	Tab
\\	Backslash
\"	Quotes
\uC	Makes C uppercase
\1C	Makes C lowercase
\Ltext**\E**	Makes all characters in text within the \L and \E pair lowercase
\Utext**\E**	Makes all characters in text within the \L and \E pair uppercase

Table 24-1. *Perl Escape Characters*

Perl Command Line Options	Function
-e	Enter one line of a Perl program
-n	Read from files listed on the command line
-p	Output to standard output any data read
Perl File Commands	
open (*file-handle*	permission-with-filename)
close (*file-handle*)	Close a file
<filename>	Read from a file
<STDIN>	Read from the standard input
<>	Read from files whose file names are provided in the argument list when the program was invoked
print *<file-handle> text;*	Write to a file. If no file handle is specified, write to standard output. If no text is specified, write contents of **$_**
printf *<handle>* "*Format-str*", *values;*	Write formatted string to a file. Use conversion specifiers to format values. If no file handle is specified, write to standard output. If no values are specified, use contents of **$_**
sprintf *str-var* "*Format-str*", *values;*	Write formatted values to a string. Use conversion specifiers to format values. If no values are specified, use contents of **$_**
Permissions for Opening Files	
< filename	Read-only
> filename	Write-only
+> filename	Read and write
>> filename	Append (written data is added to the end of the file)
command |	An input pipe, reading data from a pipe
| command	An output pipe, sending data out through this pipe

Table 24-2. *Perl File Operations and Command Line Options*

Scalar Array Operations, @*array*

push(*array*, *value-list*)	Add elements to the end of the array
pop(*array*)	Remove the last element from the end of an array
shift(*array*, *value-list*)	Add an element to the beginning of the array
unshift(*array*)	Remove an element from the beginning of an array
sort(*array*)	Sort in ascending order (alphabetic)
reverse(*array*)	Sort in descending order (alphabetic)
split(*delim*, *str*)	Split a string into an array of elements. Delimiter can be either a pattern or a string. It is used as the delimiter to separate the string into element values
join(*delim*, *array*)	Combine array elements into one string
grep(*array*, *pattern*)	Search the elements in an array for the pattern
splice (*array*, *index*)	Using splice to delete an element from an array. Index numbered from 0
splice(*array*, *index*, *num*)	Using splice to delete num consecutive number of elements from an array
splice(*array*, *num*, **0**, *str*)	Using splice to insert an element to an array with the value of str
splice(*array*, **$#argv**, **0**, *str*)	Using splice to add a new element to the end of an array

Associative Arrays Operations, %*array*

keys(%*assoc-array*)	Generate a list of all the index strings in an associative array
values(%*assoc-array*)	Generate a list of all the values of the elements in an associative array
each(%*assoc-array*)	Return both the value of the next element and its index string

Table 24-3.   *Perl Array Operations*

Associative Arrays Operations, %*array*

delete(%*assoc-array, index-string*)	Delete an element with the specified index from an associative array

General Arrays Operations

undef(*array*)	Delete an entire array (scalar or associative)

Table 24-3.   *Perl Array Operations (continued)*

Arithmetic Operators	Function
*	Multiplication
/	Division
+	Addition
–	Subtraction
%	Modulo—results in the remainder of a division
**	Power
Relational Operators	
>	Greater than
<	Less than
>=	Greater than or equal to
<=	Less than or equal to
==	Equal in let
!=	Not equal
Increment Operators	
++	Increment variable by one
--	Decrement variable by one

Table 24-4.   *Numeric Operators*

Arithmetic Operators	Function
Arithmetic Assignment Operators	
+=	Increment by specified value
-=	Decrement by specified value
/=	Variable is equal to itself divided by value
*=	Variable is equal to itself multiplied by value
%=	Variable is equal to itself remaindered by value

Table 24-4.   *Numeric Operators* (continued)

String Comparisons	Function
gt	Greater than
lt	Less than
ge	Greater than or equal to
le	Less than or equal to
eq	Equal
ne	Not equal
Logical Operations	
expression **&&** *expression* *expression* **and** *expression*	The logical AND condition returns a true 0 value if both expressions return a true 0 value; if one returns a non-zero value, then the AND condition is false and also returns a non-zero value; execution stops at the first false expression; the **and** operation is the same as **&&** but has a lower precedence

Table 24-5.   *String, Logical, File and Assignment Operators*

String Comparisons	Function
expression || *expression* *expression* **or** *expression*	The logical OR condition returns a true 0 value if one or the other expression returns a true 0 value; if both expressions return a non-zero value, then the OR condition is false and also returns a non-zero value; evaluation stops at the first true expression; the **or** operation is the same as || but has a lower precedence
! *command* **not** *command*	The logical NOT condition inverts the true or false value of the expression; the not operation is the same as **!** but has a lower precedence
File Tests	
-e	File exists
-f	File exists and is a regular file
-s	File is not empty
-z	File is empty, zero size
-r	File is readable
-w	File can be written to, modified
-x	File is executable
-d	File name is a directory name
-B	File is a binary file
-T	File is a text file
Assignment Operator	
=	Assign a value to a variable

Table 24-5. *String, Logical, File and Assignment Operators* (continued)

LABEL:**{** *statements*; **}**	Block is a collection of statements enclosed within opening and closing braces; the statements are executed sequentially; the block can be labeled
Condition Control Structures: `if, else, elsif, case`	

if(*expression*) **{**
  statements;
   }
	if executes statements if its test expression is true; statements must be included within a block

if(*expression*) **{**
  statements;
   }
else(*expression*) **{**
  statements;
   }
	if-else executes statements if the test expression is true; if false, then the else statements are executed

if(*expression*) **{**
  statements;
   }
elsif(*expression*) **{**
  statements;
   }
else(*expression*) **{**
  statements;
   }
	elsif allows you to nest if structures, enabling selection among several alternatives; at the first true if expression, its statements are executed and control leaves the entire elsif structure

unless(*expression*) **{**
  statements;
   }
	unless executes statements if its test expression is false

test **?** *stat1* **:** *stat2*	Conditional expression. If true executes *stat1*, else *stat2*
*LABEL***:{** **if**(*expr*){*statements*;**last** *LABEL*}; **}**	Simulate a switch structure by using listed if statements within a block with the last statement referencing a label for the block

Table 24-6. *Perl Conditions, Loops, and Functions*

Loop Control Structures:
`while, until, for, foreach`

LABEL:**while**(*expression*) {
    statements;
}
	while executes statements as long as its test expression is true; LABEL is optional

do{ *statements*; } **until**(*expression*)	**until** executes statements as long as its test expression is false

foreach *variable* (*list-values*)
{
    statements;
}
	foreach is designed for use with lists of values such as those generated by an array; the variable operand is consecutively assigned the values in the list

for(*init-expr*; *test-expr*; *incr-expr*)
{
    statements;
}
	The **for** control structure executes statements as long as *test-expr* is true; the first expression, *init-expr* is executed before the loop begins; the third expression, *incr-expr,* is executed within the loop after the statements

LABEL: *block-or-loop*	Label a block or loop; used with the **next**, **last**, and **redo** commands
next	Skip remainder of loop and start next iteration; like the C **continue** command; will execute any continue block
continue { *statements*; }	Execute continue block as last statements in a loop; is executed even if a next statement starts next iteration
redo *LABEL*	Re-execute loop even if test fails; skips continue block
last *LABEL*	Exit block or loop; skips continue block, if any; like the C break statement

Functions

sub *function-name* ;	Declare a function

sub *function-name* {
    statements;
}
	Define a function with the name *function-name*

Table 24-6.   *Perl Conditions, Loops, and Functions* (continued)

Functions

& *function-name* **(** *arg-list* **)**	Call a function with arguments specified in the argument list
@_	Holds the values of arguments passed to the current function. $_ and index references an argument. $[0] is the first argument
$#_	Number of arguments passed to the current function

Table 24-6. *Perl Conditions, Loops, and Functions* (continued)

String Operations	Descriptions
str **.** *str*	The dot operator concatenates strings
str **x** *num*	Repeat a string or character *num* number of times
String Functions	
chomp(*str* **)**	Remove trailing newline
substr(*str* **,** *start-pos* **,** *length* **)**	Return a substring of the specified string beginning at the start position for the length specified
substr(*str* **,** *start-pos* **,** *length* **)** **=** *string*	Replace the specified section of the string with the assigned string
length(*str* **)**	Find the length of a string
index(*str* **,** *pattern* **)**	Find the position of a pattern in a string
rindex(*str* **,** *pattern* **)**	Find the last position of a pattern in a string

Table 24-7. *String Operations*

Pattern Matching Operators	Action
var =~ /*reg-expr*/	Find the occurrence of the regular expression in the string variable
var !~ /*reg-expr*/	Check if the regular expression does not occur in string variable
/*reg-expres*/	Match a pattern using a regular expression
Pattern Matching Options	
i	Do case-insensitive pattern matching
m	Treat string as multiple lines
s	Treat string as single line
x	Extend your pattern's legibility with whitespace and comments

Table 24-8. *Pattern Matching Operators and Options*

Special Characters	Description
^	Beginning of a line
$	End of a line
c*	Match on zero or more sequential instances of the preceding character, *c*
.	Match on any single character
c+	Match on at least one or more sequential instances of the preceding character, *c*
c?	Match on zero or just one instance of the preceding character, *c*
c{*num*}	Specify the number or repeated sequential instances of the preceding character, *c*, to match on

Table 24-9. *Regular Expressions*

Special Characters	Description
c{min,max}	Specify a minimum and maximum number of repeated sequential instances of the preceding character, *c*, to match on
[*char-list*]	Classes of characters
[*char-char*]	Ranges of characters
[^*char-list*] [^*char-char*]	Any characters NOT in the character list or the range specified
reg-exp | *reg-exp*	Match on any of the specified regular expressions; the regular expressions can be a simple string; (function as a logical OR operation)
(*pattern-segment*) \ *n*	Specify a segment of a pattern that can then be referenced with the *n* code; \1 references the first segment, \2 the second, and so on; used with s/// substitution

Escape Character Regular Expressions

\w	Any alphanumeric character, [a-bA-B0-9]+
\d	Any digit (number), [0-9]+
\s	Whitespaces (spaces, tabs, newlines, form feeds), [\n\t\r\f]+
\bword	Words
\W	Characters NOT alphanumeric, [^a-bA-B0-9]+
\D	Characters NOT digits, [^0-9]+
\S	Characters NOT whitespaces, [^\n\t\r\f]+
\Bpattern	Any pattern not a word

Table 24-9.   *Regular Expressions* (continued)

Subroutine Components	Description
@_	Array to hold list of arguments. Arrays are combined into single elements of this array
sub *name* **{** *statements***;** **}**	Subroutine definition
sub *name***;**	Subroutine declaration
sub *name* **(***type-list***);**	Prototype declaration
*function-name***;**	Function call
*function-name***(***arguments***);**	Function call
&*function-name arguments***;**	Function call
my(*object-list*)	Local variable restricted to subroutine or block
local(*object-list*)	Local version of global object, known to current subroutine and block and all other subroutines called
\@*array-name*	Array reference (used in argument list to maintain integrity of an array)

Table 24-10.   *Perl Subroutines*

Chapter Twenty-Five

Tcl, Tk, and Expect

Tcl is general purpose command language developed by John Ousterhout in 1987 at the University of California, Berkeley. Originally designed to customize applications, it has become a fully functional language in its own right. As with Perl and gawk, you can write Tcl scripts, developing your own Tcl programs. Tcl is a very simple language to use.

Tcl has been enhanced by the development of several Tcl applications that extend the capabilities of the language. With these applications, a Tcl program can create graphical interfaces, communicate interactively with other programs, and manage sound recordings. The Tk application allows easy development of graphical interactive applications. You can create your own windows and dialog boxes with buttons and text boxes of your choosing. XF further enhances Tk by providing a graphical user interface to the application, allowing you to create graphical components such as windows easily. The Expect application provides easy communication with interactive programs such as ftp and telnet. Tcl-DP provides support for distributed applications. Ak provides audio capabilities such as recording, playback, and telephone control.

Tcl is often used in conjunction with Tk to create graphical applications. Tk is used to create the graphical elements such as windows and Tcl performs the programming actions such as managing user input. Like Java, Tcl and Tk are cross-platform applications. A Tcl/Tk program will run on any platform that has the Tcl/Tk interpreter installed. Currently, there are Tcl/Tk versions for Windows, the Mac, and Unix systems, including Linux. You can write a Tcl application on Linux and run the same code on Windows or the Mac. The new versions of Tcl and Tk 8.0 even support local look and feel for GUI widgets using Mac-like windows on the Mac, but Windows-like windows on the Windows 95.

Tcl is an interpreted language operating, like Perl, within its own shell. **tclsh** is the command for invoking the Tcl shell. Within this shell, you can then execute Tcl commands. You can also create files within which you can invoke the Tcl shell and list Tcl commands, effectively creating a Tcl program. A significant advantage to the Tcl language and its applications is the fact that it is fully compatible with the C programming language. Tcl libraries can be incorporated directly into C programs. In effect, this allows you to create very fast compiled versions of Tcl programs.

When you install Tk and Tcl on your system, man pages for Tcl/Tk commands are also installed. Use the **man** command with the name of the Tcl or Tk command to bring up detailed information on that command. For example, **man switch** displays the manual page for the Tcl **switch** command, and **man button** displays information on the Tk **button** widget. Once you have installed Tk, you can run a demo program called **widget** that shows you all the Tk widgets available. The **widget** program uses Tcl/Tk sample programs and can display the source code for each. You can find the **widget** program by changing to the Tk **demos** directory as shown here. (tk* here matches on directory name consisting of **tk** and its version number, **tk4.1** for version 4.1 and **tk8.0** for version 8.0.)

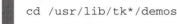

```
cd /usr/lib/tk*/demos
```

From the Xterm window just enter the command **widget**. You can also examine the individual demo files and modify them as you wish. If you have installed a version of Tk yourself into the **/usr/local/bin** directory rather than **/usr/bin**, then the **demos** directory will be located in **/usr/local/lib/tk***.

Tcl/Tk Products and Versions

Currently, both Tcl, Tk, and related software are being developed and supported by Sun Microsystems, whose Tcl/Tk research operation is led by John Ousterhout. The current release of both Tcl and Tk is 8.0. Sun also provides three other Tcl/Tk products for Internet and program development: the Tcl/Tk Web page plugin, the TclHttpd Web Server, and the SpecTcl Tcl/Tk GUI builder. Table 25-1 lists the available Tcl/Tk software. The Tcl plugin is the viewer for Tcl/Tk applications that allows you to embed Tcl/Tk programs within a Web page. Such embedded Tcl/Tk programs are called Tclets. TclHttpd is a Web Server that can be easily embedded in applications, making them Web capable. You can configure and modify the server using Tcl/Tk commands. The SpecTcl is a Tcl/Tk editor that lets you build graphical user interfaces (GUIs). Spec generates both Tcl/Tk and Java code, and can be used to create stand-alone Tcl/Tk applications or Web Tclets. SpecTcl is a window-based program with menus and icons for easily creating GUI widgets.

All these products, including current versions of Tcl and Tk, are available free of charge from the Tcl/Tk Web site listed here. Also available on this site is extensive documentation for each product in PostScript, Adobe PDF, and HTML formats. The HTML documentation can be viewed online.

```
http://sunscript.sun.com
```

Your OpenLinux CD-ROM currently only includes older versions of Tcl and Tk, versions 7.5 and 4.1. Most of the Tcl/Tk products will not run on these older versions. To use these products, you should download and install version 8.0. You can obtain RPM packages for Tcl/Tk 8.0 from the Redhat contrib directory at **ftp.redhat.com/pub/contrib/i386**. You will need both Tcl and Tk RPM packages as well as the development packages for each. The names of the current RPM packages are shown next. Once downloaded, you can install them with the **rpm-i** command as shown here. Before installing, be sure to use Lisa (or **rpm-e tk** and **rpm-e tcl**) to uninstall the older versions of Tcl/Tk if they are installed on your system (use **rpm qi tk** to check).

```
rpm -i tcl-8.0-1.i386.rpm
rpm -i tk-8.0-1.i386.rpm
rpm -i tcl-devel-8.0-2.i386.rpm
rpm -i tk-devel-8.0-2.i386.rpm
```

Before you remove the old Tcl/Tk packages, you should make a copy of their shared libraries, **/usr/lib/libtcl7.5.so** and **/usr/lib/libtk4.1.so** (give them different names). Some TclTk applications like **XF86Setup** require the old libraries. You will have to temporarily change **libtk.so** and **libtcl.so** links to link to them should you need to run **XF86Setup**. Change the links back to **/usr/lib/libtcl8.0.so** and **/usr/lib/libtk8.0.so** when you are finished.

From the Tcl/Tk Web site, you can download the most recent version of the source code files. The source code files are clearly referenced for downloading in the Tcl/Tk Web page for Unix versions. The source code files are compressed archives with a **.tar.gz** extension, one for Tcl and another for Tk. Decompress and unpack them with the **gunzip** and **tar xvf** commands. This will create subdirectories with the source code for each, **tcl8.0** and **tk8.0**. Change to the **tcl8.0** directory and check the instructions in the README file. Then change to the **unix** subdirectory and check its README file for information on compiling and installing the software. The source code uses a configure script that greatly simplifies the operation. The following commands will work on an OpenLinux system. The **-enable-gcc** option selects the gcc compiler.

```
./configure -enable-gcc
make
make install
```

First compile the Tcl application, and then perform the same operations for the Tk application. It also has a **unix** subdirectory. The **make** command for Tcl creates a program called **tclsh8.0**, and the one for Tcl creates a program called **wish8.0**. Both are installed in the **/usr/local/bin** directory. You then have to create a link called just **wish** for **wish8.0** and **tclsh** for **tclsh8.0**. You can place these links in either the **/usr/local/bin** or **/usr/bin** directories. The **make install** operations for each application will also install all the Tcl and Tk man pages, libraries, and sample programs.

```
# ln /usr/local/bin/tclsh8.0   /usr/bin/tclsh
# ln /usr/local/bin/wish8.0  /usr/bin/wish
```

Tcl

Tcl is a simple-to-use programming language. Its statements consist of a command followed by arguments, though it also has a complete set of control structures including **while** and **for** loops. Commands can be terminated either by a semicolon or by a new line. You can think of a Tcl command as a function call where the command name operates like a function name, followed by arguments to the function. However, unlike the function call, there are no parentheses or commas encasing the arguments. You simply enter the command name and then its arguments, separated only by spaces. A newline entered after the last argument will end the statement.

You can see the features in this format very clearly in the Tcl assignment command, **set**. To assign a value to a variable, you first enter the assignment command **set**. Then enter in the name of the variable, followed by the value to be assigned. The command name, variable, and value are separated only by spaces. The newline at the end of the line ends the statement. The following statement assigns a string "larisa" to the variable myname, and the next statement assigns the integer value 11 to the variable age.

```
set myname  "larisa"
set age 11
```

As in gawk and Perl, variable types are determined by their use. A variable assigned an integer will be considered an integer, and one assigned a string will be a character array.

The tclsh Shell and Scripts

You execute Tcl commands within the Tcl shell. You can do this interactively, entering commands at a Tcl shell prompt and executing them one by one, or you can place the commands in a script file and execute them all at once. To start up the Tcl shell, you enter the command **tclsh**. This starts up the Tcl shell with the % prompt. You can then enter in single Tcl commands and have them evaluated when you press ENTER. You leave the Tcl shell by entering either an exit command or a CTRL-D.

```
$ tclsh
% set age 11
% puts $age
11
% exit
$
```

You can run a Tcl script either as a stand-alone program or as a file explicitly read by the Tcl shell command **tclsh**. A Tcl script has the extension **.tcl**. For example, the **myread.tcl** Tcl script would be read and executed by the following command:

```
$ tclsh myread.tcl
```

To create a stand-alone script that operates more like a command, you need to invoke the **tclsh** command within the script. You can do this in two ways. The first uses an explicit path name for the **tclsh** command. This is placed on the first line of the script.

```
#!/usr/bin/tclsh
```

The second does not rely on an explicit path name, but will execute the **tclsh** command wherever it may be installed on a given system. This is helpful if a script is being run on different systems that may have installed tclsh in different directories.

```
#!/bin/sh
# the next line restarts using tclsh \
exec tclsh "$0" "$@"
```

The **myread** script in the sections on files uses an invocation of **tclsh** with an explicit path name, whereas the **myreport** script in that same section uses the nonexplicit approach.

Expressions

Expressions are also handled as commands. The command **expr** evaluates an expression and returns its resulting value as a string. It takes as its arguments the operands and operator of an expression. Tcl supports all the standard arithmetic, comparison, and logical operators. The result of an arithmetic expression will be the same form as its operands. If the operands are real numbers, the result will be a real number. You can mix operands of different types and Tcl will convert one to be the same as the other. In the case of real and integer operands, the integer will be converted to a real. In the next statement, the addition of 4 and 3 is evaluated by the **expr** command. The following statement multiplies 25 and 2.

```
expr 4 + 3
expr 25 * 2
```

You can create complex expressions using parentheses. The most deeply nested expressions are evaluated first. In the following example, 25 * 2 is evaluated and the result, 50, has 20 subtracted from it.

```
expr (25 * 2) - 20
```

The resulting value returned by any Tcl command is always a string. In the case of arithmetic operations, the arithmetic value is converted first to a string, which is then returned by the **expr** command.

Embedded Commands

You can combine commands by embedding one within the other. Embedding is commonly used for assigning the result of an expression to a variable. This involves two commands, the **set** command to perform the assignment, and the **expr** command to evaluate an expression. You embed commands using brackets. An embedded command is another Tcl command whose result is used as an argument in the outer Tcl command. The embedded command is executed first, and its result is used as the argument to the outer command. The following statement assigns the result of the arithmetic operation, 25 * 2, to the variable num. **expr** 25 * 2 is a command embedded within the **set** command. First the embedded command is executed, and its result, "50", is assigned to the variable num.

```
set num [expr 25 * 2]
```

Variables

Tcl supports numeric and string variables as well as arrays, including associative arrays. All variables hold as their contents a string. However, though the content of a variable is a string, that string can be used as an integer or real value in an arithmetic expression, provided that the string consists of numbers. Whenever such a variable is used as an operand in an arithmetic expression, its contents are first converted to an integer or real value. The operation is performed on the arithmetic values and the result returned by **expr** is then converted back to a string. This means that you do not have to worry about declaring the type of variable, or even defining a variable. All variables are automatically defined when they are first used in a statement.

As we have seen, variables can be assigned values using the **set** command. The **set** command takes as its argument the variable name and the value assigned. A variable's name can be any set of alphabetic or numeric characters and the underscore. Punctuation and other characters are not allowed.

When you need to use the value of a variable within a statement, you need to evaluate it. Evaluating a variable substitutes its name with its value. The **$** placed before a variable name performs such an evaluation. To use a variable's value as an operand in an expression, you need to evaluate the variable by preceding its name with the **$**. In the next example, the value 5 is assigned to the **mynum** variable. Then **mynum** is evaluated in an expression, **$mynum**, providing its value, 5, as an operand in that expression.

```
set mynum 5
expr  10 * $mynum
```

Should you want to make the value of a variable part of string, you only need to evaluate it within that string. The value of the variable becomes part of the string. In the following statement, the value of the variable **myname** is used as part of a string. In this case, the string will be "My name is Larisa".

```
set myname "Larisa"
set mystr "My name is $myname"
```

There are certain commands designed to operate on variables. The **append** command concatenates a string to a variable. The **incr** command will increment an integer, and the **unset** command will undefine a variable. The different commands that operate on variables are listed in Table 25-3.

Arrays

Array elements are defined and assigned values using the **set** command with the index encased in parentheses. The following example assigns the string "rain" as the second element in the **weather** array.

```
set weather(2) rain
```

You can then reference the element using its index encased in parentheses with the array name preceded with a **$**.

```
puts $weather(2)
rain
```

Tcl allows the use of any word string as an index, in effect, supporting associative arrays. The string used as the index is encased within parentheses next to the array name. The following statements add two elements to the **city** array with the index string **Napa** and **Alameda**.

```
set city(Napa) 34
set city(Alameda) 17
```

The elements of an associative array are referenced using a preceding **$** and the index string encased in parentheses.

```
puts $city(Napa)
34
```

Lists

Tcl supports a type of widget not found in most programming languages, the list. A list is a set of words, strings, or numbers encased in parentheses. Tcl includes a set of very flexible **list** commands that you can use to manipulate lists, combining them, separating them, or adding and deleting elements from them (see Table 25-2). To reference a list, you can either use the name of the variable it was assigned to or you can delineate the list's elements encased in parentheses.

To assign a list to a variable, you place a set of words, numbers, or strings within a set of braces and assign this list to a variable using the **set** command. The following example assigns a list of three words to the variable weather. Notice that only spaces separate the components of a list.

```
set weather {sun rain wind}
```

To access and operate on the list, you use a set of **list** commands. Many of these commands can reference a particular element according to its place in the list. The elements are indexed from 0 for the first element. The value 1 would reference the second element, and so on. In the weather list, the index for sun is 0; for rain it is 1, and for wind it is 2.

The **lindex** command returns an element from a list using its index. It takes two arguments, the list and the index for the element you want. The **lreplace** command will replace elements of a list at a specified position with new elements. **lreplace** takes the same arguments as **linsert**: the list, an index, and the new elements. The following statement replaces the second element, blue, with green (index of 1). This statement will return the list (red green yellow). Here the list is written out with its elements encased within parentheses.

```
lreplace (red blue yellow) 1 green
(red green yellow)
```

You could also assign this list to a variable and operate on the variable name. Notice the use of braces in the assignment and the **$** in the **lreplace** operation.

```
set mycolors   {red blue yellow}
lreplace $mycolors 1 green
puts $mycolors
```

You could also use array notation on the list, referencing the second element with **(1)**.

```
set mycolors(1) green
```

Control Structures

Tcl has a set of control structures similar to those used in Perl, gawk, C-shell, and C programming languages. Tcl has loops with which you can repeat commands and conditions that allow you to choose among specified commands. Table 25-3 lists the Tcl control structures. Control structures in Tcl often make use of a block of Tcl commands. A block of commands consists of Tcl commands enclosed in braces. The opening brace will begin on the same line as that of the control structure that uses it. On following lines there can be several Tcl commands, each on its own line. The block ends with a closing brace on a line by itself. A block is literally an argument to a Tcl command. The block is passed to a control structure command and the control structure will execute the commands in that block.

The **if** control structure allows you to select alternative actions. The **if** command takes two arguments, a test expression and a Tcl command or block of commands. Both are encased in their own set of braces. The test expression is used to determine if the Tcl commands will be executed. If the test expression is true, the commands are performed. If not, the commands are skipped. Below is the syntax for the **if** structure. You can specify alternative commands to execute if the expression is false by attaching an **else** block with those Tcl commands. You can nest **if** structures using the **elseif** command.

```
if {test-expression} {
    Tcl commands
    } elseif {test-expression} {
        Tcl commands
        } else {
            Tcl commands
            }
```

The switch structure chooses among several possible alternatives. The choice is made by comparing a string value with several possible patterns. Each pattern has its own block of Tcl commands. If a match is found, the associated block is executed. The **default** keyword indicates a pattern that matches anything. If all of the other matches fail, then the block associated with the **default** keyword is executed. The **switch** structure begins with the keyword **switch**, the options prefixed with **-**, and the string pattern to be matched, followed by a block containing all the patterns with their blocks. The syntax for the **switch** structure is described next.

```
switch  -options string-pattern  {
      pattern  {
            Tcl commands
            }
      pattern {
            Tcl commands
            }
      default {
            Tcl commands
            }
       }
```

Options specify the pattern-matching capabilities. The following options are supported:

-exact	Use exact matching when comparing string to a pattern. This is the default.
-glob	When matching string to the patterns, use glob style matching.
-regexp	When matching string to the patterns, use regular expression matching (i.e., the same as implemented by the **regexp** command).
--	Marks the end of options. The argument following this one will be treated as string even if it starts with a **-**.

The **-regexp** options lets you match any regular expression, whereas **-glob** lets you use the shell file name matching methods. With **-glob**, the shell special characters *, [], ?, let you easily match on part of a string. With the **-regexp** option, you can match on complex alternative strings, specifying multiple instances of characters, beginning or end of a string, and classes of characters (see Chapter 14).

The **while** loop repeats commands. In Tcl, the **while** loop begins with the **while** command and takes two arguments, an expression and either a single Tcl command or a block of Tcl commands. The expression is encased in braces. A block of Tcl commands begins with an opening brace on the same line as the **while** command. Then, on following lines are the Tcl commands that will be repeated in the loop. The block ends with a closing brace, usually on a line by itself. The syntax for the **while** loop with a single statement is described here:

```
while {expression } {
      Tcl commands
  }
```

for Loops

The **for** loop performs the same tasks as the **while** loop. However, it has a different format. The **for** loop takes four arguments, the first three of which are expressions and the last of which is a block of Tcl commands. The first three arguments are expressions that incorporate the initialization, test, and increment components of a loop. These expressions are each encased in braces. The last argument, the block of Tcl commands, begins with an opening brace and then continues with Tcl commands on the following lines, ending with a closing brace.

```
for {expression1} {expression2} {expression3} {
    Tcl commands;
    }
```

The **foreach** structure is designed to sequentially reference a list of values. It is very similar to the C-shell's **for-in** structure. The **foreach** structure takes three arguments: a variable, a list, and a block of Tcl commands. Each value in the list is assigned to the variable in the **foreach** structure. Like the **while** structure, the **foreach** structure is a loop. Each time through the loop, the next value in the list is assigned to the variable. When the end of the list is reached, the loop stops. Like the **while** loop, the block of Tcl commands is encased in braces. The syntax for the **foreach** loop is described next.

```
foreach variable ( list of values ) {
    tcl commands
    }
```

Tcl Procedures: proc

The **proc** command allows you to create your own Tcl commands for use within a program. In effect, you are creating new procedures, much like procedures or functions in other programming languages. You can think of a **proc** command as defining a Tcl command, much like you would define a function in C. The **proc** command takes three arguments: the name of the new procedure, the arguments that the procedure will take, and a block of commands that the procedure will execute. The arguments are variables that will receive the values passed to it when the procedure is used. The arguments are placed after the procedure name within braces. An opening brace then begins the block of Tcl commands for this procedure. The syntax for the **proc** command follows:

```
proc procedure-name  { arguments } {
    Tcl commands
 }
```

The following example implements the **lsearch** command that searches a list for a pattern:

```
proc mysearch { mylist pat } {
    set i 0
    set len [length $mylist]
    while { $i < $len } {
        if { [lindex $mylist $i] == $pat)
            return $i
    }
    }
```

Tcl String Commands: string

The Tcl **string** command is used to perform different operations on strings. It takes various options, depending upon the task you want to perform. You can search, substring, or obtain the length of a string. The option is entered as a word after the **string** command. Arguments will vary according to the option you choose. Table 25-3 includes the Tcl string commands.

With the **string match** command, you can perform basic search operations on a string, though regular expressions are not supported by this command. It does support *, ?, and [] special characters for simple pattern matching as used in the shell for file name matching. It takes two arguments, the pattern to match and the string to search.

```
string match report* $fname
```

The **string range** command returns a substring of a specified string. It takes three arguments: the string, and beginning and end indexes. The term "end" used for the end index will automatically copy the remainder of the string.

```
string range 4 9
string range 3 end
```

string index returns a single character from a string at a specified index. It takes two arguments: the string and index of the character to be returned.

```
string index $mystring 5
```

The **string length** command returns the length of a string.

```
string length $mystring
```

Regular expression pattern matching is implemented with the **regexp** command. **regexp** has full extended regular expression-matching capabilities, similar to **egrep**. It takes two arguments: the regular expression pattern and the string to be searched. It returns a 1 if the pattern is found in the string, and 0 if it isn't. The following looks for any numbers in **mystring**:

```
regexp [0-9]+ $mystring
```

The **regsub** command is the Tcl substitute command. It matches a regular expression like **regsub**, but then replaces the matched string with a specified replacement string, placing the entire modified string in a new variable. **regsub** takes four arguments. The first two are the same as **regexp**, the regular expression pattern and the string to be searched. The third argument is the replacement string, and the fourth the variable where the modified string will be placed.

Tcl Input and Output: gets and puts

Tcl can read input from the standard input or a file using the **gets** command, and output to the standard output with the **puts** command. The following command reads a line from the standard input, usually the keyboard. The input is placed in the variable line.

```
gets line
```

The **puts** command outputs a string to the standard output or to a file. It takes as its argument the string to be output.

```
puts $line.
```

gets reads a line into the variable specified as its argument. You can then use this variable to manipulate whatever has been read. For example, you can use **line** in a **puts** command to display what was input.

myread

```
#!/usr/bin/tclsh

gets line
puts "This is what I entered: $line"
```

```
$ myread
larisa and aleina
This is what I entered: larisa and aleina
```

You can use the **puts** command to write data to any file or to the standard output. File handle names are placed after the **print** command and before any data such as strings or variables. If no file name is specified, then **print** outputs to the standard output.

Tcl File Handles

You use the **open** command to create a file handle for a file or pipe (see Table 25-3 for a list of Tcl file commands). The **open** command takes two arguments, the name of the file name string and the file mode, and returns a file handle that can then be used to access the file. The file name string can be the name of the file or a variable that holds the name of the file. The file mode is the permissions you are opening the file with. This can be **r** for read-only, **w** for write-only, and **a** for append only. To obtain both read and write permission for overwriting and updating a file, you attach a + to the file mode. **r+** gives you read and write permission. The syntax for **open** follows:

```
open ( filename-string, file-mode );
```

You would usually use the **open** command in a **set** command so that you can assign the file handle returned by **open** to a variable. You can then use that file handle in that variable in other file commands to access the file. In the next example, the user opens the file reports with a file mode for reading, **r**, and assigns the returned file handle to the myfile variable.

```
set myfile [open  "reports" r]
```

Often, the file name will be held in a variable. You then use the **$** with the variable name to reference the file name. In this example, the file name "reports" is held in the variable filen.

```
set myfile [open  $filen r]
```

Once you have finished with the file, you close it with the **close** command. **close** takes as its argument the file handle of the file you want to close.

```
close $myfile
```

With the **gets** and **puts** commands, you can use a file handle to read and write from a specific file. **gets** takes two arguments: a file handle and a variable. It will read a line from the file referenced by the file handle and place it as a string in the variable. If there is no file handle specified, then **gets** reads from the standard input. The following command reads a line from a file using the file handle in the myfile variable. The line is read into the line variable.

```
gets $myfile line
```

The **puts** command also takes two arguments: a file handle and a string. It will write the string to the file referenced by the file handle. If there is no file handle specified, then **puts** will write to the standard output. In the following example, **puts** writes the string held in the line variable to the file referenced by the file handle held in myfile. Notice that there is a **$** before **line** in the **puts** command, but not in the previous **gets** command. **puts** operates on a string, whereas **gets** operates on a variable.

```
puts $myfile $line
```

myreport

```
#!/bin/sh
# the next line restarts using tclsh \
exec tclsh "$0" "$@"

   set reps [open "reports" r ]
   while ( gets $reps line)
      {
      puts $line;
      }
   close reps
```

Tk

The Tk application extends Tcl with commands for creating and managing graphic objects such as windows, icons, buttons, and text fields. Tk commands create graphic objects using the X-Windows systems. It is an easier way to program X-Windows objects than using the X11 toolkit directly. With Tk, you can easily create sophisticated window-based user interfaces for your programs.

The Tk language is organized according to different types of graphic objects such as windows, buttons, menus, and scroll bars. Such objects are referred to as widgets. Each type of widget has its own command with which you can create a widget. For example, you can create a button with the **button** command or a window with the **window** command. A type of widget is considered a class, and the command to create such a widget is called a class command. The command will create a particular instance of that class, a particular widget of that type. **button** is the class command for creating a button. Graphical widgets such as buttons and frames are also often referred to as widgets. Table 25-4 lists the different widgets available in Tk.

The wish Shell and Scripts

Tk operates under the X-Windows system. Within the X-Windows system, Tk uses its own shell, the **wish** shell, to execute Tk commands. To run Tk programs, you first start up your X-Windows system, then start up the **wish** shell with the command **wish**. This will open up a window in which you can then run Tk commands.

You execute Tk commands within the **wish** shell interactively, entering commands and executing them one by one, or you can place the commands in a script file and execute them all at once. Usually, Tk commands are placed in a script that is then run with the invocation of the **wish** command. Like Tcl scripts, Tk scripts usually have the extension **.tcl**. For example, a Tk script called **mydir.tcl** would be read and executed by the following command entered in an Xterm window:

```
$ wish mydir.tcl
```

To create a stand-alone script that operates more like a command, you need to invoke the **wish** command within the script. As with the **tclsh** command, you can do this two ways. The first uses an invocation of the **wish** command with its explicit path name. This is placed on the first line of the script.

```
#!/usr/bin/wish
```

The second does not rely on an explicit path name, but will execute the **wish** command wherever it may be installed on a given system. This is helpful if a script is being run on different systems that may have installed **wish** in different directories. Both the **mydir1** and **mydir2** scripts in the following sections use this nonexplicit approach.

```
#!/bin/sh
# the next line restarts using wish \
exec wish "$0" "$@"
```

When creating a stand-alone script, be sure to change its permissions with the **chmod** command to allow execution. You can then just enter the name of the script to run the program.

```
$ chmod 755 mydir1
$ mydir1
```

Tk Widgets

Tk programs consist of class commands that create various graphic widgets. The class command takes as its arguments the name you want to give the particular widget followed by configuration options with their values. Tk commands have a format similar to Tcl. You enter a Tk class command on a line, beginning with the name of the command followed by its arguments. Tk commands are more complicated than Tcl commands. Graphic interface commands require a significant amount of information about a widget to set it up. For example, a button requires a name, the text it will display, and the action it will take. Many Tk commands can take various options indicating different features of a widget. Table 25-5 lists several options commonly used for Tk widgets. In the following example, a button is created using the **button** command. The **button** command takes as its first argument the name of the button widget. Then, different options define various features. The **-text** option is followed by a string that will be the text displayed by the button. The **-command** option is followed by the command that the button executes when it is clicked. This **button** command will display a button with the text "Click Me". When you click it, the Tk shell will exit.

```
button .mybutton -text "Click Me" -command exit
```

To set up a working interface, you need to define all the widgets you need to perform a given task. Some widgets are designed to manage other widgets, such as scroll bars, are designed to manage windows. Other widgets, such as text input fields, may interact with a Tcl program. A menu choice may take the action of running part of a Tcl program.

Widgets are organized hierarchically. For example, to set up a window to input data, you may need a frame, within which may be text field widgets as well as buttons. Widget names reflect this hierarchy. The widget contained within another widget is prefixed with that widget's name. If the name of the frame is **report** and you want to call the text input field **monday**, then the text input field will have the name **report.monday**. A period separates each level in the hierarchy. A button that you want to call **ok** that is within the **report** frame would be named **report.ok**.

Once you have created your widgets, their geometry has to be defined. The geometry determines the size of each widget in relation to the others, and where they are placed in the window. Tk has three geometry managers, **pack**, **place**, and **grid**. The **pack** command is used in these examples. When you have defined your widgets, you issue a geometry manager command on them to determine their size and shape on the screen. Your widgets cannot be displayed until their geometry is determined. The following determines the geometry of the **.mybutton** widget using the **pack** command. Table 25-6 lists the different geometry commands.

```
pack .mybutton
```

The **mydir1** program is a simple Tcl/Tk program to display a list of file and directory names in a Tk listbox widget with an attached scroll bar. Figure 25-1 shows this listbox. With a listbox widget, you can display a list of items that you can then easily scroll through. Using the mouse, you can select a particular item. If a scroll bar is attached, you can scroll through the displayed items should there be more than can fit in the designated size of the listbox. First the scroll bar is defined using the **scrollbar** command, giving it the name **.scroll** and binding it with the command

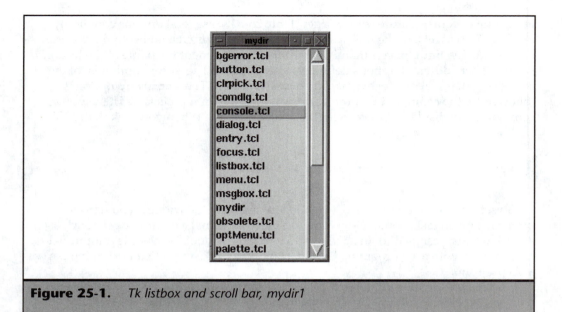

Figure 25-1. *Tk listbox and scroll bar, mydir1*

".list yview". This instructs the scroll bar to be attached to the listbox on a y
axis, vertical.

```
scrollbar .scroll -command ".list yview"
```

Then, the listbox is defined with the **listbox** command, giving it the name **.list**
and a y axis scroll capability provided by the .scroll widget. The listbox will appear
sunken with the specified width and height.

```
listbox .list -yscroll ".scroll set"  -relief sunken -width 15
-height 15 -setgrid yes
```

The two widgets are then created with the **pack** command and positioned in the
window. They are placed on the left side of the window and will always expand to fill
the window. The anchor is on the west side of the window, **w**. The listbox, **.list**, is
placed first, followed by the scroll bar, **.scroll**.

```
pack .list .scroll   -side left  -fill both -expand yes -anchor w
```

A Tcl **if** test then follows that checks if the user entered in an argument when the
program was invoked. The **if** test checks to see if there is a first element in the **argv**

list where any arguments are held. If there are no arguments, then the current directory is used, as represented by the period. This chosen directory is assigned to the **dir** variable. A Tcl **foreach** operation is then used to fill the listbox. The shell **ls** command, as executed with the **exec** command, obtains the list of files and directories. Each is then placed in the listbox with the Tk **insert** operation for the **.list** widget. The **insert** command takes a position and a value. Here, the value is a file name held in **$i** that is placed at the **end** of the list.

```
.list insert end $i
```

The CTRL-C character is then bound to the **exit** command to allow you to easily close the window.

mydir1

```
#!/bin/sh
# the next line restarts using wish \
exec wish "$0" "$@"

# Create a scroll bar and listbox
scroll bar .scroll -command ".list yview"
listbox .list -yscroll ".scroll set" -relief sunken -width 15 -height 15 -setgrid yes
pack .list .scroll  -side left -fill both -expand yes -anchor w

# If user enters a directory argument use that, otherwise use current directory.
if {$argc > 0} then {
   set dir [lindex $argv 0]
   } else {
       set dir "."
       }

# Fill the listbox (.list) with the list of files and directories obtained from ls
cd $dir
foreach i [exec ls -a ] {
   if [file isfile $i] {
   .list insert end $i
   }
   }

# Set up bindings for the file manager.  Control-c closes the window.
bind all <Control-c> {destroy .}
```

Events and Bindings

A Tk program is event driven. Upon running, it waits for an event such as a mouse event or a keyboard event. A mouse event can be a mouse click or a double-click, even a mouse down or up. A keyboard event can be a CONTROL key or meta key, even the ENTER key at the end of input data. When the program detects a particular event, it takes an action. The action may be another graphical operation such as displaying another menu, or it may be a Tcl, Perl, or shell program.

Actions are explicitly bound to given events using the **bind** command. The **bind** command takes as its arguments the name of a widget or class, the event to bind, and the action to bind to that event. Whenever the event takes place within that widget, the specified action is executed.

```
bind .myframe  <CTRL-H>   {.myframe delete insert }
```

You use the **bind** command to connect events in a Tk widget with the Tcl command you want executed. In a sense, you are dividing your Tcl program into segments, each of which is connected to an event in a Tk widget. When an event takes place in a Tk widget, its associated set of Tcl commands are executed. Other Tk commands, as well as Tcl commands, can be associated with an event bound to a Tk widget. This means that you can nest widgets and their events. The Tcl commands executed by one Tk event may, in turn, include other Tk commands and widgets with events bound to yet other Tcl commands (see Table 25-6 for a list of Tk commands).

The **mydir2** program shown in Figure 25-2 illustrates functions and widget bindings. The previous **mydir1** program is enhanced with the capability to display two listboxes, one for directories and one for files. Each has its own scroll bars. The directory listbox is named **.listdir** and its scroll bar **.scrolldir**. Each listbox and scroll bar is defined and then created, **.listdir** and **.scrolldir** first so that they will be placed on the left side of the window.

The Tcl function **listdirsfuncs** is then defined to fill both listboxes. This function takes as its argument a directory. The **cd** command will change to that directory, providing the capability of listing different directories. The **isdirectory** test checks for directories, placing them in the **.listdir** listbox. Following the definition of this function, there is a function call for it. **listdirsfuncs** needs to be called once to initially fill up the listboxes with the contents of the current directory.

There is now a binding for the **.listdir** widget. The double-click of the left mouse button, Double-Button-1, is bound to a call of the **listdirfuncs** function for the **.listdir** listbox. This binding makes any double-click on the **.listdir** listbox have the effect of calling the **listdirsfuncs** function. As there is no binding for the **.list** listbox, a double-click on that box will have no effect.

There are two actions bound to **.listdir** with the double-click. These are encased in braces. To have more than one action executed with a binding, you have to place them within braces. The first action is an operation to obtain the selected directory name

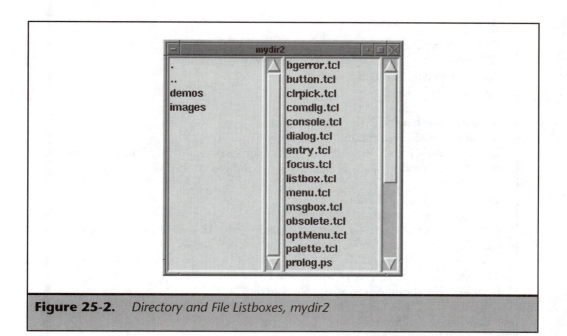

Figure 25-2.   *Directory and File Listboxes, mydir2*

from the listbox. When you click on an item in a listbox, you select it. The **[selection get]** operation will return the selected item, in this case, a directory name. The directory name is assigned to the variable **i**. This variable is then used as an argument in the function call of **listdirsfuncs**, the second action. These two actions illustrate how you can obtain values and pass them as arguments to a function, all within a binding. First you obtain the values, assigning them to variables; then, you use the contents of these variables as arguments in the function call.

Bindings are the key operational component of a Tk program. Bindings detect the events that drive a Tk program. You can think of a Tk program as an infinite loop that continually scans for the occurrence of specified events (bindings). When it detects such an event, like a mouse click or control key, then it executes the actions bound to that event. These actions can be any Tcl/Tk command or series of commands. Usually, they call functions that can perform complex operations. When finished, the program resumes its scanning, looking for other bound events. This scanning continues indefinitely until it is forcibly broken by an **exit** or **destroy** command, as is done with the CTRL-C binding. You can think of bindings as multiple entry points where different parts of the program begin. It is not really the same structure as a traditional hierarchical sequential program. You should think of a binding as starting its own sequence of commands, its own program. This means that to trace the flow of control for a Tk program, you start with the bindings. Each binding has its own path, its own flow of control.

mydir2

```
#!/bin/sh
# the next line restarts using wish \
exec wish "$0" "$@"

# Create scroll bar and listbox for directories
scroll bar .scrolldir -command ".listdir yview"
listbox .listdir -yscroll " .scrolldir set" -relief sunken -width 15 -height 15 -setgrid yes
pack .listdir .scrolldir  -side left  -fill both -expand yes -anchor w

# Create scroll bar and listbox for files
scroll bar .scroll -command ".list yview"
listbox .list -yscroll ".scroll set"  -relief sunken -width 15 -height 15 -setgrid yes
pack .list .scroll   -side left  -fill both -expand yes -anchor w

# Check to see if an argument was entered
if $argc>0 {set dir [lindex $argv 0]} else {set dir "."}

# Function to list directories and files.
#Current entries are first deleted
proc listdirsfunc dir {
   .listdir delete 0 end
   .list delete 0 end
   cd $dir
   foreach i [exec ls -a ] {
     if [file isdirectory $i] {
        .listdir insert end $i
        } else {
           .list insert end $i
           }
      }
   }

# Display directories and files the first time
listdirsfunc $dir

# Set up bindings for the browser. Directories are bound to the Mouse double-click
bind all <Control-c> {destroy .}
bind .listdir <Double-Button-1> {set i [selection get]
                  listdirsfunc  $I}
```

SpecTcl

Instead of explicitly programming Tk code to create a GUI interface, you can use the SpecTcl GUI builder. SpecTcl generates Tcl/Tk code for a user interface that you can then use in a Tcl/Tk program. You can download the Unix version of SpecTcl from the **sunscript.sun.com** Web site. SpecTcl is a Tcl/Tk program itself and requires at least Tcl 7.6 and Tk 4.7, though 8.0 for each is preferred. Your OpenLinux CD-ROM currently has only Tcl 7.5 and Tk 4.1, so to run SpecTcl you will have to first download, compile, and install version 8.0 for both Tcl and Tk.

Once you have downloaded SpecTcl and have decompressed and unpacked it, you can change to the **SpecTel1.1** directory and then to the **bin** directory. (You should unpack it in the directory where you want it installed. There you will find the commands **specTcl** and **specJava**. Run **specTcl** to start the program.) You will then be asked if you want output in the form of Tcl, Java, http, or Perl code. The Linux version of SpecTcl is an X-Windows program. It has its own GUI interface with windows, menus, and icons. You can easily create GUI widgets for a user interface with just menu selections or simple mouse operations. SpecTcl features a grid geometry manager that makes creating cross-platform GUI interfaces easy to do. Figure 25-3 shows the SpecTcl window.

The Tcl/Tk Web site contains complete documentation on using SpecTcl. Creating a widget is as simple as clicking on its icon in the palette and dragging it to the grid.

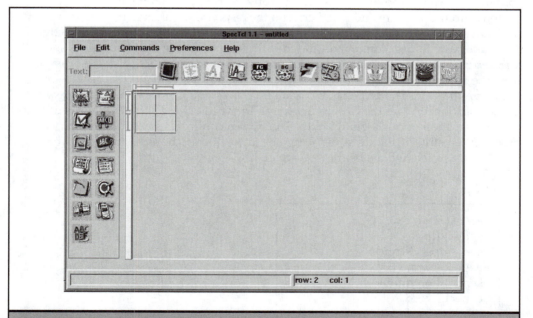

Figure 25-3.   *SpecTcl, the Tcl/Tk GUI Builder*

The palette is the double row of icons to the side. Moving a cursor over an icon will display an explanation of its operation in a small information box at the bottom of the SpecTcl window.

To configure a widget you just select it and then choose the options you want from the toolbar. The toolbar is the row of icons across the top of the window. The toolbar contains commonly used options with drop-down menus such as fonts and point sizes for text widgets. The complete set of options for a particular widget is accessible by first clicking on the widget and then selecting the **widget properties** entry in the Edit menu (for text widgets, there is a text properties entry). Click on the small box for **Additional properties** to list all the possible configuration options.

To move a widget, select and drag it. To delete one, select it and press the DEL key. You can also click on the Trash can icon in the upper-right corner. The grid organizes the interface you are building into rows and columns that you can select and then resize, copy, or delete. You can also insert new rows and columns. Once you have created your interface, you can test it by clicking on the test icon in the upper right.

Expect

Expect has several commands that you can use to automatically interact with any Unix program and utility that prompts you for responses. For example, the login procedure for different systems using ftp or telnet can be automatically programmed with Expect commands. Expect is designed to work with any interactive program. It waits for a response from a program and will then send the response specified in its script. You can drop out of the script with a simple command and interact with the program directly.

Three basic Expect commands added to Tcl scripts are the **send**, **expect**, and **interact** commands. The **expect** command will wait to receive a string or value from the application you are interacting with. The **send** command will send a string to that application. The **interact** command places you into direct interaction with the application, ending the Expect/Tcl script. In the following script, Expect is used to perform an anonymous login with ftp. The **spawn** command starts up the ftp program. The Internet address of the ftp site is assumed to be an argument to this script, and as such, will be held in the **argv** list.

myftp

```
#!/usr/bin/expect
spawn ftp
send "open $argv\r"
expect "Name"
send "anonymous\r"
expect "word:"
send "richlp@turtle.trek.com\r"
interact
```

To run Expect commands, you have to first enter the Expect shell. In the previous script, the Expect shell is invoked with the command **#!/usr/bin/expect**. Be sure to add execute permission with **chmod 755 myftp**:

```
$myftp ftp.caldera.com
```

The **expect** command can take two arguments, the pattern to expect and an action to take if the pattern is matched. **expect** can also take as its argument a block of pattern/action arguments. In this case, **expect** can match on alternative patterns, executing the action only for the pattern it receives. For example, the **ftp** command may return a "Connection refused" string instead of a "Name" string. In that case, you would want to issue this message and exit the Expect script. If you want more than one action taken for a pattern, you can encase them in braces, separated by semicolons.

Another useful Expect command is **timeout**. You can set the **timeout** command to a number of seconds, then have **expect** check for the **timeout**. To set the number of seconds for a **timeout**, you use **set** to assign it to the **timeout** variable (the default is 10 seconds). To have the **expect** command detect a **timeout**, you use the word **timeout** as the **expect** command's pattern. With the **timeout**, you can add an action to take. An example of an **expect** script follows:

```
set timeout 20
end "open $argv"
expect {
    timeout {puts "Connection timed out\N"; exit }
    "Connection refused"  {puts "Failed to connect\N"; exit}
    "Unknown host" {puts "$argv is unknown\n"; exit}
    "Name"
}
```

Tcl	The Tcl programming language and interpreter (current version 8.0) tcl8.0.tar.gz
Tk	The Tk programming language (current version 8.0) tk8.0.tar.gz

Table 25-1. *Tcl/Tk Software Products*

SpecTcl	Tcl/Tk GUI builder; creates GUI user interfaces SpecTcl1.1.tar.gz
Tcl Plugin	The Tcl/Tk Web page plugin (current version 2.0); viewer for Tcl/Tk applications (Tclets) tclplugin1.1.386.rpm
TclHttpd	Tcl/Tk Web Server tclhttpd.tar.Z
sunscript.sun.com	Tcl/Tk Web site

Table 25-1. *Tcl/Tk Software Products* (continued)

Command	**Action**
set *list values*	Create a list and assign values to it
lsearch(*list, pattern*)	Search for pattern in elements of a list
lindex(*list, index*)	Return the value of the indexed element in a list
llength(*list*)	Return the number of elements in a list
linsert(*list, index, value-list*)	Insert a new element into a list after the index
lreplace(*list, index, value-list*)	Replace element indexed with new value
lappend(*list, value-list*)	Append new values to the end of the list
concat(*lists*)	Combine elements of several lists into one list
list (*lists*)	Combine lists into a larger list whose elements are the respective lists
split(*str, delim*)	Split a string into a list, using delimiter to separate values
join(*list*)	Join elements of a list into a string
lsort(*list*)	Sort the list alphabetically or numerically

Table 25-2. *Tcl List Operations*

Assignments and Variables

`set`	Assign a value to a variable
`global`	Declare global variables
`incr`	Increment a variable by an integer value
`unset`	Delete variables
`upvar`	Reference a variable in a different scope
`variable`	Declare namespace variables
`array`	Array access operations like searches
`expr`	Math expressions

Control Structures and Procedures

`if`	Conditional command, extend with **else** and **elseif** blocks
`switch`	Switch selection structure
`while`	The **while** loop
`for`	The **for** loop, like C **for** loop
`foreach`	Loop through a list, or lists, of values
`break`	Forced loop exit
`continue`	Skip remainder of block and continue with next loop iteration
`proc`	Define a Tcl procedure
`return`	Return a value from a procedure
`source`	Read and execute Tcl commands in another file
`uplevel`	Execute a command in a different scope

Files

`file`	Obtain file information
`open`	Open a file
`close`	Close a file

Table 25-3.   *Common Tcl Commands*

Files

eof	Check for end of file
fcopy	Copy from one file to another
flush	Flush output from a file's internal buffers
glob	Match file names using glob pattern characters
read	Read blocks of characters from a file
seek	Set the seek offset of a file
tell	Return the current offset of a file
socket	Open a TCP/IP network connection

Input/Output

format	Format a string with conversion specifiers, like sprintf in C
scan	Reads and converts elements in a string using conversion specifiers, like scanf in C
gets	Read a line of input
puts	Write a string to output

Strings

binary	Convert between strings and binary data
regexp	Match on string using regular expressions
regsub	Perform substitutions using patterns with regular expressions
split	Split a string up into list elements
string	Operate on strings
subst	Perform substitutions on a string

System

catch	Trap errors
cd	Change the working directory
clock	Returns the time and formats date strings

Table 25-3. *Common Tcl Commands* (continued)

System

`error`	Raise an error
`eval`	Evaluate as a command a list of arguments
`exec`	Execute a Unix command
`exit`	End the program and exit
`pwd`	Returns the current working directory
`info`	Query the state of the Tcl interpreter
`trace`	Check values of variables

Table 25-3. *Common Tcl Commands* (continued)

Option	Description
`-anchor`	How information is displayed in the widget. Must be one of the values n, ne, e, se, s, sw, w, nw, or center
`-background`	The normal background color to use when displaying the widget
`-bitmap`	A bitmap to display in the widget
`-borderwidth`	The width of the 3D border to draw around the outside of the widget
`-cursor`	The mouse cursor to be used for the widget
`-font`	The font to use when drawing text inside the widget
`-foreground`	The normal foreground color to use when displaying the widget
`-geometry`	Specifies the desired geometry for the widget's window
`-highlightbackground`	The color to display in the traversal highlight region when the widget does not have the input focus
`-highlightcolor`	The color to use for the traversal highlight rectangle that is drawn around the widget when it has the input focus

Table 25-4. *Tk Common Standard Options*

Option	Description
-image	Specifies an image to display in the widget
-insertbackground	Color to use as background in the area covered by the insertion cursor
-justify	Justifies multiple lines of text displayed in a widget
-orient	Orientation for widgets that can position themselves, such as scroll bars
-padx	Specifies how much extra space to request for the widget in the X-direction
-pady	Specifies how much extra space to request for the widget in the Y-direction
-relief	Specifies the 3D effect desired for the widget
-selectbackground	Specifies the background color to use when displaying selected items
-text	String to be displayed inside the widget
-textvariable	Specifies the name of a variable
-troughcolor	Color to use for the rectangular trough areas in widgets, such as scroll bars and scales
-underline	Specifies the integer index of a character to underline in the widget
-xscrollcommand	Command used to communicate with horizontal scroll bars
-yscrollcommand	Command used to communicate with vertical scroll bars
Button Options	
-command	Specifies a Tcl command to associate with the button
-selectimage	Image to display when the checkbutton is selected
-height	Height for the button
-selectcolor	Background color to use when the button is selected

Table 25-4. *Tk Common Standard Options* (continued)

Option	Description
`-state`	Specifies one of three states for the radio button: normal, active, or disabled
`-variable`	Global variable to set to indicate whether or not this button is selected

Table 25-4.   *Tk Common Standard Options (continued)*

Widget	Description
`button`	A button
`canvas`	A canvas window
`checkbutton`	A checkbutton
`entry`	An input box
`frame`	A frame is a simple widget. Its primary purpose is to act as a spacer or container for complex window layouts
`image`	Create images widget for displaying pictures
`label`	Labels
`listbox`	Listboxes with selectable lists of items
`menu`	Menus
`menubutton`	A menu button to access the menu
`message`	Messages
`radiobutton`	A radio button
`scrollbar`	Scroll bar
`text`	An editable text box
`scale`	Scale

Table 25-5.   *Standard Tk Widgets*

Event Operations	Description
bind	The **bind** command associates Tcl scripts with X events
bindtags	Binds commands to tags
selection	Widget or text selected by mouse
Geometry Managers	
pack	Pack widgets next to each other
grid	Pack widgets in a grid of rows and columns
place	Place widgets in positions in frame
Window Operations	
destroy	Close a Tk window
toplevel	Select top-level window
wm	Set window features
uplevel	Move up to previous window level

Table 25-6. *Tk Operations*

Chapter Twenty-Six

gawk

The **gawk** filter differs from other filters you have seen in that it has no predefined task to perform. The filters you have examined so far were all designed to perform very specific tasks such as searching text or sorting lines. The **gawk** filter, however, has no predefined task. It is up to the user to define a task for **gawk** to perform. **gawk** has its own programming language with commands and operators that the user can choose from with which to construct a task. In this sense, **gawk** can be described as a programmable filter. You program **gawk** to perform a task. With **gawk**, you can then filter data any way you like. You can instruct **gawk** to simply display lines in a text, much like cat, or to search for patterns like grep, or even count words like wc. In each case you could add your own customized filtering capabilities. You could display only part of each line, or search for a pattern in a specific field, or count only words that are capitalized.

You can use **gawk** directly, or you can place **gawk** within a shell file that you can then execute. The name of the shell file can be thought of as a new filter that you have created. In effect, with **gawk** you can define your own filters. In this sense, there are two ways of thinking about **gawk**. **gawk** is itself a filter that you can invoke on the command line like any other filter, and **gawk** is a programmable filter that you can use to create your own filters. This chapter will examine both aspects of **gawk**. First we will examine **gawk** as a filter, with all its different features. Then we will see how you can use **gawk** to define your own filters.

The **gawk** utility has all the flexibility and complexity of a programming language. **gawk** has a set of operators that allow it to make decisions and calculations. You can also declare variables and use them in control structures to control how lines are to be processed. Many of the programming features are taken from the C programming language and share the same syntax. All of this makes for a very powerful programming tool.

gawk is the GNU version of the Unix **awk** utility. **awk** was originally created as a standard utility for the Unix operating system. One of its creators is Brian Kernighan, who developed the Unix operations system. An enhanced version of **awk**, called **nawk**, was developed later to include file handling. With **nawk**, you can access several files in the same program. **gawk** is a further enhancement, including the added features of **nawk** as well as the standard capabilities of **awk**.

The gawk Command

The **gawk** instruction takes as its arguments a **gawk** instruction and a list of file names. The **gawk** instruction is encased in single quotes and is read as one argument. The **gawk** instruction itself consist of two segments, a pattern and an action. The action is enclosed in brackets. The term 'pattern' can be misleading. It is perhaps clearer to think of the pattern segment as a condition. The pattern segment can be either a pattern search or a test condition of the type found in programming languages. The **gawk** utility has a full set of operators with which to construct complex conditions. You can think of a pattern search as just one other kind of condition for retrieving records. Instead of simply matching patterns as in the case of grep, the user specifies a condition. Records that meet that condition are then retrieved. The actions in the action segment are then applied to the record. The next example shows the syntax of a **gawk** instruction, which you can think of as **condition {***action***}**.

```
pattern {action}
```

The **gawk** utility operates on either files or the standard input. You can list file names on the command line after the instruction. If there are no file names listed, then input is taken from the standard input. The next example shows the structure of the entire **gawk** instruction. The invocation of **gawk** consists of the **gawk** keyword followed by a **gawk** instruction and file names. As with the **sed** commands, the instruction should be placed within single quotes to avoid interpretation by the shell. Since the condition and action are not separate arguments for **gawk**, you need to enclose them both in one set of quotes. The next example shows the syntax of a **gawk** command (see also Table 26-1).

```
$ gawk 'pattern {action}' filenames
```

You can think of the pattern in a **gawk** instruction as referencing a line. The **gawk** action is then performed on that line. However, both the action and pattern have defaults that allow you to leave either of them out. The print action is the default action. If an action is not specified, the line is printed. The default pattern is the selection of every line in the text. If the pattern is not specified, the action is applied to all lines. The next two examples print all lines with the pattern "Penguin." The pattern segment is a pattern search. A pattern search is denoted by a pattern enclosed in slashes. All records with this pattern are retrieved. The action segment in the first example contains the **print** command. The **print** command outputs the line to the standard output. However, in the second example there is no action segment. The default action is then used, the **print** action.

books

Tempest	Shakespeare	15.75	Penguin
Christmas	Dickens	3.50	Academic
Iliad	Homer	10.25	Random
Raven	Poe	2.50	Penguin

```
$ gawk '/Penguin/{print}' books
Tempest      Shakespeare   15.75    Penguin
Raven        Poe            2.50    Penguin
```

```
$ gawk '/Penguin/' books
Tempest      Shakespeare  15.75  Penguin
Raven        Poe           2.50  Penguin
```

Pattern Searches and Special Characters

As with the **sed** utility, **gawk** can retrieve lines using a pattern search that contains special characters. The pattern is designated with a beginning and ending slash, and placed in the pattern segment of the **gawk** instruction.

```
/pattern/ {action}
```

The pattern search is performed on all the lines in the file. If the pattern is found, the action is performed on the line. In this respect, **gawk** performs very much like an editing operation. Like **sed**, a line is treated as a line of text and the pattern is searched for throughout the line. In the next example, **gawk** searches for any line with the pattern 'Poe.' When a match is found, the line is output.

```
$ gawk '/Poe/{print}' books
Raven        Poe          2.50    Penguin
```

You can use the same special characters for **gawk** that are used for regular expressions in the **sed** filter and the Ed editor. The first example here searches for a pattern at the beginning of the line. The special character ^ references the beginning of a line. The second example searches for a pattern at the end of a line using the special character $.

```
$ gawk '/^Christmas/{print}' books
Christmas    Dickens   3.50   Academic

$ gawk '/Random$/{print}' books
Iliad        Homer    10.25   Random
```

As in Ed and Sed, you can use special characters to specify variations on a pattern. The period matches any character, the asterisk matches repeated characters, and the brackets match a class of characters: ., *, and []. In the first example here, the period is used to match any pattern in which a single character is followed by the characters "en".

```
$ gawk '/.en/{print}' books
Christmas    Dickens    3.50   Academic
Raven        Poe        2.50   Penguin
```

The next example uses the brackets and asterisk special characters to specify a sequence of numbers. The set of possible numbers is represented by the brackets enclosing the range of numeric characters, [0-9]. The asterisk then specifies any repeated sequence of numbers. The context for such a sequence consists of the characters .50. Any number ending with .50 will be matched. Notice that the period is quoted with a backslash to treat it as the period character, not as a special character.

```
$ gawk '/[0-9]*\.50/ {print}' books
Christmas    Dickens    3.50   Academic
Raven        Poe        2.50   Penguin
```

gawk also uses the extended special characters: **+**, **?**, and **|**. The **+** and **?** are variations on the ***** special character. The **+** matches one or more repeated instances of a character. The **?** matches zero or one instance of a character. The **|** provides alternative patterns to be searched. In the next example, the user searches for a line containing either the pattern "Penguin" or the pattern "Academic".

```
$ gawk '/Penguin|Academic/ {print}' books
Tempest      Shakespeare  15.75   Penguin
Christmas    Dickens       3.50   Academic
Raven        Poe           2.50   Penguin
```

Variables, Constants, and Patterns

gawk provides for the definition of variables. In **gawk**, there are three types of variables: field variables, special **gawk** variables, and user-defined variables. **gawk** automatically defines both the field and special variables. The user can define his or her own variables. You can also define arithmetic and string constants. Arithmetic constants consist of numeric characters and string constants consist of any characters enclosed within double quotes.

Field variables are designed to reference fields in a line. A field is any set of characters separated by a field delimiter. The default delimiter is a space or tab. As with other database filters, **gawk** numbers fields from 1. **gawk** defines a field variable for each field in the file. A field variable consists of a dollar sign followed by the number of the field. **$2** references the second field. The variable **$0** is a special field variable that contains the entire line. A variable may be used in either the pattern or action segment of the **gawk** instruction. If more than one variable is listed, they are separated by commas. Notice that the dollar sign is used differently in **gawk** than in the shell. In the next example, the second and fourth fields of the books file are printed out. The **$2** and **$4** reference the second and fourth fields.

books

Tempest	Shakespeare	15.75	Penguin
Christmas	Dickens	3.50	Academic
Iliad	Homer	10.25	Random
Raven	Poe	2.50	Penguin

```
$ gawk '{print $2, $4}' books
Shakespeare    Penguin
Dickens        Academic
Homer          Random
Poe            Penguin
```

In the next example, the user outputs the line with the pattern "Dickens" twice; first reversing the order of the fields and then with the fields in order. The **$0** is used to output all the fields in order, the entire line.

```
$ gawk '/Dickens/ {print $4, $3, $2, $1; print $0}' books
Academic   3.50   Dickens   Christmas
Christmas Dickens   3.50   Academic
```

gawk defines a set of special variables that provide information about the line being processed. The variable **NR** contains the number of the current line. The variable **NF** contains the number of fields in the current line. There are other special variables that hold the field and record delimiters. There is even one, **FILENAME**, that holds the name of the input file. The **gawk** special variables are listed in Table 26-1.

Both special variables and user-defined variables do not have a dollar sign placed before them. To use such variables, you only need to specify their name. The next example combines both the special variable **NR** with the field variables **$2** and **$4** to print out the line number of the line followed by the contents of fields two and four. The **NR** variable holds the line number of the line being processed.

```
$ gawk '{print NR, $2, $4}' books
1 Shakespeare    Penguin
2 Dickens        Academic
```

```
3 Homer       Random
4 Poe         Penguin
```

You can also define your own variables, giving them any name you want. Variables can be named using any alphabetic or numeric characters as well as underscores. The name must begin with an alphabetic character. A variable is defined when you first use it. The type of variable is determined by the way it is used. If you use it to hold numeric values, then the variable is considered arithmetic. If you use it to hold characters, then the variable is considered a string. You need to be consistent in the way in which you use a variable. String variables should not be used in arithmetic calculations and visa versa.

You can assign a value to a variable using the assignment operator, **=**. The left-hand side of an assignment operation is always a variable and the right-hand side is the value assigned to it. A value can be the contents of a variable such as a field, special, or other user variable. It can also be a constant, as described in the next section. In the next example, the user assigns the contents of the second field to the variable **myfield**.

```
$ gawk '{myfield = $2; print myfield}' books
Shakespeare
Dickens
Homer
Poe
```

Pattern Search Operators

You can use the special operators, **~** and **!~** to carry out pattern searches on fields. Instead of using the equality operator to compare the entire field to a string, you can use the **~** operators to see if a certain pattern exists within the field. When using these operators to search fields, the right operand is the pattern and the left operand is the field to be searched. In the next example, the first field is searched for "mas".

```
$ gawk '($1 ~ /mas/) {print}' books
Christmas   Dickens   3.50   Academic
```

The next example retrieves all records whose first field does not contain the pattern "mas".

```
$ gawk '($1 !~ /mas/) {print}' books
Tempest    Shakespeare  15.75  Penguin
```

```
Iliad        Homer        10.25   Random
Raven        Poe           2.50   Penguin
```

Just as you can use special characters in a general pattern search, you can also use special characters to search fields. In the next example, the user matches both upper and lowercase versions of "Penguin" in the fourth field. The brackets special character is used to define a class for upper and lowercase 'P'.

```
$ gawk '($4 ~ /[Pp]enguin/) {print}' books
Tempest      Shakespeare  15.75   Penguin
Raven        Poe           2.50   Penguin
```

BEGIN and END Patterns

The **gawk** instruction has two special patterns that allow the user to specify actions to be executed before and after processing lines in the input. The **BEGIN** pattern specifies actions to be performed before lines are processed. The **END** pattern specifies actions to be performed after lines are processed. In the next example, the heading " Book List " is output before any lines are processed. After processing, the value of **NR** is printed. Since **NR** increments with each line, after processing, **NR** will hold the total count of the records in the file.

```
$ gawk 'BEGIN {print "Book List"} {print} END{ print "Total records is ",
NR}' books
Book List
Tempest      Shakespeare  15.75   Penguin
Christmas    Dickens       3.50   Academic
Iliad        Homer        10.25   Random
Raven        Poe           2.50   Penguin
Total records is 4
```

gawk Instruction Files

As **gawk** instructions become more complex, it is easier to handle them by placing them in a file that can then be read by **gawk**. If you need to ever make any changes, you only need to modify the file. The **-f** option allows **gawk** to read **gawk** instructions from a file instead of the command line. In the next example, the **gawk** instructions to list books published by Penguin are placed in a file called **findbk**. **gawk** is then invoked with the **-f** option and the **findbk** file name. The **gawk** instruction will then be read from the file **findbk**.

findbk

```
BEGIN {print "Book List";
    count = 1;
    }
/$4 ~ "Penguin"/ {
    count = count + 1;
    print;
    }
END {
    print "Total records found is ", count
    }
```

```
$ gawk -f findbk   books
Book List
Tempest      Shakespeare  15.75  Penguin
Raven        Poe           2.50  Penguin
Total records found is 2
```

Notice that you do not need any single quotes around the instruction. You can organize different parts of your instruction on separate lines, making for a more readable instruction. This feature is very helpful when using control structures, as we shall see.

Control Structures

gawk operates like a programming language. You can define variables, construct expressions, and assign values. **gawk** also includes a set of control structures to provide iteration and selection capability. There are three control structures that construct loops in **gawk**: the **while**, **for**, and **for-in** loops. There is one selection control structure, the **if** structure. The **gawk** control structures are listed in Table 26-1. With the exception of the **for-in** loop, these control structures are similar to those in the C programming language. There are also various commands for reading and outputting data. Table 26-1 lists the various input and output commands used in **gawk**.

gawk as User-Defined Filters

You can use **gawk** to define your own filters by placing the whole **gawk** instruction in a script file. You can then make the file executable, and the file name becomes a new Linux command. Within the script file, **gawk** instructions must be quoted. A script file literally contains a Linux command that will be executed in the shell. Within the script file, you need to write the instruction as if you were going to execute it on the command line. You can write the **gawk** pattern and actions on their own lines, but any carriage returns need to be enclosed within the **gawk** instruction's beginning and end quotes. This means that the first line of the **gawk** operation will begin with the keyword **gawk** followed on the same line by a single quote. Then you can enter in the pattern and actions of the **gawk** instruction using different lines. However, the end of the action needs to be terminated by a single quote, followed on the same line by any file name arguments. The syntax for such a format follows:

```
gawk '
    pattern {
        gawk-actions;
    } ' filenames
```

In the next example, the user has placed the entire **gawk** instruction in a script file called **field3**. The instruction prints out the first three fields in each line. Notice that the **gawk** instruction is quoted. Once you have set the execution permission for the script file with the **chmod** command, you can then execute the file by simply entering in the script file's name.

field3

```
gawk '{
for(i=1;(i <= 3);i++)
  {
  printf("%s\t", $i);
  }
printf("\n");
}' books
```

```
$ chmod 755 field3
$ field3
Tempest      Shakespeare   15.75
Christmas    Dickens        3.50
Iliad        Homer         10.25
Raven        Poe            2.50
```

Component	Description
-f *filename*	With this option, gawk will read its commands from the file name
-Fc	This option specifies a field delimiter, c, for the input file. The default delimiter is tab or space $ gawk -F: books

Output Operations

print	Output the current line to the standard output
print *var*	Output the variable to the standard output
print *var* **>>** *filename*	Output the variable to a file

Input Operations

getline *var*	Read next input line, return 0 if at end of file. If a variable is specified, it will read the input line to it
getline *var* **<<** *filename*	Read next input line read from the specified file, return 0 if at end of file. The line will read into the specified variable

Control Structures

{ *actions* **}**	A block is formed by opening and closing braces. A block groups actions, making them subject to a control structure such as a loop or enclosing the actions in the **gawk** instruction proper

if(*expression* **)**
   action
else
   action
	The **if** control structure executes an action if its expression is true. If false, then the **else** action is executed

Table 26-1. *gawk Options, Operators, Variables, and Control Structures*

Component	Description
Control Structures	
while(*expression*) *action*	The **while** control structure executes an action as long as its expression is true
for(*exp1*; *exp2*; *exp3*) *action*	The **for** control structure executes an action as long as exp2 is true. The first expression, exp1 is executed before the loop begins. The third expression, exp3, is executed within the loop after the action
for(*variable* **in** *arrayname*) *action*	The **for-in** control structure is designed for use with associative arrays. The variable operand is consecutively assigned the strings that index the array
next	The **next** statement stops operations on the current record and skips to the next record
exit	The **exit** statement ends all processing and executes the END command if there is one
Operators	
>	Greater than
<	Less than
>=	Greater than or equal
<=	Less than or equal
==	Equal
!=	Not equal
&&	Logical AND
||	Logical OR
!	Logical NOT
str ~ *regular expr*	Matches regular expression; right operand is a regular expression
str !~ *regular expr*	Does not match regular expression; right operand is a regular expression

Table 26-1.   *gawk Options, Operators, Variables, and Control Structures* (continued)

Component	Description
Initial and Terminating Patterns	
BEGIN	Execute operations before **gawk** begins processing
END	Execute operations after **gawk** finishes processing
Variables	
NR	Record number of current record
NF	Number of fields in current record
$0	The entire current record
$*n*	The fields in the current record, numbered from 1. For example, $1
FS	Input field delimiter; default delimiter is space or tab

Table 26-1. *gawk Options, Operators, Variables, and Control Structures* (continued)

PART SEVEN

Appendixes

Appendix A

Hardware Parameters

The auto-detection feature of the Installation program should determine exactly what hardware you have and allow the installation of Caldera OpenLinux to proceed without problems.

Occasionally, however, the auto-detection feature needs some "help" to correctly locate and use your hardware. If necessary, you provide this help by entering boot parameters when you start the installation process, or kernel parameters (called *insmod* parameters) when using the Kernel Module Manager during installation.

Each parameter indicates a type of hardware (or other option) and one or more values that identify that hardware or option so that it can be correctly used. Boot parameters are entered at the boot manager prompt, before the OpenLinux installation actually starts. The insmod parameters are entered during installation, when prompted from the Kernel Module Manager menus.

For example, at the LILO boot manager prompt, you might normally enter **linux** (or press ENTER if linux is the default).

```
LILO: linux
```

If you determine during installation that boot parameters are needed, you might enter something like this instead:

```
LILO: linux cdu31a=0x340,13 eth0=11,0x260,0,0,eth0
```

This example indicates the addressing information for a Sony CD-ROM drive and an Ethernet card. The equal sign (=) separates the parameter from the value you provide. Commas separate multiple values used for a particualr parameter. Spaces separate different parameters.

You can also use boot parameters to turn off the auto-detection feature if needed. For example, if the auto-detection feature checks for some types of CD-ROM drives, it may interfere with the configuration of some network cards as a side effect. You can overcome this by providing information about your CD-ROM drive and turning off the auto-detection, thus maintaining your network card configuration.

Next are some recommended boot and insmod parameters to help you access and configure hardware that may not respond well to the auto-detection. To use parameters, you may need to know information such as the IRQ interrupt and memory address used by your hardware. Consult your hardware documentation or call your manufacturer. If you have DOS already configured on your computer, you may be able to discover some relevant hardware information by reviewing the **config.sys** file in DOS.

Items enclosed in square brackets in the syntax diagrams are optional when you enter your parameters. Items in the syntax descriptions that are in italics are variables for which you must supply a value.

A device generally has only one boot parameter, which may have several value pairs. A kernel module can have several different parameters that all apply to the same device.

After entering one of these parameters at the boot manager prompt, watch the kernel messages to see if the device was recognized correctly. Messages will generally display either "failed" or the name of the device with the correct port, IRQ, etc.

After the device-specific listings are several additional settings that you can use to control the action of the kernel and device modules during startup.

CD-ROM Parameters

ISP16/MAD16/Mozart Soft Configurable CD-ROM

* **type:** cdrom (1)
* **kernel module: isp16**
* **boot parameters:** isp16=IO[,IRQ[,DMA]]][,TYPE]
* **possible insmod parameters:**
isp16_cdrom_base={[0x340],0x320,0x330,0x360}
isp16_cdrom_irq={[0],3,5,7,9,10,11}
isp16_cdrom_dma={[0],3,5,6,7}
isp16_cdrom_type={noisp16,[Sanyo],Panasonic,Sony,Mitsumi}
(noisp16 disables driver)

Sony CDU31A/CDU33A

* **type:** cdrom (2)
* **kernel module: cdu31a**
* **boot parameters:** cdu31a=iobase,[irq[,is_pas_card]]
iobase={0x320,0x330,0x340,0x360,0x634,0x654,0x1f88}
irq={-1,[0],3,4,5,6}
-1 is to scan
0 is for no irq
is_pas_card={0,1} for Pro Audio Spectrum Card
* **possible insmod parameters:**
cdu31a_port={0x320,0x330,0x340,0x360,0x634,0x654,0x1f88}
cdu31a_irq={-1,[0],3,4,5,6}
sony_pas_init={0,1}

Mitsumi FX001S/D (non IDE/ATAPI)

* **type:** cdrom (3)
* **kernel module: mcd**
* **boot parameters:** mcd=IO,IRQ,FLAG
IO={[0x300],..,0x3FC} (in 0x04 steps)

IRQ={3,5,9,[10],11}
FLAG={[0],1}
* possible insmod parameters:
mcd_port={[0x300],..,0x3FC} (in 0x04 steps)
mcd_irq={3,5,9,[10],11}
mitsumi_bug_93_wait=

Mitsumi XA/MultiSession (non IDE/ATAPI)

* type: cdrom (4)
* kernel module: mcdx
* boot parameter: mcdx=IO
* possible insmod parameters:
mcdx=IO

Matsushita/Panasonic/Teac/CreativeLabs on SBPRO (non IDE/ATAPI)

* type: cdrom (5)
* kernel module: sbpcd
* boot parameters: sbpcd=IO,TYPE
IO={0x...} default: 0x340
TYPE={LaserMate,SoundBlaster,SoundScape,Teac16bit}
* possible insmod parameters:
IO={0x...}
TYPE={0,1,2,3}
For TYPE, 0= LaserMate, 1= SoundBlaster, 2= SoundScape, 3= Teac16bit

Aztech/Orchid/Okano/Wearnes/Conrad/TXC/CyD ROM (non IDE)

* type: cdrom (6)
* kernel module: aztcd
* boot parameters: aztcd=iobase[,magic_number]
iobase={[0x320"],?}
magic_number=0x79
* possible insmod parameters:
aztcd=iobase[,magic_number]

Sony CDU535

* type: cdrom (7)
* kernel module: sonycd535

* **boot parameters:** sonycd535=IO[,IRQ]
IO={noprobe,0x340,?}
noprobe noprobe disables driver
IRQ={...}
* **possible insmod parameters:**
sonycd535=ADR
(sonycd535_cd_base_io={0x340,?})
(sonycd535_irq_used={...}?)

GoldStar R420

* **type:** cdrom (8)
* **kernel module: gscd**
* **boot parameters:** gscd=IO
* **possible insmod parameters:**
gscd={0x300,0x310,0x320,0x330,[0x340],0x350,0x360,0x370,0x380,
0x390, 0x3A0,0x3B0,0x3C0,0x3D0,0x3E0,0x3F0}

Philips/LMS CM206/226 on CM260

* **type:** cdrom (9)
* **kernel module: cm206**
* **boot parameters:** cm206=IO,IRQ
IO={0x300,..,[0x340],..,0x370}
IRQ={3..[11]}
auto
* **possible insmod parameters:**
cm206=IO,IRQ
cm206=auto

Optics Storage DOLPHIN 8000AT

* **type:** cdrom (10)
* **kernel module: optcd**
* **boot parameter:** optcd=IO
IO={0x340,?}
* **possible insmod parameters:**
optcd=IO

Sanyo CDR-H94A

* **type:** cdrom (11)
* **kernel module: sjcd**
* **boot parameters:** sjcd=IO[,IRQ[,DMA1]]
IO={[0x340],?}

IRQ={[0]}
DMA={[0]}
* possible insmod parameters:
sjcd_base=IO

SCSI Parameters

AdvanSys ABPxxx

* type: scsi (1)
* kernel module: `advansys`
* boot parameters: advansys=IO,IO2,IO3,IO4,DEBUGLEVEL
IO=0x... IO Port of 1st adapter
IO2=0x... IO Port of 2nd adapter
IO3=0x... IO Port of 3rd adapter
IO4=0x... IO Port of 4th adapter
DEBUGLEVEL=0xdeb{0..F)
* possible insmod parameters:
asc_ioport=IO[,IO2,IO3,IO4]
asc_dbglevel=DEBUGLEVEL
asc_iopflag=(0,1) disables or enables port scanning
asc_ioport={[0x110],0x130,0x150,0x190,0x210,0230,0x250,0x330}
asc_dbglevel={0..N}
0=Errors only, 1=High-level tracing, 2+=Verbose tracing

BusLogic

* type: scsi (2)
* kernel module: `BusLogic`
* boot parameters: BusLogic=IO, TAGGED_QUEUE, BUS_SETTLE,
LOCAL_OPT, GLOBAL_OPT, STRINGS
* possible insmod parameters:
IO_Address={0x330,0x334,0x230,0x234,0x130,0x134}
TaggedQueueDepth=
BusSettleTime=
LocalOptions=
BusLogic_GlobalOptions= | = assignment
TQ:[Default,Enable,Disable] set TaggedQueuingPermitted
ER:[Default,HardReset,BusDeviceReset,None]
NoProbe
noprobe

NoProbeISA
NoSortPCI

Ultrastor 14f (ISA), 24f (EISA), 34f (VLB)

* **type:** scsi (3)
* **kernel module:** `u14-34f`
* **boot parameters:** none
* **insmod parameters:** none

UltraStore

* **type:** scsi (4)
* **kernel module:** `ultrastor`
* **boot parameters:** none
* **possible insmod parameters:**
io_ports={[0x330],0x340,0x310,0x230,0x240,0x210,0x130,0x140}
dma_list={5,6,7,0}
irq_list={10,11,14,[15]}

Adaptec AHA152X

* **type:** scsi (5)
* **kernel module:** `aha152x`
* **boot parameters:** aha152x=IO, IRQ, SCSI_ID, RECONNECT, PARITY,
SYNC, DELAY, EXT_TRANS
IO={0x140,[0x340]}
IRQ={9,10,[11],12}
SCSI_ID={0..[7]}
RECONNECT={0,[1]}
PARITY={0,[1]}
SYNC={[0],1}
DELAY={..,[100],..}
EXT_TRANS={[0],1}
* **possible insmod parameters:**
aha152x=IO, IRQ, SCSI_ID, RECONNECT, PARITY, SYNC, DELAY,
EXT_TRANS
aha152x1=IO, IRQ, SCSI_ID, RECONNECT, PARITY, SYNC, DELAY,
EXT_TRANS
(The meaning and value of items in insmod parameters are
given previously under boot parameters for this device.)
* **devices supported:**
Adaptec 152x, 151x, 1505, 282x, Sound Blaster 16 SCSI, SCSI

Pro, Gigabyte, and other AIC 6260/6360-based products
(Standard)

Adaptec 154x, AMI FastDisk VLB, DTC 329x (Standard)

* **type:** scsi (6)
* **kernel module: aha1542**
* **boot parameters:** aha1542=IO[,BUSON,BUSOFF[,DMASPEED]]
IO={0x130,0x134,0x230,0x234,[0x330],0x334,0x340}
BUSON={2,..,[7],..,15}
BUSOFF={1,..,[5],..,64}
DMASPEED={[5],6,7,8,10}
* **possible insmod parameters:** none

Adaptec AHA1740

* **type:** scsi (7)
* **kernel module: aha1740**
* **boot parameters:** none
* **possible insmod parameters:**
slot=
base=
irq_level={9,10,11,12,14,15}

Adaptec AHA274X/284X/294X

* **type:** scsi (8)
* **kernel module: aic7xxx**
* **boot parameters:** aic7xxx=extended,no_reset,irq_trigger
extended={0,[1]} 0= extended translation off
* **possible insmod parameters:**
aic7xxx_extended={0,1}
aic7xxx_no_reset={0,1}
aic7xxx_irq_trigger={-1,0,1}
-1= use board setting, 0= use edge triggered, 1= use level triggered

Future Domain 16xx

* **type:** scsi (9)
* **kernel module: fdomain**
* **boot parameters:** fdomain=IO,IRQ[,ADAPTER_ID]
* **insmod_params:**

port_base={0x140,0x150,0x160,0x170}
bios_base={0xc8000,0xca000,0xce000,0xde000,0xcc000,0xd0000,0xe0000}
interrupt_level={3,5,10,11,12,14,15}
this_id=
* **devices supported:**
Future Domain BIOS versions supported for autodetect: 2.0,
3.0, 3.2, 3.4 (1.0), 3.5 (2.0), 3.6, 3.61
Chips supported: TMC-1800, TMC-18C50, TMC-18C30, TMC-36C70
Boards supported: Future Domain TMC-1650, TMC-1660, TMC-1670,
TMC-1680, TMC-1610M/MER/MEX
Future Domain TMC-3260 (PCI)
Quantum ISA-200S, ISA-250MG
Adaptec AHA-2920 (PCI)
Possibly some IBM boards

Always IN2000

* **type:** scsi (10)
* **kernel module: in2000**
* **boot parameters:**
in2000=ioport:addr,noreset,nosync:x,period:ns,disconnect:x,debug:x,proc:x
* **possible insmod parameters:**
setup_strings=
io_ports={0x100,0x110,0x200,0x220}
irq={10,11,14,15}
addr={0xc8000,0xd0000,0xd8000}

Generic NCR5380/53c400 SCSI

* **type:** scsi (11)
* **kernel module: g_NCR5380**
* **boot_param:** ncr5380=IO,PORT[,DMA] ncr53c400=IO,IRQ
IO={[0x350],?}
IRQ={[5],...,254,255}
254 autoprobe
255 no irq
* **possible insmod parameters:**
ncr_addr=IO the port or base address (for port or memory mapped)
ncr_irq=IRQ the interrupt
ncr_dma=DMA the DMA
ncr_5380=1 to set up for a NCR5380 board
ncr_53c400=1 to set up for a NCR53C400 board

NCR53c406a

> * **type:** scsi (12)
> * **kernel module: NCR53c406a**
> * **boot parameters:** ncr53c406a=IO[,IRQ[,FAST_PIO]]
> IO={0x230,[0x330]}
> IRQ={10,11,12,15}
> FAST_PIO={0,[1]} 0: slow 1: fast
> * **possible insmod parameters:**
> port_base=IO
> irq_level=IRQ
> fast_pio=FAST_PIO
> dma_chan={[5],?}
> bios_base={0xD8000,0xc8000}

Qlogicfas Driver Version 0.45, chip ... at ..., IRQ ..., TPdma:

> * **type:** scsi (13)
> * **kernel module: glogicfas**
> * **boot parameters:** none
> * **possible insmod parameters:** none
> * **io_ports:**
> 0x230,0x330

QLogic ISP1020 Intelligent SCSI Processor Driver (PCI)

> * **type:** scsi (14)
> * **kernel module: glogicisp**
> * **boot parameters:** none
> * **possible insmod parameters:** none

Pro Audio Spektrum Studio 16

> * **type:** scsi (15)
> * **kernel module: pas16**
> * **boot parameters:** pas16=IO,IRQ
> * **possible insmod parameters:**
> io_port={0x388,0x384,0x38c,0x288}
> irq={3,5,7,10,12,14,15,255} 255= no irq
> noauto=?

Seagate ST0x/Future Domain TMC-8xx/TMC-9xx

* **type:** scsi (16)
* **kernel module: seagate**
* **boot parameters:** st0x=ADR,IRQ tmc8xx=ADR,IRQ
* **possible insmod parameters:**
controller_type={1,2} 1= SEAGATE, 2=FD
base_address={0xc8000,0xca000,0xcc000,0xce000,0xdc000,0xde000}
irq={3,[5]}

Trantor T128/T128F/T228

* **type:** scsi (17)
* **kernel module: t128**
* **boot parameters:** t128=ADR,IRQ
ADR={0xcc000,0xc8000,0xdc000,0xd8000}
IRQ={3,[5],7,10,12,14,15,-1-2} -1=no irq, -2=autoprobe
* **possible insmod parameters:**
address=ADR
irq=IRQ

DTC 3180/3280

* **type:** scsi (18)
* **kernel module: dtc**
* **boot parameters:** dtc=ADR,IRQ
* **possible insmod parameters:** none

NCR53c{7,8}xx (rel 17)

* **type:** scsi (19)
* **kernel module: 53c7, 8xx**
* **boot parameters:**
ncr53c700,ncr53c700-66,ncr53c710,ncr53c720=mem,io,irq,dma
ncr53c810,ncr53c820,ncr53c825=mem,io,irq or
pci,bus,device,function
* **possible insmod parameters:**
base=ADR
io_port=IO
irq=IRQ
dma=DMA
perm_options=BITMASK
where BITMASK is "logical or" of the following flags

```
OPTION_SYNCHRONOUS 0x400
OPTION_IO_MAPPED 0x1000
OPTION_DEBUG_TEST1 0x10000
OPTION_DISCONNECT 0x8000000
OPTION_ALWAYS_SYNCHRONOUS 0x20000000
so
normal 0x11400
disconnect 0x8011400
sync 0x20011400
sync & disconnect 0x28011400
```

NCR 53C810, 53C815, 53C820, 53C825

* **type:** scsi (20)
* **kernel module:** `ncr53c8xx`
* **boot parameters:** none
* **possible insmod parameters:** none
* **devices supported:**
NCR 53C810, 53C815, 53C820, 53C825

EATA-DMA (DPT, NEC, AT&T, SNI, AST, Olivetti, Alphatronix)

* **type:** scsi (21)
* **kernel module:** `eata_dma`
* **boot parameters:** none
* **possible insmod parameters:** none
* **io_ports:**
0x1F0,0x170,0x330,0x230 (ISA)
0x1c88 (in 0x1000 steps) (EISA)
* **devices supported:**
ISA-based EATA-DMA boards like PM2011, PM2021, PM2041, PM3021
EISA-based EATA-DMA boards like PM2012B, PM2022, PM2122,
PM2322, PM2042, PM3122, PM3222, PM3332
PCI-based EATA-DMA boards like PM2024, PM2124, PM2044,
PM2144, PM3224, PM3334

EATA-PIO (old DPT PM2001, PM2012A)

* **type:** scsi (22)
* **kernel module:** `eata_pio`
* **boot parameter:** none

* **possible insmod parameters:** none
* **io_ports:**
0x1F0,0x170,0x330,0x230

Western Digital WD 7000 (FASST/ASC/xX)

* **type:** scsi (23)
* **kernel module: wd7000**
* **boot parameters:** wd7000=IRQ,DMA
* **possible insmod parameters:**
wd7000_setupIRQ=IRQ
wd7000_setupDMA=DMA
* **io_ports:**
0x300,0x308,0x310,0x318,0x320,0x328,0x330,0x338,
0x340,0x348,0x350,0x358,0x360,0x368,0x370,0x378,
0x380,0x388,0x390,0x398,0x3a0,0x3a8,0x3b0,0x3b8,
0x3c0,0x3c8,0x3d0,0x3d8,0x3e0,0x3e8,0x3f0,0x3f8

EATA ISA/EISA (DPT PM2011/021/012/022/122/322)

* **type:** scsi (24)
* **kernel module: eata**
* **boot parameters:** none
* **possible insmod parameters:** none
* **devices supported:**
DPT SmartCache, SmartCache Plus, SmartCache III, SmartCache
IV and SmartRAID (Standard)

AM53C974

* **type:** scsi (25)
* **kernel module: am53c974**
* **boot parameters:** AM53C974=HOST_SCSI_ID, TARGET_SCSI_ID,
MAX_RATE, MAX_OFFSET
HOST_SCSI_ID ? SCSI id of the bus controller
TARGET_SCSI_ID ? SCSI id of target
MAX_RATE ? max. transfer rate
MAX_OFFSET ? max. sync. offset (0=asynchronous)
* **possible insmod parameters:** none
* **devices supported:**
AM53/79C974 PCI SCSI

PPA

> * **type:** scsi (26)
> * **kernel module: ppa**
> * **boot parameters:** ppa=IO[,SPEED_HIGH[,SPEED_LOW[,NYBBLE]]]
> IO 0x378 The base address of PPA's parallel port
> SPEED_HIGH 1 Microsecond i/o delay used in data transfers
> SPEED_LOW 6 Microsecond delay used in other operations
> NYBBLE 0 1 to force the driver to use 4-bit mode
> * **possible insmod parameters:**
> ppa_base=IO 0x378 The base address of PPA's parallel port
> ppa_speed_high=MS 1 Microsecond i/o delay used in data transfers
> ppa_speed_low=MS 6 Microsecond delay used in other operations
> ppa_nybble=N 0 1 to force the driver to use 4-bit mode
> * **devices supported:**
> IOMEGA Parallel Port ZIP drive

Network Card Parameters

Most network cards accept the following boot parameters:

```
ether=IRQ,IO,MEM_START,MEM_END,DEV_NAME
```

Most network cards accept the following insmod parameters:

```
io=IO
irq=IRQ
```

Using Other Parameters

There are many other parameters that aren't specific to certain vendors' hardware. For other parameters, see these sections in the Linux HOWTO documents:

```
* BootPrompt HOWTO
* Modules HOWTO
```

> **NOTE:** *These documents can be viewed from the Caldera_Info icon on your Desktop under Linux references, or on the Caldera internet site (**www.caldera.com**). They can also be viewed from the **/OpenLinux/doc/HOWTO** directory on the Caldera CD-ROM.*

Appendix B

Software Packages Index

The Caldera OpenLinux Base CD-ROM contains over 400MB of compressed software. The software is divided into packages based on its function. For example, one software package contains the Desktop interface and related components, another package contains the Apache World Wide Web server, and another contains the Crisplite editor.

You determined what packages are on your system by the Installation option you selected while installing OpenLinux. You can install additional packages from the CD-ROM or from another location, such as a hard disk archive of the CD-ROM, or the Caldera ftp site. Each software package can be installed or uninstalled with a single command. For instructions on installing and removing packages, see Chapter 3. All package names are case sensitive.

This apppendix lists all of the packages on the CD-ROM. Software packages that are Caldera-proprietary (and therefore cannot be freely distributed) are marked with an asterisk (*). If you need to locate a specific file or software package, you can also refer to the online index of files on the CD-ROM, in the **/col/data** directory. More recent versions for many of these software packages as well as many other Linux applications can be found in the Redhat contrib directory at **ftp.redhat.com/pub /contrib/i386** and **ftp.caldera/pub/mirrors/redhat-contrib**.

*COL	Caldera OpenLinux setup files
*COLbaseCD-doc	Caldera OpenLinux setup files
*CriSPlite	Crisplite editor for Linux
*CriSPlite-doc	The Crisplite Editor User's Manual
DEV	All necessary block and character devices for Linux
ElectricFence	Development library for the kernel malloc debugger
ImageMagick	Graphics package for displaying, converting, and manipulating various image formats under X
ImageMagick-devel	Static libraries and header files for development of graphical applications based on ImageMagick
LPRng	Enhanced replacement for the standard Unix printing tools
LPRng-lpd	Enhanced Unix print daemon compatible with the lpr standard
LSM	The Linux Software Map
NetKit-B	Various network programs

`SysVinit`	System V compatible init program
`SysVinit-scripts`	Scripts for System V init, such as 'inittab' and '/etc/rc.d'
`XFree86`	XFree86 window system servers and fundamental programs
`XFree86-8514`	XFree86 8514 server
`XFree86-AGX`	XFree86 AGX server
`XFree86-I128`	XFree86 I128 server
`XFree86-Mach32`	XFree86 Mach32 server
`XFree86-Mach64`	XFree86 Mach64 server
`XFree86-Mach8`	XFree86 Mach8 server
`XFree86-Mono`	XFree86 Mono server
`XFree86-P9000`	XFree86 P9000 server
`XFree86-S3`	XFree86 S3 server
`XFree86-S3V`	XFree86 S3 ViRGE and ViRGE/VX server
`XFree86-SVGA`	XFree86 SVGA server
`XFree86-VGA16`	XFree86 VGA16 server
`XFree86-W32`	XFree86 W32 server
`XFree86-Xnest`	XFree86 nesting server
`XFree86-Xvfb`	XFree86 Xvfb server
`XFree86-addons`	X11R6 miscellaneous programs and their man pages
`XFree86-contrib`	Additional programs for X11R6 from the 'contrib tapes'
`XFree86-devel`	X11R6 static libraries, headers, and programming man pages
`XFree86-develprof`	X11R6 profiling libraries
`XFree86-develstatic`	X11R6 static libraries

XFree86-fonts	XFree86 Window System basic fonts
XFree86-fonts100	X11R6 100dpi fonts
XFree86-fonts75	X11R6 75dpi fonts
XFree86-fontscyrillic	X11R6 Cyrillic fonts—only needed on server side
XFree86-fontserver	X11R6 font server—only needed on server side
XFree86-fontsextra	X11R6 Hebrew and Asiatic fonts—only needed on server side
XFree86-fontsscale	X11R6 scalable fonts—only needed on server side
XFree86-imake	X11R6 'imake' programming tools
XFree86-misc	X11R6 miscellaneous programs and their man pages
XFree86-programs	Additional programs for X11R6 from the 'contrib tapes'
XFree86-server	XFree86 Window System server basic stuff
XFree86-server-devel	XFree86 devel stuff for dga, misc, vidmode
XFree86-server-modules	XFree86 loadable server modules for pex, xie, dga
XFree86-setup	XFree86 setup program 'XF86Setup'
XFree86-twm	Tab window manager for X
XFree86-xdm	Display manager allowing the user to log in or out of the system under X
XFree86-xsm	X session manager
Xaw3d	The 3D Athena widget libraries version 1.3, which can replace the normal Athena widget library
Xaw3d-devel	Header files and static libraries for developing programs that use Xaw3d
Xconfigurator	X-configuration utility
abuse	A really cool X/SVGA game
acm	X-based flight combat game
adduser	User administration program

adjtimex	User-level front-end to adjtimex-syscall
amd	The auto-mounter that allows file systems to be mounted on demand
anonftp	Enables anonymous ftp access
aout-libs	Libraries for compatibility with old a.out applications
apache-docs	Documentation for the apache HTTP server
apache-httpd	Apache HTTP server to provide WWW services
archie	Information retrieval system to query special archie databases containing entries from various ftp sites all over the net
arena	Freely available, HTML-3 capable WWW browser
ash	Small Bourne shell from Berkeley (only 40K)
at	The 'at' command allows processes to be started at a predetermined time
aumix	Curses-based audio mixer
autoconf	Extendable package of GNU m4 macros that creates shell scripts to automatically configure source code packages. This package requires the GNU 'm4' package
background	Additional background pictures for the X desktop
bash	The GNU Bourne Again shell, which is functionally comparable to 'tcsh' and is the standard shell under Linux
bc	GNU binary calculator with its own calculator language
bdflush	The kernel daemon 'bdflush' is used to write altered data blocks in the cache back to the hard disk at regular intervals. This replaces the old update daemon
bin86	The assembler 'as86', linker 'ld86', and GCC front-end 'bcc' from H. J. Lu

bind	DNS nameserver used for name services in networks
bind-lib	DNS resolver library and headers
bind-utils	DNS utilities, e.g. 'host', 'dig', 'dnsquery', 'nslookup'
binutils	GNU binary development utilities
bison	GNU parser generator (mightier than 'yacc')
blt	More widgets for the tk widget set
blt-devel	Development libraries and header files for the BLT widgets
bm2font	Bm2font converts bitmaps to LaTeX fonts
bootp	Bootp/DHCP server that allows clients to automatically get their networking information
bootpc	Bootpc, a client to get networking info from bootpd
bsd-games	The BSD game collection contains classic games like backgammon, cribbage, fortune, hangman, and worms
buffer	Utility to speed up writing tapes on remote tape drives
byacc	Public-domain yacc parser generator
cdp	Full-screen text mode program for playing audio CDs
cdwrite	Writes audio or data compact discs
cmu-snmp	CMU Simple Network Management Protocol agent
cmu-snmp-devel	CMU SNMP development libs and headers
cmu-snmp-utils	CMU Simple Network Management Protocol utilities
color-ls	Color ls—patched from GNU file utils
control-panel	Redhat Control Panel

coolmail	Shows status of the mailbox
cpio	GNU 'cpio' archiving program (used by rpm)
cproto	C prototype utility
crontabs	Root crontab file
cvs	Concurrent version control system, a comprehensive front-end to 'rcs', the GNU revision control system. 'cvs' also operates on directory trees
cxhextris	X-based color version of hextris
db	BSD database library for C
db-devel	Development libraries and header files for the Berkeley database library
ddd-doc	Motif-based X interface to the GDB, DBX and XDB debuggers. Documentation and manual page
ddd-dynamic	Motif-based X interface to the GDB, DBX and XDB debuggers. Uses Motif 2.0 shared libraries
ddd-semistatic	Motif-based X interface to the GDB, DBX and XDB debuggers. With Motif 2.0 libraries statically linked in
ddd-static	Motif-based X interface to the GDB, DBX and XDB debuggers. Completely statically linked
dialog	Tool to display tty dialog boxes from shell scripts
diffutils	GNU 'diff' utilities differentiate files
dip	Allows automatic modem dialing and creation of IP connections to be controlled with a script language
dosemu	The experimental DOS emulator
dthelp	Online help for the Caldera Looking Glass desktop
dump	BSD dump/restore backup system for extended-2 file systems

e2fsprogs	Programs and utilities for the extended-2 file systems
e2fsprogs-devel	Libraries and headers for the extended-2 file system tools
easyedit	The 'easyedit' extension for Emacs
ecc	Reed-Solomon Error Correcting Coder
ed	GNU Line Editor 'ed', an 8-bit-clean POSIX line editor
edy	Edy, a German colored, window-based editor
efax	Sends and receives faxes over class 1 or class 2 modems
eject	Ejects ejectable media and controls auto ejection
elm	Menu-based mail program 'elm'
elvis	Elvis editor (Elvis is like Vi)
exmh	'exmh' mail program
expect	A 'tcl' extension that allows easy interaction between programs and scripts
expect-devel	The development and demo part of expect with man pages
ext2ed	Extended-2 file system editor (*for hackers only*)
f2c	Fortran to C converter and static libraries
f2c-libs	Shared libs for running dynamically linked Fortran programs
faces	Face-saver database tools
faces-devel	Face-saver library and header
faces-xface	Utilities to handle X-Face headers
faq	FAQs—Frequently Asked Questions and answers about Linux
fdutils	Low-level floppy disk programs

file	The GNU 'file' utility determines the type of any file with the help of '/etc/magic'
fileutils	GNU File Utilities, a collection of many fundamental Unix programs
findutils	GNU search utilities (find, xargs, and locate)
flex	GNU fast lexical analyzer generator
flying	Pool, snooker, air hockey, and other table games
fort77	A front-end driver for 'f2c'
fortune-mod	Fortune cookie program with bug fixes
free-lj4	Remote-control tool for HP LJ4 printer series
free-lj4-german	Remote-control tool for HP LJ4 printer series in German
fsstnd	Linux File System Standard documentation
fstool	File system configuration tools
ftptool	A nice ftp front-end under Xview
fvwm	Feeble (Fine?) Virtual Window Manager (including menus and configuration files)
fvwm-icons	Additional icons for the 'fvwm' window manager
fvwm-modules	Additional modules for the fvwm window manager
fwhois	A 'finger' style whois tool
g77	GNU Fortran compiler 'g77'
g77_lib	GNU Fortran 'g77' library
gawk	GNU 'awk' utility for manipulating patterns in text files
gcal	Extended calendar with highlighting, holidays, etc.
gcc	GNU 'gcc' C compiler
gcc-c++	C++ support for 'gcc'

`gcc-objc`	Objective C support for 'gcc'
`gdb`	GNU 'gdb', symbolic debugger for C and other languages
`gdbm`	GNU database library for C
`gdbm-devel`	Development libraries and header files for GNU database library
`gdbm-static`	'gdbm libraries for static linking
`gencat`	'gencat' message cataloging program (from NetBSD)
`german-docs-L-Kurs`	L-Kurs—an introduction to Linux in German
`german-docs-intro`	Linux documentation in German
`gettext`	Utilities and libraries for programming with national language support (NLS)
`getty_ps`	Getty and uugetty programs for logging in
`ghostscript`	PostScript interpreter and renderer
`ghostscript-fonts`	Fonts for GhostScript
`ghostview`	Ghostview user interface for ghostscript
`giftrans`	Converts and manipulates GIFs
`gimp-static`	General Image Manipulation Program, a Photoshop-like tool with many plug-ins
`git`	GIT—GNU Interactive Tools
`glint`	Graphical Linux Installation Tool
`gn`	Gopher server
`gnat`	GNU Ada compiler
`gnuchess`	GNU 'chess' with 'xboard'. GNU Chess is a challenging ASCII-based chess program and XBoard is its X interface
`gnuplot`	'gnuplot', an interactive tool for displaying values and functions
`gpm`	General-purpose mouse support for Linux

gpm-devel	Development libraries and headers for writing mouse-driven programs
grep	GNU 'grep' utility
groff	GNU 'groff' text-formatting utility
groff-dvi	GNU 'groff' formatter for DVI
groff-gxditview	GNU 'groff' formatter for preview under X
groff-lj4	GNU 'groff' formatter for HP Laserjet 4 printers
groff-misc	GNU 'groff' miscellaneous tools
groff-ps	GNU 'groff' formatter for PostScript
gzip	GNU 'gzip' compression utility version 1.2.4
hdparm	Hard-disk utility for reading and setting (E)IDE performance parameters
helptool	Simple help file searching tool
hman	Motif-based manual browser under X
howto-ascii	Linux HOWTO documents in ASCII format
howto-dvi	Linux HOWTO documents in dvi format
howto-html	Linux HOWTO documents in HTML format
howto-ps	Linux HOWTO documents in PostScript format
howto-sgml	Linux HOWTO documents in sgml format
html	HyperText Markup Language 3.0 documentation in HTML format
iBCS	Intel binary compliance standard (iBCS-2) module
ical	Calender application based on Tcl/Tk
illustrated-audio	Combined image and sound player for X
imap	Provides support for IMAP and POP network mail protocols
indent	GNU C indenting program for formatting C source code

inn	'internetnews' news transport system
intimed	Time server for clock synchronization
ipfwadm	IP firewall administration tool
ipx	Utilities, init scripts, man pages, and configuration files for IPX (Internetwork Packet Exchange, a Novell-centric datagram protocol)
ipxripd	IPX RIP/SAP daemon for discovering/advertising IPX routing information (RIP) and services (SAP) across an IPX internetwork
ircii	Popular Unix Internet Relay Chat client
ircii-help	Help files and documentation for ircii
isdn4k-utils	Utilities for the kernel ISDN subsystem and some contributions
ispell	GNU ispell—interactive spelling checker
jed	Editor with multiple keybindings, a C-like extension language, colors, and many other features
jed-xjed	Jed editor for X
joe	Joe, the easy-to-use editor
kbd	The loadable keyboard driver 'kbd'. Required for loading alternative keyboard layouts
koules	A well-written SVGAlib game
kterm	Xterm with Kanji (Japanese characters) support
ktzset	Sets kernel time zone at boot time
ld.so	'ld.so' dynamic linker for shared libraries with ancillary programs. Contains 'ldconfig' and 'ldd' as well
ldp-dvi	Linux Documentation Project in dvi format
ldp-ps	Linux Documentation Project in PostScript format
ldp-txt	Linux Documentation Project in ASCII format

less	The pager 'less'
*lg-eval	Caldera Looking Glass desktop evaluation
*lg-doc	Caldera Desktop User's Guide
*lg-pg	Caldera Desktop Program Groups
*lg-rules	Caldera Desktop File Typing Rules and Layouts
lha	Creates and expands lharc format archives
libc	Libc and related libraries
libc-debug	Libc with debugging information
libc-devel	Additional, for compiling essential libraries
libc-profile	Libc with profiling support
libc-static	Libraries for static linking
libelf	Library for manipulating ELF object files
libg++	GNU 'g++' library
libg++-devel	Header files and libraries for C++ development
libgnat	Ada run-time system and shared library
libgr	Graphics library set for fbm, jpeg, pbm, pgm, png, pnm, ppm, rle, and tiff
libgr-devel	Headers and static libraries for developing graphical applications
libgr-progs	Utility programs for libgr
libpam	PAM (pluggable authentication modules), a library for dynamic (re)configuration of user authentication methods like /etc/passwd, /etc/shadow, S/key, and Kerberos
libpwdb	Modular password database library
libtermcap	Library for accessing the termcap database
libtermcap-devel	Development libraries and header files for termcap library
libtiff-develdoc	Additional man pages for the functions in libtiff

lilo	'LILO', the boot loader for Linux and other operating systems from Werner Almesberger
linux-kernel-binary	Linux kernel image and modules
linux-kernel-doc	Linux kernel documentation
linux-kernel-include	Linux kernel include files (required for C programming)
linux-source-alpha	Linux kernel sources for alpha axp architecture
linux-source-common	Linux kernel sources (architecture-independent common sources)
linux-source-i386	Linux kernel sources for Intel i386 architecture
linux-source-m68k	Linux kernel sources for Motorola m68k architecture
linux-source-mips	Linux kernel sources for mips architecture
linux-source-ppc	Linux kernel sources for Power PC architecture
linux-source-sparc	Linux kernel sources for sparc architecture
linuxdoc-sgml	Text formatting system used by the Linux Documentation Project
*lisa	Linux Installation and System Administration Utility
logrotate	Log file rotator
losetup	Programs for setting up and configuring loopback devices
lout	'lout' text-formatting system
lout-doc	Full documentation for the 'lout' text-formatting system
lrzsz	Zmodem programs such as 'lzrz', 'sz', 'rz', and others
lynx	ASCII-based HTML browser
lyx	A WYSIWYG front-end to LaTeX
m4	GNU 'm4' macro processor

`macutils`	Utilities for manipulating Macintosh file formats
`mailcap`	Redhat Mailcap package
`mailx`	BSD 'mailx' mail program
`make`	The GNU 'make' utility
`man-pages`	System manual pages from the Linux Documentation Project
`man_db`	Manual page reader
`maplay`	Plays MPEG-2 audio files in 16-bit stereo
`mawk`	Mike's New/POSIX awk Interpreter
`mc`	Midnight Commander visual shell
`metamail`	Tools and programs for multimedia email
`mgetty`	Smart getty replacement for data and fax modems
`mh`	'mh' mail-handling system, with POP support, for use with 'xmh'
`minicom`	Minicom, a TTY mode communications package with support for European characters
`mkdosfs-ygg`	Creates a DOS FAT file system
`mkisofs`	Creates an ISO9660 file system image, also with Rock-Ridge extensions
`ml`	Motif-based mail-handling program, supporting POP3D newsreading, MIME, etc.
`modemtool`	Configuration tool for /dev/modem
`modules`	Utilities for the loadable Linux kernel modules by Bjorn Ekwall and Jaques Gelinas
`moonclock`	Traditional oclock with moon phase hacks
`mount`	Programs for mounting and unmounting file systems
`moxfm`	Moxfm is a full-fledged file and application manager

mpage	Places multiple pages of text onto a single PostScript page for printing
mpeg_play	X-based player for MPEG files including Red's Nightmare demo
mt-st	The 'mt' tool allows access to streamer tapes
mtools	'mtools' allows access to DOS file systems
multimedia	A CD player and audio mixer for X
mush	A comfortable interface for electronic mail
mxp	X mandelbrot set generator and explorer
ncftp	ftp client with a nice interface
ncompress	Extremely fast LZW-based file compressor by Peter Jannesen
ncsa	NCSA HTTP server daemon for providing WWW services
ncurses	'ncurses' terminal control library
ncurses-devel	Development libraries for 'ncurses'
nenscript	Converts plain ASCII to PostScript
net-tools	Basic network tools, e.g., ifconfig, route, etc.
netcfg	Network configuration tool
netpbm	Lots of image conversion and manipulation tools (hpcd support is missing due to a very restrictive redistribution clause)
nfs-server	NFS server daemons
nfs-server-clients	Client applications for use with remote NFS servers
nis-client	Network Information Service client (formerly yp)
nis-server	Network Information Service server (formerly yp)
nls	Native Language Support (NLS) files for Motif, Netscape, etc.
nvi	New Berkeley Vi editor (experimental)

open	Tools for creating and switching between virtual consoles
optprep	For installing third-party rpm packages such as Caldera's Internet Office Suite
p2c	Shared library for programs built with the 'p2c' Pascal-to-C converter
p2c-basic	A BASIC interpreter based on Pascal using the 'p2c' package
p2c-devel	Programs and headers for the Pascal-to-C translator
pam-apps	Pluggable authentication modules (PAM) for Linux
paradise	Enhanced 'netrek' client with sound and color
patch	GNU patch utilities
pcmcia-cs	PCMCIA Card Services. Tool to support 'hot-swapping' of PCMCIA cards
pdksh	Public-domain Korn shell
perf-rstatd	System monitor using rstatd services (included)
perl	PERL (practical extraction and report language)—Larry Wall's interpreted script language
perl-add	PERL extensions
perl-eg	PERL examples
perl-man	PERL man pages
perl-pod	PERL documentation
perl4	PERL (old version)
pidentd	Internet daemon authorization, user identification
pine	MIME-compliant mail reader with news support as well
pixmap	X-based, comfortable pixmap editor

plan	Motif-based scheduler/planner
playmidi	Play MIDI files on FM, GUS and MIDI devices
pmake	Berkeley's parallel make
pmirror	'mirror', a PERL script for mirroring an ftp site
popclient	POP—retrieve mail from a mailserver using post office protocol
portmap	The RPC portmapper daemon
ppp	'PPP', Point-to-Point Protocol
printtool	Tool for printer configuration under X (Tcl/Tk based)
procinfo	'/proc' file system information
procmail	'procmail', a program to filter and process email
procps	A collection of programs that evaluate the '/proc' structure of the system ('free', 'top', 'uptime' ...)
procps-X11	X-based process-monitoring utilities
project-map	Map of Linux projects in progress
psmisc	More 'ps' type tools for /proc file system
psutils	PostScript utilities
python	Very high level scripting language with X interface
pythonlib	Library of python code used by various Redhat programs
rcs	GNU 'rcs'—revision control system
rdate	Sets the system clock from a network reference. Accurate to about 1 second
rdist	Remote file distribution client that allows management of identical copies of files on multiple computers
readline	Library for reading lines from a terminal
readline-devel	Libraries and header files for developing programs that use the 'readline' library

recode	Utility for converting textfiles between different fonts according to RFC 1345
rpm	Redhat Package Manager
rpm-devel	Header files and libraries for programs that manipulate RPM packages
rxvt	'rxvt'—terminal emulator in an X window
samba	Samba is a Unix-based SMB fileserver. It enables a Linux host to become a file and printserver for WfW, OS/2, NT, or Windows 95; it also contains an SMB client and a NetBIOS nameserver
sc	Text-based spreadsheet with date support (requires ncurses-devel and bison)
screen	A screen manager with VT100/ANSI emulation, which can be used as a terminal multiplexer operating multiple virtual terminals that can be controlled from one single real terminal
sed	GNU 'sed' stream editor
sendmail	Mail transport agent 'sendmail'
sendmail-cf	'sendmail' configuration files and m4 macros
sendmail-doc	'sendmail' documentation
setup	Simple setup files
seyon	'seyon' is a complete X-based communication package for modems
sh-utils	Collection of shell programmers' utilities such as 'basename', 'date', 'dirname', 'expr', 'nohup', 'nice', and 'stty'
sharutils	GNU shar utils like 'shar', 'unshar', 'uuencode', and 'uudecode'
slang	Shared library for the C-like S-Lang language
slang-devel	Static library and header files for the C-like S-Lang language

sliplogin	Slip server (derived from BSD 'sliplogin'), which works with shadow system and mgetty
slrn	Small NNTP newsreader
slsc	Spreadsheet based on 'sc', but with many enhancements
sox	General-purpose sound file conversion tool
spice	SPICE circuit simulator
spider	X implementation of the card game Spider
stat	File information reporter
statnet	Monitors network traffic in a terminal
statserial	Displays status of the serial lines in a terminal
strace	Prints system call trace of a running process
svgalib	Library for full-screen (S)VGA graphics
svgalib-devel	Development libraries and include files for (S)VGA graphics
swatch	System log watcher and alarm
symlinks	Symbolic link sanity checker
sysklogd	Linux system and kernel logger
taper	Tape backup system (beta)
tar	GNU tape archiver 'tar'
tb	Treebrowser is a useful OpenLook (Xview) file system browser and manager
tcl	'Tool Command Language' (tcl) script language
tcl-devel	'Tool Command Language' (tcl) script language, development part with man-pages
tclx	Extensions to 'tcl' and 'tk' for POSIX systems
tclx-devel	Extensions to 'tcl' and 'tk', development part with man-pages

tcp_wrappers	Security wrapper for tcp daemons—maximum setting
tcpdump	'tcpdump' allows reading and logging of individual TCP/IP packets
tcsh	'tcsh', the extended C shell with manual pages
termcap	Terminal capability collection for GNU libtermcap
tetex	TeTeX (TeX) typesetting system and MetaFont font formatter
texinfo	'texinfo' formatter and info reader
texinfo-info	Text-based stand-alone 'info' reader
textutils	GNU text utilities like 'cat', 'cksum', head', 'join', 'pr', 'sort', 'split', and 'uniq'
tgif	Object-oriented drawing and construction program with special hyperspace mode
time	GNU time utility, which allows you to determine resource usage such as CPU-time and memory of given program executions
timetool	Redhat graphical time and date setting tool
tin	'tin', a newsreader with NNTP support
tix	Collection of many metawidgets, such as notepads, for 'Tk'
tix-devel	Metawidgets for Tk, development part with man-pages
tk	'Tk' X interface toolkit for 'Tcl'
tk-devel	'Tk' toolkit for 'Tcl', development part with man-pages
tkinfo	Tk/Tcl-based GNU Info viewer
tkman	Manual page browser with Tk front-end
tksysv	X/Tk-based System-V 'runlevel' editor
traceroute	Traces the route that packets take over a TCP/IP network

tracker	Plays Amiga MOD sound files
transfig	Converts '.fig' files (such as those from xfig) to other graphic formats
trn	A threaded newsreader with NNTP support
trojka	A falling blocks game similar to xjewels or tetris for terminals
tunelp	Configures kernel parallel port driver
typhoon	Library and utilities for relational databases
uemacs	MicroEmacs Fullscreen Editor, a small and compact version of Emacs
umb-scheme	Scheme interpreter from University of Massachusetts at Boston
umsdos_progs	The programs for the umsdos file system, which allows the installation of a Linux system within a DOS partition
unarj	A decompressor for '.arj' format archives that are widely used under DOS
units	Units conversion program
unzip	'unzip' unpacks '.zip' files such as those made by pkzip under DOS
usercfg	User and group configuration tool
util-linux	Various Linux utilities, maintained by Rik Faith
uucp	Unix to Unix Copy (UUCP) for a mail and news via modem connection. Supports HDB as well as Taylor config files; with extensive documentation and 'uupoll' script from Bodo Bauer
vga_cardgames	Card games 'klondike', 'oh hell', 'solitaire', and 'spider' for the Linux text console
vga_gamespack	'othello', 'minesweeper', and 'connect-4' for the Linux text console
vga_tetris	SVGAlib-based tetris games

vim	'vim' (Vi improved), an extended Vi editor with support for European characters
vim-X11	The 'vim' editor (Vi improved) with X support
vixie-cron	The 'cron' daemon allows processes to be started at a predetermined time
vlock	'vlock' locks one or more virtual consoles
vslick	Visual Slick Edit demo version from MicroEdge
wdiff	GNU word difference finder
which	Determines which executable would be run based on your PATH variable
words	English dictionary for ispell
workman	Graphical (OpenLook) tool for playing audio compact discs including title management for individual CDs
woven-docs-LST	Woven Goods Documentation—LST
woven-docs-RedHat	Woven Goods Documentation—Redhat
woven-docs-dlhp	Woven Goods Documentation—dlhp
woven-docs-faq	Woven Goods Documentation—FAQ
woven-docs-fsstnd	Woven Goods Doc—File System Standard
woven-docs-howto	Woven Goods Documentation—HOWTO
woven-docs-isdn	Woven Goods Documentation—ISDN
woven-docs-ldp	Woven Goods Documentation—LDP
woven-docs-llhp	Woven Goods Documentation—llhp
woven-docs-main	Woven Goods Documentation—Main
woven-docs-usenet	Woven Goods Documentation—Usenet
woven-docs-wwwhelp	Woven Goods Documentation—WWW Help
wu-ftpd	Washington University ftp daemon

x3270	X-based 3270 emulator; allows a telnet connection to an IBM host within an X window; special fonts are used
xanim	'xanim' is an animation viewer for X that supports many graphic formats
xarchie	X-based browser interface to 'archie' for querying the worldwide archie database archives
xbill	Kill the Bill
xbl	3D tetris game
xbmbrowser	Very useful X-based browser for bitmaps and pixmaps
xboing	Breakout-style video game
xcept-demo	A commercial video text decoder (BTX/Dx-J) for the X (demo version)
xchomp	PacMan-like game for X
xcolorsel	Utility to display or select colors from the RGB database
xdaliclock	An X-based 'Dali' clock
xdemineur	Another minesweeper game
xearth	The earth globe as background for X root
xemacs-base	XEmacs base package; xemacs is a powerful, extendable editor requiring X-libraries but also capable of running on plain terminals
xemacs-emul	Emulation of other editors (mainly Vi) for XEmacs
xemacs-energize	The 'energize' package for XEmacs
xemacs-hyperbole	The 'hyperbole' package for XEmacs
xemacs-lispprog	Lisp programming environment for XEmacs
xemacs-mailnews	Mail and newsreaders for XEmacs
xemacs-modes	Miscellaneous special modes for XEmacs
xemacs-oo-browse	Object browser for XEmacs

xemacs-packages	Miscellaneous packages for XEmacs
xemacs-www	WWW browser and editor for XEmacs
xevil	A fast-action, explicitly violent game for X
xf-control-panel	Icon panel with admin tools
xf-panel	XForms-based icon panel with group hierarchy
xfig	Menu-driven graphic application for drawing and manipulating objects; it is capable of saving objects in various graphic formats
xfishtank	Turns X root background into an aquarium
xfm	A comprehensive file and application manager for X
xfmail	A spiffy mail reader and editor
xfractint	Fractal-generation program for many different fractal types
xgalaga	A Galaga clone for X
xgammon	Backgammon game for one or two players
xgopher	X-based Gopher client
xjewel	A tetris-style game for X
xlander	Moon landing simulation
xlispstat	Extensible system for statistical computing and dynamic graphics
xloadimage	X-based image viewer supporting many common graphic formats; images can be displayed or loaded into the background
xlockmore	X terminal locking program including many screen savers
xmailbox	X-based mail notification tool
xmbase-grok	A simple database with graphical X front-end
xmgr	Motif-based plotting tool
xmine	Minesweeper for X

xmorph	A morphing program with an X interface
xmplay	An X MPEG video viewer
xntp	'xntp' allows a precise time synchonization utilizing a network and/or radio receivers; requires TCP/IP in the kernel, an initialized loopback device, and a correct time zone (see also ktzset from Torsten Duwe)
xosview	An X-based utility for viewing the system resources used—for example, main memory or cpu load
xpaint	'xpaint' is a user-friendly program for editing and creating pixmaps and bitmaps
xpat2	X Patience—various solitaire card games
xpdf	Portable document format (PDF) viewer for X
xpilot	Arcade-style flying game
xpm	The Xpm libraries for displaying pixmaps
xpm-devel	Development libraries and header files for handling of pixmaps
xpostit	Electronic pinboard for daily dates and important ideas
xpuzzles	Various geometry puzzles including Rubik's Cube
xrn	X-based newsreader
xscreensaver	X screen savers
xselection	Utility to get or set an X selection or cut buffer property value
xsnow	Xsnow, for those who want Christmas 12 months of the year
xsysinfo	A performance meter for X
xtar	Motif-based 'tar' tool
xteddy	The cuddly teddy bear for X—a real must for everyone!

xterm-color	ANSI (color) version of the 'xterm' terminal emulator
xtetris	X version of tetris
xtoolwait	Delayed X application launcher
xtrojka	A falling-blocks game similar to xjewels or tetris for X
xv	Great image viewer/browser for most graphic formats (shareware)
xview	Xview library and OpenLook interface for X
xview-devel	Header files and static libraries for Xview application development
xwatch	A watchdog application for log files
xwpe	Integrated X-Windows programming environment
xwpick	'xwpick' is a screen grabber that saves X windows and backgrounds in various formats
xxgdb	'xxgdb' is a graphical user interface for the GNU debugger 'gdb'
ytalk	Uses internet talk protocol to create multiuser chat sessions
zapem	A Space Invaders-like game
zgv	Console viewer for many graphics formats
zip	'zip', a compression program
zlib	The un-/compression library zlib
zlib-devel	Static version and header files for zlib
zoneinfo	Time zone utilities and data
zsh	zsh shell
zz_3dlook	3D look for all X applications

/col/contrib

`JDK_shared-1.0.2`	Java Development Kit version 1.0 (shared libraries)
`JDK_static-1.0.2`	Java Development Kit version 1.0 (static libraries)
`xfm-1.3.2-3.i386.rpm`	Xfm X-Windows File Manager

Appendix C

XFree86-Supported Chipsets for X-Windows

Standard SVGA Chipsets

Tseng ET3000, ET4000AX, ET4000/W32, ET6000
Western Digital/Paradise PVGA1
Western Digital WD90C00, WD90C10, WD90C11, WD90C24, WD90C30,
WD90C31, WD90C33
Genoa GVGA
Trident TVGA8800CS, TVGA8900B, TVGA8900C, TVGA8900CL, TVGA9000,
TVGA9000i, TVGA9100B, TVGA9200CX, TVGA9320, TVGA9400CX, TVGA9420,
TGUI9420DGi, TGUI9430DGi, TGUI9440AGi, TGUI9660XGi, TGUI9680
ATI 18800, 18800-1, 28800-2, 28800-4, 28800-5, 28800-6, 68800-3,
68800-6, 68800AX, 68800LX, 88800GX-C, 88800GX-D, 88800GX-E,
88800GX-F, 88800CX, 264CT, 264ET, 264VT, 264VT2, 264GT
NCR 77C22, 77C22E, 77C22E+
Cirrus Logic CLGD5420, CLGD5422, CLGD5424, CLGD5426, CLGD5428,
CLGD5429, CLGD5430, CLGD5434, CLGD5436, CLGD5440, CLGD5446,
CLGD5462, CLGD5464, CLGD6205, CLGD6215, CLGD6225, CLGD6235,
CLGD6410, CLGD6412, CLGD6420, CLGD6440
OAK OTI067, OTI077, OTI087
Avance Logic ALG2101, ALG2228, ALG2301, ALG2302, ALG2308, ALG2401
Chips & Technologies 65520, 65530, 65540, 65545, 65520, 65530,
65540, 65545, 65546, 65548, 65550, 65554
MX MX68000, MX680010
Video 7/Headland Technologies HT216-32
SiS 86C201, 86C202, 86C205
ARK Logic ARK1000PV, ARK1000VL, ARK2000PV, ARK2000MT
RealTek RTG3106
Alliance AP6422
Matrox MGA2064W and Mystique cards
NVidia/SGS Thomson NV1, STG2000

Accelerated SVGA Chipsets

8514/A (and true clones)
ATI Mach8, Mach32, Mach64
Cirrus CLGD5420, CLGD5422, CLGD5424, CLGD5426, CLGD5428, CLGD5429,
CLGD5430, CLGD5434, CLGD5436, CLGD5440, CGLD5446, CLGD5462,
CLGD5464
S3 86C911, 86C924, 86C801, 86C805, 86C805i, 86C928, 86C864, 86C964,
86C732, 86C764, 86C765, 86C868, 86C968, 86C325, 86C988
Western Digital WD90C31, WD90C33, WD90C24A
Weitek P9000
IIT AGX-014, AGX-015, AGX-016

IBM XGA-2
Tseng ET4000/W32, ET4000/W32i, ET4000/W32p, ET6000
Ark Logic ARK1000PV, ARK1000VL, ARK2000PV, ARK2000MT
MGA2064W

Video cards using these chipsets are supported on all bus types, including VLB and PCI.

All of these are supported in both 256-color and monochrome modes, with the exception of the Avance Logic, MX, and Video 7 chipsets, which are only supported in 256-color mode. If your video card has enough DRAM installed, many of these chipsets are supported in 16 and 32 bits-per-pixel mode (specifically, some Mach32, P9000, S3, and Cirrus boards). The usual configuration is 8 bits per pixel, that is, 256 colors.

The monochrome server also supports generic VGA cards, the Hercules monochrome card, the Hyundai HGC1280, Sigma LaserView, and Apollo monochrome cards. On the Compaq AVGA, only 64K of video memory is supported for the monochrome server, and the GVGA has not been tested with more than 64K.

Complete information on XFree86 is available at the XFree86 Web site, **www.XFree86.org**. You can always view the latest version or the XFree85-HOWTO at **sunsite.unc.edu/pub/Linux/docs/HOWTO/XFree86-HOWTO.html**. (From the Linux XFree86 HOWTO by Eric S. Raymond v5.0, 10 August 8, 1997.)

Appendix D

About the CD-ROM

The CD-ROM contains the complete Caldera OpenLinux 1.1 Linux system. Standard installation also installs and configures the Apache Web server and an ftp server, automatically configuring your OpenLinux system to be a Web and ftp site. You'll find a comprehensive set of Linux software applications, including the GNU software packages (graphics, communications, publishing, programming), as well as X-Windows applications, development tools, and Internet servers (ftp, Web, and Gopher).

You'll also find that the CD-ROM provides complete X-Windows support with a fully-configured window manager featuring program menus and a taskbar (fvwm and GoodStuff). Window-based editors such as XEmacs and CriSPLite, as well as desktops for icon-based file management, such as Xfm and a 90-day evaluation of the Caldera Desktop, are also included. Window managers, desktops, and applications are available for download from Internet sites.

Find extensive documentation including HOW-TO documents, tutorials in Web page format, and online manuals. Go to **sunsite.unc.edu/mdw** for more information.

For added functionality, unregistered versions of Netscape Navigator (3.01 and Gold) can be downloaded from **ftp.caldera.com**. You can also obtain free personal editions of the StarOffice 3.1 office suite and ADABAS-D relational database from Caldera at **www.caldera.com**. The Java Development Kit is included in OpenLinux Lite in the **contrib** directory and is available for free through **www.blackdown.org**. Numerous applications are available for download from the Redhat **contrib** directory at the Redhat ftp site and its mirror sites at **ftp.redhat.com/pub/contrib/i386**. You can both install and configure these applications with just a single **rpm -i** command. Several popular Internet sites where you can easily obtain Linux applications are listed here.

Linux Application	Internet Site
Java Development Kit	http://www.blackdown.org
Netscape Navigator	ftp://ftp.caldera.com
StarOffice and ADABAS-D	http://www.caldera.com
Tk/Tcl Applications	http://sunscript.sun.com
Perl Applications	http://www.perl.com
Window Managers and Desktops	ftp://ftp.redhat.com/pub/contrib/i386
Linux Applications	http://www.xnet.com/~blatura/linapps.shtml ftp://ftp.redhat.com/pub/contrib/i386
Linux on the World Wide Web	http://www.ssc.com/linux/resources/web.html
Caldera Linux Resources Page	http://www.caldera.com/tech-ref/linux_info.html
Redhat Linux Resources Page	http://www.redhat.com/linux-info
Linux Documentation Project	http://sunsite.unc.edu/mdw

Index

\ functions (Perl), 934-935
" (back quotes), 609-610
" (double quotes), 607-609
"" (null string), 785-786
$ (dollar sign), 161-162, 557, 593, 606-607, 928
$# special variable, 614, 620
$* special variable, 614
$@ special variable, 614
& (ampersand), 167
&& (double ampersand), 621
– (minus sign), 167, 229
+ (plus sign), 167, 229, 564
' (single quotes), 607-611
() (parentheses), 564
* (asterisk), 144-145, 558-560
< (less-than), 152-153
<< (double less-than), 611-613
= (assignment operator), 161, 606-607, 924-925
> (greater-than), 149-151
>& (greater-than ampersand), 158-160
>> (double greater-than), 149-151, 159
? (question mark), 145-147, 564
@ (at sign), 657, 926-928
@ARGV array (Perl), 932
#ARGV variable (Perl), 932
[ ] (brackets), 146, 560-563
\ (backslash), 143, 607-609
^ (caret), 557
| (vertical bar), 564
| | (double vertical bar), 621
~ (tilde), 197-199, 210-211, 287-292, 330-331

A

Absolute path names, 187, 197-199, 210-211
Absolute permissions, 228, 231-235
Accelerated SVGA chipsets for X-Windows, 1042-1043
access.conf file, 475-476
Accessing the Linux system, 59-64
Ada compiler, 897
Adaptec AHA152X SCSI parameters, 1005-1006

Adaptec AHA1740 SCSI parameters, 1006
Adaptec AHA274X/284X/294X SCSI parameters, 1006
Adaptec 154x SCSI parameters, 1006
Addresses, TCP/IP network, 769-770
Addressing, UUCP, 527-529
adduser command, 743-744
AdvanSys ABPxxx SCSI parameters, 1004
AfterStep window manager, 130-131
Aliases
    Elm, 317-319
    BASH, 583-585
    TCSH, 643-644
aliases.text (Elm), 318-319
Always IN2000 SCSI parameters, 1007
AM53C974 SCSI parameters, 1011
AMI FastDisk VLB SCSI parameters, 1006
Ampersand (&), 167
AmSTeX application, 873
AND operator (searching directories), 202-203
anonymous command (ftp), 387-388
ANSI Unix standard, 8
a.out binary file format, 896
Apache Web server, 469-478
Appending standard output (>>), 151
Applets, Java, 433-434
Applications development tools, 902-907. See also Software
apropos command, 68-69
Archie, 390-395
Archie client, 391-393
Archie command table, 406-408
Archie servers, 393-394
Archive files, 251-255
    downloading, 258-260
    installing from, 257-258
    restoring, 27
Arena Browser, 424-426
Argument arrays (argv), 656-657
Arguments, shell script, 164
Arguments (command line), explained, 141
Arguments (Linux command), 65
Arithmetic expressions (Perl), 925
Arithmetic operators (BASH), 633
Arithmetic shell operations (let), 615-616

Array management functions (Perl), 928-929
Array operations (Perl), 926-928, 938-939
Arrays (in Tcl), 956-957
Assignment operator (=), 161, 924-925
Assignments, in Tcl, 977
Associative arrays (Perl), 929-930
Asterisk (*), 144-145, 558-560
at command, 170-173
At sign (@) TCSH numeric variables, 657
AUX, 8
awk language, 12
Aztech CD-ROM parameters, 1002

B

Back quotes, 609-610
Background commands
    canceling, 166
    placing, 167-168
Background jobs, 177-179
Background processes, explained, 114
Backslashes, 143, 607-609
BACKSPACE, 142
BASH (Bourne Again Shell), 65-66, 140, 577-636
    aliases, 583-585
    arithmetic shell operations (let), 615-616
    command and file name completion, 578-579
    command line editing, 579
    commands and arguments, 631-633
    commands and comments, 604-606
    conditions and loops, 635-636
    configuring history, 582-583
    controlling command execution, 617-626
    controlling shell operations, 585-586
    environment variables and subshells, 586-588
    export variables and script shells, 614-615
    expression operators (let), 633

history, 579-583
history event editing, 581-582
initialization file, 601-602
login initialization file, 598-601
login shell configuration, 588-603
logout initialization file, 603
programming, 603-606
quoting commands (single quotes), 610-611
quoting strings, 607-609
redefinable special variables, 591-596
script command line arguments, 613-614
script input and output, 611-613
shell scripts, 604-606
special shell variables, 588
special variables and features, 630-631
summary, 627-628
system-determined special variables, 590-591
test command operations, 634
user-defined special variables, 596-598
values from Linux commands (back quotes), 609-610
variable definition/evaluation, 606-607
variable values (strings), 607-609
variables and scripts, 606-615
BASH shell prompt, configuring, 593-595
.bash_logout file, 603
.bashrc file, 601-602
Bell Labs, 6-7
bg command, 169-170
BibTeX program, 846, 873
biff utility, 325-326
Binary file formats, 896
Binary files (encoded), 367-368
Binary masks, 228, 231-235
bind command (TK), 970
.bindings file, 824
Bindings (TK), 970-972
Boot parameters, recommended, 1000-1012
Booting the computer, 34
BootPrompt HOWTO, 1012
Bourne Again Shell. See BASH
Bourne shell, 9. See also BASH
Brackets ([]), 146, 560-563
Broadcast address, 769
Browsers (Web), 417-426
BSD Unix, 7
BusLogic SCSI parameters, 1004-1005
Button command (TK), 965, 967
Byte-stream file format, 183

C compiler (gcc), 894-896, 911-912
C programming language, 6, 894-895

C shell, 9. See also TCSH shell
C++ compiler, 896-897
Caldera Desktop, 63-64, 108-110, 118-123
    with Admin_Tools window open, 63
    layouts, 123
    managing, 122-123
    with Netscape running, 115
Caldera ftp site, 13
Caldera Network Desktop, 434
Caldera OpenLinux Lite. See OpenLinux Lite
Caldera_Info icon, 417
cald1.html, 439-442
Canceling jobs, 168-169
case structure/command, 618, 621-623
cat command, 54, 148-156, 189, 220, 544-546, 578
Categories of users, 227
cd command, 121, 192-194
CDPATH special variable, 596-597
cdpath variable (TCSH), 647
CD-ROM (enclosed), 14, 1045-1046
    INN (InterNetNews) on, 343
    OpenLinux Lite on, 14-15, 22, 40-41
    software package index, 1013-1040
CD-ROM drive device name, 242
CD-ROM mounting, 241-243
CD-ROM parameters list, 1001-1004
CERN labs, 414
cfdisk command, 243
CGI programs, 442-443
CHAP (Challenge Handshake Authentication Protocol), 793-794
chat command, 89-92, 785-787, 807
Chat scripts (PPP), 785-789
chgrp command, 237
Chipsets for X-Windows, 1041-1043
chkdsk command, 29
chmod command, 98, 227-237
    chmod +x, 164
    Perl, 920
    table of options, 265-266
    TK, 966
chomp command (Perl), 925-926
chown command, 237, 750-751
clear command, 603
Click-and-drag copying, 122
Command and file name completion (BASH), 578-579
Command line, 9, 61-63, 140, 143
Command line arguments (BASH script), 613-614
Command line arguments (X-Windows), 825-826
Command line editing, 64-66
Command line editing (BASH), 579
Command line editing commands (BASH), 629-630
Command line features, 142-143
Command line installation, 81-83

Command line options (Perl), 937
Command line syntax, shell, 140-141
Command mode of Vi editor, 680-682
Command and program directories, 76-77
Command values (back quotes), 610
Commands (BASH programming), 604-606, 631-633
Commands (Linux)
    in background or foreground, 167-168
    delayed execution, 170-173
    examples of entering, 142
    format of, 65
    several on the same line, 143
Common Desktop Environment (CDE), 7, 125
Common Gateway Interface (CGI), 442
Communications, 11-12, 85-88, 326-327
Communications ports, 86-87
Communications protocols (IP), 783-800
Communications utilities, table of, 338
Compilers, 894-897
Compiling software, 260-261
Compiling X-Windows applications, 833
Comprehensive TeX Archive Network (CTAN), 846
Compressed archives
    downloading, 258-260
    installing from, 257-258
Conditional control structures. See Control structures
Configuration. See also Installation
    hardware, 999-1012
    with Lisa, 71-75
    system areas, 73
    system tools, 110-111
    UUCP, 525-527
    Web server, 471-476
    X-Windows, 47-53, 813-839
Configuration files
    restoring, 26-27
    TCP/IP, 770-772
    X-Windows, 826-831, 837-838
configure command, 260
conf.h file, 484-489
Connected systems (uname), 529-530
Connections. See Modems
Conrad CD-ROM parameters, 1002
Control structures, 617-626
    BASH, 635-636
    gawk, 991
    Perl, 930-933, 942
    Tcl, 958-960, 977
    TCSH, 658-667, 674-675
    test command, 617-618
Copying directories, 209-210
Copying files, 203-206
Copyrighted software, 13

Corel WordPerfect, 842
Counting words (wc), 548
cp command, 143, 203-206, 209-210
cr command, 132
CreativeLabs on SBPRO CD-ROM parameters, 1002
Crisplite editor, 53, 131-132
crontab command, 736
Crontab files, 735-736
Cross-references (LaTeX), 859
CSLIP connections, 794-800
CTAN sites, 846
CTRL-B, 142
CTRL-C, 143
CTRL-D, 142, 152
CTRL-F, 142
CTRL-H, 142
CTRL-U, 142
CTRL-Z, 169-170
CyD ROM CD-ROM parameters, 1002

D

Data filters, 569, 574-576
Date, for command execution, 171-172
date command, 140, 734-735
Date and time (system), 734-735
Debugger commands, 912-913
Debugger (gdb), 899-902
defaults command, 245
defrag utility, 30
DEL, 142-143
Delayed execution, 170-173
Delimiters (argument separators), 145
deliver command, 281
Dependency line (make utility), 903-904
Desktop (Caldera), 63-64, 108-110, 118-123
    with Admin_Tools window open, 63
    layouts, 123
    managing, 122-123
    with Netscape running, 115
Destructive repartitioning, hard drive, 30-32
Development tools, 902-907
Device binding fvwm configuration files, 824
Device configuration, 731-766
Device files, creating, 749
Device installation and management, 748-756
Device modules, controlling during startup, 1001
Device mounting, explained, 238
Device parameters, 999-1012
Device section of XF86Config, 820
Devices, explained, 148
Devices configuration file, 525-527
df command, 240

die command (Perl), 932-933
diff edit filter, 552, 555-557
Differences and changes (diff), 555-557
dip program, 794-800
    dynamic IP addresses with, 798-799
    script example, 795-798
    static IP addresses, 795
    table of options and commands, 809-811
    table of variables, 812
diplogin command, 799-800
Direct file copy. See UUCP
Directories, 10-11, 183-186
    adding, 76
    changing, 192-193
    complex searches, 202-203
    copying files to, 204-206
    creating, 191
    listing, 191-192
    managing, 191-199
    moving and copying, 209-210
    nested, 195
    removing, 191
    search criteria, 201-202
    searching, 199-203
    setting permissions for, 122
Directory commands, table of, 221
Directory operations, 199-217
Directory path names, 186-188
Directory permissions, 227-237, 468-469
Directory windows, 120-122
Disk space for Linux partitions, opening, 27-32
Displaying file information, 226-227
Document classes (LaTeX), 880
Document processing tools, 841-892
Documentation, 13, 71
Documentation Project (Linux), 18
Dollar sign ($), 161-162, 557, 593, 606-607
DOLPHIN 8000AT CD-ROM parameters, 1003
Domain name addresses, 382-383
Domain Name Service (DNS), 780-783
Domains, table of, 329
DOS emulators, 264
DOSemu, 264
Dot (.) files, 141, 182
Dot (.) matching character, 557-558
Dot (.) working directory, 195-197
Double ampersand (&&), 621
Double dot (..) (parent directory), 193, 195-197
Double less-than (<<), 612
Double quotes (""), 607-609
Double vertical bar (| |), 621
DOWN ARROW, 143
Downloading compressed archives, 258-260
Downloading Netscape Navigator Web Browser, 83

Drawing environments (LaTeX), 869
DTC 3180/3280 SCSI parameters, 1009
DTC 329x SCSI parameters, 1006
dvi files, 847
Dynamic IP addresses with dip, 798-799
Dynamic libraries, 898

E

EATA ISA/EISA SCSI parameters, 1011
EATA-DMA SCSI parameters, 1010
EATA-PIO SCSI parameters, 1010-1011
echo command, 162, 603, 607, 611-613, 644
Edit filters, 552-557
    summary of, 567-568
    table of, 572-574
Editors, 11-12. See also Emacs editor; Vi editor
egrep utility, 564-566
Electronic mail, 99-100, 279-338
ELF (Executable and Linking Format), 896, 898
elif command, 618, 620-621
Elm commands
    d command, 314-315
    operations on messages, 337
    receiving messages, 336
    selecting messages, 336-337
    sending messages, 335
    table of, 335-338
    u command, 314-315
.elm file, 318-319
Elm mail utility, 308-319. See also Elm commands
    aliases, 317-319
    deleting and undeleting messages, 314-315
    headers, 311
    message editing screen, 311
    options, 319
    quitting, 313-314
    reading mailbox files, 316
    receiving mail, 310, 312-313
    replying to messages, 315
    saving messages in, 315-316
    sending mail, 308-310
    sending messages from, 315
.elmrc file, 319
Emacs commands, 712-717
Emacs editor, 12, 71, 709-727
    buffers and files, 718-721
    commands, 712-717
    creating a file, 710-711
    deletions, 713
    editor commands, 723-725
    file buffer and buffer commands, 726-727
    help, 721, 727
    help commands, 727

incremental searches, 715-716
kill buffers, 714
line commands, 711-712
meta-keys, 711-712
modes, 711-712
movement commands, 713
moving text, 714-715
point and mark, 715
regions, 715
regular expression searches, 716
replace and query-replace,
    716-717
screen, 711
substitutions, 716-717
summary, 722-723
using windows, 717-718
window commands, 726
Emacs editor screen, 711
Email, 99-100, 279-338
Emergency boot disk, 46
Encoded binary files, 367-368
ENTER key, 142
env command, 589
Environment variables and subshells
    (BASH), 586-588
Environment variables (TCSH), 658
epsf files, importing in LaTeX, 868
Equations, using TeX for, 853
Error messages, 158-159
esac command, 618
ESC ? (escape question-mark), 578
Escape characters (Perl), 936
/etc/exports file, 249-251
/etc/exports options, 271
/etc/fstab file, 244-247
/etc/fstab options, 270
/etc/hostname file, 772
/etc/host.conf file, 781-782
/etc/hosts file, 770-771
/etc/mtools.conf file, 263
/etc/networks file, 771-772
/etc/passwd file, 741-742
/etc/rc.d file, 738
/etc/rc.d/init.d/inet, 772
/etc/resolv.conf file, 782-783
/etc/skel file, 742-743
/etc/XF86Config file, 47, 815-820
Events (TK), 970-972
exec command, 822
Execute permission, 227, 230, 234
Execution (remote)
    TCP/IP, 523-524
    UUCP, 534-535
EXINIT special variable, 598, 600, 696
exit command, 113, 620
Expect applications, 974-975
expect command, 974-975
export command, 586-588, 590, 598,
    615, 271
Export variables (BASH), 614-615
Exports file, 249-251
expr command (Tcl), 954-955
Expression operators (BASH), 633
Expression operators (TCSH),
    672-673

Extended special characters, 564-566
EzPPP Internet connection utility, 88,
    92-99
    domain name server panel, 96
    Login Script panel, 97
    main window, 94
    windows, 95

F

fdisk commands, 31, 36, 243-244, 268
fdisk program/utility, 28-29, 36-39
fg command, 168-170
fgrep filter, 550-552
Field variables (gawk), 987-988
figures (LaTeX), 867
File backups, 273
File buffers, 718-721
File classifications (Linux), 183-184
file command, 183-184, 218
File compression, 255-256
File copy, 122
    direct UUCP, 532-533
    remote TCP/IP, 521-523
File filters. See also Filters
    summary of, 567
    table of, 570-572
File handles (Tcl), 963-964
File information, displaying, 226-227
File links, 212-217
File management operations, 225-275
File management summary, 265
File managers, 109-111
    installing, 123-131
    starting and exiting, 109-111
    treebrowser, 127
File name arguments, 143-147
File operations, 199-217, 222, 937
File output, beginning or end of file,
    546-547
File owner or group, changing, 237
File path names, 187
File permissions, 122, 227-237,
    468-469
File structure (Linux), 8, 10-11,
    181-223, 217
File System Manager (FSM), 247-249
File systems, 237-249
    check and repair, 267
    mounting, 238
    mounting automatically, 244-247
    options (-o and /etc/fstab), 270
    types of, 269
File test (BASH), 634
File types, Linux, 183
file:, 418
Files, 10-11
    binary, 896
    C language, 896
    copying, 203-206
    creating using Emacs, 710-711
    displaying, 189, 220
    encoded binary, 367-368
    erasing, 211-212

Linux, 182-184
listing, 220
mailbox, 300-308, 316
moving, 206-209
naming, 182
permissions for, 122, 227-237,
    468-469
printing, 189-190, 220
redirection of standard output
    to, 149-151
renaming while moving, 210-211
searching with grep and fgrep,
    550-552
Files section of XF86Config, 818
Filters, 11-12, 543-557, 570-576. See
    also gawk utility
    editing, 552-557
    redirection and pipes with,
        544-547
    sed edit filter, 552-555
    summary of, 566-568
    types of output from, 547-549
    user-defined gawk, 991-992
Final configuration, 44
find command, 199-201, 223
fips utility, 30
Firewall, explained, 421
Floppy disks, mounting and
    formatting, 240-241
Floppy drive device name (fd0), 240
fmt filter (Mail), 290
folder command (Mail), 301-302, 306
Follow-up articles (trn newsreader),
    354-356, 358-359
Fonts
    LaTeX, 858, 881
    TeX, 850-852
    X-Windows, 831-833
Footnotes (LaTeX), 859
for loops, 623, 626, 960
foreach loops (Perl), 931
foreach loops (Tcl), 960
foreach loops (TCSH), 665-667
Foreground, command placed in,
    167-168
format command, 31-32
Formatting floppy disks, 240-241
Fortran compiler, 897
for-in loops, 623-626
Free Virtual Window Manager. See
    fvwm
FreeWAIS
    configuring and installing,
        508-510
    starting, 514-515
From utility, 325-326
fsck command, 240, 267
fstab command, 244-247, 270
fstool utility, 247-249
fstool window, 248
ftp, 386-390
    command table, 405-406
    configuration files, 462
    directories, 466
    files, 469

ftp://, 418
Linux sites table, 16
server, 459-460
server configuration files,
460-469
server directories, 466-467
user account, 462-466
ftpaccess file, 460-465
ftp.redhat.com/pub/contrib/386,
134-135
Full regular expressions, 564-566
Future Domain 16xx SCSI
parameters, 1006-1007
Future Domain TMC-8xx/9xx SCSI
parameters, 1009
fvwm (free virtual window
manager), 125, 821
configuration files, 822-825, 835
desktop with Netscape running,
115
GoodStuff taskbar, 116-117
keyboard bindings, 835
terminal window, 114
virtual desktops, 117-118
window manager, 115-116, 118
window manager and desktop,
115-118
workplace menu, 116
fvwm95 Web page, 128
fvwm95 window manager, 128-129,
821
fvwm2 window manager, 125

G

g++ command, 896-897
Gateway address, 769
gawk command, 984-986, 993-995
gawk utility, 983-995
BEGIN and END patterns, 990
control structures, 991
instruction files, 990-991
pattern search operators, 989-990
pattern searches, 986-987
table of options, 993-995
user-defined filters, 991-992
variables, 987-989
gcc C compiler, 71, 894-897
gcc command and options, 911-912
gdb symbolic debugger, 899-902
gdb symbolic debugger commands,
900, 912-913
Generic NCR5380/53c400 SCSI
parameters, 1007
gets command (Tcl), 962-964
Getting information (info), 847, 894
Getting started, summary of, 100-102
Ghostscript, 873-875, 891
Ghostview, 873-876, 892
glint utility, 75, 77-81
Available Packages window, 80
Installed Packages window, 79
installing software, 76
GMT time zone, using, 24, 44

GN Gopher directories, 501-502
GN Gopher server, 493-497
config file, 496
configuring, 493-495
directories, 501-502
makefile, 497
starting, 495
testing, 497-498
GNU software, 13, 71
GoldStar R420 CD-ROM parameters,
1003
GoodStuff taskbar, 116-117
Gopher, 395-402
bookmark menu, 399-402
Cap and Link files, 498-501
commands, 408-410
data directory, 480-481
directories, 498-502
example, 502-504
file types, 479
GN Gopher server, 493-497
indexes, 502
menus, 397-398
servers, 478-504
University of Minnesota
Gopher, 481-493
user account, 480
using to access services, 398-399
Gopher command table, 408-410
Gopher directories, 498-502
Gopher servers, 478-504
gopher://, 418
gopherd.conf, 482-483, 491-492
gopherdlocal.conf, 483-484, 492
gopherindex command, 502
Graphic widgets (TK), 966-969, 981
Graphical applications, with Tcl/Tk,
950
Graphical interface. See glint utility
Graphical user interface (GUI), 9-10.
See also X-Windows
Graphics card configurations, 49-50
Graphics (LaTeX), 867-870
Greenwich mean time, 24, 44
grep filter, 550-551, 563-564
groff command, 843-844
groupadd command, 747
groupdel command, 747
groupmod command, 748
Groups (user)
adding and deleting, 745-748
file permissions, 227-228
ID permissions, 230-231
managing, 763-764
gs command, 873
gunzip command, 259, 525
GV application, 875-876
gzip utility, 255-256, 274

H

Hard disk information, 24
Hard disk/drive partitions, 27
adding, 29

deleting, 28-29
Linux, 34-40
main and swap, 36
mounting, 243-244
opening disk space for, 27-32
Hard links, 212-216
Hardware administration, 74
Hardware parameters, 999-1012
Hardware requirements, minimum,
22-23
Head filter, 545-547
Headers and footers (TeX), 850
helptool utility, 69
Hidden (dot) files, 141, 182
HISTFILE special variable, 582-583
history command, 528, 579-580
History commands (BASH), 629
History event editing (BASH),
581-582
History event references (BASH), 629
History event substitutions (TCSH),
641-642
History of Linux and Unix, 6-8
History list (BASH), 66, 143
History list (Lynx), 427
History variable (TCSH), 647-648
History utility (TCSH), 639-642
HISTSAVE special variable, 582-583
HISTSIZE special variable, 582
Home directory, 185-186, 194
HOME special variable, 588, 590-591
Homesites, 13
host.conf file, 781-782
hostname command, 772
Hostnames, identifying, 770-771
Hot items (tin newsreader), 367
HotJava Web Browser, 428-429
HOWTO documents, 71, 442, 1012
HREF tag, 436-438
HTML codes for Web pages, table of,
446-449
HTML tags, 435-438
HTML 3 browser, 424-426
HTML Web pages, creating, 435-442
http (HyperText Transfer Protocol),
414
httpd command, 476-477
httpd.conf file, 471-472

I

Icons, 111-112, 121
Icon-style fvwm configuration files,
824
IDE hard drives, mounting, 243
IEEE Unix standard, 8
if control structure, 618
Perl, 932-933
Tcl, 958
ifconfig command, 281, 772-776, 805
if-else control structure, 618, 932
if-then control structure, 619-621, 660
if-then-else control structure, 661

ignoreeof variable (TCSH), 585, 644-645
imake command, 833
IMG tag, 438
Index file, ftp, 469
index.html Web page for HOWTO pages, 442
inetd daemon, 457-458, 477
info command, 847, 894
Information requirements, 24
Information sources on the Internet, 12-14
init command, 736-737
IniTeX application, 872-873
Initialization files (BASH), 601-602
Initialization files (system), 738
Initialization files (TCSH), 649-652
INN (InterNetNews), 343-344
inode number, 213
Input mode of Vi editor, 680-682
Input/output. *See* Standard input; Standard output
insmod parameters, recommended, 1000-1012
Install Disk, 46
Install disks, creating, 32-33
INSTALL files, 260
Installation program auto-detection feature, 1000
Installation
    of devices, 748-756
    of printers, 749-753
    LILO, 44-45
    Linux, 33-46
    OpenLinux Lite, 40-41
    with RPM, 81-83
    of software from compressed archives, 257-258
    of software from online sources, 83-85
    of software packages, 75-85
    of sound drivers, 54-55
    of terminals and modems, 754-755
    of trn and tin newsreaders, 342
    of UUCP, 525-527
    of window and file managers, 123-131
    of X-Windows, 47-53
Installed Linux systems, upgrading, 26-27
Integer comparisons (BASH), 634
International domains, table of, 329
Internet, information sources on, 12-14
Internet addresses, 280-281, 381-383, 414-416
Internet connections with modems, 88-99
Internet domains, table of, 329
Internet server init scripts, 454-459
Internet servers, 451-516
Internet Service Providers (ISPs), 380
Internet tools, 12, 379-411

Internet user interface (Gopher), 395-402
Interrupting a job (CTRL-Z), 169-170
IP addresses, 382-383, 414-416
IP communications protocols, 783-800
ir.h file, 508
ISP16 CD-ROM parameters, 1001
ISP1020 Intelligent SCSI Processor Driver, 1008

J

Java applets, 433-434
Java Development Kit (JDK), 430-433, 1046
Java for Linux, 13, 428-430
JDK 1.0 and 1.1 tools, 432-433
JDK 1.0.2, 431
JDK 1.1.1, 431
JDK tools and directories, 432-433
Jobs, 166
    background, 177-179
    canceling, 168-169
    controlling, 166-173
jobs command, 166-173

K

Kernel, 8, 10
Kernel Module Manager, 35, 1000
Kernel modules, controlling during startup, 1001
Keyboard configuration, 49
Keyboard events (TK), 970-972
Keyboard section of XF86Config, 818
kill command, 168-169
Korn shell, 9

L

last command (Perl), 932
Last cylinder number, 37
latex command, 847, 882-886
LaTeX program/macros, 845-847, 855-872
    character operations, 881
    counters, 861
    definition commands, 872, 890
    document classes, 855-856
    drawing environments, 869
    environments, 859-861, 886-887
    epsf files, 868
    font styles, 881
    fonts, 858, 881
    footnotes and cross-references, 859
    letter documents, 870-872
    letter environment commands, 889

lists, 861-863
    math mode, 865-867
    math operations, 888
    math symbols, 879
    packages, 857
    page format, 857
    picture environment, 869-870
    sectioning, 858-859
    tables, 863-865
Layouts, desktop, 123
LEFT ARROW, 142
LessTif window manager (mwm), 130, 821
let command, 615-616, 633
Letter documents (LaTeX), 870-872
lg command, 825
Libraries, creating and using, 897-899
Library of Congress telnet connection, 385
Library GNU Public License (LGPL), 898
lilo command, 756-757
LILO (Linux Loader), 33, 44, 60-61, 756-757
    boot manager prompt, 1000
    command line options, 765-766
    installing, 44-45
lilo.conf options, 765-766
Line buffering, explained, 151
Line-editing mode commands (Vi editor), 705-707
Line-editing mode (Vi editor), 681-682
Links (file), 212-217
Links (hard), 212-216
Links (symbolic), 215-217
Linux operating system, 3-20
    accessing, 59-64
    getting started (summary), 100-102
    history of, 6-8
    installing, 33-46
    logging into and out of, 61-63
    overview, 8-12
    releases, 14
    shutdown, 46, 59-61, 737, 762-763
    startup and setup, 57-105
    tree structure, 184-185
    types of shells for, 140
    upgrading installed, 26-27
    using as a Web server, 434-443
Linux applications, 12-14, 17
Linux command format, 65
Linux command options and arguments, 65
Linux commands, 64-66
Linux documentation, 13, 18
Linux Documentation Project, 18
Linux fdisk program, 36, 39
Linux file structure, 181-223
Linux file system manager, 247-249
Linux files, 182-184
Linux ftp sites, table of, 16

Linux installation manager. *See* glint
    utility
Linux Installation and System
    Administration. *See* Lisa utility
Linux Journal, 14
Linux Loader. *See* LILO
Linux operations, 137-275
Linux releases, 14
Linux RPM software ftp sites, 105
Linux software, 12-14, 17
Linux standard system directories, 219
Linux Usenet Newsgroups, 14, 20
Linux Web sites, 19
lisa command, 72, 773
Lisa utility, 55-56, 247-248
    initial menu, 72
    install list, 78
    installing software, 76
    main menu, 56
    mount table options, 247
    screens, 73
    software package management,
        77
    starting up, 74
    system analysis, 56
    system configuration with, 71-75
    user administration, 75
Lisp compiler, 897
List operations (Perl), 928-929
List operations (Tcl), 976
listbox command (TK), 968
Lists (LaTeX formatted), 861-863
Lists (Perl), 926-928
Lists (Tcl), 957-958
LMS CM206/226 on CM260
    CD-ROM parameters, 1003
ln command, 212-215
Local addresses, 280
Logging in as root user, 47, 72
Logging into and out of Linux, 61-63
Logical commands (&& and | |), 621
Login, remote TCP/IP, 521
.login file (TCSH), 649-650
Login initialization file (BASH),
    598-601
Login shell configuration (BASH),
    588-603
LOGNAME special variable, 591
logout command, 46, 63
.logout file (TCSH), 652
Logout initialization file (BASH), 603
Looking Glass desktop, 118
Loop control structures, 623-626
    BASH, 635-636
    Perl, 930-932, 943-944
    TCSH, 663-667
lpc commands, 764-765
lpq command, 190, 220
lpr command, 153-156, 189-190, 220
lprm command, 190, 220
lreplace command (Tcl), 957
ls command, 141-148, 150, 191-192, 220
    ls -l, 99, 213, 226-228, 236
    manual entry, 67-68
Lynx line-mode Browser, 426-428

M

Macros (LaTeX), 855-872
Macros (TeX), 845, 847, 854-872
MAD16 CD-ROM parameters, 1001
Mail, electronic, 99-100, 279-338
Mail command options, 330, 334-335
Mail commands. *See also* Mail utility
    alias, 304
    for deleting/restoring messages,
        333
    for displaying messages, 332
    for editing messages, 333
    m command, 298-299
    mail command, 284-286
    for message lists, 332-333
    p command examples, 296
    q command, 299-300
    R and r commands, 298
    for receiving messages, 331-334
    S and s commands, 300-303
    for saving messages, 333-334
    for sending messages, 330-331,
        333
    tilde commands, 287-292
    V command, 298-299
Mail file transfer (UUCP), 530-532
Mail message status codes, 331
Mail notifications with From or biff,
    325-326
Mail on remote POP servers,
    accessing, 282-284
Mail shell, 292-304
Mail shell initialization file, 304
MAIL special variable, 595-596
Mail transport agents, 281
Mail utilities. *See also* Elm mail utility
    Pine, 320-322
    table of, 338
Mail utility (Mail), 284-308. *See also*
    Mail commands
    copying a message to a file, 286
    current message marker (>),
        293-294
    deleting and undeleting
        messages, 297
    displaying messages, 294-296
    editing messages, 287-292
    fmt filter, 290
    mailbox, 292-293
    message lists, 293-294
    options, 305
    organizing mailbox files, 306-308
    quitting the Mail shell, 299-300
    receiving mail, 292-304
    replying to messages, 298-299
    saving and accessing messages,
        300-303
    saving message text in files,
        303-304
    sending mail to several users,
        285-286
    sending messages, 284-285,
        298-299

sending and receiving files,
    303-304
standard input and redirection,
    285
Mail variable (TCSH), 648
Mailbox files
    accessing, 300-303
    organizing, 306-308
    reading with Elm, 316
MAILCHECK special variable, 595
Mailing binaries and archives,
    322-324
MAILPATH special variable, 595-596
.mailrc file, 304
mailx command, 528
Main partition, 36
make utility, 833, 902-905
    make commands, 260, 508-510,
        833
    make install command, 260
Makefile, 508-510, 904-905
Makefile options, 509
Makefile.config, 484, 486-489
man utility, 67-68, 907-911
    commands and macros, 66,
        908-911, 915-916
    man documents, 66, 908-911
    man pages, 70, 815
Managing devices, 748-756
Managing directories, 191-199
Managing groups using group
    commands, 747-748
Managing groups using usercfg,
    745-747
Managing printers, 749-753
Managing terminals and modems,
    754-755
Managing user environments,
    742-743
Managing users, 738-748
Matching any character (.), 557-558
Matching beginning or end of line,
    557
Matching classes of characters ([]),
    560-563
Matching repeated characters (*),
    558-560
Math formulas
    LaTeX, 865-867
    TeX, 853-854
Math library, 897
Math symbols, TeX and LaTeX, 879
Matsushita CD-ROM parameters,
    1002
MBOX command (Mail), 306-307
mcopy command, 261
mdir command, 262
META-FAQ file, 14
Microsoft Word, 842
minicom terminal emulator, 87
Minix, 8
Minus sign (–), 167, 229
Mirror sites, 13
Mitsumi FX001S/D CD-ROM
    parameters, 1001-1002

Mitsumi XA/MultiSession CD-ROM parameters, 1002
Mkcache program, 501
mkdir command, 121, 191
mkfontdir command, 832
mkfs command, 241, 243-244, 268
mknod command, 749
mm macro package, 842
ModeLine entries (XF86Config), 819-820
Modems
    installing and managing, 754-755
    Internet connections with, 88-99
    setup, 86-87
Module section of XF86Config, 818
Modules HOWTO, 1012
Monitor configurations, 815
Monitor information, 24-25
Monitor section of XF86Config, 819-820
Monitor setup, 50-51
Monitoring frequency (Hz), 51
Monitoring a network, 778-780
Monitors file, XFree86, 815
more command/filter, 189, 220, 546
Mosaic Web Browser, 422-424
Motif window manager, 7, 130-131
mount command, 237-249
    mount -a, 244
    table of options, 267
Mount table, adding a new entry, 248
Mounting CD-ROMs, 241-243
Mounting a device, explained, 238
Mounting file systems, explained, 238
Mounting file systems automatically, 244-247
Mounting and formatting floppy disks, 240-241
Mounting hard drive partitions, 243-244
Mouse buttons, 113
Mouse events (TK), 970-972
Mouse information, 24
Mouse setup, 48-49
Moving directories, 209
Moving files, 206-209
Mozart soft configurable CD-ROM, 1001
ms macro package, 842
MS-DOS access commands, 275
msdos command, 261-264
MS-DOS hard drive partitions, mounting, 243-244
mtools utilities, 261-264
mtools.conf file, 263
mtype command, 262
Multics, 6
Multitasking, X-Windows, 114-115
MuTeX program, 846
mv command, 206-209
xmwm window manager, 130, 821

Named daemon, 783
Nameserver, setting up, 783
Nameserver addresses, 769-770
Naming Linux files, 182, 210-211
NCR53C810/15/20/25 SCSI parameters, 1010
NCR53c406a SCSI parameters, 1008
NCR53cxxx (rel 17) SCSI parameters, 1009-1010
NCR5380/53c400 SCSI parameters, 1007
NCSA, 422
Nested directories, 195
netcfg utility, 100, 773-774
netd server management, 457-459
Netmask, 770
Netscape Navigator Web Browser, 419-422, 1046
    downloading, 83
    ftp display, 86
    icon, 420
    icon bar, 421
    Linux version of, 13
    netscape command, 113
    registering, 84-85
netstat program, 778-780, 806
Network addresses, 768-770
Network administration, 767-812
    programs table, 804
    summary, 800-801
Network card parameters, 1012
Network configuration, 42-43
    getting information on, 25-26
    utility, 100
    as a Web server, 434
Network File Systems (NFSs), 249-251
Network file transfer. See ftp
Network Information Services (NIS), 251
Network initialization, 772
Network interfaces and routes, 772-778
Network monitoring, 778-780
Network name, 771-772
Network News Transport Protocol (NNTP), 340, 342
Network system information, TCP/IP, 519-520
News server software, 342-344
News servers, 340
News Transport Agents, 342-344
Newsgroups. See Usenet
Newsreaders, 339-378
NFS options, 272
nntp news servers, 340, 419
noclobber variable, 149-150, 585-586, 588, 645
noglob variable, 586, 645-646
Nondestructive repartition, 29-30
NOT operator (searching directories), 202
notify command, 168

Novell UNIX System's Group, 7
nroff document processor, 842-844
Null string (""), 785-786
Numeric operators (Perl), 939-940
Numeric operators (TCSH), 671-672
Numeric variables (@), TCSH, 657

Objective-C compiler, 896-897
Octal digits (as a mask), 231-234
od command, 184, 218
Okano CD-ROM parameters, 1002
olwm and olvwm window managers, 125-127, 821
Online documentation, 66, 71
Online manuals for applications (man), 907-911
open command (Perl), 923
open command (Tcl), 963-964
Open Directory window, 120
Open Software Foundation (OSF), 7
OpenLinux, 9
OpenLinux install disks, creating, 32-33
OpenLinux Lite, installing, 22, 40-41
OpenLinux Lite (on enclosed CD-ROM), 14-15, 22, 40-41
OpenLinux Web server, 469-478
Open-Look, 7
Operating environment, explained, 6
Operating systems, 5-6. See also Linux operating system
Operators, pattern matching, 945, 989-990
Optics Storage DOLPHIN 8000AT CD-ROM parameters, 1003
Options (command), 65, 141
OR operator (searching directories), 202-203
Orchid CD-ROM parameters, 1002
OSF Unix, 7
Ousterhout, John, 950
outfolder command (Mail), 306-307
Owner file permissions, 227-228
Ownership permissions for programs, 230

pack command (TK), 967-968
Packet routing, 776-778
Page formatting with LaTeX, 857
Pager (desktop), explained, 117
Panasonic CD-ROM parameters, 1002
Parent directory (..), 193, 195-197
Parent-child directory structure, 185
Parentheses (), 564
Partitions (hard disk), 27
    adding, 29
    deleting, 28-29

Linux, 34-40
main and swap, 36
mounting, 243-244
opening disk space for, 27-32
Pascal compiler, 897
passwd command, 62, 732-733, 742
Password
changing, 62
superuser, 44
Path names (directory), 186-188, 192, 197-199
PATH variable, 76-77, 589, 592-593, 598-600
Pattern matching operators (gawk), 989-990
Pattern matching operators (Perl), 945
Pattern searches
with gawk, 986-987
Perl, 933-934
with trn newsreader, 346-347, 359-360, 362
PDKSH shell, 577
perl command, 919-920
Perl (Practical Extraction and Report Language), 917-947
\ functions, 934-935
array management functions, 928-929
array operations, 938-939
arrays and lists, 926-928
associative arrays, 929-930
command line operations, 919
command line options, 937
control structures, 930-933, 942
escape characters, 936
file handles, 923-924
file operations, 937
input and output, 921
list operations, 928-929
loop control structures, 943-944
newsgroups, 919
numeric operators, 939-940
pattern matching, 933-934, 945
regular expressions, 945-946
scripts, 919-921
string comparisons, 940-942
string functions, 933
string operations, 944
subroutines, 934-935, 947
variables and expressions, 924-926
versions, 918
Web sites, 918
Permission symbols, 228-231
Permissions configuration file, 525-527
Permissions (file and directory), 227-237, 468-469
remote access TCP/IP, 520
script file executable, 164
setting, 122, 229-237
Permissions list, 230
Philips CD-ROM parameters, 1003
picture environment (LaTeX), 869-870

Pine Mail program, 320-322
main menu, 320
sending a message, 321
ping command, 519-520, 778
Pipes and redirection, 177
with filters, 544-547
pipe operator (|), 153-158
piping through several commands, 156
tee command, 156-158
Plus sign (+), 167, 229, 564
Pnews
posting articles with, 363-364
signature files, 364
pnp command, 35
Pointer section of XF86Config, 819
POP servers, accessing mail on, 282-284
Popclient, 282-284
PopupSMenu command, 823
POSIX, 8
Posting articles
with Pnews, 363-364
with trn newsreader, 358-359
PostScript printing, 843, 868
PPA SCSI parameters, 1012
PPP (Point-to-Point Protocol), 783
chat scripts, 785-789
options, 789-792
preparing to connect to, 784-794
providing incoming connections, 792-793
PPP security (CHAP), 793-794
pppcon command, 791
pppd program/utility, 88-92, 784-785, 788-794
options, 789-792
table of options, 808-809
print command (Perl), 920, 922
Printer management commands, 759
Printers, installing and managing, 749-753
Printing files, 189-190, 220
PrintTool utility, 749-751
Pro Audio Spektrum Studio 16 SCSI parameters, 1008
proc command (Tcl), 960-961
Procedures (Tcl), 977
Processes, explained, 166
.profile file, 598-601
Program directories, 76-77
Program managers, 109
Prompt (shell), explained, 140
Protocols (IP), 783-800
Proxies, explained, 421
ps command, 169
PS1 and PS2 special variables, 593-595
puts command (Tcl), 962-964
pwd command, 156, 192-194

Q

QLogic ISP1020 Intelligent SCSI Processor Driver, 1008
Qlogicfas Driver version 0.45 SCSI parameters, 1008
Question mark (?), 145-147, 564
Quoting commands (single quotes), 610-611
Quoting strings (BASH), 607-609
qvwm configuration file, 129
qvwm window manager, 128-129

R

rcp command, 518-519, 521-523
RCS commands, 914-915
RCS directory, 905-906
RCS files, 905-907
read command, 606, 611-613
Read permissions, 227, 235
README files, 260, 469
Redefinable special variables (BASH), 589
Redhat fstool utility, 247-249
Redhat Package Manager (RPM), 75, 81-83
modes, 102-104
runlevel system states, 761-762
Redirection, 147-153
append operator (>>), 159
file creation, 150-151
with filters, 544-547
1>&2 and 2>&1, 160
operations, 176-177
standard error (>& and 2>), 158-160
standard input (<), 152-153
standard output (> and >>), 149-151
regexp command (Tcl), 962
regsub command (Tcl), 962
Regular expressions, 557-566, 568-569
explained, 544
full, 564-566
grep and, 563-564
Perl, 945-946
summary of, 568-569
Relational operators (BASH), 633
Relative method of specifying permissions, 228
Relative path names, 187, 197-198
Remote access, 517-540
Remote access operations, TCP/IP, 518-524
Remote access permission (.rhosts), 520
Remote communications, 85-88
TCP/IP, 523-524
UUCP, 534-535
Remote file copy, TCP/IP, 521-523
Remote login
TCP/IP, 521
with telnet, 383-386

resolv.conf file, 782-783
Revision Control System (RCS),
    905-907, 914-915
.rhosts file, 520
RIGHT ARROW, 142
Ritchie, Dennis, 6
rlogin command, 519, 521
rm command, 145, 166, 211-212
rmdir command, 191
rn article list commands for trn, 374
rn newsreader article list, 361-363
root command, 72
Root directory, 11, 185-186
Root user desktop, 733-734
Root user login, 47, 72
route command, 281, 772-773
Routing, 776-778
Routing table fields, 776-777
rpm command, 75, 81-83, 525
RPM software ftp sites, 105
RPMS directory, 81
rsh command, 523-524
runlevel command, 738
ruptime command, 519
rwho command, 519

S

Sanyo CDR-H94A CD-ROM
    parameters, 1003-1004
Savehist variable (TCSH), 647-648
Scheduling tasks, 735-736
Screen section of XF86Config,
    817-818
Script command line arguments
    (BASH), 613-614
Script file executable permission, 164
Script input and output (BASH),
    611-613
scrollbar command (TK), 967
SCSI hard drives, mounting, 243
SCSI parameters, 1004-1012
Seagate STOx SCSI parameters, 1009
Search criteria, file and directory,
    201-202
Searches. *See also* Filters; gawk utility
    gawk pattern searches, 986-987,
        989-990
    grep and fgrep, 550-552
    man utility, 68
    trn newsreader, 346-347,
        359-360, 362
Searching directories, 199-203
Searching files (grep and fgrep),
    550-552
Second mouse button, 113
sed edit filter, 552-555
sendmail command, 281
set command, 161-163, 585, 606-607
    Mail, 305
    Tcl, 953-957
    Vi editor, 695-698
set prompt command (TCSH),
    646-647

Seyon telecommunications program, 88
SGML, 435
Shared libraries, 898-899
Shell, 8-10
    command line syntax, 140-141
    Linux shell types, 140
    and standard input/output, 148
Shell operations, 139-179
    summary, 173-174
    table of, 176-179
Shell prompt, 140
Shell script arguments, 164
Shell scripts, 164-166
Shell scripts (BASH), 604-606
SHELL special variable, 592
Shell symbols, table of, 175-176
Shell variables, 161-163
    BASH special, 588-603
    TCSH, 163
showrgb command, 828
Shutting down the system, 46, 59-61,
    737, 762-763
Single quotes ("), 607-611
Single quotes vs. back quotes, 610
SLIP connections, 794-800
    preparing to connect to, 784
    providing incoming, 799-800
SLIP (Serial Line Internet Protocol),
    783
smail agent, 281
Software
    compiling, 260-261
    development tools, 902-907
    installing, 75-85
    Linux, 12-14, 17
    minimum requirements, 23-24
Software package management with
    Lisa, 77
Software packages on the CD-ROM,
    1013-1040
Solaris (Sun), 7
Sony CDU535 CD-ROM parameters,
    1002-1003
Sony CDU31A/CDU33A CD-ROM
    parameters, 1001
sort filter, 155, 157-158, 167, 547, 549
Sound drivers, installing, 54-55
Special characters, 143-147
    extended, 564-566
    for filenames, 176
Special variables (BASH), 588-603,
    630-631
SpecTcl GUI builder, 973-974
Spell checking (spell), 548-549
Spell filter, 547
Spiders, explained, 429
srm.conf file, 471
srm.conf variables, 473-474
Stallman, Richard, 710
Standard C library, 897
Standard domains, table of, 329
Standard editors, 12
Standard error, 158
Standard error redirection symbols,
    175-176

Standard input, 147, 151-152
    Mail, 285
    and the shell, 148
    Tcl, 962-963, 978-979
    TCSH, 654-655
Standard output, 147-148
    appending (>>), 151
    Tcl, 962-963, 978-979
    TCSH, 654-655
Standard SVGA chipsets for
    X-Windows, 1042
Standard system directories in
    Linux, 219
Starting and exiting the window
    manager, 63-64
Starting freeWAIS, 514-515
Starting GN Gopher server, 495
Starting the Lisa utility, 74
Starting and shutting down Linux,
    60-61
Starting University of Minnesota
    Gopher, 489-490
Starting a Web server, 476-478
Startup application fvwm
    configuration files, 825
Startup kernel and device module
    control, 1001
Startup and setup, 57-105
StartupFunction, 825
startx command, 48, 59, 110, 419,
    825-826
Static IP addresses in dip scripts, 795
Static libraries, 898
Status codes for mail messages, 331
STDERR (Perl), 922
STDIN (Perl), 921
STDOUT (Perl), 922
Sticky bit, 231, 234-235
Sticky items, 118
Stream editor (sed), 553-555
string command (Tcl), 961-962
String comparisons (Perl), 940-942
String functions (Perl), 933
String operations (Perl), 944
stty command, 755
.styles file, 824
sub command, 934-935
Subroutines (Perl), 934-935, 947
SunOS, 7
Superuser, 44, 732-738
SVGA chipsets for X-Windows,
    1042-1043
Swap partition, 24, 36-37
Switch structure (Tcl), 959
Switch (TCSH condition), 662-663
Symbolic links, 215-217
Symbolic method of specifying
    permissions, 228
System administration, 74, 729-995.
    See also Lisa utility
    commands, 758-759
    configuration files, 760-761
    managing users, 738-748
    summary, 757

System configuration
  areas, 73
  with Lisa, 71-75
  tools, 110-111
System directories, 11, 76, 185-188, 219
System V release 4, 7
System V/386, 8
System initialization files, 738, 760-761
System management, 732-738
System shutdown, 46, 59-61, 737, 762-763
System states, 736-738, 761-762
System 3, 7
System time and date, 734-735
System-determined special variables (BASH), 589-591
system.fvwmdesk, 825
system.fvwmrc.bindings file, 824
system.fvwmrc.goodstuff, 822-823
system.fvwmrc.menu, 823-824
system.fvwmrc.styles file, 824
Systems configuration file, 525-527

T

Tables (LaTeX formatted), 863-865
tail command/filter, 545-547, 791
talk utility, 326-327
Tannebaum, Andrew, 8
tar utility, 251-255, 525
  options, 273
  tar t command, 259
  tar x command, 260
.tar.gz file, 257-258
Task scheduling, 735-736
Taskbar fvwm configuration files, 822-823
tb command, 127
Tcl commands, table of, 977-979
Tcl programming language, 950, 953-965
  arrays, 956-957
  control structures, 958-960
  embedded commands, 955
  expressions, 954-955
  file handles, 963-964
  input and output, 962-963
  list commands, 957-958
  list operations, 976
  procedures, 960-961
  scripts, 953-954
  set command, 953-957
  string commands, 961-962
  variables, 955-956
Tcl shell, 950, 953-954
tclsh command, 950, 954
Tcl/Tk
  GUI builder (SpecTcl), 973-974
  products, 951-952
  programs, 949-982
  software products and Web sites, 975-976

tcpd daemon, 458-459
TCP/IP, 381, 518
  configuration addresses and files, 803-804
  configuration files, 770-772
  network addresses, 768-770
  network system information, 519-520
  protocols, 768, 801-802
  remote access commands and options, 535-536
  remote access operations, 518-524
TCSH shell, 637-675
  aliases, 643-644
  argument arrays (argv), 656-657
  command line completion, 638-639
  commands and variables, 673-674
  conditions, 659-663
  control structures, 658-667, 674-675
  defining variables, 652-653
  environment variables, 658
  expression operators, 672-673
  feature variables (toggles), 644-646
  features, 670
  history commands, 669
  history event substitution, 641-642
  history utility, 639-641
  initialization files, 649-652
  input/output, 654-655
  loops, 663-667
  numeric operators, 671-672
  numeric variables (@), 657
  programming, 652-667
  scripts, 653-655
  shell variables, 653-654
  special variables, 646-648, 670-671
  summary, 667-668
  test expressions, 658-659
TCSH shell variables, 163
.tcshrc file (TCSH), 650-651
Teac CD-ROM parameters, 1002
tee command/filter, 156-158, 544-546
Telecommunications programs, 87-88
Telnet, 383-386
Telnet options and commands, table of, 404-405
TERM special variable, 597-598
Terminal emulator, 87
Terminal management commands, 759-760
Terminal name variable, 597-598
Terminal window, 112-114
Terminals, installing and managing, 754-755
test command, 617-618
Test command operations (BASH), 634
Test expressions (TCSH), 658-659

TeTeX application, 846, 872-873
TeX applications, 845-846, 848, 872-873
  math symbols, 879
  output, 848
  special characters, 878
  tools for, 841-892
TeX commands, 848-855
  fonts, 850-852
  headers and footers, 850
  math formulas, 853-854
  paragraphs, 849
  spacing, 849-850
  table of, 876-878
  tex command, 847
TeX files, 847-848
TeX macros, 854-855. *See also* LaTeX program/macros
Third mouse button, 113
Thompson, Ken, 6
Thread trees (trn newsreader), 352-356
Threads (newsgroup article), 344
Tilde (absolute path name), 197-199, 210-211
Tilde commands in Mail, 287-292, 330-331
Time configuration utility, 735
Time and date, for command execution, 171-172
Time and date (system), 734-735
Time zone, GMT as, 24, 44
timeout command (Expect), 975
tin newsreader, 364-367
  installing, 342
  table of commands, 375-378
Tk applications, 950, 965-969
  command options, 979-981
  directory and file listboxes, 971
  events and bindings, 970-972
  operations commands, 982
  widgets, 966-969, 981
Tk listbox and scrollbar, 968
Tk widgets, 966-969, 981
Tkman program, 70
TMC-8xx/TMC-9xx SCSI parameters, 1009
Torvald, Linux, 8
tr edit filter, 552
Trantor T128/T128F/T228 SCSI parameters, 1009
Tree structure, Linux, 184-185
treebrowser (Xview file manager), 127
trn commands, table of, 369-373
trn newsreader, 344-363
  article mode, 349, 351-352
  article selections, 359-361
  displaying articles, 352-356
  installing, 342
  marking articles, 359
  newsgroup list, 345-347
  newsgroup subscribing, 347
  pattern and number references, 360-362

replying to articles, 358-359
rn newsreader article list, 361-363
saving articles, 357-358
selector, 347-349
selector display modes, 349-352
subject mode, 349-350, 356
thread mode, 349, 351
thread trees, 352-356
trn options, 361
troff document processor, 842
tset command, 755
Tutorials on Linux topics, 71
TXC CD-ROM parameters, 1002
Typesetting, 845-846, 848
TZ special variable, 591

U

Ultrastor SCSI parameters, 1005
UltraStore SCSI parameters, 1005
umount command, 237-249
umount -a command, 244
uname command, 529-530
Unattached buffers, 719-721
Universal Resource Locators (URLs), 414-416
University of Minnesota Gopher server, 481-493
    configuring, 481-493
    options, 489
    starting, 489-490
Unix
    history of, 6-8
    standards, 8
Unix System V Release 4, 7
Unix System V/386, 8
Unix System Laboratories, 7
UNIX System's Group, 7
unset command, 161, 163, 606-607
UP ARROW, 143
Upgrading installed Linux systems, 26-27
URL addresses, 414-416
Usenet
    backbone sites, 340
    Linux newsgroups, 14, 20
    news, 340-341
    newsgroup article threads, 344
    newsgroups, 14, 20, 340-341, 344
    and newsreaders, 339-378
    summary, 368
User accounts, 58-59
User categories, 227
User configuration utility, 740
User directories, 11, 186
User environments, managing, 742-743
User groups
    adding and deleting, 745-748
    file permissions, 227-228
    managing, 763-764
User ID permissions, 230-231, 235
User interface, 9-10

useradd command, 744
usercfg utility, 739-741, 745-747
    group window, 746
    path names, 741
User-defined commands, 164-166
User-defined filters (gawk), 991-992
User-defined special variables (BASH), 589
User-defined variables (gawk), 988-989
userdel command, 744-745
usermod command, 744
Users
    adding with adduser, 743-744
    adding and removing, 739-741, 744
    managing, 738-748, 763-764
Utilities, 9, 11-12
uucico command, 530
uucp command, 525
UUCP (Unix to Unix CoPy), 518, 525-535, 537-540
    addressing, 527-529
    commands, 525
    commands and options table, 537-540
    installing and configuring, 525-527
    making connections, 530
uudecode program, 322-324, 368
uuencode program, 322-324, 368
uupick command, 525, 530-532
uustat command, 532-533
uuto command, 525, 530-532
uux command, 525, 534-535
uuxqt command, 530

V

Values from Linux commands, 610
Variables
    BASH, 606-615
    contents as command arguments, 162
    definition and evaluation, 161-163
    gawk, 987-989
    listing all defined, 162
    shell, 161-163
    Tcl, 955-956, 977
Variables (TCSH)
    declaring, 653-654
    feature variables, 644-646
    special variables, 646-648
    table of, 673-674
Veronica, 402
Vertical bar (|), 564
Vi editor, 12, 679-708
    / command, 692
    a command, 688-689, 691
    advanced commands, 692-694
    advanced cursor movement, 693-694
    breaking and joining lines, 691

changes, 689-690
command mode, 680-682
commands for common operations, 685-692
CTRL-Z in, 170
cursor movement, 685-687
dd command, 691
deletions, 689
.exrc command, 696-698
file creation and saving, 681-684
g command, 687-688
i command, 688-689, 691
initialization file, 696-698
input, 688-689
input mode, 680-682
line editing commands, 694-695
line editing mode, 681-682
line numbers (G command), 687-688
managing editing modes, 684
modes, 680-682
modifying text, 688-691
moving and copying lines, 691-692
moving through text, 685-688
options (.exrc), 696-698
options (set), 695-698
p command, 691-692
:q command, 684
repeat factor, 690-691
searches, 692
set command, 695-698
summary, 698-699
summary of common commands, 686
table of common commands, 687
table of line editing commands, 705-707
table of search and input options, 707-708
tables of commands, 700-707
undo, 690
:w command, 683
yy command, 691-692
zz command, 170, 682-684
Video card settings, 24-25, 820
VirTeX application, 872-873
Virtual desktop, 52-53, 117-118
Virtual screen, setting, 818
Volume label, 29

W

WAIS client commands, table of, 411
WAIS indexes, creating, 510-512
WAIS sources, 512-513
WAIS (Wide Area Information Servers), 403-404, 505-515
    starting, 514-515
    testing, 514
    z3950, 505
Waisindex options and file types, 506-508
waisserver command, 514-515

wait command, 797
wc filter, 547-548
Wearnes CD-ROM parameters, 1002
Web, 413-449
Web Browsers, 380, 417-426
    Arena, 424-426
    HotJava, 428-429
    Lynx, 426-428
    Mosaic, 422-424
    Netscape Navigator, 419-422
Web page creation (with HTML),
    435-442
    example, 439-442
    formatting text, 435-436
    images and sounds, 438
    page and text format, 435
    referencing Internet resources,
        436-438
Web page HTML codes, table of,
    446-449
Web page for online documentation,
    439-442
Web pages, 416-417
Web resource file types, table of, 444
Web search utilities, 429
Web server, 469-478
    configuring, 471-476
    directories and http options,
        460, 470
    starting, 476-478
    using Linux as, 434-443
Web site, creating, 434-435
Web sites (Linux), 19
Web tools, table of, 445
Web transfer protocols, table of, 444
WebCrawler, 429-430
Western Digital WD 7000 SCSI
    parameters, 1011
whatis command, 68-69
where command, 901
While loops, 623-624
    Perl, 930
    Tcl, 959-960
    TCSH, 663-665
who command, 739
Widgets (TK), 966-969, 981
Willow Toolkit, 264
window command (TK), 965

Window and file managers,
    installing, 123-131
Window managers, 108-109. *See also*
    fvwm; X-Windows
    AfterStep, 130-131
    fvwm95 and qvwm, 128-129
    fvwm2, 125
    LessTif, 130, 821
    Motif, 7, 130-131
    olwm and olvwm, 125-127, 8212
    starting, 124-125
    starting and exiting, 63-64
    table of, 134-135
    Web sites for, 134-135
    Xview, 125-127, 821
    X-Windows and, 821-822
Windows, 111-112
Windows emulators, 264
Wine emulator, 264
wish command (TK), 965
wish shell and scripts, 965-966
Word (Microsoft), 842
WordPerfect (Corel), 842
Working directory, 186, 195-197
Workplace menu fvwm
    configuration files, 823-824
World Wide Web (WWW), 413-449
Write permissions, 227, 235
write utility, 326-327

Xarchie, 394-395
XEmacs editor, 131-132, 721-722
Xenix, 7-8
XF86Config file, 815-820
    Device section, 820
    Files section, 818
    Keyboard section, 818
    Module section, 818
    Monitor section, 819-820
    Pointer section, 819
    Screen section, 817-818
XF86Setup, 47-48
    card list screen (video), 50
    depicting mouse setup, 48
    Keyboard Screen, 49

XFMail program, 99-100
Xfree86 package, 47
XFree86 servers, 42, 814-815, 834
Xfree86misc package, 47
XFree86-supported chipsets for
    X-Windows, 1041-1043
xfs command, 831
XFSetup86 Monitor screen, 51
xgopher client, 399
xinit command, 826
.xinitrc file, 124, 830-831
xlaunch command, 822
Xlib library, 897
Xman program, 69-70
Xman windows for displaying man
    pages, 70
xmkmf command, 261, 833
xmodmap command, 829
.Xmodmap file, 829
.Xresources file, 827
xset command, 829
xset fp rehash command, 832-833
xsetroot command, 829
xTar tar archive utility, 254-255
Xterm window, 112-114
Xview file manager (treebrowser),
    127
Xview OpenLook window manager
    (olwm), 125-127, 821
X-Windows, 9, 107-135, 814
    commands and arguments,
        825-826, 836-839
    compiling applications, 833
    configuration files, 826-831,
        837-838
    configuration summary, 833-834
    configuring, 813-839
    file managers, 110-111
    fonts, 831-833
    installing and configuring, 47-53
    multitasking, 114-115
    and Network Configuration, 100
    starting, 63-64
    and window managers, 821-822
    XFree86-supported chipsets for,
        1041-1043
xxgdb, 901-902

Caldera's OpenLinux *Lite*

OpenLinux® Lite is a complete Linux system based on the OpenLinux distribution. It includes the full-featured, 32-bit, multi-user, multi-tasking Linux operating system, installed with an easy-to-follow, quick installation with menu-based choices and auto-detection of your hardware. OpenLinux Lite uses kernel version 2.0.29 and the Apache web server for superfast TCP/IP access to the Internet. It also includes a 90-day evaluation of the CriSPLite text editor and the easy-to-use graphical Desktop with drag-and-drop features, layouts, icon bar, preferences and much more.

For even more power, upgrade to Caldera's OpenLinux Base or OpenLinux Standard commercial products. Both add functionality with additional software. Base includes the Java Development Kit (JDK) from Sun Microsystems®, Netscape Navigator, StarOffice 3.1 office suite, and ADABASE-D relational database.

OpenLinux Standard includes all the above plus the Netscape FastTrack commercial Web server with SSL, Netscape Navigator 3.0 Gold, full Novell Netware support, and Caldera's OpenDOS, a fully-functional DOS.

Check us out at http://www.caldera.com or call us at 800-850-7779.

(Note that the OpenLinux Lite CD does not include technical support.)